HANDBOOK OF
ADOLESCENT PSYCHOLOGY

THIRD EDITION

HANDBOOK OF ADOLESCENT PSYCHOLOGY

THIRD EDITION

Volume 1: Individual Bases of Adolescent Development

Edited By

RICHARD M. LERNER

LAURENCE STEINBERG

WILEY

John Wiley & Sons, Inc.

This book is printed on acid-free paper. ∞

Copyright © 2009 by John Wiley & Sons, Inc. All rights reserved.

Published by John Wiley & Sons, Inc., Hoboken, New Jersey.

Published simultaneously in Canada.

For general information on our other products and services please contact our Customer Care Department within the U.S. at (800) 762-2974, outside the United States at (317) 572-3993 or fax (317) 572-4002.

Wiley also publishes its books in a variety of electronic formats. Some content that appears in print may not be available in electronic books. For more information about Wiley products, visit our website at www.wiley.com.

Library of Congress Cataloging-in-Publication Data:

Handbook of adolescent psychology / edited by Richard M. Lerner, Laurence Steinberg.—3rd ed.
    p. cm.
    Includes index.
    ISBN 978-0-470-14921-8 (cloth : v. 1 : alk. paper)
    ISBN 978-0-470-14922-5 (cloth : v. 2 : alk. paper)
    ISBN 978-0-470-14920-1 (set)
    1. Adolescent psychology. I. Lerner, Richard M. II. Steinberg, Laurence D., 1952-
BF724.H33 2009
155.5—dc22
                                              2008038561

Printed in the United States of America

10 9 8 7 6 5 4 3 2 1

Contributors

Joseph P. Allen
Department of Psychology
University of Virginia
Charlottesville, Virginia

Iris Beltran
Department of Psychology
Arizona State University
Tempe, Arizone

Sheri A. Berenbaum
Department of Psychology
The Pennsylvania State University
University Park, Pennsylvania

Edmond P. Bowers
Lynch School of Education
Boston College
Chestnut Hill, Massachusetts

Linda M. Burton
Department of Sociology
Duke University
Durham, North Carolina

Noel A. Card
Division of Family Studies and Human
    Development
University of Arizona
Tucson, Arizona

Laurie Chassin
Department of Psychology
Arizona State University
Tempe, Arizona

Bruce E. Compas
Department of Psychology and Human
    Development
Vanderbilt University
Nashville, Tennessee

James E. Côté
Department of Sociology
University of Western Ontario
London, Ontario

Lisa M. Diamond
Department of Psychology
University of Utah
Salt Lake City, Utah

Lorah D. Dorn
Cincinnati Children's Hospital Medical
    Center
College of Medicine
University of Cincinnati
Cincinnati, Ohio

Sherry Eaton
Department of Psychology
North Carolina Central University
Durham, North Carolina

Jacquelynne S. Eccles
Institute for Social Research on
Research Center for Group Dynamics
    Achievement Research Lab
University of Michigan
Ann Arbor, Michigan

Nancy Eisenberg
Department of Psychology
Arizona State University
Tempe, Arizona

David P. Farrington
Institute of Criminology
Cambridge University
Cambridge, England

Yulika E. Forman
Eliot-Pearson Department of Child
   Development
Tufts University
Medford, Massachusetts

Nancy L. Galambos
Department of Psychology
University of Alberta
Edmonton, Alberta

Raymond Garrett-Peters
Center for Social Demography and
   Ethnography
Duke University
Durham, North Carolina

Julia A. Graber
Department of Psychology
University of Florida
Gainesville, Florida

Amanda L. Hare
Department of Psychology
University of Virginia
Charlottesville, Virgina

Penny Hauser-Cram
Lynch School of Education
Boston College
Chestnut Hill, Massachusetts

Andrea Hussong
Department of Psychology
University of North Carolina
Chapel Hill, North Carolina

Charles E. Irwin, Jr.
Department of Pediatrics
University of California, San Francisco
San Francisco, California

Pamela Ebstyne King
School of Psychology
Fuller Theological Seminary
Pasadena, California

Joanne Kersh
Center for Social Development and
   Education
University of Massachusetts at Boston
Boston, Massachusetts

Marty Wyngaarden Krauss
Provost and Senior Vice President for
   Academic Affairs
Brandeis University
Waltham, Massachusetts

Deanna Kuhn
Teachers College
Columbia University
New York, New York

Jacqueline V. Lerner
Lynch School of Education
Boston College
Chestnut Hill, Massachusetts

Richard M. Lerner
Eliot-Pearson Department of Child
   Development
Tufts University
Medford, Massachusetts

Todd D. Little
Department of Psychology
University of Kansas
Lawrence, Kansas

Elizabeth McConnell
Department of Psychology
University of Kansas
Lawrence, Kansas

Brenda McDaniel
Oklahoma State University
Tempe, Arizona

Kathleen Boykin McElhaney
Department of Psychology
University of Virginia
Charlottesville, Virginia

Susan M. McHale
Department of Human Development and
   Family Studies
Pennsylvania State University
University Park, Pennsylvania

Amanda Sheffield Morris
Department of Human Development and
   Family Sciences
Oklahoma State University
Tulsa, Oklahoma

Elizabeth M. Ozer
Department of Pediatrics
University of California, San Francisco
San Francisco, California

Tomáš Paus
Brain & Body Centre
University of Nottingham
Nottingham, United Kingdom
Montreal Neurological Institute
McGill University
Montreal, Canada

Erin Phelps
Eliot-Pearson Department of Child
    Development
Tufts University
Medford, Massachusetts

Kristopher J. Preacher
Department of Psychology
University of Kansas
Lawrence, Kansas

Robert W. Roeser
Department of Psychology
Portland State University
Portland, Oregon

Kristen L. Reeslund
Department of Psychology and Human
    Development
Vanderbilt University
Nashville, Tennesee

Ritch C. Savin-Williams
Department of Human Development
Cornell University
Ithaca, New York

Judith Smetana
Department of Clinical & Social Sciences
    in Psychology
University of Rochester
Rochester, New York

Lisa M. Sontag
Department of Psychology
University of Florida
Gainesville, Florida

Tracy L. Spinrad
School of Social and Family Dynamics
Arizona State University
Tempe, Arizona

Laurence Steinberg
Department of Psychology
Temple University
Philadelphia, Pennsylvania

J. Claire Stephenson
Department of Psychology
University of Virginia
Charlottesville, Virginia

Elizabeth J. Susman
Department of Biobehavioral Health
Pennsylvania State University
University Park, Pennsylvania

Myriam Villalobos
Department of Clinical & Social Sciences
    in Psychology
University of Rochester
Rochester, New York

Contents

Preface

In 2004, in our preface to the second edition of the *Handbook of Adolescent Psychology*, we noted that 24 years separated the first and second editions of this work. At the time of the publication of the first edition, the field was one where relatively little empirical work was being conducted and where, as well, the major theoretical frame was psychoanalytic. There was also present a little cognitive developmental theory, a touch of behaviorism, and just the beginnings (in the prescient chapter by Elder, 1980) of a dynamic, developmental systems model.

By 2004, 852 pages and 25 chapters (plus an afterword) were needed to summarize the vast empirical literature that had developed in the previous quarter-century. The chapters of the second edition revealed that the role of grand theories of adolescence, whether psychoanalytic or not, had waned, and that the sorts of mutually influential, person ←→ context relational models of development that Elder had discussed (represented as individual ←→ context relations) had become the predominant theoretical lens in the study of adolescent development, as they had within the field of human development more broadly (Damon & Lerner, 2006, 2008). In the second edition, the contexts in which adolescent development takes place received considerably more attention than had been the case previously. Moreover, the second edition reflected a growing interest in how theoretically-predicated, empirically-based knowledge about adolescence could be used to capitalize on the strengths of young people and promote their positive development.

We suggested in 2004 that the quality and quantity of the ongoing work in the scientific study of adolescence indicated that the field was remarkably active; that the increasing numbers of high-quality researchers drawn to the study of adolescent development portended an even greater growth in knowledge than had taken place between the publication of the first and second editions of the *Handbook*; and that it was likely that the field's future would be marked by the rapid evolution of the theoretical and empirical emphases represented in the second edition of the *Handbook*. Our expectations have been confirmed, but the expansion of the field took place with a breadth and depth of scholarship that we could not have fully anticipated.

The publication of the third edition of the *Handbook of Adolescent Psychology* in 2009 represents only a five-year period between the present and prior edition, about 25% of the time between the first and the second editions. However, within this relatively short period, the knowledge base within the field has exploded. The number of chapters we have included in this edition in order to fairly represent the range of high-quality scholarship defining the cutting edge of the contemporary study of adolescent development has increased by more than 50% and now fills two volumes.

Framing this scientific work are both theoretical models that stress processes of systemic, individual ←→ context relations (see our opening chapter on the history of scientific research on adolescence in Volume 1) and scientific methods that include both sophisticated quantitative techniques to study change (Little, Card, Preacher, & McConnell) and rich qualitative, ethnographic procedures that give voice to the developing adolescent and insight into the nature of his or her social, cultural, and historical context (Burton, Garrett-Peters, & Eaton). The contemporary study of individual development reflects this dynamic between person and context—whether the focus of analysis is brain development (Paus), puberty (Susman & Dorn), thinking (Kuhn), social cognition (Smetana & Villalobos), moral cognition and prosocial behavior (Eisenberg, Morris, McDaniel, & Spinrad), identity and self (Côté), gender and gender role development (Galambos, Berenbaum, & McHale), autonomy and attachment (McElhaney, Allen, Stephenson, & Hare), academic motivation (Eccles & Roeser), spirituality and religious development (King & Roeser), or sex (Diamond & Savin-Williams).

The study of interpersonal relationships in adolescence—involving those with parents (Laursen & Collins), siblings (East), peers (Brown & Larson), romantic partners (Connolly & McIsaac), or mentors (Rhodes & Lowe)—illustrate that the process of adolescent development involves dynamic, mutually influential exchanges between the developing youth and significant others. Indeed, even when the focus of developmental analysis is on the features of the institutional or cultural contexts of adolescence, the relations between the characteristics of the young person and the features of the settings in which he or she develops constitute the basic process of change during this period of life. These relational processes unfold in schools (Elmore), after-school settings (Mahoney, Vandell, Simpkins, & Zarrett), workplaces (Staff, Messersmith, & Schulenberg), and neighborhoods (Leventhal, Dupere, & Brooks-Gunn), and are influenced by poverty (McLoyd, Kaplan, Purtell, Bagley, Hardaway, & Smalls), the structure of the transition to adulthood within the United States and internationally (Hamilton & Hamilton), ethnicity and immigration (Fuligni, Hughes, & Way), mass media (Roberts, Henricksen, & Foehr), the legal system (Woolard & Scott), globalization (Larson, Wilson, & Rickman), and culture (Schlegel).

Theory and research about individual development, interpersonal relationships, and contextual influences on these processes underscore that the adolescent years are marked by both opportunity and vulnerability. This potential for intraindividual variation in the course and outcomes of individual ←→

context relations is brought into high relief in the burgeoning scholarship applying developmental science to help youth confront the normative and nonnormative challenges of the period and, as well, to promote their positive, healthy development. Scholarship about adolescent risk and resilience (Compas & Reeslund), positive youth development (Lerner, Phelps, Forman, & Bowers), and citizenship (Sherrod & Lauckhardt) rely on these bidirectional models to frame research. Similar use of these dynamic conceptions of development occurs in studies of internalizing problems (Graber & Sontag), externalizing problems (Farrington), substance use (Chassin, Hussong, & Beltran), developmental disabilities (Hauser-Cram, Krauss, & Kersh), and physical health (Ozer & Irwin), as well as in efforts to promote positive development through community-based programs and social policies (Balsano, Theokas, & Bobek). Together, then, the two volumes of the third edition of the *Handbook of Adolescent Psychology* depict a field that is enriching our understanding of the basic, relational process shaping trajectories of development across the adolescent period; providing important leadership in the study of human development over the entire life span; and offering innovative and scientifically grounded means to promote healthy development among young people in the United States and abroad.

There are numerous people to thank for their contribution to this edition of the *Handbook*. First and foremost, we owe our greatest debt of gratitude to the colleagues who wrote the chapters for the *Handbook*. Their careful scholarship and commitment to the field have allowed us to produce a volume that will benefit scientists, practitioners, and policy makers alike.

We are deeply grateful also to Lauren White, Editor at the Institute for Applied Research in Youth Development. Her expertise and tenacity in overseeing the day-to-day management of this work through all phases of manuscript development and production were invaluable to us. The overall quality of the *Handbook* is a direct result of her impressive ability to track and coordinate the myriad editorial tasks associated with a project of this scope, her astute editorial skills and wisdom, and her unfailing good humor and patience (with the editors as well as the contributors).

We also appreciate greatly the important contributions to this book made by Jennifer Davison, managing editor at the Institute. Her knowledge of the manuscript development and production process, and her talents for enhancing the efficiency and quality of the editing, were enormous assets that enabled this work to be completed in a timely and high-quality manner.

We are indebted to our editor at John Wiley and Sons, Patricia Rossi. Her enthusiasm for our vision for the *Handbook*, unflagging support, and collegial and collaborative approach to the development of this project were vital bases for the successful completion of the *Handbook*.

Several organizations that supported our scholarship during the time we worked on the *Handbook* also deserve our thanks. Tufts University and Temple University have provided the support and resources necessary to undertake and complete this project. In addition, Richard M. Lerner thanks the National 4-H Council, the Philip Morris USA Youth Smoking Prevention Department, and the John Templeton Foundation. Laurence Steinberg is especially indebted to Temple University for supporting a sabbatical leave during which most of his work on this book was completed.

Finally, we want to once again dedicate this *Handbook* to our greatest sources of inspiration, both for our work on the *Handbook* and for our scholarship in the field of adolescence: our children – Justin, Blair, Jarrett, and Ben. Now all in their young adulthood, they have taught us our greatest lessons about the nature and potentials of adolescent development.

R.M.L.
L.S
July, 2008

REFERENCES

Damon, W., & Lerner, R. M. (2006). *Handbook of child psychology* (6th ed., Vols. 1–4). Mahwah, NJ: Lawrence Erlbaum.

Damon, W., & Lerner, R. M. (2008). *Child and adolescent development: An advanced course*. Hoboken, NJ: John Wiley & Sons.

Elder, G. H. Jr. (1980). Adolescence in historical perspective. In J. Adelson (Ed.), *Handbook of adolescent psychology* (pp. 3–46). New York: John Wiley & Sons.

PART I

Conceptual and Methodological Foundations

CHAPTER 1

The Scientific Study of Adolescent Development

Historical and Contemporary Perspectives

RICHARD M. LERNER AND LAURENCE STEINBERG

In the opening sentence of the preface to the first edition of his classic, *A History of Experimental Psychology*, Edwin G. Boring (1929) reminded readers that "psychology has a long past, but only a short history" (p. ix), a remark he attributed to the pioneer of memory research, Hermann Ebbinghaus. A similar statement may be made about the study of adolescents and their development.

The first use of the term *adolescence* appeared in the fifteenth century. The term was a derivative of the Latin word *adolescere*, which means to grow up or to grow into maturity (Muuss, 1990). However, more than 1,500 years before this first explicit use of the term *adolescence,* both Plato and Aristotle proposed sequential demarcations of the life span, and Aristotle in particular proposed stages of life that are not dissimilar from sequences that might be included in contemporary models of youth development. He described three successive, seven-year periods (infancy, boyhood, and young manhood) prior to the full, adult maturity.

About 2,000 years elapsed between these initial philosophical discussions of adolescence and the emergence within the twentieth century of the scientific study of this period of life (with the publication in 1904 of

G. Stanley Hall's two-volume work on adolescence). Across the subsequent (at this writing) 106 years, the history of the scientific study of adolescence has had three overlapping phases (Steinberg & Lerner, 2004). These phases in the history of the field, which we discuss in the pages that follow, are illustrated in Figure 1.1.

THE FIRST PHASE OF THE SCIENTIFIC STUDY OF ADOLESCENCE

G. Stanley Hall's (1904) two-volume work, *Adolescence*, launched the scientific study of adolescence as a field framed by an evolutionary (Darwinian) conception of the basic process accounting for change across this period of life. As explained by Overton (2006), the approach to understanding development that was epitomized by Hall's theory reflected a nativist, and hence split, view of change (wherein nature, as opposed to nurture, is regarded as the fundamental basis of development). Hall's view also established the field for years to come as one that adhered to a biologically based, deficit view of adolescence.

Fancying himself as the "Darwin of the mind" (White, 1968), Hall sought to translate the ideas

The preparation of this chapter was supported in part by grants to Richard M. Lerner from the National 4-H Council, the Philip Morris USA Youth Smoking Prevention Department, and the John Templeton Foundation, and through a sabbatical leave granted to Laurence Steinberg by Temple University.

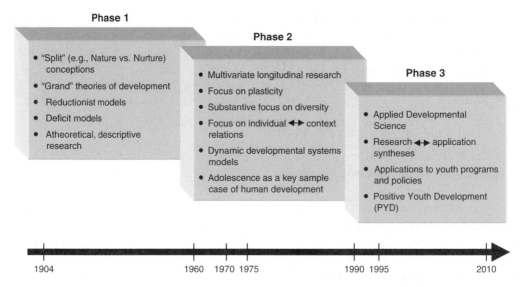

FIGURE 1.1   Three phases in the history of the scientific study of adolescent development

of Ernst Haeckel (e.g., 1868, 1891), an early contributor to embryology, into a theory of lifespan human development. Haeckel advanced the idea of recapitulation, that the adult stages of the ancestors comprising a species' evolutionary (phylogenetic) history were repeated in compressed form as the embryonic stages of the organism's ontogeny. Hall extended Haeckel's idea of recapitulation beyond the prenatal period in order to fashion a theory of human behavioral development. To Hall, adolescence represented a phylogenetic period when human ancestors went from savagery to civilization. This transition, according to Hall, made adolescence a period of storm and stress, a time of universal and inevitable upheaval.

Although other scholars of this period (e.g., Thorndike, 1904) quickly rejected Hall's recapitulationism on both empirical and methodological grounds (e.g., see Lerner, 2002, for a discussion), other theorists of adolescent development used a conceptual lens comparable to Hall's, at least insofar as his biological reductionism and his deficit view of adolescence were concerned. Anna Freud (1969), for instance, saw adolescence as a biologically based, universal developmental disturbance. Erik Erikson (1950, 1959) viewed the period as

one wherein an inherited maturational ground plan resulted in the inescapable psychosocial crisis of identity versus role confusion. When theorists rejected the nature-based ideas of psychoanalysts or neopsychoanalysts, they proposed equally one-sided, nurture-oriented ideas (and hence also used split conceptions) to explain the same problems of developmental disturbance and crisis. For example, McCandless (1961, 1970) presented a social-learning, drive-reduction theory to account for the developmental phenomena of adolescence (e.g., regarding sex differences in identity development) that Erikson (1959) interpreted as associated with maturation (see Lerner & Spanier, 1980, for a discussion).

Although the developmental theory of cognition proposed by Piaget (e.g., 1969, 1970, 1972) involved a more integrative view of nature and nurture than these other models, he also saw nature and nurture as separable (and hence split) sources of development, ones that just happened to interact (but, because they were separate and split, did not alter the status or quality of each other over the course of their interaction). The predominant focus of Piaget's (1970) ideas was on the emergence of formal logical structures, and not on the adolescent period per se. The absence of concern in Piaget's theory with the broader array of biological, emotional, personality, social, and societal concerns that had engaged other theorists' discussion of adolescence did not stop a relatively minor and historically transitory interest in Piaget's ideas as a frame for empirical understanding of the adolescent period (Steinberg & Morris, 2001). However, as Steinberg and Morris (2001) have explained, only a short while after this period of heightened interest in using the onset of formal operations as an explanation for everything adolescent, the influence of Piaget's theory on mainstream empirical work in the study of adolescence would become as modest as that associated with the other grand theories of the period, such as those authored by Erikson or McCandless.

The waning of these grand theories across the first phase of the study of adolescence, a phase that lasted about 70 years, was due—at least in part—to the fact that the sorts of Cartesian "splits" (see Overton, 2006) emphasized in the ideas of these theorists created false dichotomies—not only nature versus nurture, but also continuity versus discontinuity, stability versus instability, constancy versus change, or basic versus applied—that limited the intellectual development of the field. Seen through the contemporary, postmodern lens of relational models of development (e.g., Overton, 2006), conceptions that recognize the fundamental, integrative character of influences across the levels of organization comprising the ecology of human development (Bronfenbrenner, 2005; Bronfenbrenner & Morris, 2006; Collins, Maccoby, Steinberg, Hetherington, & Bornstein, 2000; Elder & Shanahan, 2006), scholarship-pursuing unidimensional conceptions of human development focused on, at best, ecologically invalid assessments of components of youth behavior or, at worst, counterfactual characterizations of the bases of individual structure and function (Gottlieb, Wahlsten, & Lickliter, 2006; Hirsch, 2004).

However, these theories were limited by the fact that they either focused exclusively on nature (e.g., genetic or maturational) (e.g., Freud, 1969; Hall, 1904), focused exclusively on nurture (e.g., McCandless, 1961), or weakly combined multiple sources of influence in ways that retained an emphasis on one or the other sources of development (usually on nature) as the prime basis of development (e.g., Erikson, 1959, 1968). As such, these theories were becoming increasingly out of step with empirical evidence indicating that variation associated with complex relations between organismic (biological) and contextual (proximate to distal) ecological variation, including culture and history, were involved in the course of adolescent development. While this evidence began to accumulate during the first phase in the scientific study of adolescence, it would not be until the end of the second phase and the emergence of the third phase of development of the field that these data, and other findings related to them, would be integrated into dynamic, integrative models of development (Steinberg & Lerner, 2004). Indeed, during the first phase of the field, the major empirical studies of adolescence were not primarily theory-driven, hypothesis-testing investigations. Instead, they were atheoretical, descriptive studies (McCandless, 1970). As such, even theory and research were split into separate enterprises. Moreover, there was also a split between scholars whose work was focused on basic developmental processes and practitioners whose focus was on community-based efforts to facilitate the healthy development of adolescents.

In other words, the divergence between the "grand" theories of the adolescent period and the range of research about adolescence that would come to characterize the field at the end of the twentieth century actually existed for much of the first phase of the field's development. The "classic" studies of adolescence conducted between 1950 and 1980 were not investigations derived from the theories of Hall, Anna Freud, McCandless, Piaget, or even Erikson (work associated with the ideas of Marcia, 1980, notwithstanding). Instead, this research was directed to describing (note, *not* explaining;

McCandless, 1970; Petersen, 1988) patterns of covariation among pubertal timing, personal adjustment, and relationships with peers and parents (e.g., Jones & Bayley, 1950; Mussen & Jones, 1957), both within and across cultural settings (e.g., Mussen & Bouterline Young, 1964); the diversity in trajectories of psychological development across adolescence (e.g., Bandura, 1964; Block, 1971; Douvan & Adelson, 1966; Offer, 1969); and the influence of history or temporality (i.e., as operationalized by time of testing– or cohort-related variation) on personality development, achievement, and family relations (e.g., Elder, 1974; Nesselroade & Baltes, 1974). Petersen (1988, p. 584) described the quality of the classic empirical work on adolescence by noting that:

> Most . . . research fell into one of two categories: (a) studies on behavioral or psychological processes that happened to use adolescent subjects, or (b) descriptive accounts of particular groups of adolescents, such as high school students or delinquents.

Despite its separation from the grand theories of adolescence that dominated the field during its first phase of scientific development, this body of early research, and the subsequent scholarship it elicited (e.g., see reviews by Lerner & Galambos, 1998; Petersen, 1988; and Steinberg & Morris, 2001), made several important contributions to shaping the specific character of the scientific study of adolescence between the early 1980s and late 1990s. As elaborated later in this chapter, this character involved the longitudinal study of individual–context relations among diverse groups of youth, the deployment of innovative quantitative and qualitative, ethnographic methods (see chapters 2 and 3, this volume), and the use of such scholarship for purposes of both elucidating basic developmental processes and applying developmental science to promote positive youth development across the adolescence period and within the diverse settings of their lives (e.g., Hamburg, 1974; Lerner, 2004,

2005; Steinberg, 1996; Steinberg & Levine, 1997).

These contributions to the study of adolescence acted synergistically with broader scholarly activity within developmental science pertinent to the theoretical, methodological, and applied features of the study of human development across the life span. A classic paper by Hamburg (1974) did much to provide the foundation for this integration, making a compelling case for viewing the early adolescent period as a distinct period of the life course and providing an exemplary ontogenetic window for understanding the key individual–context relational processes involved in coping and adaptation (processes that, we will explain, were conceptualized as bidirectional and mutually influential and that provided the potential for systematic change, for plasticity, across the adolescent period). Based on such evidence, Petersen (1988, p. 584) noted:

> Basic theoretical and empirical advances in several areas have permitted the advance of research on adolescence. Some areas of behavioral science from which adolescence researchers have drawn are life-span developmental psychology, life-course sociology, social support, stress and coping, and cognitive development; important contributing areas in the biomedical sciences include endocrinology and adolescent medicine. The recent maturation to adolescence of subjects in major longitudinal studies . . . has also contributed to the topic's empirical knowledge base.

The emergence of the relationship between the specific study of adolescence and more general scholarship about the overall course of human development provided the bridge to the second phase in the study of adolescent development. Indeed, in a review of the adolescent development literature written during this second phase, Petersen (1988, p. 601), predicted that, "Current research on adolescence will not only aid scientific understanding of this particular phase of life, it also may illuminate development more generally." Future events were consistent with Petersen's prognostication.

THE SECOND PHASE OF THE SCIENTIFIC STUDY OF ADOLESCENCE

From the late 1970s through this writing, the adolescent period has come to be regarded as an ideal "natural ontogenetic laboratory" for studying key theoretical and methodological issues in developmental science (Lerner & Steinberg, 2004; Steinberg & Lerner, 2004). There are several reasons for the special salience of the study of adolescent development to understanding the broader course of life-span development.

The Emergence of Adolescence as the New Focal Period Within the Life Span

The prenatal and infant periods exceed adolescence as ontogenetic periods of rapid physical and physiological growth. Nevertheless, a first reason for the adolescent period emerging in the 1970s as a time in ontogeny engaging the focused interest of developmental scientists was that the years from approximately 10 to 20—"the adolescent decade"—not only include the considerable physical and physiological changes associated with puberty but also mark a time when the interdependency of biology and context in human development is readily apparent (see chapters 4 and 5, this volume). Second, and in a related vein, as compared to infancy, the cognitive abilities, social relationships, and motivations of adolescents can, through reciprocal relations with their ecology, serve as active influences on their own development.

Third, the study in adolescence of these relations between active individuals and their varied and changing contexts serves as an ideal means to gain insight about bidirectional, mutually influential person–context relations. In post-Cartesian, postmodern conceptions of development, these relations were regarded as constituting the basic process of human development (Overton, 2006). Indeed, Overton (1973), as well as other developmental scientists working during the 1970s and early to mid-1980s (for instance, Baltes, 1979; Baltes & Schaie, 1973; Bronfenbrenner, 1979; Lerner, 1978; Dixon & Nesselroade, 1983; Riegel, 1975, 1976; Sameroff, 1983), began to forward developmental models that rejected reductionist biological or environmental accounts of development and, instead, focused on the variables from interdependent, or fused, levels of organization as constituting the developmental system and its multilayered context (e.g., Collins et al., 2000; Gottlieb et al., 2006; Thelen & Smith, 2006).

These developmental systems models have provided a metatheory for research on adolescent development, and have been associated with more midlevel (as opposed to grand) theories, models that have been generated to account for transformations in individual–context relations within selected domains of development. Instances of such midlevel developmental systems theories are the stage–environment fit model used to understand achievement in classroom settings (e.g., see chapter 12, this volume), the goodness-of-fit model used to understand the importance of temperamental individuality in peer and family relations (Lerner et al., 2003), and models linking the developmental assets of youth and communities in order to understand positive youth development (Benson, 2006; Damon, 2004).

A fourth and related reason for the focus by developmental scientists on the study of the adolescent period arose because of the growing emphasis on developmental systems theoretical models. By the end of this second phase in the study of adolescence (during the second half of the 1990s), these dynamic, developmental systems models were regarded as defining the cutting edge of theory in developmental science (Damon & Lerner, 2006, 2008). The multiple individual and contextual transitions into, throughout, and out of the adolescent period involve the major institutions of society (e.g., family, peers, schools, the workplace, and the neighborhood or community). As such, the study of the individual's relations to these contexts engaged scholars interested in the dynamics of both ecological and individual levels of organization. Focus on adolescents' varied relations across the ecology of human development afforded a rich opportunity for understanding the nature of multilevel systemic change.

Finally, there was also a practical reason for the growing importance of adolescence in the broader field of developmental science: As noted by Steinberg and Morris (2001), the longitudinal samples of many developmental scientists who had been studying infancy or childhood had aged into adolescence. Applied developmental scientists were also drawn to the study of adolescents because of the historically unprecedented sets of challenges to the healthy development of adolescents that arose during the latter decades of the twentieth century (Dryfoos, 1990; Lerner, 2007). In addition, scholars became engaged in the study of adolescents because of interests in age groups other than adolescents! For example, interest in infants often entailed the study of teenage mothers, and interest in middle and old age frequently entailed the study of the "middle generation squeeze," wherein the adult children of aged parents cared for their own parents while simultaneously raising their own adolescent children (Steinberg & Steinberg, 1994).

The Emerging Structure of the Field of Adolescent Development

The scholarly activity that emerged at about the close of the 1970s was both a product and a producer of a burgeoning network of scholars from multiple disciplines. In 1981, the late Herschel Thornburg launched a series of biennial meetings (called the "Conference on Adolescent Research") at the University of Arizona. During these meetings (which occurred also in 1983 and 1985), the idea for a new scholarly society, the Society for Research on Adolescence (SRA), was born. The first meeting of the SRA was held in Madison, Wisconsin, in 1986, and Thornburg was elected the first president of the organization.

Across more than the next two decades, with biennial conventions in Alexandria, Virginia (1988); Atlanta (1990); Washington (1992); San Diego (1994); Boston (1996); again in San Diego (1998); Chicago (2000); New Orleans (2002); Baltimore (2004); San Francisco (2006); and again Chicago (2008), and through the leadership of the SRA presidents that succeeded Thornburg—John P. Hill, Anne C. Petersen, E. Mavis Hetherington, Sanford M. Dornbusch, Jeanne Brooks-Gunn, Stuart T. Hauser, Laurence Steinberg, W. Andrew Collins, Jacquelynne Eccles, Elizabeth Susman, Vonnie McLoyd, and Reed Larson—the organization and the field it represented flourished. Between 1986 and 2008, attendance at SRA biennial meetings rose from a few hundred to nearly 2,000. The Society launched its own scholarly journal in 1991, the *Journal of Research on Adolescence* (Lerner, 1991), grew from approximately 400 members in 1986 to more than 1,200 members in 2008, and attracted disciplinary representation from scholars and practitioners in psychology, sociology, education, family studies, social work, medicine, psychiatry, criminology, and nursing.

Impetus to this growth in scholarly interest in the study of adolescence also was stimulated by the publication in 1980 of the first handbook for the field. Edited by Joseph Adelson (1980), the *Handbook of Adolescent Psychology* was published as part of the Wiley Series on Personality Processes. The volume reflected the emerging multidisciplinary interest in the field (with chapters discussing levels of organization ranging from biology through history, including an interesting historical chapter on youth movements), the growing interest in systems models of adolescent development (e.g., in the chapters by Elder, 1980, and by Petersen & Taylor, 1980), the importance of longitudinal methodology (Livson & Peskin, 1980), and the increasing interest in diversity (i.e., there was a five-chapter section on "Variations in Adolescence"). Importantly, as reflected in several chapters on the problems of adolescence, there was still ample representation in the volume of the deficit view of adolescence. Nevertheless, the 1980 *Handbook* included information pertinent to normative development and to developmental plasticity, that is, to the potential for systematic change across development—change that, within developmental systems models, was regarded to derive from individual–context relations. Finally, presaging an emphasis on positive youth development that would crystallize during the third phase in the history of the field (Damon, 2004; Lerner, 2005, 2007), there were several chapters that discussed the positive individual and social features of youth development.

The publication of a handbook, the organization of a successful scholarly society, and the initiation of that society's scholarly journal all underscored the growing interest in and the scientific maturity of research on adolescent development. This intellectual milieu and the scholarly opportunities it provided attracted a broad range of scholars to the field, some for reasons that had little to do with adolescence per se, but others because they came to see themselves as experts on the second decade of life. By the mid-1980s, a growing cadre of scientists would identify themselves as adolescent developmentalists.

The Study of Adolescence as a Sample Case for Understanding Plasticity and Diversity in Development

Scholars interested primarily in the instantiation of developmental processes within other periods of the life span (e.g., infancy; Easterbrooks & Graham, 1999; or adult development and aging; Brim, 1966; Nesselroade & Baltes, 1974) or in disciplines other than developmental psychology (e.g., life course sociology; Burton, 1990; Elder, 1974, 1980) became adolescent developmentalists as well. This attraction inheres in the "window" that the period provides to understanding how development, at any point across the life span, involves the relations of diverse and active individuals and diverse, active, and multitiered ecologies (Bronfenbrenner, 1979, 2005; Bronfenbrenner & Morris, 2006).

As suggested by Steinberg and Morris (2001), the one scientific concern that arguably was most significant in transforming the field of adolescent development beyond a focus on this single developmental period into an exemplar for understanding the breadth of the human life span was the emerging focus within developmental science on the ecology of human development (e.g., Bronfenbrenner, 1979, 2005; Bronfenbrenner & Morris, 2006). The integrated, designed, and natural ecology was of interest because its study was regarded as holding the key to understanding the system of relations between individuals and contexts that is at the core of the study of human development and to providing evidence that theories about the character of interactions within the developmental system (e.g., Collins et al., 2000; Horowitz, 2000; Gottlieb, 1997, 1998; Gottlieb et al., 2006; Thelen & Smith, 2006) were more useful in accounting for the variance in human ontogeny than theories whose grounding is exclusively nature (e.g., behavioral genetic or sociobiological; e.g., Plomin, 2000; Rowe, 1994) or exclusively nurture (e.g., social learning or functional analysis; Gewirtz & Stingle, 1968; McCandless, 1970).

A second set of broader issues that engaged developmental science in the study of adolescence pertained to understanding the bases, parameters, and limits of the plasticity of human development (which, as we have noted, reflects the potential across ontogeny for systematic change in the structure or function of attributes of the individual). The presence of plasticity across the life span legitimates an optimistic view about the potential for interventions into the course of life to enhance human development. In the second phase of the history of the field, the focus on plasticity encouraged growth in scientific activity in the application of developmental science to improve life outcomes, and gave impetus to the idea that positive development could be promoted among all people (Lerner, Fisher, & Weinberg, 2000) and, in regard to the adolescent period, among diverse youth (Lerner, 2005).

This idea of "positive youth development" (PYD) flourished in the third phase of the history of this field. That is, because plasticity means that the particular instances of human development found within a given sample or period of time are not necessarily representative of the diversity of development that might potentially be observed under different conditions, the PYD perspective is based on the belief that the potential for plasticity among all youth constitutes a fundamental resource for healthy development; if supportive families, schools, communities, programs, and policies could be created for youth, their potential for plasticity could be actualized as change in positive directions (chapter 14, this volume).

Finally, while the coalescing of developmental scientists interested in positive youth development would not occur until the third phase of the history of the field, within the second phase developmentalists pursuing an interest in the developmental system and the plasticity in ontogenetic change that it promoted recognized the need to develop and deploy methods that could simultaneously study changes in (at least a subset of) the multiple levels of organization involved in the development of diverse individuals and contexts. Accordingly, multivariate longitudinal designs were promoted as key to the study of the relatively plastic developmental system, as were the development of empirical tools, such as change-sensitive measures, sophisticated data analysis techniques, and strategies such as triangulation of observations within and across both quantitative and qualitative domains of inquiry.

Defining Features of the Study of Adolescence During Its Second Phase

Three defining features of the second phase of the scientific history of adolescent development are worth noting. First, during its second phase, the empirical study of adolescence emerged as a "relational" field of inquiry. That is, it became an area of scholarship wherein, implicitly (e.g., Block, 1971; Mussen & Bouterline Young, 1964) or, at times, explicitly

(e.g., Nesselroade & Baltes, 1974), the key unit of analysis in understanding the development of the person was his or her relation with both more molecular (e.g., biological) and more molar (social group, cultural, and historical) levels of organization (Overton, 2006). In such a relational frame, no one level of organization was seen as the "prime mover" of development.

A second distinctive feature of the field of adolescence within this second phase derived from its relational character. The confluence of the multiple levels of organization involved in the developmental system provide the structural and functional bases of plasticity and of the inevitable and substantively significant emergence of systematic individual differences; that is, such individuality serves as a key basis of the person's ability to act as an agent in his or her own development (Brandtstädter, 2006; Lerner, 2002). Accordingly, the field of adolescence has become an exemplar within the broader study of human development for the study of individual differences and for the person-centered approach to research on human development (Magnusson, 1999a, 1999b; Magnusson & Stattin, 2006).

Third, although there remains a focus within the contemporary adolescent literature on problems of this developmental period (Steinberg & Morris, 2001), the focus on plasticity, diversity, and individual agency—and the strength or capacity of an adolescent to influence his or her development for better or for worse—means that problematic outcomes of adolescent development are now regarded as just one of a larger array of outcomes (e.g., Hamburg, 1974; Hamburg, 1992). Indeed, it is this plasticity that provides the theoretical basis of the view that all young people possess strengths or, more simply, the potential for positive development (Damon, 2004; Damon & Gregory, 2003).

In sum, the second phase in the scientific study of adolescence arose in the early to mid-1970s, as developmental scientists began to make use of the burgeoning empirical research on adolescents; that is, because this work involved the study of both individual and contextual variation, developmental scientists began to see that the adolescent years provided a "natural developmental laboratory" for elucidating issues of interest across the entire life span (Petersen, 1988). Indeed, while, at the beginning of the 1970s, the study of adolescence—like the comedian Rodney Dangerfield—"got no respect," the reliance on adolescence research to inform fundamental questions in developmental science about how links between diverse individuals and changing contexts textured the course of change across individuals, families, and generations, research on adolescent development began to emerge as a dominant force in developmental science. By the end of the 1970s, the study of adolescence had finally come of age.

To help place this turning point in the context of the actual lives of the scientists involved in these events, it may be useful to note that the professional careers of the editors of this *Handbook* began just as this transition was beginning to take place. Across our own professional lifetimes, then, the editors of this *Handbook* have witnessed a sea change in scholarly regard for the study of adolescent development. Among those scholars whose own careers have begun more recently, the magnitude of this transformation is probably hard to grasp. To those of us with gray hair, however, the change has been nothing short of astounding. At the beginning of our careers, adolescent development was a minor topic within developmental science, one that was of a level of importance to merit only the publication of an occasional research article within prime developmental journals or minimal representation on the program of major scientific meetings. Now, about four decades later, the study of adolescent development is a distinct and major field within developmental science, one that plays a central role in informing, and, through vibrant collaborations with scholars having other scientific specialties, being informed by other areas of focus.

In essence, then, the study of adolescence in its second phase was characterized by an interest in developmental plasticity among diverse youth. Because of this focus, interest also arose in the application of science to real-world problems, a focus that would burgeon in the next phase of the history of the field. Finally, however, the second phase also was marked by the development and use of more nuanced and powerful developmental methods, ones aimed at providing sensitivity to the collection and analysis of longitudinal data pertinent to the multiple levels of organization involved in adolescent development (e.g., Baltes, Reese, & Nesselroade, 1977; Baltes & Schaie, 1973). Together, these intellectual facets of the second phase in the study of adolescent development created the scientific bases for the emergence of a subsequent phase, one that—at this writing—characterizes the contemporary status of the field.

THE THIRD PHASE OF THE SCIENTIFIC STUDY OF ADOLESCENCE

When we wrote the opening chapter of the second edition of the *Handbook of Adolescent Psychology*, this third stage seemed to have just crystallized. Now, as a consequence of the unprecedented growth in theoretically informed research about the adolescent period, the vantage point of writing the opening chapter of the third edition of this work, albeit only six years later, enables us to see clearly that the field is unequivocally embedded within this third period of its growth, one that we have noted involves burgeoning interest in applied developmental science, that is, in evidence-based applications of research about adolescent development. Nevertheless, as we have explained, the roots of this third phase were established within the second phase, by some of the scientific innovators whose work in this phase we have noted.

For instance, more than a third of a century ago, Bronfenbrenner (1974) explained the importance of a science of development that involved the full and bidirectional collaboration between the producers and consumers of scientific knowledge. In turn, Hamburg (1992;

Hamburg & Takanishi, 1996) proposed that the quality of life of adolescents, and their future contributions to civil society, could be enhanced through collaboration among scholars, policy makers, and key social institutions, for instance, community-based youth-serving organizations (e.g., 4-H, Boys and Girls Clubs, scouting), schools, and the media. In our view, Hamburg's (1992; Hamburg & Takanishi, 1996) vision has been actualized.

The idea that the adolescent period provides the ideal time within life to study the bases of positive human development frames what has become a defining feature of the field in its current, third phase. As shown in Figure 1.1, the study of adolescent development is today characterized by a synthetic interest in basic and applied concerns about youth development.

In sum, in what has emerged as the third phase in the history of the scientific study of adolescence, the field of adolescent development serves as an exemplar of developmental science that is of service to policy makers and practitioners seeking to advance civil society and promote positive development (Lerner, 2004, 2007). Indeed, as evidenced by the contributions of this third edition of the *Handbook*, we are in a phase of science defined by theoretically framed, research-based applications to programs and policies that advance understanding of the basic, individual–context relational process of adolescent development and, as well, that enables policy makers and practitioners to collaborate with scientists to enhance the course of development. Evidence-based practice, policy, and advocacy aimed at understanding the bases of, and as well promoting, positive, healthy development among all youth may be the hallmark of this third period.

CONCLUSIONS: ADOLESCENCE AS A FIELD OF SCIENTIST–PRACTITIONER–POLICY MAKER COLLABORATION

The chapters in this *Handbook* both reflect and extend the emphases on individual–context

relations, developmental systems, plasticity, diversity, longitudinal methodology, and application that were crystallized and integrated within the second phase of the development of the scientific study of adolescence and that, in turn, are being extended, both quantitatively and qualitatively, in its current, third phase. As evident within each of the chapters in this *Handbook*, the study of adolescence today represents the exemplar within developmental science of excellent conceptual and empirical work being undertaken with a collaborative orientation to making a contribution both to scholarship and to society.

These collaborations, involving the understanding and support of young people, are vital endeavors – for both science and society. The future of civil society in the world rests on the young. Adolescents represent at any point in history the generational cohort that must next be prepared to assume the quality of leadership of self, family, community, and society that will maintain and improve human life. Scientists have a vital role to play in enhancing, through the generation of basic and applied knowledge, the probability that adolescents will become fully engaged citizens who are capable of, and committed to, making these contributions.

The chapters in this *Handbook* demonstrate that high-quality scientific work on adolescence is in fact being generated at levels of study ranging from the biological through the historical and sociocultural. Above all, this *Handbook* demonstrates that the study of adolescent development at its best both informs and is informed by the concerns of communities, practitioners, and policy makers. It is our hope that we have assembled the best information possible to be used to promote and advocate for the healthy and positive development of young people everywhere and to advance developmental science.

REFERENCES

Adelson, J. (Ed.). (1980). *Handbooks of adolescent psychology.* New York: John Wiley & Sons.

Baltes, P. B. (1979). Life-span developmental psychology: Some converging observations on history and theory. In P. B. Baltes &

O. G. Brim, Jr. (Eds.), *Life-span development and behavior*, Vol. *2*, New York: Academic Press.

Baltes, P. B., Reese, H. W., & Nesselroade, J. R. (1977). *Life-span developmental psychology: Introduction to research methods.* Monterey, CA: Brooks/Cole.

Baltes, P. B., & Schaie, K. W. (1973). On life-span developmental research paradigms. In P. B. Baltes & K. W. Schaie (Eds.). *Life-span developmental psychology: Personality and socialization* (pp. 365–395). New York: Academic Press.

Bandura, A. (1964). The stormy decade: Fact or fiction? *Psychology in the School, 1*, 224–231.

Benson, P. L. (2006). All kids are our kids: What communities must do to raise caring and responsible children and adolescents (2nd ed). San Francisco: Jossey-Bass.

Block, J. (1971). *Lives through time.* Berkeley, CA: Bancroft.

Boring, E. G. (1929). *A history of experimental psychology.* New York: Century.

Brandtstädter, J. (2006). Action perspectives on human development. In R. M. Lerner (Ed.), *Handbook of child psychology*, Vol. 1: *Theoretical models of human development* (6th ed.; pp. 516–568). Editors-in-chief: W. Damon & R. M. Lerner. Hoboken, NJ: John Wiley & Sons.

Brim, O. G., Jr. (1966). Socialization through the life cycle. In O. G. Brim, Jr. & S. Wheeler (Eds.), *Socialization after childhood: Two essays* (pp. 1–49). New York: John Wiley & Sons.

Bronfenbrenner, U. (1974). Developmental research, public policy, and the ecology of childhood. *Child Development, 45*, 1–5.

Bronfenbrenner, U. (1979). *The ecology of human development: Experiments by nature and design.* Cambridge, MA: Harvard University Press.

Bronfenbrenner, U. (2005). *Making human beings human.* Thousand Oaks, CA: Sage.

Bronfenbrenner, U., & Morris, P. A., (2006). The bioecological model of human development. In R. M. Lerner (Ed.), *Handbook of child psychology*, Vol. 1: *Theoretical models of human development* (6th ed.; pp. 793–828). Editors-in-chief: W. Damon & R. M. Lerner. Hoboken, NJ: John Wiley & Sons.

Burton, L. M. (1990). Teenage childbearing as an alternative life-course strategy in multigeneration black families. *Human Nature, l*, 123–143.

Collins, W. A., Maccoby, E. E., Steinberg, L., Hetherington, E. M., & Bornstein, M. H. (2000). Contemporary research on parenting: The case for nature and nurture. *American Psychologist, 55*, 218–232.

Damon, W. (2004). What is positive youth development? *Annals of the American Academy of Political and Social Science, 591*, 13–24.

Damon, W., & Gregory, A. (2003). Bringing in a new era in the field of youth development. In R. M. Lerner & P. L. Benson (Eds.), *Developmental assets and asset-building communities: Implications for research, policy, and practice* (pp. 47–64). Norwell, MA: Kluwer Academic Publishers.

Damon, W., & Lerner, R. M. (Eds.). (2006). *Handbook of Child Psychology* (6th ed.). Hoboken, NJ: John Wiley & Sons.

Damon, W., & Lerner, R. M. (2008). *Child and adolescent development: An advanced course.* Hoboken, NJ: John Wiley & Sons.

Dixon, R. A., & Nesselroade, J. R. (1983). Pluralism and correlational analysis in development psychology: Historical commonalities. In E. M. Lerner (Ed.), *Developmental psychology: Historical and philosophical perspectives* (pp. 113–145). Hillsdale, NJ: Lawrence Erlbaum.

Douvan, J. D., & Adelson, J. (1966). *The adolescent experience.* New York: John Wiley & Sons.

Dryfoos, J. G. (1990). *Adolescents at risk: Prevalence and prevention.* New York: Oxford University Press.

Easterbrooks, M. A., & Graham, C. A. (1999). Security of attachment and parenting: Homeless and low-income housed mothers and infants. *American Journal of Orthopsychiatry, 69*, 337–346.

Elder, G. H. (1974). *Children of the Great Depression.* Chicago: University of Chicago Press.

Elder, G. H., Jr. (1980). Adolescence in historical perspective. In J. Adelson (Ed.), *Handbooks of adolescent psychology* (pp. 3–46). New York: John Wiley & Sons.

Elder, G. H., Jr., & Shanahan, M. J. (2006). The life course and human development. In R. M. Lerner (Ed.). *Handbook of child psychology*, Vol. *1*: *Theoretical models of human development* (6th ed.; pp. 665–715). Editors-in-chief: W. Damon & R. M. Lerner. Hoboken, NJ: John Wiley & Sons.

Erikson, E. H. (1950). *Childhood and society.* New York: Norton.

Erikson, E. H. (1959). Identity and the life cycle. *Psychological Issues, 1*, 50–100.

Erikson, E. H. (1968). *Identity, youth, and crisis.* New York: Norton.

Freud, A. (1969). Adolescence as a developmental disturbance. In G. Caplan & S. Lebovici (Eds.), *Adolescence* (pp. 5–10). New York: Basic Books.

Gewirtz, J. L., & Stingle, K. G. (1968). Learning of generalized imitation as the basis for identification. *Psychological Review, 75*, 374–397.

Gottlieb, G. (1997). *Synthesizing nature–nurture: Prenatal roots of instinctive behavior.* Mahwah, NJ: Laurence Erlbaum.

Gottlieb, G. (1998). Normally occurring environmental and behavioral influences on gene activity: From central dogma to probabilistic epigenesis. *Psychological Review, 105*, 792–802.

Gottlieb, G., Wahlsten, D., & Lickliter, R. (2006). The significance of biology for human development: A developmental psychobiological systems perspective. In R. M. Lerner (Ed.), *Handbook of child psychology*, Vol. 1: *Theoretical models of human development* (6th ed.; pp. 210–257). Editors-in-chief: W. Damon & R. M. Lerner. Hoboken, NJ: John Wiley & Sons.

Hall, G. S. (1904). *Adolescence: Its psychology and its relations to physiology, anthropology, sociology, sex, crime, religion, and education*, Vols. 1 & 2. New York: Appleton.

Haeckel, E. (1868). *Naturliche schopfungsgeschichte.* Berlin: Georg Reimer.

Haeckel, E. (1891). *Anthropogenie oder entwickelungsgeschichte des menschen* (4th rev. and enlarged ed.). Leipzig: Wilhelm Engelmann.

Hamburg, B. (1974). Early adolescence: A specific and stressful stage of the life cycle. In G. Coelho, D. A. Hamburg, & J. E. Adams (Eds.), *Coping and adaptation* (pp. 101–125). New York: Basic Books.

Hamburg, D. A. (1992). *Today's children: Creating a future for a generation in crisis.* New York: Times Books.

Hamburg, D. A., & Takanishi, R. (1996). Great transitions: Preparing American youth for the 21st century—The role of research. *Journal of Research on Adolescence, 6*, 379–396.

Hirsch, J. (2004). Uniqueness, diversity, similarity, repeatability, and heritability. In C. Garcia Coll, E. Bearer, & R. M. Lerner (Eds.), *Nature and nurture: The complex interplay of genetic and environmental influences on human behavior and development* (pp. 127–138). Mahwah, NJ: Lawrence Erlbaum.

Horowitz, F. D. (2000). Child development and the PITS: Simple questions, complex answers, and developmental theory. *Child Development, 71*, 1–10.

Jones, M. C., & Bayley, N. (1950). Physical maturing among boys as related to behavior. *Journal of Educational Psychology, 41*, 129–148.

Lerner, R. M. (1978). Nature, nurture, and dynamic interactionism. *Human Development, 21*, 1–20.

Lerner, R. M. (1991). Editorial: Continuities and changes in the scientific study of adolescence. *Journal of Research on Adolescence, 1*, 1–5.

Lerner, R. M. (2002). *Concepts and theories of human development* (3rd ed.). Mahwah, NJ: Lawrence Erlbaum.

Lerner, R. M. (2004). *Liberty: Thriving and civic engagement among America's youth.* Thousand Oaks, CA: Sage.

Lerner, R. M. (2005, September). *Promoting positive youth development: Theoretical and empirical bases.* White paper prepared for the Workshop on the Science of Adolescent Health and Development, National Research Council/Institute of Medicine. Washington, DC: National Academies of Science.

Lerner, R. M. (2007). *The good teen: Rescuing adolescents from the myths of the storm and stress years.* New York: Crown.

Lerner, R. M., Anderson, P. M., Balsano, A. B., Dowling, E. M., & Bobek, D. L. (2003). Applied developmental science of positive human development. In R. M. Lerner, M. A. Easterbrooks, & J. Mistry (Eds.), *Handbook of psychology: Vol. 6, Developmental psychology* (pp. 535–558). Editor-in-chief: I. B. Weiner. New York: John Wiley & Sons.

Lerner, R. M., Fisher, C. B., & Weinberg, R. A. (2000). Toward a science for and of the people: Promoting civil society through the application of developmental science. *Child Development, 71*, 11–20.

Lerner, R. M., & Galambos, N. (1998). Adolescent development: Challenges and opportunities for research, programs, and policies. In J. T. Spence (Ed.), *Annual Review of Psychology* (Vol. 49; pp. 413–446). Palo Alto, CA: Annual Reviews.

Lerner, R. M., & Spanier, G. B. (1980). *Adolescent development: A life-span perspective.* New York: McGraw-Hill.

Lerner, R. M., & Steinberg, L. (Eds.). (2004). *Handbook of adolescent psychology.* New York: John Wiley & Sons.

Livson, N., & Peskin, H. (1980). Perspectives on adolescence from longitudinal research. In J. Adelson (Ed.), *Handbook of adolescent psychology* (pp. 47–98). New York: John Wiley & Sons.

Magnusson, D. (1999a). Holistic interactionism: A perspective for research on personality development. In L. A. Pervin & O. P. John (Eds.), *Handbook of personality: Theory and research* (2nd ed.; pp. 219–247). New York: Guilford Press.

Magnusson, D. (1999b). On the individual: A person-oriented approach to developmental research. *European Psychologist, 4*, 205–218.

Magnusson, D., & Stattin, H. (2006). The person in the environment: Towards a general model for scientific inquiry. In R. M. Lerner (Ed.), *Handbook of child psychology*, Vol. 1: *Theoretical models of human development* (6th ed.; pp. 400–464). Editors-in-chief: W. Damon & R. M. Lerner. Hoboken, NJ: John Wiley & Sons.

Marcia, J. E. (1980). Identity in adolescence. In J. Adelson (Ed.), *Handbook of adolescent psychology*, (pp. 159–187) New York: John Wiley & Sons.

McCandless, R. R. (1961). *Children and adolescents.* New York: Holt, Rinehart, & Winston.

McCandless, B. R. (1970). *Adolescents.* Hinsdale, IL: Dryden Press.

Mussen, P. H., & Bouterline Young, H. (1964). Personality characteristics of psychically advanced and retarded adolescents in Italy and the United States. *Vita Humana, 7*, 186–200.

Mussen, R. H., & Jones, M. C. (1957). Self-conceptions, motivations, and interpersonal attitudes of late- and early-maturing boys. *Child Development, 28*, 242–256.

Muuss, R. E. (1990). *Adolescent behavior and society: A book of readings* (4th ed.). New York: McGraw-Hill.

Nesselroade, J. R., & Baltes, P. B. (1974). Adolescent personality development and historical changes: 1970–72. *Monographs of the Society for Research in Child Development, 39*.

Offer, D. (1969). *The psychological world of the teen-ager.* New York: Basic Books.

Overton, W. F. (1973). On the assumptive base of the nature–nurture controversy: Additive versus interactive conceptions. *Human Development, 16*, 74–89.

Overton, W. F. (2006). Developmental psychology: Philosophy, concepts, methodology. In R. M. Lerner (Ed.), *Handbook of child psychology*, Vol. 1: *Theoretical models of human development.* (6th ed.; pp. 18–88). Editors-in-chief: W. Damon & R. M. Lerner. Hoboken, NJ: John Wiley & Sons.

Petersen, A. C. (1988). Adolescent development. In M. R. Rosenzweig (Ed.), *Annual review of psychology* (Vol. 39; pp. 583–607). Palo Alto, CA: Annual Reviews.

Petersen, A. C., & Taylor, B. (1980). The biological approach to adolescence: Biological change and psychological adaptation. In J. Adelson (Ed.), *Handbook of adolescent psychology* (pp. 117–155). New York: John Wiley & Sons.

Piaget, J. (1969). The intellectual development of the adolescent. In G. Caplan & S. Lebovici (Eds.), *Adolescence: Psychosocial perspective* (pp. 22–26). New York: Basic Books.

Piaget, J. (1970). Piaget's theory. In P. H. Mussen (Ed.), *Carmichael's manual of child psychology* (3rd ed., Vol. 1; pp. 703–723). New York: John Wiley & Sons.

Piaget, J. (1972). Intellectual evolution from adolescence to adulthood. *Human Development, 15*, 1–12.

Plomin, R. (2000). Behavioural genetics in the 21st century. *International Journal of Behavioral Development, 24*, 30–34.

Riegel, K. F. (1975). Toward a dialectical theory of human development. *Human Development, 18*, 50–64.

Riegel, K. F. (1976). The dialectics of human development. *American Psychologist, 31*, 689–700.

Rowe, D. C. (1994). *The limits of family influence: Genes, experience, and behavior.* New York: Guilford Press.

Sameroff, A. J. (1983). Developmental systems: Contexts and evolution. In W. Kessen (Ed.), *Handbook of child psychology, Vol. 1: History, theory, and methods* (pp. 237–294). New York: John Wiley & Sons.

Steinberg, L. (1996). *Beyond the classroom: Why school reform has failed and what parents need to do.* New York: Simon & Schuster.

Steinberg, L., & Lerner, R. M. (2004). The scientific study of adolescent development: A brief history. *Journal of Early Adolescence, 23*, 45–54.

Steinberg, L., & Levine, A. (1997). *You and your adolescent: A parent's guide for ages 10 to 20.* New York: HarperPerennial.

Steinberg, L., & Morris, A. S. (2001). Adolescent development. In S. T. Fiske, D. L.Schacter, & C. Zahn-Waxler (Eds.), *Annual review of psychology* (Vol. 52; pp. 83–110). Palo Alto, CA: Annual Reviews.

Steinberg, L., & Steinberg, W. (1994). *Crossing paths: How your child's adolescence triggers your own crisis.* New York: Simon & Schuster.

Thelen, E., & Smith, L. B. (2006). Dynamic systems theories. In R. M. Lerner (Ed.). *Theoretical models of human development.* Volume *1* of *Handbook of Child Psychology* (6th ed., pp. 258–312). Editors-in-chief: W. Damon & R. M. Lerner. Hoboken, NJ: John Wiley & Sons.

Thorndike, E. L. (1904). The newest psychology. *Educational Review, 28*, 217–227.

White, S. H. (1968). The learning-maturation controversy: Hall to Hull. *Merrill-Palmer Quarterly, 14*, 187–196.

CHAPTER 2

Modeling Longitudinal Data from Research on Adolescence

TODD D. LITTLE, NOEL A. CARD, KRISTOPHER J. PREACHER, AND ELIZABETH McCONNELL

The study of adolescent development generally relies on two types of study, cross-sectional and longitudinal. Cross-sectional studies are quite common and involve comparing two or more cohorts of youth who are assessed at a single, concurrent measurement occasion. Longitudinal studies, in contrast, involve collecting data at two or more occasions, with the interval between occasions allowing for some sort of meaningful change to occur. As we describe next, there are several advantages associated with longitudinal designs and the analysis of longitudinal data.

ADVANTAGES OF LONGITUDINAL DATA

Longitudinal data offer several advantages over cross-sectional data in the study of adolescent development. The first advantage is that longitudinal data allow us to draw more valid conclusions regarding developmental changes in levels (i.e., means) and processes (i.e., associations) of phenomena than can be drawn with cross-sectional data. Researchers may try to infer such changes from concurrent data collected from participants over a

developmental range (e.g., across age from early, middle, and late adolescence). However, in cross-sectional designs, age effects are confounded with cohort effects, leading to ambiguity in interpretation (Baltes, 1968; Schaie, 1965). For instance, if concurrent data reveal that a phenomenon is more prevalent or frequent among older than middle adolescents and among middle than early adolescents, these differences *may* be due to developmental differences. However, they also may be due to cohort differences, such that those born earlier (i.e., the late adolescents) experience different sociohistorical inputs and exhibit higher levels of the phenomenon than those born later (i.e., the early adolescents). With longitudinal data, we can hold constant the cohort effect so that changes can be attributed to developmental differences (see Baltes, 1968; Schaie, 1965). Some longitudinal designs (i.e., accelerated longitudinal designs, described later) can be used to identify and separate both developmental and cohort effects.

A second advantage of a longitudinal study is that it allows for inferences regarding various estimates of the cross-time relations among

Correspondence regarding this chapter should be addressed to Todd D. Little (yhat@ku.edu), Department of Psychology, University of Kansas, 1415 Jayhawk Blvd., Lawrence, KS 66045-7555; Noel A. Card (ncard@email.arizona.edu), Division of Family Studies and Human Development, University of Arizona, Tucson, AZ 85721-0033; or Kristopher J. Preacher (preacher@ku.edu), Department of Psychology, University of Kansas, 1415 Jayhawk Blvd., Lawrence, KS 66045-7555.

This work was supported in part by grants from the NIH to the University of Kansas Intellectual and Developmental Disabilities Research Center (5 P30 HD002528). Its contents are solely the responsibility of the authors and do not necessarily represent the official views of the NIH.

a set of variables. These cross-time relations have many forms, including stability, stationarity, and equilibrium of the individual differences associations, as well as mean changes and intraindividual differences. Generally speaking, *stability* refers to the strength of the relation between the relative standing of a person on the same construct measured at two or more measurement occasions. These associations are often referred to as autoregressive paths, or interindividual stability. *Stationarity* refers to whether the autoregressive paths are equal in magnitude over multiple time intervals (e.g., two or more intervals among three or more measurement occasions, assuming equal length intervals; Kenny, 1979). For example, if the stability coefficient is of the same magnitude between Times 1 and 2 and Times 2 and 3, stationarity holds. A third cross-time relation of interest is the stability in the pattern of associations among two or more constructs across two or more measurement occasions. Termed *equilibrium*, this cross-time relation refers to the equality or homogeneity of the within-time covariances (Cole & Maxwell, 2003; Dwyer, 1983; Kessler & Greenberg, 1981).

Each of these three terms (stability, stationarity, and equilibrium) refers to across-time associations among constructs; however, they do not address the across-time similarity or change in mean levels of a construct (i.e., is the typical developmental trend one of increase or decrease in a construct across adolescence?). To address this issue, we need to consider within-person, or intraindividual, stability or change across time. Fully understanding these different conceptualizations of stability can be confusing, so we discuss these further in the context of panel models and growth curve models below. Regardless of the form considered, knowing the degree of stability is important because it helps us understand whether certain phenomena are transient (less stable) or persistent (more stable) across adolescent development. The key point here is that addressing any conceptualization of stability versus change requires longitudinal data.

The third advantage of a longitudinal study is that it allows us to make qualified inferences regarding the cause–effect relations among constructs. Although causality can be inferred only within properly conducted experimental designs, it is less often recognized that such designs are necessarily longitudinal in that some time must elapse between the experimental manipulation and measured outcome. As Gollob and Reichardt (1987) stated simply: "Causes take time to exert their effects" (p. 81). For many aspects of adolescent development, experimental manipulation is difficult or not ethically possible, and in these situations longitudinal naturalistic research provides our best basis for inference regarding directions of influence. These issues will be further discussed later in this chapter (in the section on panel designs), but the point here is that directions of causal influence from nonexperimental data can be evaluated legitimately only within longitudinal designs.

A fourth advantage of a longitudinal study is the ability to model the processes through which effects are expressed over time. With multiple observation occasions, both direct and indirect pathways of influence can be modeled and, in multivariate growth curve models, dynamic associations can be modeled. Often, the patterns of indirect influence over time provide the most meaningful information for theoretical consideration. For example, Cole and Maxwell (2003) describe how indirect processes of associations over time, when equilibrium of within time associations is achieved, allows one to make strong inferences of mediation (we discuss this model in more detail in the section on mediation and moderation below). Similarly, Greenwood and Little (2008) describe how the regression discontinuity design for intervention evaluations, when coupled with longitudinal designs, allows inferences of intervention effectiveness that are as valid and strong as those obtained with the gold standard of the randomized clinical trial (which also incorporates longitudinal data in its inferential arsenal; see Shadish, Cook, & Campbell, 2002).

Given the value of longitudinal data, it is not surprising that they are frequently used in developmental research. Card and Little (2007a) examined the prevalence of longitudinal designs in six premier developmental journals during a one-year publication period, finding that only 41% of studies published in these journals analyzed longitudinal data. Many developmental journals give preference to longitudinal studies, and at least one of the leading journals of adolescent development, *Journal of Research on Adolescence*, explicitly requests that submitted manuscripts include analyses of longitudinal data. Although such policies may dismiss the value of many cross-sectional studies, and we certainly do not want to deemphasize the value of a well-conceived and executed concurrent study, the advantages of longitudinal analyses highlight the merits of collecting and analyzing longitudinal data. However, the advantages and benefits of longitudinal data can be realized only if the theoretical rationale, measurement operations, and statistical model are coordinated.

Rationale for Longitudinal Data

Notwithstanding the many advantages of longitudinal data, we emphasize that researchers should not collect longitudinal data just to get longitudinal data. Too often, longitudinal data are collected with little thought devoted to the rationale, and lack of forethought can lead to poor design decisions and wastes precious resources on collecting data that are unable to deliver the sought-for answers. In studying adolescence, longitudinal data are very useful for understanding mechanisms of change and processes of influence as well as the interplay of the adolescent and the context (see Card, Little, & Bovaird, 2007; Little, Bovaird, & Card, 2007). However, studies that collect large batteries of questionnaire protocols annually or semiannually often lack correspondence with either a well-considered theoretical model or the needs of the underlying statistical model. In fact, we will consistently echo Collins's (2006) call for integrating

the theoretical model, the temporal design, and the statistical model (see also Ram & Grimm, 2007).

The kinds of answers that state-of-the-science methods can glean from longitudinal data are only as good as the theoretical rationale and design of the study itself. A number of considerations must go into planning for longitudinal data. In the next section, we highlight a number of considerations that are particularly relevant to understanding developmental mechanisms and processes in adolescence.

DESIGN AND DATA CONSIDERATIONS

In this section, we will discuss a number of important design and data issues that need to be carefully considered before a statistical model is adopted and specified.

Design Considerations

The first critical issue, of course, is the theoretical model driving the research. As found throughout this *Handbook*, many theoretical models exist that make explicit the mechanisms and processes of change. However, many theoretical models are not sufficiently developed to provide clear guidance. Longitudinal data are best suited for testing hypotheses derived from well articulated models of change. In this regard, theory is an analyst's best friend. Key theoretical considerations that need to be addressed include: what changes, what drives change, what is the functional form of change, what mediating and/or moderating mechanism are impacting change, how quickly change occurs, and whether the available measures are sufficiently calibrated and sensitive to capture all of these features. Explicitly addressing these and related considerations in the planning stages of a study provides the optimal basis for designing a useful and informative longitudinal investigation.

Well-articulated models of change and the theoretical expectations derived from them will drive a number of key design considerations. As we describe next, some key considerations include the interval of measurement, the functional form of change, how we might represent time, several issues of measurement, and whether we will rely on manifest or latent variable analyses.

Interval of Measurement

The first issue is the interval of measurement. The vast majority of studies on adolescent development conduct annual or semiannual assessments with little thought to whether the change process under study will be captured adequately. For example, many studies of the dynamics of adolescent social development hypothesize fluid and relatively rapid transmission of influence. Measurements that do not occur at the pace of (or faster than) the change process cannot yield much meaningful information about it. Figure 2.1 illustrates the problem. Measurement intervals that do not keep pace with the change process provide, at best, a static replication of the cross-sectional information identified at a first measurement occasion. Any associations with change from one time point to the next do not reflect true change but rather are likely to reflect common contextual features associated with the timing of the measurement. For example, an annual school-based study that assesses indicators of affect at each measurement occasion (fall semester of a school year), may find modest stability of affect and may find that increases or decreases in affect are reliably predicted

across the one-year interval. Attributing causal processes to such findings is likely unwarranted because the observed associations are confounded with the context of the fall semester of a school year (i.e., beginning of new school year with new classes, teachers, and peers). The true processes of change associated with affect likely operate over much shorter intervals and the observed associations are therefore spurious.

Functional Form of Change

Another consideration is the functional form of the change process. Many theoretical models propose a functional form that is generally nonlinear in nature (e.g., initially rapid growth dampened by a deceleration with age). Globally speaking, across the life span, nonlinear change functions are likely and perhaps common. However, depending on the adequacy of the study design, the functional form of the process under study may not be captured sufficiently to model it with a nonlinear statistical model. Locally speaking, an adequate statistical model may in fact fit quite adequately as a linear function. Figure 2.2 illustrates this issue. Here, the appropriate statistical model may very well be a simple linear approximation even though the underlying theoretical model is explicitly nonlinear. In order to statistically capture the expected nonlinear nature of the growth pattern, measurements need to be taken well before and well after the expected bend of a curve. These extra measurements provide stability for estimating the "tails" accurately so that the bend can be modeled. Extra

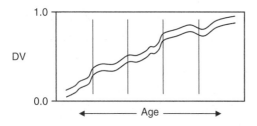

FIGURE 2.1 When measurement interval does not capture rate of change. *Note:* At a given age range, the overall nonlinear pattern can be reasonably approximated with a linear trend. If one measured across the entire age range, then a nonlinear model could be fit to the data.

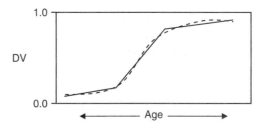

FIGURE 2.2 Comparison of local linear change and global nonlinear change.

measurements at the bend of the expected curve can also provide more stable estimates of the functional form.

However, researchers should not be dismayed if their theory suggests nonlinear growth. If they are not able to collect data at sufficient numbers of time points, their data may well be reasonably approximated with a linear trajectory. Local linear approximations can be quite powerful in capturing the information found in a narrow band of otherwise nonlinear change. However, we encourage researchers to design data collection intervals that allow one to adequately test a theoretical model that hypothesizes nonlinear growth (see e.g., Blozis, Conger, & Harring, 2007).

Representing Time

A third issue involves the unit of time used to index the developmental process. Age in years is a common index for representing developmental processes. However, age alone may not be the optimal index. Rather than automatically thinking of time in terms of age in years, we encourage adolescence researchers to consider what the true index of time is over which change occurs. Next, we offer just a few possibilities to highlight the various ways that time can be represented in longitudinal models—these are just some of a few interesting and innovative ways in which time can be conceptualized and utilized in longitudinal studies (see Wohlwill, 1973).

One alternative index of development is experiential time. This type of index of time is common in studies of childhood and adolescence in which researchers use grade in school to reflect the "time" axis. Here, the developmental changes of participants are assumed to be mostly determined by grade-related experiences and not the underlying maturational age of the adolescent. For some phenomena, this assumption is probably reasonable, particularly for academic-related outcomes. For other outcomes, grade in school may not be an optimal index of development. Other examples of experiential time include amount of experience

in extracurricular activities (e.g., first versus fourth year in club) or number of relationships (e.g., first versus later boyfriend/girlfriend), to suggest just a few.

Another alternative index of development is time to or since a key developmental episode. Puberty is a good example of a meaningful episode that has significant implications for understanding development. Here, the index of development would be time leading up to the episode (pubertal onset) and time after the episode. So, we might consider "time" as being two years before puberty, one year before, year of pubertal transition, one year after, and so on. Other relevant episodes during adolescence and emergent adulthood on which we might index time include school transitions (e.g., transition to high school, graduation from high school), moving out of the home, or marriage.

In these alternative conceptualizations of developmental processes, the chronological age of individuals can, and probably should, also be included as a context covariate. For example, research on pubertal onset has shown that early versus late onset, relative to adolescents' chronological age, has implications for adjustment (e.g., Zehr, Culbert, Sisk, & Klump, 2007). However, models of the change process prior to and following puberty that give rise to the adjustment difficulties are not possible if chronological age is used as the primary index of time. The data can be reorganized to center on the episode (e.g., pubertal onset) and how the repeated measurements before and after the episode can be used to model the dynamics of change both before and after the event. Note that such rearrangements of the data lead to a number of unobserved measurement occasions for each individual. Later, we discuss why the unobserved occasions can be effectively treated as a simple missing data problem whereby the missing information can be accurately and validly imputed.

Measurement Across Time

A fourth issue involves measurement. In this context, a number of features of measurement

TABLE 2.1   A Simple Taxonomy of the Nature of the Measured Variables Crossed with the Nature of the Latent Variables Found in General SEM Models

		Nature of the Unobserved, Latent Variables	
		Categorical	Metrical
Nature of the Observed, Manifest Variables	Categorical	Latent Transition Analysis	Latent Trait Analysis; IRT
	Metrical	Latent Class; Mixture Modeling	Latent Variable Analysis; CFA

Note: *Categorical* refers to variables that reflect nominal or polytomous categories. *Metrical* refers to variables that reflect ordinal, interval, or ratio-level properties. Many models for longitudinal data can contain more than one of these kinds of variables.

need to be considered. The first feature is the nature of the observed variable (our measures) and the nature of the latent variable (the underlying construct about which we wish to draw conclusions). Table 2.1 shows a general taxonomy of the kinds of analyses that are appropriate given the nature of the observed and latent variables. Quite often, a given project will contain a mix of nominal (or polytomous) and metrical (e.g., interval, ratio) manifest and latent variables. Mapping these measurements onto the appropriate statistical tool is important for ensuring valid conclusions. Commonly, a given study will have a combination of types of variables at both the manifest and latent levels. Most modern statistical programs can readily estimate models that contain such combinations (e.g., Muthén & Muthén, 2007), but often do so by either correcting for the restrictions of the noncontinuous measures or imposing assumptions in the estimation phase that may or may not be reasonable. Our advice is to consider carefully the nature of the variables to be collected and spend both thought and time to develop better and more precise measures. In our view, many researchers do not prepare thoroughly enough before embarking

on a study. Examining a battery of measures and attempting to improve on their fidelity of measurement, for example, would enhance the overall ability of a longitudinal study to detect change. For a list of resources on innovations in measurement, visit www.Quant.KU.edu.

A second measurement feature is the developmental appropriateness of the measures. Embretson (2007), for example, outlines some serious measurement problems that can occur when trying to model developmental change processes. When measures are not appropriately calibrated for age-related differences in the phenomenon under study, they can provide dramatically biased estimates of the true growth function. Embretson's simulations are based on the logic of item response theory (IRT). Instead of an item's being appropriate for a person of low ability or high ability, items are appropriate for persons who are more or less developed in the skill, attitude, belief, trait, or behavior that the item is intended to measure. In this regard, measurement instruments need to provide sufficient sensitivity across the low to high levels of the qualities that individuals in a study may possess. The sensitivity and appropriateness of a measure are dependent on both the developmental age of the person and the person's individual characteristics. The broader implication here is that IRT methodology should be applied much more regularly across the developmental, social, and behavioral sciences in order to evaluate the breadth of item coverage of a measure.

A related measurement issue is the homotypic versus heterotypic expression of a construct across time (Sears, 1947). In many developmental studies, the expression of the underlying construct changes over time; this changing expression of a common underlying construct is referred to as heterotypic continuity (in contrast to homotypic continuity, or the same expression of the construct across time). Many of the behaviors that indicate aggression, for example, change as the child matures through adolescence into adulthood. To account for this heterotypic continuity, it is necessary to change the measures used to assess the construct across time. However, this change should not be an all-or-nothing decision; too often, researchers implement a wholesale switch from one measurement battery to another when the participants reach an age at which the former instrument is no longer deemed developmentally appropriate. Such decisions in the design of measurement protocols can have disastrous effects on the ability to model change over time. The key problem here is the lack of a linking function to allow one to map the meaning of a score on the earlier measure to a score on the later measure. A simple remedy to this problem is to phase in the new instrument and to phase out the old. Having one or more measurement occasions in which all items (or a key subset of items) from both instruments are assessed allows one to statistically calibrate the scores across the two instruments, which then allows one to model growth trends across the measures used in a different span of the study. Here, again, IRT methodology is ideally suited to provide the calibration that would allow one to model growth in circumstances when the item pool for measuring a construct must change.

Another related issue has to do with the cross-time factorial invariance (i.e., measurement equivalence) of the constructs. In all studies that do not use latent variable structural equation modeling (SEM) procedures, factorial invariance is simply assumed. Factorial invariance refers to the idea that a construct's indicators retain their relative relation with the construct, in terms of their pattern of intercepts and factor loadings, across time (and across groups; Card & Little, 2006; Little, Card, Slegers, & Ledford, 2007; Meredith, 1993; Selig, Card, & Little, 2008; Vandenberg & Lance, 2000; Widaman & Reise, 1997). Fortunately, with SEM procedures, the assumption that the construct's relative measurement characteristics have not changed over time (i.e., factorial invariance) can be readily assessed. Demonstrating the measurement equivalence of a set of indicators over time is

critically important for the quality of generalizations that one can draw. If invariance of the loadings and the intercepts holds, then one can attribute all observed changes to changes in the latent constructs; that is, the potential confound of changes in the relative measurement properties of the items has been ruled out. If one does not establish measurement invariance, then this potential confound of changes in the measurement properties remains a very real threat to validity (Shadish et al., 2002).

Partial measurement invariance refers to the idea that one or more loadings or intercepts are not proportionally invariant over time. Although rules of thumb vary, if a reasonable number of items or indicators show invariance while a minority of items do not, one can compare and discuss changes that reflect true changes in the underlying construct (Reise, Widaman, & Pugh, 1993; Byrne, Shavelson, & Muthén, 1989). Finding noninvariance of a few of the indicators of a construct reflects an important outcome of a study that should be examined and discussed in some detail, because the lack of invariance likely was caused by some developmental process or external factor. Here, the sensitivity of the indicator may have changed or the composition of the construct may have changed.

Latent versus Manifest Variables
Longitudinal data have their advantages, and so, too, do particular methods of data analysis. Although we will discuss some manifest (observed) variable techniques for the analysis of longitudinal data, we will emphasize the latent variable approaches encompassed the class of techniques termed *structural equation modeling* (SEM; Bollen, 1989), which encompasses confirmatory factor analysis (CFA; latent variable analysis with unstructured bivariate associations among latent variables; Brown, 2006) and mean and covariance structures (MACS; latent variable analysis including information about variable means; Little, 1997). Latent variable analyses are advantageous for a number of important reasons. First,

when multiple indicators of a construct are employed, the common variance among the indicators provides information about the construct that is (in theory) free of measurement error (Little, Lindenberger, & Nesselroade, 1999). Measurement error is a nefarious problem in manifest variable approaches because it contributes to the unreliability of a measure and contaminates the true score information that one seeks to measure. The assumptions and accuracy of inferences based on classical manifest variable analyses (e.g., regression, analysis of variance [ANOVA]) are undermined when variables are measured with some degree of error (i.e., classical techniques assume that variables are measured without error). In the behavioral and social sciences, measurement is replete with different degrees of unreliability. Unreliability leads to systematic under- or overestimation of the true relations or associations among the constructs analyzed, which can lead to various errors of inference and generalizability (for a detailed discussion of these issues, see Cole & Maxwell, 2003; and Widaman, Little, Preacher, & Sawalani, in press).

In addition to estimating and correcting for unreliability, latent variable SEM approaches provide a wealth of important validity information. For example, the degree to which the multiple indicators converge on the measurement of a common construct provides information about the content validity of the indicators. When multiple constructs, each with multiple indicators, are included in an SEM analysis, the convergent and discriminant patterns of validity in both the indicators and the constructs are fully exposed. Well-fitting models signify, for example, that indicators converge on the constructs they are intended to measure and the pattern of latent correlations among the constructs informs the degree of discrimination among the focal constructs as well as the criterion-related validity of each construct.

Another major assumption of classical techniques is that a measure provides equivalent measurement across time and across subgroups

of individuals. As mentioned, this assumption of factorial invariance is one that can be easily specified and tested in the context of latent variable SEM approaches.

We raise the values of latent variable analysis in this section because these techniques require proper planning at the design stage. Specifically, researchers need to plan to collect multiple indicators of the constructs of interest. At a minimum, these multiple indicators might be multiple items from one scale. Ideally, these multiple indicators might come from different scales or be based on different information sources, so as to reduce the specific yet undesired shared components of these multiple indicators (e.g., shared reporter variance). In order to produce what is known as a just-identified measurement structure, we recommend that researchers collect at least three indicators of a construct (see Little, Slegers, & Card, 2006). If more than three indicators are obtained, researchers can use parceling techniques to include all of this information within this just-identified measurement structure (see Little, Cunningham, Shahar, & Widaman, 2002). The key points here are that latent variable analyses have definite advantages over manifest variable approaches, but researchers need to plan to have multiple indicators of constructs in their designs in order to conduct such analyses.

MISSING DATA

It is often said that the best way to handle missing data is to not have missing data. There is some truth to this adage, and researchers should make every effort to collect all data from all participants (e.g., repeatedly visiting schools to obtain data from students absent on testing days). In reality, however, data will be missing no matter how Herculean the effort to collect complete data. As we describe next, ample evidence points to the conclusion that full information maximum likelihood (FIML) estimation and iterative imputation algorithms (e.g., expectation maximization, EM; Markov chain Monte Carlo, MCMC) are the best approaches to handling missing data (Enders, in press; Little & Rubin, 2002; Schafer & Graham, 2002).

In longitudinal research, the reasons why data may be missing are numerous. Each of these reasons would reflect a missing data mechanism. One critical missing data mechanism in longitudinal research is attrition. Participants drop out from a study for various reasons such as family mobility, lack of interest in further participation, or unfavorable circumstances that coincide with a measurement occasion. Clearly, all reasonable effort should be taken to retain participants in a study. Using appropriate incentives, staying in contact, and providing "something" in return are each useful in maximizing retention. When efforts such as these fail, however, the missing observations are not to be viewed as a complete loss of information from the study, as they would be treated using classical methods of pairwise or listwise deletion. Instead, one can utilize all available information from each participant in a study to inform the estimation of parameters of the statistical model employed (Little, Lindenberger, & Maier, 2000).

Before describing the ways to manage missing data, it is useful to consider the three common terms used to describe patterns of missingness. As outlined in Table 2.2, data can be missing completely at random (MCAR), missing functionally at random (MAR), or not missing at random (NMAR). As the name implies, MCAR data are missing due to a completely random process. Examples of how this might arise are if some questionnaires were accidentally destroyed or a pesky gremlin randomly deleted cells within our database (and we were unable to replace these scores). The unrealistic nature of these examples speaks to the likely unreality of the MCAR pattern. The second pattern, MAR, is somewhat misleading in its label. Data that are MAR are not technically missing at random. Instead, there is a relation between the missing data mechanism and information contained in the dataset (variables that have been measured), but *no relation* between the missing data mechanism and information not contained in the dataset (variables that have not been measured). For example, if missing data are highly predicted by absenteeism (students who frequently miss school are less likely to complete questionnaires at that time point) and we have a measure of attendance (e.g., access to school records), then missingness would be considered MAR. Finally, NMAR implies that the missingness is associated with some variable

TABLE 2.2   Types of missing data patterns

	No Association with *any* observed variable(s)	An association with *Analyzed* variables	An association with *Unanalyzed* variables
	MCAR	**MAR**	**MAR**
No Association with unobserved/unmeasured variables	Fully recoverable Fully unbiased	Mostly recoverable Mostly unbiased	Mostly recoverable Mostly unbiased
	NMAR	**NMAR + MAR**	**NMAR + MAR**
An Association with unobserved/unmeasured variables	Not recoverable As biased as not imputing	Partly recoverable Less biased than not imputing	Partly recoverable Less biased than not imputing

Note: 'Recoverable' refers to recovering the missing data processes and 'bias' refers to the accuracy of conclusions relative to analyzing complete case data only. In all instances, power will be maximized by estimating missing data. The 'association' here refers to the reliable relation between the measured or unmeasured variables and the missing data process. In most cases, this association is assumed to be linear. The distinction between analyzed vs. unanalyzed variables refers to the variables selected for a given analysis vs. the variables on the dataset that are not selected for a given analysis.

that is *not* contained in the dataset. From the previous example, if the researcher did not have a measure of attendance, then the pattern would be considered NMAR.

Data can be missing for many reasons and at many levels and, for the most part, each of these possible mechanisms (MCAR, MAR, and NMAR) will contribute to the missing data found in a longitudinal study. In each situation, it is better to use FIML procedures or impute missing data than to rely only on complete case analysis (i.e., listwise or pairwise deletion). When data are MCAR, any approach (imputation or deletion) will yield unbiased parameter estimates (i.e., means, standard deviations, and associations); however, as we describe later, imputation (or FIML) will provide the maximum statistical power. In the more common cases of MAR or NMAR, imputation (or FIML) is also preferable to deletion. Inferences become compromised when the missing data process results from, or is associated with, variables that are unmeasured (NMAR). Here, the reasons for the missingness, because they are unmeasured, cannot be used to help inform the estimation algorithms, and the missing data process will not be recovered. However, the inferences to the population based on the sample will be just as biased as those based on complete case analyses (i.e., using listwise or pairwise deletion). When there is a relation between information contained in the dataset (variables that have been measured) and the missing data mechanism (MAR), the best-practice techniques for handling missing data do a very good job of recreating the missing data process so that inferences are less biased than otherwise.

Because missing data are almost always missing due to processes that arise from all three of these mechanisms, utilizing all the information in the dataset in the estimation or imputation process will lead to two significant advantages: (1) the full power of the original sample will be retained, and (2) inferences will be as generalizable as possible. Here, an important distinction needs to be made between

analyses that use FIML estimation of a reduced set of the possible variables contained in the dataset versus imputation procedures that utilize all variables in the dataset (analyzed and unanalyzed). If a variable that is associated with the missing data process is not included in an analysis, then it cannot inform the estimation process, and the missing data process associated with the unanalyzed variable will not be recovered. In such situations, the bias that could have been corrected by including the unanalyzed variable will not be corrected. Because longitudinal datasets often contain a broad array of variables in the data set (including many that are not relevant to a particular analysis or research question), we recommend that researchers use all available variables in the data set and use a multiple imputation procedure such as Norm (see Schafer, 1997), SAS PROC MI (www.SAS.com), or the R module Amelia II (Honaker, King, & Blackwell, 2008) (for information on these and other imputation software, visit www.Quant.KU.edu).

In longitudinal data, a number of aspects of imputation must be considered. First, all imputation algorithms assume that the association between the observed data and the missing data process are linear. Potential nonlinearities can be included by creating additional variables such as interaction terms and powered polynomials and using these informative variables in the missing data imputation process. Even if these informative variables are not to be utilized to address any theoretical questions, they can provide more refined information to better condition the imputation of missing data.

Collecting and analyzing data from an initial wave of data collection is common practice when embarking on a longitudinal study. Any missing data at this initial stage would be imputed, and analyses based on these data would be subsequently reported. A question emerges, however, when the second wave of data is collected. Should the missing data at Wave 1 be reestimated using the information from Wave 2? In our view, the answer is yes. The logic for this answer is that information about how an individual changes at Wave 2 provides additional information that increases the likelihood of accurately recovering the missing data process. Keep in mind that modern missing data imputation is an agnostic affair when it comes to causality or time-ordered relations (Enders, in press). All that a missing data procedure attempts to accomplish is to optimize a variance–covariance matrix and mean vector that looks as much like the population as possible given all the available information provided by the sample at hand. To do so, the procedures impute likely values where data are missing and then estimates sufficient statistics; it then uses these sufficient statistics to reevaluate the likely values imputed into the missing data cells, reestimates these likely values, and then reestimates the sufficient statistics. This process continues until the change from one iteration to the next is trivially small. Investigators should not worry about whether a variable in the data set is an outcome, predictor, or a diagnostic category.

The agnostic process of estimation means that one can estimate missing information for any type of variable. Gender, for example, can be estimated in this manner. If an estimated value for gender comes out to be 0.7 and gender is coded 0 and 1, then the most likely gender of this individual is the sex coded as 1 (male). For categorization purposes (e.g., in multiple-group analyses), this case can be treated as if gender were male, but for analytic purposes the imputed value can be left as 0.7 in order to minimize any bias (Enders, in press).

Because dropout and attrition often lead to a significant percentage of missing data, longitudinal studies should routinely utilize multiple imputations. As described above, a single imputation is an iterative process. This iterative process is somewhat dependent on the initial guesses plugged in for the missing data. Multiple imputations allow the uncertainty and potential influence of the starting point on the standard errors of estimation to be minimized. Early work on multiple imputation suggested that a small number of imputations would be sufficient to capture this uncertainty. More recently, however, work in this area indicates that a larger number of imputations (>20) are needed in order to accurately capture the true information and inherent variability. With the increase in computational capabilities and the availability of software routines to easily combine and summarize the results from the multiple analyses of the multiple imputations, we recommend that researchers err on the side of more rather then fewer imputations (software routines and links to routines that summarize imputation results can be found at www.Quant.KU.edu). Graham, Olchowski, and Gilreath (2007) provide sound guidance for determining the appropriate number of imputations given the fraction of missing data present in a given sample (see also Enders, in press).

One key implication of this discussion of missing data is that one should carefully attend to, and plan to assess, important potential predictors of the missing data mechanism. Measuring those variables that consistently associate with missingness helps inform the imputation process such that the missing data are more likely to be MAR (recoverable) than NMAR (unrecoverable). A comprehensive review of the literature on adolescent development would provide a solid list of variables that show consistent associations with missing data processes and reasons for attrition. These variables should be routinely measured for their use in the imputation stages of a project (a partial list of recommended variables can be found at www.Quant.KU.edu).

One consequence of the ability to recover missing data using modern techniques has to do with intentionally missing data collection designs (see Graham, Taylor, Olchowski, & Cumsille, 2006). Such designs involve randomly assigning participants to different patterns of data collection occasions and/or variables in the protocol. As long as each possible pairwise association has sufficient coverage to accurately estimate the population covariance, the random nature of the missing data design will yield a missing data process that is fully recoverable.

ANALYSIS TECHNIQUES

Given that one has carefully considered the design needs for answering the questions of interest, the theoretical model should be matched with the appropriate statistical model. Many different considerations are involved in choosing the appropriate statistical model. Rosel and Plewis (2008) provide a taxonomy of statistical models that all fall under the broad umbrella of SEM. A first consideration is whether the model should be univariate or multivariate. Given that models of a single measure are relatively simple and specific to circumscribed questions, we will focus on multivariate models (models that include two or more constructs). A second consideration is whether the constructs should be modeled as observed, manifest variables or as unobserved, latent variables. We outlined the various advantages of latent variable approaches above, and focus more of our discussion below on latent variable applications (though we will give some consideration to manifest variable approaches). Other dimensions that can be considered include the presence or absence of covariates, interactions, multiple levels, and nonlinear effects (Rosel & Plewis, 2008). In addition to these considerations, models can be applied to categorical or metrical variables (Collins, 2006).

In the next three sections, we describe the basic features and issues in specifying panel models, growth curve models, and intensive time series models. We also address, when applicable, inclusion of covariates, handling multiple levels, and modeling nonlinear effects. We devote the Conclusions section to a discussion of mediation and moderation in the context of the three general classes of technique for modeling longitudinal data (for thorough treatments of these techniques, see, e.g., Bijleveld & van der Kamp, 1998; Cairns, Bergman, & Kagan, 1998; Collins & Horn, 1991; Collins & Sayer, 2001; Hedeker & Gibbons, 2006; Little,

Schnabel, & Baumert, 2000; Magnusson, Bergman, Rudinger, & Törestad, 1991; Menard, 1991; Moskowitz & Hershberger, 2002; Nesselroade & Baltes, 1979; Saldaña, 2003).

PANEL MODELS

The first type of longitudinal model that we address is termed the *panel model*. Panel models are also referred to as autoregressive models. We prefer panel models to emphasize that data for these models usually reflect multiple measures at a few assessment occasions. In this regard, panel models consist, at a minimum, of data collected at two time points in which the presumed antecedent(s) is measured at Time 1 and the presumed consequence(s) is measured at Time 2. We emphasize that this is a minimum condition, and there are substantial advantages to measuring both antecedents and consequences at both times, measuring alternative predictor variables at Time 1 (and preferably also at Time 2), and obtaining data from more than two time points. We elaborate on each of these considerations in the next subsection, describing the logic of panel models and the kinds of questions that can be answered. We also note that it is possible to analyze panel data using either manifest (i.e., multiple regression) or latent variable analysis, as described in the second and third subsections (respectively) below.

Logic of and Questions Answered by Panel Models

As mentioned, panel models involve measuring the presumed antecedents and consequences at two (or more) time points. The focus of panel models is on interindividual (i.e., between person) differences. Specifically, analyses of panel models answer the question of whether (and to what extent) interindividual differences in the presumed antecedent at Time 1 are predictive of later (Time 2) interindividual differences in the presumed consequent. In other words, does a person's relative standing on variable X at one time point relate to that person's relative standing on variable Y at a later time point?

The key analytic consideration of panel models is the presence of associations among variables across time. Three aspects of these associations (e.g., correlations) merit attention. First, as alluded to earlier, associations involve the covariation of interindividual differences among variables, in this case among variables over time. These covariances or correlations tell us nothing about whether the mean level of a variable or set of variables is increasing, decreasing, or staying the same. To address these questions, growth curve models are preferred (see next section). Second, there are several ways to assess correlations, including a manifest variable (i.e., regression) framework as well as a latent variable (i.e., structural equation) framework. Although there are several advantages of the latter approach, which we highlight throughout, we want to emphasize that there is not a single right way to analyze panel models. As with all statistical models, the important issue is whether the analytic model answers the questions the researcher wants to ask (see preceding discussion). The third consideration of our initial statement is that there is intentional breadth in terms of variables included. Examining the across-time correlation of a single variable provides important information regarding the interindividual (but not intraindividual, or within-person) stability of that variable. More commonly, researchers think of panel models involving two variables, in which associations between X and Y across time are of interest. However, panel models are not restricted to just two variables, and it is often valuable to compare the relative predictive strength of multiple variables across time, or whether these longitudinal associations are mediated or moderated (see the section, *Mediation and Moderation in Longitudinal Data*).

Imagine that a researcher believes that X causes Y over time. More explicitly, imagine that this researcher believes that an adolescent's level of X relative to peers (i.e., interindividual differences in X) leads to an adolescent's being high or low (relative to peers) on Y at some specific later time. The first task of the researcher is to explicate the amount of time over which the presumed influence is expected to occur (see Gollob & Reichardt, 1987). Then, the researcher collects data measuring (at a minimum) X at one time, waits the expected amount of time over which the influence occurs, and then collects data measuring (at a minimum) Y at this second time point. The researcher then analyzes these data to determine the existence and magnitude of the association between Time 1 X and Time 2 Y.

Imagine that the researcher does indeed find an association between Time 1 X (denoted X_1) and Time 2 Y (denoted Y_2), as shown in Figure 2.3, situation A. Based on this association, can it be concluded that X causes Y? Although many researchers might be tempted to jump to this conclusion, such a conclusion would *not* be appropriate. A failure to find this association would refute the researcher's hypothesis that X causes Y over the specified time period (to the extent that there was adequate statistical power to detect an effect of a certain size). A finding that X_1 is associated with Y_2 *might* mean that X causes Y, but there are at least two alternative explanations.

The first alternative explanation is that, instead of X causing Y, Y actually causes X. This possibility is illustrated in Figure 2.3, situation B, where we have shown earlier values of Y (denoted Y_0) causing X (at Time 1, X_1). If Y is also stable across time (in terms of interindividual differences), then an association between Y_0 and Y_2 is also likely. Based on these two associations, the detected association between X_1 and Y_2 can be considered spurious, in that it is due *not* to X causing Y, but rather Y causing X and Y being stable across time. One way to account for this alternative explanation is to measure X and Y at both occasions, and evaluate the extent to which X_1 predicts later Y_2 (controlling for Y_1) *and* the extent to which Y_1 predicts later X_2 (controlling for X_1). This evaluation is depicted in Figure 2.3, situation C. If the researcher finds that X_1 predicts later

Situation A. Researcher finds longitudinal association of X with later Y

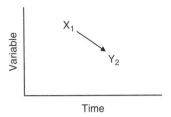

Situation B. Y causing X accounts for longitudinal association of X with later Y

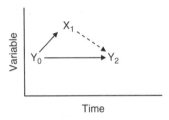

Situation C. Researcher evaluates longitudinal associations of both X and Y

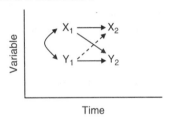

Situation D. Causal variable Z produces longitudinal association of X predicting Y

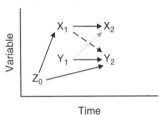

Situation E. Researcher controls for third variable(s) Z in evaluating longitudinal associations of X and Y

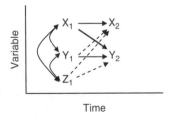

FIGURE 2.3 An illustration of different panel models in longitudinal research.

Y_2 but Y_1 does not predict later X_2 (which is why this path is indicated with a dashed line in Figure 2.3, situation C), then it is plausible to rule out this alternative explanation if two assumptions can be made.

The first assumption is that the time span of influence between measurements of the two variables is equal. In this hypothetical example, we emphasized that the researcher carefully considered the time span over which X was expected to influence Y (i.e., the researcher has measured the variables at the "correct" interval to detect this association). There is no guarantee, however, that this time span is also that over which Y might influence X. Analysis of data in which an inappropriate time span for the influence of Y on X would not provide an appropriate test of this explanation; therefore, the failure to find a predictive relation of Y_1 toward X_2 among these data would not provide a convincing case for ruling out this direction of influence. Researchers who wish to evaluate competing directions of influence between X and Y must carefully consider the time span over which *both* processes occur. If it can be convincingly (and not just conveniently) argued that the two processes occur across the same period of time, then the analyses depicted in Figure 2.3, situation C can compare these two directions of influence. If this argument cannot be made, then more than two occasions of measurement are needed, as described below.

The second assumption that must be made is even more difficult to support. This assumption is that no third variable causes both X and Y. This threat to inferences of causality is pervasive and can never fully be ruled out in a naturalistic (i.e., nonexperimental) study; it is known as the "third variable problem." This problem is illustrated in Figure 2.3, situation D, in which variable Z represents a third variable, potentially causing both X and Y. The threat is that the observed relation between X and Y may not be due to X causing Y, but rather to the mutual reliance of X and Y on the same third variable Z. Specifically, the threat is that some third variable Z causes X_1 as well as Y_2, and this common cause is what accounts for the spurious longitudinal association between X and Y. The third variable problem is widely invoked by critics of research attempting to draw causal inferences from longitudinal naturalistic data. We propose two rebuttals to these sorts of critique.

The first rebuttal is to ask critics to explicate the time span of influence of the third variable Z. Given the existence of the pattern of associations shown in Figure 2.3, situation C, the critique of a potential third variable as the true cause should specify one of two conditions. First, a critic invoking the third variable threat should be pressed to specify that the influence of Z on X occurs more quickly than the influence of Z on Y. Alternatively, one invoking the third variable critique might specify that the third variable Z causes Y but not X, and that X is merely associated with Z. Too often, the third variable critique is raised in a nonspecific way that does not consider the specifics of influence. Although it is the researcher's responsibility to rule out competing explanations, we believe that those raising this critique should offer a reasonable explication of this differential time span of influence.

The second—and more authoritative—rebuttal to the third variable problem is to actually measure and include the third variable in one's model. Although there is a potentially infinite number of third variables (i.e., multiple Zs) that could be invoked, the researcher should plan to address the most theoretically defensible possibilities by including measures of these third variables (at a minimum, at Time 1 to evaluate the prediction of later X and Y from earlier Zs). If X_1 is found to predict later Y_2 even after controlling for relevant Z_1s, this offers evidence against the threat of the third variable as the true causal mechanism (this scenario is depicted in Figure 2.3, situation E). Of course, the effectiveness of controlling for Zs in ruling out the third variable threat depends on the expected influence of Z occurring over the same time span as the $X \rightarrow Y$ relation.

Despite these methods of evaluating competing $X \rightarrow Y$ versus $Y \rightarrow X$ explanations and potential rebuttals to third variable problem critiques, analysis of panel models cannot conclusively demonstrate causality. There is always the possibility that Y causes X over time spans other than those studied, which limits our conclusions regarding the direction of influence between X and Y to the particular time span investigated. The third variable problem can never be fully ruled out, as there are potentially infinite Zs that we have not considered that could account for the observed longitudinal associations. At the same time, analysis of panel models with adequate consideration of these potential problems allows us to build a strong case for causality (especially if we control for most theoretically viable third variable causes), and certainly the strongest case that can be made without experimental manipulation. Like all statistical models, panel models allow us to evaluate only whether the data are consistent (or not) with our theoretical predictions.

Manifest Variable Analysis of Panel Data

Manifest variable analysis of panel models is typically performed using a series of multiple regressions. We will describe these analyses in a way paralleling the increasing sophistication of analyses described in the previous subsection (and Figure 2.3).

Consider first the simplest, but least optimal, case in which the researcher measures X at Time 1 and Y at Time 2. The regression model is straightforward:

$$Y_2 = B_0 + B_1 X_1 + e \qquad (1)$$

Here, the estimate of interest is B_1, the regression coefficient of X_1. Specifically, one is interested in the statistical significance of this coefficient (does X predict later Y?) as well as its sign (does X predict higher or lower Y?) and magnitude (how strongly does X predict Y?). Magnitude can be evaluated using the standardized regression coefficient.

When researchers have measures of both X and Y at both time points, the regression analyses yield much more convincing information. Consider first the evaluation that X predicts Y from the following equation (for alternative possibilities, see Duncan, 1969):

$$Y_2 = B_0 + B_1 Y_1 + B_2 X_1 + e \qquad (2)$$

Here, Y_2 is predicted by two variables. The first variable is the earlier value of the variable itself (Y_1). Inclusion of this predictor is important in two ways. First, the regression coefficient of this predictor (B_1) indicates the magnitude of interindividual stability in Y (usually evaluated in terms of significance and the magnitude of the standardized regression coefficient). Second, including the initial level of the dependent variable (often termed the autoregressive component) means that B_1 is interpreted as the extent to which X_1 predicts Y_2 above and beyond the stable variability of Y. In other words, the regression coefficient of X_1 (B_2) represents the extent to which X_1 predicts instability, or interindividual change, in Y_2.

A key value of including both X and Y at both time points is the ability to evaluate both directions of prediction, that is, X → Y and Y → X. Therefore, it is common to evaluate a second regression analysis in addition to that described earlier (Equation 2), assuming such an effect is theoretically tenable:

$$X_2 = B_0 + B_1 X_1 + B_2 Y_1 + e \qquad (3)$$

The coefficients of this regression are interpreted in a way parallel to those just described. Namely, B_1 is interpreted as the interindividual stability in X, and B_2 is interpreted as the prediction of change in X from Y. We stated earlier that direction of influence between X and Y is indicated by finding that one variable predicts the other (e.g., X predicts change in Y) but that the other variable does not predict the first (e.g., Y fails to predict change in X). This interpretation suggests one of the critical limitations to using manifest variable regression analyses to analyze panel models—substantive decisions are based on inferential conclusions that are not easily comparable. An illustration should clarify this point. Imagine that the

researcher found that X significantly predicts change in Y, with $B = 0.30$ and $p = 0.049$. In a separate regression predicting X, the researcher found that Y fails to predict change in X, with $B = 0.29$ and $p = 0.051$. Although letter-of-the-law hypothesis testing would lead to conclusions that X predicts Y but not vice versa, this example shows clearly that X's ability to predict Y is not substantially stronger than Y's ability to predict X. Statistically, methods of comparing these two predictions within a multiple regression framework are difficult (see Widaman, 2000), and are much more easily accomplished within an SEM framework as described below.

Consider next the situation in which the researcher wishes to control for one or more additional variables in order to rule out alternative causal explanations. Following from previous equations (for alternatives, see Duncan, 1969), the researcher would fit two regression equations, one with each Time 2 X and Y serving as dependent variables:

$$Y_2 = B_0 + B_1 Y_1 + B_2 X_1 + B_3 Z_{a1} \\ + B_4 Z_{b1} + \cdots + e \qquad (4)$$

$$X_2 = B_0 + B_1 X_1 + B_2 Y_1 + B_3 Z_{a1} \\ + B_4 Z_{b1} + \cdots + e \qquad (5)$$

These equations make clear that the researcher can control for as many potential alternative causal variables as desired.

Latent Variable Analysis of Panel Data

Analyzing panel models in a latent variable framework has several advantages over analysis in a multiple regression framework (e.g., Anderson, 1987; Little, Preacher, Selig & Card, 2007; see Figure 2.4 for an example of a latent variable panel model). In this subsection, we will first describe these advantages. We will then briefly describe the practice of fitting latent variable path models. However, space constraints preclude a full description of these practices, and we refer interested readers to Little, Preacher, et al. (2007) for further description.

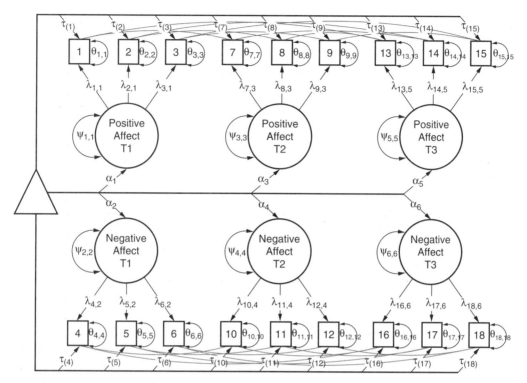

FIGURE 2.4   A detailed model of a three-wave panel model of two constructs, including all relevant para-meter estimates.

The first advantage of latent variable panel analysis over manifest variable regression techniques is simply the correction for unreliability. It is well known that unreliability attenuates (i.e., diminishes the estimated values of) correlations among variables; what is less often recognized is the unpredictable biases this causes in manifest variable regression analyses, such as the analysis of panel models. If we consider the longitudinal association between X_1 and Y_2, we know that unreliability of either of these variables will attenuate the longitudinal correlation between these variables. However, if we also consider unreliability of Y_1, the picture becomes more complex: now we have an attenuated stability estimate of Y and an attenuated estimate of the concurrent correlation between X_1 and Y_1. The net result of these two attenuations will be to inflate the unique association of X_1 predicting Y_2. We have no way of knowing if this regression coefficient is underestimated

(due to attenuated correlation between X_1 and Y_2), overestimated (due to attenuated control of Y_1), or the competing attenuations balance each other to produce an unbiased estimate (the possibility that most researchers using regression seem to hope for, but that is probably least likely). If we also add additional third variables (i.e., Zs) to the equation, the problem is even further compounded. In short, attenuation due to unreliability biases parameter estimates in manifest variable regression in ways that are difficult to predict. The extent to which this problem has led to inappropriate substantive conclusions in regression analyses of panel models is frightful to consider. In contrast, latent variable representations of panel models correct for this unreliability to produce unbiased parameter estimates.

A second advantage of latent variable panel models is that they allow for evaluation of measurement equivalence across time. This is a considerable advantage when we consider the impact of changing measurement properties across time. Using manifest variable regression, one might regress Y_2 onto Y_1 and X_1. If we conclude that X predicts change in Y, we are really concluding that there is a change in the *construct* of Y that is predictable from earlier levels of X. An alternative possibility, if we do not establish equivalence of measurement across time, is that change in the *measurement* of Y is predictable from earlier levels of X. One possible cause of this alternative possibility is that some aspect of Y is becoming increasingly salient to the measurement of Y across time, and X is simply associated (not necessarily in a causal manner) with that particular aspect.

The remaining advantages are aspects of the general modeling tools of SEM, but also apply to manifest variable path analysis. However, if one were to go to the trouble of using these modeling programs, it would be advisable to conduct latent variable analyses given the advantages just described (assuming that one has multiple measured indicators of the constructs).

A third advantage of latent variable panel analysis is that paths within the model can be easily directly compared. We described earlier the challenges of comparing competing prediction paths across separate regression equations. This problem is solved within a latent variable framework. To compare whether an $X \rightarrow Y$ path is stronger than a $Y \rightarrow X$ path, one can statistically compare a model in which these two paths are freely estimated to a model in which these are constrained equally. If this constraint significantly worsens model fit (as evaluated by a significant increase in χ^2), then we can conclude that these two paths are significantly different from one another. This formal statistical comparison allows much greater clarity in decisions regarding direction of influence. Such a comparison, however, would have to be performed estimating the paths as standardized path coefficients if X and Y are measured on different scales; this is achieved through the use of phantom variables (Little, 1997; Rindskopf, 1984).

Latent variable panel models also allow for the evaluation of complex data. One complexity is the addition of more than two time points. This addition not only provides a replication of two time-point results (i.e., do Time 1 $\rightarrow$ Time 2 relations also emerge at Time 2 $\rightarrow$ Time 3?), but also allows for greater flexibility in evaluating various time spans of influence. This flexibility might allow researchers to detect, for example, not only whether X predicts change in Y over a shorter time frame (e.g., between Times 1 and 2) but also whether Y predicts X over a longer time frame (e.g., between Times 1 and 3). Increasing the number of time points also allows for evaluation of more complex longitudinal processes, such as longitudinal mediation (e.g., $X_1 \rightarrow M_2 \rightarrow Y_3$; see Cole & Maxwell, 2003; Gollob & Reichardt, 1991; Little, Card, Bovaird, Preacher, & Crandall, 2007; and discussion of mediation below).

Finally, multiple-group latent variable panel models allow several opportunities that are difficult or impossible in manifest variable regression. One opportunity is to evaluate whether the longitudinal predictions are moderated across different groups (e.g., differences by sex or ethnicity). This method of assessing moderation is accomplished by fitting the longitudinal model in multiple groups simultaneously, and then evaluating whether parameters (e.g., $X \rightarrow Y$) differ across groups. Although such interactions can be evaluated in multiple regression with the use of product terms, inclusion of these product terms quickly becomes cumbersome and the statistical power to detect these interactions with unreliable variables is often inadequate. Moreover, analysis of moderation via multiple-group SEM avoids the often unrealistic assumption of multiple regression of homoskedasticity (that the residual variances are equal across moderator groups; multiple-group SEM allows these residual variances to be freely estimated). A second opportunity afforded in multiple-group latent variable panel models is in the analysis of accelerated longitudinal designs (see Bell, 1953; Little, Card et al., 2007; Schaie, 1965). These designs involve collecting longitudinal data from several cohorts so that the cohort groups partially overlap in age. Treating these cohorts as groups in a multiple-group analysis allows one to evaluate whether the longitudinal predictions are similar or different across a wide range of age and cohort (for details, see Little, Card et al., 2007).

In addition to these basic considerations, users of SEM panel models might consider several recent advances not described in detail here. One of these issues involves the method of scaling the latent variable. In longitudinal studies in which the measures have a meaningful scale (e.g., frequency ratings), a recently proposed effects coding approach might be a useful method of scale setting (see Little, Slegers, & Card, 2006; Marsh, Wen, Hau, Little, Bovaird, & Widaman, 2007). In addition, Widaman and Thompson (2003) have described the necessity of specifying alternative null models for the computation of relative fit indices (e.g., comparative fit index [CFI], Tucker-Lewis index [TLI]) for cases in which the usual null model of independence is not nested within the theoretical model. It is appropriate to use these alternative null models in repeated-measures SEM applications, such as the latent variable panel model.

GROWTH CURVE MODELS

As mentioned, panel models focus on interindividual differences in changes over time. In the next section, we will describe techniques for modeling within-person, or intraindividual, changes over time.

The Logic of Growth Curve Models

Many modeling paradigms have a tendency to lose sight of the individual in an attempt to accurately model nomothetic laws guiding the relations among variables. Panel models are useful for modeling the temporal stability of (inter-)individual differences in constructs and the longitudinal causal linkages among different constructs. However, other models are required for modeling within-person (i.e., intraindividual) change over time, as well as interindividual differences in this intraindividual change. For

example, throughout the adolescent years, individuals tend to steadily increase in affiliation with peers (time spent with friends rather than family; e.g., Rubin, Bukowski, & Parker, 2006). However, some adolescents likely increase in affiliation more quickly than others, and some individuals begin adolescence with lower or higher levels of affiliation relative to their peers. For example, the data may appear as in Figure 2.5, where each line represents the measurements of a single adolescent from ages 11 to 18.

For situations in which both the mean trajectory and variability in individual trajectories are of interest, *growth curve modeling* has become very popular. Unlike panel models, growth curve models focus on trajectories of change within the individual (*intraindividual change*) and individual differences in trajectories of change (*interindividual differences in interindividual change*). Depending on what is being measured, the appropriate unit of time may be minutes, weeks, months, or even years. A single study may be characterized by anywhere from 2 measurements to 50 or more. Measurements may occur simultaneously or at different times, and spacing among occasions may differ from occasion to occasion and from case to case. The researcher may be interested not only in modeling change, but in modeling the antecedents (predictors) and sequelae (outcomes) of change in several variables measured simultaneously. For example, a researcher may be interested in investigating potential predictors of change in teen affiliation and alcohol use in the same sample of high school students, as well as the potential for aspects of these trajectories to predict SAT scores. Such data characteristics would be difficult or impossible to address using older analyses such as analysis of covariance (ANCOVA), but growth curve modeling can be used to model change under all of these circumstances and more.

We briefly discuss two multivariate approaches to modeling change over time: (a) the multilevel model for repeated measures and (b) the latent growth curve model. Subsequently,

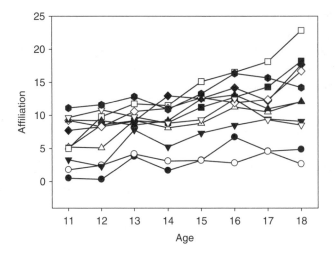

Note: Affiliation is measured as the average number of meaningful social
encounters per day over the course of one 2-week period at roughly
the same time every year.

FIGURE 2.5 Individual observed trajectories of affiliation for 11 fictitious adolescents, followed from age 11 to age 18.

we discuss the pros and cons of a recent extension of the latent growth curve model that is intended to identify latent classes characterized by unique trajectories—the growth mixture model.

The Multilevel Modeling Approach

Multilevel modeling (MLM), or hierarchical linear modeling (HLM), is an extension of regression analysis applied to hierarchically organized data that would otherwise violate the independence assumption of ordinary regression. For example, students "nested within" the same classroom likely are more similar on key educational outcomes than are students drawn from different classrooms; a shared environment can be expected to lead to increased similarity. MLM is very useful for analyzing repeated measures data, because repeated measures can be seen as nested within individuals in the same way that students are nested within classrooms.

The basic *level 1* equation for repeated measures data is:

$$y_{ij} = \beta_{0j} + \beta_{1j} time_{ij} + \varepsilon_{ij} \qquad (6)$$

where y_{ij} is the measurement on some outcome y for individual j at time i, β_{0j} and β_{1j} are, respectively, the intercept and slope, and ε_{ij} is a residual term. The residuals are assumed to be normally distributed with mean 0 and variance σ_ε^2. Unlike intercepts and slopes in ordinary regression, the intercepts and slopes in multilevel regression can be treated as *random effects* with their own *level 2* equations:

$$\beta_{0j} = \gamma_{00} + u_{0j} \qquad (7)$$

$$\beta_{1j} = \gamma_{10} + u_{1j} \qquad (8)$$

where γ_{00} and γ_{10} are the means of the distributions of β_{0j} and β_{1j}, u_{0j} and u_{1j} are level 2 residuals representing the deviations of individuals from those means, and u_{0j} and u_{1j} are assumed to be multivariate normally distributed with means 0, variances τ_{00} and τ_{11}, and covariance τ_{10}. That is, each individual is implicitly allowed to have his or her own intercept and slope. These individual coefficients are not actually estimated; rather, their means, variances, and covariances are estimated.

We could expand this basic linear model in many ways. For example, we could add predictors to the level 1 equation that are assessed at each occasion, in which case they are termed *time-varying covariates*. Returning to our affiliation example:

$$Affil_{ij} = \beta_{0j} + \beta_{1j}time_{ij} + \beta_{2j}mood_{ij} + \varepsilon_{ij} \quad (9)$$

We could also, or instead, add student-level predictors of intercepts and slopes (*time-invariant covariates*) to the level 2 equations, for example:

$$\beta_{0j} = \gamma_{00} + \gamma_{01}IQ_j + u_{0j} \quad (10)$$

$$\beta_{1j} = \gamma_{10} + \gamma_{11}IQ_j + u_{1j} \quad (11)$$

Substitution of Equations 10 and 11 into Equation 9 demonstrates that models with level 2 predictors of slopes lead to cross-level interaction effects, which are often of great interest to researchers:

$$y_{ij} = \gamma_{00} + \gamma_{01}IQ_j + \gamma_{10}time_{ij} + \gamma_{11} \underbrace{IQ_j \times time_{ij}}_{\substack{\text{cross-level} \\ \text{interaction term}}} + u_{0j} + u_{1j}time_{ij} + \varepsilon_{ij}$$

$$(12)$$

Multilevel models are advantageous for many reasons. Foremost, they avoid the parameter bias that occurs from mistakenly assuming independence. They also grant the researcher the ability to model regression weights as dependent variables in their own right, and to partition variance in meaningful ways to shed light on developmental phenomena. Software for fitting multilevel models is plentiful and can now be found in all major general statistics packages, including SPSS, SAS (PROC MIXED), R, Stata, and others, and in more specialized applications such as HLM, MLwiN, LISREL, and Mplus. Good introductions to MLM can be found in Hofmann (1997), Luke (2004), and Singer and Willett (2003). Many

book-length treatments are available, including Bickel (2007), Hox (2002), Snijders and Bosker (1999), Kreft and de Leeuw (1998), and Raudenbush and Bryk (2002).

The Latent Growth Curve Approach

Latent growth curve modeling (LGM) is the application of SEM to the study of trajectories. LGM has its roots in factor analysis (Rao, 1958; Tucker, 1966), in which the aim was to recover polynomial trends in repeated measures data as factors. The main development leading to modern LGM occurred with the application of confirmatory factor analysis to repeated measures data (Meredith & Tisak, 1990). This development allowed scientists to test theory-based models of change in a confirmatory mode.

Because individuals are hypothesized to vary in terms of individual intercepts and slopes, and these aspects of change are not directly observable, it is natural to model these random effects as latent variables, or factors. Each of these *aspects of change* (e.g., intercept, linear slope, quadratic slope, and so on) is modeled as a latent variable, with the growth trend reflected in the pattern of loadings. The latent variables are often permitted to vary, indicating that individuals are permitted by the model to differ in their trajectories.

Consider the case of a simple linear model where individuals are hypothesized to differ in terms of both intercept and slope. A simple linear growth curve is depicted in the path diagram in Figure 2.6. Using standard SEM notation, yearly assessments of affiliation from ages 11 to 18 are arrayed as squares from left to right in chronological order. Circles represent latent variables and residual terms, and the triangle represents a constant. Affiliation at time j is modeled as a function of all the variables from which it receives arrows, weighted by the value of the associated path coefficient. For example, "Affil. Age 14" receives arrows from the intercept and slope factors, and from the random disturbance term δ_{14}. Its equation is therefore:

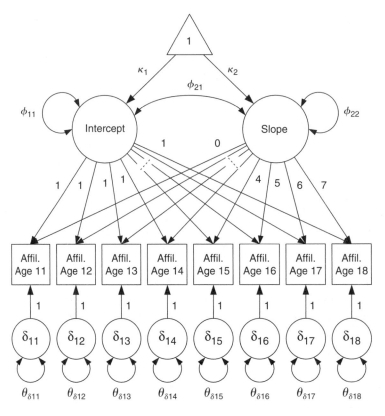

Note: Greek symbols represent parameters to be estimated, including κ_1 (mean intercept); κ_2 (mean slope); ϕ_{11}, ϕ_{22}, and ϕ_{21} (intercept and slope variances and covariance); and $\theta_{\delta 11} - \theta_{\delta 18}$ (occasion-specific disturbance variances).

FIGURE 2.6   A latent growth curve model specifying linear change in affiliation.

$$Affil_{14} = Intercept + Slope \times 3 + \delta_{14} \qquad (13)$$

More generally, affiliation at time j can be modeled as a function of time as:

$$Affil_j = Intercept + Slope \times time_j + \delta_j \quad (14)$$

where $time_j$ is simply the value assigned to the factor loading associated with slope. In matrix notation, all of the equations can be summarized as:

$$\mathbf{Y} = \mathbf{\Lambda}\xi + \delta \qquad (15)$$

where $\mathbf{Y}$ is a vector containing the repeated measures of affiliation, $\mathbf{\Lambda}$ is a matrix of factor loadings containing a column for each aspect of change (1s for intercept and linear

increasing integers for slope), ξ is a vector containing the intercept and slope factors, and δ is a vector of disturbance residuals. The elements of $\mathbf{\Lambda}$ should be chosen with care, because any model parameters associated with the Intercept are conditional on the point at which the time metric equals "0." See our earlier discussion of how to choose an appropriate metric of time.

This model is termed an *unconditional* growth model because no predictors of intercepts or slopes are included. So the model for the observed means is very simple:

$$\mathbf{\mu}_y = \mathbf{\Lambda}\mathbf{\kappa} \qquad (16)$$

where $\mathbf{\mu}_y$ is a vector of modeled means and $\mathbf{\kappa}$ is a vector of latent variable means containing the mean intercept and slope. The associated covariance structure explaining the variances and covariances among the repeated measures is:

$$\Sigma = \Lambda \Phi \Lambda' + \Theta_\delta \tag{17}$$

where Φ contains the variances and covariance of intercept and slope and Θ_δ is a diagonal matrix of disturbance variances. These models can be extended to include predictors of intercepts and slopes, but our purpose here is to provide an introduction to these models.

The primary benefit of LGM is its flexibility. For example, researchers are not limited to modeling equally spaced occasions—the factor loadings in Λ can be adapted to reflect any well-defined functional trend. Some software applications (Mplus and Mx) can even fit models to data in which each individual is assessed using his or her own unique measurement schedule. Missing data pose no obstacle in LGM (unless they are NMAR). Change in multiple variables may be assessed simultaneously, which permits estimation of covariances of intercepts and slopes across variables. LGM permits the assessment of change in latent variables with multiple indicators. Because aspects of change are treated as variables in LGM, the entire model in Figure 2.6 can be included in a larger structural model in a modular fashion. Furthermore, because LGM is a special application of SEM, researchers have access to an array of fit indices to aid in assessing model fit.

Numerous introductions to growth curve modeling are now available. Some of the more accessible ones include Byrne and Crombie (2003), Chan (1998), Curran (2000), Curran and Hussong (2003), Hancock and Lawrence (2006), and Willett and Sayer (1994). For more comprehensive treatments of LGM, we refer the reader to Bollen and Curran (2006); Preacher, Wichman, MacCallum, and Briggs (2008), and Duncan, Duncan, and Strycker (2006).

Interestingly, the basic form of both the multilevel model of change and the latent growth curve model are identical for a broad class of applications. Random effects in repeated measures of MLM are equivalent to latent aspects of change in LGM, and for many models the parameter estimates are identical across these two general methods (e.g., γ_{00} in Equation 7 is equivalent to κ_1 in Figure 2.6; see Bauer, 2003; Chou, Bentler, & Pentz, 1998; Curran, 2003; MacCallum, Kim, Malarkey, & Kiecolt-Glaser, 1997; Preacher et al., 2008; Rovine & Molenaar, 2000; Willett & Sayer, 1994).

Growth Mixture Modeling: Identifying Subgroups of Growth

One increasingly popular model for treating longitudinal data in developmental research is the *latent growth mixture model* (LGMM; see Muthén, 2008). Mixture modeling involves identifying subgroups or classes of individuals characterized by different patterns of model parameters. Rather than manually dividing the sample into groups, the researcher simply specifies the number of groups, and separate sets of model parameters are estimated for each group, along with probabilities of class membership. An LGMM, then, is mixture modeling applied to longitudinal data in an attempt to identify K subgroups (or latent classes) characterized by different latent growth trajectories (e.g., intercepts, slopes; see e.g., Barker, Tremblay, Nagin, Vitaro, & Lacourse, 2006; Muthén & Muthén, 2000).

Approaches to LGMM include those popularized by Nagin and colleagues (1999, 2005; Nagin & Tremblay, 1999) in which no heterogeneity is permitted in growth trajectories within classes, and those by Muthén and colleagues (Muthén, 2001; Muthén & Shedden, 1999) in which variability both within and between classes is permitted. Currently, the most flexible and popular software packages for fitting LGMMs are Mplus (Muthén & Muthén, 2007) and Proc TRAJ (Jones, Nagin, & Roeder, 2001; Nagin, 1999).

The rapid increase in the use of LGMM in developmental research has arguably outpaced careful consideration of the pros and cons of this method. Next, we describe both (1) the arguments against LGMMs, which should caution researchers against the uninformed use of these models; and (2) suggestions for using LGMMs, in which we describe some basic principles to follow if one feels theoretically justified in using LGMMs.

Arguments Against LGMM

Despite the rapidly increasing popularity of growth mixture modeling, Bauer (2007) offers a sobering litany of both methodological and theoretical concerns that, when carefully considered, should make developmental researchers very reluctant to apply such models without ample justification. First, the data to which LGMMs are applied are often nonnormal. Yet, because of the assumption of within-class normality, it is often easy for LGMMs to recover several artifactual classes, within each of which the assumption of normality is satisfied. In other words, nonnormal data can easily lead to the retention of spurious latent classes (Bauer, 2007; Bauer & Curran, 2003a, 2003b; Tofighi & Enders, 2007). Second, the specific growth model specifications within classes can give rise to spurious compensatory retention of too many classes as the model attempts to recover the observed variability in the data (Bauer & Curran, 2004). Class retention depends on the proper specification of a within-class model of growth. For example, if the effects of exogenous predictors of growth are actually nonlinear but are modeled as linear, spurious classes may result (Bauer, 2007). Third, if missing data are not missing at random (NMAR; see earlier discussion of missing data types) but are assumed to be MAR or MCAR, the number of classes can be underestimated (if multiple classes do exist). Fourth, in complex (e.g., stratified) samples, sampling probabilities need to be considered during parameter estimation, or else bias will result. It follows that if the researcher does not properly consider sample weights (the rule rather than the exception), then the number of classes, class proportions, and within-class parameter estimates can be considerably off the mark (for details of these issues, see Bauer, 2007).

Beyond purely methodological concerns, there are also theoretical and practical concerns that limit the current usefulness of LGMM. For example, LGMM is often used in cases where there is no reasonable basis for suspecting the existence of latent classes. Through random slopes, latent growth curve models already allow for the possibility of variability in trajectories. To justify LGMM, theory would have to predict the existence of discrete classes, each characterized by a different mean growth trajectory. Justifying the existence of latent taxa can be very difficult when continua provide a more parsimonious and (usually) more realistic alternative (Bauer, 2007; MacCallum, Zhang, Preacher, & Rucker, 2002).

Practically speaking, LGMMs are difficult to understand and use (though software advances are ameliorating this problem), improper solutions frequently occur, spurious classes are routinely extracted even in homogeneous populations, parameters tend to be very sensitive to starting values, and very large samples are required for accurate estimation. Furthermore, the question of how to properly apply fit statistics and model selection criteria to LGMMs is not entirely settled. We believe the nearly immediate popularity of LGMMs so soon after their introduction has done more harm than good. With time, many of the issues described above may be addressed and resolved by methodologists. Until then, however, we recommend that researchers employ extreme caution and conservatism when using LGMMs. To use LGMMs the researcher must appropriately address nonnormality (either by transforming variables or by properly modeling nonnormality) and have very strong theoretical reasons to suspect the existence of discrete classes. However, Bauer and Shanahan (2007) provide a sound example of how these techniques can be fruitfully employed that does not rely on a class interpretation, but instead they emphasize their use to approximate an unknown nonlinear function.

Suggestions If One Uses LGMM

Given the methodological difficulties and potential pitfalls of LGMM, researchers should exercise extreme restraint and caution if using LGMMs. If one feels amply justified on the basis of strong theory to employ LGMMs, one needs to follow the principles of replicability, interpretability, and predictability. These principles are general ones that cannot replace very strong theory that clearly states (1) why qualitatively distinct classes should exist, (2) how many classes should exist, and (3) what the functional form of the growth trajectories within each class should be. These principles also cannot replace quality measurement to provide data that meet the estimation needs of LGMMs. Nevertheless, these principles can strengthen the validity of conclusions drawn on the basis of LGMM.

Because of the susceptibility and tendency to find groups where groups may not exist, replicate the subgroup compositions using either cross-validation techniques (if sample sizes are very large; Browne & Cudeck, 1989) or independent samples (or subsamples). One form of replication that may be fruitful in this context is to employ an $N-k$ resampling technique (i.e., sample size, N, minus a sample fraction, k; called group jackknife; see Efron, 1979; Efron & Tibshirani, 1993) to derive subgroups and to compare the profiles and probabilities of group memberships across the repeated subsamples. This criterion, however, is the weakest supporting evidence because if the data that one analyzes have problematic characteristics that give rise to spurious classes, then these spurious classes are likely to reemerge. The best use of this criterion is to collect new data with improved measures that clearly satisfy the estimation needs of LGMMs.

Interpretability refers to the theoretical basis for the expectation of subgroups that emerge from LGMMs. Here, specifying a priori, and grounding in sound theory, the number and expected nature of all groups that should emerge would provide a basis to feel encouraged that the derived groups are meaningful. Too often

researchers succumb to the tendency to "Label After Results Are Known" (LARKing; c.f. HARKing, Kerr, 1998). Post hoc labeling of subgroups encourages reification of the potentially random subgroups that emerge. The more that theory can be brought to bear in LGMMs, the more the technique has a confirmatory nature to it and the more likely it is that the identified groups are meaningful.

The third key to supporting the validity of the LGMM results is predictability. Again, on the basis of *very strong predictions grounded in theory*, specifying a set of variables that can predict and reliably differentiate the subgroup characteristics would add the strength of criterion validity information to the work. Moreover, specifying a set of criterion variables with which the subgroups show reliable associations would further strengthen the validity arguments in favor of meaningful subgroups. These criterion associations also need to be grounded in theory and should provide clear statements of both the direction and magnitude of associations.

These basic principles can provide a broad set of methodologically grounded arguments to support the results of LGMMs. For the most part, however, we strongly encourage researchers to resist the temptation to apply these models simply because of their intuitive appeal. Unlike other statistical methods in which violations of assumptions do not completely undermine the utility of the procedures, LGMMs are quite sensitive to assumption violations.

Combining Panel Models With Latent Growth Curve Models

Bollen and Curran (2004, 2006) and Curran and Bollen (2001) emphasize that panel models and latent growth curve models need not be treated as mutually exclusive choices for modeling longitudinal data. They propose an *autoregressive latent trajectory* (ALT) model (Figure 2.7) that incorporates aspects of both kinds of models. The ALT model includes factors representing aspects of change (intercept, slope, etc., as in Figure 2.6) but also

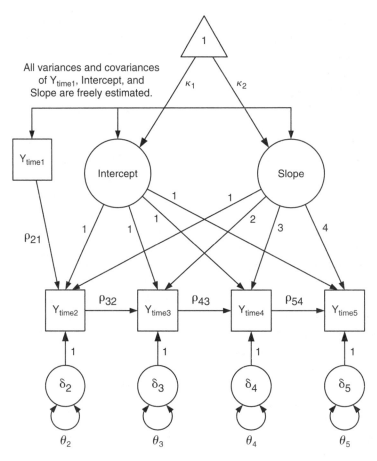

FIGURE 2.7   An autoregressive latent trajectory model with five repeated measurements.

directional paths linking adjacent measurements, as in Figure 2.3. An example of this
ALT model is displayed in Figure 2.7.

In the ALT model, y at time t is modeled as
a function of (1) an underlying latent trajectory that determines growth over time *and* (2)
y at time $t-1$. Thus, one can think of the ALT
model as a special case of LGM with time-
varying covariates, where the covariate at each
occasion after the first is simply the repeated
measure at the previous occasion. One could
also think of the panel model and the standard
latent growth curve model as nested within the
ALT model as special cases. The ρ coefficients
are autoregressive parameters that reflect the
degree of association between adjacent measurements after controlling for the growth curve.

The ρ coefficients are sometimes constrained
to equality. Because the panel model treats the
first measurement as exogenous to the system, in ALT models the initial measure is also
treated as exogenous and permitted to covary
with the latent curve factors.

TIME SERIES AND RELATED MODELS

The methods for analyzing longitudinal
data discussed thus far are generally implemented in data collection designs involving
a large sample of participants and a small but
adequate number of repeated observations.
Often, research questions involve longitudinal
designs where a small number of individuals
(perhaps even one) are measured repeatedly

over a large number of intervals. In time series analysis, numerous (often 50 or more) observations provide the basis for estimating key parameters depicting the associations of the measures over time (Box & Pierce, 1970). Designs such as this are the ideal longitudinal design for many questions in the social and behavioral sciences (Velicer & Fava, 2003). Tracking key variables at intensive intervals is relatively easy using handheld devices or daily diary data, providing a long series of measurements (Walls & Schafer, 2006). The goal of time series (and related) designs and analyses are to identify time-related patterns in the sequence of numbers where the patterns are correlated, but offset in time.

Manifest Variable Time Series Analysis

The need for specific techniques of time series analysis arises when considering the problems of classical methods, such as multiple regression, in analyzing these intensive repeated data. The primary rationale for use of time series procedures rather than multiple regression analysis is the inherent dependency that results from making repeated observations of the same participant or group of participants, referred to as autocorrelation. Use of multiple regression in the presence of autocorrelation is an explicit violation of the assumption of independence of errors. As a result, Type I error rates would be substantially increased. In addition, false patterns may either obscure or spuriously enhance effects of predictors (e.g., onset of a contextual change) unless the autocorrelation is accounted for in the model.

There are several classes of time series analysis (see Hershberger, Molenaar, & Corneal, 1996). The most common time series application in behavioral research (Velicer & Fava, 2003) is the autoregressive integrated moving average (ARIMA; Box, Jenkins, & Reinsel, 1994) class of models in which the pattern of change in a dependent variable is assessed over time (see also Boker, Deboeck, Edler, & Keel; 2008; Hershberger et al., 1996; van Buuren, 1997). The basic properties of

an ARIMA model are characterized by three parameters. The key elements of an ARIMA (p, d, q) time series analysis are the lingering effects of preceding scores called *autoregressive* elements (p), trends in the data called *integrated* elements (d), and the lingering effects of preceding shocks called the *moving average* element (q). All ARIMA models also have random process error terms called *shocks*, but differ in the *order* (how many preceding observations must be considered when determining the dependency) of the p, d, and q parameters.

A time series analysis consists of three steps. The first step is to identify which mathematical model best represents the data, focusing on the autocorrelation function, potential cyclic patterns, autoregressive components (p), and moving-average components (q). Here, the task is to specify values of the p, d, and q parameters that adequately fit the pattern of change over time. One typically begins by identifying d, the integrative element, representing the average pattern of no change in mean ($d = 0$), linear increase or decrease ($d = 1$), or linear and quadratic change ($d = 2$) (or potentially higher order change processes, although these are rare) across the *entire* time span. Once this overall pattern is identified, it is removed (in time series terminology, the series is made *stationary*), and the next two parameters are estimated. These parameters specify whether scores (p) or moving averages (q) are unrelated to previous scores (e.g., $p = 0$), related only to the previous score (i.e., simple autocorrelation, $p = 1$), or related to even earlier scores or shocks (p or $q > 1$). The second step, *estimation*, is to reconfigure the dependent observed variable into a serially independent variable through a transformation appropriate for the identified model. The third step, *diagnosis*, is to estimate the model parameters through generalized least squares and examine the residuals for unaccounted patterns.

Time series analysis can be used to answer several types of research questions. First, time series analysis can be used to evaluate patterns of overall trends and autocorrelation, such as whether there are linear increases or decreases over time, or whether previous scores/shocks impact later scores. Time series analyses can also be used to evaluate potential cycles and trends, therefore identifying potential seasonal or other periodic patterns (e.g., patterns of substance use across a week that are high near weekends and lower during the middle weekdays), and whether longer trends are distinct from (or similar to) "local" patterns. Time series analyses are sometimes used for forecasting, or attempting to predict value of observations in the future; this use is more common in the field of economics, but might be considered in adolescent research (e.g., predicting patterns of school violence across the school year).

Time series analyses can also consider covariates of change (see McDowell, McCleary, Meidinger, & Hay, 1980). When considering presumed causes of change, the field of time series analysis often uses the term *interventions* to reference these predictors of change. Following this tradition, we use here the term *intervention* broadly to refer to any event (or shock) expected to impact the adolescent across time, whether intentionally introduced by the researcher (e.g., social skills training) or naturally occurring (e.g., an adolescent joins a school club). The impact of these interventions or events is evaluated after accounting for other change patterns (e.g., cyclical waves). Similarly, we can evaluate whether this impact is abrupt and permanent (e.g., disasters, parental divorce that permanently affects the adolescent's family environment) or abrupt but temporary (e.g., parental separation that resolves to a stable family environment). It is also possible to evaluate the impact of multiple interventions, assuming there is some separation of these interventions in time (e.g., parental divorce and later transition to a different school). Similarly, one can evaluate the impact of introduction, then removal, of an intervention (e.g., an adolescent joins and then leaves a school club).

Although time series analyses often use data from a single person, they can also incorporate data from multiple participants or compare across individuals or groups to assess the degree of similarity in the patterns for different populations. Several options for combining time series data across participants exist. In *pooled* time series analysis (Hsiao, 1986), all observations for all participants are included in a single vector, and a patterned transformation matrix is utilized to convert the serially dependent variable into a serially independent variable. Another alternative parallels meta-analysis. Here, individual participant time series are combined rather than individual studies. However, the meta-analytic approach is difficult in that there is a lack of statistical time series information in the published literature (many reports still rely on visual analysis) and an appropriate definition of effect size is needed for time series data. Multilevel or mixed modeling, as described in the previous sections, can be considered as a means of utilizing data from multiple participants, where the elements of the time series are nested within individuals, resulting in a two-level hierarchy. A multilevel approach to time series analysis is easily conducted using traditional multilevel software (for example, HLM or SAS PROC MIXED). In SEM packages, specifying a time series model can be more challenging because of the large number of observation occasions (e.g., typically > 50) and the need to model such data in "wide" format.

Multivariate time series models involve measuring multiple variables at each time point for the same individual. A basic approach can be to determine the cross-lagged correlational structure between the multiple variables, where *lag* refers to the time relation between two variables. If one variable can be conceptualized as a dependent variable and the remaining variables can be considered covariates, then a *concomitant variable time series analysis* (Glass, Willson, & Gottman, 1975) can be conducted as a direct analog to the ANCOVA. We discuss the possibilities of multivariate time series models in the next section on latent variable analyses.

Latent Variable Time Series Analysis

Most techniques described as "time series" models are applied to manifest variable relations and often to a single variable. In the early developments of factor analysis, however, p-technique factor analysis was introduced to provide a basis for modeling multivariate time series data as a reduced set of latent factors (Cattell, 1952, 1963, 1988). Simply stated, p-technique factor analysis utilizes factor extraction methods for a set of variables, but rather than factor across multiple individuals, the cases used to generate the analyzed covariance matrix are intensively repeated observations of one or a few individuals. In this regard, the "sample size" used in the analysis is the number of repeated observations, and the actual number of participants may be only a single individual. P-technique factor analysis, as originally conceived, has some known limitations. For example, if there is any serial dependency inherent in the time series, it can result in underestimated factor loadings (i.e., due to positive autocorrelations; Wood & Brown, 1994). When there is little or no dependency in the time series data, p-technique can provide useful factors that can inform important research questions (see Hawley & Little, 2003, for example).

The basic idea of p-technique SEM analysis is that indicators of a construct will ebb and flow over time in a consistent manner such that they will reflect an underlying latent construct that is defined on the basis of the change patterns among the indicators (Nesselroade, McArdle, Aggen, & Meyers, 2001). The relations among multiple constructs can then be assessed and compared on the basis of their cross-time changes with one another. For example, asking a person to rate his or her mood by providing ratings on three indicators of positive affect (e.g., happy, glad, up) and three indicators of negative affect (e.g., sad, down, blue) every day for, say, 100 days would yield a covariance matrix among the indicators that would allow one to test a model in which two constructs, each with three indicators, underlie

the data. Such a model would be a simple CFA specifying two constructs, and the appropriateness of the model would be evaluated using standard model fit criteria.

A time-ordered data matrix such as this easily captures contemporaneous relations among the indicator processes, but it does not capture lagged dynamic influences. To address this limitation, dynamic p-technique SEM utilizes the inherent time-ordered information of such a data matrix to analyze a lagged covariance matrix wherein the effects of the constructs at occasion o can be evaluated for their influence on the latent constructs at occasion $o + 1$ (Hawley & Little, 2003). In other words, the data set can be lagged such that concurrent covariation and lagged covariation among a set of variables can be modeled. Because SEM is a covariance structure modeling technique, covariance matrices of this nature can be analyzed in much the same way that a covariance matrix derived from multiple individuals can be analyzed. Both panel-like and growth curve–like models are perfectly suited to model dynamic covariance matrices. Because the dynamic version of p-technique SEM analysis explicitly models any serial dependency in the data (Hershberger, 1998), the dependency issue no longer presents a potentially biasing influence on model parameters.

Figure 2.8 depicts a basic block Toeplitz covariance matrix that is modeled in a dynamic p-technique SEM (see Hawley & Little, 2003; Little, Bovaird, & Slegers, 2006). A lagged covariance matrix contains three distinct structural features. The first feature is the simultaneous or synchronous relations among the variables. In this example, these simultaneous relations among the variables are represented twice, within Lag 0 and again within Lag 1, in the triangles directly below the major diagonal. The variances of the variables are located along the major diagonals and covariances are located off the diagonals. For the most part, the corresponding elements between these two sections would be nearly or exactly identical (see Hawley & Little,

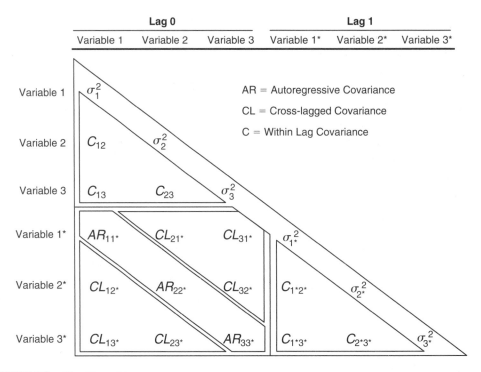

FIGURE 2.8   Toeplitz matrix.

2003). The lower quadrant of a lagged covariance matrix contains the lagged information among the variables, which reflects two sources of lag information. The autoregressive lagged relations between each pair of variables are located on the subdiagonal of this lower quadrant (denoted $AR_{1,1*}$, $AR_{2,2*}$, and $AR_{3,3*}$; see Figure 2.8). This information reflects a variable's correlation with itself between lag 0 and lag 1. Cross-lagged relations among the variables are represented in the upper and lower triangles of this quadrant (e.g., $CL_{1,2*}$, $CL_{1,3*}$, and $CL_{2,3*}$). $CL_{1,2*}$, for example, represents the covariation between variable 1 at lag 0 (V_1) and variable 2 at lag 1 (V_{2*}) (see e.g., Molenaar, 1985, 1994; Molenaar, De Gooijer, & Schmitz, 1992; Wood & Brown, 1994). With dynamic p-technique models the structural relations specified for the variables within lag 0 would be identical for lag 1 because these two parts of the block Toeplitz dynamic matrix are essentially identical. The key feature of dynamic p-technique

SEM models therefore is the unique parameters that link the constructs estimated within lag 0 with their lagged counterparts within lag 1. These parameters reflect the dynamic relations among the constructs.

Dynamic p-technique SEM is a very powerful technique to model developmental phenomena (Little, Bovaird & Slegers, 2006). Dynamic p-technique factor analysis has been applied in the domains of mood, personality, and locus of control (see Jones & Nesselroade, 1990, for a review). Unfortunately, the technique has yet to be fully utilized as a potentially powerful research tool in adolescent developmental research. Given that the intensive study of a single individual allows one to model the truly dynamic interplay among a set of constructs (Nesselroade & Molenaar, 1999), this lack of utilization is disappointing. Dynamic p-technique SEM is particularly well suited to examine questions regarding topics such as the person–situation debate and the social–personality nexus (see Fleeson & Jolley, 2006).

Dynamic p-technique SEM has the additional advantages of traditional applications of SEM such as the ability to model change relations as error-free constructs. Moreover, the lagged covariance matrix depicted in Figure 2.8 can be extended to include multiple potential lags.

Although dynamic p-technique SEM models can be fit to a single individual, the broader usefulness of this approach emerges when one compares the resulting dynamic models of change across a sample of individuals. With this approach, the key sample size issue is ensuring sufficient data points for each individual to establish a well-conditioned model for each individual. In such situations, the models can be compared across a relatively small number of individuals to draw conclusions about similarities and differences in the modeled dynamic processes. In this regard, the number of persons needed to make reasonably sound nomothetic generalizations is relatively small. In situations in which the number of observations for a given subject is not sufficiently large to allow estimation of a well-conditioned covariance matrix, data from a number of participants can be chained. In particular, Nesselroade and Molenaar (1999) proposed combining pooled time series data with dynamic factor analysis to overcome the limitation of the number of observations in the time series needed for stable estimation of the population covariance matrices.

In short, dynamic p-technique SEM is particularly useful for intensive repeated measures designs that are geared to understand dynamic change processes. Advantages of the dynamic p-technique include accounting for the autocorrelation among indicators, allowing cross-lagged influences, and correcting for measurement error (when multiple indicators of latent variables are employed). Dynamic p-technique SEM enjoys nearly limitless expandability to be able to incorporate static covariates, time-varying effects, and static outcomes (Little, Bovaird, & Slegers, 2006). With multiple-group capabilities of SEM programs, comparing models across groups of individuals allows nomothetic assessments of the

similarities and differences in the dynamic patterns among individuals.

MEDIATION AND MODERATION IN LONGITUDINAL DATA

Questions about mediation and moderation abound, but these terms are often misused or misunderstood. *Mediation* is said to occur when part of the effect of X on Y occurs indirectly through some intermediate variable M. That is, X causes Y because X causes M, which in turn causes Y, or M is one mechanism through which X exerts its effect on Y. A question about mediation, therefore, generally takes the form of "by what means does variable X exert influence on variable Y?" In other words, is there a potential causal chain that links X to Y via some mediating influence M? Here, M is the "delivery agent" or "carrier" that transmits the influence of X to Y.

Moderation, however, occurs when the magnitude or direction of the effect of X on Y depends on some third variable W. A question about moderation generally takes the form of "is the relation between variable X and variable Y impacted by some moderating influence, W?" Here, W is the "changer" of a relation between two (or more) variables; in other words, a question about moderation typically is answered with an "it depends on"–type statement: The relation between X and Y depends on the level of variable W.

Mediation and moderation are often confused, despite repeated attempts to educate researchers on the difference (e.g., Baron & Kenny, 1986; Frazier, Tix, & Barron, 2004). In this section we assume the reader is already familiar with the basic concepts of—and distinctions between—mediation and moderation. A good understanding of the basic concepts involved in mediation can be gained from Frazier et al. (2004); MacKinnon (2008); MacKinnon, Fairchild, and Fritz (2007); MacKinnon, Lockwood, Hoffman, West, and Sheets (2002); Preacher and Hayes (2008b); and Shrout and Bolger (2002). Basic material on modeling moderation (interaction) effects is provided by Aiken and West (1991); Cohen, Cohen, West, and Aiken (2003); Jaccard, Turrisi, and Wan (1990); and Aguinis (2004). Here, we discuss some ways in which mediation and moderation effects may be incorporated into models for longitudinal data. In what follows, we assume that the *indirect effect* (the product of the X → M and M → Y paths) has been adopted to represent mediation (e.g., Dearing & Hamilton, 2006).

Mediation in Longitudinal Settings

The first questions to ask regarding mediation are "What effect is hypothesized to be mediated?" and "By what?" The object of a mediation analysis is to determine by what intermediate steps an effect unfolds (or by what mechanism the effect occurs). Once potential mediators (mechanisms) are identified, attention can be devoted to modeling the effect. Traditional cross-sectional models provide a weak basis for causal inference (and hence inferences of mediation effects) because they allow no time for effects to unfold. Thus, panel models are ideally suited for investigating mediation effects. Gollob and Reichardt (1991) and Cole and Maxwell (2003) strongly advocate using models like that in Figure 2.9 to address hypotheses of mediation. Such models have many advantages relative to other models used to assess mediation. First, the temporal separation necessary for establishing causal effects is considered. Second, because repeated measures of each variable are

included, more precise estimates of key path coefficients are obtained. Third, panel models can easily incorporate latent variables to correct for measurement error. Fourth, by controlling for previous measurement of M and Y, only the portions of the variances of M and Y that do not remain stable over time contribute to the estimation of the mediation effect. This serves to reduce bias and paint a more realistic picture of the indirect process by which X effects change in Y via M.

Gollob and Reichardt (1991) argue that there is no single mediation effect characterizing a set of variables X, M, and Y. Rather, a potentially different mediation effect exists for every choice of lag separating the assessments of X and M, and M and Y (see also Cole & Maxwell, 2003; Maxwell & Cole, 2007). Thus, serious attention should be devoted to choosing the optimal lags to separate measurement of key variables involved in the mediation effect. It is important to note that this optimal lag may not correspond to the lag associated with the largest effect. The best lag to use instead may be dictated by theory or context. For example, if the researcher is interested in gauging how (and by what means) an intervention initiated at the beginning of the school year affects grades at the end of the school year, the beginning and end points of the study are predetermined. It remains only to choose the appropriate occasion (or preferably occasions) to measure the mediator. Detailed instructions for how to estimate and test mediation effects in panel models, as well as other important design and modeling issues to consider, can be found in Cole and Maxwell (2003), Maxwell and Cole (2007), and Little et al. (2007).

Moderation in Longitudinal Settings

As with mediation, the first questions to ask with regard to moderation are "What effect is hypothesized to be moderated?" and "By what?" Once these questions are answered, the appropriate modeling strategy follows naturally. In the context of panel models, for

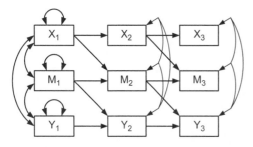

FIGURE 2.9 A longitudinal mediation panel model.

example, the lagged effect of X_1 on Y_2 may depend on W_1 (in order for W to influence this lagged effect, W necessarily must be measured before Y_2, hence the "1" subscript), in which case the researcher may consider using W_1 and the product of X_1 and W_1 as additional predictors of Y_2. There are numerous ways in which moderation can be examined with longitudinal data. We focus on two examples to give readers an idea of the many possibilities.

Moderated Autoregressive Effects

Consider first a (univariate) time series consisting of four equally spaced repeated measurements of affiliation. The simplex model depicted in Figure 2.10 could be applied to these data. Coefficients a_1, b_1, and c_1 may or may not be constrained to equality, depending

on how stationary the researcher believes the process to be.

One way to incorporate a moderation effect, assuming it is justified by theory, would be to hypothesize that the autoregressive weights a_1, b_1, and c_1 are moderated by self-monitoring (SM), which might be assumed to be a trait characteristic and so measured only once, at Time 1. Moderation by SM may be incorporated by computing the product SM × affiliation at Time $j - 1$ and including this interaction term as a predictor at Time $j - 1$, as in Figure 2.11. The significance of the a_3, b_3, and c_3 coefficients can be used as a basis for deciding whether the autoregressive effect of affiliation at Time $j - 1$ on affiliation at Time j is moderated by SM.

As with many interaction effects, if the interaction is found to be significant, the researcher

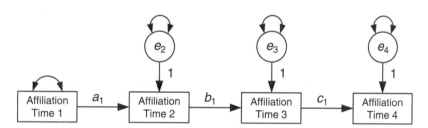

FIGURE 2.10   A simplex model for four repeated measurements.

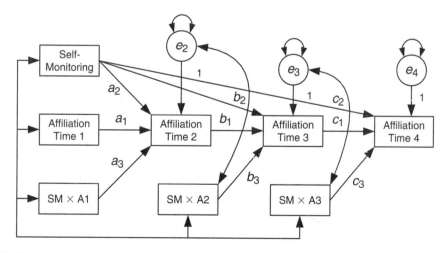

FIGURE 2.11   A moderated simplex model in which the autoregressive effect depends on the moderator self-monitoring.

may wish to explore the effect further by (1) plotting the interaction effect for various interesting conditional values of SM (say, ±1 SD and the mean) and (2) testing the *simple slope* of affiliation at Time j regressed on affiliation at Time $j - 1$ (i.e., the *simple autoregression*) for significance at conditional values of SM. Methods for accomplishing this are exactly analogous to well-known methods for plotting and probing significant interaction effects in ordinary regresssion (see Aiken & West, 1991; Preacher & Rucker, 2005; Preacher, Curran, & Bauer, 2006). For example, if we wished to test the significance of the autoregression of affiliation at Time 3 on affiliation at Time 2 when SM = 3, the simple autoregression is:

$$\hat{\omega} = \hat{b}_1 + \hat{b}_3 (3)$$

(18)

and the standard error for this estimate is:

$$se_{\hat{\omega}} = \sqrt{\hat{s}_1^2 + 2(3)\hat{s}_{31} + (3^2)\hat{s}_3^2}$$

(19)

where $\hat{s}_1^2$, $\hat{s}_3^2$, and $\hat{s}_{31}$ are the asymptotic variances and covariance of the parameter estimates $\hat{b}_1$ and $\hat{b}_3$. The critical ratio $\hat{\omega}/se_{\hat{\omega}}$ can be compared to the standard normal distribution (assuming a large sample size) to determine whether the autoregression is significant when SM = 3. All of the requisite coefficient estimates can be found in standard SEM output, and the asymptotic (co)variances are provided by special request in most SEM programs.

Predictors of Slopes in MLM and LGM

Moderation effects can also be modeled as part of the growth curve models discussed earlier, although these effects may not be immediately recognizable as moderation. Recall that any variable that affects the relation between two other variables can be considered a moderator. In LGM, the slope factor represents the relation between time and the outcome variable

(this latent variable itself may or may not vary across people). Thus, including predictors of the slope factor amounts to including moderators of the effect of time. See Curran, Bauer, and Willoughby (2004) and Preacher et al. (2006) for more detailed discussions and worked examples. By the same token, including level 2 predictors of slopes in MLM qualifies as moderation (Bauer & Curran, 2005). In both the LGM and MLM contexts, if predictors of slopes are included, the same variables must also be included as predictors of intercepts.

Extensions

Clearly, the concepts of mediation and moderation have many potential applications in models for longitudinal data. We illustrated a few here, but the precise way in which mediators or moderators are included in specific applications will depend on the research context. Some studies may require multiple mediating variables (MacKinnon, 2000; Preacher & Hayes, 2008a). Multiple-group analysis can be construed as a kind of moderation analysis, in which some model parameters can vary according to the moderating group variable. Polynomial growth functions (e.g., quadratic trajectories) can be considered moderation effects, in which one variable (e.g., time) moderates its own linear influence on the outcome. Interactions among three or more variables may be entertained.

Mediation and moderation may even be combined into one model. For example, a given mediation effect may be hypothesized to vary across levels of a moderator (*moderated mediation*; see Bauer, Preacher, & Gil, 2006; Edwards & Lambert, 2007; Preacher, Rucker, & Hayes, 2007). Or a moderation effect may be hypothesized to be mediated (*mediated moderation*). Latent moderation effects, in which either the independent variable or the moderator is latent (or both) are beyond the scope of this chapter, but interested readers can consult Schumacker and Marcoulides (1998) and Little, Bovaird, and Widaman (2006) to learn more.

CONCLUSIONS

In this chapter, we have provided a broad overview of issues and techniques in modeling longitudinal data during adolescence. As we have indicated throughout, a number of detailed resources are available to delve more deeply into these issues and techniques. We close by discussing some opportunities and future directions for longitudinal data analysis.

Opportunities

As should be clear, longitudinal data can provide extremely rich information to inform our understanding of developmental mechanisms and processes. Of course, issues of causality are more challenging in the context of nonexperimental methodology, but when coupled with a broad-based program of research that includes experimentation and rigorous inferential designs, the basis for causal inference can be significantly strengthened. In fact, each of the techniques and issues that we have highlighted herein can be appropriately coupled with rigorous experimental designs such as randomized intervention trials and regression discontinuity designs (Greenwood & Little, 2008). In situations in which it is not possible or ethical to manipulate the presumed cause, longitudinal studies without experimental manipulation often represent our best approaches to evaluating presumed causal relations (or at least the temporal primacy of constructs; Card & Little, 2007).

We emphasize again that the opportunities afforded by longitudinal research will not be realized if researchers do not attend carefully to the critical design and measurement issues we outlined above. Moreover, the statistical model that one chooses to employ must match the theoretical model in order to capitalize on the strong inferential capabilities of modern analytic procedures. Quite often, researchers will need to utilize more than one statistical approach to fully exploit the available information contained in longitudinal data. Panel analyses, for example, can inform the direct and indirect pathways by which antecedent variables influence consequent variables, while multivariate growth curve models can reveal different information such as the strength of the dynamic relations in the changes over time.

Future Directions

In terms of future directions, we highlight some that are particularly promising for use in the study of adolescent development. First, Bayesian estimation methods have emerged as useful tools for estimating a variety of models, including complex growth curve models that can be difficult or impossible to estimate using current maximum likelihood estimation (MLE)-based software. Bayesian methods for analyzing longitudinal data in the study of adolescent development are particularly useful because of their ability to incorporate prior information in estimating both simple and complex models. In addition to being an alternative to the MLE method, Bayesian methods also have unique strengths, such as systematically incorporating prior information from previous studies. Bayesian methods are also particularly well-suited to analyze small sample data (Zhang, Hamagami, Wang, Grimm, & Nesselroade, 2007; Wang & McArdle, 2008).

A second important direction in the development of tools for the analysis of longitudinal data is in the use of bootstrap estimation of sampling distributions of parameter estimates (and corresponding confidence intervals). Bootstrap estimation has been around for some time but is only recently receiving the attention that the approach deserves. Although various methods of bootstrapping exist, the basic idea is that one resamples from the original sample a very large number of replicate samples (e.g., 2,000 to 5,000 resamples). These resamples have the same sample size as the original sample, but the key is that the resamples are drawn from the original sample *with replacement*. Because the sampling is done with replacement a given observational record might occur many times in a given resample and not occur at all in another resample.

The inherent variability across the large number of resamples provides an empirical basis to estimate the confidence intervals for each estimated parameter of a given model. The model is run using each of the large number of replicate samples and the estimated parameters are stored. The estimated parameters from the original sample provide the point estimate for a given analysis. The values demarcating the lower and upper 2.5% of the distribution of estimated parameters from the bootstrapped samples provide an empirical calculation of the 95% confidence interval of each model parameter. A nice feature of such empirically derived distributions is that they do not need to be symmetric and the inherent degree of sampling variability is fully captured. When the collected data do not meet the assumptions of the analytic procedure (e.g., normality), the quality of generalizations made from bootstrapped estimation of confidence intervals often are significantly better than those derived from the theoretical distributions used in other estimation methods such as maximum likelihood and least squares estimation.

Final Thoughts

Given the lack of training opportunities found in many universities, students and researchers often must rely on self-guided learning. A chapter such as this cannot substitute for in-depth training, but it can provide a guide to the directions and issues that one should cover. In this chapter we provided a broad overview of issues in, and techniques for, longitudinal data analysis. Because a handbook chapter such as this cannot provide the details or address the nuances of any of the topics we have presented, we have attempted to provide a wealth of readings and resources to help readers find the additional information needed. We have also highlighted a number of web-based resources (e.g., www.Quant.KU.edu) that provide updated guidance and information relevant to the techniques we have described here. Because these techniques continue to develop and become more capable as well as more refined, we encourage all researchers to focus concerted efforts to stay informed with the state-of-the-science in quantitative methodology.

REFERENCES

Aguinis, H. (2004). *Regression analysis for categorical moderators.* New York: Guilford Press.

Aiken, L. S., & West, S. G. (1991). *Multiple regression: Testing and interpreting interactions.* Thousand Oaks, CA: Sage.

Anderson, J. G. (1987). Structural equation models in the social and behavioral sciences: Model building. *Child Development, 58,* 49–64.

Baltes, P. B. (1968). Longitudinal and cross-sectional sequences in the study of age and generation effects. *Human Development, 11,* 145–171.

Barker, E. D., Tremblay, R. E., Nagin, D. S., Vitaro, F., & Lacourse, E. (2006). Development of male proactive and reactive physical aggression during adolescence. *Journal of Child Psychology and Psychiatry, 47,* 783–790.

Baron, R. M., & Kenny, D. A. (1986). The moderator–mediator variable distinction in social psychological research: Conceptual, strategic, and statistical considerations. *Journal of Personality and Social Psychology, 51,* 1173–1182.

Bauer, D. J. (2003). Estimating multilevel linear models as structural equation models. *Journal of Educational and Behavioral Statistics, 28,* 135–167.

Bauer, D. J. (2007). Observations on the use of growth mixture models in psychological research. *Multivariate Behavioral Research, 42,* 757–786.

Bauer, D. J., & Curran, P. J. (2003a). Distributional assumptions of growth mixture models: Implications for overextraction of latent trajectory classes. *Psychological Methods, 8,* 338–363.

Bauer, D. J., & Curran, P. J. (2003b). Over-extracting latent trajectory classes: Much ado about nothing? Reply to Rindskopf (2003), Muthén (2003), and Cudeck and Henly (2003). *Psychological Methods, 8,* 384–393.

Bauer, D. J., & Curran, P. J. (2004). The integration of continuous and discrete latent variable models: Potential problems and promising opportunities. *Psychological Methods, 9*(1), 3–29.

Bauer, D. J., & Curran, P. J. (2005). Probing interactions in fixed and multilevel regression: Inferential and graphical techniques. *Multivariate Behavioral Research, 40,* 373–400.

Bauer, D. J., & Shanahan, M. J. (2007). Modeling complex interactions: Person-centered and variable-centered approaches. In T. D. Little, J. A. Bovaird, & N. A. Card (Eds.), *Modeling contextual effects in longitudinal studies* (pp. 255–284). Mahwah, NJ: Lawrence Erlbaum.

Bauer, D. J., Preacher, K. J., & Gil, K. M. (2006). Conceptualizing and testing random indirect effects and moderated mediation in multilevel models: New procedures and recommendations. *Psychological Methods, 11,* 142–163.

Bell, R. Q. (1953). Convergence: An accelerated longitudinal approach. *Child Development, 24,* 145–152.

Bickel, R. (2007). *Multilevel analysis for applied research: It's just regression!* New York: Guilford Press.

Bijleveld, C. C. J. H., & van der Kamp, L. J. T. (1998). *Longitudinal data analysis: Designs, models and methods.* Thousand Oaks, CA: Sage.

Blozis, S. A., Conger, K. J., & Harring, J. R. (2007). Nonlinear latent curve models for multivariate longitudinal data. *International Journal of Behavioral Development, 31,* 340–346.

Boker, S. M., Deboeck, P. R., Edler, C., & Keel, P. K. (2008). Generalized local linear approximation of derivatives from time series. In S. Chow, E. Ferrer, & F. Hsieh (Eds.), *Statistical methods for modeling human dynamics: An interdisciplinary dialogue.* Boca Raton, FL: Taylor & Francis.

Bollen, K. A. (1989). *Structural equations with latent variables.* New York: John Wiley & Sons.

Bollen, K. A., & Curran, P. J. (2004). Autoregressive latent trajectory (ALT) models: A synthesis of two traditions. *Sociological Methods and Research, 32,* 336–383.

Bollen, K. A., & Curran, P. J. (2006). *Latent curve models: A structural equation perspective.* Hoboken, NJ: John Wiley & Sons.

Box, G. E. P., Jenkins, G. M., & Reinsel, G. C. (1994). *Time series analysis: Forecasting and control.* (3rd ed.). Englewood Cliffs, NJ: Prentice Hall.

Box, G. E. P., & Pierce, D. A. (1970). Distribution of residual autocorrelations in autoregressive-integrated moving average time series models. *Journal of the American Statistical Association, 65,* 1509–1526.

Brown, T. A. (2006). *Confirmatory factor analysis for applied research.* New York: Guilford Press.

Browne, M. W., & Cudeck, R. (1989). Single sample cross-validation indices for covariance structures. *Multivariate Behavioral Research, 24,* 445–455.

Byrne, B. M., & Crombie, G. (2003). Modeling and testing change: An introduction to the latent growth curve model. *Understanding Statistics, 2,* 177–203.

Byrne, B. M., Shavelson, R. J., & Muthén, B. (1989). Testing for the equivalence of factor covariance and mean structures: The issue of partial measurement invariance. *Psychological Bulletin, 105,* 456–466.

Cairns, R. B., Bergman, L. R., & Kagan, J. (Eds.) (1998). *Methods and models for studying the individual.* Thousand Oaks, CA: Sage.

Card, N. A. & Little, T. D. (2007). Longitudinal modeling of developmental processes. *International Journal of Behavioral Development, 31,* 297–302.

Card, N. A., & Little, T. D. (2006). Analytic considerations in cross-cultural research on peer relations. In X. Chen, D. C. French, & B. Schneider (Eds.), *Peer relations in cultural context* (pp. 75–95). New York: Cambridge University Press.

Card, N. A., Little, T. D., & Bovaird, J. A. (2007). Modeling ecological and contextual effects in longitudinal studies of human development. In T. D. Little, J. A. Bovaird, & N. A. Card (Eds.), *Modeling contextual effects in longitudinal studies* (pp. 1–11). Mahwah, NJ: Lawrence Erlbaum.

Cattell, R. B. (1952). The three basic factor-analytic research designs—their interrelations and derivatives. *Psychological Bulletin, 49,* 499–551.

Cattell, R. B. (1963). The structuring of change by P- and incremental R- technique. In C. W. Harris (Ed.), *Problems in measuring change* (pp. 167–198). Madison: University of Wisconsin.

Cattell, R. B. (1988). The data box. In J. R. Nesselroade & R. B. Cattell (Eds.), *Handbook of multivariate experimental psychology* (pp. 69–130). New York: Plenum.

Chan, D. (1998). The conceptualization and analysis of change over time: An integrative approach incorporating longitudinal mean and covariance structures analysis (LMACS) and multiple indicator latent growth modeling (MLGM). *Organizational Research Methods, 1,* 421–483.

Chou, C.-P., Bentler, P. M., & Pentz, M. A. (1998). Comparisons of two statistical approaches to study growth curves: The multi-level model and the latent curve analysis. *Structural Equation Modeling, 5,* 247–266.

Cohen, J., Cohen, P., West, S. G., & Aiken, L. S. (2003). *Applied multiple regression/correlation analysis for the behavioral sciences* (3rd ed.). Mahwah, NJ: Lawrence Erlbaum.

Cole, D. A., & Maxwell, S. E. (2003). Testing mediational models with longitudinal data: Questions and tips in the use of structural equation modeling. *Journal of Abnormal Psychology, 112,* 558–577.

Collins, L. M. (2006). Analysis of longitudinal data: The integration of theoretical models, temporal design, and statistical model. *Annual Review of Psychology, 57,* 505–528.

Collins, L. M., & Horn, J. L. (Eds.) (1991). *Best methods for the analysis of change: Recent advances, unanswered questions, future directions.* Washington, DC: American Psychological Association.

Collins, L. M., & Sayer, A. G. (Eds.) (2001). *New methods for the analysis of change.* Washington, DC: American Psychological Association.

Curran, P. J. (2000). A latent curve framework for the study of developmental trajectories in adolescent substance use. In J. S. Rose, L. Chassin, C. C. Presson, & S. J. Sherman (Eds.), *Multivariate applications in substance use research.* Mahwah, NJ: Lawrence Erlbaum.

Curran, P. J. (2003). Have multilevel models been structural equation models all along? *Multivariate Behavioral Research, 38,* 529–569.

Curran, P. J., Bauer, D. J., & Willoughby, M. T. (2004). Testing main effects and interactions in latent curve analysis. *Psychological Methods, 9,* 220–237.

Curran, P. J., & Bollen, K. A. (2001). The best of both worlds: Combining autoregressive and latent curve models. In L. M. Collins, & A. G. Sayer (Eds.), *New methods for the analysis of change,* (pp. 105–136). Washington, DC: American Psychological Association.

Curran, P. J., & Hussong, A. M. (2003). The use of latent trajectory models in psychopathology research. *Journal of Abnormal Psychology, 112,* 526–544.

Dearing, E., & Hamilton, L. C. (2006). Contemporary advances and classic advice for analyzing mediating and moderating variables. *Monographs of the Society for Research in Child Development, 71,* 88–104.

Duncan, O. D. (1969). Some linear models for two-wave, two-variable panel analysis. *Psychological Bulletin, 72,* 177–182.

Duncan, T. E., Duncan, S. C., & Strycker, L. A. (2006). *An introduction to latent variable growth curve modeling: Concepts, issues, and applications* (2nd ed.). Mahwah, NJ: Lawrence Erlbaum.

Dwyer, J. H. (1983). *Statistical models for the social and behavioral sciences.* New York: Oxford University Press.

Edwards, J. R., & Lambert, L. S. (2007). Methods for integrating moderation and mediation: A general analytical framework using moderated path analysis. *Psychological Methods, 12,* 1–22.

Efron, B. (1979). Bootstrap methods: Another look at the jackknife. *The Annals of Statistics, 7,* 1–26.

Efron, B., & Tibshirani, R. J. (1993). *An introduction to the bootstrap.* New York: Chapman & Hall.

Embretson, S. E. (2007). Impact of measurement scale in modeling development processes and ecological factors. In T. D. Little, J. A. Bovaird, & N. A. Card (Eds.), *Modeling contextual effects in longitudinal studies* (pp. 63–87). Mahwah, NJ: Lawrence Erlbaum.

Enders, C. K. (in press). *Applied missing data analysis.* New York: Guilford Press.

Fleeson, W., & Jolley, S. (2006). A proposed theory of the adult development of intraindividual variability in trait-manifesting behavior. In D. K. Mroczek & T. D. Little (Eds.), *Handbook of personality development* (pp. 41–60). Mahwah, NJ: Lawrence Erlbaum.

Frazier, P. A., Tix, A. P., & Barron, K. E. (2004). Testing moderator and mediator effects in counseling psychology research. *Journal of Counseling Psychology, 51,* 115–134.

Glass, G. V., Willson, V. L., & Gottman, J. M. (1975). *Design and analysis of time-series experiments.* Boulder, CO: Colorado Associated University Press.

Gollob, H. F., & Reichardt, C. S. (1987). Taking account of time lags in causal models. *Child Development, 58,* 80–92.

Gollob, H. F., & Reichardt, C. S. (1991). Interpreting and estimating indirect effects assuming time lags really matter. In L. M. Collins & J. L. Horn (Eds.), *Best methods for the analysis of change: Recent advances, unanswered questions, future directions.* Washington, DC: American Psychological Association.

Graham, J. W., Olchowski, A. E., & Gilreath, T. D. (2007). How many imputations are really needed? Some practical clarifications of multiple imputation theory. *Prevention Science*, *8*, 206–213.

Graham, J. W., Taylor, B. J., Olchowski, A. E., & Cumsille, P. E. (2006). Planned missing data designs in psychological research. *Psychological Methods*, *11*, 323–343.

Greenwood, C. R., & Little, T. D. (2008). *Use of regression discontinuity designs in special education research*. Paper commissioned as one in a series of invited NCSER, IES papers devoted to special education research methodology topics Hyattsville, MD: Optimal Solutions Group.

Hancock, G. R., & Lawrence, F. R. (2006). Using latent growth models to evaluate longitudinal change. In G. R. Hancock & R. O. Mueller (Eds.), *Structural equation modeling: A second course*. Greenwich, CT: Information Age.

Hawley, P. H., & Little, T. D. (2003). Modeling intraindividual variability and change in biobehavioral developmental processes. In B. Pugesek, A. Tomer, & A. von Eye (Eds.), *Structural equations modeling: Applications in ecological and evolutionary biology research* (pp. 143–170). Cambridge, UK: Cambridge University Press.

Hedeker, D., & Gibbons, R. D. (2006). *Longitudinal data analysis*. Hoboken, NJ: John Wiley & Sons.

Hershberger, S. L. (1998). Dynamic factor analysis. In G. A. Marcoulides (Ed.), *Modern methods for business research* (pp. 217–249). Mahwah, NJ: Lawrence Erlbaum.

Hershberger, S. L., Molenaar, P. C. M., & Corneal, S. E. (1996). A hierarchy of univariate and multivariate structural time series models. In G. A. Marcoulides & R. E. Schumaker (Eds.), *Advanced structural equation modeling: Issues and techniques* (pp. 159–194). Mawah, NJ: Lawrence Erlbaum.

Hofmann, D. A. (1997). An overview of the logic and rationale of hierarchical linear models. *Journal of Management*, *23*, 723–744.

Honaker, J., King, G., & Blackwell, M. (2008). *Amelia II: A program for missing data*. Accessed on 10/25/2008 at http://gking.harvard.edu/amelia/.

Hox, J. (2002). *Multilevel analysis: Techniques and applications*. Mahwah, NJ: Lawrence Erlbaum.

Hsiao, C. (1986). *Analysis of panel data*. Cambridge University Press.

Jaccard, J., Turrisi, R., & Wan, C. K. (1990). *Interaction effects in multiple regression*. Newberry Park, CA: Sage.

Jones, B., Nagin, D., & Roeder, K. (2001). A SAS procedure based on mixture models for estimating developmental trajectories. *Sociological Methodology Research*, *29*, 374–393.

Jones, J. C., & Nesselroade, J. R. (1990). Multivariate, replicated, single-subject, repeated measures designs and P-technique factor analysis: A review of intraindividual change studies. *Experimental Aging Research*, *16*, 171–183.

Kenny, D. A. (1979). *Correlation and causality*. New York: John Wiley & Sons.

Kerr, N. L. (1998). HARKing: Hypothesizing after the results are known. *Personality and Social Psychology Review*, *2*, 196–217.

Kessler, R. C., & Greenberg, D. F. (1981). Linear panel analysis: *Models of quantitative change*. New York: Academic Press.

Kreft, I. G. G., & de Leeuw, J. (1998). *Introducing multilevel modeling*. London: Sage.

Little, R. J. A., & Rubin D. B. (2002). *Statistical analysis with missing data* (2nd ed.). New York: John Wiley & Sons.

Little, T. D. (1997). Mean and covariance structures (MACS) analyses of cross-cultural data: Practical and theoretical issues. *Multivariate Behavioral Research*, *32*, 53–76.

Little, T. D., Bovaird, J. A., & Card, N. A. (Eds.) (2007). *Modeling contextual effects in longitudinal studies*. Mahwah, NJ: Lawrence Erlbaum.

Little, T. D., Bovaird, J. A., & Slegers, D. W. (2006). Methods for the analysis of change. In D. K. Mroczek & T. D. Little (Eds.),

Handbook of personality development (pp. 181–211). Mahwah, NJ: Lawrence Erlbaum.

Little, T. D., Bovaird, J. A., & Widaman, K. F. (2006). On the merits of orthogonalizing powered and product terms: Implications for modeling interactions among latent variables. *Structural Equation Modeling*, *13*, 497–519.

Little, T. D., Card, N. A., Bovaird, J. A., Preacher, K. J., & Crandall, C. S. (2007). Structural equation modeling of mediation and moderation with contextual factors. In T. D. Little, J. A., Bovaird, & N. A. Card (Eds.), *Modeling contextual effects in longitudinal studies* (pp. 207–230). Mahwah, NJ: Lawrence Erlbaum.

Little, T. D., Card, N. A., Slegers, D. W., & Ledford, E. C. (2007). Representing contextual effects in multiple-group MACS models. In T. D. Little, J. A., Bovaird, & N. A. Card (Eds.), *Modeling contextual effects in longitudinal studies* (pp. 121–147). Mahwah, NJ: Lawrence Erlbaum.

Little, T. D., Cunningham, W. A., Shahar, G., & Widaman, K. F. (2002). To parcel or not to parcel: Exploring the question, weighing the merits. *Structural Equation Modeling*, *9*, 151–173.

Little, T. D., Lindenberger, U., & Maier, H. (2000). Selectivity and generalizability in longitudinal research: On the effects of continuers and dropouts. In T. D. Little, K. U. Schnabel, & J. Baumert (Eds.), *Modeling longitudinal and multilevel data: Practical issues, applied approaches, and specific examples* (pp. 187–200). Mahwah, NJ: Lawrence Erlbaum.

Little, T. D., Lindenberger, U., & Nesselroade, J. R. (1999). On selecting indicators for multivariate measurement and modeling with latent variables: When "good" indicators are bad and "bad" indicators are good. *Psychological Methods*, *4*, 192–211.

Little, T. D., Preacher, K. J., Selig, J. P., & Card, N. A. (2007). New developments in latent variable panel analysis of longitudinal data. *International Journal of Behavioral Development*, *31*, 357–365.

Little, T. D., Schnabel, K. U., & Baumert, J. (Eds.) (2000). *Modeling longitudinal and multilevel data: Practical issues, applied approaches, and specific examples*. Mahwah, NJ: Lawrence Erlbaum.

Little, T. D., Slegers, D. W., & Card, N. A. (2006). A non-arbitrary method of identifying and scaling latent variables in SEM and MACS models. *Structural Equation Modeling*, *13*, 59–72.

Luke, D. A. (2004). *Multilevel modeling*. Thousand Oaks, CA: Sage.

MacCallum, R. C., Kim, C., Malarkey, W. B., & Kiecolt-Glaser, J. K. (1997). Studying multivariate change using multilevel models and latent curve models. *Multivariate Behavioral Research*, *32*, 215–253.

MacCallum, R. C., Zhang, S., Preacher, K. J., & Rucker, D. D. (2002). On the practice of dichotomization of quantitative variables. *Psychological Methods*, *7*, 19–40.

MacKinnon, D. P. (2000). Contrasts in multiple mediator models. In J. S. Rose, L. Chassm, C. C. Presson, & S. J. Sherman (Eds.), *Multivariate applications in substance use research: New methods for new questions* (pp. 141–160). Mahwah, NJ: Lawrence Erlbaum.

MacKinnon, D. P. (2008). *Introduction to statistical mediation analysis*. New York: Lawrence Erlbaum.

MacKinnon, D. P., Fairchild, A. J., & Fritz, M. S. (2007). Mediation analysis. *Annual Review of Psychology*, *58*, 593–614.

MacKinnon, D. P., Lockwood, C. M., Hoffman, J. M., West, S. G., & Sheets, V. (2002). A comparison of methods to test the significance of the mediated effect. *Psychological Methods*, *7*, 83–104.

Magnusson, D., Bergman, L. R., Rudinger, G., & Törestad, B. (Eds.) (1991). *Problems and methods in longitudinal research: Stability and change*. New York: Cambridge University Press.

Marsh, H. W., Wen, Z., Hau, K-T., Little, T. D., Bovaird, J. A., & Widaman, K. F. (2007). Unconstrained structural equation models of latent interactions: Contrasting residual- and mean-centered approaches. *Structural Equation Modeling*, *14*, 570–580.

Maxwell, S. E., & Cole, D. A. (2007). Bias in cross sectional analysis of longitudinal mediation. *Psychological Methods*, *12*, 23–44.

McDowell, D., McCleary, R., Meidinger, E. E., & Hay, R. A. (1980). *Interrupted time series analysis*. Thousand Oaks, CA: Sage.

Menard, S. W. (1991). *Longitudinal research*. Newbury Park, CA: Sage.

Meredith, W. (1993). Measurement invariance. factor analysis and factorial invariance. *Psychometrika*, *58*, 525–543.

Meredith, W., & Tisak, J. (1990). Latent curve analysis. *Psychometrika*, *55*, 107–122.

Molenaar, P. C. M. (1985). A dynamic factor model for the analysis of multivariate time series data. *Psychometrika*, *57*, 333–349.

Molenaar, P. C. M. (1994). Dynamic latent variable models in developmental psychology. In A. von Eye & C. C. Clogg (Eds.), *Latent variables analysis* (pp.155–180). Thousand Oaks, CA: Sage.

Molenaar, P. C. M., De Gooijer, J. G., & Schmitz, B. (1992). Dynamic factor analysis of nonstationary multivariate time series. *Psychometrika*, *57*, 333–349.

Moskowitz, D. S., & Hershberger, S. L. (Eds.). (2002). *Modeling intraindividual variability with repeated measures data: Methods and applications*. Mahwah, NJ: Lawrence Erlbaum.

Muthén, B. O. (2001). Latent variable mixture modeling. In G. A. Marcoulides & R. E. Schumaker (Eds.), *New developments and techniques in structural equation modeling* (pp. 1–33). Mahwah, NJ: Lawrence Erlbaum.

Muthén, B. O. (2008). Latent variable hybrids: Overview of old and new models. In G. R. Hancock & K. M. Samuelsen (Eds.), *Advances in latent variable mixture models*. Charlotte, NC: Information Age.

Muthén, B. O., & Muthén, L. K. (2000). Integrating person-centered and variable-centered analyses: Growth mixture modeling with latent trajectory classes. *Alcoholism: Clinical and Experimental Research*, *24*, 882–891.

Muthén, B. O., & Shedden, K. (1999). Finite mixture modeling with mixture outcomes using the EM algorithm. *Biometrics*, *55*, 463–469.

Muthén, L. K., & Muthén, B. O. (2007). *Mplus user's guide* (version 5). Los Angeles: Muthén & Muthén.

Nagin, D. S. (1999). Analyzing developmental trajectories: A semi-parametric, group-based approach. *Psychological Methods*, *4*, 139–157.

Nagin, D. S. (2005). *Group-based modeling of development*. Cambridge, MA: Harvard University Press.

Nagin, D. S., & Tremblay, R. E. (1999). Trajectories of boys' physical aggression, opposition, and hyperactivity on the path to physically violent and nonviolent juvenile delinquency. *Child Development*, *70*, 1181–1196.

Nesselroade, J. R., & Baltes, P. B. (Eds.). (1979). *Longitudinal research in the study of behavior and development*. New York: Academic Press.

Nesselroade, J. R., McArdle, J. J., Aggen, S. H., & Meyers, J. (2001). Dynamic factor analysis models for representing process in multivariate time-series. In D. M. Moskowitz & S. L. Hershberger (Ed.), *Modeling intraindividual variability with repeated measures data: Methods and applications* (pp. 235–265). Mahwah, NJ: Lawrence Erlbaum.

Nesselroade, J. R., & Molenaar, P. C. M. (1999). Pooling lagged covariance structures based on short, multivariate time series for dynamic factor analysis. In R. H. Hoyle (Ed.), *Statistical strategies for small sample research* (pp. 223–250). Thousand Oaks, CA: Sage.

Preacher, K. J., Curran, P. J., & Bauer, D. J. (2006). Computational tools for probing interaction effects in multiple linear regression, multilevel modeling, and latent curve analysis. *Journal of Educational and Behavioral Statistics*, *31*, 437–448.

Preacher, K. J., & Hayes, A. F. (2008a). Asymptotic and resampling strategies for assessing and comparing indirect effects in multiple mediator models. *Behavior Research Methods*, *40*, 879–891.

Preacher, K. J., & Hayes, A. F. (2008b). Contemporary approaches to assessing mediation in communication research. In A. F. Hayes, M. D. Slater, & L. B. Snyder (Eds.), *The Sage sourcebook of advanced data analysis methods for communication research* (pp. 13–54). Thousand Oaks, CA: Sage.

Preacher, K. J., & Rucker, D. D. (2005, January). *Probing significant interaction effects in path analysis*. Poster presentation, the annual meeting of the Society for Personality and Social Psychology, New Orleans, LA.

Preacher, K. J., Rucker, D. D., & Hayes, A. F. (2007). Addressing moderated mediation hypotheses: Theory, methods, and prescriptions. *Multivariate Behavioral Research*, *42*, 185–227.

Preacher, K. J., Wichman, A. L., MacCallum, R. C., & Briggs, N. E. (2008). *Latent growth curve modeling*. Thousand Oaks, CA: Sage.

Ram, N., & Grimm, K. J. (2007). Using simple and complex growth models to articulate developmental change: Matching theory to method. *International Journal of Behavioral Development*, *31*, 303–316.

Rao, C. R. (1958). Some statistical models for comparison of growth curves. *Biometrics*, *14*, 1–17.

Raudenbush, S. W., & Bryk, A. S. (2002). *Hierarchical linear models: Applications and data analysis methods* (2nd ed.). Thousand Oaks, CA: Sage.

Reise, S. P., Widaman, K. F., & Pugh, R. H. (1993). Confirmatory factor analysis and item response theory: Two approaches for exploring measurement invariance. *Psychological Bulletin*, *114*, 552–566.

Rindskopf, F. (1984). Using phantom and imaginary latent variables to parameterize constraints in linear structural models. *Psychometrika*, *49*, 37–47.

Rosel, J., & Plewis, I. (2008). Longitudinal data analysis with structural equations. *Methodology*, *4*, 37–50.

Rovine, M. J., & Molenaar, P. C. M. (2000). A structural modeling approach to a multilevel random coefficients model. *Multivariate Behavioral Research*, *35*, 51–88.

Rubin, K. H., Bukowski, W. M., & Parker, J. G. (2006). Peer interactions, relationships, and groups. In N. Eisenberg, W. Damon, & R. M. Lerner (Eds.), *Handbook of child psychology*, Vol. 3: *Social, emotional, and personality development* (6th ed.; pp. 571–645). Hoboken, NJ: John Wiley & Sons.

Saldaña, J. (2003). *Longitudinal qualitative research: Analyzing change through time*. Walnut Creek, CA: Alta Mira.

Schafer, J. L. (1997). *Analysis of incomplete multivariate data*. London: Chapman & Hall.

Schafer, J. L., & Graham, J. W. (2002) Missing data: Our view of the state of the art. *Psychological Methods*, *7*, 147–177.

Schaie, K. W. (1965). A general model for the study of developmental problems. *Psychological Bulletin*, *64*, 92–107.

Schumacker, R. E., & Marcoulides, G. A. (1998). *Interaction and nonlinear effects in structural equation modeling*. Mahwah, NJ: Lawrence Erlbaum.

Sears, R. R. (1947). Child psychology. In W. Dennis (Ed.), *Current trends in psychology* (pp. 50–74). Pittsburgh, PA: University of Pittsburgh Press.

Selig, J. P., Card, N. A., & Little, T. D. (2008). Latent variable structural equation modeling in cross-cultural research: Multigroup and multilevel approaches. In F. J. R. van de Vijver, D. A. van Hemert, & Y. H. Poortinga (Eds.), *Individuals and Cultures in Multilevel Analysis* (pp. 93–119). Mahwah, NJ: Lawrence Erlbaum.

Shadish, W. R., Cook, T. D., & Campbell, D. T. (2002). *Experimental and quasi-experimental designs for generalized causal inference*. Boston: Houghton, Mifflin and Company.

Shrout, P. E., & Bolger, N. (2002). Mediation in experimental and nonexperimental studies: New procedures and recommendations. *Psychological Methods*, *7*, 422–445.

Singer, J. D., & Willett, J. B. (2003). *Applied longitudinal data analysis: Modeling change and event occurrence*. New York: Oxford University Press.

Snijders, T., & Bosker, R. (1999). *Multilevel analysis: An introduction to basic and advanced multilevel modeling*. London: Sage.

Tofighi, D., & Enders, C. K. (2007). Identifying the correct number of classes in a growth mixture model. In G. R. Hancock & K. M. Samuelsen (Eds.), *Advances in latent variable mixture models* (pp. 317–341). Greenwich, CT: Information Age.

Tucker, L. R. (1966). Learning theory and multivariate experiment: Illustration by determination of parameters of generalized learning curves. In R. B. Cattell (Ed.), *Handbook of multivariate experimental psychology* (pp. 476–501). Chicago: Rand McNally.

van Buuren, S. (1997). Fitting ARMA time series by structural equation models. *Psychometrika, 62*, 215–236.

Vandenberg, R. J., & Lance, C. E. (2000). A review and synthesis of the measurement invariance literature: Suggestions, practices, and recommendations for organizational research. *Organizational Research Methods, 3*, 4–70.

Velicer, W. F., & Fava, J. L. (2003). Time series analysis. In W. F. Velicer & J. A. Schinka (Ed.), *Handbook of psychology: Research methods in psychology*, vol. 2; (pp. 581–606). New York: John Wiley & Sons.

Walls, T. A., & Schafer, J. L. (Eds.) (2006). *Models for intensive longitudinal data*. New York: Oxford University Press.

Wang, L., & McArdle, J. J. (2008). A simulation study comparison of Bayesian estimation with conventional methods for estimating unknown change points. *Structural Equation Modeling, 15*, 52–74.

Widaman, K. F. (2000). Testing cross-group and cross-time constraints on parameters using the general linear model. In T. D. Little, K. U. Schnabel, & J. Baumert (Eds.), *Modeling longitudinal and multilevel data: Practical issues, applied approaches, and specific examples* (pp. 163–186). Mahwah, NJ: Lawrence Erlbaum.

Widaman, K. F., & Thompson, J. S. (2003). On specifying the null model for incremental fit indices in structural equation modeling. *Psychological Methods, 8*, 16–37.

Widaman, K. F., Little, T. D., Preacher, K. J., & Sawalani, G. (in press). Creating and using short forms in archival data. In B. Donnellen & K. Trzesniewski (Eds.), *Archival data analysis*. Washington, DC: American Psychological Association.

Widaman, K. F., & Reise, S. P. (1997). Exploring the measurement invariance of psychological instruments: Applications in the substance use domain. In K. J. Bryant, M. Windle, & S. G. West (Eds.), *The science of prevention: Methodological advances from alcohol and substance abuse research* (pp. 281–324). Washington, DC: American Psychological Association.

Willett, J. B., & Sayer, A. G. (1994). Using covariance structure analysis to detect correlates and predictors of individual change over time. *Psychological Bulletin, 116*, 363–381.

Wohlwill, J. F. (1973). *The study of behavioral development*. New York: Academic Press.

Wood, P., & Brown, D. (1994). The study of intraindividual differences by means of dynamic factor models: Rationale, implementation, and interpretation. *Psychological Bulletin, 116*, 166–186.

Zehr, J. L., Culbert, K. M., Sisk, C. L., & Klump, K. L. (2007). An association of early puberty with disordered eating and anxiety in a population of undergraduate women and men. *Hormones and Behavior, 52*, 427–435.

Zhang, Z., Hamagami, F., Wang, L., Grimm, K. J., & Nesselroade, J. R. (2007). Bayesian analysis of longitudinal data using growth curve models. *International Journal of Behavioral Development, 31*, 347–383.

CHAPTER 3

"More Than Good Quotations"

How Ethnography Informs Knowledge on Adolescent Development and Context

LINDA M. BURTON, RAYMOND GARRETT-PETERS, AND SHERRY C. EATON

In their attempts to advance understanding of [youth] development under such circumstances, the researchers found themselves seeking a firmer grasp on the settings in which the transactions of daily life took place, and on the meanings those transactions and settings had for the young people involved. The reach of traditional surveys and formal face-to-face interviews for such purposes is limited, so there was impetus to explore more observational and interpretive procedures that might supplement those already in hand. (Jessor, Colby, & Shweder, 1996, p. xi)

In the critically-acclaimed volume, *Ethnography and Human Development,* editors Jessor, Colby, and Shweder (1996) direct our attention to the importance of ethnography in discerning the impact of diverse settings and the nuances of everyday life on the developmental experiences of adolescents. This classic work moved ethnography to the foreground of developmental science such that even skeptics of ethnographic research asked the question: "Could ethnography be one of the most important methods in the study of human development?" (Weisner, 1996, p. 305). As 25-year veterans of using ethnographic methods to study adolescents across diverse contexts (e.g., families, schools, neighborhoods), and racial, ethnic, and socioeconomic groups, we contend, as have others, that ethnography is central to any research effort aimed at discerning how context and culture shape the developmental experiences of teens (James, 2001). In fact, we could not imagine a meaningful and informative science of adolescent development without the thoughtful

integration of knowledge generated by high-quality ethnographic research.

In this chapter we discuss the value of ethnography and the ways in which it contributes to scientific knowledge about adolescent development and context. Indeed, ethnography has occasionally been characterized as a seductive and scientifically questionable methodology among social scientists with little experience or knowledge about the conceptual and analytic labor and rigor that are hallmarks of the method (Hammersley & Atkinson, 1995). Some social scientists ask whether ethnography can deliver insights beyond "illustrative quotes," while others are convinced about the value of ethnography in informing developmental theories and praxis (James, 2001; Qvortrup, 2000). To be sure, scientifically rigorous ethnography is about much more than "good quotations." Our goal in this chapter is to lend further credence to that point.

This chapter is organized to address three ambitious objectives. First, we discuss the value of ethnography, describing in some detail what ethnographic research is and what we can learn by using it to study adolescents across various settings. Second, using adolescent development and school contexts as an exemplar research focus, we provide a brief summary of how existing ethnographies have enhanced our understanding of adolescence and school settings beyond what quantitative studies have offered. Third, we take the liberty of creating a "teachable moment" in this chapter by providing an account of how ethnographic research is used to formulate an alternative life-course model of adolescent development that has practical implications for school programs. Specifically, we use ethnographic research on adolescent adultification to illustrate how the knowledge gleaned from these studies has contributed to the emergence of an alternative conceptual model of adolescent development with practical implications for school-based service learning programs. The goal of this exercise is to provide the reader with a concrete demonstration of ethnography's utility in studying adolescents and their contexts—an application, we contend, that takes us beyond attributing the value of ethnography to generating "good quotations."

THE VALUE OF ETHNOGRAPHY IN THE STUDY OF ADOLESCENCE AND CONTEXTS

What is the value of using ethnographic research methods to study adolescents? And, by extension, how does ethnography help us to better understand adolescent development and the context in which it occurs? We argue that ethnography is an especially valuable form of research for studying adolescents, precisely because it allows us better access to the worlds in which adolescents live, to uncover the various cultural logics they use, and to see and define the world as they see it (Becker, 1996; Geertz, 1973; Weisner, 1996). An ethnographic approach enables us to view adolescents as competent actors, situated, as Lofland and Lofland (1995) have aptly put it, in "the context of social practice." Ethnographic inquiry also allows us, as both researchers and nonadolescents, to gain better access to the actions of adolescents across time and to the meanings they ascribe to themselves and social others as they navigate the transition from childhood to the world of adulthood. Such a meaning-centered approach can shed light on the circumstances that enable and constrain adolescents as they conform to, modify, and at times challenge social arrangements in worlds controlled largely by adults. By studying adolescents up

close, ethnographic research can help us realize what it means to be one of a class of social actors inhabiting an inherently liminal social status (Fine, 2004; James, 1986; Thorne, 1986) between the more clearly defined poles of childhood and adulthood.

Ethnographic Inquiry and Analysis

As typically practiced, *ethnography* refers to some combination of participant observation and interviewing (structured or unstructured, formal or informal) as the primary modes of data collection. Participant observation, the close-up and intensive study of some social group or social world through human group activities, is the hallmark of ethnographic research (for excellent guides to ethnographic fieldwork and analysis, see, e.g., Agar, 1980; Emerson, Fretz, & Shaw, 1995; Hammersley & Atkinson, 1995; Lofland & Lofland, 1995; Spradley, 1979, 1980). One of the primary aims of ethnographic researchers is to describe a particular social–cultural world in detail. This means to record and recreate, typically through written narrative, as accurate a picture as possible of the social setting(s) being studied and the cultural meanings, practices, and analytic categories humans employ there (see Lofland, 1972; Spradley, 1979, 1980). It is in this vein that ethnography is often broadly translated as "the writing of culture."

At its base, ethnographic research is descriptive and is aimed at recreating a more or less comprehensive picture of some setting, community, or behaviors of a particular group of social actors. All ethnographic description, by virtue of parsing up a social world, naming the people involved, and chronicling their activities and beliefs, simultaneously entails some degree of interpretation and analysis. A good deal of ethnographic research takes interpretation as a primary analytic goal. The work of anthropologist Clifford Geertz (1973, 1983) stands out as the prototypical example of interpretive ethnography—work that explicitly moves beyond description and aims to identify and interpret the whole complex of meanings behind the activities of the particular human community being studied. Building on this interpretive thrust, much of contemporary ethnographic research, particularly in sociology, is explicitly analytic in design. Such "analytic" ethnography (Lofland, 1972, 1995) is research that aims to: (1) provide a close-up and detailed description of social life, and (2) articulate patterns and regularities of behavior and social circumstance.

One way in which ethnographers achieve this sort of analysis is by highlighting social processes—what it is, for example, that adolescents actually do with one another, family members, teachers, and so on, as they respond to situations, engage in joint accomplishments (e.g., schooling) and simultaneously adapt and develop as human beings in socially circumscribed worlds. In a succinct description of the whole of ethnographic research practice, Schwalbe (1995) goes beyond the aims of description, interpretation, and explicit analysis to identify an additional strength of ethnographic research:

> Traditional ethnography has its large and small aims. A small aim is to develop detailed accounts of how groups of people think and feel and behave. This is ethnography's classic aim of documenting culture, of creating a record of the beliefs and customs of people in different places. . . . The ethnographic accounts that best serve these aims are not only accurate, detailed, and thorough, they also conjure vivid images in our minds and induce in us feelings that mirror those of the studied others. To experience these images and feelings is to move toward understanding the studied others, to appreciate the different sensibility of their world, and, as a result, to expand our own sensibilities. The craft of ethnography is thus not only to see and record, or even to represent faithfully; it is to *create* human experience, echoes of the original, through semiotic artifice. (p. 395)

Thus, good ethnographic description and analysis cannot only vividly recreate a social and cultural world for readers, but it can provide the opportunity to move readers to take the perspective of the actors in question, to see their social worlds and realize the attendant pressures, joys, and dangers that impinge on their actions.

In accomplishing all these tasks, ethnographic inquiry enables a much more nuanced understanding of contextual conditions (via observation of behaviors, informal questioning during the flow of activities, and formal interviewing) in ways that other methods of studying adolescents often do not. Doing ethnographic fieldwork also allows us, as both cultural outsiders and hypothesis-testing researchers, to press these individuals for explanations of their and others' behaviors in these settings. Coupled with observational data on these same goings-on, ethnographers can gain a fuller understanding of what people think, feel, and do as situated members of some class of social actors (e.g., as children, parents, friends, bosses, coworkers, etc.).

Ethnography and Context

As hinted at earlier, ethnographic research sensitizes both the practitioner and reader to context. Social scientists are compelled to consider the conditions under which people act, if not make outright attempts to embed those being studied in a particular and meaningful context, in order to make sense of human action and human experience. Ascertaining the *meaning* of human action—and this extends to human thought and feeling that undergirds such action—is virtually impossible without some reference to context. This contextualizing bent applies to survey and experimental researchers as much as it does to ethnographers, as each operates according to a relational ontology that situates the person(s), phenomenon, or problem under study relative to other features of that object's environment (see chapter 1, this volume; Overton, 2006).

For most of us, *context* is synonymous with "circumstances" or "situation" or "setting" or "surroundings." For child researchers Graue and Walsh (1998), context is "a culturally and historically situated place and time, a specific here and now" (p. 9). Sociologists Glaser and Strauss (1964, p. 670) provide a more generic meaning, defining context as "a structural unit of an encompassing order larger than the other unit under focus." Taken together these definitions point to the sum of circumstances that physically, temporally, socially, and ideologically bracket and inform some defined human activity. The boundaries of such circumstances, of course, are not absolute. They are shaped by both our perceptual equipment and social experience. Ultimately, though, these are socially learned and agreed-upon matters defined by our participation and membership in cultural and social groups (e.g., as middle-class adolescents, academic social scientists, members of U.S. society). Exactly where we learn to draw contextual boundaries, just as the ways in which we learn to define reality and cut the world into conceptual categories, is a social and cultural matter (see Zerubavel, 1993, 1997) and, hence, intersubjective (cf. Schlecker and Hirsh, 2001).

For ethnographic and qualitative researchers, the importance of context is linked especially to the perceived capacity of lived experience to provide some insight into how and why human actors behave as they do. As both symbol users and social scientists, in order to report and analyze such experience we are first compelled to embed it in some meaningful context, at least implicitly. Thus, the task of understanding what was experienced, how it was experienced, and the like requires some reference to the perceived and (potentially) objective conditions under which it occurred (e.g., when, where, with whom, etc.). Context also entails circumstances that somehow shape the *meaning* of some action, event, or situation from the point of view of the social actor. By this we mean the various definitions that may be attributed to situations from the perspective of the differently situated actors (e.g., adolescent versus adult) that arguably influence their definition of the situation and

potential lines of action (Ball, 1972; Blumer, 1969; Perinbanayagam, 1974).

These conditions under which humans act have an apparent range of identifiable types. Most obvious are physical contexts, whether immediate (e.g., a home or a school classroom) or more diffuse (e.g., an economically poor and dangerous neighborhood). We can also speak of contexts that are social, cultural, historical, or political in nature. Contexts can be familial, educational, literary, developmental, communication based, interactional, emotional, racialized, and even surveillant in nature. These latter contexts are analytic creations in the sense that we, whether social scientists or lay theorists, are necessarily compelled to frame (cf. Goffman, 1974) or contextualize a question, problem of study, or social situation to even begin talking about it or acting toward it. The common protest against an interpretation of some action or statement that was "taken out of context" illustrates the weight we give to context in shaping the meaning of something that was said or done.

Most ethnographic researchers are unavoidably attuned to context, whether as a component of research design or in coming to understand, in the course of performing fieldwork, how behaviors and cultural rules are contingent on setting and situation. Social experience, whether fieldwork based or not, is often a guide here. So, for example, in describing how she came to focus on a particular high school—and thus employ a fuller ethnographic research approach—in her study of teenage girls' experiences of race and social class, Bettie (2003) highlighted the central role that context and contextualization play in providing ethnographically produced knowledge:

> But it wasn't long into the process of interviewing community college women that I became frustrated by the fact that their descriptions of themselves and their high school peers were devoid of context for me. I had to rely on what each of them could *tell* me of their respective high school experiences. . . . Through their

narratives they constructed race and class identities for themselves which were relational, clearly defined by the context of the communities from which they came. But I could not *see* for myself what they meant and where they fit in to the high school and community hierarchy they described. (p. 8)

Recognizing the limitations of data gained solely from interviews, Bettie realized the value of studying teenage girls in the immediate context of their high school. A broader ethnographic approach provided opportunities to make sense of what these young women were saying in their interviews about a consequential social world—school—and their relationships and daily interactions therein. In particular, participant observation also provided data on what these teens actually *did* in their daily school rounds as students and friends, in the context of relations with teachers, administrators, same-sex friends, disliked others, and the like. Ethnographic fieldwork, in other words, can provide valuable and, hence, more credible data by considering not only what people *say*, but what they *do* as well (see Becker, 1996; Blumer, 1955; Deutscher, 1966).

The experience of ethnographic fieldwork itself can sensitize researchers to the importance of context as they are able to follow individuals and come to understand the various (i.e., contextual) conditions under which certain behaviors, social rules, and lines of action are appropriate, rewarded, and/or penalized. Understanding the world from the perspectives of those being studied—gaining an emic perspective, in the language of anthropologists—is such an example of trying to understand adolescent behavior by attention to the "context of lived experience." With regard to adolescent development, this work can entail taking adolescents seriously as social actors (cf. Baker, 1982; Fine and Sandstrom, 1988; James, 2001; Qvortrup, 2000; Waksler, 1986), as competent societal members, rather than unformed (and hence, not fully credible) adults.

Virtues of Ethnographic Research (aka, "Things to Consider When Studying Adolescents")

An ethnographic approach to studying the lives of adolescents is not limited to just documenting teens' experiences and perspectives on their worlds, although this is an important aim in its own right. Rather, doing ethnography with adolescents also allows us to analyze how they create and organize their own social worlds (e.g., peer structures), drawing from and building on available materials in the larger social environment (e.g., class and racial hierarchies, gender ideologies, cultural and social capital, etc.) in the process of simultaneously navigating adolescence and developing into full-fledged adults (see for example, Bettie, 2003; Fine, 2004).

And, unless our research focus is limited solely to the cognitive or affective inner workings of some socially isolated individual, ethnographic fieldwork in settings such as schools or families enables us to better understand adolescents. It does so in at least three ways: (1) by describing empirical features of the settings being studied; (2) by gaining local actors' perspectives on self, others, and their environments; and (3) by building a bigger picture of these social worlds by gathering data from all participants involved and triangulating such information to see what is at stake for these actors, how they interact with one another, with what resources, and with what consequences (cf. Becker, 1996, on "ethnography and breadth of information"). In doing ethnographic research on adolescent development, we point out below three particular areas to consider: contexts of adolescence, "shadowing" adolescents, and researcher–adolescent relations.

Attention to Contexts of Adolescence

While some contexts of adolescent development are identical to those of adults, many are peculiar to youth populations, from the shared problems and constraints they face at certain points in the period of adolescence, to the physical spaces they often inhabit apart from adult supervision (cf. Fine, 2004, on the interstitial social location of adolescents). While adolescents are in many ways reflections of the adult actors under whom they learn and develop, the former also can create and inhabit subcultural worlds physically and ideationally distinct from those of adults. So, for instance, we might consider the kinds of physical and social settings in which adolescents play out their daily lives. What are the various cultural worlds that adolescents inhabit as students, family members, athletes, workers, or even gang members? Furthermore, in the context of what sort of political relations do they interact with peers, family members, school officials, and the like? What, in more broadly construed terms, are the identifiable conditions under which adolescents think, feel, and act as members of an age-graded category of individuals on the path to adulthood? To even begin answering that question requires us to appeal to a larger, often unrealized context— the broader cultural circumstances under which we ourselves act as social scientists, teachers, parents, and, yes, even former adolescents. Thus, unless we engage in too much ethnocentrism here, we need to acknowledge our own cultural (i.e., socially shared) understandings of "adolescence" as, say, middle-class, twenty-first-century North American academics. This identification can entail reflecting on where we draw the boundaries of adolescence and asking how this definition is historically specific relative to other definitions, both in the U.S. context and elsewhere (cf. Burton 1997, 2007; Mead, 1928).

Studying adolescents in context, then, involves paying close attention to both the local settings in which they typically act (see Graue & Walsh, 1998) and the implied circumstances, such as risk taking (Lightfoot, 1992), transitioning to adulthood, and so on, under which they act (for a detailed discussion of his point, see Colby, 1996). This emphasis can mean, for example, focusing on the political nature of adolescent life. Similar to children, adolescents are not full, legally recognized adults in most

regards and thus live and develop in contexts (e.g., families and schools) under at least some degree of control and supervision by adults (see, e.g., Everhart, 1983; Ferguson, 2000; Fine, 2004). Thus, we can take seriously the broader jural context framing adolescents' lives. One defining feature of adolescence, therefore, as Fine and Sandstrom (1988) have noted, involves adolescents' social position with respect to adult abilities and normative and legal rights:

> The actions of adolescents, more than is true for younger children, are consequential to the community. Adolescents have the opportunity to make important decisions for themselves, and may do each other grievous harm. Adolescents are in a position in which they have the skills to do virtually all those things that adults do, but they don't have the social right to do them or they don't have the judgment (according to adults) to make the right choices. (p. 71)

By observing adolescents in context and asking who does what to whom, with whom, under what circumstances, and with what resources, ethnographic research gets at so-called lived experience, the empirical stuff of everyday life. While not the only way of arriving at such knowledge, doing ethnographic research with adolescents can push us to consider the political and jural contexts within which they act and develop. Thus, by doing participant observation with adolescents, we are more likely to perceive how they stand out as a social category of individuals, otherwise indistinguishable (e.g., physically) from adults.

As we argue later in this chapter, family and school contexts are two of most salient settings for understanding influences on adolescent development. A partial list of ethnographic research on adolescents in the last few decades attests to the arguable importance of family and school contexts, particularly as these have generated important knowledge on a range of adolescent-related phenomena, such as: "accelerated" development and truncated adolescence (Allison et al., 1999; Burton, 2007);

adaptation to dangerous environments and limited opportunity structures (Anderson, 1990; Burton & Jarrett, 2000; Everhart, 1982, 1983; Jarrett, 1998; MacLeod, 1995; Rubin, 1994; Willis, 1981); role conflicts as students, family members, and workers (Burton, Obeidallah, & Allison, 1996; Stack, 2001); schools as sites of identity development (Eckert, 1989; Fine, 2004; Gaines, 1990); and the impact of race, class, and gender on development and performance (Anderson, 1990; Bettie, 2003; Boggs, 1985; Clark, 1984; Eder, Evans, & Parker,1995; Fine, 2004; Fordham, 1996; Fordham & Ogbu, 1986; Jarrett, 2003; MacLeod, 1987; Romo & Falbo, 1996; Stack, 2001; Suarez-Orozco & Suarez-Orozco, 1995; Swain, 2006; Valdes, 1996; Vigil, 1997). These contexts are notable due to the sheer amount of time adolescents spend in each and because of the formative interactions and socialization processes that take place there (around formal and informal education, gender socialization, etc.) with parents, close friends, peers, and teachers.

School settings in particular provide an important locale for studying adolescence, because school is a prominent location, a "natural" experimental setting where adolescents come together and interact, crafting gender performances, co-constructing peer culture, and being socialized within a formalized educational curriculum (see, e.g., Eder, Evans, & Parker, 1995; Everhart, 1983). In addition, schools are valuable as sites where adolescent–adult power relations are played out, specifically in the context of teens' physical, emotional, social, and cultural development. Family contexts are likewise important as settings in which to learn about adolescence, to glean information about similarities or differences in both the content of what is learned at home and the actual resources parents or other caregivers may or may not have to assure positive developmental outcomes for adolescents in their care (see Kreppner, 1992). Close-up, ethnographic research can sensitize us to the potential differences that may exist, for instance, between low-income or nonWhite, middle-class families

and those with ample resources and the requisite cultural capital needed to succeed across multiple areas of mainstream social life. In doing so, ethnographic research in family contexts enables us to see the possible differences in cultural and social capital (Anderson, 1990; Boggs, 1985; Lareau, 1987), temporal resources (Roy, Tubbs, & Burton, 2004), and so on, that shape adolescents' developmental trajectories as, say, "adultified" children (Burton, 2007) or unsuccessful students (Ferguson, 2000; Fordham, 1996; Fordham & Ogbu, 1986; Stack, 2001).

Even with an eye on the importance of family and school contexts in the lives of adolescents, attention to context is not limited to the immediate social setting. Rather, a thorough ethnographic data collection and analysis design (or any social science analysis, for that matter; see chapter 2, this volume) should be attentive to the larger contexts within which the setting or actors of interest are located. Bettie (2003), again, has pointed to a set of overarching contexts that can help us better understand the actions and experiences of the cohort of high school girls she followed over the course of a school year:

> This book, then, presents an ethnographic portrait of working-class white and Mexican American girls in their senior year of high school. . . . The context of these young women's lives includes a deindustrializing economy, the growth of service-sector occupations held largely by men and women of color and by white women; the related family revolutions of the twentieth century; the elimination of affirmative action; a rise in anti-immigrant sentiment; and changing cultural representations and iconographies of class, race, and gender meanings. . . . My goal was to learn how these young women experience and understand class differences in their peer culture and how their and their parents' class location and racial/ethnic identity shaped the girls' perceptions of social differences at school and the possibilities for their futures. (p. 7)

With this list of background conditions, Bettie has identified a range of potential classed, raced, and gendered contexts that shape the beliefs and actions of these young women, from the kinds of teens with whom they formed friendships, to the kinds of jobs and aspirations they perceived as open to them based on their class position. Importantly, she has identified the broader societal conditions impacting not only these adolescents' educational experiences and opportunities, but their family lives as well. Only in the world of analysis are specific contexts such as family and school—and the interactions that take place within—discrete and isolated entities. At the level of experience, these realms always inform each other, with adolescents bringing the cultural tools they gain at home to bear on their school experiences, and vice versa. The extent to which they do so, of course, is always an empirical question.

"Shadowing" Adolescents

Ethnography is a particularly valuable method of data collection and analysis because the method enables researchers, through participant observation and close-up study, to shadow those studied across settings to wherever they go (see James, 1986). In the first instance, this method allows researchers to glean information from what adolescents do and say in actual social settings, in interaction with children, adults, and one another. Using ethnographic methods to follow adolescents across the various social worlds they inhabit can also attune researchers to contexts different from those that may be central in adult life.

Thus, ethnographic researchers also are exposed to potentially new and unconsidered social spaces and analytic contexts that matter for adolescents' social, biological, and psychological development. These contexts include subcultural worlds and practices, both familiar and emergent (e.g., youth gangs, sports and drug cliques, etc.), as well as less visible analytic contexts, such as fast-paced and far-reaching communication contexts (Kritt, 1992) made possible by cell phones, e-mail, and the Internet (e.g., web spaces such as Facebook

and MySpace). In this same vein, ethnographic research also allows us to get at such individuals' understandings of these worlds and to examine sites of interaction either hidden from or largely misunderstood by the larger society (see, e.g., Anderson, 1990; Ferguson, 2000; MacLeod, 1987; Vigil, 1997; Whyte, 1955). Given the often sensitive nature of activities by such "vulnerable" populations, data—and credible data at that—can be difficult to collect (see Dodson & Schmalzbauer, 2005; Taylor, 1990). And, while not foolproof as a method, ethnography, with its emphasis on studying groups up close and over time, provides greater opportunity for those studied to reveal information they would typically guard closely.

This ability to shadow adolescents across settings is even applicable in bounded contexts such as schools, where ethnographic researchers are potentially able to observe and interact with adolescents and others in a range of situations, from classroom (Everhart, 1982, 1983; Ferguson, 2000; Tyson, 2003) and playground settings (Eder, Evans, & Parker, 1995; Thorne, 1986), to unsupervised hallway encounters (Bettie, 2003; Everhart, 1982, 1983) and special disciplinary spaces (Ferguson, 2000). The value of ethnographic research in this sense comes from "being there" (Becker, 1996), over time and in as many situations as possible, when the action (i.e., social interaction) unfolds. Thus, ethnographers are able to observe adolescents—and often pose questions in the process—as they go about their everyday routines or encounter novel situations. Such an approach allows us to amass a breadth of data within a given social world, such as schools, and enables us to observe new patterns of behavior, bolster earlier observations, and at times disconfirm previous findings, building a body of analytic knowledge in the process (cf. Lofland, 1972, 1995).

Ferguson's (2000) study of young Black males labeled as troublemakers in a public school offers a good illustration of how shadowing research participants across physical contexts can shed valuable light on the social shaping of adolescents' development. Through the course of her fieldwork, Ferguson was able to follow relevant actors across a variety of settings within the school proper, from classrooms and hallways to the library, cafeteria, and teachers' lounge. So, for example, by observing and interacting with the overwhelmingly Black and male students who were removed from class for disciplinary reasons, Ferguson came across what she came to call "the punishing room." This was an isolated space intentionally set off from the regular flow of school activities, a place designed by administrators in which to punish and reform problem students (but one that unintentionally reinforced larger societal notions of punishment, criminality, and race, and gave the students there valued opportunities away from the boredom of daily class routines). By following the students assigned to this setting and observing them and adults in interaction, Ferguson gained access to additional data that helped her produce a more comprehensive picture of the larger disciplinary context of the school and see how this multifaceted context specifically impacted one group of youth.

Researcher-Adolescent Relations

Another valuable feature of ethnographic research derives from the capacity of ethnographers and those researched to form social relationships over the course of any research project. In this sense, ethnographic fieldwork is, relative to other forms of research, a decidedly social practice. By engaging in participant observation and qualitative interviewing, ethnographers unavoidably enter into and cultivate social relationships with research participants (see Asher & Fine, 1991; Gans, 1968; Gold, 1958; Stebbins, 1972; Vidich, 1955). This is not to say that all ethnographers create close relationships with each of those they study, but that, at a minimum, the act of inserting oneself into the flow of others' daily activities, interviewing them, and so on, entails forming and maintaining some degree of social relationship. For

ethnographic research projects that are longitudinal in nature, this means fieldworkers face the additional demand of navigating and maintaining relations with those they are studying over some span of time, whether weeks, months, or years. In part, these relationships, like any other successful social relationship, are built on some degree of reciprocal exchange (Wax, 1956). Thus, from the perspective of fieldworkers, research participants are integral sources of information, providing ethnographers with observable data, interpretations, and access to often hidden cultural worlds. Without research participants, in other words, there would be no ethnography.

Those studied also gain something from these relationships, although the relative value of such interactions may not always be balanced. So for those studied, researcher–participant relationships can be therapeutic, with field researchers providing a sympathetic ear during interviews, a source of valuable information, and/or a willing audience for whom participants can perform a valued version of self. Beyond the therapeutic benefits it might offer, mere involvement in a research study can also be important for what it symbolizes about participants—that someone cares about their lives; that they are involved in something larger than themselves; that they are important (see, e.g., Van Maanen's [1983] ethnography of policemen). Such an impact may account for the positive role of mentors in youth development as well (e.g., see chapter 5, volume 2 of this *Handbook*).

Like any other set of relations between ethnographic researchers and those being studied, the relationships between adult ethnographers and adolescent research participants are important to consider. What sets adolescents and adults apart as research participants is the former's often subordinate status relative to those in the adult world and to adult researchers in particular (for exceptions to this rule, see Fine & Sandstrom, 1988). For certain adolescents, this power differential can compel them to more fully reveal information to adult researchers whom they "rightly" define into an authoritative role. For other adolescents, this perceived social distance can motivate them to disclose less information, whether as an oppositional act or as a way of guarding potentially damaging information from those they perceive as having power to penalize them (via disapproval, direct punishment, etc.). To the extent that these factors can impede data collection, some ethnographers advocate various strategies to downplay such age and status differentials, from dressing in fashionably acceptable and innocuous ways (Bettie, 2003) to affecting the most "least-adult role" available in that setting (Mandell, 1988).

The social relationships that potentially develop between ethnographers and research participants are also noteworthy because of the trust that can be generated over time between researcher and participant. Trust, a basic feature of all social interactions and relationships, is likewise a key component of successful ethnographer–participant relationships. All ethnographic fieldworkers aim to cultivate some measure of rapport and trust with those they are studying (see Asher & Fine, 1991; Harrington, 2003; Wax, 1956). This goal is the case, whether participating in a group's daily activities as a tolerated outsider, a welcome and interested observer, or someone who has been accepted and redefined, to varying degrees, as a "friend" (see, e.g., Bourgois, 1995; Liebow, 1993; MacLeod, 1995; Stack, 1974). Because adolescents often inhabit cultural worlds apart from those of adults and navigate subordinate positions relative to adults, the former have good reason to guard sensitive information. Such forms of sensitive data are rarely disclosed immediately by those studied, at least not until some measure of trust has been earned by researchers (Dodson & Schmalzbauer, 2005; Wax, 1956; Wolcott, 2001). Here, the long-term nature of ethnographic research is invaluable, increasing the likelihood that those studied will reveal sensitive information over the course of time and through the development of closer social relations.

VALUE ADDED: ETHNOGRAPHIC INSIGHTS ON ADOLESCENTS AND SCHOOL CONTEXTS

Our nuts-and-bolts discussion of the value of ethnography underscores its importance in generating knowledge about adolescent development and context. We now provide an overview of themes in several exemplar ethnographic studies on adolescents and schools to illustrate some specific ways in which ethnography contributes to our understanding of adolescent development and contexts (for more extensive reviews of the ethnographic literature on adolescence across a variety of contexts, see Burton, Obeidallah, & Allison, 1996; Burton & Jarrett, 2000; or Jarrett, 1998, 2003). As noted in the previous section, ethnographies provide detailed descriptions of what adolescents and their parents, teachers, and peers actually do with one another, as well as insights on the nuanced understandings that are shared among parties involved in these encounters. Ethnography also sensitizes researchers to the unique cultural and spatial elements, in this case, in school contexts, and how the dynamics of class, race, ethnicity, and gender shape the developmental experiences of youth in these environments (Carter, 2005; Clark, 1983; Dodson, 1998; Gandara, 1995; Gaines, 1990; Hebert, 2000; Hebert & Reis, 1999). Three themes, which consistently emerged in most of the existing ethnographies on adolescents and schools that we have reviewed, are addressed. The themes concern the impact of parental involvement, peer networks, and school influences (i.e, tracking programs) on adolescents' academic outcomes (also see chapter 12, this volume).

Parental Involvement

Numerous studies have documented that parents' involvement in their children's education matters greatly (see chapter 1, volume 2 of this *Handbook*). Indeed, parental involvement is correlated with children's academic successes across grades (Eccles & Harold, 1993, 1996;

Epstein, 1987; Epstein & Saunders, 2002) and across ethnic groups (Delgado-Gaitan, 1991; Hill, 2001; Rosier & Corsaro, 1993). The research in this area, which is largely quantitative, has focused on school-based and home-based activities such as the frequency of parents' attendance at school events and conferences, how often parents are in contact with teachers and other school personnel, and whether parents assist their children with homework and other learning activities (Pomerantz, Moorman, & Litwack, 2007). What ethnographic studies add to this literature is an in-depth sense of the social processes and specific strategies parents use to facilitate their children's progress through the school system (Suarez-Orozco & Suarez-Orozco, 1995; Rosier & Cosaro, 1993; Valdes, 1996).

In their ethnographic study, Falbo, Lein, and Amador (2001) have examined the ways in which parents were involved in their children's academic lives as they transitioned from middle to high school. Several parental strategies were identified and found to be associated with adolescents' academic achievement, including parents' active monitoring of adolescents' academic and social activities; the ways in which parents evaluated information about their children from teachers; how parents assisted their children with homework; and whether parents could create positive social networks for their children in the contexts of home and school environments. To be sure, several of these factors have been identified and deemed important in quantitative research on parental involvement and schools. However, ethnographic research has provided "finer-grained" detail on how these factors operate in the lives of adolescents and their parents.

For example, the Falbo, Lein, and Amador (2001) work extends what we know about parental involvement through their observations of the precise strategies parents use to monitor their children. Consider this mother's approach: "We do embarrassing things [to him]. Like if he can't manage to come in before 12:00 [midnight], then the next round, I'll be going to get him and knocking on the door of this house where all these people are having a good time and there I am, his mother, picking him up. Believe me, the threat of that ... He doesn't want that!" (Falbo, Lein, & Amador, 2001, p. 521). This mother also actively influenced whom her son would interact with by having him participate in school activities such as the swim team. This strategy ensured that he would associate with peers who were serious about their athletic and academic performance.

In addition to the importance of monitoring peer associations, ethnographic studies have shown that, in some contexts, parents keep track of their children to the point of hypervigilance. Ferguson's (2000) ethnographic study of African American males attending an ethnically diverse school demonstrates this point. The mother of one of the students in the study describes the steps she takes to monitor her son's time after school:

> He doesn't have time for anything like that (rap music) after school. He has one free afternoon—Monday. Otherwise, he's playing baseball, soccer, or he goes to tutoring. When he comes home he has homework, then the chores he has to do. Thursday evening he's singing in the church choir. He doesn't have time left over for all this bebop stuff and just hanging out with friends. (pp. 128–129)

Ethnographies also make us aware of what parents are thinking when they do not take a proactive role in monitoring their children. The mother of Fran, a student in the Falbo, Lein, and Amador (2001, p. 522) study describes her ineffectiveness in setting limits on Fran's behaviors:

> I'm very lenient, my husband's probably not. What happens is I forget and end up giving in. So remembering that she's being punished becomes a big problem with me sometimes, so I try not to make long-range punishments anymore.

In this case, the mother's lack of vigilant monitoring and her inability to nest her daughter in an academically engaged and positive peer group contributed, as she saw it, to her daughter's failing three courses.

A number of ethnographies have described, in great detail, the plans of actions parents take to ensure that their children complete high school (see Jarrett, 1998). For example, Romo and Falbo (1996), in their ethnographic study of Hispanic youth attending a large southwestern school, examined the strategies parents employed to help their children graduate. The participants in their study were high school students who had been labeled "at risk" for dropping out and their families. In four years of ethnographic work, which involved in-depth interviews with the parents and students, home visits and observations, and gathering contextual data from the school district, Romo and Falbo (1996) identified seven strategies that parents employed to help their children achieve academic success. Parents took charge of their children; openly communicated with them; set limits on their children's behaviors; actively monitored their children's activities in and outside of school; took actions to make sure their children did not associate with peers who either did not attend or did not take school seriously; communicated messages to their children about the importance of school; and were actively involved in their children's schooling. Active parental involvement is duly noted in the efforts of one father's efforts to ensure that his son was enrolled in the courses he needed for college: "One thing I didn't like about the school was that Robert wanted to take Algebra and they wouldn't let him take Algebra because they said his seventh-grade scores showed that he did not have the ability. So I went down there and talked to 'em about it." (Romo & Falbo, 1996, p. 21). Because the father had attended college, he knew which courses were needed for college matriculation. He was able to effectively advocate for his child and, ultimately, assure that his son was placed in the proper course. This case shows how the nature and, subsequently, the effectiveness of parental involvement is in part shaped by the parent's educational background. Parents

with college experience often feel more confident about their ability to impact their child's schooling and, as such, take a more direct, assertive approach with school personnel.

Another value of ethnographic studies is that they provide insights into what does not work concerning parents' involvement in schools. Some parents who want their children to succeed may not have the confidence, experience, time, or resources to assist their children's learning. As such, they tend to be less directive, deferring to teachers and other school officials as the experts on education, in general, and their child's education, in particular. This approach is evidenced in Lareau's (2003) ethnographic work on child inequality in school and home settings. In response to her daughter's low grades, one mother said of her daughter: "Her spelling and reading are like F's. And they keep telling me not to worry, because shes in the Special Ed class. But besides that, she does good. I have no behavior problems with her at all" (Lareau, 2003, p. 210). As this statement shows, parents' trust in the decisions of school personnel may sometimes compel them not to be as assertive in intervening on their child's behalf. Ogbu (2003, p. 70) terms this the "allocation of educational responsibility to others." In his ethnography of African American students attending an affluent suburban school he identified this behavior as one of the primary reasons parents were not more involved in the school system. Ogbu (2003) asserts that many parents felt that teachers were primarily responsible for educating their children. A teacher in his study commented: "Many Black parents just expect that the school will do everything necessary to make sure that their children get an education. (p.236)"

Ethnographic studies have uncovered a host of other reasons why parents may not be as involved in their child's education both at school and at home. The reasons include: limited parental education; parental mistrust of the school system; the generation gap; inappropriate societal role models; lack of awareness of academic problems; and employment constraints on parents' time (Ogbu, 2003). The felt demands presented by employment and time allocated to children's educational needs is expressed by the adolescent child of working-class parents:

> The students don't see [their parents]. They don't come home until ten o'clock and [the students], you know. They might not even get dinner. They might have to make dinner for themselves. They . . . don't ever see [their parents] for a week. And by the time they get up and go to school, their mother's at work already. They don't even see [their parents] for a week. I see my mother on like, maybe Monday, and I might see her [again on] Friday, Friday night. You know what I'm sayin'? So, there's not even thinkin' of my schoolwork, 'cause I don't even see my mom for, I mean, a week. (Ogbu, 2003, pp. 248–249)

Even when parents attempt to comply with school standards and are actively involved in their child's schooling, the actions of the parents can be misinterpreted by teachers and school professionals when parental messages about what constitutes proper behavior is at odds with school expectations. Lareau (2003) has noted the efforts of a working-class mother of a male student to monitor her son's homework, attend school conferences, and contact the school if needed. However, when the boy was suspended for defending himself from a bully—a response that had been instilled at him in the home—the school counselor made the following comment about the family's child-rearing practices:

> I felt he was being given the wrong message . . . that this was acceptable behavior. And I said that to her [the mother]. That's really giving him the wrong message. . . . I tried to explain that even though I could appreciate the fact that she wanted him to stand up for himself, that this kind of behavior—fighting—is against school rules. There are people here, if he is having a problem, who will help him. By the same token, Billy has to take responsibility for how he triggers aggressive behavior in other children. (p. 226)

In this instance the child was caught in the middle between differing expectations at home and school (cf. Anderson, 1990).

In very detailed ways, ethnographic studies also illustrate the effects of parental involvement on children's academic achievement as seen through the messages and beliefs parents transmit to their children about the importance of education (Eccles & Harold, 1996; Epstein, 1987). This influence is apparent in the comments of a parent in Delgado-Gaitan's (1992) ethnographic study of the socialization practices of Mexican American families:

> We tell them that we as children did not have the opportunity to study in Mexico because we had too much work to do on the ranch. But, they have the opportunity to study here for a good career. They [the children] need to prepare themselves to obtain a good job, better than we have right now. Sometimes, the children prefer to play outside rather than to study, and we have to remind them how it is to live without education. We also encourage them to pay attention to their studies and to do their homework nightly and to go bed early because they often want to watch television until it is late. (p. 507)

This same view holds, as indicated in Ferguson's (2000, p. 110) articulation below, but with regard to race, specifically:

> It is important that black male children, or even black children period, are taught to be prepared. Prepare yourself the best way you possibly can. That means doing well in school academically. . . . [But] to be your best . . . cause there's one thing that's never going to change about you and that's your skin color and you can't change people's perceptions based on that. Even as a black professional, my colleagues, their perception of me doesn't change just because I'm educated. Constantly, you have to prove who you are or that you're worthy, if you choose to do so. It's a constant thing. Racial attitudes are embedded in the person and there's really not a heck of a lot that the individual who's subjected to the negative racial attitudes can do about it other than to be the very best that you can be at anything you desire to be. . . . And I think kids need to learn that.

Parental messages and attitudes about the value of education are shaped by income and social class. In her ethnographic study of upper-middle- and lower-class parents' involvement in their children's schools, Lareau (2000) found that working-class parents were less likely to initiate contact with teachers, were less familiar with the school curriculum, and were more awkward and strained in their contacts with school personnel than middle-class parents. The author noted that "Parent's actions were not tied to how strongly they wanted their children to graduate from high school. Instead parent's performance was linked to their educational competence, their social confidence, the information they had about their children's schooling, their conception of parent's proper role in education and their children's classroom performance. These social forces forged a closer alignment between family life and school life for upper-middle class families than for working class families . . . Working-class families lacked the social resources upper-middle class families had to facilitate parent's involvement in schooling (Lareau, 2000, pp. 145–146)". In other words, these parents exhibited behaviors that were congruent with the school's expectations and culture.

Gorman's (1998) ethnographic study of working and middle-class parents' attitudes toward education indicated that parents' social class and whether or not they had experienced "hidden injuries of class" would influence the attitudes and subsequently the messages they would relay to their children about the value of a college education. Gorman found that parents who felt somehow victimized due to their working-class status were less involved in their child's schooling and were less likely to see the value of education beyond high school. This effect is seen in the comments of a store clerk about her daughter's present and future schooling:

> [My daughter's teacher] knows me, [but] I don't bug her. I'm not like that. College isn't the only thing. I think if [children] have common sense they can accomplish anything. I think she'll probably go to college. I'm not going to push it. Two years of college, I'd be happy with that. (p. 22)

However, a lack of resources, parental education, difficulty understanding the cultural climate of the school, and work demands can impinge on contributions made by parents who value education and attempt to provide support and assist their children's schooling. Such a commitment to the education of her children is evidenced by the mother of a high schooler in the Romo and Falbo (1996) ethnographic study, who notes:

> . . . Like I would get up early in the morning and drop some of the kids off at my dad's and mom's, one of them off at a place to catch the bus, and then I would take off and catch the bus, go to school in the afternoons, pick them up after school from my mom, go home, and go to night school. (pp. 46–47)

This example highlights the sacrifices this mother made to not only obtain an education for herself, but to provide for her children. The extent of this mother's commitment to education and the processes involved in her making things work would more than likely not have been detected by quantitative measures on parental involvement.

The exemplar studies mentioned to this point demonstrate how ethnographically generated knowledge about social processes and nuanced behaviors extend our understanding of the influence of certain factors, in this case parental involvement, on adolescents' developmental outcomes. The information derived from these studies add texture to quantitatively generated insights and illuminate details about the "engines" driving the effects of parental involvement on adolescent's academic achievement. Ethnographies also have drawn attention to dimensions of peer and school (i.e., tracking programs) influences on adolescents' academic success. We briefly review several examples of those studies below.

Peer Networks

Ethnographic studies have been particularly adept at identifying the nuanced characteristics of peer networks that impact adolescents' performance in school (Gibson, Gandara, & Koyama, 2004). For example, Stanton-Salazar Spina's (2005) ethnography of peer socialization practices among Mexican American adolescents attending an urban high school revealed that the peer networks of "macho" males were not limited to same-sex peers. Rather, as this male student indicates in his description of his nonromantic relationship with a same-aged female, girls are involved, too: "*De todo*. She supports me to do better in school. She tells me to do good in football and try to get a scholarship. . . . *Cuando me siento deprimido, hablo con ella*" [When I feel depressed, I talk to her]" (p. 399). He goes on to describe how the relationship helps him deal with his anger:

> You know, I'm the kind of guy that can go around and like, you know, get mad and know . . . *siento como que quiero chingar a alguien*. [I feel like I wanna fuck somebody up (i.e., to hit and seriously injure someone)]. She's the person that when she looks at me, you know [giggles], all those mad feelings go to, like, Oh God!, you know. Like she can control me, like she's holding me back, just by looking at me [laughs]. (pp. 399–400)

The effects of peers in keeping adolescents in line as members of some social category (e.g., as a "good" student) is noted comparably in Conchas and Noguera's (2004) ethnographic study of high school students. According to one male teen:

> I mean, we develop relationships where . . . they inspire me to do my work. . . . I mean, its just like they're just there, it's an inspiration. When I have one of those days when I just don't feel like doing no work, if I see them doing their work, I start working. I think to myself, "man, I'm slipping in this class. I need to take . . . start doing my work. (p. 327)"

The peer groups cited in this work encouraged, assisted, and supported each other in their academic pursuits. Conversely, ethnographic studies also reveal that just as peers can influence behaviors and actions that promote excellence in school, they can also have negative effects. Such is the case with Ramona, a student in the Romo and Falbo (1996) study. Ramona was a member of the high school marching band. She described the others in the band as "good" friends because they helped her with her homework and other assignments. However, her interaction with these "good" friends ended when she was removed from the band due to missed band trips and practices (had to work) and poor grades. As a result, she began to hang out with "bad" friends (i.e., girls whose boyfriends were gang members.) Thus, when students are not a part of peer groups that are an integral part of the school, their sense of wanting to belong may cause them to gravitate toward peers who, like them, are not integrated in the school's culture.

Moreover, ethnographic studies have shown that involvement in peer groups that operate outside of the school's culture is often the case among low-income and minority students. For many of these students, the parental or financial support that is required to be involved in many school-related activities or organizations may not be available. These peer groups, although seen as outside and at odds with the school culture, do provide a measure of social support and are composed of individuals with similar racial and economic backgrounds. The need for group affiliation, if not met in the corridors of school, is often met through associations elsewhere. An example of this can be seen in the experiences of a female high school student in the Falbo, Lein, and Amador (2001) study:

> I have a bunch of friends that like to go crazy. They skip school and go smoke pot and stuff. I met them before, when they were good kids. When I first got into middle school, I didn't know anybody and that was when I was in seventh grade and they helped me out. They helped me

adjust and get my work done. Now, they're just totally changed. I hope I can get at least one of my friends back into class because she goes to class with me and I want her to go back. (p.524)

As this adolescent's experience shows, peer relations are consequential, both for the ways in which they constrain and enable adolescents to behave (e.g., by attending school versus skipping school and engaging in potentially problematic behaviors). Thus, the influence of peers cannot be underestimated (see chapter 3, volume 2 of this *Handbook*).

Along similar lines, ethnographic research is particularly insightful with regard to uncovering issues about racial identity and peer-group association (Fordham, 1996). For example, several ethnographies show that for many ethnic minority high-achieving students, choosing between belonging to pro-school groups or their own ethnic groups can lead to the pressure-filled experience of being caught between two worlds (e.g., identifying with "White" cultural values or maintaining a connection with their cultural peer group, in the case of many African American students). This situation has been termed by Fordham and Ogbu (1986) as "acting White." According to Fordham and Ogbu, minority high achievers hide or play down school achievements because not do so would leave them open to hostility and rejection by their same race group peers who are failing. Although more quantitatively oriented researchers have criticized this explanation for the low achievement of minority students (Bergin & Cooks, 2002; Carter, 2003, 2005), it cannot be discounted out of hand. Students in the Romo and Falbo (1996) study, for example, talked about how peers in the neighborhood thought that anyone who did well in school was a nerd, thus compelling them to hide achievement in order to avoid ridicule and rejection.

Flores-Gonzales's (2005) ethnography of peer group membership and its relationship to academic achievement among a primarily low-income and Latino student body provides another telling example The author concluded

that academic achievement is related to peer group membership and that practices in the schools determine in which peer groups students will align themselves. The two peer groups identified in this ethnography—"school kids" (high achievers)" and "street kids" (low achievers)—were separated by the school through the use of space, access to extracurricular activities, and special programs. As such, the high achievers did not have to "act White" because there was little interaction between them and the "street kids." The impact of being in a particular group has ramifications for how one is viewed by others and how one views self, as revealed in the comments of this female high school student:

> You could say they [nonscholars] call us nerds because we are in scholars. They separate us. You're [non-scholars] *por cortar* [into cutting], you're like the bad people. You've got the honor students, and usually scholars I see hang out with those who have the same aspirations. They associate with other people. Don't get me wrong, but I think that they hang around people that have the same aspirations. (p. 638)

These examples highlight ways in which peer group membership can impact developmental outcomes for adolescents. Membership in school groups, such as athletics, honor societies, band, and so on, also are highly visible, and thus belonging to one of these group gives its members high status among the school population. Having high status due to membership in these school-sanctioned groups can lead to positive academic-related outcomes and healthy psychological adjustment for teens. Conversely, not being a member of a high status group can lead to feelings of alienation and disconnectedness. In addition, students who are not part of a peer group in school have less opportunity to learn and practice the behaviors and social skills that are vital for the development of a healthy self-image. Consider the experience of Jenny, a student in the Evans and Eder (1993) ethnographic study of middle school "social isolates":

Immediately after Jenny sat down, Patty—who was sitting next to her—sort of went "Ooooh!" and scooted far away from her. She made a facial expression indicating revulsion. Janice and the other girls got into the act right away. They kept telling each other to "Say, 'Hey Jenny!' and then bark." And they kept doing it too. (p. 154)

Students who experience this type of ridicule and rejection are less likely to ever become a part of positive peer groups within the school, and are thus more likely to become disengaged from the learning environment.

Because peer groups are formed based on similarity of interests and backgrounds, it is not surprising that most peer groups are also comprised of individuals sharing the most salient and visible of characteristics—race and gender. Although in any high school, one finds the groups based on common interests are diverse in gender and ethnicity, the preponderance of peer groups are composed of adolescents with the same racial or ethnic background. Gandara (2002) contends that peer groups are first defined by race and ethnicity and later by other attributes. Although gender groupings are prevalent from childhood through adulthood, race may supersede other characteristics, such as academic status, class, and gender, in the selection of peers, especially for students of color.

Bettie (2003) found this racial effect to be the case in her ethnographic study of middle and working-class White and Mexican American teens. Working-class students of both ethnicities were enrolled in college preparatory classes, which were predominantly White and middle-class. However, whereas the White girls focused on differences from the other students in terms of class, the more salient feature for differentiation for the Mexican American girls was race, as seen in the observations of one of the Mexican American girls:

I think it is harder for Mexican American students, because I think most white people have, like, money, like their parents they went to college, and they have money. They have an education. . . . The white students don't understand because, you know, their parents got to go to college, you know, had an education, they all have jobs. (p. 156)

Outside of the classroom, White girls tended to associate with peers of their same class, as opposed to the Mexican American girls, whose associations were with others of similar racial background of differing abilities and social status. Although there are common experiences shared by all when attempting upward mobility, for girls of diverse racial backgrounds, Bettie (2003) notes that:

This experience differs, of course, for whites and people of color, as racial/ethnic groups of color are more consciously aware of themselves as a community of people because of a common history of colonization and oppression that results from being historically defined as a racial group. Alternatively, an aspect of whiteness is that whites often do not immediately experience themselves as members of the racial/ethnic category "white," but as individuals, and, without a cultural discourse of class identity, they do not readily experience themselves as members of a class community either. (p. 161)

Thus, for low-achieving students who may not have other sources for building positive self-images or self-esteem, negative school experiences may cause them to develop a failure identity.

As noted earlier in our discussion, ethnography is particularly useful in highlighting the aspects of social encounters that go undetected or unmeasured in quantitative investigations of schools and peer relations, and yet may have a profound impact on the developmental outcomes of adolescents. The ethnographies discussed here highlight the ways in which race and class shape the daily experiences of teens and how educational institutions are complicit in creating divisive environments. By extension, we now provide examples of how ethnographies can inform our understanding of impact of school policies and procedures on adolescent development.

School Influences: Tracking and Encounters with School Personnel

A common theme in the ethnographies we reviewed is the impact of the practice of educational tracking on student academic and personal development (Bettie, 2003; Ferguson, 2000; Ogbu, 2003; Oakes, 1992; Romo & Falbo, 1996). Tracking is the assignment of students to courses and programs based on measured ability. The fundamental assertion for tracking is that it allows schools to meet student needs by providing low-achieving students with needed remediation while allowing high-achieving students to engage in more challenging courses. Usually, the data used to determine what track a student should be placed in are standardized tests scores and/or teacher recommendations. However, this attempt at grouping students according to ability most often leads to the perpetuation of racial and class inequities, as students in lower-track courses tend to be of minority and/or lower class status.

For example, in Ogbu's (2003) study of academic disengagement, the majority of the students in the high school honors and advanced placement classes were White, while most students in the general education and college prep courses were Black. Based on their work with Hispanic students and their families, Romo and Falbo (1996) concluded that "many of our high school students dropped out because they correctly perceived that the education the schools were providing them was at such a low level that they would not be able to achieve their goal of a good life even after graduation" (p. 38). In addition, tracking has a negative impact on low achievers as they are often exposed to lower teacher expectations and less academically able peers and a low quality of instruction (Mills, 1997). This final point is highlighted when specific classroom practices are observed.

In order to more clearly understand how schools affect student development, it is important to look at the school/institutional policies, personnel and classroom practices, and how students interpret what happens in school (see chapter 12, this volume). Ethnographic methods are particularly appropriate for this type of scientific inquiry (see Tyson, 2003). A look into what actually occurs in the classroom is provided by Ferguson's (2000) detailed observations of the classroom environment for students placed in the school's compensatory education program. Students were assigned to this track based on standardized test scores. Although there was a low student-to-teacher ratio and more access to technology, the students mainly engaged in rote learning experiences. The following field note excerpt vividly illustrates this effect:

> The classroom has a long table down the center. Big sunny windows face out on the street. Two rows of ten computers sit on the table back to back. All of the kids sitting at the terminals are either Black, Hispanic or Asian. This year one hundred seventy-nine children are in comp ed. One hundred and thirty-four of them are African American. Most of the others in the program speak English as a second language and need to practice English language skills. On each computer is a paper cup. When the children come into the room, they take a folder from Mrs. Alvarez and sit in front of a computer terminal. Each program is personalized so that each child is greeted at the terminal by name when they log on and at the end of the exercise is given their score by name. But this individualization is more apparent than real since the children are all pretty much kept working in the same program at the same level. (pp. 56–57)

In this setting, Ferguson describes minimal interaction between the teachers and the students, except that needed to ensure that students are staying on task and with the group. Students who attempt to move more rapidly are discouraged from doing so. The effect of such a learning environment is that students who have been identified as at risk for failure or low achieving have little opportunity to move out of this classification, as the type of learning they are engaged in does not encourage the attainment of higher-order, critical thinking skills.

Now, compare the comments below to those made about Ogbu's (2003) observations of a math enrichment class:

> During the lesson, students answered and discussed the teacher's questions. The students themselves asked the teacher several questions. Toward the end of the math period the teacher asked the class to help her choose a question she would ask the incoming fifth grade graders in order to select students for the same math enrichment program. At first she asked if she could use the same questions she had used to select the current students. The students were enthusiastic and very involved in the discussion that followed. (p. 102)

The students in this classroom were required to think analytically and creatively. Not only were these students gaining valuable practice using the type of cognitive skills that would enable them to tackle more difficult material, the teachers' inclusion of them in the learning process served to enhance self-esteem and confidence and, thus, their continued academic success.

Once students leave home and enter the context of schools, it is the school personnel (i.e., principals, counselors, and teachers) that directly determine how children and adolescents experience the process of education. Through explicit actions and implicit messages, these school-based actors influence the ways students perceive the educational system and their value in society as a whole. Students are keenly perceptive and responsive to both subtle and not-so-subtle messages about their own ability and worth, as well as those of others. As a result, these perceptions influence important aspects of development such as self-esteem and self-worth. Thus, viewing the school experience from a student perspective, which is what ethnography allows researchers to do, can assist in understanding possible causes of student behavior (Everhart, 1982, 1983; Swain, 2006; Tatum, 2004).

Lee's (1999) ethnographic study of low-achieving inner city students highlights ways in which students' school-based experiences can contribute to their academic failure or success. The students interviewed in the study came from varied grade levels, racial and linguistic backgrounds, and gender. Students were employed as researchers to assist with conducting and analyzing the interviews. From the students' perspective, low achievement was partially due to factors in the home and peer pressures, but primarily the students attributed poor school performance to school-related factors, such as teacher-centered classrooms, perceived racism and discrimination, and lack of personal teacher–student relationships (cf. Steele, 1992). Students interviewed felt that problems with behavior and achievement were evident among all the racial groups, but that school personnel tended to see these difficulties among certain groups of students. This view was expressed by a biracial (Asian and African American) female student:

> I guess the reason why some teachers say that Asians are doing best academically in the school is that, in my opinion, because I am half Black, Black people can get an attitude. Asians can do what's expected from them, I guess, probably. But there is that side of them that I see that they're the ones cutting and everything. But the Black people can be doing their work and everything but they just don't like being told. . . . Teachers think that Asians do all the work, they do this, they do that, they're good in school, they're very smart in math. In my opinion, most of the Asian students are the ones who cut!. . . I think that every race in this school is doing well. I don't think that they should categorize only the Asians as doing the best in this school because it's not true. Asians themselves would not say Asians are doing well. (p. 227)

Student reactions to these perceptions can result in feelings of frustration and acts of deviance, especially toward those who they feel exemplify these attitudes. As another student put it, "Teachers need to start paying attention to us [African Americans] and realize that students got feelings too instead of them giving their little attitude 'cuz students gonna turn around and do something" (Lee, 1999, p. 228).

Students also attribute academic success or failure to aspects of their own personality. This is exemplified in Way's (1998) five-year ethnographic study of students attending a large, ethnically diverse urban high school. Self-blame is evident as this student engages in self-attributions to make sense of his apparent shortcomings in school:

> You know I haven't been doing as well as I want to because I do get lazy sometimes and I be like, "Oh, I do this tomorrow, I do that tomorrow." ... I'm more lazy, it's all in my mind. 'Cause I know I could do it. But see, I'm kind of lazy 'cause I be like I don't progress that fast. Then when I think about it in my head, I'm like "Damn," you know, "Let's start doing it." I always try to put things off a day later and stuff, and the next thing you know it's the next month. (p.186)"

Interestingly, this student does not cite the fact that, in addition to attending school, he worked outside of school to help with family finances. This student's assumption of adult-like responsibilities in his family would not have been detected if not for the type of inquiry enabled by ethnographic methods. This vital piece of information provides important insight on the "unspoken forces" that are having a strong influence on his academic performance.

FROM CONCEPTUALIZATION TO APPLICATION: ETHNOGRAPHY, ADOLESCENT ADULTIFICATION, AND SCHOOL-BASED SERVICE-LEARNING PROGRAMS

Our third objective in this chapter is to provide a practical example of how ethnographic research can inform both the framing of a contextually-relevant conceptual model of adolescent development, as well as practices in school-based programs. The purpose of this example is to demonstrate a key reason why ethnography is of value. Ethnography enables emergent nuanced developmental knowledge about youth and their

contexts to be brought to the forefront of scientific attention. Nuanced understandings of adolescents and the various settings they navigate can provide critically important insights for shaping the successful development and implementation of programs promoting positive youth development (e.g., see chapter 15, this volume). Accordingly, we use ethnographic research on adultification in childhood and adolescence to illustrate how the knowledge gleaned from these studies contributed to the formulation of an alternative life-course model of adolescent development that has practical implications for school-based service-learning programs.

This section of the chapter leads the reader through a three-stage process. First, we present the logic of how research questions involving adultification and school-based service-learning programs emerged from our ethnographic work. The specific questions that were raised are: (1) Why should service-learning professionals be interested in acquiring insights on adolescent adultification? and (2) What should service-learning professionals know about adolescent adultification and how families, as developmental contexts, shape the consequent behaviors of teens? Second, we demonstrate how an ethnographically derived conceptual model on adultification became useful in identifying and interpreting certain adolescent behaviors observed in school-based service-learning programs. Third, we summarize the service-learning program recommendations we developed based on ethnographically-generated insights.

Building a Case for Using Ethnographic Data to Inform Program Practices

For well over a decade we have used ethnographic methods to study the experiences of childhood adultification and how the processes involved create developmental opportunities and constraints for youth. Adultification comprises social and developmental processes in which youth are prematurely exposed to adult knowledge, or assume adult roles and responsibilities in their families (e.g., household financial manager) (see Burton, 2007). Approximately six years ago, we were asked to apply findings from our ethnographic research on childhood adultification to practices in school-based service-learning programs (Burton, Brooks, & Clark, 2004), an effort that we continue to engage in through this writing. Service-learning programs involve teaching methods that include students' performing community service in order to learn knowledge and skills connected to curricular objectives. "It usually involves meeting authentic community needs, student involvement in planning and implementing service activities, reflection to gain greater insight and learning from the service experience, and celebration or recognition of accomplishments" (Billig, 2002, p. 1; National and Community Service Act of 1990).

Our foray into applying ethnographic insights to school-based service-learning programs began with this question: Why should service-learning professionals be interested in acquiring insights on adultification? To address this question, we reviewed the conceptual literature on this topic and also consulted the ethnographic studies of others as well as our own (see Burton, 2007). Through this process, we determined that there were a number of important reasons to integrate knowledge on adultified children and teens in the conceptualization, implementation, and evaluation of service-learning programs.

First, our review of the service-learning literature suggested that very little was known about the diversity of individual and contextual attributes that influence outcomes for certain subgroups of youth involved in service-learning programs, particularly adultified children (Anderson, 1998; Billig, 2000a, 2000b; Billig & Furco, 2002; Conrad, 1980; Furco, 2003; Waterman, 2003). And our ethnographic data indicated that adultified youth represent a special population of children who often evidence social and emotional behaviors that are developmentally "out of sync" with the expectations of social service-learning programs (McLaughlin, Irby, & Langman, 1994; National Research Council, 2002). These children's behaviors required attention to and an understanding of the contextual meanings of their actions as well as the forces that shaped what they do. For example, some adultified children enter and progress through service-learning programs with well-entrenched, "hyper" forms of the same personal qualities these programs are designed to engender (e.g., responsibility, life skills, advocacy, empowerment). However, prior to entering these programs, the external impetuses of these children's qualities are not often discerned, meaning that erroneous interpretations are potentially made in evaluating the true impact of service-learning experiences on their developmental outcomes. An ethnographic case study of 12-year-old Candace illustrates this point (Burton, 2007):

> Candace is described by her mother as having been the official *"woman of the house"* since the age of seven. When Candace was six years old, her parents divorced and her father, who had a severe illicit drug addiction, moved out of the house, out of the area, and out of her life. Upon his departure, Candace "stepped up to the plate," taking on the care of her younger brother, cleaning the house preparing meals, and "making sure that the family was well-taken care of" while her mother worked. With every year that followed, Candace took on more and more of the day-to-day household responsibilities, as well as caring for her younger brother and ailing grandparents who moved in with the family when Candace was 11 years old. According to Candace's mother, by the time Candace was 12 years old, she had "the social, language, and life skills of a mature 30-year-old woman and the empathy and sensitivity of Gandhi." Consequently, it was quite a surprise to Candace's mother when, after Candace completed a school-based service-learning program, the program director said to her, "Candace has grown so much from participating in this program … she has learned quite a bit about taking on responsibility and caring for others." Stunned by the comment, Candace's mother replied, *"Are you talking about my child?*

Didn't you notice that she already had those skills before she started this program?"

Waterman (2003), a service-learning evaluation researcher, would likely comment that Candace's mother's reply to the program director represents the "confounding life events problem." In defining this problem, Waterman (2003, p. 97) states that:

> Because maturational timetables throughout childhood and adolescence are variable among students, what the students initially bring to a service-learning program may be quite different. For a service-learning program designed to promote particular forms of student development, minimal impacts may be observed among students who are maturationally advanced [due to collateral events arising outside of school, for example, with respect to physical health, family circumstances, and social relationships, p. 96] at the time the service program is initiated. Since they will have already made the advances anticipated to be an outcome of the education program, pre-/post-test assessments can reveal little change. Such students will look as good at the start of a program as they are expected to look at the end.

In further responding to Candace's mother's point, Waterman might have noted that the confounding life events problem extends beyond making errors in attributing service-learning program effects on children. He has argued that positive behavioral outcomes for children also may not be observed in evaluations as a consequence of confounding life events (e.g., adultification) actively interfering with the behaviors service-learning programs are designed to promote. Thus, given that adultified children are likely to occupy a unique "confounding" behavioral niche within broader youth populations, a comprehensive understanding of adultification by researchers and practitioners became important for accurately assessing children's progress in and promoting optimal outcomes for them in service-learning programs.

A second and equally important reason for integrating ethnographic knowledge on adultification into service-learning practices involved practitioners' experiences in identifying and working directly with adultified youth. Practitioners with limited experience in these matters are often ill-prepared to foster optimal service-learning experiences for adultified children, given that the strengths and weakness of adultified children do not necessarily conform to normative expectations of "appropriate" behaviors for children of similar ages (Ferguson, 2000). As such, professionals who are not sensitized to adultification issues misinterpret an adultified child's behavior. For example, an adultified child's aggressive leadership style could be viewed by an undiscerning eye as disrespectful to adults. A child's excessive worry and anxiety about his/her siblings' well-being and safety might be labeled peculiar. And a child who was consistently late for or absent from service-learning activities could be considered irresponsible. Indeed, these children required much less in the way of a contextual evaluations of their behavior, but rather, they may have needed well-informed constructive assistance in shaping their adultification experiences within the broader contexts of service-learning activities. Without ethnographic information, these insights about the different developmental course of adultified youth would not be available to practitioners and perhaps compromise their abilities to meet the program needs of these teens.

A third consideration involved the integration of social and emotional learning (SEL) and service learning (SL) in school-based programs. Prevailing research on integrated SEL/SL approaches reports that such programs are particularly beneficial for children in that "social and emotional learning provides the skills that help children and youth to act according to core ethical values such as caring, respect, responsibility and honesty, and service learning provides the opportunities for children and youth to apply these skills (in real world activities) and the values they represent"

(Kathleen Beland, Creative Director for the Character Education Partnership in Washington D.C., cited in Education Commission of the States, 2003, p. 4). By extension, conventional wisdom suggests that knowledge about adultified adolescents growing up in families with considerable emotional needs is critical for integrated SEL/SL programs that are likely to involve adultified youth. SEL/SL programs could potentially teach adultified teens social and emotional "tempering techniques" in tandem with practical real-world experiences, thus providing significant opportunities for positive development for youth with "hyper" social, emotional, and life skills. Stated another way, through appropriate mentorship, instruction, and activities, integrated SEL/SL programs could provide the "checks and balances strategies" hyper-adultified teens needed to shape and refine their social and emotional skills in ways that are appropriate for what the contexts or circumstances in their day-to-day lives actually demand (Rhoads, 1997). For instance, in an SEL/SL program, adultified youth who, because of their adult responsibilities, are overly concerned about the well-being of others or who exhibit personally harmful levels of self-sacrificing behaviors might learn more about setting appropriate social and emotional boundaries around their efforts (Valleau, Bergner, & Horton, 1995). These lessons might keep adultified children from being taken advantage of, or distill their propensity for engaging in potentially harmful codependent caregiving relationships (Burton, 2007).

Finally, our ethnographic research suggested that knowledge concerning adultification is important for service-learning programs because of the potential opportunities for growth adultified youth can provide for other children. When adultified children's social and emotional skills and strengths are channeled properly, these children can be very helpful in mentoring their "nonadultified" peers about responsibility and being caring of others. However, service-learning professionals' recognition of the value of these children's assets and their

potential as mentors are important precursors to developing relevant social and emotional learning opportunities for adultified youth and their nonadultified peers. Without ethnographic information about these youth, such insights would not likely prevail and the value of these youth for enhancing the lives of their nonadultified peers would be missed.

What Should Service-Learning Practitioners Know About Adolescent Adultification?

Based on the rationale we developed about the importance of adultification knowledge for service-learning programs, we then asked the question: What should service-learning practitioners know about adolescent adultification, and what can ethnographic knowledge contribute to their understanding of this phenomenon? To address this question, we consulted an emergent conceptual model on childhood adultification. We used the model, which is featured in Figure 3.1 (see Burton, 2007, for a detailed discussion of the model) to: (1) delineate the characteristics of families who are likely to have adultified children; (2) outline the forms and features of adultification, relative to families' needs, cultural practices, and child attributes; and (3) describe the potential developmental, behavioral, and health outcomes of adultification for children and adolescents. The model was developed primarily using ethnographic data collected across a number of longitudinal multisite studies and provides valuable insights on the meanings and mechanisms involved in adultified adolescents' behaviors. We highlight the insights below.

Family Contexts and Adultified Children

Our research indicated that a critical source of information for service-learning practitioners involved knowledge about the family context of adultified children. By definition, adultification implies children's taking on of fairly extensive adult roles and responsibilities before they are necessarily developmentally ready to do so. Certain family attributes and circumstances

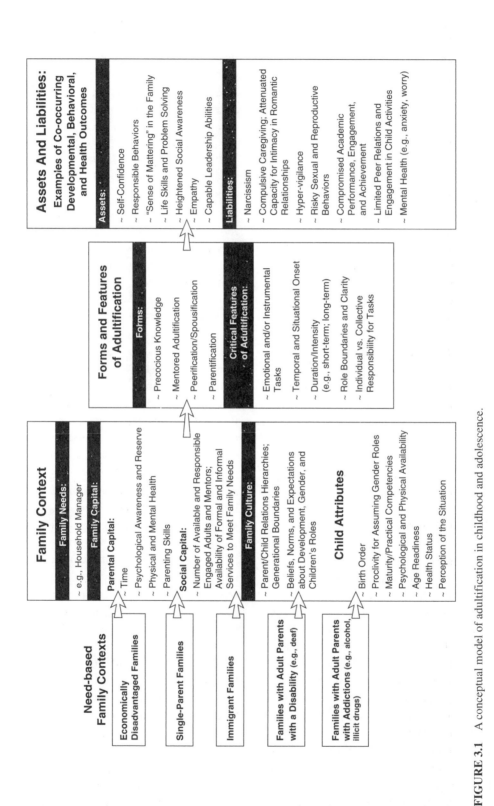

FIGURE 3.1 A conceptual model of adultification in childhood and adolescence.

are particularly conducive to producing an adultified child (Anderson, 1990; Burton, 1990; Dodson, 1998; East, Weisner, & Reyes, 2006; Ferguson, 2000; Fine & Weis, 1998; MacLeod, 1995; Menjivar, 2000; Stack, 1996; Stack & Burton, 1993). Family environments in which adults' capacities to perform certain critical tasks are severely limited by compromised capital, including time, psychological awareness and reserve in raising children, physical and mental health, and involvement in their children's day-to-day lives, will be more apt to lead to the adultification of children. Households that are financially challenged, have few responsible adults present, have multiple family members with mentally or physically disabling conditions, and have ineffective ties to formal and informal services to meet family needs would be expected to also show higher levels of children who are "growing up a little faster" (Burton, 1991; Kotlowitz, 1991; Orellana, 2001; Preston, 1994; Wallerstein, 1983).

Understanding family culture, which comprises specific beliefs about accelerated child development, kinship rules and regulations that mandate children's early assumptions of certain responsibilities, and ambiguous definitions of parent/child relational hierarchies also is important (Stack & Burton, 1993). Moreover, the ethnographic data suggested that in some families the need to have "specialty tasks" performed by children to ensure communication in a dominant culture fosters adultification. For example, the special needs around communication in the family environments of hearing children of deaf parents and children in immigrant families increase children's likelihood of being adultified. In both cases, children may be called upon to bridge the language barrier between the adults in their families and the outside world by serving as a translator for adults in the family (Valenzuela, 1999; Preston, 1994).

Our guiding premise in applying ethnographic research to service-learning programs is that ethnographically generated knowledge can inform service-learning professionals'

understanding of the different developmental circumstances of these youth, that is, of the specific family contexts of adultified children. Armed with this ethnographically-derived, new knowledge of the nature of the development of these youth, there would be an enhancement of practitioners' abilities to accurately assess children's service-learning outcomes, as well as identify the social and emotional needs of, and create opportunities for, this special population of youth. In line with this premise, the discussion that follows describes specific family circumstances using ethnographic data, and how each circumstance may be expected to lead to particular child or adolescent adultification outcomes that are relevant for service-learning programs.

Single-Parent Families

Many researchers have stressed the greater reliance by parents on children in single-parent families (Hetherington, 1999; Nock, 1988; Weiss, 1979). Indeed, a number of social scientists have suggested that single parents often rely so heavily on their children for instrumental and emotional support that these families experience a breakdown in family hierarchy, with children and parents playing much more egalitarian roles, and in some instances, children actually "parenting" their parents (Glenwick & Mowry, 1986; Nock, 1988; Weiss, 1979). Children in these families are often afforded greater power and influence in both more menial family tasks, such as keeping house, and in more complex areas of family life, such as determining family routines and helping parents work through important family decisions. Weiss (p. 99) discusses the implications of a general loosening of the family hierarchy describing the "absence of an echelon structure" in single-parent families, in which "children have rights and responsibilities not very different from their parents."

According to Nock, this recalibration of hierarchies and increased power results in youth understanding hierarchies in ways which often leads to them having less success and greater difficulty in institutions operating under a well-defined hierarchy, such as the educational system. The comments of Jason, a 15-year-old adultified participant in one ethnographic study (Burton, Obeidallah, & Allison, 1996, p. 404) illustrates this phenomenon:

> Sometimes I just don't believe how this school operates and thinks about us. Here I am grown man. I take care of my mother and have raised my sisters. Then I come here and this know-nothing teacher treats me like I'm some dumb kid with no responsibilities. I am so frustrated. They are trying to make me something that I am not. Don't they understand I'm a man and have been a man longer than they have been women?

Jason, in fact, participated in a service-learning activity at his school for two weeks. He curtailed his participation after the second week because, as he states, "I can't deal with these people telling me what to do all the time." Jason's service-learning facilitator characterized his behavior in the program as "rude and always challenging authority." According to the school counselor, however, the facilitator had not taken the time to explore the reasons why Jason was questioning and rejecting authority in his service-learning activities. The school counselor cogently argued that Jason's challenging authority was related to the "grown-up" responsibilities he had at home and urged the facilitator to be "patient with him."

In addition to challenges in navigating adult hierarchies, children in some single-parent families may also be more likely to take on greater responsibility for providing emotional support to their parents. The increased psychological stress and feelings of isolation that many single parents experience may lead children to act as a confidant to their parent, consoling and offering advice when their parent is feeling depressed or overwhelmed. These circumstances accelerate children's development of the very core competencies that SEL/SL programs attempt to foster in youth. Adultified youth growing up in need-based families often,

out of necessity, demonstrate more advanced forms of social awareness, self-management, responsible decision making, and relationship skills. However, what many of these children lack, given their often hyper form of altruism, is a strong sense of self-awareness. Thus, developing a sense of self-awareness may be a domain for potential intervention in the lives of adultified children participating in SEL/SL programs. Elucidating these developmental issues through ethnographic information enables practitioners to design programs that better fit the needs of these youth.

Economic Hardship

As is the case of single-parent families, many researchers have suggested that children in families experiencing economic hardship are more often needed to provide economic support and household labor than their economically advantaged peers (see East, Weisner, & Reyes, 2006; Elder, 1974; Weisner & Gallimore, 1977; Willis, 1981; Williams & Kornblum, 1994). For, example, Shimahara and Condon's (1983, p. 159) ethnographic study depicts instances of child migrant workers' extensive work responsibilities in their families:

> The average migrant child is expected to assume his share of family responsibilities as soon as he is able to do so; accordingly, he is often an accomplished bean or strawberry picker by the time he is six, and an expert baby nurse at seven.

MacLeod (1995, p. 51) describes the experiences of 16-year-old Joe, who is the family's primary breadwinner:

> My brother Joe had to quit school when he was sixteen years old, just because my father was an alcoholic. He had to go out and get a job. My (other) brother, he was a bikey. . . . But Joe was out gettin' a job at sixteen to support all the kids. . . . He's our father. That's what he really is—he's our father. Every fucking penny that my brother got he threw right into the family, right into the house. Cuz my mother can't work."

And in yet another example, a 12-year-old boy becomes the primary advocator for services for his unemployed mother, who is critically ill, and his eight younger siblings (Burton, 2007):

> Kevin entered the social worker's office with visible resolve. He said, "My family needs food, housing, and health care now. What do I have to do to get it?"

Based on ethnographic data and the conceptual model (see Figure 3.1), we argue that what is important for service-learning professionals to recognize about children growing up in these family contexts is that, in contrast to some of the negative implications of adultification for youths' emotional well-being, these children may learn a great deal about responsibility from their accountability and obligations within the family. Adultified youth can often handle taxing leadership positions, take charge of situations, and outwardly display competent behaviors, even though their family responsibilities may sometime compromise their school attendance, academic performance, and participation in service-learning activities. Children who bear heavy responsibilities in families may also have a strong sense that they matter in families, feel needed and appreciated by their parents, and value and gain confidence from useful economic, domestic, and social skills they garner in their family roles (Dodson & Dickert 2004).

Indeed, as revealed by ethnographic information, the expertise and experiences of adultified children growing up in economically disadvantage households raise several important challenges for service learning professionals:

1. How do the life skills these adultified children bring to the table enhance or hinder the service-learning experiences of these youth?

2. What role can these children play in enhancing the life skills of their "nonadultified" peers?

3. How can service-learning programs assist these children in using their skills effectively in contexts beyond their own family?

4. How can service-learning programs help these children recognize their potential for "mattering" in the roles they play outside of those they perform for their families?

These questions, elicited arguably uniquely by ethnography, will lead to answers that may enhance services for adultified youth.

Parental Incapacitation Due to Substance Abuse or Chronic Illness

The incapacitation of a parent due to substance abuse such as alcoholism or a severe chronic illness might also affect a child's role within his or her family (Ackerman, 1983; Brisbane, 1989; Deutsch, 1982). Children may be called on to take over the responsibilities that the incapacitated parent cannot perform (Bekir, McLellan, Childress, & Gariti, 1993). This situation would likely involve an increased role in the performance of basic household tasks, such as cooking and cleaning, as well as possible increased involvement in the general management of the family. The child might be expected to watch over his or her siblings, performing both caretaking responsibilities and more parental duties, such as limit setting and discipline. Further, depending on the presence and status of a second parent, children in these families might feel a responsibility to help encourage and support their well parent, who may experience difficulty in coping with his or her partner's condition.

Indeed, many of the social and emotional experiences of the adultified children of substance-dependent parents are similar to those of children in single-parent and economically disadvantaged families, and service-learning professionals would do well to incorporate this knowledge about the development of adultified youth into service-learning program development and evaluation. In addition to these developmental issues, however, service learning professionals must be sensitive to still other individual and contextual factors that may impact the service-learning experiences of children with substance-abusing parents. Evan's story illustrates this point:

> By the time he was 14 years old, Evan was already the man of the house. Both of his parents are disabled (his father had been exposed to Agent Orange during the Vietnam War, and his mother has mental health problems and is addicted to drugs), so Evan started working to take care of his parents and two younger siblings while still going to school full time. In school, Evan was required to take credits in "experiential learning" that required him to work in the community in which he lived. Evan shared that he often "knocked heads" with his activity leader because "she was cramping his style . . . always bossing him, telling him how to be a leader, how he had to learn how to care for others." She didn't seem to have a clue that Evan already did that every day of his life. Moreover, Evan found working in his own neighborhood an embarrassment. He was always scared he would see his mother at the crack house on his way to the homeless shelter. He was also afraid that "folks in the 'hood knew all his business" and would not take his efforts seriously because, after all, he was from "the 'hood" himself. (Burton, Brooks, & Clark, 2004, p. 20)

The location of service-learning activities is indeed an important consideration, but ethnographic data and the conceptual model also suggest that service-learning professionals must consider the hypercaregiver behaviors of the adultified children of substance abusers, and, comparably, the children of parents with severe chronic illnesses (e.g., HIV) (Stein, Riedel, & Rotheram-Borus, 1999). Melissa's situation provides some perspective about this issue:

> Melissa, now 17 years old, has been providing care for her mother and siblings since she was five years old. She describes herself as a "quick study." Because of all of the work she has had to do in balancing the needs of her family and school, she is incredibly capable at multi-tasking and succeeding in whatever she does. According

to her instructor, in her service-learning experience Melissa was considered a star volunteer, "providing empathy, caring, and guidance" for those she worked with." In fact although she was encouraged by her instructor to do so, she may have provided a little too much caring because she didn't seem to be able to "turn it off." In addition to her responsibilities at home, she continued to work many, many hours in the community even after the service-learning experience was completed. (Burton, Brooks, and Clark, 2004, p. 21)

The examples of Evan and Melissa punctuate the importance of understanding the impact of adultification on the service-learning experiences of children. Evan's story suggests that his experience was compromised by his instructor's having him work in a neighborhood where the problems of his mom are known and where his "skills" and knowledge as a leader were challenged rather than being further developed. Melissa's situation suggests that while her service-learning experience was deemed a success by her instructor, no attention was given to her compulsive caregiving behaviors. In some instances, caregiving may be a positive consequence of adultification, with the adultified youth demonstrating a great deal of warmth and concern for others. Circumstances also may play out in a less positive way, with the adultified child selecting into relationships where his or her needs and wants are completely disregarded. These children may not ever learn the skills necessary to ask for their needs to be met, and thus may be continually involved in relationships that are one-sided, with the child ignoring his or her own needs in order to meet those of others.

Indeed, Melissa's service-learning experience was a missed opportunity for her to garner insights about setting boundaries in providing care for others. While the majority of service-learning professionals we have worked with have had "aha" moments, when ethnography makes them aware of the specific developmental circumstances of adultified children, that did not occur in Melissa's case. As such, the program experiences she needed were not provided for her.

Children in Immigrant Families and the Hearing Children of Deaf Parents

Unlike the family circumstances described so far, the increased need of assistance from children in immigrant families and the hearing children of deaf parents are often more specific to interactions with the "*outside world.*" Children in immigrant families, for example, often serve as the family's translator or cultural bridge to the society in which they are living (Baptiste, 1993). Immigrant children often learn the language and culture of a new society much more quickly than their parents; hence, their parents often rely on them to navigate through their new environment. As a result, these children are likely to be privy to a great deal of information that is unavailable to most children. They may be present during legal negotiations or interactions with service providers, such as utility companies or insurance agents. The comments of an adultified Asian immigrant teen in Sun Hee Park's (2005, p. 68) ethnographic study illustrates the situation:

> I was my parents' translator since the age of eight or nine when my dad told me to talk to the plumber guy. That was a scary experience cause I realized that I knew something more than my dad did. It was a weird superficial sense of superiority. From then on, I translated most of their legal papers—I remember my mom dragging me to her lawyer a couple of years ago and telling me to literally decipher a mass of 40 documents for her within the hour. I also talked to my dad's credit card companies, deal with phone bills, gas bills, etc., etc., etc.

Similar to children of immigrant families, hearing children of deaf parents are often required to act as both a translator and a cultural bridge to mainstream society. The difficulty in finding an interpreter and the desire to keep private information from individuals outside the family often results in children's being asked to accompany parents on errands or meetings to interpret for them. Yet, as is true for children of immigrant families, the child's role as translator is often more complicated than a simple word-for-word interpretation of the other person's message. Differences in the patterns of thinking and communicating between what ethnographers term the *deaf* and *hearing* cultures also require children to translate the broader message coming from hearing adults (Preston, 1994).

While many immigrant children and the hearing children of deaf parents develop highly specialized life skills that are potentially advantageous for them and others when participating in service-learning programs, it is important to note that mastering these skills at a young age often comes at an expensive emotional price. These children tend to exhibit high levels of performance anxiety and worry and low levels of self-awareness. Involvement in SEL/SL programs could be particularly beneficial to these children if the programs helped them to appropriately build their social and emotional competencies. Moreover, these children could provide valuable growth opportunities to their nonadultified peers by mentoring them in specialized life skills (e.g., sign language).

Forms and Features of Adultification

Furthermore, as the ethnographic model (see Figure 3.1) displays, it is not sufficient for service-learning professionals only to understand the family contexts of adultification. They also must have an appreciation for the forms and features of adultification. Understanding the forms and features of childhood adultification or having a sense of "a child's level of adultification" can provide critical insights—or "aha" moments—when assessing the impact of service-learning programs on adultified youth. Such insights can inform the "action plans" professionals develop for optimizing the service-learning experience of these children.

Depicted in Figure 3.1 are four levels of adultification, ranging from basic to increasingly complex forms. Precocious knowledge, the first and perhaps the most innocuous form, involves the acquisition of knowledge that is advanced for the child's age. With precocious knowledge, children are often privy to adult conversations and transactions, visually exposed to types of behaviors from which children are often shielded (e.g., adult sexual acts), or consistently witness the harsh realities of life in high-risk environments, as seen in a description of a 12-year-old's grasp of "correct battlefield conduct" (Kotlowitz, 1991, p. 9):

> Suddenly, gunfire erupted. The frightened children fell to the ground. "Hold your head down!" Lafeyette snapped, as he covered Dede's head with her pink nylon jacket. If he hadn't physically restrained her, she might have sprinted for home, a dangerous action when the gangs started warring. "Stay down," he ordered the trembling girl. The two lay pressed to the beaten grass for half a minute, until the shooting subsided. Lafeyette held Dede's hand as they cautiously crawled through the dirt toward home.

Although precocious knowledge is the most basic form of adultification, it is also the most subtle and slippery to measure. In fact, this construct is identifiable only because it emerges from the nuances of the ethnographic literature; it likely evades detection by more quantitatively -oriented methods of data collection.

Mentored adultification is the action phase of precocious knowledge and involves a child's prematurely assuming an adult-like role with very limited adult supervision. In some instances, as noted in Smith's (1991) ethnographic study, mentored adultification may arise less from the urgency of family needs than from an encouragement of early independence in general:

> One three-year-old I observed could generally choose what to wear without help, fix a simple breakfast for herself, make sandwiches and pour milk for lunch. Both boys and girls are introduced to household chores—separating the laundry, making beds, matching socks, dusting,

etc.—around the age of four. . . . Virtually all the women I talked to told me that by the time they were eight years old, they could, and often did, clean the house, do the laundry and fix dinner—as well as care for younger children" (Smith, 1991, p. 100).

This sort of training for a "junior homemaker" role is the most common form of mentored adultification.

With mentored adultification, although the child has precocious knowledge and takes on adult-like responsibilities, a parent–child hierarchy is in place. However, adultification takes the form of peerification/spousification, the third form, when the child behaves in some way more like a parent's peer than like a parent's subordinate. For example, a child may become peerified in protecting a parent when the family situation demands it, as Dodson's (1998, p. 116) ethnographic research illustrates: "Maria . . . recalls that she developed her [coping] skills as 'my mother's social worker for her welfare benefits. I had to fight her battles, she was too weak.'"

A peerified/spousified child may periodically step into and out of a parental role, but a parentified child, the fourth form, is a fulltime quasi-parent. Parentification offers the extreme example of the loosening of family hierarchies and the assumption of adult roles by children. One of Fine and Weis's (1998, p. 200) ethnographic respondents notes:

> My father's an alcoholic, and my mom is mentally ill, she's schizophrenic and it was tough. . . . I was kind of the caretaker. I did the cooking from, I can remember seven years old, making dinner and cleaning. . . . It was more or less, I was to take care of my mother instead of her taking care of me.

With respect to the four forms of adultification, what is important for service-learning professionals to know about is what factors the ethnographic research suggest matter most in how the forms impact youth outcomes that are related to service-learning experiences. What appears to matter most for the developmental outcomes of adultified children are:

- The temporal (e.g., early childhood, late adolescence) and situational (e.g., parental illness, parental divorce) onset of the adultification experience
- How long the child is engaged in adultified behaviors
- Whether the experience involves a light versus a heavy load of adult responsibilities
- The degree to which role boundaries, expectations, and hierarchies are clear between the parents and children
- Whether more than one sibling is adultified in the family

How these factors operate in producing outcomes is most clear in extreme cases of parentification. Essentially, children who become parentified around age 4 or 5, remain in that situation consistently through their teen years, and have an extensive repertoire of adult responsibilities with no help from other siblings evidence the most hyper forms of social and emotional outcomes.

The circumstances of children with alcoholic families shed further light on the discussion. In these families, the alcoholic parent and the nonalcoholic parent may be inconsistent in their ability to play the parental role. Thus, a child may be expected to play the role of an adult and manage the household at one point in time and may be punished for the same behavior during times when the parents are functioning well enough. In addition, the age at which these roles are taken on may impact whether and how they alter the child's course of development (Chase, Deming, & Wells, 1998). For instance, the adultified child in the alcoholic family is expected to ignore his or her own needs in order to meet those of the family. According to Deutsch (1982, p. 56), "The process of becoming individuated is subordinated to that of meeting the family's needs." This process may

be particularly harmful for adolescents who are attempting to build their autonomy from their families but are prevented from doing so by their roles as the "Family Hero." Moreover, it may be a process that is in direct conflict with the outcomes SEL/SL programs are attempting to foster in adultified adolescents.

Child Attributes

To be sure, the attributes of the child influence the forms and features of adultification as well as developmental outcomes. Children who tend to be more mature, have certain competencies (e.g., language skills), are in better health, see their roles as "mattering" or important to family survival, and are physically available are the most likely to be "recruited" for higher forms of adultification (e.g., mentored adultification, peerification, parentification) based on family needs. Birth order and gender are also important factors, particularly in families with an alcoholic parent.

In families with an alcoholic parent, the "Family Hero," or adultified child, is often expected to be the oldest female in the family (Brisbane, 1989; Deutsch, 1982). However, it is unclear whether this role is typically occupied by the oldest female or whether this has simply been the conceptual perspective of the researchers involved, and thus the role of males has been ignored. Deutsch (1982) discusses the differences in the assumption of this role by males and females, describing how this role might be more difficult for boys. He states that while the oldest boy may be groomed for this responsibility, his identity and masculinity may be confused by the lack of masculinity in his role and responsibilities at home, thus making this situation quite stressful. Thus, while girls may be more likely to take on this role, boys may also perform it and may find it more stressful than girls. This issue underscores the importance of devoting special attention to gender issues in devising social and emotional learning opportunities for adultified children.

Ethnographic Insights Informing Program Recommendations

After using the knowledge derived from ethnographic studies and the conceptual model to identify and describe elements of adultification that are relevant to service-learning programs, we have been able to develop practical recommendations that service-learning professionals can consider in their program assessment and teaching practices. The recommendations are as follows:

- The specific roles adultified children take in their families (e.g., caregiver) may immeasurably impact the social and emotional outcomes of their service-learning experiences. It is important for service-learning practitioners to accurately assess the "skills" adultified children bring to the table and consider their preentry social and emotional repertoire before evaluating program outcomes.
- When working with adultified children in service-learning programs, it is important that practitioners help these children "widen their lens" or contextualize their experiences beyond their personal situations. Many adultified children and teens have limited experience in applying their skills in contexts outside of environments that provide services necessary to meet family needs. Assisting these children in learning to appropriately use their skills (e.g., advocacy) across a range of contexts may help them in navigating diverse environments as they move to adulthood.
- In Evan's case, we see a young teen whose experiential learning activities occurred in the neighborhood he lived in. This created a personal dilemma for Evan, and he received no assistance from his service-learning facilitator in reconciling it. It is important that service-learning practitioners take into account the issues some economically disadvantaged children, in particular, face in working in their own neighborhoods where "everybody knows your business."

- Many adultified children become compulsive life-course caregivers, in large part, because they have considerable caregiving responsibilities. In working with adultified children, service-learning practitioners should consider how these caregiving responsibilities might impact a child's ability to participate fully in activities and also how their "overflow caregiving attributes" impact the ways in which they interact with other program participants and the "targeted" service-learning populations (e.g., families in a homeless shelter).
- Service-learning practitioners, particularly those implementing SEL/SL programs, may be in unique situations to assist adultified children in fine-tuning their social and emotional competencies. In particular, they can help adultified children learn how to set boundaries around exchanges and reciprocity with others. Adultified children tend to be "hypergivers." Assisting adultified children in learning how to receive could be particularly beneficial as they learn how to balance responsibilities and relationships in their lives.
- Many adultified children develop a sense that they "matter" in the context of what they do for their families. Service-learning programs can be particularly instrumental in helping these children develop a sense that what they do matters beyond the immediate needs of their families and that they have much to offer their school and community environments.
- Adultified children, because of familial circumstances, often assume leadership roles at very young ages in their families. Service-learning professionals can help these children refine, diversify, and optimize their leadership skills by creating activities that allow them to effectively use their skills in peer team efforts and in activities that are distinct from those expected in their families.
- Children who grow up in families with considerable needs and who assume adultified

roles within them often have a greater sense of social awareness and execute more responsible behaviors than their peer counterparts. With the proper guidance, adultified children can serve as effective "coaches," helping their nonadultified peers to develop efficacious, caring, and responsible behaviors toward others. Such activities are indeed consistent with the philosophies and practice of social and emotional learning and service-learning programs.

In sum, using ethnography-derived knowledge for recasting the service-learning experiences of adultified youth would enhance considerably the potential of these programs for creating a fit with the unique set of individual and contextual circumstances shaping their development. Such enhancement, which in this case is predicated on the ethnographic study of the lives of these youth, illustrates the special role of ethnography in discerning the unique circumstances of adolescents' developmental milieu and, in so doing, affording value for the application of developmental science to promote their positive development (see chapter 18, volume 2 of this *Handbook*; and chapter 15, this volume).

CONCLUSIONS

In this chapter we attempted three very ambitious objectives aimed at presenting readers with a brief tutorial about ethnography and providing concrete examples of how ethnographically-generated knowledge can provide important insights about adolescent development and context. We began with a discussion of the value of ethnography, noting that while illustrative quotations are one of the ways in which ethnographers provide examples of the meanings individuals attach to behaviors and contexts, the nuances of their social interactions, or relevant cultural processes, ethnography also makes important contributions to scientific knowledge in many other ways. For example, culturally relevant theoretical models can be derived from ethnographic research as well as policy and program recommendations. These theories and policy recommendations take into account the developmental experiences adolescents have as they traverse multiple contexts and whether adults' sense of the developmental experiences of youth fit with how adolescents see those experiences. In essence, ethnographically derived theories and policy and program recommendations represent the lived experiences of adolescents.

Using several exemplar ethnographic studies of adolescent development and school contexts, we also provided examples of how ethnography renders fine-grained descriptions of processes that influence adolescent outcomes but may not be easily identified or measured in quantitative research. Through these descriptions, we demonstrated how parents implement their unique brands of monitoring their children's academic activities; how unsuspecting peer relationships, such as those between boys and girls, influence academic success; and how multiple strands of racial discrimination in school tracking programs compromise adolescents' school performance. Findings such as those reported in the chapter expand the interpretation of results from quantitative studies in very important ways.

Finally, we took the liberty of creating a "teachable moment" in this chapter by providing an account of how ethnographic research can be used to formulate an alternative life-course model of adolescent development that has practical implications for school programs. Specifically, we use ethnographic research on adolescent and child adultification to illustrate how the knowledge gleaned from ethnographic studies has contributed to the emergence of an alternative conceptual model of adolescent development, one with practical implications for school-based service-learning programs. The goal of this exercise was to provide the reader with a "start-to-finish" example of the full range of knowledge building that ethnography is capable of.

We do not consider ourselves pied pipers of ethnography, but we do recognize its value and contributions to the science of adolescent development. It is our hope that this chapter stimulates further interest in ethnography and its application to building theory and developing culturally and contextually sensitive programs that reflect the realities of the adolescent experience.

REFERENCES

Ackerman, R. J. (1983). *Children of alcoholics: A guidebook for educators, therapists, and parents.* Holmes Beach, FL: Learning Publications.

Agar, M. (1980). *The professional stranger: An informal introduction to ethnography.* San Diego: Academic Press.

Allison, K. W., Burton, L. M., Marshall, S., Perez-Febles, A., Yarrington, J., Kirsh, L. B., & Merriwether-DeVries, C. (1999). Life experiences among urban adolescents: Examining the role of context. *Child Development, 70,* 1017–1029.

Anderson, E. (1990). *Streetwise: Race, class, and change in an urban community.* Chicago: University of Chicago Press.

Anderson, S. M. (1998). Service-learning: A national strategy for youth development. A position paper issued by the Education Policy Task Force, Institute for Communitarian Policy Studies, George Washington University.

Asher, R. A. & G.A. Fine. (1991). Fragile ties: Shaping relationships with women married to alcoholics. In W. B. Shaffir and R.A. Stebbins (Eds.), *Experiencing fieldwork: An inside view of qualitative research* (pp. 196–205). Newbury Park, CA: Sage.

Baker, C. D. (1982). The adolescent as theorist. *Journal of Youth and Adolescence, 11,* 167–181.

Ball, D. (1972). The definition of situation: Some theoretical and methodological consequences of taking W.I. Thomas seriously. *Journal for the Theory of Social Behavior, 2,* 61–82.

Baptiste, D. A. (1993). Immigrant families, adolescents, and acculturation: Insights for therapists. *Marriage and Family Review, 19,* 341–363.

Becker, H.S. (1996). The epistemology of qualitative research. In R. Jessor, A. Colby, and R. A. Shweder (Eds.), *Ethnography and human development: Context and meaning in social inquiry* (pp. 53–71). Chicago: University of Chicago Press.

Bekir, P., McLellan, T., Childress, A. R., & Gariti. P. (1993). Role reversals in families of substance misusers: A transgenerational phenomenon. *International Journal of the Addictions, 28,* 613–630.

Bergin, D. A., & Cooks, H. C. (2002). High school students of color talk about accusations of "acting white." *Urban Review, 34,* 113–134.

Bettie, J. (2003). *Women without class: Girls, race, and identity.* Los Angeles: University of California Press.

Billig, S. (2000a). Research on K–12 school-based service-learning. The evidence builds. *Phi Delta Kappan, 81,* 659–664.

Billig, S. (2000b). *Service-learning impacts on youth, schools, and communities: Research on K–12 school-based service-learning.* Denver: RMC Research Corporation.

Billig, S. (2002). Support for K–12 service-learning practice: A brief review of the research. *Educational Horizons, 80,* 184–189.

Billig, S., & Furco, A. (2002). Research agenda for K–12 service-learning: A proposal to the field. In A. Furco & S. Billig (Eds.), *Service-learning: The essence of the pedagogy.* Greenwich, CT: Information Age.

Blumer, H. (1955). Attitudes and the social act. *Social Problems, 3,* 59–65.

Blumer, H. (1969). *Symbolic interaction: Perspective and method.* Berkeley: University of California Press.

Boggs, S. T. (1985). *Speaking, relating, and learning: A study of Hawaiian children at home and at school.* Norwood, NJ: Ablex.

Bourgois, P. (1995). *In search of respect: Selling crack in el barrio.* New York: Cambridge University Press.

Brisbane, F. L. (1989). The family hero in Black alcoholism families. *Journal of Alcohol and Drug Education, 34,* 29–37.

Burton, L. M. (1990). Teenage childbearing as an alternative life-course strategy in multi-generation black families, *Human Nature, 1,* 123–143.

Burton, L. M. (1991). Caring for children: Drug shifts and their impact on families. *American Enterprise, 2,* 34–37.

Burton, L. M. (1997). Ethnography and the meaning of adolescence in high-risk neighborhoods. *Ethos, 25,* 208–217.

Burton, L. M. (2007). Childhood adultification in economically disadvantaged families: A conceptual model. *Family Relations, 56,* 329–345.

Burton, L. M., Brooks, J., & Clark, J. (2004). *Adultified children in need-based families: A discourse for service-learning.* Denver, CO: RMC Corporation.

Burton, L. M., & Jarrett, R. L., (2000). In the mix, yet on the margins: The place of family in urban neighborhood and child development research. *Journal of Marriage and the Family, 62,* 1114–1135.

Burton, L. M., Obeidallah, D. A., & Allison, K. (1996). Ethnographic insights on social context and adolescent development among inner-city African-American teens. In R. Jessor, A. Colby, and R. A. Shweder (Eds.), *Ethnography and human development: Context and meaning in social inquiry* (pp. 395–418). Chicago: University of Chicago Press.

Carter, P. L. (2003). "Black" cultural capital, status positioning, and schooling conflicts for low-income African American youth. *Social Problems, 50,* 136–155.

Carter, P. L. (2005). *Keepin' it real: School success beyond black and white.* New York: Oxford University Press.

Chase, N. D., Deming, M. P., & Wells, M. C. (1998). Parentification, parental alcoholism, and academic status among young adults. *American Journal of Family Therapy, 26,* 105–114.

Clark, R. M. (1983). *Family life and school achievement: Why poor black children succeed or fail.* Chicago: University of Chicago Press.

Colby, A. (1996). The multiple contexts of human development. In R. Jessor, A. Colby, and R. A. Shweder (Eds.), *Ethnography and human development: Context and meaning in social inquiry* (pp. 327–338). Chicago: University of Chicago Press.

Conchas, G. Q., & Noguera, P. A. (2004). Understanding the exceptions: How small schools support the achievement of academically successful black boys. In N. Way and J. Chu (Eds.), *Adolescent boys: Exploring diverse cultures of boyhood* (pp. 313–337). New York: New York University Press.

Conrad, D., & Hedin, D. (1980). *High school community service: A review of research and programs.* Madison, WI: National Center for Effective Secondary Schools.

Delgado-Gaitan, C. (1991). Involving parents in the schools: A process of empowerment. *American Journal of Education, 100,* 20–46.

Delgado-Gaitan, C. (1992). School matters in the Mexican-American home: Socializing children to education. *American Education Research Journal, 29,* 495–513.

Deutsch, C. (1982). *Broken bottles, broken dreams: Understanding and helping children of alcoholics.* New York: Teachers College Press.

Deutscher, I. (1966). Words and deeds: Social science and social policy. *Social Problems, 13,* 235–254.

Dodson, L. (1998). *Don't call us out of name: The untold lives of women and girls in poor America.* Boston: Beacon Press.

Dodson, L., & Dickert, J. (2004). Girls' family labor in low-income households: A decade of qualitative research. *Journal of Marriage and Family, 60,* 318–332.

Dodson, L., & Schmalzbauer, L. (2005). Poor mothers and habits of hiding: Participatory methods in poverty research. *Journal of Marriage and Family, 67,* 949–959.

East, P. L. Weisner, T. S., & Reyes, B. T. (2006). Youth's caretaking of their adolescent sisters' children: Its cost and benefits for youths' development. *Applied Developmental Science, 10*, 86–95.

Eccles, J. S., & Harold, R. D. (1993). Parent–school involvement during the early adolescent years. *Teachers College Record, 94*, 568–587.

Eccles, J. S., & Harold, R. D. (1996). Family involvement in children's and adolescents' schooling. In A. Booth & J. F. Dunn (Eds.), *Family school links: How do they affect educational outcomes?* (pp. 3–34). Mahwah, NJ: Lawrence Erlbaum.

Eckert, P. (1989). *Jocks and burnouts: Social categories and identities in high school*. New York: Teachers College Press.

Eder, D., Evans, D. C., & Parker, S. (1995). *School talk: Gender and adolescent culture*. New Brunswick, NJ: Rutgers University Press.

Education Commission of the States. (2003). *Making the case for social and emotional learning and service-learning*. Denver, CO: Education Commission of the States.

Elder, G. H., Jr. (1974). *Children of the great depression. Social change in life experience*. Chicago: University of Chicago Press.

Emerson, R. M., Fretz, R. I., & Shaw, L. L. (1995). *Writing ethnographic fieldnotes*. Chicago: University of Chicago Press.

Epstein, J. L. (1987). Toward a theory of family–school connections: Teacher practices and parent involvement. In K. Hurrelman, F. X. Kaufmann, & F. L. Sel (Eds.), *Social intervention: Potential and constraints* (pp. 121–136). Berlin: Walter de Gruyer.

Epstein, J. L., & Sanders, M. G. (2002). Family, school, and community partnerships. In M. H. Bornsten (Ed.), *Handbook of parenting*, Vol. 5: *Practical issues in parenting* (pp. 407–437). Mahwah, NJ: Lawrence Erlbaum.

Evans, C., & Eder, D. (1993). "No exit": Processes of social isolation in the middle school. *Journal of Contemporary Ethnography, 22*, 139–170.

Everhart, R. B. (1982). The nature of "goofing off" among junior high school adolescents. *Adolescence, 65*, 177–188.

Everhart, R. B. (1983). *Reading, writing, and resistance: Adolescence and labor in a junior high school*. Boston: Routledge.

Falbo, T., Lein, L., & Amador, N. A. (2001). Parental involvement during transition to high school. *Journal of Adolescent Research, 16*, 511–529.

Ferguson, A. A. (2000). *Bad boys: Public schools in the making of Black masculinity*. Ann Arbor: University of Michigan Press.

Fine, G. A. (2004). Adolescence as cultural toolkit: High school debate and the repertoires of childhood and adulthood. *Sociological Quarterly, 45*, 1–20.

Fine, G. A., and Sandstrom, K. L. (1988). *Knowing children: Participant observation with minors*. Newbury Park, CA: Sage.

Fine, M. (1991). *Framing dropouts: Notes on the politics of an urban public high school*. Albany: State University of New York Press.

Fine, M., & Weis, L. (1998). *The unknown city: The lives of poor and working class young adults*. Boston: Beacon Press.

Fordham, S. (1996). *Blacked out: Dilemmas of race, identity, and success at Capital High*. Chicago: University of Chicago Press.

Fordham, S., & Ogbu, J. (1986). Black students' school success: Coping with the "burden of 'acting white.'" *Urban Review, 18*, 176–206.

Flores-Gonzales, N. (2005). Popularity versus respect: School structure, peer groups and Latino academic achievement. *International Journal of Qualitative Studies, 18*, 625–642.

Furco, A. (2003). Issues of definition and program diversity in the study of service-learning. In S. Billig & A. S. Waterman (Eds.), *Studying service-learning: Challenges and solutions*. Mahwah, NJ: Lawrence Erlbaum.

Gaines, D. (1990). *Teenage wasteland: Suburbia's dead end kids*. New York: Pantheon Books.

Gandara, P. (1995). *Over the ivy walls: The educational mobility of low-income Chicanos*. Albany: State University of New York Press.

Gandara, P. (2002). A study of high school Puente: What we have learned about preparing Latino youth for postsecondary education. *Educational Policy, 16*, 474–495.

Gans, H.J. (1968). The participant-observer as a human being: Observations on the personal aspects of fieldwork. In H.S. Becker, B. Geer, D. Riesman, and R. S. Weiss (Eds.), *Institutions and the person* (pp. 300–317). Chicago: Aldine.

Geertz, C. (1973). *The interpretation of cultures*. New York: Basic Books.

Geertz, C. (1983). *Local knowledge*. New York: Basic Books.

Gibson, M.A., Gandara, P., & Koyama, J.P. (2004). The role of peers in the schooling of U.S. Mexican youth. In M. A. Gibson, P. Gandara, & J. P.Koyama (Eds.). *School connections: U.S. Mexican youth, peers, and school achievement* (pp. 1–17). New York: Teachers College Press.

Glaser, B. G., & Strauss, A. L. (1964). Awareness contexts and social interaction. *American Sociological Review, 29*, 669–679.

Glenwick, D. S. & Mowerey, J. D. (1986). When parent becomes peer: Loss of intergenerational boundaries in single parent families. *Family Relations, 35*, 57–62.

Gold, R.L. (1958). "Roles in sociological field observations. *Social Forces, 36*, 217–223.

Goffman, E. (1974). *Frame analysis: An essay on the organization of experience*. New York: Harper-Colophon.

Gorman, T. J. (1998). Social class and parental attitudes toward education. *Journal of Contemporary Ethnography, 27*, 10–44.

Graue, M., & Walsh, D. J. (1998). *Studying children in context: Theories, methods, and ethics*. London: Sage.

Hammersley, M., & Atkinson, P. (1995). *Ethnography: Principles in practice*. London: Routledge.

Harrington, B. (2003). The social psychology of access in ethnographic research. *Journal of Contemporary Ethnography, 32*, 592–625.

Hebert, T. P. (2000). Defining belief in self: Intelligent young men in an urban high school. *Gifted Child Quarterly, 44*, 91–112.

Hebert, T. P., & Reis, S. M. (1999). Culturally diverse high-achieving students in an urban high school. *Urban Education, 34*, 428–457.

Hetherington, E. M. (1999). *Coping with divorce, single parenting, and remarriage: A risk and resiliency perspective*. Mahwah, NJ: Lawrence Erlbaum Associates.

Hill, N. E. (2001). Parenting and academic socialization as they relate to school readiness: The roles of ethnicity and family income. *Journal of Educational Psychology, 95*, 74–83.

Honora, D. (2003). Urban African American adolescents and school identification. *Urban Education, 38*, 58–76.

James, A. (1986). Learning to belong: The boundaries of adolescence. In A. P. Cohen (Ed.), *Symbolising boundaries* (pp. 155–171) Manchester, UK: Manchester University Press.

James, A. (2001). Ethnography in the study of children and childhood. In P. Atkinson, A. Coffey, S. Delamont, J. Lofland, & L. Lofland (Eds.), *Handbook of ethnography* (pp. 246–257). Thousand Oaks, CA: Sage.

Jarrett, R. L. (1998). African American children, families, and neighborhoods: Qualitative contributions to understanding developmental pathways. *Applied Developmental Science, 2*: 2–16.

Jarrett. R. L. (2003). Worlds of development: The experiences of low-income African American youth. *Journal of Children and Poverty, 9*, 45–76.

Jessor, R., Colby, A., & Shweder, R. A. (Eds.). (1996). *Ethnography and human development*. Chicago: University of Chicago Press.

Kotlowitz, A. (1991). *There are no children here: The story of two boys growing up in the other America*. New York: Doubleday.

Kreppner, K. (1992). Development in a developing context: Rethinking the family's role for children's development. In L. T. Winegar & J. Valsiner (Eds.), *Children's development within social context*, Vol. 1: *Metatheory and theory* (pp. 161–182). Hillsdale, NJ: Lawrence Erlbaum.

Kritt, D. (1992). The mass media as a symbolic context for socio-emotional development. In L. T. Winegar & J. Valsiner (Eds.), *Children's development within social context*, Vol. 1: *Metatheory and theory* (pp. 183–201). Hillsdale, NJ: Lawrence Erlbaum.

Lareau, A. (1987). Social class differences in family-school relation-ships: The importance of cultural capital. *Sociology of Education*, *60*, 73–85.

Lareau, A. (2000). *Home advantage: Social and parental intervention in elementary education*. MD: Rowman & Littlefield, Inc.

Lareau, A. (2003). *Unequal childhoods: Class, race, and family life*. Berkeley, CA: University of California Press.

Lee, P. W. (1999). In their own voices: An ethnographic study of low-achieving students within the context of school reform. *Urban Education*, *34*, 214–244.

Liebow, E. (1993). *Tell them who I am: The lives of homeless women*. New York: Free Press.

Lightfoot, C. (1992). Constructing self and peer culture: A narra-tive perspective on adolescent risk taking. In L. T. Winegar & J. Valsiner (Eds.), *Children's development within social context*, Vol. 2: *Research and methodology* (pp. 229–245). Hillsdale, NJ: Lawrence Erlbaum.

Lofland, J. (1972). Editorial introduction. *Urban Life and Culture*, *1*, 3–5.

Lofland, J. (1995). Analytic ethnography: Features, failings, and futures. *Journal of Contemporary Ethnography*, *24*, 30–67.

Lofland, J., & Lofland, L. H. (1995). *Analyzing social settings: A guide to qualitative observation and analysis*. Belmont, CA: Wadsworth Publishing.

MacLeod, J. (1995). *Ain't no makin' it: Aspirations and attain-ment in a low-income Neighborhood* (2nd ed.). Boulder, CO: Westview Press.

Mandell, N. (1988). The least-adult role in studying children. *Journal of Contemporary Ethnography*, *12*, 3–27.

Mead, M. (1928). *Coming of age in Samoa*. New York: Morrow.

McLaughlin, M. W., Irby, M. A., & Langman, J. (1994). *Urban sanctuaries: Neighborhood organizations in the lives and futures of inner-city youth*. San Francisco: Jossey-Bass.

Menjívar, C. (2000). *Fragmented ties: Salvadoran immigrant networks in America*. Berkeley: University of California Press.

Mills, R. (1997). Grouping students for instruction: Issues of equity and effectiveness. In J. L. Ervin (Ed.), *What current research says to the middle level practioner* (pp. 87–94). Columbus, OH: National Middle School Association.

National and Community Service Act of 1990. 42 U.S. Code 12511.

National Research Council (2002). *Community programs to promote youth development*. Washington, DC: National Academy Press.

Nock, S. L. (1988). The family and hierarchy. *Journal of Marriage and the Family*, *50*, 957–966.

Oakes, J. U. (1992). Can tracking research inform practice? Technical, normative, and political considerations. *Educational Researcher*, *21*, 12–21.

Ogbu, J. (2003). *Black American students in an affluent suburb: A study of academic disengagement*. Mahwah, NJ: Lawrence Erlbaum.

Orellana, M. F. (2001). The work kids do: Mexican and Central American immigrant children's contributions to households and schools in California. *Harvard Educational Review*, *71*, 336–389.

Overton, W. F. (2006). Developmental psychology: Philosophy, concepts, methodology. In R. M. Lerner (Ed.), *Handbook of Child Psychology* (6th ed.), Vol. 1: *Theoretical models of human development*. Editors-in-chief: W. Damon & R. M. Lerner. Hoboken, NJ: John Wiley & Sons.

Sun Hee Park, L. (2005) *Consuming citizenship: Children of Asian Immigrant entrepreneurs*. Palo Alto, CA: Stanford University Press.

Perinbanayagam, R. S. (1974). The definition of the situation: An analysis of the ethnomethodological and dramaturgical view. *Sociological Quarterly*, *15*, 521–541.

Pomerantz, E. M., Moorman, E. A., & Litwack, S. D. (2007). The how, whom and why of parents' involvement in children's aca-demic lives: More is not always better. *Review of Educational Research*, *77*, 373–410.

Preston, P. (1994). *Mother father deaf: Living between sound and silence*. Cambridge, MA: Harvard University Press.

Qvortrup, J. (2000). Macroanalyis of childhood. In P. Christensen & A. James (Eds), *Research with children* (pp. 77–98). London: Falmer.

Rhoads, R. A. (1997). *Community service and higher learning: Explorations of the caring self*. Albany, NY: State University of New York Press.

Romo, H. D. & Falbo, T. (1996). *Latino high school graduation: Defying the odds*. Austin: University of Texas Press.

Rosier, K. B., & Corsaro, W. A. (1993). Competent parents, com-plex lives: Managing parenthood in poverty. *Journal of Contemporary Ethnography*, *22*, 171–204.

Roy, K. M., Tubbs, C. Y., & Burton, L. M. (2004). Don't have no time: Daily rhythms and the organization of time for low-income families. *Family Relations*, *53*, 168–178.

Rubin, L. B. (1994). *Families on the fault line: America's working class speaks about the family, the economy, race, and ethnicity*. New York: HarperCollins.

Schlecker, E., & Hirsch, E. (2001). Incomplete knowledge: Ethnography and the crisis of context in studies of media, science and technology. *History of the Human Sciences*, *14*, 69–87.

Schwalbe, M. (1995). The responsibilities of sociological poets. *Qualitative Sociology*, *18*, 393–413.

Shimahara, N. K., & Condon, E. (1983). *Seasonal life: Farmworkers, children and socialization*. New Brunswick, NJ: Rutgers University.

Smith, P. (1991). Social reproduction and transformation in two urban minority populations. Doctoral dissertation, The New School for Social Research. *Dissertation Abstracts International*, *52*(3), 982.

Spradley, J. P. (1979). *The ethnographic interview*. New York: Holt, Reinhart, and Winston.

Spradley, J. P. (1980). *Participant observation*. New York: Holt, Reinhart, and Winston.

Stack, C. (1974) *All our Kin: Strategies for survival in a Black community*. New York: Harper & Row.

Stack, C. B. (1996). *Call to home: African Americans reclaim the rural south*. New York: Basic Books.

Stack, C. B. (2001). Coming of age in Oakland. In J. Goode and J. Maskovsky (Eds.), *The new poverty studies: The ethnography of power, politics, and impoverished people in the United States*. New York: New York University Press.

Stack, C. B., & Burton, L. M. (1993). Kinscripts. *Journal of Comparative Family Studies*, *24*, 157–170.

Stanton-Salazar, R. D., & Spina, S. U. (2005). Adolescent peer networks as a context for social and emotional support. *Youth and Society*, *36*, 379–417.

Stebbins, R. A. (1972). The unstructured interview as incipient interpersonal relationship. *Sociology and Social Research*, *56*, 64–179.

Steele, C. M. (1992, April). Race and the schooling of black Americans. *The Atlantic*, *269*, 68–78.

Stein, J. A., Riedel, M., and Rotheram-Borus, M. J. (1999). Parentification and its impact on adolescent children of parents with AIDS. *Family Process*, *38*, 193–208.

Suarez-Orozco, C., & Suarez-Orozco, M. M. (1995). *Transforma-tions: Immigration, family life, and achievement motivation among Latino adolescents*. Stanford, CA: Stanford University Press.

Swain, J. (2006). An ethnographic approach to researching children in junior school. *International Journal of Social Research Methodology*, *9*, 199–213.

Tatum, B. D. (2004). Family life and school experience: Factors in the racial identity development of black youth in white communities. *Journal of Social Issues*, *60*, 117–135.

Taylor, C. S. (1990). *Dangerous society*. East Lansing, MI: Michigan State University Press.

Thorne, B. (1986). *Gender play: Boys and girls in school*. New Brunswick, NJ: Rutgers University Press.

Tyson, K. (2003). Notes from the back of the room: Problems and paradoxes in the schooling of young Black students. *Sociology of Education, 76*, 326–343.

Valdes, G. (1996). *Con respeto: Bridging the distances between culturally diverse families and schools: An ethnographic portrait*. New York: Teachers College Press.

Valenzuela, A. (1999). Gender roles and settlement activities among children and their immigrant families. *American Behavioral Scientist, 42*, 720–742.

Valleau, M. P., Bergner, R. M., & Horton, C. B. (1995). Parentification and caretaker syndrome: An empirical investigation. *Family Therapy, 22*, 157–164.

Van Maanen, J. (1983). The moral fix: On the ethics of field work. In R. M. Emerson (Ed.), *Contemporary field research: A collection of readings* (pp. 269–287). Boston: Little, Brown, and Company.

Vidich, A. J. (1955). Participant observation and the collection and interpretation of data. *American Journal of Sociology, 60*, 354–360.

Vigil, J. D. (1997). *Personas Mexicanas: Chicano high schoolers in a changing Los Angeles*. Fort Worth, TX: Harcourt Brace College Publishers.

Waksler, F. C. (1986). Studying children: Phenomenological insights. *Human Studies, 9*, 71–82.

Wallerstein, J. S. (1983). Children of divorce: The psychological tasks of the child. *American Journal of Orthopsychiatry, 53*, 230–243.

Waterman, A. S. (2003). Issues regarding the selection of variables for study in the context of the diversity of possible student outcomes of service learning. In S. Billig & A. S. Waterman (Eds.), *Studying service-learning: Innovations in education research methodology*. Mahwah, NJ: Lawrence Erlbaum.

Wax, R. (1956). Reciprocity as a field technique. *Human Organization, 11*, 34–41.

Way, N. (1998). *Everyday courage: The lives and stories of urban teenagers*. New York: New York University Press.

Weisner, T. S. (1996). Why ethnography should be the most important method in the study of human development. In R. Jessor, A. Colby, and R. A. Shweder (Eds.), *Ethnography and human development: Context and meaning in social inquiry* (pp. 305–324). Chicago: University of Chicago Press.

Weisner, T. S., & Gallimore, R. (1977). My brother's keeper: Child and sibling caretaking. *Current Anthropology, 18*, 169–190.

Weiss, R. S. (1979). Growing up a little faster: The experience of growing up in a single-parent household. *Journal of Social Issues, 35*, 97–111.

Whyte, W. F. (1955). *Street corner society* (2nd ed.). Chicago: University of Chicago Press.

Williams, T., & Kornblum, W. (1994). *The uptown kids: Struggle and hope in the projects*. New York: Grosset/Putnam.

Willis, P. (1981). *Learning to labor*. New York: Columbia University Press.

Wolcott, H. F. (2001). *The art of fieldwork*. Walnut Creek, CA: AltaMira Press.

Zerubavel, E. (1993). *The fine line: Making distinctions in everyday life*. Chicago: University of Chicago Press.

Zerubavel, E. (1997). *Social mindscapes: An introduction to cognitive sociology*. Cambridge, MA: Harvard University Press.

PART II

Domains of Individual Development in Adolescence

CHAPTER 4

Brain Development

TOMÁŠ PAUS

Does the human brain continue developing during adolescence? This chapter will describe the main features of brain structure and function that continue to change during this period of human development. I will focus on empirical findings acquired with magnetic resonance imaging (MRI) over the past 15 years in studies of typical development. I will start by reviewing the basic concepts essential for the understanding of this field, including brain anatomy and neurochemistry, MRI, and computational neuroanatomy, and provide an overview of relevant findings. Given a number of popular concepts used to interpret structural and functional MRI findings, I will point out the lack of direct evidence supporting some of these interpretations. I will conclude by discussing the role of genes and environment in shaping the human brain and the emergence of population neuroscience as a discipline relevant for future studies of adolescence.

BASIC BRAIN ANATOMY AND NEUROCHEMISTRY

Based on embryonic and evolutionary development, the mammalian brain is typically divided into the forebrain, midbrain, and hindbrain. The *forebrain* consists of the cerebrum (the cerebral cortex and basal ganglia) and diencephalon (thalamus, hypothalamus, and other gray-matter nuclei). The *midbrain* includes the substantia nigra and tectum (superior and inferior colliculi). The *hindbrain* consists of the cerebellum, pons, and medulla oblongata. Figure 4.1 points out some of the brain structures on a T1-weighted MR scan.

The *cerebral cortex* is the outermost layer of the cerebrum; it is a 2–4-mm-thick sheath of gray matter, with two thirds of the cortex being buried in the cerebral sulci (or folds). The surface area of the cortex increases with increasing brain size more than one would expect from a simple geometric relationship between the surface and volume; this is particularly the case for the prefrontal cortex (Toro et al., 2008). The outermost area, the neocortex, has six cortical layers that differ in the mixture of the different types of neurons (e.g., pyramidal and granular cells); based on the so-called cytoarchitecture, a number of cortical areas can be distinguished (e.g., Brodmann, 1909). The archicortex, which includes the hippocampus, is evolutionary older and has only three cortical layers.

Brain tissue can be divided into gray and white matter; this distinction is simply based on the visual appearance of a fresh brain. *Gray matter* consists of a number of cellular elements, including the cell bodies of nerve cells (neurons) and their treelike extensions (dendrites), glial cells (e.g., astrocytes, microglia), and blood vessels. The adult human brain contains over 100 billion neurons (Sholl, 1956).

The author's work is supported by the Canadian Institutes of Health Research, the Royal Society (United Kingdom), and the National Institutes of Health (United States). I am grateful to my collaborators, students, and research fellows for their intellectual contributions and hard work.

Figure 4.2 provides a breakdown of the relative number of various cellular elements found in the mouse cerebral cortex (Braitenberg & Schüz, 1998). *White matter* owes its appearance to the high content of a fatty substance called myelin that wraps around axons, the long projections of neurons. The white mat-

ter of a 20-year-old man contains a staggering 176,000 km of myelinated axons (Marner, Nyengaard, Tang, & Pakkenberg, 2003).

Transmission of information from one neuron to the next involves several steps. Local excitatory and inhibitory postsynaptic potentials (EPSPs and IPSPs) are continuously being summed at the axonal hillock and, once a threshold value is reached, an action potential is generated. The action potential then travels along the axon and, at the synapse, causes a release of neurotransmitters. The so-called conduction velocity is higher in myelinated versus nonmyelinated axons and in axons with larger versus smaller diameter (Hursh, 1939; Rushton, 1951; Schmidt-Nielsen, 1997).

Neurotransmitters are chemicals that either relay action potentials or modulate (e.g., amplify or moderate) this process. Neurotransmitters include amino acids (e.g., glutamate and gamma-aminobutyric acid [GABA]), monoamines (e.g., dopamine, serotonin, norepinephrine), acetylcholine, and many neuropeptides (e.g., oxytocin). Glutamate and GABA are the main excitatory and inhibitory neurotransmitters, respectively, and dopamine is one of the most studied neuromodulators. The action of a particular neurotransmitter is mediated by a receptor; a given neurotransmitter can bind to a number of receptor subtypes that are found in different brain regions, or different layers of the cerebral cortex, with varied densities (Eickhoff, Schleicher, Scheperjans,

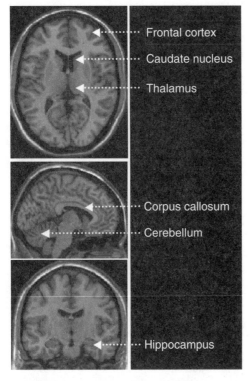

FIGURE 4.1　T1-weighted MR image of the human brain. Top, axial section; Middle, sagittal section; Bottom, coronal section.

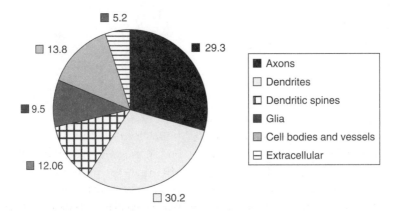

FIGURE 4.2　Cellular composition of the cerebral cortex (based on data from Braitenberg & Schüz, 1998).

Palomero-Gallagher, & Zilles, 2007; Zilles, Palomero-Gallagher, & Schleicher, 2004). The very complex interaction between different neurotransmitters released at any given time at the synapse determines the number of EPSPs and IPSPs generated on the postsynaptic membrane and, in turn, firing of the neuron.

The basic principles of the brain's functional organization are those of *specialization and integration*. Information is computed in highly specialized but often spatially segregated regions of the cortex and subcortical gray-matter nuclei. This information is, in turn, integrated by being shared across the various cortical and subcortical regions via cortico-cortical and cortico-subcortical projections, hence the importance of structural and functional connectivity.

MAGNETIC RESONANCE IMAGING

Brain Mapping

A number of techniques are available for mapping the human brain. Magnetic resonance imaging is, however, the only method that allows the researcher to map both structure and function of the human brain in a noninvasive manner. For this reason, this chapter focuses on findings obtained with MRI. It should be noted that other techniques—namely, electroencephalography (EEG) and magnetoencephalography (MEG)—have high temporal resolution and are therefore particularly useful for evaluating developmental changes in the *speed* of neural processing. We have compared the different brain-mapping techniques and described the basic principles guiding their use in studies of brain–behavior relationship elsewhere (Paus, 2003).

Principles of MRI

MRI revolutionized the way we can study the structure and function of the human brain in living human beings throughout the entire life span (Bushong, 2003). The principles of MRI are relatively straightforward. In most applications, the MR signal is based on magnetic properties of the hydrogen atoms, which are a component of the most abundant substance in the human body—water. By placing the human body in a strong static magnetic field (B_0; 0.5 to 7.0 T) and applying a brief pulse of electromagnetic energy, we can make the little dipoles formed by the hydrogen nuclei rotate away from their axes and, in turn, measure the time it takes for the nuclei to "relax" back to their original position. By changing slightly the static magnetic field at different positions along/across the B_0, we can establish the spatial origin of the signal and, eventually, create a three-dimensional (3D) image of the measurement. What is measured depends on the combination of various imaging parameters or, in the terminology of the MR physicists, on the acquisition sequence.

Imaging Brain Structure

For imaging *brain structure*, the most common acquisition sequences include T1-weighted (T1W) and T2-weighted (T2W) images, diffusion-tensor images (DTIs) and magnetization-transfer (MT) images. The T1W and T2W images are typically used for quantifying the volume of gray and white matter (both global and regional), and estimating the cortical thickness or other morphological properties of the cerebral cortex, such as its folding. Using DTI and MT imaging, one can assess different properties of white matter, again, both globally and regionally. The various features of brain structure that can be extracted from these four types of images are described below. In addition to the above sequences, less common but often even more informative acquisitions include T1 and T2 relaxometry (i.e., measurement of the actual relaxation times; Roberts & Mikulis, 2007) and magnetic resonance spectroscopy (MRS; Hope & Moorcraft, 1991).

Imaging Brain Function

For imaging *brain function*, the most common MR parameter to measure is the blood oxygenation level–dependent (BOLD) signal. The BOLD signal reflects the proportion of oxygenated and deoxygenated blood in a given brain region at a given moment. A strong correlation between the amount of synaptic activity and regional cerebral blood flow is the reason why the BOLD signal is a good, albeit indirect, measure of brain "function" (Logothetis, Pauls, Augath, Trinath, & Oeltermann, 2001). In the majority of functional MRI (fMRI) studies, one measures *changes* in BOLD signal in response to various sensory, motor, or cognitive stimuli. Therefore, only brain regions that are likely to respond to such stimuli can be examined using a given paradigm.

Imaging Neurotransmission

For imaging *neurotransmission*, one must resort to positron emission tomography (PET). To assess the distribution of a particular receptor, a small amount of a specific radioactive tracer is injected into the bloodstream. Mainly for reasons of radiation safety, this approach is not used in studies of healthy children and adolescents. Therefore, our knowledge of age-related changes in neurotransmitter systems during development relies on postmortem data and studies carried out in experimental animals.

Computational Neuroanatomy

As pointed out earlier, the different acquisition sequences capture various properties of gray and white matter and, in turn, provide a wealth of information that can be extracted from the images using an ever-growing array of computational algorithms. Here, I provide an overview of the most common techniques used in developmental studies.

Computational analysis of high-resolution structural brain MR images (typically T1W and T2W images) is used to extract in a fully automatic fashion two types of measurements: (1) voxel- or vertex-wise features derived for each X, Y, and Z (i.e., 3D) location (e.g., gray- and white-matter "density" maps, cortical thickness, cortical folding); and (2) volumetric measures (volumes of gray or white matter in particular brain regions, or the area of specific brain structures, etc).

Density maps are generated by (1) registering T1W images with a template brain (e.g., the average MNI-305 atlas; Evans et al., 1993); (2) classifying the brain tissue into gray matter (GM), white matter (WM), and cerebrospinal fluid (CSF); and (3) smoothing the binary 3D images (i.e., GM, WM and CSF) to generate 3D maps of GM/WM "density." These maps are then used in voxel-wise analyses of age- or group-related differences in GM or WM density (see Ashburner & Friston, 2000, for a methodological overview).

Cortical thickness can be measured, for example, using FreeSurfer; this is a set of automated tools for reconstruction of the brain cortical surface (Fischl & Dale, 2000). For every subject, FreeSurfer segments the cerebral cortex, WM, and other subcortical structures, and then computes triangular meshes that recover the geometry and the topology of the pial surface and the gray/white interface of the left and right hemispheres. The local cortical thickness is measured based on the difference between the position of equivalent vertices in the pial and gray/white surfaces. A correspondence between the cortical surfaces across subjects is then established using a nonlinear alignment of the principal sulci in each subject's brain with an average brain (Fischl, Sereno, Tootell, & Dale, 1999). Local estimates of *cortical folding* can be obtained by measuring, for every point x on the cortical surface, the area contained in a small sphere centred at x. If the brain were lissencephalic (i.e., without convolutions), the area inside the sphere would be approximately that of the disc. Using this approach, one can estimate the local degree of folding throughout the cortex (Toro et al., 2008).

The *volume of brain tissues* (GM or WM) can be estimated by registering nonlinearly the native T1W images to a labeled template brain on which lobes (or other predefined brain regions) have been defined *a priori* (usually traced by an expert). Information about anatomical boundaries from the template brain can then be back-projected onto each subject's brain, in native space, and intersected with the tissue-classification map. One can then count the number of GM and WM voxels belonging to a given anatomical region, such as the frontal lobe (Collins, Neelin, Peters, & Evans, 1994; Collins, Holmes, Peters, & Evans, 1995). More sophisticated algorithms are often developed to segment small structures with poorly defined boundaries, such as the hippocampus and amygdala (Chupin et al., 2007).

In addition to the density maps and volumetric measurements of WM structures, such as the corpus callosum, two other techniques are used to evaluate structural properties of white matter: DTI and MT imaging. Using DTI, one can estimate local differences in the magnitude (apparent diffusion coefficient [ADC]) and directionality (fractional anisotropy [FA]) of the (fast) diffusion of water in the extracellular space around the axons (in most common acquisition protocols). The more unidirectional the water diffusion is in a given fiber tract, the higher the FA value in that location. It is assumed that FA varies as function of structural properties of white matter, such as myelination and fiber arrangement of a given WM tract (e.g., Laule et al., 2007; Mädler, Drabycz, Kolind, Whittall, & Mackay, 2008). Values of FA can be calculated, for example, using FMRIB's Diffusion Toolbox (www.fmrib.ox.ac.uk/fsl). The tract-based spatial statistics (TBSS) can be used to compare statistically the FA values between individuals by aligning the individual subjects to the average WM tract "skeleton" (Smith et al., 2006).

The *magnetization transfer ratio* (MTR) is another measure employed for the assessment of WM properties; it provides information on the macromolecular content and structure of the tissue (McGowan, 1999). Given that the macromolecules of myelin are the dominant source of MT signal in white matter (Kucharczyk, Macdonald, Stanisz, & Henkelman, 1994; Schmierer, Scaravilli, Altmann, Barker, & Miller, 2004), one can use MTR as an index of myelination. Note, however, that myelin is not likely to be the sole factor influencing MTR

(see Laule et al., 2007). The MT ratio is calculated as the percent signal change between two acquisitions, MT pulse on and off (Pike, 1996). To obtain mean MTR values for WM, one can calculate MTR across all WM voxels constituting a given lobar volume of WM in that subject.

The preceding techniques provide a wealth of information about structural properties of the human brain. The next section will review findings obtained with some of these approaches in studies of typically developing adolescents.

BRAIN STRUCTURE DURING ADOLESCENCE

Age Differences in Brain Structure

The overall volume of WM increases in a linear way during childhood and adolescence, although there are several interesting regional variations. These include age-related increases in WM density in the internal capsule and the putative arcuate fasciculus (Paus et al., 1999); regional variations in the growth of the corpus callosum, where the splenium continues to increase whereas the genu does not (Giedd et al., 1996a, 1999b; Pujol, Vendrell, Junque, Marti-Vilalta, & Capdevila, 1993); and an age-related increase in the WM volume of the left inferior frontal gyrus in boys but not girls (Blanton et al., 2004). DTI has been employed more recently to assess age-related changes in magnitude and directionality of the diffusion of water in the human brain during childhood and adolescence. Overall, DTI-based studies reveal age-related decreases in ADC and increases in FA in a number of white matter regions, many of which are identical to those revealed by the previous structural MR studies (Klingberg, Vaidya, Gabrieli, Moseley, & Hedehus, 1999; Schmithorst, Wilke, Dardzinski, & Holland, 2002; Snook, Paulson, Roy, Phillips, & Beaulieu, 2005).

The monotonic nature of the developmental changes in brain maturation observed for WM does not appear to hold in the case of GM. GM volume in the frontal and parietal lobes appears to peak between 10 and 12 years and decreases slightly afterwards; in the temporal lobes, the peak occurs around the age of 16 years (Giedd et al., 1999a). Other investigators found similar age-related GM "loss" in the frontal, parietal, and temporal lobes; it appears to start around puberty in the sensorimotor areas and spreads forward over the frontal cortex and back over the parietal and then temporal cortex (Gogtay et al., 2004; Sowell, Thompson, Tessner, & Toga, 2001). The dorsolateral prefrontal cortex and the posterior part of the superior temporal gyrus appear to "lose" grey matter last of all (Gogtay et al., 2004). More recently, similar age-related "loss" of the cortical GM has been observed using cortical thickness as the parameter of interest (Shaw et al., 2006). It has been often suggested that such age-related changes in cortical GM during adolescence reflect "synaptic pruning." Whether or not this might be the case is discussed later.

Knowledge of the functional organization of the human brain, gleaned from lesion studies and functional imaging work, provides a foundation for the initial functional interpretations of the preceding structural observations. For example, changes in WM volume along the arcuate fasciculus and in the left inferior frontal gyrus are likely to correlate with changes in language, while the late maturational changes in GM within the prefrontal cortex and the superior temporal gyrus/sulcus may be related, respectively, to executive functions and processing of biological motion (discussed later in this chapter). Only a handful of studies have acquired structural and functional (e.g., neuropsychological assessment) data sets in the same group of individuals, however. In these studies, significant correlations were found between IQ and GM volume of the prefrontal cortex (Reiss, Abrams, Singer, Ross, & Denckla, 1996), between IQ and fractional anisotropy in the WM of the frontal lobes (Schmithorst, Wilke, Dardzinski, & Holland, 2005), between IQ and cortical thickness (Shaw et al., 2006), and between reading skills and fractional anisotropy in the left

temporo-parietal WM (Beaulieu et al., 2005; Deutsch et al., 2005).

Sex Differences in Brain Structure During Adolescence

Given the presence of sex differences in cognitive abilities (Hall, 1978; Kimura, 1996) and affect-related processes (Herba & Phillips, 2004), as well as in the incidence of certain psychopathologies (e.g. depression; Angold, Costello, & Worthman, 1998; Angold, Costello, Erkanli, & Worthman, 1999), an important question is whether girls and boys show different trajectories in their brain maturation. This section will review the current literature on this topic. I will start by describing sex differences in the adult brain, and, with this background, I will then evaluate the current knowledge of the presence or absence of such differences at different stages of brain development and maturation.

In biology, *sexual dimorphism* typically refers to apparent sex differences in external features such as body size, color of feathers, or presence of horns. In humans, there are few qualitative physical differences between men and women other than in the genitalia and in secondary sexual characteristics (e.g., breast development). Most physical sex differences are quantitative and show a considerable overlap between men and women (e.g., in distributions of height and weight). In a broad sense, this is also true about sex differences in the structure of the human brain.

Overall, the male brain is larger (by ~10%) than the female brain; it contains a greater absolute volume of both GM and WM (Carne, Vogrin, Litewka, & Cook, 2006; Good et al., 2001; Gur, Gunning-Dixon, Bilker, & Gur, 2002; Luders, Steinmetz, & Jancke, 2002). This difference remains even after accounting for sex differences in overall body height or weight (Ankney, 1992; Peters et al., 1998; Skullerud, 1985). When expressed as a percentage of total brain (or cranial) volume, sex differences in the volume of WM disappear (Gur et al.,

2002; Luders et al., 2002); whether the same is true with respect to GM is unclear. Some studies indicate that the differences remain (Good et al., 2001), whereas others indicate that they disappear (Gur et al.), and still others find that the pattern reverses (i.e., female > male; Luders et al.).

Moving beyond global volumes of GM and WM, only a handful of regions are *relatively* (i.e., after removing the effect of brain size) larger in the male than in the female brain, including the amygdala and hippocampus (Good et al., 2001; Gur et al., 2002) and the paracingulate sulcus (Paus et al., 1996a, 1996b; Yucel et al., 2001). In fact, there are many more brain structures that are relatively larger in the female than in the male brain, including the lateral orbitofrontal cortex (Good et al.; Gur et al.), anterior (Good et al.; Paus et al., 1996b) and posterior (Good et al.) cingulate cortex, and the inferior frontal gyrus (Good et al.). Compared with the male brain, the female brain also appears to contain more WM constituting the corpus callosum (Bermudez & Zatorre, 2001; Cowell, Allen, Zalatimo, & Denenberg, 1992; Steinmetz, et al., 1992; Steinmetz, Staiger, Schlaug, Huang, & Jancke, 1995), internal and external capsule, and optic radiation (Good et al.), and shows a greater extent of interhemispheric connections between the posterior temporal regions (Hagmann et al., 2006).

When do these sex differences emerge? Answering this question would further our understanding of the mechanisms underlying sexual dimorphism in the human brain and may help us in distinguishing between genetic and environmental influences on these differences. Sex differences in overall brain size appear to be present even before birth. Using head circumference as a proxy for brain size, male infants showed slightly higher (2%) values than female infants with comparable femur length, both prenatally and during the first year of life (Joffe et al., 2005). Using autopsy material, sex differences in brain weight are seen as early as infancy (Dekaban, 1978). Matsuzawa

and colleagues (2001) found, however, no sex differences in MR-derived measures of total brain volume, but as noted by the authors, their study was underpowered and hampered by the fact that the girls were slightly older than the boys. Regarding regional sex differences after birth, an ultrasound-based study examined the total area and subdivisions of the corpus callosum in neonates (Hwang et al., 2004) and observed sex differences (F > M) in the thickness of the splenium. Overall, brain weight is about 90% of the adult brain by about the age of 5 years (Dekaban) and it reaches the adult size by about the age of 10 years (Dekaban; Pfefferbaum et al., 1994). The rather sparse amount of *in vivo* data available regarding the brain growth during the first 5 years of life does not allow us, however, to make any conclusions regarding sex differences in the rate of the growth during this period.

Much richer literature exists on sex differences in brain structure during childhood and adolescence. On a global level, it appears that males show larger age-related increases than females in the total volume of WM (Giedd et al., 1999a; De Bellis et al., 2001). This sexual dimorphism is particularly striking during adolescence (Perrin et al., 2008a). The presence of sex differences in testosterone is an obvious candidate for the underlying mechanism. How can we move beyond mere correlations and strengthen the inference as to whether this is the case? In one study, my colleagues and I examined the relationship between testosterone levels and WM volume in individuals who differ in a functional polymorphism in the relevant hormonal pathway. The androgen receptor (AR) gene was the first candidate gene we selected using this simple logic; the relevant functional polymorphism is the number of CAG repeats in exon 1, which influences the "effectiveness" of the receptor (Perrin et al., 2008a). Figure 4.3 shows that male adolescents with the more "effective" AR gene (short AR; right panel) show a much stronger relationship between testosterone and WM volume (Perrin et al., 2008a).

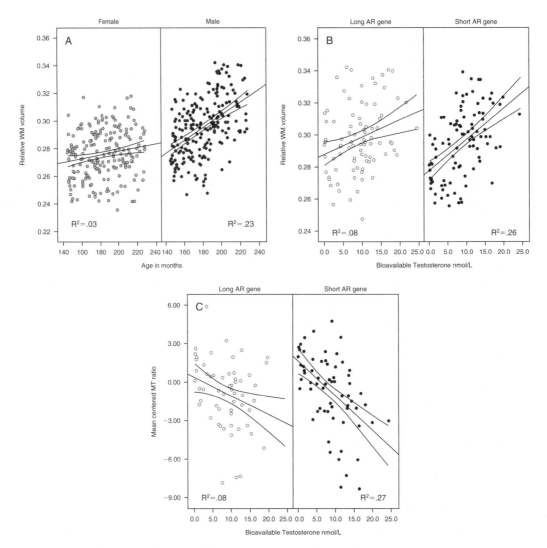

FIGURE 4.3 Relative (brain-volume corrected) volume of white matter (WM) plotted as a function of age in female (left) and male (right) adolescents; **B,** Relative volume of WM plotted as a function of plasma levels of bioavailable testosterone in male adolescents with low (short AR gene) and high (long AR gene) number of CAG repeats in the androgen-receptor gene; **C,** mean-centred values of magnetization-transfer ratio (MTR) in white matter plotted as a function of bioavailable testosterone in male adolescents with short and long AR. The WM volumes and MTR values have been summed across all four lobes. From Perrin et al. 2008a.

Are sex differences in age-related global increases in WM also seen regionally? This question has been asked in several morphometric studies of the corpus callosum, but findings from this work are inconsistent. Two studies reported no sex differences in the rate of age-related increases in the area of the corpus callosum (Giedd et al., 1999b; Rauch & Jinkins, 1994), whereas two other studies found sex differences in the rate of growth over a 2-year period during late adolescence and early adulthood, with males growing faster than females (Pujol et al., 1993), and in the age at which the maximum width of certain parts of the corpus callosum is attained during adulthood (among males, 20 years, but among females, 40–50 years; Cowell et al., 1992). It thus seems that, at least in the case of the corpus callosum, maturation of WM continues through early and middle adulthood, with sex differences emerging during these later periods of maturation.

Changes in GM also seem to follow different timetables in males and females. Between the ages of 5 to 21 years, the volume of GM in all but the occipital lobe increases with age and then declines. The peak of these changes occurs, however, at different ages in different lobes and, within a given lobe, at different ages in males and females (for the frontal lobe, peak GM volume is 11.0 years among females and 12.1 years among males; for the parietal lobe, 10.2 years among females and 11.8 years among males; for the temporal lobe, 16.7 years among females and 16.5 years among males; Giedd et al., 1999a). This timetable suggests that girls are ahead of boys during the early (10–12 years) stages of adolescent cortical maturation, but that this sex difference disappears at the later stages (around 16 years). Obviously, one needs to keep in mind that this statement applies only to those biological processes that could be captured by the rather gross MR-based estimates of GM volume available at the time of this particular study.

As described above, adult females and males differ in the size of several GM structures, including the amygdala and hippocampus (with these structures larger among males than females), and the different regions of the frontal cortex (with these areas larger among females than males). The available data also suggest that amygdala volume increases more with age among males than females (Giedd et al., 1996c). This is also the case for the hippocampus (Suzuki et al., 2005); but it is important to note that the opposite trend was reported in another study, namely, age-related increase in the hippocampal volume seen in females but not males (Giedd et al., 1996c). Boys but not girls also seem to show an age-related increase in the volume of the caudate nucleus and the putamen between ages 5 and 18 (Giedd et al., 1996b).

Overall, then, the female and male brains differ in several respects before, during, and after adolescence. Most of the differences are quantitative in nature and rather subtle. These include, for example, differences in brain size, total WM volume, and the size of brain regions such as the amygdala and hippocampus (M > F), or the orbitofrontal and anterior cingulate cortices, and corpus callosum (F > M). The available data suggest that some of these sex differences continue to develop during childhood and adolescence. Most notably, this is the case for age-related increases in global and local (i.e., corpus callosum, inferior frontal gyrus) WM, as well as in the size of some brain regions, such as the amygdala and the hippocampus. It is also clear that the timing of cellular processes influencing the overall cortical volume of different lobes varies not only as a function of location (e.g., frontal versus temporal) but also as a function of sex.

Whether changes in the hormonal environment play a causal role in the emergence of sex differences in brain structure and function during puberty is difficult to ascertain. The complexity of age-related changes in hormone levels, and the often tight correlation between hormone levels and age, limit the usefulness of correlational analyses. For example, in a large sample of male adolescents ($n = 204$; $12-18$ years), we observed very little effect of testosterone on the volume of WM above and beyond the effect of age (Perrin et al., 2008a). Given the cycle-related changes in hormone levels in female adolescents, only studies that acquire data during different phases of the menstrual cycle longitudinally may provide some answers about the influence of female sex hormones on the brain (Perrin, Herve, Pitiot, Totman, & Paus, 2008b). Nonetheless, several alternative approaches are available. As described earlier (Figure 4.3), one can take advantage of a functional polymorphism in a gene involved in transmitting hormonal signals and evaluate the relationship between plasma levels of a particular hormone and the brain phenotype in individuals with the different variants of the gene. In this manner, we can inject a certain level of causality into the analysis and overcome the influence of confounders, such as age, that are unrelated to the genetic polymorphism. Another strategy involves studies of individuals who suffer from conditions that influence their hormonal environment, such as congenital adrenal hyperplasia or Klinefelter (XXY) syndrome (e.g., Giedd et al., 2006, 2007). Finally, as with studies of other environmental effects, experimental manipulations in animal models (*in vivo* and *in vitro*) are essential for dissecting the complex nature of hormonal influences on the adolescent brain.

BRAIN FUNCTION DURING ADOLESCENCE

Functional imaging studies pose both technical (reviewed in Davidson, Thomas, & Casey, 2003) and conceptual challenges. The latter involve a confounding interaction between age and performance. In other words, when studying age-related changes in brain activity during the performance of a given task, how do we interpret fMRI findings against the background of concomitant age-related differences in task performance? Is brain activity different because the behavior (performance) is different, or vice versa? One of the approaches used to overcome this issue is that of matching subjects either by age or by performance, and examining the differences in fMRI response in these matched groups; this approach has been used extensively in studies of verb generation, for example (Brown et al., 2004; Schlaggar et al., 2002). In the domain of executive function, Kwon, Reiss, and Menon (2002) used this approach in a study of visuospatial working memory and found age-related (from age 7 to 22 years) increases in the BOLD signal in the prefrontal and parietal cortex even after factoring

out interindividual differences in performance. Similar BOLD increases were also observed in these regions during the performance of a variety of tasks involving some form of response inhibition, including the Stroop task (Adleman et al., 2002), antisaccade task (Luna et al., 2001), the stop task (Rubia et al., 2000) and, to a certain extent, during performance on a go/no-go task (Tamm, Menon, & Reiss, 2002) and the Eriksen flanker task (Bunge, 2002).

During adolescence, high demands are placed not only on the executive systems but also on the interplay between cognitive and affect-related processes. Such cognition–emotion interactions are particularly crucial in the context of peer–peer interactions and the processing of verbal and nonverbal cues. It is therefore of interest to note that the cortex of the superior temporal sulcus (STS) contains a set of regions engaged during the processing of nonverbal cues such as those carried by eye and mouth movements (e.g., Puce, Allison, Bettin, Gore, & McCarthy, 1998), hand movements/actions (e.g., Beauchamp, Lee, Haxby, & Martin, 2002; Decety et al., 1997; Grezes, Costes, & Decety, 1999), or body movements (e.g., Bonda, Petrides, Ostry, & Evans, 1996). As suggested by Allison, Puce, and McCarthy (2000), feedforward and feedback interactions between the STS and amygdala may be critical for the discrimination of various facial expressions and for the attentional enhancement of the neural response to socially salient stimuli. Consistent with such an "amplification" mechanism, Kilts and colleagues (2003) observed a significantly stronger neural response to dynamic, as compared with static, facial expressions of anger in both the STS and amygdala. My colleagues and I have also observed a strong BOLD response in the amygdala not only while adult subjects viewed video clips of angry hand movements or angry faces, but also during viewing of (dynamic) neutral facial expressions (Grosbras & Paus, 2006). Although basic aspects of face perception are in place shortly after birth (Goren, 1975), both the quantity and quality of face processing continues to increase throughout adolescence (e.g., Carey, 1992; McGivern, 2002; Taylor, McCarthy, Saliba, & Degiovanni, 1999). Developmental fMRI studies of the processing of facial expressions are consistent with this pattern. For example, happy, but not sad, faces elicit significant BOLD response in the amygdala in adolescent subjects (Yang et al., 2003). Studies of fearful facial expressions suggest that an increase in the BOLD signal in the amygdala can be detected in adolescents (Baird et al., 1999) but it is relatively weak (Thomas et al., 2001).

Adolescence has been traditionally associated with risk-taking and sensation-seeking behavior (reviewed in Steinberg, 2008). In this context, several investigators have used fMRI to examine possible differences between children, adolescents, and young adults in brain activity while they experienced gains or losses of various rewards. Given its role in reward and motivation (Robbins & Everitt, 1996), the nucleus accumbens (or ventral striatum) has been the focus of the majority of these studies. If adolescents were "driven" by rewards, one would expect heightened engagement of this structure during tasks that involve reward seeking. This appeared to be the case in some (Ernst et al., 2005; Galvan et al., 2006) but not other (Bjork et al., 2004) studies. In the latter report, Bjork and colleagues described an age-related increase (from 12 to 28 years) in the BOLD signal in the nucleus accumbens during anticipation of gains; this was the case even when self-reported level of excitement was taken into account. It is worthwhile pointing out that, in the same study, self-reported excitement was positively correlated with the BOLD signal in the accumbens even when age was taken into account. This observation highlights the importance of multidimensional approach to the interpretation of fMRI findings (discussed later in this chapter).

The aforementioned studies evaluated age-related differences in the presence and/ or magnitude in task-related changes in the BOLD signal. As pointed out earlier, however, information computed in the various specialized and spatially segregated regions must be integrated to give rise to behaviors as complex as the choice of an appropriate action in an emotionally laden context. Hence, it is also important in imaging studies to evaluate possible age differences in functional connectivity. Only a handful of investigators have included such assessments in their analyses. In a study of memory encoding, Menon, Boyett-Anderson, and Reiss (2005) observed an age-related *decrease* in the fMRI signal between 11 and 19 years in the left medial temporal lobe while subjects viewed a series of novel photographs of natural outdoor scenes, as compared with viewing the same scene repeatedly (control condition). They then used voxel-wise regression analysis to identify brain regions that showed correlation in the fMRI signal with that measured in two subregions of the left medial temporal lobe, namely, the hippocampus and the entorhinal cortex. This analysis revealed an age-related *increase* in the correlation between activation in the left entorhinal cortex and the left dorsolateral prefrontal cortex. This work nicely illustrates the importance of including the analysis of functional connectivity in developmental studies; although the fMRI signal decreased in one of the memory-relevant structures (entorhinal cortex), the hypothesized interaction between this structure and other brain regions (prefrontal cortex) actually increased.

In a different developmental study, Schmithorst and Holland (2006) investigated the relationship between intelligence and functional connectivity in a large sample of typically developing children and adolescents, aged 5–18 years. They measured fMRI signal during a task requiring the child to generate silently appropriate verbs in response to hearing nouns, every 5 seconds. After identifying brain regions engaged during this task, as compared with simply tapping fingers in response to a warble tone, they correlated fMRI signal in all such voxels with the subjects' full-scale intelligence quotient (FSIQ). This analysis revealed a positive fMRI–FSIQ correlation in five regions of the left hemisphere: Broca's area, the middle temporal gyrus, the anterior cingulate, the precuneus, and the medial frontal gyrus (putative supplementary motor area). Next, the authors computed the connectivity coefficient, defined as a weighted sum of the pairwise covariances between these regions. Using this coefficient as a measure of functional connectivity, Schmithorst and Holland found several age and sex differences in the relationship between intelligence and connectivity. In boys, functional connectivity appeared to increase as a function of intelligence between 5 and 9 years; no such relationship was present in older boys (10–12 years), and a negative correlation was observed in the oldest boys (13–18 years). In girls, however, no relationship was found in younger girls (age 5–13 years) but a strong positive correlation between functional connectivity and intelligence was clearly present in older girls (13–18 years). It is of note that the preceding effects were found in the time series measured during both the verb-generation and the control task, while some other effects were only found in the verb-generation task. As the authors point out, the observed sex differences in the relationship between intelligence and functional connectivity are consistent with some structural findings in adults, such as significant correlations between intelligence and regional WM volumes in women but GM volumes in men (Haier, Jung, Yeo, Head, & Alkire, 2005).

My colleagues and I have investigated functional connectivity in the context of possible neural substrate of resistance to peer influence (RPI) in early adolescence (Grosbras et al., 2007). In these studies, we asked whether the probability with which an adolescent follows the goals set by peers or those set by himself/herself might depend on the interplay between three neural systems: the frontoparietal network (responsible for bottom-up imitation of actions), the STS network (responsible

for processing social cues), and the prefrontal network (responsible for top-down regulation of actions). In the scanner, we asked 10-year-old children to watch brief video clips containing face or hand/arm actions, executed in neutral or angry ways, while measuring changes in fMRI signals. Outside the scanner, we administered a questionnaire assessing RPI (Steinberg & Monahan, 2007). We found that children with high versus low scores on the RPI measure showed stronger interregional correlations in brain activity across the three networks while watching angry hand actions. The pattern of interregional correlations identified by this method included both: (1) regions involved in action observation—the frontoparietal as well as temporo-occipital systems; and (2) regions in the prefrontal cortex.

Overall, studies of functional connectivity during adolescence are in their infancy. The preceding three examples illustrate the power of this approach but also indicate that large numbers of subjects of both genders in different age groups may be necessary to reach valid conclusions. Acquiring high-resolution structural MRI and/or DTI in the same individuals would greatly facilitate the identification of possible similarities and differences between functional, effective, and structural connectivity in the same sample (reviewed in Paus, 2007). As discussed in the following section, interpretation of fMRI data is challenging and should be approached cautiously.

INTERPRETING IMAGING-BASED EVIDENCE OF BRAIN MATURATION DURING ADOLESCENCE

A number of conceptual frameworks have been put forward to interpret some of the findings reviewed in this chapter vis-à-vis underlying neurobiology. Unfortunately, the indirect nature of the available measures makes it very difficult to verify the validity of some of these propositions. Here, I will raise questions about some of the underlying assumptions implicit in these frameworks in order to clarify the distinction between established facts and hypotheses.

Cortical Gray Matter and Synaptic Pruning

MR-based estimates of the volume of cortical GM and cortical thickness appear to decrease during adolescence. This has been often interpreted as an indication of "synaptic pruning," a process by which "redundant" synapses overproduced in the early years of life are being eliminated (see Purves, White, & Riddle, 1996, for a critical appraisal of neural Darwinism).

The initial evidence for accelerated synaptic pruning during postnatal development came from postmortem studies by Huttenlocher, who described a decrease in the number of synapses in the human cerebral cortex during childhood and adolescents (Huttenlocher, 1984; Huttenlocher & de Courten, 1987). It should be noted that these initial studies were limited by the low number of specimens available for the different stages of human development. A more definite evidence of synapse elimination during adolescence was provided by studies carried out by Rakic and colleagues in nonhuman primates (e.g., Bourgeois and Rakic, 1993; Rakic, Bourgeois, Eckenhoff, Zecevic, & Goldman-Rakic, 1986). Using electron microscopy, they observed a dramatic decrease in the number of synapses in the monkey visual cortex during puberty (between the age of 2.5 and 5 years), whether expressed as a number of synapses per neuron or per cubic millimeter of neuropil (about a 45% loss). But it is unlikely that this decrease in synaptic density translates into a decrease in cortical volume. Bourgeois and Rakic (1993) commented that "changes in the density of synapses affect very little either the volume or surface of the cortex because the total volume of synaptic boutons . . . is only a very small fraction of the cortical volume" and concluded that ". . . a decline of synaptic number during puberty should have a rather small effect on the overall volume of the cortex" (Bourgeois & Rakic).

If the number of synapses per se is unlikely to change the cortical volume/thickness, then what other cellular elements could affect it? As illustrated in Figure 4.2, about 10% of the (mouse) cortex is occupied by glial cells and about 60% by neuropil, the latter consisting of dendritic and axonal processes. It is conceivable that a reduced number of synapses, and a corresponding decrease in metabolic requirements, would be accompanied by a reduction in the number of glial cells, leading to a decrease in the cortical GM volume or thickness. But it is perhaps even more likely that the apparent loss of GM reflects an increase in the degree of myelination of intracortical axons. As shown in Kaes (1907) and (Conel, 1967), myelination of intracortical fibers progresses gradually from birth to adulthood (Figure 4.4). The higher the number of myelinated fibers in the cortex, the less "gray" the cortex would appear on regular T1W images. Such a "partial-volume" effect could result in an apparent loss of cortical GM (see also Paus, 2005).

White Matter and Myelination

Given the well-documented histology-based increase in the degree of myelination during the first two decades of human life (e.g., Yakovlev & Lecours, 1967), it is perhaps not surprising that any changes in the volume or "density" of white matter revealed by computational analyses of T1W images are attributed to changes in myelination. Again, assumptions based on previous knowledge are influencing interpretation of new data. Quite often, articles reporting age-related changes in myelination have merely measured volumes of WM. Is this only a matter of semantics, or could other, myelination-independent processes affect the volume and/or other features of WM?

Figure 4.3 provides a clear example of dissociation between age-related changes in the volume of white matter during adolescence and changes in MTR, an indirect index of the amount of myelin in WM. Although WM volume increased with age during adolescence among males (Figure 4.3a), MTR values decreased (Figure 4.3c), thus indicating a decrease in the amount of myelin in the unit of volume (Perrin et al., 2008a). If

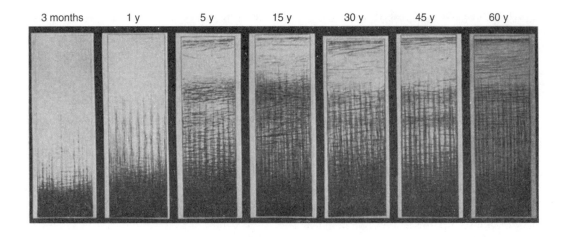

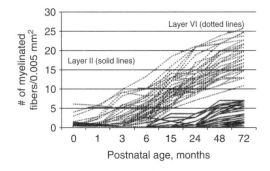

FIGURE 4.4 *Top.* Post-mortem intracortical myelin stain data from Kaes (1907), [adapted and reproduced in Kemper (1994)]. *Bottom.* Plot of Conel's uncorrected post-mortem data on layer II (solid lines) and layer VI (dashed lines) myelinated fiber density (no. per 0.005 mm^2) versus postnatal age (months) for the Von Economo areas he studied. From Shankle et al. 1998.

not increases in myelin, what could be driving the observed increase in WM volume during male adolescence? Our tentative answer is that this may be due to changes in axonal caliber. The larger the caliber, the fewer axons fit in the same unit of the imaged volume, producing a relative decrease in the myelination index. Although more work is needed to confirm this initial observation, it serves as a reminder that most of the MR sequences from which inferences are often drawn are not specific enough to interpret MR-based findings as reflecting a single neurobiological process, such as myelination.

Functional "Activations"

Interpretations of group differences in task-related brain activity indexed by the BOLD signal are fraught with difficulties. When evaluating differences between, for example, children and adolescents performing a "reward" task, one can observe a number of possible outcomes. Compared with children, adolescents may "activate" additional brain regions, show stronger "activations" in the same brain regions, or present a more focused "pattern" of activations. How should we interpret such findings? Cautiously, with a number of factors in mind.

We should first consider the possibility that the two groups may differ in the task performance and/or strategy employed to solve the task at hand. As noted earlier, when age-related differences in fMRI response are found, these can be removed by matching participants of different age on their performance (e.g., Kwon et al., 2002; Schlaggar et al., 2002). Clearly, the more sensitive the performance measure used and the higher the number of participants, the easier it would be to deal with this potential confounder.

The next factor to consider is the emotional and motivational state of the participant. Depending on the familiarity with the task, scanning environment, or the duration of the scanning session, participants are likely to experience varied levels of anxiety and arousal in the scanner. These and other external factors may have different effects on participants of different ages. In addition to minimizing the effect of such confounders, one could collect measures of autonomic (e.g., heart rate, pupil diameter) or central (EEG) arousal during scanning and include these as covariates in subsequent analyses of fMRI data.

Importantly, state-related changes are accompanied by release of neurotransmitters, such as dopamine and norepinephrine (Arnsten & Li, 2005), that modulate task-related changes in brain "activation." In fact, age-related differences in dopaminergic neurotransmission have often been invoked when interpreting fMRI findings obtained in the context of reward processing, often comparing adolescents with young adults. Two recent postmortem studies reported, however, that there are no differences between adolescents (14–18 years) and young adults (20–24 years) in the levels of different dopamine receptors or in the activity of enzymes involved in the synthesis (tyrosine hydroxylase) and metabolism (catechol-O-methyl transferase [COMT]) of dopamine in the human prefrontal cortex (Turnbridge et al., 2007; Wickert et al., 2007).

At the analytical level, it is, of course, essential to support claims about the presence or absence of "activations" by proper statistical analysis. It is not sufficient to demonstrate that a particular brain region shows a statistically significant increase in the BOLD signal in one group while it fails to reach the threshold in another group. One should be also aware of possible imaging artifacts. For example,

when counting the number of "activated" voxels and/or regions, a possibility exists that any subtle misregistrations of images acquired over time may give rise to apparent "activations" that may mimic true changes in brain activity; for example, small "nodding" movements of the head may affect especially midline structures, such as the anterior cingulate cortex. Subtle misregistration, however, may lead to an apparent decrease in the magnitude of the BOLD response at a "peak" location. Again, age may modulate the probability of such confounders.

Overall, interpretation of findings obtained with functional MRI is challenging and needs to take into account both the experimental design and physiology underlying the fMRI signal. Even when all possible experimental variables are perfectly controlled, the indirect nature of the BOLD signal and the complexity of the underlying neurophysiology prevent one from drawing conclusions about developmental processes such as synaptic pruning or dopaminergic neurotransmission.

Brain Images and Causality

The use of structural and functional neuroimaging provides a powerful tool for the study of brain maturation and cognitive development during adolescence. In addition to the need to keep in mind the many specific challenges associated with the interpretation of structural and functional findings discussed in the previous section, one also needs to be cautious about the general meaning of "brain images." In particular, we should not confuse a manifestation with a cause.

Observing a difference between children and adolescents in the size (or "activation") of a particular structure simply points to a possible neural mechanism mediating the effect of age on a given behavior; it is not the "cause" of this behavior. For example, a stronger activation of the ventral striatum during the performance of a "reward" task by adolescents, as compared with adults, should not be interpreted as "causing" the adolescent's reward-seeking behavior; it merely indicates possible age-related differences in the probability of engaging this structure during this particular task. In this sense, neuroimaging-based assessment should be treated in the same way, and at the same level, as any other quantitative phenotype describing cognitive, emotional, endocrine, or physiological characteristics of an individual. To look for causes of a given behavior and its higher or lower probability during adolescence, we need to turn our attention to the individual's environment and his/her genes.

ROLE OF GENES AND ENVIRONMENT IN SHAPING THE BRAIN

It is clear that both genes and experience influence many structural features of the human brain. In a special issue of *Human Brain Mapping* on genomic imaging (Glahn, Paus, & Thompson, 2007), a number of articles reported high heritability of regional volumes of GM estimated from twin studies carried out in adults, as well as in children and adolescents. At a single-gene level, several previous reports revealed differences between (adult) individuals with different allelic variations in brain morphology (e.g., Pezawas et al., 2004, 2005).

Findings of genetic influences on brain morphology are often seen as the consequence of a *direct* effect of the genes on brain structure, perhaps occurring as early as *in utero*. But it is also possible—in fact, quite likely—that these effects are mediated by the different level of *functional* engagement of given neural circuits in individuals with different genes and experiences. Several studies have confirmed that a repeated (functional) engagement of a particular neural circuit leads to changes in its structural properties, which can be detected *in vivo* with MR (e.g., in musicians: Gaser & Schlaug, 2003; Sluming et al., 2002; London taxi drivers: Maguire et al., 2000; bilingual subjects: Mechelli et al., 2004; initially inexperienced jugglers: Draganski et al., 2004). Although determining directionality of such structure–function relationships is impossible

in the majority of current studies (with the exception of the "juggler" study), the existing animal experimental literature confirms the possibility of experience impacting brain structure (e.g., Sirevaag & Greenough, 1988).

Overall, there is an increasing body of evidence that challenges a simple, deterministic view of genes influencing the brain directly and, in turn, the individual's behavior. As indicated by a number of studies on the effect of experience on brain structure, MRI-derived anatomical measures may very well reflect a cumulative effect of the differential experience (behavior) rather than the other way around. This point speaks directly to the issue of biological determinism. Quite often, we view developmental changes in brain structure as (biological) prerequisites of a particular cognitive ability. For example, the common logic assumes that cognitive/executive control of behavior emerges in full only after the prefrontal cortex reaches the adult-like level of structural maturity. But given the role of experience in shaping the brain, it might also be that high demands on cognitive control faced, for example, by young adolescents assuming adult roles due to family circumstances may facilitate structural maturation of their prefrontal cortex. This scenario, if proven correct, will move us away from the "passive" view of brain development into one that emphasizes an active role of the individual and his/her environment in modulating the "biological" (e.g., hormonal) developmental processes.

Given the variety of environmental factors and the challenges of genetics of complex traits, the role of genes and environment are best addressed at a population level, that is, by studying large numbers of individuals. In this context, population neuroscience is emerging where social (Wilkinson, 2005) and genetic (Davey-Smith et al., 2005) epidemiology intersect with cognitive neuroscience (Gazzaniga, 2004).

The wide availability of MR scanners in both clinical and research settings has made it relatively easy and affordable to carry out population-based studies with this brain

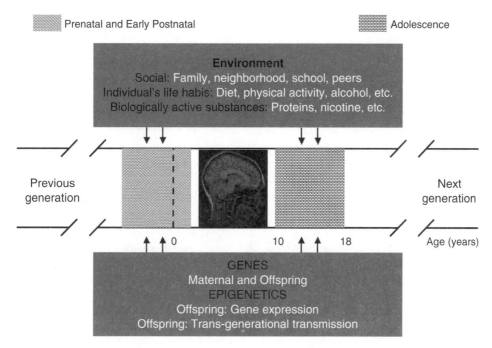

FIGURE 4.5   Population neuroscience and studies of brain development.

mapping technique. According to the European Magnetic Resonance Forum (www.emrf.org/), the number of MR scanners (1T and higher) sold per year increased from about 100 scanners sold in 1985 to 1,500 sold in 2001. By 2006, there were more than 11,000 scanners in the United States, 5,600 in Japan, 3,500 in China, 1,195 in Germany and 480 scanners in the United Kingdom.

Using MRI, several studies of brain development are on the way. In the early 1990s, the Child Psychiatry Branch of the National Institute of Mental Health initiated the first large-scale effort in this domain; over the past 15 years, more than 1,500 cross-sectional and longitudinal images of brain structure have been collected in typically developing children and adolescents (Lenroot & Giedd, 2006). In 2000, the National Institutes of Health funded the NIH Pediatric MRI project (Evans & Brain Development Cooperative Group, 2006); over a period of 6 years, a longitudinal dataset (three time points two years apart) has been collected in a sample of about 400 children and

adolescents. Several years later, my colleagues and I started the Saguenay Youth Study; a rich dataset containing information about brain, behavior, cardiovascular and metabolic health, as well as DNA, has been collected in over 560 adolescents (Pausova et al., 2007). Overall, the hope is that large-scale studies that collect MR images of the developing brain, along with detailed information about participants' environments as well as genetic background, will further our understanding of the genetic and environmental determinants of brain maturation and cognitive development during adolescence (Figure 4.5).

CONCLUSIONS

The second decade of human brain development is as dynamic as the preceding one; the human brain continues to grow and change in both a structural and functional sense. MRI has contributed a wealth of information about the adolescent brain, documenting, in particular, its continuing structural maturation and beginning to elucidate interesting changes in its functional organization. Several large-scale MR-based studies of childhood and adolescence are under way, promising to deliver new insights into neural mechanisms underlying cognitive and emotional development during adolescence and, most importantly, to identify possible genetic and environmental influences on brain maturation and on cognitive and socioemotional development during adolescence. Together with other techniques not covered in this chapter, such as electro- and magnetoencephalography, we are continuing to learn a great deal about the adolescent brain in space and time.

REFERENCES

Adleman, N.E., Menon, V., Blasey, C.M., White, C.D., Warsofsky, I.S., Glover, G. H., et al. (2002). A developmental fMRI study of the Stroop color-word task. *Neuroimage, 16*, 61–75.

Allison, T., Puce, A., & McCarthy, G. (2000). Social perception from visual cues: Role of the STS region. *Trends in Cognitive Sciences, 4*, 267–278.

Angold, A., Costello, E. J., Erkanli, A., & Worthman, C. M. (1999). Pubertal changes in hormone levels and depression in girls. *Psychological Medicine, 29*, 1043–1053.

Angold, A., Costello, E. J., & Worthman, C. M. (1998). Puberty and depression: The roles of age, pubertal status and pubertal timing. *Psychological Medicine, 28*, 51–61.

Ankney, C. D. (1992). Differences in brain size. *Nature, 358*, 532.

Arnsten, A. F., & Li, B. M. (2005). Neurobiology of executive functions: catecholamine influences on prefrontal cortical functions. *Biological Psychiatry, 57*, 1377–1384.

Ashburner, J., & Friston, K. J. (2000). Voxel-based morphometry—the methods. *Neuroimage, 11*, 805–821.

Baird, A. A., Gruber, S. A., Fein, D. A., Maas, L. C., Steingard, R. J., Renshaw, P. F., et al. (1999). Functional magnetic resonance imaging of facial affect recognition in children and adolescents. *Journal of the American Academy of Child and Adolescent Psychiatry, 38*, 195–199.

Beauchamp, M. S., Lee, K. E., Haxby, J. V., & Martin, A. (2002). Parallel visual motion processing streams for manipulable objects and human movements. *Neuron, 34*, 149–159.

Beaulieu, C., Plewes, C., Paulson, L. A., Roy, D., Snook, L., Concha, L., et al. (2005). Imaging brain connectivity in children with diverse reading ability. *Neuroimage, 25*, 1266–1271.

Bermudez, P., & Zatorre, R. J. (2001). Sexual dimorphism in the corpus callosum: methodological considerations in MRI morphometry. *Neuroimage, 13*, 1121–1130.

Bjork, J.M., Knutson, B., Fong, G.W., Caggiano, D.M., Bennett, S.M., & Hommer, D. W. (2004). Incentive-elicited brain activation in adolescents: Similarities and differences from young adults. *Journal of Neuroscience, 24*, 1793–1802.

Blanton, R. E., Levitt, J. G., Peterson, J. R., Fadale, D., Sporty, M. L., Lee, M., et al. (2004). Gender differences in the left inferior frontal gyrus in normal children. *Neuroimage, 22*, 626–636.

Bonda, E., Petrides, M., Ostry, D., & Evans, A. (1996). Specific involvement of human parietal systems and the amygdala in the perception of biological motion. *Journal of Neuroscience, 16*, 3737–3744.

Braitenberg, V., & Schüz, A. (1998). *Cortex: Statistics and geometry of neuronal connectivity* (2nd ed.). Heidelberg, Germany: Springer.

Brodmann, K. (1909/1994). *Localisation in the cerebral cortex.* London: Smith-Gordon.

Brown, T.T., Lugar, H. M., Coalson, R. S., Miezin, F. M., Petersen, S. E., & Schlaggar, B. L. (2004) Developmental changes in human cerebral functional organization for word generation. *Cerebral Cortex, 15*, 275–290.

Bunge, S. A. (2002) Immature frontal lobe contributions to cognitive control in children: Evidence from fMRI. *Neuron, 33*, 301–311.

Bourgeois, J.P. & Rakic, P. (1993) Changes in synaptic density in the primary visual cortex of the macaque monkey from fetal to adult stage. *Journal of Neuroscience, 13*, 2801–20.

Bushong, S. C. (2003). *Magnetic resonance imaging* (3rd ed.) St. Louis, MO: Mosby.

Carey, S. (1992) Becoming a face expert. *Philosophical Transactions of the Royal Society of Biological Sciences, 335*, 95–102.

Carne, R. P., Vogrin, S., Litewka, L., & Cook, M. J. (2006). Cerebral cortex: An MRI-based study of volume and variance with age and sex. *Journal of Clinical Neuroscience, 13*, 60–72.

Chupin, M., Hammers, A., Bardinet, E., Colliot, O., Liu, R. S. N., Duncan, J. S., et al. (2007). Fully automatic segmentation of the hippocampus and the amygdala from MRI using hybrid prior knowledge. In *Medical image computing and computer-assisted intervention,* vol. *4791* (pp. 875–882). Berlin, Germany: Springer.

Collins, D. L., Holmes, C. J., Peters, T. M., & Evans, A. C. (1995). Automatic 3D model-based neuroanatomical segmentation. *Human Brain Mapping, 3*, 190–208.

Collins, D. L., Neelin, P., Peters, T. M., & Evans, A. C. (1994). Automatic 3D intersubject registration of MR volumetric data in standardized Talairach space. *Journal of Computer Assisted Tomography, 18*, 192–205.

Conel, J. L. (1967) *Postnatal development of the human cerebral cortex: The cortex of the seventy-two-month infant,* vol. *8.* Cambridge, MA: Harvard University Press.

Cowell, P. E., Allen, L. S., Zalatimo, N. S., & Denenberg, V. H. (1992). A developmental study of sex and age interactions in the human corpus callosum. *Developmental Brain Research, 66*, 187–192.

Davidson, M. C., Thomas, K. M., & Casey, B. J. (2003). Imaging the developing brain with fMRI. *Mental Retardation and Developmental Disabilities Research Reviews, 9*, 161–167.

Davey Smith, G., Ebrahim, S., Lewis, S., Hansell, A. L., Palmer, L. J, & Burton, P. R. (2005). Genetic epidemiology and public health: Hope, hype, and future prospects. *Lancet, 366*, 1484–1498.

De Bellis, M. D., Keshavan, M. S., Beers, S. R., Hall, J., Frustaci, K., & Masalehdan, A., et al. (2001). Sex differences in brain maturation during childhood and adolescence. *Cerebral Cortex, 11*, 552–557.

Decety, J., Grezes, J., Costes, N., Perani, D., Jeannerod, M., & Procyk, E. (1997). Brain activity during observation of actions. Influence of action content and subject's strategy. *Brain, 120*, 1763–1777.

Dekaban, A. S. (1978). Changes in brain weights during the span of human life: Relation of brain weights to body heights and body weights. *Annals of Neurology, 4*, 345–356.

Deutsch, G.K., Dougherty, R.F., Bammer, R., Siok, W.T., Gabrieli, J.D., & Wandell, B. (2005). Children's reading performance is correlated with white matter structure measured by diffusion tensor imaging. *Cortex, 41*, 354–363.

Draganski, B., Gaser, C., Busch, V., Schuierer, G., Bogdahn, U., & May, A. (2004). Neuroplasticity: Changes in grey matter induced by training. *Nature, 427*, 311–312.

Eickhoff, S. B., Schleicher, A., Scheperjans, F., Palomero-Gallagher, N., & Zilles, K. (2007). Analysis of neurotransmitter receptor distribution patterns in the cerebral cortex. *Neuroimage, 34*, 1317–1330.

Ernst, M., Nelson, E. E., Jazbec, S., McClure, E. B., Monk, C. S., Leibenluft, E., et al. (2005). Amygdala and nucleus accumbens in responses to receipt and omission of gains in adults and adolescents. *Neuroimage, 25,* 1279–1291.

Evans, A. C., Collins, D. L., Mills, S. R., Brown, E. D., Kelly, R. L., & Peters, T. M. (1993). 3D statistical neuroanatomical models from 305 MRI volumes. *Proceedings of the IEEE–Nuclear Science Symposium and Medical Imaging Conference,* 1813–1817.

Evans, A. C. & Brain Development Cooperative Group. (2006). The NIH MRI study of normal brain development. *NeuroImage, 30,* 184–202.

Fischl, B., & Dale, A. M (2000). Measuring the thickness of the human cerebral cortex from magnetic resonance images. *Proceedings of the National Academy of Sciences, 297,* 11050–11055.

Fischl, B., Sereno, M. I., Tootell, R. B., & Dale, A. M. (1999). High-resolution intersubject averaging and a coordinate system for the cortical surface. *Human Brain Mapping, 8,* 272–284.

Galvan, A., Hare, T. A., Parra, C. E., Penn, J., Voss, H., Glover, G., & Casey, B. J. (2006). Earlier development of the accumbens relative to orbitofrontal cortex might underlie risk-taking behavior in adolescents. *Journal of Neuroscience, 26,* 6885–6892.

Gaser, C., & Schlaug, G. (2003). Brain structures differ between musicians and non-musicians. *Journal of Neuroscience, 23,* 9240–9245.

Gazzaniga, M. S. (2004). *The cognitive neurosciences III.* Cambridge, MA: MIT Press.

Giedd, J. N., Blumenthal, J., Jeffries, N. O., Castellanos, F. X., Liu, H., Zijdenbos, A., et al. (1999a). Brain development during childhood and adolescence: A longitudinal MRI study. *Nature Neuroscience, 2,* 861–863.

Giedd, J. N., Blumenthal, J., Jeffries, N. O., Rajapakse, J. C., Vaituzis, A. C, Liu, H., et al. (1999b). Development of the human corpus callosum during childhood and adolescence: A longitudinal MRI study. *Progress in Neuro-Psychopharmacology & Biological Psychiatry, 23,* 571–588.

Giedd, J. N., Rumsey, J. M., Castellanos, F. X., Rajapakse, J. C., Kaysen, D., Vaituzis, A. C., et al. (1996a). A quantitative MRI study of the corpus callosum in children and adolescents. *Developmental Brain Research, 91,* 274–280.

Giedd, J. N., Snell, J. W., Lange, N., Rajapakse, J. C., Casey, B. J., & Kozuch, P. L. (1996b). Quantitative magnetic resonance imaging of human brain development: Ages 4–18. *Cerebral Cortex, 6,* 551–560.

Giedd, J. N., Vaituzis, A. C., Hamburger, S. D., Lange, N., Rajapakse, J. C., Kaysen, D., et al. (1996c). Quantitative MRI of the temporal lobe, amygdala and hippocampus in normal human development: Ages 4–18 years. *Journal of Comparative Neurology. 366,* 223–230.

Giedd, J. N., Clasen, L. S., Lenroot, R., Greenstein, D., Wallace, G. L., Ordaz, S., et al. (2006). Puberty-related influences on brain development. *Molecular and Cellular Endocrinology, 254–255,* 154–162.

Giedd, J. N., Clasen, L. S., Wallace, G. L., Lenroot, R. K., Lerch, J. P., Wells, E. M., et al. (2007). XXY (Klinefelter syndrome): A pediatric quantitative brain magnetic resonance imaging case-control study. *Pediatrics, 119,* e232–e240.

Glahn, D. C., Paus, T., & Thompson, P. M. (2007). Imaging genomics: Mapping the influence of genetics on brain structure and function. *Human Brain Mapping, 28,* 461–463.

Gogtay, N., Giedd, J. N., Lusk, L., Hayashi, K. M., Greenstein, D., Vaituzis, A. C., et al. (2004). Dynamic mapping of human cortical development during childhood through early adulthood. *Proceedings of the National Academy of Sciences U S A, 101,* 8174–8179.

Good, C. D., Johnsrude, I., Ashburner, J., Henson, R. N., Friston, K. J., & Frackowiak, R. S. (2001). Cerebral asymmetry and the effects of sex and handedness on brain structure: A voxel-based morphometric analysis of 465 normal adult human brains. *Neuroimage, 14,* 685–700.

Goren, C. C. (1975) Visual following and pattern discrimination of face-like stimuli by newborn infants. *Pediatrics, 56,* 544–549.

Grezes, J., Costes, N., & Decety, J. (1999) The effects of learning and intention on the neural network involved in the perception of meaningless actions. *Brain, 122,* 1875–1887.

Grosbras, M. H., & Paus, T. (2006). Brain networks involved in viewing angry hands or faces. *Cerebral Cortex, 16,* 1087–1096.

Grosbras, M. H., Osswald, K., Jansen, M., Toro, R., McIntosh, A. R., Steinberg, L., et al. (2007). Neural mechanisms of resistance to peer influence in early adolescence. *Journal of Neuroscience, 27,* 8040–8045.

Gur, R. C., Gunning-Dixon, F., Bilker, W. B., & Gur, R. E. (2002). Sex differences in temporo-limbic and frontal brain volumes of healthy adults. *Cerebral Cortex, 12,* 998–1003.

Hagmann, P., Cammoun, L., Martuzzi, R., Maeder, P., Clarke, S., Thiran, J. P., et al. (2006). Hand preference and sex shape the architecture of language networks. *Human Brain Mapping, 27,* 828–835.

Haier, R. J., Jung, R. E., Yeo, R. A., Head, K., & Alkire, M. T. (2005). The neuroanatomy of general intelligence: Sex matters. *Neuroimage, 25,* 320–327.

Hall, J. A. (1978). Gender effects in decoding nonverbal cues. *Psychological Bulletin, 85,* 845–857.

Herba, C., Phillips, M. (2004). Annotation: Development of facial expression recognition from childhood to adolescence: Behavioural and neurological perspectives. *Journal of Child Psychology and Psychiatry, 45,* 1185–1198.

Hope, P. L., & Moorcraft, J. (1991) Magnetic resonance spectroscopy. *Clinics in Perinatology, 18,* 535–548.

Hursh, J. B. (1939). Conduction velocity and diameter of nerve fibers. *American Journal of Physiology, 127,* 131–139.

Huttenlocher, P. R. (1984). Synapse elimination and plasticity in developing human cerebral cortex. *American Journal of Mental Deficiency, 88,* 488–496.

Huttenlocher, P. R., & de Courten, C. (1987). The development of synapses in striate cortex of man. *Human Neurobiology, 6,* 1–9.

Hwang, S. J., Ji, E. K., Lee, E. K., Kim, Y. M., Shin, D. Y., Cheon, Y. H., et al. (2004). Gender differences in the corpus callosum of neonates. *Neuroreport, 15,* 1029–1032.

Joffe, T. H., Tarantal, A. F., Rice, K., Leland, M., Oerke, A. K., Rodeck, C., et al. (2005). Fetal and infant head circumference sexual dimorphism in primates. *American Journal of Physical Anthropology, 126,* 97–110.

Kaes, T. (1907). *Die grosshirnrinde des menschen in ihren massen und ihrem fasergehalt.* Jena: Gustav Fisher.

Kimura, D. (1996). Sex, sexual orientation and sex hormones influence human cognitive function. *Current Opinions in Neurobiology, 6,* 259–263.

Kilts, C. D. (2003) Dissociable neural pathways are involved in the recognition of emotion in static and dynamic facial expressions. *Neuroimage, 18,* 156–168.

Klingberg, T., Vaidya, C. J., Gabrieli, J. D. E., Moseley, M. E., & Hedehus, M. (1999). Myelination and organization of the frontal white matter in children: A diffusion tensor MRI study. *NeuroReport, 10,* 2817–2821.

Kucharczyk, W., Macdonald, P. M., Stanisz, G. J., & Henkelman, R. M. (1994). Relaxivity and magnetization transfer of white matter lipids at MR imaging: Importance of cerebrosides and pH. *Radiology, 192,* 521–529.

Kwon, H., Reiss, A. L., & Menon, V. (2002). Neural basis of protracted developmental changes in visuo-spatial working memory. *Proceedings of the National Academy of Sciences Online, 99,* 13336–13341.

Laule, C., Vavasour, I. M., Kolind, S. H., Li, D. K., Traboulsee, T. L., Moore, G. R., et al. (2007). Magnetic resonance imaging of myelin. *Neurotherapeutics, 4,* 460–484.

Lenroot, R. K., & Giedd, J. N. (2006). Brain development in children and adolescents: Insights from anatomical magnetic resonance imaging. *Neuroscience and Biobehavorial Review, 30,* 718–729.

Logothetis, N. K., Pauls, J., Augath, M., Trinath, T., & Oeltermann, A. (2001). Neurophysiological investigation of the basis of the fMRI signal. *Nature, 412,* 150–157.

Luders, E., Steinmetz, H., & Jancke, L. (2002). Brain size and grey matter volume in the healthy human brain. *Neuroreport, 13,* 2371–2374.

Luna, B., Thulborn, K. R., Munoz, D. P., Merriam, E. P., Garver, K.E., Minshew, N. J., et al. (2001) Maturation of widely distributed brain function subserves cognitive development. *Neuroimage, 13,* 786–793.

Mädler, B., Drabycz, S. A., Kolind, S. H., Whittall, K. P., & Mackay, A. L. (2008). Is diffusion anisotropy an accurate monitor of myelination? Correlation of multicomponent T(2) relaxation and diffusion tensor anisotropy in human brain. *Magnetic Resonance Imaging,* June 3 [Epub ahead of print].

Maguire, E. A., Gadian, D. G., Johnsrude, I. S., Good, C. D., Ashburner, J., Frackowiak, R. S., et al. (2000). Navigation-related structural change in the hippocampi of taxi drivers. *Proceedings of the National Academy of Sciences Online U S A, 97,* 4398–4403.

Marner L., Nyengaard J. R., Tang, Y., & Pakkenberg, B. (2003). Marked loss of myelinated nerve fibers in the human brain with age. *Journal of Compartive Neurology, 462,* 144–152.

Matsuzawa, J., Matsui, M., Konishi, T., Noguchi, K., Gur, R. C., Bilker, W., et al. (2001). Age-related volumetric changes of brain gray and white matter in healthy infants and children. *Cerebral Cortex, 11,* 335–342.

McGivern, R. F. (2002) Cognitive efficiency on a match to sample task decreases at the onset of puberty in children. *Brain Cognition, 50,* 73–89.

McGowan, J. C. (1999). The physical basis of magnetization transfer imaging. *Neurology, 53,* S3–S7.

Mechelli, A., Crinion, J. T., Noppeney, U., O'Doherty, J., Ashburner, J., Frackowiak, R. S., et al. (2004). Neurolinguistics: Structural plasticity in the bilingual brain. *Nature, 431,* 757.

Menon, V., Boyett-Anderson, J. M., Reiss, A. L. (2005). Maturation of medial temporal lobe response and connectivity during memory encoding. *Cognitive Brain Research, 25,* 379–385.

Paus, T. (2003). Principles of functional neuroimaging. In R. B.Schiffer, S. M.Rao, & B. S.Fogel (Eds.), *Neuropsychiatry* (2nd ed.; pp. 63–90). Philadelphia: Lippincott, Williams & Wilkins.

Paus, T. (2005). Mapping brain maturation and cognitive development during adolescence. *Trends in Cognitive Science, 9,* 60–68.

Paus, T. (2007). Maturation of structural and functional connectivity in the human brain. In V.Jirsa & A. R.McIntosh (Eds.). *Handbook of brain connectivity.* Heidelberg, Germany: Springer-Verlag.

Paus, T., Otaky, N., Caramanos, Z., MacDonald, D., Zijdenbos, A., D'Avirro, D., et al. (1996a). In vivo morphometry of the intrasulcal gray matter in the human cingulate, paracingulate, and superior-rostral sulci: Hemispheric asymmetries, gender differences and probability maps. *Journal of Comparative Neurology, 376,* 664–673.

Paus, T., Zijdenbos, A., Worsley, K., Collins, D. L., Blumenthal, J., Giedd, J. N., et al. (1999). Structural maturation of neural pathways in children and adolescents: In vivo study. *Science, 283,* 1908–1911.

Paus, T., Tomaiuolo, F., Otaky, N., MacDonald, D., Petrides, M., Atlas, J., et al. (1996b). Human cingulate and paracingulate sulci: Pattern, variability, asymmetry, and probabilistic map. *Cerebral Cortex, 6,* 207–214.

Pausova, Z., Paus, T., Abrahamowicz, M., Almerigi, J., Arbour, N., Bernard, M., et al. (2007). Genes, maternal smoking and the offspring brain and body during adolescence: Design of the Saguenay Youth Study. *Human Brain Mapping, 28,* 502–518.

Perrin, J. S., Leonard, G., Perron, M., Pike, G. B., Pitiot, A., Richer, L., et al. (2008a). Growth of White Matter in the Adolescent Brain: Role of Testosterone and Androgen Receptor. *Journal of Neuroscience, 28,* 9519.

Perrin, J. S., Herve, P. Y., Pitiot, A., Totman, J., & Paus, T. (2008b). Brain structure and the female menstrual cycle. *Neuroimage Supplement1,* 41, 638 M-PM.

Peters, M., Jancke, L., Staiger, J. F., Schlaug, G., Huang, Y., & Steinmetz, H. (1998). Unsolved problems in comparing brain sizes in Homo sapiens. *Brain and Cognition, 37,* 254–85.

Pezawas, L., Verchinski, B. A., Mattay, V. S., Callicott, J. H., Kolachana, B. S., Straub, R. E., et al. (2004). The brain-derived neurotrophic factor val66met polymorphism and variation in human cortical morphology. *Journal of Neuroscience, 24,* 10099–10102.

Pezawas, L., Meyer-Lindenberg, A., Drabant, E. M., Verchinski, B. A., Munoz, K. E., Kolachana, B. S., et al. (2005). 5-HTTLPR polymorphism impacts human cingulate-amygdala interactions: A genetic susceptibility mechanism for depression. *Nature Neuroscience, 8,* 828–834.

Pfefferbaum, A., Mathalon, D. H., Sullivan, E. V., Rawles, J. M., Zipursky, R. B., & Lim, K. O. (1994). A quantitative magnetic resonance imaging study of changes in brain morphology from infancy to late adulthood. *Archives of Neurology,* 51, 874–887.

Pike, G. B. (1996). Pulsed magnetization transfer contrast in gradient echo imaging: A two-pool analytic description of signal response. *Magnetic Resonance in Medicine, 36,* 95–103.

Puce, A., Allison, T., Bettin, S., Gore, J. C., & McCarthy, G. (1998). Temporal cortex activation in humans viewing eye and mouth movements. *Journal of Neuroscience, 18,* 2188–2199.

Pujol, J., Vendrell, P., Junque, C., Marti-Vilalta, J. L. & Capdevila, A. (1993). When does human brain development end? Evidence of corpus callosum growth up to adulthood. *Annals of Neurology, 34,* 71–75.

Purves, D., White, L. E., Riddle, D. R, (1996). Is neural development Darwinian? *Trends in Neuroscience, 19,* 460–464.

Rakic, P., Bourgeois, J. P., Eckenhoff, M. F., Zecevic, N., & Goldman-Rakic, P. S. (1986). Concurrent overproduction of synapses in diverse regions of the primate cerebral cortex. *Science, 232,* 232–235.

Rauch, R. A., & Jinkins, J. R. (1994). Analysis of cross-sectional area measurements of the corpus callosum adjusted to brain size in male and female subjects from childhood to adulthood. *Behavior and Brain Research, 64,* 65–78.

Reiss, A. L., Abrams, M. T., Singer, H. S., Ross, J. L., and Denckla, M. B. (1996). Brain development, gender and IQ in children. A volumetric imaging study. *Brain, 119,* 1763–1774.

Robbins, T. W., & Everitt, B. J. (1996). Neurobehavioural mechanisms of reward and motivation. *Current Opinion in Neurobiology, 6,* 228–236.

Roberts T. P., & Mikulis, D. (2007). Neuro MR: Principles. *Magnetic Resonance Imaging, 26,* 823–837.

Rubia, K., Overmeyer, S., Taylor, E., Brammer, M., Williams, S. C., Simmons, A., et al. (2000). Functional frontalisation with age: Mapping neurodevelopmental trajectories with fMRI. *Neuroscience and Biobehavioral Review, 24,* 13–19.

Rushton, W. A. H. (1951). A theory of the effects of fibre size in the medullated nerve. *Journal of Physiology, 115,* 101–122.

Schlaggar, B. L., Brown, T. T., Lugar, H. M., Visscher, K. M., Miezin, F. M., & Petersen, S. E. (2002). Functional neuroanatomical differences between adults and school-age children in the processing of single words. *Science, 296,* 1476–1479.

Schmidt-Nielsen, K. (1997). *Animal physiology: Adaptation and environment* (5th ed.). Cambridge: Cambridge University Press.

Schmierer, K., Scaravilli, F., Altmann, D. R., Barker, G. J., & Miller, D. H. (2004). Magnetization transfer ratio and myelin in postmortem multiple sclerosis brain. *Annals of Neurology, 56,* 407–415.

Schmithorst, V. J., & Holland, S. K. (2006). Functional MRI evidence for disparate developmental processes underlying intelligence in boys and girls. *Neuroimage, 31,* 1366–1379.

Schmithorst, V. J., Wilke, M., Dardzinski, B. J., & Holland, S. K. (2005). Cognitive functions correlate with white matter architecture in a normal pediatric population: A diffusion tensor MRI study. *Human Brain Mapping, 26,* 139–147.

Schmithorst, V. J., Wilke, M., Dardzinski, B. J., & Holland, S. K. (2002). Correlation of white matter diffusivity and anisotropy with age during childhood and adolescence: A cross-sectional diffusion-tensor MR imaging study. *Radiology, 222*, 212–218.

Shaw, P., Greenstein, D., Lerch, J., Clasen, L., Lenroot, R., Gogtay, N., et al. (2006). Intellectual ability and cortical development in children and adolescents. *Nature, 440*, 676–679.

Sholl, D. A. (1956). *The organization of the cerebral cortex.* London: Methuen & Co.

Sirevaag, A. M., & Greenough, W. T. (1988). A multivariate statistical summary of synaptic plasticity measures in rats exposed to complex, social and individual environments. *Brain Research, 441*, 386–392.

Skullerud, K. (1985). Variations in the size of the human brain. Influence of age, sex, body length, body mass index, alcoholism, Alzheimer changes, and cerebral atherosclerosis. *ACTA Neurologica Scandinavica, Suppl. 1002*, 1–94.

Sluming, V., Barrick, T., Howard, M., Cezayirli, E., Mayes, A., & Roberts, N. (2002). Voxel-based morphometry reveals increased gray matter density in Broca's area in male symphony orchestra musicians. *Neuroimage, 7*, 1613–1622.

Smith, S. M., Jenkinson, M., Johansen-Berg, H., Rueckert, D., Nichols, T. E.Mackay, C. E., et al. (2006). Tract-based spatial statistics: Voxelwise analysis of multi-subject diffusion data. *NeuroImage, 31*, 1487–1505.

Snook, L., Paulson, L. A, Roy, D., Phillips, L., & Beaulieu, C. (2005). Diffusion tensor imaging of neurodevelopment in children and young adults. *Neuroimage, 6*, 1164–1173.

Sowell, E. R., Thompson, P. M., Tessner, K. D., Toga, A.W. (2001). Mapping continued brain growth and gray matter density reduction in dorsal frontal cortex: Inverse relationships during post-adolescent brain maturation. *Neuroscience, 21*, 8819–8829.

Steinberg, L. (2008). A neurobehavioral perspective on adolescent risk-taking. *Developmental Review, 28*, 78–106.

Steinberg, L., & Monahan, K. (2007). Age differences in resistance to peer influence. *Developmental Psychology, 43*, 1531–1543.

Steinmetz, H., Jancke, L., Kleinschmidt, A., Schlaug, G., Volkmann, J., & Huang, Y. (1992). Sex but no hand difference in the isthmus of the corpus callosum. *Neurology, 42*, 749–752.

Steinmetz, H., Staiger, J. F., Schlaug, G., Huang, Y., & Jancke, L. (1995). Corpus callosum and brain volume in women and men. *Neuroreport, 6*, 1002–1004.

Suzuki, M., Hagino, H., Nohara, S., Zhou, S. Y., Kawasaki, Y., Takahashi, T., et al. (2005). Male-specific volume expansion of the human hippocampus during adolescence. *Cerebral Cortex, 15*, 187–193.

Tamm, L., Menon, V., & Reiss, A. L. (2002). Maturation of brain function associated with response inhibition. *Journal of the American Academy of Child and Adolescent Psychiatry, 41*, 1231–1238.

Taylor, M. J., McCarthy, G., Saliba, E., & Degiovanni, E. (1999). ERP evidence of developmental changes in processing of faces. *Clinical Neurophysiology, 110*, 910–915.

Thomas, K. M., Drevets, W. C., Whalen, P. J., Eccard, C. H., Dahl, R. E., Ryan, N. D., et al. (2001). Amygdala response to facial expressions in children and adults. *Biological Psychiatry, 49*, 309–316.

Toro, R., Perron, M., Pike, B., Richer, R., Veillette, S., Pausova, Z., et al. (2008). Brain size and folding of the human cerebral cortex. *Cerebral Cortex.* Feb 10, 2008; [Epub ahead of print]

Turnbridge, E. M., Wickert, C. S., Kleinman, J. E., Herman, M. M., Chen, J., Kolachana, B. S., et al. (2007). Catechol-O-methyl-transferase enzyme activity and protein expression in human prefrontal cortex across the postnatal lifespan. *Cerebral Cortex, 17*, 1206–1212.

Wickert, C. S., Webster, M. J., Gondipalli, P., Rothmond, D., Fatula, R. J., Herman, M. M., et al. (2007). Postnatal alterations in dopaminergic markers in the human prefrontal cortex. *Neuroscience, 144*, 1109–1119.

Wilkinson, R. G. (2005). *The impact of inequality: How to make sick societies healthier.* London: Routledge.

Yakovlev, P. I., Lecours, A-R. (1967). The myelogenetic cycles of regional maturation of the brain. In A. Minkowski (Ed.), *Regional development of the brain in early life* (pp. 3–70). Oxford, UK: Blackwell Scientific.

Yang, T. T., Menon, V., Eliez, S., Blasey, C., White, C., Gotlib, I. H., et al. (2002). Amygdalar activation associated with positive and negative facial expressions: A 3T functional magnetic resonance imaging experiment. *Neuroreport, 13*, 1737–1741.

Yucel, M., Stuart, G. W., Maruff, P., Velakoulis, D., Crowe, S. F., Savage, G., et al. (2001). Hemispheric and gender-related differences in the gross morphology of the anterior cingulate/paracingulate cortex in normal volunteers: An MRI morphometric study. *Cerebral Cortex, 11*, 17–25.

Zilles, K., Palomero-Gallagher, N., & Schleicher, A. (2004). Transmitter receptors and functional anatomy of the cerebral cortex. *Journal of Anatomy, 205*, 417–432.

CHAPTER 5

Puberty

Its Role In Development

ELIZABETH J. SUSMAN AND LORAH D. DORN

What is this mystical, dreaded, and shrouded period of development, labeled *puberty,* that is accompanied by rapid morphological body changes, including physical growth and hormonal changes as well as a myriad of psychological and social contextual changes? Puberty has intrigued scholars, artists, parents, and adolescents alike for centuries, and cultures have ritualized puberty to varying degrees. In some instances rituals feast the reproductive transition of puberty, whereas in other instances religious and social aspects of puberty are celebrated. At its core, puberty is the period of development through which its passage endows an adolescent with reproductive competence. At an even more basic analysis, puberty is a brain–neuroendocrine process that provides a stimulus for all the physical changes and putative psychological changes that accompany this period of development. How, then, does a biologically based process come to be so compacted with social and psychological significance?

Puberty's significance likely derives to some extent from its mistaken identity and overlap with the adolescent passage. Adolescence is a wider concept that encompasses the time and terrain that includes both puberty and the social, emotional, and wider psychological changes that characterize the chronological transition from childhood to adulthood. The primary functions of puberty and adolescence are principally nonoverlapping; puberty entails brain development consisting of neuroendocrine changes, characterized by activation of

gonadotropin-releasing hormone (GnRH) and elevated secretion of gonadotropins and sex steroids, resulting in sexual maturation and related physical growth changes (Rockett, Lynch, & Buck, 2004; Sisk & Zehr, 2005). Adolescence entails the acquisition of adult cognition, emotions, and social roles that are possible through maturation of brain functions and dynamic interactions with varying family, educational, and social contexts. How the biological and psychological processes interact to influence one another has been the challenge to scientists for decades. The goal of this chapter is to present a perspective on the neuroendocrinology of puberty and the implications of these brain changes for psychological development. The chapter begins with a historical and theoretical perspective on the role of puberty in development followed by a review of the major neuroendocrine changes that occur at puberty and how these changes affect physical morphological characteristics. Then, the literature is condensed to present an overview of the relations between pubertal status and pubertal timing and psychological development. Finally, we conclude with research and intervention recommendations for the future.

HISTORICAL PERSPECTIVE

A classic perspective on adolescence is that it is a period characterized by "storm and stress" (Hall, 1904). This view portrays adolescents as oppositional, emotionally labile, and in need of constant monitoring so as to mold the adolescent's developing character to prevent adult psychopathology. The biological changes of puberty were considered a major influence on the storm and stress of adolescence (Freud, 1958). This viewpoint has been significantly reconceptualized and now adolescents are presented in a more balanced and positive perspective. Adolescence now is viewed as a transitional period that is characterized by storm and stress for only a fraction of boys and girls (Offer & Offer, 1975; Offer & Schonert-Reichl, 1992). If it even does exist, the storm and stress of adolescence currently can be conceptualized as neither a universal phenomenon nor an exclusively biologically based aspect of development.

Changes in this perspective on adolescence evolved primarily from two distinct lines of evidence. First, parents, teachers, and others endowed with the responsibility to care for youth were aware that all adolescents are not the stormy and stressed-out persons who were portrayed in the literature and past popular press reports. Offer and Offer (1975) published a seminal study showing that about 80% of adolescent boys remain well adjusted during this transitional period. Adolescents do have problems, and multiple studies of mental health problems have shown prevalence rates of about 20% for mental health problems (Costello et al., 1996; Kashani, Orvaschel, Burk, & Reid, 1985; Offord et al., 1987). Collectively, adolescence now seems to be viewed as a more positive period of development, and newer research focuses on positive youth development (Catalano, Haggerty, Oesterle, Fleming, & Hawkins, 2004; Larson, 2000; Lerner, Brentano, Dowling, & Anderson, 2002) rather than the negative perspective in past eras. In brief, adolescents are not consistently characterized by emotional distress and behavioral disruption and they are known to be competent to interact seamlessly with family, friends and others in their wider ecology. The socially valuable movement toward positive youth development is designed to foster growth potential along favorable directions.

Theories of Puberty and Psychological Development

Puberty as a biological process that deterministically influenced psychological functioning and social behavior was a view derived from evolutionary (Parker, 2000) and psychodynamic theories (Blos, 1962; Freud, 1958; Freud, 1998; Hall, 1904) that dominated the early twentieth century. Sigmund and Anna Freud were instrumental in advancing a perspective that merged the biological–sexual and psychological aspects of pubertal development. For Sigmund Freud, the arrival of puberty signaled the end of infantile sexual life and the beginning of normal adult sexual life (Freud, 1998). In infancy, the oral phase, the sexual instinct was predominantly autoerotic; at puberty, the genital phase, the search becomes for a sexual object. The autoerotic zones of infancy become subordinated to the genital zone. The two sexes are considered to diverge as the basic anatomy of sexuality is different between males and females. Freud considered male sexuality as straightforward and understandable, whereas sexuality in females became a combination of an affectional and a sensual current. The sexual aim of males becomes discharge of the sexual products, and the sexual aim is subordinate to the reproductive function.

Anna Freud (1958) carried on and expanded the traditional psychoanalytic perspective of her father with regard to puberty and adolescence. She developed the notion that defense mechanisms are critical to understanding adolescent adjustment. Defense mechanisms ward off pregenital urges that are reawakened or new urges arising from endogenous biological changes. Unconsciously, adolescents call on defense mechanisms to protect the ego and reduce anxiety.

After the analytically oriented era waned, behavioral and contextually oriented models of development became predominant in the mid to late twentieth century. This period might aptly be described as the dark ages of empiricism with regard to puberty and psychological development. Skinnerian behaviorism (Skinner, 1953), social learning theory (e.g., Bandura, 1978), ecological theories (Bronfenbrenner, 1979), and life-course perspectives gave virtually no attention to puberty or biology more broadly. The rich inner psychological life and sexual fantasies and urges of adolescents became as repressed by late twentieth century scientists as by the Victorian adolescent. However, a minority perspective erupted in the 1980s that had been brewing among developmental psychologists. A foundation for the rise of a new era of interdisciplinary models of the biological and psychological aspects of puberty sprung out of the now classic Petersen and Taylor (1980) chapter on pubertal development in Adelson's (1980) *Handbook of Adolescent Development*. Petersen and Taylor suggested that the biological changes during puberty play a major role in psychological development. Furthermore, they suggested that being off time in pubertal development was a risk for adjustment problems.

The publication was followed in the early 1980s, parallel to the rise of the Society of Research in Adolescence, by a movement originating from a small group of scholars (Jeanne Brooks-Gunn, Richard M. Lerner, David Magnusson, Anne Petersen, Laurence Steinberg, Elizabeth Susman, and others) who put forth a paradigm that had parallels with a phoenix rising from the ashes. Like the risen phoenix, puberty and its psychological correlates took on a new form as a period of development characterized by *integrated* biological, psychological, and contextual features. The role of puberty in development then began to receive moderate attention given its potential as a mechanism involved in the etiology of adolescent adjustment and psychopathological problems. Several of these scholars began or continued the first longitudinal studies that focused on the integration of biopsychosocial processes inherent in adolescent development. The more integrated perspective became the norm for considering puberty and psychological development. This perspective is now viewed as essential for understanding the fragmented findings regarding the role of puberty in psychological development.

It follows that the current chapter presents a perspective on puberty as a biopsychosocial transition that is initiated by major neuroendocrine changes and is accompanied by psychological and behavior changes that simultaneously initiate changes in the social contexts in which adolescents find themselves. This theoretical approach is referred to as *dynamic integration* and refers to the essential and changing fusion of processes across psychological, biological, and contextual levels of analysis (Susman & Rogol, 2004). The neuroendocrine changes that initiate and control the progression of puberty now will be reviewed.

PUBERTY: A BRAIN–NEUROENDOCRINE EVENT

Puberty consists of a coordinated series of hormone and physical growth changes that form the core of the transition from childhood to adolescence. An increasing sophistication of brain and neuroendocrine changes has led scientists to consider the primacy of the neurobiological basis of puberty. The brain undergoes extensive remodeling at puberty and these changes form the basis for reproductive maturation (Sisk & Foster, 2004). These neurobiological changes are responsible for both the biological hormone and physical morphological changes and likely contribute to the social, cognitive, and emotional changes that occur during puberty. The structural and functional changes of the brain first will be considered, followed by neuroendocrine changes responsible for the onset and progression of puberty.

Structure and Function of Brain Development

Coming to know the structure of human brain during adolescence is the result largely of the implementation of new imaging technologies. Much of what we know about adolescent brain development is derived from studies using magnetic resonance imaging (MRI) or functional MRI (fMRI). The yield from imaging changes in the brain is revolutionary as these studies show both structural and functional changes during puberty. Much of the richest work has come from the laboratories of Giedd (Giedd et al., 1999; Giedd, 2008), Casey (Casey, Jones, & Hare, 2008) and Paus (Paus, 2005). Importantly, some changes in the brain occur prior to puberty, some during puberty and some after puberty (Dahl, 2004).

Major changes in gray matter volume develop in a U-shaped function (Giedd, 2004; Gogtay et al., 2004). Motor and sensory systems mature earlier, in general, compared to the higher order functions that are responsible for associative areas of the cortex (Galvin et al., 2006; Gogtay et al.; Sowell, Thompson, & Toga, 2004). Specifically, the limbic system is proposed to develop earlier than the prefrontal control areas of the brain. The prefrontal cortex (PFC) is one of the last changes to occur in brain development (Lewis, 1997). Based on this model, the adolescent is considered to be biased more toward functional limbic activity relative to prefrontal control activity. With advancing development there is a functional connectivity between the limbic and prefrontal regions. Nonetheless, Casey and colleagues (Casey et al., 2008) propose a model indicating that bottom-up limbic and prefrontal top-down control regions should be considered together, even though they have different developmental trajectories. In brief, findings to date are interpreted to suggest differential development of bottom-up limbic systems, which are implicated in incentive and emotional processing, and top-down control systems during adolescence as compared to childhood and adulthood. Adolescents are assumed to have a heightened responsiveness to incentives and socioemotional contexts simultaneous with the period when impulse control is still relatively immature. This perspective has direct implications for social and emotional development and behavior. The relatively late development of the prefrontal cortex may be an underlying process related to risk-taking behavior in adolescents (Steinberg, in press). In addition, Casey et al. (2008) note that the sequence of developmental events may be exacerbated in adolescents prone to emotional reactivity, increasing the likelihood of poor mental health outcomes. Finally, given the major brain changes at puberty, the adolescent brain may be more vulnerable to the effects of substance use and abuse or other environmental insults that predispose youth to a trajectory of cognitive, emotional, and behavioral problems.

Neuroendocrine Changes and Reproduction

In spite of the new knowledge about the brain presented earlier regarding the puberty-related structural and functional aspects of brain development, there is virtually no overlap in the literature between this newly derived knowledge and neuroendocrine, puberty-related brain changes. The neuroendocrine changes responsible for the onset and progression of puberty consist of reactivation of the hypothalamic–pituitary–gonadal (HPG) axis and are referred to as gonadarche. Reactivation of GnRH via the GnRH pulse generator is the primary component of the neurobiology of puberty. We refer to "reactivation" because the initial activation of GnRH occurs in the fetal and neonatal period.

GnRH is a decapeptide secreted in a pulsatile fashion by specialized neurons in the median eminence of the hypothalamus. GnRH stimulates the pituitary to secrete gonadotropins, luteinizing hormone (LH) and follicle-stimulating hormone (FSH). LH and FSH travel via peripheral circulating blood to affect target cells in the testes in males and ovaries in females. Vital to reproduction, gonadal hormones are stimulated by gonadotropins and regulate ovulation and spermatogenesis in females and males, respectively. Sisk and Foster (2004) suggest that in the brain gonadal steroids control GnRH secretion by way of neuroendocrine feedback loops and facilitate sexual behavior.

Much of what we know about the GnRH pulse generator and the onset of puberty derives from animal models, primarily from the rhesus monkey (see Plant, 2000; Knobil, 1988). The regulation of GnRH pulse frequency is responsible for producing a pattern of gonadotropin and steroid hormone secretion that is necessary for gonadal function and reproductive competence. The specific neural mechanism regulating GnRH secretion is not known in spite of decades of research. What is known is that activation of the HPG axis has a defined developmental history from the prenatal period to midadolescence. In prenatal and early postnatal life there is an increase in gonadal steroids that is responsible for sexual differentiation and organizing of the nervous system. In early infancy, GnRH pulse frequency declines and remains quiescent until puberty. At that time, GnRH secretion gradually increases and remains high, stimulating gonadotropin and gonadal hormone secretion during the reproductive years. In approximately the third decade of life, testosterone and estrogen begin to decline, reaching low but detectable levels within the older adult. The multiple species-specific signals for puberty are integrated in such a way as to allow for the increase in GnRH at puberty. Sisk and Zehr (2005) go on to suggest that permissive signals cannot fully explain the onset of reproductive competence, as such signals are not unique to puberty. For instance, GnRH pulse frequency goes from low to high in the resumption of fertility after lactation. It was suggested that an innate developmental clock senses the unfolding of primary genetic programs that produce signals that in turn determine responses to endogenous and exogenous signals (e.g., the environment) that bring about high-frequency GnRH pulses. There exists the notion that a master regulatory gene allows for programming of the multiple permissive genes, but to date, this master gene remains elusive.

The trigger that determines the timing of pubertal onset and the resurgence of GnRH pulses is not known. The logical explanation that a specific gene triggers the onset of puberty has led to a search for a gene specific to the initiation of puberty. The identification of kisspeptin and its receptor, G protein coupled receptor 54 (GPR54), held promise as the gene responsible for the initiation of puberty (Seminara, 2003). GPR54 is a promising candidate, as the absence of this gene is associated with the absence of GnRH activity at puberty. But, to date, no single gene has been positively identified as a precipitant for the initiation of the complex pubertal process. Sisk and Foster (2004) suggest that there are multiple permissive signals rather than a singular cause of the onset of puberty: melatonin, leptin, ghrelin, body fat, and a complex of genes. Rather than a single trigger, it is likely the case that multiple triggers work in unison to bring about a resurgence of GnRH secretion.

Sex Differences in Pubertal Triggers

Males and females differ in permissive signals of puberty, and most of the triggers in women are related to energy balance. Sex differences likely stem from the different demands involved in reproduction. The beginning of the reproductive period is energy expensive for both males and females, given the rapid physical growth and metabolic changes that occur. In subhuman primates, males and females must defend the territory in which they will rear their young. However, females bear the added energy-intense period of pregnancy and childbirth and then must lactate to feed and rear offspring. Sisk and Foster (2004) suggest that organisms must determine whether growth is sufficient to reproduce (via metabolic cues), relationships with possible mates are possible (through social cues) and whether the conditions are conducive to reproducing (via environmental cues). In females, for successful reproduction, there must be, for example, insulin, glucose and leptin present in quantities sufficient to support pregnancy and lactation. Consider the case of leptin, an adipocyte-derived hormone that has been demonstrated to be a pivotal regulator for the integration of energy homeostasis and repro-duction (Fernandez-Fernandez et al., 2006). Leptin is necessary, but not sufficient to trig-ger the onset of puberty. When the permissive signals collectively bring about metabolic and growth conditions, reproduction becomes pos-sible and is partially observable in secondary sexual characteristics.

Other Regulators of the Timing of Puberty

Neurotransmitters also have an impact on GnRH. For example, gamma-aminobutyric acid (GABA) has primarily inhibitory control on GnRH (McCarthy, Davis, & Mong, 1997) and glutamate has excitatory control over GnRH (Grumbach, 2002). The system and its feedback loops are complex and are beyond the scope of this chapter. The reader is referred to Styne and Grumbach (2007). Figure 5.1 (Banerjee & Clayton, 2008) shows genetic and neurobiological pathways and other factors influencing puberty.

Adrenarche

The neurobiological and peripheral processes of gonadarche and the reproductive axis were described above. A second component of puberty, adrenarche, begins earlier than gonadarche at around age 6–8 years of age. Adrenarche reflects maturation of the adrenal glands, although the trigger for its initiation is unknown (Parker, 1991). Adrenal androgens such as dehydroepi-androsterone (DHEA), its sulfate (DHEAS), and androstenedione are products of the adre-nal glands whose concentrations begin to rise at adrenarche and continue on an upward trajec-tory through the third decade of life (Saenger & Dimartino-Nardi, 2001). Adrenarche and gona-darche are two independent, yet overlapping, components of puberty.

Concentrations of adrenal androgens pri-marily have an impact on the development of axillary and pubic hair as well as acne and body odor. However, these concentrations generally are not high enough to act on peripheral target tissues until later, often after gonadarche. Pubic

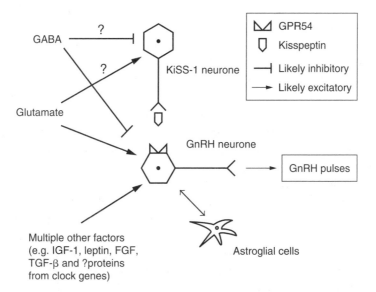

FIGURE 5.1   Neurobiological pathways and other factors influencing the activity of gonadotropin-releasing hormone neurons: Genetic variation in the components of these pathways and the other factors are likely to influ-ence the time of onset and tempo of human puberty. GnRH, gonadotropin-releasing hormone; IGF-I, insulin-like growth factor-I; FGF, fibroblast growth factor; TGF, transforming growth factor. (Reprinted from Banerjee, I., & Clayton, P. (2007). The genetic basis for the timing of human puberty. *Journal of Neuroendocrinology, 19*(11), 831–838, with permission from Wiley-Blackwell Publishing Ltd.)

hair generally is not evident at age 6 when adrenarche alone has occurred. DHEA also serves as a precursor for the development of other androgens such as testosterone. In girls, much of the exposure of androgens comes from DHEA or its conversion. Concentrations of these hormones also have been associated with behavior problems and mood disturbances (Goodyer, Herbert, Tamplin, & Altham, 2000a, 2000b; Goodyer, Herbert, & Altham, 1998; Goodyer et al., 1996; Dorn, Hitt, & Rotentstein, 1999; Dorn et al., 2008). It is yet to be identified whether adrenal androgens have effects similar to testosterone on aggressive or other behaviors.

A third axis, the growth axis, also is involved in puberty. Growth, primarily linear growth, also involves neuroendocrine changes. Growth hormone (GH) increases, but there are also other growth factors that are key contributors to growth. Linear growth has been the focus of the psychology of youth as changes in linear growth, along with secondary sex characteristics, constitute the signal for adolescents themselves and others around them that the adolescent years have arried.

Physical Changes at Puberty

External changes in height and weight and secondary sexual characteristics provide visible ways of marking the progress of pubertal development. These growth changes include increases in linear growth and body composition and development of primary sexual characteristics (ovaries, testes), as well as secondary sexual characteristics (pubic hair, genital and breast development). Collectively, all the changes are a result of the neuroendocrine development described earlier. Early descriptions of growth and pubertal changes in girls and boys were first described by Tanner (Tanner, 1962; Marshall & Tanner, 1969, 1970). Generally, the height spurt begins earlier in girls, at approximately age 12, than in boys, at about age 14 (Marshall & Tanner 1969, 1970). In girls the earliest external change evident at puberty is an increase in breast tissue (Tanner & Whitehouse, 1976; Parent et al.,

2003). Girls usually begin the development of secondary sex characteristics with breast development followed by pubic hair development, whereas boys generally begin genital growth with an increase in testicular volume followed by appearance of pubic hair. Girls tend to mature physically earlier than boys by approximately 18–24 months (Patton & Viner, 2007). Menarche is a relatively late event in the pubertal process, occurring after the growth spurt and after breast development and pubic hair growth has begun. The average age of menarche for White, African American, and Latino girls is: 12.6–12.9, 12.1–12.2, and 12.2–12.3 years, respectively (Wu, Mendola, & Buck, 2002; Chumlea et al., 2003). The rising gonadal and adrenal hormone (DHEA, DHEAS, and androstenedione) concentrations as a result of GnRH secretion result in the changes in primary and secondary sexual characteristics previously described. These hormones increase across puberty, but there are large individual differences resulting in overlap of hormones across adjacent stages of puberty (Styne & Grumbach, 2008; Nottelmann et al., 1987). The result of wide individual variations in hormone levels is that hormone levels cannot be matched to a specific pubertal stage. It follows that hormone levels to determine sexual maturity stage is not an option in research (See Dorn, Dahl, Woodward, & Biro, 2006, for further discussion).

Assessing Pubertal Maturation

Tanner and Marshall described methods of quantifying breast and pubic hair development for girls and genital and pubic hair for boys (Tanner, 1962; Marshall & Tanner, 1969, 1970). A five-stage rating system (1 = prepubertal to 5 = full maturation) was developed for each secondary sex characteristic, and the characteristics were originally adapted from Reynolds and Wines (1948). Photographs are available of these stages in endocrinology (e.g., Kronenberg, Melmed, Polonsky, & Larsen, 2008) or adolescent medicine textbooks (Neinstein, 2008), as well as psychology-related textbooks focusing on adolescent development (Steinberg, 2007). Additional photographs showing these same stages were published later (van Wieringen, Roede, & Wit, 1985) and most recently appear in Biro and Dorn (2005). It is important to note that Tanner criteria for assessing pubertal maturation were developed from a relatively small sample of boys and girls (less than 400) housed in an institution in England. Thus, the sample is representative neither of the United Kingdom nor of other world populations. Further, the sample included only Caucasians youth. To our knowledge there are no photographs describing the stages in boys and girls of different ethnic groups.

Components of Change

Three characteristics of changes in puberty may have important implications for health and development in adolescence and beyond. These include timing, sequence, and tempo. Timing refers to being earlier or later compared to a normative age group. For example, breast development at age 3 signals the need to conduct an appropriate evaluation for precocious puberty. Alternatively, a 14- or 15-year-old boy with short stature (e.g., low percentile in height compared to norms) signals the need for an evaluation to determine a diagnosis of delayed puberty. A critical question is whether a developmental clock that determines the timing of GnRH maturation also determines gonadal maturation (Sisk & Foster, 2004). The majority of psychological research on puberty has focused on the importance of timing of puberty. This literature is briefly reviewed later in this chapter.

The sequence of pubertal components, that is, the order in which growth or development of secondary sex characteristic occurs, has received little empirical attention. Generalities of the sequence have been described by Tanner (1962) and others showing that in girls, breast development is often the first change, followed by the height spurt and pubic hair growth. Menarche is a relatively late event during the pubertal process. If this sequence deviates

substantially from the norm, it should set into motion further concerns by a parent or health care provider. For instance, early pubic hair development in the absence of breast development may reflect early adrenarche. In a recent paper, Biro and colleagues (2003) reported that most White girls with asynchronous maturation were more likely to begin puberty with breast development (thelarche) compared to initiation with pubic hair (adrenarche). Of interest is that the reported age of onset of puberty in both groups was 10.7 years. Specifically, girls in the thelarche pathway had a greater sum of skin folds, percent body fat, waist-to-hip ratio, and body mass index (BMI) at menarche, andmany of these differences held across a 10-yearlongitudinal study. In this pathways paper, Biro et al. proposed that the sequence in which pubertal changes are experienced in girls may have long-term ramifications for health. For example, girls with breast development first, stimulated by gonadal axis activation, may be more at risk for obesity and breast cancer than girls with pubic hair development first. To our knowledge there are no studies that examine the psychological import of the sequence of pubertal development.

Finally, the tempo of puberty, that is, the rate of progression through puberty, also has received little empirical attention from either a medical or psychological perspective. Nonetheless, there have been citations indicating that the tempo of puberty has not really changed in the last several decades (Reiter & Lee, 2001). The tempo of puberty varies across adolescents, and differences in tempo will determine the later progression through puberty. For instance, at one time of measurement, one adolescent may be more advanced in physical maturation than another adolescent who began puberty at the same time, but one adolescent's maturational progression may slow so that measurement at a second time point finds the same adolescent as average in terms of tempo. In African American children aged 10–12 years old, Ge and colleagues (2003) found that males who experienced accelerated pubertal maturation from the first to second assessment showed the highest increase in depressive symptoms. Does it follow then that a faster tempo constitutes a risk for depressive symptoms in males? The answer may be no. In a study of 327 male and female adolescents (aged 10–12 years at first assessment and 12–14 years at second assessment), boys with accelerated pubertal maturation had a *lower* isk of depression (Laitinen-Krispijn, van der Ende, & Verhulst, 1999). An unanswered question is whether age of onset of puberty is correlated with tempo of puberty or age of menarche. It seems appropriate to suggest, given the opposing findings above, the need to consider pubertal tempo when examining pubertal influences and depressive affect.

Timing of Puberty: Its Psychological Significance

The biological changes of puberty are universal, but the timing and social significance of these changes to adolescents themselves, societies, and scientific inquiry vary across historical time, individuals and families, and cultures. The psychological significance of the timing of puberty is one of the most populartopics examined by scholars of adolescent development.

Secular Trends in the Timing of Puberty

The last decade evidenced a renewed interest in secular changes in the timing of puberty (Buck Louis et al., 2008; Euling et al., 2008; Golub et al., 2008; Kaplowitz, 2008). The increase in interest was sparked partially by a controversial paper by Herman-Giddens et al. (1997) showing that girls were entering puberty at an earlier age than was the norm in U.S. girls. Specifically, signs of puberty were evident in African American girls, on average, at age 7 and in Caucasian girls, on average, at age 9. The study was conducted on more than 17,000 girls, yet the report has been controversial based primarily on methodological issues (see Emans & Biro, 1998; Reiter & Lee, 2001; Rosenfield

et al., 2000). In another sample, Sun and colleagues reported older ages of onset of puberty based on breast development than did Herman-Giddens and colleagues (Sun et al., 2002). Other studies of girls showing earlier maturation (particularly by age at menarche) include findings from the National Health Examination Survey (Anderson, Dallal, & Must, 2003), the National Health and Nutrition Examination Survey (Chumlea et al., 2003), the Bogalusa Heart Study (Freedman et al., 2002), and the Fels Longitudinal Study (Demerath et al., 2004). Importantly, age at menarche was not reported to be earlier than in the past. Maturation in boys also is reported to be earlier than in previously described cohorts, as reported in a secondary data analysis from a cross-sectional survey of the National Health and Nutrition Examination Survey (Herman-Giddens, Wang, & Koch, 2001). The analysis included 2,114 boys who were identified as White, African American, or Mexican American. In all racial groups, boys matured earlier than reported in previous studies based on Tanner criteria for genital and pubic hair development. Further, African American boys had the earliest age of onset of puberty (age 11.2 years; Tanner 2) based on pubic hair and age 9.5 for genital development. The African American sample also reached full maturity of genital development (Tanner 5) at an earlier age than the other groups. Importantly, age at menarche, compared to age of onset of puberty, has not varied in recent history. Nonetheless, secular trends have shown dramatic differences in timing of puberty across time (Gluckman & Hanson, 2006) and may be changing too slowly to show an evolutionary change in the time period assessed (see Figure 5.2). In conclusion, Biro and colleagues (Biro, Huang, et al., 2006) note that the correlation is low between age of menarche and age of onset of puberty, and this correlation has gotten progressively lower across the decades. The divergence in the correlation between age of onset of puberty and age of menarche may result from the increase in weight in both boys and girls.

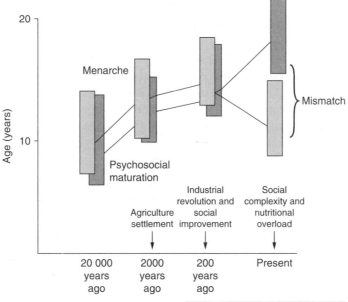

FIGURE 5.2   The relationship between the likely range of ages of menarche (light gray) and achievement of psychosocial maturity (dark gray) from 20,000 years ago to the present day. The mismatch in timing between these two processes is a novel phenomenon. (Reprinted from Gluckman, P. D., & Hanson, M. A. (2008). Evolution, development and timing of puberty. *Trends in Endocrinology & Metabolism, 17*(1), 7–12, with permission from Elsevier.)

Not all recent findings support the divergence of age of onset of puberty and age of menarche. Current speculation is that secular trends in the timing of puberty now may be characterized by stability rather than change. In Europe, Parent et al. (2003) reported that the downward trend in age of maturation is decreasing or is even slightly increasing in some instances. Similarly, Sun et al. (2005) noted no convincing evidence for earlier age of pubertal maturation from 1966 to 1994. Evidence to the contrary is that menarche, as opposed to pubertal maturation, also is decreasing in two longitudinal studies (Anderson & Must, 2005). A recent panel concluded that the findings for girls are sufficient to suggest a secular trend toward an earlier age of onset of breast development and age of menarche (Euling et al., 2008). In contrast, the panelists concluded that the data for boys were insufficient to make a conclusion about a secular trend in boys' development.

Recently, Biro (2006) raised the important question, "Whither goest puberty?" And what are the causes of the changes in timing of puberty? Although the exact cause of early timing of puberty is unknown, there are several plausible explanations. Several environmental factors beyond heritability could influence the earlier onset of puberty: nutritional status, chronic diseases, migration to a healthy environment, infectious diseases, pollution and exposure to environmental toxins (Delemarre-van de Waal, 2005). It is of note that we, and most of the literature on timing of puberty, are referring to a small variation in timing that is well within the normal range of timing of puberty or menarche from a health care perspective. Pediatric endocrinologists would likely not see these smaller differences as abnormal. Nonetheless, even minor variations in the timing of puberty may have implications for health and behavior. Following is a discussion regarding endogenous and exogenous influences on the timing of puberty.

Obesity and Timing of Puberty

Obesity as an initiator of early timing of puberty is now a major concern given the epidemic of obesity that is rampant in North America and is spreading to other nations. The concern is that the obesity observed during adolescence will persist into adulthood. This concern was warranted in a prospective study of boys and girls (Bratberg, Nilsen, Holmen, & Vatten, 2007). The study examined the influence of early sexual maturation on subsequent overweight in late adolescence and found that timing did relate to later obesity, but this relation was modified by central adiposity in early adolescence.

A question in the past was whether early puberty initiates weight gain or whether heavier weight is an initiator of earlier puberty. The latter explanation has received recent support. Girls who were heavier at age 5 had an earlier timing of puberty based on both estradiol levels and Tanner stage (Davison, Susman, & Birch, 2003). In a similar vein, higher weight status even in young children was related to earlier timing of puberty (Lee et al., 2007). Surprisingly, infants' weight at 36 months and higher rate of change in BMI between 36 months and grade 1, earlier age of mothers' menarche, and non-White race each consistently and positively was associated with an earlier onset of puberty (Lee et al.). In a recent review, Biro and colleagues reported relatively consistent evidence for the relations of timing of puberty and obesity (Biro, Khoury, & Morrison, 2006) in older children and adolescents. Kaplowitz (2008) suggests that obesity may be causally related to earlier puberty in girls rather than earlier puberty causing an increase in body fat. Much of the research on timing of puberty and obesity is in girls and also shows that these relations are more evident in Black compared to White girls (Biro et al., 2006). These relations do not hold in boys for unknown reasons.

Endocrine Disruptors

One of the proposed mechanisms of earlier timing of puberty focuses on endocrine disruptors. Endocrine disruptors include a variety of substances that could be natural or synthetic environmental chemicals that disrupt or change normal endocrine functions (Nebesio & Pescovitz, 2007). Examples include such things as harsh pesticides or chemicals that come from industry processing or waste (e.g., polychlorinated biphenyls [PCBs], phthalates) that are converted to natural estrogens or phytoestrogens. Effects of these disruptors may be on the HPG axis concurrently or may result from accumulation over time, in turn contributing to later reproduction problems. Examination of the mechanisms involved in endocrine disruptors and timing of puberty has been carried out in both lower animal and human models.

There are extensive animal model studies showing the impact of environmental chemicals on pubertal timing, yet there is less empirical evidence in human models (see review by Buck Louis et al., 2008). Some of these studies report earlier timing of puberty as a result of exposure to disruptors, whereas others report later timing. It also seems that males may not be as affected by endocrine disruptors as females. Most of these studies using animals report on development following a known exposure to a chemical. Few studies of healthy children have included measures of endocrine disruptors. In studies that have found putative disruptor effects on timing of puberty, speculation is that endocrine disruptors may have played a role. For example, one of the proposed mechanisms involved in earlier puberty in African Americans was the use of hair products containing natural estrogens (Herman-Giddens et al., 1997). Exposure to specific chemicals in hair products, however, was not measured. In earlier reports, early puberty (precocious puberty, premature thelarche, premature adrenarche) in children in Puerto Rico was thought to be related to significant amounts of estrogen from the food supply (Bongiovanni, 1983; Comas, 1982; Saenz de Rodriguez, Bongiovanni, & Conde de Borrego, 1985). The amount of estrogen in the food supply was not determined.

Caution is warranted regarding the potential effect of these endocrine disruptors on health as well as on timing of puberty. Progress in the development of household and industrial products in our modern society, where there is also an increased use of household chemicals, pesticides, and plastics, may have a higher risk–benefit ratio than in the past.

Measurement of Puberty: Pubertal Status and Pubertal Timing

Pubertal status and pubertal timing are key variables in both biological and behavioral studies. Whether puberty is considered a cause or a consequence of the outcome at hand or whether it must be controlled for in a statistical analysis, both are variables deserving of considerable attention. Assessment of puberty is often missing in studies in which it is relevant or puberty may be measured in an inappropriate method with respect to the research question. Currently, the "gold standard" for measuring pubertal stage is by Tanner criteria (Marshall &Tanner, 1969, 1970) as assessed by a physical examination by a trained examiner. Frequently, psychosocial studies of adolescents measure pubertal maturation using self- or parent report of adolescents' maturation. The most widely used self-report measure is the Petersen Pubertal Development Scale (PDS; Petersen, Crockett, Richards, & Boxer, 1988). Adolescents report on specific puberty-related physical or auditory changes (e.g., voice, skin changes, body hair, linear growth). Other studies have used photographs or line drawings (Morris & Udry, 1980). Self-ratings are not perfectly related to assessments by physical examinations (i.e., by kappa coefficients) but in some cases can be strongly correlated with actual physical examinations. Although not perfectly correlated, there are some instances where self-report is an appropriate measure of puberty. The measure of puberty should match the research question. The reader is referred to a recent and more in-depth publication outlining methods of measuring puberty and their respective strengths and limitations

(Dorn et al., 2006). In that report, the more frequently used measures of pubertal status and pubertal timing are evaluated for strengths and weaknesses.

Age at menarche is another index frequently used to reflect pubertal development. This measure is most often obtained by self-report but also has been obtained via parent report using either a questionnaire or an interview. As mentioned previously, menarche is a relatively late event in the pubertal process. Thus, it can be equated neither with "pre- versus postpubertal" nor can it be used to determine the exact stage of pubertal development. Menarche does occur when the majority of girls are Tanner 4 (nearly two-thirds) but about 25% are Tanner 3, 5% Tanner 2, and 10% Tanner 5 when becoming menarcheal (Neinstein, 2008). Further, the consistency of reporting age at menarche across many years is not perfect. Correlations range from 0.60 to 0.81 (Bergsten-Brucefors, 1976; Casey et al., 1991; Damon & Bajema, 1974; Livson & McNeill, 1962; Must et al., 2002). In brief, age of menarche is an index of just that— age of menarche; it reveals little about pubertal maturation other than that gonadotropins and sex steroids are at levels essential for the beginning of the menstrual cycle.

The methods for estimating timing of puberty are varied. In some instances, indices of puberty are used to reflect adolescents as early, on time, or late with respect to a same-age cohort. Comparisons can be made to sex-specific national norms or the peer group to answer the question of whether a particular adolescent is on time, early, or late. Frequently, age at menarche or Tanner stage for age is categorized in this manner. For example, distributions of pubertal stage have been trichotomized or cut points have been determined by a specified number of standard deviations to estimate timing of puberty. Importantly, one needs to articulate the rationale for defining the method of timing of puberty in each instance.

Other studies have used a pubertal status (stage) measure to reflect pubertal timing as a continuous measure. For example, pubertal stage has been regressed on chronological age and the residuals then used in analyses as an index of timing (Dorn, Ponirakis, & Susman, 2003; Ellis & Garber, 2000; Ellis et al., 1999). This methodology of considering the continuum of timing of puberty tends to be useful for smaller samples that are not population based. The use of stage residual scores allows for considering the relative age of pubertal stage or "earlier timing" rather than "early timing" as defined by a categorical variable.

Does Pubertal Status or Timing Make a Difference in Psychological Development?

This section presents a brief review of major findings on the relation between pubertal status and pubertal timing and psychological development. It first considers differences in psychological parameters between adolescents at different pubertal stages. Second, the section discusses the relation between psychological parameters and timing of puberty (earlier, later, or on time).

Pubertal Status   The relationship between pubertal status and psychological functioning has not been as thoroughly examined as timing of puberty and psychological dimensions. Noteworthy are three reports from the Great Smokey Mountain longitudinal study that are relevant to pubertal status and psychological development (Costello et al., 1996). First, after the transition to midpuberty (Tanner Stage III and above), girls were more likely than boys to be depressed (Angold, Costello, & Worthman, 1998). Second, Angold, Costello, Erkanli, & Worthman (1999) examined whether the morphological changes associated with Tanner stage or the hormonal changes were more strongly associated with increased rates of depression in adolescent girls. Models that included testosterone and estradiol eliminated the seemingly strong Tanner stage differences and depression. The effect of testosterone on depression was nonlinear. These findings were interpreted as arguing against theories that explain the emergence of the female excess of depression in terms of changes in body morphology and resultant psychosocial effects on social interactions and self-perception. The authors conclude that causal explanations of the increase in depression should focus on factors associated with changes in androgen and estrogen levels rather than the morphological changes of puberty.

Third, a later report from the Great Smokey Mountain study showed that after controlling for age, Tanner stage predicted alcohol use and alcohol use disorder (AUD) in both boys and girls (Costello, Sung, Worthman, & Angold, 2007). The effect of morphological development was strongest in early-maturing girls. Early pubertal maturation predicted alcohol use in boys and girls and AUD in girls. The highest level of excess risk for alcohol use was in early-maturing youth with conduct disorder and deviant peers. Lax supervision predicted alcohol use in early-maturing girls. In contrast, poverty and family problems predicted alcohol use in early-maturing boys. The dearth of recent studies on pubertal status differences in either internalizing or externalizing behavior problems prevents drawing definitive conclusions about pubertal status differences and psychological development. The need for assessment of stage differences is especially acute in studies that use sexual maturity ratings by a trained health care provider.

Pubertal Timing   Pubertal timing and its connection to psychological adjustment has received significantly more attention than pubertal status. The literature on the psychological significance of timing of puberty has been extensively (See Alsaker, 1995) or partially reviewed in various publications (Mendle, Turkheimer, & Emery, 2007; Susman & Rogol, 2004). The next section presents representative studies showing the association between timing of puberty and internalizing and externalizing behavior problems.

When scientists began to consider the timing of the impact of physical maturation on mental health and adjustment, primarily two hypotheses were articulated. First, the maturational deviance hypothesis, also coined the "off-time" hypothesis, suggested that those either early or late pubertal changes compared to same age peer group will likely experience more stress and adjustment difficulties than on-time developers (Brooks-Gunn, Petersen, & Eichorn, 1985; Caspi & Moffitt, 1991; Petersen & Taylor, 1980; Tschann et al., 1994). Off-time pubertal development may be more difficult in the absence of the necessary social support or resources to cope with earlier or later maturation. That is, if maturation is early, emotional and social resources may not yet be in place for the younger age adolescent. Alternatively, if maturation is late, social and family resources might be available but not at the time when they were most needed by the adolescent. In turn, adjustment problems may be more likely for either the earlier or the later maturer. Few studies focus on positive effects of either earlier or later timing of puberty.

The second hypothesis is the early-maturational or early timing hypothesis (Brooks-Gunn et al., 1985; Caspi & Moffitt, 1991; Petersen & Taylor, 1980; Tschann et al., 1994). This hypothesis suggests that early maturation, particularly in girls, is a disadvantage because girls bypassed the opportunity to complete the normative tasks of development that facilitate coping with the issues and problems associated with puberty. Adding to the stress of puberty, there are more advanced social role expectations for early maturers since their appearance is more physically mature, and in turn they are expected to act more maturely. Early-maturing girls also face more social pressures at a time when they are cognitively and emotionally unprepared to deal with abstractions and complex emotional issues. In brief, there is a mismatch between physical development and cognitive and emotional development. The findings from studies of timing of puberty and adjustment are not consistent in terms of whether earlier or later timing of puberty is good or bad for boys or girls.

Early Maturation and Internalizing Problems

Early maturation for girls fairly consistently is associated with negative psychological and behavioral consequences (Ge, Brody, Conger, Simons, & Murry, 2002; Ge, Conger, & Elder, 2001a, 2001b; Graber, Lewinsohn, Seeley, & Brooks-Gunn, 1997; Hayward, Gotlib, Schraedley, & Litt, 1999). Representative findings are that early-maturing girls report more negative emotions than on-time or later maturing peers. For instance, Ge and colleagues (2001a) report findings showing that seventh-grade girls who experienced menarche at younger ages subsequently experienced a higher level of depressive symptoms than on-time and later maturing peers. The gender differences disappeared when pubertal transition indices (pubertal status and menarche) were included in the model. The finding is important as it indicates that pubertal maturation may explain the often reported gender difference in depressive symptoms. The effects of early maturation are true for boys as well as for girls. Early-maturing boys reported more hostile feelings and internalized distress symptoms compared to on-time and later maturing boys (Ge et al., 2001b). The negative effects of early maturation for boys are inconsistent with the earlier findings reporting positive effects of early timing of puberty on boys.

Early Maturation and Externalizing Problems

The early-maturational hypothesis suggests that earlier maturing girls engage in more acting-out behavior than on-time or later maturing peers (Ge et al., 2001a). Studies such as those of Ge and colleagues do report that earlier maturing girls tend to exhibit more behavior problems and adjustment difficulties than their on-time or later maturing peers. But the relationship between earlier timing and externalizing behavior problems can be moderated by a history of vulnerability (Caspi & Moffitt, 1991). Early maturers with a history of behavior problems later reported more behavior problems than on-time or later maturers without a history of behavior problems. In addition, earlier maturing girls with no history of behavior problems experienced fewer behavior problems than girls with a history of behavior problems who matured on time.

A consistent finding related to pubertal timing is the link between earlier maturation and substance use. Substance use is more prevalent in both earlier maturing boys and girls (Dick, Rose, Kaprio, & Viken, 2000; Orr & Ingersoll, 1995; van Jaarsveld, Fidler, Simon, & Wardle, 2007; Wilson, Killen, & Hayward, 1994). Specifically, early timing of maturation is linked to a higher incidence of smoking (Martin et al., 2001). Early timing of maturation and substance use also occurs across cultures. In East and West German youth, earlier timing was associated with more frequent cigarette and alcohol use (Wiesner & Ittel, 2002). On-time and later maturation was not associated with substance use. Similarly, in Norwegian and Swedish youth, earlier puberty was associated with alcohol use, alcohol intoxication, drunkenness onset, and number of units consumed (Andersson & Magnusson, 1990; Wichstrøm, 2001). The mechanisms relating early timing of puberty and substance use have received a moderate amount of attention. Substance use may lower resistance to peer pressure to use various substances increasing both substance use and other health-compromising behaviors, such as risky sexual behavior. In brief, the growing body of literature indicates that early pubertal maturation in girls is generally associated with negative psychological and health outcomes in Western societies. The findings are strong enough at this date to suggest to policy makers that programs to reduce externalizing behavior, principally substance use and risky behavior, should be initiated earlier than in the past for adolescent girls who exhibit early signs of puberty. The findings to date are deemed insufficient to make a similar recommendation for boys.

Timing of Puberty and Health

A new set of findings shows that timing of puberty has potentially serious implications for health problems, either during adolescence or later in the life span. Adolescents with earlier puberty are at risk for accelerated skeletal maturity and short adult height, earlier sexual debut, and a higher risk for sexual abuse (Golub et al., 2008). An even more serious implication of earlier timing of puberty is its association with reproductive tract cancers later in life. Earlier age of menarche is a risk for breast cancer and lower age of puberty in boys is associated with a higher incidence of testicular cancer (Golub et al., 2008). One explanation for the link between earlier timing of puberty and reproductive cancer is a longer duration of exposure to estrogen in girls and testosterone in boys. Estrogen and testosterone are growth factors that putatively contribute to reproductive cancer.

In the earlier discussion, the focus was on timing of gonadarche and health risks. Early adrenarche also carries a risk for health problems as well: metabolic syndrome or ovarian hyperandrogenism/polycystic ovarian syndrome (PCOS) in adulthood (Ibáñez, Dimartino-Nardi, Potau, & Saenger, 2000). PCOS is a disorder characterized by infertility, hirsutism, obesity, menstrual disorders, and ovarian atretic follicles. These problems in turn put females at risk for obesity, type 2 diabetes, cardiovascular disease, and infertility (Golub et al., 2008). Obesity and reproductive problems additionally are associated with mood and affect problems, and there is speculation that depression and mood problems may play a role in the onset of these disorders. Premature adrenarche also is associated with mood and behavioral problems (Dorn, Hitt, & Rotenstein, 1999; Dorn, 2007). Longitudinal studies to establish the connection between timing of gonadarche and adrenarche and metabolic and psychiatric disorders are not yet available.

Earlier timing of puberty has negative implications for lifestyle and health behaviors. In addition to the well-known relationship between earlier timing of puberty and smoking, earlier maturers reported more sedentary behavior, but earlier maturation was offset by physical activity (van Jaarsveld et al., 2007). The same study also reported lower rates of breakfast eating and higher reported stress, especially among early-maturing girls. To date, no policy recommendations are available regarding education of adolescents and their families regarding timing of puberty and health risks.

Spermarche as an Index of Timing of Puberty

Spermarche (oigarche) is rarely used as an index of timing in boys compared to age of menarche as an index of timing in girls. Reaching spermarche at 11 years or younger was associated with higher levels of depression (Kaltiala-Heino, Marttunen, Rantanen, & Rimpela, 2003). But later timing of spermarche also was associated with depression. A second paper from the same sample yielded different results as the adolescents were grouped based on age at menarche or spermarche (10 or younger, 11 years, 12 years, 13 years, 14 years, and 15 years or older) (Kaltiala-Heino, Kosunen, & Rimpela, 2003). In boys, only early maturation increased the risk of depression. It is not surprising that spermarche is an infrequent index of timing of puberty given that the presence of sperm in urine is a preferred way to assess spermarche. But urine is difficult to accurately collect as it is an embarrassing and sensitive procedure for some youth. Nonetheless, indices of the timing of spermarche provide a potentially valid and needed index of pubertal maturation.

Family Influences on Timing of Puberty and Menarche

The evolution of puberty occurred so as to maximize the probability for successful procreation. Puberty-related mutations in successive generations have favored biological qualities fostering survival in particular geographic and cultural settings. Draper & Harpending (1982) proposed that individuals have evolved to be sensitive to features of their early childhood environment that may affect later reproductive competence. Belsky, Steinberg, & Draper (1991) extended this perspective to consider family disruption/father absence and early timing of puberty or menarche. Psychosocial acceleration theory and life history theory have been used to explain the unusual connection between family disruption/father absence and timing of puberty. The psychosocial acceleration theory was proposed first by Belsky et al. to explain the role of family disruption/father absence and early timing of menarche. Specifically, Belsky et al. proposed an evolutionary function of family ecology and psychosocial influences to explain earlier timing of puberty. From an early age, children are socialized to develop an understanding of the availability and predictability of resources, the trustworthiness of meaningful others, and the enduring quality of close relationships. In brief, individuals are presumed to become sensitive to qualities of the environment that enhance or suppress reproductive tendencies. For instance, family stressors create conditions that undermine parental functioning, such as parental conflict, and lower parental investment in girls. Girls from families characterized by father absence or discordant male–female relationships perceive males as less salient to family relationships and lack parental investment in offspring. Given the perceived instability of relationships with males, girls accelerate the timing of menarche and subsequently engage in early sexual activity and unstable pair bonding. Mendle et al. (2006) later similarly proposed that unstable parental relationships subsequently lead girls to believe that resources are limited, people are untrustworthy, and relationships opportunistic. Further, parents' mating reproductive behavior characterized by multiple sexual partners and erratic relationships contribute to a girl's sense of a transient family situation.

In a somewhat similar perspective to the psychosocial acceleration theory, Ellis and Essex (2007) proposed a life history theory linking family structure and processes and timing of puberty. They emphasize the importance of life history traits, that is, the constellation of maturational and reproductive characteristics that influence speed of reproduction and population turnover. A key assumption of the life history approach is that individuals make trade-offs in distribution of metabolic resources to sustain vital functions: growth, reproduction, and maintenance, given that resources are finite and unpredictable. Individuals choose evolutionarily relevant features of the environment as a basis for altering the timing and tempo of pubertal maturation (Ellis, 2004). A life history perspective asks questions about when individuals should stop converting surplus energy related to growth and begin to shift resources to reproduction.

Published studies based on acceleration and the life history perspectives show support for the hypotheses regarding timing of puberty or menarche and family structure or processes (see also Ellis et al., 2004). One notable and consistent finding is that menarche occurs at an earlier age among girls raised in stressful family circumstances (Doughty & Rodgers, 2000; Jones, Leeton, McLeod, & Wood, 1972; Kim & Smith, 1998a, 1998b; Kim, Smith, & Palermiti, 1997; Moffitt, Caspi, Belsky, & Silva, 1992; Surbey, 1990). The majority of the studies use father absence as a marker of family disruption in relation to timing of menarche. Other studies assess father absence, family dysfunction, or qualities of parenting (Belsky et al., 2007; Ellis & Essex, 2007; Surbey, 1998) or family composition (e.g., stepbrothers) (Matchock & Susman, 2006). Thus, it is difficult to separate the effects of family disruption as indexed by father absence and family disruption. Table 5.1 shows representative findings from father absence and family disruption studies.

Father Absence

The absence of a biological figure and its effects on timing of puberty or menarche was the original focus of studies of the sociobiology of puberty. The general conception was that father absence or some permutation of father absence (i.e., stepparent) was related to earlier menarche in father-absent homes. For instance, Surbey (1990) reported that girls achieved earlier menarche in father-absent homes than in father-present homes. The girls in the survey who also experienced high levels of stress also achieved earlier menarche. Since the early Surbey (1990) study, more and more family and contextual measures have been added to the analyses of family structure and function and timing of puberty or menarche (See also Bogaert, 2008). The inclusion of family functioning as in the case of parental investment and early predictors of timing of puberty (e.g., Belsky et al., 2007) has enriched the wealth of findings on the sociobiology of puberty. Nonetheless, specific mechanism and pathways linking timing of puberty and menarche to contextual and individual level variables have not been identified.

Family stress or disruption refers to events that are considered stressors in families and include mental health problems of parents, family conflict, and financial and employment problems. The psychosocial acceleration and life history evolution-based perspectives propose that family disruption and father absence play a causal role in early timing of puberty (Belsky et al., 1991). Girls in these families engage in early sexual behavior and early reproduction (Draper & Harpending, 1982; Ellis, 2004). In one of the first tests of the psychosocial acceleration theory, Moffitt, Caspi, Belsky, and Silva (1992) showed that family conflict, divorce and father absence in childhood predicted earlier age of menarche. Weight also contributed to the influence on earlier menarche. Similarly, in a retrospective study of college age girls, earlier menarche was related to family stress in later childhood (age 7–11), conflict with mother and anxiousness and internalizing symptoms (anxiousness/depression) in early childhood (birth to age 6), and earlier age at dating boys and more boyfriends (Kim & Smith, 1998a). Other studies report that greater marital and family conflict is associated with primarily early timing of puberty in girls (Ellis & Garber, 2000; Graber, Brooks-Gunn, & Warren, 1995). Longer durations of father absence also correlate with an

Table 5.1 Studies Examining Family Contextual Correlates of Pubertal Timing.

Authors	Sample	Puberty Measures	Family/adolescent Characteristic	Findings	
				Males	Females
Belsky, Steinberg, Houts, Friedman, DeHart, Cauffman, Roisman, Halpern-Felsher, Susman, NICHD Early Child Care Research Network (2007).	N = 756 Boys and Girls	Tanner Stage	Rearing experiences Mother's age of menarche Infant negative emotionality Rearing by emotionally interaction	Pubertal onset was not significantly predicted by maternal age of menarche, any rearing variables, or by infant negativity.	Mothers with earlier menarche had daughters with earlier puberty. Insensitive parenting earlier in childhood, predicted earlier pubertal development. Maternal harsh control predicted earlier menarche
Bogaert (2008).	N = 5913 Girls	Menarche	Father absence Siblings		Earlier age of puberty was predicted by father absence
Ellis & Essex (2007).	N = 756 Girls	Pubertal Timing Menarche	Rearing experiences.	Pubertal onset was not predicted by maternal age of menarche, rearing variables or infant negativity.	Mothers who reported an earlier age of menarche had daughters who reported earlier age of menarche and initiated pubertal development earlier than did girls whose mothers reported later age of menarche. Infant negative emotionality did not significantly predict pubertal outcome.
Ellis, Bates, Dodge, Fergusson, Horwood, Pettit, & Woodward (2003).	N = 281 Girls	Pubertal Timing	Father absence Early sexual activity Teenage pregnancy		Greater exposure to father absence was strongly associated with elevated risk for early sexual activity and adolescent pregnancy. Elevated risk was either not explained or only partly explained by familial, ecological, and personal disadvantages associated with father absence. After controlling for covariates, there was stronger and more consistent evidence of effects of father absence on early sexual activity and teenage pregnancy than on other behavioral or mental health problems or academic achievement.

Study	N	Measure	Predictors	Findings
Ellis, Bates, Dodge, Fergusson, Horwood, Pettit, & Woodward (2003).	N = 630 Girls	Petersen Development Scale	Father absence	Father absence was associated with earlier sexual activity and teenage pregnancy. Father absence earlier in the girl's life was associated with sexual activity and teenage pregnancy
Ellis & Garber (2000)	N = 87 Girls	Menarche	Maternal psychopathology Discordant family relationships and father/stepfather absence. Stress in mothers' romantic relationships	History of mood disorders in mothers predicted earlier pubertal timing in daughters. Relation was mediated by dyadic stress and biological father absence; step father presence was best accounted for earlier pubertal maturation in girls
Ellis, McFadyen-Ketchum, Dodge, Pettit, & Bates (1999).	N = 173 Girls	Pubertal timing	Negative-coercive parenting	Negative-coercive (or less positive-harmonious) family relationships in early childhood provoked earlier puberty. Fathers' presence in the home, more time spent by fathers in child care, greater supportiveness in the parental dyad, more father-daughter affection, and more mother-daughter affection, prior to kindergarten, each predicted later pubertal timing by daughters
Graber, Brooks-Gunn, & Warren (1995)	N = 75 Girls	Pubertal Timing Menarche	Heredity Transmission Weight and weight for height Stressful life events Family relationships Absence or present of an adult male	Breast development, weight, family relations, and depressive affect were predictive of age at menarche; family relations predicted age of menarche above the influence of breast development or weight.
Kim & Smith (1998a)	N = 28 Daughters N = 21 Mothers	Menarche	Childhood stress Conflict in family environment	Earlier menarche correlated with family stress at late childhood; more conflict with mother in early childhood; more rejection from, and less closeness to, mother throughout childhood; more anxious and internalizing symptoms in late childhood; earlier age at dating boys and more boyfriends.

(Continued)

Table 5.1 (Continued)

Authors	Sample	Puberty Measures	Family/adolescent Characteristic	Findings	
				Males	Females
Kim & Smith (1998b).	N = 357 Boys and girls	Age at Menarche and Spermarche		Earlier spermarche was associated with father absence; more stress in quality of family life, parental marital unhappiness and parental marital conflict in early childhood; more independence from mother and father in late childhood; earlier age at dating women, more girlfriends, and earlier age at sexual intercourse.	Earlier menarche was associated with parental marital conflict in early childhood; more parental marital unhappiness throughout childhood; more independence from mother and father in late childhood; less anxiousness or internalizing symptoms (anxiousness/depression) in late childhood; earlier age at dating men and more boyfriends.
Kim, Smith, & Palermiti (1997).	N = 380 Boys and Girls	Menarche and spermarche	Early childhood stress or conflict in the family environment	Earlier spermarche was associated with more parental marital conflict, less emotional closeness to father; more aggressiveness, unruliness, and externalizing symptoms in early or late childhood. Earlier spermarche was associated with earlier age at dating women, having more girlfriends, having had intercourse and having more total frequency of intercourse partners.	Earlier menarche was associated with stress in quality of family life; unhappiness in parental marital relations during childhood; more conflict with mother; less emotional closeness to mother; and behavioral independence from mother or father in late childhood. Earlier menarche was associated with earlier age at dating men and older age of first sexual intercourse partner relative to own age at first intercourse.
Matchock & Susman (2006).	N = 1938 Women	Menarche	Absence of Biological Father Presence of half or step-brothers Living in an urban environment Body weight Race Siblings		Absence of the biological father, presence of half or step-brothers and living in an urban environment were all predictors of earlier menarche. Body weight and race were also related to menarche timing. The number of siblings and the birth order had no effect on menarche. Although presence of a sister showed delay in menarche, especially if they were older.

Author	N	Measure	Factors	Findings
Mendle, Turkheimer, D'Onofrio, Lynch, Emery, Slustke, & Martin (2006).	N = 1284 Girls	Menarche	Childhood stress	Within the discordant MZ twin pairs, children raised by the twin providing a stepfather had an age of menarche slightly earlier than children raised by the co twin without a stepfather. The opposite pattern occurred in children of the discordant DZ pairs.
Moffitt, Caspi & Silva (1992).	N = 1037 Girls	Menarche	Family Stress; Behavioral and Psychological Problems	Family conflict and father absence in childhood predicted an earlier age of menarche and these factors combined with weight showed some evidence of an additive influence on menarche.
Mustanski, Viken, Kaprio, Pulkkinen, & Rose (2004).	N = 1891 Boys and Girls	Pubertal Development Scale	Father absence; Environmental influences	Genetic influences made the largest contribution to variance common to PDS items. In girls, common environmental influences were added for growth spurt and menarcheal status. For both common and item-specific variation, genetic effects were partially sex specific. Subsidiary analyses found accelerated maturation in for girls who at age 14 were reared in father-absent homes. Genetic influences made the largest contribution to variance common to PDS items. Genetic and non shared environmental factors accounted for variation specific to PDS items in boys. Genetic effects were partially sex specific. Subsidiary analyses found accelerated maturation in boys who at age 14 were reared in father-absent homes.
Romans, Martin, Gendall, Herbison (2003).	N = 2225 Girls	Menarche	Father absence; Family conflict; Genetic determination of early puberty	Early menarche was predicted by low family socio-economic status, absence of father, family conflict, poor relationships between the girl and either/both parents, a self-rated childhood personality style as a loner, and childhood physical and sexual abuse.

(Continued)

Table 5.1 (Continued)

Authors	Sample	Puberty Measures	Family/adolescent Characteristic	Findings	
				Males	Females
Surbey (1998).	N = 1200 Girls	Pubertal Timing Menarche	Father absence Heightened levels of childhood stress		Menarche was earlier in girls from father-absent households and those reporting high levels of stress during childhood. The mothers of the father-absent girls also were early matures, began dating early, tended to have their first child at an earlier age and have more children, and had more negative attitudes toward males and the family than mothers of father present girls.
Wierson, Long, & Forehand (1993).	N = 71 Girls	Menarche	Divorced Families Interparental Conflict		Earlier menarche in girls from divorced families. Earlier menarche in families with maternal reported interparental conflict.
Wierson, Long, & Forehand (1993).	N = 71 Girls	Menarche	Environmental Stress Divorce Interparental conflict		Compared to girls with intact families, those from divorced families had earlier onset of menarche. Higher maternal reports of interparental conflict were significantly related to earlier menarche in the total sample.

earlier menarcheal onset (Moffitt et al., 1992; Romans, Martin, Gendall, & Herbison, 2003; Surbey, 1990; Wierson, Long, & Forehand, 1993). Studies of family stress and timing of puberty in males are more rare than studies of girls.

Others have argued that the posited causal relationship between family structure and functioning and timing of puberty can be explained by uncontrolled genetic and environmental influences (Mendle et al., 2006). Girls who experience early menarche are more likely to be from lower socioeconomic status (SES) families, experience psychological difficulties, and transmit the likelihood of earlier development to children (e.g., Mustanski, Viken, Kaprio, Pulkkinen, & Rose, 2004; Stattin & Magnusson, 1990; Udry, 1979). These are potential confounds that cannot be controlled in research that compares age of menarche among unrelated individuals. Mendle et al. (2006) did a comparison of the stepparenting effects in the children of monozygotic (MZ) and dizygotic (DZ) twins and determined that this design can potentially discriminate whether confounds in the association between stepfathering and menarche are mediated via genetics or shared environment. A within-pair difference between the daughters of discordant DZ pairs but not between daughters of discordant MZ pairs suggests that the confound is primarily genetic. This is because DZ twins differ in genetic endowment and shared environment, whereas MZ twins differ only in their shared environment. A comparison of the stepparenting effects in the children of MZ and DZ twins can potentially discriminate whether confounds in the association between stepfathering and menarche are mediated via genetics or shared environment.

Variables indicative of stress were included by Mendle and colleagues (2006): divorce, being raised by both biological parents in the household, presence of a stepfather in the household, and absence of a biological father in child rearing. Results show that girls reared in families with stepfathers exhibit a significantly earlier age of menarche than girls raised without stepfathers. Of note is that the presence of a step-uncle was as predictive of early menarche as the presence of a stepfather. That is, it was not necessary for a child to experience the direct environmental influence of a stepfather to experience an accelerated age of menarche, if she is genetically related to someone who does have a stepfather. In brief, in a pair of twin mothers, of which only one raises her children with a stepfather, the offspring of both twins are equally likely to exhibit early age of menarche. Mendle et al. conclude that some genetic or shared environmental confound accounts for the earlier menarche found in female children living with stepfathers. However, it is also possible that earlier menarche results from some shared environmental quality.

Parental Investment

Parental investment refers to the quantity and quality of parenting of offspring. For example, father investment as indexed by qualities of parenting and timing of puberty was considered (Moffitt et al., 1992). Negative aspects of family environment (family conflict, maternal harsh control) and earlier timing of menarche were related to timing of puberty. Recently, Ellis and Essex (2007) used a life history approach and proposed that humans have evolved to be sensitive to specific features of early childhood environments and that exposure to different parental environments bias children toward development of alternative reproductive strategies, including differential pubertal timing. Ellis (2004) extended the Belsky et al. (1991) perspective to parental investment by positing a unique and central role for fathers in the regulation of female offspring sexual development, separate from the effects of other dimensions of psychosocial stress and family support in the child's ecology. Higher quality parental investment in the preschool years and greater parental supportiveness predicted lower rates of evidence of adrenarche, the early aspect of puberty, in boys and girls in the first grade and less development of secondary sexual characteristics in girls in the fifth grade (Ellis & Essex, 2007). Higher quality mother and father parental investment and less father-reported maternal conflict or depression predicted later adrenarche, the early phase of puberty. Older age at menarche in mothers, higher SES, greater mother-based supportiveness, and lower third-grade body mass index also uniquely and significantly predicted later sexual maturity in daughters. Ellis and Essex (2007) concluded that, consistent with a life history perspective, quality of parental investment emerged as a central dimension of the proximal family environment and pubertal timing.

These findings are consistent with the previous Ellis et al. (1999) findings. Parental warmth, positive family relationships, and paternal involvement in child rearing were related to a later age of menarche. The quality of the father's investment in the family emerged as the most important feature of the proximal family environment as a correlate of daughters' pubertal timing. Parenting qualities consisted of greater supportiveness in the parental dyad, more time spent by fathers in child care, more father–daughter affection, and more mother–daughter affection. Positive parenting characteristics, according to the child development theory (CDT), reap a longer childhood (later sexual maturation and onset of reproduction) and that high-investing family contexts foster development of sociocompetitive competencies. In contrast, the costs of truncating childhood are reduced in low-investing family contexts that do not meaningfully facilitate competitive competencies.

The argument proposed by Ellis and Essex (2007) regarding early age at adrenarche and family processes and the ecology of development has good internal consistency. Nonetheless, the logic is not consistent with the biology of reproduction. Adrenarche is independent of gonadarche; children can experience gonadarche without adrenarche and children

enter adrenarche in the absence of activation of the GnRH system. Specifically, adrenarche is not accompanied by increases in gonadal steroids, testosterone and estradiol, hormones that are essential for ovulation, spermatogenesis, and reproduction. Thus, the evolutionary significance of the timing of adrenarche is irrelevant to reproduction. In brief, family environment appears to affect a puberty-related event, adrenarche, that is not related to reproduction suggesting a reconsideration of the role of family environment and early timing of puberty as a reproductive strategy.

A limitation of many of the studies on family and contextual influences on age of onset of puberty or menarche is that they are cross-sectional or short-term longitudinal. Belsky et al. (2007) overcame this limitation by capitalizing on a 12-year longitudinal design to assess the effects of family influences on timing of puberty. Other major strengths of the study were that it included boys *and* girls and mothers and fathers, the adolescents had annual repeated assessments of pubertal development by trained nurses and physicians during puberty, and both family structure and process were considered. The results were both consistent and inconsistent with earlier findings. Rearing experiences predicted pubertal timing among girls but not boys. There are too few studies that included boys to know how to evaluate the consistency of this finding. Maternal age at menarche was a stronger predictor of girls' pubertal development than were early rearing conditions suggesting the strength of the genetic influence on timing of menarche. A unique finding was that early maternal harsh control at 54 months and at first and third grade predicted earlier menarche. An additional novel finding was that negative experiences with fathers and mothers predicted earlier age of menarche. In summary, the study yielded multiple novel findings supporting the influence of parenting characteristics on timing of puberty and menarche. A prominent limitation of the study is the small effect size and the limited number of significant findings.

Nonetheless, it is noteworthy that any effects emerged given the extended time frame of the study and the major genetic influences on timing of puberty.

Explanations are varied regarding the mechanisms involved in father absence, family disruption and timing of puberty. The studies based on the evolutionary model imply a causal relation between family disruption/ father absence and timing of age at menarche or timing of puberty. One explanation is that a stressful family environment characterized by family conflict, absence of a biological father, poverty, and accompanying low parental investment creates an internalizing disorder that lowers metabolism, thereby inciting a weight gain that in turn accelerates menarche (Belsky, et al., 1991; Ellis & Essex, 2007). Recent evidence raises questions regarding mechanisms involved in weight and earlier puberty. Heavier weight status even during the preschool- and school-age period predicted earlier timing of puberty (Davison et al., 2003; Lee et al., 2007). The question, then, is: How does this early weight gain affect timing of puberty? To test the hypothesis that family environment and weight status in combination are mechanisms involved in early timing of puberty, future studies need to be longitudinal from infancy to the onset of puberty.

Family influences on acceleration of timing of puberty and menarche are based on the assumption that the family environment is stressful, likely arising from the unpredictability of parental absence, psychopathology, and other forms of family disruption. However, objectively measured stress is not part of the design of the studies, for the most part. Stress is merely implied by family conflict, poverty, and father absence or stepparenting. What is needed are good measures of subjective aspects of stress as well as the neuroendocrine indices of stress in family members to establish the mechanisms involved in stress and timing of puberty.

Noteworthy is that the acceleration and life history perspectives on stress and reproduction are at odds with the neuroendocrinology of reproduction. Cortisol exerts inhibitory effects on reproduction at the levels of the GnRH neuron, the pituitary gonadotroph (responsible for secreting LH and FSH), and the gonad itself, thereby suppressing sex steroids (T and estrogen) and delaying maturation of reproductive function and physical growth (See Susman, Reiter, Ford, & Dorn, 2002). That is, CRH, ACTH, and cortisol suppress the reproductive axis. In brief, theories regarding putative family stress and timing of puberty or menarche run counter to the well-known physiology of stress and reproduction. The two sets of evidence can be reconciled nonetheless. Although acute stress may suppress reproductive functioning, chronic stress may release gonadotropins and sex steroids from the downregulating effects of CRH, ACTH, and cortisol. Family stress is likely to be of long duration, thus attenuating the classic acute response to stress. To advance the field, future studies would benefit from including: (1) objective indices of family stress, family structure and interactions, and reliable and valid measures of timing of puberty and menarche; and (2) longitudinal assessment of early family adversity and the neurobiology of stress and reproduction for long periods prior to the onset of puberty.

Genetics can be an alternative explanation to the evolutionary model of family relations and timing of puberty (See Mendle et al., 2006). Girls who mature early tend to have earlier sexual activity, and earlier age of first marriage and first birth, which increases the probability of divorce and lower quality paternal investment. Puberty, sexual, and reproductive timing may be genetically programmed (Ellis et al., 1999). Mothers who are early maturers tend to have daughters who are early maturers (Brooks-Gunn & Warren, 1989), suggesting a genetic linkage. In addition, the androgen receptor (AR) gene has been used as an explanation of the effect of father absence on age of menarche (Comings, Muhleman, Johnson, & MacMurray, 2002). Shorter alleles of the X-linked AR gene are associated with aggression, greater numbers of sexual partners, impulsivity, and divorce in males, and with early age of menarche in females (Comings et al.). The same genes may predispose children to early timing and early sexual activity. Comings et al. also reminded the field that there are paternal as well as maternal influences on age of menarche. The same genetic factors that influence a man's likelihood to abandon marriages may also contribute to an earlier age of menarche in female offspring.

Mendle et al. (2006) tested an alternative hypothesis that nonrandom selection into step-fathering families related to shared environmental and/or genetic predispositions leads to a spurious relation between stepfathering and earlier menarche (also discussed earlier in this chapter). Using the controls for genetic and shared environmental experiences offered by the children-of-twins design, cousins discordant for stepfathering were found not to differ in age of menarche. Moreover, controlling for mother's age of menarche eliminated differences in menarcheal age associated with stepfathering in unrelated girls. These findings strongly suggest that selection and not causation accounts for the relationship between stepfathering and early menarche.

As an argument counter to genetic influences, it could be proposed that the effect is still there between family environmental factors and timing of puberty when mothers' age of menarche is controlled. Mothers' age of menarche could be considered a poor control for genetic influences. Age of menarche is a broad proxy for a genetic influence, and there is significant error of measurement in retrospective recall of age of menarche. Molecular genetics approaches yielding new genetic markers will likely be illustrative of the complexity of genetic influences on timing of puberty in functional and disruptive families.

Mechanisms Involved in Timing of Puberty and Adjustment

The mechanisms relating timing of puberty and psychosocial adjustment, as discussed here and elsewhere, remain an empirical largely unknown. The findings are based on not well-articulated theories and few mechanisms are proposed to explain the authenticated connection between timing of puberty and a diverse array of behaviors, emotions, and disorders and family structure and functioning. What then are the possible explanations for the long-standing connection between timing of puberty and psychological development? The explanation can be separated into two broad categories: social/contextual and brain development. Social/contextual explanations include peers, family, school, and the broader social ecology of youth. A fairly consistent explanation of earlier maturation and deviant behavior is that early maturers tend to associate with older and deviant peers. Older deviant peers may perceive the early-maturing adolescent as older than his/her stated age and include the early-maturing adolescent in adult-like deviant behaviors that include substance use and risky sexual activity. In the case of sexually risky behaviors, early-maturing girls also may be preyed upon by older boys and men, as these males perceive the girls as inexperienced and vulnerable to sexual coercion. Later maturing boys and girls may be protected by their childish appearance and are excluded by older, deviant peers.

Family members and teachers exert influences on an off-time maturing adolescent via expectations and social roles. The juvenile appearance of a late-maturing adolescent can lead to assigning less responsibility and independence to the childlike-appearing adolescent with the consequence to the adolescent of not being allowed to participate in peer activities that may lead to deviance or result in fewer opportunities to develop competencies. Similarly, institutions in the wider social environment, such as church groups and clubs, may assign less independent and challenging tasks to the immature-appearing adolescents.

The relationship between brain development, timing of puberty, and adjustment is now only beginning to be considered. Briefly, the question is whether there is asynchrony between higher order functions like decision making and impulse control and emotional areas of the brain and hypothalamic functioning and the reactivation of the GnRH axis. Steinberg (in press) suggests an explanation for the association of brain development and risk taking that can be applied to timing of puberty and risk taking as well. As previously discussed, early-maturing adolescents may not have the social decision-making skills and impulse control required to avoid risky situations.

Puberty and Obesity

The higher weight status of early timing adolescents, as previously discussed, has led to the suggestion that the increase in obesity is responsible for the earlier timing of puberty. Adolescents worldwide are now considered overweight or obese, and there is virtually no evidence that the epidemic is subsiding, which is an alarming trend, given the association of obesity with cardiovascular disease and diabetes and other chronic diseases (Dietz, 1998; Katzmarzyk, Tremblay, Pérusse, Després, & Bouchard, 2003). The increase in BMI in the United States in particular may be related to various eating behaviors characterized by high-energy dense foods. For example, in a review by Biro, Khoury, and Morrison (2006), calorie consumption has increased across the last three or so decades with high increases in soft drinks and snacks that are salty and lower intake of milk. Further, overweight adolescents seem to be particularly vulnerable to consumeing more in a fast-food setting. With respect to activity, the Biro, Khoury et al. review also provides evidence that physical activity decreases across adolescence, and there is some evidence that the amount of television viewing and computer-related games may have an impact on weight status.

Puberty is a sensitive period for the development of overweight and obesity, since body fat increases secondary to pubertal development (Dietz, 1997). Early sexual maturation is related to obesity and overweight in adolescence and is carried over to the young adult years (Bratberg et al., 2007) and appears to have a heritable intergenerational component (Ong et al., 2007). Environmental factors may

also play a role in weight status during puberty. For example, Belsky et al. (1991) proposed that a stressful family environment, characterized by family conflict, absence of a biological father, poverty, and resultant insufficient parenting, predisposes girls to develop an internalizing disorder that lowers metabolism, thereby inciting weight gain that accelerates the timing of menarche. Overall, the psychological consequences of weight status are only beginning to be addressed, but it is increasingly clear that another negative consequence of early puberty is overweight and obesity.

Puberty and Bone Health

In this section we provide an example of the importance that puberty can have on accrual of bone mineral density (BMD) or bone mineral content (BMC) and, in turn, how depression may play a role in bone health. Over 40% of BMD is accrued in adolescence, with the majority of accrual occurring in the two years surrounding menarche (Glastre et al., 1990). During these two years, as much bone is laid down as is lost in the last four decades of life (Bailey, Mirwald, McKay, & Faulkner, 2000). Thus, building an adequate store of bone mineral is crucial during this period to decrease the chance of becoming osteoporotic in the post-menopausal years. Optimum accrual depends on one's genetic and familial background, but lifestyle and behavioral factors such as exercise, nutrition, and smoking also influence accrual. Timing of puberty has been shown to have an impact on bone accrual. Later pubertal timing (later menarche) girls had lower BMD (Galuska & Sowers, 1999). The explanation is that later maturing girls have less estrogen exposure, and estrogen produces strong bones. In brief, a later maturer has fewer ovulations and menstrual cycles and in turn, less lifetime estrogen exposure.

Where does depression fit into the puberty–bone density model? In the adult literature, there is generally a strong association between depression and BMD. Individuals with depression or who report depressive symptoms are more likely to have osteoporosis or lower BMD (Eskandari et al., 2007; Jacka et al., 2005; Schweiger, Weber, Deuschle, & Heuser, 2000; Yazici, Akinci, Sütçü, & Ozçakar, 2003; Michelson et al., 1996). It is not known if this relationship holds true in adolescents. If one considers that rates of depression become higher in girls during puberty (Costello, Mustillo, Erkanli, Keeler, & Angold, 2003) and that early maturers are more vulnerable to depression (Hayward et al., 1997; Kaltiala-Heino, Marttunen, Rantanen, & Rimpela, 2003), early timing of puberty may also contribute to bone density. Recognized is that other factors may influence both bone health and depression during puberty, and these include smoking and change in exercise and eating habits.

Puberty and Sleep

The media frequently describes findings on the sequelae of lack of sleep in adolescents. Factors responsible for this lack of sleep are lack of parental monitoring, peer interactions and influences, pervasive use of television and communication media (cell phones and text messaging), music devices, and Internet surfing. Sleep characteristics of adolescence began to receive systematic attention in the last two decades. Carskadon, Acebo, & Jenni (2004) have produced seminal work showing the systematic changes that occur in the sleep patterns of adolescents. This research showed that there is a major shift in sleep characteristics during the pubertal period. The total amount of sleep decreases, and there is an increase in daytime sleepiness (Carskadon & Acebo, 2002; Dahl & Lewin, 2002). There is also a major shift in time of onset of sleep and time of awakening, referred to as phase delay. Phase delay is related to stage of puberty independent of age, suggesting that the biological changes of puberty have links to changes in sleep patterns (Carskadon, Vieira, & Acebo, 1993; see also Carskadon et al., 1997; Carskadon, Wolfson, Acebo, Tzischinskky, & Seifer, 1998; Carskadon & Acebo, 2002). The preference

for later onset and offset of sleep and societal demands for early school attendance results in an asynchrony in the biological and social needs of adolescents.

Changes in sleep quality and duration during puberty can be justified based on biological and social changes that occur at puberty. First, sleep is associated with the same hormones involved with endocrine changes of puberty (Knutson, 2005). For example, growth hormone–releasing hormone that is produced in abundance during puberty appears to be important in the regulation of sleep (Steiger & Holsboer, 1997). Ghrelin improves slow-wave sleep, which is the deeper stages of non-rapid eye movement (REM) sleep (Steiger, 2003). Sleep deprivation resulted in a stronger increase of slow-wave activity in Tanner 5 (39% above baseline) than in Tanner 1–2 adolescents (18% above baseline). Additional findings show that the buildup of homeostatic sleep pressure during wakefulness was slower in Tanner 5 adolescents compared with Tanner Stage 1–2 children (8.9 +/– 1.2 hours) (Jenni, Achermann, & Carskadon, 2005). The social changes of adolescence, such as increasing interaction with peers, have not been examined in relation to the changes in sleep quality and duration. An unfortunate side effect of lower duration of sleep is its association with obesity. Shorter sleep duration in third and sixth grade was independently associated with obesity at sixth grade (Lumeng et al., 2007).

A contributing factor to sleep problems during adolescence is morningness/eveningness (M/E) preference. M/E refers to a preference for activities in the morning or evening. Support was found for the hypothesis that trait circadian preference mediates mood, daytime functioning, and academic grades through its effect on sleep variables at school time. It was concluded that whereas the imposition of school schedules negatively impacted mood and daytime functioning for the sample as a whole, evening-oriented adolescents were the most vulnerable to poorer outcomes (Warner, Murray, & Meyer, in press). Eveningness students obtained poorer quality and less sleep than morning-oriented students and were more likely to exhibit antisocial behavior (Warner et al., in press; Susman et al., 2007). The evening-preference adolescent gets less sleep and, as a result, has difficulty concentrating and controlling impulses.

What Do We Know for Sure About Puberty and Development?

It is a given that puberty is an essential stage of reproductive development that has challenged scholars and scientists, communities and teachers, as well as parents and adolescents themselves. The degree to which adolescents experience mood and behavior changes during puberty varies considerably. Across time, much has become known about both the biological and psychological changes that occur at puberty. First, in the past several decades, discoveries have documented the neuroendocrine processes of puberty due primarily to technological advances in molecular biology and other life sciences, hormone assay development, and strong empirical studies in lower animal models, as well as in studies of humans. Second, in the psychosocial literature, studies are relatively consistent in pointing to early pubertal development as being behaviorally and psychologically problematic, primarily for girls. Such studies have generally focused on negative outcomes related to mood disturbances and risky behaviors and have used timing of puberty variables in associative or predictive models. Third, the measurement of pubertal progression has been examined in detail so that investigators now have access to assessments of the appropriateness of different measures of pubertal development, depending on the research question. Fourth, research on the psychological effects of pubertal development has become based on more complex theoretical and statistical models than in the past. These complex models are characterized by multiple levels of analysis that combine "protein to population" levels. Recent work on identification of genes and proteins that are responsible for the onset of puberty represent

the most basic level of analysis. At the population level, the ADD Health study has produced an abundance of information on sexual, psychological, and social influences on the U.S. population of adolescents. In addition, contextual variables are now being examined as mediators or moderators that may impact associations of biological pubertal processes on psychological outcomes. These multiple-level studies offer a richness of detail that has never before been available to scientists of adolescent development.

What We Would Like to Know in the Future and Some Conclusions

Although the knowledge regarding puberty and its role in psychological development has certainly expanded, much is left to be uncovered. Puberty's "effects on health and wellbeing are considered profound and paradoxical" (Patton & Viner, 2007, p. 1130). Thus, the topic warrants further attention as a way of improving psychological and physical health and developmental outcomes in youth. Some of the gaps in the literature are as follows:

1. There is an asynchrony between medical and psychological research with regard to biological and psychological issues inherent in the consequences of pubertal status and pubertal timing. However, the medical research community has identified the significant impact of altered timing of puberty (e.g., precocious puberty and premature adrenarche) on current health or later adult health problems (Golub et al., 2008; see review by Dorn, 2007). For instance, there is now a growing recognition of the association between timing of puberty and adult disease, particularly reproductive cancers. There is also growing recognition in the medical community that the downward secular trend in timing of puberty may precipitate psychosocial and health problems by compromising growth, increasing the risk of early and

risky sexual activity, potential sexual abuse, and inappropriate expectation by others (Golub et al.). What we would like to know is whether these early psychosocial problems have adult psychological sequelae. As a beginning, basic knowledge on the mechanisms involved in early or late timing of puberty and psychosocial functioning is needed. As an additional issue, there is a continuing need for health policy that continues surveillance of human adolescents to define and refine the mechanisms of altered timing of puberty. For instance, screening for exposure to endocrine disruptors is a promising trend for the future. There is also asynchrony between the psychological and medical community in the precision of measuring puberty; its measurement has often lacked rigor in psychological studies. Whether puberty is a cause, correlate, or confound of the outcomes of interest, it can play a leading role in study outcomes and therefore deserves scrutiny in both the medical and psychological community.

2. Health and developmental problems of adolescence are complex and require an interdisciplinary focus. The roots of psychological and behavioral problems stem from, or contribute to, brain–behavior interactions, family dysfunction, reproduction and physical morphological changes, and peers. These inherent complex features of puberty mandate that research scientists are obligated to collaborate across disciplinary lines. The richness and expertise of each discipline in terms of methods, measures, and theoretical and empirical–statistical models could ultimately lead to an empirically based body of research to enhance prevention and intervention efforts. An area of inquiry with rich interdisciplinary attention is that of brain development. Cognitive functioning research from a neurobiological perspective appears to be an area already beginning to develop. Such functioning as

assessed by neuropsychologists and functional and structural brain imaging neuroscientists and neurologists, in combination with behavioral scientists, holds much promise for understanding adolescent behavior. A challenge for the scientific community is to garner funding support for such valuable interdisciplinary efforts.

3. Longitudinal studies with rigorous methodology for measuring puberty as well as other biological and psychological parameters are an additional necessary step in solving complex research problems encountered in pubertal-age adolescents. Several sources have commented on appropriate measures and methodologies for studies of pubertal development (Dorn et al., 2006; Euling et al., 2008). Future longitudinal studies will yield the most payoff by beginning to assess the biological and behavioral roots of pubertal processes by beginning at an early age so as to capture pubertal onset and the range of pubertal changes through adrenarche and gonadarche. Needed in these longitudinal assessments are better biomarkers of onset and progression of puberty, such as genomic and hormone assay studies. A collateral consideration is that to understand the role of puberty on psychological development, longer term perspectives are essential. We do not know for certain whether the links between internalizing and externalizing behavior are a result of puberty per se or whether they represent continuity from earlier phases of development.

4. Fourth, mechanisms impacting puberty and, in turn, its effect on psychological development need further examination. For example, we know little about why pubertal timing is early or late and whether timing is a consequence of genetics, environmental factors, other influences, or a combination of these processes. In turn, we do not know why early pubertal timing is generally negative for girls but positive or neutral for boys. Nor do we know why timing of

puberty seems to have less of an impact on boys than on girls, at least in the psychosocial arena. Importantly, there is a very small amount of knowledge on the positive effects of puberty on development. The majority of studies to date have focused on negative outcomes of puberty with a minority focused on positive youth development. For some adolescents, puberty is a positive sign of emerging adolescence, adulthood, independence, and respect. For others, puberty and its rapid physical growth may enhance self-esteem and vigor and be a protective influence for depression and anxiety.

5. Much more research needs to be carried out regarding structure and function of brain development across puberty. Since most studies have measured change only across chronological age rather than pubertal stage, appropriately little can be said about neuroendocrine changes and brain development as they relate to the external manifestations of puberty. Briefly, we need to know if pubertal status and pubertal timing are related to brain structure and function and, in turn, how those changes may or may not be related to emotions and cognitions as well as behavioral outcomes.

A concluding note is not complete without mentioning the current state of prevention and intervention to reduce problems of youth and increase positive youth development. The current state of knowledge regarding puberty and timing of puberty offers insights into prevention and intervention efforts. One issue is that most parents and school systems have not caught up with the importance of earlier timing of puberty in the health and development of adolescents. As previously indicated, earlier timing, especially for girls, is associated with and predictive of internalizing and externalizing problems, interactions with older and perhaps deviant peers, and early and risky sexual behavior. Thus, earlier maturing adolescents require earlier risk education efforts than their on-time peers on issues of

normal sexual development, risky behaviors, relationships, and Internet safety. Parents, the educational system, and health care providers also are encouraged to undertake earlier health promotion and disease prevention efforts with the aim of assisting adolescents to cope with peer expectations, early sexual development, and expectations for mature behavior.

It also may be advantageous to approach adolescents in a more creative manner than in educational programs that currently are available. For instance, adolescents are likely to be interested in new information about brain development during puberty and adolescence, especially if it is presented via the Internet. Specifically, adolescents should be assured that decision making will be difficult in some instances as brain structures and functions are still developing and adult decisions may be beyond their grasp. Adolescents need to be provided with the assurance that asking others for help is healthy and expected. Within this neurobiological approach, an aim could be to familiarize the adolescent with the awareness that since brains are still developing, they may be highly vulnerable to insults (e.g., negative effect of substance use) that have the potential for affecting academic performance and emotions later in life. In brief, an adolescent-friendly approach that emphasizes the developing brain and decision making is warranted. The effort to mount such an approach is daunting to consider but offers a novel approach to adolescent health promotion.

Finally, scientists, clinicians, and policy makers have not had an established venue for sharing new scientific information that is relevant to pubertal neurobiological processes and the psychological, health, and societal implications of timing of puberty and its wide-ranging impact on development. Similarly, funding agencies tend not to adopt an interdisciplinary approach to basic science, health promotion, or social policy regarding puberty and adolescence more broadly. Conversations and formal organizational structures to guarantee cross discipline and interagency collaboration is most assuredly guaranteed to improve the health and development of adolescents and their families in the next decade.

REFERENCES

Adelson, J. (1980). *Handbook of adolescent development*. New York: John Wiley & Sons.

Alsaker, F. (1995). Is puberty a critical period for socialization? *Journal of Adolescence, 18*, 427–444.

Anderson, S. E., Dallal, G. E., & Must, A. (2003). Relative weight and race influence average age at menarche: Results from two nationally representative surveys of U.S. girls studied 25 years apart. *Pediatrics, 111*, 844–850.

Anderson, S. E., & Must, A. (2005). Interpreting the continued decline in the average age at menarche: Results from two nationally representative surveys of U.S. girls studied 10 years apart. *Journal of Pediatrics, 147*, 753–760.

Andersson, T., & Magnusson, D. (1990). Biological maturation in adolescence and the development of drinking habits and alcohol abuse among young males: A prospective longitudinal study. *Journal of Youth and Adolescence, 19*, 33–41.

Angold, A., Costello, E. J., & Worthman, C. W. (1998). Puberty and depression: The role of age, pubertal status, and pubertal timing. *Psychological Medicine, 28*, 51–61.

Angold, A., Costello, E. J., Erkanli, A., & Worthman, C. (1999). Pubertal changes in hormone levels and depression in girls. *Psychological Medicine, 29*, 1043–1053.

Bailey, D. A., Mirwald, R. L., McKay, H. A., & Faulkner, R. A. (2000). Adolescent bone mineral gain compared to postmenopausal loss. *Journal of Bone and Mineral Research, 15*, S202.

Bandura, A. (1978). Social learning theory of aggression. *Journal of Communication, 28*, 12–19.

Banerjee, I., & Clayton, P. (2008). The genetic basis for the timing of human puberty. *Journal of Neuroendocrinology, 19*, 831–838.

Belsky, J., Steinberg, L., & Draper, P. (1991). Childhood experience, interpersonal development, and reproductive strategy: An evolutionary theory of socialization. *Child Development, 62*, 647–670.

Belsky, J., Steinberg, L. D., Houts, R. M., Friedman, S. L., DeHart, G., Cauffman, E., et al. (2007). Family rearing antecedents of pubertal timing. *Child Development, 78*, 1302–1321.

Bergsten-Brucefors, A. (1976). A note on the accuracy of recalled age at menarche. *Annals of Human Biology, 3*, 71–73.

Biro, F. M. (2006). Puberty—whither goest? *Journal of Pediatric & Adolescent Gynecology, 19*, 163–165.

Biro, F., Huang, B., Crawford, P., Lucky, A., Stiegel-Moore, R., Barton, B. A., et al. (2006). Pubertal correlates in Black and White girls. *Journal of Pediatrics, 148*, 234–240.

Biro, F. M., Khoury, P., & Morrison, J. A. (2006). Influence of obesity on timing of puberty. *International Journal of Andrology, 29*, 272–277.

Biro, F. M., & Dorn, L. D. (2005). Puberty and adolescent sexuality. *Pediatric Annals, 34*, 777–784.

Biro, F. M., Lucky, A. W., Simbartl, L. A., Barton, B. A., Daniels, S. R., Striegel-Moore, R. H., et al. (2003). Pubertal maturation in girls and the relationship to anthropometric changes: Pathways through puberty. *Journal of Pediatrics, 142*, 643–646.

Blos, P. (1962). *On adolescence: A psychoanalytical interpretation*. New York: Free Press.

Bogaert, A. F. (2008). Menarche and father absence in a national probablity sample. *Journal of Biosocial Science, 40*, 623–36.

Bongiovanni, A. M. (1983). An epidemic of premature thelarche in Puerto Rico. *Journal of Pediatrics, 103*, 245–246.

Bratberg, G. H., Nilsen, T. I., Holmen, T. L., & Vatten, L. J. (2007). Early sexual maturation, central adiposity and subsequent overweight in late adolescence. A four-year follow-up of 1605 adolescent Norwegian boys and girls: The Young HUNT study. *BMC Public Health, 7*, 54.

Bronfenbrenner, U. (1979). *The ecology of human development*. Cambridge, MA: Harvard University Press.

Brooks-Gunn, J., Petersen, A. C., & Eichorn, D. (1985). The study of maturational timing effects in adolescence. *Journal of Youth and Adolescence, 14*, 149–161.

Brooks-Gunn, J., & Warren, M. P. (1989). Biological and social contributions to negative affect in young adolescent girls. *Child Development, 60*, 40–55.

Buck Louis, G. M., Gray, L. E. J., Marcus, M., Ojeda, S. R., Pescovitz, O. H., Witchel, S. F., et al. (2008). Environmental factors and puberty timing: Expert panel research needs. *Pediatrics, 121*, S192–S207.

Carskadon, M. A., & Acebo, C. (2002). Regulation of sleepiness in adolescents: Update, insights, and speculation. *Sleep, 25*, 606–614.

Carskadon, M. A., Acebo, C., & Jenni, O. G. (2004). Regulation of adolescent sleep: Implications for behavior. *Annals of the New York Academy of Sciences, 1021*, 276–291.

Carskadon, M. A., Acebo, C., Richardson, G. S., Tate, B. A., & Seifer, R. (1997). An approach to studying circadian rhythms of adolescent humans. *Journal of Biological Rhythms, 12*, 278–289.

Carskadon, M. A., Vieira, C., & Acebo, C. (1993). Associations between puberty and delayed phase preference. *American Sleep Disorders Association and Sleep Research Society, 16*, 258–262.

Carskadon, M. A., Wolfson, A. R., Acebo, C., Tzischinsky, O., & Seifer, R. (1998). Adolescent sleep patterns, circadian timing, and sleepiness at a transition to early school days. *Sleep, 21*, 871–881.

Casey, B. J., Jones, R. M., & Hare, T. A. (2008). The adolescent brain. *Annals New York Academy of Sciences, 1124*, 111–126.

Casey, V. A., Dwyer, J., Colman, K. A., Krall, E. A., Gardner, J., & Valadian, I. (1991). Accuracy of recall by middle-aged participants in a longitudinal study of their body size and indices of maturation earlier in life. *Annals of Human Biology, 18*, 155–166.

Caspi, A., & Moffitt, T. (1991). Individual differences are accentuated during periods of social change: The sample case of girls at puberty. *Journal of Personality and Social Psychology, 61*, 157–168.

Catalano, R. F., Haggerty, K. P., Oesterle, S., Fleming, C. B., & Hawkins, J. D. (2004). The importance of bonding to school for healthy development: Findings from the Social Development Research Group. *Journal of School Health, 74*, 252–261.

Chumlea, W. C., Schubert, C. M., Roche, A. F., Kulin, H. E., Lee, P. A., Himes, J. H., et al. (2003). Age at menarche and racial comparisons in U.S. girls. *Pediatrics, 111*, 110–113.

Comas, A. P. (1982). Precocious sexual development in Puerto Rico. *Lancet, 1*, 1299–1300.

Comings, D., Muhleman, D., Johnson, J., & MacMurray, J. (2002). Parent–daughter transmission of androgen receptor gene as an explanation of the effect of father absence on age of menarche. *Child Development, 73*, 1046–1051.

Costello, E. J., Angold, A., Burns, B. J., Stangl, D. K., Tweed, D. L., Erkanli, A., et al. (1996). The Great Smokey Mountains Study of Youth: Goals, design, methods, and the prevalence of DSM-III-R disorders. *Archives of General Psychiatry, 53*, 1129–1136.

Costello, E. J., Mustillo, S., Erkanli, A., Keeler, G., & Angold, A. (2003). Prevalence and development of psychiatric disorders in childhood and adolescence. *Archives of General Psychiatry, 60*, 837–844.

Costello, E. J., Sung, M., Worthman, C., & Angold, A. (2007). Pubertal maturation and the development of alcohol use and abuse. *Drug & Alcohol Dependence. 88*(Suppl 1), S50–S59.

Dahl, R. E. (2004). Adolescent brain development: A period of vulnerabilities and opportunities *Annals of the New York Academy of Sciences, 1021*, 1–22.

Dahl, R. E., & Lewin, D. S. (2002). Pathways to adolescent health sleep regulation and behavior. *Journal of Adolescent Health, 31*(6 Suppl), 175–184.

Damon, A., & Bajema, C. J. (1974). Age at menarche: Accuracy of recall after thirty-nine years. *Human Biology, 46*, 381–384.

Davison, K. K., Susman, E. J., & Birch, L. L. (2003). Percent body fat at age 5 predicts earlier pubertal development among girls at age 9. *Pediatrics, 111*, 815–821.

Delemarre-van de Waal, H. A. (2005). Secular trend of timing of puberty. *Endocrine Development, 8*, 1–14.

Demerath, E., Li, J., Sun, S. S., Chumlea, W. C., Remsberg, K. E., Czerwinski, S. A., et al. (2004). Fifty-year trends in serial body mass index during adolescence in girls: The Fels Longitudinal Study. *American Journal of Clinical Nutrition, 80*, 441–446.

Dick, D. M., Rose, R. J., Kaprio, J., & Viken, R. (2000). Pubertal timing and substance use: Associations between and within families across late adolescence. *Developmental Psychology, 36*, 180–189.

Dietz, W. H. (1997). Periods of risk in childhood for the development of adult obesity—what do we need to learn? *Journal of Nutrition, 127*, 1884S–1886S.

Dietz, W. H. (1998). Health consequences of obesity in youth: Childhood predictors of adult disease. *Pediatrics, 101*, 518–525.

Dorn, L. D., Hitt, S. F., & Rotenstein, D. (1999). Biopsychological and cognitive differences in children with premature vs. on-time adrenarche. *Archives of Pediatrics and Adolescent Medicine, 153*, 137–146.

Dorn, L. D. (2007). Psychological abnormalities associated with premature adrenarche and precocious puberty. In O. Pescovitz & E. Walvoord (Eds.), *When puberty is precocious: Scientific and clinical aspects* (pp. 309–330). Totowa, NJ: Humana Press.

Dorn, L. D., Dahl, R. E., Woodward, H. R., & Biro, F. (2006). Defining the boundaries of early adolescence: A user's guide to assessing pubertal status and pubertal timing in research with adolescents. *Applied Developmental Science, 10*, 30–56.

Dorn, L. D., Rose, S. R., Rotenstein, D., Susman, E. J., Huang, B., Loucks, T. L., et al. (2008). Differences in endocrine parameters and psychopathology in girls with premature adrenarche versus on-time adrenarche. *Journal of Pediatric Endocrinology & Metabolism, 21*, 439–448.

Dorn, L. D., Ponirakis, A., & Susman, E. J. (2003). Pubertal timing and adolescent adjustment and behavior: Conclusions vary by rater. *Journal of Youth and Adolescence, 32*, 157–167.

Doughty, D., & Rodgers, J. L. (Eds.). (2000). *Behavior genetic modeling of menarche in U.S. females*. Boston: Kluwer Academic Publishers.

Draper, P., & Harpending, H. (1982). Father absence and reproductive strategy: An evolutionary perspective. *Journal of Anthropological Research, 58*, 255–273.

Ellis, B. J. (2004). Timing of pubertal maturation in girls: An integrated life history approach. *Psychological Bulletin, 130*, 920–958.

Ellis, B. J., Bates, J. E., Dodge, K. A., Fergusson, D. M., Horwood, L. J., Pettit, G. S., et al. (2003). Does father absence place daughters at special risk for early sexual activity and teenage pregnancy? *Child Development, 74*, 801–821.

Ellis, B. J., & Essex, M. J. (2007). Family environments, adrenarche, and sexual maturation: A longitudinal test of a life history model. *Child Development, 78*, 1799–1817.

Ellis, B. J., & Garber, J. (2000). Psychosocial antecedents of variation in girls' pubertal timing: Maternal depression, stepfather presence, and marital and family stress. *Child Development, 71*, 485–501.

Ellis, B. J., McFadyen-Ketchum, S., Dodge, K. A., Pettit, G. A., & Bates, J. E. (1999). Quality of early family relationships and individual differences in the timing of pubertal maturation in girls: A longitudinal test of an evolutionary model. *Journal of Personality and Social Psychology, 77*, 387–401.

Emans, S. J., & Biro, F. (1998). Secondary sexual characteristics and menses in young girls. *Pediatrics, 101*, 949–950.

Eskandari, F., Martinez, P., Torvik, S., Phillips, T., Sternberg, E., Mistry, S., et al. (2007). Low bone mass in premenopausal women with depression. *Archives of Internal Medicine, 167*, 2329–2336.

Euling, S. Y., Herman-Giddens, M. E., Lee, P. A., Selevan, S. G., Juul, A., Sørensen, T. I., et al. (2008). Examination of U.S. puberty—timing data from 1940 to 1994 for secular trends: Panel findings. *Pediatrics, 121*, S172–S191.

Fernandez-Fernandez, R., Martini, A. C., Navarro, V. M., Castellano, J. M., Dieguez, C., Aguilar, E., et al. (2006). Novel signals for the integration of energy balance and reproduction. *Molecular & Cellular Endocrinology, 254–255*, 127–132.

Freedman, D. S., Khan, L. K., Mei, Z., Dietz, W. H., Srinivasan, S. R., & Berenson, G. S. (2002). Relation of childhood height to obesity among adults: The Bogalusa Heart Study. *Pediatrics, 109*, E23–E29.

Freud, A. (1958). Adolescence. *Psychoanalytic Study of the Child, 13*, 255–278.

Freud, S. (1998). The transformations of puberty. In M. Perret-Catipovic & F. Ladame (Eds.), *Adolescence and psychoanalysis: The story and the history* (pp. 16–42). London: Karnac Books.

Galuska, D. A., & Sowers, M. R. (1999). Menstrual history and bone density in young women. *Journal of Women's Health and Gender-Based Medicine, 8*, 647–656.

Ge, X., Conger, R. D., & Elder, G. H. (2001a). The relation between puberty and psychological distress in adolescent boys. *Journal of Research on Adolescence, 11*, 49–70.

Ge, X., Conger, R. D., & Elder, G. H., Jr. (2001b). Pubertal transition, stressful life events, and the emergence of gender differences in depressive symptoms during adolescence. *Developmental Psychology, 37*, 404–417.

Ge, X., Brody, G. H., Conger, R. D., Simons, R. L., & Murry, V. (2002). Contextual amplification of pubertal transitional effect on African American children's problem behaviors. *Developmental Psychology, 38*, 42–54.

Ge, X., Kim, I. J., Brody, G. H., Conger, R. D., Simons, R. L., Gibbons, F. X., et al. (2003). It's about timing and change: Pubertal transition effects on symptoms of major depression among African American youths. *Developmental Psychology, 39*, 430–439.

Giedd, J. N. (2004). Structural magnetic resonance imaging of the adolescent brain. *Annals of the New York Academy of Sciences, 77*.

Giedd, J. N. (2008). The teen brain: Insights from neuroimaging. *Journal of Adolescent Health, 42*, 335–343.

Giedd, J. N., Blumenthal, J., Jeffries, N. O., Castellanos, F. X., Liu, H., Zijdenbos, A., et al. (1999). Brain development during childhood and adolescence: A longitudinal MRI study. *Nature Neuroscience, 2*, 861–863.

Glastre, C., Braillon, P., David, L., Cochat, P., Meunier, P. J., & Delmas, P. D. (1990). Measurement of bone mineral content of the lumbar spine by dual x-ray absorptiometry in normal children: Correlations with growth parameters. *Journal of Clinical Endocrinology and Metabolism, 70*, 1330–1333.

Gluckman, P. D., & Hanson, M. A. (2006). Changing times: The evolution of puberty. *Molecular Cell Endocrinology, 254–255*, 26–31.

Gogtay, N., Giedd, J. N., Lusk, L., Hayashi, K. M., Greenstein, D., Vaituzis, A. C., et al. (2004). Dynamic mapping of human cortical development during childhood through early adulthood. *Proceeding of the National Academy of Science, 101*, 8174–8179.

Golub, M. S., Collman, G. W., Foster, P. M., Kimmel, C. A., Rajpert-De Meyts, E., Reiter, E. O., et al. (2008). Public health implications of altered puberty timing. *Pediatrics, 121*, S218–S230.

Goodyer, I. M., Herbert, J., & Altham, P. M. E. (1998). Adrenal steroid secretion and major depression in 8- to 16-year-olds, III. Influence of cortisol/DHEA ratio at presentation on subsequent rates of disappointing life events and persistent major depression. *Psychological Medicine, 28*, 265–273.

Goodyer, I. M., Herbert, J., Altham, P. M. E., Pearson, J., Secher, S. M., & Shiers, H. M. (1996). Adrenal secretion during major depression in 8- to 16-year-olds, I. Altered diurnal rhythms in salivary cortisol and dehydroepiandrosterone (DHEA) at presentation. *Psychological Medicine, 26*, 245–256.

Goodyer, I. M., Herbert, J., Tamplin, A., & Altham, P. M. E. (2000a). First-episode major depression in adolescents: Affective, cognitive and endocrine charactersitics of risk status and predictors of onset. *British Journal of Psychiatry, 176*, 142–149.

Goodyer, I. M., Herbert, J., Tamplin, A., & Altham, P. M. E. (2000b). Recent life events, cortisol, dehydroepiandrosterone and the onset of major depression in high-risk adolescents. *British Journal of Psychiatry, 177*, 499–504.

Graber, J. A., Brooks-Gunn, J., & Warren, M. P. (1995). The antecedents of menarcheal age: Heredity, family environment, and stressful life events. *Child Development, 66*, 346–359.

Graber, J. A., Lewinsohn, R. M., Seeley, J. R., & Brooks-Gunn, J. (1997). Is psychopathology associated with the timing of pubertal development? *Journal of the American Academy of Child and Adolescent Psychiatry, 36*, 1768–1776.

Grumbach, M. M. (2002). The neuroendocrinology of human puberty revisited. *Hormone Research, 57*, 2–14.

Hall, G. S. (1904). *Adolescence: Its psychology and its relations to psychology, anthropology, sociology, sex, crime, religion, and education.* New York: Appelton.

Hayward, C., Gotlib, I., Schraedley, P., & Litt, I. F. (1999). Ethnic differences in the association between pubertal status and symptoms of depression in adolescent girls. *Journal of Adolescent Health, 25*, 143–149.

Hayward, C., Killen, J. D., Wilson, D. M., Hammer, L. D., Litt, I. F., Kraemer, H. C., et al. (1997). Psychiatric risk associated with early puberty in adolescent girls. *Journal of the American Academy of Child and Adolescent Psychiatry, 36*, 255–262.

Herman-Giddens, M. E., Slora, E. J., Wasserman, R. C., Bourdony, C. J., Bhapkar, M. V., Koch, G. G.,et al. (1997). Secondary sexual characteristics and menses in young girls seen in office practices: A study from the Pediatric Research in Office Settings Network. *Pediatrics, 99*, 505–512.

Herman-Giddens, M. E., Wang, L., & Koch, G. (2001). Secondary sexual characteristics in boys. *Archives of Pediatric and Adolescent Medicine, 155*, 1022–1028.

Ibáñez, L., Dimartino-Nardi, J., Potau, N., & Saenger, P. (2000). Premature adrenarche—normal variant or forerunner of adult disease. *Endocrine Reviews, 21*, 671–696.

Jacka, F. N., Pasco, J. A., Henry, M. J., Kotowicz, M. A., Dodd, S., Nicholson, G. C., et al. (2005). Depression and bone mineral density in a community sample of perimenopausal women: Geelong Osteoporosis Study. *Menopause, 12*, 88–91.

Jenni, O. G., Achermann, P., & Carskadon, M. A. (2005). Homeostatic sleep regulation in adolescents. *Sleep, 28*, 1446–1454.

Jones, B., Leeton, J., McLeod, I., & Wood, C. (1972). Factors influencing the age of menarche in a lower socio-economic group in Melbourne. *Medical Journal of Australia, 2*, 533–535.

Kaltiala-Heino, R., Kosunen, E., & Rimpela, M. (2003). Pubertal timing, sexual behaviour and self-reported depression in middle adolescence. *Journal of Adolescence, 26*, 531–545.

Kaltiala-Heino, R., Marttunen, M., Rantanen, P., & Rimpela, M. (2003). Early puberty is associated with mental health problems in middle adolescence. *Social Science & Medicine, 57*, 1055–1064.

Kaplowitz, P. B. (2008). Link between body fat and the timing of puberty. *Pediatrics, 121*, S208–S217.

Kashani, J. H., Orvaschel, H., Burk, J. P., & Reid, J. C. (1985). Informant variance: The issue of parent–child disagreement.

Journal of the American Academy of Child Psychitary, 24, 437–441.

Kaltiala-Heino, R., Marttunen, M., Rantanen, P., & Rimpela, M. (2003). Early puberty is associated with mental health problems in middle adolescence. *Social Science & Medicine, 57*, 1055–1064.

Katzmarzyk, P. T., Tremblay, A., Pérusse, L., Després, J. P., & Bouchard, C. (2003). The utility of the international child and adolescent overweight guidelines for predicting coronary heart disease risk factors. *Journal of Clinical Epidemiology, 56*, 456–462.

Kim, K., & Smith, P. K. (1998a). Childhood stress, behavioural symptoms and mother–daughter pubertal development, *Journal of Adolescence, 21*, 231–240.

Kim, K., & Smith, P. K. (1998b). Retrospective survey of parental marital relations and child reproductive development. *International Journal of Behavioral Development, 22*, 729–751.

Kim, K., Smith, P. K., & Palermiti, A. L. (1997). Conflict in childhood and reproductive development. *Evolution and Human Behavior, 18*, 109–142.

Knobil, E. (1988). The hypothalamic gonadotropic hormone releasing hormone (GnRH) pulse generator in the rhesus monkey and its neuroendocrine control. *Human Reproduction, 3*, 29–31.

Knutson, K. L. (2005). Sex differences in the association between sleep and body mass index in adolescents. *Journal of Pediatrics, 147*, 830–834.

Kronenberg, H. M., Melmed, S., Polonsky, K. S., & Larsen, P. R. (Eds.). (2008). *Kronenberg: Williams Textbook of Endocrinology* (11th ed.; pp. 969–1166). Philadelphia: Elsevier.

Laitinen-Krispijn, S., van der Ende, J., & Verhulst, F. C. (1999). The role of pubertal progress in the development of depression in early adolescence. *Journal of Affective Disorders, 54*, 211–215.

Larson, R. W. (2000). Toward a psychology of positive youth development. *American Psychologist, 55*, 170–183.

Lee, J. M., Appugliese, D., Kaciroti, N., Corwyn, R. F., Bradley, R. H., & Lumeng, J. C. (2007). Weight status in young girls and the onset of puberty. *Pediatrics, 119*, e624–e630.

Lerner, R. M., Brentano, C., Dowling, E. M., & Anderson, P. M. (2002). Positive youth development: Thriving as the basis of personhood and civil society. *New Directions in Youth Development, 95*, 11–33.

Lewis, D. H. (1997). Functional brain imaging with cerebral perfusion SPECT in cerebrovascular disease, epilepsy, and trauma. *Neurosurgery Clinics of North America, 8*, 337–344.

Livson, N., & McNeill, D. (1962). The accuracy of recalled menarche. *Human Biology, 34*, 218–221.

Lumeng, J. C., Somashekar, D., Appugliese, D., Kaciroti, N., Corwyn, R. F., & Bradley, R. H. (2007). Shorter sleep duration is associated with increased risk for being overweight at ages 9 to 12 years. *Pediatrics, 120*, 1020–1028.

Marshall, W. A., & Tanner, J. M. (1969). Variations in patterns of pubertal change in girls. *Archives of Disease in Childhood, 44*, 291–303.

Marshall, W. A., & Tanner, J. (1970). Variations in the pattern of pubertal change in boys. *Archives of the Disease in Childhood, 45*, 13–23.

Martin, C. A., Logan, T. K., Portis, C., Leukefled, C. G., Lynam, D., & Staton, M. (2001). The association of testosterone with nicotine use in young adult females. *Addictive Behaviors, 26*, 279–283.

Matchock, R. L., & Susman, E. J. (2006). Family composition and menarcheal age: Anti-inbreeding strategies. *American Journal of Human Biology, 18*, 481–491.

McCarthy, M. M., Davis, A. M., & Mong, J. A. (1997). Excitatory neurotransmission and sexual differentiation of the brain. *Brain Research Bulletin, 44*, 87–95.

Mendle, J., Turkheimer, E., & Emery, R. E. (2007). Detrimental psychological outcomes associated with early pubertal timing in adolescent girls. *Developmental Review, 27*, 151–171.

Mendle, J., Turkheimer, E., D'Onofrio, B. M., Lynch, S. K., Emery, R. E., Slutske, W. S., et al. (2006). Family structure and age at menarche: A children-of-twins approach. *Developmental Psychology*, *42*, 533–542.

Michelson, D., Stratakis, C., Hill, L., Reynolds, J., Galliven, E., Chrousos, G., et al. (1996). Bone mineral density in women with depression. *New England Journal of Medicine*, *335*, 1176–1181.

Moffitt, T. E., Caspi, A., Belsky, J., & Silva, P. A. (1992). Childhood experience and onset of menarche: A test of a sociobiological model. *Child Development*, *63*, 47–58.

Morris, N. M., & Udry, J. R. (1980). Validation of a self-administered instrument to assess stage of adolescent development. *Journal of Youth and Adolescence*, *9*, 271–280.

Must, A., Phillips, S. M., Naumova, E. N., Blum, M., Harris, S., Dawson-Hughes, B., et al. (2002). Recall of early menstrual history and menarcheal body size: After 30 years, how well do women remember? *American Journal of Epidemiology*, *155*, 672–679.

Mustanski, B. S., Viken, R. J., Kaprio, J., Pulkkinen, L., & Rose, R. J. (2004). Genetic and environmental influences on pubertal development: Longitudinal data from Finnish twins at ages 11 and 14. *Developmental Psychology*, *40*, 1188–1198.

Nebesio, T. D., & Pescovitz, O. H. (2007). The role of endocrine disruptors in pubertal development. In O. H.Pescovitz & E. C. Walvoord (Eds.), *When puberty is precocious* (pp. 425–432). Totowa, NJ: Humana Press.

Neinstein, L. S. (2008). *Adolescent health care: A practical guide* (5th ed.). Baltimore: Lippincott , Williams, & Wilkins.

Nottelmann, E. D., Susman, E. J., Inoff-Germain, G. E., Cutler, G. B., Jr., Loriaux, D. L., & Chrousos, G. P. (1987). Developmental processes in American early adolescence: Relations between adolescent adjustment problems and chronologic age, pubertal stage and puberty-related serum hormone levels. *Journal of Pediatrics*, *110*, 473–480.

Offer, D., & Offer, J. (1975). *From teenage to young manhood: A psychological study*. New York: Basic Books.

Offer, D., & Schonert-Reichl, K. A. (1992). Debunking the myths of adolescence: Findings from recent research. *Journal of the American Academy of Child and Adolescent Psychiatry*, *31*, 1003–1014.

Offord, D. R., Boyle, M. H., Szatmari, P., Rae-Grant, N. I., Links, P. S., Cadman, D. T., et al. (1987). Ontario Child Health Study. II. Six-month prevalence of disorder and rates of service utilization. *Archives of General Psychiatry*, *44*, 832–836.

Ong, K. K., Northstone, K., Wells, J. C., Rubin, C., Ness, A. R., Golding, J., et al. (2007). Earlier mother's age at menarche predicts rapid infancy growth and childhood obesity. *PLoS Medicine*, *4*, e132.

Orr, D. P., & Ingersoll, G. M. (1995). The contribution of level of cognitive complexity and pubertal timing to behavioral risk in young adolescents. *Pediatrics*, *95*, 528–533.

Parent, A. S., Teilmann, G., Juul, A., Skakkebaek, N. E., Toppari, J., & Bourguignon, J. P. (2003). The timing of normal puberty and the age limits of sexual precocity: Variations around the world, secular trends, and changes after migration. *Endocrine Reviews*, *24*, 668–693.

Parker, L. N. (1991). Adrenarche. *Endocrinology and Metabolism Clinics of North America*, *20*, 71–83.

Parker, S. T. (2000). Comparative developmental evolutionary biology, anthropology, and psychology. In S. T. Parker, J. Langer, & L. M.McKinney (Eds.), *Biology, brains, and behavior* (pp. 1–24). Sante Fe: SAR Press.

Patton, G. C., & Viner, R. (2007). Pubertal transitions in health. *Lancet*, *369*, 1130–1139.

Paus, T. (2005). Mapping brain maturation and cognitive development during adolescence. *Trends in Cognitive Sciences*, *9*, 60–68.

Petersen, A. C., Crockett, L., Richards, M., & Boxer, A. (1988). A self-report measure of pubertal status: Reliability, validity, and initial norms. *Journal of Youth and Adolescence*, *17*, 117–133.

Petersen, A. C., & Taylor, B. (1980). *The biological approach to adolescence: Biological change and psychosocial adaptation*. In J. Adelson (Ed.), *Handbook of the Psychology of Adolescence* (pp. 115–155). New York: John Wiley & Sons.

Plant, T. M. (2000). Ontogeny of GnRH gene expression and secretion in primates. In J. P. Bourguignon & T. M. Plant (Eds.), *The onset of puberty in perspective* (pp. 3–13). Amsterdam: Elsevier Science B. V.

Reiter, E. O., & Lee, P. A. (2001). Have the onset and tempo of puberty changed? *Archives of Pediatric and Adolescent Medicine*, *155*, 988–989.

Reynolds, E. L., & Wines, J. V. (1948). Individual differences in physical changes associated with adolescence in girls. *American Journal of Diseases of Children*. *75*, 329–350.

Rockett, J. C., Lynch, C. D., & Buck, G. M. (2004). Biomarkers for assessing reproductive development and health: Part 1—Pubertal development. *Environmental Health Perspectives*, *112*, 105–112.

Romans, S. E., Martin, M., Gendall, K. A., & Herbison, G. P. (2003). Age of menarche: The role of some psychosocial factors. *Psychological Medicine*, *33*, 933–939.

Rosenfield, R. L., Bachrach, L. K., Chernausek, S. D., Gertner, J. M., Gottschalk, M., Hardin, D. S., et al. (2000). Current age of onset of puberty [Letters to the Editor]. *Pediatrics*, *106*, 622.

Saenger, P., & DiMartino-Nardi, J. (2001). Premature adrenarche. *Journal of Endocrinological Investigation*, *24*, 724–733.

Saenz de Rodriguez, C. A., Bongiovanni, A. M., & Conde de Borrego, L. (1985). An epidemic of precocious development in Puerto Rican children. *Journal of Pediatrics*, *107*, 393–396.

Schweiger, U., Weber, B., Deuschle, M., & Heuser, I. (2000). Lumbar bone mineral density in patients with major depression: Evidence of increased bone loss at follow-up. *American Journal of Psychiatry*, *157*, 118–120.

Seminara, S. (2003). The GPR54 gene as a regulator of puberty. *New England Journal of Medicine*, *349*, 1614–1627.

Sisk, C. L., & Foster, D. L. (2004). The neural basis of puberty and adolescence. *Nature Neuroscience*, *7*, 1040–1047.

Sisk, C. L., & Zehr, J. L. (2005). Pubertal hormones organize the adolescent brain and behavior. *Frontiers in Neuroendocrinology*, *26*, 163–174.

Skinner, B. F. (1953). *Science and human behavior*. New York: Macmillan.

Sowell, E. R., Thompson, P. M., & Toga, A. W. (2004). Mapping changes in the human cortex throughout the span of life. *Neuroscientist*, *10*, 372–392.

Stattin, H., & Magnusson, D. (1990). *Pubertal maturation in female development*. Hillsdale, NJ: Lawrence Erlbaum.

Steiger, A. (2003). Sleep and endocrinology. *Journal of Internal Medicine*, *254*, 13–22.

Steiger, A., & Holsboer, F. (1997). Neuropeptides and human sleep. *Sleep*, *20*, 1038–1052.

Steinberg, L. (in press). The social neuroscience of risk taking in youth. *Developmental Review*.

Steinberg, L. (2007). *Adolescence* (8th ed.). Columbus, OH: McGraw-Hill.

Styne, D. M., & Grumbach, M. M. (2007). Control of puberty in humans. In O. H. Pescovitz & E. C. Walvoord (Eds.), *When puberty is precocious* (pp. 51–82). Totowa, NJ: Humana Press.

Styne, D. M., & Grumbach, M. M. (2008). Puberty: Ontogeny, neuroendocrinology, physiology, and disorders. In H. M. Kronenberg, S. Melmed, K. S. Polonsky, & P. R. Larsen (Eds.), *Kronenberg: Williams Textbook of Endocrinology* (11th ed.; pp. 969–1166). Philadelphia: Elsevier.

Sun, S. S., Schubert, C. M., Chumlea, W. C., Roche, A., Kulin, H., Lee, P., et al. (2002). National estimates of the timing of sexual maturation and racial differences among U.S. children. *Pediatrics*, *110*, 911–919.

Sun, S. S., Schubert, C. M., Liang, R., Roche, A. F., Kulin, H. E., Lee, P. A., et al. (2005). Is sexual maturity occurring earlier among U.S. children? *Journal of Adolescent Health, 37,* 345–355.

Surbey, M. K. (1990). Family composition, stress, and the timing of human menarche. In T. E. Ziegler & F. B. Bercovitch (Eds.), *Socioendocrinology of primate reproduction* (pp. 11–32). New York: Wiley-Liss.

Surbey, M. K. (1998). Parent offspring strategies in the transition at adolescence. *Human Nature, 9,* 67–94.

Susman, E., Reiter, E., Ford, C., & Dorn, L. D. (2002). Work Group I: Developing models of healthy adolescent physical development. *Journal of Adolescent Health, 31,* 171–174.

Susman, E., & Rogol, A. D. (Eds.). (2004). *Puberty and psychological development.* Hoboken, NJ: John Wiley & Sons.

Susman, E., Dockray, S., Schiefelbein, V. L., Herwehe, S., Heaton, J., & Dorn, L. D. (2007). Morningness and eveningness, morning to afternoon cortisol ratio, and antisocial behavior problems during puberty. *Developmental Psychology, 43,* 811–822.

Tanner, J. M. (1962). *Growth at adolescence.* Springfield, IL: Charles C. Thomas.

Tanner, J. M., & Whitehouse, R. H. (1976). Clinical longitudinal standards for height, weight, height velocity, weight velocity, and stages of puberty. *Archives of Disease in Childhood, 51,* 170–179.

Tschann, J. M., Adler, N. E., Irwin, C. E., Jr., Millstein, S. G., Turner, R. A., & Kegeles, S. M. (1994). Initiation of substance use in early adolescence: The roles of pubertal timing and emotional distress. *Health Psychology, 13,* 326–333.

Udry, J. R. (1979). Age at menarche, at first intercourse, and at first pregnancy. *Journal of Biosocial Science, 11,* 433–441.

van Jaarsveld, C. H., Fidler, J. A., Simon, A. E., & Wardle, J. (2007). Persistent impact of pubertal timing on trends in smoking, food choice, activity, and stress in adolescence. *Psychosomatic Medicine, 69,* 798–806.

van Wieringen, J. C., Roede, M. J., & Wit, J. M. (1985). Growth diagrams for patient care. *Tijdschrift voor kindergeneeskunde, 53,* 147–152.

Warner, S., Murray, G., & Meyer, D. (2008). Holiday and school-term sleep patterns of Australian adolescents. *Journal of Adolescence, 31, 595–608.*

Wichstrøm, L. (2001). The impact of pubertal timing on adolescents' alcohol use. *Journal of Research on Adolescence, 11,* 131–150.

Wierson, M., Long, P. J., & Forehand, R. L. (1993). Toward a new understanding of early menarche: The role of environmental stress in pubertal timing. *Adolescence, 28,* 913–924.

Wiesner, M., & Ittel, A. (2002). Relations of pubertal timing and depressive symptoms to substance use in early adolescence. *Journal of Early Adolescence, 22,* 5–23.

Wilson, D. M., Killen, J. D., & Hayward, C. (1994). Timing and rate of sexual maturation and the onset of cigarette and alcohol use among teenage girls. *Archives of Pediatric Adolescent Medicine, 148,* 789–795.

Wu, T., Mendola, P., & Buck, G. M. (2002). Ethnic differences in the presence of secondary sex characteristics and menarche among U.S. girls: The third national health and nutrition examination survey, 1988–1994. *Pediatrics, 110,* 752–757.

Yazici, K. M., Akinci, A., Sütçü, A., & Ozçakar, L. (2003). Bone mineral density in premenopausal women with major depressive disorder. *Psychiatry Research, 117,* 271–275.

CHAPTER 6

Adolescent Thinking

DEANNA KUHN

It is striking to look at the tables of contents of the many textbooks on adolescence as a life stage and notice that at most a single chapter, and sometimes only part of a chapter, is devoted to the cognition of adolescents. There are a number of ways to explain this, but perhaps the major one is that a great deal is going on during this life period. Adolescents are coping with challenging changes in their bodies, their emotions, their family roles, their peer relationships, and their school activities. So much needs to be addressed that is clearly central and consequential in adolescents' lives that adolescents' thinking perhaps does not stand out as a centerpiece of adolescent life. Yet, adolescents' thinking, whether more or less proficient, and explicit or only implicit, stands to influence adolescent life in all of these other areas of activity and change. Adolescents need to make sense of what is happening to them, and what they are doing about it, as they encounter at a rapid pace the many new experiences, challenges, and choices that are characteristic of the period. They are, in fact, thinking beings, even in settings where it may not appear so. Prompted to some degree by their elders, teens begin to anticipate their own futures to a much greater extent than they did as children, but they also pay more attention to the past, in the form of regret over lost opportunities or actions and aspirations that had outcomes different than expected. They have begun to construct their own, often life-lasting identities.

Just as it is with children, then, key to understanding adolescents is understanding their thinking. Yet the study of adolescent cognition and cognitive development differs from the study of cognitive development in children in at least one crucial way. By the later years of childhood, researchers begin to encounter cognitive achievements that may or may not develop, in contrast to the largely universal developments of younger children. By adolescence, enormous individual variability in cognitive functioning is apparent. In this chapter I probe the factors that contribute to this variability, among them not just environmental diversity but the greater role that older children and adolescents play in choosing what they will do, hence assuming the role of producers of their own development (Lerner, 2002).

We examine here the thinking competencies and dispositions of adolescents from the dual perspectives of how they differ both from those of children and those of adults—and hence what is likely to be undergoing change during this period. Also, we consider the role that these competencies and dispositions are likely to play in the affairs of adolescent life. What we learn from close study of this sort can make significant differences in how we as educators and parents attempt to intervene in effective ways in adolescents' lives. As an example, the admonition "It only takes once" has been widely regarded as an appropriate message to convey to adolescents regarding the risks of unprotected sex. In truth, however, the majority of single instances of unprotected sexual activity do not result in pregnancy. An adolescent girl who has unprotected sex on a single occasion and does not become pregnant may struggle with how to explain this phenomenon and may reach the conclusion that she is infertile, a conclusion that could lead to riskier subsequent behavior (Bruine de Bruin, Downs, & Fischhoff, 2007).

Throughout the chapter, I highlight the practical implications of what we know about adolescent thinking, with the goal of better understanding adolescents and identifying the most effective ways to support their transition from being children to responsible adults. In addition, however, I situate current knowledge in a historical framework—the only framework in which it can be fully appreciated and understood. The study of adolescents' thinking, as both unique to this life stage and undergoing development, does not have a long history, a milestone being the publication of Inhelder and Piaget's volume, *The Growth of Logical Thinking in Childhood and Adolescence*, in the 1950s. Influenced by this work, subsequent efforts for some time focused on the mastery of logical reasoning, narrowly defined as deductive or syllogistic (if–then) reasoning, as well as efforts to replicate and further examine the particular cognitive skills described in the Inhelder and Piaget volume (Kuhn, 2008). As described later, more recent empirical study of adolescent thinking has to some extent evolved in reaction to this earlier work.

Although the bulk of research in the field of cognitive development, especially in recent years, has been focused on the first decade, and indeed the first few years, of life, enough has by now been learned about developments in the second decade to make it challenging to examine all of them in a single chapter. In undertaking to do so, we examine the historical evolution I've noted and where it has led. Yet we will begin with the present, by considering first what has been the most dramatic new evidence to appear in the field of adolescence in some time—evidence that development of the brain is incomplete at the end of the first decade of life and continues to develop throughout the second decade and even into the third. Is this, then, where we should be focusing our attention to understand adolescent thinking and its development?

IS IT ALL ABOUT THE BRAIN?

Neuroimaging techniques are now available that allow precise longitudinal examination of changes in brain structure over time. These studies make it clear that the brain continues to develop into and through the adolescent years. The area of greatest change after puberty is the prefrontal cortex. It is implicated in what have come to be called "executive" functions (Nelson, Thomas, & deHaan, 2006), which include monitoring, organizing, planning, and strategizing—indeed any mental activity that entails managing one's own mental processes— and is also associated with increase in impulse control.

Modern longitudinal neuroimaging research reports two kinds of change, one in the so-called gray matter, which undergoes a wave of overproduction (paralleling one occurring in the early years) at puberty, followed by a reduction, or "pruning," of those neuronal connections that do not continue to be used. A second change, in so-called white matter, is enhanced myelination, that is, increased insulation of established neuronal connections, improving their efficiency (Giedd et al., 1999). By the end of adolescence, then, this evidence suggests, teens have fewer, more selective, but stronger, more effective neuronal connections than they did as children. In addition to growth in the prefrontal cortex regions during adolescence, there has also been reported exaggerated activation of limbic subcortical regions (implicated in reward-related learning) and delayed functional connectivity between these and prefrontal regions, leaving the prefrontal regions with insufficient control of such activity during this period (Casey, Getz, & Glavan, in press).

The news about adolescent brain development has attracted the interest and imagination of the media, with authors not hesitating to draw wide-ranging conclusions, and this development in risk of becoming an explanation for anything and everything about teenagers (Kuhn, 2006). In *The Primal Teen: What the New Discoveries About the Teenage Brain*

Tell Us About Our Kids, for example, Strauch (2003) points to incomplete brain development as an explanation for just about everything about adolescents that adults have found perplexing, from sleep patterns to risk taking and mood swings. In the cognitive realm, Strauch quotes approvingly a middle-school teacher's comment that it is good to know that "if you have an adolescent in a seventh-grade science class and he or she is having difficulty with abstract concepts, it may . . . have to do with brain development and developmental readiness" (p. 214). Such an inference warrants concern because it absolves less-than-optimal instruction as a possible contributor, among other reasons.

Should an immature adolescent brain carry such explanatory burdens? This chapter is not the appropriate place to delve deeply into the developmental neuropsychology literature in search of an answer to this question. Yet we can answer the question in a clear and simple way by noting what is by now a widely accepted conclusion among developmental neuropsychologists (Huttenlocher, 2002; Nelson et al., 2006; Thomas & Johnson, 2008; see also chapter 5, this volume): Development of the brain is dependent on experience. A consequence is that brain development cannot by itself be used to explain that experience. In other words, there cannot exist a simple, unidirectional causal relation between brain developments and outcomes at a behavioral or psychological level. Sufficient amounts and kinds of experience are necessary for anticipated neurological developments to occur. These developments in turn create potentialities for new kinds of experiences. The relations between neurological and psychological change are thus complex, bidirectional ones.

Neuropsychologists have studied such brain–behavior relations in animals as well as humans, beginning very early in life. These relations have been relatively less studied as of yet at the adolescent life stage of interest to us here. Yet the broad conclusion of an interactive, bidirectional relationship between brain and behavior is perhaps even more compelling at this stage, due to the great experiential variability that we have already noted emerges at this stage. Adolescents are producers of their own development to a greater extent than are children, and this claim applies at the level of the brain as well as that of experience and behavior. The activities in which a young adolescent chooses to engage and not to engage affect which neuronal connections will be strengthened and which will wither. These neurological changes, in turn, further support the activity specialization in a genuinely interactive process that helps to explain the widening individual variation that appears in the second decade of life, which there will be a good deal more to say about as we proceed.

DEVELOPING PROCESSING SKILLS

Although changes at the level of the brain cannot fully explain them, all indications are that significant advances continue to occur during the second decade of life in the skills involved in registering and processing basic information. These are particularly important to examine given suggestions that they may underlie advances in more complex, higher order kinds of cognition.

Processing Speed

The most basic of these is processing speed. How quickly is new information taken in? The most common tasks that researchers have used to measure processing speed require naming or matching numbers or familiar words presented as pictures or text. Processing speed can also be measured simply as the time it takes an individual to respond "yes" or "no" to a stimulus (Luna, Garver, Urban, Lazar, & Sweeney, 2004)—a basic reaction-time measure of clear importance to adolescent activities such as driving. The findings in this case are clear. Response time has been found to decrease on measures of processing speed from early childhood through mid-adolescence (Demetriou, Christou, Spanoudis, & Platsidou, 2002; Kail,

1991, 1993; Luna et al., 2004), with change best fitting a quadratic model of decreasing rate of change. The most recent work by Kail and Ferrer (2007) adds valuable longitudinal data to previous cross-sectional evidence. Importantly, however, as Kail and Ferrer note, this finding is qualified by the fact that number- and figure-matching tasks of the sort they employed cannot be taken as "pure" measures of processing speed. A number of other perceptual, cognitive, and motor processes are involved in their execution.

Response Inhibition

While reaction time is a measure of how rapidly one can make a response, another cognitive function that is at least as important in its implications, especially in the case of adolescents, is the ability to inhibit a response. Although they are related, it is useful to make a distinction between two types of inhibition, especially as different research paradigms have been employed to investigate them.

In the first type, emphasis is on irrelevant stimuli that have the potential to interfere with processing and the challenge is to ignore them, that is, inhibit any attention to them, in favor of attending to stimuli relevant to the task at hand. This type of inhibition is typically referred to under the heading of selective attention. In an early classic study, Maccoby and Hagen (1965) demonstrated that the superior performance of adolescents over children on a learning task was attributable not only to their greater attention to the stimuli that were to be remembered but also to their reduced attention to irrelevant stimuli that were also present. Older participants performed more poorly than younger ones on a test of memory for the irrelevant stimuli. Increasing ability to ignore attention to irrelevant stimuli during the childhood years has also been reported in other studies (Hagen & Hale, 1973; Schiff & Knopf, 1985). A different kind of interference from competing stimuli arises not from simultaneous but from previously presented material. Kail (2002) reports a decline between middle childhood and adulthood in proactive interference—the interference of previously presented material in present recall. Adolescents and adults are better able than children to screen out and disregard the previous material.

A second type of inhibition has received less attention, despite its potential importance. It is the ability to inhibit an already established response when told not to exhibit it. For example, an individual may be instructed to inhibit a motor response that has become routine whenever a particular signal is given. Performance on these tasks improves with age until mid-adolescence (Luna et al., 2004; Williams, Ponesse, Schacher, Logan, & Tannock, 1999). In another paradigm, a "directed forgetting" technique has been used in studies of memorization of word lists. The individual is instructed to forget words that have already been presented and hence to inhibit them in subsequent free recall. During recall, improvement occurs into adolescence in the ability to inhibit words under "forget" instructions, as well as to withhold production of incidentally learned words (Harnishfeger, 1995). Young children, in contrast, typically display no difference in frequencies of production of words they were instructed to forget and those they were instructed to remember.

In sum, the evidence is ample that both resistance to interfering stimuli and inhibition of unwanted responses develop across the childhood years and into adolescence. It has even been suggested they may play a role in the developmental advances observed in basic memory tasks, notably digit span, that have been employed as measures of processing capacity (Harnishfeger, 1995; Harnishfeger & Bjorklund, 1993). It is important to note, however, that the evidence regarding inhibition of responses comes from paradigms in which the individual is instructed to inhibit the unwanted response. We have less information about response inhibition in the important condition in which individuals must make their own decisions regarding the desirability of a behavior and hence decide and regulate which behaviors to exhibit and which to inhibit. We will have more to say about this form of inhibition as we explore further the topic of cognitive self-regulation in its broader aspect, or what has come to be referred to as executive control.

Processing Efficiency

Response inhibition leads us to the construct of processing efficiency. An individual who inhibits responding to stimuli that are inappropriate or irrelevant is likely to function with greater cognitive efficiency than one who does not. Recent work suggests that processing efficiency involves not simply passive reactions (or inhibition of reactions) to stimuli but a more dynamic activity that can be called "action monitoring" (Hogan, Vargha-Khadem, Kirkhan, & Baldeweg, 2005; Ladouceur, Dahl, & Carter, 2007). In the Hogan et al. study, for example, adolescents performed less well than young adults on a task in which participants were instructed to press the left button in response to a left-pointing green arrow and the right button in response to a right-pointing green arrow. When arrows were red, however, they were to make the opposite responses. In both the Hogan et al. and Ladoceur et al. studies, moreover, participants' brain activity was monitored via functional magnetic resonance imaging while performing such a task and correspondences found between task performance and neurological event-related potentials associated with incorrect responses, specifically an "error-related negativity" brain wave that has been shown to increase in amplitude with age through adolescence (Davies, Segalowitz, & Gavin, 2004). Authors of these studies speculate that this brain activity is associated with cognitive control mechanisms involved in monitoring tasks.

Another aspect of action monitoring has been studied under the heading of prospective memory (Ceci & Bronfenbrenner, 1985; Kerns, 2000; Mantyla, Carelli, & Forman, 2007). In Ceci and Bronfenbrenner's study, for example, children and adolescents were instructed to turn off a battery charger after 30 min to avoid overcharging, while playing a video game during the 30-min period—a "multitasking" demand of clear relevance to adolescent life. An observer monitored how often an available clock was checked (which required interrupting the game), as well as temporal accuracy. These studies showed teens to do better than children but worse than adults. Also significant in the Mantyla et al. study was a relation between performance and skill in both response inhibition and a related skill of "updating" (Miyake, Friedman, Emerson, et al., 2000)—in this case, for example, matching a letter to one that appeared two items earlier.

Processing Capacity

Still another processing dimension that it has been speculated may undergo developmental change is processing capacity. Here, things become decidedly less clear, the primary reason being that different researchers operationalize this construct in different ways. At least two different components are involved. One, emphasized by Pascual-Leone (1970), is short-term storage space. The other, emphasized by Case (1992), is operating space, which arises when the individual must manipulate the information rather than only store and reproduce it. The familiar construct "working memory" in some contexts has been used in the operating space sense and in others in the storage sense.

Developmentally increasing processing speed, Case proposed (1992; Case, Kurland, & Goldberg, 1982; Case & Okamoto, 1996), reduces the space required for operations, leaving more space available for short-term storage. The net result is greater processing efficiency, rather than any absolute increase in capacity. Others (Cowan, 1997; Demetriou et al., 2002), however, dispute Case's claim that processing speed and processing capacity are causally related, as opposed to independently increasing or mediated by a third variable such as increasing knowledge.

Whether processing capacity increases in an absolute sense or only as a by-product of increased efficiency, there remains the question of how to measure it. Pascual-Leone (1970), Case (1992, 1998; Case & Okamoto, 1996), and more recently, Halford (Halford, Wilson, & Phillips, 1998; Halford & Andrews, 2006) have all proposed systems to identify the processing demands of a task, and, by implication, the processing capacity of an individual based on performance on the task. Case, for example, identified progress from tasks requiring attention to a single dimension to tasks requiring the coordination of two dimensions (Case & Okamoto, 1996). Halford and Andrews invoke a construct of structural complexity, indexed by the number of dimensions that must be simultaneously represented if their relations are to be understood. They present data for a number of tasks, suggesting that this number increases developmentally from early childhood into adolescence.

In sum, there is general agreement across studies that processing continues to improve in the second decade of life, but there is little agreement about the particulars. There are several distinct components of processing ability, and there is no universal agreement as to how they are related. Inhibition, as already noted, is a construct of critical relevance, particularly in adolescence, and is in need of further elucidation (Lustig, Hasher, & Zacks, 2007). The connection between capacity and efficiency needs to be clarified, but so do the relations between speed and capacity (Kail, 2007) and between speed and inhibition (Luna et al., 2004). Do processing improvements take place in a domain-general manner, as some researchers maintain (Gathercole, Pickering, Ambridge, & Wearing, 2004; Swanson, 1999), or do improvements differ across domains, as others claim (Demetriou et al., 2002)? The primary challenge is arguably one of achieving agreed-upon measures of processing constructs, if we are to make headway in understanding their developmental course and interrelation. Tasks involving capacities to represent versus store versus manipulate mental symbols are likely to produce divergent capacity estimates, and the

goal of producing "pure" measures of capacity remains elusive and may be impossible to achieve. Supporting the latter conclusion is the fact that we have yet to identify conclusively the set of factors that contribute to developmentally increasing performance on what might appear to be the simplest, most straightforward measure of capacity of all—digit span. Indeed, all the factors we have noted—capacity, efficiency, speed, and inhibition—as well as several others—familiarity, knowledge, strategy—have been implicated (Case et al., 1982; Harnishfeger, 1995; Bjorklund & Harnishfeger, 1990).

Brain Development, Processing Capability, and Reasoning

For all the attention and excitement they have generated, then, discoveries related to continuing brain developments during the second decade of life by no means answer the important questions regarding the cognitive capacities of adolescents. Further investigation of these developments is, of course, of critical importance to pursue, but at the moment, as we have seen, they are no more than suggestive regarding the developmental course of the most basic cognitive processes, much less more complex ones (Kuhn, 2006).

The claim is rarely made that development at the neurological level or an increase in the number of pieces of information that can be simultaneously processed is the direct and sole cause of a qualitatively new form of thinking. The emergence and development of the new form must be accounted for at the psychological level. Still, processing increases may function as necessary conditions that create the potential for the emergence of new capabilities, allowing, for example, solution of a previously insoluble problem or construction of a new approach to a familiar situation.

Kail (2007) assessed processing speed (number and figure matching), working memory (for words), and reasoning (Raven matrices) longitudinally in 8- to 13-year-old girls and reported a structural equation model in which processing speed is associated with increased working memory, which is associated with superior reasoning. Demetriou et al. (2002) report a wide-ranging empirical investigation of the relations between developing information-processing capacities and developing reasoning skills in a cross-sequential design in which children 8–14 years of age were assessed initially and again at two subsequent yearly intervals. Assessments included processing speed, capacity, and inhibition, as well as several kinds of reasoning; each skill was examined in three domains—verbal, numerical, and spatial. The authors' conclusion is that of a necessary-but-not-sufficient relation. Processing improvements, they say, ". . . open possibilities for growth in other abilities. In other words, changes in these functions may be necessary but not sufficient for changes in functions residing at other levels of the mental architecture." (p. 97)

Unfortunately, however, the measurement uncertainties we have noted make it difficult to definitively rule out any directions of causality. Performance improves with age on all of the various tasks Demetriou et al. administer. But even the sophisticated analytic methods they use do not allow them to conclude with certainty what causal relations may exist. The reasoning tasks in particular are necessarily brief and arbitrarily chosen—for example, four syllogisms and four analogies in the verbal domain—and even the authors acknowledge in their discussion that an improved "yardstick for specifying differences between concepts or problems" (p. 132) is needed. A further complication is the varying patterns they obtain in the three content domains, leading them to conclude that processing capabilities are specific to the kind of information being processed.

As does Kail (2007), Demetriou et al. (2002) make it clear that processing capabilities can be no more than necessary conditions for thinking, and they stress the importance of what they label "top-down" as well as "bottom-up" influences. In particular, they emphasize the role of a "hypercognitive" or executive operator, which ". . . may participate and contribute to the relations between all other processes and abilities" (p. 127). Thus, in turning now to an examination of these high-order forms of thinking, we must keep in mind developing information-processing capabilities without expecting that they will by themselves explain what is observed to develop in the higher order realm.

PROPOSITIONAL AND DEDUCTIVE REASONING

Formal Operations

Widespread interest in adolescent cognition as having unique characteristics absent in children's thinking began in the context of Piaget's stage theory. Inhelder and Piaget (1958) proposed a final stage of formal operations as supported by a unique logical structure emerging at adolescence and manifesting itself in a number of different capabilities. In the context of their stage theory, formal operations are significant as a reflection of the emergence of a structure that Piaget characterized as operations on operations. With attainment of this stage, according to Inhelder and Piaget, thought becomes able to take itself as its own object—adolescents become able to think about their own thinking, hence the term *operations on operations*, or, more precisely, mental operations on the elementary operations of classification and relation characteristic of the preceding stage of concrete operations. The formal operational thinker becomes able, for example, not only to categorize animals according to physical characteristics and according to habitats but also to operate on these categorizations, that is, to put them into categories, and on this basis to draw inferences regarding relations that hold among animals' physical characteristics and habitats. The formal operational thinker is thus said to reason at the level of *propositions* that specify relations between one category (or relation) and another. As aspects of this second-order operatory structure, according to the theory, there emerge other reasoning capabilities, notably systematic combination and isolation of variables, which we return to later, as well as several others such as proportional and correlational reasoning, also thought to involve second-order operations.

Much of the empirical research on adolescent cognition carried out during the latter part of the twentieth century arose in response to Inhelder and Piaget's work. This work began as simple efforts to replicate their findings and went on from there to studies that critically assessed their claims, in particular the claim of synchronous emergence at adolescence of multiple competencies reflective of a new stage structure. Subsequent cross-sectional research generally upheld Inhelder and Piaget's (1958) claim that adolescents on average do better than children in tasks purported to assess these competencies (Keating, 1980, 2004; Neimark, 1975). Piaget, however, hypothesized these capabilities to appear in early adolescence as a tightly linked, integrated whole, a manifestation of the emergence of the formal operational stage structure. In this respect, subsequent research has been less supportive, yielding little evidence for a unified or abrupt transition from a childhood stage of concrete operations to an adolescent stage of formal operations.

Three kinds of variability contribute to this conclusion. One is interindividual variability in the age of emergence of the different alleged behavioral manifestations of the formal operational structure, for example, combinatorial and isolation-of-variables reasoning. A second is intraindividual variability in the emergence of formal operations skills. There is little evidence to support the claim that these skills emerge synchronously within an individual. Third, and most serious, is task variability. As is the case with respect to virtually all reasoning skills, whether one is judged to possess or not possess the skill is very much a function of the manner in which it is assessed, in particular the amount of contextual support provided (Fischer & Bidell, 1991). Indeed, task variance is so pronounced that we confront in this chapter the phenomenon we call the paradox of early competence and later failures of competence. In other words, there are some tasks in which a particular form of reasoning can be identified as present in children as young as preschool age. In other forms of the same task, however, even adults appear deficient.

These findings make it doubtful that emergence of a singular cognitive structure at a specific point in time—whether Piaget's formal operational structure or some other structure—can account adequately for the progress along multiple fronts that we examine in this chapter. Nonetheless, to anticipate our conclusions, we will maintain that Piaget was on the right track in identifying thinking about one's own thought as a hallmark of cognitive development in the second decade of life. We can assign such a capability a modern-sounding name, like *metacognition* or *executive control*. But what needs to be abandoned is the idea that we can pinpoint its emergence to some narrow window of months or years in late childhood or early adolescence, or indeed any time (Keating, 2004). Even preschoolers can be metacognitive when, for example, they recognize an earlier false belief that they no longer hold, while examples of adolescents' and adults' failures to be sufficiently metacognitive are myriad.

Deductive Reasoning

Historically, formal operations theory has had two major influences on the directions that the study of adolescent cognition has taken in the now half-century since the appearance of Inhelder and Piaget's book. One, which we turn to later, is the study of scientific reasoning, in particular the control-of-variables strategy. The other, which we consider now, is propositional reasoning. Inhelder and Piaget's theory was interpreted as claiming the formal operational stage to mark the advent of propositional reasoning, and drawing inferences from the propositions that make up formal syllogisms was taken as an index of this ability.

Most extensively studied have been classical syllogisms that assert conditional relations between categories, that is, *if p, then q*. In the traditional syllogistic reasoning task, the initial major premise—*if p, then q*—is presented, followed by one of four secondary premises, either *p* (known as the *modus ponens* form), *q*, *not-p*, or *not-q* (known as the *modus tollens* form). The respondent is asked if a conclusion follows. The *modus ponens* form allows the conclusion *q*: If *p* is asserted to be the case and it is known that *if p, then q*, it follows that *q* must be the case. Similarly, the *modus tollens* form allows the conclusion *not-p*: If *not-q* is asserted and it is known that *if p, then q*, it follows that *p* cannot be the case (because if it were, *q* would be the case and we know it is not). The other two forms, however, having *q* or *not-p* as secondary premises, allow no definite conclusion. Another extensively researched task is the selection task (Wason, 1966). In this case, instead of a secondary premise, the reasoner is asked to indicate which of the four cases (*p*, *not-p*, *q*, and *not-q*) would need to be examined in order to verify the truth of the major premise (*if p, then q*). (Here, the answer is the two determinate cases—*p*, to verify that *q* follows, and *not-q*, to verify that *p* is not the case.)

In reviews of research on the development of deductive inference skills (Braine & Rumain, 1983; Klaczynski, 2004; Markovits & Barrouillet, 2002; O'Brien, 1987), two conclusions emerge consistently. Provided the content and context are facilitative, even quite young children can respond correctly at least to the two determinate syllogism forms (Dias & Harris, 1988; Hawkins, Pea, Glick, & Scribner, 1984; Kuhn, 1977; Rumain, Connell, & Braine, 1983). The majority of adults, in contrast, do not respond correctly in the standard form of the selection task (Wason, 1966). The evidence, then, does not support any sudden onset, or even marked transition, in competence in propositional reasoning.

The other consistent conclusion is the sizable effect of proposition content on performance. In short, what is being reasoned about makes a great deal of difference (Klaczynski, Schuneman, & Daniel, 2004; Klaczynski & Narasimham, 1998; Markovits & Barrouillet, 2002). These consistent findings have led investigators to reject as implausible the acquisition of a general, content-free set of rules applicable across any content.

The Critical Role of Meaning

Contemporary investigators have turned their efforts to theories in which problem content is critical and mediates performance. Klaczynski (2004), for example, claims that availability of mental representations of alternatives accounts for most of the performance variance. Consider, for example, the two propositions, "If Tom studies, he'll pass the exam," and "If Tom cheats, he'll pass the exam." Respondents of all ages are more likely to respond correctly to the two indeterminate syllogism forms when they occur in an example like the second proposition, compared to the first. For affirming the consequent, *q* (Tom passed the exam), respondents may correctly note in the second example that it is indeterminate whether Tom cheated. In the example of the first proposition, by contrast, they are more likely to falsely conclude that Tom studied hard. The likely reason is that in the case of the cheating proposition, they can readily represent alternative antecedents, that is, possible causes of Tom's success other than cheating, leading to recognition that the antecedent does not follow from the consequent and that the true antecedent remains indeterminate. In the first (Tom studies) proposition, these alternatives come to mind less readily. Similarly for the other indeterminate syllogism form, denying the antecedent (*not-p*)—Tom didn't study hard or Tom didn't cheat—respondents are more likely to recognize that no conclusion follows when presented the second proposition (because not cheating leaves open multiple alternative consequents). Thus, semantic content, or meaning, significantly enhances or impedes deductive reasoning.

What Develops?

In contrast to the two determinate forms (*modus ponens* and *modus tollens*), on which performance is very good (75% correct) by early adolescence (Klaczynski et al., 2004), on the indeterminate syllogism forms a low level of correctness in early adolescence increases only modestly by late adolescence, with content effects remaining strong (Barrouillet, Markovits, & Quinn, 2001; Klaczynski et al., 2004; Klaczynski & Narasimham, 1998). What accounts for the modest improvement that does occur? Even preschoolers (Fay & Klahr, 1996). have been shown to be willing to suspend judgment, so it does not appear to be willingness to make an indeterminacy judgment that is the stumbling block.

Another possibility is increased awareness of alternatives due to an expanding knowledge base (Klaczynski et al., 2004), leading to the correct recognition of indeterminacy. This remains a potential contributor, but, again, seems not to tell the whole story. It is worthy of note in this respect that content familiarity by itself does not determine performance on syllogistic problems. Klaczynski (2004). offers the example of the two propositions, "If a person eats too much, she'll gain weight" and "If a person grows taller, she'll gain weight." The former is more familiar, but performance on the latter is superior, presumably due to the greater availability of alternative antecedents.

Consistent with this possibility is the likelihood that incorrect responders terminate processing prematurely, with the tendency to do so diminishing into and through adolescence. Premature terminators rely first on the inference rule that is simplest and most readily available in their repertoires, the biconditional—*p* and *q* "go together"—and consider the problem no further. Klaczynski (2004) points to more developed metacognitive skill as key in the adolescent's increasing likelihood of inhibiting premature termination and

continuing processing long enough to contemplate alternatives and recognize their implications. Ready availability of such alternatives, of course, supports doing so.

When Knowledge and Reasoning Conflict

Another respect in which adolescents outperform children in deductive reasoning is the ability to draw conclusions irrespective of belief in the truth or falsity of the premises being reasoned about (Markovits & Vachon, 1989; Morris & Sloutsky, 2002; Moshman & Franks, 1986). This capability extends beyond syllogistic reasoning and indeed was identified by Inhelder and Piaget (1958) as a foundation of the stage of formal operations. Consider the following:

> All wrestlers are police officers.
> All police officers are women.

> Assume the two previous statements are true; is the following statement true or false?

> All wrestlers are women.

Children rarely are able to judge such conclusions as valid deductions from the premises, despite their empirical falsity, and fail to see their logical necessity (Moshman & Franks, 1986; Pillow, 2002). By early adolescence, the distinction between truth and validity begins to appear. But even older adolescents and adults continue to make errors in deductive reasoning when the premises are counterfactual (Markovits & Vachon, 1989).

Inhelder and Piaget (1958) maintained that children, having not reached the stage of formal operations, are unable to reason about the hypothetical and are confined to mental operations on the empirical world. But the distinction is not as clear-cut as they implied. Children are able to exercise their imaginative capabilities in creative ways: "Imagine a world in which . . ." and simple counterfactuals are a routine part of the school curriculum; for example, "Suppose you had nine marbles and gave four to a friend." As the deductive operations get more complex, however, as in the above example, a conflict arises between trusting the deductive operations (which seem trustworthy enough when content is neutral) and trusting one's knowledge.

Overcoming this conflict implicates the executive, or metacognitive, processes that have been suggested to play a role in improvements in performance on deductive reasoning problems involving indeterminacy. In the present case, two meta-level components may be involved. One is increasing meta-level understanding of the deductive inference form, that is, its validity, dependability, independence from content, and utility. The other is increasing meta-level awareness and management of one's own system of beliefs, making it possible to "bracket," that is, temporarily inhibit, these beliefs, in order to allow the deductive system to operate, with the understanding that this suspension of belief is only temporary. Inhibition capacities are implicated here (Handley, Capon, Beveridge, Dennis, & Evans, 2004; Simoneau & Markovits, 2003), a fact we return to in further examination of executive processes.

The importance of belief inhibition is also supported by findings that deductive reasoning performance is susceptible to improvement in children by introducing a fantasy context (Dias & Harris, 1988; Kuhn, 1977; Leevers & Harris, 1999; Morris, 2000). If belief is suspended by the fantasy context, it can't conflict with the conclusions reached through deductive reasoning, and the practice in suspending belief stands to benefit the reasoning process once the fantasy context is withdrawn. From each of these perspectives, then, belief inhibition appears key.

Deduction and Thinking

Is the development of deductive reasoning competence central to the development of mature, effective thinking among adolescents? In this chapter I take the position that it is not. The role of the deduction paradigm in research on thinking has been debated in recent years, leading one prominent researcher to speculate that deductive tasks may involve simply the "application of strategic problem solving in which logic forms part of the problem definition" (Evans, 2002). Evans recommends that the deduction paradigm be supplemented with other methods of studying reasoning.

Developmentally, mastery of the indeterminate syllogistic forms appears secondary to development of ability to reason independently of the truth status of the premises—a broad, flexible, and powerful mental skill that allows one to "disembed" a representation of meaning from its context. Adolescents and adults have learned to use the indeterminate syllogistic forms in practical, if not strictly logical, ways, drawing on their real-world knowledge. Thus, "If you drive too fast, you'll have an accident" readily invokes alternative antecedents and hence interpretation as the formal logical conditional. "If you drink too much, you'll have a hangover," in contrast, invokes the simpler (logically incorrect) biconditional. Little confusion arises over this difference in everyday reasoning.

When knowledge and deduction conflict, however, real-world knowledge does not scaffold reasoning. To the contrary, it must itself be managed and controlled, enabling the deductive system to function. Weak executive control, we see in the remainder of this chapter, makes it difficult to temporarily inhibit one's beliefs, so as to enable the reasoning process to operate independently of them, causing a number of different kinds of limitations. This skill does show improvement in the years between late childhood and late adolescence, but its absence remains an obstacle to good thinking throughout adolescence and adulthood. We turn now to inductive reasoning, where we find its role is crucial.

INDUCTIVE REASONING AND CAUSAL INFERENCE

There is simply no question about the fundamental role that inductive reasoning plays in the thinking of people of all ages. We daily confront enormous amounts of data, some consistent and some inconsistent over time, and must construct meaning out of this wealth of input. Most often, the inductive reasoning of adolescents and adults concerns relations between concepts, relations that are commonly construed as causal. Does alcohol affect a person's judgment? Does this clothing style make one popular? A set of existing ideas is brought to contemplation of the topic, and the task becomes one of achieving coordination between these ideas and new information that becomes available.

Much of the literature on causal inference in early childhood emphasizes the impressive skills young children display. Research on adolescents' causal inference, in contrast, highlights limitations in skill that remain characteristic into and throughout adulthood. Our task in this section, then, is to take account of both of these literatures and formulate a portrayal of the development of inductive inference skills in the years in between.

Evidence for Early Competence

Schulz and Gopnik (2004) present evidence of 4-year-olds' ability to isolate causes in a multivariable context (ones in which multiple events co-occur with an outcome and are potential causes). Children observed a monkey hand puppet sniffing varying sets of three plastic flowers, one red, one yellow, and one blue. An adult first placed the red and blue flowers in a vase and brought the monkey up to sniff them. The monkey sneezed. The monkey backed away, returned to sniff again, and again sneezed. The adult then removed the red flower and replaced it with the yellow one, leaving the yellow and blue flowers together in the vase. The monkey came up to smell the flowers twice and each time sneezed. The adult then removed the blue flower and replaced it with the yellow flower, leaving the red and yellow flowers together in the vase. The monkey came up to smell the flowers, and this time did not sneeze. The child was then asked, "Can

you give me the flower that makes Monkey sneeze?" Seventy-nine percent of 4-year-olds correctly chose the blue flower.

In this study, associations between flower color and sneezing were arbitrary; children had no preconceived ideas about them. When new information must be coordinated with prior expectations, as is usually the case, causal inference becomes more challenging. Here, the findings of numerous investigators show the influence of theoretical expectation on the interpretation of data and the ubiquity of faulty causal inference (Ahn, Kalish, Medin, & Gelman, 1995; Amsel & Brock, 1996; Cheng & Novick, 1992; Chinn & Brewer, 2001; Klaczynski, 2000; Klahr, 2000; Klahr, Fay, & Dunbar, 1993; Koslowski, 1996; Kuhn, Amsel, & O'Loughlin, 1988; Kuhn, Garcia-Mila, Zohar, & Andersen, 1995; Kuhn, Schauble, & Garcia-Mila, 1992; Schauble, 1990, 1996; Stanovich & West, 1997). When theoretical expectations are strong, individuals may ignore the evidence entirely and base inferences exclusively on theory. Or they may make reference to the evidence but represent it in a distorted manner, characterizing it as consistent with their theoretical expectations when it in fact is not. Or they may engage in "local interpretation" of the data (Klahr et al., 1993; Kuhn et al., 1992), recognizing only those pieces of data that fit their theory and failing to acknowledge the rest.

Coordinating Theory and Evidence

Biased processing of information about the world remains commonplace among adults as well as adolescents. Is this deliberate, for example, when a teen tells a parent what "all" the other kids are allowed to do? It may be, but another explanation is insufficient control over the interaction of theory and evidence in one's thinking (Kuhn, 1989). Under such conditions of weak control, thinking is based on a singular representation of "the way things are" with respect to the phenomena being contemplated, and new information is seen only as supporting—or, more aptly, "illustrating"—this reality. New information is not encoded as distinct from what is already known.

Under such conditions, new information can still modify understanding, but the individual may not be aware that this has taken place. A consequence is that individuals remain largely unaware regarding the source of their knowledge. When asked, "How do you know (that A is the cause of O)?," they make mistakes in attributing the inference to the new information they are contemplating, versus their own prior understanding (Kuhn & Pearsall, 2000; Kuhn et al., 1988, 1992, 1995; Schauble, 1990, 1996).

Is there evidence of developmental progress in this respect? Kuhn et al. (1988, 1995). compared children, early adolescents, and adults with respect to evidence evaluation and inference skills and found some improvement in the years between middle childhood and early adulthood, despite the far-from-ideal performance of adults. Among sixth graders, for example, the proportion of evidence-based inferences was about 25%, compared to roughly 50% for noncollege young adults.

Interpreting Evidence of Covariation

Even if the data are faithfully registered, the opportunity for inferential error remains strong. Much evidence exists of unjustified inductive inferences of a relation, usually causal, between two variables, based on minimal evidence, notably as minimal as a single co-occurrence of two events (Klahr et al., 1993; Kuhn et al., 1988, 1992, 1995; Schauble, 1990, 1996). Because the events occurred together in time and/or space, one is taken to be the cause of the other, despite the presence of other covariates. This "false inclusion" is, of course, common in everyday thought at all ages. Thus, when community college students were told about an effort to improve student performance in which a new curriculum, teacher aides, and reduced class size were all introduced in various combinations (Kuhn, Katz, & Dean, 2004), they sometimes relied on as little as a single instance

in which multiple factors were introduced as evidence for the role that one or more of the factors had played in the outcome. A typical example: "Yes a new curriculum is beneficial, because here, where they had it, the class did well."

False inclusion based on a single instance shows some decline in frequency in the years from late childhood to early adulthood (Kuhn et al., 1988, 1995, 2004). Adults are more likely than children to base their causal inferences on a comparison of two instances, rather than a single instance of co-occurrence of antecedent and outcome. Even inferences based on comparisons of multiple instances can be fallacious if additional covariates are not controlled and causality is attributed to the wrong variable, although again we see age-related improvement between late childhood and adulthood (Kuhn et al., 1988). These kinds of errors are ubiquitous in everyday life. An example is that of the author's teenaged son needing to be picked up late one night from a party that had gotten out of hand and listening to his frustrated father lament, "Drinking and trouble—haven't you figured out the connection?" Despite the late hour and his shaky state, the teenager advanced a lengthy argument to the effect that his father had the causality all wrong and the trouble should be attributed to other covariates, among them bad luck.

Notable, finally, is the extent to which the factors we have identified as important in this context are similar to those we identified as important in the case of deductive inference. One is the ability to inhibit the premature responding that terminates processing and prevents considering alternatives (in this case, additional covariates). The other is the ability to "bracket" (i.e., temporarily inhibit) one's beliefs, in order to accurately represent evidence and enable the inference system to operate. Both of these abilities, in turn, involve meta-level, or executive, control of mental processes, which we can accordingly hypothesize is increasing during the age period in which we see improvements in reasoning performance.

Coordinating Effects of Multiple Variables

Inductive inference about causal status is one important kind of reasoning essential to everyday life. Another is prediction of outcomes, based on causal knowledge. Here, an individual must consider the causal status not just of a single variable but of all relevant variables, and integrate their individual (as well as interactive) effects in order to make an outcome prediction. Kuhn and colleagues (Kuhn, 2007; Kuhn & Pease, 2006; Keselman, 2003; Kuhn, Black, Keselman, & Kaplan, 2000; Kuhn & Dean, 2004; Kuhn et al., 2004) identify an inadequate mental model of multivariable causality as a further source of error affecting causal reasoning. (Here, we use the *mental model* terminology in this more generic sense, rather than its typical usage referring to mental representations of particular physical phenomena.)

We might assume that understanding of multiple causality reflects a standard scientific model: Multiple effects contribute to an outcome in an *additive* manner; as long as background conditions remain constant, these effects are expected to be *consistent* (i.e., the same antecedent does not affect an outcome on one occasion and fail to do so on another). Data from the reasoning of both adolescents and adults, however, bring into question assumptions regarding both additivity and consistency (Kuhn, 2007; Kuhn, Iordanou, Pease, & Wirkala, 2008; Keselman, 2003; Kuhn et al., 2000; Kuhn & Dean, 2004). Keselman (2003), for example, asked sixth graders to investigate and make inferences regarding the causal role of five variables on an outcome (earthquake risk), as well as asking them to make outcome predictions for two new cases representing unique combinations of levels of the variables. Three of the five variables had additive effects on the outcome, and the remaining two had no influence. After each prediction, the question was asked, "Why did you predict this level of risk?" All five variables were listed, and students were instructed to indicate as many of them as had influenced their prediction judgment.

Over half of the students justified one or more predictions by implicating a variable they had explicitly judged to be noncausal in making earlier judgments of causal status. More than 80% failed to implicate as contributing to the outcome one or more variables they had previously explicitly judged to be causal. Overall, fewer features were implicated as contributing to a prediction than had been explicitly stated to be causal, and attributions were inconsistent across predictions. Most often, students justified their predictions by appealing to the effect of only a single (usually shifting) variable. Adults do better in each of these respects (Kuhn & Dean, 2004), but their performance remains far from the normative scientific model of multivariable causality.

We can thus point to an inadequate mental model of multivariable causality as a constraint on adolescents', as well as many adults', ability to reason about the simultaneous, additive effects of multiple variables. Additional challenges, we have seen, come into play when individuals bring new evidence to bear on their causal models and to coordinate them with theoretical expectations. An adolescent, then, may be satisfied with a single causal factor as an explanation for an unsatisfactory outcome—for example, "the teacher didn't explain well"—and be unconcerned about other potential causal influences or about other situations with the same outcome (e.g., another teacher's class) for which this explanation cannot be invoked.

Does experience in coordinating effects of multiple variables improve this mental model? This question is one part of the more general question to which we now turn. As children progress into and through adolescence, do they improve in their ability to integrate the new information they encounter with their existing understandings? In other words, do children become better learners in their transition from childhood into and through adolescence?

LEARNING AND KNOWLEDGE ACQUISITION

Comparing Young Adolescents and Adults

A study by Kuhn and Pease (2006) asks most directly the question of concern to us in this section: Do young adolescents learn differently than adults? Sixth graders and young adults were shown a teddy bear that they helped the interviewer to outfit with seven accessories (e.g., jacket, backpack, keychain). The interviewer presented the situation of a charity group raising funds and having teddy bears to give to donors as token gifts. To improve donations, it was explained, the charity wanted to try dressing the bears up a bit. They could afford to add a few accessories and had to choose which ones. Participants were asked to choose the two they thought most likely to increase donations and the two least likely to do so. This content domain was selected to make it unlikely that either age group could be regarded as more knowledgeable in making these choices.

The participant was then presented results of some "test runs" involving these four accessories. A sequence of five instances, presented cumulatively, involving different combinations of the accessories, established that two accessories (one the participant believed effective and one the participant believed ineffective) increased donations and the other two did not. The most successful combination was presented as the fifth instance, such that the correct answer could simply be "read off" from this instance and no complex inferential reasoning was required. Nonetheless, neither group was entirely successful in learning the information presented. Adults, however, showed a higher rate of success than the 12-year-olds: 75% reported the correct answer, versus 35% of the younger group.

Kuhn and Pease's (2006) findings of less effective learning by preadolescents compared to adults were substantiated in a more extensive microgenetic study (Kuhn et al., 1995). Participants were observed over multiple occasions spanning several months as they sought to learn which variables were effective and which were not in contexts involving both physical content (e.g., the speed of model boats down a canal) and social content (e.g., the popularity of children's TV programs). Again, in both physical and social domains, an adult group was more effective in acquiring the new information than was a young adolescent group. Both children and adults drew conclusions virtually from the outset, on the basis of minimal or no data, and then changed their minds repeatedly. But the children remained more strongly wedded to their initial theories and drew on them more than on the new evidence they accessed as a basis for their conclusions.

How, then, should one account for superior learning on the part of adults? Kuhn and Pease (2006) propose that the older participants made better use of a meta-level executive to monitor and manage learning. This executive allowed them to maintain dual representations, one of their own understanding (of the relations they expect or see as most plausible) and the other of new information to be registered. It is this executive control that enables one to temporarily set aside or "bracket" existing beliefs and thereby effectively inhibit their influence on the interpretation of new data. In the absence of this executive control, there exists only a singular experience of "the way things are" as a framework for understanding the world. This executive control, manifested in response inhibition and bracketing, is, of course, exactly what we identified earlier as a central factor in the development of deductive and inductive inference.

Microgenetic analysis in the Kuhn et al. (1995) research made possible the dual objectives of tracing not only the acquisition of knowledge over time but also the evolution of the knowledge-acquisition strategies that were responsible for generating that knowledge. Here, the now widely observed findings from microgenetic research apply (Kuhn et al., 1995; Siegler, 2006). At both ages, individuals displayed not just one but a variety of different strategies, ranging from less to more effective. Over time, what changes is the frequency of usage of these strategies, with a general decline over time in the usage of less effective strategies and increase in the use of more powerful ones.

Comparing Children and Adolescents

Despite the findings just described suggesting that adolescents do not yet learn as efficiently as do young adults, there is evidence that adolescents do better than children in monitoring and managing learning, even in simple rote learning tasks. In a study by Crone, Somsen, Zanolie, and Van der Molen (2006), for example, 8- to 10-year-olds were compared to 12- to 14-year-olds and 16- to 18-year-olds, performing a task that required sorting a sequence of stimuli appearing on a computer screen according to a rule. Plus and minus signs appeared following the response to each stimulus, providing feedback as to correctness. After a number of correct responses, the sorting rule changed without explanation and the respondent had to learn through trial and error how to modify responses to conform to the new rule. Frequency of perseverative errors declined with age. Moreover, only the two older groups showed a physiological response (heart rate slowing) following errors, suggesting improvement with age in the ability to monitor performance, as similarly found in the studies by Hogan et al. (2005) and Ladoceur et al. (2007) described earlier.

Another study of children and adolescents that similarly suggests a developing ability to monitor performance involves a very different, but critically important kind of learning: learning by analogy. Counter to Piaget's early claims that analogical reasoning ability was a manifestation of the formal operational structure and hence did not appear until adolescence, subsequent research has shown that even preschool children can reason by analogy under highly facilitative conditions (Goswami, 2001). Analogy is a powerful learning mechanism that

allows one to apply structural relations understood in one domain to another, perhaps less familiar domain in a way that enhances understanding. For example, in coming to appreciate that verbal assaults can cause psychological wounds, the analogy of physical assaults and resulting wounds can be a powerful device. To benefit, however, the learner must see the deeper structural parallel across the two domains and not be distracted by surface similarities across domains. Richland, Morrison, and Holyoak (2006) examined children's and adolescents' ability to detect these deeper structural relations and avoid distraction by superficial similarities. One of the simplest items, for example, involved a dog chasing a cat in one scene and a boy chasing a girl in another, with an additional girl in the second scene functioning as a distractor. The respondent is asked to "figure out what the pattern is that happens in both pictures. . . . Which one is in the same part of the pattern in the second picture?" The most common error on the part of children was choice of the distractor. By age 13–14, such errors were greatly reduced (though not eliminated). The authors implicate enhanced inhibitory control as a key factor in this age-related change, as well as other factors such as the degree of familiarity with the content. The broad implication is that the effectiveness of learning by analogy improves with age, at least into adolescence.

The Development of Learning

Should it be concluded, then, that the learning process undergoes developmental change? Some years ago, Carey (1985) answered this question with a categorical no, claiming there was no reason to believe that the learning process operated any differently in children than in adults. The findings described here suggest that Carey's sweeping claim, while likely true with respect to some kinds of learning, is not categorically correct. A great deal of the learning that children, adolescents, and adults engage in, both in and out of school, is simple associative learning. It is not mindful learning, and there is no evidence to indicate that the nature of associative learning processes undergoes developmental change. In contrast, learning that is conceptual—that is, entailing a change in understanding—requires cognitive engagement on the part of the learner, and hence an executive that must allocate, monitor, and otherwise manage the mental resources involved. These executive functions, and the learning that requires them, do show evidence of developing, although Kuhn and Pease's data show that developmental change of this sort is highly variable. In that study, some 12-year-olds performed as well as the typical adult, and some adults performed no better than most 12-year-olds.

The microgenetic method of examining repeated engagement with a task over time has been held responsible for blurring the distinction between development and learning (Kuhn, 1995, 2001a; Siegler, 2006). While the distinction between the two may not be as rigid as theorists of the Piagetian era in the 1960s and 1970s held it to be, it does not follow that there remain no useful distinctions at all. Learning what recordings are on this week's "Top 100" list and learning that conflicting ideas can both be right are different kinds of learning in numerous important respects (among them generalizabilty, reversibility, and universality of occurrence). What is important is recognizing the process of change as one that has multiple parameters. When the process is examined microgenetically, it becomes possible to begin to characterize it in terms of many such parameters. It is more research of this sort that is required to support the claim that these change processes themselves undergo change as individuals mature. We return to this possibility in further discussion of the development of executive control, or, in different language, the development of mental self-management, as an attainment critical to the adolescent years.

INQUIRY AND SCIENTIFIC THINKING

Increasingly today, the view is being expressed that the most important thing young people need to learn is how to become effective, independent learners in their own right. This view leads to a discussion of inquiry skills, with early adolescence regarded as an auspicious time for development of these skills. If well learned, they stand to serve an adolescent outside of school and well beyond the formal schooling years.

Inquiry skills lie at the heart of scientific thinking. Modern research in developmental psychology on the development of scientific thinking began very narrowly, in the form of replication studies seeking to confirm the findings reported by Inhelder and Piaget (1958). The bulk of these replication studies focused even more narrowly on the "isolation of variables" or "controlled comparison" investigative strategy, which Inhelder and Piaget reported did not appear until adolescence. Using Piagetian tasks in which participants were required to investigate simple physical phenomena such as a pendulum or the flexibility of rods, Inhelder and Piaget's findings were upheld with respect to children's difficulty with these tasks and evidence of improvement from childhood to adolescence, but it was also found that even older adolescents and adults did not always perform successfully (Keating, 1980). Relatively little discussion has occurred, however, regarding the broader educational or practical significance of these findings. Assuming these tasks are valid indicators of the ability to engage in scientific thinking, is it important for most people to be able to think scientifically?

Does Adolescent Thinking Need to Become "Scientific"?

Today, this question can be answered affirmatively with assurance (Trefil, 2008). What has come to be called "inquiry" has found its way into the American national curriculum standards for science for every grade and often appears in social studies and even language arts standards as well (Levstik & Barton, 2001). In the national science standards, the goals of inquiry learning for grades 5–8, for example, are the following (National Research Council, 1996):

- Identify questions that can be answered through scientific investigations.
- Design and conduct a scientific investigation.
- Use appropriate tools and techniques to gather, analyze, and interpret data.
- Develop descriptions, explanations, predictions, and models using evidence.
- Think critically and logically to make the relationships between evidence and explanations.

Under "Design and conduct a scientific investigation," subskills identified include " . . . systematic observation, making accurate measurements, and identifying and controlling variables." Note that these skills are very closely related to what Inhelder and Piaget (1958) introduced as the isolation-of-variables competency, as the cornerstone of experimental investigation. Do young people need to be able to design and carry out experiments? Very few will grow up to become professional scientists, few enough certainly that educating all of them toward this end is questionable.

The claim I make here is that the skills involved in scientific thinking are essential tools for all adolescents. Scientific thinking is central to science but not specific to it. The definition of scientific thinking I have adopted is *intentional knowledge seeking* (Kuhn, 2002). This definition encompasses any instance of purposeful thinking that has the goal of enhancing the seeker's knowledge. As such, scientific thinking is a human activity engaged in by most people, rather than a rarefied few. It connects to other forms of thinking studied by psychologists, such as inductive inference and problem solving. We characterize its goals and purposes as more closely aligned with argument than with experimentation (Kuhn, 1993; Lehrer, Schauble, & Petrosino, 2001).

It is the intention to seek knowledge that transforms the implicit theory revision even young children engage in, as they learn about the world, into scientific thinking. Theory revision becomes something one *does*, rather than something that happens outside of conscious awareness. To seek knowledge is to recognize that one's existing knowledge is incomplete, possibly incorrect—that there is something new to know. The process of theory–evidence coordination accordingly becomes explicit and intentional. Newly available evidence is examined with regard to its implications for a theory, with awareness that the theory is susceptible to revision and that its modification may be an outcome of the process. Research evidence is by now plentiful that children execute this process less skillfully than most adults and certainly less skillfully than professional scientists (Zimmerman, 2007). The adolescent years, then, are a period of growth in these vital skills.

The Process of Inquiry

As Klahr (2000) notes, very few studies of scientific thinking encompass the entire cycle of scientific investigation, a cycle we characterize as consisting of four major phases: inquiry, analysis, inference, and argument. A number of researchers have confined their studies to only a portion of the cycle, most often the evaluation of evidence (Amsel & Brock, 1996; Klaczynski, 2000; Koslowski, 1996), a research design that links the study of scientific reasoning to research on inductive causal inference. We postpone discussion of argument to a later section, and we focus here on studies in which young people direct their own investigations and seek their own data as a basis for their inferences, hence involving at least the first three phases of the cycle (Dean & Kuhn, 2007; Keselman, 2003; Klahr, 2000; Klahr et al., 1993; Kuhn et al., 1992, 1995; Kuhn, Cheney, & Weinstock, 2000; Kuhn & Dean, in press; Kuhn & Pease, in press; Kuhn & Phelps, 1982; Penner & Klahr, 1996; Schauble, 1990, 1996). These studies offer a picture of how the strategies associated with each phase of scientific investigation are situated within a context of all the others and how they influence one another.

The studies by Klahr and his associates (Klahr, 2000; Klahr et al., 1993) have followed children, teens, and adults asked to conduct investigations of the function of a particular key in controlling the behavior of an electronic robot toy, or, in another version, the behavior of a dancer who performs various movements in a computer simulation. To do this, individuals need to coordinate hypotheses about this function with data they generate, or, in Klahr's (2000) terminology, to coordinate searches of a hypothesis space and an experiment space.

The microgenetic studies by Kuhn and associates, as well as those by Schauble (1990, 1996), Keselman (2003), and Penner and Klahr (1996) examine what we regard as a prototypical form of scientific inquiry—the situation in which a number of variables have potential causal connections to an outcome and the investigative task is to choose instances for examination and on this basis to identify causal and noncausal variables, with the goals of predicting and explaining variations in outcome. Examined in these studies in their simplest, most generic form, at the same time these are common objectives of professional scientists engaged in authentic scientific inquiry.

Studies originating in both Klahr's and Kuhn's laboratories have portrayed similar overall pictures. Adults on average exhibit more skill than children or young adolescents at each stage of the process. The younger group is more likely to seek to investigate all factors at once, to focus on producing outcomes rather than analysis of effects, to fail to control variables and, hence, to choose uninformative data for examination, and to engage in what Klahr refers to as "local interpretation" of fragments of data, ignoring other data that may be contradictory. Klahr (2000) concludes that, ". . . adult superiority appears to come from a set of domain-general skills that . . . deal with the coordination of search in two spaces" (p. 119).

Kuhn et al. (1995) compared the progress of children and adults as they continued their investigations in multiple content domains over a period of months. Although the strategies of both groups improved, adults both started at a slightly higher level and progressed further. Yet microgenetic analysis of the change process confirmed the now common finding that individuals of both ages display not just one but a variety of different strategies ranging from less to more effective. Kuhn et al. (1995) concluded, "Rather than a unidimensional transition from a to b, the change process must be conceptualized in terms of multiple components following individual (although not independent) paths" (p. vi). This was the case with respect to *inquiry* strategies, which range from "generate outcomes" to "assess the effect of X on outcome"; with respect to *analysis* strategies, which range from "ignore evidence" to "choose instances that allow an informative comparison"; and with respect to *inference* strategies, which range from "unsupported claims" to "representations in relation to both consistent and inconsistent evidence" (Kuhn, 2002; Kuhn & Pease, in press). Strategic progress with continued engagement not only occurred in both age groups, Kuhn et al. (1995). found, but was maintained when new problem content was introduced midway through the sessions. And, importantly, the most prevalent change to occur overall was not the emergence of any new strategies but the inhibition and decline of ineffective ones, in particular the inhibition of invalid causal inference. Inhibition of less competent strategies, then, warrants its own attention as a developmental challenge at least on a par with achieving more frequent use of more competent strategies (Kuhn & Pease, in press).

Supporting the Development of Inquiry Skills

Inquiry skills have become a focus of very wide concern to educators, with growing attention being devoted to how they might be promoted. Exercise of such skills in a rich problem environment, as we have noted, is typically productive in strengthening them (Dean & Kuhn, 2007; Kuhn & Pease, in press). And weaknesses in the inquiry process arise long before one gets to the phase of designing and interpreting experiments. A first, critical phase is formulating a question to be asked. Unless the student understands the purpose of the activity as seeking information that will bear on a question whose answer is not already known, inquiry often degenerates into an empty activity of securing observations for the purpose of illustrating what is already believed to be true (Kuhn, 2002). Students may initially pose ineffective questions, for example, by intending to discover the effects of all variables at once. And it may be this ineffective intention that then leads them to experimentation flaws, for example, simultaneously manipulating multiple variables (in effect overattending to them, rather than underattending by failing to control them, as is often assumed).

Kuhn and Dean (2005), in the context of an extended intervention otherwise confined to exercise, added the simple suggestion to students that they choose a single variable to try to find out about. ("Let's try to find out about just one feature" to see if it makes a difference.") This simple intervention had a pronounced effect on their investigation and inference strategies, greatly enhancing mastery of controlled comparison and valid inference. The understanding associated with the initial phase of the inquiry process is most critical because it gives meaning and direction to what follows. If a question is identified that seems worth asking and the ensuing activity seems capable of answering, the stage is set for what is to follow. In the multivariable context of isolation of variables and controlled comparison, the student may cease to vary other variables across two-instance comparisons because of an increasing sense that they are not relevant to the comparison being made. Once they are left alone, and thereby "neutralized" as Inhelder and Piaget (1958) described it, the way is prepared for increased usage and increasing metastrategic understanding of the power of controlled comparison.

But the most important message here is that we need to look beyond the control-of-variables strategy as a narrow procedure to teach students to execute. Rather, it should be conveyed as a tool for them to draw on in seeking answers to the questions that arise. Furthermore, gaining the competence to execute a particular cognitive strategy is only one part of what needs to be acquired. At least as important is developing understanding of what the strategy buys one, of why it is worth employing. It is this understanding that will play a major role in whether an individual is disposed to ever use the strategy outside of the narrow context in which it was acquired.

This raises the topic of intellectual dispositions and values, which we turn to before concluding the chapter. First, we consider some other broad cognitive skills that we would hope to see develop during the adolescent years. Inquiry is not the only general-purpose intellectual skill that will serve teens well and requires nurturing during the adolescent years, if it is to develop to its fullest. Another vital skill is argument, which similarly, the evidence indicates, develops to its fullest only in a context of consistent engagement and nurturing.

ARGUMENT

Even more than inquiry, argument brings us squarely into the realm of everyday, informal reasoning. If there were a single intellectual skill that would serve adolescents well in their lives within, outside of, and beyond the classroom, this would seem to be it. To participate fully in an adult role in a democratic society, a young person should be able to take reasoned positions on controversial matters and to engage in productive discourse with those who take contrasting positions. How well can average adolescents perform these skills? Indeed, adolescents are known to be argumentative at times. But—a different question—can they argue well? The existing evidence is not encouraging.

Individual Arguments

Educators at all levels have long lamented students' weaknesses in producing a cogent argument in support of a claim in their expository writing. By asking adolescents and adults to generate arguments in individual verbal interviews, Kuhn (1991) probed whether these weaknesses reflect poorly developed writing skills or deficits that are more cognitive in nature. Individual argument skills remained poor among adolescents even when the possibly inhibiting factor of producing written text was removed. Only on average about one third of a teen sample was able to offer a valid supporting argument for their claim regarding an everyday topic (e.g., why prisoners return to crime when they're released), a percentage that increased only very modestly to near one half among adults. Others tended to offer pseudo-evidence for their claims, in the form of an example or script (e.g., of a prisoner returning to crime), rather than any genuine evidence to support the claim. Similarly, in the minority were those adolescents or adults who were able to envision counterarguments or rebuttals to their claims. Although chronological age (from adolescence through the sixties) was not a strong predictor of skill, education level was.

Other research is consistent with a picture of poorly developed argument skills (Brem & Rips, 2000; Glassner, Weinstock, & Neuman, 2005; Knudson, 1992; Means & Voss, 1996; Perkins, 1985; Voss & Means, 1991). In particular there is a consistent picture of arguments that are confined to the merits of one's own position, without attention to alternatives or opposing arguments. Kuhn, Shaw, and Felton (1997) compared young teens' and young adults' arguments for or against capital punishment. The two groups were equally likely to address both sides of the argument (31% of teens and 34% of adults did so); the remainder confined their arguments to supporting their own position. Overall, the available research indicates at most slight improvement during adolescent years in ability to produce sound arguments.

In other studies, adolescents have been asked to evaluate the strength or soundness of arguments presented to them (Kuhn, 2001a;

Neuman, 2002; Weinstock, Neuman, & Tabak, 2004). Kuhn (2001a) reported a tendency on the part of eighth graders to focus on the content of the claim rather than the nature of the argument supporting it, hence producing the typical justification, "This is a good argument because it [the claim] is true." A comparison group of community college students were better able to separate their belief in the truth or falsity of the claim from their evaluation of the strength of the argument.

Several authors have examined the influence of one's belief regarding the claim on the evaluation of arguments supporting or opposing it (Klaczynski, 2000; Koslowski, 1996; Stanovich & West, 1997). These studies report that the same arguments are scrutinized more thoroughly and evaluated more stringently if they contradict the evaluator's beliefs than if they are supportive of these beliefs, paralleling findings from the scientific reasoning literature that individuals evaluate identical evidence differently if it is belief-supportive vs. belief-contradictory (Kuhn et al., 1988; Kuhn et al., 1995; Schauble, 1990, 1996). Klaczynski (2000), for example, studied early adolescents (mean age 13.4). and middle adolescents (mean age 16.8). classified by self-reported social class and religion. They were asked to evaluate fictitious studies concluding that one social class or one religion was superior to another on some variable. At least one major and several minor validity threats were present in each study. The older group was superior in critiquing the studies. Both groups, however, exhibited a positive bias toward studies that portrayed their group favorably, critiquing these studies less severely, although only for the religion grouping—a bias that did not diminish with age, and, indeed, is commonplace in adults as well.

Argumentive Discourse

Why do skills in producing or identifying sound arguments generally remain poor throughout adolescence? Graff (2003) makes the claim that developing arguments to support a thesis in expository writing is difficult for students because the task fails to reproduce the conditions of real-world argument, which is dialogic. Most often, two people engage in discourse in which they debate a claim, an activity we can refer to as *argumentation*, to distinguish it from argument, as the product of an individual mind. Nonetheless, implicit in argument as product is the advancement of a claim in a framework of evidence and counterclaims that is characteristic of argumentive discourse, and the two kinds of argument are closely related (Billig, 1987; Kuhn, 1991).

In the absence of the physically present interlocutor characteristic of argumentive discourse, Graff (2003) suggests, the student takes the writing task to be one of stringing together a sequence of true statements, avoiding the complication of stating anything that might not be true. The result is often a communication in which both reader and writer are left uncertain as to why the argument needs to be made at all. Who would want to claim otherwise? If students plant a "naysayer"—an imaginary opponent—in their written arguments, Graff suggests, as a scaffold for the missing interlocutor, their argumentive essays become more authentic and hence more meaningful.

Felton and Kuhn (2001) asked junior high school and community college students to engage in a discussion of the merits of capital punishment with a peer whose view opposed theirs. Each of the utterances in the dialog was classified according to whether its function was (1) to advance exposition of the speaker's claims or arguments, or (2) in some way to address the partner's claims or arguments. Among teens, an average of 11% of utterances address the partner's claims or arguments, compared to 24% among adults. Thus, while some improvement appears during adolescence, the weaknesses observed in dialogic argument resemble those observed in individual arguments, with only a minority of arguers going beyond exposition of their own position. Why might this be? Felton and Kuhn suggest that attention to the other's ideas

and their merits may create cognitive overload, or it simply may not be recognized as part of the task. Supporting the latter explanation, Kuhn and Udell (2007) found that young teens had no difficulty producing arguments against the opposing position when these were explicitly solicited. Thus, they had the competence to address opposing positions, but did not see a need to do so. Most likely, then, meta-level, as well as procedural, limitations constrain performance.

Supporting the Development of Argument Skills

Efforts to enhance teens' argument skills (as distinguished from writing skills) have focused on dialogic argument as the most promising context. Kuhn et al. (1997) asked young teens to engage in dialogic arguments on capital punishment with a series of different classmates over a period of weeks. Felton (2004) had students alternate roles of dialog participants and peer advisers, the latter role intended to heighten students' reflective awareness of their argumentive discourse. In more recent studies (Iordanou, 2008; Kuhn, Goh, Iordanou, & Shaenfield, 2008), students conducted their discourse via a computer-network chat program, allowing them to reflect on the written transcription of the interchange, which remained in view. Pre–post differences in these studies were encouraging, especially as they mirror the cross-sectional differences between teens and adults observed by Felton and Kuhn (2001). Gains transferred to dialogs on a new topic, as well as to individual arguments.

One limitation of the dialogic practice method is that it engages young people in the relevant activity without offering them a reason to be engaged in it. Kuhn and Udell (2003) thus devised a more structured intervention in which students were organized into pro and con teams (based on their initial opinions) and engaged in various activities over a 10-week period toward a goal of a "showdown" debate with the opposing team. After several sessions devoted to developing and evaluating their own arguments, the teams exchanged arguments and then generated counterarguments to the opposing team's arguments, related evidence to both their own and the opposing team's arguments, and, finally, generated rebuttals to the opposing team's counterarguments. Progress occurred in the same directions as observed in the preceding studies, particularly a sizeable increase in counterargument against the opponents' claims. A comparison group that participated only in the initial phase of developing their own arguments showed some, but more limited, progress. Udell (2007) extended this design to a topic of personal relevance (teen pregnancy) as well as a more impersonal one (capital punishment) and found that gains following the personal-topic intervention transferred to the impersonal topic, but transfer did not occur in the reverse direction. In a similar design, Iordanou (2008) observed transfer from a science to a social domain, but not the reverse. Finally, DeFuccio, Kuhn, Udell, and Callender (in press) extended this team approach to older teen males who were residents of a state detention facility and awaiting trial. They, too, despite their initial skepticism, showed significant increases in argumentation skill over a period of several months.

At the beginning of these interventions, all of these students clearly wanted to win. By the end, they still wanted to win, but by now they cared deeply about their topic and had developed a richer understanding surrounding it, even though none of the participants had much initial knowledge. But had students learned anything about argument itself? Had they come to see a point to arguing, beyond prevailing— being the winner? Had they progressed from winning to knowing as a conceptual justification for their activity? Had they constructed an understanding of argument itself? The only possible answer is incompletely, at best. But we return to this question shortly in taking up the question of what adolescents think about their own and others' knowing and thinking.

DECISION MAKING

We come now to the topic that many readers have perhaps been looking for. It is well and good, it can be said, to learn what we can about how adolescents think. But the vital question is, "What can this knowledge tell us about adolescents' decision making, very often about life-risking matters?" How can we help adolescents to make better decisions? If we could just get them to *think*, would that be the answer?

Unfortunately, but unsurprisingly, these questions lack simple answers. The weaknesses in adolescents' inductive and argumentive reasoning that have been highlighted in this chapter might tempt us to conclude that this is where the answer lies. In fact, however, any strong conclusions about the nature of adolescent decision making would be premature. Relatively little research is available on adolescent decision making, especially outside of the laboratory and in the real-life domains of greatest significance to adolescents and the adults close to them. In this section we examine what tentative conclusions might be drawn from the available research, first with respect to decisions involving simple choices (of one well-identified alternative over another) in laboratory settings of limited consequence, and then with respect to the more complex real-life decisions that adolescents face.

Integrating Dimensions to Make Preference Judgments

Consider the following problem, presented to 8-year-old and 12-year-old children by Bereby-Meyer, Assor, and Katz (2004):

In a computer store, Ron is offered four computer games that he can afford:

1. The first one is interesting, has not-so-good voice quality, and comes with an option to add players.

2. The second is not interesting, has not-so-good voice quality, and comes with an option to add players.
3. The third one is not interesting, has good voice quality, and lacks an option to add players.
4. The fourth one is interesting, has not-so-good voice quality, and lacks an option to add players.

Which computer game is the best choice for Ron?

In a similar study (Capon & Kuhn, 1980), preferences of kindergarteners, fourth graders, eighth graders, and young adults were solicited regarding real, physically present objects—pocket-sized notebooks of two colors, binding types (side or top), shapes, and surfaces. At the end of the study, they were given their most preferred notebook to keep. They were also asked for separate preference judgments regarding the four dimensions themselves.

Results of the two studies are similar. Bereby-Meyer et al. (2004) observed some improvement with age, but they found frequent use at both ages of what they term the *lexicographic error*, in which judgment is based on a single dimension. Similarly, Capon and Kuhn (1980) found that rarely before adulthood did participants take more than a single dimension into account in making preference judgments for the notebooks, despite the fact that at all ages the majority indicated preferences on at least three of the four dimensions in making dimension preference judgments.

Related findings come from the now frequently studied Iowa Gambling Task (Crone & Van der Molen, 2007; Hooper, Luciana, Conklin, & Yarger, 2004; Huizenga, Crone, & Jansen, 2007; Overman, et al., 2004). Respondents in this task are asked to repeatedly choose a card from any of four decks. Two decks result in consistent high gains but unpredictable high losses. The other two yield low constant gains and low unpredictable losses

and are favorable in the long run. Huizenga et al. report improved performance from age 10–12 to 13–15 and again from 13–15 to 18–25 years. These gains they attribute to a developmental shift in choice behavior from focusing only on frequency (of outcome) to considering both frequency and amount. In a related task, Figner, Mackinlay, Wilkening, & Weber, 2008) similarly found a difference between adolescents, who focused only on likelihood of gain/loss, and adults, who also took amounts of gain and loss into account. This is the case even though we know from other research that under the right circumstances even young children are able to take into account the joint effects of two variables (Dixon & Tuccillo, 2001; Wilkening & Anderson, 1982).

The parallel between the data from these studies and the findings reported earlier regarding coordinating effects of multiple variables (Keselman, 2003; Kuhn, 2007; Kuhn & Dean, 2004) is notable. Recall that a large majority of sixth graders failed to implicate as contributing to an outcome as many variables as they had previously explicitly claimed to be causal, and half justified their predictions by appealing to the effect of only a single variable. The fact that in the inductive inference context, where it is clearly normative to do so, sixth graders (and even older individuals) do not attend to all dimensions they implicate as causal suggests that they may experience difficulty in attending to and integrating all of the multiple dimensions they would, in fact, wish to enter into preference judgments of objects, and that developmental factors may be relevant.

Performance on Decision-Making Scenarios from the Adult Literature

Further evidence regarding adolescents' decision-making capabilities comes from administering to adolescents some of the widely employed scenarios from the adult decision-making literature. Klaczynski (2001a, 2001b) reported results for a number of these scenarios, including this one:

Ken and Toni are teachers who are arguing over whether students enjoy the new computer-based teaching method used in some math classes. Ken's argument is, "Each of the 3 years that we've had the computer class, about 60 students have taken it. They have written essays on why they liked or didn't like the class. Over 85% of the students say they have liked it. That's more than 130 of 150 students." Toni's argument is, "Stephanie and John (the two best students in the school, both high-honors students) have complained about how much they hate the computer-based class and how much more they like regular math classes. They say a computer can't replace a good teacher."

To this scenario, which assesses the relative weight given to statistically based versus anecdotal evidence, respondents were asked which course to choose. The proportion of adolescents basing their choice on the statistical evidence increased from 18% at age 12 to 42% at age 16.

Another scenario assessed the "sunk cost" effect:

A. You are staying in a hotel room on vacation. You paid $10.95 to see a movie on pay TV. After 5 minutes, you are bored and the movie seems pretty bad. How much longer would you continue to watch the movie?

B. You are staying in a hotel room on vacation. You turn on the TV and there is a movie on. After 5 minutes, you are bored and the movie seems pretty bad. How much longer would you continue to watch the movie?

Because sunk costs are irretrievable, they should be ignored and decisions in the two situations should be the same. Here, Klaczynski found, all age groups, including an adult group, were susceptible to the sunk-cost fallacy (choosing to watch longer in situation A than in situation B), with only 16% of young adolescents (age 12), 27% of older adolescents (age 16), and 37% of adults responding correctly.

In sum, then, the picture is one of modest improvement during the teen years toward an asymptote characteristic of the adult population—an asymptote itself of a very modest level, with the average adult at least as likely to make an incorrect judgment as a correct one in response to most such scenarios from the adult literature.

Implications for Real-Life Decision Making

Parker and Fischhoff (2005) presented to young male teens the sunk-cost scenario and several others from the adult decision-making literature, such as susceptibility to framing effects (inconsistency in responses to formally equivalent choices, depending, for example, whether they are framed in terms of gains or losses). Their study does not examine developmental change, but it goes beyond those reported thus far in investigating relations between performance and self- and parent-report measures of antisocial behavior, delinquency, alcohol and drug use, and sexual behavior. They report modest correlations between poor performance in response to these scenarios and high incidence of the noted behaviors.

How, then, should we conceptualize the factors that contribute to adolescent decision making? Some argue for a direct link between decision-making capacity and maturation of the prefrontal cortex (Baird & Fugelsang, 2004). Others, such as Parker and Fischhoff (2005; Fischhoff, in press), see enhanced decision making with age largely in cognitive terms, as a component of more general cognitive competence, and they note in this regard the substantial correlations between performance on their decision-making items and standard intelligence measures such as Wechsler Intelligence Scale for Children (WISC) vocabulary. Still, they claim, performance on their decision-making scenarios has something to contribute, above and beyond general intelligence, to prediction of real-life decision-making competence.

Another view, advocated by Klaczynski (2001a) and by Reyna and Farley (2006), derives from dual-process theories of cognition (Sloman, 1996; Evans, 2002). Present throughout development are two cognitive systems: an experiential system and an analytic system. The two are thought to be in competition with one another, especially in contexts like the decision scenarios illustrated here, in which they yield opposing judgments. The experiential system is useful and adaptive; were it not for its rapidity and automaticity, information processing would be overburdened. Developmental change may occur, however, in the degree to which the experiential system predominates. In the process of becoming more prominent with age are increasingly powerful metacognitive operators that have the potential to invoke the analytic system. Once invoked, the analytic system has the dual tasks of inhibiting the experiential system and doing its own primary work, which entails extracting the decontextualized representations that will lead to correct judgments.

The dual-process model fits well with much of the data on reasoning examined thus far in this chapter. Figuring prominently in interpreting the relevant phenomena were response inhibition capability, particularly the premature termination of processing that precludes consideration of alternatives, and the ability to bracket, or temporarily inhibit, one's beliefs, in order to accurately represent data and allow the inference system to operate. Both of these involve competing systems, one effortless and intuitive and the other deliberate and reflective.

Taken to its limits, the dual-process model applied to decision making holds that sufficient analytic competence is not the only or even major constraining factor in sound decision making; rather, it is the experiential system that must be monitored and managed (Steinberg, 2008), so as to inhibit its nonreflective application, leading to premature closure and poor performance. Numerous kinds of evidence can be marshaled in support of this model. Figner et al. (2008), for example, showed that teens' performance on their card task deteriorated when an affect-laden "hot" version was presented, emphasizing what the respondent had to win or lose. Similarly, Seguin, Arseneault, and Tremblay (2007) demonstrate the role of both cognitive and affective factors in young adolescents' performance on a card-playing task, in particular the effects of "hot" processes on response perseveration. Huizenga et al. (2007) interpret their findings of inferior performance among younger teens on the Iowa Gambling Task in terms of the need to inhibit focus on a single dimension, and the resulting premature closure, that arises from attending only to the immediate reward and ignoring longer term consequences.

The sort of cognitive control implicated in managing the experiential system may itself involve dual processes. Iselin (in press) examined reactive control (the ability to activate goal-related information in response to an external trigger) and proactive control (the ability to maintain a mental representation of goal-related information in preparation for a behavioral response) and found that both improve between adolescence and young adulthood. These findings are based on a laboratory task, but there are indications that similar distinctions may apply in real-life contexts. In self-reports, for example, adolescents regard themselves less likely than do young adults to anticipate the future consequences of their actions and less likely to plan ahead (Steinberg et al., in press). Steinberg et al. take these indications of increasing future orientation during adolescence as implying that impulse control is one, but not the only, factor responsible for improvement with age in adolescent decision making.

Reyna and colleagues (Reyna & Farley, 2006; Rivers, Reyna, & Mills, 2008) go furthest in discounting the importance of analytic competence in adolescent decision making, pointing to evidence suggesting that teens are already engaging in ample cognitive analysis—specifically, cost–benefit analysis (and particularly benefit) of engaging in risky behavior as the basis for their decisions (Benthin, Slovic, & Severson, 1993); Goldberg, Halpern-Felsher, & Millstein, 2002; Halpern-Felsher, Biehl, Kropp, & Rubinstein, 2004; Parsons, Halkitis, Bimbi, & Borkowski, 2000; Shapiro, Siegel, Scovill, & Hays, 1998). Rather than cognitive competence, Reyna and Farley argue, it is performance, and the variables that control it, that warrant the attention. Teens need to learn, for example, that some behaviors are so dangerous that they are not susceptible to cost–benefit analysis and should be categorically avoided. In this vein, Mills, Reyna, and Estrada (2008) address the conflicting findings regarding whether perceived risk decreases or increases teens' decisions to take risk. It depends, Mills et al. say, on how the risk is conceptualized by the adolescent—either in absolute ("avoid risk") or relative (quantitative cost–benefit analysis) terms. In the latter case, they suggest, engaging in analysis of potential risk may actually lead the teen to greater risk taking.

Reyna and Farley (2006) cast in an either/or framework their own recommendations for strengthening teen decision making, opposing their view to approaches that advocate promoting development of teens' cognitive skills as a basis for sound decision making. Developing a categorical "no-risk" stance, they imply, with a minimum of detailed analysis, optimizes teens' decision making. At this stage in our knowledge, however, this either/or stance seems unwarranted. Why not work on both fronts, exploring ways to enhance intellectual, analytic skills relevant to decision making, while at the same time exploring the additional cognitive and noncognitive factors that arise in accounting for the often considerable gap between competence and performance? Indeed, even those teens likely to be at the lowest levels on measures of inhibition and self-management—the teen residents of a correctional facility in the earlier described study

by DeFuccio et al. (in press)—showed themselves amenable to an intervention designed to enhance their cognitive skills.

EPISTEMOLOGICAL UNDERSTANDING AND INTELLECTUAL VALUES

Analytic thinking competencies provide an essential foundation for sound decision making. But they are not the only relevant intellectual factors in predicting how adolescents will handle the challenges that confront them. Another aspect of intellectual functioning that we have not yet addressed explicitly is that of intellectual values. Does an adolescent *believe* that reasoning and analysis are helpful in addressing issues? Does the adolescent see them as the soundest path to making up one's mind in the face of competing claims or to influencing the minds of others? These are intellectual values, ones educators hope to see develop and become solidified during the adolescent years (Kuhn, in press; Resnick & Nelson-Le Gall, 1997).

Kuhn and Park (2005) presented questions like these to adolescents and their parents, in the United States and elsewhere around the world, and observed striking diversity in the stances taken:

> Many social issues, like the death penalty, gun control, or medical care, are pretty much matters of personal opinion, and there is no basis for saying that one person's opinion is any better than another's. So there's not much point in people having discussions about these kinds of issues. Do you agree, somewhat agree, or disagree?

Many teens agreed, giving such reasons as "It's not worth it to discuss it because you're not going to get anywhere; everyone has a right to think what they want to"; or "It's not worth it to discuss it because it's not something you can get a definite answer to."

These are statements of value, and yet underlying them is a set of beliefs regarding the nature of knowledge and knowing, or *epistemology*.

In studies of adolescents' epistemological beliefs, the most common stance is the *multiplist*, or relativist, stance reflected in the preceding quotes (see Hofer & Pintrich, 1997, 2002, Moshman, 2005, in press, for review of research). Knowledge claims are personal opinions, like pieces of clothing, that people are free to choose for themselves and accordingly are not open to criticism. These adolescents have renounced a developmentally earlier, and radically different, *absolutist* stance, in which knowledge is taken to be a direct reflection of an objective reality, with no intervening role accorded to the human knower. But they have not yet achieved the *evaluativist* level, in which it is understood that even though everyone has a right to their opinion, not all opinions are equally right, when contemplated in a framework of argument and evidence. Only at this level has one achieved a coordination between the subjective and objective elements of knowing (Kuhn, Cheney, & Weinstock, 2000).

A number of authors have focused specifically on the relation between level of epistemological understanding and argument skill, reporting a relation between the two (Kardish & Scholes, 1996; Kuhn, 1991; Kuhn, Iordanou, Pease, & Wirkala, 2008; Mason & Boscolo, 2004; Weinstock & Cronin, 2003; Weinstock et al., 2004). Kuhn et al. (in press) make a conceptual case for this relation: If facts can be ascertained with certainty and are readily available to anyone who seeks them, as the absolutist understands, or, alternatively, if any claim is as valid as any other, as the multiplist understands, there is little reason to expend the intellectual effort that argument entails. One must see the point of arguing to engage in it. This connection extends well beyond but certainly includes science, and in the field of science education, a number of authors have made the case for the connection between productive science learning and a mature epistemological understanding of science as more than the empirical verification of facts (Carey & Smith, 1993; Metz, 2004; Smith, Maclin, Houghton, & Hennessey, 2000). In order for

scientific inquiry to be valued as a worthwhile enterprise, it must be understood to occupy an epistemological ground other than the accumulation of undisputed facts dictated by absolutism or the suspension of judgment dictated by multiplism.

Mason and Boscolo (2004) assessed the level of epistemological understanding of 10th and 11th graders. They found students on average to be at the multiplist level. Students were divided into three groups—those who scored lower than average (hence, showing at least some absolutist thinking), those at the average level, and those above average (hence, showing at least some evaluativist thinking). On a separate occasion, argument skill was assessed by asking students to write a concluding paragraph to an essay that presented two opposing views regarding genetically modified food. The authors also assessed students' level of interest, degree of knowledge, and beliefs regarding the topic. Only epistemological level was predictive of the quality of the concluding paragraph the student produced. Only students in the highest epistemological group were likely to undertake any sort of reconciliation of the two positions, even the minimal one of suggesting that more information was needed. Students at the lower epistemological levels were likely to refer to only one position or to simply consecutively list the two contrasting positions in their summary.

With the examination of epistemological understanding and intellectual values, then, we come to a convergence between the concerns of developmental psychologists and those of educators. As in other of the domains we have examined, the thinking of many adolescents does not achieve the potential it might. In the case of epistemological understanding and intellectual values, the implications for educational achievement are direct and critical ones. Like everyone, adolescents need a reason to invest themselves in intellectual pursuits. Social recognition for academic achievement, as an end in itself, may temporarily serve this purpose, but in the long run it does not (Kuhn,

2005). Educators, then, need to be concerned not only with developing adolescents' intellectual skills, but with helping them to find purpose in what they are doing in their intellectual pursuits. This sense making is a critical aspect of what needs to develop and one likely to have major consequences for the individual pathways an adolescent chooses to follow.

CONCLUSIONS

What Does and Can Develop Cognitively in Adolescence?

The opening section of this chapter suggested that the task at hand was to characterize adolescent thinking by identifying how it differs from the thinking of children, on the one hand, and that of adults, on the other. As is often the case, on examining the particulars we can now see that a seemingly well-defined question such as this one not only lacks simple answers but may be the wrong question entirely. We need now to reformulate it.

Although certain basic processing capacities appear to develop universally and reach an asymptote during adolescence, we cannot say the same about any higher order cognitive competencies. Enormous individual variability in cognitive competencies is already evident at the beginning of the second decade of life. The "good enough" intellectual environment that suffices to support the transitions common to childhood cognitive development apparently is not good enough to support universal attainment of the cognitive capabilities that have the potential to develop during the second decade. In many, perhaps most, adults, this potential is never fully realized.

An implication is that we should not use some measure of average adult performance as a standard against which to compare teens. Rather, the question we should be asking is how the maximum intellectual potential of adolescents can be realized. The implications are strong ones in terms of policy, as well as research. We need to identify the critical

components of environments that will support the intellectual development of each individual to full potential.

Adolescents, however, as was emphasized in the preceding section, are not passive recipients of environmental input. At the very least, they are partners in effecting their own development and defining the paths they will follow. A few things, however, we can count on to happen. Young adolescents begin to acquire much more control over their activities and lives than they experienced as children. Modern culture has introduced them to the art of dividing attention among multiple kinds of input. In short, they have more discretion over how and where their cognitive resources will be deployed.

Nurturing a Developing Executive

Evidence we have examined in this chapter supports the view that as children enter their second decade, a stronger executive is likely to develop that assists them in managing their cognitive resources in the face of multiple, often conflicting task demands and personal goals. Emergence and strengthening of this executive is arguably the single most consequential intellectual development to occur in the second decade of life. It fills a much needed role in determining how attention and effort will be allocated. A stronger executive implies that development is increasingly governed from the "top down." This is not to say that most adults, as well as children and teens, don't apply "bottom-up" habitual patterns of thinking and behaving much of the time. But during the second decade of life, young people increasingly develop the potential to manage and deploy their cognitive resources in consciously controlled and purposefully chosen ways.

Strengthening of executive function can be identified at all levels, from the brain to social networks. At each of these levels, it is important to keep in mind, two different components of executive function can be distinguished, one dedicated to allocation and execution and the other to inhibition (Kuhn & Pease, in press).

At the level of the brain, development of these two components may not be in synchrony, resulting in a period during which inhibitory control is inadequate (Casey, Getz, & Glavan, in press). At the behavioral level, growing inhibitory control is at least as critical to adolescent functioning as is control of execution. Although there is evidence of origins in early childhood (Duckworth & Seligman, 2005), it is not until the second decade that we are likely to see consistent, fully conscious and reflective inhibitory control. Adolescents are truly capable of "thinking twice."

Inhibition of initial responses creates the potential to process further, when one judges doing so to be worth the effort. In the absence of this inhibition, processing stops. No further alternatives are envisioned. Such inhibition, recall, is essential if one is to temporarily "bracket" the perspective dictated by one's own beliefs or understanding, in order to extract decontextualized representations, disembedded from a particular context, and to determine their implications. Without this skill, deductive, inductive, and argumentive reasoning are all impaired, as we have seen.

Realizing Potential Along Divergent Pathways

The developing executive figures importantly in the greatly increased individual variability that we have emphasized becomes evident by early adolescence. Brain and behavior both become more specialized and hence individualized, with increased specialization of brain functions guided by the activities in which the adolescent engages, as well as creating new potentials for action, in a truly interactive process (Thomas & Johnson, 2008).

It is thus especially important to reflect on what kinds of experiences we wish the developing adolescent brain to have. To do this we need to conduct more studies of adolescent cognition in the situated contexts of the activities in which teens in fact choose to invest their intellectual resources. We are certainly taking a risk in drawing conclusions from investigations confined to artificial problems, constructed for research purposes, that bear no clear relation to the kinds of thinking that adolescents do in their daily lives. At the same time, the ability to decontextualize—to extract a generalized representation distinct from its specific context—remains a critical developmental achievement that needs to be studied further (Stanovich, 1999, 2004).

How do young teens choose to invest the many discretionary hours they have available? The choices that earlier were made by parents are now made by teens themselves. With concentrated engagement in the activities they choose, adolescents get even better at what they are already good at, thus increasing the range and diversity of individual pathways. To a greater extent than children, teens attribute meaning and value (both positive and negative) to what they do. Positively valued activities lead to behavioral investment, which leads to greater expertise and hence greater valuing, in a circular process that has taken hold by early adolescence. A consequence is an increasingly firm sense of personal identity—"This is who I am"—and, particularly, "This is what I'm good at" (and its even more potent complement, "This is what I'm no good at"). The selfless curiosity and exploration characteristic of early childhood have likely gone underground and become difficult to detect. An implication is that valuing intellectual engagement can certainly be supported by those who work with young adolescents, but better results can be expected to the extent the way has been laid by activities involving genuine intellectual engagement in the years leading up to the second decade (Kuhn, 2005).

Early adolescence is increasingly being recognized as a second critical period, akin to what has been widely regarded as the critical period of early childhood, when patterns are established that will be resistant to change later on. In the case of early adolescence, it is a period marked by diverging developmental pathways. How do universal and individual trajectories intersect? And how can each best be supported? There may be opportunities to develop potential during this period that will not remain available indefinitely. During this second critical period, it is arguably disposition—to do or not to do x or y—as much or more than competence, that ought to be the focus of those concerned with supporting adolescents' intellectual development (Kuhn, 2001a; Perkins, Jay, & Tishman, 1993; Stanovich & West, 1997, 1998, 2000).

In the sense of being free agents—able to decide what they will attend to and what they will not, what they will invest themselves in and what they will not, what they will value and what they will not—adolescents are more like adults than they are like children. The competencies adolescents develop will count for little if they choose not to use them. Dispositions and values thus join competence as critical aspects of the study of adolescent thinking.

The thinking that adolescents do in connection with each of these constructs is central. Adolescents can and frequently do think about every aspect of their life experience, as this experience expands and increases in complexity and challenge. In seeking to understand any domain of adolescent experience, it is prudent, then, that we consider the kinds of thinking the adolescent brings to it.

REFERENCES

Ahn, W., Kalish, C., Medin, D., & Gelman, S. (1995). The role of covariation versus mechanism information in causal attribution. *Cognition, 54,* 299–352.

Amsel, E., & Brock, S. (1996). Developmental changes in children's evaluation of evidence. *Cognitive Development, 11,* 523–550.

Baird, A., & Fugelsang, J. (2004). The emergence of consequential thought: Evidence from neuroscience. *Philosophical Transactions of the Royal Society of London, Series B: Biological Sciences, 3359,* 1797–1804.

Barrouillet, P., Markovits, H., & Quinn, S. (2001). Developmental and content effects in reasoning with causal conditionals. *Journal of Experimental Child Psychology, 81,* 235–248.

Benthin, A., Slovic, P., & Severson, H. (1993). A psychometric study of adolescent risk perception. *Journal of Adolescence, 16,* 153–168.

Bereby-Meyer, Y., Assor, A., & Katz, I. (2004). Children's choice strategies: the effects of age and task demands. *Cognitive Development, 19,* 127–146.

Billig, M. (1987). *Arguing and thinking: A rhetorical approach to social psychology.* Cambridge: Cambridge University Press.

Bjorklund, D., & Harnishfeger, K. (1990). The resources construct in cognitive development: Diverse sources of evidence and a theory of inefficient inhibition. *Developmental Review, 10,* 48–71.

Braine, M., & Rumain, B. (1983). Logical reasoning. In J. Flavell & E. Markman (Eds.), *Handbook of child psychology, Vol. 3: Cognitive development* (4th ed.). New York: John Wiley & Sons.

Brem, S., & Rips, L. (2000). Explanation and evidence in informal argument. *Cognitive Science, 24,* 573–604.

Bruine de Bruin, W., Downs, J., & Fischhoff, B. (2007). Adolescents' thinking about the risks of sexual behaviors. In M. Lovett & P. Shah (Eds.), *Thinking with data.* Mahwah, NJ: Lawrence Erlbaum.

Capon, N., & Kuhn, D. (1980). A developmental study of consumer information-processing strategies. *Journal of Consumer Research, 7,* 225–233.

Carey, S. (1985). Are children fundamentally different kinds of thinkers and learners than adults? In S. Chipman, J. Segal, & R. Glaser (Eds.), *Thinking and learning skills* (Vol. 2). Hillsdale, NJ: Lawrence Erlbaum.

Carey, S., & Smith, C. (1993). On understanding the nature of scientific knowledge. *Educational Psychologist, 28,* 235–251.

Case, R. (1992). *The mind's staircase: Exploring the conceptual underpinnings of children's thought and knowledge.* Hillsdale, NJ: Lawrence Erlbaum.

Case, R. (1998). The development of conceptual structures. In D. Kuhn & R. Siegler (Eds.), (W. Damon, series ed.), *Handbook of Child Psychology,* Vol. 2: *Cognition, Perception, and Language.* (5th ed.). New York: John Wiley & Sons.

Case, R., Kurland, D., & Goldberg, J. (1982). Operational efficiency and the growth of short-term memory span. *Journal of Experimental Child Psychology, 33,* 386–404.

Case, R., & Okamoto, Y. (1996). The role of central conceptual structures in the development of children's thought. *Monographs of the Society for Research in Child Development* (Vol. 61, whole no. 246).

Casey, B., Getz, S., & Glavan, A. (in press). The adolescent brain. *Developmental Review.*

Ceci, S., & Bronfenbrenner (1985). Don't forget to take the cupcakes out of the oven: Prospective memory, strategic time-monitoring and context. *Child Development, 56,* 152–164.

Cheng, P., & Novick, L. (1992). Covariation in natural causal induction. *Psychological Review, 99,* 365–382.

Chinn, C., & Brewer, W. (2001). Models of data: A theory of how people evaluate data. *Cognition and Instruction, 19,* 323–393.

Cowan, N. (1997). The development of working memory. In N. Cowan (Ed.), *The development of memory in childhood.* East Sussex, UK: Psychology Press.

Crone, E., Somsen, R., Zanolie, K., & Van der Molen, M. (2006). A heart rate analysis of developmental change in feedback processing and rule shifting from childhood to early adulthood. *Journal of Experimental Child Psychology, 95,* 99–116.

Crone, E., & Van der Molen, M. (2007). Development of decision making in school-aged children and adolescents: Evidence from heart rate and skin conductance analysis. *Child Development, 78,* 1288–1301.

Davies, P., Segalowitz, S., & Gavin, W. (2004). Development of response-monitoring ERPs in 7–25 year olds. *Developmental Neuropsychology, 25,* 355–376.

Dean, D., & Kuhn, D. (2007). Direct instruction vs. discovery: The long view. *Science Education, 91,* 384–397.

De Fuccio, M., Kuhn, D., Udell, W., & Callender, K. (in press). Developing argument skills in severely disadvantaged adolescents in a residential correctional setting. *Applied Developmental Science.*

Demetriou, A., Christou, C., Spanoudis, G., & Platsidou, M. (2002). The development of mental processing: Efficiency, working memory, and thinking. *Monographs of the Society for Research in Child Development,* Vol. 67 (serial no. 268xxx).

Dias, M., & Harris, P. (1988). The effect of make-believe play on deductive reasoning. *British Journal of Developmental Psychology, 6,* 207–221.

Duckworth, A., & Seligman, M. (2005). Self-discipline outdoes IQ in predicting academic performance of adolescents. *Psychological Science, 16*, 939–944.

Evans, J. St. (2002). Logic and human reasoning: An assessment of the deduction paradigm. *Psychological Bulletin, 128*, 978–996.

Felton, M. (2004). The development of discourse strategies in adolescent argumentation. *Cognitive Development, 19*, 35–52.

Felton, M., & Kuhn, D. (2001). The development of argumentive discourse skills. *Discourse Processes, 32*, 135–153.

Figner, B., Mackinlay, R., Wilkening, F., & Weber, E. (2008). Affective and deliberative processes in risky choice: Accounting for age differences in risk taking. Unpublished ms., Columbia University.

Fischer, K., & Bidell, T. (1991). Constraining nativist inferences about cognitive capacities. In S. Carey & R.Gelman (Eds.), *The epigenesis of mind: Essays on biology and cognition* (pp. 199–235). Hillsdale, NJ: Lawrence Erlbaum Associates.

Fischhoff, B. (in press). Assessing adolescent decision-making competence. *Developmental Review*.

Gathercole, S., Pickering, S., Ambridge, B., & Wearing, H. (2004). The structure of working memory from 4 to 15 years of age. *Developmental Psychology, 40*, 177–190.

Giedd, J., Blumenthal, J., Jeffries, N., Castellanos, F., Lui, H., Zijdenbos, A., et al. (1999). Brain development during childhood and adolescence: A longitudinal MRI study. *Nature Neuroscience, 2*, 861–863.

Glassner, A., Weinstock, M., & Neuman, Y. (2005). Pupils' evaluation and generation of evidence and explanation in argumentation. *British Journal of Educational Psychology, 75*, 105–118.

Goldberg, J., Halpern-Felsher, B., & Millstein, S. (2002). Beyond invulnerability: The importance of benefits in adolescents' decision to drink alcohol. *Health Psychology, 21*, 477–484.

Goswami, U. (2001). Analogical reasoning in children. In D. Gentner, K.Holyoak, & B. Kokinov (Eds.), *The analogical mind: Perspectives from cognitive science* (pp. 437–470). Cambridge MA: MIT Press.

Graff, G. (2003). *Clueless in academe: How schooling obscures the life of the mind*. New Haven: Yale University Press.

Hagen, J., & Hale, G. (1973). The development of attention in children. In A. Pick (Ed.), *Minnesota symposium on child psychology* (Vol. 7). Minneapolis: University of Minnesota Press.

Halford, G.S. & Andrews, G. (2006). Reasoning and problem solving. In D. Kuhn & R. S. Siegler (Eds.), Cognition, Perception, and Language, Volume 2 of *Handbook of Child Psychology* (6th ed.) (pp. 557–608). Editors-in-chief: W. Damon & R. M. Lerner. Hoboken, NJ: Wiley.

Halford, G. S., Wilson, W. H., & Phillips, S. (1998). Processing capacity defined by relational complexity: Implications for comparative, developmental, and cognitive psychology. *Behavioral and Brain Sciences, 21*, 803–864.

Halpern-Felsher, B., Biehl, M., Kropp, R., & Rubinstein, M. (2004). Perceived risks and benefits of smoking: Differences among adolescents with different smoking experiences and intentions. *Preventive Medicine, 39*, 559–567.

Handley, S., Capon, A., Beveridge, M., Dennis, I., & Evans, J. (2004). Working memory, inhibitory control and the development of children's reasoning. *Thinking and Reasoning, 10*, 175–196.

Harnishfeger, K. (1995). The development of cognitive inhibition: Theories, definition, and research evidence. In F. Dempster & C. Brainerd (Eds.), *Interference and inhibition in cognition*. San Diego, CA: Academic Press.

Harnishfeger, K., & Bjorklund, D. (1993). The ontogeny of inhibition mechanisms: A renewed approach to cognitive development. In M. Howe & R. Pasnak (Eds.), *Emerging themes in cognitive development, Vol. 1: Foundations*. New York: Springer-Verlag.

Hawkins, J., Pea, R., Glick, J., & Scribner, S. (1984). "Merds that laugh don't like mushrooms": Evidence for deductive reasoning by preschoolers. *Developmental Psychology, 20*, 584–594.

Hofer, B., & Pintrich, P. (1997). The development of epistemological theories: Beliefs about knowledge and knowing and their relation to learning. *Review of Educational Research, 67*, 88–140.

Hofer, B., & Pintrich, P. (2002). *Epistemology: The psychology of beliefs about knowledge and knowing*. Mahwah, NJ: Lawrence Erlbaum.

Hogan, A., Vargha-Khadem, F., Kirkham, R., & Baldeweg, T. (2005). Maturation of action monitoring from adolescence to adulthood: an ERP study. *Developmental Science, 8*, 525–534.

Hooper, C., Luciana, M., Conklin, H., & Yarger, R. (2004). Adolescents' performance on the Iowa Gambling Task: Implications for the development of decision-making and ventromedial prefrontal cortex. *Developmental Psychology, 40*, 1148–1158.

Huizenga, H., Crone, E., & Jansen, B. (2007). Decision-making in healthy children, adolescent and adults explained by the use of increasingly complex proportional reasoning rules. *Developmental Science, 10*, 814–825.

Huttenlocher, P. (2002). *Neural plasticity: The effects of the environment on the development of the cerebral cortex*. Cambridge, MA: Harvard University Press.

Inhelder, B., & Piaget, J. (1958). *The growth of logical thinking from childhood to adolescence*. New York: Basic.

Iordanou, K. (2008). Developing argument skills across scientific and social domains. Unpublished doctoral dissertation, Teachers College Columbia University.

Iselin, A.M. (in press). Reactive and proactive control in incarcerated and community adolescents and young adults. *Cognitive Development*.

Kail, R. (1991). Development of processing speed in childhood and adolescence. In R. Hayne (Ed.), *Advances in child development and behavior* (Vol. 23). San Diego, CA: Academic Press.

Kail, R. (1993). Processing time decreases globally at an exponential rate during childhood and adolescence. *Journal of Experimental Child Psychology, 56*, 254–265.

Kail, R. (2002). Developmental change in proactive interference. *Child Development, 73*, 1703–1714.

Kail, R. (2007). Longitudinal evidence that increases in processing speed and working memory enhance children's reasoning. *Psychological Science, 18*, 312–313.

Kail, R., & Ferrer, E. (2007). Processing speed in childhood and adolescence: Longitudinal models for examining developmental change. *Child Development, 78*, 1760–1770.

Kardash, C., & Scholes, R. (1996). Effects of pre-existing beliefs, epistemological beliefs, and need for cognition on interpretation of controversial issues. *Journal of Educational Psychology, 88*, 260–271.

Keating, D. (1980). Thinking processes in adolescence. In J. Adelson (Ed.), *Handbook of adolescent psychology*. New York: John Wiley & Sons.

Keating, D. (2004). Cognitive and brain development. In R. Lerner & L. Steinberg (Eds.), *Handbook of adolescent psychology*. Chichester: John Wiley & Sons.

Kerns, K. (2000). The CyberCruiser: An investigation of development of prospective memory in children. *Journal of the International Neuropsychological Society, 6*, 62–70.

Keselman, A. (2003). Supporting inquiry learning by promoting normative understanding of multivariable causality. *Journal of Research in Science Teaching, 40*, 898–921.

Klaczynski, P. (2000). Motivated scientific reasoning biases, epistemological beliefs, and theory polarization: A two-process approach to adolescent cognition. *Child Development, 71*, 1347–1366.

Klaczynski, P. (2001). The influence of analytic and heuristic processing on adolescent reasoning and decision making. *Child Development, 72*, 844–861.

Klaczynski, P. (2004). A dual-process model of adolescent development: Implications for decision making, reasoning, and identity. In R. Kail (Ed.), *Advances in Child Development and Behavior* (Vol. 31). San Diego, CA: Academic Press.

Klaczynski, P., Schuneman, M., & Daniel, D. (2004). Development of conditional reasoning: A test of competing theories. *Developmental Psychology.*

Klaczynski, P. A., & Narasimham, G. (1998). Representations as mediators of adolescent deductive reasoning. *Developmental Psychology, 5,* 865–881.

Klahr, D. (2000). *Exploring science: The cognition and development of discovery processes.* Cambridge: The MIT Press.

Klahr, D., Fay, A., & Dunbar, K. (1993). Heuristics for scientific experimentation: A developmental study. *Cognitive Psychology, 25,* 111–146.

Knudson, R. (1992). Analysis of argumentative writing at two grade levels. *Journal of Educational Research, 85,* 169–179.

Koslowski, B. (1996). *Theory and evidence: The development of scientific reasoning.* Cambridge, MA: MIT Press.

Kuhn, D. (1977). Conditional reasoning in children. *Developmental Psychology, 13,* 342–353.

Kuhn, D. (1989). Children and adults as intuitive scientists. *Psychological Review, 96,* 674–689.

Kuhn, D. (1991). *The skills of argument.* Cambridge, UK: Cambridge University Press.

Kuhn, D. (1993). Science as argument: Implications for teaching and learning scientific thinking. *Science Education, 77,* 319–337.

Kuhn, D. (1995). Microgenetic study of change: What has it told us? *Psychological Science, 6,* 133–139.

Kuhn, D. (2001a). How do people know? *Psychological Science, 12,* 1–8.

Kuhn, D. (2002). What is scientific thinking and how does it develop? In U. Goswami (Ed.), *Handbook of childhood cognitive development.* Oxford, UK: Blackwell.

Kuhn, D. (2005). *Education for thinking.* Cambridge, MA: Harvard University Press.

Kuhn, D. (2006). Do cognitive changes accompany developments in the adolescent brain? *Perspective on Psychological Science, 1,* 59–67.

Kuhn, D. (2007). Reasoning about multiple variables: Control of variables is not the only challenge. *Science Education, 91,* 710–716.

Kuhn, D. (2008). Formal operations from a twenty-first century perspective. *Human Development, 51,* 48–55.

Kuhn, D. (in press). The importance of learning about knowing: Creating a foundation for development of intellectual values. *Perspectives on Child Development,*

Kuhn, D., Amsel, E., & O'Loughlin, M. (1988). *The development of scientific thinking skills.* San Diego, CA: Academic Press.

Kuhn, D., Black, J., Keselman, A., & Kaplan, D. (2000). The development of cognitive skills to support inquiry learning. *Cognition and Instruction, 18,* 495–523.

Kuhn, D., Cheney, R., & Weinstock, M. (2000). The development of epistemological understanding. *Cognitive Development, 15,* 309–328.

Kuhn, D., & Dean, D. (2004). Connecting scientific reasoning and causal inference. *Journal of Cognition & Development, 5,* 261–288.

Kuhn, D., & Dean, D. (2005). Is developing scientific thinking all about learning to control variables? *Psychological Science, 16,* 866–870.

Kuhn, D., & Dean, D. (in press). Scaffolded development of inquiry skills in academically-disadvantaged middle-school students. *Journal of the Psychology of Science and Technology.*

Kuhn, D., Garcia-Mila, M., Zohar, A., & Andersen, C. (1995). Strategies of knowledge acquisition. *Society for Research in Child Development Monographs, 60* (serial no. 245).

Kuhn, D., Goh, W., Iordanou, K., & Shaenfield, D. (2008). Arguing on the computer: A microgenetic study of developing argument skills in a computer-supported environment. *Child Development, 79,* 1311–1329.

Kuhn, D., Iordanou, K., Pease, M., & Wirkala, C. (2008). Beyond control of variables: What needs to develop to achieve skilled scientific thinking? *Cognitive Development, 23.*

Kuhn, D., Katz, J., & Dean, D. (2004). Developing reason. *Thinking & Reasoning, 10,* 197–219.

Kuhn, D., & Park, S. (2005). Epistemological understanding and the development of intellectual values. *International Journal of Educational Research, 43,* 111–124.

Kuhn, D., & Pearsall, S. (2000). Developmental origins of scientific thinking. *Journal of Cognition and Development, 1,* 113–129.

Kuhn, D., & Pease, M. (2006). Do children and adults learn differently? *Journal of Cognition and Development, 7,* 279–293.

Kuhn, D., & Pease, M. (in press). What needs to develop in the development of inquiry skills? *Cognition and Instruction.*

Kuhn, D., & Phelps, E. (1982). The development of problem-solving strategies. In H. Reese (Ed.), *Advances in child development and behavior* (Vol. 17). New York: Academic Press.

Kuhn, D., Schauble, L., & Garcia-Mila, M. (1992). Cross-domain development of scientific reasoning. *Cognition and Instruction, 9,* 285–332.

Kuhn, D., Shaw, V., & Felton, M. (1997). Effects of dyadic interaction on argumentive reasoning. *Cognition and Instruction, 15,* 287–315.

Kuhn, D., & Udell, W. (2003). The development of argument skills. *Child Development, 74,* 1245–1260.

Kuhn, D., & Udell, W. (2007). Coordinating own and other perspectives in argument. *Thinking and Reasoning, 13,* 90–104.

Ladouceur, C., Dahl, R., & Carter, C. (2007). Development of action monitoring through adolescence into adulthood: ERP and source localization. *Developmental Science, 10,* 874–891.

Leevers, H., & Harris, P. (1999). Transient and persisting effects of instruction on young children's syllogistic reasoning with incongruent and abstract premises. *Thinking and Reasoning, 5,* 145–174.

Lehrer, R., Schauble, L., & Petrosino, A. J. (2001). Reconsidering the role of experiment in science education. In K. Crowley, C. Schunn & T. Okada (Eds.), *Designing for science: Implications from everyday, classroom, and professional settings* (pp. 251–277). Mahwah, NJ: Lawrence Erlbaum.

Lerner, R. (2002). *Concepts and theories of human development* (3rd ed.). Mahwah, NJ: Lawrence Erlbaum.

Levstik, L., & Barton, K. (2001). *Doing history: Investigating with children in elementary and middle schools.* Mahwah, NJ: Lawrence Erlbaum.

Luna, B., Garver, K., Urban, T., Lazar, N., & Sweeney, J. (2004). Maturation of cognitive processes from late childhood to adulthood. *Child Development, 75,* 1357–1372.

Lustig, C., Hasher, L., & Zacks, R. (2007). Inhibitory deficit theory: Recent developments in a "new view." In D. Gorfein & C. MacLeod (Eds.), *Inhibition in cognition.* Washington, DC: American Psychological Association.

Maccoby, E., & Hagen, J. (1965). Effects of distraction upon central versus incidental recall: Developmental trends. *Journal of Experimental Child Psychology, 2,* 280–289.

Mantyla, T., Carelli, M. G., & Forman, H. (2007). Time monitoring and executive functioning in children and adults. *Journal of Experimental Child Psychology, 96,* 1–19.

Markovits, H., & Barrouillet, P. (2002). The development of conditional reasoning: A mental model account. *Developmental Review, 22,* 5–36.

Markovits, H., & Vachon, R. (1989). Reasoning with contrary-to-fact propositions. *Journal of Experimental Child Psychology, 47,* 398–412.

Mason, L., & Boscolo, P. (2004). Role of epistemological understanding and interest in interpreting a controversy and in topic-specific belief change. *Contemporary Educational Psychology, 29,* 103–128.

Means, M., & Voss, J. (1996). Who reasons well? Two studies of informal reasoning among students of different grade, ability, and knowledge levels. *Cognition & Instruction, 14,* 139–178.

Metz, K. (2004). Children's understanding of scientific inquiry: Their conceptualization of uncertainty in investigations of their own design. *Cognition and Instruction, 22,* 219–290.

Mills, B., Reyna, V., & Estrada, S. (2008). Explaining contradictory relations between risk perception and risk taking. *Psychological Science*, *19*, 429–433.

Miyake, A., Friedman, N., & Emerson, M. et al., (2000). The unity and diversity of executive functions and their contributions to complex frontal lobe tasks: A latent variable analysis, *Cognitive Psychology*, *41*, 49–100.

Morris, A. (2000). Development of logical reasoning: Children's ability to verbally explain the nature of the distinction between logical and nonlogical forms of argument. *Developmental Psychology*, *36*, 741–758.

Morris, B., & Sloutsky, V. (2002). Children's solutions of logical versus empirical problems: What's missing and what develops? *Cognitive Development*, *116*, 907–928.

Moshman, D. (2005). *Adolescent psychological development: Rationality, morality, and identity* (2nd ed.). Mahwah, NJ: Lawrence Erlbaum.

Moshman, D. (in press). Epistemic development and the perils of Pluto. In M. Shaughnessy, M. Vennemann, & C. K. Kennedy (Eds.), *Metacognition*. Hauppauge, NY: Nova.

Moshman, D., & Franks, B. A. (1986). Development of the concept of inferential validity. *Child Development*, *57*, 153–165.

National Research Council. (1996). *The National Science Education Standards*. Washington, DC: National Academy Press.

Neimark, E. (1975). Intellectual development during adolescence. In F. Horowitz (Ed.), *Review of child development research* (Vol. 4). Chicago: Chicago University Press.

Nelson, C.A., Thomas, K.M. & de Haan, M. (2006). Neural bases of cognitive development. In D. Kuhn & R. S. Siegler (Eds.). *Cognition, Perception, and Language*, Volume 2 of *Handbook of Child Psychology* (6th ed.) (pp. 3–57). Editors-in-chief: W. Damon & R. M. Lerner. Hoboken, NJ: Wiley.

Neuman, Y. (2002). Go ahead, prove that God does not exist! On students' ability to deal with fallacious arguments. *Learning and Instruction*, *13*, 367–380.

O'Brien, D. (1987). The development of conditional reasoning: An iffy proposition. In H. Reese (Ed.), *Advances in child development and behavior* (Vol. 20). Orlando, FL: Academic Press.

Overman, W., Frassrand, K., Ansel, S., Trawalter, S., Bies, B., & Redmond, A. (2004). Performance on the Iowa card task by adolescents and adults. *Neuropsychologia*, *42*, 1838–1851.

Parker, A., & Fischhoff, B. (2005). Decision-making competence: External validation through an individual-differences approach. *Journal of Behavior Decision Making*, *18*, 1–27.

Parsons, J., Halkitis, P., Bimbi, D., & Borkowski, T. (2000). Perceptions of the benefits and consts associated with condom use and unprotected sex among late adolescent college students. *Journal of Adolescence*, *23*, 377–391.

Pascual-Leone, J. (1970). A mathematical model for transition in Piaget's developmental stages. *Acta Psychologica*, *32*, 301–345.

Penner, D., & Klahr, D. (1996). The interaction of domain-specific knowledge and domain-general discovery strategies: A study with sinking objects. *Child Development*, *67*, 2709–2727.

Perkins, D. (1985). Postprimary education has little impact on informal reasoning. *Journal of Educational Psychology*, *77*, 562–571.

Perkins, D., Jay, E., & Tishman, S. (1993). Beyond abilities: A dispositional theory of thinking. *Merrill-Palmer Quarterly*, *39*, 1–21.

Pillow, B. (2002). Children's and adults' evaluation of the certainty of deductive inferences, inductive inferences, and guesses. *Child Development*, *73*, 779–792.

Resnick, L., & Nelson-Le Gall, S. (1997). Socializing intelligence. In L. Smith, J. Dockrell, & P. Tomlinson (Eds.), *Piaget, Vygotsky and beyond*. London: Routledge.

Reyna, V., & Farley, F. (2006). Risk and rationality in adolescent decision-making: Implications for theory, practice, and public policy. *Psychological Science in the Public Interest*, *7*, 1–44.

Richland, L., Morrison, R., & Holyoak, K. (2006). Children's development of analogical reasoning; Insights from scene analogy problems. *Journal of Experimental Child Psychology*, *94*, 249–273.

Rivers, S., Reyna, V., & Mills, B. (2008). Risk taking under the influence: A fuzzy-trace theory of emotion in adolescence. *Developmental Review*, *28*, 107–144.

Rumain, B., Connell, J., & Braine, M. (1983). Conversational comprehension processes are responsible for reasoning fallacies in children as well as adults: If is not the biconditional. *Developmental Psychology*, *19*, 471–481.

Schauble, L. (1990). Belief revision in children: The role of prior knowledge and strategies for generating evidence. *Journal of Experimental Child Psychology*, *49*, 31–57.

Schauble, L. (1996). The development of scientific reasoning in knowledge-rich contexts. *Developmental Psychology*, *32*, 102–119.

Schiff, A., & Knopf, I. (1985). The effect of task demands on attention allocation in children of different ages. *Child Development*, *56*, 621–630.

Schulz, L., & Gopnik, A. (2004). Causal learning across domains. *Developmental Psychology*, *40*, 162–176.

Seguin, J., Arseneault, L., & Tremblay, R. (2007). The contribution of "cool" and "hot" components of decision-making in adolescence: Implications for developmental psychopathology. *Cognitive Development*, *22*, 530–543.

Shapiro, R., Siegel, A., Scovill, L., & Hays, J. (1998). Risk-taking patterns of female adolescents: What they do and why. *Journal of Adolescence*, *24*, 143–159.

Siegler, R.S. (2006). Microgenetic Analyses of Learning. In D. Kuhn & R. S. Siegler (Eds.). Cognition, Perception, and Language, Volume 2 of *Handbook of Child Psychology* (6th ed.) (pp. 464–510). Editors-in-chief: W. Damon& R. M. Lerner. Hoboken, NJ: Wiley.

Simoneau, M., & Markovits, H. (2003). Reasoning With premises that are not empirically true: Evidence for the role of inhibition and retrieval. *Developmental Psychology*, *39*, 964–975.

Sloman, S. (1996). The empirical case for two systems of reasoning. *Psychological Bulletin*, *119*, 3–22.

Smith, C., Maclin, D., Houghton, C., & Hennessey, M. (2000). Sixth-grade students' epistemologies of science: The impact of school science experiences on epistemological development. *Cognition and Instruction*, *18*, 349–422.

Stanovich, K. (1999). *Who is rational? Studies of individual differences in reasoning*. Mahwah, NJ: Lawrence Erlbaum.

Stanovich, K. (2004). *The robot's rebellion*. Chicago: University of Chicago Press.

Stanovich, K., & West, R. (1997). Reasoning independently of prior belief and individual differences in actively open-minded thinking. *Journal of Educational Psychology*, *89*, 342–357.

Stanovich, K., & West, R. (1998). Individual differences in rational thought. *Journal of Experimental Psychology: General*, *127*, 161–188.

Stanovich, K., & West, R. (1999). Individual differences in reasoning and the heuristics and biases debate. In P. Ackerman & P. Kyllonen (Eds.), *Learning and individual differences: Process, trait, and content determinants* (pp. 389–411). Washington, DC: American Psychological Association.

Stanovich, K., & West, R. (2000). Individual differences in reasoning: implications for the rationality debate? *Behavioral and Brain Sciences*, *23*, 645–665.

Steinberg, L. (2008). A social neuroscience perspective on adolescent risk-taking. *Developmental Review*, *28*, 78–106.

Steinberg, L., Graham, S., O'Brien, L., Woolard, J., Cauffman, E., & Banich, M. (in press). Age differences in future orientation and delay discounting. *Child Development*.

Strauch, B. (2003). *The primal teen: What the new discoveries about the brain tell us about our kids*. New York: Doubleday.

Swanson, H. L. (1999). What develops in working memory? A life span perspective. *Developmental Psychology*, *35*, 986–1000.

Thomas, M., & Johnson, M. (2008). New advances in understanding sensitive periods in brain development. *Current Directions in Psychological Science, 17*, 1–5.

Trefil, J. (2008). *Why science?* New York: Teachers College Press.

Udell, W. (2007). Enhancing adolescent girls' argument skills in reasoning about personal and non-personal decisions. *Cognitive Development, 22*, 341–352.

Voss, J., & Means, M. (1991). Learning to reason via instruction in argumentation. *Learning and Instruction, 1*, 337–350.

Wason, P. (1966). Reasoning. In B. Foss (Ed.), *New Horizons in Psychology*. New York: Penguin.

Weinstock, M., & Cronin, M. (2003). The everyday production of knowledge: Individual differences in epistemological understanding and juror-reasoning skill. *Applied Cognitive Psychology, 17*, 161–181.

Weinstock, M., Neuman, Y., & Tabak, I. (2004). Missing the point or missing the norms? Epistemological norms as predictors of students' ability to identify fallacious arguments. *Contemporary Educational Psychology, 29*, 77–94.

Williams, B., Ponesse, J., Schacher, R., Logan, G., & Tannock, R. (1999). Development of inhibitory control across the life span. *Developmental Psychology, 35*, 205–213.

Zimmerman, C. (2007). The development of scientific thinking skills in elementary and middle school. *Developmental Review, 27*, 172–223.

CHAPTER 7

Social Cognitive Development in Adolescence

JUDITH G. SMETANA AND MYRIAM VILLALOBOS

Social cognitive development is typically defined as the study of children's and adolescents' understanding of their social world. While this definition appears relatively straightforward, there is a long-standing schism in the field in terms of who has appropriated the topic and how it has been approached. Some researchers have defined social cognitive development as pertaining to the social origins of cognition (e.g., Hala, 1997; Lewis & Carpendale, 2002). Over the past 20 years, this research has focused on children's developing understanding of others' internal psychological states, including beliefs, desires, emotions, and intentions (typically referred to as *theory of mind*). Thus, researchers have primarily examined the social and cognitive factors that may facilitate a mature understanding of mind (with varying definitions of what this entails) and the role of theory of mind in children's developing social competence. Other researchers have viewed social cognitive development as pertaining primarily to cognitive approaches to social development (e.g., Lapsley, 1990) and have focused on age-related achievements in children's and adolescents' thinking about diverse social topics, including the developing understanding of social institutions (like society and government), rights and freedoms, social relationships, and self and others as psychological systems.

While we attempt to bridge the gap between these two approaches, our focus in the present chapter is more consistent with the second orientation. In part, this is because very little

research on theory of mind has extended into adolescence. But in addition, adolescence is characterized by an increasing involvement in the world of peers and in social institutions beyond the family. It is also a developmental period when adolescents become increasingly interested in ideology and abstraction, and, thus, it is important to understand how adolescents' reasoning reflects the expansion of their social worlds and cognitive capacities. Thus, we examine a range of topics that have been examined from social cognitive perspectives.

We begin the chapter with a brief historical overview of the major theoretical frameworks that have guided much of the research on adolescent social cognitive development. Next, we focus on adolescents' reasoning about rights and civil liberties, followed by a section examining adolescents' thinking about society, government and other social institutions, and adolescents' engagement in civic and community life. Then, we discuss social cognitive approaches to adolescents' social relationships, including friendships, exclusion from social groups, and aggression. The self and self-system processes also can be objects of social cognition (Mead, 1934), and in the following section, we consider adolescents' understanding of self and personal jurisdiction, ethnic identity, their understanding of others' perspectives, and egocentrism. As we shall see, these categories are somewhat arbitrary and overlap in many instances, but they provide a framework for the types of social cognitive studies that have been conducted. The chapter concludes with a consideration of the strengths and limitations of the current research and directions for future research.

HISTORICAL AND THEORETICAL OVERVIEW

Research on many of the topics considered here was at its zenith in the 1970s, driven by the emergence of organicism as the prevailing metatheoretical orientation in the developmental sciences and more specifically, by the increased interest in structural–developmental theory. However, as described below, other theoretical perspectives also responded to the increased interest in social cognitive processes.

Structural Developmental Approaches

Global Stage Theories

Kohlberg's theory of the development of moral judgment (Colby & Kohlberg, 1987; Kohlberg, 1984) and Selman's theory of the development of perspective taking (Selman, 1971; Selman & Jacquette, 1977) both had enormous appeal during the 1980s and stimulated a great deal of research. Central to both theories was the proposition that thinking develops through a series of sequential, hierarchical, and increasingly abstract and inclusive stages.

Based on an extensive program of research, Kohlberg (Colby & Kohlberg, 1987; Kohlberg, 1984) proposed that moral judgments develop through a series of six universal stages that entail a progressive integration of concepts of justice as differentiated from social conventions, societal norms, punishment, laws, and pragmatic concerns. Through analyses of individuals' responses to hypothetical dilemmas that opposed conflicting concerns with respect to law, life, interpersonal obligations, trust, and authority, Kohlberg asserted that moral judgments shift from an external focus on obedience, punishment avoidance, and instrumental needs in middle and late childhood to a conventional understanding during early and middle adolescence that entails broader interpersonal and then societal perspectives. The attainment of

Piagetian formal operational thought was seen as providing adolescents with the ability to develop principled or "postconventional" reasoning, where moral judgments are seen as universal and entailing an understanding of rights and justice that is independent of societal conventions or rules.

Researchers also have looked at qualitative changes in perspective taking. Kohlberg asserted that the development of perspective-taking abilities, as described by Selman (1980) is necessary but not sufficient for moral judgment development. Selman hypothesized that social perspective taking develops through a series of four sequential stages, the first two of which develop during childhood. By early adolescence, teens were described as acquiring the ability to simultaneously consider their own and others' perspectives and understand that others can do the same. In middle adolescence, they were seen as able to compare their own and others' perspectives against the social system in which they live. At this point, adolescents understand how societal forces affect their own and others' perspectives. As discussed later in the chapter, these perspective-taking levels were seen as structuring reasoning about other social concepts, like friendship and ethnic identity.

These theoretical formulations led to an enormous number of studies examining the validity and generalizability of these stages. Gilligan (1982) was one of the most prominent critics of Kohlberg's theory. She argued that whereas Kohlberg's theory adequately characterized the development of boys' moral judgments (indeed, the model was originally developed on a sample of boys), the model was biased against females. Gilligan asserted that Kohlberg's scoring system led to an underestimation of girls' moral reasoning capacities and that girls' moral reasoning may be underscored as Stage 3 interpersonal morality, in comparison to boys, whose reasoning is typically scored as Stage 4 law and order morality. Furthermore, she asserted that girls' moral reasoning is different from boys, not less mature, and that the differences are not adequately captured by Kohlberg's scoring system. Gilligan asserted that for girls, morality is structured by care, responsibility to others, and the self as embedded in relationships, whereas for boys, morality is structured by concepts of justice and fairness; the self as seen as separate from others.

However, extensive reviews, as well as a meta-analysis of 80 studies that included males' and females' moral reasoning, scored for Kohlberg's moral judgment stages, have provided little support for Gilligan's claims. These reviews have revealed few sex differences in moral stages, particularly when educational and occupational levels are controlled (Walker, 1984). Furthermore, Gilligan's (1982) claim that girls' moral reasoning is oriented toward care rather than justice has received a great deal of research attention, but has not received strong empirical support. Adolescent males and females use both justice and care orientations, although females focus somewhat more on care than do males. The results also vary according to the situational contexts in which justice and care are assessed. Scrutinizing two decades of research on the issue, Walker (2006) concluded that when sex differences in moral reasoning are found, they can be attributed primarily to differences in dilemma content, particularly when participants reason about self-generated moral issues.

By the mid- to late 1980s, further questions emerged about the applicability of Kohlberg's theory of moral judgment across social classes and cultures, and interest in Kohlberg's approach waned.

Local and Domain-Specific Stage Theories

The research on moral judgment and perspective taking also generated a cottage industry of studies describing a proliferation of stages of thinking about different aspects of social development. For instance, and as described in more detail later in this chapter, researchers proposed that thinking about law and government

(Gallatin & Adelson, 1971), tolerance (Enright & Lapsley, 1981; Enright, Lapsley, Franklin, & Steuck, 1984), economic inequality (Leahy, 1983), friendship (Bigelow, 1977), and interpersonal negotiation (Selman, Beardslee, Schultz, Krupa, & Podorefsky, 1986) was progressively restructured through development.

Even among researchers who were engaged in the social cognitive research enterprise, however, questions were raised about this "ad-hoc empirical" approach, where a narrow sequence of developmental stages was described on a topic of interest to a particular investigator. The concerns focused on whether thinking really developed separately in each topic or content area or whether individuals' knowledge could be described as developing in different social knowledge domains, much as researchers studying cognitive development have proposed (Carey, 1985; Gelman, 2003; Keil, 2007).

For instance, Turiel (1983) asserted that children's and adolescents' social knowledge develops in three conceptually and developmentally distinct domains: the moral (prescriptive understanding of others' welfare, rights, fair distribution), the societal and social conventional (descriptive understanding of empirical uniformities and norms that structure social interactions in different settings), and the psychological (understanding of self and others as psychological systems). Whereas Kohlberg proposed that concepts of justice become differentiated from a global confusion of social concepts, Turiel (1983, 2002, 2006) proposed that concepts of society and social convention are differentiated from concepts of justice in early childhood and follow different developmental trajectories, based on qualitatively different types of social experiences and social interactions. As described in several sections of this chapter, much of the research from the social domain perspective has focused on how individuals distinguish between moral and social conventional concepts and apply these concepts in their reasoning about different social and moral issues.

Social Learning Approaches

Social learning theory, which predominated in the 1970s, also took a social cognitive turn in the 1980s. Expanding on the original formulation emphasizing the importance of observational learning and modeling, Bandura (1989, 1991; Bandura & Wood, 1989) reformulated social cognitive theory to emphasize the integration into individuals' behavioral repertoires of learned behaviors and the rules and strategies for where and when those behaviors are appropriate. According to Bandura, individuals set goals for themselves, which are then translated cognitively into representations that both motivate and self-regulate their behavior. Once behaviors become routinized, individuals' perceived self-efficacy in enacting the behavior, as well as their outcome expectancies, or their beliefs about the likely outcomes of engaging in a behavior, become important. Thus, social cognitive research has focused on enhancing the knowledge and skills necessary to effectively self-regulate one's own behavior (Bandura & Wood, 1989). As described in a subsequent section, Bandura's approach has been particularly relevant in the understanding of the development and maintenance of aggressive behavior.

Social Information Processing Approaches

Dodge's social information processing model has been the focus of much research, particularly in the study of aggressive behavior. In his initial model, Dodge (1986) described a five-step sequence, later expanded by Crick and Dodge (1994), of the on-line information processing steps involved in deciding to engage in and then enact social behaviors. Initially, individuals are seen as selectively attending to and interpreting internal and external cues (encoding). Next, the individual must mentally represent the meaning of the cues, especially others' intentions and threats. Then, individuals must access possible behavioral responses from memory. Once they have accessed potential responses, individuals must evaluate them and

decide on which response to employ. The final step entails the enactment of the behavior. As described in more detail later in the chapter, this model has been applied to understand the social cognitive biases that lead to and maintain aggressive behavior.

Current Approaches

With the rise of contextualist approaches (e.g., Bronfenbrenner, 1986), many researchers abandoned their interest in social cognitive studies and shifted their attention to examining adolescent behavior in different ecological niches. Nevertheless, as the research reviewed in this chapter indicates, interest in and research on adolescents' social reasoning has continued. The newer studies continue to focus on normative age trends, but they also have incorporated a focus on reasoning in more delimited and circumscribed ways that attend to contextual and cultural differences. The research has expanded to consider contextual variations in adolescents' social reasoning and how adolescents in different contexts and cultures coordinate different types of concepts in their social reasoning. In the following sections, we consider trends in social cognitive research on specific topics.

ADOLESCENTS' CONCEPTIONS OF CIVIL LIBERTIES AND RIGHTS

There has been long-standing interest in examining changes during the second decade of life in individuals' thinking about broader social institutions, like government, laws, and society, and the rights of individuals within those institutions. A large-scale cross-national study by Gallatin and Adelson (1971; Adelson, 1972) has been influential. These researchers interviewed 330 American, British, and German teens between the ages of 11 and 18. They presented their participants with a hypothetical situation: 1,000 people move to a Pacific island to form a new society and must establish a political order. This hypothetical context allowed Gallatin and Adelson to ask a wide range of open-ended questions about the nature of law and government, the answers to which were analyzed for developmental changes as well as gender, cross-national, and socioeconomic status differences.

Gallatin and Adelson (1971) found a dramatic increase with age in viewing some types of laws (for instance, requiring men over 45 years of age to have annual medical exams) as infringements on personal freedoms. They also found small age-related increases in viewing other types of civil liberties (like freedom of speech) as rights that government should guarantee. The authors asserted that adolescent development entails an increased understanding of governmental functions, including certain principles of democracy. Generalizing from the findings, Adelson (1972) concluded that findings reflected age-related increases from early to middle adolescence in abstraction (due to increases in hypothetico-deductive reasoning, as conceptualized within a Piagetian framework), time perspective (entailing a move from a focus on the present to a more historically rooted viewpoint), and ideology. As Helwig and Turiel (2002) have noted, these conclusions are similar to those drawn from Kohlberg's research on moral judgment.

Kohlberg's theory has been criticized on many fronts, but of interest here is the robust finding that principled moral reasoning, as defined by Kohlberg and his colleagues, rarely emerges during adolescence, if at all (Colby & Kohlberg, 1987). Thus, the findings from Kohlberg's research, like those of Gallatin and Adelson (1971), suggest that the majority of American adolescents (and even most adults) rarely develop abstract or principled conceptions of rights and civil liberties. This conclusion has been criticized on both conceptual and methodological grounds (Helwig, 2006; Helwig & Turiel, 2002). For instance, in Kohlberg's hypothetical situations, rights were presented in conflict with other social issues, laws, or public welfare in contextualized situations. In the global stage model structuring these studies, adolescents were only credited as having principled, abstract, and generalized concepts of rights if the respondent judged that rights override these other types of concerns across different situations. Thus, to be scored as having a mature understanding of rights, individuals must uphold or give priority to moral principles without exception (a position more extreme than that held by many moral philosophers, who allow that there are circumstances or situations where other moral or social concerns can take priority over rights). Furthermore, in some of the assessments (e.g., in Gallatin & Adelson, 1971), adolescents were asked to articulate definitions of abstract terms like rights or produce examples, for instance, of laws that should be guaranteed. Thus, the interviews had very strong production demands with respect to participants' verbal abilities.

In more recent research on conceptions of rights and civil liberties reviewed below, adolescents' thinking about rights and freedoms in abstract situations has been separated from their evaluations of situations in which rights are in conflict with other moral and social concerns. The results suggest that when different components of adolescents' reasoning are separated and examined abstractly or in contextualized situations, adolescents demonstrate a much more complex and differentiated understanding of civil liberties and rights than the previous research indicated. Thus, the more recent research suggests that the complexity of Kohlberg's dilemmas may have led to an underestimation of adolescents' understanding.

Freedom of Speech and Religion

Helwig (1995, 1997, 1998) has conducted programmatic research to examine age-related changes in conceptions of specific civil liberties, like freedom of speech and religion, which are often considered to be prototypic examples of rights in philosophical writing. In his studies, he has examined differences in adolescents' judgments when rights are presented abstractly and in more contextualized situations. Helwig (1995) found that nearly all adolescents (primarily White, middle-class American 7th and 11th graders and college students) viewed freedom of speech and religion as universally applicable rights and judged that they are not contingent on existing rules or laws (e.g., that it would be wrong for the government to prohibit them), both when they were presented abstractly and in a decontextualized manner and when they were presented in contextualized situations where there were no other competing moral concerns.

These rights were much less likely to be affirmed, however, when the same freedoms were presented as in conflict with other moral concerns pertaining to psychological harm, physical harm, and equality, particularly when physical harm was seen as a consequence. Thus, adolescents subordinated rights to other moral concerns, such as preventing harm or promoting equality. With age, adolescents increasingly coordinated different principles and concerns in their social judgments. Early adolescents were more likely than older adolescents and college students to view issues of equality as overriding civil liberties (e.g., they were less accepting of speech advocating the exclusion of low-income people from political parties) and also were less likely to uphold civil liberties when they conflicted with a law. Thus, although younger students could evaluate laws and social systems using abstract concepts of rights, nearly half of the participants used a purely legalistic perspective to evaluate the legitimacy of violating existing rules in situations where the social system was described as restricting individuals' civil liberties.

On the surface, these findings appear similar to Kohlberg's law-and-order (Stage 4) perspective, yet Helwig's (1995) findings do not accord with Kohlberg's conclusion that individuals who support compliance with laws do not have concepts of rights, that their judgments are made solely on the basis of convention or authority, or that they see rights as deriving solely from laws. Rather, the findings suggest that adolescents hold abstract concepts of rights that can be applied in straightforward

and contextualized situations and that override some but not all moral and nonmoral concerns in some situations. Thus, with age, adolescents become better able to integrate and coordinate their understanding of laws restricting civil liberties and judgments of compliance with concepts of rights. A subsequent study included younger children as well as early adolescents and college students and asked individuals to evaluate the same rights in the context of authority restrictions in different contexts such as home and school. Helwig (1997) found increases with age from early adolescence to young adulthood in grounding rights in evaluations of the agents' competencies (whether they were mature enough or mentally or physically competent). This research also indicated that, in contrast to Kohlberg's conclusions, younger children had concepts of rights, which were grounded in personal prerogatives to make their own choices.

Most of the research on adolescents' conceptions of rights and civil liberties has been conducted in Western cultures, which are often described as having an orientation toward rights and a view of individuals as autonomous agents (Shweder, Goodnow, Hatano, LeVine, Markus, & Miller, 2006). Thus, it is of interest to examine whether similar findings are obtained in other cultures, particularly those that are described as collectivist and as subordinating freedoms and rights to duties (Shweder et al.). Several recent studies in diverse cultures have revealed a similar pattern of results to the studies just described; adolescents endorse rights and freedoms in some situations but subordinate rights to other moral and social concerns in others.

For instance, Turiel and Wainryb (1998) examined these issues in a sample of Druze Arab (a small, hierarchically organized, patriarchal, and highly inbred Arab community in northern Israel) early and late (13- and 17-year old) adolescents and adults. When evaluating three rights (freedom of speech, religion, and reproduction) presented abstractly, participants overwhelmingly endorsed the freedoms for individuals in their own country (although more for freedom of speech and religion than reproduction). They also negatively evaluated laws that restricted these freedoms. Age differences paralleled Helwig's (1995) findings; late adolescents and adults viewed it as more acceptable to violate unjust laws restricting civil liberties than did early adolescents. Also similar to Helwig's (1995) findings, when Druze participants applied the same rights in conflicting situations, they sometimes subordinated those rights to other social and moral concerns, suggesting that rights can be legitimately restricted in some circumstances. Moreover, reflecting the hierarchical structure of their society, rights were applied differentially to males and females. Participants judged that it was wrong for husbands and fathers to restrict their wives', sons', and daughters' freedoms, but judged that it was more wrong to restrict sons than wives or daughters.

Using methods similar to Helwig (1995), Verkuyten and Slooter (2008) examined Dutch 12- to 18-year-old Muslim minority and non-Muslim majority adolescents' reasoning about freedom of speech and minority rights. Participants were only moderately accepting of freedom of speech and minority rights in concrete and realistic situations (unlike Helwig, they did not include an assessment of abstract situations), but endorsement varied according to the type of situation, whose rights they were asked to endorse, and the group membership of the participant and hypothetical actor. Muslims were more likely than non-Muslims to reject freedom of speech that pertained to Islam or entailed offending God and religion, whereas non-Muslims rejected minority rights entailing separate schools and burning the national flag in a demonstration, particularly for Muslim actors. Thus, as with previous research, the study demonstrated that individuals apply different forms of social reasoning to evaluate complex social issues of free speech and minority rights, but they also showed the importance of considering individuals' social identities, including their group memberships and the intergroup context.

While these studies examined the moral judgments of individuals in other cultures, Wainryb (1993) examined whether American adolescents believe that moral judgments can be generalized to other cultures described as having different moral or informational beliefs (defined as descriptive beliefs about aspects of reality). Most early, middle, and late adolescents evaluated moral acts entailing harm or injustice in other cultures as wrong, based on concerns with harm, coercion, or injustice, even when the opposing moral belief was described as part of the culture or tradition. Nevertheless, when applying moral evaluations across cultures, a considerable number of teenagers struggled to coordinate nonrelativistic moral judgments with concerns about the integrity of the culture and the need to respect other cultural traditions and beliefs. When individuals in other cultures were described as holding different informational beliefs (e.g., that children misbehave because they are possessed by evil spirits that can only be exorcised by spanking), the majority of adolescents changed their evaluation of the acts (viewing hitting as acceptable, for instance, because the intentions of a father spanking his child in such a culture would be different, or that the consequences might be different, because children might believe that spanking is helping rid them of their evil spirits). Although global stage theories of moral judgment development would predict a shift across adolescence from relativistic judgments to more generalized nonrelativistic judgments (e.g., Colby & Kohlberg, 1987), no significant age differences in evaluations were observed. Rather, adolescents at all ages made both relativistic and nonrelativistic judgments and rarely displayed a consistent orientation.

Concepts of Harm and Welfare

These findings can be further elucidated by recent research examining adolescents' reasoning and ability to weigh situations in which there is moral ambiguity about the harm caused and individuals' personal choices to behave in their own self-interest. In an ongoing study, Nucci and Turiel (2007) examined the development of children's and adolescents' reasoning about situations entailing moral concerns with either helping someone in need or refraining from engaging in harm (either direct or indirect) to the other person, as depicted in conflict with self-interest. The scenarios varied both the nature of the act and the characteristics of the child (neutral, provoked, or vulnerable) depicted in the situation.

The results of the study are complex, but generally, the researchers found that nearly all children and adolescents judged it to be wrong to harm another when harm was presented in a direct and unambiguous way. As Damon (1977) has described, the "tit-for-tat" direct reciprocity of middle childhood was found to be replaced in early adolescence by notions of equality, and concepts of fairness shifted during adolescence from a focus on direct equality to a coordination of equality with equity (Nucci & Turiel, 2007). However, along with this developing understanding of fairness, adolescents also developed a greater capacity to incorporate ambiguous aspects of moral situations. Rather than finding a linear progression of moral thinking, Nucci and Turiel found a U-shaped pattern of moral growth in children's and adolescents' ability to integrate divergent aspects of situations. They observed periods of transition in which adolescents were more able to consider aspects of moral situations but where they applied moral criteria unevenly. In particular, in early adolescence, their attempts to establish boundaries of personal jurisdiction resulted in an overapplication of conceptions of rights in morally ambiguous contexts. As adolescence progressed, adolescents were better able to distinguish personal choices from conceptions of rights and to coordinate the moral, conventional, and personal aspects of multifaceted moral situations.

Nurturance and Self-Determination Rights

Another line of research has drawn heavily on policy concerns, as reflected in the United Nations' Convention on the Rights of the Child, and the need to establish universal rights that can be used to guide policy in different countries. This research has examined conceptions of rights in terms of distinctions between children's nurturance and self-determination rights. Nurturance rights are defined broadly as society's obligation to consider the best interests of the child, and more narrowly, as children's right to care and protection, whereas self-determination rights are defined as children's ability to exercise control over different areas of their own lives (even when they might conflict with supervising adults' views) and their right to freedom of expression.

One of the earliest studies to draw this distinction was conducted by Rogers and Wrightsman (1978); although their sample included participants ranging in age from 18 to 41, participants evaluated scenarios focusing on early adolescents. More recently, Ruck and colleagues have conducted an ambitious program of research that has examined children's and adolescents' evaluations of nurturance and self-determination rights (Ruck, Abramovitch, & Keating, 1998; Ruck, Keating, Abramovitch, & Koegl, 1998). In Ruck and colleagues' initial studies, Canadian, mostly White children and adolescents responded to hypothetical vignettes describing examples of each type of rights as well as a standardized interview. When asked in an open-ended and abstract way to describe the rights that children have, adolescents gave relatively concrete responses, demonstrating the limitations of an unstructured interview to assess adolescents' knowledge. There was a shift with age from not being able to describe rights at all or focusing on recreation and play in pre- and early adolescence to an increased focus on rights to education and decision-making in middle adolescence (Ruck, Keating et al., 1998). Legal rights were not mentioned until early adolescence, and civil liberties were not mentioned until middle adolescence.

When the same participants were asked to evaluate specific vignettes depicting the two types of rights (Ruck, Abramovitch, et al., 1998), a more complex picture emerged. Nearly all participants supported children's nurturance rights (e.g., that parents have an obligation to provide food and clothing or to help with homework), based on an increased understanding with age of parental duty and responsibility (an age trend that was also evident in the unstructured interviews). In contrast, endorsement of self-determination rights (e.g., to be able to keep a secret diary or express opinions in a school newspaper) increased dramatically with age. This was accompanied by a shift with age from viewing these as entitlements to seeing them as specific self-determination rights and from supporting nurturance over self-determination rights to prioritizing self-determination, a shift that was complete by middle adolescence.

When nurturance and self-determination rights were examined specifically within the context of the home and using a more ethnically diverse sample, adolescents strongly endorsed both types of rights across ages and did not differ in their support of self-determination versus nurturance rights (Ruck, Peterson-Badali, & Day, 2002). Nevertheless, adolescents' justifications for rights took into consideration contextual differences in the vignettes. Like Helwig (1995), Ruck, Abramovitch et al. (1998) concluded that their findings do not support a global stage interpretation but rather indicate that adolescents' understanding of rights is strongly influenced by the specific contexts and situations being evaluated. Moreover, more authoritative parenting and greater responsiveness were associated with Canadian middle class mothers'—but not adolescents'—endorsement of nurturance rights; contrary to predictions, less authoritative parenting was associated with teens' endorsement of greater self-determination (Day, Peterson-Badali, & Ruck, 2006).

Ruck, Tenenbaum, and Sines (2007) examined British adolescents' evaluations of nurturance and self-determination rights for a marginalized group (political asylum seekers); in this study, rights were described as potentially in violation of authority or government practices (e.g., right to privacy versus carrying an ID card for the former; not having money for food and clothes versus government provision for the latter). From early to late adolescence, participants endorsed asylum-seekers' nurturance rights over their self-determination rights. While nurturance rights were primarily justified using moral reasons, justifications for self-determination rights focused on social conventions (references to group functioning, authority, or tradition) and personal choice or individuals' maturity.

Again, cross-cultural studies help to inform whether reasoning reflects particular cultural orientations towards rights. Early adolescents' evaluations of nurturance and self-determination rights have been examined in two cross-national studies comparing Malaysian ethnic Chinese, Canadian, American, and Swiss early adolescents (Cherney & Shing, in press). Using vignettes and open-ended interviews similar to those used by Ruck and his colleagues, Cherney and Shing found that regardless of country of origin, all early adolescents advocated rights, based on concerns with fairness, autonomy, and democratic decision making. Cross-cultural differences in individuals' emphasis on nurturance versus self-determination rights also were found, but these were not explainable by broad cultural orientations like individualism and collectivism. Rather, participants considered the features of the different situations in their judgments and reasoning, and adolescents also rejected existing cultural practices under certain circumstances. Interestingly, the researchers found that across cultures, Buddhist children advocated more for self-determination rights than did Christian children, a finding that the researchers attributed to the paternalistic nature of Christianity. Furthermore, consistent with Helwig's (1997) findings, evaluations of whether adolescents should be granted rights were based on their evaluations of children's developmental competence.

Finally, Lahat, Helwig, Yang, Tan, and Liu (in press) examined rural and urban mainland

Chinese early and late adolescents' judgments and justifications about children's nurturance and self-determination rights. Adolescents responded in writing to nine scenarios, three each entailing self-determination and nurturance rights in conflict with authorities' desires and three describing conflicts between nurturance and self-determination. Late adolescents and urban youth were more likely than early adolescents and rural youth to endorse self-determination, both when it was in conflict with authority's desires and with nurturance rights, based on concerns with personal choice and autonomy. In contrast, adolescents' justifications for nurturance rights focused on the adolescent's psychological and physical well-being. Thus, the results of this study are in accord with the findings of earlier studies of self-determination and nurturance rights in the United States (Ruck, Abramovitch, et al., 1998) and with other studies suggesting that the endorsement of rights is not restricted to individuals in Western cultures (Turiel, 2002).

Summary

The results of these studies suggest that well before adolescence, children in different cultures develop concepts of rights in abstract situations. By adolescence, they are also willing to generalize their moral evaluations to individuals in other cultures, even when those cultures are described as having opposing moral beliefs (but not when they are described as having different informational assumptions that change the meaning of the moral events). Across ages, adolescents as well as adults balanced concerns with rights with other social and moral considerations, although the ways in which these are coordinated and the types of concerns that are seen as overriding appear to vary by culture. In addition, beyond cultural variations, the results vary as a function of the specific questions asked.

Some generalizable developmental patterns in adolescents' social reasoning do emerge across the different studies, however. The ability to consider and coordinate a broader array of

different conflicting moral and social concerns, to view rights as overriding laws, to be sensitive to social contexts, and to consider the competence of the agent to exercise their rights all appear to increase with age across adolescence, even among youth in cultures commonly described as collectivist. Consistent with the emphasis on normative patterns, however, thus far, this research has focused on describing age-related changes in reasoning. Individual differences in reasoning or correlates with behavior have not been examined. It is also worth noting that despite the debates about gender differences in moral reasoning and Gilligan's (1982) claim that girls are more oriented toward care and responsibility than justice and rights, few gender differences in reasoning have been found.

ADOLESCENTS' POLITICAL, SOCIETAL, AND CIVIC CONCEPTS

A large body of research by political scientists, sociologists, and psychologists has focused on political socialization. Although the topic is large and diffuse (Gallatin, 1980), much of the earlier research on this topic adopted (at least implicitly) a social learning perspective and focused on the influence of parents and schools on children's and adolescents' political attitudes, beliefs, and behaviors. Of particular concern to understanding adolescent social cognitive development, however, is research that has examined adolescents' knowledge of politics, law, and government. (Adolescents' conceptions of rights, discussed in the previous section, also are considered an aspect of political socialization.)

In an early review, Gallatin (1980) asserted that other research (Greenstein, 1965; Hess & Torney, 1967), as well as her own cross-national research (Gallatin & Adelson, 1971), yields a consistent picture of dramatic changes from childhood to late adolescence in children's views of government. She identified a three-stage sequence in the growth of political thinking. Gallatin proposed that prior to adolescence, children view government and law as coercive; government's function is to keep individuals in line, and children's reasoning is concretely pragmatic or punitive. With the onset of adolescence, children develop a more benign but rudimentary and fragmented notion of the political system. By the end of the second decade, late adolescents espouse a more conceptual view in which government is seen as providing services and ensuring the smooth operation of society. As discussed previously, these earlier studies typically asked children and adolescents to describe terms presented abstractly and placed heavy demands on children's verbal production. When the scope of the studies has been more restricted and methods have been less open-ended, a more differentiated picture has emerged.

Adolescents' Concepts of Social Organization and Convention

Based on semi-structured interviews about hypothetical conventional dilemmas, Turiel (1978, 1983) found that social conventional understanding is structured by concepts of social organization and develops through seven levels of progressively more sophisticated understanding of social conventions as important in structuring social life. Rather than a straightforward progression, however, Turiel asserted that development entails oscillations between affirmation and negations of the importance of conventions.

Thus, preadolescents' affirmation of the importance of conventions based on a concrete understanding of rules and authority expectations is rejected in early adolescence, because conventions are seen as arbitrary, changeable regardless of the rules, and "nothing but" social expectations. Systematic concepts of social structure emerge during middle adolescence, when adolescents first understand that conventions are normatively binding because they exist within a social system with fixed roles and a hierarchical structure. This is followed in late adolescence by a negation phase where uniformity in conventions is seen as "nothing but" adherence to arbitrary societal standards

that have been codified through habitual use. Finally, and similar to Gallatin's (1980) description of late adolescents' views of government, Turiel (1978) claimed that young adults develop an understanding of conventions as uniformities that coordinate social interactions and that facilitate the smooth functioning and operation of the social system.

Few studies have examined the validity of this developmental progression in different contexts and cultures, but several studies have investigated associations between social conventional reasoning and behavior. Geiger and Turiel (1983) found that level of social conventional reasoning in early adolescence was associated both concurrently and longitudinally with conventionally disruptive behavior, such as talking back to teachers, eating in class, or talking during class. At the beginning of the study, students who were not disruptive (as identified by school counselors) all affirmed social conventions as aspects of hierarchical social systems, whereas the disruptive students were more likely to negate the importance of social conventions. A year later, all of the initially disruptive students who had begun to affirm social conventions as aspects of hierarchical social systems were no longer disruptive, but students whose reasoning had not progressed still evidenced disruptive behavior, suggesting that some disruptive behavior may be due to developmental immaturity in thinking. Similarly, Smetana (1988b) examined associations between developmental levels of social conventional reasoning and adolescents' reasoning about disagreements with parents. As discussed in a later section, adolescents' reasoning about conflicts was primarily personal rather than conventional, but nevertheless, there were some continuities between reasoning about conflicts and level of social conventional reasoning.

Reasoning About Fair Government

Much of the research on political socialization focuses on mixtures of moral and conventional concepts. For instance, Helwig (1998) examined children and adolescents' evaluative (moral) judgments of democratic political systems. He compared Canadian children and adolescents' conceptions of the fairness of different governmental systems, including different forms of democracy (consensual, direct, and representative), oligarchy (rule based on wealth), and meritocracy (where the most intelligent and knowledgeable individuals make decisions). All participants were found to evaluate the three democratic systems of national government as more fair than nondemocratic systems, but by early adolescence, direct democracy was seen as more fair than other democratic systems as well, based on appeals to democratic principles such as majority rule and representation.

These results are not surprising, given that Canadian children grow up in a democratic form of government. However, this research has been extended to compare mainland Chinese and Canadian adolescents' conceptions of different forms of government (Helwig, Arnold, Tan, & Boyd, 2007). Few differences in judgments and reasoning were found between urban, middle class teens in Canada and Nanjing, China; middle-class urban adolescents in both cultures viewed representative democracy as most fair, followed by direct democracy, based on appeals to democratic principles. To determine whether these cross-cultural similarities were due to their shared middle-class, urban status, however, the researchers also examined the evaluations of youth in two additional locations in China that varied in their degree of modernization, exposure to Western influences, and urban versus rural status. Teenagers in Canada and China, including Chinese youth in rural, less modernized villages far removed from Western influence, all asserted that democratic systems were better and fairer than oligarchy of the wealthy or meritocracy. These judgments were based on rationales that people should have a voice or "say," that they allow different segments of society to be represented in governance, and that these systems provide accountability. Moreover, Chinese youth viewed representative democracy as

better than democracy by consensus based on concerns with practicality and utility. Thus, these findings suggest that adolescents in different cultures evaluate the features of political organizations independent of official cultural ideologies and connect them to judgments of political fairness.

These findings are in accord with the results of several cross-national surveys of adolescents' civic attitudes (Torney-Purta, Lehmann, Oswald, & Schultz, 2001; Torney-Purta, Oppenheim, & Farnen, 1975). Surveying youth in 10 diverse countries, including the United States, Sweden, Iran, and Israel, Torney-Purta et al. (1975) found striking similarities in adolescents' political and civic attitudes and knowledge. In a more recent survey of political and civic attitudes and knowledge among 14-year-olds in 28 countries, Torney-Purta et al. (2001) found a great deal of diversity in adolescents' civic knowledge, but attitudes did not vary systematically as a function of whether they were living in countries with long-established democratic traditions or not. Trust in government-related institutions was lower among students from countries with less than 40 years of a democratic tradition, however.

Reasoning About Economic Inequalities

Researchers interested in political thinking also have examined adolescents' conceptions of economic inequalities. Situations of economic inequality can be seen as entailing both knowledge of economic systems and evaluative judgments of fairness. For instance, in a large study of 6- to 17-year-old African American and White students varying in social class, Leahy (1983) found that with age, adolescents attributed acquisition of wealth to individual effort, although poverty was not blamed on a lack of effort. Early adolescents reasoned in terms of equality and equity and appeared to have a "closed-system" view of wealth, viewing transformations in one dimension, such as poverty, as compensated by a transformation of the second dimension (wealth). Sociocentric views entailing changes in the social structure increased across adolescence. Although there were few differences in reasoning according to social class and race, upper-middle-class and White participants were more likely to deny the possibility of change in the social structure than were lower class and Black participants.

More recent studies have focused on social class differences in adolescents' understanding of unemployment, homelessness, poverty, and affluence (Flanagan, Ingram, Gallay, & Gallay, 1997; Flanagan & Tucker, 1999). Flanagan et al. (1997) found that inner city 7th through 12th graders were more likely than same-age teens living in the urban ring or in wealthy suburbs to attribute both poverty and affluence to personal factors such as lack of effort, lack of motivation, or failure to work hard in school, all factors that are under the individual's control. In contrast, youth living in the urban ring or in wealthy suburbs were more likely than inner city youth to offer systemic or structural explanations that attributed responsibility to social institutions, conditions, or forces beyond the individual's control. Urban (both ring and inner city) also offered more personal and individual attributions for unemployment than did suburban teens (Flanagan et al., 1997). In addition to social class differences, older teens also were more likely than early adolescents to offer both personal and situational explanations (Flanagan & Tucker). In turn, teens who gave more societal, situational explanations for poverty and unemployment were less likely to believe in the United States as an equitable society and were more likely to report that their families adhered to a compassionate ethic (Flanagan & Tucker). Thus, Flanagan et al. (1997) asserted that teenagers' differential access to societal opportunities led to differences in their understanding of the social contract and the extent to which it offered opportunities for changing economic circumstances. Although few age differences were found in the types of explanations teenagers used, other research has shown that the integrative complexity of sociopolitical

reasoning, as assessed in mother–adolescent interactions, increases with age during adolescence (Santoloupo & Pratt, 1994).

Tolerance

Dissent and tolerance for dissent are considered important characteristics of democratic societies, and political scientists have examined tolerance extensively, primarily through large survey studies of attitudes. These surveys generally show that although most American adults are tolerant when rights are presented abstractly (i.e., the right to free speech), they are much less tolerant when those same rights are presented in particularized situations (e.g., the right of Ku Klux Klan members to speak at a rally). There has been substantially less developmental research on children's thinking about tolerance, however, although several studies in the 1980s adopted a cognitive–developmental approach to examine developmental changes in children's and adolescents' beliefs about tolerance, as reflected in their reasoning about others who disagree with them (Enright & Lapsley, 1981; Enright et al., 1984).

In Enright's studies, children and adolescents responded to dilemmas focusing on diverse topics (e.g., returning money to someone who dropped it and whether to accept a party invitation from a popular girl). The results were seen as supporting a developmental progression of tolerance, which was associated with moral judgment stage development (Enright & Lapsley, 1981). Once children acquired an understanding that others' beliefs can be judged differently from their own, they shifted from being relatively intolerant (during childhood) to greater tolerance toward disagreeing others (in early adolescence) to being willing to suspend evaluations of disagreeing others without more information about the beliefs or interaction with the disagreeing other (found only among late adolescents). This sequence was observed in cross-sectional studies using different methods, although the modal ages varied somewhat according to the specific methods that were employed (Enright & Lapsley, 1981).

The sequential nature of the stages also was confirmed in a one-year longitudinal study of American students (Enright et al., 1984) that also included a cross-cultural comparison of youth in Zaire (Enright et al., 1984).

Rather than focusing on tolerance for dissenting beliefs, Avery (1988, 1992) examined adolescents' tolerance for dissenting groups, focusing specifically on teenagers' evaluations of their least liked sociopolitical groups. She selected groups of highly tolerant and highly intolerant youth, based on their extreme scores on an attitude survey administered to a large sample of high school students. While tolerant students professed dislike for their most disliked groups' beliefs, they also displayed a broader knowledge and understanding of the groups than did the intolerant students, and they were more likely than intolerant students to ground their beliefs about the right to dissent in individual rights. Evaluative judgments were found to be more important in intolerant than tolerant students' thinking, and they were more certain about the negative effects of dissent. Avery's findings are consistent with Verkuyten and Slooter (2008) in suggesting that the more negative the perception of a group, the less likely adolescents are to view that group as having rights. She invoked both developmental processes and social learning (increased exposure leading to increased role taking) to account for her results.

More recently, Wainryb, Shaw, and Maianu (1998) critiqued Enright's studies for their lack of attention to the diverse content of the dilemmas, which mixed moral and nonmoral issues. They also noted that the previous research on tolerance, which focused only on disagreeing others, provides a limited assessment, as tolerance also may include tolerance for others' beliefs and for particular acts. Taking these factors into account, Wainryb et al. found that judgments and justifications about tolerance varied according to whether dissenting beliefs pertained to moral or informational beliefs, whether beliefs were depicted as in a culture that shared or did not share those beliefs, and whether tolerance was assessed toward different beliefs, acts based on the beliefs, and individuals engaged in the acts. Adolescents in their study (primarily White, middle-class youth) were found to demonstrate patterns of both tolerance and intolerance depending on how these different features were combined. Judgments reflected an attempt to coordinate an understanding and appreciation of cultural conventions with moral issues. Adolescents were more tolerant when beliefs or acts were presented as embedded in cultural traditions than when they were not grounded in cultural practice. At all ages, adolescents were more tolerant of holding dissenting beliefs (what Enright & Lapsley, 1981, assessed) than of publicly expressing those beliefs, but tolerance for both increased across adolescence. Teens also were more tolerant of public expression of dissenting beliefs (on the grounds that expressing the beliefs does not, in itself, harm others) than of individuals engaging in the acts based on those beliefs. In turn, they were more tolerant of the persons than the acts. All adolescents were largely intolerant of actual practices based on those dissenting beliefs, although adolescents (but not children) were somewhat more tolerant when the practices were described as part of a cultural tradition. Thus, rather than indicating a general age-related trend toward greater tolerance, both tolerance and intolerance were found to coexist during adolescence. While tolerance increased with age, it did not extend to practices that were seen as coercive, unfair, or causing harm to others.

A further study examining college students' judgments of tolerance for social practices in other cultural contexts found that students generally made more positive judgments of cultural practices entailing features that individuals in the students' culture might view as immoral (e.g., harmful or unjust; for instance, an African cultural practice of knocking out the front teeth when boys turn 14) when the participants in the practice (perpetrator and victim) were seen as sharing the same informational assumptions about the meaning of the practice.

When informational assumptions were shared, the perpetrator was evaluated as a good person. Students evaluated both the practice and the perpetrator more negatively when the participants shared the same moral beliefs or when perpetrator and victim differed in moral beliefs or informational assumptions (Shaw & Wainryb, 1999). Thus, the findings suggest that young adults are tolerant of practices that seem unfair or unjust when they believe that individuals in other cultures interpret and share an understanding of the acts as beneficial and consensual, but they are not tolerant when they believe the acts are harmful or unjust or when there is perceived dissent about the acts. In general, then, the findings from these studies suggest that tolerance increases across adolescence but that late adolescents interpret practices in other cultures in terms of their moral meaning (e.g., their potential harm or injustice) in that particular cultural context. These findings also cast doubt on the assertion (Colby & Kohlberg, 1987) that late adolescents go through a stage of ethical relativism.

Civic Competence and Civic Engagement

The past decade has seen a resurgence of interest in studying adolescents' civic engagement, which has been viewed as an index of adolescents' civic competence and political and civic commitment (see reviews by Flanagan, 2005; Youniss, Bales, Christmas-Best, Diversi, McLaughlin, & Silbereisen, 2002). Indeed, one purpose of Torney-Purta et al.'s (2001) recent 28-nation study was to examine civic engagement in different societies. Although most of this research has focused on behavioral variables such as involvement in different civic activities like voting, volunteering, and participating in youth organizations, some research has examined adolescents' reasoning about their involvement.

Yates and Youniss (1996) have shown that inner city, primarily African American middle adolescents' involvement in community service increased their understanding of the social and political order and their relationship to it. Working in a soup kitchen over a three-month period was associated with increases in seeing the humanity of homeless persons. The experience also led to increases in students' consciousness of the homelessness experience (e.g., greater reflection on how it would feel to be homeless) and at a more sophisticated level, greater reflection on justice, responsibility, and homelessness as a sociopolitical issue. The authors hypothesized that even the short duration of involvement had beneficial effects on adolescents' reasoning. As service learning becomes a normative experience for American high school students, more research on its long-term influence in facilitating teens' moral and political reasoning or civic attitudes is needed.

Most of the research on civic involvement has focused on single (and typically, varying) indicators of involvement, such as voting or engaging in service activities. Metzger and Smetana (in press) examined whether late adolescents have differentiated conceptions of involvement in different civic and community activities, as examined in terms of moral, conventional, and personal judgments and justifications. Studying an ethnically diverse sample of lower-middle-class high school students, these researchers found that adolescents treated involvement in standard political activities (like voting, joining a political party, or keeping up with current affairs) as more obligatory (assessed on several dimensions) than other activities, but for conventional reasons (e.g., that it is important to follow customs and do what is expected of one or because it is important for things to run smoothly). In contrast, they viewed community service activities (e.g., feeding the homeless or working at a fund raiser aiding victims of a natural disaster) as more worthy of respect than other issues and as relatively obligatory, based on moral justifications (that it helps or benefits other people). Political activities like protesting against a law with which one disagrees or boycotting a company's products or services were rated as less obligatory, less worthy of respect, and less important than standard political or community service activities but higher on each of these dimensions than involvement in community social activities, such as joining a community sports or music club or attending a community social event or dance, which were judged to be personal choices. Furthermore, involvement in organized activities was uniquely associated with beliefs concerning similar forms of civic involvement. Involvement in volunteering and service activities was associated with viewing community service as more obligatory and more worthy of respect (e.g., more moral), while greater involvement in political activities was associated with evaluating involvement in both standard political activities and social movement activities as more obligatory and more worthy of respect. Thus, adolescents' civic beliefs were associated with their civic involvement. Because the study was cross-sectional, however, the causal direction of the findings could not be tested.

Reasoning About Other Social Practices

Decision Making in Different Contexts

Using a design similar to Helwig et al. (2007) and studying adolescents from the same three regions of China, Helwig, Arnold, Tan, and Boyd (2003) also examined Chinese adolescents' judgments and reasoning about the best way to make decisions in peer groups, families, and classrooms. In different hypothetical vignettes, Chinese adolescents evaluated the appropriateness of using group consensus, majority rule, or adult authority to decide about issues in each context that either pulled for adult involvement or autonomous decisions (e.g., the content of the curriculum or the destination of a class field trip). The results indicated that Chinese adolescents' reasoning about appropriate decision making differed by context and type of decision. Overall, teens from more rural and traditional environments

were more supportive of adult involvement in decision making, and across ages, teenagers rated adult involvement in decision making more positively for the school context than the other contexts, especially with respect to decisions about the curriculum. The developmental pattern reflected an increasing sensitivity with age to the social context and type of decision. Chinese youth viewed consensus as more appropriate to the family context and majority rule as more appropriate to the peer context. Based on their results, Helwig et al. (2003) asserted that social cognitive research should attend more to local contexts and situations rather than search for broad cultural differences in reasoning.

Learning Practices

Thorkildsen (1989, 1993) has conducted programmatic research to examine conceptions of the fairness of other social practices, focusing on different learning practices to facilitate student learning. She found a convergent pattern of responses in adolescents' reasoning about fairness in the treatment of slow versus fast learners. Overall, peer tutoring was generally seen as most fair. During adolescence (from about age 10 to about 16 years of age), students reasoned about fair educational practices in terms of equality (i.e., allowing fast and slow learners to learn the same things). At around age 18, however, there was a shift to an equity view that favored practices that would allow acceleration rather than keep everyone learning the same thing. Similar results were obtained in a sample of average-ability and high-ability youth attending university-sponsored gifted programs (Thorkildsen, 1993). With age, adolescents shifted toward a more meritocratic view of learning, where acceleration for fast learners was seen as fair. Thorkildsen viewed these findings as supporting a cognitive–developmental rather than a cultural transmission view in that similar patterns were found in youth with different social experiences.

More recently, this work has been extended to examine how high school students attending different types of schools evaluated the fairness and efficacy of three different instructional practices (modeling, lecturing, and inventing) for teaching controversial and noncontroversial science topics (Thorkildsen, Sodonis, & McNulty, 2004). Having teachers model the process of scientific inquiry was viewed as most effective, autonomy supportive, and fair for both types of topics, although students varied in their ranking of lecturing and having students invent their own ideas according to whether the topic was controversial. Thorkildsen et al. concluded that middle adolescents coordinated knowledge of epistemology, fairness, and motivation in their conceptions of procedural justice.

Summary

Global stage views of the development of political thinking, which described thinking as progressing from a view of government as coercive to an understanding of the functions of government in structuring society, have given way to more nuanced views that have examined reasoning about different aspects of government. More recent research has demonstrated that earlier conclusions about the limits of adolescents' understanding were partially due to the methods employed, as they relied heavily on adolescents' verbal production in response to abstract and open-ended questions.

Across the different areas of research reviewed in this section, the findings indicate that adolescents also take an evaluative stance on government, economic systems, and social practices. Adolescents' increased understanding of social systems is accompanied by a greater tolerance for divergent social practices and an increased ability to evaluate the fairness of different social and governmental practices. With age, adolescents in both Western and Eastern cultures endorse more democratic government (particularly direct democracy) but more meritocratic learning practices. As demonstrated in research on social inequality (and also in the preceding section, in research on rights), adolescents' reasoning is influenced

by where in the social hierarchy they sit, and with age, they contextualize their judgments of harm and fairness to evaluate social practices in terms of their cultural context. Finally, research on civic engagement suggests that adolescents differentiate among moral, conventional, and personal aspects of civic life and that these conceptualizations are associated with involvement in different civic and community activities.

ADOLESCENTS' REASONING ABOUT SOCIAL RELATIONSHIPS

Adolescents' reasoning about their social relationships has been a persistent topic of interest over the past 30 years, but as the review of research in this section will demonstrate, the focus of this work has expanded from an interest in friendships, broadly considered, to a focus on the more negative aspects of peer relationships, including peer exclusion, harassment, and aggression.

Friendship

Based on content analyses of students' friendship expectations, Bigelow (1977; Bigelow & LaGaipa, 1975) proposed that friendship conceptions develop through a three-stage sequence that entails shifts from viewing friendships in terms of propinquity and common activities in middle childhood to a normative focus (being "nice" or "good") in preadolescence and importantly, to a focus on intimacy and self-disclosure in early adolescence. Although Bigelow's studies confirmed an age-related progression in Canadian and Scottish children's reasoning, he also found that many 13- to 14-year-olds (the upper age in his samples) were still reasoning at the lower levels as well. Berndt (1982) found a similar pattern of responses. Focusing specifically on adolescents' conceptions of friendship, LaGaipa (1979) found that from early and middle to late adolescence, friendships were increasingly described in terms of authenticity and intimacy and that by late adolescence, normative descriptions of friendships declined. Sex differences, with girls more likely than boys to describe friendship in terms of self-disclosure and loyalty and commitment, also became more pronounced in late adolescence. The increased importance of intimacy in self-descriptions of friendships in early adolescence has been confirmed in other research (Berndt, 1982; Selman, 1981).

Selman (1981; Selman & Jacquette, 1977) applied his social perspective-taking model (described in an earlier section) to describe adolescents' understanding of close dyadic relationships. Focusing on six different dimensions of friendships, such as friendship formation, closeness and intimacy, trust, and conflict, and asking open-ended questions such as why are friends important, what type of person makes a good friend, and what makes friendship really close, Selman and his colleagues found that interpersonal reasoning about these different aspects of friendship changed qualitatively with age in ways that paralleled his perspective-taking levels. The focus during middle childhood on the more concrete aspects of friendships, such as sharing toys, enlarges during early adolescence. These more concrete dimensions remain important, but early adolescents also demonstrate a greater awareness of the psychological aspects of friendships. They stress the importance of more abstract dimensions, including trust, intimacy, and faithfulness, and also become more aware of their friends' personalities. Thus, trust is described as the mutual and intimate sharing of personal experiences in an ongoing relationship. With further development, adolescents understand that a satisfying relationship entails trust and a need to balance intimacy and independence. Selman hypothesized that social perspective taking was necessary but not sufficient for the development of interpersonal reasoning.

Using Selman's friendship interview, some researchers have found a great deal of heterogeneity in adolescents' reasoning about the different friendship issues (Keller & Wood, 1989; Pellegrini, 1986), although evidence for the validity of the sequence has been obtained. Keller and Wood followed a sample of 9-year-old Icelandic children longitudinally for six years and found that reasoning about interpersonal relationships progressed about one stage during this period. They also found relatively stable gender and social class effects, with lower class males evincing lower levels of friendship reasoning than lower class females or all higher social class teens.

In subsequent research, Keller and colleagues (Keller, Edelstein, Schmid, Fang, & Fang, 1998; Keller, Fuxi, Ge, Edelstein, Cecora, & Eckert, 2004) used an action–theoretical framework to examine reasoning about moral norms like promise keeping in friendship contexts. Comparing a cross-sectional sample of adolescents in Beijing with their Icelandic sample (which has been followed longitudinally through adolescence), Keller and colleagues (Keller et al., 1998, 2004) confirmed the importance and salience of friendships for adolescents in both cultures and found increasing consistency with age between practical judgments about what hypothetical story characters would do in friendship contexts and what they ought to do.

Peer Exclusion

Adolescents' reasoning about peer inclusion and exclusion from social groups has been heavily researched in the last decade. Drawing on social domain theory, Killen and colleagues have examined how gender or racial stereotypes influence adolescents' reasoning about exclusion. The consistent finding, which accords with Helwig's (1995) findings regarding rights, is that when acts are presented in straightforward contexts with no other competing concerns, most participants (regardless of age) evaluate exclusion as wrong, based on moral concerns. When stereotype information is presented in conflict with threats to group functioning, however, early adolescents are more likely than younger children to coordinate moral concerns with fairness and social conventional concerns with group processes, with greater emphasis given to group processes among early adolescents. These findings were obtained in an initial study of middle-class, European American children (Killen & Stangor, 2001) and were largely replicated in a sample of Korean, Japanese, and American children and adolescents (Park, Killen, Crystal, & Watanabe, 2003). Cultural variations depended on the particular situation; overall, and contrary to the notion that individuals from cultures characterized by a collectivist orientation would respond similarly, Japanese and Korean teens differed in their evaluations more than did American and Japanese teens. Although social judgments about exclusion varied according to the dilemma context, with age, adolescents were increasingly able to coordinate moral and conventional concerns in conflicting situations.

Using a grounded theory approach, Leets and Sunwolf (2005) examined a large sample of urban, ethnically, culturally, and socioeconomically diverse high school students' reasons for excluding others from their social groups. Unlike Killen and colleagues, who assessed adolescents' reasoning about hypothetical situations, students in this study responded to open-ended questions about actual exclusion, and the response categories were inductively generated. The most common reason for actual exclusion pertained to the unattractiveness of the excluded individual, which was viewed in terms of developing social identity, followed by concerns with punishment (retribution for previous behavior), the dangers the individual posed to the group or to individuals, and group loyalty. There was moderate consistency between adolescents' stated reasons for exclusion and their exclusionary behavior.

Reasoning About Exclusion from Social Reference Groups

Killen and Stangor's (2001) findings have been extended to demonstrate that adolescents' moral and social reasoning also is influenced by stereotypes about adolescents' social reference groups (peer crowds; Horn, Killen, & Stangor, 1999). Horn et al. examined middle adolescents' evaluations of appropriate punishment for other teens accused of hypothetical transgressions that were either depicted as consistent or inconsistent with their reference group (e.g., either football players or computer club members breaking expensive sound equipment at a school dance while drunk or breaking into the school Internet system and damaging expensive software). Overall, making unsubstantiated accusations and punishing a group for an act of vandalism based on stereotypic attributions were seen as morally wrong, but the extent to which the acts were seen as consistent with stereotypes influenced judgments. When transgressions were inconsistent with stereotypes, adolescents viewed retribution as more unjustified and unfair and decisions to punish as more severe than when the same events were depicted as consistent with stereotyped expectations for the reference group. Social conventional reasons pertaining primarily to social organizational concerns like keeping social order were applied more in these latter situations. Thus, the findings suggest that reference group stereotypes influence adolescents' social decision making in ambiguous situations.

Horn (2003) found that middle adolescents' (9th and 11th graders') identification with either high-status (cheerleaders, jocks, or preppies) versus low-status (dirties, druggies, and gothics) peer groups also influenced their judgments of peer group exclusion. Adolescents who belonged to high-status groups judged exclusion from peer groups as less wrong than did adolescents who either belonged to low-status groups or did not belong to a group. Thus, moral concepts of fairness or equal treatment were influenced both by the moral parameters of the situation as well as adolescents' position in the social hierarchy. With age, adolescents were more likely to judge exclusion as wrong.

Reasoning About Peers Based on Gender and Sexual Nonconformity

Research has shown the importance of adherence to gender-based conventions during adolescence; violations of gender norms regarding activities or appearance can lead to ridicule and harassment. In several studies, Horn and colleagues (2006a, 2006b, 2006c; Horn & Nucci, 2003) have examined how evaluations of gender nonconformity influence adolescents' judgments of the acceptability of heterosexual and gay and lesbian peers. In these studies, heterosexual, ethnically diverse 10th and 12th graders evaluated hypothetical peers who were described as straight or gay and as either conforming to or violating gender norms regarding activities or appearance and mannerisms. Horn (2006b) found that regardless of their sexual orientation, high school students viewed peers who are nonconforming to gender roles as less acceptable than gender-conforming individuals. Males in this study rated gay or lesbian youth who conformed to gender norms as more acceptable than straight teens who were nonconforming to gender norms regarding appearance and mannerisms.

Horn and Nucci (2003) found that adolescents are relatively accepting of homosexuality in particular situations but that acceptance was greater with age, among teens with more benign attitudes toward homosexuality, and in contexts entailing more limited interaction. Among girls, there was an increase with age in acceptance of homosexuality, regardless of sexual identity or gender nonconformity. Adolescents who reported more negative attitudes toward homosexuality justified their beliefs on the basis of societal and religious conventions, norms, or rules. More positive attitudes toward gay and lesbian youth were associated with evaluations that teasing, harassing, or excluding based on sexual orientation or gender nonconformity in school is wrong, based on moral concerns with fairness and rights. However, adolescents viewed excluding (but not teasing or harassing) as less wrong when the excluded individual was described as gay or lesbian than heterosexual. Horn and Nucci (2003) suggested that high school students are comfortable granting rights to gay or lesbian peers, particularly in contexts with minimal social interaction, but they are less comfortable in situations that demand more personal interactions. Adolescents and young adults appear to distinguish between their personal beliefs about the permissibility of homosexuality and their conceptions of the fair treatment of others.

Reasoning About Exclusion Based on Race/Ethnicity

Adolescents' reasoning about peer exclusion on the basis of race also has been the focus of much recent research. Phinney and Cobb (1996) interviewed Hispanic and European American pre- to middle adolescents about the permissibility of excluding another teen from a school club on the basis of their ethnicity. The majority of teens viewed intergroup exclusion based on race as wrong, and judgments did not differ as a function of participants' race, gender, or age. Reasons supporting inclusion focused on fairness, welfare, social principles, and cultural diversity, and appeals to social principles increased with age. A small minority (about 10%) endorsed exclusion, based on individuals' right to choose their own friends and cultural barriers; European American students' reasons for exclusion focused more on rights and rules than did Hispanic students, while Hispanics reasoned about cultural barriers more than did Anglos.

Subsequent research has examined reasoning about racial exclusion among U.S. youth of different ethnicities (Killen, Lee-Kim, McGlothlin, & Stangor, 2002) and in different relationship contexts, including relationships varying in intimacy (Killen, Henning, Kelly, Crystal, & Ruck, 2007; Killen, Stangor, Price, Horn, & Sechrist, 2004). Consistent with Killen and Stangor (2001) and Phinney and Cobb (1996), interviews with a large sample of European American, African American, Latino, and Asian American students about explicit racial exclusion indicated that most students viewed exclusion as wrong based on moral reasons such as unfairness, and moral reasoning about exclusion increased with age during adolescence. However, there were contextual differences in reasoning, with students also using personal reasons when evaluating friendship decisions and social conventional (e.g., group functioning) reasons when evaluating exclusion from a school club.

Similar results were obtained in studies with racially and ethnically mixed pre- and early adolescents (Killen et al., 2007) and college students (Killen et al., 2004). However, these studies also indicated that decisions about intimate relationships (e.g., dating) typically were seen as personal choices, based on personal preferences for romantic partners, and less often were seen as entailing moral concerns. Moreover, adolescents were more likely than children to view exclusion from friendships based on race as wrong (Killen et al., 2007), and minority (African American) participants were more likely than majority teens to view race-based exclusion from interracial friendship contexts as wrong when non-race-based reasons for exclusion were given. Adolescents were more likely than children to reject parental discomfort as a legitimate reason for a European American child not to bring an African American child home for a sleepover, but there also was an increase with age in tolerating peer disapproval as a legitimate reason not to bring an African American friend as a date to a dance. These findings may reflect the increasing importance of the peer context during adolescence for decisions about racial exclusion that are seen as personal choices (e.g., Killen et al., 2004) and, more generally, the ways in which nonmoral considerations are applied, particularly by majority adolescents, to justify racial exclusion. (It is also possible that the results reflect a more general shift in who adolescents view as an acceptable reference group for all of their decisions.)

Research also has shown that personal experiences with peer exclusion (both race-based and otherwise) influences minority but not majority youths' reasoning about exclusion from interracial friendships (Margie, Brenick, Killen, Crystal, & Ruck, 2006). For minority (African American, Latino, Asian American, and other) adolescents, more personal experience with peer exclusion was associated with a greater likelihood of evaluating race-based exclusion as morally wrong.

Reasoning About Aggression

As Tisak, Tisak, and Goldstein (2006) noted in their review, social cognitive theory (Bandura, 1989, 1991), Dodge's social information processing model (Crick & Dodge, 1994), and social domain theory all have been prominent in studying adolescents' social reasoning about aggression.

Social cognitive researchers have focused on the role of beliefs and values in the acquisition, maintenance, and escalation of aggressive behavior. More specifically, research from this perspective has examined beliefs about individuals' self-efficacy to enact aggressive behavior, their expectations that aggression will increase status or produce tangible rewards, the beliefs that aggression will lead to the victim's pain or suffering, and the value placed on these outcomes. Numerous cross-sectional studies (see Tisak et al., 2006, for a review) have shown that these beliefs differentiate aggressive and nonaggressive adolescents' aggressive behavior. However, Egan, Monson, and Perry (1998) further found that social cognitions influenced pre- and early adolescents' aggressive behavior as assessed longitudinally over the school year, although the effects varied by gender. For boys, different cognitions associated with aggression led to greater physical aggression over time, but only when boys initially were above average in aggression and low in victimization. Social cognitions about aggression were not very influential in predicting changes over time in physical aggression for girls, but unlike for boys, beliefs predicted increases in aggression only when girls were victimized. Much less research from a social cognitive perspective has examined adolescents' beliefs about relational aggression, although Goldstein and Tisak (2004) found that relationally aggressive adolescents had positive outcome expectancies for their aggressive behavior.

As reviewed in detail by Dodge, Coie, and Lynam (2006), Dodge's social information processing model (Crick & Dodge, 1994) has been used extensively to study aggressive and nonaggressive children and adolescents' interpretation of ambiguous cues. Numerous studies (primarily focused on children, not adolescents) have examined hostile attribution biases and have shown that aggressive children are more likely than nonaggressive children to infer hostile intent in ambiguous situations.

In a classic study, Slaby and Guerra (1988) combined the social information processing and social cognitive approaches to examine antisocial aggressive youth (who were incarcerated in a juvenile correctional facility for having committed a violent crime, such as rape, murder, or assault) and highly aggressive and low-aggressive high school students. They found that adolescents who were high in aggression had poor information processing skills (specifically, problem-solving skills) and also had beliefs that supported aggression. Thus, low, high, and antisocial aggressive youth, respectively, had evinced increasing levels of aggression, which in turn was associated with fewer social problem-solving skills and greater endorsement of nonnormative beliefs concerning aggression. For instance, antisocial aggressive youth were more likely than other teens to believe that aggression was legitimate, that their victims do not suffer, and that engaging in aggression helped them to avoid a negative self-image of themselves.

In a large sample of over 2,000 Black, White, Asian, and Latino early adolescents, Bellmore, Witkow, Graham, and Juvonen (2005) demonstrated that adolescents' aggressive normative beliefs (the latent knowledge structures that are presumed to guide the selection of appropriate responses) and hostile responses were both associated with their aggressive reputation, as rated by teachers and classmates. There also were ethnic differences in beliefs; for instance, Black adolescents approved of aggressive retaliation toward peers more than did other teens, while Black and Latino youth approved

of aggressive retaliation in response to victimization more than did White youth. Although levels of aggressive beliefs varied by gender (with boys more approving of aggressive retaliation, choosing more hostile responses, and seen as more aggressive than girls) as well as ethnicity, similar links between social cognitions and aggressive behaviors were found among all youth.

Finally, the social domain model has been used to examine differences in reasoning about moral, conventional, and personal acts. Crane-Ross, Tisak, and Tisak (1998) found that adolescents who held stronger beliefs that aggression is acceptable were more aggressive, while adolescents who believed that violations of conventions are acceptable engaged in more conventional misconduct. Tisak and Jankowski (1996) compared evaluations of adjudicated adolescents who were convicted of either felonies or misdemeanors and found that their judgments about moral and conventional transgressions were similar to those made by nonadjudicated samples, although offenders justified their moral evaluations with greater references to laws, authority, and punishment than did other youth. In addition, felons rated rules regarding personal issues to be more important and viewed conventional violations as more deserving of punishment than did misdemeanants (Tisak & Jankowski).

Peer Victimization

A related line of research has examined adolescents' social reasoning about peer harassment and victimization. Graham and Juvonen (1998) focused on the victims' attributions and construals of the causes of peer harassment. These researchers distinguished between characterological self-blame, which pertains to stable, uncontrollable causes of victimization, and behavioral self-blame, which pertains to unstable and controllable causes. In response to hypothetical incidents of peer harassment, early adolescent victims employed significantly more characterological self-blame attributions than did nonvictims, but they did not differ in their behavioral self-blame attributions, which are potentially less maladaptive. Exploratory data, described in Graham and Juvonen (2001), indicated that about two thirds of the middle school students they sampled attributed peer victimization to characteristics of the victims, with about half of all the responses attributing victimization to causes controllable by the victim (e.g., annoying behavior), and a smaller proportion attributing victimization to causes that are not controllable by the victim (e.g., physical unattractiveness). Only about a third of the responses attributed victimization to characteristics of the aggressor or the school environment. Furthermore, Graham and Juvonen (1998) found that early adolescents who perceived themselves as targets of others' harassment but who were not perceived as victims by peers made similar characterological attributions as did teens who were identified by peers as victims of harassment. Thus, these authors suggest that the perception that they are singled out for harassment leads victims to come to blame themselves for their abuse.

In an interesting analysis of ethnic variation in victimization, Graham and Juvonen (2001) suggest that being in the numerical minority in a school is an important antecedent of victimization; they found that students of different ethnicities who were numerical minorities in a multiethnic school were over-represented as (peer nominated) victims than would be expected by chance. But the victims who were part of the numerical ethnic majority of the school experienced lower self-esteem, more loneliness, and greater rejection by peers than victims belonging to the numerical ethnic minority groups in the school. They assert that students who were deviant from the dominant ethnic group norms were especially vulnerable to maladjustment as a consequence of victimization because they were more likely to experience characterological self-blame. Thus, Graham and Juvonen (2001) argue for the importance of examining the effects of ethnicity within the context of school composition

on victimization rather than the effects of ethnicity in and of itself.

Summary

Research on reasoning about friendships indicates that with age, adolescents—and particularly girls—increasingly conceptualize friendships in terms of intimacy, closeness, and trust. Moreover, there is some evidence that similar age-related changes in reasoning are found across cultures. As the research reviewed in this section suggests, however, social cognitive research has largely shifted from studying adolescents' conceptualizations of friendships to focus on the more problematic aspects of adolescents' social relationships, including peer harassment, victimization, and peer group exclusion.

When asked to evaluate peer exclusion abstractly and with no competing concerns, most adolescents evaluate exclusion from social groups (in nonintimate contexts, like school clubs) on the basis of gender or race as wrong, based on moral concerns with fairness. Compared to younger children, however, early adolescents also demonstrate an increased ability to consider group processes, and concerns with group processes override moral concerns in some circumstances (e.g., when peer disapproval is anticipated). Adolescents' social reasoning also is influenced by social reference group stereotypes; adolescents are better able to comprehend the morally troubling aspects of peer group exclusion when it is inconsistent with reference group stereotypes than when it is consistent with those stereotypes.

Moreover, across the different topics studied, the evidence strongly suggests that personal experience influences adolescents' social reasoning, with those who benefit more from exclusion less likely to view exclusion as wrong. For instance, individuals' location within peer reference groups influences adolescents' evaluations of peer exclusion, with lower status individuals viewing exclusion from social groups as more wrong than higher status youth. Likewise, minority youth (and especially minority youth with relatively more personal experience with exclusion) view race-based exclusion as more wrong than do majority youth. Adolescents also appear to differentiate between the types of settings and view exclusion in more intimate settings (such as dating) as more of a personal choice. With age, however, there is an increasing tendency to judge peer group exclusion as wrong regardless of context or circumstance. As this suggests, the research on peer exclusion has focused primarily on normative age trends in evaluating peer group exclusion in different contexts and by different groups.

In contrast, research on social reasoning about aggression and peer victimization has focused primarily on individual differences, with the aim of predicting the biased social cognitions that influence aggressive behavior or victimization. This work has consistently shown that different biased social cognitions and beliefs differentiate aggressive and non-aggressive teens, while the research on peer victimization indicates that characterological and self-blame attributions are implicated in peer victimization. Group composition rather than ethnicity alone (whether one is in a numerical majority or minority group) moderates the effects of victimization on adjustment.

ADOLESCENTS' CONCEPTIONS OF SELF, IDENTITY, AND PERSONAL ISSUES

At first blush, adolescents' self-conceptions may not appear to be within the same realm as adolescents' reasoning about their social worlds, but research considering the self as an object of thought (e.g., self-conceptions) and adolescents' ability to apprehend others' psychological states have been enduring topics of social cognitive research. In the following sections, we review research on adolescents' thinking about the self and the boundaries of personal jurisdiction, adolescents' perspective taking, ethnic identity, egocentrism, and finally, theory of mind.

Self-Conceptions

Several researchers (Broughton, 1978; Damon, 1988; Damon & Hart, 1982; Harter, 1999, 2006; Harter, Bresnick, Bouchey, & Whitesell, 1997) have provided integrative descriptions of developmental changes in self-conceptions during childhood and adolescence (see also chapter 9, this volume). Across the different research programs, the evidence suggests that the more traitlike understanding of the self in middle childhood is transformed during early adolescence to more abstract, integrated, and psychological notions. Broughton's cross-age interviews about mind, self, and reality indicated that early adolescents begin to distinguish between mental and physical reality. The mind is increasingly seen as volitional and independent of physical activity, and the self is seen in primarily mental terms. Broughton described the self as having thorough and private access to inner processes and also able to evaluate the self's actions. Yet both Broughton (1978) and Harter and Monsour (1992) have found that early adolescents' self-descriptions remain compartmentalized and not yet fully integrated in that they express but do not appear to recognize contradictory statements. Harter and Monsour (1992) further claim that early adolescence marks the emergence of different role-related selves, where adolescents also report different levels of self-esteem in different relationships, as well as the emergence of false-self behavior (Harter et al., 1997).

Middle adolescence brings an increased focus on introspection (which is thought to be related to egocentrism, as discussed in a later section) and a further proliferation—but also some integration—across multiple selves (Damon, 1988; Harter, 2006; Harter & Monsour, 1992). Nevertheless, middle adolescents' (and according to Harter et al., 1997, especially females') increased recognition of their contradictory self-descriptions and their inability to coordinate them leads to considerable intrapsychic confusion and conflict (Harter & Monsour, 1992). In late adolescence and early adulthood, both Broughton (1978) and Damon and Hart (1982) have proposed that different personal beliefs and moral values become more integrated and internalized. Furthermore, Harter and Monsour (1992) asserted that the contradictory aspects of adolescents' self-portraits are no longer seen as in opposition to each other as they become integrated into a more abstract, higher order construction.

Concepts of Personal Choice and Personal Jurisdiction

Extensive research from the social domain perspective has examined adolescents' developing conceptions of personal choice and personal jurisdiction. Personal issues have been defined as issues that are beyond the realm of justifiable social or parental regulation and moral concern because they pertain to privacy, control over one's body, and personal preferences and choices (Nucci, 1981, 1996, 2001). Among American adolescents, personal issues include choice of friends, appearance, and preferences about leisure activities. Personal issues have been described as an aspect of individuals' developing sense of agency, effectance, and uniqueness and thus as a universal developmental need (Nucci, 1996).

Numerous studies (Smetana, 1988a, 1989, 2000; Smetana & Asquith, 1994; Smetana & Gaines, 1999; Smetana, Daddis, & Chuang, 2003) have shown that American parents believe that it is important for their teenagers to have some areas of personal freedom and that the boundaries of teenagers' personal freedoms increase with age; nevertheless, adolescents and parents disagree about just how much personal freedom teenagers should have. Research has shown that American adolescents typically affirm the legitimacy of parental authority over moral, conventional, and prudential issues, but they reject parental authority over personal issues (Smetana, 1988a, 2000; Smetana, Crean, & Campione-Barr, 2005). Both cross-sectional (Fuligni, 1998; Smetana, 1988a; Smetana & Asquith, 1994) and longitudinal studies (Smetana, 2000; Smetana, Campione-Barr, & Daddis, 2004; Smetana et al., 2005)

have indicated that adolescents' claims to personal jurisdiction increase with age. Moreover, similar findings have been obtained among American adolescents from European, Filipino, Mexican, Chinese (Fuligni, 1998) and African (Smetana, 2000) backgrounds, although differences were found in the specific ages at which autonomy over different issues was expected; autonomy generally develops later in minority teens. While parents also agree that teenagers should have more personal jurisdiction as they get older, parents' judgments consistently lag behind adolescents', suggesting that the push for more personal freedom comes from "the bottom up."

Personal Reasoning and Adolescent–Parent Conflict

Smetana (1988b, 1995a) has claimed that these discrepancies between parents' and adolescents' views of adolescents' personal freedoms lead to the increases in adolescent–parent conflicts typically observed in early to middle adolescence. For example, research examining adolescents' and parents' reasoning about family conflicts and disagreements has shown that adolescents may assert that cleaning their room, deciding what to wear or how to look, who their friends should be, when to do their homework, and what music or television shows to watch are personal issues. In contrast, parents typically view the same issues as family or cultural conventions or as prudential and pertaining to the teen's health, safety, or comfort and, thus, legitimately decided by parents. Moreover, longitudinal analyses indicated that middle-class African American adolescents' personal reasoning about disagreements with parents increases significantly from early to middle adolescence, coinciding with normative increases in conflict intensity (Smetana et al., 2003). Thus, adolescent–parent conflict appears to entail adolescents' attempts to expand their autonomy by renegotiating the boundaries of legitimate parental authority.

Whether adolescents view some behaviors as personal or prudential also has been associated with their involvement in risk behavior. High school students are more likely to view illegal drug and alcohol use as an issue of personal discretion or prudence than a moral or conventional issue (Nucci, Guerra, & Lee, 1991), but (self-reported) high drug users were more likely to view drug and alcohol use as a personal issue and as less harmful and less wrong than were low drug users. Whereas low-drug-using adolescents viewed parents and the law as having the legitimate authority to regulate drug use, high-drug-using teenagers viewed only themselves as having legitimate authority over this issue. Whether these different conceptualizations of drug use antecede or are a consequence of drug use merits further attention.

School and Teacher Authority

The age-related changes observed in American adolescents' concepts of legitimate parental authority also have been observed in adolescents' judgments of school and teacher authority (Smetana & Bitz, 1996). In a study of lower-middle-class, ethnically diverse students, adolescents of varying ages (from pre- to late adolescence) were found to uphold school and teacher authority to regulate hypothetical school moral, conventional, and prudential issues, but they rejected teachers' authority to regulate personal issues in school, such as deciding which friends to sit next to in class, how to spend lunch money, and with whom to have lunch. Compared to their view of authority at home, adolescents were more accepting of teacher and school authority to regulate school issues that entailed overlapping conventional and personal concerns (referred to as contextually conventional issues); adolescents recognized and were accepting of the need for schools to restrict their personal freedom in the service of maintaining social order. Of practical significance, this and other research (Eccles et al., 1993; Eccles, Wigfield, & Schiefele, 1998) has suggested the importance of the "stage–environment" fit between the adolescents' developmental needs for autonomy and the organization of the school environment.

That is, the structure of many junior high school classrooms restricts adolescents' personal jurisdiction just at the time when their claims for greater autonomy are on the rise, perhaps resulting in decreases in intrinsic motivation for school.

Parenting, Family, and Peer Influences on Personal Reasoning

Several studies have shown that parenting styles are associated with how adolescents draw boundaries between legitimate social and moral regulation and personal issues (Darling, Cumsille, & Pena-Alampay, 2005; Smetana, 1995b). Permissive and undifferentiated parents appear to overextend the boundaries of adolescents' personal domains and view more issues as personal for their teens than do other parents (Smetana, 1995b). Findings from a large cross-national study (Darling et al., discussed in more detail below) also indicted that adolescents from more authoritative families viewed parental authority as more legitimate, although authoritative parenting was not associated with differences in actual autonomy. In contrast, Smetana found that parents' reports of less authoritative parenting were associated with adolescents' greater emotional autonomy (which has been linked with detachment rather than healthy adjustment), while more authoritarian and less authoritative parenting was associated with more frequent and more intense adolescent–parent conflict.

More recent longitudinal research has shown the importance of age-appropriate parental autonomy granting. In a five-year longitudinal study, Smetana et al. (2004) found that African American middle-class adolescents who were granted more unilateral decision-making control over personal issues in early adolescence reported more depressed mood five years later, while increases in adolescents' decision-making autonomy from middle to late adolescence were associated with better adjustment. Likewise, in a cross-national study of American and Japanese youth, parental overcontrol of the personal domain was associated with greater internalized distress (Hasebe, Nucci, & Nucci, 2004).

Siblings also may influence expectations for autonomy and judgments of personal issues. Comparing American, lower-middle-class, primarily White early and middle adolescents with younger and older siblings, Campione-Barr and Smetana (2007) found that later-born adolescents expected more autonomy over personal issues at earlier ages and reported more conflict with parents than same-age, first-born teens. This may be because, as also found in this study, parents of later-borns viewed fewer issues as personal for their adolescents than did parents of first-borns. Family structure also moderated these judgments; later-born adolescents in single-parent and step-parent families viewed a greater number of hypothetical issues as within their personal domains than did first-born adolescents, but two-parent biological families did not differ.

Daddis (2008, in press) has proposed that peers also may influence adolescents' push for greater personal jurisdiction from parents. That is, adolescents may compare the extent of their personal freedoms with what their close friends are allowed to do, leading to disagreements with parents. Examining American middle class, early and middle adolescents and their reciprocally nominated best friends, Daddis (2008, in press) found that best friends were more similar than nonfriends in their reasoning about legitimate parental authority and that best friends were perceived as influential in deciding what types of issues should be personal, particularly in middle adolescence.

Daddis, Driscoll, and Thacker (2007) also have found that peer reference groups influenced adolescents' beliefs about the legitimacy of parental authority regarding personal issues. Among teens in the "normal" crowd, evaluations of the legitimacy of parental authority for personal, prudential, and moral issues were similar to those observed in previous research, with teens affirming parents' legitimate authority to regulate moral and prudential issues and rejecting parents' legitimate authority over

personal issues. Comparing across crowd membership, however, "normals" affirmed legitimate parental authority over prudential issues more than did "jocks," "preps," or "outcasts" ("nerds" and "loners"), who, in turn, viewed parental authority as more legitimate than did teens in the alternative ("skaters" and "goths") or hip-hop crowds. Similar findings were obtained in evaluations of the legitimacy of parental authority over moral issues, except that "normals" and "preps" did not differ significantly. Surprisingly, however, "jocks," "preps," "normals," and "alternatives" rejected parental authority over personal issues more than did teens in the hip-hop and outcast crowds. While the sample size for this study was relatively large (more than 500 high school students), further research will be needed to determine why youth in the hip-hop and outcast crowds were more accepting of parental authority over personal issues than youth in the other reference groups.

Cultural Influences on Personal Reasoning

Most studies of adolescents' conceptions of autonomy and personal jurisdiction have been conducted in Western contexts, but several studies have been conducted in different cultural contexts. For instance, replicating the studies of American adolescents' reasoning about disagreements with parents, Yau and Smetana (1996, 2003) found that lower socioeconomic status Chinese adolescents in Hong Kong and Shenzen (in the People's Republic of China) primarily reasoned about conflicts with parents (particularly over doing homework and choice of activities) in terms of personal jurisdiction. The age-related patterns were similar to those found in American samples; across contexts, appeals to personal jurisdiction, as assessed in individual interviews, were greater among older than younger adolescents. The findings suggested, however, that Chinese teenagers may have fewer and less intense conflicts and that conflicts may be less likely to be resolved in terms of transfers of power from parents to children than has been observed among European American families.

Appeals to personal prerogatives and personal entitlements also have been observed among adolescents in northeastern Brazil (Nucci, Camino, & Sapiro, 1996) and between Druze Arab and Jewish adolescents in Israel (Wainryb & Turiel, 1994), although social class (lower versus middle) effects in interaction with age were found among Brazilian youth, and cultural differences were found among Israeli youth. The study of Brazilian youth (Nucci et al., 1996) indicated that regardless of age, autonomy over personal acts was seen as more acceptable than autonomy over prudential acts. Prior to adolescence, however, middle-class children viewed personal issues as personal prerogatives based on justifications pertaining to privacy, autonomy, and rights, while lower class children evaluated these same issues in terms of norms and parental authority constraints. The acceptability of engaging in personal choices increased during adolescence so that by middle adolescence, all youth primarily justified their judgments of personal issues in terms of personal preferences, prerogatives, and rights. Thus, early developing social class differences were moderated by developmental processes. A subsequent study of mothers and daughters in Brazil (discussed in Nucci, Hasebe, and Lins-Dyer, 2005) indicated that across age and social class, Brazilian adolescents evaluated personal issues as legitimately subject to teens' control. Their judgments of actual control reflected social class differences, whereas their evaluations of ideal control did not. Lower class girls viewed their mothers as having more control, particularly over prudential and conventional issues, than did middle-class girls, and these findings were mirrored in mothers' judgments. In addition to social class effects, judgments of parental control regarding overlapping issues also has been found to vary as a function of immigration status and acculturation in a Mexican immigrant and Mexican American sample (Lins-Dyer, 2003, as discussed in Nucci et al., 2005), with

less American-acculturated parents exerting more control.

Beliefs about legitimate parental authority and obligations to obey parental rules have been examined among a large sample of teens in Chile, the Philippines, and the United States (with the U.S. sample consisting primarily of Hispanic teens in Miami; Darling et al., 2005). The normative patterns were very similar across cultures; in all three countries, adolescents' demands for autonomy increased with age. Adolescents clearly differentiated among domains in their beliefs regarding the legitimacy of parental authority, with parental regulation of prudential issues seen as most legitimate. Interestingly, across contexts, adolescents were least accepting of parental authority and exerted autonomy most regarding multifaceted issues, such as where teens go with friends, which are seen as personal by teens but prudential by parents. Nevertheless, the fit between teens' autonomy demands and parents' autonomy granting varied by culture. Chilean and Filipino parents granted autonomy more slowly than adolescents wanted, while American parents granted autonomy at earlier ages than adolescents demanded.

Likewise, in a large sample including nearly 3,500 adolescents in Chile, Cumsille, Darling, Flaherty, and Martinez (2006) replicated the domain differences and age trends (toward rejection of parental authority over personal issues) found in previous research. In a study employing a different Chilean sample, and controlling for parenting, adolescents' issue-specific beliefs about legitimate parental authority and obligations to obey parents (but not their global beliefs) were found to predict obedience (Darling, Cumsille, & Martinez, 2007). However, Cumsille et al. also identified three distinct patterns of beliefs about parental authority. The most frequent pattern entailed acceptance of legitimate parental control over most prudential, multifaceted, and personal items. A smaller number differentiated parental authority according to domains (e.g., acceptance of parental authority over prudential items and rejection over personal items). Least frequently, Chilean adolescents rejected parental authority over both prudential and personal items. Thus, as Daddis et al. (2007) found in his study of American adolescents' reference groups, within normative, age-related changes, there were individual variations in the patterning of adolescents' autonomy beliefs that may have different developmental implications.

Reasoning About Adolescent Disclosure and Nondisclosure

Finally, an emerging area of research has focused on adolescents' social reasoning about disclosure and secrecy in adolescent–parent relationships. This research is based on recent findings by Stattin and Kerr (2000) (Kerr & Stattin, 2000) suggesting that parents' knowledge of adolescents' behavior and activities outside of the home comes from adolescents' voluntary disclosure of information, rather than from parents' attempts to monitor adolescents' behavior. Accordingly, several studies have examined adolescents' justifications for disclosing and not disclosing information to their parents. Darling, Cumsille, Caldwell, and Dowdy (2006) reported that adolescents fully disclosed to parents about their activities and whereabouts primarily because they felt obligated to and, less frequently, because they hoped to change their parents' minds or because they could not get away with not disclosing. In a primarily European American, lower-middle-class sample, Smetana, Villalobos, Tasopoulos-Chan, Gettman, and Campione-Barr (in press) found that middle adolescents reported not disclosing to parents about their prudential activities (like attending parties where teens are drinking or drinking alcohol themselves) due to concerns with parental disapproval or punishment, whereas they did not disclose about personal activities because they viewed them as private matters or as not causing harm. Adolescents' reasons for not disclosing about peer issues focused on both concerns about parental disapproval and punishment and the assertion that these were private matters.

Similar patterns in reasoning were found in a large study of American high school students from Chinese, Mexican, and European backgrounds (Yau, Tasopoulos-Chan, & Smetana, 2007), although some gender and ethnic differences in reasoning were found. For instance, across groups, girls were more likely than boys to not disclose to parents about prudential behavior (such as drinking alcohol, smoking cigarettes, or having unprotected sex) because of fear of parental disapproval or punishment. Concerns about parental disapproval or punishment for disclosing about behaviors like watching R-rated movies or their communications in instant messaging (which were referred to as multifaceted issues) were voiced more by Mexican American than Chinese American teens, whereas for multifaceted and personal issues, concerns that parents would not listen or understand were reported more by American adolescents from Chinese than either Mexican or European backgrounds.

Summary

The research reviewed in this section indicates that among American adolescents of different ethnicities and among youth in different cultures, reasoning about personal choices and personal jurisdiction increases with age during adolescence, although there is some cultural and ethnic variation in the timing, boundaries, and content of the personal domain. Furthermore, person-centered approaches suggest that there is also variability in the patterning of adolescents' appeals to personal freedoms.

Social Perspective Taking

For more than 30 years, Selman and colleagues' program of research has focused on describing the development of perspective-taking ability, or the ability to understand and coordinate one's own and others' perspectives. As described at the outset of the chapter, Selman originally described four qualitatively distinct developmental levels of perspective taking, the last two of which were seen as developing during adolescence. Early adolescents develop the ability to simultaneously consider one's own and others' perspectives and to understand that others can do the same. Middle adolescents are able to evaluate their own and others' perspectives in a broader, social systemic context. The sequential nature of the hypothesized scheme was supported in a small, 5-year longitudinal study using a socioeconomically diverse, primarily European American (but 25% African American) sample of boys (Gurucharri & Selman, 1982). Moreover, a 4-year longitudinal follow-up of a small sample of disturbed boys, compared with a matched control sample of typically functioning boys, indicated that the disturbed boys progressed through the same sequence as the control boys, although at a slower pace, as would be expected theoretically (Guracharri, Phelps, & Selman, 1984). However, the developmental lag evidenced by boys in the disturbed group diminished over time.

Research has shown that adolescents who have more mature social perspective-taking skills do not necessarily have better interpersonal relationships, however (Selman & Adalbjarnardottir, 2000). In an attempt to explain this discrepancy, Selman's program of research has shifted over time from an exclusive focus on social perspective taking to examining the association between social perspective taking and actual behavior. The notion of interpersonal negotiation skills, described as a psychosocial competence that entails individuals' thinking about and strategies for solving social conflicts, was incorporated in the model (Selman et al., 1986). Thus, Selman and Schultz (1990) proposed that interpersonal negotiation skills develop sequentially, in tandem with the development of social perspective taking. Research has shown that the developmental level of interpersonal negotiation, as assessed in hypothetical situations, increases in maturity with age from childhood to adolescence (Burack et al., 2006; Selman et al., 1986), is more mature among girls than boys (Selman et al., 1996), and is more developmentally mature among nonmaltreated youth

than among adolescents with a history of maltreatment (Burack et al., 2006).

In attempting to account for the observed discrepancies between perspective-taking levels and negotiation skills, Selman and his colleagues have found that levels of interpersonal negotiation are influenced by both context and experience. Shultz and Selman (1990) found that self-reported interpersonal negotiation abilities as assessed in real-life situations were inversely associated with socioeconomic status. Moreover, in their sample of early adolescents from urban schools, more than a third of the sample showed a discrepancy between interpersonal negotiations in hypothetical versus real-life dilemmas, with the vast majority at higher developmental levels when reasoning about hypothetical than actual situations (as would be expected from Selman and colleagues' model). Further, controlling for socioeconomic status, interpersonal negotiation in hypothetical dilemmas and emotional maturity (assessed in terms of defense mechanisms and object representation), both alone and in combination, significantly predicted self-reported interpersonal negotiation strategies in real-life situations. Finally, Selman et al. (1986) found that adolescents' interpersonal negotiation strategies are more developmentally mature when reasoning about situations involving peers than about situations involving adults and when the dilemmas pertained to personal rather than work-related issues. The most mature interpersonal negotiations were found when adolescents reasoned about dilemmas pertaining to personal issues with peers.

Other studies have examined the utility of Selman's developmental model of interpersonal negotiation for understanding typically developing and atypical samples, but hypothesized differences in developmental levels of negotiation have not been consistently obtained. For instance, developmental level of reasoning about interpersonal negotiation (as assessed using hypothetical dilemmas) did not differ among White, middle-class adolescents with and without bipolar disorder, although adolescents with bipolar disorder reported having poorer social skills than their healthy counterparts (Goldstein, Miklowitz, & Mullen, 2006). In addition, the Burack et al. (2006) study described previously did not find a significant association between early to late adolescents' developmental level of reasoning about interpersonal negotiation and either internalizing or externalizing behaviors, although they did find an association between reasoning about interpersonal negotiation and internalizing behaviors among nonmaltreated children. In contrast, Zahed, Im-Bolter and Cohen (2007) found that the developmental maturity of interpersonal negotiation as assessed on hypothetical dilemmas was negatively associated with externalizing behaviors in a sample of 7- to 14-year-olds.

The inconsistencies in the findings and the lack of clear associations between developmental levels of reasoning about negotiation and adolescents' behaviors led Levitt and Selman (1996) to incorporate personal meaning into their framework. They asserted that personal meaning adds an emotional component to the framework and integrates the psychosocial competencies of interpersonal understanding and skills with individuals' developmental histories to influence behavior (Levitt & Selman). In their revised model, social perspective taking is seen as the basis for personal meaning. Personal meaning is not proposed to differ qualitatively with age, because it is influenced by contextual variables, such as family and peer factors, and biological factors like temperament and neurological development. Thus, Levitt and Selman suggested that personal meaning, along with interpersonal understanding and skills, mediates associations between contextual and biological variables and social behavior.

Reasoning About Ethnicity

Quintana and colleagues (Quintana, 1994; Quintana, Casteneda-English, & Ybarra, 1999) have applied Selman's original social perspective-taking stages to the development of Mexican American children and adolescents' ethnic perspective-taking ability, which refers to how individuals understand ethnicity. Based on semistructured interviews administered to Mexican American children and youth, Quintana described four levels of ethnic perspective taking that develop from childhood to adulthood; the last two developmental levels were seen as occurring during adolescence. Starting around early adolescence, Quintana asserted that teens develop a group perspective regarding ethnicity; they abandon the idea that ethnicity is defined by concrete characteristics such as color of skin or language spoken and become more aware of subjective variables that distinguish ethnic groups, such as background experiences related to ethnicity. They also begin to understand that views of ethnicity are influenced by contextual variables like parenting and their ethnic rearing environment. Minority youth also develop more of a group consciousness that involves criticizing the status quo by blaming the (majority) group in power for the minority group's disadvantaged position. Therefore, stereotypes of their group shift from negative to positive.

According to Quintana (1994), late adolescents develop a multicultural perspective on ethnicity. They begin to appreciate the value of ethnic diversity and understand the perspective of individuals in both the dominant and oppressed groups. As hypothesized, ethnic perspective-taking levels have been found to be associated with the developmental maturity of social perspective taking and with ethnic knowledge and identity among Mexican American children and adolescents (Quintana, 1994; Quintana et al., 1999), but not with ethnic socialization (Quintana et al., 1999).

Karcher and Fisher (2004) criticized Quintana's research for not considering how both the immediate and more distal environment influence development. Based on dynamic skill theory, they proposed that adolescents' intergroup understanding develops toward increasing complexity and that adolescents differentiate and coordinate multiple abstract thoughts or beliefs about ethnic groups (like the characteristics of individuals in an ethnic group, the experiences particular to a certain ethnic group, and adolescents' feelings toward an ethnic group) to form a more complex understanding that ultimately incorporates all of these beliefs. These researchers examined Caucasian and Mexican American early, middle, and late adolescents' ethnic understanding, evaluated in terms of both probed responses and spontaneous, unstructured responses. They found support for their model, as interpersonal understanding skills increased with age. Congruent with Vygotsky's zone of proximal development, they also found that adolescents in the high-support (probed) condition described their own ethnic group in more complex terms than they described other ethnic groups. Karcher and Fisher (2004) found that the difference between optimal and functional skills also increased with age. Furthermore, more complex intergroup understanding was associated with both prior exposure to other ethnic groups and with higher levels on Quintana's (1994) ethnic perspective-taking interview.

Adolescent Egocentrism

Most of the research discussed thus far has viewed age-related changes in adolescents' social reasoning in terms of increased developmental maturity. However, the research on adolescent egocentrism suggests that social cognitive development also has limitations that can bring about distortions in social reasoning. In an initial formulation, Elkind (1967) hypothesized that the transition to formal operational thought in early adolescence leads to two social cognitive biases, or forms of adolescent egocentrism, the *imaginary audience* and the *personal fable*. According to Elkind, the imaginary audience entails adolescents' mistaken belief that others are constantly paying attention, watching, and/or criticizing them, while the personal fable refers to adolescents' beliefs that they are unique and invulnerable. Both beliefs were thought to emerge during the early development of formal operations,

leading to biases or errors in judgments that are resolved once formal operational thought is consolidated in middle to late adolescence.

A great deal of research has examined the evidence for age-related changes in the personal fable and egocentrism, but this research has not supported Elkind's theory. Regardless of how egocentrism is assessed, age-related changes have not been observed (Frankenberger, 2000; Greening, Stoppelbein, Chandler, & Elkin, 2005; Jahnke & Blanchard-Fields, 1993; Quadrel, Fishhoff & Davis, 1993; Vartanian & Powlishta, 1996), nor have significant associations been obtained between formal operations and adolescent egocentrism either in adolescence (Jahnke & Blanchard-Fields) or young adulthood (Rycek, Stuhr, McDermott, Benker, & Swartz, 1998). Moreover, numerous studies have found sex differences in egocentrism, with imaginary audience thinking and uniqueness as assessed on the personal fable subscale more prevalent among adolescent females than males (Frankenberger, 2000, 2004; Goossens, Beyers, Emmen, & van Aken, 2002; Greening et al., 2005; Ryan & Kuczkowski, 1994; Rycek et al., 1998; Schonert-Reichl, 1994). These gender differences are not consistent with the hypothesis that the emergence of adolescent egocentrism is due to the onset of formal operations, as sex differences in formal operational ability typically have not been found (Vartanian, 2000). In addition, according to Elkind's original theoretical formulation, adolescent egocentrism should decline later in adolescence, but the available research indicates that egocentrism is present in childhood and continues into adulthood. These anomalies have led to several reformulations of the construct and a new set of measures.

As discussed by Vartanian and Powlishta (1996), Lapsley and Murphy (1985) proposed that adolescent egocentrism was the result of problems with interpersonal understanding. More specifically, they linked egocentrism to Selman's (1971; Selman & Jacquette, 1977) levels of interpersonal understanding, and more specifically, to Level 3 understanding.

However, the empirical evidence has not supported this reinterpretation either, although social perspective taking has been found to be associated with the personal fable (but not the imaginary audience; Jahnke & Blanchard-Fields, 1993; Vartanian & Powlishta, 1996). As would be predicted, adolescents who were at Selman's Level 3 had higher scores on assessments of the personal fable than did adolescents who were at Level 2.

A second reinterpretation, called the "new look" (Lapsley, 1993), considered adolescent egocentrism as the result of the separation–individuation process, as described by Blos (1962, 1979). The personal fable and imaginary audience were proposed to have different adaptive functions in this process. The personal fable was thought to promote assertion and individuation through an active focus on the self, whereas the imaginary audience was thought to promote connectedness by replacing the now-lost parental introjects. Some support for the "new look" has been obtained. Contrary to Elkind's theory, supporters of the "new look" claimed that this approach may accommodate evidence of gender and age differences in egocentrism. As there are individual differences in the timing of separation–individuation, the timing of egocentrism also can vary and therefore can expand into adulthood for some individuals. In addition, research has found that as expected, separation–individuation is associated with egocentrism as assessed on some subscales of the revised measure. Goossens et al. (2002) found support for the "new look," but only for the invulnerability and omnipotence subscales of the personal fable scale. As expected, they were inversely associated with connectedness, although they were not positively related to separation, as would be expected. Furthermore, associations between separation–individuation and egocentrism have been found only when using new measures of adolescent egocentrism that stem from the 'new look' perspective (Vartanian, 1997).

Although none of the explanatory theories about the nature and development of adolescent egocentrism have received strong support, empirical research has suggested that higher scores on specific adolescent egocentrism subscales are associated with poorer adjustment, including greater depression and loneliness (Goossens et al., 2002; Schonert-Reichl, 1994), and lower self-esteem (Ryan & Kuczkowski, 1994). More specifically, greater depression has been associated with higher scores on the imaginary audience subscales among females and with higher personal fable responses for males (Schonert-Reichl). In addition, poorer self-concept among German adolescents has been associated with greater imaginary audience responses but lower personal fable scale scores (Goossens, Seiffge-Krenke, & Alfons, 1992).

Furthermore, adolescent egocentrism is associated with socioeconomic status, suggesting the influence of social experiential factors. Higher invulnerability (as assessed on a personal fable subscale) has been found to be associated with higher levels of parental education (Greene, Kremer, Walters, Rubin, & Hale, 2000). Higher social class among females was associated with more imaginary audience behavior and lower scores on the personal fable scale, while higher social class among males was associated with stronger endorsement of the personal fable (Schonert-Reichl, 1994).

Adolescent egocentrism also has been associated with involvement in risk behaviors. For instance, higher scores on assessments of the personal fable have been associated with greater risk taking (Alberts, Elkind, & Ginsberg, 2007), and when coupled with high sensation seeking, greater participation in risky sexual behavior, alcohol consumption, and drug use (Greene et al., 2000). Lower scores on assessments of the imaginary audience have been associated with greater contraceptive use (Holmbeck, Crossman, Wandrei, & Gasiewski, 1994), while higher scores on assessments of both the imaginary audience and the personal fable have been associated with the number of peers who smoke, suggesting that adolescents who are high in egocentrism are more likely to smoke in the future (Frankenberger, 2004). However, Greening et al. (2005) did not find support for associations between egocentrism and biased risk perception in middle and late adolescents. Imaginary audience has been positively associated with externalizing and problem behaviors among boys without behavioral disorders, whereas among boys with behavioral disorders, greater invulnerability and personal uniqueness as assessed on the personal fable subscale were associated with fewer internalizing problems (Beaudoin & Schonert-Reichl, 2006). Nevertheless, the field still lacks a compelling theoretical explanation for adolescent egocentrism, nor is it clear whether it is a developmental or an individual difference variable. Thus, these links between egocentrism scores and problem behavior are not as useful as they might be.

More recently, the notion of adolescent egocentrism as reflecting bias or errors in social cognition has been challenged altogether (Bell & Bromnick, 2003; Vartanian, 2000, 2001). Vartanian (2000) claimed that both the old and new measures of adolescent egocentrism do not assess biased perceptions, as the imaginary audience measures suggest to the adolescent that there *is* an audience. In addition, it has been noted that these measures do not assess positive or admiring biases (Ryan & Kuczkowski, 1994; Vartanian, 2000). When adolescent egocentrism was examined with alternative measures that address these issues, no support was obtained for the notion that adolescents have biased social cognition (Vartanian & Powlishta, 2001). Furthermore, Bell and Bromnick found that adolescents cared about what others think because there are real personal and social consequences for one's behaviors. This research points to the need for careful methodology in studying adolescent egocentrism and leaves unresolved the question of whether egocentrism is a normal consequence of adolescent development or an aspect of psychological functioning that simply varies among individuals regardless of age.

Theory of Mind

Taking the perspective of another (mind reading) is quintessentially a mentalizing task. Although rarely referenced in contemporary discussions, Selman's extensive program of research predates the current interest in theory of mind and assesses the abilities typically studied in adolescence. Despite a recent call for more studies of adolescents' theory of mind (Carpendale & Chandler, 1996), there is still a surprising paucity of empirical studies that examine the normative development of theory of mind during adolescence. The few available studies have not been developmentally focused, and, therefore, the developmental trajectory of theory of mind during adolescence remains uncharted. Only one study (Choudhury, Blakemore, & Charman, 2006) has showed developmental changes in theory of mind during adolescence, although this study employed a reaction time task (assessing how much time it took adolescents to identify a face depicting how either self or other would feel) rather than a reasoning task. There were developmental changes in adolescents' but not adults' responses for first person versus third person stimuli, leading Choudhury et al. to speculate that perspective taking develops during adolescence, perhaps in parallel with the underlying neural circuitry.

O'Connor and Hirsch (1999) examined inter- as well as intraindividual variability in theory of mind among a high-risk sample of White and minority early adolescents. In semi-structured interviews, participants responded to four vignettes focusing on common school situations. The vignettes manipulated the protagonists' liking for the teacher and whether the protagonist was the self or another student. More advanced responses in judging the hypothetical teacher's and student's thoughts involved more references to context and fewer references to internal, enduring characteristics. On average, the researchers found that theory of mind was not fully developed by early adolescence. Mentalizing about the teacher's behavior, however, was more advanced when adolescents responded to vignettes involving a liked than a disliked teacher, suggesting that the developmental sophistication of theory of mind varies according to the quality of social relationships. Consistent with these findings, Humfress, O'Connor, Slaughter, Target, and Fonagy (2002) found that adolescents' mentalizing is relationship specific. Early adolescents with more secure attachment relationships to parents had more sophisticated mentalizing abilities. Furthermore, adolescents with more avoidant attachments to parents provided more sophisticated mentalizing when presented with vignettes that did not include parents.

Finally, Gonzalez Cuenca, Barajas Esteban, and Fernandez Molina (2005) found evidence for intraindividual variation in theory of mind, as assessed in terms of understanding of nonliteral utterances and false beliefs among adopted, Spanish, early through late adolescents. Greater verbal ability and less time spent in the child protection system were associated with more advanced theory of mind. Overall, these studies suggest that individual and contextual variables influence theory of mind in adolescence, although there is still much to be learned about its development during this period.

CONCLUSIONS

As this review suggests, social cognition has been extensively investigated during adolescence. Topics of study have included adolescents' understanding of rights and civil liberties, society and government, social relationships, and self-system processes, including perspective taking and egocentrism. Research on some topics—notably social cognitive biases in aggression and attributions regarding victimization—has focused primarily on identifying individual differences in responses and has not focused on developmental changes during adolescence. In most of the other areas reviewed here, however, the research has sought to identify normative developmental patterns either within or across different social contexts and with some focus as well on intraindividual variations in reasoning.

As noted throughout this review, the global stage theories of development, including Kohlberg's theory of moral judgment development (1984; Colby & Kohlberg, 1987), Selman's original theory of perspective-taking levels (Selman & Jacquette, 1977), and the parallel account of the development of adolescents' friendship concepts (Selman, 1981), as well as narrower stage theories (e.g., Gallatin's 1980 model of concepts of government), have been largely abandoned or substantially reworked, although, sadly, they still prevail in most textbook accounts of adolescent development. The continued prominence of these theoretical accounts, at least in what students are taught—despite the weight of evidence against them—is no doubt due to the desire for a straightforward and relatively simple account of development. These theories all offer a view of adolescent social cognitive development in which social reasoning progresses from more concrete, authority-oriented, or personality trait–like responses to more abstract, inclusive, generalizable, autonomous, or psychological responses. But the research reviewed here suggests that social cognitive development is considerably more complex and contextually variable than these accounts propose.

Although the research discussed here does not lend itself to a description of a single or even several developmental trajectories, the findings across multiple content areas do support some general conclusions about developmental processes. For instance, even early adolescents appear to have relatively mature understandings of different social concepts (such as rights, tolerance, exclusion, or personal choices) when those concepts are presented abstractly or in decontextualized ways and the production demands of the interviews are minimized. Thus, changes in reasoning during adolescence appear primarily in adolescents' ability to reason about and coordinate complex or multifaceted concepts (involving conflicting or different concerns), to handle disparities and incongruities in their thinking (for instance, to resolve the inconsistency of having multiple role-related selves, to be both tolerant about some social practices and intolerant of others), and to reason about specific situations and social contexts. There is substantial evidence that adolescents' reasoning becomes both more broadly inclusive and more situated and sensitive to the social and cultural context with age.

Rather than showing a pattern of straightforward improvement in social reasoning, as most of the earlier theoretical perspectives have proposed, the research reviewed in this chapter suggests that the development of different types of social reasoning shows patterns of fluctuation, detours, and regression. For instance, along with the more complex and differentiated understanding of society and social organization that develops during adolescence, adolescents also go through phases where they reject the understanding they had earlier achieved (Turiel, 1978). Nucci and Turiel's (2007) recent and ongoing analyses of how concepts of harm and welfare develop during adolescence indicate that there is a U-shaped pattern of growth entailing transitional periods in which moral criteria are applied unevenly and uncertainly, as adolescents attend to new features of moral situations and grope toward more complex integrations of moral thought. Harter and colleagues (Harter, 2006; Harter et al., 1997; Harter & Monsour, 1992) have elegantly described how the emergence and proliferation of different role-related selves, combined with increased introspective abilities (and thus the ability to recognize contradictions), brings with it the potential for significant intrapsychic distress and concerns with inauthenticity. And social cognitive advances during adolescence also have been credited with the onset of egocentrism (although the processes that lead to egocentrism remain unclear). In all of these areas, the process of development appears to resolve incongruities and contradictions in reasoning and lead to increased integration and coordination of social concepts. Thus, as Nucci and Turiel (2007) have proposed in their analyses of concepts of harm, the research on diverse

social cognitive topics suggests that social cognitive development is not linear but has more of the characteristics of dynamic systems (Smith & Thelen, 2003).

It also should be noted that there is considerably more overlap and interconnections among the content areas reviewed here than the structure of this chapter, with its separation of topics, suggests. For example, judgments of civil liberties (Helwig, 1995, 1997, 2006) and adolescents' claims to personal jurisdiction (Smetana, 2002) are intertwined at various points of development; adolescents' attempts to establish agency through asserting claims to personal jurisdiction form the basis of more abstract notions of individual (or self-determination) rights, including civil liberties like freedom of expression and freedom of religion (Nucci, 1996). Likewise, although they have been researched separately, adolescents' reasoning about tolerance for cultural practices (Wainryb et al., 1998) is certainly relevant to understanding adolescents' beliefs and reasoning about homosexuality (Horn, 2006a, 2006b; Horn & Nucci, 2003), and could be fruitfully integrated. The research reviewed here also suggests that adolescents' understanding of societal practices and government, including issues like civic involvement, economic inequality, and decision-making practices, involve complex coordinations of justice and welfare concerns with an understanding of social systems, including hierarchies, social roles, and power relationships. Similarly, the research indicates that adolescents' understanding of social relationships sometimes involves competing concerns with welfare, fairness, and group processes. Thus, part of the developmental story involves understanding how different concepts are interwoven, overlap, and become distinguished or coordinated in development.

The social cognitive research reviewed here generally has been attentive to gender variations in social reasoning, although few consistent gender effects have been found, except in Harter's program of research on adolescent self-conceptions, the research on friendship conceptions, and the investigations of adolescent egocentrism. These findings suggest that adolescent girls are more likely than boys to reason about self-disclosure, intimacy, loyalty, and commitment as salient aspects of adolescent friendships; at the same time, girls also appear to be more vulnerable to egocentrism and to the negative consequences of recognizing contradictions in their self-portraits. Widely accepted popular conceptualizations of gender differences in moral judgment, however, have not been supported by empirical study. Further research is needed to understand the bases for those gender differences that do exist and to determine if they are associated with other vulnerabilities (e.g., the greater incidence of depression among adolescent girls than boys).

Relatively less research has focused on differences in or effects of socioeconomic status, race, and ethnicity on adolescents' social reasoning. The available research (e.g., Cherney & Shing, in press; Flanagan et al., 1997; Graham & Juvonen, 2001; Margie et al., 2006) suggests, however, that sociodemographic background may influence social reasoning insofar as it affords adolescents with different social experiences and opportunities. Much of the research, for instance, on the effects of working in a homeless shelter (Yates & Youniss, 1996), on urban versus suburban youths' reasoning about poverty and homelessness (Flanagan & Tucker, 1999), on minority teenagers' personal experience with racial exclusion (Margie et al.), and on ethnic minority adolescents' intergroup reasoning (Karcher & Fisher, 2004), suggests that adolescents' social experiences are associated with or lead to greater sensitivity to unfair social conditions and the plight of others. However, other research, for instance, Horn's (2003) findings about the effects of peer reference groups on reasoning about peer exclusion, Wainryb and Turiel's (1994) research on the different judgments of Druze Arab women and men, and Verkuyten and Slooten's (2008) research on Muslim minority and non-Muslim majority Dutch adolescents suggest the

opposite; these studies have found that those at the top of the social hierarchy are more likely to assert privileges and personal choices and are less sensitive to the needs or rights of others. These findings are not inconsistent, however, as the first set of studies all focused on minority teens or youth living in poverty (and thus those less privileged in society). Thus, the findings suggest that the effects of race and social class appear to be moderated by one's location in the social hierarchy, with those at the top having more to lose and thus potentially viewing privileges and rights differently from others. These findings suggest that societal and power hierarchies may be socially reproduced through the different meanings that individuals ascribe to rights, privileges, and personal choices. Graham and Juvonen's (2001) analysis of ethnicity in the context of school composition further underscores the importance of context for social understanding. Although more research is needed on these effects, the studies demonstrate that adolescents actively interpret their social experiences and that this is done from adolescents' particular vantage points in society.

The studies reviewed in this chapter indicate that social cognitive research has become more contextual both in terms of considering reasoning among adolescents reared in different social contexts and circumstances (as just discussed) and in examining adolescents' reasoning about varying and specific situations. In contrast to the social cognitive research of 30 years ago, there also has been a greater emphasis on the role of family, peers, and schools in the development of adolescents' social understanding, but more research is needed on how adolescents' social interactions in different familial, social, and cultural contexts influence their construction and interpretation of their social worlds. Research that examines individual variations in social reasoning (e.g., Cumsille et al., 2006; Daddis et al., 2007) as well as normative patterns also would contribute to our understanding of adolescents' social cognitive development. Finally, research in numerous content areas has demonstrated correspondences between adolescents' social reasoning and social behavior (e.g., Geiger & Turiel, 1983; Metzger & Smetana, in press; Nucci et al., 1991; Selman & Schultz, 1990), but surprisingly little longitudinal research has examined the reciprocal influences of social reasoning and social behavior over time. A richer and more complete account of adolescent social cognitive development would be obtained by further research on how adolescents' social reasoning influences and is influenced by their choices, decisions, social interactions, and behaviors in different cultural and social contexts.

REFERENCES

Adelson, J. (1972). The political imagination of the young adolescent. In Kagan, J., & Coles, R. (Eds.), *12 to 16: Early adolescence* (pp. 106–143). New York: Norton.

Alberts, A., Elkind, D., & Ginsberg, S. (2007). The personal fable and risk-taking in early adolescence. *Journal of Youth and Adolescence, 36,* 71–76.

Avery, P. G. (1988). Political tolerance among adolescents. *Theory and Research in Social Education, 16,* 183–201.

Avery, P. G. (1992). Political tolerance: How adolescents deal with dissenting groups. In H. Haste & J. Torney-Purta (Eds.), *The development of political understanding: A new perspective* (pp. 39–51). San Francisco: Jossey-Bass.

Bandura, A. (1989). Regulation of cognitive processes through perceived self-efficacy. *Developmental Psychology, 25,* 729–735.

Bandura, A. (1991). Social cognitive theory of moral thought and action. In W. M. Kurtines & J. L.Gewirtz (Eds.), *Moral behavior and development: Advances in theory, research, and applications,* Vol. 1 (pp. 45–103). Hillsdale, NJ: Lawrence Erlbaum.

Bandura, A., & Wood, R. E. (1989). Effect of perceived controllability and performance standards on self-regulation of complex decision making. *Journal of Personality and Social Psychology, 56,* 805–814.

Bell, J. H., & Bromnick, R. D. (2003). The social reality of the imaginary audience: A grounded theory approach. *Adolescence, 38,* 205–219.

Bellmore, A. D., Witkow, M. R., Graham, S., & Juvonen, J. (2005). From beliefs to behavior: The mediating role of hostile response selection in predicting aggression. *Aggressive Behavior, 31,* 453–472.

Berndt, T. J. (1982). The features and effects of friendships in early adolescence. *Child Development, 53,* 1447–1460.

Beaudoin, K. M., & Schonert-Reichl, K. A. (2006). Epistemic reasoning and adolescent egocentrism: Relations to internalizing and externalizing symptoms in problem youth. *Journal of Youth and Adolescence, 35,* 999–1014.

Bigelow, B. (1977). Children's friendship expectations: A cognitive-developmental study. *Child Development, 48,* 246–253.

Bigelow, B., & LaGaipa, J. J. (1975). Children's written descriptions of friendships: A multidimensional analysis. *Developmental Psychology, 11,* 857–858.

Blos, P. (1962). On adolescence: A psychoanalytic interpretation. New York: Free Press.

Blos, P. (1979). *The adolescent passage: Clinical studies.* Madison, CT: International Universities Press.

Bronfenbrenner, U. (1986). Ecology of the family as a context for human development: Research perspectives. *Developmental Psychology, 22,* 723–742.

Broughton, J. (1978). The development of concepts of mind, self, reality, and knowledge. In W. Damon (Ed.), *Social cognition* (pp. 75–100). San Francisco: Jossey-Bass.

Burack, J. A., Flanagan, T., Peled, T., Sutton, H. M., Zygmuntowicz, C., & Manly, J. T. (2006). Social perspective-taking skills in maltreated children and adolescents. *Developmental Psychology, 42,* 207–217.

Campione-Barr, N., & Smetana, J. G. (2007). *The impact of sibling ordinal status on adolescents' negotiation, expectations, and actual behavioral autonomy.* Unpublished manuscript, University of Missouri.

Carey, S. (1985). *Conceptual change in childhood.* Cambridge, MA: MIT Press.

Carpendale, J. I., & Chandler, J. (1996). On the distinction between false belief understanding and subscribing to an interpretive theory of mind. *Child Development, 67,* 1686–1706.

Cherney, I. D., & Shing, Y. L. (in press). Children's nurturance and self-determination rights: A cross-cultural perspective. *Journal of Social Issues.*

Choudhury, S., Blakemore, S., & Charman, T. (2006) Social cognitive development during adolescence. *Social Cognitive and Affective Neuroscience, 3,* 165–174.

Colby, A., & Kohlberg, K. (Eds.). (1987). *The measurement of moral judgment,* Vols. 1–2. New York: Cambridge University Press.

Crane-Ross, D. A., Tisak, M. S., & Tisak, J. (1998). Aggression and conventional rule violation among adolescents: Social-reasoning predictors of social behavior. *Aggressive Behavior, 24,* 347–365.

Crick, N. R., & Dodge, K. A. (1994). A review and reformulation of social Information-processing mechanisms in children's social adjustment. *Psychological Bulletin, 115,* 74–101.

Cumsille, P., Darling, N., Flaherty, B. P., & Martinez, M. L. (2006). Chilean adolescents' beliefs about the legitimacy of parental authority: Individual and age-related differences. *International Journal of Behavioural Development, 30,* 97–106.

Daddis, C. (2008). Influence of close friends on the boundaries of adolescent personal authority. *Journal of Research on Adolescence, 18,* 75–98.

Daddis, C. (in press). Similarity between early and middle adolescent close friends' beliefs about personal jurisdiction. *Social Development.*

Daddis, C., Driscoll, A., & Thacker, A. (2007). *Peer group membership and adolescent beliefs about parental authority.* Paper presented at the Biennial Meetings of the Society for Research in Child Development, Boston, MA.

Damon. W. (1977). *The social world of the child.* San Francisco: Jossey-Bass.

Damon, W. (1988). *Self understanding in childhood and adolescence.* San Francisco: Jossey-Bass.

Damon, W., & Hart, D. (1982). The development of self-understanding from infancy through adolescence. *Child Development, 53,* 841–864.

Darling, N., Cumsille, P., Caldwell, L. L., & Dowdy, B. (2006). Predictors of adolescents' disclosure to parents and perceived parental knowledge: Between- and within-person differences. *Journal of Youth and Adolescence, 35,* 667–678.

Darling, N., Cumsille, P., & Martinez, M. L. (2007). Adolescents as active agents in the socialization process: Legitimacy of parental authority and obligation to obey as predictors of obedience. *Journal of Adolescence, 30,* 297–311.

Darling, N., Cumsille, P., & Pena-Alampay, L. (2005). Rules, obligations to obey, and obedience in three cultures: Age-related differences and the development of autonomy. In J. G. Smetana (Ed.), *Changing boundaries of parental authority* (pp. 47–60). San Francisco: Jossey-Bass.

Day, D. M., Peterson-Badali, M., & Ruck, M. D. (2006). The relationship between maternal attitudes and young people's attitudes towards children's rights. *Journal of Adolescence*, *29*, 193–207.

Dodge, K. A. (1986). A social information-processing model of social competence in children. In M. Perlmutter (Ed.), *Minnesota Symposia on Child Psychology*, Vol. *18* (pp. 77–125). Hillsdale, NJ: Lawrence Erlbaum.

Dodge, K. A., Coie, J. F., & Lynam, D. (2006). Aggression and antisocial behavior in youth. In N.Eisenberg (Ed.), *Handbook of child psychology* 6th ed.), Vol. *3*: *Social, emotional, and personality development* (William Damon, series editor; pp. 719–788). Hoboken, NJ: John Wiley & Sons.

Eccles, J. S., Midgley, C., Wigfield, A., Buchanan, C. M., Reuman, D., Flanagan, C., et al. (1993). Development during adolescence: The impact of stage-environment fit on adolescents' experiences in schools and families. *American Psychologist*, *48*, 90–101.

Eccles, J. S., Wigfield, A., & Schiefele, U. (1998). Motivation to succeed. In W. Damon (Ed.), *Handbook of child psychology* 5th ed.), Vol. *3*: *Social, emotional, and personality development* (pp. 1017–1095; N. Eisenberg [ed.]). New York: John Wiley & Sons.

Egan, S. K, Monson, T. C., & Perry, D. G. (1998). Social-cognitive influences on change in aggression over time. *Developmental Psychology*, *34*, 996–1006.

Elkind, D. (1967). Egocentrism in adolescence. *Child Development*, *38*, 1025–1034.

Enright, R. D., & Lapsley, D. K. (1981). Judging others who hold opposite beliefs: The development of belief-discrepancy reasoning. *Child Development*, *52*, 1053–1063.

Enright, R. D., Lapsley, D. K., Franklin, C. C., & Steuck, K. (1984). Longitudinal and cross-cultural validation of the belief-discrepancy reasoning construct. *Developmental Psychology*, *20*, 143–149.

Flanagan, C. (2005). Volunteerism, leadership, political socialization, and civic engagement. In M.Gazzaniga (Ed.), *The new cognitive neurosciences* (2nd ed.; pp. 721–745). Cambridge, MA: MIT Press.

Flanagan, C. A., Ingram, P., Gallay, E. M., & Gallay, E. E. (1997). Why are people poor?: Social conditions and adolescents' interpretations of the social contract. In R. W. Taylor & M. C. Wang (Eds.), *Social and emotional adjustment and family relations in ethnic minority families* (pp. 53–63). Mahwah, NJ: Lawrence Erlbaum.

Flanagan, C., & Tucker, C. J. (1999). Adolescents' explanations for political issues: Concordance with their views of self and society. *Developmental Psychology*, *35*, 1198–1209.

Frankenberger, K. D. (2000). Adolescent egocentrism: A comparison among adolescents and adults. *Journal of Adolescence*, *23*, 343–354.

Frankenberger, K. D. (2004). Adolescent egocentrism, risk perceptions, and sensation seeking among smoking and nonsmoking youth. *Journal of Adolescent Research*, *19*, 576–590.

Fuligni, A. J. (1998). Authority, autonomy, and parent–adolescent conflict and cohesion: A study of adolescents from Mexican, Chinese, Filipino, and European backgrounds. *Developmental Psychology*, *34*, 782–792.

Gallatin, J. (1980). Political thinking in adolescence. In J. Adelson (Ed.), *Handbook of adolescent psychology* (pp. 344–382). New York: John Wiley & Sons.

Gallatin, J., & Adelson, J. (1971). Legal guarantees of individual freedom: A cross-national study of the development of political thought. *Journal of Social Issues*, *27*, 93–108.

Geiger, K. M., & Turiel, E. (1983). Disruptive school behavior and concepts of social convention in early adolescence. *Journal of Educational Psychology*, *75*, 677–685.

Gelman, S. A. (2003). *The essential child: Origins of essentialism in everyday thought*. New York: Oxford University Press.

Gilligan, C. (1982). *In a different voice*. Cambridge, MA: Harvard University Press.

Goldstein, T. R., Miklowitz, D. J., & Mullen, K. L. (2006). Social skills knowledge and performance among adolescents with bipolar disorder. *Bipolar Disorders*, *8*, 350–361.

Goldstein, S. E., & Tisak, M. S. (2004). Adolescents' outcome expectancies about relational aggression within acquaintanceships, friendships, and dating relationships. *Journal of Adolescence*, *27*, 283–302.

Gonzalez Cuenca, A. M., Barajas Esteban, C., & Fernandez Molina, M. (2005). Understanding false beliefs and non-literal utterances in adopted adolescents. *Psicothema*, *17*, 43–48.

Goossens, L., Beyers, W., Emmen, M., & van Aken, M. (2002). The imaginary audience and personal fable: Factor analyses and concurrent validity of the "new look" measures. *Journal of Research on Adolescence*, *12*, 193–215.

Goossens, L., Seiffge-Krenke, I., & Alfons, M. (1992). The many faces of adolescent egocentrism: Two European replications. *Journal of Adolescent Research*, *7*, 43–58.

Graham, S., & Juvonen, J. (1998). Self-blame and peer victimization in middle school: An attributional analysis. *Developmental Psychology*, *34*, 587–538.

Graham, S., & Juvonen, J. (2001). An attributional approach to peer victimization. In J. Juvonen & S. Graham (Eds.), *Peer harassment in school: The plight of the vulnerable and victimized* (pp. 49–71). New York: Guilford Press.

Greene, K., Kremar, M., Walters, L. H., Rubin, D. L., & Hale, J. L. (2000). Targeting adolescent risk-taking behaviors: The contributions of egocentrism and sensation-seeking. *Journal of Adolescence*, *23*, 439–461.

Greening, L., Stoppelbein, L., Chandler, C. C., & Elkin, T. D. (2005). Predictors of children's and adolescents' risk perception. *Journal of Pediatric Psychology*, *30*, 425–435.

Greenstein, F. (1965). *Children and politics*. New Haven, CT: Yale University Press.

Gurucharri, C., Phelps, E., & Selman, R. (1984). Development of interpersonal understanding: A longitudinal and comparative study of normal and disturbed youths. *Journal of Consulting and Clinical Psychology*, *52*, 26–36.

Gurucharri, C., & Selman, R. L. (1982). The development of interpersonal understanding during childhood, preadolescence, and adolescence: A longitudinal follow-up study. *Child Development*, *53*, 924–927.

Hala, S. (1997). *The development of social cognition*. East Sussex, UK: Psychology Press, Ltd.

Harter, S. (1999). *The construction of the self*. New York: Guilford Press.

Harter, S. (2006). The self. In N. Eisenberg (Ed.), *Handbook of child psychology* (6th ed.), Vol. 3: *Social, emotional, and personality development* (William Damon, series editor; pp. 505–570). Hoboken, NJ: John Wiley & Sons.

Harter, S., Bresnick, S., Bouchey, H. A., & Whitesell, N. R. (1997). The development of multiple role-related selves during adolescence. *Development and Psychopathology*, *9*, 835–854.

Harter, S., & Monsour, A. (1992). Developmental analysis of conflict caused by opposing attributes in the adolescent self-portrait. *Developmental Psychology*, *28*, 251–260.

Hasebe, Y., Nucci, L., & Nucci, M. S. (2004). Parental control of the personal domain and adolescent symptoms of psychopathology. *Child Development*, *75*, 815–828.

Helwig, C. C. (1995). Adolescents' and young adults' conceptions of civil liberties: Freedom of speech and religion. *Child Development*, *66*, 152–166.

Helwig, C. C. (1997). The role of agent and context in judgments of freedom of speech and religion. *Child Development*, *68*, 484–495.

Helwig, C. C. (1998). Children's conceptions of fair government and freedom of speech. *Child Development*, *69*, 518–531.

Helwig, C. C. (2006). Rights, civil liberties, and democracy across cultures. In M. Killen & J. G. Smetana (Eds.), *Handbook of Moral Development* (pp. 185–210). Mahwah, NJ: Lawrence Erlbaum.

Helwig, C. C., Arnold, M. L., Tan, D., & Boyd, D. (2003). Chinese adolescents' reasoning about democratic and authority-based decision-making in peer, family, and school contexts. *Child Development, 74,* 783–800.

Helwig, C. C., Arnold, M. L., Tan, D., & Boyd, D. (2007). Mainland Chinese and Canadian adolescents' judgments and reasoning about the fairness of democratic and other forms of government. *Cognitive Development, 22,* 96–109.

Helwig, C. C., & Turiel, E. (2002). Civil liberties, autonomy, and democracy: Children's perspectives. *International Journal of Law and Psychiatry, 25,* 253–270.

Hess, R., & Torney, J. (1967). *The development of political attitudes in children.* Garden City, NY: McGraw-Hill.

Holmbeck, G. N., Crossman, R. E., Wandrei, M. L., & Gasiewski, E. (1994). Cognitive development, egocentrism, self-esteem, and adolescent contraceptive knowledge, attitudes, and behaviors. *Journal of Youth and Adolescence, 23,* 169–193.

Horn, S. S. (2003). Adolescents' reasoning about exclusion from social groups. *Developmental Psychology, 39,* 71–84.

Horn, S. S. (2006a). Adolescents' acceptance of same-sex peers based on sexual orientation and gender expression. *Journal of Youth and Adolescence, 36,* 363–371.

Horn, S. S. (2006b). Heterosexual students' attitudes and beliefs about same-sex sexuality and the treatment of gay, lesbian, and gender non-conforming youth. *Cognitive Development, 21,* 420–440.

Horn, S. S. (2006c). Group status, group bias, and adolescents' reasoning about the treatment of others in school contexts. *International Journal of Behavioral Development, 30,* 208–218.

Horn, S. S., Killen, M., & Stangor, C. (1999). The influence of group stereotypes on adolescents' moral reasoning. *Journal of Early Adolescence, 19,* 98–113.

Horn, S. S., & Nucci, L. (2003). The multidimensionality of adolescents' beliefs about and attitudes toward gay and lesbian peers in school. *Equity and Excellence in Education, 36,* 136–147.

Humfress, H., O'Connor, T. G., Slaughter, J., Target, M., & Fonagy, P. (2002). General and relationship-specific models of social cognition: Explaining the overlap and discrepancies. *Journal of Child Psychology and Psychiatry, 43,* 873–883.

Jahnke, H. C., & Blanchard-Fields, F. (1993). A test of two models of adolescent egocentrism. *Journal of Youth and Adolescence, 22,* 313–326.

Karcher, M. J., & Fisher, K. W. (2004). A developmental sequence of skills in adolescents' intergroup understanding. *Applied Developmental Psychology, 25,* 259–282.

Keil, F. C. (2007). Biology and beyond: Domain specificity in a broader developmental context. *Human Development, 50,* 31–38.

Keller, M., Edelstein, W., Schmid, C., Fang, F., & Fang, G. (1998). Reasoning about responsibilities and obligations in close relationships: A comparison across two cultures. *Developmental Psychology, 34,* 731–741.

Keller, M., Fuxi, F., Ge, F., Edelstein, W., Cecora, L., & Eckert, U. (2004). Self in relationship. In D. K. Lapsley & D. Narvaez (Eds.), *Moral development, self, and identity* (pp. 267–298). Mahwah, NJ: Lawrence Erlbaum.

Keller, M., & Wood, P. (1989). Development of friendship reasoning: A study of interindividual differences in intraindividual change. *Developmental Psychology, 25,* 820–826.

Kerr, M., & Stattin, H. (2000). What parents know, how they know it, and several forms of adolescent adjustment: Further support for a reinterpretation of monitoring. *Developmental Psychology, 36,* 366–380.

Killen, M., Henning, A., Kelly, M. C., Crystal, D., & Ruck, M. (2007). Evaluations of interracial peer encounters by majority and minority U.S. children and adolescents. *International Journal of Behavioral Development, 31,* 491–500.

Killen, M., Lee-Kim, J., McGlothlin, H., & Stangor, C. (2002). *Monographs of the Society for Research in Child Development* (serial no. 271. Vol. 67, No. 4).

Killen, M., & Stangor, C. (2001). Children's social reasoning about inclusion and exclusion in gender and race peer group contexts. *Child Development, 72,* 174–186.

Killen, M., Stangor, C., Price, B. S., Horn, S., & Sechrist, G. (2004). Social reasoning about racial exclusion in intimate and non-intimate relationships. *Youth & Society, 35,* 252–283.

Kohlberg, L. (1984). *Essays on moral development,* Vol. 2: *The psychology of moral development.* San Francisco: Harper & Row.

LaGaipa, J. J. (1979). A developmental study of the meaning of friendship in adolescence. *Journal of Adolescence, 2,* 201–213.

Lahat, A., Helwig, C. C., Yang, S., Tan, D., & Liu, C. (in press). Mainland Chinese adolescents' judgments and reasoning about self-determination and nurturance rights. *Social Development.*

Lapsley, D. K. (1990). Continuity and discontinuity in adolescent social cognitive development. In R. Montemayor, G. R. Adams, & T. P. Gullotta, (Eds.), *From childhood to adolescence: A transitional period?* (pp. 183–204). Thousand Oaks, CA: Sage.

Lapsley, D. K. (1993). Toward an integrated theory of adolescent ego development: The "new look" at adolescent egocentrism. *American Journal of Orthopsychiatry, 63,* 562–571.

Lapsley, D. K., & Murphy, M. N. (1985). Another look at the theoretical assumptions of adolescent egocentrism. *Developmental Review, 5,* 201–217.

Leahy, R. L. (1983). Development of the conception of economic inequality: II. Explanation, justifications, and concepts of social mobility and change. *Developmental Psychology, 19,* 111–125.

Leets, L., & Sunwolf. (2005). Adolescent rules for social exclusion: When is it fair to exclude someone else? *Journal of Moral Education, 34,* 343–362.

Levitt, M. Z., & Selman, R. L. (1996). The personal meaning of risk behavior: A developmental perspective on friendship and fighting in early adolescence. In G. G. Noam & K. Fischer (Eds.), *Development and vulnerability in close relationships* (pp. 201–233). Mahwah, NJ: Lawrence Erlbaum.

Lewis, C., & Carpendale, J. (2002). Social cognition. In P. K. Smith & C. H. Hart (Eds.), *Blackwell handbook of childhood social development* (pp. 375–393). Oxford, UK: Blackwell.

Margie, N. G., Brenick, A., Killen, M., Crystal, D., & Ruck, M. (2006). *Peer victimization and moral judgments about interracial peer encounters.* Poster presented at the annual meeting of the Association for Psychological Science, New York.

Mead, G. H. (1934). *Mind, self, and society: From the standpoint of a social behaviorist.* Chicago: University of Chicago Press.

Metzger, A., & Smetana, J. G. (in press). Adolescent civic and political engagement: Associations between domain-specific beliefs and behavior. *Child Development.*

Nucci, L. (1981). The development of personal concepts: A domain distinct from moral or societal concepts. *Child Development, 52,* 118–121.

Nucci, L. P. (1996). Morality and personal freedom. In E. S. Reed, E.Turiel, & T. Brown (Eds.), *Values and knowledge* (pp. 41–60). Mahwah, NJ: Erlbaum.

Nucci, L. P. (2001). *Education in the moral domain.* Cambridge, UK: Cambridge University Press.

Nucci, L. P., Camino, C., & Sapiro, C. M. (1996). Social class effects on Northeastern Brazilian children's conceptions of areas of personal choice and social regulation. *Child Development, 67,* 1223–1242.

Nucci, L. P., Guerra, N., & Lee, J. (1991). Adolescent judgments of the personal, prudential, and normative aspects of drug usage. *Developmental Psychology, 27,* 841–848.

Nucci, L. P., Hasebe, Y., & Lins-Dyer, M. T. (2005). Adolescent psychological well-being and parental control over the personal. In J. G. Smetana (Ed.), *Changing boundaries of parental authority* (pp. 17–30). San Francisco: Jossey-Bass.

Nucci, L. P., & Turiel. E. (2007). *Development in the moral domain: The role of conflict and relationships in children's and adolescents' welfare and harm judgments.* Paper presented at the Biennial Meetings of the Society for Research in Child Development, Boston, MA.

O'Connor, T. G., & Hirsch, N. (1999). Intra-individual differences and relationship-specificity of mentalising in early adolescence. *Social Development, 8*, 256–274.

Park, Y., Killen, M., Crystal, D., & Watanabe, H. (2003). Korean, Japanese, and American children's evaluations of peer exclusion: Evidence for diversity. *International Journal of Behavioral Development, 27*, 555–565.

Pellegrini, D. S. (1986). Variability in children's level of reasoning about friendship. *Journal of Applied Developmental Psychology, 7*, 341–354.

Phinney, J. S., & Cobb, N. J. (1996). Reasoning about intergroup relations among Hispanic and Euro-American adolescents. *Journal of Adolescent Research, 11*, 306–324.

Quadrel, M. J., Fishhoff, B., & Davis, W. (1993). Adolescent (in)vulnerability. *American Psychologist, 48*, 102–116.

Quintana, S. (1994). A model of ethnic perspective-taking ability applied to Mexican-American children and youth. *International Journal of Intercultural Relations, 18*, 419–448.

Quintana, S. M., Castaneda-English, P., & Ybarra, V. C. (1999). Role of perspective-taking abilities and ethnic socialization in development of adolescent ethnic identity. *Journal of Research on Adolescence, 9*, 161–184.

Rogers, C. M., & Wrightsman, L. S. (1978). Attitudes towards children's rights: Nurturance or self determination? *Journal of Social Issues, 34*, 59–68.

Ruck, M. D., Abramovitch, R., & Keating, D. P. (1998). Children's and adolescents' understanding of rights: Balancing nurturance and self-determination. *Child Development, 64*, 404–417.

Ruck, M. D., Keating, D. P., Abramovitch, R., & Koegl, C. J. (1998). Adolescents' and children's knowledge about rights: Some evidence for how young people view rights in their own lives. *Journal of Adolescence, 21*, 275–289.

Ruck, M. D., Peterson-Badali, M., & Day, D. M. (2002). Adolescents' and mothers' understanding of children's rights in the home. *Journal of Research on Adolescence, 12*, 373–398.

Ruck, M. D., Tenenbaum, H., & Sines, J. (2007). British adolescents' views about the rights of asylum-seeking children. *Journal of Adolescence, 30*, 687–693.

Ryan, R., & Kuczkowski, R. (1994). The imaginary audience, self-consciousness, and public individuation in adolescence. *Journal of Personality, 62*, 219–238.

Rycek, R., Stuhr, S. L., McDermott, J., Benker, J., & Schwartz, M. D. (1998). Adolescent egocentrism and cognitive functioning during late adolescence. *Adolescence, 33*, 745–749.

Santoloupo, S., & Pratt, M. W. (1994). Gender and parenting style variations in mother-adolescent dialogues and adolescent reasoning about political issues. *Journal of Adolescent Research, 9*, 241–261.

Schonert-Reichl, K. (1994). Gender differences in depressive symptomatology and egocentrism in adolescence. *Journal of Early Adolescence, 14*, 49–65.

Schultz, L. H., & Selman, R. L. (1990). Relations among interpersonal action-related thought, self-reported social action, and emotional maturity in early adolescents. In C. Vandenplas-Holper & B. P. Campos (Eds.), *Interpersonal and identity development: New directions* (pp. 23–33). Oporto, Portugal: Instituto de Consulta Psicologica, Formacao e Desenvolvimento.

Selman, R. L. (1971). Taking another's perspective: Role-taking development in early childhood. *Child Development, 42*, 1721–1734.

Selman, R. L. (1980). *The growth of interpersonal understanding: Developmental and clinical analyses.* New York: Academic Press.

Selman, R. L. (1981). The child as a friendship philosopher. In S. R. Asher & J. M. Gottman (Eds.), *The development of children's friendships* (pp. 242–272). Cambridge, UK: Cambridge University Press.

Selman, R. L., & Adalbjarnardottir, S. (2000). A developmental method to analyze the personal meaning adolescents make

of risk and relationship: The case of "drinking." *Applied Developmental Science, 4*, 47–65.

Selman, R. L., Beardslee, W., Schultz, L. H., Krupa, M., & Podorefsky, D. (1986). Assessing adolescent interpersonal negotiation strategies: Toward the integration of structural and functional models. *Developmental Psychology, 22*, 450–459.

Selman, R. L., & Jacquette, D. (1977). Stability and oscillation in interpersonal awareness: A clinical-developmental analysis. *Nebraska Symposium on Motivation, 25*, 261–304.

Selman, R. L., & Schultz, L. H. (1990). *Making a friend in youth: Developmental theory and pair therapy.* Chicago: University of Chicago Press.

Shaw, L., & Wainryb, C. (1999). The outsider's perspective: Young adults' judgments of social practices of other cultures. *British Journal of Developmental Psychology, 17*, 716–792.

Shweder, R. A., Goodnow, J. J., Hatano, G., LeVine, R. A., Markus, H., & Miller, P. (2006). The cultural psychology of development: One mind, many mentalities. In R. M. Lerner (Ed.), *Handbook of Child Psychology* (6th ed.), Vol. 1: *Theoretical models of human development* (William Damon, series editor; pp. 865–937). Hoboken, NJ: John Wiley & Sons.

Slaby, R. G., & Guerra, N. G. (1988). Cognitive mediators of aggression in adolescent offenders I: Assessment. *Developmental Psychology, 24*, 580–588.

Smetana, J. G. (1988a). Adolescents' and parents' conceptions of parental authority. *Child Development, 59*, 321–335.

Smetana, J. G. (1988b). Concepts of self and social convention: Adolescents' and parents' reasoning about hypothetical and actual family conflicts. In M. R. Gunnar & W. A. Collins (Eds.), *21st Minnesota Symposium on child psychology: Development during the transition to adolescence* (pp. 77–122). Hillsdale, NJ: Lawrence Erlbaum.

Smetana, J. G. (1989). Adolescents' and parents' reasoning about actual family conflict. *Child Development, 60*, 1052–1067.

Smetana, J. G. (1995a). Conflict and coordination in adolescent–parent relationships. In S. Shulman (Ed.), *Close relationships and socioemotional development* (pp. 155–184). Norwood, NJ: Ablex.

Smetana, J. G. (1995b). Parenting styles and conceptions of parental authority during adolescence. *Child Development, 66*, 299–316.

Smetana, J. G. (2000). Middle class African American adolescents' and parents' conceptions of parental authority and parenting practices: A longitudinal investigation. *Child Development, 71*, 1672–1686.

Smetana, J. G. (2002). Culture, autonomy, and personal jurisdiction in adolescent–parent relationships. In H. W. Reese & R. Kail (Eds.), *Advances in child development and behavior*, Vol. 29 (pp. 51–87). New York: Academic Press.

Smetana, J. G., & Asquith, P. (1994). Adolescents' and parents' conceptions of parental authority and adolescent autonomy. *Child Development, 65*, 1143–1158.

Smetana, J. G., & Bitz, B. (1996). Adolescents' conceptions of teachers' authority and their relations to rule violations in school. *Child Development, 67*, 1153–1172.

Smetana, J. G., Campione-Barr, N., & Daddis, C. (2004). Developmental and longitudinal antecedents of family decision-making: Defining health behavioral autonomy for African American adolescents. *Child Development, 75*, 1418–1434.

Smetana, J. G., Crean, H. F., & Campione-Barr, N. (2005). Adolescents' and parents' changing conceptions of parental authority. In J. G. Smetana (Ed.), *Changing boundaries of parental authority* (pp. 31–46). San Francisco: Jossey-Bass.

Smetana. J. G., Daddis, C., & Chuang, S. S. (2003). "Clean your room!" A longitudinal investigation of adolescent–parent conflict and conflict resolution in middle class African American families. *Journal of Adolescent Research, 18*, 631–650.

Smetana, J. G., & Gaines, C. (1999). Adolescent-parent conflict in middle class African American families. *Child Development, 70*, 1447–1463.

Smetana, J. G., Villalobos, M., Tasopoulos-Chan, M., Gettman, D. C., & Campione-Barr, N. (in press). Early and middle adolescents' disclosure in different domains. *Journal of Adolescence*.

Smith, L. B., & Thelen, E. (2003). Development as a dynamic system. *Trends in Cognitive Sciences*, *7*, 343–348.

Stattin, H., & Kerr, M. (2000). Parental monitoring: A reinterpretation. *Child Development*, *71*, 1072–1085.

Thorkildsen, T. A. (1989). Justice in the classroom: The student's view. *Child Development*, *60*, 965–972.

Thorkildsen, T. A. (1993). Those who can, tutor: High-ability students' conceptions of fair ways to organize learning. *Journal of Educational Psychology*, *8*, 182–190.

Thorkildsen, T. A., Sodonis, A., & White-McNulty, L. (2004). Epistemology and adolescents' conceptions of procedural justice in school. *Journal of Educational Psychology*, *96*, 347–359.

Tisak, M. S., & Jankowski, A. M. (1996). Societal rule evaluations: Adolescent offenders' reasoning about moral, conventional, and personal rules. *Aggressive Behavior*, *22*, 195–207.

Tisak, M. S., Tisak, J., & Goldstein, S. E. (2006). Aggression, delinquency, and morality: A social-cognitive perspective. In M. Killen & J. G. Smetana (Eds.), *Handbook of Moral Development* (pp. 611–629). Mahwah, NJ: Lawrence Erlbaum.

Torney-Purta, J., Lehmann, H. Oswald, W., & Schultz, W. (2001). *Citizenship and education in twenty-eight countries: Civic knowledge and engagement at age fourteen*. Amsterdam: International Association for the Evaluation of Educational Achievement (IEA).

Torney-Purta, J. V., Oppenheim, A. N., & Farnen, R. F. (1975). *Civic education in ten countries: An empirical study*. New York: John Wiley & Sons.

Turiel, E. (1978). The development of concepts of social structure: Social convention. In J. Glick & K. A. Clarke-Stewart (Eds.), *The development of social understanding* (pp. 25–108). New York: Gardner Press.

Turiel, E. (1983). *The development of social knowledge: Morality and convention*. Cambridge, UK: Cambridge University Press.

Turiel, E. (2002). *The culture of morality: Social development, context, and conflict*. New York: Cambridge University Press.

Turiel, E. (2006). The development of morality. In N. Eisenberg (Ed.), *Handbook of child psychology* (6th ed.), Vol. 3: *Social, emotional, and personality development* (William Damon, series editor; pp. 789–857). Hoboken, NJ: John Wiley & Sons.

Turiel, E., & Wainryb, C. (1998). Concepts of freedoms and rights in a traditional, hierarchically organized society. *British Journal of Developmental Psychology*, *16*, 375–395.

Vartanian, L. R. (1997). Separation-individuation, social support, and adolescent egocentrism: An exploratory study. *Journal of Early Adolescence*, *17*, 245–270.

Vartanian, L. R. (2000). Revisiting the imaginary audience and personal fable constructs: A conceptual review. *Adolescence*, *35*, 639–661.

Vartanian, L. R. (2001). Adolescents' reactions to hypothetical peer group conversations: Evidence for imaginary audience? *Adolescence*, *36*, 347–380.

Vartanian, L. R., & Powlishta, K. K. (1996). A longitudinal examination of the social-cognitive foundations of adolescent egocentrism. *Journal of Early Adolescence*, *16*, 157–178.

Vartanian, L. R., & Powlishta, K. K. (2001). Demand characteristics and self-report measures of imaginary audience sensitivity: Implications for interpreting age differences in adolescent egocentrism. *Journal of Genetic Psychology*, *162*, 187–200.

Verkuyten, M., & Slooter, L. (2008). Muslim and non-Muslim adolescents' reasoning about freedom of speech and minority rights. *Child Development*, *79*, 514–528.

Wainryb, C. (1993). The application of moral judgments to other cultures: Relativism and universality. *Child Development*, *64*, 924–933.

Wainryb, C., Shaw, L., & Maianu, C. (1998). Tolerance and intolerance: Children's and adolescents' judgments of dissenting beliefs, speech, persons, and conduct. *Child Development*, *69*, 1541–1555.

Wainryb, C., & Turiel, E. (1994). Dominance, subordination, and concepts of personal entitlements in cultural contexts. *Child Development*, *66*, 390–401.

Walker, L. J. (1984). Sex differences in the development of moral reasoning: A critical review. *Child Development*, *55*, 677–691.

Walker, L. J. (2006). Gender and morality. In M. Killen & J. G. Smetana (Eds.), *Handbook of Moral Development* (pp. 93–115). Mahwah, NJ: Lawrence Erlbaum.

Yates, M., & Youniss, J. (1996). Community service and political-moral identity in adolescents. *Journal of Research on Adolescence*, *6*, 271–284.

Yau, J., & Smetana, J. G. (1996). Adolescent-parent conflict among Chinese adolescents in Hong Kong. *Child Development*, *67*, 1262–1275.

Yau, J., & Smetana, J. G. (2003). Adolescent–parent conflict in Hong Kong and Shenzhen: A comparison of youth in two cultural contexts. *International Journal of Behavioral Development*, *27*, 201–211.

Yau, J., Tasopoulos-Chan, M., & Smetana, J. G. (2007). *Disclosure to parents about their everyday activities among American adolescents from Mexican, Chinese, and European backgrounds*. Unpublished manuscript, Azusa Pacific University.

Youniss, J., Bales, S., Christmas-Best, V., Diversi, M., McLaughlin, M., & Silbereisen, R. (2002). Youth civic engagement in the Twenty-First Century. *Journal of Research on Adolescence*, *12*, 121–148.

Zahed, Z. Y., Im-Bolter, N., & Cohen, N. J. (2007). Social cognition and externalizing psychopathology: An investigation of the mediating role of language. *Journal of Abnormal Child Psychology*, *35*, 141–152.

CHAPTER 8

Moral Cognitions and Prosocial Responding in Adolescence

NANCY EISENBERG, AMANDA SHEFFIELD MORRIS, BRENDA McDANIEL, AND TRACY L. SPINRAD

From the late 1960s through the 1980s, research on moral judgment flourished, especially work shaped by Kohlberg's (1981, 1984) influential cognitive developmental approach to moral judgment. In addition, there was a marked upsurge in empirical research on prosocial development from the early to mid-1970s until approximately the early 1990s. Much of the early research on moral judgment included adolescent participants; moreover, in recent years there has been a large amount of research on adolescents' aggression and anti-social behavior (see chapter 20 in this *Volume*). Nonetheless, as noted by Hoffman in 1980 and Eisenberg in 1990, studies of the prosocial aspects of moral development during adolescence have been limited in quantity. Indeed, in 1987, Hill commented that "capability for relatedness, connectedness, communion, and for what Gilligan has termed 'caring morality' have . . . been little studied (p. 24)." Perhaps the relative dearth of research on adolescents' prosocial tendencies is not surprising, given that social science researchers and the popular press have tended to emphasize the negative aspects of adolescence, painting a picture of this developmental period as one of emotional turmoil, hormones, and delinquency (Steinberg & Morris, 2001), despite the increasing theory and research in recent years about positive youth development (see chapter 15, this volume; Gestsdóttir & Lerner, 2007; Lerner, 2005, 2007).

It is our perception that the focus on aggression has continued in recent years, perhaps with increasing work on delinquency (e.g., Stams et al., 2006). Research on moral reasoning has continued to be quite limited in quantity in the last decade or two, although it is our impression that research on prosocial behavior has increased somewhat since the late 1990s.

Nonetheless, there is a body of research on adolescents' moral reasoning and prosocial behavior that is informative for researchers and practitioners interested in adolescent development. In this chapter, we review findings on adolescents' moral reasoning or attributions, as well as prosocial behaviors and emotional reactions (e.g., empathy and sympathy). We begin with a brief discussion of some of the reasons why one would expect morality to continue to develop in adolescence. Next, findings on moral cognitions (e.g., moral judgment and attributions) are discussed, including those pertaining to justice-oriented and prosocial issues. Then data on adolescents' prosocial behavior (including volunteer/civic activities) and empathy-related responding are reviewed. Normative development (i.e., age-related changes) and variables related to individual differences in moral development are considered. Research conducted with children in late elementary school and high school is emphasized in this chapter, rather than work with college students. Moreover, more recent findings and trends

Work on this chapter was supported by grants from the National Institutes of Mental Health (1 R01 MH 60838) and the National Institute of Drug Abuse (DA05227).

in conceptual and empirical work often are highlighted; readers can access earlier reviews for detailed summaries of prior work (e.g., Hoffman, 1980; Eisenberg, 1990; Eisenberg & Morris, 2004).

THE FOUNDATIONS FOR MORAL COGNITIONS AND PROSOCIAL DEVELOPMENT IN ADOLESCENCE

During the preschool and elementary school years, major advances are evident in moral judgment and in regard to the frequency of some types of morally relevant behaviors (e.g., some positive behaviors; e.g., Eisenberg & Fabes, 1998; Rest, 1983). Nonetheless, there are reasons to expect further change in moral cognitions and prosocial tendencies in adolescence. First, moral judgment and prosocial behaviors such as helping, sharing, and comforting have been linked both conceptually and empirically with perspective-taking skills (Eisenberg, 1986; Kohlberg, 1981, 1984), which continue to develop in adolescence. For example, it is not until preadolescence (ages 10–12) that individuals are "aware of the infinite regress (I know that you know that I know that you know, etc.) characteristic of dyadic relations; that each person is simultaneously aware of his own and others' subjective abilities . . . (and begin) to view his own interactions with and subjective perspectives of others from a third person perspective" (Selman, 1975, p. 40). Moreover, later in adolescence, the individual may become aware that in taking another's perspective, "the mutuality of perspectives includes a view of both self and other as complex psychological systems of values, beliefs, attitudes, etc. [and] . . . further awareness that the mutuality of understanding of each other's point of view can take place at different qualitative levels—for example, persons can 'know' each other as acquaintances, friends, closest friends, lovers, etc." (Selman, 1975, p. 40). Selman (1980) reported a linear pattern of change in social perspective taking from childhood to adulthood, including advances for many individuals from adolescence into

adulthood (Selman, 1980). Given the conceptual importance of understanding another's perspective for sympathy, other-oriented prosocial behaviors, and higher level moral reasoning, advances in perspective-taking skills in adolescence would be expected to be associated with further development of these capabilities during the same period (Colby, Kohlberg, Gibbs, & Lieberman, 1983; Eisenberg, 1986; Kohlberg, 1984). Furthermore, the motivation to take another's perspective has been found to increase from mid-adolescence into early adulthood (Eisenberg, Cumberland, Guthrie, Murphy, & Shepard, 2005), which is likely to contribute to both the quality of moral reasoning and adolescents' tendencies to want to assist others.

Similarly, the advances in social problem-solving skills and interpersonal negotiation skills noted during adolescence (e.g., Berg, 1989; Brion-Meisels & Selman, 1984) would be expected to contribute to the development of other-oriented social interaction, as would advances in conceptions of friendship and relationships (Brown & Gilligan, 1992; Rubin, Bukowski, & Parker, 1998; Selman, 1980) and in the ability to make accurate attributions about others' motives (Crick & Dodge, 1994; also see Eisenberg, 1986). In addition, changes in conceptions of the self from childhood into adolescence likely promote moral and prosocial development. In childhood, the self is defined primarily in terms of nonmoral properties (e.g., bodily properties, material possessions, or typical behavior); in contrast, by late adolescence, the self is defined in terms of social and psychological aspects of the self, and morality is the major regulator of social interactions, whereas belief systems are central to characterizing the psychological self (see Damon & Hart, 1988; Harter, 1999, 2006).

Changes in the quality of moral reasoning and in the likelihood of sympathetic responding during adolescence that are discussed in this chapter also have been conceptually linked to the development of altruistic tendencies (e.g., Eisenberg, 1986; Eisenberg, Fabes, & Spinrad, 2006). For example, Hoffman (2000) argued that the ability to sympathize with the distresses of others who are abstract (i.e., are not in the immediate situation) and with the chronic distress of others (including disadvantaged social groups) develops in late childhood or early adolescence, based on early adolescents' new-found ability to view others as having continuing personal identities and life experiences beyond the immediate situation. This change in sympathy is believed to promote adolescents' willingness to assist abstract individuals or groups (who are not immediately present).

Finally, recently researchers have documented the advances in cortical functioning that occur in adolescence. Toga, Thompson, and Sowell (2006) reviewed data indicating that changes in areas of the brain relevant to executive functioning and regulation occur throughout adolescence (e.g., changes in the white and gray matter in frontal, temporal, and parietal lobes; and myelination). Changes in multiple areas of the prefrontal cortex throughout adolescence are believed to contribute to improvements in executive functioning (long-term planning, self-evaluation, self-regulation, and the coordination of affect and cognition; e.g., Sowell, Trauner, Gamst, & Jernigan, 2002; see Keating, 2004). In addition, substantial changes in neurological systems that regulate how individuals process and respond to social stimuli, including facial displays of affective states, appear to occur during adolescence (Nelson, Leibenluft, McClure, & Pine, 2005). Individual differences in these brain changes would be expected to relate to adolescents' self-regulation and, hence, their moral behavior.

In brief, during late childhood and adolescence there are significant changes in sociocognitive skills, motivation, and regulatory capacities that are believed to foster the development of moral reasoning and altruistic tendencies. Therefore, adolescence would be expected to be a period of growth for moral and prosocial dispositions, cognitions, and behaviors.

Adolescents' Moral Reasoning

As mentioned previously, one reason to expect change in moral behavior in adolescence is that moral reasoning continues to mature during adolescence and into adulthood. Moral reasoning (or judgment), depending on its conceptualization, reflects the structure and/or content of an individual's reasoning about hypothetical or real-life moral dilemmas—that is, how an individual justifies his or her moral decisions (Eisenberg, 1986; Kohlberg, 1981; Rest, 1979; see Lapsley, 2006). In some studies, scores of moral reasoning may reflect the actual decision made by a person as much or more than his or her reasoning (e.g., Piaget, 1932/1965).

Space does not permit an in-depth review of the basic findings on the development of moral reasoning and recent changes in its measurement (see Gibbs, Basinger, Grime, & Snarney, 2007; Lapsley, 2006; Rest, Narvaez, Bebeau, & Thoma, 1999a, 1999b; Thoma, 2006; Walker, 2002). Nor can we review recent arguments regarding the nature of moral reasoning more generally (see, for example, Gibbs, 2006; Krebs & Denton, 2005, 2006). Rather, focal issues in recent research on adolescents' moral judgment are briefly summarized. These include findings on adolescents' level of moral reasoning and its structure and the relations of moral reasoning to adolescents' adjustment, social competence, and risky behaviors, as well as to socialization correlates.

Justice Moral Reasoning

The type of moral reasoning that has received the most empirical attention is Kohlberg's justice-oriented reasoning (Kohlberg, 1981). According to Colby et al. (1983), although Stage 2 (individualism, instrumental purpose, and exchange) reasoning is predominant in early adolescence, at about age 13, and throughout adolescence, Stage 3 (mutual interpersonal expectations, relationships, and interpersonal conformity reasoning) moral reasoning is the most common, dominant mode of moral reasoning. In this type of reasoning, the "right" includes living up to what is expected by people close to you or what others generally expect of people in your role (as son, wife, etc.). "Being good" is important and is reflected in having good motives, showing concern for others, and in maintaining mutual relationships through trust, loyalty, respect, and gratitude (Colby et al., 1983). At this stage, the focus in moral reasoning shifts from self-interest (Stage 2) to fulfilling others' expectations and concern with one's position in others' eyes, as well as maintaining positive interpersonal relationships with others. Gibbs et al. (2007), in a review of research, concluded that by late adolescence, Stage 3 normally becomes the typical moral reasoning stage, not only in North America, but also globally. Stage 4 (social system and conscience) reasoning also is used by some adolescents, but generally is used infrequently. Stage 4 reasoning increases with age from early adolescence into adulthood. Stage 4 reasoning emphasizes fulfilling the duties to which one has agreed, upholding of laws except in extreme cases in which they conflict with other fixed social duties, and contributing to the society, group, or institution (Colby et al. 1983).

More recent research is consistent with earlier findings (e.g., Dawson, 2002; Pratt, Arnold, Pratt, & Diessner, 1999; Walker, Gustafson, & Hennig, 2001; also see Narvaez, 1998) in regard to the nature of adolescents' moral reasoning. However, it has been argued that what has been coded as Stage 3 might actually be two different stages (Dawson, 2002) or that there are really only three distinct developmental schemas or levels, personal interest (Stages 2 and 3), maintaining norms (Stage 4) and postconventional (Stages 5 and 6) after age 12 (the age at which people can respond to the Defining Issues Test [DIT]; Rest, Narvaez, Bebeau, & Thoma, 1999b). Moreover, there is debate regarding the best way to assess moral judgment and how to quantify it (see Gibbs et al., 2007; Lapsley, 2006). Thus, currently there is not consensus on the nature of moral stages in adolescence.

In recent years, there has been some research in which adolescents have been asked to reason about real life rather than hypothetical moral dilemmas (e.g., Trevethan & Walker, 1989). Walker, Pitts, Hennig, and Matsuba (1995) found that there was not a significant difference between 16–19 year-olds' moral reasoning about real-life moral conflicts (coded using Kohlberg's stages) and 18- to 25-year-olds' reasoning, although 35- to 48- and 65- to 84-year-olds' reasoned at higher levels than did the two younger groups. Thus, change in moral reasoning in late adolescence about real-life moral dilemmas (as well as hypothetical dilemmas) appears to be relatively gradual.

Consistent with Kohlberg's theory (1981), it also appears that for justice reasoning, at least as traditionally coded and for reasoning in reaction to vignettes (rather the preference measures such as the DIT; see Lapsley, 2006), there is a cycle of consolidation and then transition upward from stage to stage (with a mix of reasoning, especially higher level reasoning and one's modal level of reasoning during the transition). These findings at least partly support a structural model in which moral reasoning during late childhood and adolescence advances from lower to more mature levels, with periods of apparent disequilibrium between them (Walker et al., 2001). However, this pattern of structural change likely does not characterize moral judgment as assessed with other instruments (e.g., pencil and paper measures of moral judgment) or moral reasoning about issues besides justice (Lapsley, 2006). In addition, it appears that both adolescents and adults are more likely to use alternative ethical systems (other than Kohlberg's) such as religious prescriptions, community norms, professional codes, and care reasoning when they are in a period of transition between stages (Thoma & Rest, 1999).

Prosocial Reasoning

As was noted by Thoma and Rest (1999), individuals sometimes use moral reasoning that is not well represented in Kohlberg's (1981) justice-oriented moral reasoning. One type of reasoning used by adolescents is care-oriented reasoning (Perry & McIntire, 1995; Skoe et al., 1999). According to Gilligan (1982), the focus of care reasoning is on not turning away from others rather than not treating others unfairly (i.e., justice concerns). Gilligan's care reasoning is similar to the stages of prosocial moral reasoning delineated by Eisenberg (1986), who has defined prosocial moral reasoning as reasoning about moral dilemmas in which one person's needs or desires conflict with those of others in a context in which the role of prohibitions, authorities' dictates, and formal obligations is minimal.

In the last two decades, Eisenberg and colleagues (Eisenberg, Miller, Shell, McNalley, & Shea, 1991; Eisenberg, Carlo, Murphy, & Van Court, 1995; Eisenberg et al., 2005) have followed children through adolescence into early adulthood to delineate the development of their prosocial moral reasoning. In general, they have found that some self-reflective and internalized modes of moral reasoning (e.g., reasoning pertaining to role taking, positive or negative affect based on the consequences of behavioral choices; positive affect related to living up to internalized values; internalized norm, rule, and law reasoning; generalized reciprocity) increased in use, whereas stereotypic reasoning (e.g., references to expected or normative behavior, such as, "it's nice to help") continued to decrease in use from childhood until the late teens. The linear increases in references to positive affect/values and negative affect about consequences were not found until late adolescence. However, hedonistic reasoning (i.e., reasoning in which the justification is one's own desires, e.g., "She wouldn't help because she would rather go to the party"), which had decreased from childhood into early mid-adolescence, increased modestly in mid-, and then again, late adolescence, primarily for males. Moreover, direct reciprocity and approval-oriented reasoning, which had begun to decline in mid-adolescence, showed little evidence of declining in the late teens (and even increased somewhat). Although there was a linear increase in overall level of reasoning throughout adolescence (also see Eisenberg-Berg, 1979a), moral reasoning at age 19 to 20 was not predicted from moral reasoning at earlier points in adolescence,

apparently because of substantial declines in reasoning (due to increases in direct reciprocity and hedonistic reasoning) for some people and substantial increases in reasoning due to the use of higher level categories of reasoning for some others. In contrast, there was some continuity in moral reasoning from age 13–14 years to 17–18 years.

Eisenberg et al. (2005) examined changes in moral reasoning from age 15–16 to 25–26; they focused on changes in level of moral judgment (assessed through interviews) rather than individual types of moral reasoning. They found that both moral judgment composite scores computed from all levels of reasoning and Level 4 (self-reflective empathic reasoning, for females only) generally increased from late adolescence into the early 20s but then leveled off or declined slightly, whereas rudimentary needs-oriented reasoning (Level 2) showed the inverse pattern of change. Level 1 (hedonistic, self-focused orientation) and Level 5 (strongly internalized orientation), both of which were not highly used, did not change over this period, whereas Level 3 reasoning (stereotypic or approval/interpersonal) increased with age.

Findings somewhat similar to those described above have been obtained by researchers using a variety of methods (Carlo, Eisenberg, & Knight, 1992). For example, in a study of Israeli 12- to 13-, 14- to 15-, and 16- to 17-year-olds' self-reported motives for their own volunteering to help, reports of altruistic motives (i.e., personal willingness to assist without any expectation of reward or approval, and without reference to compliance) increased with age (Bar-Tal & Nissim, 1984). Further, in work on attributions about the value of others' prosocial actions, investigators have found that from early adolescence into early adulthood, students increasingly devalue prosocial actions done for self-related reasons (e.g., tangible rewards, returning a favor), approval or praise, or to avoid criticism and punishment, and increasingly value prosocial actions due to empathy (see Eisenberg, 1986, 1990, for reviews).

In one of the few cross-cultural studies on the topic, Boehnke, Silbereisen, Eisenberg, Reykowski, and Palmonari (1989) examined German, Polish, Italian, and American elementary, middle, and/or high school students' attributions for why story characters' engaged in prosocial actions. Interest in others was a relatively favored motive at all ages, whereas self-focused motives were chosen infrequently by the preadolescents and junior and senior high school students. Conformity-related reasons decreased with age in Italian, German, and Polish samples across grades 6, 9, 10, and 12, whereas task-oriented reasons (i.e., pragmatic concerns related to the completion of a task) increased. In another sample of German students in grades 5–6 or 7–9, preference for hedonistic motives (i.e., motives related to an individual's feelings of physical well-being but not other aspects of self-interest) decreased with age and preference for task-oriented motives (e.g., "because I know if I helped, the work would get done more quickly") increased. For American children in grades 2–3, 5–6, and 7–8, selection of hedonistic motives decreased with age in early adolescence (Boehnke et al., 1989). Thus, adolescents preferred other-oriented or task-oriented motives for assisting, and conformity and hedonistic motives were somewhat less preferred with age. The lack of an age-related change in other-oriented motives may have been due to the format of the measure.

Gilligan (1982) argued that care-related moral reasoning is somewhat more common among females, and there is some support for this assertion. In a meta-analysis, Jaffe and Hyde (2000) found a small sex difference in care-related reasoning (broadly defined) favoring females (effect size = 0.28). Of particular interest, this difference was much larger in adolescents (0.53) than in children (0.08), university students (0.18), or young adults who were not university students (0.33) compare with Pratt, Skoe, & Arnold (2004) who found no gender differences in adolescence in care reasoning.

In adolescence, whether girls score higher than boys in care-related reasoning may depend on the country or culture. For example, in a study with young adolescents, a sex difference was found in Canada but not in Norway (Skoe et al., 1999). In the United States, however, the sex difference favoring females' higher use of care-oriented reasoning was replicated in a study of African American seventh graders' reasoning about dating dilemmas (Weisz & Black, 2002).

In regard to prosocial moral reasoning, Eisenberg et al. (1987) found that a sex difference in types of reasoning reflecting another orientation seemed to emerge in early adolescence and generally was maintained throughout adolescence (for at least some higher level modes of other-oriented moral reasoning and for the overall level of prosocial moral reasoning; Eisenberg et al., 1991, 1995). Similarly, Boehnke et al. (1989) found modest evidence of females providing more other-oriented and less self-interested reasons for hypothetical story characters' prosocial actions.

Thus, in general, investigators have found that moral reasoning and attributions regarding motives for prosocial behavior tend to stabilize or become more other-oriented and higher level with age during the adolescent years. Moreover, females tend to express more of these types of reasoning/attributions than do males.

Relations of Higher Level Moral Reasoning to Adolescents' Adjustment and Social Competence

Adolescents' levels (and type) of moral reasoning are important in part because they relate to differences in their behavior (or attitudes toward various behaviors), including externalizing problems, prosocial behaviors, adjustment, and risky behaviors. Moreover, adolescents' moral reasoning has been linked to their political attitudes and tolerance of others.

Externalizing Problems

Adolescents' moral reasoning has been relatively consistently related to their antisocial behavior.

In a meta-analysis of 50 studies, moderate to large effect sizes indicate that juvenile delinquents use a lower stage moral judgment compared to nondelinquent peers (Stams et al., 2006). Similarly, in reviews a decade apart, Nelson, Smith, and Dodd (1990) and Jurkovic (1980) found that juvenile delinquents use less mature moral reasoning than their nondelinquent peers. Additional studies not in those reviews generally are consistent with their conclusions (e.g., Carlo, Koller, & Eisenberg, 1998; Lardén, Melin, Holst, & Långström, 2006), although self-reported offending was not related to justice-related moral reasoning within a group of convicted young male offenders (Aleixo & Norris, 2000) or in a recent study of 12- to 15-year-olds (Tarry & Emler, 2007; see Brusten, Stams, & Gibbs, 2007, for a critique of this study, and Emler & Tarry, 2007, for their response). Further, adolescents who score lower on moral judgment are more aggressive (for boys but not girls; Schonert-Reichl, 1999), hold more positive attitudes toward violent groups (Sotelo & Sangrador, 1999), and are more likely to perceive intentionally injurious sport actions as legitimate (Bredemeier, 1985). Acting-out preadolescent and adolescent males are also more accepting in their judgments about others' aggressive actions (Sanvitale, Saltzstein, & Fish, 1989; also see Berkowitz, Mueller, Schnell, & Padberg, 1986). Further, gains in moral reasoning due to an intervention with delinquents have been linked to lower recidivism in adolescents (although the gains in moral reasoning due to the intervention were not significant; Gibbs, Potter, Barriga, & Liau, 1996).

Conversely, adolescents who reason at more mature levels tend to be more prosocial and socially competent. For example, higher level and/or other-oriented (and sometimes low hedonistic reasoning) prosocial moral judgment generally has been positively related to humanitarian political attitudes (Eisenberg-Berg, 1979b; Eisenberg-Berg & Mussen, 1980), as well as self- and/or other-reported prosocial tendencies and sympathy across the teen years (Carlo, Eisenberg, & Knight, 1992;

Carlo, Hausmann, Christiansen, & Randall, 2003; Eisenberg et al., 1991, 1995, 2002; Eisenberg, Zhou, & Koller, 2001; also see Wentzel, Filisetti, & Looney, 2007). Sixth and eight graders' reported internal (reflecting personal valuing of prosocial behavior) and self-focused (avoiding negative feelings of guilt or shame) reasons for performing various prosocial behaviors were also related to high levels of empathy, perspective taking, perceived competence (Wentzel et al., 2007). Moreover, measures of moral reasoning tapping a justice orientation more than a care orientation have been associated with Italian adolescents' involvement in volunteer activities (Comunian & Gielen, 1995) and with 10- to 13-year-old Canadian girls' (but not boys') prosocial nominations by peers (Schonert-Reichl, 1999), as well as with tolerance of others' views or lifestyle (Breslin, 1982; Raaijmakers, Verbogt, & Vollebergh, 1998). In regard to social competence, level of justice-oriented moral reasoning has been related to pre- and young adolescents' peer sociometric status and peer nominations for leadership (girls only) (Schonert-Reichl, 1999). Socially withdrawn behavior or shyness with peers has been negatively related to level of justice-related moral reasoning for boys in early adolescence (Schonert-Reichl, 1999) and for emotionally disturbed individuals in early and mid-adolescence (Sigman & Erdynast, 1988; Sigman, Ungerer, & Russell, 1983). Further, justice-related moral judgment has been linked to higher level social problem-solving skills in 14- to 18-year-old inner city youth (Kennedy, Felner, Cauce, & Primavera, 1988) and with mature ego functioning (inter- and intrapersonal strategies for coping; Matsuba & Walker, 1998). Mature ego defense mechanisms at ages 13–14 and 16–18 also have been associated with higher level justice reasoning 10 to 20 years later (sometimes even when controlling for moral reasoning in adolescence; Hart & Chmiel, 1992). Thus, although, of course, the findings have not always been significant and the percent of variance accounted for by these relations generally is modest, adolescents who are more advanced in their moral reasoning appear to be not only more moral in their behavior, but also better adjusted and higher in social competence.

The Relation of Moral Judgments to Adolescents' Attitudes About Risky Behavior

A special concern in adolescence is the rise in risky behaviors such as drug use, sexual activity, and suicide. Although very limited, there is some evidence of links between cognitions about morality and adolescents' tendencies to endorse or engage in such behaviors.

Some investigators have examined the relation of level of moral judgment to adolescents' risky behavior. There appear to be weak but not very consistent relations between the two (Berkowitz et al., 1995). For example, in a study of undergraduates, Hubbs-Tait and Garmon (1995) found that risk taking during sexual intercourse (i.e., lower likelihood of using condoms) and anal sex were inversely related with level of justice-related moral reasoning (on Rest's, 1979, Defining Issues Test or DIT). In contrast, in a study of sexually active teenage girls, Jurs (1984) found no relation between moral reasoning (also on the DIT) and the responsible use of birth control, getting pregnant, and the decision to abort (although adolescents reasoning at higher levels were more likely to have taken a sex education course).

However, whether or not an individual considers a given risky behavior to be a moral issue or not may moderate the relation of moral judgment to risky behaviors. Some investigators have examined adolescents' tendencies to categorize risky behaviors as involving moral, social conventional, personal, or prudential decisions. *Moral* judgments involve categorical and prescriptive judgments of right and wrong about interpersonal issues such as harm and justice. *Social conventional* issues pertain to customs or regulations intended to ensure social coordination and social organization, such as choices about modes of dress,

table manners, and forms of greeting. *Personal* choices refer to issues of private behavior that impinge primarily on the self. For example, within Western culture, the choice of friends or recreational activities usually is considered a personal choice, whereas *prudential* issues involve actual or potential self-harm (but do not involve others' welfare; Nucci, Guerra, & Lee, 1991; Tisak, Tisak, & Rogers, 1994).

Many high school students consider the use of legal drugs such as nicotine, caffeine, and alcohol, as well as premarital sex, as a personal or prudential choice (especially the latter, if assessed) rather than a behavior that should be controlled by authorities or as a moral issue (Killen, Leviton, & Cahill, 1991; Kuther & Higgins-D'Alessandro, 2000; Nucci et al., 1991). In contrast, the use of illegal drugs such cocaine, crack, and marijuana is less likely to be viewed as an issue under personal jurisdiction and is more likely to be viewed as "wrong," regardless of authority or laws (Killen et al., 1991). Risky behaviors are seldom viewed as social conventional issues (Killen et al., 1991; Nucci et al., 1991; see Tisak et al., 1994, for data on adolescents' views on the legitimacy of parents' attempts to prohibit contact with drug-using friends). Of importance, students who are higher in the use of drugs are more likely than their low-using students to view the drug use as a personal choice (Kuther & Higgins-D'Alessandro, 2000), and less likely to view it as harmful and a prudentially unacceptable choice (wrong only because it hurts the self; Nucci et al., 1991). High drug users also are more likely to view themselves as the only authority with regard to the choice to use drugs and are less likely than their peers to view parents or the law as legitimate authorities (Nucci et al., 1991). Moreover, in one study, adolescents' views regarding the nature of decisions regarding drug use were found to moderate the relation of level of justice-related moral reasoning to drug use. When adolescents considered drug use a moral decision, a higher degree of substance use was related to lower level justice-oriented moral reasoning, whereas moral reasoning was unrelated to the use of drugs for adolescents who considered it to be a personal decision (similar findings were not obtained for sexual behavior or suicide; Kuther & Higgins-D'Alessandro, 2000). Findings such as these suggest that moral reasoning is related to some risky behaviors, but only for adolescents who view them as having moral relevance. However, it is not clear if moral reasoning actually affects risky behavior or if participation in risky behavior affects how adolescents categorize risky behaviors.

Socialization of Moral Reasoning

Different socialization agents, such as parents, peers, teachers, and other adult role models (e.g., coaches, religious leaders), likely influence adolescent' moral reasoning. However, most research to date has focused on parents as the primary socialization influence, with some research on peers.

Parental Influences

Socialization by parents typically has been assigned a circumscribed role in moral development by cognitive developmental theorists such as Kohlberg (Walker & Hennig, 1999). Thus, it is not surprising that the contributions of parenting to the development of moral reasoning have not been studied extensively. Some aspects of socialization that have received the most attention in studies with adolescents are parental moral reasoning, parental warmth, and aspects of parent–child discussions that might stimulate perspective taking or autonomous moral thinking.

Based on cognitive developmental theory, one would expect parenting practices that create cognitive conflict about moral issues to be linked to higher level moral judgment. Somewhat consistent with this notion, there is evidence that a Socratic style of discussion (encouraging the child to form opinions and to use reasoning) between parents and children, combined with other variables (such as parental support), is most conducive to the development of justice-related moral reasoning in

late childhood and adolescence. Based on studies in which parents and their child discussed hypothetical and real-life moral dilemmas (sometimes one in the child's life) and attempted to reach a consensus, Walker and Hennig (1999) concluded that:

> Parents who engage in cognitively challenging and highly opinionated interactions, who are hostile, critical, and interfering, and who display poor ego functioning (defensiveness, rigidity, rationalization, insensitivity, inappropriate emotional expression) provide a context that hinders children's opportunities to move toward more mature moral understandings. In contrast, effective parents are more child-centered and scaffold their child's development by eliciting the child's opinions, drawing out the child's reasoning with appropriate probing questions, and checking for understanding; all in the context of emotional support and attentiveness and with the challenging stimulation of advanced moral reasoning (pp. 271–272).

In Walker's studies, parent behaviors such as critiquing and directly challenging the child (especially in a hostile manner), presenting of counter-considerations, and simply providing information were not associated with children's moral growth. Direct challenges to the child's reasoning may have been viewed as hostile by the child and, consequently, may have been counterproductive, whereas simple provision of information may have been viewed as lecturing (Walker & Hennig, 1999; Walker, Hennig, & Krettenauer, 2000; see Walker & Taylor, 1991).

Similar findings in regard to style of interactions have been found in other studies of preadolescents or adolescents, although there are some inconsistencies in the literature. Buck, Walsh, and Rothman (1981) examined the relation of 10- to 13-year-old boys' moral reasoning to parental behaviors during a discussion with thier son of how to handle their son's aggression. Boys with higher moral reasoning had parents who considered their sons' view and tended to encourage their son to express his views. Similarly, Holstein (1972) found that parents who encouraged their children's participation in discussion and decision making were more likely to have children who reasoned at relatively high levels. In contrast to Walker and Hennig (1999), Pratt et al. (1999) observed that fathers' tendencies to extend, challenge, or clarify the reasoning of their adolescents were positively related to adolescents' concurrent moral reasoning and reasoning two years later. Similar findings were not obtained for mothers, although mothers' tendencies to consider their children's perspectives when recalling social-ization encounters were related to higher level moral reasoning at the 2-year follow-up.

Other investigators besides Walker and Hennig (1999) have obtained associations between parental warmth or involvement and high-level moral reasoning in adolescents (e.g., Buck et al., 1981; McDevitt, Lennon, & Kopriva, 1991; Palmer & Hollin, 1996; Powers, 1988; Speicher, 1992). In some relevant studies, researchers found relations between parental nurturance and moral reasoning for one par-ent or for one group of children (e.g., age or sex group) but not the other (e.g., Bakken & Romig, 1994; Hart, 1988). Inconsistencies may occur because parental warmth by itself probably is not sufficient to stimulate higher level moral reasoning. As noted by Hoffman (2000), parental warmth provides an optimal environment for socialization because children are more likely to attend to parents and care about pleasing them when the relationship generally is supportive. Thus, parental warmth may not have a direct effect on children's moral reasoning, but may moderate the effec-tiveness of other parental practices in fostering the growth of moral reasoning. A combination of warmth and other productive parental practices, such as using a Socratic method in discussions and holding high standards for children, may be necessary to foster adolescents' moral reasoning. In support of this premise, authoritative parenting (which includes sup-port, demands for appropriate behavior and control, and practices such as induction) has been linked to higher level moral judgment,

more parent–adolescent value agreement, and higher generativity/concern for the next gen-eration (Boyes & Allen, 1993; Lawford, Pratt, Hunsberger, & Pancer, 2005; Pratt et al., 1999) (although democratic parenting has not always been associated with adolescents' moral reasoning; Speicher, 1992). Parental use of autonomy-promoting practices at age 16 also has been associated with caring moral reasoning concurrently and at age 20 (Pratt et al., 2004).

Authoritative parenting has also been linked to moral values, which are relevant for moral judgment. Pratt, Hunsberger, Pancer, and Alisat (2003) examined authoritative parenting in rela-tion to moral values (e.g., fair, honest), moral motivation, and the moral ideal self in a lon-gitudinal study of adolescents. Authoritative parenting was associated with more parent–adolescent agreement concerning both moral and nonmoral values. Among boys, parental monitoring and strictness were associated with moral self-values, and this link was explained by adolescents' perceived parent and peer emphasis on the importance of moral values. Thus, these findings support the significance of both parents' and peers' valuing of moral behavior on the development of adolescents' moral values.

Consistent with the relation of authoritative parenting to higher level moral reasoning, there appears to be a modest relation between parental use of inductions (reasoning) during discipline and older children and adolescents' mature moral judgment (Janssen, Janssens, & Gerris, 1992), although such relations often vary across parent, social class, or age group (e.g., Eisikovits & Sagi, 1982; Parikh, 1980; see Eisenberg & Valiente, 2002, for more details). Moreover, parental emphasis on prosocial behavior and caring as a goal has been associ-ated with higher level prosocial moral reason-ing (McDevitt et al., 1991; Pratt et al., 2004). Further, agreement between parents in regard to child-rearing practices, attitudes, and values at age 3 has predicted higher moral reasoning for 14-year-old males (but not females; Vaughn, Block, & Block, 1988).

Consistent with these findings, White and Matawie (2004) found that components of the family environment (e.g., cohesion, communication) were associated with adolescent morality, specifically content of moral thought (i.e., reasons for making a moral judgment), assessed via the revised Moral Authority Scale (White, 1997; assessing internal, external, and principled moral sources of reasoning). Adolescents' reports of both mothers' and fathers' morality were associated with their own reports of morality (external [family and educator source] and principle sources [society and equality sources]), and in general, family cohesion, adaptability, and positive communication predicted adolescents' external morality. These findings indicated that family processes and both mother and father influences are important in adolescent reasoning, particularly when adolescents view their family influence as an important reason for their moral decision making.

In summary, higher level reasoning in adolescence is related to parenting that is supportive and stimulates adolescents to question and expand on their reasoning, as well as to an authoritative parenting style (including inductive discipline). Moreover, research suggests that overall family processes are influential in determining the source for adolescent moral decision making. However, findings are limited in number and sometimes inconsistent (e.g., Leahy, 1981; see Eisenberg & Valiente, 2002). Although infrequently examined, it is possible that the parenting behaviors/characteristics associated with adolescents' moral judgment vary across adolescence. For example, based on her finding that moral judgment was predicted by reports of comfort with, and frequency of family moral and political discussions in later adolescence and early adulthood, but not earlier adolescence, Speicher (1992) suggested that the quality of interpersonal family relationships may be more important for the development of moral reasoning in early adolescence, whereas aspects of the family environment related to cognitive stimulation and perspective taking may be important at an older age. Currently, there are too few data to test such a prediction. Moreover, because all the extant data with adolescents are correlational, it is unclear to what degree parental behaviors actually cause changes in adolescents' moral reasoning rather than adolescents varying in their moral reasoning eliciting different parenting styles and practices (or some other factor such as genetics affecting both parenting and adolescents' moral judgment).

Peer Influences

Cognitive developmental theorists have argued that interactions with peers are a more important influence on moral development than are interactions with parents or other adults because peer relations are more egalitarian and provide opportunities for social interaction among equals. The equal status in peer interactions is viewed as encouraging peers to cooperate and deal with moral conflicts by balancing self and other interests at comparable levels (Kohlberg, 1969; Piaget, 1932/1965). Moreover, interactions with peers also may provide opportunities for self-exploration and allow adolescents to discuss identity issues, such as beliefs and aspirations, among a supportive group of equals, which might affect their moral identity. In general, research indicates that peers do play a role in the development of adolescent moral reasoning, although most relevant work has been conducted with children rather than adolescents.

Of the researchers who have examined peer influences on moral reasoning, most find that moral discussions with peers do have a positive effect on moral development. At least one study found that peers may even have a greater influence than parents. Using an experimental design, Kruger (1992) found that girls who engaged in a conflict discussion with a peer had higher levels of moral development on a posttest compared to girls who engaged in a parent–child discussion.

Similarly, Walker et al. (2000) examined parent and peer effects on moral reasoning by having parent–adolescent and friend–adolescent dyads discuss moral conflicts. The sample included a group of adolescents in late childhood and mid-adolescence, and moral reasoning was assessed yearly using Kohlberg's Moral Justice Interview (MJI), over four years. Walker et al. found evidence for both parent and peer influences on moral reasoning, but patterns of influence differed. For peers, they found that friends' interfering speech (which interfered with discussion and indicated negative affect) was associated with higher levels of moral development; this finding is in line with the cognitive developmental notion that some degree of conflict among peers supports moral development. Contrary to this idea and to previous findings (Berkowitz & Gibbs, 1983), Walker et al. also found that peers' high-powered, dominant challenges to moral thinking (coded as highly operational speech that operates on the reasoning of another, for example, critiques or competitive clarification) were related to minimal moral development. This contradiction in Walker et al.'s findings suggests that a moderate degree of conflict in discussion with a friend may promote moral development, as long as the conflict is not overly challenging and dominant (see also Schonert-Reichl, 1999). Walker et al. hypothesized that the difference between their findings and those of Berkowitz and Gibbs, who found positive relations between operational/challenging conversation and moral reasoning among peers, likely was due to the nature of the peers used in the two studies. In the Berkowitz and Gibbs study, the peer was an unacquainted peer, and in the Walker et al. study, the peer was a friend.

Walker et al. also found that for both parent and peer dyads, a Socratic style of discussion predicted more mature moral development. In contrast, for both parents (as mentioned previously) and peers, highly informative interactions (sharing opinions, agreement or disagreement), which may have been perceived as intrusive and lecturing, were associated with lower levels of moral reasoning.

The quality of peers' relationships may also play a role in youth moral development. Schonert-Reichl (1999) examined associations

of peer relationships and friendship quality to moral reasoning in youth aged 10 through 13. Youths' completed sociometric measures of peer acceptance, questionnaires about their friendships, and Kohlberg's moral reasoning measure. Having a greater number of close friends and being perceived as a leader/high peer acceptance were associated with higher levels of moral reasoning. In addition, the relation between moral reasoning and peer acceptance was mediated by social behavior, suggesting that links between moral judgment and behavior are important in peer acceptance.

Moreover, Schonert-Reichl's findings suggested that time spent with friends and the quality of such interaction were related to moral reasoning, although findings differed for males and females. For example, females' socializing and agentic activities with friends were both associated with higher levels of moral reasoning, indicating that more interaction with peers in general has a positive impact on moral judgment. For boys, those who did not resolve conflicts with friends quickly and easily were higher in moral reasoning, again highlighting the importance of some level of conflict in the development of moral judgment. Pratt et al. (2003) found that male (but not female) adolescents' perceptions of peers' beliefs about specific moral values (e.g., being honest, fair, a good citizen) were important in moral values for the self. This finding supports the conclusion that peers as well as families are important in the moral socialization process and that gender differences in such associations may exist.

In summary, research findings are consistent with the view that peers influence adolescents' moral reasoning through friendship, peer group qualities, and dialogue about moral conflicts. It also appears that a moderate degree of conflict among friends may be associated with higher levels of moral reasoning, perhaps due to challenges to the adolescents' thinking. However, because most relevant studies are correlational in design (or could not control the quality of peer interactions), it is difficult to ascertain the direction of effects.

Culture and Moral Reasoning

It is unclear if the findings reviewed above generalize to non-Western countries; relatively little of the research on moral judgment has been conducted in non-Western societies and much of that work is not easily accessible (e.g., the studies are unpublished, dissertations, or published in a language besides English; see, e.g., the Gibbs et al., 2007, review). Moreover, there is debate regarding the degree to which systems for coding moral judgment developed in the United States accurately represent the development of moral judgment in non-Western, nonindustrialized countries. Some researchers argue for the universal application of Kohlberg's coding systems because these basic stages have been found in 23 different countries (Gibbs et al., 2007). However, others have refuted the universality of Kohlberg's moral judgment stages across cultures. For instance, Baek (2002) compared 7- to 16-year-old Korean and British children on Kohlberg's moral dilemmas and found cultural differences in the use of moral orientations as well as the inability to match some Korean children's responses to Kohlberg's stages. Other discrepant cross-cultural findings have appeared within a sample of mainland Chinese 7- to 15-year-old children. With this sample, there was evidence for both universal stage-like progression and culture-specific moral development (Fang et al., 2003). In the Gibbs et al. review of 23 countries, China was represented; however, Korea was not.

Other cross-cultural work has shown similar mixed findings. Fang, Fang, Keller, Edelstein, and Shuster (2002) explored moral reasoning in friendships in Western (Iceland) and Eastern (China) children and adolescents. In general, culture-specific differences (e.g., self- versus other-focused differences) were noted until the age of 15 when universally an overall importance of close friendships was found. Thus, it is possible that cross-cultural

differences and similarities in moral judgment change with age.

In one interesting cross-national study, Ferguson and Cairns (2002) studied adolescents in Northern Ireland, Scotland, and the Republic of Ireland to assess the relation between the violent environment of Northern Ireland and level of moral reasoning. No significant differences were found among the three countries, despite differences in the social environments to which the adolescents were exposed.

Subcultural differences in values may also affect adolescents' moral reasoning. In a within-group study of African American adolescents, those higher in African cultural values (i.e., communalism, spirituality, and an emphasis on affect [integration of affect with thought and behavior, emphasis on emotional expression and attending to emotional cues]) were relatively high in moral reasoning; an emphasis on interpersonal competition and material well-being (Anglo values) were not related to moral reasoning (Woods & Jagers, 2003). Given the prosocial nature of the African values in this study, it is likely that the same values in other cultural groups would predict higher levels of moral judgment. However, there is little research examining if adolescents' acceptance of subcultural (or cultural) values is linked with moral reasoning and how the nature of the given values may moderate this relation.

The cross-cultural work has been conducted with a variety of instruments and methods, and the findings may vary accordingly. Indeed, more published research is needed to examine the universality of adolescents' moral judgment and its correlates.

PROSOCIAL BEHAVIOR

Prosocial behavior is defined as voluntary behavior intended to benefit another (e.g., Eisenberg, 1986; Staub, 1979). Prosocial behaviors based on moral emotions and values rather than factors such as self-interest or the desire for approval are generally labeled as altruistic. Unfortunately, it often is impossible to know if a person's motives for performing prosocial behaviors are altruistic or not.

In this section, age-related changes in prosocial behavior from childhood into adolescence are examined. Then we review the consistency of prosocial tendencies in adolescence, followed by a discussion of gender differences in adolescents' prosocial behavior. Next, other correlates of prosocial behavior in adolescence are briefly discussed, including personality or personal characteristics (e.g., regulation, social competence, and adjustment), and characteristics of the family or parental practices. Finally, correlates and possible consequences of adolescents' involvement in voluntary and/or civic activities are reviewed, and the possible role of adolescents' volunteering or civic service in their prosocial development is examined.

Age Trends in Prosocial Behavior and Empathy-Related Responding

If adolescents' moral reasoning is more sophisticated and other-oriented than that of younger children, one would expect prosocial behavior to increase with age throughout childhood and into adolescence. According to a meta-analysis (Eisenberg & Fabes, 1998), prosocial behavior does increase across childhood, and adolescents tend to be higher in prosocial behavior than preschoolers (on a variety of measures of prosocial behavior, mostly observed measures) and children aged 7 to 12 (on sharing/donating, but not instrumental helping or comforting). Adolescents and children did not differ in their self-reported prosocial behavior; however, they differed on observations of prosocial behavior and on others' reports thereof. Differences between adolescents and both preschoolers and young children held for comparison of early adolescents (age 13 to 15) and older adolescents (age 16 to 18) (Fabes, Carlo, Kupanoff, & Laible, 1999). However, there was limited evidence of an increase in prosocial responding across adolescence (from age 12 to 17 or 18), although prosocial behavior did increase in adolescence in experimental/structured studies (but not naturalistic/correlational studies), and

when the recipient of aid was a child rather than an adult (Eisenberg & Fabes). Thus, although adolescents exhibit more prosocial behavior than younger children, change in adolescence was noted only for particular recipients or types of studies. However, the number of studies that compared older and younger adolescents was surprisingly small (11), so the findings must be viewed as merely suggestive.

Recent studies also are inconclusive. Carlo, Crockett, Randall, and Roesch (2007) found a decline in adolescents' self-reported prosocial behavior from 7th to 11th grade, with a slight rebound in 12th grade. Moreover, Kokko, Tremblay, Lacourse, Nagin, and Vitaro (2006) found gradual declines in prosocial behavior from age 6 to 12. Helping victims of aggression may also decline across adolescence (Lindeman, Harakka, & Keltikangas-Jarvinen, 1997). Eisenberg et al. (2005) examined self-reported helping behavior from age 15–16 into the 20s and found a cubic trend, with helping increasing from 15–16 to 17–18, then declining in the early 20s, and then increasing in the mid-20s.

In the aforementioned meta-analysis, prosocial behavior directed toward adults did not change with age in adolescence. This may particularly be true in the family setting. Eberly and Montemayor (1998) found that adolescents' reports of prosocial behaviors directed at parents (e.g., helping with various tasks) were higher in 8th graders than either 6th or 10th graders (who did not differ from one another); there were no age-related differences in parents' reports of helpfulness. In a 2-year follow-up of the same sample, adolescents' self-reported prosocial behavior directed toward their parents did not change for 6th graders who became 8th graders, declined over the 2 years for 8th graders who became 10th graders, and increased for 10th graders who became 12th graders. Thus, there seemed to be a sort of regression to the mean; 8th graders, who initially were high in self-reported helpfulness declined over the 2 years, whereas 10th graders, who were low, increased. In contrast, parents' reports of adolescents' helpfulness did not change. Self-reported prosocial behavior directed toward fathers increased over the 2 years; Youths' helpfulness toward their mothers (and parent-reported helpfulness toward each parent) did not change (Eberly & Montemayor, 1999). In another study of 5th to 9th graders, parents generally reported a decline in helpfulness with age (Eberly, Montemayor, & Flannery, 1993). Moreover, Keith, Nelson, Schlabach, and Thompson (1990) found no change with age among a sample of 10- to 14-year olds in their family responsibilities (e.g., doing chores for the family). Thus, there seems to be no clear pattern of change in adolescence in helping of parents. Perhaps the inconsistencies in the literature are partly due to the fact that many adolescents spend less time at home than when younger, and this variable has not been considered in analyses of helpfulness directed at parents (Larson & Richards, 1991).

As was mentioned previously, empathy-related responding has been linked in theory and empirically to prosocial behavior. Based on Hoffman's theory, one would expect an age-related increase in empathy-related responding, especially in situations in which empathy/sympathy is toward abstract groups (e.g., needy individuals). Eisenberg and Fabes (1998) reported an age-related increase in empathy-related responding (empathy/sympathy); however, they did not break down the findings by age. In early studies of empathy-related responding (before about 1986), findings regarding age-trends in empathy-related responding in adolescence were inconsistent, although there was some evidence of an increase from childhood into adolescence (Eysenck, Easting, & Pearson, 1984; Saklofske & Eysenck, 1983; see Lennon & Eisenberg, 1987). There is additional evidence of an increase in empathy-related responding, especially for sympathy, since the 1980s. For example, in a longitudinal study of 9th or 10th graders, Davis and Franzoi (1991) found an increase in sympathy and a decline in personal distress over 2 years. In a cross-sectional study of 6th to 12th graders, Olweus and Endresen

(1998) found an increase in girls' empathic distress (likely primarily personal distress), whereas boys' empathy did not change. Girls' sympathetic concern toward male and female targets increased with age, as did boys' sympathy with female targets; however, males' sympathy toward male targets declined somewhat with age, particularly between grades 8 and 9 (also see Szagun, 1992). In another cross-sectional study, Strayer and Roberts (1997) found that both reported empathic sadness and facial concerned reactions to evocative videotapes increased with age (although there was no age difference in affective matching of the emotion in the film). In contrast, in a cross-sectional study of 8th and 11th graders in Israel, Karniol, Gabay, Ochion, and Harari (1998) found no change in self-reported sympathy or personal distress, and empathy with fantasy stimuli (e.g., films, books) declined with age. Nor did Eisenberg et al. (2005) find a change in sympathy from mid-adolescence into early adulthood, although personal distress reactions decreased and cognitive perspective taking increased. In general, then, there seems to be a modest increase in sympathy with age (which may vary with the recipient), whereas the few findings for personal distress were inconsistent. The fact that such change apparently is modest is consistent with the lack of consistent change in prosocial behavior during adolescence, although as discussed shortly, researchers have found that volunteering does increase from childhood to adolescence.

Consistency in Prosocial Responding

There is considerable evidence that individual differences in preadolescents' and adolescents' prosocial behavior and empathy/sympathy show modest to moderate consistency across contexts (e.g., Dlugokinski & Firestone, 1973; Small, Zeldin, & Savin-Williams, 1983; Zeldin, Savin-Williams, & Small, 1984; see Eisenberg, 1990; cf. Payne, 1980) and across 2 years or more time (e.g., Bandura, Caprara, Barbaranelli, Gerbino, & Pastorelli, 2003; Bar-Tal & Raviv, 1979; Davis & Franzoi, 1991;

Eberly & Montemayor, 1999; Eisenberg et al., 1995; Wentzel et al., 2004; contrast with Murphy, Shepard, Eisenberg, Fabes, & Guthrie, 1999). For example, Michalik et al. (2007) found consistency in sympathy from approximately age 4.5–7 to 8 years later. Eisenberg and colleagues (1999) found consistency in prosocial behavior from the preschool years until adolescence and early adulthood. This consistency was partially mediated by individual differences in sympathy; it is likely that consistency across adolescence is also partly due to the stability of sympathetic responding. The consistency in prosocial tendencies in adolescence suggests that individual differences in prosocial values, goals, and/or self-schema are fairly stable. by adolescence (Eisenberg et al., 2002).

Because moral behavior seems to be more consistent if it is based on higher level moral values and orientations (Rholes & Lane, 1985), one would expect more consistency in prosocial behavior in adolescence than at younger ages. Unfortunately, although consistency in prosocial tendencies appears to be higher in adolescence than at younger ages (Caprara, Barbaranelli, Pastorell, Bandura, & Zimbardo, 2000; Eisenberg & Fabes, 1998), the degree of consistency across age groups has not been systematically compared.

Gender Differences in Prosocial Behavior and Empathy-Related Responding

The common stereotype is that females are more caring, other oriented, and helpful than are males. Clearly, this stereotype is not entirely accurate; prosocial behavior in childhood and adulthood appears to vary with the degree to which a prosocial action is consistent with gender roles (e.g., Eagly & Crowley, 1986; Zarbatany, Hartmann, Gelfand, & Vinciguerra, 1985). Nonetheless, there appears to be a kernel of truth to the stereotype, at least in childhood and adolescence. In a meta-analysis of gender differences in prosocial behavior, Eisenberg and Fabes (1998) found that across childhood and adolescence, females were higher

on prosocial behavior, and this difference held to varying degrees across types of prosocial behavior, method of data collection and study design, and the target of prosocial behavior (e.g., a child or an adult). The biggest gender difference was for kind/considerate behavior; differences were considerably smaller for sharing/donating, instrumental help, and comforting. The size of the gender difference increased with age but was reduced to nonsignificance when the effects of other study qualities were controlled in the analyses (correlational/naturalistic studies increased with age and stronger gender differences were obtained in them than in structured/experimental contexts). Further analysis of these studies indicated that the sex difference was significantly stronger in early (13 to 15 years) and late (16 to 18 years) adolescence than in early or middle childhood (Fabes et al., 1999). It was not reported if this pattern held when controlling for study characteristics.

Findings in recent studies generally have been consistent with the conclusion that there is a gender difference favoring females in prosocial behavior (e.g., Barry & Wentzel, 2006; Bosacki, 2003; Carlo, Crockett, et al., 2007; Estrada, 1995; Michalik et al., 2007; Scourfield et al., 2004). For example, in a study of 7- to 13-year-olds in Italy, Caprara, Barbaranelli, and Pastorelli (2001) found that children rated girls in their grade as more prosocial (e.g., helpful, likely to share, likely to try to cheer up a sad person) than boys at ages 11, 12, and 13, but not at ages 7 to 10; teachers rated girls as more prosocial at ages 9, 10, 11, and 13. In both childhood and early adolescence, females reported more prosocial behavior. In addition, some investigators (e.g., Jones & Dembo, 1989), but not all (e.g., Berndt & Perry, 1986), have found that females are more prosocial in intimate friendship relationships. Adolescent females, in comparison to adolescent males, report more helpful or caring activities at both home and work (Call, Mortimer, & Shanaham, 1995), although reports of helpfulness directed toward adolescents' parents sometime have (Eberly et al., 1993), and sometimes have not, (Eberly & Montemayor, 1998, 1999) differed by sex of the adolescent. Female adolescents do more traditionally female household tasks whereas males do more masculine tasks (Keith et al., 1990), and it is likely that many female tasks (e.g., caring for younger children, helping in the kitchen or with laundry) are considered to be more prosocial than masculine tasks such as working in the yard or washing the car. More generally, female adolescents (and young adults), in comparison to males, report that it is more important to help others (the difference seemed to hold across close and distant relationships; Killen & Turiel, 1998) and have been found to engage in more volunteer activities (Keith et al., 1990).

Nonetheless, the sexes may differ in some types of prosocial behaviors but not others. Carlo et al. (2003) found that sex differences varied with type of reported prosocial behavior: Adolescent girls were more likely to report altruistic and emotional prosocial behaviors than were boys, whereas boys were more likely to report prosocial tendencies in public situations. No sex differences were found in situations involving anonymous or compliant prosocial behavior or helping in dire circumstances.

Similarly, gender differences have been found in empathy-related responding in childhood and adolescence. In their meta-analysis, Eisenberg and Fabes (1998) found that the difference in self-reported empathy/sympathy was significant for self-reported and observational measures of empathy-related responding (including combined behavioral and facial reactions), but not for nonverbal facial and physiological measures. The gender difference in self-reported empathy/sympathy increased with age across childhood and adolescence (there are few studies using other methods in adolescence). Other relatively recent work using adults' reports or self-report measures of sympathy is consistent with prior research in finding that female adolescents report more sympathy (Eisenberg et al., 1995; Estrada,

1995; Karniol, Gabay, Ochion, & Harari, 1998; Laible, Carlo, & Raffaelli, 2000; Michalik et al., 2007; Olweus & Endresen, 1998; Strayer & Roberts, 1997) and personal distress (Eisenberg et al., 1995; Olweus & Endresen, 1998) than do males, are viewed as more sympathetic by adults (Murphy et al., 1999), and also show more facial empathy (matching of emotions; Strayer & Roberts, 1997).

Thus, it appears that in adolescence, females view themselves as more prosocial and empathic/sympathetic, and also enact more prosocial, caring behaviors than do males. This difference may be partly due to the types of prosocial behaviors measured in adolescence and the characteristics of the studies; the sex difference is smaller when experimental studies of instrumental helping (especially on masculine tasks) are examined (Eisenberg & Fabes, 1998). However, in adolescence, both parents (Power & Shanks, 1989) and adolescents (McDevitt, et al., 1991) report that parents (or just mothers; McDevitt et al., 1991) emphasize prosocial behavior more with daughters than sons. For example, in a large study of 18-year-olds in seven countries (Australia, United States, Sweden, Hungary, Czech Republic, Bulgaria, and Russia), Flannagan, Bowes, Jonsson, Csapo, and Sheblanova (1998) found that females in all countries reported higher levels of families' encouragement of an ethic of social responsibility than did males (and they volunteered more in five of the seven countries). Thus, prosociality and caring are likely more basic to females' self-image and values. Individual differences in femininity have been found to account for the sex difference in sympathy in adolescence (Karniol et al., 1998), and emotional expressiveness and caring behavior are part of the feminine stereotype (and most measures of femininity). Thus, even if males and females both experience empathic emotion, females may be more likely than males to interpret it as sympathy and link it to prosocial goals and values. Moreover, because females in early adolescence have been found to have more prosocial self-schema than males, one would expect these schema to heighten their prosocial responding, at least if the schema are made salient to them in the situation (see Froming, Nasby, & McManus, 1998) or perhaps when the situation offers opportunities for assisting in ways that are consistent with a feminine gender role.

The Relation of Adolescents' Dispositional Characteristics to Their Prosocial Responding

Prosocial behavior in adolescence has been related to a variety of other aspects of functioning, including empathy-related responding, moral behavior, social competence, level of social cognition, and academic performance. There are, however, relatively few studies on most correlates of prosocial responding and often the data are all self-reported. Thus, many of the findings require further verification, although the fact that they generally are consistent with findings for children and/or adults supports their veracity.

Consistent with theory (Eisenberg, 1986; Hoffman, 2000; Staub, 1979), adolescents' empathy-related responding, especially sympathetic concern, has been positively related to measures of prosocial goals, attitudes, and behavior, for both self-report and occasionally behavioral or other-report measures (Eisenberg et al., 1991, 1995; Eisenberg, Zhou, & Koller, 2001; Estrada, 1995; Krevans & Gibbs, 1996; Wentzel, 2003; Wentzel et al., 2004; Wentzel, Filisetti, & Looney, 2007; see Eisenberg & Fabes, 1998). This relation held for boys, but not girls, in a sample of African American youth (McMahon, Wernsman, & Parnes, 2006). Sympathetic youth also report being high in having a social conscience (Lerner et al., 2005). I contrast, adolescents' (and preadolescents') personal distress tends to be unrelated or negatively related to empathy-related responding (Eisenberg et al., 1991, 1995; Estrada, 1995).

Sympathetic/prosocial early adolescents also are viewed as well-regulated by parents and/or teachers (Eisenberg, Liew, & Pidada, 2004; Murphy et al., 1999); report high

intentional self-regulation (Gestsdottir & Lerner, 2007) and self-efficacy in regard to emotional and behavioral regulation, as well as academic competence (Bandura et al., 2003); and do well in school (Lerner et al., 2005; Wentzel et al., 2004). Conversely, empathy or sympathy (e.g., Carlo, Roesch, & Melby, 1998; Cohen & Strayer, 1996; Laible, Carlo, & Raffaelli, 2000; Murphy et al., 1999; Robinson, Roberts, Strayer, & Koopman, 2007; also see de Wied, Goudena, & Matthys, 2005) and prosocial behavior (Caprara et al., 2000; Rigby, 1993; not Carlo, Roesch, et al., 1998) usually have been negatively related to measures of delinquency, bullying, and externalizing problems, as well as with dispositional anger and negative emotionality (Bandura et al., 2003; Carlo, Roesch, et al., 1998; Gini, Albiero, Benelli, & Altoe, 2007; Lim, Khoo, & Wong, 2007; Ma, Cheung, & Shek, 2007; Murphy et al., 1999; also see Muris, Meesters, & van den Berg, 2003). Sometimes prosocial values or responding has been linked with low psychological distress (Lawford et al., 2005; Wentzel et al., 1999), although findings in regard to internalizing problems are less common than for externalizing problems. These findings are relatively consistent and sometimes based on behavioral measures or multiple reporters (e.g., Caprara et al., 2001; Cohen & Strayer, 1996). However, the relation of prosocial responding to aggression likely varies depending on the actor's motive for engaging in prosocial behavior. For example, reports of prosocial actions performed for personal gain have been positively related to reported aggressive actions and the acceptance of aggression (Boxer, Tisak, & Goldstein, 2004).

Prosocial behavior and empathy-related responding have not been consistently related to sociability in adolescence (Carlo, Roesch, et al., 1998) or shyness (Eisenberg, Liew, et al., 2004), although sociability/low shyness seems to predict prosocial responding at a younger age (Eisenberg et al., 2006). Extroverted and introverted early adolescents tend to differ in the degree to which their prosocial behaviors are affected by the presence of other people (Suda & Fouts, 1980). Prosocial adolescents tend to be well liked by peers (Caprara et al., 2000; Pakaslahti & Keltikangas-Jarvinen, 2001; Wentzel, 2003; Wentzel & McNamara, 1999) and have supportive peer relationships (de Guzman & Carlo, 2004; Markiewicz, Doyle, & Brendgen, 2001; Wentzel, 2003), and popular adolescents tend to engage in more helping involving peers whereas less popular adolescents tend to help in situations that do not involve interaction with peers (Hampson, 1984). Similarly, teachers' reports of early adolescents' sympathy have been correlated with peer nominations of high social status and with teachers' antecedent and concurrent ratings of socially competent and appropriate behavior at school (Eisenberg, Liew, et al., 2004; Murphy et al., 1999). Adolescents' reports of their own sympathy also tend to relate to high social competence (Laible & Carlo, 2004), their number of friends (Coleman & Byrd, 2003), and a positive connection/attachment with peers, school, and/or the community (Laible et al., 2000; Lerner et al., 2005). Prosocial adolescents also have been found to be high in self-reported (perceived) social competence (Wentzel et al., 2007) and have a positive identity (Lerner, et al., 2005), but are not especially high in dominant behavior (Small et al., 1983).

There is some evidence that prosocial and/or sympathetic adolescents are more mature in their social cognition, including their perspective taking (Bosacki, 2003; Carlo et al., 2003; Estrada, 1995; Eisenberg et al., 1991, 2001; Karniol & Shomroni, 1999; Wentzel et al., 2007; contrast with Emler & Rushton, 1974; Marsh, Serfica, & Barenboim, 1981), emotional intelligence (Charbonneau & Nicol, 2002), self-understanding (Bosacki, 2003), means-end thinking (Marsh et al., 1981), and moral reasoning (see prior review and Eisenberg, 1986). Preadolescents who are viewed as prosocial by their peers also are less likely than less prosocial peers to attribute hostile intent to others (an attribution style generally associated with low aggression) or feel distressed in provocative situations, tend to evaluate aggressive responses to provocation more negatively (and prosocial responses more positively), and are more likely to endorse relational rather than instrumental goals for dealing with peer provocation (Nelson & Crick, 1999). Prosocial adolescents also have been found to be high in self-esteem (Johnson, Beebe, Mortimer, & Snyder, 1998; Laible & Carlo, 2004; Lawford et al., 2005; Lerner et al., 2005; also see Bronstein et al., 2007), although this relation was evident only for females in one study (Laible, Carlo, & Roesch, 2004).

Finally, prosocial behavior predicts concurrent grades, intrinsic motivation toward school, educational aspirations (Johnson et al., 1998), and mastery motivation (Gilman & Anderman, 2006), as well as future grades at school (Caprara, et al., 2000). Some of these relations may be mediated by the quality of prosocial children's and adolescents' behavior at school.

SITUATIONAL FACTORS

Of course, adolescents' sympathy and prosocial behavior are affected by situational factors, as well as by dispositional characteristics. However, there is little systematic research on any given situational variable. One that has received attention is the target of a potential prosocial action. Young adolescents are more likely to share with or assist friends than acquaintances and disliked peers (Berndt, 1985; Buhrmester, Goldfarb, & Cantrell, 1992) and perceive friends as more supportive than nonfriends (Berndt & Perry, 1986). This is not surprising, given the importance to adolescents of intimacy and helping one another in friendships (e.g., Youniss, 1980). In addition, in contexts in which peers or teachers expect prosocial behavior, adolescents are likely to behave more prosocially (Wentzel et al., 2007). Moreover, there likely is an interaction between personality and situational factors in terms of which situations evoke prosocial responding from which individuals.

For example, as already noted, popular and less popular eighth graders preferred to help in different situations (Hampson, 1984), as do extroverted and introverted sixth graders (Suda & Fouts, 1980). Finally, the social context may affect opportunities for prosocial behavior, as well as the development of prosocial values and motives. For example, in poor neighborhoods and neighborhoods with a high percentage of the population being children, youth are relatively unlikely to develop a moral identity or engage in civic activities (Hart, 2005; Hart, Atkins, & Ford, 1998). In such neighborhoods youth interact primarily with peers and may be exposed to relatively few opportunities for adult-guided or assisted prosocial behaviors.

The Socialization of Prosocial Behavior and Empathy/Sympathy

Although the genetic contribution to individual differences in prosocial tendencies may be larger in adolescence than childhood (and the shared environment contribution smaller; Scourfield et al., 2004), it is likely that important socializers influence adolescents' prosocial and sympathetic responding.

Family Influences

In the larger literature on the socialization of prosocial behavior in childhood, high levels of prosocial behavior and empathy/sympathy have been related to supportive parenting, especially in combination with parental modeling of prosocial, caring behavior and/or parental discipline that is not punitive but involves the use of inductions (reasoning) and the setting of high standards for children (Eisenberg & Fabes, 1998). The limited findings in studies with adolescents generally are consistent with this pattern. For example, although findings often were statistically significant for only one sex or the other, parental use of inductive discipline (usually reported by parents or their adolescent children) has been positively related to preadolescents' or adolescents' prosocial behavior (e.g., Bar-Tal, Nadler, &

Blechman, 1980; Hoffman & Saltzstein, 1967; Krevens & Gibbs, 1996) and empathy/sympathy (Krevans & Gibbs, 1996), especially for individuals with a history of inductive discipline (Dlugokinski & Firestone, 1974). Similarly, there is some evidence that parental conversations about others with problems that emphasize empathy and sympathy, are associated with prosocial behavior (Carlo, McGinley, Hayes, Batenhorst, & Wilkinson, 2007). In contrast, power assertive discipline (e.g., punishment or threats thereof) has been negatively related to adolescents' sympathy/empathy and prosocial behavior (Krevens & Gibbs, 1996). Moreover, adolescents' prosocial behavior has been correlated with parental emphasis on autonomy (Bar-Tal et al., 1980), as well as adolescents' reports of parent–adolescent interdependency (i.e., shared time, engaging in mutual activities, and strength of parental influence; Eberly & Montemayor, 1998). Authoritative parenting (i.e., supportive parenting combined with appropriate control) during adolescence predicts young adults' concern for the next generation (Lawford et al., 2005). Moreover, parental demands and expectations for socially responsible and moral behavior have been associated with adolescents' endorsement of caring values (Pratt et al., 2003) and caring moral reasoning (Pratt, Skoe, & Arnold, 2004). Consistent with findings on the modeling of prosocial behavior and the importance of parental expectations for prosocial/moral behavior, adolescent exemplars of prosocial commitment have been found to have identities that incorporate parent-related representations (e.g., "what my mother is like," "what I am like with my father," "what my mother expects me to be"; Hart & Fegley, 1995). Because adolescents report that they share values with their parents (Hill, 1987), it is likely that parental prosocial values contribute to adolescents' prosocial tendencies. Indeed, in a recent study, adolescents' accurate perceptions and acceptance of maternal prosocial values were related to adolescents' prosocial behavior indirectly through the adolescents' personal values (Padilla-Walker, 2007), indicating that parenting may first influence values and then prosocial behavior.

Consistent with the relation between adolescents' prosocial tendencies and their interdependency with parents, supportive parenting has been positively related to prosocial characteristics or sympathy in adolescence in some studies (Bar-Tal et al., 1980; Bronstein, Fox, Kamon, & Knolls, 2007; Eberly & Montemayor, 1993, 1998; Laible & Carlo, 2004; Mussen, Harris, Rutherford, & Keasey, 1970), although findings in other studies have been nonsignificant or inconsistent (Carlo McGinley, et al., 2007; Carlo, Roesch, et al., 1998; Eberly & Montemayor, 1999). Adolescents who report prosocial tendencies also tend to describe their parents in positive terms and report positive relationships with parents (Ma et al., 2007; Rigby, 1993) and being attached to their parent (Markiewicz et al., 2001). There is initial evidence that this relation may be more consistent for maternal than paternal support (Laible & Carlo, 2004; Markiewicz et al., 2001). Using latent growth curve analyses, Carlo, Crockett, et al. (2007) found that supportive parenting in grade 7 was associated with seventh graders' prosocial tendencies; however, trajectories of the two variables from across the high school years were not related. Supportive parenting may set an affective climate that moderates the degree to which adolescents are responsive to parental discipline, demands, values, and teachings (Hoffman, 2000). Thus, parental support may be positively related to prosocial development only when parents use inductions, model prosocial tendencies, and/or have high expectations regarding prosocial or moral behavior (Eisenberg & Fabes, 1998).

It is noteworthy that similar findings have been obtained in a study of adolescents' moral courage—the ability to stand up for values, especially those of fairness and justice (often for others). Bronstein et al. (2007) found that supportive parenting (reported and observed) in 5th grade predicted 12th grade girls' moral courage, whereas harsh restrictive parenting predicted both girls' and boys' reticence to take a stand. Self-esteem in 12th grade and peer competence (for girls only) mediated the relations of parenting to moral courage and/or reticence, indicating that parenting may affect peer relations and, in turn, moral courage.

Consistent with the findings on supportive parenting, Michalik et al. (2007) found that adolescents' prosocial behavior and/or sympathy was correlated with concurrent parental positive expressivity in the home, as well as with parental positive expressivity in childhood. However, there was not a consistent pattern between parents' (mostly mothers') expression of negative emotion in the home during adolescence and youths' sympathy or prosocial behavior. Parents' observed negative emotionality when interacting with their child eight years earlier was negatively related to adolescents' prosocial behavior. In contrast, parents' reports of expressing negative emotion in the family during the adolescents' childhood were positively related to girls' sympathy in adolescence. The authors noted that parents' negative and positive expressivity were not negatively interrelated in childhood for daughters (but were for sons) and that early parental expression of negative emotions, if not overwhelming, may help daughters to understand and sympathize with others' distress.

It is also possible that siblings contribute to adolescents' development. For example, Tucker, Updegraff, McHale, and Crouter (1999) found that older early-adolescent female siblings' (ages 10 to 12) empathy was positively related to their younger sisters' (2 to 3 years younger) empathy. The author posited that younger sisters may model or identify with older sisters; however, it should be noted that findings are correlational and not longitudinal so causality could go both ways. Findings also varied for sister–brother relationships (see Tucker et al, 1999), but nevertheless support the idea that siblings may have an influence on moral development.

Unfortunately, most of the research on the socialization of adolescents' prosocial tendencies is correlational, and much is based solely on adolescents' reports (although some include parents' reports; e.g., Eberly & Montemayor, 1998, 1999; Eberly, Montemayor, & Flannery, 1993; Krevans & Gibbs, 1996). In addition, much of the existing research has been conducted with young adolescents. Thus, we know relatively little about the socialization correlates of prosocial behavior in older adolescents and variables that mediate or moderate relations between quality of parenting and youths' prosocial behavior (e.g., adolescents' sympathy has been found to mediate the relations of some parenting practices to adolescents' reported prosocial behavior; Carlo, McGinley, et al., 2007). In addition, we know relatively little about the influence of other adult socializers such as teachers, with whom supportive relationships may be associated with adolescents' prosociality (see Ma, Shek, Cheung, & Tam, 2002).

Peer Influences

There is very little research on the relation of prosocial behavior to peer interactions. As already noted, it has been found that popular, well-adjusted peers tend to be more prosocial than rejected peers (e.g., Coie, Dodge, & Kupersmidt, 1990; Wentzel & Caldwell, 1997; Wentzel, 2003). It is likely that prosocial behavior affects peer acceptance, and that the quality of peer relationships affects prosocial behavior. For example, in a study of Chinese adolescents, youths who reported that their close friends engaged in prosocial rather than delinquent behavior, and encouraged them to engage in prosocial rather than negative behaviors, were relatively prosocial (Ma et al., 2007). Similarly, in a study in the United States, positive peer relationships generally were correlated with 7th to 12th graders' prosocial tendencies (although an increase in positive peer relationships was associated with a decline in prosocial behavior; Carlo, Crockett, et al., 2007). Moreover, secure attachment relationships with peers were related to high levels of empathy in a sample of older adolescents (Laible et al., 2004). In addition, Wentzel et al. (2004) found that having at least one

reciprocated friendship was related to higher levels of prosocial behavior. Students with initially low levels of prosocial behavior relative to those of their reciprocated friend improved when exposed to their more prosocial peers, and students with initially higher levels of prosocial behavior decreased their levels of prosocial behavior when exposed to a less prosocial friend. The prosociality of a close friend predicted change in youths' prosocial goals, which predicted more prosocial behavior across time (Wentzel et al., 2004). However, this path of potential influence appears to apply only if the adolescent views his or her relationship with the friend as positive (Barry & Wentzel, 2006) and held across time only if the frequency of interaction between the friends was relatively high (findings within time were different; Barry & Wentzel, 2006).

Wentzel and McNamara (1999) posited that peers may affect prosocial behavior both directly and through their influence on emotional functioning. Children who are accepted by peers would be expected to have opportunities to learn and practice prosocial skills. Moreover, adolescents in a supportive emotional environment may be less likely to experience emotional distress, thus leading to more positive, prosocial behavior. In a study of sixth graders, Wentzel and McNamara found that peer acceptance was associated with prosocial behavior, and that adolescent's low emotional distress mediated concurrent relations between perceived support from peers and prosocial behavior. These findings support Wentzel and her colleagues' hypotheses, although it is also possible that prosocial early adolescents were more likely to garner peer acceptance and support, and that this fact affected their emotional distress.

Initial evidence also suggests that the centrality (visibility) of one's peer group may moderate the effects of peers' prosociality. Ellis and Zarbatany (2007) found that higher levels of the group's prosocial behavior at an initial assessment predicted higher levels of the average individual's prosocial behavior months later if the group was visible; in contrast, higher levels of group prosocial behavior at the first assessment predicted lower average levels of prosocial behavior later if the group was not visible (the interaction was significant but not the simple slopes).

VOLUNTEERING AND COMMUNITY SERVICE

An important prosocial behavior that has received a great deal of attention in the last two decades is volunteering and community service (also see chapter 11, volume 2 of this *Handbook*.). Adolescence is a time when youth are beginning to engage in adult-like activities and behaviors that reflect adult society. Community service is one type of activity in which many teens participate; indeed, approximately half of all adolescents engage in some type of community service or volunteer activity (see Yates & Youniss, 1996a), and many high schools are requiring community service as part of their curriculum (Reinders & Youniss, 2006). Involvement in such activities, which provides meaningful exposure to adult society, creates an opportunity for adolescents to explore their identity and potential roles in the community and greater society (Reinders & Youniss, 2006; Youniss & Yates, 1997; Youniss, McLellan, Su, & Yates, 1999).

Individual Characteristics Associated With Volunteering

Adolescent volunteers tend to share certain characteristics, such as extraversion, a commitment to others, and a high degree of self-understanding (see below). Some of these characteristics exist prior to adolescence; however, many may become solidified during this developmental period in conjunction with identity development (Yates & Youniss, 1996a). Moreover, developmental characteristics, such as cognitive development, and background characteristics, such as parental education, gender, and socioeconomic status (SES), also are related to adolescents' propensities to engage

in community service (Mustillo, Wilson, & Lynch, 2004; Yates & Youniss, 1996a).

Similar to findings for prosocial behavior more generally, gender differences in volunteering behavior have been examined in several studies. Studies indicate that females tend to volunteer more than males, and adolescents from families with higher levels of socioeconomic status are also more likely to volunteer (Mustillo et al., 2004; Nolin, Chaney, Chapman, & Chandler, 1997; Youniss, McLellan, Su, et al., 1999; cf. Johnson et al., 1998). However, youths from families at higher income levels may have more opportunities to volunteer and more free time (Smetana & Metzger, 2005).

In regard to personality characteristics, in contrast to some other types of prosocial behavior, individuals who volunteer tend to be more extraverted and social compared to nonvolunteers (e.g., Knapp & Holzberg, 1964), which is logical because of the social interaction involved in most volunteer activities. Children with resilient personalities are also more likely to volunteer as an adolescent (Atkins, Hart, & Donnelly, 2005). Similarly, individuals (e.g., college students) involved in community service tend to be involved in a variety of clubs and activities (e.g., 4-H, YMCA, church; Fitch, 1987). There is also evidence suggesting that community service participation actually lowers adolescents' levels of alienation and isolation (Calabrese & Schumer, 1986), and that volunteers tend to have a greater desire to help others, a strong sense of social responsibility, and have more malleable beliefs about disadvantaged groups (Karafantis & Levy, 2004; Magen & Aharoni, 1991; see also Yates & Youniss, 1996a).

Identity Development

Adolescence has traditionally been viewed as a developmental period in which youth struggle to establish their own identity, and separate from their parents. Researchers studying volunteering and community service often link identity development to civic involvement (see Hart, 2005; Yates & Youniss, 1996a; see also Hardy & Carlo, 2005a; Youniss, McLellan, Su, et al., 1999; Youniss & Yates, 1997). In a review of 44 articles on community service, Yates and Youniss (1996a) emphasized three components of identity development that are associated with volunteer behavior: *agency*, which emphasizes Erikson's (1968) concept of industry reflecting an individuals' self-concept of ability and future capabilities, and *social relatedness* and *moral–political awareness,* which refer to individuals' understandings of the self in relation to sociohistorical context. In a recent longitudinal study of late adolescents, Lawford et al. (2005) found that volunteering in the teenage years predicted concern for future generations (i.e., generativity).

Studies on agency indicate that volunteering is associated with increased self-understanding and higher levels of perceived competence and self-esteem (Yates & Youniss, 1996a). For example, Serow (1990) found that grade point average, measures of mastery, and number of goal-oriented activities were associated with volunteering behavior. Similarly, Johnson et al. (1998) found that adolescents involved in volunteer activities have higher educational plans and aspirations, grade point averages, academic self-esteem, and intrinsic motivation toward school work. In addition, adolescent volunteers tend to have higher levels of internal locus of control (Bensen et al., 1980).

Similar characteristics have been related to youth being designated as care exemplars, that is, individuals committed to the care of others in the community. For example, Hart and Fegley (1995) studied teens nominated by community leaders as care exemplars. Compared to matched controls, care exemplars were more likely to describe themselves in terms of moral goals and personality characteristics, and were more likely to have self-concepts involving the importance of personal beliefs. Care exemplars were also more likely to express a close connection between their "actual" and "ideal" selves, indicating that care exemplars were more driven by their ideals and beliefs. Interestingly, controls did not differ from the

care exemplars in moral judgment or cognitive complexity, suggesting that differences in self-understanding and self-concept were more related to volunteering and moral behavior.

Studies examining *social relatedness and moral political-awareness* suggest that, in general, adolescents who volunteer provide moral reasons for their behavior and are more likely to engage in political and civic activities in adulthood (also see chapter 11, volume 2, of this *Handbook* Fendrich, 1993; Yates & Youniss, 1996b). There also is some evidence that community service actually enhances adolescents' thinking about societal values and social order. For example, Yates and Youniss (1998) examined the narratives of Black adolescents who participated in a soup kitchen for the homeless. They found that over time, adolescents' narratives reflected more transcendence—values that supersede the family and self and have historical continuity—suggesting that the youths became more aware of values such as justice and social responsibility as a result of their experience (see also Lawford et al., 2005; and Karafantis & Levy, 2004).

In addition, several recent studies indicate that regardless of whether or not volunteering is required by school or engaged in by choice, it is still associated with positive outcomes such as future volunteering, voting, and prosocial moral values in adolescence and early adulthood (Hart, Donnelly, Youniss, & Atkins, 2007; Pratt, et al., 2003; Reinders & Youniss, 2006). Thus, there is ample evidence to indicate that the actual experience of volunteering increases prosocial and civic behavior, suggesting that such effects are not merely due to prosocial individuals choosing to volunteer.

The Socialization of Volunteering and Community Service

The socialization of volunteer/community service likely occurs in the home, peer group, and religious institutions. Indeed, research indicates that parents, peers, and community institutions, such as a church or synagogue, all are associated with adolescent volunteering.

However, many studies are correlational, so it is impossible to determine causality.

Parental Influences

Despite increases in peer influence during adolescence, research suggests that parents also have an important impact on adolescents during this developmental period (Collins, Maccoby, Steinberg, Hetherington, & Bornstein, 2000). Parents influence adolescent volunteering in a variety of ways. Mechanisms of influence could include, but are not limited to, the transmission of SES, modeling/setting an example, the transmission of values, and active recruitment into community service (Janoski & Wilson, 1995; Mustillo et al., 2004). Moreover, parents have the ability to demonstrate and teach youth that service can be a meaningful part of life, impacting others in important ways (Yates & Youniss, 1996a).

Consistent with the notion that parental modeling influences adolescents' service-related activities, youth who participate in community service tend to have one or both parents involved in community service (e.g., Keith et al., 1990; Mustillo et al., 2004). There also is some evidence suggesting that parental volunteering is more closely linked to girls' than boys' volunteering. Stukas, Switzer, Dew, Goycoolea, & Simmons (1999) found that adolescent girls with parents involved in volunteering/community service were more likely to have altruistic self-images compared to girls without parents involved in volunteering. There was no effect of parental volunteering on boys' altruistic self-images. Nevertheless, both boys and girls who had parents engaged in some form of community service were more likely to perceive themselves as engaging in volunteer work in the future compared to adolescents without parents involved in community service. Similarly, in a sample of late adolescent African Americans, Smetana and Metzger (2005) found that mothers', not fathers', community involvement was positively associated with adolescent community involvement and future intentions to be involved in community service.

Parenting styles also may contribute to volunteering or community service. Gunnoe, Hetherington, and Reiss (1999) found that authoritative parenting was positively related to adolescents' social responsibility, measured as a composite of prosocial behavior, concern for right and wrong, and responsibility for actions. In addition, parental religiosity had direct and indirect effects (through authoritative parenting) on adolescent social responsibility.

Peer Influences

Although there is not much research about peer influences on volunteering behavior, the presence of peers and the nature of peers' activities and expectations may play an important role in adolescent community service. Involvement in extracurricular activities—many of which involve peers—has been linked to adolescent community service (e.g., Youniss, McLellan, Su, et al., 1999). Youniss, McLellan, Su, et al. (1999) hypothesized that this effect is due to peer group influences, and the fact that many groups/clubs engage in community service as a part of their group activities. It is likely that the nature of the club and the group's values are important. Moreover, mere involvement in the peer group (rather than clubs) may undermine the likelihood of engaging in civic and voluntary activities (see Hart, 2005).

In one study examining the effects of peer crowds on adolescent volunteering, teens in *school* crowds (which value achievement and involvement in school clubs) were more likely to volunteer than fun crowd (e.g., popular) members. School, all around, and average crowd members were more likely to report the intention to be involved in future community service compared to disengaged and fun crowd members (Youniss, McLellan, & Mazer, 2001).

Pugh and Hart (1999) explored adolescents' peer group orientation and their expectations regarding future community service. They found that increased studying and decreased peer group informal reward orientation/identity (valuing a fun/delinquent subculture) were related to higher levels of expected future volunteerism. There was no relation between formal peer group orientation/identity (which reflects a commitment to being well-rounded and participating in extracurricular activities and valuing academics) and perceptions of future volunteering. Nevertheless, adolescents' perceptions of the activities that they engage in with peers may have some influence on moral identity development.

Religious Influences

The social institution that has been most often associated with volunteering is the church or synagogue (Youniss, 1993). In general, adolescents who view religion as important, compared to adolescents who do not, are more likely to engage in volunteering and community service (Youniss, McLellan, & Yates, 1999; Marris et al., 2000), and religious identity in youth has been positively linked with prosocial concerns (Furrow, King, & White, 2004). For example, Smetana and Metzger (2005) found that African American adolescents' spirituality and religiosity were associated with higher levels of current community service and community service three years later. These results are in line with other studies of European American adolescents (Bachman, Johnston, & O'Malley, 1993; Bensen et al., 1980). Moreover, volunteers tend to attend church more frequently (e.g., Bensen et al., 1980) and, in college, score higher on measures of religiosity (e.g., Fitch, 1987).

One large scale study of fifth through ninth graders (N = 8,165; Bensen et al., 1980) found that volunteering was predicted by adolescents' intrinsic religious orientation, which reflects an open, flexible religious system in which internalized values guide behavior. These findings suggest that religious identity and community service are somewhat intertwined. Youniss, McClellan, and Yates (1999) argued that religiosity affects youth volunteering because religious organizations typically sponsor service, and actions involving service and goodwill is grounded in most religious belief systems.

It should be noted that it is difficult to determine direction of effects, in that religious participation often involves volunteering activities, and more research is needed to disentangle church/temple/mosque going, religiosity, and volunteering in youth (Smetana & Metzger, 2005). Moreover, although religiosity seems to be related to adolescents' prosocial tendencies more generally (e.g., French, Eisenberg, Vaughan, Purwono, & Ari, 2008; Furrow et al., 2004), it may be related to some types of prosocial actions more than to others. For example, Hardy and Carlo (2005b) found that a composite measure of religiosity (assessing the importance of religion, religious practice, religious identity, and spirituality) was related to adolescents' self-reports of kindness that was compliant, anonymous, and altruistic, but not public prosocial behaviors, those based on dire needs, or those performed in a highly emotional context. Thus, religiosity might be related to prosocial behaviors that are requested by others and those that involve a cost to the self, but may be less often related to helping with emergency situations or helping in highly emotional situations. In addition, religiosity might sometimes be expected to preclude some types of helping or volunteering—for example, if the recipients in need are deemed as having committed an unforgivable offense by the religious group (see Cohen, Malka, Rozin, & Cherfas, 2005) or as holding values contrary to the religion. It is likely that the relation between religiosity and prosocial behaviors, including volunteering, is nuanced and varies with the values of the religion and the nature of the prosocial opportunity (i.e., the identity of the recipient of helping; see Lerner, in press; and Oman, Flinders, & Thoresen, in press, for further discussion of religiosity and adolescents' religiosity/spirituality and positive development and purpose).

Outcomes Associated With Volunteering and Community Service

Regardless of the empirical evidence, many individuals believe that involvement in community service inherently is associated with positive youth development. Indeed, state and federal laws have been passed that encourage youth volunteering based on this underlying assumption (e.g., the National Community Service Trust Act of 1993). For example, the state of Maryland now requires service hours as a requirement for high school graduation (see also *The Campaign for the Civic Mission of Schools,* 2008). Moreover, judicial systems often require youth who have been convicted of a crime to participate in community service programs. Do these types of programs affect adolescent adjustment? There is evidence suggesting that these programs do make a difference.

For example, adolescents who volunteer in high school are more likely to volunteer later in life and value the need for community service (Janoski, Musick, & Wilson, 1998; Reinders & Youniss, 2006). Of course, correlational studies cannot prove causal relations. However, as a step toward firmer inferences about causality, some studies examining the effects of volunteering and service have used a pre–post design with volunteering as the intervening factor. Of these studies, few have used random assignment (for an exception, see Allen, Philliber, Herrling, & Kuperminc, 1997), but most have included a comparison control group see Moore & Allen, 1996; Yates & Youniss, 1996a). For example, using a pre–post test design, researchers have found that community service was associated with increases in adolescents' self-esteem (Conrad & Hedin, 1982), self-confidence (Cognetta & Sprinthall, 1978), self-image (Switzer, Simmons, Dew, Regalski, & Wang, 1995) and personal responsibility and competence (Conrad & Hedin, 1982; Hamilton & Fenzel, 1988). In a panel design of youth volunteers and nonvolunteers in which initial levels of a variety of variables correlated with volunteering were taken into account, volunteering was related to gains in subsequent intrinsic work values, anticipated importance of career, and the anticipated importance of community involvement (Johnson et al., 1998).

There is also evidence that service participation is related to decreases in truancy, deviant school behavior, disciplinary problems, and lower rates of pregnancy (Allen et al., 1997; Calabrese & Schumer, 1986; Switzer et al., 1995; also see Yates & Youniss, 1996a). Similarly, involvement in prosocial activities such as church and volunteer activities is associated with higher educational trajectories and lower levels of risky behavior (Eccles & Barber, 1999). Moreover, studies using a pre–post test, control group design also indicate that working with marginalized populations may increase levels of empathy (Hobfoll, 1980) and tolerance (Karafantis & Levy, 2004; Riecken, 1952). In a comprehensive review of volunteering programs aimed at intervention, many of which were mentioned above, Moore and Allen (1996) concluded that volunteer programs for adolescents reduce rates for course failure, suspension from school, school dropout, and teen pregnancy, and improve reading skills, self-concept and attitudes toward society. However, they note that quality of the program (e.g., allowing adolescents autonomy and choice), length of the program (programs 12 weeks or more tended to be more successful than shorter programs), and age of adolescents (in some programs older youth benefited more) all affect potential benefits of volunteering.

Involvement in community service has been associated with prosocial and deviant behavior in expected directions, even when controlling for background characteristics such as SES and gender. For example, in a study of 13,000 high school seniors discussed previously, Youniss, McLellan, Su, et al. (1999) controlled for gender, religion (Catholic or not), and SES. Youniss et al. reported that service was positively associated with a conventional political orientation (e.g., voting) and conventional religious orientation (church attendance and judging religion as an important part of life) among adolescents. In contrast, service was negatively associated with marijuana use. Service was also associated with unconventional political acts such as boycotting and demonstrating, suggesting that community service does not merely reflect an adherence to adult societal norms. The effects of service on outcomes remained significant when controlling for background characteristics, suggesting that service does impact adjustment.

In one of the few studies to find sex differences associated with the effects of volunteering (most studies find a positive impact on males and females), Stukas et al. (1999) examined seventh-grade students who were involved in a mandatory service-learning program (e.g., tutors for younger students, volunteers at a senior center) as part of their school curriculum. Girls felt more positively than did boys about volunteering, and were more likely to report wanting to help in the future as a result of the program. The authors suggested that these variations may have been due to socialization differences between boys and girls that emphasize females' focus on prosocial goals of the program whereas males might have focused more on the "mandatory" nature of the program (see Miller, 1994).

Unfortunately, almost all research on volunteering/community service has been correlational or used a pre–post-design without random assignment. Moreover, it is possible that in many of the studies volunteers differed from nonvolunteers not only in their characteristics but also in their ongoing developmental trajectories. To better assess the effects of participating in service, studies are needed in which adolescents who wish to volunteer are assigned to groups that either do so or engage in some other, less prosocial activity.

CONCLUSIONS AND FUTURE DIRECTIONS

Although there is an accumulating data base on adolescents' moral reasoning and prosocial behaviors and emotion, it is meager compared to that for preadolescent children. Thus, many of the findings presented in this chapter have not been replicated and some of the conclusions are based on only one or a few studies. Clearly, there is much to be learned. In regard to moral reasoning, there is not yet consensus on the stages of moral reasoning and the degree to which they are qualitative in nature and universal. This is a larger issue in moral reasoning research, as findings differ for different content domains and methods of coding. Moreover, although work using real-life (rather than hypothetical) moral dilemmas seems particularly appropriate for adolescents, we do not yet know much about factors that affect reasoning about real-life moral dilemmas that have already occurred. In addition, although there sometimes is a relation between moral reasoning and behavior, we know little about variables that moderate the degree of this relation. It also is possible that any relation between moral judgment (or labeling a behavior as moral) and behavior is at least partly due to post hoc construction of moral reasoning based on the adolescents' justifications of their own behavior (Haidt, 2001). A valuable approach would be to determine if successful moral reasoning interventions also influence adolescents' risky behaviors, as well as their amoral or antisocial behavior.

Relatively little is known about the socialization of moral reasoning in adolescence, both in the family and outside of it. Due to the increasing role of peers and other extrafamilial individuals in adolescents' lives (Larson & Richards, 1991), it would be useful to know more about the ways in which extrafamilial influences combine with familial factors to affect moral cognitions, and if familial influences change in magnitude with age in adolescence (or change in a nonlinear manner). It is likely that peers and involvement in extrafamilial activities influence adolescents' moral development in both positive and negative ways, but it is difficult to disentangle the extent to which these factors actually shape adolescents' moral development or whether adolescents self-select into peer groups and activities that are consistent with their moral values and behavior.

There is somewhat more work (especially in the last decade) on adolescents' prosocial behavior (including volunteering/civic involvement) and empathy-related responding than on their moral cognitions. However, little is known about how the context (social or otherwise), including the peer group, affects adolescents' prosocial tendencies. Given the importance of identity formation in adolescence, it also would be useful to know if prosocial predispositions, which seem to be relatively stable across adolescence, undergo further change or consolidation in late adolescence. Similarly, it is possible that changes in identity, values, or perspective taking in middle or late adolescence affect people's tendencies to sympathize with others, although little is known about the development of sympathy in adolescence. In recent years, it has been argued that emerging adolescence (e.g., approximately age 18 to 25) is a unique and important state of life (see Arnett, 2004, 2007) and it is likely that at least some of the developmental changes, correlates, and processes related to prosocial behavior continue to emerge or change in emerging adulthood.

A future direction of adolescent moral research includes exploring the empirical influence of moral role models. The philosophical argument of the emulation of role models being central to moral education has been made (Kristjansson, 2006); however, few empirical studies test this claim (also see Oman et al., in press). For instance, Owens and Ascione (1990) explored how models can facilitate the prosocial behavior of sharing certificates in third, fourth, and fifth graders. Children watched videotapes of different models sharing, which affected their later sharing behavior. Familiar child models, described as similar to the child, increased sharing behavior. However, unfamiliar, child models described as dissimilar increased sharing behavior when compared to parent models. Furthermore, sharing behavior was greatest when watching a best friend as opposed to a least preferred peer. Currently, research is being conducted that explores urban adolescents' moral role models (McDaniel & Morris, 2008). Using a computerized methodology (see McDaniel & Grice, 2005, 2008), names of various role models are gathered from the youth such as a family member, a friend, a teacher, and a famous individual. The youth then rate these individuals, along with their actual (right now) and ideal (how one would truly like to be) selves, on moral descriptors such as *friendly versus unfriendly, fair versus unfair, and honest versus tells lies* and complete adjustment questionnaires. Results from this work will provide insight into the influence of different moral role models on the development of the self as well as adjustment and maladjustment.

Another topic that has received inadequate attention is adolescents' emotions in regard to morally relevant behaviors (other than empathy-related responding). Numerous individuals have examined children's beliefs about actors' emotions (e.g., anger, happiness) after transgressions (e.g., the "happy victimizer"; see Arsenio, Gold, & Adams, 2006). For example, Arsenio et al., 2006) found that behaviorally disturbed adolescents tend to report greater happiness after provoked and unprovoked aggression (also see Cimbora & McIntosh, 2003). In a study in Germany, Krettenauer and Eichler (2006) studied adolescents' self-attributed moral emotions when asked to imagine they had committed a transgression (e.g., "Imagine you did . . . How would you feel?" Scored "Not Bad" to "Extremely Bad"). Adolescents' delinquent behavior was associated with lower intensity of self-attributed moral emotions. Moreover, guilt has been related to low levels of adolescents' self-reported antisocial attitudes (Robinson et al., 2007; Tangney, Wagner, Hill-Barlow, Marschall, & Gramzow, 1996) and behaviors, marginally differentiated delinquent and non-delinquent adolescents (Robinson et al., 2007), and is related to low levels of conduct disorder (Cimbora & McIntosh, 2003). In contrast, shame has been positively related to adolescents' reported aggression (Tangney et al., 2006). Thus, it appears adolescents' emotional reactions to enacting or viewing transgressions likely contribute to their moral motivation and behavior.

Much of the work reviewed in this chapter has been correlational, so few firm conclusions can be drawn in regard to causality. Alternative explanations—including ones involving heredity—often are possible. Even in many of the studies involving pre/post tests, it is possible that factors other than the targeted variables (e.g., volunteer experience) account for effects. For example, adolescents who choose to be volunteers may have a number of personal and background characteristics that could account for positive developmental changes over time. More experimental and longitudinal research across the adolescent years is an obvious need.

As is true in much of the moral development research, most of the data involving adolescents have been collected in North America or perhaps Europe. Little is known about the generalizability of many of the findings to ethnic minorities or other cultures. Moreover, ethnic identity and acculturation may be important factors in the development of moral emotions and behavior (see Schwartz, Zamboanga, & Jarvis, 2007). Especially for morality, culture is likely to be an important influence on development, and this may be especially true for adolescents, who are preparing for entry into their adult culture.

Finally, unlike two or three decades ago, there is not a grand theory (e.g., psychoanalytic or social learning theory) that is typically used to try to tie together work on moral development. Although grand theories likely cannot account for the complexity of moral development, often mini-theories are not available to guide our thinking about adolescents' moral development (see, however, Hoffman, 2000). Clearly, some of the central issues in adolescence, such as the development of identity, the importance of adolescents' obtaining some psychological autonomy while still retaining a strong connection to socializers (Allen, Hauser, Eickholt, Bell, & O'Connor, 1994), and the

central role of peers in adolescents' development require additional conceptual (as well as empirical) attention in work on moral development. Moreover, additional emphasis on mediating processes, factors that moderate the nature of relations between moral functioning and other variables, and developmental trajectories of different aspects of moral responding would deepen our understanding of adolescents' moral development. Thus, there is much work to be done if we are to truly grasp the nature of adolescents' moral thought and behavior and to develop ways to prevent and ameliorate deficits in moral development.

REFERENCES

Aleixo, P. A., & Norris, C. E. (2000). Personality and moral reasoning in young offenders. *Personality and Individual Differences, 28*, 609–623.

Allen, J. P., Hauser, S. T., Eickholt, C., Bell, K. L., & O'Connor, T. G. (1994). Autonomy and relatedness in family interactions as predictors of expressions on negative adolescent affect. *Journal of Research on Adolescence, 4*, 535–552.

Allen, J. P., Philliber, S., Herrling, S., & Kuperminc, G. P. (1997). Preventing teen pregnancy and academic failure: Experimental evaluation of a developmentally based approach. *Child Development, 64*, 729–742.

Arnett, J. J. (2004). *Emerging adulthood: The winding road from the late teens through the twenties.* New York: Oxford University Press.

Arnett, J. J. (2007). Emerging adulthood: What is it and what is it good for? *Child Development Perspectives, 1*, 68–70.

Arsenio, W. F., Gold, J., Adams, E. (2006). Children's conceptions and displays of moral emotions. In M. Killen & J. Smetana (Eds.), *Handbook of moral development* (pp. 581–609). Mahwah, NJ: Lawrence Erlbaum Associates.

Atkins, R., Hart, D., & Donnelly, T. M. (2005). The association of childhood personality type with volunteering during adolescence. *Merrill-Palmer Quarterly, 51*, 145–162.

Bachman, G. G, Johnston, L. D., & O'Malley, P. M. (1993). *Monitoring the future: A continuing study of the life styles and values of American youth.* Ann Arbor, MI: Survey Research Center.

Baek, H. (2002). A comparative study of moral development of Korean and British children. *Journal of Moral Education, 31*, 373–391.

Bakken, L., & Romig, C. (1994). The relationship of perceived family dynamics to adolescents' principled moral reasoning. *Journal of Adolescent Research, 9*, 442–457.

Bandura, A., Caprara, G. V., Barbaranelli, C., Gerbino, M., & Pastorelli, C. (2003). Role of affective self-regulatory efficacy in diverse sphere of psychosocial functioning. *Child Development, 74*, 769–782.

Barry, C. M., & Wentzel, K. R. (2006). Friend influence on prosocial behavior: The role of motivational factors and friendship characteristics. *Developmental Psychology, 42*, 153–163.

Bar-Tal, D., Nadler, A., & Blechman, N. (1980). The relationship between Israeli children's helping behavior and their perception on parents' socialization practices. *Journal of Social Psychology, 111*, 159–167.

Bar-Tal, D., & Nissim, R. (1984). Helping behavior and moral judgment among adolescents. *British Journal of Developmental Psychology, 2*, 329–336.

Bar-Tal, D., & Raviv, A. (1979). Consistency in helping-behavior measures. *Child Development, 50*, 1235–1238.

Bensen, P., Dehority, J., Garman, L., Hanson, E., Hochschwender, M., Lebold, C., Rohr, R., & Sullivan, J. (1980). Intrapersonal correlates of nonspontaneous helping behavior. *Journal of Social Psychology, 110*, 87–95.

Berg, C. A. (1989). Knowledge of strategies for dealing with everyday problems from childhood through adolescence. *Developmental Psychology, 25*, 607–618.

Berkowitz, M W., Begun, A. L., Zweben, A., Giese, J. K., Mulry, G., Horan, C., Wheeler, T., Gimenez, J., & Piette, J. (1995). Assessing how adolescents think about the morality of substance use. *Drugs and Society, 8*, 111–124.

Berkowitz, M. W., & Gibbs, J. C. (1983). Measuring the developmental features of moral discussion. *Merrill-Palmer Quarterly 29*, 399–410.

Berkowitz, M. W., Mueller, C. W., Schnell, S. V., & Padberg, M. T. (1986). Moral reasoning and judgments of aggression. *Journal of Psychology and Social Psychology, 51*, 885–891.

Berndt, T. J. (1985). Prosocial behavior between friends in middle childhood and early adolescence. *Journal of Early Adolescence, 5*, 307–317.

Berndt, T. J., Perry, T. B. (1986). Children's perceptions of friendships as supportive relationships. *Developmental Psychology, 22*, 640–648.

Boehnke, K., Silbereisen, R. K., Eisenberg, N., Reykowski, J., & Palmonari, A. (1989). The development of prosocial motivation: A cross-national study. *Journal of Cross Cultural Psychology, 20*, 219–243.

Bosacki, S. L. (2003). Psychological pragmatics in preadolescents: Sociomoral understanding, self-worth, and school behavior. *Journal of Youth and Adolescence, 32*, 141–155.

Boxer, P., Tisak, M. S., & Goldstein, S. E. (2004). Is it bad to be good? An exploration of aggressive and prosocial behavior subtypes in adolescence. *Journal of Youth and Adolescence, 33*, 91–100.

Boyes, M. C., & Allen, S. G. (1993). Styles of parent-child interaction and moral reasoning in adolescence. *Merrill-Palmer Quarterly, 39*, 551–570.

Bredemeier, B. J. (1985). Moral reasoning and the perceived legitimacy of intentionally injurious sport acts. *Journal of Sport Psychology, 7*, 110–124.

Breslin, A. (1982). Tolerance and moral reasoning among adolescents in Ireland. *Journal of Moral Education, 11*, 112–127.

Brion-Meisels, S., & Selman, R. L. (1984). Early adolescent development of new interpersonal strategies: Understanding and intervention. *School Psychology Review, XIII*, 278–291.

Bronstein, P., Fox, B. J., Kamon, J. L., & Knolls, M. L. (2007). Parenting and gender as predictors of moral courage in late adolescence: A longitudinal study. *Sex Roles, 56*, 661–674.

Brown, L. M., & Gilligan, C. (1992). *Meeting at the crossroads: Women's psychology and girls' development*. Cambridge, MA: Harvard University Press.

Brusten, C., Stams, G. J., & Gibbs, J. C. (2007). Missing the mark. *British Journal of Developmental Psychology, 25*, 185–189.

Buck, L. Z., Walsh, W. F., & Rothman, G. (1981). Relationship between parental moral judgment and socialization. *Youth and Society, 13*, 91–116.

Buhrmester, D., Goldfarb, J., & Cantrell, D. (1992). Self-presentation when sharing with friends and nonfriends. *Journal of Early Adolescence, 12*, 61–79.

Calabrese, R. L., & Schumer, H. (1986). The effects of service activities on adolescent alienation, *Adolescence, 21*, 675–687.

Call, K. T., Mortimer, J. T., & Shanahan, M. J. (1995). Helpfulness and the development of competence in adolescence. *Child Development, 66*, 129–138.

Campaign for the civic mission of schools. Retrieved September 16, 2008, from http://civicmissionofschools.org

Caprara, G. V., Barbaranelli, C., & Pastorelli, C. (2001). Prosocial behavior and aggression in childhood and pre-adolescence. In A. C. Bohart & D. J. Stipek (Eds.), *Constructive & destructive behavior: Implications for family, school, & society* (pp. 187–203). Washington, DC: APA Books.

Caprara, G. V., Barbaranelli, C., Pastorelli, C., Bandura, A., & Zimbardo, P. G. (2000). Prosocial foundations of children's academic achievement. *Psychological Science, 11*, 302–306.

Carlo, G., Crockett, L. J., Randall, B. A., & Roesch, S. C. (2007). A latent growth curve analysis of prosocial behavior among rural adolescents. *Journal of Research on Adolescence, 17, 2*, 301–324.

Carlo, G., Eisenberg, N., & Knight, G. P. (1992). An objective measure of adolescents' prosocial moral reasoning. *Journal of Research on Adolescence, 2*, 331–349.

Carlo, G., Hausmann, A., Christiansen, S., & Randall, B. A. (2003). Sociocognitive and behavioral correlates of a measure of prosocial tendencies for adolescents. *Journal of Early Adolescence, 23*, 107–134.

Carlo, G., Koller, S., & Eisenberg, N. (1998). Prosocial moral reasoning in institutionalized delinquent, orphaned, and non-institutionalized Brazilian adolescents. *Journal of Adolescent Research, 13*, 363–376.

Carlo, G., McGinley, M., Hayes, R., Batenhorst, C., & Wilkinson, J. (2007). Parenting styles or practices? Parenting, sympathy, and prosocial behaviors among adolescents. *Journal of Genetic Psychology, 168*, 147–176.

Carlo, G., Roesch, S. C., & Melby, J. (1998). The multiplicative relations of parenting and temperament to prosocial and anti-social behaviors in adolescence. *Journal of Early. Adolescence, 18*, 266–290.

Charbonneau, D., & Nicol, A. A. M. (2002). Emotional intelligence and prosocial behaviors in adolescents. *Psychological Reports, 90*, 361–370.

Cimbora, D. M., & McIntosh, D. N. (2003). Emotional responses to antisocial acts in adolescent males with conduct disorder: A link to affective morality. *Journal of Clinical Child and Adolescent Psychology, 32*, 296–301.

Cognetta, P. V., & Sprinthall, N. A. (1978). Students as teachers: Role taking as a means of promoting psychological and ethical development during adolescence. In N. A. Sprinthall & R. L. Mosher (Eds.), *Value development . . . as the aim of education*. Schenectady, NY: Character Research Press.

Cohen, A. B., Malka, A., Rozin, P., & Cherfas, L. (2005). Religion and unforgiveable offenses. *Journal of Personality, 74*, 85–117.

Cohen, D., & Strayer, J. (1996). Empathy in conduct-disordered and comparison youth. *Developmental Psychology, 32*, 988–998.

Coie, J. D., Dodge, K. A., & Kupersmidt, J. B. (1990). Peer group behavior and social status. In S. R. Asher & J. D. Coie (Eds.), *Peer rejection in childhood* (pp. 17–59). Cambridge, UK: Cambridge University Press.

Colby, A., Kohlberg, L., Gibbs, J., & Lieberman, M. (1983). A longitudinal study of moral judgment. *Monographs of the Society for Research in Child Development, 48*(1–2, serial no. 200).

Coleman, P. K., & Byrd, C. P. (2003). Interpersonal correlates of peer victimization among young adolescents. *Journal of Youth and Adolescence, 32*, 301–314.

Collins, W. A., Maccoby, E., Steinberg, L., Hetherington, E. M., & Bornstein, M. (2000). Contemporary research on parenting: The case for nature *and* nurture. *American Psychologist, 55*, 218–232.

Comunian, A. L., & Gielen, U. P. (1995). Moral reasoning and prosocial action in Italian culture. *Journal of Social Psychology, 135*, 699–706.

Conrad, D., & Hedin, D. (1982). The impact of experiential education on adolescent development. In D. Conrad & D. Hedin (Eds.), *Youth participation and experiential education*. New York: Haworth Press.

Crick, N. R., & Dodge, K. A. (1994). A review and reformulation of social information-processing mechanisms in children's social adjustment. *Psychological Bulletin, 115*, 74–101.

Damon, W., & Hart, D. (1988). *Self-understanding in childhood and adolescence*. Cambridge, UK: Cambridge University Press.

Davis, M. H., & Franzoi, S. L. (1991). Stability and change in adolescent self-consciousness. *Journal of Research in Personality 25*, 70–87.

Dawson, T. L. (2002). New tools, new insights: Kohlberg's moral judgment stages revisited. *International Journal of Behavioral Development, 26*, 154–166.

De Guzman, M. R. T., & Carlo, G. (2004). Family, peer, and acculturative correlates of prosocial development among Latino youth in Nebraska. *Great Plains Research, 14*, 185–202.

De Wied, M., Goudena, P. P., & Matthys, W. (2005). Empathy in boys with disruptive behavior disorders. *Journal of Child Psychology and Psychiatry, 46*, 867–880.

Dlugokinski, E., & Firestone, I. J. (1973). Congruence among four methods of measuring other-centeredness. *Child Development, 44*, 304–308.

Dlugokinski, E. L., & Firestone, I. J. (1974). Other centeredness and susceptibility to charitable appeals: Effects of perceived discipline. *Developmental Psychology, 10*, 21–28.

Eagly, A. H., & Crowley, M. (1986). Gender and helping behavior: A meta–analytic review of the social psychological literature. *Psychological Bulletin, 100*, 283–308.

Eberly, M. B., Montemayor, R., & Flannery, D. J. (1993). Variation in adolescent helpfulness toward parents in a family context. *Journal of Early Adolescence, 13*, 228–244.

Eberly, M. B., & Montemayor, R. (1998). Doing good deeds: An examination of adolescent prosocial behavior in the context of parent–adolescent relationships. *Journal of Adolescent Research, 13*, 403–432.

Eberly, M. B., & Montemayor, R. (1999). Adolescent affection and helpfulness toward parents: A 2-year follow-up. *Journal of Early Adolescence, 19*, 226–248.

Eccles, J. S., & Barber, B. L. (1999). Student council, volunteering, basketball, or marching band: What kind of extracurricular involvement matters? *Journal of Adolescent Research, 14*, 10–43.

Eisenberg, N. (1986). *Altruistic emotion, cognition, and behavior*. Hillsdale, N.J: Lawrence Erlbaum.

Eisenberg, N. (1990). Prosocial development in early and mid adolescence. In R. Montemayor, G. R. Adams, & T. P. Gullotta (Eds.), *From childhood to adolescence: A transitional period? Advances in adolescence*, Vol. 2 (pp. 240–269). Newbury Park, CA: Sage.

Eisenberg, N., Carlo, G., Murphy, B., & Van Court, P. (1995). Prosocial development in late adolescence: A longitudinal study. *Child Development, 66*, 1179–1197.

Eisenberg, N., Cumberland, A., Guthrie, I. K., Murphy, B. C., & Shepard, S. A. (2005). Age changes in prosocial responding and moral reasoning in adolescence and early adulthood. *Journal of Research in Adolescence, 15*, 235–260.

Eisenberg, N., & Fabes, R. A. (1998). Prosocial development. In W. Damon (series ed.) & N. Eisenberg (vol. ed), *Handbook of child psychology*, Vol. 3: *Social, emotional, and personality development* (pp. 701–778; 5th ed.). New York: John Wiley & Sons.

Eisenberg, N., Fabes, R. A., & Spinrad, T. L. (2006). Prosocial behavior. In N. Eisenberg (Vol. Ed) and W. Damon & R. M. Lerner (Series Eds.), *Handbook of child psychology*, Vol. 3: *Social, emotional, and personality development* (6th ed.; 646–718). Hoboken, NJ: John Wiley & Sons.

Eisenberg, N., Guthrie, I., Cumberland, A., Murphy, B. C., Shepard, S. A., Zhou, Q., et al. (2002). Prosocial development in early adulthood: A longitudinal study. *Journal of Personality and Social Psychology, 82*, 993–1006.

Eisenberg, N., Guthrie, I. K., Murphy, B. C., Shepard, S. A., Cumberland, A., & Carlo, G. (1999). Consistency and development of prosocial dispositions: A longitudinal study. *Child Development, 70*, 1360–1372.

Eisenberg, N., Liew, J., & Pidada, S. (2004). The longitudinal relations of regulation and emotionality to quality of Indonesian children's socioemotional functioning. *Developmental Psychology, 40*, 790–804.

Eisenberg, N., Miller, P. A., Shell, R., McNalley, S., & Shea, C. (1991). Prosocial development in adolescence: A longitudinal study. *Developmental Psychology, 27*, 849–857.

Eisenberg, N., & Morris, A. S. (2004). Moral cognitions and prosocial responding in adolescence. In L. Steinberg & R. Lerner (Eds.), *Handbook of adolescent psychology* (pp. 155–188). Hoboken, NJ: John Wiley & Sons.

Eisenberg, N., Shell, R., Pasternack, J., Lennon, R., Beller, R., & Mathy, R. M. (1987). Prosocial development in middle childhood: A longitudinal study. *Developmental Psychology, 24*, 712–718.

Eisenberg, N., & Valiente, C. (2002). Children's prosocial and moral development. In M. Bornstein (Ed.), *Handbook of parenting* (2nd ed., Vol. 5, pp. 111–142). Hillsdale, NJ: Lawrence Erlbaum.

Eisenberg, N., Zhou, Q., & Koller, S. (2001). Brazilian adolescents' prosocial moral judgment and behavior: Relations to sympathy, perspective taking, gender-role orientation, and demographic characteristics. *Child Development, 72*, 518–534.

Eisenberg-Berg, N. (1979a). The development of children's prosocial moral judgment. *Developmental Psychology, 15*, 128–137.

Eisenberg-Berg, N. (1979b). The relationship of prosocial moral reasoning to altruism, political liberalism, and intelligence. *Developmental Psychology, 15*, 87–89.

Eisenberg–Berg, N., & Mussen, P. (1980). Personality correlates of socio-political liberalism and conservatism in adolescence. *Journal of Genetic Psychology, 137*, 165–177.

Eisikovits, Z., and Sagi, A. (1982). Moral development and discipline encounter in delinquent and nondelinquent adolescents. *Journal of Youth and Adolescence, 11*, 217–246.

Ellis, W. E., & Zarbatany, L. (2007). Peer group status as a moderator of group influence on children's deviant, aggressive, and prosocial behavior. *Child Development, 78*, 1240–1254.

Emler, N. P., & Rushton, J. P. (1974). Cognitive-developmental factors in children's generosity. *British Journal of Social and Clinical Psychology, 13*, 277–281.

Emler, N., & Tarry, H. (2007). Clutching at straws; is it time to abandon the moral judgment deficit explanation for delinquency? *British Journal of Developmental Psychology, 25*, 191–195.

Erikson, E. H. (1968). *Identity: Youth and crisis*. New York: W. W. Norton.

Estrada, P. (1995). Adolescents' self-reports of prosocial responses to friends and acquaintances: The role of sympathy-related cognitive, affective, and motivational processes. *Journal of Research on Adolescence, 5*, 173–200.

Eysenck, S. B. G., Easting, G., & Pearson, P. R. (1984). Age norms for impulsiveness: Venturesomeness and empathy in children. *Personality and Individual Differences, 5*, 315–321.

Fabes, R. A., Carlo, G., Kupanoff, K., & Laible, D. (1999). Early adolescence and prosocial/moral behavior I: The role of individual processes. *Journal of Early Adolescence, 19*, 5–16.

Fang, G., Fang, F., Keller, M., Edelstein, W., Kehle, T. J., & Bray, M. A. (2003). Social moral reasoning in Chinese children: A developmental study. *Psychology in the Schools, 40*, 125–138.

Fang, F., Fang, G., Keller, M., Edelstein, W., & Shuster, P. (2002). A cross cultural study on the development of moral reasoning in friendship in Western and Eastern children and adolescents. *Acta Psychologica Sinica, 34*, 67–73.

Ferguson, N. & Cairns, E. (2002). The impact of political conflict on moral maturity: A cross-national perspective. *Journal of Adolescence, 25*, 441–451.

Fendrich, J. (1993). *Ideal citizens*. Albany: State University of New York Press.

Fitch, R. T. (1987). Characteristics and motivations of college students volunteering form community service. *Journal of College Student Personnel*, 424–431.

Gestsdóttir, S., Lerner, R. M. (2007). Intentional self-regulation and positive youth development in early adolescence.: Findings from the 4-H study of positive youth development. *Developmental Psychology*, *43*, 508–521.

Flannagan, C. A., Bowes, J. M., Jonsson, B., Csapo, B., & Sheblanova, E. (1998). Ties that bind: Correlates of adolescents' civic commitment in seven countries. *Journal of Social Issues*, *54*, 457–475.

French, D., Eisenberg, N., Vaughan, J., Purwono, U., & Ari, T. (2008). Religious involvement and competence in Indonesian Muslim adolescents. *Developmental Psychology*, *44*, 597–611.

Froming, W. J., Nasby, W., & McManus, J. (1998). Prosocial self-schemas, self-awareness, and children's prosocial behavior. *Journal of Personality and Social Psychology*, *75*, 766–777.

Furrow, J. L., King, P. E., & White, K. (2004). Religion and positive youth development: Identity, meaning, and prosocial concerns. *Applied Developmental Science*, *8*, 17–26.

Gibbs, J. C. (2006). Should Kohlberg's cognitive developmental approach to morality be replaced with a more pragmatic approach? Comment on Krebs and Denton (2005). *Psychological Review*, *113*, 666–671.

Gibbs, J. C., Basinger, K. S., Grime, R. L., & Snarey, J. R. (2007). Moral judgment development across cultures: Revisiting Kohlberg's universality claims. *Developmental Review*, *27*, 443–500.

Gibbs, J. C., Potter, G. B., Barriga, A.Q., & Liau, A. K. (1996). Developing the helping skills and prosocial motivation of aggressive adolescents in peer group programs. *Aggression and Violent Behavior*, *1*, 283–305.

Gilligan, C. (1982). *In a different voice: Psychological theory and women's development*. Cambridge, MA: Harvard University Press.

Gilman, R., & Anderman, E. M. (2006). The relationship between relative levels of motivation and intrapersonal, interpersonal, and academic functioning among older adolescents. *Journal of School Psychology*, *44*, 375–391.

Gini, G., Albiero, P., Benelli, B., & Altoe, G. (2007). Does empathy predict adolescents' bullying and defending behavior? *Aggressive Behavior*, *33*, 467–476.

Gunnoe, M. L., Hetherington, E. M., & Reiss, D. (1999). Parental religiosity, parenting style, and adolescent social responsibility. *Journal of Early Adolescence*, *19*, 199–225.

Haidt, J. (2001). The emotional dog and its rational tail: A social intuitionist approach to moral judgment. *Psychological Review*, *108*, 814–834.

Hamilton, S. F., & Fenzel, L. M. (1988). The impact of volunteer experience on adolescent social development: Evidence of program effects. *Journal of Adolescent Research*, *3*, 65–80.

Hampson, R. B. (1984). Adolescent prosocial behavior: Peer-group and situational factors associated with helping. *Journal of Personality and Social Psychology*, *46*, 153–162.

Hardy, S. A., & Carlo, G. (2005a). Identity as a source of moral motivation. *Human Development*, *48*, 232–256.

Hardy, S. A., & Carlo, G. (2005b). Religiosity and prosocial behaviours in adolescence: The mediating role of prosocial values. *Journal of Moral Education*, *34*, 231–249.

Hart, D. (1988). A longitudinal study of adolescents' socialization and identification as predictors of adult moral judgment development. *Merrill-Palmer Quarterly*, *34*, 245–260.

Hart, D. (2005). The development of moral identity. In G. Carlo & C. P. Edwards (Eds.), *Nebraska Symposium on Motivations: Moral motivation through the life span*, Vol. 51 (pp. 165–196). Lincoln, NE: University of Nebraska Press.

Hart, D., Atkins, R., & Ford, D. (1998). Urban America as a context for the development of moral identity in adolescence. *Journal of Social Issues*, *54*, 513–530.

Hart, D., & Chmiel, S. (1992). Influence of defense mechanisms on moral judgment development: A longitudinal study. *Developmental Psychology*, *28*, 722–730.

Hart, D., & Fegley, S. (1995). Altruism and caring in adolescence: Relations to self-understanding and social judgment. *Child Development*, *66*, 1346–1359.

Hart, D., Donnelly, T. M., Youniss, J., & Atkins, R. (2007). High school predictors of adult civic engagement: The roles of volunteering, civic knowledge, extracurricular activities, and attitudes. *American Educational Research Journal*, *44*, 197–219.

Harter, S. (1999). *The cognitive and social construction of the developing self*. New York: Guilford Press.

Harter, S. (2006). The self. In N. Eisenberg (Vol. Ed.) and W. Damon & R. M. Lerner (Series Eds.), *Handbook of child psychology*, Vol. 3 (6th ed.): *Social, emotional, and personality development* (pp. 505–570). Hoboken, NJ: John Wiley & Sons.

Hill, J. P., (1987). Research on adolescents and their families: Past and prospects. *New Directions in Child Development*, *37*, 13–31.

Hobfoll, S. E. (1980). Personal characteristics of the college volunteer. *American Journal of Community Psychology*, *8*, 503–506.

Hoffman, M. L. (1980). Moral development in adolescence. In J. Adelson (Ed.), *Handbook of adolescent psychology* (pp. 295–343). New York: John Wiley & Sons.

Hoffman, M. L. (2000). *Empathy and moral development: Implications for caring and justice*. Cambridge, UK: Cambridge University Press.

Hoffman, M. L., Saltzstein, H. D. (1967). Parent discipline and the child's moral development. *Journal of Personality and Social Psychology*, *5*, 45–57.

Holstein, C. (1972). The relation of children's moral judgment level to that of their parents and to communication patterns in the family. In R. C. Smart and M. S. Smart (Eds.), *Readings in child development and relationships*. New York: Macmillan.

Hubbs-Tait, L., & Garmon, L. C. (1995). The relationship of moral reasoning and AIDS knowledge to risky sexual behavior. *Adolescence*, *30*, 539–564.

Jaffe, S., & Hyde, J. S. (2000). Gender differences in moral orientation: A meta-analysis. *Psychological Bulletin*, *126*, 703–726.

Janoski, T., Musick, M., & Wilson, J. (1998). Being volunteered? The impact of social participation and pro-social attitudes on volunteering. *Sociological Forum*, *13*, 495–519.

Janoski, T., Wilson, J. (1995). Pathways to volunteerism: Family socialization and status transmission models. *Social Forces*, *74*, 271–292.

Janssen, A. W. H., Janssens, J. M. A. M., & Gerris, J. R. M. (1992). Parents' and children's levels of moral reasoning: Antecedents and consequences of parental discipline strategies. In J. M. A. M. Janssens and J. R. M. Gerris (Eds.), *Child rearing: Influence on prosocial and moral development* (pp. 169–196). Amsterdam: Swets and Zeitlinger.

Johnson, M. K., Beebe, T., Mortimer, J. T., & Snyder, M. (1998). Volunteerism in adolescence: A process perspective. *Journal of Research on Adolescence*, *8*, 309–332.

Jones, G.P., & Dembo, M. H. (1989). Age and sex role differences in intimate friendships during childhood and adolescence. *Merrill-Palmer Quarterly*, *35*, 445–462.

Jurkovic, G. J. (1980). The juvenile delinquent as a moral philosopher: A structural–developmental perspective. *Psychological Bulletin*, *88*, 709–727.

Jurs, J. (1984). Correlation of moral development with use of birth control and pregnancy among teenage girls. *Psychological Reports*, *55*, 1009–1010.

Karafantis, D. M., & Levy, S. R. (2004). The role of children's lay theories about malleability of human attributes in beliefs about and volunteering for disadvantaged groups. *Child Development*, *75*, 236–250.

Karniol, R., Gabay, R., Ochion, Y., & Harari, Y. (1998). Is gender or gender-role orientation a better predictor of empathy in adolescence? *Sex Roles*, *39*, 45–59.

Karniol, R., & Shomroni, D. (1999). What being empathic means: Applying the transformation rule approach to individual differences in predicting the thoughts and feelings of prototypic and nonprototypic others. *European Journal of Social Psychology*, *29*, 147–160.

Keating, D. (2004). Cognitive and brain development. In R. Lerner & L. Steinberg (Eds.), *Handbook of adolescent psychology* (2nd ed., pp. 45–84). Hoboken, NJ: John Wiley & Sons.

Keith, J. G., Nelson, C. S., Schlabach, J. H., & Thompson, C. J. (1990). The relationship between parental employment and three measures of early adolescent responsibility: Family-related, personal, and social. *Journal of Early Adolescence*, *10*, 399–415.

Kennedy, M. G., Felner, R. D, Cauce, A., & Primavera, J. (1988). Social problem solving and adjustment in adolescence: The influence of moral reasoning level, scoring alternatives, and family climate. *Journal of Clinical Child Psychology*, *17*, 75–83.

Killen, M., Leviton, M., & Cahill, J. (1991). Adolescent reasoning about drug use. *Journal of Adolescent Research*, *6*, 336–356.

Killen, M., & Turiel, E. (1998). Adolescents' and young adults' evaluations of helping and sacrificing for others. *Journal of Research on Adolescence*, *8*, 355–375.

Knapp, R. H., & Holzberg, J. D. (1964). Characteristics of college students volunteering for service to mental patients. *Journal of Consulting Psychology*, *28*, 82–85.

Kohlberg, L. (1969). Stage and sequence: The cognitive–developmental approach to socialization. In D. A. Goslin (Ed.), *Handbook of socialization theory and research* (pp. 347–480). Chicago: Rand McNally.

Kohlberg, L. (1981). *The philosophy of moral development: Moral stages and the idea of justice.* San Francisco: CA: Harper and Row.

Kohlberg, L. (1984). *Essays on moral development*, Vol. II. *The psychology of moral development.* San Francisco, CA: Harper & Row.

Kokko, K., Tremblay, R. E., Lacourse, E., Nagin, D. S., & Vitaro, F. (2006). Trajectories of prosocial behavior and physical aggression in middle childhood: Links to adolescent school dropout and physical violence. *Journal of Research on Adolescence*, *16*, 403–428.

Krebs, D. L., & Denton, K. (2005). Toward a more pragmatic approach to morality: A critical evaluation of Kohlberg's model. *Psychological Review*, *113*, 672–675.

Krebs, D. L., & Denton, K. (2006). Explanatory limitations of cognitive-developmental approaches to morality. *Psychological Review*, *113*, 672–675.

Krettenauer, T. & Eichler, D. (2006). Adolescents' self-attributed moral emotions following a moral transgression: Relations with delinquency, confidence in moral judgment and age. *British Journal of Developmental Psychology*, *24*, 489–506.

Krevans, J., Gibbs, J. C. (1996). Parents' use of inductive discipline: Relations to children's empathy and prosocial behavior. *Child Development*, *67*, 3263–3277.

Kristjansson, K. (2006). Emulation and the use of role models in moral education. *Journal of Moral Education*, *35*, 37–49.

Kruger, A. C. (1992). The effect of peer and adult–child transactive discussions on moral reasoning. *Merrill-Palmer Quarterly*, *38*, 191–211.

Kuther, T. L., & Higgins-D'Alessandro, A. (2000). Bridging the gap between moral reasoning and adolescent engagement in risky behavior. *Journal of Adolescence*, *23*, 409–422.

Laible, D., & Carlo, G. (2004). The differential relations of maternal and parental support and control to adolescent social competence, self-worth, and sympathy. *Journal of Adolescent Research*, *19*, 759–782.

Laible, D. J., Carlo, G., & Raffaelli, M. (2000). The differential relations of parent and peer attachment to adolescent adjustment. *Journal of Youth and Adolescence*, *29*, 45–59.

Laible, D. J., Carlo, G., & Roesch, S. C. (2004). Pathways to self-esteem in late adolescence: The role of parent and peer attachment, empathy, and social behaviours. *Journal of Adolescence*, *27*, 703–716.

Lapsley, D. K. (2006). Moral stage theory. In M. Killen & J. G. Smetana (Eds.), *Handbook of moral development* (pp. 37–66). Mahwah, NJ: Lawrence Erlbaum.

Lardén, M., Melin, L., Holst, U., &Långström, N. (2006). Moral judgment, cognitive distortions and empathy in incarcerated delinquent and community control adolescents. *Psychology, Crime & Law*, *12*, 453–462.

Larson, R., & Richards, M. H. (1991). Daily companionship in late childhood and early adolescence: Changing developmental contexts. *Child Development*, *62*, 284–300.

Lawford, H., Pratt, M. W., Hunsberger, B., Pancer, S. M. (2005). Adolescent generativity: A longitudinal study of two possible contexts for learning concern for future generations. *Journal of Research on Adolescence*, *15*, 261–273.

Leahy, R. L. (1981). Parental practices and the development of moral judgment and self-image disparity during adolescence. *Developmental Psychology*, *17*, 580–594.

Lennon, R., & Eisenberg, N. (1987). Gender and age differences in empathy and sympathy. In N. Eisenberg & J. Strayer (Eds.), *Empathy and its development* (pp. 195–217). New York: Cambridge University Press.

Lerner, R. M. (2008). Spirituality, positive purpose, wisdom, and positive development in adolescence: Comments on Oman, Flinders, and Thoresen's ideas about "integrating spiritual modeling into education." *International Journal of the Psychology of Religion*, *18*, 108–118.

Lerner, R. M., Lerner, J. V., Almerigi, J. B., Theokas, C., Phelps, E., Gestsdottir, S., et al. (2005). Positive youth development, participation in community youth development programs, and community contributions of fifth-grade adolescents: Findings from the first wave of the 4-H study of positive youth development. *Journal of Early Adolescence*, *25*, 17–71.

Lim, K. M., Khoo, A., & Wong, M. Y. (2007). Relationship of delinquent behaviors to prosocial orientations of adolescents. *North American Journal of Psychology*, *9*, 183–188.

Lindeman, M., Harakka, T., & Keltikangas-Jarvinen, L. (1997). Age and gender differences in adolescents' reactions to conflict situations: Aggression, prosociality, and withdrawal. *Journal of Youth and Adolescence*, *26*, 339–351.

Ma, H. K., Cheung, P. C., & Shek, D. T. L. (2007). The relation of prosocial orientation to peer interactions, family social environment and personality of Chinese adolescents. *International Journal of Behavioral Development*, *31*, 12–18.

Ma, H. K., Shek, D. T. L., Cheung, P. C., & Tam, K. K. (2002). A longitudinal study of peer and teacher influences on prosocial ad antisocial behavior or Hong Kong Chinese adolescents. *Social Behavior and Personality*, *30*, 157–168.

Magen, Z., & Aharoni, R. (1991). Adolescents' contributing toward others: Relationship to positive experiences and transpersonal commitment. *Journal of Humanistic Psychology*, *31*, 126–143.

Markiewicz, D., Doyle, A. B., & Brendgen, M. (2001). The quality of adolescents' friendships: Associations with mothers' interpersonal relationships, attachments to parents and friends, and prosocial behaviors. *Journal of Adolescence*, *24*, 429–445.

Marris, J. S., Jagers, R. J., Hatcher, C. A., Lawhon, G. D., Murphy, E. J., Murray, Y. F. (2000). Religiosity, volunteerism, and community involvement among African American men: An exploratory analysis. *Journal of Community Psychology*, *28*, 391–406.

Marsh, D. T., Serfica, F. C., & Barenboim, C. (1981). Interrelations among perspective taking, interpersonal problem solving, and interpersonal functioning. *Journal of Genetic Psychology*, *138*, 37–48.

Matsuba, M. K., & Walker, L. J. (1998). Moral reasoning in the context of ego functioning. *Merrill-Palmer Quarterly*, *44*, 464–483.

McDaniel, B. L., & Grice, J. W. (2005). Measuring self-discrepancies on the Big Five personality traits with the repertory grid. *Personal Construct Theory & Practice*, *2*, 18–31.

McDaniel, B. L., & Grice, J. W. (2008). Predicting psychological well-being from self-discrepancies: A comparison of idiographic and nomothetic measures. *Self and Identity, 7,* 243–261.

McDaniel, B. L., & Morris, A. S. (2008). *Tulsa Family and Youth Development Project.* Data collection in progress.

McDevitt, T. M., Lennon, R., Kopriva, R. J. (1991). Adolescents' perceptions of mothers' and fathers' prosocial actions and empathic responses. *Youth & Society, 22,* 387–409.

McMahon, S. D., Wernsman, J., & Parnes, A. L. (2006). Understanding prosocial behavior: The impact of empathy and gender among African American adolescents. *Journal of Adolescent Health, 39,* 135–137.

Michalik, N., Eisenberg, N., Spinrad, T. L., Ladd, B., Thompson, M., & Valiente, C. (2007). Longitudinal relations among parental personality, emotional expressivity, youths' sympathy, and prosocial behavior. *Social Development, 16,* 286–309.

Miller, F. (1994). Gender differences in adolescents' attitudes toward mandatory community service. *Journal of Adolescence, 17,* 381–393.

Moore, C. W., & Allen, J. P. (1996). The effects of volunteering on the young volunteer. *Journal of Primary Prevention, 17,* 231–258.

Muris, P., Meesters, C., & van den Berg, F. (2003). The Strengths and Difficulties Questionnaire (SDQ): Further evidence for its reliability and validity in a community sample of Dutch children and adolescents. *European Child and Adolescent Psychiatry, 12,* 1–8.

Murphy, B. C., Shepard, S. A., Eisenberg, N., Fabes, R. A., & Guthrie, I. K. (1999). Contemporaneous and longitudinal relations of young adolescents' dispositional sympathy to their emotionality, regulation, and social functioning. *Journal of Early Adolescence, 19,* 66–97.

Mussen, P., Harris, S., Rutherford, E., & Keasey, C. (1970). Honesty and altruism among preadolescents. *Developmental Psychology, 3,* 169–194.

Mustillo, S., Wilson, J., & Lynch, S. M. (2004). Legacy volunteering: A test of two theories of intergenerational transmission. *Journal of Marriage and Family, 66,* 530–541.

Moore, C. W., & Allen, J. P. (1996). The effects of volunteering on the young volunteer. *The Journal of Primary Prevention, 17,* 231–259.

Narvaez, D. (1998). The influence of moral schemas on the reconstruction of moral narratives in eighth graders and college students. *Journal of Educational Psychology, 90,* 13–24.

Nelson, E., Leibenluft, E., McClure, E., & Pine, D. (2005). The social re-orientation of adolescence: A neuroscience perspective on the process and its relation to psychopathology. *Psychological Medicine, 35,* 163–174.

Nelson, J. R., Smith, D. J., & Dodd, J. (1990). The moral reasoning of juvenile delinquents: A meta-analysis. *Journal of Abnormal Child Psychology, 19,* 231–239.

Nelson, D. A., & Crick, N. R. (1999). Rose-colored glasses: Examining the social information-processing of prosocial young adolescents. *Journal of Early Adolescence, 19,* 17–38.

Nolin, M. J., Chaney, B., Chapman, C., & Chandler, K. (1997). *Student participation in community service.* Washington, DC: U.S. Department of Education.

Nucci, L., Guerra, N., & Lee, J. (1991). Adolescent judgments of the personal, prudential, and normative aspects of drug usage. *Developmental Psychology, 27,* 841–848.

Olweus, D., & Endresen, I. M. (1998). The importance of sex-of-stimulus object: Age trends and sex differences in empathic responsiveness. *Social Development, 7,* 370–388.

Oman. D., Flinders, T., & Thoresen, C. (2008). Integrating spiritual modeling into education: A college course for stress management and spiritual growth. *International Journal of the Psychology of Religion, 18,* 79–107.

Owens, C. R., & Ascione, F. R. (1990). Effects of the model's age, perceived similarity, and familiarity on children's donating. *The Journal of Genetic Psychology, 152*(3), 341–357.

Padilla-Walker, L. M. (2007). Characteristics of mother–child interactions related to adolescents' positive values and behaviors. *Journal of Marriage and Family, 69,* 675–686.

Pakaslahti, L., & Keltikangas-Jarvinen, L. (2001). Peer-attributed prosocial behavior among aggressive/preferred, aggressive/non-preferred, non-aggressive/preferred, and non-aggressive/non-preferred adolescents. *Personality and Individual Differences, 30,* 903–916.

Palmer, E. J., and Hollin, C. R. (1996). Sociomoral reasoning, perceptions of own parenting, and self-reported delinquency. *Personality and Individual Differences, 21,* 175–182.

Parikh, B. (1980). Development of moral judgment and its relation to family environment factors in Indian and American families. *Child Development, 51,* 1030–1039.

Payne, F. D. (1980). Children's prosocial conduct in structural situations and as viewed by others: Consistency, convergence and relationships with person variables. *Child Development, 51,* 1252–1259.

Perry, C. M., & McIntire, W. G. (1995). Modes of moral judgment among early adolescents. *Adolescence, 30,* 707–715.

Piaget, J. (1932/1965). *The moral judgment of the child.* New York: Free Press.

Power, T. G., & Shanks, J. A. (1989). Parents as socializers: Maternal and paternal views. *Journal of Youth and Adolescence, 18,* 203–220.

Powers, S. I. (1988). Moral judgment development within the family. *Journal of Moral Education, 17,* 209–219.

Pratt, M. W., Arnold, M. L., Pratt, A. D., & Diessner, R. (1999). Predicting adolescent moral reasoning from family climate: A longitudinal study. *Journal of Early Adolescence, 19,* 148–175.

Pratt, M. W., Hunsberger, B., Pancer, S. M., & Alisat, S. (2003). A longitudinal analysis of personal values socialization: Correlates of a moral self-ideal in late adolescence. *Social Development, 12,* 563–585.

Pratt, M. W., Skoe, E. E., & Arnold, M. L. (2004). Care reasoning development and family socialization patterns in later adolescence: A longitudinal analysis. *International Journal of Behavioral Development, 28,* 139–147.

Pugh, M. J., & Hart, D. (1999). Identity development and peer group participation. *New Directions in Child and Adolescent Development, 84,* 55–70.

Raaijmakers, Q. A. W., Verbogt, T. F. M. A., & Vollebergh, W. A. M. (1998). Moral reasoning and political beliefs of Dutch adolescents and young adults. *Journal of Social Issues, 54,* 531–546.

Reinders, H. & Youniss, J. (2006). School-based required community service and civic development in adolescents. *Applied Developmental Science, 10,* 2–12.

Rest, J. R. (1979). *Development in judging moral issues.* Minneapolis: University of Minnesota Press.

Rest, J. R. (1983). Morality. In P. Mussen (Ed.), *Handbook of child psychology,* Vol. 3: *Cognitive development* (pp. 556–629). New York: John Wiley & Sons.

Rest, J. R., Narvaey, D., Bebeau, M. J., & Thoma, S. J. (1999a). A neo-Kolhlbergian approach: The DIT and schema theory. *Educational Psychology Review, 11,* 291–324.

Rest, J. R., Narvaez, D., Bebeau, M.J., & Thoma, S. J. (1999b). *Postconventional moral thinking: A neo-Kohlbergian approach.* Mahwah, NJ: Lawrence Erlbaum.

Rholes, W. S., & Lane, L. W. (1985). Consistency between cognitions and behavior: Cause and consequence of cognitive moral development. In J. B.Pryor & J. D. Day (Eds.), *The development of social cognition* (pp. 97–114). New York: Springer-Verlag.

Riecken, R. W. (1952). *The volunteer work camp: A psychological evaluation.* Cambridge: Addison-Wesley.

Rigby, K. (1993). School children's perceptions of their families and parents as a function of peer relations. *Journal of Genetic Psychology, 154,* 501–513.

Robinson, R., Roberts, W. L., Strayer, J., & Koopman, R. (2007). Empathy and emotional responsiveness in delinquent and non-delinquent adolescents. *Social Development, 16*, 555–579.

Rubin, K. H., Bukowski, W., & Parker, J. G. (1998). Peer interactions, relationships, and groups. In W. Damon (Series Ed.) & N. Eisenberg (Vol. Ed.), *Handbook of Child Psychology* (pp. 619–700), Vol. 3: *Social, emotional, and personality development* (5th ed.). New York: John Wiley & Sons.

Saklofske, D. H., & Eysenck, S. B. G. (1983). Impulsiveness and venturesomeness in Canadian children. *Psychological Reports, 52*, 147–152.

Sanvitale, D., Saltzstein, H. D., & Fish, M. (1989). Moral judgments by normal and conduct-disordered preadolescent and adolescent boys. *Merrill-Palmer Quarterly, 35*, 463–481.

Schonert-Reichl, K. A. (1999). Relations of peer acceptance, friendship adjustment, and social behavior to moral reasoning during early adolescence. *Journal of Early Adolescence, 19*, 249–279.

Schwartz, S. J., Zamboanga, B. L., & Jarvis, L. H. (2007). Ethnic identity and acculturation in Hispanic early adolescents: Mediated relationships to academic grades, prosocial behaviors, and externalizing symptoms. *Cultural Diversity and Ethnic Minority Psychology, 13*, 364–373.

Scourfield, J., John, B., Martin, N., & McGuffin, P. (2004). The development of prosocial behaviour in children and adolescents: A twin study. *Journal of Child Psychology and Psychiatry, 45*, 927–935.

Selman, R. L. (1975). Level of social perspective taking and the development of empathy in children: Speculations from a social–cognitive viewpoint. *Journal of Moral Education, 5*, 35–43.

Selman, R. L. (1980). *The growth of interpersonal understanding: Developmental and clinical analysis.* New York: Academic Press.

Serow, R. C. (1990). Volunteering and values: An analysis of participation in community service. *Journal of research and Development in Education, 23*, 198–203.

Sigman, M., & Erdynast, A. (1988). Interpersonal understanding and moral judgment in adolescents with emotional and cognitive disorders. *Child Psychiatry and Human Development, 19*, 36–44.

Sigman, M., Ungerer, J. A., & Russell, A. (1983). Moral judgment in relation to behavioral and cognitive disorders in adolescents. *Journal of Abnormal Child Psychology, 11*, 503–512.

Skoe, E. A., Hansen, K. L., Morch, W-T., Bakke, I., Hoffmann, T., Larsen, B., & Aasheim, M. (1999). Care-based moral reasoning in Norwegian and Canadian early adolescents: A cross-national comparison. *Journal of Early Adolescence, 19*, 280–291.

Small, S. A., Zeldin, R. S., & Savin-Williams, R. C. (1983). In search of personality traits: A multimethod analysis of naturally occurring prosocial and dominance behavior. *Journal of Personality, 51*, 1–16.

Smetana, J. G., & Metzger, A. (2005). Family and religious antecedents of civic involvement in middle class African American late adolescents. *Journal of Research on Adolescence. Special Issue: Moral Development, 15*, 325–352.

Sotelo, M. J., & Sangrador, J. L. (1999). Correlations of self-ratings of attitude towards violent groups with measures of personality, self-esteem, and moral reasoning. *Psychological Reports, 1999*, 558–560.

Sowell, E. R., Trauner, D. A, Gamst, A., & Jernigan, T. L. (2002). Development of cortical and subcortical brain structures in childhood and adolescence: A structural MRI study. *Developmental Medicine and Child Neurology, 44*, 4–16.

Speicher, B. (1992). Adolescent moral judgment and perceptions of family interaction. *Journal of Family Psychology, 6*, 128–138.

Stams, G. J., Brugman, D., Dekovic, M., van Rosmalen, L., van der Laan, P., & Gibbs, J. C. (2006). The moral judgment of juvenile delinquents: A meta-analysis. *Journal of Abnormal Child Psychology, 34*, 697–713.

Staub, E. (1979). *Positive social behavior and morality*, Vol. 2: *Socialization and development.* New York: Academic Press.

Steinberg, L., & Morris, A. S. (2001). Adolescent development. *Annual Review of Psychology, 52*, 83–110.

Strayer, J., & Roberts, W. (1997). Facial and verbal measures of children's emotions and empathy. *International Journal of Behavioral Development, 20*, 627–649.

Stukas, A. A., Switzer, G. E., Dew, M. A., Goycoolea, J. M., & Simmons, R. G. (1999). Parental helping models, gender, and service-learning. *Journal of Prevention and Intervention in the community, 18*, 5–18.

Suda, W., & Fouts, G. (1980). Effects of peer presence on helping in introverted and extroverted children. *Child Development, 51*, 1272–1275.

Switzer, G. E., Simmons, R. G., Dew, M. A., Regalski, J. M., & Wang, C. (1995). The effect of a school-based helper program on adolescent self-image, attitudes, and behavior. *Journal of Early Adolescence, 15*, 429–455.

Szagun, G. (1992). Children's understanding of the feeling experience and causes of sympathy. *Journal of Child Psychology and Psychiatry, 33*, 1183–1191.

Tangney, J. P., Wagner, P. E., Hill-Barlow, D., Marschall, D. E., Gramzow, R. (1996). Relation of shame and guilt to constructive versus destructive responses to anger across the lifespan. *Journal Personality Social Psychology, 70*, 797–809.

Tarry, H., & Emler, N. (2007). Attitude, values and moral reasoning as predictors of delinquency. *British Journal of Developmental Psychology, 25*, 169–183.

Thoma, S. J. (2006). Research on the Defining Issues Test. In M. Killen & J. G.Smetana (Eds.), *Handbook of moral development* (pp. 67–91). Mahwah, NJ: Erlbaum. (Read pp. 57 to bottom of 80 well; quickly get a sense of pp. 81–88).

Thoma, S. J., & Rest, J. R. (1999). The relationship between moral decision making and patterns of consolidation and transition in moral judgment development. *Developmental Psychology, 35*, 323–334.

Tisak, M. S., Tisak, J., & Rogers, M. J. (1994). Adolescents' reasoning about authority and friendship relations in the context of drug usage. *Journal of Adolescence, 17*, 265–282.

Toga, A. W., Thompson, P. M. & Sowell, E. R. (2006). Mapping brain maturation. (2006). *Trends in Neuroscience, 29*, 148–159,

Trevethan, S. D., & Walker, L. J. (1989). Hypothetical versus real-life moral reasoning among psychopathic and delinquent youth. *Development and Psychopathology, 1*, 91–103.

Tucker, C. J., Updegraff, K. A., McHale, S., & Crouter, A. C. (1999). Older siblings as socializers of younger siblings' empathy. *Journal of Early Adolescence, 19*, 176–198.

Vaughn, B. E., Block, J. H., & Block, J. (1988). Parental agreement on child rearing during early childhood and the psychological characteristics of adolescents. *Child Development, 59*, 1020–1033.

Walker, L. J. (2002). The model and the measure: An appraisal of the Minnesota approach to moral development. *Journal of Moral Education. 31*, 353–367.

Walker, L.J., Gustafson, P., & Hennig, K. H. (2001). The consolidation/ transition model in moral reasoning development. *Developmental Psychology, 37*, 187–197.

Walker, L. J., & Hennig, K. H. (1999). Parenting style and the development of moral reasoning. *Journal of Moral Education, 28*, 359–374.

Walker, L. J., Hennig, K.H., & Krettenauer, T. (2000). Parent and peer contexts for children's moral reasoning development. *Child Development, 71*, 1033–1048.

Walker, L. J., Pitts, R. C., Hennig, K. H., & Matsuba, M. K. (1995). Reasoning about morality and real-life moral problems. In M. Killen & D. Hart (Eds.), *Morality in everyday life* (pp. 371–407). Cambridge, UK: Cambridge University Press.

Walker, L. J., & Taylor, J. H. (1991). Family interactions and the development of moral reasoning. *Child Development, 62*, 264–283.

Weisz, A. N., & Black, B. M. (2002). Gender and moral reasoning: African American youth respond to dating dilemmas. *Journal of Human Behavior in the Social Environment, 5*, 35–52.

Wentzel, K. R. (2003). Sociometric status and adjustment in middle school: A longitudinal study. *Journal of Early Adolescence, 23*, 5–28.

Wentzel, K. R., & Caldwell, K. C. (1997). Friendships, peer acceptance, and group membership: Relations to academic achievement in middle school. *Child Development, 68*, 1198–1209.

Wentzel, K. R., Barry, C. M., & Caldwell, K. A. (2004). Friendship in middle school: Influences on motivation and school adjustment. *Journal of Educational Psychology, 96*, 195–203.

Wentzel, K. R., Filisetti, L., & Looney, L. (2007). Adolescent prosocial behavior: The role of self-processes and contextual cues. *Child Development, 78*, 895–910.

Wentzel, K. R., & McNamara, C. C. (1999). Interpersonal relationships, emotional distress, and prosocial behavior in middle school. *Journal of Early Adolescence, 19*, 114–125.

White, F. A. (1997). Measuring the content of moral thought: The Revised Moral Authority Scale (MAS-R). *Social Behavior and Personality, 25*, 321–333.

White, F. A., & Matawie, K. M. (2004). Parental morality and family processes as predictors of adolescent morality. *Journal of Child and Family Studies, 13*, 219–233.

Woods, L. N., & Jagers, R. J. (2003). Are cultural values predictors of moral reasoning in African American adolescents? *Journal of Black Psychology, 29*, 102–118.

Yates, M., & Youniss, J. (1996a). A development perspective on community service in adolescence. *Social Development, 5*, 85–111.

Yates, M., & Youniss, J. (1996b). Community service and political-moral identity in adolescents. *Journal of Research on Adolescence, 6*, 271–284.

Yates, M., & Youniss, J. (1998). Community service and political identity development in adolescence. *Journal of Social Issues, 43*, 495–512.

Youniss, J. (1980). *Parents and peers in social development: A Sullivan–Piaget perspective*. Chicago: University of Chicago Press.

Youniss, J. (1993). Integrating culture and religion into developmental psychology. *Family Perspective, 26*, 171–188.

Youniss, J., McLellan, J. A., Mazer, B. (2001). Voluntary service, peer group orientation, and civic engagement. *Journal of Adolescent Research, 16*, 456–468.

Youniss, J., McLellan, J. A., Su, Y., & Yates. M. (1999). The role of community service in identity development: Normative, unconventional, and deviant orientations. *Journal of Adolescent Research, 14*, 248–261.

Youniss, J., McLellan, J. A., & Yates, M. (1999). Religion, community service, and identity in American Youth. *Journal of Adolescence, 22*, 243–253.

Youniss, J., & Yates, M. (1997). *Community service and social responsibility in youth*. Chicago: University of Chicago Press.

Zarbatany, L., Hartmann, D. P., Gelfand, D. M., & Vinciguerra, P. (1985). Gender differences in altruistic reputation: Are they artifactual? *Developmental Psychology, 21*, 97–101.

Zeldin, R. A., Savin-Williams, R. C., & Small, S. A. (1984). Dimensions of prosocial behavior in adolescent males. *Journal of Social Psychology, 123*, 159–168.

CHAPTER 9

Identity Formation and Self-Development in Adolescence

JAMES E. CÔTÉ

The study of identity and self in adolescence has proven to be a formidable task. A major stumbling block is definitional. Both concepts are higher-order abstractions of myriad psychological and social processes, so no single definitions can be identified, operational or theoretical. In turn, these psychological and social processes can be identified at different levels of analysis and have different properties related to their rates and types of potential change. In addition, these concepts have been approached from a variety of disciplinary and epistemological perspectives (Côté, 2006a), and research efforts based on these differing perspectives have sometimes produced different empirical measures of the same constructs. The result has been two rather large areas of study—ego psychology in the case of identity and self psychology in the instance of the self—both of which are characterized by academic enclaves and disputed territories, with different researchers sometimes using the same terminology to refer to clearly different phenomena (Côté & Levine, 2002). At the same time, both concepts represent humanistically grounded, holistic attempts to understand the very essence of what makes us human, and as such deserve the attention of the best minds in the academic community.

Given these two very large bodies of literature, to give some coherence to this chapter, the focus will be on those works that are most relevant to *development* during adolescence, as opposed to those that simply describe correlates of the concepts, especially during periods of the life course other than adolescence. That is, the concentration will be on the fundamental processes that represent qualitative changes, or potential changes, during adolescence. In addition, because the two literatures have developed as distinct research traditions with different theoretical roots, each will be treated separately, overlapping only when studies employ both constructs.

To set the stage for discussing each research tradition, the definitional architecture of each concept will be discussed first in an attempt to show how these traditions differ at their most fundamental levels. The literature in each tradition then will be critically analyzed in terms of how well the issue of (identity and self) development have been theoretically formulated and empirically investigated. This analysis involves first identifying the theoretical roots of each tradition, then elaborating their methodologies, and, finally, evaluating their major developmental findings. The chapter ends with an assessment of how well these two traditions have empirically investigated the issue of (identity and self) development, beginning with how to better integrate the self and identity approaches to adolescent development. This concluding section then moves to a discussion of the most promising research directions.

DEFINITIONAL ISSUES

Both concepts—identity and self—are multidimensional, and as noted have no single or simple definitions. For that reason, and to show how the identity literature differs from the self literature, it is useful to begin by providing a definitional checklist that specifies a taxonomy of the processes, structures, and contents associated with the architecture of each concept.

In the identity literature, *identity* refers to the *sameness and continuity* of the person's psychological functioning, interpersonal behavior, and commitments to roles, values, and beliefs. As we see in the case of Erik Erikson's work, sameness and continuity are the sine qua non of identity. Moreover, the *sense* of sameness and continuity is the signature of the "identity of the ego"—a person with a strong sense of identity experiences herself or himself as being the same entity over time and in various contexts, while at the same time is capable of clearly differentiating her/himself from others and from the contexts in which relations with others are experienced. From this Eriksonian viewpoint, which dominates the identity field, we can characterize the architecture of identity in terms of three key defining aspects:

- **Process**—ego identity: the sense, and behavioral demonstration, of continuity in functioning over time and across contexts; ego strengths enabling this are derived from resolutions of each of the eight psychosocial stages: trust, autonomy, initiative, industry, identity, intimacy, generativity, and integrity.
- **Content**—social roles (self-constructed or based on others' expectations), personal identifications, and shared values (including personal variants in beliefs and attitudes), which form the basis of enduring commitments that are internalized as being "part" of the person.
- **Structure**—the organization of roles, identifications, and values into stable configurations (i.e., how content is organized by and for the person); these configurations vary in terms of how open or closed they are to change, as they provide the filters through which information about the world is synthesized.

In the literature on the self, the self is defined in terms of consciousness, reflective awareness, and stimulated self-regulation (impulse control and other forms of conformity). Clearly, this is not a simple definition; indeed, an agreed-upon definition of the self continues to be an open question. In fact, on its web site, the International Society for Self and Identity posts a page titled "What *is* the Self?" This source admits that there is no "widely accepted definition or description of the self." However, it does offer the following "best attempt" at a definition:

> The human self is a self-organizing, interactive system of thoughts, feelings, and motives that characterizes an individual. It gives rise to an enduring experience of physical and psychological existence—a phenomenological sense of constancy and predictability. The self is reflexive and dynamic in nature: responsive yet stable. (Hoyle, n.d., www.psych.neu.edu/ISSI/daily.htm)

This source goes on to note that "skeptics might argue that the description fails to resolve, even address . . . fundamental issues . . . and they would be correct. Yet the description captures what we know about the activity of the self from decades of scientific inquiry and, in that sense, provides a credible, if not complete, account of it." In spite of these ambiguities, I offer the following characterization of the architecture of the self as conceptualized in the literature on adolescence:

- **Process**—an ongoing monitoring and reflected appraisal of how one is perceived by others, culminating in an "interior sense-of-being" that can be enduring and unified.
- **Content**—self-concepts pertaining to various spheres social functioning, such as family, school, and peer group.
- **Structure**—the salience hierarchy of self-concepts into a configuration based on reflected appraisals and cultural expectations concerning independence from, and interdependence with, others.

Before proceeding, several further comparisons of the terminology used in self and identity literatures are useful. The use of similar terminology stands to reason to the extent that self psychology addresses a variety of concerns having to do with the interactional and social structural levels of analysis, and touches on the executive and synthetic functions that are prominent in Erikson's psychoanalytic approach to identity. However, self psychology has placed more emphasis on the *maintenance* of self-structures and identities, than on identity *formation* and the *development* of self during adolescence. Part of the tendency to focus on maintenance issues seems to stem from the equation of self with personal and social identities in the work on interpersonal aspects of the self, which has dominated work in self psychology. When the executive functions of the self are brought into focus, it becomes clearer that research is needed into how these functions grow and become more differentiated with age. However, the point to be taken here is that self psychology tends to conflate the notions of self and identity, whereas the ego psychology approach more clearly differentiates these.

In sorting out the terminological differences in this field, it useful to note that Erikson (1968, pp. 216–221) developed an elaborate model of the personality, including a more differentiated view of the ego than did the Freudian model. Erikson reserved the term *ego* for the most "active" but largely *unconscious* agency of the personality, which performs the *synthetic functions* of the personality (i.e., actively defines situations and develops constructions of reality) as well as the *executive functions* (i.e., produces deliberate presentations of self and management of impressions). In developing the concept of ego identity, Erikson observed how people are able to maintain, or often lose, their sense of temporal–spatial continuity over time and across social situations—the sine qua non of ego identity. In other words, he studied how people can maintain or lose their sense inner continuity in reference to reality construction and behavioral management.

At the same time, Erikson posited that the personality also contains a "global" self that is comprised of a number of "specific" selves, each of which more or less corresponds to social roles played by the individual. These role-specific selves develop on the basis of learning and repeated experience across similar circumstances. Erikson justified this modification of Freudian tri-partite theory of personality (i.e., id, ego, superego) in the following way:

> Only after we have separated . . . the selves from the ego can we consign to the ego that domain which it has had ever since . . . Freud's earliest days: the domain of an inner "agency" safeguarding our coherent existence by screening and synthesizing, in any series of moments, all the impressions, emotions, memories, and impulses which try to enter our thought and demand our action, and which would tear us apart if unsorted and unmanaged by a slowly grown and reliabiy watchful screening system. (1968, p. 218)

Thus, Erikson postulated that the personality possesses an agentic structure in the ego, as well as content-based structure in the self, with the self constituting the repository of role-playing and role-making contents. We can now consider Erikson's contributions to the field in more detail.

THE ERIKSONIAN APPROACH TO IDENTITY FORMATION

Erikson is the recognized pioneer of identity theory in the social sciences, with enduring influences for many contemporary formulations of identity (Weigert, Teitge, & Teitge, 1986). Upon his passing in 1994, he was described as a "psychoanalyst who profoundly reshaped views of human development" ("Psychoanalyst coined identity crisis," 1994). Erikson honed the concept of identity in the 1950s and 1960s, based on Sigmund and Anna Freud's later works on the ego (their ego psychology). It was not until the 1970s, though, that the social scientific community took widespread interest in the concept of identity; since then, the identity literature has burgeoned, particularly in psychology and sociology (Côté, 2006a).

Erikson also postulated an eight-stage theory of psychosocial development over the life cycle as part of his attempt to build a unified theory of human development. Others of his generation also sought to develop comprehensive theories that would unify our understandings of human development, but subsequent generations have either fed off these efforts or turned away from using so-called "grand" theoretical frameworks to guide their research (cf. Sorell & Montgomery, 2001). However, it was not his "grand" theory that was to stimulate the most empirical research, but his more middle-range work on the identity stage.

Erikson's influence on the study of identity in adolescence in psychology includes the proposition that the key psychosocial task of this stage involves developing a viable sense of identity that links childhood with adulthood by consolidating identifications rooted in childhood into a coherent adult identity. Thus, the psychosocial task of identity formation was identified as a "normative event" of adolescence in the sense that it typically occurred for the majority of the population (Erikson, 1963). However, Erikson also pointed out ways in which significant prolongations of the identity stage take place for certain people in particular cultural and historical contexts (e.g., 1958). At the height of his writings some 40–50 years ago, these extensions of the identity stage were thought to be exceptions, found only in some cultures and then mainly among the affluent and others who could "afford" a prolonged identity stage, as in the case of college attendance. As we see later, the extension of the identity stage beyond the late teens now appears to be a normative event in many societies.

Erikson (1968) postulated that the transition to adulthood could constitute an "institutionalized moratorium." This postulate was derived from his general theory of the life cycle (*his* preferred term), which proposed that in most cultures *each stage* has some sort of psychosocial moratorium that gives each novitiate ample

time to master that stage. He also contended that some cultures also provide structured or institutionalized contexts to provide guidance during each psychosocial moratorium. Erikson wrote most about the moratorium of the identity stage, though, arguing that nearly all cultures provide their new members with some sort of institutional guidance to take them from childhood to adulthood (the "institutionalized" part of the concept), as well as a "time out" from certain social responsibilities that constitutes a "delay" in the transition (the "moratorium" part). Accordingly, Erikson argued that most cultures have provided their young people with some sort of structured delay from adult responsibilities, during which novitiates can take time to develop their adult identities within guiding social structures. In his words:

> Societies offer, as individuals require, a more or less sanctioned intermediary period between childhood and adulthood, *institutionalized moratoria*, during which a lasting pattern of "inner identity" is scheduled for relative completion. (1980, p. 110)

These institutionalized moratoria usually grant young people the license to experiment with various roles, if they so wish, without their being expected to accept or carry permanent responsibilities and commitments. This experimentation can take various forms of exploration, including military service (or programs like the Peace Corps), travel (the *Wanderschaft*), schooling, or even just "dropping out" for a while (cf. Erikson, 1968, p. 157). In the 1950s, Erikson (1958) believed that this moratorium could sometimes last until age 24, especially among college students, but at that time it was seen more commonly a late-teen phenomenon. Erikson (in Evans, 1969) also acknowledged that societies vary in terms of the degree to which they structure identity moratoria and how much conformity they demand to the norms and values of adult society during that moratorium. For example, military service is highly structured, whereas the *Wanderschaft* is loosely structured.

Erikson also postulated that each of the eight psychosocial stages presents people with a potential crisis as they pass through the stage and are faced with challenges associated with the stage. It is in this light that he argued that a moratorium period can provide an essential interlude during which a crisis can be resolved in ways compatible with the specific needs of the person experiencing it, in relation to the social context precipitating the crisis. Erikson referred to a variety of forms that identity crises can take, pointing out that they can vary in terms of their prolongation (e.g., 1968, p. 17), severity (e.g., 1958, p. 47), and aggravation (e.g., 1975, pp. 20–22). The *severity* of an identity crisis is manifested in a heightened sense of identity confusion and an unstable personal and social role repertoire. A *prolonged* crisis is evident when the role repertoire remains unstable over a long period. And, an *aggravated* identity crisis involves repeated but unsuccessful attempts to establish a stable role repertoire.

Given common misconceptions regarding his work, it is worth stressing that Erikson did *not* believe that the identity crisis must be severe for subsequent ego development to take place. Indeed, contrary to common conceptions of his work, Erikson argued that a severe identity crisis is not a cultural norm, even in American society. In his words, "the vast majority of young people . . . can go along with their parents in a kind of fraternal identification" (1968, p. 33). In this respect, he argued that the identity crisis is least severe among those who invest their sense of identity in the "technological ethos" of their culture (whatever the type of technology). Instead of severe, prolonged, or aggravated identity crises, Erikson believed that most young people work through an identity "crisis" in a muted and barely discernible form, even in modern societies. In premodern and tribal societies, where the productive contribution of all members of the community is needed from an early age, the adult community guides most young people through the stage with rites and initiations to ensure that it takes place over a relatively short period of time and with maximum assurance of a successful resolution (thereby minimizing the chances of severe crises).

Formulated in the above manner, we can see how Erikson was able to study a variety of cultures, finding great variation in both the structure of adolescence and the tasks associated with identity formation. However, it is not widely recognized that he slanted his formulations toward contemporaneous American culture (in which he lived as an adult), where resolution of the identity stage was predicated around choice and individuality during a relatively protracted and loosely structured adolescence, especially for majority group, middle class, and affluent males. For example, in a chapter entitled "Reflections on the American Identity," Erikson (1963, p. 286) wrote:

> The process of American identity formation seems to support an individual's ego identity as long as he can preserve a certain element of deliberate tentativeness of autonomous choice. The individual must be able to convince himself that the next step is up to him and that no matter where he is staying or going he always has the choice of leaving or turning in the opposite direction if he chooses to do so.

It is upon this choice-based type of identity crisis that most empirical formulations of ego identity have been based, not surprisingly in the United States (i.e., Marcia's identity status paradigm, discussed later). However, Erikson never endorsed this empirical approach, presumably because it represents only one, culturally specific reaction to the identity stage. Other forms of the identity crisis involve conscious and unconscious inner-conflict resolutions, or an emotional shift in identifications from a dependent child to an authority-bearing adult, and these may be more prevalent and more significant developmentally in other cultures (see Côté, 1986, for an operationalization of a more conflict-based identity crisis). The conflict-based crisis may be more emotional than cognitive (involving ambivalence and resentment), but may still result in a realignment and consolidations of identifications (cf. Erikson, 1968, 1979). Another form of "crisis" is well institutionalized, as in cases where the young person is guided through an identity transformation based on community-sanctioned rituals and apprenticeships. In the case of rites of passage, the precipitated crisis involves a potential loss of nerve or inability to withstand pain and discomfort (see Côté & Levine, 1987, for a discussion of various types of crises and stage resolutions). A little-cited quotation from Erikson (1959, pp. 105–106) helps highlight different forms of identity crises and their import:

> The identity development of an individual is always anchored in the identity of his group; although through his identity he will seal his individual style. Of individual differences we may often not have the fullest perception. Especially in an alien culture we may see somebody going slowly through an identity crisis, in which conformity seems more emphasized than individuality. This very conformity may keep some aspects of the crisis from verbalization or awareness; only closer study could reveal it. Or the individual's experience may seem entirely submerged in rituals and procedures which seem to exaggerate the horror of individual decision and to offer, as a way out, the narrowest choice of models. We will not know the nature of this process until we have learned to study its variations.

In spite of Erikson's extensive writings on the identity crisis and its variations, social scientists seem to have left the empirical study of this concept behind (Baumeister & Muraven, 1996; Honess & Yardley, 1987). In addition to non-Eriksonian interpretations of the concept of "crisis," the lack of attention to these sorts of conflicts may be because the choice-based identity crisis has become so common and prolonged in Western countries like the United States that it is deemed to be "normal" for adolescents and young adults to go a decade or more without stable roles anchored in the

adult community (Côté, 2000, 2006b). Erikson himself realized that the meaning behind his concept of identity crisis might be lost on those who interpret it only in its most severe connotations implying impending catastrophe, rather than in its meaning of a time when preparations for an uncertain future must be decided upon and undertaken. Erikson endorsed the conception of crisis as involving both danger and opportunity (e.g., Erikson, 1968).

Finally, it should be noted that Erikson did not advance any operational definitions or develop his own empirical measures of identity-related concepts. Instead, he preferred a clinical approach to case studies and an inductive method of theory construction based on case studies. This idiographic approach was especially well suited to his acclaimed psychohistorical studies (e.g., 1958). Still, his writings were rich and suggestive enough to have stimulated hundreds of empirical studies of identity formation, to which we now turn.

THE EMPIRICAL STUDY OF IDENTITY FORMATION

Stimulated by Erikson's writings, the earliest empirical studies of identity formation assessed resolution of the identity stage (e.g., Constantinople, 1969; Simmons, 1973) and strength of ego identity (e.g., Rasmussen, 1964) with paper-and-pencil measures, treating these constructs as a continuum. However, this line of enquiry was eclipsed by Marcia's (1964) operationalization of identity formation. Had this first line of research continued and garnered the attention of more researchers, these instruments might have been further refined to develop population norms that would identify the type of normative development postulated by Erikson and threshold points below which problematic identity formation could be identified. This would have followed Erikson's view that most people adequately resolve the identity stage, but a certain percentage of the population experiences difficulties resolving the identity crisis. In the concluding section, after evaluating the Marcian approach that has dominated the study of identity formation over the past 40 years, recommendations are made regarding a return to this approach, especially in light of the prolongation in the transition to adulthood that has occurred since the introduction of the Marcian approach.

This first line of approach to operationalizing Erikson's work was a more standard psychometric approach that gave way to what Kroger (1993) calls a "dimensional" approach that formed the basis of Marcia's operationalization. This approach involves crosstabulating two dimensions postulated to underlie identity formation—crisis and commitment—to create four identity statuses, which we will now consider.

The Identity Status Approach to Identity Formation

Marcia's (1964, 1966, 1980) identity status paradigm has produced the largest body of research—hundreds of studies—rooted in Erikson's work. Based on his reading of Erikson, Marcia postulated that four identity statuses characterize progress through the identity stage: identity diffusion, identity foreclosure, identity moratorium, and identity achievement. These statuses are operationalized in terms of (1) the conscious deliberation of alternative goals, beliefs, and values (representing the identity crisis, but referred to as "choice"); and (2) consolidations of these deliberations as probable courses of future action, expressed in "commitments." The original measure was a semistructured interview that assesses three domains of identity: occupation, politics, and religion. Subsequently, paper-and-pencil measures operationalizing these two dimensions were developed to allow for mass data collections (see Adams, Bennion, & Huh's [1989] Extended Objective Measure of Ego Identity Status—the EOM-EIS; Balistreri, Busch-Rossnagel, and Geisinger's [1995] Ego Identity Process Questionnaire—the EIPQ; and Bosma's [1985] Groningen Identity Development Scale—the GIDS).

The areas or "domains" of commitment formation were expanded to increase the relevance and inclusiveness of the typology. For example, to be more inclusive of women, premarital intercourse (Marcia & Friedman, 1970) and sex roles (Matteson, 1977) have been added; to include younger samples, dating and friendships were operationalized (Grotevant & Cooper, 1981); to be sensitive to minority groups, ethnicity has been studied (Phinney, 1989); and to understand European samples (specifically Dutch), lifestyle concerns were measured (Bosma, 1985).

Although based on the cross-tabulation of the two dimensions of choice and commitment, the statuses were originally theorized to vary hierarchically in terms of levels of maturity of self-regulation and complexity of social functioning (Marcia, 1964). Identity diffusion (low choice, low commitment) is generally considered the least mature and least complex status, reflecting a lack of concern about directing one's present and future life. Individuals who remain diffused beyond early or middle adolescence have been found to be prone to drug abuse, risky sexual behavior, and academic failure (Jones, 1992, 1994; Jones & Hartmann, 1988; White, 2000). Kroger (2003) describes diffusions as having low levels of self-esteem and autonomy, difficulties adapting to new environments (like university settings), and more self-focus. Cognitively, the diffusion tends to have disorganized thinking, an external locus of control, and a tendency toward procrastination and defensive avoidance of issues. Their moral reasoning and ego development also tend to be at the lowest levels among the identity statuses (Kroger).

Foreclosure (low choice, high commitment) is thought to be a somewhat more mature status than diffusion in that commitments are embraced. However, foreclosed individuals have been found to have low developmental complexity associated with a conformist and obedient orientation, as evidenced by such tendencies as authoritarianism, closed-mindedness, and rigidity (Berman et al., 2001; Marcia, 1980), and overidentifying with their parents (Adams, Dyk, & Bennion, 1987; Côté & Levine, 1983).

Moratorium (high crisis—making choices, low commitment) is often considered a more functionally complex status than both diffusion and foreclosure because the individual is purportedly taking proactive steps in autonomously considering identity alternatives during an ongoing identity crisis. However, the higher level of functioning implied in the moratorium status has been found to be hampered by higher levels of anxiety (Kidwell, Dunham, Bacho, Pastorino, & Portes, 1995) and uncertainty (Meeus, 1996; Meeus, Iedema, Helsen, & Vollebergh, 1999).

Resolution of the identity stage, in turn, is operationalized by the fourth identity status, identity achievement (past crisis producing autonomous choices, high commitment), considered the most mature and functionally complex status. Assignment of people to this identity status has been empirically associated with, among other things, balanced thinking (Boyes and Chandler, 1992), mature interpersonal relationships (Dyk & Adams, 1990; Orlofsky, Marcia, & Lesser, 1973), and higher levels of personal agency (on a measure comprised of the following subscales: self-esteem, internal locus of control, ego strength, and purpose in life; Côté, 1996). Kroger (2003) summarizes the correlates in terms of (1) personality characteristics (high achievement motivation and self-esteem; low neuroticism and use of defense mechanisms), (2) cognitive processes (functioning best under stress; more purposeful, higher levels of moral reasoning and ego development), and (3) interpersonal skills (high intimacy, self-disclosure, and most secure attachments).

General Assessments of the Identity Status Paradigm

Numerous recent reviews are available of the identity status paradigm (e.g., Kroger, 1993, 2003; LaVoie, 1994; Marcia, Waterman, Matteson, Archer, & Orlofsky, 1993; Schwartz, 2001; van Hoof, 1999). These reviews reveal that Marcia's elaboration of Erikson's formulations of identity, and subsequent methodological and

conceptual elaborations of Marcia's formulations, provide an empirically useful method of studying how the interplay of choice and commitment affects various dimensions of personality and social behavior, at least among "lower middle to upper middle class ethnic majorities in North America, Northern Europe, and parts of the British Commonwealth" (Marcia, 1989, p. 402). Antecedent socialization experiences, especially in the family and educational contexts, are also associated with the choice/commitment cross-tabulation that underlies the identity statuses (e.g., Waterman, 1993). The success of this conceptual model in providing verifiable predictions attests to its usefulness in studying certain aspects of (Western) identity formation. However, additional components of identity formation have been identified as in need of study, and questions have been raised about how adequately the identity status paradigm represents Erikson's theoretical formulations in terms of adhering to its developmental claims about the interrelationships of the identity statuses (e.g., Côté & Levine, 1987, 1988; van Hoof, 1999).

Marcia (1980, p. 161) has maintained that the identity statuses are useful partly because they provide for "a greater variety of styles in dealing with the identity issue than does Erikson's simple dichotomy of identity versus identity confusion." The statuses were originally based on the developmental hypothesis that a "continuum of ego identity based upon proximity of an individual to identity achievement . . . [underlies] the statuses" (Marcia, 1967, p. 119). A developmental progression through the statuses was postulated to be a dominant pattern, with identity achievement and identity diffusion as "polar alternatives of status inherent in Erikson's theory," and identity foreclosure and identity moratorium as "roughly intermediate in this distribution" (Marcia, 1966, pp. 551–552). Thus, it appears that the identity statuses were thought of as akin to substages of the identity stage (Côté & Levine, 1988). Other than the distinction between diffusion and achievement, revisions to these assumptions have been made, and there are no longer structural claims to sequential progress through the statuses, or even that the domains progress in unison (see also Marcia et al., 1993; Waterman, 1988).

Criticisms of the identity status approach also include its narrowness (van Hoof, 1999) and lack of attention to broader social-contextual factors affecting identity development (Côté & Levine, 1988). Its referents—choice and commitment— are operationalized primarily as intrapsychic processes and, theoretically speaking, are not necessarily connected to the social circumstances in which the identity is formed (van Hoof, 2001). What has been called for is the integration of more contextually oriented elements into the psychological study of identity, to bring the Marcia approach closer to the multidimensionality and scope that Erikson envisioned (Côté & Levine, 1987, 2002; Schwartz, 2001).

We return to these issues later when we discuss the studies that have examined the developmental properties of the identity statuses. First, however, it is useful to acknowledge other empirical neo-Eriksonian approaches, including the specialized study of ethnic identity formation.

Other Empirical Approaches to Identity Formation

In tracing the evolution of the Eriksonian approach to identity, Schwartz (2001) classified approaches into extensions and expansions: Extensions complement the Marcian approach, while expansions move beyond the Marcian crisis/commitment approach in ways that draw more from Erikson's original formulations. Four extension models are identified by Schwartz: Berzonsky's (1992) social–cognitive, identity-styles approach, which identifies diffuse-avoidant, normative, and informational ways of processing identity-relevant information; Grotevant's (1987) exploration-process model, which emphasizes the abilities and orientations people use in exploring identities; Waterman's (1990) self-discovery, personal expressiveness approach to commitment formation; and Kerpelman and

Lamke's (1997) identity control theory, which emphasizes reciprocal causation and mutual influence of the microprocesses stimulating or inhibiting identity explorations.

In addition, Schwartz identifies three expansion models: Kurtines's (1999) co-constructivist model, with its emphasis on choice, personal responsibility, and moral-ethical consistency; Adams's (Adams & Marshall, 1996) developmental social psychological model, with its emphasis on the complementary processes of integration and differentiation as part of resolution of the identity stage; and Côté's (1997, 2002) identity capital model, where the social and psychological resources at people's disposal are assessed as predictors of the outcomes of identity formation, particularly personal agency in the formation of adult identities and acceptance into specific adult communities.

Ethnic Identity Formation

The preceding approaches to identity formation have been developed to investigate what are believed to be universal forms of identity formation, with the acknowledgment that differences in timing and emphasis may be found among various population segments, like women and ethnic minorities. However, this logic does not work very well when the content of identity formation differs among subpopulations, as in the case of ethnic identity (and gender identity). Initial attempts to study how social contexts affect ethnic identity formation operationalized ethnicity in terms of respondents' ethnic group "membership." However, Phinney and Rosenthal (1992, p. 148) argued that "ethnic identity . . . [is] a multifaceted, dynamic construct . . . with complex and subtle interactions between different elements of ethnic identity and external forces." They went on to note that simply treating ethnicity as group membership fails to distinguish ethnicity from ethnic identity, confusing the social and psychological dimensions of identity:

> [W]hile purporting to measure ethnic identity, researchers simply use ethnic group membership as a variable of interest, without assessing the

adolescent's sense of belonging to the group (self-identification), evaluation of his or her group membership (ethnic pride), or any other aspect of ethnic identity. (Phinney & Rosenthal, 1992, p. 161)

Clearly, assessing the effect of social context on ethnic identity formation is extremely complex. The difficulties include whether ethnicity or race is related to minority or majority status; whether minority status is disparaged or admired; whether the larger society is assimilationist or multicultural; and how ethnicity/race interact with other factors like gender (Phinney & Rosenthal, 1992). Accordingly, every adolescent has an "ethnicity," but its salience is society dependent, as are the combinations and permutations of relations when the social context includes numerous ethnic groups (as in multicultural cities like Miami, Los Angeles, and Toronto; Côté, 2006c). Moreover, race and ethnicity are more social constructions than genetic realities, suggesting that there are great individual variations in how they are perceived, and therefore how they affect the psychological elements of identity. As we see, it sometimes takes significant experiences to create an epiphany to trigger a conscious deliberation of the implications of one's ethnicity.

To date, there is no sustained empirical investigation of ethnic identity formation in adolescence that is independent of the Erikson–Marcia tradition, although some useful alternatives to the crisis/commitment dimensions are being assessed (e.g., Spencer's [2006] model that integrates the "identity-focused cultural ecology" [ICE] perspective with her "phenomenological variant of ecological systems theory" [PVEST]).[1] Several measures of racial and ethnic identity development have been developed (see Cross, 1991; Helms, 1990), but the Multigroup Ethnic Identity Measure (MEIM) developed by Phinney (1989) has been the most widely used in the study of adolescent development. The MEIM comprises three dimensions: self-identification of a sense of belongingness to a particular group, ethnic affirmation and belonging, and ethnic identity achievement.

More recently, Umaña-Taylor, Yazedjian, and Bámaca-Gómez (2004) developed the Ethnic Identity Measure, which more specifically distinguishes among ethnic identity exploration, commitment, and affirmation. Both of these instruments allow for the measurement of general ethnic identity, and are therefore useful in the assessment of any ethnic group, as well as with members of multiple racial/ethnic groups.

Phinney defines ethnic identity as a self-constructed internalization of the meaning and implications of a person's group membership based on that person's attitudes and feelings toward his or her cultural background, ethnic heritage, and racial phenotype (Phinney, 2006). In Phinney's model, ethnic identity develops like Marcia's identity statuses, through the Marcian processes of exploration and commitment. However, Phinney is careful to note that ethnic identity is a component of social identity, unlike the identity statuses, which ostensibly represent ego identity (Phinney & Rosenthal, 1992). While identity status implies choice, ethnic identity involves choice limitations to the extent that one cannot choose one's heritage. Moreover, this heritage can take on differing degrees of salience, and people vary in terms of how much they deliberate upon the relevance of this heritage for their overall sense of identity. Ethnic identity formation involves the task of resolving positive and negative understandings and feelings about the one's own group in relation to other groups that impinge upon one's life. During childhood, these understandings tend to be concrete and oriented to physical attributes like skin color and food preferences, but during adolescence they become more abstract, involving issues associated with ethnic group consciousness (Phinney, 2006).

Phinney proposes a three-stage model of ethnic identity formation that parallels development through the identity statuses. In the first stage, ethnicity remains unexamined, having been internalized from significant others in the family and/or local community.

If these internalizations do not reflect concerns about issues arising from an ethnic background, the person would be classifiable as diffused in terms of an ethnic identity status. If the internalizations are based on stronger views about conflicts or salient experiences associated with ethnic background, the person would be classified as foreclosed for ethnic identity status. The unexamined stage is presumed by Phinney to be characteristic of early adolescence (Phinney & Rosenthal, 1992).

It usually takes a significant experience of prejudice or discrimination to make a person's ethnicity salient in identity formation, by triggering a period of exploration and leading the person to question what it means to have that ethnicity in his or her society. Phinney equates this exploration with the identity crisis identified by Erikson, and the moratorium status postulated by Marcia. A person experiencing this crisis will explore cultural differences between his or her ethnic group and the dominant group in the society, or among the various groups in the society, along with the images, stereotypes, and obstacles that confront members of certain groups.

As with the identity status paradigm, in Phinney's model it is a positive development for this crisis to be "followed by a resolution of the conflicts and contradictions posed by minority status in society" (Phinney & Rosenthal, 1992, p. 150), resulting in ethnic identity achievement. This resolution entails a "commitment to a particular way of being a member of their group" (Phinney & Rosenthal, pp. 150–151), involving a secure sense of who people are in terms of their ethnic background. With this review of conceptual bases of the empirical approaches to identity formation complete, we now turn to the findings they have produced.

DEVELOPMENTAL PATTERNS OF IDENTITY FORMATION

In this section, we first examine the research that has been carried out based on the assumption that identity formation processes are universally applicable—normative—with person–context

variation of degree as a result of certain socialization experiences, and among subpopulations (or demographic groups). The person–context variations are examined, respectively, in terms of education and family settings, and gender, ethnicity, and social class. Given that the identity status paradigm has been the most widely used operationalization of identity formation, discussion will be limited to these studies.

Identity Statuses: Normative Development

Readers will recall that the identity statuses were originally postulated to represent a developmental sequence mapping the identity stage as laid out by Erikson, where crisis-precipitated explorations during adolescence would be normative (i.e., the norm, and therefore widespread) occurrences leading to commitments to an occupation, belief system, and lifestyle. In this section, we examine these findings with an eye to assessing how well this operationalization of Erikson's theory matches his original formations of identity formation. What we find is that many researchers have voiced disappointment with the findings and many have acknowledged that, despite its extensive usage, the identity status paradigm falls short in terms of both its original postulates about how the individual identity statuses represent developmental trajectories and how well the identity status paradigm captures the essence of the identity stage as theorized by Erikson.

In terms of the longitudinal studies that have examined developmental patterns and shifts, Kroger (1993) notes that "the Foreclosure to Moratorium to achievement shift [is] . . . the most common pathway of movement" (p. 10). However, while this may be the most common and "desirable" pathway among contemporary American youth, it does *not* seem to describe the development of a *majority* of young people: only between 30% and 40% of college seniors have been classified as identity achievement (up from about 20% in first year; Waterman, Greary, & Waterman, 1974; Waterman & Waterman, 1971). Moreover, studies of adult populations have found a preponderance of foreclosures (estimated at 30%–40% of the adult population), and a minority of achievements (about 20% of fathers of college students, according to Waterman & Waterman, 1975). Apparently, diffusion characterizes an estimated 25% of college students (and 10%–20% of the adult population), and only between 10% and 30% of young (Western) people temporarily experience the moratorium status (Kroger, 2000; Meeus et al., 1999; van Hoof, 1999; Waterman, 1982, 1999). Based on the identity status paradigm's conceptualization of identity formation, then, it would appear that a significant proportion of the population does *not* mature to the most "advanced" level of achievement, which was postulated to represent the successful resolution of Erikson's identity stage (cf. van Hoof, 1999).

In the most extensive review of the developmental significance of the identity statuses, Meeus (1996) argues that the identity status literature has not sufficiently documented the developmental validity of the statuses as a sufficient operationalization of the identity stage. Only 49 out of 163 studies he reviewed actually address developmental concerns, and then mostly by inference. Instead, most studies looked at cross-sectional concomitants of the statuses. The most robust, replicated finding from this paradigm involves the differences between identity diffusion and identity achievement, supporting Erikson's original postulates about the bipolar processes associated with the identity crisis and its resolution (cf. Côté & Schwartz, 2002). However, the correlates of the moratorium and foreclosure statuses do not reveal a picture of developmental significance.

These accumulated findings reinforced the doubts that have been raised over time about the validity of the identity status paradigm as an operationalization of "substages" of the identity stage. The contention that the only "successful" resolution of the identity stage is identity achievement, in conjunction with the finding that few adults are identity achieved raises the issue of whether the identity status

paradigm is more prescriptive than descriptive. That is, is this an outcome that identity status researchers think people *ought to do* (i.e., form an identity along the lines of the choice/commitment cross-tabulation); and, in conceiving it this way, have they missed what most people *actually do*?

Not only is a clear picture not readily apparent of how the identity statuses constitute developmentally progressive resolutions of the identity stage, even a more basic assumption that identity grows in strength during adolescence for most people is not supported. Certainly, there is a trend revealed in the identity status literature that during adolescence the population-level incidence of diffusion and foreclosure decreases while moratorium and achievement increases in ways one would assume as young people move toward adult maturity (e.g., Archer & Waterman, 1990). However, it is surprising that this tendency is not stronger. Not only are myriad patterns evident as some adolescents move among the statuses and their domains at different rates, but by the end of adolescence, about one half are still in the diffusion and foreclosure statuses (Kroger, 2003).

Others have commented on the question of the developmental relevance of the identity status paradigm. Grotevant (1986, p. 176) argues that "because there does not appear to be one single developmental sequence for the identity statuses . . . the statuses are less useful than might be desired for making developmental comparisons." LaVoie (1994, pp. 23–26) also comments on this problem, noting a "failure to address the mechanisms involved in the transition between statuses even though . . . identity [is recognized] as a developmental process." LaVoie further argues that "available data are not supportive of a common structure" that might link possible identity domains, and he concludes that the "structural components of identity are still in question, especially the matter of a deep structure." This observation suggests that we should look to the context of development, rather than only to the "inner workings" of the individual, to see if there are social influences militating against the formation of a "deep structure" of identity. More specifically, we need to investigate whether cultural forces are creating a disarray of identity domains and a muddled identity formation (Fadjukoff & Pulkkinen, 2005).

This last point warrants further consideration. If the identity statuses represented a normative course toward resolution of the identity stage (in Western countries), self-conscious identity explorations should constitute a major transformative life event of which most adults would have explicit memories (e.g., Marcia, 1976a). However, as noted, some 40 years of research suggests that far fewer exploration-based commitments can be found among those who appear to have resolved the identity stage in purely Eriksonian terms (i.e., among those who are functioning adults with apparently low levels of identity confusion). Accordingly, it has not been established that active, conscious exploration (the moratorium status) is *the* normative (i.e., most widely used) route to the formation of adult identities constituting resolution of the identity stage (the identity achievement status).

Defending the developmental validity of the identity status paradigm, Waterman (1999, p. 610) argues that more people make their way to the identity achievement status than is the case in other developmental areas like moral reasoning (postconventional stage), or ego development (integrated stage). Similarly, Kroger (2000, 2003) suggests that this lack of identity development during adolescence leaves considerable scope for later identity formation in adulthood. However, these explanations only serve to highlight how the logic of the identity status paradigm diverges from Erikson's normative approach, where he saw the bulk of the population as routinely resolving the identity stage by developing a functional adult identity in a timely fashion, even if some difficulties are experienced along the way.

However, there is a useful way to interpret these accumulated empirical findings of the identity status literature without being forced to choose between a wholesale acceptance or rejection of the paradigm. This is to return to Erikson's original postulation that the resolution of the stage can be viewed in terms of a bipolar continuum between identity confusion and identity consolidation (the formation of a resilient sense of ego identity). When this is done, in older populations of young adults or adults, the diffusion and moratorium statuses would be viewed in terms of persisting identity confusion, while foreclosure and achievement would be seen as two forms of identity consolidation. In the case of the latter two statuses, foreclosure would correspond to Erikson's proposition that most young people have muted identity crises and can "can go along with their parents in a kind of fraternal identification" (cited above from Erikson, 1968, p. 33) in finding a resolution to the identity stage, while achievement would represent a successful resolution of more active identity crises involving more serious realignment of identifications. When these two groups are considered together, the identity status literature provides an estimate that between 60% and 80% of the adult population has resolved the identity stage in functionally adequate ways (combining percentages cited above). This combined estimate is much more reasonable than the 30%–40% estimate obtained if only the achievement status is used to represent successful resolution of the identity stage.

Adopting this conciliatory view, however, would require rejecting the position among some theorists that identity achievement is synonymous with "having" an identity (e.g., Marcia, 1993). The miscalculation of this position is revealed in the above-noted findings that only a minority of adults appear to be identity achieved, which would leave most Westerners "without an identity." I do not believe most developmental psychologists could accept such a position.

We return to this issue in the concluding section, where we consider a return to methodologies involving the continuum concept of identity stage resolution and a return to some of "pre-Marcian" interpretations of Erikson's writings. Next we examine differences in normative development attributable to person–context mediations and interactions.

Identity Statuses: Person–Context Effects

The issue of how social contexts affect human development constitutes perhaps the greatest challenge facing researchers (e.g., Lerner, 2002). The challenge is indeed great in the cases of identity formation. In the early 1990s, Kroger (1993, p. 11) observed that research exploring "the roles of culture, social class, ethnicity, and historical ethos . . . [in identity formation] has only just begun." A problem has been that psychological approaches to identity formation have tended to undertheorize "the social" in its broadest sense (but see Spencer's [2006] proposed model). Instead, early efforts were devoted mainly to immediate context variables like family background and educational settings. Since then, interest has increasingly turned to more general issues that have occupied public policy agendas, particularly ethnicity and gender. It needs to be stressed, however, that "ethnicity" and "gender" are not social contexts per se. Rather, they are social identities attributed to individuals by others that take on particular meanings within socially constructed cultural contexts; at the same time, individuals experiencing these social identities have different subjective experiences of them that have different meanings in different contexts. Moreover, as we discuss later, the experience of social identities such as gender and ethnicity can compound, producing complex interaction effects, especially when social class is added to the mix.

At the same time, it is useful to distinguish social contexts whose functions are explicitly to socialize people into certain identities, as in the case of schools and families, from the more demographically based attributes such as gender, ethnicity, and social class (or socioeconomic status). Although socialization is associated with these demographically based characteristics, these are attributes of the individual that are often associated with differential social statuses, while schools and families represent socialization contexts that exist at the institutional level, rather than the level of individual. We begin, then, by examining identity formation in two socialization contexts, educational settings and the family, and then move on to look at identity formation in terms of gender, ethnicity, and social class origins. In these socialization contexts, identity formation processes are mediated in the sense that development is potentially affected positively or negatively by certain experiences.

Educational Settings

It is widely assumed that attending college or university has dramatic effects on personality development, including identity formation. Indeed, several decades of research on college effects have explored the ways in which college might stimulate forms of human development. For example, researchers have explored psychosocial developmental models such as vectors of student development (Chickering, 1969), ego strength (Adams, Ryan, & Keating, 2000), and identity status (Berzonsky & Kuk, 2000; Marcia, 1966; Waterman, 1993) to look for ways in which college enhances student psychosocial development. And, as noted above, the percentage of college students classified as identity achieved has been found to increase from about 20% in first year to between 30% and 40% in the senior year (at least for Baby Boomers: Waterman, Greary, & Waterman, 1974; Waterman & Waterman, 1971). However, in the largest review ever of these studies, Pascarella and Terenzini (1991) concluded that the evidence of widespread (main effect) identity development that is directly attributable to college attendance is inconclusive because few controls have been employed to account for maturation effects (i.e., whether the identity formation would have taken place among those not attending college). In their recent update to this research review, Pascarella and Terenzini (2005) still could not identify any "studies that examined the extent to which such development could be attributed to the college experience rather than to other maturational or sociocultural forces" (p. 228).

The evidence of change in response to the college experience is strongest for variables like political liberalism, various forms of self-concept, personal adjustment and psychological well being, with effect sizes similar to the cognitive variables (about one-third to one-half of a standard deviation). However, as noted, net of competing explanations like maturation effects, there has been little demonstrable effect of college attendance for variables like identity and ego development, interpersonal relationships, maturity, and general personality development. This may be because deep-seated characteristics underpinning identity are resistant to change during this period (Côté & Allahar, 1996; Côté & Levine, 2000), or simply that these factors are not targeted in any systematic way at most colleges (whereas the cognitive variables are directly targeted), so expectations of substantive changes may be unrealistic.

Family

Research into how identity formation is affected by characteristics of the family dates back to the early research on identity status (see Adams, Côté, & Marshall, 2001, for a review). Much of this research focused on parenting styles, and the extent to which parents grant psychological autonomy to their children: thinking for themselves and exploring their potentials and social opportunities. Adolescents who are granted more psychological autonomy, but who abide by parental guidance, tend to show the best outcomes in many areas of functioning, including identity formation.

The most popular framework for understanding parent–adolescent relationships is the parenting style model based on Baumrind (1968). Maccoby and Martin (1983) later extended

Baumrind's work by defining parenting styles in terms of two underlying dimensions: demandingness and responsiveness. Demandingness refers to parents' expectations about their children's maturity and the parents' demands for their children to comply with them. Responsiveness is parents' sensitivity to their children's signals, needs, and states. Cross-tabulating the two dimensions produces four parenting styles: The *authoritative* style is high on both responsiveness and demandingness, which set the stage for the effective granting of psychological autonomy. The *authoritarian* style exhibits high demandingness but low responsiveness. The *indulgent* style, in contrast, is low on demandingness but high on responsiveness. And the *indifferent* style is low on both responsiveness and demandingness. These last two styles constitute permissive styles of parenting.

The empirical literature provides evidence for predictable associations of parenting styles, and associated practices, with the identity statuses and their associated characteristics. Parental warmth and support—responsiveness (Adams & Jones, 1983; Jackson, Dunham, & Kidwell, 1990)—and parental encouragement and companionship (Adams, 1985), have been found to be positively associated with the moratorium and achievement statuses. However, excessively high levels of responsiveness can apparently impede identity explorations if the parental warmth and support leads to enmeshment with others (Cooper, Grotevant, & Condon, 1983; Dyk, 1990). At the same time, moderate demandingness or democratic paternal parenting (Lee, Kobayashi, & Adams, 1988) enhances identity exploration while excessive parental attempts to control adolescent behaviors can discourage identity explorations (Bosma & Gerritts, 1985).

Consistent with the research reported to date, Hess and McDevitt (1984) predicted that authoritative parents encourage independent problem solving and critical thinking. This parenting style involves a form of communication that seems to enhance the development of more mature forms of identity because it provides opportunities for adolescents to engage in the active exploration of ideas (Gecas & Seff, 1990). Berzonsky and Kinney (1998) found that adolescents who are informationally oriented tend to report their parents' style as more authoritative, while normatively oriented adolescents rate their parents as more authoritarian. In addition, the diffuse–avoidant style is associated with the perception that parents are either permissive or authoritarian, and less likely to be authoritative. Aunola, Stattin, and Nurmi (2000) assessed the relationship between parenting styles and adolescent employment of coping strategies, finding those socialized by authoritative parents tend to employ adaptive, task-oriented strategies that are associated with identity moratorium and achievement. Over- and undercontrolled adolescents are more likely to engage in task-irrelevant or passive behaviors that characterize the coping strategies of identity diffusions. Consistent with the research specifically addressing identity formation, adolescents raised by parents employing permissive and neglectful styles are not socialized to become self-regulating, and the result can be greater impulsivity (Barber, 1996) and lower self-reliance and orientation to work (Lamborn, Mounts, Steinberg, & Dornbusch, 1991; Wintre & Yaffe, 2000).

As one would expect, authoritarian parents can discourage the active exploration of ideas and independent problem solving, instead encouraging an unquestioning dependence on their control and guidance (Hess & McDevitt, 1984). Enright, Lapsley, Drivas, and Fehr (1980) contrasted autocratic with democratic, permissive families, and found that the former discouraged more mature identity explorations. Kerpelman and Smith (1999) report that the majority of delinquent adolescent daughters among 25 mother–daughter pairs had relationships in which the mother invalidated the daughter's positive identity statements or contradicted the daughter's positive and negative assertions about her identity. Consistently negative or ambiguous feedback from a parent does not reflect a responsive relationship and is unlikely to encourage identity exploration. For example, Hauser et al. (1991) found that adolescent ego identity level was positively associated with styles of interaction that are supportive, but was negatively associated with constraining styles.

Thus, the empirical literature appears to show that adolescents who are overcontrolled by authoritarian parents or undercontrolled by permissive or neglectful parents are not provided with opportunities to practice exploration of ideas and self-regulation of behavior. The result can be the development of maladaptive strategies to problem solving concerning personal goals. The literature suggests that a moderate degree of connectedness, reflected through shared affection and an acceptance of individuality, provides the psychological foundation and security for adolescents to begin the searching process for self-defined commitments (e.g., Cooper et al., 1983; Grotevant, 1983; Grotevant & Cooper, 1985). In contrast, weak affectionate bonding with parents and poor communication levels, reflected by rejection or psychological withdrawal, seems to provide an insecure or constricted psychological base for self-exploration. In addition, extreme affection (enmeshment) between adolescents and their parents and limited family tolerance for individuality might enmesh adolescents and discourage identity explorations.

Ethnic Identity Development

Research based on Phinney's model and her Multigroup Ethnic Identity Measure shows that there is significant movement through these three stages between the ages 16 and 19, and that college students score higher on questionnaire scales of ethnic identity achievement than do high school students (Phinney & Rosenthal, 1992). However, research also finds that only about one-quarter of ethnic minority adolescents can be classified as achieved on ethnic identity by the end of high school (Phinney, 2006). At the same time, issues that appear to have been previously resolved can reemerge if circumstances stimulate their reconsideration. Those who explore their ethnicity and have a greater understanding of their ethnic group's history and traditions also have a more secure sense of their ethnic identity and commitment to their ethnic group (Phinney, 2005).

Little systematic research has been carried out on postadolescent youth, especially among those who do not attend college. However, those who attend college are more likely to explore their ethnicity. And ethnic identity achievements are more likely to become involved in cultural activities that strengthen their ethnic identity, while those with a weaker sense of ethnic identity may withdraw from these cultural activities and experience a further weakening of their ethnic identity (Phinney, 2006). Those classified as achieved on ethnic identity have also been found to have higher self-esteem (Phinney & Alipuria, 1990), and as enjoying better psychological well-being in terms of coping ability, mastery, self-esteem and optimism, and lower levels of loneliness and depression (Roberts et al., 1999). In addition, those classified as achieved have more positive attitudes toward other groups, and more mature intercultural thinking, than those classified as diffused (Phinney, Jacoby, & Silva, 2007), along with the highest scores on psychological adjustment and ego identity (Kroger, 2003).

Finally, Phinney's (2005) research finds that the meaning and strength of ethnic identity differs among ethnic groups, with African Americans having the strongest ethnic identities, presumably in response to the negative stereotypes and discrimination to which they are exposed. Asians and Latinos also have strong ethnic identities, but score lower than African Americans. European Americans have the lowest scores, even those living in diverse communities and attending mixed schools.

Gender

The identity status literature reveals a certain amount of confusion in terms of how to characterize gender differences. The earliest research from the 1970s reported gender differences that seem to have disappeared during the 1980s (Patterson, Sochting, & Marcia, 1992). Whether this was due to changing sociohistorical circumstances or changing methodologies is not known (Marcia, 1993), but the general consensus seems to be that among contemporary (American, high school and college attending) youth, there are no significant differences in *how* and *when* females and males consolidate their commitments. That is, there appears to now be agreement that there are no meaningful differences in the *processes* by which psychological aspects of identity come together (i.e., the frequencies and subjective meanings of the identity statuses), and when they come together (Archer, 1993; Marcia, 1993; Sorell & Montgomery, 2001; Waterman, 1993). Recently, Kroger (2003, p. 219) concluded, "there has been little evidence of gender differences regarding questions of identity structure, domain salience, or developmental processes."

However, reliable differences seem to have been identified in terms of the "domains" or content areas around which identity issues are explored. Archer (1993, p. 85) summarized these findings as follows:

> Gender differences were found in the domains of sexuality (Waterman & Nevid, 1976), family/career prioritizing (Archer, 1985), and friendship (Thorbecke & Grotevant, 1982), but not on vocation, religious beliefs, sex roles, values, dating, and so forth. In each case of significant gender differences, females have been more likely to be identity achieved or in moratorium and males, foreclosed or diffuse, reinforcing the female self-in-relation expectation. But females have been as likely as males to be self-defined in the intrapersonal domains as well.

In other words, more females appear to be exploring issues related to real-life concerns (in a world of changing gender roles), thereby increasing the complexity of their identity formation (while fewer males appear to be as concerned with these gender-related issues). As Waterman (1993, p. 62) puts it:

> [T]he task of identity formation is more complex for females than for males in that they endeavour to work out for themselves their goals, values, and beliefs in more domains than do males. Not only do females experience the desire to establish their sense of identity in vocational choice, religious beliefs, political ideology, and sex-role attitudes in the same manner as males, but they engage in more active reflection and decision-making regarding identity in a relational context than do their male counterparts.

When the concept of gender is expanded to the more complex concept of *gender identity*, or *gender-role orientation*, consistent differences among the identity statuses have been found on measures of gender identity. Gecas and Burke (1995, p. 54) define gender identity as "the socially defined self-meanings of masculinity/ femininity one has as a male or female member of society and are inherently derived from and tied to social structure." In a recent review of the literature, Marcia (1993) concluded, "across various measures of identity, intimacy, and sex-role typing, the relationships among androgyny, high intimacy, and high identity, as well as between masculinity and identity and femininity and intimacy are fairly well established" (p. 40). Kroger (2003, p. 219) summarizes research in this area, noting that "gender-role orientation, rather than gender per se, is an important predictor of difference in resolutions to questions of identity, moral reasoning, and intimacy."

The future to this line of research seems to clearly lie not with mere categorizations of people as male or female, but in assessments of how they experience masculinity and femininity, along with the various combinations and permutations of these experiences, as with shades of androgyny. The same logic likely applies to the importance of experiences of sexuality, rather than mere classifications of its variations (e.g., Cass, 1979; D'Augelli, 1994; Halverson, 2005).

Social Class

Phillips and Pitman (2003) recently pointed out that "a review of the literature indicates that studies investigating identity processes among the poor are not only sparse, they are virtually nonexistent" (p. 116). They go on to observe that studies of economically disadvantaged adolescents has confounded social class with ethnic minority status, and have thus used the ethnic identity formation model of development rather than the more general identity status model, or developed a model specific to social class issues (but see Schwartz, Montgomery, & Briones, 2006). Phillips and Pitman attribute this confounding to the lack of attention among identity theorists and researchers with respect to "the effect of external sociocultural influences on identity formation" (p. 116).

In an attempt to rectify this gap in the literature, Phillips and Pittman developed a model that identifies the types of "identity work" that economically disadvantaged adolescents might undertake in coping with disparaging self-relevant information, limited opportunities, and chronic exposure to high levels of stress and negative life events. They predict that those who are unsuccessful in overcoming these problems may avoid or prematurely end any identity explorations, or adopt a "negative identity" (Erikson, 1968) that sets them up for future failures and underachievement.

Yoder (2000) offered a model with which to understand how the barriers to identity status formation could be conceptualized within the identity status paradigm. She argues that most models of identity formation adopt a static view of the environments in which identity exploration might take place. These models tend to assume that social structure is clearly defined for all adolescents, there are few physical or economic limitations confronting them, and that all adolescents understand the work and life options ostensibly available to them. She offers a model in which each of the four identity statuses can be subdivided in terms of whether the barriers to exploration and commitment are absent, present, or have been overcome.

To date, these suggestions for conceptualizing economic disadvantage and undertaking empirical research to investigate its effects have not been heeded by researchers, perhaps because of the convenience of conducting research on middle class young people in high schools and colleges. At the same time, the basic assumption remains that identity formation among the disadvantaged is hampered by forms of discrimination and underprivilege that create difficulties in the transition to adulthood (e.g., in the United States and Canada it is assumed that everyone who is not middle class, Anglo, and male will encounter special and/or more severe problems). However, in one of the few statements about this assumption, Rotheram-Borus and Wyche (1994, p. 67) argue that "empirical support for . . . lowered expectations for identity achievement among minority group members has been mixed."

As useful as these research efforts have been into the complexities of ethnicity, gender, and class, the situation is even more complex when the combinations and permutations of these three contexts are considered, as we see next.

Interactions among Contextual Factors

Little research has been devoted to two- and three-way interactions among demographic background variables like gender, ethnicity, and social class (Schwartz, Montgomery, & Briones, 2006). This research is important to undertake because it is possible, for example, that ethnicity may be more important for certain dimensions of identity formation than gender, such that depending on their social class and age, women of a given ethnicity may subjectively experience more in common with men of their own ethnic group than with women of another ethnic group, as they form their sense of identity; moreover, in terms of actual social identity (as per their social location), they may objectively have more in common with their brothers (cf. Brand, 1987; Espin & Gawelek, 1992). (We see below that in the United States,

self-esteem appears to develop quite differently for minority group adolescent females than it does for White adolescent females.) Rotheram-Borus and Wyche (1994, p. 68) refer to this general issue in the following manner:

> [S]ome evidence exists that gender and ethnicity interactively influence personality development. . . . It also appears that minority adolescents are socialized into gender roles that differ from those of European-American males and females, . . . and that gender stereotyping is less salient within some ethnic groups than within the European-American group. . . . Because the gender roles of a youth's ethnic group and socioeconomic status will define the context of his or her search to a significant extent, research in this area is greatly needed in the future.

Similarly, working-class women may experience more in common with their male class counterparts than their middle-class sisters. However, in the social sciences, an earlier interest in social class issues appears to have been eclipsed by the more recent interest in gender and ethnicity, in spite of the fact that "class"*qua* material resources underlies much of the gender and ethnic disparity being debated in the public forum (Allahar & Côté, 1998). Consequently, it is unlikely that we will find much research directly addressing the relationship between social class and identity formation in the near future. However, research paralleling identity formation, as in the case of educational research attempting to understand the experiences of first-generation university students, may shed some light on this important area (Côté, 2007).

THE SELF PSYCHOLOGY APPROACH TO SELF-DEVELOPMENT

Much of this literature on the adolescent self has emerged out of social psychology, in the field of self psychology. Self psychology stems from the pioneering works of William James (1948/1892), G. H. Mead (1934), and Charles

Horton Cooley (1902). In particular, James's and Mead's distinctions between the "I" and the "Me" have generated much of the theory and research on the self, and its postulated key attributes, especially self-concept and self-esteem. However, this research tradition is not focused specifically on adolescent development. Accordingly, the theoretical basis of self psychology will be briefly described, and only those empirical studies most illustrative of the nature of adolescent development will be reviewed subsequently.

Self psychology has focused on the distinction between the self "as knower" and the self as "known," in a way that is homologous to Erikson's distinction between the ego and the self. With this distinction between two moments of self-epistemology in mind, Baumeister (1998) distinguishes among three major research concerns in this field: reflexive consciousness, the interpersonal self, and the executive functions of the self.

Research into the area of reflexive consciousness stems directly from the "I"/"Me" distinction in the work of James and G. H. Mead. This research has investigated relationships among reflexive cognition, self-esteem (e.g., Steele, 1988; Baumeister, 1990), external and internal standards for self-comparison (e.g., Higgins, 1987), and the acquisition of self-knowledge as a function of age and cognitive development (Harter, 1993; Hart, Maloney, & Damon, 1987; Honess & Yardley, 1987). Researchers have investigated the internal consistency of self-knowledge (e.g., Broughton, 1981; Rosenberg, 1997) and the organization of self-schemas (Byrne, 1996; Byrne & Shavelson, 1996; Marsh & Hattie, 1996). Interest can also be found in how personal self-conceptions are coordinated with more social and ethnic identities (Roberts, Phinney, Romero, & Chen, 1996; Thoits & Virshup, 1997), as well as in broader questions about the historical and cultural origins of the self-knowledge system (Baumeister, 1997; Danziger, 1997; Holland, 1997; Mageo, 1997).

Investigations of the interpersonal self involve the extent to which others' perceptions of self influence a person's self-concept. This concern with "reflected appraisal" (Felson, 1989) has stimulated the study of the accuracy of perception of the impressions made on others and as well as the functions of self-deception (DePaulo, Kenny, Hoover, Webb, & Oliver, 1987). Research involving self-presentation and the management of impressions has focused on the relevance of self-motives, such as supplication and ingratiation (Jones & Pittman, 1982), self-monitoring abilities (Snyder, 1987), and threats to the self (Heatherton & Vohs, 2000). In addition, some theorists have examined cultural processes involved in self-identity (e.g., Shotter & Gergen, 1989; Worchel, Morales, Paez, & Deschamps, 1998).

Finally, Baumeister's (1998) study of the executive functions of the self highlights the potentially agentic aspects of human functioning. However, there is a reticence in the literature to develop a more fully articulated view of agency equivalent to that which is latent in Erikson's work and manifest in the recent work of some sociologists (e.g., Emirbayer & Mische, 1998).

From this general background of self psychology, we now move to a consideration of theoretical approaches to self-development during adolescence.

Theoretical Approaches to Self-Development

According to most theoretical models of the development of the self, the self is formed during childhood (e.g., through the Meadian play and game stages; Hewitt, 2000), and potentially undergoes a strengthening, consolidation, and differentiation during adolescence (Honess & Yardley, 1987; Shapka & Keating, 2005). Harter (1999) argues that this differentiation involves a greater focus on abstract traits than is the case among children. Markus and Nurius (1986) have researched ways in which these abstractions can involve differentiating between actual and possible selves as part of developing self-schemas—cognitive structures that arrange self-concepts and process information through them.[2] Moreover, adolescents differentiate between future ideal selves and feared selves (Oyserman & Markus, 1990). While this ability to abstract one's self has growth-enhancing potentials, discrepancies between actual selves and ideal abstractions of selves can be a source of self-esteem problems and can lead to depressive states (e.g., Choi & Lee, 1998). In addition, a lack of balance between, and clear conception of, ideal and feared selves has been found to be associated with delinquency, with delinquents having sets of more intensely negative feared selves (Oyserman & Markus). An imbalance of ideal and feared selves has also been found to be a stronger predictor of delinquency than lower self-esteem.

Unlike identity research, no qualitatively different stagelike "statuses" have been researched in the adolescence literature (although Hart, Maloney, & Damon, 1987, postulated four developmental levels of self-understanding representing the senses of continuity of self and distinctiveness from others). Instead, in general, studies have examined whether various domains of self-concept increase in positive valence and strength during this age period (the sum of which equals global self-esteem). As one would expect, this is the case, although as we will see later, the increase in their strength varies by factors associated with contextually specific experiences. First, we examine the empirical findings investigating normative development.

Normative Self-Development

The earliest measures in self psychology assessed levels and changes in self-esteem (e.g., Coopersmith, 1967) and self-concept (Fitts, 1965). These studies suggested that self-concept becomes more differentiated and abstract during adolescence, and self-esteem strengthens overall.

During the 1960s there was an explosion of research based on the Tennessee Self-Concept Scale (TSCS; Fitts, 1965), a 100-item scale that provides a normative profile of five domains of self-concept: physical self,

moral–ethical self, personal self, family self, and social self. The sum of these items yields a measure of global self-esteem (P scores). In addition, the TSCS provides an estimate of the differentiation of self-concept (D scores), with low scores suggesting "an uncertain, poorly-differentiated image" (Thompson, 1972, p. 3). Other measures of self-esteem were developed and extensively used in the 1960s and 1970s (e.g., Coopersmith, 1967; Rosenberg, 1965). While useful, this potpourri of measures creates difficulties in comparing studies and developing a consistent picture of changes in self-esteem, as well as the relationships of self-esteem to socialization influences and social context (Dusek & McIntyre, 2003).

In addition to this problem of multiple instruments of the same concept, Dusek and McIntyre (2003) argue that it is important to differentiate self-concept from self-esteem, with the former being a qualitative category (e.g., "I am a student"), and the latter being a variable assessment of self-concept (e.g., "I am a good student/poor student"). In addition, self-esteem can be measured in (less accurate) global terms, as well as in (more accurate) terms that are specific to self-concepts. They further argue that most self-research has assumed that global measures of self-esteem give accurate assessments of adolescents' senses of competence in the various domains of functioning that produce self-concepts (e.g., student, athlete, attractive). However, they argue this is a highly dubious assumption because adolescents do not necessarily summarize their self-esteem across these domains. Moreover, separate domains are of differing importance for each person, and this importance can shift from day to day and situation to situation.

Based on population norms derived from a database of over 400 studies using the TSCS, Thompson concluded that self-esteem increases with age, with high school samples having below average scores, college students and adults having average scores, and the elderly having above average scores. Thompson also found that self-concept becomes more certain and differentiated with age, but that the dividing line is between college students and adults. That is, high school and college students have below average D scores (and high school students are more uncertain about their self-concepts than college students), while adults and the elderly have above-average scores.

Research based on other approaches supports the finding based on the TSCS that self-concept becomes less certain during early to mid-adolescence. Harter (1986) found that early adolescents have more contradictory self-concepts than late adolescents, but that the ability to understand why these contradictions exist is part of developing a behavioral repertoire for functioning in a variety of societal contexts. The adolescent learns that different contexts can evoke a range of subjective reactions and require different forms of impression management. Adolescents can thus come to intuit that there can be differences between a "real self" and a "role self" (Harter, 1997; Harter, Waters, & Whitesell, 1997).

At the same time, there is evidence that declines in self-esteem during early adolescence are limited to a subpopulation of adolescence, with most young adolescents maintaining a consistent level of self-esteem or increasing in self-esteem (e.g., Palh, Greene, & Way, 2000). In relation to the "on-time" onset of puberty, early-maturing females can experience a decline in self-esteem, while early-maturing males can experience an increase (Dusek & McIntyre, 2003). One longitudinal study identified four patterns of self-esteem development in a sample followed from grade 6 to grade 8 in the United States (Hirsch & DuBois, 1991), and only one pattern involved a steep decline in self-esteem (among 21% of the sample).

Rosenberg's (1986) self-esteem measure has yielded some results that speak to the issue of emotional turbulence during adolescence. He distinguished between "baseline self-esteem" and "barometric self-esteem." The former refers to the level at which people maintain a stable, global view of themselves, while the latter characterizes a sense of self-esteem that

is situation dependent. Rosenberg's research supports the conclusion that the self-esteem of adolescents fluctuates more than that of either children or adults, being more determined by the characteristics of the situation encountered and the nature of relationships with people in those situations.

Finally, Harter (1989) developed the Self-Perception Profile for Adolescents, which measures eight facets of adolescent self-image (e.g., scholastic competence and physical appearance). This scale allows for an assessment of global self-esteem by not including scores for facets that are not part of the adolescent's self-concept (e.g., athletic competence), thereby providing a more accurate assessment of the adolescent's overall self-appraisal. Research with this scale, while based primarily on White, middle-class American samples finds that females rate themselves lower than males on their physical appearance, but higher on close friendships, but that most domains increase with age (Shapka & Keating, 2005). At the same time, females' global scores are lower than those of males'.

Person–Context Effects in Self-Development

The literature on social context and subpopulation differences in the development of the self is more straightforward than is the case for research on identity because there are no theories of "substages" of development, so this literature requires less analysis than is the case for identity research. At the same time, more studies have examined multiple contexts, so subsections will not be used in this section to separate the studies on the basis of gender, ethnicity, and social class. However, studies examining educational settings and the family will be dealt with separately.

Thompson (1972) reported that findings from the TSCS indicate that delinquents had lower self-concepts than nondelinquent adolescents. In comparing Black and White adolescents, Black high school students scored lower on overall self-concept, but not in the areas of physical self and personal self. In addition, studies of economically disadvantaged youth have not found significant differences on the TSCS, although differences do emerge in the adult population. Age may thus be a more important factor in self-concept than socioeconomic status, although none of these studies is based on longitudinal research. Results with the TSCS in terms of gender differences have been inconsistent (e.g., Chiam, 1987; Putnam, Hosie, & Hansen, 1978; Sharpley & Hattie, 1983).

Other measures of self-esteem have not necessarily supported the findings of the TSCS program. Rosenberg (1965) found that among adolescents social class was weakly related to self-esteem on his measure, and ethnicity was unrelated. More recently, African Americans have been found to have higher self-esteem than White adolescents, who in turn had higher self-esteem than Latinos, Asian Americans, and Native Americans (Twenge & Crocker, 2002). Further, within these non-White ethnic groups, females had been found to have higher self-esteem than males.

Longitudinal research suggests that self-esteem plays different roles in the development of White males and females in the United States (Block & Robins, 1993), with females experiencing a lowering of self-esteem during adolescence, in contrast to increases experienced by males. Part of this difference in self-esteem development may involve physical self-concept, with males being more positive about their bodies as part of a less differentiated physical self-conception. In contrast, these adolescent females may have a more differentiated body image that would be more prone to dissatisfaction with different parts of the body (Koff, Rierdan, & Stubbs, 1990; Perkins & Lerner, 1995). The extreme sexualization of the female body in American culture may play a role in a greater self-consciousness of the physical self, as well as dissatisfaction when the unrealistic ideals promulgated by the media are internalized as points of reference for self-development (cf. Stice, Spangler, & Agras, 2001).

These apparently robust gender differences, which have become well known outside of academic circles (e.g., in some popular books like Wolf, 1991), are tempered when non-White ethnic groups are included in studies. These studies find that African American females judge their own physical appearance quite differently, feeling far more satisfaction with their body image. One study found that most African American females were satisfied with their bodies (70%), while almost none of the White females were (10%) (Parker, Nichter, Vuckovic, Sims, & Ritenbaugh, 1995). African American females are also more likely to endorse being overweight as acceptable, as part of a greater flexibility in their self-acceptance. Consequently, the self-esteem difficulties found among White adolescent females are not found among other ethnic groups in which extreme body image ideals are not internalized. Indeed, there is some evidence that females in these groups have higher self-esteem than their male peers (Dubois, Felner, Brand, Phillip, & Lease, 1996).

Educational Settings

On the issue of the educational contexts, school transitions have often been the focus of research. Studies generally find that those who move to a new school, as in the transition to a junior high school, experience a decline in self-esteem, greater instability in their self-concept, and more self-consciousness (e.g., Simmons & Blyth, 1987; Wigfield & Eccles, 1994). Those who are younger than their classmates during such transitions seem to be particularly vulnerable to these experiences (Fenzel, 1992). These types of effects have been found in other countries, such as Japan (Kozumi, 1995). However, subsequent analyses reveal that the decline is not experienced equally across all ethnic groups, with African American females actually experiencing an increase in self-esteem in these transitions (Dusek & McIntyre, 2003). Dusek and McIntyre review a number of hypotheses that have been offered to explain this tendency for a drop in self-esteem in school transitions, as well as differences by subgroups, calling for more research using better designs and instrumentation.

Other school contexts appear to affect self-esteem. One study found that those attending rural schools had lower self-esteem and less ambitious educational plans than urban adolescents (Sarigiani, Wilson, Petersen, & Vicary, 1990). Other research finds that supportive, better quality teaching can enhance self-esteem, even among those with low self-esteem to begin with (Smith & Smoll, 1990; Stefanich, Wills, & Buss, 1991), as can supportive and validating peer relationships (Kramer, 1991; Robinson, 1995). However, adolescents who are preoccupied with gaining the approval of peers have more school difficulties than those whose self-worth is more independent of peer approval (Harter, Stocker, & Robinson, 1996).

In their massive review of effects of college on development, Pascarella & Terenzini (2005) concluded that sufficient research been carried out to draw conclusions about the effects of college attendance on self-concept. Several studies using "large, representative, national samples" have concluded that academic self-concept and social self-concept (self-confidence) is enhanced "independent of effects attributable to precollege characteristics and to normal maturation" (p. 263). Those who are more engaged in their learning develop a stronger sense of themselves as scholars. However, in the case of self-esteem research, the results are contradictory and afford no reliable conclusions that those who attend college develop higher levels of self-esteem than those who do not.

One final school effect is worth mentioning in light of what has been called the "cult of self-esteem" that has gripped schools in the United States and Canada over the past few decades (Côté & Allahar, 2007). That is, educators increasingly targeted students' self-esteem, often with inflated grades, to entice them to become more engaged in school. However, the research conducted on the relationship between self-esteem and academic achievement (grades) reveals a weak statistical relationship (Dusek & McIntyre, 2003). The more recent and sophisticated research employing structural-equation modeling has looked for reciprocal, causal effects, but it has concluded that these effects are even weaker than the earlier correlational studies suggested, although grades may have a greater effect on self-esteem than self-esteem has on grades (Dusek & McIntyre, 2003).

Family

The research on family and parenting effects on self-esteem generally reveals the same patterns as identity research has found (above). Higher self-esteem is associated with authoritative parenting, as well as with acceptance and warmth provided by other family members (e.g., Dusek & McIntyre, 2003; Luster & McAdoo, 1995). Similarly, the active promotion of both the individuality of adolescents and their connection to parents is associated with more positive forms of self-development (e.g., Cooper, Grotevant, & Condon, 1983; Grotevant & Cooper, 1985). In addition to parenting style, some early research suggested that adolescents in single-mother households had lower self-esteem, especially if both the adolescent and the single-mother were relatively young. However, authoritative parenting skills apparently can offset this effect (Dusek & McIntyre).

Summary

There appears to be some consistency in the research findings from the self psychology approach to adolescent development, both developmentally and when applied to subgroups of the adolescent population. However, inconsistencies abound, in part because of methodological issues associated with the use of differing instrumentation, and in part because of research designs. In fact, this area of research remains controversial from the point of view of some psychologists who feel that self-esteem is a mere epiphenomenon, and not the "vaccine" to positive development that some have contended (DuBois & Tevendale, 1999).

Still, some recent research suggests that self-esteem has certain "essential" properties. For example, using the Japanese version of the Rosenberg Self-Esteem Scale in a longitudinal study on 100 pairs of Japanese adolescent twins (68 pairs of monozygotic twins and 32 pairs of dizygotic twins), Kamakura, Ando, and Ono (2007) calculated that the heritability of self-esteem was 31% at their first data collection and 49% at their second data point. In addition, stability in self-esteem between these two data points was due to both genetic and nonshared environmental effects (unique experiences within the same family), while change in self-esteem was explained only by nonshared environmental influences.

New Directions

In this final section, suggestions are made for compensating for some of the shortcomings identified above in both traditions, and strengthening our understanding of how humans come to understand themselves as "whole persons" in differing cultural contexts, beginning with suggestions for a rapprochement between the two approaches. This section ends with conclusions about the policy implications of identity research.

Reconciling the Identity and Self Approaches to Adolescent Development

Given the separate study of self and identity discussed earlier, the most obvious direction future efforts might take is toward an integration of certain aspects of the self literature with the identity literature. As noted above, the chief obstacle to this is definitional: many of the same terms are used differently in these two bodies of literature. Côté and Levine (2002) argue that an amalgamation such as this would require the development of an agreed-upon taxonomy. One avenue that may be useful in developing this taxonomy is a "division of labor," in which it is acknowledged that the self literature is best applied to early adolescence, the age period when the

most changes in self-esteem and self-concept appear to take place, and the identity literature is best applied mainly to late adolescence (and beyond), the age period(s) during which most identity explorations, commitment formations, and other types of identity consolidations appear to take place. This latter point is further supported by the fact that the empirical measures of identity do not work well in early adolescence, suffering especially in terms of internal consistency estimates, presumably because identities are not sufficiently consolidated to produce acceptable intercorrelations among scale items (cf. Roberts, 2001).

Toward this end, a case has been made that self-concept refers to a person's subjective experiences of concrete behaviors involved in role enactments. When these experiences are the object of reflection, they become first-order schema content for the second-order domains of personal and social identities. In other words, self-concepts are not "identities," when an identity is defined as the second-order consolidation of the first-order reflective experiences of behavior that become the basis for self-concepts. Indeed, the research consistently shows that self-concepts become consolidated during early to mid-adolescence, providing the foundation for identity formation in which these are further consolidated with more abstract beliefs, values, and commitments. It follows, then, that self-concept consolidations are part of what the identity researchers have studied as the early foundations of the personal and social identities that eventually contribute to resolutions of the identity stage (cf. Côté & Levine, 2002).

This logic suggests that in the subjective, experiential realm, personal and social identities are based on cognitive operational structures of self-concepts. This distinction parallels the more generic distinction between cognitive process and cognitive content. In distinguishing between first-order self-concepts and second-order identities, "levels" of reflexive consciousness are explicitly specified, and a basis is laid for postulating that a form of personal agency is involved in identity formation during late adolescence and beyond, which is not involved in early forms of self-concept development.

In addition to attention to taxonomic issues, these two fields need to become more relevant to the real-world experiences of people in various social and cultural contexts. Although the general self and identity literatures have been striving to be more relevant cross-culturally, they have achieved only limited success, as we see in the next two sections. Becoming more relevant means more than just adding variables to represent a widening radius of influence beyond the family and school. It means developing a more macro theoretical orientation that includes a conceptual framework about the nature of cultural and societal effects on identity and self-development (cf. Spencer, 2006). Without some sort of macro orientation, researchers will continue to grope about for ways to make their field more relevant to the realities people face.

This need for a macro orientation applies to all age groups, not just adolescence, so it is useful to examine these broader efforts. The efforts of some self-theorists to broaden this field to include other cultures can be used as a basis for further developments in this regard. The place to start is with reconsidering the "conventional wisdom" that is the product of research conducted in the highly individualistic societies like the United States, where high self-esteem and choice-based identities are considered by many people to constitute optimal outcomes of adolescent development.

Culture Reconsidered: Collectivism, Individualism, and the Self

Both the identity and self literatures are vulnerable to the criticism of ethnocentrism, or even "Ameri-centrism" to the extent that studies have been largely carried out in the United States, and to a lesser extent in Europe following methodologies developed in the United States. Criticism can even find purchase in the narrow focus taken in studies

conducted on adolescents in the United States, to the extent that White, middle-class young people have been the focus of investigation. For example, as we saw, there has been great concern for some time that adolescent females have self-esteem problems, but there is some evidence that this applies mainly to White females, and then only to the extent that they have modeled their behaviors after advertisements portraying unrealistic standards of beauty and sexuality.

It has been further noted that the focus of self psychology on self-esteem appears to be a distinctly American preoccupation. As Arnett (2004) argues, since the 1960s there has been a self-esteem movement in the United States, especially in schools, based on the assumption that if young people value themselves more they will have better academic achievement and peer relations. This movement was fueled in the 1980s by concerns that the self-esteem of females dropped during adolescence, a finding that we now see as suspect from a normative point of view. Arnett further contends that the United States stands out from other Western countries with this concern about self-esteem, attributing it to American individualism. Moreover, while there is a gap between the United States and other Western countries in terms of the value placed on adolescent self-esteem, the gap is even greater in non-Western countries, where self-criticism is valued over self-esteem (e.g., in Japan). The findings reported in this chapter thus need to be viewed in light of the fact that the research has been almost entirely carried out on American adolescents.

This issue is brought into sharper focus when we consider the work of Markus and Kitayama (1991), who postulate that the self varies in terms of schema contents on the dimension "independence–interdependence." The independent self-schema involves a sense of autonomy and separateness from others, and the right to choose the duties and obligations that will form the basis of allegiances with others. The self is perceived as being "whole unto itself," comprised of its own thoughts, beliefs, and feelings. "Others" and social contexts are perceived as outside the self and are utilized as sources of reflected appraisals. Relationships can be situationally variable, but the self is perceived as maintaining a unitary core and as being, more or less, constant. Markus and Kitayama identify this construal of the self as more common in Western societies.

The interdependent self-schema, in contrast, is more likely to be found in the more duty-bound cultures of the Orient, in premodern Western societies, and to some extent more family-oriented modern Western cultures (Schwartz, Montgomery, & Briones, 2006). Here, the self is defined as more context specific and part of a complex set of duties and obligations. While an interdependent self may hold personal beliefs, values, and desires, they are subordinate to these complex duties and obligations. These personal preferences must be controlled and often inhibited if the self is to maintain connection, so the conception of a "whole self unto itself" is not influential in the interdependent self-schema (cf. Mageo, 1997).

Markus and Kitayama (1991) review a substantial amount of literature documenting the cognitive, emotional, and motivational consequences of these two forms of self-schemas. As one would expect, those using an interdependent self-schema are more likely to process self-relevant information in a situationally specific manner and to be attentive to the expectations and needs of others. For example, in a situation requiring decisions about the distribution of property, the interdependent self would likely consider its obligation not to exclude the other from distribution, whereas the independent self would more likely focus on the acquisition rights of the self. It follows that the interdependent self is more likely to experience and utilize "other-focused" emotions and cognitive operations such as empathy, sympathy, and shame, and identify these feelings as properties of context and relationship with the other. Finally, those with the interdependent self-schema can understand their motives and

goals, and thus their sense of personal agency, in terms of accommodating and cooperating with others, with the expectation of reciprocation. In contrast, the independent self can perceive certain others and contexts as objects to be avoided, manipulated, or controlled if the self is to be fulfilled. Duties and obligations are thus seen as matters of individual choice that are part of self-fulfillment.

Future research needs to reevaluate the accumulated findings in the literature on adolescence regarding self-esteem and self-concept (drops, changes, group differences, etc.) in terms of how much they represent the formation of the independent self rather than the interdependent self, with the caveat that these ideas should not be overextended (Oyserman, Coon, & Kemmelmeier, 2002). For an example, see Takata (2002, 2007) who published empirical findings suggesting that in contemporary Japanese society, interdependent self-schemas are passively acquired in late childhood, actively internalized in adolescence, and then re-arranged into more independent self-schemas in adulthood (presumably as part of the formation of adult identities now functional in contemporary Japanese society).

Identity in Cross-Cultural Perspective

A similar logic about independence–interdependence can be applied to identity, although there has not been a sustained effort to develop a theoretical framework based on this logic. Accordingly, it is necessary to piece together seemingly disparate sources.

On the question of cross-cultural applicability of the identity status paradigm, we can consult the historical record provided by anthropologist Margaret Mead during the 1920s—one of the few such records regarding non-Western forms of adolescence (Côté, 1994). In her pioneering book on the nature of adolescence, *Coming of Age in Samoa* (1928), Mead provided an ethnography of adolescence in Polynesian Samoan culture as it was becoming Westernized.

Samoan culture before contact with the West would be called a "foreclosed society" from the point of view of the identity status paradigm (cf. Marcia, 1976b). In foreclosed societies, of which precontact Samoa would have been a case, choice-based identities would not have been common; in fact, it would have been culturally inappropriate to form an autonomous identity that involved a questioning and potential rejection of parental values and beliefs (cf. Mead, 1928, with Marcia, 1993). Instead, Mead described how passage through the identity stage was well structured and orderly for most Samoan adolescents as they appropriated parental beliefs and cultural roles into a consolidated adult identity based on cultural identifications. As this structure broke down over the history of contact with the West, identity formation became more conflict-based, the transition to adulthood became more problematic (including epidemic suicide rates), and the intergenerational transmission of culture became more problematic (Côté, 1994).

In cultures in which identity formation is less choice based, child-rearing techniques and cultural conditioning can emotionally prepare children and adolescents for this social convention, by effecting a high degree of conformity-oriented behavior and a low degree of individualized or "creative" behavior. Indeed, child-rearing techniques similar to those in precontact Samoa prevailed in other South Pacific cultures as well, and continue to do so in certain respects. Crocombe (1989) argues many South Pacific cultures typically socialize young people "not to 'push' themselves . . . much of their cultural conditioning has taught them not to innovate, not to work out their own destiny, not to strive to improve their position" (p. 40). Erikson (1959, p. 78) touched on this issue in reference to the "dilemma of choice" being "a particular problem in a culture in which there seems to be a great deal of choice." He contrasted choice- and conformity-oriented cultures, noting that choice and conformity are:

. . . relative matters and we need to examine . . . the specific relationship of choice to conformity in various cultures. Inner identity . . . is a combination of the two; for I cannot feel identical with myself if I do not feel identical with something that has been created and distilled in my culture over a long period. To be firmly told by tradition who one is can be experienced as freedom; while the permission to make original choices can feel like enslavement to some dark fate.

Chapman and Nicholls (1976) empirically tested this cultural difference in identity formation in 1970s' New Zealand by assessing *occupational* identity status among Maori (Polynesian descent) and Pakeha (European descent) high school students. They found that more Maori adolescents were identity diffused, while more Pakeha youth were identity achieved (p. 61). These findings were interpreted to mean that "Maoris typically see occupation as a means of providing the necessities of life and of making it possible to extend hospitality while Pakeha more commonly see occupations as a vehicle to and index of success" (p. 65). Noting differing cultural meanings regarding choice and commitment around occupation, Chapman and Nicholls argue that the "greater frequency of identity diffusion among Maoris may indicate that this is an adaptive, role-appropriate status for Maoris" (p. 69).

The Chapman and Nichols study raises several questions. For example, just why might identity diffusion be adaptive for one group and not another? If it is adaptive, then certain forms of ego and self development must be associated with it. What are these forms of development and how do they take place (cf. Mageo, 1997)? The reader is reminded that from Erikson's perspective, people in all societies, including "foreclosed" ones, should have a generally good sense of ego identity if their community effectively supports them in their roles. Hence, a specific research question that can be pursued is what is substituted for *conscious decision making* as a source of self and identity development in conformity-oriented cultures. One avenue to explore in this regard is the *guidance* the culture may provide the young that makes conscious decision-making unnecessary as a stimulus to development. Erikson (1959, p. 76) alluded to this when he wrote that:

> Ego Identity also rests on the inner continuity between what one was as a child and what one is going to be as an adult. Such inner continuity and sameness are supported by cultural processes so long as they function with great sagacity. Rites, rituals, and traditions seek to give the individual a sense that, on each stage of his long childhood and apprenticeship, everything occurred in pre-ordained steps, so that he who looks into his future and tests his opportunities will perceive his past stages as adding up to something.

We see from these considerations that when one attempts to apply the identity status paradigm cross-culturally, its implications are undertheorized and underresearched. Because of this, the paradigm does not provide the theoretical concepts with which to understand the types of development that might be linked with specific social and cultural contexts, such as those that are not choice-based and self-focused. In contrast, in Erikson's general theory, people of all cultures can develop a strong sense of ego identity based on role validation and community integration, especially when there is a lack of ambiguity regarding beliefs (cf. Côté & Levine, 1987). In speaking to this general issue, Erikson (1963, pp. 185–186) wrote that:

> [E]ven the most "savage" culture must strive for what we . . . call a "strong ego" in its majority or at least in its dominant minority—i.e., an individual core firm and flexible enough to reconcile the necessary contradictions in any human organization, . . . and above all to emerge from…infancy with a sense of identity and an idea of integrity.

Marcia (1993, p. 41) commented on this issue by arguing that cross-cultural validity "does not mean identical behavior. Foreclosures in a 'foreclosed' setting ought not to be found behaving exactly like Foreclosures in a setting that encourages [choice-based] moratoria."

While this may be true, the following position by Marcia does not take us out of the above-identified conceptual dilemma: "Rather, cross-cultural validity means that, taking into account the processes underlying an identity status, one ought to be able to make verifiable predictions about that status's behavior in a given cultural context" (Marcia, 1993, p. 41). As the Chapman and Nichols study suggests, the problem is that in many cultural settings Western-style "identity status" has little variation—it is either diffused or foreclosed depending on the identity domain (occupation and ideology, respectively). The question then becomes what variation exists with identity formation in, say, a "foreclosed setting." For example, in a conformity-oriented (foreclosed) culture are there developmental changes based on ritualized realignments of identifications, which would be overlooked when identity formation is defined in terms of choice making? These are the types of questions that need to be posed and explored in cross-cultural research, and Erikson's writings are rich with clues as to how to proceed, as suggested above in the discussion of the varieties of identity crisis he identified. If we approach a culture only with a paradigm based on choice-driven development, we will not be sensitive to other forms of self and identity development (cf. Kroger, 1993, pp. 11–12).

Questions about the cross-cultural sensitivity of our theories and measures can be extended to issues of social and historical change (see chapter 17, vol. 2 of this *Handbook*). Erikson and Marcia formulated their frameworks in the mid-1900s, as did the pioneers in self-esteem and self-concept research. The possibility emerges that some fundamental societal conditions have changed that affect both identity formation and self-development, the implications of which we now turn.

New Societal Conditions in Western Societies

Interview questions about religion and politics formed the original basis of the identity status assessment of respondents' ideological values and beliefs. However, in contrast to adolescents of the mid-twentieth century, it is possible that religious and political issues have an entirely different relevance for many young people today. In many countries, current cohorts are at a historical low level of involvement in organized religion and the mainstream political process (e.g., Gidengil, Blais, Nevitte, & Nadeau, 2003); among many of those who take an interest, involvements tend to be more individualized, based on a cafeteria-style picking and choosing of various elements that they find personally appealing (Côté, 2000). For example, in Canada, only 12% of young people attended services regularly in the 1990s, down dramatically from midcentury (e.g., Clark, 1998).

According to Statistics Canada, the percentage of Canadians reporting "no religion" on their census forms increased from less than 1% prior to 1971 to 16% in 2001, and 40% of those reporting no religion were 24 or younger (Statistics Canada, 2003). Moreover, about one-quarter of children 14 and younger were listed on their 2001 census forms (by their parents) as having no affiliation to an organized religion. Given the growing ambivalence, and the consequent low level of community pressure to explore these issues, we should no longer expect these belief systems to be a source of normative explorations that are pivotal in terms of forging or adopting a worldview.

Accordingly, we may need to consider that there are new sources of identity crisis focused on different issues and belief systems, especially among college-attending youth. While it remains to be empirically verified, one type could be called the "postmodern identity crisis," not because we might be moving into a postmodern society (Chandler, 1995; Côté, 2000), but because some people embrace and celebrate fluid identities associated with superficial interpersonal displays of appearance, a lack of core character and consistency, and eschewing social commitments in favor of contextual allegiances (cf. Gergen, 1991).

In Erikson's terms, some young people can *lack* a sense of fidelity—something "larger than themselves" to have faith in—and will experience a sense of identity confusion as a result.

Currently, postmodern philosophy (e.g., Hollinger, 1994) provides a convenient but paradoxical solution to this dilemma—to have faith that there is nothing in which to have faith. This dilemma appears to be commonplace among university students in the arts and humanities, where their curriculum can teach them to think this way and where they may find inspiration from professors who have embraced academic postmodernism. Others may pick up a moral position akin to this from Western secular society, which has become increasingly relativistic (cf. Jacoby, 2008). Those experiencing this form of crisis are reminiscent of what Marcia (1980) once called "alienated Achievements" in the 1960s and 1970s, who were committed to a lack of commitment as a form of social protest. Erikson (1968) identified a similar group of youth in the 1960s as "Protean youth."

This source, and other sources of identity conflicts and explorations, needs to be identified and researched if we are to bring this area of research into the twenty-first century. At the same time, this new research paradigm will need to take account of the prolonged transition to adulthood that now appears to be normative, an issue to which we now turn.

New Measures to Assess the Prolonged Transition to Adulthood

Based on Erikson's postulations regarding the moratorium period embedded in the identity stage, and his inclusion of college attendance as a form of moratorium, we would expect identity formation to proceed at variable rates for people, depending on their circumstances and opportunities. Given the increasing rates of postsecondary attendance in most developed countries (Côté & Allahar, 2007), it should now be common for resolution of the identity stage to be delayed until well into the 20s—especially in reference to the primary tasks associated with the adoption of identities with which to function in the adult world. Following Erikson, Arnett (2000) contends that three areas of identity exploration are relevant during this age period, which he calls "emerging adulthood": worldview, work, and love. While the concept of emerging adulthood has stimulated considerable research, the question that remains to be answered empirically is just how much *active* identity exploration takes place during this extended transition to adulthood. The issue of *active exploration* is important because of Arnett's claims that emerging adulthood is a new developmental stage. If the transition is delayed for economic or social reasons, many young people may simply be waiting for age-based opportunities to become available, and may not be active in their identity formation beyond what they experienced during their teens. Instead, identity changes may be more on a trial-and-error basis than as a result of deliberate explorations (e.g., Côté & Bynner, 2008).

In fact, the literature is sparse concerning identity formation in the 20s independent of the research conducted on college students, who have been treated as (late) adolescents. As noted above, Pascarella and Terenzini (1991, 2005) report that there is little demonstrable effect of college attendance for variables such as identity formation, ego development, maturity, and other aspects of personality development, net of maturational effects (i.e., changes in these variables might take place without someone attending college). At the same time, some research based on the identity status paradigm reveals instabilities in identity status following adolescence. For example, Fadjukoff and Pulkkinen (2003) followed over 200 Finnish adults from ages 27 to 36, and again to 42. They report that because of the piecemeal approach to identity issues that most adults in their sample took, they had a difficult time determining an overall identity status for most adults, even when based on same-status classifications for only three or more domains out of five (politics, religion, occupation, relationships, and lifestyle).

Fewer than 10% of those studied shared all five domains in the same status at any of the three data collection points. Overall, only one-half of the sample had the same overall identity status at all three points, even with the three out of five criterion. Because diffusion was more common than achievement in the ideological areas, and cohort diffusion level actually increased with age, Fadjukoff and Pulkkinen speculated that this may be a reflection of "postmodern" trends. Occupational identity status was the most stable of the domains, showing the most progression toward achievement and the least regression to "less mature" statuses, especially between ages 36 and 42.

One problem in studying older age groups may be that the identity statuses were developed to characterize adolescent development around expressions of present commitments and future courses of action. While these results may provide gross estimates of identity activities, from the Eriksonian view, any commitments expressed during the identity moratorium should be viewed as experimental, and therefore unstable, unless there is evidence that the person has put them into concrete courses of action. For example, a 17-year-old stating that she is committed to becoming a lawyer needs to be taken lightly, because it is quite likely that those plans will change depending on ensuing circumstances (like getting into a university, getting good grades there, getting into a law school, passing the bar exams, and so forth). A 27-year-old stating that he is a lawyer would be a much more convincing indicator of identity achievement in the area of occupation.

With respect to ideological identity, Côté (2006b) found in a 10-year longitudinal study very little activity in religious and political identity formation during the 20s, suggesting that most young people make up their minds in their adolescence, or avoid the issues entirely and then stick with that position. Instead, it appears that this period can indeed constitute a prolonged identity moratorium in the Eriksonian sense, which for many is not over, even by the late 20s or later. With regard to the progress of the cohort in terms resolving the identity stage (as measured by the Identity Stage Resolution Index—ISRI),[3] some normative gains were observed during the early 20s in terms of forming a sense of adult identity, but none were evident for the sense of societal identity. In fact, most of the cohort progress in resolving the identity stage was made between the early and late 20s, not between the late teens and early 20s, as Arnett postulates regarding emerging adulthood (e.g., 2000, p. 469).

Based on the ISRI, a more multidimensional measure of identity formation during the prolonged transition to adulthood has been developed with items relevant to the life circumstances of 20- and 30-year-olds (Identity Issues Inventory—III; Côté & Roberts, 2005; Roberts, 2007). It shows that key forms of identity formation in the areas of self-identity (integration and differentiation) and societal identity (worldview and work roles) at three levels of identity (ego, personal, and social identity) extend well into the 30s for many people, and that a significant proportion appear to be stalled or arrested on key identity issues associated with the assumption of an adult identity. Initial results with this measure suggest that identity formation (now) continues beyond adolescence, but stagnates in the late 20s and early 30s for a significant proportion of the population. Gains in identity resolution then appear to made after the age of 35, suggesting that identity development and the acquisition of adult roles is now stretching into the late 30s.

Findings based on the Identity Issues Inventory support neither Arnett's claims that the early 20s is now the prime phase of identity formation, nor postmodernists' claims that identities are now fluid, fragmented, and "de-centered" as a "normal" state of affairs (cf. Chandler, 1995; Gergen, 1991).

Finally, as new research is undertaken to understand this more prolonged identity formation, it may be worth noting Côté and Levine's (1988) argument that the identity statuses may have a strong characterological component, such that some people have

personality dispositions that may change during the identity stage, but others have dispositions that are likely to remain much the way they were before that stage (cf. Schwartz, 2001). For example, a personality type that is conformist and deferent to authority, like the prototypical foreclosure (Marcia, 1980), is not likely to be radically affected by opportunities for nonconformity and rejection of authority, even during their college years. Similarly, a diffused personality type is not likely to suddenly become focused and searching, even if given the freedom to do so in college. Other personality or character types are more open to change, and these are ones we would expect to be most affected by opportunities to explore themselves and their world, as permitted by an institutionalized moratorium. This "character-type hypothesis" helps explains why many adults score as foreclosure and diffusion, as noted above, while only a minority has a history of in-depth and active identity explorations.

CONCLUSIONS: EXPLORING POLICY IMPLICATIONS

After a half century of theorizing and research, what can be concluded about how much this area can contribute to practical matters in people's lives and by implication in the applied, policy realm?

To begin, it needs to be acknowledged that these fields are not as well respected as other areas of adolescent psychology in terms of their practical implications. Many social scientists do not appear to see these efforts as sufficiently rigorous to warrant their attention (see discussions by Côté, 2006a; DuBois & Tevendale, 1999). This has had the unfortunate effect of reducing the types of funding opportunities that could lead to the groundbreaking studies that would gain the attention of policy makers. Pascarella & Terenzini (2005) are somewhat critical of this area because of its lack of methodological rigor, with no studies controlling for maturation effects when examining identity formation in college (this would require a comparison group on non–college attendees). Admittedly, there is a cause-and-effect problem here, because if funding agencies provided the money to conduct this (expensive) research, these fields would garner more respect, assuming that more and more impressive research were published from this funding.

Policy makers need viable frameworks if they are to apply academic concerns to real-world problems. Accordingly, more self and identity research needs to move from the pure to applied realm. This is not to abandon pure research, which is essential in testing theoretical frameworks, but very little self and identity research has been carried out in applied settings, so we have little idea of the practical utility of most of the concepts used in these fields (cf. Ferrer-Wreder, Montgomery, & Lorente, 2003). A model that can be consulted for this purpose is the "applied developmental science" model (Lerner, Fisher, & Weinberg, 2000), which proposes that scholars and communities become partners in the knowledge-generation process and that multiple methods be used to triangulate on the processes under scrutiny.

There are many obstacles to taking self and identity research into a more applied realm, especially in individualistic societies where ideas of freedom of choice are virtually sacred. Given the increasingly choice-based nature of identity formation in Western—and other—societies, an obvious obstacle is proposing applications that influence people's choice making. For example, although we know that there are considerable drawbacks in Western contexts to identity diffusion in terms of school failure, risk behaviors, and the like, a sizable proportion of the population can be thus characterized, even in adulthood, as noted earlier. Given the magnitude of the population that could be characterized as diffused (and perhaps they are happily so as part of a characterological disposition), and the "rights" of people to adopt whatever stances they like to the commitments in their lives, what can we recommend to policy makers? And why would

policy makers want to "interfere" with people's choices? Moreover, as we saw in the case of some South Pacific societies, forms of identity diffusion appear to be functional in these non-Western cultures.

While this might seem like an intractable problem for modern democracies, it needs to be recognized that modern democracies *have* developed and continue to support institutions that directly and deliberately affect people's choices in their identity formation, most notably educational systems. It is within the logic of existing educational systems that we perhaps have the most hope of positively affecting identity formation in the area of choice making. Such efforts need to be informed by a sophisticated view of choice making itself, and the recent work of Schwartz (2000, 2004) helps to bring to light the complex, potentially negative aspects of unguided self-determination, a problem about which Erikson wrote as a potential form of "enslavement to some dark fate" (1959, p. 78). Schwartz argues that people in individualistic societies face a "tyranny of choice" by the very nature of excessive choice-making requirements for which they are not necessarily equipped. Certainly, there are liberating potentials to a greater freedom of choice, but ostensibly unconstrained choice can be paradoxically constraining, as in situations of having too many choices with too little information, living with the consequences of poor choices, and experiencing the various negative psychological consequences routinely associated with facing numerous choices on a daily basis.

More generally, the identity and self fields may contribute to policy concerns by investigating the wider benefit of learning and education for identity formation (cf. Dreyer, 1994). Work in this area has already begun in England through the efforts of the British government in funding the Centre for the Wider Benefits of Learning at the University of London (Schuller, Preston, Hammond, Brassett-Grundy, & Bynner, 2004). The wider benefits of learning, in general, are myriad, including better health and more involvements in community enhancing activities. Some of these benefits are sustaining of the person's capacities, while others are transformative, enhancing the person's capabilities. The identity benefits of learning potentially include greater satisfaction with the course of one's life and success in one's life project (Côté, 2002), as well as better self-understanding, independent and critical thought, and a reflexive awareness of one's place in the world (Schuller et al.), but work in this area has just begun. Of course, "education" varies in quality, and much mass education has become perfunctory, even at the tertiary level (Côté & Allahar, 2006, 2007). For example, the high school diploma in the United States has recently been called no more than an "attendance certificate" (American Diploma Project, 2004). Thus, it is clear that there is ample room in the curriculum to experiment with innovations that yield returns in more aspects of people's lives beyond an obligatory academic education, including their identity formation. As Dreyer aptly notes:

[T]he need for educational reform in the U.S. public schools is clearly recognized. What remains to be seen is whether developmental psychologists, such as identity theorists, will play a role in that reform or will retire to the world of abstract research. . . . (1994, p. 137)

Thus, we already have an institutional context in place in which to seek to direct self and identity development in positive ways. If researchers are creative enough in what they study, and convincing enough in disseminating their results, identity and self development may come to be seen at least as important as the academic curriculum in influencing students' future life chances, and this field may become one of the more important policy vehicles taking us into the twenty-first century.

ENDNOTES

1. This is a promising framework that incorporates an Eriksonian-based model of identity as a mediating factor in the coping abilities of diverse youth to their stressors and vulnerabilities.

2. Dunkel and Anthis (2001) argue that the creation of possible selves is a mechanism involved in identity formation, based on their findings that identity exploration is correlated with the number of possible selves a person generates and identity commitments are associated with the consistency of hoped-for selves.

3. The ISRI is a 6-item scale that taps identity-based markers representing the degree to which individuals feel they have (a) matured into adulthood (Adult Identity Resolution Scale; AIRS) and (b) found a more or less permanent niche (lifestyle and community) in life (Societal Identity Resolution Scale; SIRS). High scores can be taken as an indicator that a person has settled key aspects of identity formation in the conventional/traditional sense of accepting mature and committed roles in an adult community. Low scores can be taken to mean that a person does not feel mature and does not have stable roles in an adult community.

REFERENCES

Adams, G. R. (1985). Family correlates of female adolescents' ego identity development. *Journal of Adolescence, 8,* 69–82.

Adams, G. R., Bennion, L., & Huh, K. (1987). *Objective measure of ego identity status: A reference manual.* Unpublished manuscript: Guelph University, Ontario, Canada.

Adams, G. R., Côté, J. E, & Marshall, S. (2001). *Parent–adolescent relationships and identity development: A literature review and policy statement.* Ottawa: Health Canada.

Adams, G. R., Dyk, P. A. H., & Bennion, L. D. (1987). Parent–adolescent relationships and identity formation. *Family Perspective, 21,* 249–260.

Adams, G. R., & Jones, R. M. (1983). Female adolescents' identity development: Age comparisons and perceived child-rearing experience. *Developmental Psychology, 19,* 2, 249–256.

Adams, G. R., & Marshall, S. K. (1996). A developmental social psychology of identity: Understanding the person-in-context. *Journal of Adolescence, 19,* 429–442.

Adams, G. R., Ryan, B., & Keating, L. (2000). Family relationships, academic environments, and psychosocial development during the university experience: A longitudinal investigation. *Journal of Adolescent Research, 15,* 99–122.

Allahar, A, & Côté, J. E. (1998). *Richer and poorer: The structure of social inequality in Canada.* Toronto: Lorimer Press.

American Diploma Project (2004). *Ready or not: Creating a high school diploma that counts.* Washington, DC: Achieve, Inc. Retrieved December 9, 2004, from www.achieve.org.

Archer, S. L. (1993). Identity in relational contexts: A methodological proposal. In J. Kroger (Ed.), *Discussions on ego identity* (pp. 75–99). Hillsdale, NJ: Lawrence Erlbaum.

Archer, S. L., & Waterman, A. S. (1990). Varieties of diffusions and foreclosures: An exploration of subcategories of the identity statuses. *Journal of Adolescent Research, 5,* 96–111.

Arnett, J. J. (2000). Emerging adulthood: A theory of development from the late teens through the twenties. *American Psychologist, 55,* 469–480.

Arnett, J. J. (2004). *Adolescence and emerging adulthood: A cultural approach* (2nd ed). Upper Saddle River, NJ: Prentice Hall.

Aunola, K., Stattin, H., & Nurmi, J. (2000). Parenting styles and adolescents' achievement strategies. *Journal of Adolescence, 23,* 205–222.

Balistreri, E., Busch-Rossnagel, N. A., & Geisinger, K. F. (1995). Development and preliminary validation of the Ego Identity Process Questionnaire. *Journal of Adolescence, 18,* 179–190.

Barber, B. K. (1996). Parental psychological control: Revisiting a neglected construct. *Child Development, 67,* 3296–3319.

Baumrind, D. (1968). Authoritarian vs. authoritative control. *Adolescence, 3,* 255–272.

Baumeister, R. F. (1990). Suicide as escape from self. *Psychological Review, 97,* 90–113.

Baumeister, R. F. (1997). The self and society: Changes, problems, and opportunities. In R. D. Ashmore & L. Jussim (Eds.), *Self and identity: Fundamental issues* (pp. 191–217). New York: Oxford University Press.

Baumeister, R. F. (1998). The self. In D. T. Gilbert, S. T. Fiske & G. Lindzey (Eds.), *The handbook of social psychology* (4th ed.) (pp. 680–740). New York: McGraw-Hill.

Baumeister, R. F., & Muraven, M. (1996). Identity as adaptation to social, cultural, and historical context. *Journal of Adolescence, 19*, 405–416.

Berman, S., Montgomery, M., & Kurtines, W. (2004). The development and validation of a new measure of identity distress. *Identity: An International Journal of Theory and Research, 4*, 1–8.

Berzonsky, M. D. (1992). A process perspective on identity and stress management. In G. R. Adams, T. P. Gullota, & R. Montemayor (Eds.), *Adolescent identity formation* (pp. 193–215). Newbury Park: Sage.

Berzonsky, M., & Kinney, A. (1998, March). *Identity commitment, identity style and parental authority.* Paper presented at the biennial meetings of the Society for Research on Adolescence, San Diego, California.

Berzonsky, M. D., & Kuk, L. S. (2000). Identity status, identity processing style, and transition to university. *Journal of Adolescent Research, 15*, 81–98.

Block, J. H., & Robins, R. W. (1993). A longitudinal study of consistency and change in self-esteem from early childhood to early adulthood. *Child Development, 64*, 909–923.

Bosma, H. A. (1985). *Identity development in adolescence: Coping with commitments.* Groningen, Netherlands: University of Groningen Press.

Bosma, H. A., & Gerritts, R. S. (1985). Family functioning and identity status in adolescence. *Journal of Early Adolescence, 5*, 69–80.

Boyes, M. C, & Chandler, M. J. (1992). Cognitive development, epistemic doubt, and identity formation in adolescence. *Journal of Youth and Adolescence, 21*, 277–304.

Brand, D. (1987). Black women and work: The impact of racially constructed gender roles in the sexual division of labour. *Fireweed, 25*, 28–37.

Broughton, J. (1981). The divided self in adolescence. *Human Development, 24*, 13–32.

Byrne, B. M. (1996). Academic self-concept: Its structure, measurement, and relation with academic achievement. In B. A. Bracken (Ed.), *Handbook of self-concept* (pp. 287–316). New York: John Wiley & Sons.

Byrne, B. M., & Shavelson, R. J. (1996). On the structure of social self-concept for pre-, early, and late adolescents: A test of the Shavelson, Hubner, and Stanton (1976) model. *Journal of Personality and Social Psychology, 70*, 599–613.

Cass, V. (1979). Homosexual identity formation: A theoretical model. *Journal of Homosexuality, 9*, 105–126.

Chandler, M. J. (1995). Is this the end of "The age of development," or what? or: Please wait a minute Mr. Post-man. *The Genetic Epistemologist, 23*, 1–11.

Chapman, J. W., & Nicholls, J. G. (1976). Occupational identity status, occupational preference, and field dependence in Maori and Pakeha boys. *Journal of Cross-Cultural Psychology, 7*, 61–72.

Chiam, H-K. (1987). Change in self-concept during adolescence. *Adolescence, 22*, 69–76.

Chickering, A. W. (1969). *Education and identity.* San Francisco: Jossey-Bass.

Choi, J. W., & Lee, Y. H. (1998). The effects of actual self, ideal self, and self-discrepancy on depression. *Korean Journal of Clinical Psychology, 17*, 69–87.

Clark, W. (1998, Autumn). Religious observance: Marriage and family. *Canadian Social Trends*, 2–7.

Constantinople, A. (1969). An Eriksonian measure of personality development in college students. *Developmental Psychology, 1*(4), 357–372.

Cooley, C. H. (1902). *Human nature and the social order.* New York: Scribner's.

Cooper, C. R., Grotevant, H. D., & Condon, S. M. (1983). Individuality and connectedness in the family as a context for adolescent identity formation and role-taking skill. In H. D. Grotevant & C. R. Cooper (Eds.), *Adolescent development in the family* (New Directions in Child Development, No. 22). San Francisco: Jossey-Bass.

Coopersmith, S. (1967). *The antecedents of self-esteem.* San Francisco: Freeman.

Côté, J. E. (1986). Identity crisis modality: A technique for assessing the structure of the identity crisis. *Journal of Adolescence, 9*, 321–335.

Côté, J. E. (1994). *Adolescent storm and stress: An evaluation of the Mead–Freeman controversy.* Hillsdale, NJ: Lawrence Erlbaum.

Côté, J. E. (1996). Identity: A multidimensional analysis. In G. R. Adams, R. Montemayor, & T. P. Gullotta (Eds.), *Psychosocial development during adolescence: Progress in developmental contextualism* (pp. 130–180). Thousand Oaks, CA: Sage.

Côté, J. E. (1997). An empirical test of the identity capital model. *Journal of Adolescence, 20*, 577–597.

Côté, J. E. (2000). *Arrested adulthood: The changing nature of maturity and identity.* New York: New York University Press.

Côté, J. E. (2002). The role of identity capital in the transition to adulthood: The individualization thesis examined. *Journal of Youth Studies, 5*, 117–134.

Côté, J. E. (2006a). Identity studies: How close are we to developing a social science of identity? An appraisal of the field. *Identity: An International Journal of Theory and Research, 6*(1), 3–25.

Côté, J. E. (2006b). Emerging adulthood as an institutionalized moratorium: Risks and benefits to identity formation. In J. J. Arnett & J. Tanner (Eds.), *Emerging adults in America: Coming of age in the 21st century* (pp. 85–116). Washington, DC: American Psychological Association.

Côté, J. E. (2006c). Acculturation and identity: The role of individualization theory. *Human Development, 49*, 31–35.

Côté, J. E. (2007, October). *Capital ideas: Mass education and agency.* Keynote address for the conference *International Congress on Social Capital and Networks of Trust*, Agora Centre, University of Jyväskylä, Finland.

Côté, J. E., & Allahar, A. (1996). *Generation on hold: Coming of age in the late twentieth century.* New York: New York University Press.

Côté, J. E., & Allahar, A. (2006). *Critical youth studies: A Canadian focus.* Toronto: Pearson Education.

Côté, J. E., & Allahar, A. (2007). *Ivory tower blues: A university system in crisis.* Toronto: University of Toronto Press.

Côté, J. E., & Bynner, J. (2008). Changes in the transition to adulthood in the UK and Canada: The role of structure and agency in emerging adulthood. *Journal of Youth Studies, 11*, 251–268.

Côté, J. E. & Levine, C. (1983). Marcia and Erikson: The relationships among ego identity status, neuroticism, dogmatism, and purpose in life. *Journal of Youth and Adolescence, 12*, 43–53.

Côté, J. E., & Levine, C. (1987). A formulation of Erikson's theory of ego identity formation. *Developmental Review, 9*, 273–325.

Côté, J. E., & Levine, C. (1988). A critical examination of the ego identity status paradigm. *Developmental Review, 8*, 147–184.

Côté, J. E, & Levine, C. (2000). Attitude versus aptitude: Is intelligence or motivation more important for positive higher educational outcomes? *Journal of Adolescent Research, 15*, 58–80.

Côté, J. E, & Levine, C. (2002). *Identity formation, agency, and culture: A social psychological synthesis.* Mahwah, NJ: Lawrence Erlbaum.

Côté, J. E., & Roberts, S. E. (2005). *The Identity Issues Inventory: Preliminary manual.* Unpublished manuscript. London: University of Western Ontario.

Côté, J. E., & Schwartz, S. (2002). Comparing psychological and sociological approaches to identity: Identity status, identity capital, and the individualization process. *Journal of Adolescence, 2002, 25,* 571–586.

Crocombe, R. (1989). *The South Pacific: An introduction* (5th ed.). Suva, Fiji: University of the South Pacific.

Cross, W. E., Jr. (1991). *Shades of Black: Diversity in African-American identity.* Philadelphia: Temple University Press.

Danziger, K. (1997). The historical formation of selves. In R. D. Ashmore & L. Jussim (Eds.), *Self and identity: Fundamental issues* (pp. 137–159). New York: Oxford University Press.

D'Augelli, A. (1994). Identity development and sexual orientation: Toward a model of lesbian, gay, and bisexual development. In E. Trickett, R. Watts, & D. Birman (Eds.), *Human diversity: Perspectives on people in context* (pp. 312–333). San Francisco: Jossey-Bass.

DePaulo, B. M., Kenny, D. A., Hoover, C. W., Webb, W., & Oliver, P. V. (1987). Accuracy of person perception: Do people know what kinds of impressions they convey? *Journal of Personality and Social Psychology, 52,* 303–315.

Dreyer, P. H. (1994). Designing curricular identity interventions for secondary schools. In S. L. Archer (Ed.), *Interventions for adolescent identity development* (pp. 121–140). Thousand Oaks, CA: Sage.

Dubois, D., Felner, R., Brand, S., Phillip, R., & Lease, A. (1996). Early adolescent self-esteem: A developmental–ecological framework and assessment strategy. *Journal of Research on Adolescence, 6,* 543–579.

DuBois, D. L., & Tevendale, H. D. (1999). Self-esteem in childhood and adolescence: Vaccine or epiphenomenon? *Applied and Preventative Psychology, 8,* 103–117.

Dunkel, C. S., & Anthis, K. S. (2001). The role of possible selves in identity formation: A short-term longitudinal study. *Journal of Adolescence, 24,* 765–776.

Dusek, J. B., & McIntyre, J. G. (2003). Self-concept and self-esteem development. In G. R. Adams, & M. D. Berzonsky (Eds.), *Blackwell handbook of adolescence* (pp. 290–309). Malden, MA: Blackwell Publishing.

Dyk, P. (1990). *Family relations factors that facilitate or inhibit middle adolescent identity development.* Unpublished doctoral thesis. Logan: Utah State University.

Dyk, P. H., & Adams, G. R. (1990). Identity and intimacy: An initial investigation of three theoretical models using cross-lag panel correlations. *Journal of Youth and Adolescence, 19,* 91–110.

Emirbayer, M., & Mische, A. (1998). What is agency? *American Journal of Sociology, 103,* 962–1023.

Enright, R., Lapsley, D., Drivas, A., & Fehr, L. (1980). Parental influences on the development of adolescent autonomy and identity. *Journal of Youth and Adolescence, 9,* 529–545.

Erikson, E. H. (1958). *Young man Luther.* New York: Norton.

Erikson, E. H. (1959). Late adolescence. In D. H. Funkenstein (Ed.), *The student and mental health: An international view* (pp. 66–106). Cambridge, MA: Riverside Press.

Erikson, E. H. (1963). *Childhood and society* (2nd ed.). New York: Norton.

Erikson, E. H. (1968). *Identity: Youth and crisis.* New York: Norton.

Erikson, E. H. (1975). *Life history and the historical moment.* New York: Norton.

Erikson, E. H. (1979). Report from Vikram: Further perspectives on the life cycle. In S. Kakar (Ed.), *Identity and adulthood* (pp. 13–34). Bombay: Oxford University Press.

Erikson, E. H. (1980). *Identity and the life cycle: A reissue.* New York: Norton.

Espin, O. M., & Gawelek, M. A. (1992). Women's diversity: Ethnicity, race, class, and gender in theories of feminist psychology. In L. S. Brown & M. Ballou (Eds.), *Personality and psychopathology: Feminist reappraisals* (pp. 88–107). New York: Guilford Press.

Evans, R. I. (1969). *Dialogue with Erik Erikson.* New York: Dutton.

Fadjukoff, P., & Pulkkinen, L. (2005). Identity processes in adulthood: Diverging domains. *Identity: An International Journal of Theory and Research, 5,* 1–20.

Felson, R. B. (1989). Parents and the reflected appraisal process: A longitudinal analysis. *Journal of Personality and Social Psychology, 56,* 965–971.

Fenzel, L. M. (1992). The effect of relative age on self-esteem, role strain, GPA, and anxiety. *Journal of Early Adolescence, 12,* 253–266.

Ferrer-Wreder, L., Montgomery, M. J., & Lorente, C. C. (2003). Identity promotion, adolescence. In T. P. Gullotta & M. Bloom (Eds.), *Encyclopedia of Primary Prevention and Health Promotion* (pp. 600–606). New York: Kluwer Academic.

Fitts, W. H. (1965). *The Tennessee Self-Concept Scale.* Nashville, TN: Counsellor Recordings and Tests.

Gecas, V., & Burke, P. J. (1995). Self and identity. In K. S. Cook, G. A. Fine, & J. S. House (Eds.), *Sociological perspectives on social psychology* (pp. 41-67). Boston: Allyn and Bacon.

Gecas, V., & Seff, M. A. (1990). Families and adolescents: A review of the 1980s. *Journal of Marriage and the Family, 52,* 941–958.

Gergen, K. J. (1991). *The saturated self: Dilemmas of identity in contemporary life.* New York: Basic Books.

Gidengil, E., Blais, A., Nevitte, N., & Nadeau, N. (2003). Turned off or tuned out? Youth participation in politics. *Electoral Insight, 5,* 9–14.

Grotevant, H. D. (1983). The contribution of the family to the facilitation of identity formation in early adolescence. *Journal of Early Adolescence, 3,* 225–237.

Grotevant, H. D. (1986). Assessment of identity development: Current issues and future directions. *Journal of Adolescent Research, 1,* 175–182.

Grotevant, H. D. (1987). Toward a process model of identity formation. *Journal of Adolescent Research, 2,* 203–202.

Grotevant, H. D., & Cooper, C. (1981). Assessing adolescent identity in the areas of occupation, religion, politics, friendship, dating, and sex roles: Manual for administration and coding of the interview. *JSAS Catalog of Selected Documents in Psychology, 11,* 52–53 (Ms. No. 2295).

Grotevant, H. D., & Cooper, C. R. (1985). Patterns of interaction in family relationships and the development of identity exploration in adolescence. *Child Development, 56,* 415–428.

Halverson, E. R. (2005). Insideout: Facilitating gay youth identity development through a performance-based youth organization. *Identity: An International Journal of Theory and Research, 5,* 67–90.

Hart, D., Maloney, J., & Damon, W. (1987). The meaning and development of identity. In T. Honess & K. Yardley (Eds.), *Self and identity: Perspectives across the lifespan* (pp. 121–133). London: Routledge & Kegan Paul.

Harter, S. (1986). Processes underlying the enhancement of the self-concept of children. In J. Suis & A. Greenald (Eds.), *Psychological perspectives on the self,* vol. 3. Hillsdale, NJ: Lawrence Erlbaum.

Harter, S. (1989). Causes, correlates, and the functional role of global worth: A life-span perspective. In J. Kolligian & R. Sternberg (Eds.), *Perceptions of competence and in competence across the life-span.* New Haven, CT: Yale University Press.

Harter, S. (1993). Causes and consequences of low self-esteem in children and adolescents. In R. Baumeister (Ed.), *Self-esteem: The puzzle of low self-regard* (pp. 87–116). New York: Plenum Press.

Harter, S. (1997). The personal self in context: barriers to authenticity. In R. D. Ashmore & L. Jussim (Eds.), *Self and identity: Fundamental issues* (pp. 81–105). New York: Oxford University Press.

Harter, S. (1999). *The construction of self: A developmental perspective.* New York: Guilford Press.

Harter, S., Stocker, C., & Robinson, N. S. (1996). The perceived directionality of the link between approval and self-worth: The liabilities of a looking glass orientation among young adolescent. *Journal of Research on Adolescence, 6,* 285–308.

Harter, S., Waters, P. L., & Whitesell, N. R. (1997). Lack of voice as a manifestation of false-self behavior among adolescents: The school setting as a stage upon which the drama of authenticity is enacted. *Educational Psychologist, 32,* 153–173.

Hauser, S., Houlihan, J., Powers, S., Jacobson, A., Noam, G., Weiss-Perry, B., et al. (1991). Adolescent ego development within the family: Family styles and family sequences. *International Journal of Behavioral Development, 14,* 165–193.

Heatherton, T. F., & Vohs, K. D. (2000). Interpersonal evaluations following threats to self: Role of self-esteem. *Journal of Personality and Social Psychology, 78,* 725–736.

Helms. J. (1990). *Black and White racial identity: Theory, research, and practice.* New York: Greenwood Press.

Hess, R. D., & McDevitt, T. M. (1984). Some cognitive consequences of maternal intervention techniques: A longitudinal study. *Child Development, 55,* 2017–2030.

Hewitt, J. P. (2000). *Self and society: A symbolic interactionist social psychology* (7th ed.). Boston: Allyn and Bacon.

Higgins, E. T. (1987). Self-discrepancy: A theory relating self and affect. *Psychological Review, 94,* 319–340.

Hirsch, B., & DuBois, D. (1991). Self-esteem in early adolescence: The identification and prediction of contrasting longitudinal trajectories. *Journal of Youth and Adolescence, 20,* 53–72.

Holland, D. (1997). Selves as cultured: As told by an anthropologist who lacks a soul. In R. D. Ashmore & L. Jussim (Eds.), *Self and identity: Fundamental issues* (pp. 160–190). New York: Oxford University Press.

Honess, T., & Yardley, K. (1987). *Self and identity: Perspectives across the lifespan.* London: Routledge & Kegan Paul.

Hollinger, R. (1994). *Postmodernism and the social sciences: A thematic approach.* Thousand Oaks, CA: Sage.

Jackson, E. P., Dunham, R. M., & Kidwell, J. S. (1990). The effects of gender, family cohesion, and adaptability on identity status. *Journal of Adolescent Research, 5,* 161–174.

Jacoby, S. (2008). *The age of American unreason.* New York: Pantheon.

James, W. (1948). *Psychology.* Cleveland, OH: World Publishing (original work published in 1892).

Jones, R. M. (1992). Identity and problem behaviors. In G. R. Adams, T. P. Gullotta, & R. Montemayor (Eds.), *Adolescent identity formation: Advances in adolescent development* (pp. 216–233). Newbury Park, CA: Sage.

Jones, R. M. (1994). Curricula focused on behavioral deviance. In S. L. Archer (Ed.), *Interventions for adolescent identity development* (pp. 174–190). Newbury Park, CA: Sage.

Jones, R. M., & Hartmann, B. R. (1988). Ego identity: Developmental differences and experimental substance use among adolescents. *Journal of Adolescence, 11,* 347–360.

Jones, E. E., & Pittman, T. S. (1982). Toward a general theory of self-presentation. In J. Suls (Ed.), *Psychological perspectives on the self* (pp. 231–262). Hillsdale, NJ: Lawrence Erlbaum.

Kamakura, T., Ando, J., & Ono, Y. (2007). Genetic and environmental effects of stability and change in self-esteem during adolescence. *Personality and Individual Differences, 42,* 181–190.

Kerpelman, J. L., & Lamke, L. K. (1997). Anticipation of future identities: A control theory approach to identity development within serious dating relationships. *Personal Relationships, 4,* 47–62.

Kerpelman, J. L., & Smith, S. L. (1999). Adjudicated adolescent girls and their mothers: Examining identity perceptions and processes. *Youth and Society, 30,* 313–347.

Kidwell, J. S., Dunham, R. M., Bacho, R. A., Pastorino, E., & Portes, P. R. (1995). Adolescent identity exploration: a test of Erikson's theory of transitional crisis. *Adolescence, 30,* 185–193.

Koff, E., Rierdan, J., & Stubbs, M. L. (1990). Gender, body image, and self-concept in early adolescence. *Journal of Early Adolescence, 10,* 56–68.

Kozumi, R. (1995). Feelings of optimism and pessimism in Japanese students' transition to junior high school. *Journal of Early Adolescence, 15,* 412–428.

Kramer, L. R. (1991). The social construction of ability perceptions: An ethnographic study of gifted adolescent girls. *Journal of Early Adolescence, 11,* 340–362.

Kroger, J. (1993). Ego identity: An overview. In J. Kroger (Ed.), *Discussions on ego identity.* Hillsdale, NJ: Lawrence Erlbaum.

Kroger, J. (2000). Ego identity status research in the new millennium. *International Journal of Behavioral Development, 24,* 145–148.

Kroger, J. (2003). Identity development during adolescence. In G. R. Adams, & M. D. Berzonsky (Eds.), *Blackwell handbook of adolescence* (pp. 205–226). Malden, MA: Blackwell Publishing.

Kurtines, W. M. (1999). *A co-constructivist perspective on human behavior and development.* Unpublished manuscript. Miami: Florida International University.

Lamborn, S., Mounts, N., Steinberg, L., & Dornbusch, S. (1991). Patterns of competence and adjustment among adolescents from authoritative, authoritarian, indulgent, and neglectful homes. *Child Development, 62,* 1049–1065.

LaVoie, J. C. (1994). Identity in adolescence: Issues of theory, structure and transition. *Journal of Adolescence, 17,* 17–28.

Lee, T., Kobayashi, N. J., & Adams, G. R. (1988). Family influences on adolescent development in non-problematic L.D.S. families. *Association for Mormon Counselors and Professionals Journal, 14,* 15–29.

Lerner. R. (2002). *Concepts and theories of human development* (3rd ed.). Mahwah, NJ: Lawrence Erlbaum.

Lerner, R. M., Fisher, C. B., & Weinberg, R. A. (2000). Applying developmental science in the 21st century: International scholarship for our times. *International Journal of Behavioral Development, 24,* 24–29.

Luster, T., & McAdoo, H. P. (1995). Factors related to self-esteem among African-American youths: A secondary analysis of the High/Scope Perry Preschool data. *Journal of Research on Adolescence, 5,* 451–467.

Maccoby, E., & Martin, J. (1983). Socialization in the context of the family: Parent-child interaction. In E. M. Hetherington (Ed.), *Handbook of child psychology: Socialization, personality, and social development* (Vol 4). New York: Wiley.

Mageo, J. M. (1997). The reconfiguring self. *American Anthropologist, 97,* 282–296.

Marcia, J. E. (1964). *Determination and construct validation of ego identity status.* Unpublished doctoral dissertation, Ohio State University.

Marcia, J. E. (1966). Development and validation of ego identity status. *Journal of Personality and Social Psychology, 3,* 551–558.

Marcia, J. E. (1967). Ego identity status: Relationship to change in self-esteem, "general maladjustment," and authoritarianism. *Journal of Personality, 35,* 119–133.

Marcia, J. E. (1976a). Identity six years after: A follow-up study. *Journal of Youth and Adolescence, 5,* 145–160.

Marcia, J. E. (1976b). *Studies in ego identity.* Unpublished manuscript. Burnaby, BC, Canada: Simon Fraser University.

Marcia, J. E. (1980). Identity in adolescence. In J. Adelson (Ed.), *Handbook of adolescent psychology* (pp. 159–187). New York: John Wiley & Sons.

Marcia, J. E. (1989). Identity and intervention. *Journal of Adolescence, 12,* 401–410.

Marcia, J. E. (1993). The ego identity status approach ego identity. In J. E. Marcia, A. S. Waterman, D. R. Matteson, S. L. Archer, & J. L. Orlofsky (Eds.), *Ego identity: A handbook for psychosocial research* (pp. 3–41). New York: Springer-Verlag.

Marcia, J. E., & Friedman, M. (1970). Ego identity status in college women. *Journal of Personality, 38,* 249–262.

Marcia, J. E., Waterman, A. S., Matteson, D. R., Archer, S. L., & Orlofsky, J. L. E. (Eds.). (1993). *Ego identity: A handbook for psychosocial research*. New York: Springer-Verlag.

Markus, H. R. & Kitayama, S. (1991). *Culture and the self: Implications for cognition, emotion, and motivation. Psychological Review, 98*, 224–253.

Markus, H., & Nurius, R. (1986). Possible selves. *American Psychologist, 41*, 954–969.

Marsh, H. W., & Hattie, J. (1996). Theoretical perspectives on the structure of self-concept. In B. A. Bracken (Ed.), *Handbook of self-concept* (pp. 38–90). New York: John Wiley & Sons.

Matteson, D. R. (1977). Exploration and commitment: Sex differences and methodological problems in the use of the identity status categories. *Journal of Youth and Adolescence, 6*, 353–379.

Mead, G. H. (1934). *Mind, self, and society*. Chicago: University of Chicago Press.

Mead, M. (1928). *Coming of age in Samoa: A psychological study of primitive youth for Western civilization*. New York: Morrow Quill Paperbacks.

Meeus, W. (1996). Studies on identity development in adolescence: An overview of research and some new data. *Journal of Youth and Adolescence, 25*, 569–598.

Meeus, W., Iedema, J., Helsen, M., & Vollebergh, W. (1999). Patterns of adolescent identity development: Review of literature and longitudinal analysis. *Developmental Review, 19*, 419–461.

Orlofsky, J. L., Marcia, J. E., & Lesser, I. M. (1973). Ego identity status and the intimacy versus isolation crisis of young adulthood. *Journal of Personality and Social Psychology, 27*, 211–219.

Oyserman, D., & Markus, H. (1990). Possible selves and delinquency. *Journal of Personality and Social Psychology, 59*, 112–125.

Oyserman, D., Coon, H. M., & Kemmelmeier, M. (2002). Rethinking individualism and collectivism: Evaluation of theoretical assumptions and meta-analyses. *Psychological Bulletin, 128*, 3–72.

Palh, K., Greene, M., & Way, N. (2000, April). *Self-esteem trajectories among urban, low income, ethnic minority high school students*.Poster presented at the biennial meeting of the Society for Research on Adolescence, Chicago.

Parker, S., Nichter, M., Vuckovic, N., Sims, C., & Ritenbaugh, C. (1995). Body image and weight concerns among African American and White adolescent females: Differences which make a difference. *Human Organization, 54*, 103–114.

Pascarella, E. T., & Terenzini, P. T. (1991). *How college affects students: Findings and insights from 20 years of research*. San Francisco: Jossey-Bass.

Pascarella, E. T., & Terenzini, P. T. (2005). *How college affects students, vol. 2: A third decade of research*. San Francisco: Jossey-Bass.

Patterson, S. J., Sochting, I., & Marcia, J. E. (1992). The inner space and beyond: Women and identity. In G. R. Adams, T. P. Gullota, & R. Montemayor (Eds.), *Adolescent identity formation* (pp. 9–24). Newbury Park, CA: Sage.

Phillips, T. M., & Pittman, J. F. (2003). Identity processes in poor adolescents: Exploring the linkages between economic disadvantage and the primary task of adolescence. *Identity: An International Journal of Theory and Research, 3*, 115–129.

Phinney, J. S. (1989). Stages of ethnic identity development in minority group adolescents. *Journal of Early Adolescence, 9*, 34–49.

Phinney, J. S. (2005). Ethnic identity development in minority adolescents. In C. B. Fisher & R. M. Lerner (Eds.), *Encyclopedia of Applied Development Science*, vol. *1* (pp. 420–422). Thousand Oaks, CA: Sage.

Phinney, J. S. (2006). Ethnic identity exploration in emerging adulthood. In J. J. Arnett & J. Tanner (Eds.), *Emerging adults in America: Coming of age in the 21st century* (pp. 117–134). Washington DC: American Psychological Association.

Phinney. J. S., & Alipuria, L. (1990). Ethnic identity in college students from four ethnic groups. *Journal of Adolescence, 13*, 171–184.

Phinney, J. S., Jacoby, B., & Silva, C. (2007). Positive intergroup attitudes: The role of ethnic identity. *International Journal of Behavioral Development, 31*, 478–490.

Phinney, J. S., & Rosenthal, D. A. (1992). Ethnic identity in adolescence: Process, context, and outcome. In G. R. Adams, T. P. Gullotta, & R. Montemayor (Eds.), *Adolescent identity formation: Advances in adolescent development* (pp. 145–172). Newbury Park, CA: Sage.

Perkins, D. F. & Lerner, R. M. (1995). Single and multiple indicators of physical attractiveness and psychosocial behaviors among young adolescents. *Journal of Early Adolescence, 15*, 269–298.

Psychoanalyst coined identity crisis. (1994, May 13). *The Globe and Mail*, E8.

Putnam, B. A., Hosie, T. W., & Hansen, J. C. (1978). Sex differences in self-concept variables and vocational attitude maturity of adolescents. *Journal of Experimental Education, 47*, 23–27.

Rasmussen, J. E. (1964). The relationship of ego identity to psychosocial effectiveness. *Psychological Reports, 15*, 815–825.

Roberts, R. E., Phinney, J. S., Romero, A., & Chen, Y. W. (1996, March). *The structure of ethnic identity across ethnic groups*.Paper presented at the meeting of the Society for Research on Adolescence, Boston, MA.

Roberts, R. E., Phinney, J. S., Masse, L. C., Chen, Y., Roberts, C. R., & Romero, A. (1999). The structure of ethnic identity of young adolescents from diverse ethnocultural groups. *Journal of Early Adolescence, 19*, 301–322

Roberts, S. E. (2001). *Risk behaviors in adolescence: Parenting styles and identity*. Unpublished master's thesis. London: University of Western Ontario..

Roberts, S. E. (2007). *Identity stage resolution in the prolonged transition to adulthood: Development and validation of the Identity Issues Inventory*. Unpublished doctoral dissertation. London: University of Western Ontario.

Robinson, N. S. (1995). Evaluation of the nature of perceived support and its relation to perceived self-worth in adolescence. *Journal of Research on Adolescence, 5*, 253–280.

Rosenberg, M. (1965). *Society and the adolescent self-image*. Princeton, NJ: Princeton University Press.

Rosenberg, M. (1986). Self-concept from middle childhood through adolescence. In J. Suls & A. Greenwald (Eds.), *Psychological perspectives on the self*, vol. *3*). Hillsdale, NJ: Lawrence Erlbaum.

Rosenberg, S. (1997). Multiplicity of selves. In R. D. Ashmore & L. Jussim (Eds.), *Self and identity: Fundamental issues* (pp. 23–45). New York: Oxford University Press.

Rotheram-Borus, M. J., & Wyche, K. F. (1994). Ethnic differences in identity formation in the United States. In S. L. Archer (Ed.), *Interventions for adolescent identity development* (pp. 62–83). Thousands Oaks, CA: Sage.

Sarigiani, P. A., Wilson, J. L., Petersen, A. C., & Vicary, J. R. (1990). Self-image and educational plans of adolescents from two contrasting communities. *Journal of Early Adolescence, 10*, 37–55.

Schuller, T., Preston, J., Hammond, C., Brassett-Grundy, A., & Bynner, J. (2004). *The benefits of learning: The impact of education on health, family life and social capital*. London: RoutledgeFalmer.

Schwartz, B. (2000). Self-determination: The tyranny of freedom. *American Psychologist, 55*, 79–88.

Schwartz, B. (2004). *The paradox of choice: Why more is less*. New York: HarperCollins.

Schwartz, S. J. (2001). The evolution of Eriksonian and neo-Eriksonian identity theory and research: A review and integration. *Identity: An International Journal of Theory and Research, 1*, 7–58.

Schwartz, S. J., Montgomery, M. J., & Briones, E. (2006). The role of identity in acculturation among immigrant people: Theoretical propositions, empirical questions, and applied recommendations. *Human Development, 49,* 1–30.

Shapka, J. D., & Keating, D. P. (2005). Structure and change in self-concept during adolescence. *Canadian Journal of Behavioural Science/Revue canadienne des Sciences du comportement, 37,* 83–96.

Sharpley, C. F., & Hattie, J. A. (1983). Cross-cultural and sex differences on the Tennessee Self Concept Scale: A challenge to Fitts' original data. *Journal of Clinical Psychology, 39,* 717–721.

Shotter, J., & Gergen, K. J. (1989). *Texts of identity: Inquiries in social construction.* London: Sage.

Simmons, D. D. (1973). Development of an objective measure of identity achievement status. *Journal of Projective Techniques and Personality Assessment, 34,* 241–244.

Simmons, R. G., & Blyth, D. A. (1987). *Moving into adolescence: The impact of pubertal change and school context.* Hawthorne, NJ: Aldine.

Smith, R. E., & Smoll, F. L. (1990). Self-esteem and children's reactions to youth support coaching behaviors: A field study of self-enhancement process. *Developmental Psychology, 26,* 987–993.

Snyder, M. (1987). *Public appearances, private realities: The psychology of self-monitoring.* New York: Freeman.

Sorell, G. T., & Montgomery, M. J. (2001). Feminist perspectives on Erikson's theory: Its relevance for contemporary identity development research. *Identity: An International Journal of Theory and Research, 1,* 97–128.

Spencer, M. B. (2006). Phenomenology and ecological systems theory: Development of diverse groups. In W. Damon & R. Lerner (Eds.), *Handbook of Child Psychology* (6th ed.), vol. *1* (pp. 829–893). New York: John Wiley & Sons.

Statistics Canada. (2003). *2001 Census: Analysis Series Religion in Canada,* Cat. No. 96F0030XIE2001015. Ottawa: Author.

Steele, C. M. (1988). The psychology of self-affirmation: Sustaining the integrity of the self. In L. Berkowitz (Ed.), *Advances in experimental social psychology,* vol. *1* (pp. 261–302). New York: Academic Press.

Stefanich, G. P., Wills, F. A., & Buss, R. R. (1991). The use of interdisciplinary teaming and its influence on student self-concept in middle schools. *Journal of Early Adolescence, 11*(4), 404–419.

Stice, E., Spangler, D., & Agras, W. S. (2001). Exposure to media-portrayed thin-ideal images adversely affects vulnerable girls: A longitudinal experiment. *Journal of Social and Clinical Psychology, 20,* 270–288.

Takata, T. (2002). Internalization of the Japanese cultural view of self through social comparison: A developmental analysis based on cross-sectional data. *Japanese Journal of Educational Psychology, 50,* 465–475.

Takata, T. (2007). Independent and interdependent self-schema in Japanese adolescents and elders. *Japanese Journal of Psychology, 78,* 495–503.

Thoits, P. & Virshup, L. K. (1997). Me's and we's: Forms and functions of social identities. In R. D. Ashmore & L. Jussim (Eds.), *Self and identity: Fundamental issues* (pp. 106–136). London: Oxford University Press.

Thompson, W. (1972). *Correlates of the self concept.* Nashville, TN: Counselor Recordings and Tests.

Thorbecke, W., & Grotevant, H. D. (1982). Gender differences in interpersonal identity formation. *Journal of Youth and Adolescence, 11,* 479–492.

Twenge, J. M., & Crocker, J. (2002). Race and self-esteem: Meta-analyses comparing Whites, Blacks, Hispanics, Asians, American Indians and comment on Gray-Little and Hafdahl. *Psychological Bulletin, 128,* 371–408.

Umaña-Taylor, A. J., Yazedjian, A., & Bámaca-Gómez, M. (2004). Developing the ethnic identity scale using Eriksonian and social identity perspectives. *Identity: An International Journal of Theory and Research, 4,* 9–38.

van Hoof, A. (1999). The identity status field re-reviewed: An update of unresolved and neglected issues with a view on some alternative approaches. *Developmental Review, 19,* 497–556.

Waterman, A. S. (1982). Identity development from adolescence to adulthood: An extension of theory and a review of research. *Developmental Psychology, 18,* 341–358.

Waterman, A. S. (1988). Identity status theory and Erikson's theory: Communalities and differences. *Developmental Review, 8,* 185–208.

Waterman, A. S. (1990). Personal expressiveness: Philosophical and psychological foundations. *Journal of Mind and Behavior, 11,* 47–74.

Waterman, A. S. (1993). Developmental perspectives on identity formation: From adolescence to adulthood. In J. E. Marcia, A. S. Waterman, D. R. Matteson, S. L. Archer, & J. L. Orlofsky (Eds.), *Ego identity: A handbook for psychosocial research* (pp. 42–68). New York: Springer-Verlag.

Waterman, A. S. (1999). Identity, the identity statuses, and identity status development: A contemporary perspective. *Developmental Review, 19,* 591–621.

Waterman, A. S., Geary, P. S., & Waterman, C. K. (1974). Longitudinal study of changes in ego identity status from the freshman to the senior year at college. *Developmental Psychology, 10,* 387–392.

Waterman, A. S., & Waterman, C. K. (1971). A longitudinal study of changes in ego identity status during the freshman year at college. *Developmental Psychology, 5,* 167–173.

Waterman, C. K., & Waterman, A. S. (1975). Fathers and sons: A study of ego identity across two generations. *Journal of Youth and Adolescence, 4,* 331–338.

Weigert, A. J., Teitge, J. S., & Teitge, D. W. (1986). *Society and identity: Toward a sociological psychology.* Cambridge: Cambridge University Press.

White, J. M. (2000). Alcoholism and identity development: A theoretical integration of the least mature status with the typologies of alcoholism. *Alcoholism Treatment Quarterly, 18,* 43–59.

Wigfield, A., & Eccles, J. S. (1994). Children's competence beliefs, achievement values, and general self-esteem: Change across elementary and middle school. *Journal of Early Adolescence, 14,* 107–138.

Wintre, M. G., & Yaffe, M. (2000). First-year students adjustment to university life as a function of relationships with parents. *Journal of Adolescents Research, 15,* 9–37.

Wolf, N. (1991). *The beauty myth: How images of beauty are used against women.* New York: Anchor.

Worchel, S., Morales, J. F., Paez, D., & Deschamps, J.-C. (1998). *Social identity: International perspectives.* London: Sage.

Yoder, A. E. (2000). Barriers to ego identity status formation: A contextual qualification of Marcia's identity status. *Journal of Adolescence, 23,* 95–106.

CHAPTER 10

Gender Development in Adolescence

NANCY L. GALAMBOS, SHERI A. BERENBAUM, AND SUSAN M. McHALE

GENDER DEVELOPMENT IN ADOLESCENCE

How do we understand gender development in adolescence? The expression of gender in adolescence is both an extension of characteristics present or shaped in childhood and a reflection of change brought about by puberty and its physical transformations, advances in cognitive development, and the widening social world of adolescents. The aim of this chapter is to describe the role of gender in adolescent development, to review research on gender development in adolescence, to consider explanatory perspectives on gender development, and to identify opportunities for research.

Terminology is a first concern: In research on gender development, different terms have been used to refer to the same quality, and different definitions have often been applied to the same term. In particular, there has been controversy about the terms *sex* and *gender*, with some scholars arguing that biologically based differences should be called sex differences and experientially based differences should be referred to as gender differences (Lippa, 2002). But, biological and experiential influences are intertwined throughout development, and it is difficult to know *a priori* the relative influences of biology and experience. We primarily use the term *gender*, but make no assumptions about the sources of observed effects.

We ground our discussion in work that has brought order to the different terms, definitions, and operationalizations found in the literature on gender development (Huston, 1983; Ruble & Martin, 1998; Ruble, Martin, & Berenbaum, 2006). In an early handbook chapter, Huston (1983) developed a matrix of gender constructs by content categories, with individual cells of the matrix defining specific gender-related phenomena that are, have been, or could be the foci of research. Huston's matrix was subsequently modified by Ruble and Martin (1998) and by Ruble et al. (2006). As shown in Table 10.1, the matrix underscores the multidimensionality of gender: Individuals are not necessarily consistent in their gender typing across domains; different gender phenomena may develop under different influences and along distinct trajectories. This complexity is a challenge for researchers interested in gender development. Because much less is known about gender development in adolescence than in childhood, we cannot comment on all cells in the matrix; instead, our review is organized around the six content areas or rows of the matrix.

We begin by reviewing evidence on gender development during adolescence, including whether and how girls and boys differ in particular gender-related characteristics and whether and how they change across childhood through adolescence in these gendered qualities and behaviors. In the second half of this chapter, we consider sources of influence on gender development, including factors that produce differences between girls and boys, and differences among girls and among boys

TABLE 10.1   A Multidimensional Matrix for Organizing Gender-related Constructs

| Content | Constructs | | | |
	Concepts or Beliefs	Identity or Self-Perception	Preferences	Behavioral Enactment
1. Biological/ categorical sex	Gender awareness, labeling, and constancy	Personal sense of self as male or female	Wish to be male or female	Displaying bodily attributes of one's gender (e.g., clothing, body type, or hair); transvestism, transsexualism
2. Activities and interests: Toys, play activities, occupations, household roles, or tasks	Knowledge of gender stereotypes or beliefs about toys, activities, and so on	Self-perception of interests and activities as related to gender	Preference for toys, games, or activities	Engaging in gender-typed play, activities, occupations, or achievement tasks
3. Personal-social attributes: Personality traits, social behaviors, and abilities	Knowledge of gender stereotypes or beliefs about personality or role-appropriate social behavior	Perception of own traits and abilities (e.g., on self-rating questionnaires)	Preference or wish to have gender-linked attributes	Displaying gender-typed traits (e.g., aggression, dependence) and abilities (e.g., math)
4. Social relationships: Sex of peers, friends, lovers; or play qualities	Concepts about norms for gender-based relationships	Self-perception of own patterns of friendships, relationships, or sexual orientation	Preference for social interactions or judgments about social relationships based on sex or gender	Engaging in social activity with others on the basis of sex or gender (e.g. same-sex peer play)
5. Styles and symbols: Gestures, speech patterns (e.g., tempo), appearance, or body image	Awareness of gender-related symbols or styles	Self-perception of non-verbal stylistic characteristics or body image	Preference for gender-typed stylistic or symbolic objects or personal characteristics	Manifesting gender-typed verbal and nonverbal behavior
6. Values regarding gender	Knowledge of greater value attached to one sex or gender role than the other	Self-perceptions associated with group identification	In-group/out-group biases, prejudice, or attitudes toward egalitarian roles	In-group/out-group discrimination

Source: Ruble, Martin, & Berenbaum, 2006. Reprinted with permission of John Wiley & Sons, Inc.

in their gendered characteristics. Toward this end, we describe and evaluate three major perspectives on gender development: biological, cognitive, and socialization (Ruble et al., 2006). Throughout, we identify gaps in the literature and suggest directions for future research. We note that these

The major approaches to gender development will be discussed in detail later in the chapter. We introduce them here to provide a backdrop for our investigation of age-related changes in gender-related characteristics and behaviors in adolescence. We note that these

approaches have generally been focused on childhood, so we discuss them in general, consider the limited evidence that is directly relevant to adolescence, and suggest opportunities for research that could help to explain gender development at adolescence.

Biological approaches emphasize the parallels between physical and psychological sexual differentiation, focusing on the roles of evolution, genes, and hormones present from prenatal life. Puberty (see chapter 5, this volume) has been of special interest in understanding gender development in adolescence: The outward physical changes that occur during puberty reflect underlying hormonal changes that have taken place over several years and serve notice to the world that adolescence has begun. But gender development is affected by hormones present during other developmental periods (particularly prenatal life) and by other biological factors.

Cognitive theories emphasize the ways in which children's thoughts about gender facilitate their development in gender-related ways. Gender-related cognitions emerge and develop in childhood, shape how information in the environment is perceived and assimilated, and motivate gender-related behavioral choices and preferences. Cognitive approaches have been applied less often in studies of adolescent than of childhood gender development. The cognitive changes of adolescence, however, suggest that this should be an important focus of study. For example, aspects of executive functioning (cognitive skills guiding goal-directed behavior) increase from early to middle adolescence (Demetriou, Christou, Spanoudis, & Platsidou, 2002) and probably reflect brain maturation (e.g., Giedd et al., 1999).

Socialization theories focus primarily on social learning processes. Between- and within-sex variations in gender development are hypothesized to result from observation of and reinforcement for gender-typed roles, behaviors, and attitudes, as well as from differential treatment of girls and boys in the course of everyday social exchanges and in the opportunities and resources provided to each. Recent formulations have incorporated cognitive, motivational, affective, and self-regulatory elements, emphasizing youth as active agents in their own development (Bussey & Bandura, 1999).

An integrative perspective uniquely focused on adolescence is the *gender intensification hypothesis* (Hill & Lynch, 1983). Hill and Lynch built on early writings suggesting that the developmental trajectories of girls and boys increasingly diverge in adolescence, and proposed that a convergence of biological,

social, and even cognitive changes was responsible for this pattern. They argued that the physical changes of puberty mark the onset of sexual maturity and direct attention to looming adult roles. These changes elicit reactions from socialization agents and also alter adolescents' self-perceptions in ways that accentuate gender-stereotypical activities, interests, and self-perceptions. In their review, Hill and Lynch documented gender differences in a variety of domains during the second decade of life, including internalizing symptoms (greater anxiety and self-esteem problems in girls than in boys), achievement (favoring boys), and social relationships and social behavior (with girls more than boys oriented to relationship intimacy and boys more than girls inclined to exhibit physical aggression). They noted, however, that there was a lack of longitudinal data needed to document the hypothesized patterns of *change* from childhood to adolescence or the sources of those changes. As our review suggests, 25 years later we are only a little closer to data-based conclusions about patterns of gender development in adolescence, and researchers have not yet achieved the kind of integrated analysis of biological, social, and cognitive forces in gender development that Hill and Lynch proposed.

AGE-RELATED TRENDS IN GENDER DIFFERENTIATION ACROSS ADOLESCENCE

Are there changes from childhood through adolescence in the gender-related thoughts, characteristics, and actions of girls and boys? Focusing on the rows—content areas—of the matrix, we address this question.

The Content of Gender Development: Biological Sex

The focus of gender developmental research on biological sex concerns concepts or beliefs about gender, particularly the acquisition of gender labeling and gender constancy, which occur in childhood. Of relevance to adolescence are the other constructs in this content area: a person's gendered sense of self, desire to be a particular gender, and the display of attributes consistent with one's gender. Critical questions concern changes with age in contentedness with one's gender and whether and how gender identity changes from childhood through adolescence.

Most children express satisfaction with their own sex, although more girls than boys wish to be the other sex (Antill, Cotton, Russell, & Goodnow, 1996). Among typical children, gender-contentedness is higher in boys than in girls and decreases across the adolescent transition (Egan & Perry, 2001). Individuals who show both gender identity problems (distress about assigned sex and expressed wish to be the other sex) and extreme (and exclusive) cross-gender behavior are considered to have gender identity disorder (GID). There are separate criteria for GID for children versus for adolescents and adults, reflecting developmental differences in clinical presentation. Boys are referred more often than girls for evaluation, but the bias is greater in childhood than in adolescence (Zucker, 2004). This may reflect referral bias due to cultural factors; for example, beliefs that girls may outgrow cross-gender behavior, and less tolerance of cross-gender behavior in boys than in girls. Consistent with this argument, girls display more extreme cross-gender behavior than boys before a clinical assessment is obtained (Zucker & Bradley, 1995). Individuals diagnosed with GID in adolescence are more likely than those diagnosed in childhood to show persistence into adulthood (Zucker, 2004), suggesting reduced plasticity of gender identity with age, and perhaps some misdiagnoses.

Outcome studies of children with extreme cross-gender identity show that the overwhelming majority develops gender-typical identity in adolescence and adulthood, although some may continue to display gender-atypical characteristics. An early study of boys showed that most developed a homosexual orientation without gender dysphoria (Green, 1974). A recent study of girls showed

that most developed a heterosexual orientation without gender dysphoria, but there were higher-than-typical rates of both nonheterosexual orientation (32% in fantasy, 24% in behavior) and gender dysphoria (12%; Drummond, Bradley, Peterson-Badali, & Zucker, 2008).

Not all adolescents and adults with GID desire a change in secondary sex characteristics; those who do are considered transsexual. Among adult males with GID, there is heterogeneity in other aspects of gender-related behavior; for example, there is an equal distribution of those sexually attracted to biological males or females (Blanchard, 1989).

The Content of Gender Development: Activities and Interests

There has been considerable study of gender differences in activities and interests across the life span, with most research examining knowledge and expressed preferences, and less focused on behavioral enactment of male- versus female-typed activities. This work suggests that children's knowledge about, interests/preferences for, and behavioral enactment of sex-typed activities are among the earliest expressions of gender development and gender differences (Huston, 1983).

Most research on gender development in this broad domain focuses on early and middle childhood and examines children's conceptions or stereotypes about and their interests and behavioral engagement in activities ranging from play with toys and leisure-time pursuits to instrumental activities such as household chores, academics, and occupations (Liben & Bigler, 2002; Lippa, 1998; McHale, Crouter, & Tucker, 1999). Across childhood, there is an age-related increase in knowledge of stereotypes regarding activities and in flexibility regarding children's own interests and activity involvement. Some work also suggests gender differences in these patterns, with girls exhibiting greater flexibility than boys in their concepts, interests, and activity involvement (Ruble et al., 2006). Such results are consistent with the idea that male-typed activities have more social value than female-typed ones (e.g., Ferree, 1990) and with evidence that boys are considerably more likely than are girls to exhibit intense, focused interests (DeLoache, Simcock, & Macari, 2007; Johnson, Alexander, Spencer, Leibham, & Neitzel, 2004).

Studies of adolescents' gendered interests and activities are rarer than those of children and focus on testing competing theories, specifically, whether cognitive developmental advances promote continuing flexibility in activities and interests in adolescence (e.g., Liben & Bigler, 2002) or whether increasing gender socialization pressures at puberty promote more stereotypicality in this domain (e.g., Katz & Ksansnak, 1994; McHale, Shanahan, Updegraff, Crouter, & Booth, 2004). We begin by discussing research on youth's interests and preferences for activities and then review what is known about youth's behavioral enactment of gendered activities.

In contrast to theories of gender development during adolescence, the best evidence available suggests that both stereotypical *and* counter-stereotypical activity interests decline over time. For example, one large-scale longitudinal study of youth's "subjective values" for activities (i.e., ratings of how fun, interesting, and important an activity was) revealed declines between first and twelfth grade in ratings of math, sports, and reading among both girls and boys (e.g., Jacobs, Lanza, Osgood, Eccles, & Wigfield, 2002); gender differences persisted across this period, with boys valuing sports and math, and girls valuing reading. The age-related declines were suggested to reflect increasing specialization given constraints on opportunities, such as tryouts or grade point requirements. Indeed, declines in interests were linked to changes in youth's perceptions of their skill in each activity domain. This pattern—of stable gender differences in activity interests but decline in both male- and female-typed interests in both sexes—has been replicated in a longitudinal study from age 7 to age 19 (McHale, Kim, Dotterer, Crouter, & Booth, in press). In contrast, two short-term longitudinal studies showed little systematic change in middle childhood or early adolescence in stereotyped concepts about or self-reported interests in gendered activities (Liben & Bigler, 2002; Serbin, Powlishta, & Gulko, 1993), suggesting that a longer time frame is needed to detect developmental change in this broad arena.

Youth's activity interests also have been studied in terms of occupational preferences, which have been argued to be among the largest gender differences in adolescence and adulthood (Lippa, 1998, 2002). In high school and college students, there are large gender differences in occupational preferences that correspond to a "people versus things" continuum: Girls and young women systematically express greater interest in occupations such as teaching and social work (a "people" orientation), and boys and young men express more interest in occupations such as builder and auto mechanic (a "things" orientation). Importantly, within-sex variations in occupational interests were related to gendered personal qualities. For example, young women and men who rated themselves as more feminine on the Bem Sex Role Inventory reported stronger interests in people-oriented occupations relative to same-sex others.

Research on youth's activity involvement or behavioral enactment confirms the gender differences in interests and preferences. Beginning in middle childhood, girls around the world spend more time than boys in work, and boys spend more time than girls in leisure. This difference is most pronounced in preindustrialized societies where youth are heavily involved in the family economy (Larson & Verma, 1999), but even in industrial and postindustrialized societies, girls are more involved in work than boys, especially paid work, across the high school years (Shanahan & Flaherty, 2001) and girls do more household chores and spend more time on homework than do boys (Bowes & Goodnow, 1996; U.S. Department of Education, 1993). Girls and boys also differ in the kinds of work they undertake.

With respect to domestic work, for example, girls spend more time on food preparation and house cleaning, and boys spend more time on home repairs and taking out trash (Bowes & Goodnow, 1996; McHale et al., 1999). In the case of paid work, adolescent girls' jobs tend to be focused around work with people, such as waitressing and babysitting, whereas boys' jobs are likely to involve manual labor (Steinberg & Cauffmann, 1995).

Turning to youth's time in leisure activities, some research shows that girls and boys spend their time in different ways, although findings of gender differences are not entirely consistent. When gender differences emerge, boys tend to spend more time playing sports and watching television, whereas girls spend more time in sedentary hobbies such as artwork and reading. Boys also watch different kinds of shows on television (cartoons and sports versus sitcoms) and enjoy different kinds of reading (comics) than girls (novels; Coles & Hall, 2002; Larson & Verma, 1999; McHale, Crouter, & Tucker, 2001).

Few studies have measured age differences or age-related *changes* in youth's activities, and evidence of developmental patterns is mixed. Consistent with a gender-intensification process, an early cross-sectional study of time use revealed that gender differences in sports involvement were more pronounced in adolescence than in middle childhood (Timmer, Eccles, & O'Brien, 1985), and another study showed that, compared to young adolescent girls, girls in middle adolescence spent less time in sports but more time socializing (a female-typed activity; Richards & Larson, 1989). But other data show more complex change patterns: A combined cross-sectional and longitudinal study of girls showed that time in female-typed structured activities (dance, handicrafts, reading) declined from a high point in middle childhood, that time in male-typed activities (particularly sports) peaked in early adolescence and then declined, and that time spent socializing, specifically talking on the phone, increased between about age 8 and

about age 16 (McHale, Shanahan, et al., 2004). Taken together, the evidence supports neither a cognitive developmental nor a gender intensification perspective but instead converges with research on youth's interests to suggest that, for both sexes, time in most kinds of structured activities declines across adolescence.

Conclusions about the normative development of gendered activities and interests must be understood in light of several methodological and conceptual issues. First, conclusions vary depending on how gender development is operationalized. That is, some researchers have focused on changes in the extent of sex differences, others have studied within-person changes in involvement in specific activity (male- or female-typed) categories, and still others have assessed gendered patterns in youths' relative involvement in stereotypically masculine versus feminine activities. Somewhat different patterns emerge depending on measurement choices (McHale, Kim, Whiteman, & Crouter, 2004). Second, the gendered nature of activities differs across time and place. With respect to secular changes, for example, girls' involvement in some sports has increased substantially since the passage of Title IX, the Educational Amendment Act (Fredricks & Eccles, 2004); girls have shown increasing interest and involvement in some subfields of science (e.g., Eccles, Barber, & Jozefowicz, 1998); and there has been a reversal in the past decade of the balance of male versus female college students, suggesting that educational achievement is becoming a female-typed domain (Hamilton & Hamilton, 2006). Different cultures also may define gendered activities in different ways: In cultures that emphasize the importance of family ties, for example, the stereotypical activities of the father may include more parental involvement than in more individualistic-oriented cultural groups, and in poor and minority families, the "traditional" roles of father as breadwinner and mother as homemaker never fit the stereotype that was evident in mainstream U.S. culture (Coontz, 1992). Third, there are within-sex variations in interests and activities that may be due to individual and social contextual factors (e.g., Berenbaum & Snyder, 1995; Crouter, Helms-Erikson, Updegraff, & McHale, 1999; Jacobs et al., 2002). These will be highlighted later in our discussion of theories of gender development, but they do cast doubt on whether there exists a universal pattern in the development of interests and activities. That is, individual and group differences make it difficult to draw generalizations about the development of gendered interests and activities.

An important direction for research is to examine the developmental *implications* of youth's interest and involvement in gendered activities. From both ecological (e.g., Bronfenbrenner, 1979) and social cognitive (Eccles, Wigfield, & Schiefele, 1998; Wigfield, Eccles, Schiefele, Roeser, & Davis-Kean, 2006) perspectives, interest and involvement in gendered activities will have a significant influence on opportunities and choices later in life, such as in the areas of educational and occupational achievement and family formation and roles. With some important exceptions such as Eccles and colleagues' research on achievement motivation, we have little data on long-term effects of youth's gendered interests and activity involvement.

The Content of Gender Development: Personal–Social Attributes

There has been substantial research directed at individuals' knowledge about, possession of, and display of gender-linked traits, behaviors, and abilities, although much of this work is focused on children and adults. Of particular interest in adolescence are three broad sets of attributes that are hypothesized to exhibit emerging or increasing gender differences around adolescence: internalizing and externalizing behaviors; temperament, personality, and self-concept; and cognitive abilities.

Internalizing and Externalizing Behaviors

In adolescence, girls are more likely than boys to show internalizing problems (e.g., anxiety, depression) whereas boys are more likely than

girls to evidence externalizing problems (e.g., physical aggression, delinquency). It is well documented that gender differences in depressive symptoms and depressive disorders emerge at about age 13 and increase to age 18, with girls surpassing boys (e.g., Angold, Erkanli, Silberg, Eaves, & Costello, 2002; Ge, Conger, & Elder, 2001; Ge, Lorenz, Conger, Elder, & Simons, 1994; Twenge & Nolen-Hoeksema, 2002). Social phobias also emerge and begin to rise in girls at about age 13 (Costello, Mustillo, Erkanli, Keeler, & Angold, 2003).

Although conduct disorders, violent crime, and delinquency are considerably more prevalent in boys than girls at most points in adolescence (Costello et al., 2003; Farrington, 2004), longitudinal studies suggest a high level of stability in externalizing problems in boys; for many, externalizing behaviors were present in childhood and continued into adolescence (Crick & Zahn-Waxler, 2003). But girls do not show this stability. For example, even when girls were diagnosed with conduct disorders in childhood, they were less likely to persist into adolescence. Furthermore, the prevalence of conduct disorders increased from age 10 to 14 among girls, but remained at similar, higher levels among boys, showing more gender convergence than divergence by mid-adolescence; then by age 17, it decreased in girls, resulting in an increasing gender gap in prevalence rates (Moffitt, Caspi, Rutter, & Silva, 2001).

Several caveats limit conclusions about gender-linked, age-related changes in internalizing and externalizing behaviors in adolescence. First, for many girls, depression is comorbid with anxiety in adolescence. In fact, there is mounting evidence that childhood anxiety may be a precursor of adolescent girls' depression (Costello et al., 2003). This heterotypic continuity points to the possibility that depression and anxiety are not necessarily distinct problems (Crick & Zahn-Waxler, 2003), but they have not typically been examined in tandem in studies of adolescent gender development. Second, although the distinction between internalizing and externalizing behaviors seems clear, the problems are often comorbid. For example, in one study, 25% of young women with diagnosed depression at age 21 had a previous diagnosis of conduct disorder; moreover, conduct disorders appeared to precede the onset of depression (Moffitt et al., 2001). Third, the pattern of gender differences in any study varies with definitions of behavior, measurement, sample, and research design (Costello et al., 2003; Crick & Zahn-Waxler, 2003).

Temperament, Personality, and Self-Concept

A recent meta-analysis of gender differences in temperament considered data up to age 13 on the three main dimensions of temperament (effortful control, negative affectivity, and surgency) and their components (Else-Quest, Hyde, Goldsmith, & Van Hulle, 2006). Findings revealed a large gender difference in effortful control in childhood, favoring girls, which may reflect greater developmental maturity of girls compared to boys. The absence of data for adolescents, however, means that we do not know whether boys catch up to girls. The meta-analysis showed few differences in negative affectivity except for small differences in fear (higher in girls than in boys) and difficulty and intensity of negative affect (higher in boys than in girls). There was, however, a moderate gender difference in overall surgency, with boys higher in some components (impulsivity, activity level, and high-intensity pleasure), and girls higher in others (positive mood, approach, and shyness). Links between gender differences in childhood temperament and gender differences in adult personality, however, are not obvious.

There has been considerable attention to the gendered personality traits of instrumentality and expressivity, which are the main characteristics tapped in measures of masculinity and femininity such as Bem's Sex Role Inventory. By age 8, children describe themselves in terms of such gender-typed traits (Ruble & Martin, 1998), and this continues into adolescence (Galambos, Almeida, &

Petersen, 1990; Klingenspor, 2002; Washburn-Ormachea, Hillman, & Sawilowsky, 2004). In one study, Swedish boys and girls aged 11–18 years endorsed several instrumental and expressive qualities, with the importance of expressive characteristics increasing and instrumental traits decreasing with age (Intons-Peterson, 1988).

A recent longitudinal study of the development of gendered personality characteristics charted changes in expressivity (female-typed qualities such as sensitivity and kindness) and instrumentality (male-typed qualities such as competitiveness and independence) from about age 7 to about age 19 (McHale, Kim, Dotterer, Crouter, & Booth, in press). Findings revealed average gender differences at age 13, with girls reporting higher levels of expressivity and boys reporting higher levels of instrumentality. Instrumentality increased in both girls and boys from early in middle childhood through adolescence, however. Expressivity, in contrast, showed different changes in girls and boys: there were no changes across time for girls, but boys showed declines in expressivity from early to middle adolescence, followed by a "recovery" of sensitivity and kindness by late adolescence, consistent with gender intensification. These gendered personality characteristics may contribute to sex differences in adjustment (Ruble et al., 2006). For example, in adolescents, instrumentality partially mediated the relation between gender and internalizing symptoms, and expressivity fully mediated the relation between gender and externalizing symptoms (Hoffman, Powlishta, & White, 2004).

Research on gender differences in the "big five" personality characteristics has generally focused on adults, but there is some information about gender differences in these dimensions of personality in adolescence. In two samples of adolescents, girls were reliably higher than boys on neuroticism, extraversion, openness, and agreeableness, but there was no gender difference in conscientiousness; the sample followed from early to late adolescence showed increases in neuroticism among girls but not boys, paralleling patterns for gender intensification in depression (McCrae et al., 2002). Cross-cultural meta-analysis (Costa, Terracciano, & McCrae, 2001) revealed a number of differences between adult men and women, but most were small. There were small to moderate differences in three of the big five factors, with women higher than men in neuroticism, agreeableness, and extraversion, but there were no overall differences in openness or conscientiousness. There also were cross-cultural similarities in patterns of sex differences, and differences were largest in European and North American countries, and smallest in African and Asian countries.

Meta-analytic studies of aggression reveal it to be higher in male than in female adults, with small to moderate overall effect sizes (Bettencourt & Miller, 1996; Eagly & Steffen, 1986). Gender differences in physical aggression emerge early in childhood, are present in virtually all cultures, are found in many species, and are related in men to higher levels of testosterone (Lippa, 2002), although there are important social moderators of such effects (e.g., Booth, Granger, Mazur, & Kivlighan, 2007). Boys are consistently more aggressive than girls, but longitudinal studies from multiple sites show that from kindergarten through middle adolescence, the developmental course of physical aggression is similar: physical aggression exhibits considerable rank-order stability but decreases across time within each sex. Chronic childhood aggression (i.e., consistently high levels) predicts violent and nonviolent offending in boys but not in girls in adolescence, suggesting gender differences in the implications of early physical aggression for adolescent functioning and in the etiology of delinquency (Broidy et al., 2003).

Whereas boys are more physically aggressive than girls, girls may engage in as much or more relational aggression as boys (e.g., spreading rumors, shunning; Cairns & Cairns, 1994; Crick et al., 1998). Still, physical aggression and relational aggression are positively correlated in both sexes (Cillessen & Mayeux, 2004). A longitudinal study following students from grades 5 to 9 showed that girls' (but not boys') relational aggression became increasingly linked to or reinforced by higher status (perceived popularity) among peers, although this was at the expense of sociometric popularity, or actually being liked (Cillessen & Mayeux).

Gender differences in global self-esteem (overall feelings of self-worth) are found from early adolescence through at least young adulthood, with males scoring higher than females, but it is not clear whether there are differences in childhood. There are cultural moderators of these differences, with gender differences evident in Whites but not in African Americans (Kling, Hyde, Showers, & Buswell, 1999; Major, Barr, Zubek, & Babey, 1999). Compared with European American early adolescent girls, African American girls have higher self-esteem and do not show declines in self-esteem. Latinas, however, have high self-esteem prior to early adolescence but show a steep drop beginning in high school (American Association of University Women, 1992). Higher self-esteem in African American girls and Latinas has been linked to stronger ethnic identity (Phinney & Alipuria, 1990; Phinney & Chavira, 1992).

Gender differences in self-concept (self-evaluations of skills in specific domains) are small and follow expected patterns (e.g., Wilgenbusch & Merrell, 1999), with boys' self-concepts higher in math, sports, and physical appearance, and girls' self-concepts higher in music, and verbal/reading ability, and sometimes social competence (Klomsten, Skaalvik, & Espnes, 2004; Watt, 2004). Gender differences in self-concept develop early and remain relatively consistent over time, with few exceptions (Cole et al., 2001; Jacobs et al., 2002).

Cognitive Abilities

There are no gender differences in overall intellectual ability, but the sexes differ in *patterns* of cognitive abilities: males have better spatial and mathematical skills than do females, whereas females are better than males in verbal fluency, writing, perceptual speed, and verbal memory (Blakemore, Berenbaum, & Liben, 2009; Halpern, 2000; Kimura, 1999). The most reliable evidence about cognitive gender differences comes from adolescents and adults because of the difficulty in measuring these skills in children. For all abilities that show gender differences, the size of the difference varies by component ability and often by age.

The largest cognitive gender difference is in spatial ability, with males outperforming females in most aspects (Halpern, 2000; Linn & Petersen, 1985); sex differences are most pronounced in mental rotation, and are moderate to large on tasks involving rotation of three-dimensional objects (Blakemore et al., 2009; Halpern, 2000). There are also moderate to large differences in spatial perception, which requires recognition of the vertical or horizontal, targeting (i.e., hitting a target with a ball; Kimura, 1999), and abilities related to navigating in the real world (Blakemore et al., 2009; Halpern, 2000). There is a very large gender disparity in National Geography Bee winners. Although boys and girls participate at equal rates in the initial stages, boys are increasingly more successful than girls at each level of competition, so that in most years, all 10 finalists are boys (Liben, 1995). In one spatial domain, memory for spatial location, females outperform males, and the difference is large (Blakemore et al., 2009; Kimura, 1999).

There are gender differences in some mathematical abilities. Meta-analyses show a greater male advantage in selected samples (Hyde, Fennema, & Lamon, 1990) and on certain standardized tests (e.g., SAT; Hyde & Frost, 1993). There is no gender difference in mathematical concepts, but females have a small advantage over males in computation, especially before puberty, and males have a small to moderate advantage over females on problem-solving tasks, especially at older ages (Hyde et al., 1990).

An important question concerns the age at which gender differences in math emerge. Data from two large, longitudinal, nationally representative U.S. studies from age 4 to 18 years (Leahy & Guo, 2001) showed a small male advantage that emerged at about age 16. For comparison to other studies with more selected samples (and larger gender differences), the researchers restricted the sample to high-scoring students, and found that the gender difference emerged at about the same age, with a larger difference in the restricted than in the full sample for geometry (but not math reasoning).

Gender differences in math performance have been hypothesized to result from differences in mathematics affect (e.g., attitudes toward and beliefs about math) through effects on test performance and selection of math courses. In a study examining trajectories in mathematics affect in a U.S. nationally representative sample of 7th graders tracked through 12th grade, boys started out with more positive attitudes toward math and less math anxiety than did girls, with mathematics affect becoming more negative in both sexes over the next six years, but girls' math anxiety accelerating faster than boys', thereby increasing the gender gap (Ma & Cartwright, 2003).

The gender difference on verbal tasks is in the opposite direction, with females outperforming males in many domains. Meta-analyses (Hyde & Linn, 1988) show that males are somewhat better than females in analogies, but females have a small to moderate advantage over males in other verbal skills, including overall and general verbal skills, vocabulary, reading comprehension, essay writing, and speech production. A summary of several large studies of adolescents showed larger gender differences than reported in meta-analyses in reading comprehension and writing (Hedges & Nowell, 1995); this is consistent with national data on writing proficiency (Halpern, 2000). Females also do better than males on verbal abilities not included in meta-analyses, with moderate to large differences on phonological processing (Majeres, 1997, 1999), verbal fluency (Halpern), and verbal learning and memory (Halpern; Hedges & Nowell; Kimura, 1999; Kramer, Delis, & Daniel, 1988). Females' superior learning and recall of lists of common objects is largely due to their use of efficient clustering strategies. Females also outperform males on perceptual speed, with small to moderate differences.

Some have argued that cognitive sex differences have declined across time (e.g., Feingold, 1988; but cf. Hedges & Nowell, 1995), but methodological issues make it difficult to draw firm conclusions. Historical trends might reflect factors correlated with publication year, such as sampling (e.g., college enrollment shifted from more men than women to a preponderance of women, changing selection effects), publishing trends (e.g., greater likelihood that nonsignificant findings are published now than previously), and use of tests that never showed large gender differences (Halpern, 2000).

The Content of Gender Development: Social Relationships

Adolescence is a period in which relationships focus increasingly on the world beyond the family, and especially on the peer group. These changes are facilitated by adolescents' increasing autonomy, identity development, and sexuality associated with physical maturation. Our review of this content area, social relationships, considers the development of adolescents' relationships with mothers, fathers, siblings, friends, and romantic partners—relationships that have received the most research attention.

Parent–Adolescent Relationships

How relationships with parents change across adolescence has been a focus of substantial study, in part because of interest in the effects of adolescent development on family dynamics, and in part because of established links between parent–offspring relationships and youth well-being (e.g., Collins & Laursen, 2006; Steinberg & Silk, 2002). Research on parent–adolescent relationships has not tended to focus explicitly on gender, but the available evidence allows us to piece together a picture of gendered relationship patterns. To understand the role of gender in parent–adolescent relationships, we consider two issues: whether youth have different experiences with mothers versus fathers, and whether parents treat their sons and daughters differently.

Regarding the first issue, there is substantial evidence that mothers and fathers have different parental roles and relationships with their children (Leaper, Anderson, & Saunders, 1998; Maccoby, 1998; Russell & Saebel, 1997). The potential importance for gender development of complementarity in mothers' and fathers' roles was highlighted in early theoretical work, including psychoanalytic theory, social role theory, and social learning theory (Chodorow, 1978; Collins & Russell, 1991; Parsons & Bales, 1955). Most of the empirical research has been grounded in social learning theories (e.g., Mischel, 1966), which explain how youth acquire the social relational behaviors and roles of their same-sex parent. To the extent that mothers' and fathers' behaviors are complementary, the unique attributes and roles of females versus males may be especially salient and easy to learn. Despite secular increases in egalitarianism in many segments of U.S. society, there are still marked differences in mothers' and fathers' family roles that persist through adolescence: Mothers tend to be more involved with their children than fathers; fathers' involvement tends to center around leisure as opposed to the caregiving and teaching activities in which mothers spend their time; youth feel closer to mothers than to fathers and converse with them about a range of topics, including feelings, while focusing conversations with fathers on instrumental issues and concerns; and youth tend to have more conflicts and disagreements with mothers than with fathers and show them less deference (Maccoby; McHale, Crouter, &

Whiteman, 2003; Smetana, Metzger, & Campione-Barr, 2004; Steinberg & Silk, 2002).

With respect to the second issue—whether boys and girls are treated differently by parents—the evidence is nuanced. Most research has focused on young children, and studies that consider the development of parent–offspring relationships in adolescence tend to highlight parents' roles as relationship partners (e.g., relational warmth and conflict). However, parents also serve other roles for their children: instructors; sources of advice, help, and material resources; and opportunity providers (Parke & Buriel, 1998). As we elaborate in our discussion of family socialization influences on gender development, there is evidence that parents treat their sons and daughters differently in many of these domains (Fredricks & Eccles, 2004; McHale et al., 2003). Some work also suggests that fathers, in particular, place different value on sons versus daughters. For example, fathers spend more time in parenting when they have sons (Harris & Morgan, 1991) and are less likely to divorce when they have sons (Diekmann & Schmidheiny, 2004).

A limitation of existing research on parents' differential treatment of daughters versus sons is its reliance on between-family comparisons, that is, comparisons of boys in one group of families with girls in another group of families. Within-family comparisons of the experiences of girls and boys in the same families, however, provide a more powerful test of gender differences and a clearer understanding of the family circumstances within which gendered differential treatment emerges (McHale et al., 2003; Russell & Saebel, 1997; Siegal, 1987). In such research, family members serve as their own "controls" and thus, for example, comparing an adolescent's feelings of closeness toward her mother versus her father corrects for that adolescent's overall tendency toward relationship intimacy. Further, having a child of each sex affords parents the opportunity to exhibit sex-typed differential behavior toward different family members if they are so inclined, or

to be more scrupulous about equal treatment if they hold egalitarian ideals (McHale et al., 2003).

Our understanding of the role of gender in parent–offspring relationships during adolescence has been limited by a lack of longitudinal data and a focus on childhood. Some research, however, has been aimed at testing a gender intensification hypothesis. From this perspective, gender differences in parent–offspring relationships should become pronounced at puberty, with parents taking on increased responsibility for socializing same-sex offspring, and adolescents collaborating in this process as they identify with the gendered characteristics, interests, and activities of a same-sex parent. Some evidence of gender intensification comes from a longitudinal within-family study by Crouter and McHale and colleagues. An early study documented increases in youths' time spent with their same-sex parent from about age 10 to about age 12, but this pattern emerged only for youth with an opposite-sex younger sibling (Crouter, Manke, & McHale, 1995). The investigators reasoned that the presence of a younger sibling of the other sex provided mothers and fathers with the opportunity to display complementary and sex-typed involvement with their offspring, but data on younger siblings' time with parents were not collected in the initial study. In a follow-up study of both first- and second-born siblings, the development of warmth and conflict in the parent–child relationship was studied from about age 7 to about age 19 (Shanahan, McHale, Osgood, & Crouter, 2007). Overall, warmth in both mother– and father–offspring relationships peaked at the end of middle childhood, declined until about age 16, and then showed some recovery. But, there was evidence for gender intensification in families with both a boy and a girl: same-sex parent–youth dyads (i.e., mother–daughter and father–son dyads) became increasingly warmer in their relationships from middle childhood through middle adolescence *relative to* the opposite sex dyads (i.e., mother–son and father–daughter) in the same family. In contrast, gender intensification was not apparent in families with same-sex first- and second-borns. Analyses regarding parent–offspring conflict revealed no gendered patterns, but there were declines in the frequency of conflict beginning in early to middle adolescence (Shanahan, McHale, Crouter, & Osgood, 2007).

These studies did not directly compare mothers and fathers, and focused on conflict frequency rather than its emotional intensity. A meta-analysis of 53 studies of conflict in early adolescence (Laursen, Coy, & Collins, 1998), however, revealed that mother–child conflict declined more in early adolescence than did father–child conflict, and that increases in the intensity of emotion in conflicts were evident only in father–son relationships. Greater declines in conflicts with mothers during adolescence may be apparent because mothers tend to be more involved with their children and so have more conflicts with them to start. The intensity of father–son conflict is suggestive of fathers' pronounced investment in this relationship and clearly requires further scrutiny. It is also important to test whether there are gendered patterns in the *content* of parent–adolescent conflict, that is, in what parents and offspring fight about. Such a domain approach (e.g., Smetana & Daddis, 2002) may provide for an appropriately nuanced picture of the role of gender in the development of parent–adolescent conflict.

In sum, the weight of the evidence suggests that parent–child relationships are indeed gendered, and that in some contexts, gender differences in some elements of parent–offspring relationships become more pronounced across the course of adolescence. An important direction for research is to learn more about contextual factors that afford or constrain gender-typed parent–offspring relationships. As we elaborate in our discussion of family gender socialization influences, it is also important to assess directly the consequences of gender-typing in parent–offspring relationships for adolescents' gender development.

Sibling Relationships

Most youth grow up in a household with at least one sibling, and sibling relationships are the longest lasting relationships in most individuals' lives (Bank & Kahn, 1997; Hernandez, 1997). As such, study of sibling relationships could provide a unique forum for life-span study of gender in close relationships. As in the larger literature on the development of social relationships, however, siblings have been relatively neglected by gender development researchers. Much of what we know about these relationships comes from studies of children, studies that use cross-sectional designs, and studies that include only one member of the sibling dyad.

Like parent–child relationship researchers, investigators who study sibling relationships have been interested in how these change between childhood and adolescence. Youths' increasing interest in the world outside the home may result in lower levels of sibling involvement in adolescence (e.g., Brody, Stoneman, & McCoy, 1994; Buhrmester & Furman, 1990). Increasing social cognitive skills, however, also may enhance intimacy and mutual understanding in adolescent sibling relationships even as siblings pursue their own paths outside the family (Bigner, 1974; Cole & Kerns, 2001). Most evidence suggests that sibling conflict declines from childhood through adolescence and into adulthood, although findings rely heavily on cross-sectional data and are not entirely consistent (Buhrmester & Furman; Cole & Kerns; Stewart et al., 2001).

What is the role of gender in the development of sibling relationships during adolescence? Attributing findings to differences in boys' versus girls' orientations to close relationships, early cross-sectional research suggested that middle childhood and adolescent-age sisters have closer and more affectionate sibling relationships than brothers (e.g., Furman & Buhrmester, 1992; McCoy, Brody, & Stoneman, 1994). These early studies also suggested that the gender constellation of the dyad might be important, such that same-sex dyads experience higher levels of positivity than mixed-sex dyads (Buhrmester, 1992), although other research documented such a tendency only in sister–sister dyads (Cole & Kerns, 2001). Most research on siblings has focused on European American youth, but a study of 245 Mexican American adolescent sibling dyads (Updegraff, McHale, Whiteman, Thayer, & Delgado, 2005) showed that dyads that included a sister reported more positive relationships than dyads with only brothers, and that sister–sister pairs spent more time together than mixed-sex pairs. In contrast, a study of 172 African American sibling dyads revealed no effects of gender constellation on warmth, conflict, and control (McHale, Whiteman, Kim, & Crouter, 2007). Some literature suggests that compared to European American families, Mexican American families are more traditional in their gender role orientations, whereas African American families are less so, and this pattern of results directs attention to a topic that has been neglected by gender researchers, that is, the interface of gender and culture.

As noted, most research on siblings is cross-sectional and provides only a snapshot of sibling relationships. But there is one longitudinal study of the development of sibling relationships in about 200 European American families that followed youth from about age 7 to about age 19 (Kim, McHale, Osgood, & Crouter, 2006). Gendered patterns in sibling relationships changed across adolescence: Although sisters reported higher levels of intimacy on average, longitudinal analyses revealed that mixed-sex, but not same-sex, dyads showed increases in intimacy from middle childhood through late adolescence; by late adolescence, sister–brother dyads reported levels of intimacy that were as high as sister–sister pairs, whereas brother–brother pairs reported lower levels of intimacy than other dyads. These findings are consistent with the broader literature on gender in relationships: In close relationships, "happiness is a feminine partner" (Ickes, 1993), and females

tend to play the role of "kin-keepers" within the family (Eagly, 1987).

In sum research shows sibling relationships gendered. The data however, are congruent with neither a cognitive developmental model, predicting decreases in sex-typing across age nor gender intensification models, predicting increases in sex-typing in adolescence. They do, however, underscore the role of adolescent development in increasing intimacy between sister–brother dyads across adolescence: Interest in and involvement with the other sex increases at puberty, and youth may look to a sibling of the other sex for advice and information as they begin to negotiate heterosexual relationships.

Friendships and Romantic Partners

Friendships are gendered in many ways. Children see relationships with girls and boys to be different, and in actuality, they are different. Adolescence marks a transition from extreme engagement with same-sex others to other-sex friendships (Brown, 2004). In childhood, the tendency to segregate with same-sex others is extremely large (gender accounts for 70%–85% of the variance in children's play partners, Martin & Fabes, 2001), shows stable individual differences (Martin & Fabes, 2001), and is found across cultures (Whiting & Edwards, 1988) and settings (Maccoby, 1998).

During adolescence, gender-based peer preferences begin to change. Small cliques of same-sex peers in early adolescence give way to both same-sex friendships and heterosexual dating couples and other types of other-sex relationships (Brown, 2004). About 40%–50% of youth in mid-adolescence have romantic relationships, increasing to almost 100% by late adolescence (Connolly, Craig, Goldberg, & Pepler, 1999). Girls (but not boys) still report feeling more comfortable with same-sex peers (Lundy, Field, & McBride, 1998). Longitudinal data across grades 9–11 show that children's same-sex peer networks remain about the same, but that their other-sex peer networks increase in size (Richards, Crowe, Larson, & Swarr, 1998).

Different activities and qualities character-ize relationships with girls versus boys (Ruble et al., 2006), with most information coming from studies of preadolescents. Interactions among boys are characterized by rough-and-tumble play, activity, and attempts to attain dominance, whereas interactions among girls are more often cooperative and enabling of others (Di Pietro, 1981; Eaton & Enns, 1986; Pellegrini & Smith, 1998). Boys often play fur-ther away from adults than do girls (Benenson, Morash, & Petrakos, 1998), so their play may be more peer- than adult-oriented (Martin & Fabes, 2001). Boys are more likely than girls to associate in larger groups (Maccoby, 2002), and sex differences in play are exaggerated in groups versus dyads (Fabes, Martin, Hanish, Anders, & Madden-Derdich, 2003). These differences continue and increase with age: In middle childhood, boys more than girls are involved in physical and fantasy games and aggression, whereas girls more than boys are involved in conversations, verbal games, and emotional exchange (Buhrmester, 1996; Lansford & Parker, 1999). Children's activities are influenced by their play partners. Boylike behavior may result, not from the direct influence of individual boys' personali-ties, but from boys' tendencies to respond in particular ways in boy groups (Maccoby). In contrast, girls' behavior is more similar than boys' across play contexts (Benenson et al., 2002). Both boys and girls, however, engage in more active play with boys than with girls. Both sexes adjust their behavior somewhat to fit their play partners' styles, but, because other-sex group encounters are relatively rare, they may have little overall impact during childhood (Fabes, Martin, & Hanish, 2003).

In adolescence, there are sex differences in the topic and content of friendships: Girls' friendships focus on issues of intimacy, love, and communion, whereas boys' friendships tend to focus on agency, power, and excitement (Rose, 2002). Because of greater intimacy, girls' relationships are more fragile and prone to disruption through divulging of confidential information (Benenson & Christakos, 2003). As children grow older, their peer relationships increasingly reflect sexual interests.

Sibling interactions may influence ado-lescent friendships, especially for girls. For example, girls with a brother are more likely to report using control strategies with friends than girls with a sister (Updegraff, McHale, & Crouter, 2000). More generally, in a period of sex segregation, sibling interactions may pro-vide otherwise unavailable opportunities for learning about other-sex interactions (McHale et al., 1999).

Few children report preferences for other-sex relationships. Girls with gender-atypical inter-ests have some preference for other-sex peers (Bailey, Bechtold, & Berenbaum, 2002; Berenbaum & Snyder, 1995). Sexual minority youth report predominantly same-sex peers, but both sexes report more friendships with girls than boys (Diamond & Dube, 2002).

Work of the past decade has highlighted developmental patterns of sexual attraction and behavior. This work is discussed in detail else-where in this *Handbook* (see chapter 14, this volume) so is briefly summarized here. With few exceptions (e.g., Hyde & Jaffee, 2000), most work concerns sexual minorities, although a complete picture requires understanding sex-ual development in all individuals (Diamond, 2003). Same-sex sexual orientation is thought to develop in stages marked by awareness of same-sex attractions in late childhood/early adolescence, followed by testing and explo-ration, and finally the adoption of a sexual minority label, disclosing sexual identity to others, and involvement in same-sex romantic relationships. Different models are needed to describe the development of sexual orienta-tion in men versus women, but these have yet to be fully articulated (Diamond, 2000; Savin-Williams & Diamond, 2000). Intriguing lon-gitudinal data from nonheterosexual women show fluidity in identity labels (Diamond, 2008). Precursors to sexual orientation have been identified. For example, early gender atypicality is apparent in individuals who grow up to identify themselves as homosexual or bisexual (Bailey & Zucker, 1995).

The Content of Gender Development: Styles and Symbols

Adolescent girls and boys differ in mannerisms, ways of dressing and appearing, body image, and communication styles (verbal and nonverbal). Research on the stylistic and symbolic aspects of gender differences in adolescence has largely focused on body image and its correlates. We also review the limited literature on verbal and nonverbal behaviors.

Body Image

Awareness of appearance, particularly of current cultural ideals for body size and shape, has received a great deal of empirical attention. Adolescents are well aware that thinness is the standard for the female body, whereas muscularity is the standard for the male body (Phelps et al., 1993). Adolescent girls, who are at particular risk for eating disorders, not only know that "thin is in" but recognize that the media, fashion models, and peers reinforce this standard and associate its attainment with attractiveness, happiness, and success (Tiggemann, Gardiner, & Slater, 2000). There is some variability, however, in this awareness. White girls, for example, are more aware of a thinness standard than are African American girls, but African American girls who hang out in mixed-ethnicity peer groups have higher awareness scores than their counterparts with primarily African American friends (Abrams & Stormer, 2002).

Girls' and boys' self-perceptions of their bodies (i.e., body image) show internalization of masculine and feminine body standards. By early adolescence, some girls show heightened concern about their appearance, which is associated with body dissatisfaction (Lindberg, Grabe, & Hyde, 2007; Sinton & Birch, 2006). Compared to adolescent boys, adolescent girls are generally more dissatisfied with their bodies and express more concerns about their weight (Barker & Galambos, 2003; Phelps et al.,

1993). A longitudinal study found that girls' weight concerns increased from age 11 to 16 and then decreased to age 18, whereas boys' weight concerns decreased from age 11 to 18 (May, Kim, McHale, & Crouter, 2006). These results echo those of a cross-sectional study in which body distortion (perceiving oneself as heavier than one's actual weight) was highest in girls age 15 or 16 compared to younger or older girls; there was no age-related difference in boys' body distortion (Phelps et al.). Peer sexual harassment and being teased about body size and shape are related to increased body dissatisfaction in both adolescent girls and boys, pointing to contextual effects (Barker & Galambos; Lindberg et al.). Increases in body image concerns, in turn, may put girls at risk for the development of eating disorders.

Preferences concerning body shape and size are believed to influence body image as adolescents mature physically and gain weight as a matter of course. Compared to their current status, the ideal figure preference for adolescent girls is a thinner body, while for adolescent boys it is a slightly heavier build (Phelps et al., 1993). The natural course of physical development takes girls away from their preference as their body mass index (BMI) increases; it brings boys closer to their preference as they gain weight and muscle mass. In fact, in one study, a higher BMI was related to body dissatisfaction only in girls (Barker & Galambos, 2003), but in another, BMI predicted body shame in both sexes (Lindberg et al., 2007). Ultimately, adolescents may engage in behaviors to bring their body images in line with preferences. Girls report engaging in more weight control behaviors than do boys (Barker & Galambos, 2003) and girls exhibit significantly higher prevalences of eating problems and disorders compared to boys (Crick & Zahn-Waxler, 2003).

Verbal and Nonverbal Behaviors

Studies of the verbal and nonverbal behaviors of adolescents are rare. One study of 11- to

14-year-olds in summer camp found that boys were more assertive and argumentative than were girls, whereas girls were more complimentary and advice seeking and giving than were boys (Savin-Williams, 1979). Another study found that 15-year-old unacquainted girl–boy pairs were more similar than different with respect to verbal behaviors (number of questions asked, interruptions, and shows of uncertainty; Kolaric & Galambos, 1995). Amount of speaking time, however, was higher for boys when the topic was a masculine task (changing oil) but higher in girls when the topic was feminine (babysitting). With respect to nonverbal behaviors, girls engaged in more smiling, coy smiling, hair flipping, and appearing smaller, whereas boys did more chin touching. There were no gender differences in gestures, head–facial touching, gazing, and head tilts. The authors speculated that girls engaged in nonverbal-display behaviors that communicated their femininity. Although these studies point to gender differences in adolescence, they do not indicate when the differences develop.

A study of the nonverbal behaviors of 10- and 13-year-old girls and boys in an interaction with an adult found that, although there was no gender difference in smiling or talking, girls looked more at their adult partners than did boys. Girls also engaged in more-back-channel behaviors (indications of interest without interrupting, e.g., "yes," "uhhuh") than did boys, but only at age 13 (van Beek, van Dolderen, & Dubas, 2006). Another study contrasting 13- and 16-year-olds in interactions with same-age, same-sex nondepressed peers found that older adolescent girls looked more at their partners while listening and while speaking and smiled more compared to younger adolescent girls; older adolescent boys, however, looked less at partners when listening and speaking and smiled less compared to younger adolescent boys (van Beek et al.). These results are suggestive of increases in gender-typed behaviors from early to middle adolescence (i.e., eye contact while listening and speaking, smiling).

A meta-analysis of gender differences in smiling indicates that females smile more than males, with the largest difference in adolescents, compared to young, middle-aged, and older adults (La France, Hecht, & Levy Paluck, 2003). Another meta-analysis examining talkativeness, affiliative speech, and assertive speech in children from age 1 to 17 years (Leaper & Smith, 2004) shows the subtlety of gender differences. Overall, girls were significantly more talkative than were boys, but only in early childhood; the sexes did not differ in affiliative behavior in middle childhood (5–9 years), but girls were significantly more affiliative than boys in adolescence (10–17 years). Assertive speech did not differentiate adolescent girls and boys. There appear to be selected gender differences in smiling and affiliation that may emerge in adolescence, but considerably more research is needed before we understand the nature and extent of gendered verbal and nonverbal behaviors.

The Content of Gender Development: Values Regarding Gender

Are there changes across adolescence in the evaluation of gender, including gender categories and the personal qualities and roles of females and males? What are adolescents' own preferences and biases regarding gender, and do these change in adolescence? As with other domains of gender, there has been far less research attention paid to development during adolescence compared to childhood. Developments in adolescence, including increasing social cognitive abilities that may allow for more flexibility in thinking and greater awareness of values held in the broader society, pubertal changes that transform the experience of being a girl or a boy, and the possibility of intensification of gender socialization pressures all mean, however, that the study of gender-oriented values in adolescence can provide important insights into our understanding of gender development. As we highlight below, recent research on adolescents' gender values does provide an important qualification to theories of gender development in showing that developmental patterns may differ as a function of the social ecologies within which youth are embedded. That is, there may not be a universal developmental course in the expression of gender values across adolescence. Instead, the development of values and their correlates may vary across contexts, and an important direction for research is to identify contextual moderators of the development of gendered values.

Although all societies mark the differential roles and status of women and men, conceptions of gender roles vary across time and place (e.g., Glick & Fiske, 2001). We know little, however, about the development of adolescents' concepts and beliefs regarding the status of gender categories (Ruble et al., 2006). Early research indicated that, by early adolescence, youth in more egalitarian societies (Sweden and the United States) recognize gender-based discrimination (Intons-Petersen, 1988). Recent cross-sectional research has shown that perceptions of gender inequality increase from middle childhood through late adolescence; with age, youth are more likely to report such inequality in the spheres of politics and business, but not in the home (Neff, Cooper, & Woodruff, 2007). Another line of research on youths' concepts and beliefs about gender focuses on age-related changes in reasoning about the bases for gender differences and gender discrimination (Killen, Lee-Kim, McGlothlin, & Stangor, 2002). This work suggests, for example, that with age, youth exhibit fewer essentialist and more socialization explanations for sex differences, though girls are more likely to focus on socialization explanations than boys (Neff & Terry-Schmidt, 2002). Research on attributions about gender and gender roles lies at the interface of developmental and social psychology, and such cross-disciplinary work is an important direction for future studies.

Another important direction for research concerns the implications for self-views of gender of perceptions of societal values regarding masculine and feminine attributes. From the perspective of social identity theory, membership in a social category such as male versus female has implications for an individual's self-perceptions to the extent that such categories vary in their prestige (Ruble et al., 2006). Research showing increasing gender differences in internalizing symptoms in early adolescence (e.g., Angold et al., 2002; Ge et al., 2001) is consistent with the possibility that increasing awareness of the differential status of men and women has implications for girls' mental health. With respect to achievement, girls rate themselves as lower in ability than boys in stereotypically masculine domains of achievement (even when they exhibit similar or higher levels of achievement), possibly reflecting their awareness of societal values about competence and achievement in men and women (e.g., Eccles, Wigfield, & Schiefele, 1998). Such studies provide only indirect evidence of the developmental significance of youths' perceptions, however (Ruble et al., 2006).

Most research on gender values has focused on preferences regarding gender, including gender role attitudes, or youths' beliefs about the activities that women and men should engage in and the attributes that they should portray. Perhaps because traditional values support higher status and prestige for the male role, most of this research shows that girls express more flexible and less stereotypic attitudes than boys (Ruble et al., 2006). When researchers use more subtle strategies for assessing implicit beliefs, however, sex differences are not as clear. A study of college-age youth, for example, found that women who are parents are seen as less agentic and committed to their jobs than men who are parents, and young men and women did not differ in these stereotyped judgments (Fuegan, Biernat, Haines, & Deaux, 2004).

A handful of studies has focused on the development of gender attitudes in adolescence. In one study of the development of gender role flexibility (Katz & Ksansnak, 1994), four possible trajectories of change from late middle childhood through late adolescence were identified, with the trajectories corresponding to major theoretical perspectives on gender development. From a social learning perspective, which highlights adolescents' increasing awareness of social models of the different roles of women and men, one possible trajectory is marked by increasingly traditional values across adolescence. From the perspective of gender schema theory (e.g., Martin & Halverson, 1981), gender attitudes should become more flexible (less traditional) over time as youths' reasoning skills develop and they become aware of and make efforts to account for observations that do not fit stereotypes. Two additional trajectories congruent with gender intensification are described by curvilinear patterns across adolescence and imply increasing flexibility in middle childhood followed by increasing traditionality in adolescence. Data from a cross-sectional study of three age groups of youth (in middle childhood, early adolescence, and later adolescence; Katz & Ksansnak, 1994) and short-term longitudinal studies that followed youth in middle childhood (Serbin et al., 1993) and in early adolescence (Liben & Bigler, 2002) revealed results that were most consistent with a gender schema perspective, with flexibility in attitudes increasing with age. In contrast, a longitudinal study of young adolescents found different patterns for girls and boys: from grade 6 to 8, girls became less traditional, a pattern consistent with a gender schema perspective, but boys became more traditional, consistent with gender intensification (Galambos et al., 1990). Discrepant results may reflect the use of somewhat different measures, and youth studied at different ages.

It seems most likely, however, that inconsistencies reflect the reality that there is not a universal pattern in the development of attitudes, but rather that developmental patterns differ across individuals and social contexts (Crouter, Whiteman, McHale, & Osgood, 2007): From an ecological perspective

(Bronfenbrenner, 1979), different processes may emerge in different social ecologies, such that youth living in contexts with egalitarian models will espouse increasingly flexible gender attitudes consistent with a cognitive developmental perspective, whereas those living in traditional contexts may exhibit increases in traditionality, consistent with social learning and gender intensification predictions. Trajectories of gender role attitude development from about age 7 to about age 19 are consistent with such an ecological model (Crouter, et al.). In this study, the overall or "normative" pattern of change showed declines in traditionality until middle adolescence, followed by increases in traditionality through later adolescence, a pattern consistent with a gender intensification hypothesis. But there were several moderators of these patterns, particularly parents' gender role attitudes, youth gender, and youths' position in the family structure. Girls with less traditional parents, particularly those with brothers, showed a pattern consistent with gender schema theory: continuous declines in traditionality from middle childhood through late adolescence. Boys from traditional families, however, showed a pattern at the other extreme: consistently high or increasing levels of traditionality from middle childhood through adolescence, a pattern congruent with a social learning model (Katz & Ksansank, 1994). Finally, boys from less traditional families and girls from traditional families showed patterns consistent with gender intensification: They displayed increasing flexibility until middle adolescence, followed by increases in traditionality. Studies like this one highlight the importance of examining gender development in context.

Much work has been directed at identifying social influences on individual differences in gender attitudes of youth, from family factors such as parents' attitudes, family roles, and family structure (e.g., Booth & Amato, 1994; Kiecolt & Acock, 1988; Tennenbaum & Leaper, 2002), to situations, culture, geography, and historical time (Harris & Firestone, 1998; Rice & Coates, 1995; Vogel, Tucker, Wester, & Heesacker, 1999). It also seems likely that development is driven in part by youth themselves, for example, through their own gendered characteristics. For example, girls who are gender atypical in their interests or identity might have consistently flexible attitudes and be less subject to gender socialization pressures at adolescence than are girls with traditional interests. The use of long-term longitudinal designs to study individual and group differences in developmental patterns of gender role attitudes and values about gender is an important direction for research.

The Content of Gender Development: Summary of Developmental Trends in Adolescence

There is much less evidence about development in adolescence than in childhood, and few researchers have used the multidimensional matrix of gender typing (Huston, 1983; Ruble et al., 2006) to study the ways in which different aspects of gender change. In nearly all content areas, some gender differences are well established by adolescence and persist throughout this developmental period (e.g., sex-typed activity interests; occupational interests; involvement in paid work, housework, and homework; parent–adolescent relations and activities; spatial ability), although average levels decline through the teens for both sexes in some characteristics (e.g., gender contentedness, activity interests, physical aggression). Some gender differences first emerge in adolescence (e.g., depression, eating problems) whereas others exist at entry into adolescence and escalate (e.g., math anxiety). Other gender gaps narrow across adolescence (e.g., relationship intimacy). In the case of yet other dimensions, such as values regarding gender, findings reveal that change patterns vary across context. There also are gender differences in cross-time stability, as in the case of conduct problems, which are stable for

boys but not for girls from childhood through adolescence. The great diversity of paths across adolescence in the gender-linked constructs highlighted by the matrix demonstrates that gender development does not follow a single path. In the second half of this chapter, we consider the array of influences that are responsible for these diverse patterns.

INFLUENCES ON GENDER DEVELOPMENT

Much has been written on the causes of gendered characteristics. It is beyond the scope of this chapter to present this work in detail. Instead, we review key propositions and supporting research pertaining to contemporary theoretical perspectives on gender development during adolescence, specifically biological, cognitive, and socialization perspectives.

Biological Influences

Biological explanations of adolescent development have generally been narrowly focused on the role of pubertal sex hormones. As discussed by Susman and Dorn (chapter 5, this volume), pubertal hormones are powerful influences on adolescent development. But they are not the only type of biological influence. Biological approaches to gender development provide explanations of gendered psychological characteristics using the same biological processes that explain gender-related *physical* characteristics. This includes immediate or proximal causes—sex chromosomes, genes, and sex hormones—and historical or distal ones— evolutionary processes. In addition, biological approaches include the study of sex differences in the brain, but the brain changes in response to experience, so sex differences in brain structure and function might either cause gender-related behavior or result from it.

Biological perspectives on gender development have become increasingly visible and accepted. Converging data from multiple methods (facilitated by methodological and technological advances) provide compelling support for biological contributors to gender development. Most of this work concerns children and adults rather than adolescents, but the similarity of results across childhood and adulthood suggests that biological factors likely contribute to adolescent gender development as well. Questions no longer concern whether behavior is influenced by nature or nurture, but the mechanisms by which biology and the social environment work together to produce behavior. There is sophisticated understanding of the malleability of biological processes, which means that biological influences on gender development are not deterministic.

Evolutionary Psychology Perspectives

Evolutionary psychologists view behavior as the result of adaptive pressures, and thus that brains—and, therefore, behaviors—developed to solve the problems faced by our ancestors, with good solutions enabling them to survive and reproduce. Through natural and sexual selection, psychological characteristics that increase reproductive success become increasingly common. There are different specific challenges for men and women related to their different roles in reproduction, so, according to evolutionary psychologists, sex differences in reproductive tasks result in psychological sex differences (Trivers, 1972). Women can have only a limited number of children, so they want to ensure that each child is "high quality" and will survive to reproduce him- or herself; this is considered to account for women's preferences for men with characteristics likely to reflect "good genes" and the ability to provide resources. Men cannot be certain about paternity, and this has been interpreted to account for men's preferences for multiple partners (increasing the likelihood of fathering children).

Thus, sex differences in adaptive pressures related to differences in reproduction are hypothesized to result in behavioral gender differences seen today. Consider the example of an evolutionary perspective applied to spatial ability, which shows an increasing gender difference in adolescence. Traditional evolutionary explanations have focused on the nature of the work done by the two sexes, with males hunting and females gathering. An alternative evolutionary explanation emphasizes the importance of good spatial skills for males' ability to traverse large territories and encounter many females, with corresponding opportunities to mate and produce offspring (Gaulin, 1995).

There are many appeals of an evolutionary approach for understanding behavioral sex differences. It places behavior on an equal footing with other (physical) traits, correctly conceptualizes behavior (as other traits) as adaptation to problems faced by ancestors, and provides a single explanation for a range of behavioral sex differences. There is some evidence that evolution can account for physiological and neurochemical differences between the sexes that underlie differences in psychological characteristics.

Nevertheless, evolutionary theories are controversial as scientific explanations of psychological sex differences (Eagly & Wood, 1999; Newcombe, 2007). The main concerns relate to (1) the difficulty of inferring adaptive significance—a specific behavior may have "evolved" because it was adaptive or as a by-product of another trait that was crucial to survival; (2) the difficulty of providing empirical evidence that evolutionary theory uniquely explains the phenomena of interest—for example, sex differences in interest in multiple sex partners might arise from modeling; and (3) the failure to consider the complexity of selection—for example, fitness depends not just on the number of offspring produced, but on the number who survive to reproduce themselves, so both sexes need to invest in their offspring. These concerns have led to the development of an alternative biosocial perspective which focuses on the origin of sex differences in the different placements of women and men in the social structure, rather than in evolved dispositions (Eagly & Wood; Wood & Eagly, 2002).

Perspectives from Physical Sexual Differentiation

Considerable work focuses on the ways in which gender development parallels physical sexual differentiation, a process governed by sex chromosomes, genes, and sex hormones. Genetic sex is determined at conception by the composition of the sex chromosomes (XX or XY). The sexes start out with the same sets of structures that differentiate into male or female gonads, internal reproductive organs, and genitals (Grumbach, Hughes, & Conte, 2002). Male development is initiated by the *SRY* gene on the Y chromosome and then largely depends on hormones secreted by the testes, particularly high levels of androgen, and functioning androgen receptors. Female-typical development is seen as a default process, occurring when *SRY* is absent and androgen is low (estrogen has little role during prenatal development), although completely normal female development requires other genes. Sex hormones continue to exert physical effects after birth, primarily at puberty and into adolescence and adulthood; they are responsible for the development of secondary sex characteristics and the achievement of reproductive capacity. Disorders of sex development (formerly called "intersex" conditions) provide opportunities to study effects on gender development of genes and hormones, as described below.

Genetic Influences on Gender Development: Sex Chromosome Effects

It is not easy to study whether gender development is directly influenced by genes on the sex chromosomes, because there are very few conditions in which effects of those genes can be studied in isolation. Most evidence about the behavioral effects of genes on the X chromosome comes from individuals with Turner syndrome who develop as females but have an absent or poorly formed second X chromosome. Girls and women with Turner syndrome have normal verbal abilities, but deficits in specific cognitive abilities, including visual–spatial ability, executive function, and social cognition (e.g., recognizing emotion in faces; Ross, Roeltgen, & Zinn, 2006). It is difficult to determine whether these deficits are directly due to their chromosomal abnormalities or to the low levels of hormones that result from the deficient X chromosome, but intriguing molecular genetic data have tied the visuospatial deficits to genes on a specific region of the X chromosome (Ross, Roeltgen, Kushner, Wei, & Zinn, 2000).

Behavioral effects of genes on the Y chromosome can be studied in people with complete androgen insensitivity syndrome (AIS), who have normal male sex chromosomes with a functional *SRY* gene, normal testes that make male-typical levels of androgen, but defective androgen receptors, which makes them unable to respond to the androgens they produce, so they develop a female body and are reared as females. If genes on the Y chromosome affect gender-related behavior, then people with AIS should be male-typical (in contrast with their female rearing and low androgen levels). Extant data show that they are female-typical, for example, in gender role (such as recalled childhood activities), sexual orientation, gender identity, and marital status (Hines, Ahmed, & Hughes, 2003; Wisniewski et al., 2000).

Genetic Influences on Gender Development: Autosomal Effects

Gendered characteristics may also be influenced by genes that are shared by the sexes but are differently expressed in them due to sex differences in other aspects of physiology, such as sex hormones. The genes involved in baldness, for example, are on the autosomes, but their expression requires the presence of high levels of testosterone (Otberg, Finner, & Shapiro, 2007). Sex differences in environmental exposure might also affect gene expression (Wizemann & Pardue, 2001). For example, sex differences in skin cancer rates might be due to modification of gene expression by sex differences in sun exposure.

Gene expression also applies to psychological traits, and there is some evidence that puberty regulates genes that influence gendered characteristics, specifically eating disorders. A longitudinal twin study showed that some genes become important only after puberty: Genetic factors accounted for a small proportion of the variation in disordered eating at age 11, but almost half the variation at ages 14 and 18 years, and the authors suggested that "the transition from early to mid adolescence (is) a critical time for the emergence of a genetic diathesis for disordered eating" (Klump, Burt, McGue, & Iacono, 2007). In general, the triggers for gene expression are both intrinsic (e.g., hormones) and extrinsic (e.g., diet, maternal care), so gene regulation can help us to understand both biological and social influences on adolescent gender development. It is likely that research efforts over the next few years will identify the ways in which the physical and psychological changes of adolescence "turn on" specific genes related to gender.

Hormonal Influences on Behavior and Brain

The same hormones that produce physical sexual differentiation also affect sexual differentiation of the brain and behavior (Becker, Breedlove, Crews, & McCarthy, 2002; Cohen-Bendahan, van de Beek, & Berenbaum, 2005). Hormones affect behavior in two ways: by producing permanent changes to brain structures and the behaviors they subserve, usually early in life ("organizational" effects) and by producing temporary alterations to the brain and behavior (through ongoing changes to neural circuitry) as the hormones circulate in the body, primarily throughout adolescence and adulthood ("activational" effects); the distinction between organizational and activational hormone effects is not absolute. The key sensitive period for human brain and behavioral sexual differentiation has been considered to occur during weeks 8–24 of gestation, but other times may be important. There is increasing attention to puberty as another sensitive period for permanent brain changes (discussed later).

It is not possible to investigate the effects of hormones in people by manipulating their levels, but much has been learned from individuals whose hormone levels were atypical for their sex during early development as a result of genetic disease or maternal ingestion of drugs during pregnancy to prevent miscarriage. Evidence from these natural experiments has been supplemented by data from normal individuals with typical variations in hormones. Most of this work has been conducted in preschool and school-aged children and adults, so we discuss only a sample of this work here (for additional information, see Berenbaum, 2006; Cohen-Bendahan et al., 2005; Ruble et al., 2006). Nevertheless, the similarity of results across age groups suggests that similar findings will be obtained in adolescents.

Prenatal Hormones and Gender Development: Experiments of Nature

The most extensively studied natural experiment, congenital adrenal hyperplasia (CAH) is a genetic disease that results in exposure to high levels of androgens beginning early in gestation because of an enzyme defect affecting cortisol production. Females with CAH have external genitalia masculinized to varying degrees, but they have ovaries and a uterus and are fertile. Most girls are diagnosed at birth and treated with cortisol to reduce androgen excess (or they will experience rapid growth and early puberty) and surgically to feminize their genitalia. If androgens that are present during sensitive periods of development affect later gender development, then females with CAH should be more male typical and less female-typical than a comparison group of females without CAH (discussed later). Males with CAH have few prenatal effects and are treated postnatally with cortisol to maintain growth and prevent early puberty and other consequences of the disease. They are reared as boys, develop male gender identity, and generally display male-typical behavior (Berenbaum, 2001; Cohen-Bendahan et al., 2005).

Considerable evidence shows girls and women with CAH to be masculinized and defeminized in aspects of their feelings, preferences, and behavior. The largest and most consistent effects (more than one standard deviation) concern gendered interests and activities: from childhood through adolescence into adulthood, girls and women with CAH report being more interested in male-typed occupations than in female-typed occupations, and they report liking and engaging more in male-typed activities and less in female-typed activities than do typical girls and women (usually their unaffected sisters; Berenbaum, 1999; Berenbaum & Snyder, 1995; Meyer-Bahlburg, Dolezal, Baker, Ehrhardt, & New, 2006; Servin, Nordenström, Larsson, & Bohlin, 2003). Observational studies in children confirm the increased boy-typed toy play of girls with CAH (Berenbaum & Snyder; Nordenström, Servin, Bohlin, Larsson, & Wedell, 2002). There is, unfortunately, no study of time use in adolescent girls with CAH.

The masculinized interests and activities characteristic of females with CAH appear to result directly from prenatal androgen. For example, time spent playing with boys' toys is correlated with degree of prenatal androgen excess (Berenbaum, Duck, & Bryk, 2000; Nordenström et al., 2002); parents do not seem to socialize girls with CAH in a masculine way, and may, in fact, pressure them to behave in feminine ways (Nordenström et al.; Pasterski et al., 2005). In light of the subtlety of parent socialization of gender (as described later), it will be interesting to examine gender development in girls with CAH in family context.

Girls and women with CAH are masculinized and defeminized in other domains, with effects moderate to large in size (Cohen-Bendahan et al., 2005). Females with CAH are more aggressive than their unaffected sisters, as revealed in parent reports of children (Pasterski et al., 2007) and self-reports of adults (Berenbaum & Resnick, 1997). Girls with CAH are reported by their parents to be less interested in babies than are their sisters. At several ages from late childhood to adulthood, females with CAH scored higher on spatial tasks than unaffected females; meta-analysis shows the effects to be small to moderate in size (Puts, McDaniel, Jordan, & Breedlove, 2008). Women with CAH are more likely than typical women to have bisexual or homosexual orientation, although about 65% are exclusively heterosexual (Hines, Brook, & Conway, 2004; Zucker et al., 1996).

Gender identity is typical in the majority of girls and women with CAH, although degree of identification may be reduced compared to typical females (Berenbaum & Bailey, 2003). Degrees of prenatal androgen excess and genital appearance do not appear to contribute to variations in gender identity. Gender change in females with CAH is uncommon but still more common than in the general population; it is equally likely in those few reared male and those reared female (Dessens, Slijper, & Drop, 2005).

Findings from girls and women with CAH have been confirmed when they have been tested in other natural experiments, although such studies are limited by the rarity of these other conditions. For example, individuals with male-typical prenatal development (chromosomes and androgens) who were reared as girls because of a birth defect (called cloacal exstrophy) resulting in an absent or poorly formed penis have male-typed activity interests and sexual attraction to women (consistent with exposure to high prenatal androgens), but most have female gender identity (consistent with rearing; Meyer-Bahlburg, 2005).

Prenatal Hormones and Gender Development: Normal Variations

Considerable work has been directed to examining the generalizability of results obtained in clinical populations, through studies of gender-related behavior in typical individuals in relation to prenatal hormones obtained from amniotic fluid or mother's blood during pregnancy (none directly measure fetal hormones) or to markers of prenatal hormones (Cohen-Bendahan et al., 2005). Associations between indicators of amniotic prenatal hormones and early childhood behavior are found sometimes (Lutchmaya, Baron-Cohen, & Raggatt, 2002) but not always (Knickmeyer et al., 2005). It is unclear whether negative findings indicate lack of association between behavior and testosterone within the normal range or study limitations (e.g., small samples, single measure, limited variability in testosterone). Two studies have found links between hormones in mother's blood during pregnancy and behavior in daughters, including parent-reported boy-typed activities in childhood (Hines et al., 2002) and a broad measure of gender roles in adulthood (Udry, 2000). There are currently no studies of adolescent behavior in relation to prenatal hormones assessed in amniotic fluid or mother's blood, but these data will likely become available as children already studied are followed into adolescence.

There has been increasing study of associations between behavior and morphological measures considered "markers" of prenatal hormone exposure. For example, fingerprint patterns, finger lengths, and otoacoustic emissions (sounds produced by the ear) have been related to sexual orientation, spatial ability, personality, and activity interests. These markers are nonintrusive, easily collected, and potentially valuable as retrospective measures of prenatal hormone exposure that can be used at all ages, but they are not sufficiently validated to ensure that they truly reflect within-sex variations in hormones present during sensitive periods of brain development (Cohen-Bendahan et al., 2005).

Pubertal Hormones and Gender Development

The main biological focus of adolescent gender development has concerned effects of changes in sex hormones and physical appearance at puberty. There is particular emphasis on characteristics that become increasingly gendered in adolescence and that relate to behavioral risk (e.g., substance use and mental health problems).

Hormonal increases at pubertal onset appear to increase girls' risk for serious depression, especially for those with genetic vulnerability (Angold, Costello, Erkanli, & Worthman, 1999), but not to increase negative affect in the normal range (Buchanan, Eccles, & Becker, 1992). As discussed elsewhere (chapter 5, this volume), associations between hormones and affect across the entire pubertal transition are neither simple nor large. Hormone effects are clearer in studies linking hormones to aggression and behavior problems, particularly in boys (Buchanan et al.; Susman et al., 1998). Hormones both affect and are affected by behavior. For example, testosterone levels increase in adult sports players who win and in their fans (e.g., Bernhardt, Dabbs, Fielden, & Lutter, 1998). Behavioral effects of testosterone also depend on social context (e.g., Rowe, Maughan, Worthman, Costello, & Angold, 2004).

Circulating hormones also appear to be weakly associated with patterns of cognitive abilities, although the links are not always found and the strongest evidence comes from observational studies in adults (Hampson, 2002). Verbal fluency and memory are enhanced by circulating estrogens beginning in adolescence. Spatial ability is enhanced by moderate levels of androgen in adults (i.e., levels high for normal females, low for normal males).

Some of the inconsistencies about hormonal influences on adolescent behavior reflect the complexity and challenges of assessing pubertal hormones and the physical changes that accompany them (Dorn, Dahl, Woodward, & Biro, 2006). Even direct hormone assays are limited unless they are repeated to capture intraindividual variability. Because biology does not operate in a vacuum, it is important to study how hormones are mediated through and modified by social context to produce gender-related changes during adolescence. For example, links between testosterone and child gendered adjustment outcomes (risky behavior, depression) were found to depend on the quality of parent–child interactions: Hormone–behavior associations were found only when relationship quality was poor, suggesting that relationships buffer hormonal effects (Booth, Johnson, Granger, Crouter, & McHale, 2003).

Timing of pubertal maturation relates to behavioral risk, especially in girls (see chapter 5, this volume). Early-maturing girls have more emotional distress and problem behavior (e.g., delinquency, substance use, early sexuality) than on-time peers (e.g., Ge, Conger, & Elder, 1996) and these problems persist into adulthood (Weichold, Silbereisen, & Schmitt-Rodermund, 2003). There is good evidence that these effects are mediated and moderated by socialization. For example, girls who mature early associate with older and male peers who expose them to risky substances and activities (Weichold et al., 2003); early maturers' higher rate of externalizing behavior has been linked to parents' use of harsh inconsistent discipline (Ge, Brody, Conger, Simons, & Murry, 2002). These effects vary by social context. For example, early-maturing children living in disadvantaged neighborhoods were significantly more likely to affiliate with deviant peers (Ge et al., 2002); problem behaviors were higher in early-maturing girls who attended coeducational schools than in their counterparts in all-girl schools (Caspi, Lynam, Moffitt, & Silva, 1993).

Interestingly, however, recent work in rodents suggests that behavioral changes at puberty might reflect permanent changes to the brain induced by hormones (e.g., Sisk & Zehr, 2005). Given cross-species continuities in hormone–behavior links, it is likely that similar effects operate in human adolescents, and an exciting area of current inquiry concerns the ways in which the behavioral risks associated with early puberty are mediated by permanent changes in the brain.

Neural Substrates of Gender Development

Ultimately, all aspects of gender development—as all psychological functions—are mediated through the brain. Studies of brain sex differences have generally been based on the premise that these differences are responsible for behavioral differences observed, but the brain changes in response to the environment, so brain sex differences could result from behavioral differences. Information about brain sex differences has increased dramatically with the availability of imaging techniques, including structural magnetic resonance imaging (MRI) to observe details of brain structure, and functional MRI (fMRI) to measure brain activation to specific tasks (Resnick, 2006).

There is a sex difference in brain size (about 10% larger in men than in women), which is largely attributable to the difference in body size (Halpern, 2000). There are also sex differences in fine-grained aspects of brain structure that relate to function, such as the relative amounts of gray and white matter, which contain cell bodies and fiber tracts, respectively. Some studies suggest that females have more cortical gray matter (e.g., Good et al., 2001; Witelson, Glezer, & Kigar, 1995), whereas males have more white matter (e.g., De Bellis et al., 2001; Giedd et al., 1999), differences that might have implications for task performance and processes involving coordination among multiple brain areas, respectively.

A well-replicated finding concerns sex differences in cerebral lateralization (also known as hemispheric specialization). In most people, the left hemisphere is specialized for language tasks and the right for perceptual and spatial processing, with some variation among individuals and groups (e.g., handedness) in the extent of this specialization. Women are somewhat less lateralized than men (Voyer, 1996) in terms of both brain structure and function (Resnick, 2006); there may also be sex differences in brain organization within hemispheres (Kimura, 1999). Sex differences in lateralization have been suggested to represent neural underpinnings of sex differences in cognition and behavior, but there is little direct evidence for this association, and the sex difference in lateralization is smaller than most psychological sex differences, so lateralization cannot be the main basis for these differences.

Contemporary research focuses on specific aspects of brain structure associated with specific behaviors, asking whether brain sex differences underlie sex differences in psychological functions that are subserved by those regions. There is not a consistent pattern of sex differences in specific brain regions; some of this may reflect methodological issues (Raz et al., 2004; Resnick, 2006). Further, it is unclear what significance should be attached to sex differences in the size of specific areas (Lenroot & Giedd, 2006; Paus, 2005): Brain sex differences are generally small; a large brain size does not always mean optimal function; brain size differences have seldom been explicitly related to behavioral differences; and brain structure changes in response to experience. Thus, even if reliable sex differences in brain structure emerge, it will be difficult to determine whether they are the causes or the consequences of sex differences in behavior.

Developmental changes in the structure of the brain, including sex differences, are only beginning to be understood (Giedd, 2004; Giedd et al., 1999). Some of the most exciting work has come from a long-term longitudinal study tracking brain development in individual children, and the ways in which development differs for boys and girls (Lenroot et al., 2007). This work, using MRI, has shown the subtleties of sex differences in brain development. Girls appear to reach a peak earlier in brain development than do boys. In the cerebral cortex, the volume appears to peak at age 10.5 in girls and age 14.5 in boys. Gray matter increases and then decreases in both sexes, with the peak occurring 1–2 years earlier in girls than in boys. White matter increases in both sexes throughout ages 3–27, but boys have a steeper rate of increase during adolescence. These data suggest that the key brain sex differences occur in developmental trajectory, rather than in final end points.

Paralleling structural MRI studies examining sex differences in the size of specific brain regions are fMRI studies examining sex differences in the activation of specific regions in response to psychologically relevant stimuli or tasks. As with studies of structure, most of these studies have been conducted in adults. We provide examples of brain activation during gender-related tasks of cognition and emotion; see Resnick (2006) for additional information. In a rhyming task, the sexes differentially activated the left and right frontal regions: Men used the left only, whereas women used both the left and right hemispheres (Shaywitz et al., 1995). There was little overlap between the sexes, but the activation difference did not translate into a performance difference, perhaps because the task was easy. In navigating a virtual-reality maze, men performed more quickly than women, and the sexes activated different regions: Men were more likely to use the left hippocampus and women the right parietal and prefrontal regions, and this difference was suggested to reflect men's use of geometric cues versus women's use of landmarks (Grön, Wunderlich, Spitzer, Tomczak, & Riepe, 2000). This finding parallels one in rats showing that females preferentially use landmarks and males use geometric cues in solving a spatial task, and that these sex differences are produced by early sex hormones (Williams & Meck, 1991).

The amygdala has received a lot of attention because of its role in processing emotion (Hamann & Canli, 2004). Meta-analysis suggests no sex difference in overall activation to emotional stimuli, but a sex difference in lateralization of activation (men greater than women) (Wager, Phan, Liberzon, & Taylor, 2003). The amygdala may also mediate sex differences in sexual arousal: In response to sexual stimuli, the amygdala and hypothalamus were more strongly activated in men than in women (Hamann, Herman, Nolan, & Wallen, 2004).

Hormones and the Brain

Hormonal effects on behavior most likely occur through effects on the brain, but there are only a few relevant studies. Circulating estrogens appear to affect gender-related cognition through effects on brain activity (Maki & Resnick, 2001). For example, there are menstrual cycle changes in women's brain activity while solving mental rotation tasks, and estrogen-associated changes in brain activation for memory tasks in postmenopausal women. Interesting questions concern the ways in which changes in sex hormones at puberty affect behavior through effects on the brain. For example, how does estrogen affect the brain to increase the likelihood of depression in teenage girls but not boys, and how does testosterone affect the brain to increase the display of aggression in teenage boys more than in girls? Further, in light of suggestions from animal work that variations in pubertal timing affect behavior through changes to the organization of the brain (Sisk & Zehr, 2005), it will be interesting to study whether early-maturing girls' increased risk of psychological problems is associated with specific brain changes, particularly in regions known to mature at puberty.

Biological Influences: Summary and Directions for Research

It is clear that biology plays a role in gender development, with particular evidence that hormones present during early development affect gendered activities and interests and some personal–social attributes, that hormone effects at adolescence are moderated by social context, and that brain development occurs on a different timetable for girls and boys. But there is much still to be known about biological influences on adolescent development, including early hormone effects on adolescents' time use, how hormonally influenced characteristics change adolescents' transactions with the environment, and brain mediators of cognitive and social changes at adolescence (and their dependence on or independence from hormonal changes at puberty). Biology operates in social context, and the most exciting questions concern the ways in which the social environment regulates genetic and hormonal processes to bring about adolescent gender development.

Cognitive Influences

A key perspective on gender development concerns the central role of cognitions or thoughts about gender. We focus on three prominent cognitive theories of gender development: cognitive developmental, gender schemas, and group identity.

Cognitive Developmental Theory

A chapter by Kohlberg (1966) heralded the cognitive approach to understanding gender development. Kohlberg was largely focused on explaining gender development in childhood, and proposed the radical idea that children socialize *themselves* in gendered ways, by categorizing individuals (including themselves) and actively processing information according to gender (Ruble et al., 2006). Of importance to his theory is the child's acquisition of gender knowledge, which was thought to develop in stages from gender identity (knowing that one is male or female) to gender stability (knowing that gender is maintained over time), and then to gender consistency (knowing that gender identity is stable over changes in gender-linked traits, behaviors, and/or appearances). These achievements, which together comprise gender constancy, enable the child to seek information concerning sex-appropriate behaviors (i.e., to construct the meaning of gender) and then to behave accordingly (in a gender-typed manner) to achieve consistency between the self and the environment. Aspects of gender constancy do indeed seem to facilitate children's gendered behavior and understanding of gender but the relative roles of each stage of gender constancy need to be clarified, and gender constancy does not precede all aspects of gender development (Martin, Ruble, & Szkrybalo, 2002).

Kohlberg's theory has less to say about gender development in adolescence than in the early years, although advances in cognitive development that occur with age are expected to shape children's understandings of gender as well as their own gender-typed behaviors. A growing body of brain research shows changes in the prefrontal cortex, improved connectivity among different regions of the brain through increased myelination, and selective synaptic pruning in adolescence (e.g., Giedd, 2004; Giedd et al., 1999), which may underlie enhanced executive functioning, including more rapid processing of information (e.g., Demetriou et al., 2002), formal reasoning skills, and judgment and decision-making (Keating, 2004; see chapters 4 and 6, this volume). Indeed, Keating argued that the brain changes of adolescence likely transform the adolescent into a conscious being who actively self-guides and self-regulates emotion, attention, and behavior, all of which imply improved cognitive flexibility. As a result of such cognitive changes, increased flexibility in gender-related attitudes and behaviors is expected in middle childhood to adolescence (Serbin et al., 1993).

Gender Schema Theory

Kohlberg's cognitive developmental theory paved the way for other cognitive theories, including the gender schema theories of Bem (1981), which focused on individual differences, and Martin and Halverson (1981), which focused on developmental changes. Gender schemas are beliefs, cognitions, and ideas related to sex differences and to masculinity and femininity that organize the way that people, situations, and events are interpreted and can influence and bias behavior (Martin et al., 2002). From Bem's perspective, individuals were considered to vary in their use of gender schemas, or naive theories about gender, through which they view the world and themselves, with gender-schematic individuals seeing the world and themselves in terms of gender stereotypes (males should be masculine and act in masculine ways, whereas females should be feminine and act in feminine ways), and gender-aschematic individuals less attuned to noticing and interpreting their own and others' behavior in gendered terms.

Martin and Halverson (1981) emphasized the role of gender schemas in children's own gender development. Schemas serve several functions, regulating behavior by providing scripts for acting in ways consistent with one's gender, pointing to information to be attended to, encoded, and recalled, and facilitating inferences and interpretations about the social world. Whereas cognitive developmental theory emphasizes the need for complete gender constancy before gender development can occur, gender schema theory focuses on the importance of early gender knowledge (children's recognition that there are two gender groups and that they belong to one) and the ways in which this knowledge motivates gender-related behavior and thinking early in childhood (Martin & Ruble, 2004).

Cognitive developmental theory leads to the search for general or universal patterns of age-related changes in sex typing, whereas gender schema theories focus more on individual differences in cognitive processes, including effects of the social environment (Serbin et al., 1993). Gender schema theory does also address universal patterns of early gender development, however, leading to predictions about the acquisition of knowledge and beliefs in childhood: Learning about the genders is believed to start in the toddler years; additional knowledge and beliefs about the genders solidify and become rigidly applied by age 5–7 years, and then are used in a flexible way until age 12 or so (Martin & Ruble, 2004). With the focus on early gender development, gender schema theorists have paid less attention to changes in adolescence, although, as noted earlier, cognitive developmental theory proposes increased gender flexibility due to increased cognitive flexibility.

A rare longitudinal study of children's beliefs about stereotypic differences between the sexes (Trautner et al., 2005) indicated that rigidity of beliefs was highest between the ages of 5 and 7, but decreased steadily and significantly between ages 7 and 10 (i.e., flexibility increased in this period). Interestingly, these changes were normative, and individual differences in rigidity were not maintained across time; although there was variation in the age at which children became flexible, there was little variation by age 10. Cross-sectional research with 3- to 7-year-olds confirmed the general pattern of increasing rigidity followed by flexibility; peak rigidity was reached by age 5, but decreased by age 7 (Ruble et al., 2007). Consistent with Kohlberg's ideas, some relations between age and rigidity, however, were mediated by gender constancy (i.e., stability or consistency), which increased with age and was associated with lower rigidity (Ruble et al.). These studies suggest a universal pattern of development of stereotypic beliefs in the early years, with the timing of changes in these beliefs connected to cognitive changes.

A consideration of trajectories of gender flexibility into adolescence is important given competing hypotheses, with cognitive theories suggesting an increase in flexibility and gender intensification predicting a decrease at least for a time around puberty. As reviewed earlier, several studies suggest that flexibility in some personal preferences and attitudes toward gender nontraditionality in others increases with age from middle childhood into early and middle adolescence (e.g., Liben & Bigler, 2002; Katz & Ksansnak, 1994; Serbin et al., 1993), although there are exceptions. For example, flexibility increased after the transition to junior high school, followed by a decrease through high school (Alfieri, Ruble, & Higgins, 1996). Inconsistencies may be attributable to individual and contextual characteristics that affect whether flexibility is expressed. These include at least adolescent gender and birth order, sibling gender, parents' gender attitudes and household and occupational activities, and timing of school transitions (e.g., Alfieri et al.; Crouter et al., 2007; Katz & Ksansnak, 1994). A broader set of biological, social, and cognitive factors (and their interactions) that explain variability about the average trajectory should be considered. It would be interesting, for example, to study directly how flexibility is affected by hormonally influenced characteristics (e.g., whether, compared to typical girls, girls with CAH are less flexible and whether this reflects their male-typed interests) and by brain changes subserving cognitive changes (e.g., executive

functioning), and to observe whether social context affects these relations.

Few, if any, studies have examined the extent to which changes in gender flexibility in adolescence are dependent on normative cognitive development, or whether there are meaningful individual differences that are influenced by variations in cognition. A study of 5- to 12-year-olds showed that greater gender flexibility was related to one aspect of cognitive maturity—conservation ability—suggesting that cognitive advances may accompany decreases in stereotyped beliefs, as cognitive developmental theory suggests (Serbin et al., 1993). Research is needed to examine the extent to which brain changes and improvements in executive functioning covary with changes in gender flexibility across adolescence.

Whether flexibility changes during the transition into adulthood is also an interesting developmental question. Some limited experimental evidence suggests that gender schemas are similar in adolescents and young adults. In a study that included comparisons of 11- to 13-year-olds with young adults, male participants had better incidental (unintentional) memory for male-stereotyped toy pictures than for female- or neutral-typed, whereas female participants remembered both male- and female-typed toys better than neutral; there were no age differences in memory for gender-schematic information (Cherney, 2005). In other work, gender stereotypes for activities or psychological traits were shown to be activated in 11-year-olds and in adult females and males, and stereotypes could be inhibited in both age groups by introducing new evidence (Barberá, 2003). Gender-schematic encoding for occupations was similar in female and male sixth graders and college students (Kee, Gregory-Domingue, Rice, & Tone, 2005). Although these cross-sectional studies suggest that automatic gender schematic processing may operate in the same way in early adolescence and adulthood, more studies spanning the periods from childhood through adolescence and into adulthood are needed in order to draw conclusions about age differences or age-related changes in processing of information about gender. Whether gender-schematic processing relates to general improvements in executive functioning across adolescence would be an interesting avenue of research.

How do gender cognitions relate to behavior in adolescence? Given the proposed importance of gender schemas for motivating behavior (Martin & Halverson, 1981), another direction for research is to investigate how gender schemas guide gender-linked self-evaluations and behaviors in adolescence. In two rare exemplary studies, there was evidence for such links. In 9- to 12-year-old girls, appearance schemas (cognitive investment in physical appearance) predicted body dissatisfaction more than did appearance media exposure and conversations with friends about appearance (Clark & Tiggemann, 2007). In middle adolescence, appearance schematicity at age 15 years predicted increases in body dissatisfaction by age 17 among girls but not boys (Hargreaves & Tiggemann, 2002). If gender schemas provide scripts for behavior, as gender schema theory and these studies of body dissatisfaction suggest, then it would be particularly worthwhile to examine how gender schemas influence behaviors in other prominent domains of adolescent development. For example, adolescents have sexual (Krahé, Bieneck, & Scheinberger-Olwig, 2007) and academic (Grabill et al., 2005) scripts that could be examined as predictors of gender differences in sexual and academic behaviors.

Group Identity Theory

Another cognitive perspective on gender development derives from work in social psychology concerned with effects of group membership on individuals' behavior, particularly effects of social identity (Tajfel & Turner, 1986). Individuals use cognitive processes to categorize themselves as members of particular groups (e.g., gender, ethnicity), and then use these categories to establish a social or collective identity (e.g., identifying with the male or female gender). Collective identities enhance self-concepts by facilitating positive comparisons with the in-group (the group with which one identifies) and sometimes negative comparisons with out-group members; these comparisons are associated with stereotyping, prejudice, and derogation (Ruble et al., 2006; Tajfel & Turner). The categorization process and resulting collective identity serve important functions. First, the sense of "we-ness" facilitates belongingness and connectedness with others in the group, in turn enhancing self-esteem. Second, collective identity has motivational significance, as it enables the formation of values and interests congruent with beliefs about the in-group, and ultimately shapes behavior. Group status is important, as members of high-status groups (e.g., boys) take positions that maintain their perceived superiority (Ruble et al., 2006). Indeed, sex differences in attitudes in early adolescence—with boys' attitudes toward women becoming less egalitarian and girls' attitudes becoming more egalitarian (Galambos et al., 1990)—may reflect gender intensification resulting from social identity and power differentials.

Social identity concepts have been used to understand the development of stereotypes and prejudices about gender (e.g., Bigler & Liben, 2007). This process involves children's noticing that people are implicitly and explicitly grouped in the social environment on the basis of person attributes such as gender (so that the grouping attribute becomes psychologically salient), then categorizing individuals on these salient dimensions, and finally developing stereotypes and prejudices associated with these groups, exaggerating differences between the in-group and out-group.

There is ample evidence that children group people by gender and use this information to make judgments about them. Not only do they show in-group bias, but by 5 years some may actively reject and become hostile to the other sex, a phenomenon that continues into early adolescence (Maccoby & Jacklin, 1987;

Powlishta, Serbin, Doyle, & White, 1994; Yee & Brown, 1994). For example, when 8- to 10-year-old children rated unfamiliar target boys and girls in a videotape, they showed bias for their own sex and against the other sex (Powlishta, 1995): Girls rated the qualities of the target girls more favorably than did boys, both girls and boys indicated that they liked targets of their own sex more than members of the other sex, and girls and boys exaggerated perceived similarities of same-sex targets to themselves (intragroup similarities) and differences with other-sex targets (intergroup differences). In a separate mixed-sex group puzzle task, children chose to interact more with others of their own sex. The extent to which adolescents evidence in-group and out-group biases and whether their social behavior is shaped by such biases are intriguing issues, considering the importance of peer groups and romantic relations to adolescents in general.

In this regard, self-report data show that group bias and social identity processes concerning peers are apparent in adolescence (Tarrant, 2002; Tarrant, North, & Hargreaves, 2004), although there are few studies specific to gender group bias. In one exceptional study (Eckes, Trautner, & Behrendt, 2005), high school students aged 16–19 years evaluated peer crowds to which they belonged and did not belong. Participants showed clear evidence of intergroup bias, but it transcended gender: Both girls and boys favored own-gender in-groups but evaluated out-groups (whether same- or other-gender) more negatively; they rated own-gender out-groups more negatively than they rated other-gender out-groups; for example, "athletic" girls found "prissy" girls to be less attractive than boys in the "macho" or "poser" crowds. Adolescents evidenced more ambivalence in their ratings of the attributes of other-gender out-groups (seeing both unfavorable and favorable attributes) than in same-gender out-groups, perhaps as a result of attractions that are inevitable between the sexes in adolescence (Eckes et al.). Other questionnaire studies have documented intergroup bias

and hostility toward the other sex in adolescents, with intergroup bias higher in childhood than in early to middle adolescence (Egan & Perry, 2001; Sherriff, 2007; Verkuyten & Thijs, 2001). Adolescent girls' gender bias is stronger than adolescent boys' (Egan & Perry, 2001), and this gender difference may be magnified in cultures with more gender segregation and defined gender roles (Verkuyten & Thijs, 2001).

In a study of status effects on intergroup phenomena, fourth-, sixth-, and eighth-grade Black and White girls and boys rated the competence of gender and ethnic groups in academic domains, sports, and music (Rowley, Mistry, & Feagans, 2007). Girls (who are of lower status) showed in-group bias by holding stereotypes favorable to their gender (girls were seen to be good at music and reading/writing) and by not seeing advantages for boys (e.g., in math and science). Black girls and boys (also of lower status) also held favorable in-group biases and were less likely to note advantages for out-groups. High-status groups (Whites and boys), however, endorsed the most traditional stereotypes (positive or negative) when it came to evaluating their social group. In addition, some stereotypes were stronger in the older age groups.

These studies show that intergroup phenomena operate in adolescence but there is not enough research to draw conclusions about age-related change or differences in group bias and social identity pertaining to gender. Evidence about age effects is inconsistent, with some studies showing less intergroup bias in adolescence than in childhood (Egan & Perry, 2001; Verkuyten & Thijs, 2001), consistent with cognitive developmental perspectives, but others showing more intergroup bias in adolescence (e.g., Rowley et al., 2007). Inconsistency may be due to methodological differences or to social contextual effects involving, for example, status and culture (Rowley et al.; Verkuyten & Thijs). How cognitions concerning gender change in adolescence, as well as their roots in cognitive development, in attractions to the other sex, and in the social context, can be addressed only with longitudinal research. Such research can identify cognitive, biological, and social mechanisms that cause group differences to be noticed, exaggerated, and followed as examples for behavior in adolescence.

Cognitive Influences: Summary and Directions for Research

Gender-related cognitions—about the self and about others—emerge early in childhood and persist into adolescence, but change over time as the child develops cognitively and is exposed to different social environments. Gender schemas serve important functions by organizing the adolescent's social world ("us" and "them") and by providing scripts for behavior in unfamiliar situations, but they can also restrict choices that might be beneficial for development, as when group bias eliminates activities with the other sex that could be informative and rewarding. The biological, cognitive, and social transitions of adolescence as they relate to gender cognitions are vastly understudied. For example, are there changes in gender group bias that occur as a result of increased peer affiliation, time spent with the other sex, and sexual attractions brought about by hormonal changes? Can changes in the brain be linked to changes in executive functions as well as to gender schemas and flexibility across adolescence? Is the identity development process that is natural to adolescence connected with gender cognitions and the timing of increase in gender flexibility? Is gender-schematic processing different in adolescence compared to childhood and adulthood? Longitudinal research examining covariations of gender cognitions with prenatal hormones, and adolescent changes in the brain, body, and social relations is needed so that gender development is understood in relation to the transitions unique to adolescence.

Socialization Influences

In contrast to biological and cognitive perspectives, which highlight within-individual forces, socialization perspectives target external influences on gender development. These influences range from experiences in everyday life—interactions with parents and peers, school activities, and role models observed on television and in other media—to larger societal forces such as cultural norms and the legal system that promote egalitarianism or establish and sanction differential opportunities and constraints for males versus females. Research on socialization influences on adolescents' gender development has focused heavily on family and peer influences, and our review highlights this work. We also consider the more limited research on the roles of schools and the media in adolescent gender development. Gender socialization research tends to focus on such proximal influences, but it is important to remember that macrolevel societal forces also can exert an impact on gender development by shaping opportunities and constraints in the social/economic/political environment, and in turn, girls' and boys' everyday activities and experiences. Indeed, cross-cultural research highlights the nature of male and female roles as a key property of cultural "niches," a property that is tied on the one hand to subsistence demands, and on the other to attitudes and practices around child socialization (e.g., Weisner, 2002). A consideration of cross-cultural research is beyond the scope of this chapter. This is an area rich in theory and data, however, and may inform our understanding of the role of larger social and cultural forces in adolescent gender development, a topic that has received minimal research attention to date.

The extant data on adolescent gender development focuses largely on European American youth and provides substantial evidence that girls and boys have different socialization experiences. There is less evidence, however, that the sex-typed experiences of girls and boys explain either the sex differences or the developmental changes in gendered qualities and behaviors that we described in the first half of this chapter. Instead, most research on gender socialization influences has been directed at explaining individual differences among girls' and among boys' gendered qualities and behaviors. Even here, causal inferences are tenuous because most studies are based on correlational data. These findings provide a first step, but experimental studies are an important direction in efforts to test gender development theories. A complete understanding of socialization influences also requires research that links sex-typed treatment to both sex differences and developmental differences.

Gender Socialization by Parents

Most work in this area is grounded in social learning theories and focuses on parents' differential treatment of girls versus boys and parents' modeling of gender roles. Early reviews revealed few differences in the ways that parents treated boys and girls, with the important exception of parents' encouragement of their children's involvement in gender-typed activities (Maccoby & Jacklin, 1975; Lytton & Romney, 1991). These reviews, however, focused on young children and their mothers, with little known about the role of fathers or about parental socialization in adolescence (Block, 1983; Lytton & Romney, 1991). From our current vantage point, differential parent treatment of sons and daughters was underestimated. Recent research provides a more nuanced picture of parents' gendered treatment of offspring, including that some effects become more pronounced in early adolescence (Crouter et al., 1995; Shanahan, McHale, Crouter, et al., 2007). With some important exceptions, described below (e.g. Eccles et al., 1998; Wigfield et al., 2006), the links between parents' treatment and offspring gendered outcomes in adolescence have not been well documented.

The larger social context appears to influence the extent to which parents provide differential treatment to boys and girls, including effects of parents' attitudes, cultural values, social class, and family structure. For example, parent gender role attitudes affect monitoring, allocation of responsibilities, and time spent with children: European American mothers with more traditional attitudes intensified their monitoring of postmenarcheal daughters, whereas mothers with less traditional attitudes granted older daughters more autonomy; and parents with traditional attitudes were more gender-typed in allocation of household chores to daughters versus sons, and spent more time with same- versus opposite-sex offspring (McHale et al., 1999). Culture also affects gendered parenting: Mexican American parents with strong orientations toward traditional Mexican culture were more likely than acculturated parents to show gendered differential treatment, such as assigning more household chores and fewer privileges to daughters than to sons (McHale, Updegraff, Shanahan, & Killoren, 2005).

Situational factors are also important in gendered behavior; as social psychologists have argued, gender is constructed in the context of ongoing social interactions (Deaux & Major, 1987). In support of these ideas, a meta-analysis of how parents talk to their children (Leaper et al., 1998) identified situational factors moderating mothers' language use with daughters versus sons. For example, although there was no overall difference in mothers' directive speech toward girls and boys, the effect size was greater (suggesting more directive speech toward sons) when mother–child pairs were observed in problem-solving tasks than when they were observed in unstructured settings.

Our understanding of the effects of parents' gender-typed differential treatment could benefit from expanding efforts beyond the current focus on parents as interaction partners. In gender, as in other areas of parenting effects on youth development, research primarily concerns the nature of parents' and children's interpersonal exchanges such as affection, control, and language use. But, as Parke and colleagues have emphasized, parents also influence their children's development when they act as instructors and opportunity providers (Parke &

Buriel, 1998; Parke, Ornstein, Rieser, & Zahn-Waxler, 1994).

Research by Eccles and colleagues targets a broad range of parental socialization influences (e.g., Eccles et al., 1998; Wigfield et al., 2006). This work, grounded in social cognitive theories of achievement motivation, is focused on understanding gender differences in education and occupation achievement through study of parental influences on youths' self-efficacy and competence beliefs, as well as youths' interests and activity involvement. Interest and involvement in activities are seen to develop as parents and other socialization agents instill beliefs that boys and girls have different competencies, which are differentially valued. The transmission by parents of this information then has consequences for children's current and future opportunities and achievements. In a series of studies, Eccles and her colleagues highlighted the academic domain, especially parents' attitudes about boys' and girls' abilities in math and science and their links with youths' academic efficacy beliefs and academic performance. Their findings show that parents' attitudes are more important contributors to youth achievement-related interests and choices than are youths' measured abilities. For example, youths' beliefs about their academic competencies and their ideas about their future involvement in particular academic domains were more closely tied to parents' gender stereotypes than to youths' test scores or grades (e.g., Jacobs, 1991; Jacobs & Eccles, 1992). Further, young adults' actual career choices were predicted by parents' (gendered) perceptions of their child's ability to succeed in math (Bleeker & Jacobs, 2004). The authors suggested that youths' gendered interests and activities may mediate the links between socialization experiences and later life choices and achievements.

The work of Eccles and colleagues has also highlighted other roles for parents, as models, interpreters of experiences, and providers of opportunities (e.g., Fredricks & Eccles, 2004). Parents are thought to actualize their beliefs about gender in their behavior, such as explicit training or instruction around their beliefs, guiding offspring toward involvement in particular kinds of activities, and providing resources and opportunities. For example, parents are more likely to orchestrate boys' than girls' involvement in programs for gifted children, computer classes, and sports teams (Eccles & Harold, 1992; Fredricks & Eccles, 2004). From the way that bedrooms are decorated (Rheingold & Cook, 1975), to the gifts that youth are given (Fisher-Thompson, 1993), to the allocation of household chores (Bowes & Goodnow, 1996) and family privileges (McHale et al., 2005), parents exhibit differential treatment of girls and boys in ways that have not been captured by studies that focus on parent–child interactions. Research on gender development should be extended to capture the many tangible ways in which parents treat boys and girls differently and link these patterns of treatment to gender development and gender differences.

Parents also socialize their children around gender by serving as models of gender attitudes and stereotypes, gendered personal qualities, and gender roles. There have been explicit efforts to establish links between parents' characteristics and youth gender development, and research shows clear associations between parents and their children with respect to cognitive and attitudinal variables. A meta-analysis of gendered cognitions about appropriate roles for women and men, for example (Tenenbaum & Leaper, 2002), found moderate parent–child associations, with the links between attitudinal variables stronger than links between parents' and offspring's self-perceptions of their own femininity and masculinity. Longitudinal evidence confirms that parents serve as role models for their children's developing gender role attitudes (Crouter et al., 2007; Cunningham, 2001). Parents' attitudes also can have indirect effects on their offspring's development over the long term. For instance, mothers' gender role attitudes were linked to their daughters' attitudes, which in turn were related to daughters' gendered career aspirations in early adulthood (Steele & Barling, 1996). Although links between parents' and offspring's gendered personality qualities are generally weaker than links between gender role attitudes (Tenenbaum & Leaper, 2002), these may be stronger when both parents display gender stereotypical traits (Klein & Shulman, 1981), perhaps reflecting a dosage effect. Modeling effects also may differ across development. Combined cross-sectional and short-term longitudinal data on girls' sex-typed personality qualities and interests showed that mothers' sex-typed qualities were more consistent predictors of girls' qualities in middle childhood, but that fathers' qualities were more consistent predictors in adolescence (McHale, Shanahan, et al., 2004).

Parents also socialize their children through their own gender roles in the family (i.e., involvement in paid and domestic labor; child care responsibilities). The division of housework between mothers and fathers, for example, has been linked to youths' involvement in sex-typed chores in middle childhood and adolescence (Blair, 1992; Crouter et al., 1995). Although most research on the division of child care has focused on young children, some evidence shows effects on adolescents of gendered patterns of parental involvement. Data from a short-term longitudinal study (Updegraff, McHale, & Crouter, 1996) revealed, for example, that girls from egalitarian families (defined by mothers and fathers' relative time spent in child-oriented activities) maintained high levels of performance in math and science across the transition to middle school, whereas those from traditional families (mother more involved than father) showed declines in their grades over time. Mothers' involvement in the labor force also has been a focus of study. Young adolescent girls reported more egalitarian gender attitudes when their mothers were employed and their fathers were supportive of mothers' employment (Nelson & Keith, 1990). These effects are long lasting: Mothers' work involvement

in adolescence was linked to daughters' gender role ideology in adulthood (Moen, Erickson, & Dempster-McClain, 1997). Selection effects almost certainly affect these patterns, and thus it is essential to study the processes through which maternal employment affects offspring gender development. For example, employed mothers may hold egalitarian gender attitudes, and mothers' attitudes may explain the link between maternal employment and gender role attitudes of adolescent and young adult daughters (Ex & Janssens, 1998).

Gender Socialization by Siblings

We know less about the role of siblings in gender development than about the roles of parents and peers. The lack of attention to siblings is surprising given that some of the earliest studies of sibling influences focused on gender development (Brim, 1958; Koch, 1956; Sutton-Smith & Rosenberg, 1970). This early work was directed at testing a social learning hypothesis that children growing up with a sibling of the other sex—particularly an older sibling—would be less sex-typed than children with a same-sex sibling. Some studies found support for this prediction (see Rust et al., 2000, for a more recent example), but effects have been inconsistent due, at least in part, to the methodological limitations of this work (Huston, 1983; Ruble & Martin, 1998). Among the most important of these is that the sex-typed personal qualities of siblings were not measured directly; instead the assumption was that brothers would invariably display more stereotypically masculine characteristics and behaviors, and sisters, more feminine ones.

A burgeoning literature on the links between the behaviors and characteristics of adolescent-age siblings provides a model for studying siblings' role in gender development. Most of this research focuses on risky behavior, showing that, beyond parent and family background characteristics and in some studies, peer group characteristics, older siblings' involvement in delinquent activities, substance use, and risky sex behaviors is associated with similar behaviors in their younger sisters and brothers (e.g., Brook, Whiteman, Gordon, & Brenden, 1983; Rodgers & Rowe, 1988; Slomkowski, Rende, Novak, Lloyd-Richardson, & Niaura, 2005). McHale and colleagues applied this paradigm to study siblings as agents of gender socialization (e.g., McHale, Updegraff, Helms-Erikson, & Crouter, 2001). Focusing on first- and second-born sibling dyads, they found that older adolescent siblings' gender role attitudes, personality qualities, and involvement in sex-typed leisure activities predicted those of younger siblings over a two-year period, controlling for both younger siblings' earlier qualities and the gendered qualities of both mothers and fathers. Indeed, older siblings' gendered qualities were more consistent predictors of younger siblings' qualities than were parent predictors. Especially at a time of change in norms about gender, older siblings may be more relevant and salient role models than parents.

Although older siblings' qualities were positive predictors of younger siblings' gendered qualities, this study also revealed some evidence of older siblings' deidentification from their younger sisters and brothers. For example, the more time younger siblings spent in feminine leisure in early adolescence, the less time older sisters spent in these same activities two years later. As proposed by Alfred Adler (Ansbacher & Ansbacher, 1956; see also Sulloway, 1996), sibling deidentification refers to a dynamic whereby siblings develop different attributes and interests in an effort to establish their own niches in the family and reduce sibling rivalry. Some investigators have suggested that sibling deidentification is more pronounced in early adolescence when identity formation processes are salient (Brody et al., 1994; Grotevant, 1978). The operation of two competing kinds of influences, social learning and deidentification, makes it difficult to detect sibling influences, and an important direction for research on the role of siblings in gender development is to identify the family conditions under which siblings serve as models versus as foils in one another's development.

Siblings also indirectly influence one another's gender development through their impact on larger family dynamics. The constellation of the sibling subsystem helps to define the family's structure and thereby affords opportunities for patterns of daily activities, roles, and relationships in the family including the allocation of household chores, family caregiving, and time spent with fathers and mothers. Within-family comparisons provide for a more powerful test of parents' gender-differential treatment than do more typical between-family comparisons. Having both a daughter and a son affords parents the opportunity to treat their children in sex-typed ways, but factors ranging from situational demands and culture, to child characteristics, to parents' attitudes and values will help determine whether parents engage in sex-typed differential treatment. Norms in the U.S. for equal treatment of offspring (Parsons, 1974/1942), for example, mean that some parents may be less likely to engage in sex-typed treatment when they have both a daughter and a son given everyday opportunities for social comparison. That is, parents may be more sensitive to the gendered nature of their treatment when they have both a daughter and son, and their children also have the opportunity to monitor whether their parents' treatment is equitable. These kinds of dynamics direct attention to the way families work as systems and provide new directions for studying the family's role in gender socialization.

Gender Socialization by Peers

It is common to observe that in adolescence more leisure time is spent in the company of peers than ever before (Brown, 2004; see also chapter 3, vol. 2 of this *Handbook*). There is no doubt that the peer context influences adolescent behavior; for instance, adolescents who associate with deviant peers are more likely to get into trouble (Galambos, Barker, & Almeida, 2003). But the potential influence of peers on gender-related behavior is not as well documented, and it is often difficult to separate effects of peers from characteristics of children that draw them to specific peers (Rubin, Bukowski, & Parker, 2006).

Beginning in early childhood and evidenced in many cultures, boys and girls segregate themselves into same-sex peer groups, continuing until about age 12 (Maccoby, 1990). Within these same-sex groups, girls tend to form dyadic or triadic friendships, whereas boys tend to form larger friendship networks. The quality of girls' and boys' same-sex interactions in these groups differs as well, with competition and conflict present in the all-male groups and nurturance and empathy characterizing all-girl groups (Maccoby). The intimacy that is present in girls in adolescence may have a basis in these earlier all-girl groups. Maccoby (1990, 2002) argued that gender-typed behavior is observed, learned, and reinforced in these groups.

It is not clear, however, to what extent peer groups in adolescence form a context for and shape gendered behaviors. We provide examples of studies of adults and children that suggest interesting possibilities for observational studies of adolescents. Research on dyadic interactions in young adults demonstrates that different behaviors are elicited in same- versus mixed-sex dyads. For example, women's language use has been shown to be more tentative than men's only in mixed-sex dyads; women were more effective in changing men's (but not women's) opinions when they used tentative language than when they used assertive language (Carli, 1990). The peer context also affects children. A study of young children found that girls' expression of their own perspectives was more frequent in all-girl playgroups than in playgroups in which boys were present (Benenson, Del Bianco, Philippoussis, & Apostoleris, 1997). A rare study comparing self-perceptions of adolescent seventh- and eighth-grade boys and girls who were paired to play a game with a same-sex or an other-sex partner on separate occasions found that boys scored higher on femininity

after they were paired with a girl rather than a boy. Girls also reported greater femininity after interacting with a girl as compared to a boy partner (Leszczynski & Strough, 2008). One way to observe how the peer group shapes gendered characteristics is to conduct studies of male and female adolescents interacting with same- and other-sex peers, as the enactment of gender roles comes alive (or not) in these situations.

Questionnaire studies suggest that peer interactions may contribute to gender differentiation in adolescence, particularly in emotion processes. For example, adolescent girls engage in significantly more corumination (talking excessively with a same-sex close friend about problems) than do adolescent boys, with the gender difference larger in adolescence than in childhood, and corumination is associated with increased internalizing symptoms (Rose, 2002). Across a 6-month period, girls (but not boys) who coruminated showed increased depression and anxiety (Rose, Carlson, & Waller, 2007). These results suggest that the gender difference in depression that emerges by middle adolescence could be partly explained by girls' corumination in the context of close friendships.

The extent to which adolescents feel accepted by peers could be one link in the chain by which peers reinforce adolescents' engagement in gender-typical or atypical behaviors. Some data suggest that the adjustment consequences of gender atypicality are mediated by peer behavior: Better outcome is associated with peer acceptance than rejection (Smith & Leaper, 2005). Other data show that popularity in grade 10 was linked to increases in alcohol use and sexual experience by grade 12 (Mayeux, Sandstrom, & Cillessen, 2008). The effects on gender development of peer acceptance and popularity is worthy of investigation in longitudinal research.

Given speculation about gender intensification in adolescence, in part due to peers as important socializing agents, it is surprising that there is not more research on whether, how much, and how peers influence gender-related behavior and development. Research following preschoolers across 6 months showed a social dosage effect of peers on gender-linked behavior (Martin & Fabes, 2001). Aggression, rough-and-tumble play, activity level, and gender-typed play increased among boys in proportion to the amount of time spent with same-sex peers at baseline; similarly, aggression and activity level decreased but gender-typed play increased among girls with higher baseline levels of same-sex interactions.

Reviewing the literature on gender differences in peer relationship processes in childhood and adolescence, Rose and Rudolph (2006) proposed a peer socialization model by which exposure to same-sex peers facilitates the learning of gender-linked behaviors and styles (e.g., cooperative behavior in girls, competitive behavior in boys), which ultimately leads to gendered adjustment outcomes (internalizing and externalizing symptoms); they noted the need for direct empirical support to test the model.

Gender Socialization in Schools

Given where adolescents spend their time, schools can be salient sources of influence on development. Teacher efficacy, teacher-student relationships, organizational structures, and the timing and nature of school transitions are among the important characteristics of school environments thought to be relevant for gender development (Eccles et al., 1993; Eccles, 2004). Early research focused on teacher expectation influences on gender differences in math and science performance and interests (e.g., Parsons, Kaczala, & Meece, 1982), whereas recent research includes the study of school influences on functioning in both academic and psychological (e.g., self-esteem, depressive symptoms, behavior problems) domains (Roeser, Eccles, & Sameroff, 1998). The value of this type of work is illustrated in a short-term longitudinal study of children followed from sixth through eighth grade, with repeated assessments of their perceptions of school climate (teacher and peer support, opportunities for student autonomy, and clarity and consistency of school rules) and adjustment (self-esteem, depressive symptoms, behavior problems; Way, Reddy, & Rhodes, 2007). Girls started sixth grade with more positive perceptions of school climate, but both girls and boys reported increasingly negative perceptions of school climate and declining adjustment across middle school. Associations between declining school climate and worsening self-esteem, depressive symptoms, and behavior problems were not different for girls and boys in this or a similar study (Roeser et al.), but further work including potential moderators (e.g., parent attitudes, school context) might show gender-related trajectories.

An interesting question is whether adolescents' school attendance and dropout relate to gender socialization, especially in developing countries where school enrollment rates are lower than in developed nations. For example, a study in five selected developing countries (India, Kenya, Nicaragua, Pakistan, South Africa) examined noneconomic household work, labor market work, and leisure-time activities of adolescent girls and boys ages 15 through 19 who were either enrolled in school or not (Lloyd, Grant, & Ritchie, 2008). School tended to be an equalizer: Although girls spent more time in household work and less in leisure than did boys regardless of enrollment status, gender differences were smallest among children in school. Thus, despite concerns that schools can contribute to gender differentiation, this cross-cultural research shows that schooling may reduce such effects by removing adolescents from situations in which gender roles are more highly differentiated and circumscribed.

The effects of single-sex versus coeducational schools or classrooms have been the subject of both education research and (sometimes heated) public dialogue. Although there is strong advocacy for single-sex schooling to redress gender gaps such as lower reading achievement in boys and lower math achievement in girls (e.g., Sax, 2005), there is no clear consensus on benefits of gender segregation in education (Bracey, 2006). Empirical evidence does not conclusively support positive effects of single-sex education (e.g., Mael, Alonso, Gibson, Rogers, & Smith, 2005; Thompson & Ungerleider, 2004). Although it might be quite some time before the debate is resolved, it draws attention to schools as contexts in which gender socialization can occur.

Gender Socialization in the Media

Adolescents are great users of the media, including television, movies (in theater or home), music, print, electronic games, and the Internet. They spend an average of 7–8 hours per day using media for leisure purposes, with television and audio media consuming the largest proportions of their time. Boys and girls are not entirely similar in their media use: Boys report devoting more time to television and to playing video games, whereas girls report more time listening to music (Gentile, Lynch, Linder & Walsh, 2004; Roberts & Foehr, 2004). Adolescent boys also engage in more frequent use of media with violent content, in electronic games, television shows, movies, and Internet activities (Funk, Baldacci, Pasold, & Baumgardner, 2004; Krahé & Möller, 2004).

Mass media have come under fire from academics and members of the public for its sexualization of young girls, the portrayal of violence, and the perpetuation of gender stereotypes and unrealistic expectations for body weight and appearance. Despite a very long history of concern about the impact of media on youth, however, there is surprisingly little research on this topic (Roberts, Henriksen, & Foehr, 2004).

One domain of behaviors likely to be affected by media pertains to body image and eating problems. Situation comedies, for instance, have different representations of weight in men and women, overrepresenting underweight women, whose bodies are admired, and evaluating overweight women more negatively than overweight men (Fouts &

Burggraf, 1999, 2000; Fouts & Vaughan, 2002). These studies show how television distorts reality and perpetuates gender stereotypes (e.g., "thinner is better"). From a social learning perspective, we would expect harm to viewers who receive and internalize these messages.

In general, research shows an association between television viewing and stereotypical attitudes across the life span (Signorielli, 2001). In adolescence, high levels of television watching are associated with traditional gender role attitudes and stereotypes (Morgan, 1987). Girls were more likely than boys to perceive that the media influenced their body images (Polce-Lynch, Myers, Kliewer, & Kilmartin, 2001), but higher levels of entertainment television viewing were linked to poorer body images in both adolescent girls and boys (Anderson, Huston, Schmitt, Linebarger, & Wright, 2001). More exposure to appearance-related television was related to increased body dissatisfaction in 5- to 8-year-old girls followed for 1 year (Dohnt & Tiggemann, 2006). Twelve-year-old girls with increased eating disorder symptoms across 16 months also increased reading of fashion magazines (but decreased television viewing); girls with decreased symptoms reported decreased reading of fashion magazines and television viewing (Vaughan & Fouts, 2003). Correlational and experimental data show that higher exposure to music videos is related to adolescents' more traditional gender attitudes and sexual stereotypes (e.g., women want relationships, while men want sex; Ward, Hansbrough, & Walker, 2005).

Another domain of behavior linked to media involvement is aggression. The high level of violence shown on television, movies, and video games is well documented. A large body of evidence shows a connection between violent and aggressive behavior and exposure to television violence (Roberts et al., 2004), and evidence is mounting for a link with violent electronic games, used more by boys than girls (Funk et al., 2004; Gentile et al., 2004; Krahé & Möller, 2004). To the extent that adolescent boys immerse themselves in technology that reinforces violence, gender differences in physical aggression may be magnified.

Other areas of concern regarding socialization effects of the media include exposure to sex-related content on the Internet, on television, in the movies, and in music videos, and exposure to depictions of substance use (smoking, drinking, other drugs). Studies are limited, and the evidence linking adolescents' exposure to sex in the media with sexual behavior is equivocal, as is evidence linking substance use in the media to adolescents' attitudes and behavior (Greenfield & Yan, 2006; Roberts et al., 2004).

It is important to note that, with the exception of data on aggression, most evidence about associations between media exposure and behavior come from correlational studies, with potential effects of selection (e.g., girls at risk for eating problems might selectively read fashion magazines) and confounds. Therefore, it is important to collect longitudinal and intervention data.

Socialization Influences: Summary and Directions for Research

As our review suggests, girls and boys grow up in different social worlds. In some cases, differences between girls' and boys' experiences are subtle and nuanced, but in other cases those differences are stark. Importantly, most of the relevant research has been conducted with middle-class European American youth, that is, youth who grow up in democracies that espouse egalitarian values. We know very little about the differential treatment and development of girls and boys in contexts where values, norms, and political and legal systems promote sex-differential treatment. Taken together and extended over a lifetime, however, even in a democratic society, established differences between the socialization experiences of males and females can make for profound gender differences in self-perceptions, preferences, and behaviors.

The larger literature defines adolescence as a period of social transition, and a changing social world has implications for adolescents' gender development. For example, an expanding social world exposes adolescents to an increasingly broader range of social influences, and adolescents' growing autonomy means they can make more of their own choices from the range of opportunities provided by their social contexts. Importantly, adolescents' physical, cognitive, and emotional maturation also means that their choices have increasingly clear implications for gendered roles, relationships and activities in adulthood. The gender intensification hypothesis proposed that social changes in adolescence operate to promote gender stereotyping, but the picture that emerges from the admittedly limited empirical data is more complex and multifaceted.

Acknowledging the range and complexity of social influences makes it less surprising that a single trajectory does not capture the totality of gender development in adolescence. Indeed, an ecological perspective highlights that patterns of gender development are likely to vary across context, and directs attention to examining how social-contextual factors operate in gender development. Although a body of research has established gender differences in girls' versus boys' social experiences, and some work links socialization to individual differences in youths' gendered qualities, much less has been done to document links between gender socialization and gender differences or gender development. And, even when such studies are undertaken and connections established, the causal roles of socialization forces in individual differences, gender differences, and gender development are not clear. For example, selection effects, including youths' choices regarding their socialization experiences and the ways in which girls and boys elicit reactions from the social environments because of their characteristics and behaviors, mean that firm conclusions about the causal role of social influences are not possible. An agenda for investigating the role of socialization influences in gender development includes studying youth from a broad range of social environments and conducting research that integrates the study of socialization influences with an examination of the roles of biological and cognitive factors in gender development.

Influences on Gender Development: Summary

Our review reveals some evidence for biological, cognitive, and socialization influences on gender development in adolescence. Most of the research focused on adolescence targets young adolescents, and more generally, there is much less known about influences on gender development in adolescence than in childhood. Clearly, more work remains to be done, and in the final section of this chapter we describe some directions this work might take.

What we know about biological factors—especially prenatal sex hormones—is that these explain some of the differences between the sexes in some characteristics, especially activities and interests, but do not have as much to say about variations within sex or about change across development. Future biological work in adolescent gender development is likely to focus on brain changes (including effects of pubertal hormones and consequences for gendered risk behavior and mental health problems), and on social and hormonal modification of gene expression.

Cognitive approaches have generally focused on early childhood and the role of gender cognitions in acquiring gendered characteristics. Developments in adolescence include changes in the brain, hormones, physical appearance, cognitive capacity, identity formation, peer networks, family roles, schools, and civic engagement, and all of these can affect youths' views of themselves and their worlds. We know very little about changes in adolescents' gender cognitions, however, including the ways in which these covary with, result from, or influence biological, cognitive, and social changes.

Socialization approaches have generally received the most attention as causes of adolescent gender development. There is evidence for associations between gendered actions of social agents and between-person differences in adolescents' gendered characteristics, but we know less about whether socialization processes are linked to differences between girls and boys or how they affect gender development over time. Recent research has provided a clearer picture of the multifaceted nature of parent and family socialization influences, but an important step in studies of socialization effects is to incorporate the role of adolescents in their own development. Another important direction is examination of the interplay of culture and gender in adolescent development.

SUMMARY AND INTEGRATION

In this final section, we provide a summary of key issues in the study of gender development in adolescence. In light of the gaps in the evidence on gender development in adolescence, we also highlight areas in need of further study and promising directions for research. Finally, we point to the need for an integration of perspectives in the study of adolescents' gender development.

Understanding Gender Development in Adolescence

Studying gender development in adolescence involves studying development in most of the domains represented in this volume, drawing from the matrix presented in Table 10.1 (initially developed by Huston, 1983, and modified by Ruble and colleagues [Ruble & Martin, 1998; Ruble et al., 2006]). As our review has shown, gendered characteristics at any single point in time are influenced by biological, cognitive, and social factors. Studying the sources and development of these characteristics before, during, and after adolescence challenges us conceptually and methodologically in several ways, and these challenges create opportunities to understand gender development. We offer six general conclusions derived from our review that can provide direction for future research.

Understanding Gender Development Requires Study of Sex Differences

The classic approach to studying gender involves between-sex comparisons, that is, boys versus girls and men versus women contrasted on one or more variables. From a single *t*-test in one study to meta-analyses of results from many studies, this approach tells us about differences between the sexes. We know less about these differences in adolescence than at other ages; how they unfold across development; how biological, cognitive, and social influences change with age; and how these influences work in concert to explain sex differences.

Understanding Gender Development Requires Study of Individual Differences

There is substantial variability across individuals in the expression of gender-related characteristics. Indeed, for many characteristics, there is as much variability within sex as there is between the sexes, and the distributions of males' and females' characteristics largely overlap. We know little about developmental change in this variation. Across development, do individuals maintain their rank order relative to age mates? Or is there a lack of stability in individual differences as mean levels of gendered qualities change? It seems likely that answers to these questions will vary across gendered behaviors and characteristics, and the matrix can provide researchers with a map of what is known and what remains to be studied. As we have implied, an important research question is whether the same processes account for both within-sex and between-sex variation.

If we take seriously the importance of individual differences, we also must move beyond the search for universal patterns of development to consider the many possible sources of influence on gendered characteristics, and how these influences interact to promote divergent developmental patterns. Some of the data we have described show how trajectories of gender development depend on youths' social ecologies—and these deserve additional study. We also need to recognize and understand adolescents' own roles in their gender development, including the reactions that they elicit from the social world by virtue of their characteristics and behaviors, their reactions to and interpretations of their experiences, and the choices that they make within the contexts of defined opportunity structures.

Understanding Gender Development Requires Longitudinal Investigations

Studies of change across age show that gender is not static or immutable, but we have little basic information about normative trajectories of development for most gendered characteristics. At present, we also know little about how gender differences wax and wane across time or whether individual differences are stable across important developmental transitions. Longitudinal studies that consider the possibility of varying trajectories are essential for illuminating the nature and correlates of gender development. Such studies should include measures of multiple dimensions of gender so as to illuminate the extent of covariation across time in different domains of gender. The identification of interlinked patterns of development is essential for obtaining a more comprehensive picture of age-related change in gender differentiation.

Understanding Gender Development Requires Attention to the Construction of Gender in Interpersonal Contexts

Within-individual variability in gendered attributes and behaviors across settings has been highlighted by social psychologists but rarely studied by developmentalists. There is evidence in adults (e.g., Carli, 1990; Leaper et al., 1998) and some evidence in children (e.g., Benenson et al., 1997, 2002; Leaper & Smith, 2004) that gendered behavior can be evoked or dampened in different situations, defined by task demands or the social composition of the setting, for example. It is surprising that more attention has not been paid to situational effects in adolescentce. One study showed that gender differences can be elicited and even reversed in direction in adolescents, depending on situational factors (e.g., Kolaric & Galambos, 1995). Situational variability provides information about motivations to act in gendered ways, and ignoring situational factors introduces error into conceptual and statistical models, error that may be responsible for inconsistent findings of gender effects across studies.

Understanding Gender Development Requires a Multidimensional Focus

The matrix of gender content and constructs presented in Table 10.1 has served as a guide for research on gender development in childhood. Our application of the matrix to adolescent research has allowed us to identify areas of previous research focus, areas needing attention, and areas of neglect. The matrix also serves as a guide for measurement development, and as an opportunity to clarify constructs as evidence is accrued.

Understanding Gender Development Requires an Integration of Perspectives

Over the past several decades of theorizing and research on gender development, biological, cognitive, and socialization approaches have become more nuanced. There is clear recognition that gender development cannot be explained through a single set of processes, but instead, that biology, cognitions, and socialization all play a role individually and in concert. Despite this recognition, most studies have been limited by the search for a single source of influence. Examples of the way in which two sources of influence have been studied together include research on how early pubertal timing and stressful life events (i.e., biological and social influences) combine to predict the development of depression, a sex-typed mental health problem, across adolescence (Ge et al., 2001) and how attributional style and stressors (i.e., cognitive and social factors) together increase depression in adolescent girls (Garber, Keiley, & Martin, 2002). An integrated explanation of depression

would consider biological factors, including genetic predispositions, prenatal exposures, and the physical and hormonal changes of adolescence; cognitive factors, including perceptions of self and the social world, tendency to ruminate, and social problem-solving ability; and social factors, including the ways in which social agents react to adolescents' developing characteristics and aspects of friendships (e.g., corumination) that might reinforce depressive symptoms, to understand how these influences interact in the development of depression. Such an explanation would also include possible developmental antecedents of depression (e.g., childhood anxiety). And, such an integrated model can be applied to any of the gendered characteristics reviewed in this chapter.

Recent methodological advances (e.g., multilevel modeling, growth mixture modeling with latent trajectory classes) allow us to address key questions about gender development that in the past we could pose but not answer. By collecting longitudinal data on the varied dimensions of gender, we can model average trajectories for a single aspect of gender development over time (e.g., gender attitudes), and we can also examine covariations among multiple constructs as they develop together across time. In this way, the coupling of diverse constructs in the matrix can be observed. Consider some examples. Do girls for whom gender attitudes become more traditional over time also evidence change in gender-typed behaviors, such as reduced interest in math or increased expressivity? How does increasing gender flexibility in interests and preferences coincide with change in the quantity and quality of time spent with same- and other-sex peers? How do high prenatal androgens characteristic of girls with CAH relate to or stimulate changes in adolescents' gender-related cognitions (e.g., concepts about male–female activities), and to what extent is the link mediated by the girls' own gender nonnormative characteristics? How does adolescent brain maturation trigger change in cognitive and affective processes involved in gendered risk behavior, including substance use? How do social experiences affect expression of genes contributing to gendered characteristics?

The application of new statistical methods coincides with the growing recognition that it is essential to consider biological, cognitive, and social influences on individual trajectories of gender development, and makes it possible to examine stable (e.g., gender, birth order) as well as changing (e.g., hormonal levels, cognitive functioning, social stressors) sources of influence on variations around normative patterns. This work is exciting because of its implications for establishing temporal associations and precedence. For instance, trajectories of gender flexibility could be examined as they are accompanied or preceded by a school transition, a particular aspect of the pubertal process, increased distance from a parent, or a change in executive functioning. Such research could tell us how flexibility is affected by cognitive changes in executive function mediated through hormonally induced changes to frontal regions of the brain, and whether these links are modified by social context, such as parents' gendered attitudes. These are only a few of the many possibilities for learning more about the course and causes of gender development in adolescence.

REFERENCES

Abrams, L. S., & Stormer, C. C. (2002). Sociocultural variations in the body image perceptions of urban adolescent females. *Journal of Youth and Adolescence, 31,* 443–450.

Alfieri, T., Ruble, D. N., & Higgins, E. T. (1996). Gender stereotypes during adolescence: Developmental changes and the transition to junior high school. *Developmental Psychology, 32,* 1129–1137.

American Association of University Women. (1992). *The AAUW report: How schools short-change girls.* Washington, DC: Author.

Anderson, D. R., Huston, A. C., Schmitt, K. L., Linebarger, D. L., & Wright, J. C. (2001). Early childhood television viewing and adolescent behaviors: The recontact study. *Monographs of the Society for Research in Child Development, 66* (1, Serial No. 264).

Angold, A., Costello, E. J., Erkanli, A., & Worthman, C. M. (1999). Pubertal changes in hormone levels and depression in girls. *Psychological Medicine, 29,* 1043–1053.

Angold, A., Erkanli, A., Silberg, J., Eaves, L., & Costello, E. J. (2002). Depression scale scores in 8–17-year-olds: Effects of age and gender. *Journal of Child Psychology and Psychiatry, 43,* 1052–1063.

Ansbacher, H. L., & Ansbacher, R. R. (1956). *The individual psychology of Alfred Adler: A systematic presentation in selections from his writings.* Oxford, UK: Basic Books.

Antill, J. K., Cotton, S., Russell, G., & Goodnow, J. J. (1996). Measures of children's sex-typing in middle childhood, II. *Australian Journal of Psychology, 48,* 35–44.

Bailey, J. M., & Zucker, K. J. (1995). Childhood sex-typed behavior and sexual orientation: A conceptual and quantitative review. *Developmental Psychology, 31,* 43–55.

Bailey, J. M., Bechtold, K. T., & Berenbaum, S. A. (2002). Who are tomboys and why should we study them? *Archives of Sexual Behavior, 31,* 333–341.

Bank, S. P., & Kahn, M. D. (1997). *The sibling bond.* New York: Basic Books.

Barberá, E. (2003). Gender schemas: Configuration and activation processes. *Canadian Journal of Behavioural Science, 35,* 176–184.

Barker, E. T., & Galambos, N. L. (2003). Body dissatisfaction of adolescent girls and boys: Risk and resource factors. *Journal of Early Adolescence, 23,* 141–165.

Becker, J. B., Breedlove, S. M., Crews, D., & McCarthy, M. M. (Eds.). (2002). *Behavioral endocrinology* (2nd ed.). Cambridge, MA: MIT Press.

Bem, S. L. (1981). Gender schema theory: A cognitive account of sex typing. *Psychological Review, 88,* 354–364.

Benenson, J. F., & Christakos, A. (2003). The greater fragility of females' versus males' closest same-sex friendships. *Child Development, 74,* 1123–1129.

Benenson, J. F., Del Bianco, R., Philippoussis, M., & Apstoleris, N. H. (1997). Girls' expression of their own perspectives in the presence of varying numbers of boys. *International Journal of Behavioral Development, 21,* 389–405.

Benenson, J. F., Meaiese, R., Dolenszky, E., Dolensky, N., Sinclair, N., & Simpson, A. (2002). Group size regulates self-assertive versus self-deprecating responses to interpersonal competition. *Child Development, 73,* 1818–1829.

Benenson, J. F., Morash, D., & Petrakos, H. (1998). Gender differences in emotional closeness between preschool children and their mothers. *Sex Roles, 38,* 975–985.

Berenbaum, S. A. (1999). Effects of early androgens on sex-typed activities and interests in adolescents with congenital adrenal hyperplasia. *Hormones and Behavior, 35,* 102–110.

Berenbaum, S. A. (2001). Cognitive function in congenital adrenal hyperplasia. *Endocrinology and Metabolism Clinics of North America, 30,* 173–192.

Berenbaum, S. A. (2006). Psychological outcome in children with disorders of sex development: Implications for treatment and understanding typical development. *Annual Review of Sex Research, 17,* 1–38.

Berenbaum, S. A., & Bailey, J. M. (2003). Effects on gender identity of prenatal androgens and genital appearance: Evidence from girls with congenital adrenal hyperplasia. *Journal of Clinical Endocrinology and Metabolism, 88,* 1102–1106.

Berenbaum, S. A., Duck, S. C., & Bryk, K. (2000). Behavioral effects of prenatal versus postnatal androgen excess in children with 21-hydroxylase-deficient congenital adrenal hyperplasia. *Journal of Clinical Endocrinology and Metabolism, 85,* 727–733.

Berenbaum, S. A., & Resnick, S. M. (1997). Early androgen effects on aggression in children and adults with congenital adrenal hyperplasia. *Psychoneuroendocrinology, 22,* 505–515.

Berenbaum, S. A., & Snyder, E. (1995). Early hormonal influences on childhood sex-typed activity and playmate preferences: Implications for the development of sexual orientation. *Developmental Psychology, 31,* 31–42.

Bernhardt, P. C., Dabbs, J. M., Fielden, J. A., & Lutter, C. D. (1998). Testosterone changes during vicarious experiences of winning and losing among fans at sporting events. *Physiology & Behavior, 65,* 59–62.

Bettencourt, B. A., & Miller, N. (1996). Gender differences in aggression as a function of provocation: A meta-analysis. *Psychological Bulletin, 119*, 422–447.

Bigler, R. S., & Liben, L. S. (2007). Developmental intergroup theory: Explaining and reducing children's social stereotyping and prejudice. *Current Directions in Psychological Science, 16*, 162–166.

Bigner, J. J. (1974). A Wernerian developmental analysis of children's description of siblings. *Child Development, 45*, 317–323.

Blair, S. L. (1992). The sex-typing of children's household labor: Parental influence on daughters' and sons' housework. *Youth & Society, 24*, 178–203.

Blakemore, J. E. O., Berenbaum, S. A., & Liben, L. S. (2009). *Gender development*. New York: Taylor & Francis Group, Psychology Press.

Blanchard, R. (1989). The classification and labeling of nonhomosexual gender dysphorias. *Archives of Sexual Behavior, 18*, 315–334.

Bleeker, M. M., & Jacobs, J. E. (2004). Achievement in math and science: Do mothers' beliefs matter 12 years later? *Journal of Educational Psychology, 96*, 97–109.

Block, J. H. (1983). Differential premises arising from differential socialization of the sexes: Some conjectures. *Child Development, 54*, 1335–1354.

Booth, A., & Amato, P. R. (1994). Parental gender role nontraditionalism and offspring outcomes. *Journal of Marriage and the Family, 56*, 865–877.

Booth, A., Granger, D., Mazur, A., & Kivlighan, K. (2007). Testosterone and social behavior. *Social Forces, 85*, 167–191.

Booth, A., Johnson, D. R., Granger, D. A., Crouter, A. C., & McHale, S. (2003). Testosterone and child and adolescent adjustment: The moderating role of parent–child relationships. *Developmental Psychology, 39*, 85–98.

Bowes, J. M., & Goodnow, J. J. (1996). Work for home, school, or labor force: The nature and sources of changes in understanding. *Psychological Bulletin, 119*, 300–321.

Bracey, G. W. (2006). Single sex education: No easy answer. *Principal Leadership, 7*, 52–55.

Brim, O. G., Jr. (1958). Family structure and sex role learning by children: A further analysis of Helen Koch's data. *Sociometry, 21*, 1–16.

Brody, G. H., Stoneman, Z., & McCoy, J. K. (1994). Forecasting sibling relationships in early adolescence from child temperaments and family processes in middle childhood. *Child Development, 65*, 771–784.

Broidy, L. M., Nagin, D. S., Tremblay, R. E., Bates, J. E., Brame, B., Dodge, K. A., et al. (2003). Developmental trajectories of childhood disruptive behaviors and adolescent delinquency: A six-site, cross-national study. *Developmental Psychology, 39*, 222–245.

Bronfenbrenner, U. (1979). *The ecology of human development: Experiments by nature and design*. Cambridge, MA: Harvard University Press.

Brook, J. S., Whiteman, M., Gordon, A. S., & Brenden, C. (1983). Older brother's influence on younger sibling's drug use. *Journal of Psychology: Interdisciplinary and Applied, 114*, 83–90.

Brown, B. (2004). Adolescents' relationships with peers. In R. M. Lerner & L. Steinberg (Eds.), *Handbook of adolescent psychology* (2nd ed., pp. 363–394). Hoboken, NJ: John Wiley & Sons.

Buchanan, C. M., Eccles, J. S., & Becker, J. B. (1992). Are adolescents the victims of raging hormones: Evidence for activational effects of hormones on moods and behavior at adolescence. *Psychological Bulletin, 111*, 62–107.

Buhrmester, D. (1992). The developmental courses of sibling and peer relationships. In F. Boer & J. Dunn (Eds.), *Children's sibling relationships: Development and clinical issues* (pp. 19–40). Hillsdale, NJ: Lawrence Erlbaum.

Buhrmester, D. (1996). Need fulfillment, interpersonal competence and the developmental contexts of early adolescent friendship. In W. M. Bukowski, A. F. Newcomb, & W. W. Hartup (Eds.), *The company they keep: Friendship in childhood and adolescence* (pp. 158–185). New York: Cambridge University Press.

Buhrmester, D., & Furman, W. (1990). Perceptions of sibling relationships during middle childhood and adolescence. *Child Development, 61*, 1387–1398.

Bussey, K., & Bandura, A. (1999). Social cognitive theory of gender development and differentiation. *Psychological Review, 106*, 676–713.

Cairns, R. B., & Cairns, B. D. (1994). *Lifelines and risks: Pathways of youth in our time*. New York: Harvester Wheatsheaf.

Carli, L. L. (1990). Gender, language, and influence. *Journal of Personality and Social Psychology, 59*, 941–951.

Caspi, A., Lynam, D., Moffitt, T. E., & Silva, P. A. (1993). Unraveling girls' delinquency: Biological, dispositional, and contextual contributions to adolescent misbehavior. *Developmental Psychology, 29*, 19–30.

Cherney, I. D. (2005). Children's and adults' recall of sex-stereotyped toy pictures: Effects of presentation and memory task. *Infant and Child Development, 14*, 11–27.

Chodorow, N. (1978). *The reproduction of mothering: Psychoanalysis and the sociology of gender*. Berkeley: University of California Press.

Cillessen, A. H. N., & Mayeux, L. (2004). From censure to reinforcement: Developmental changes in the association between aggression and social status. *Child Development, 75*, 147–163.

Clark, L., & Tiggemann, M. (2007). Sociocultural influences and body image in 9- to 12-year-old girls: The role of appearance schemas. *Journal of Clinical Child and Adolescent Psychology, 36*, 76–86.

Cohen-Bendahan, C. C. C., van de Beek, C., & Berenbaum, S. A. (2005). Prenatal sex hormone effects on child and adult sex-typed behavior: Methods and findings. *Neuroscience and Biobehavioral Reviews, 29*, 353–384.

Cole, A., & Kerns, K. A. (2001). Perceptions of sibling qualities and activities of early adolescents. *Journal of Early Adolescence, 21*, 204–226.

Cole, D. A., Maxwell, S. E., Martin, J. M., Peeke, L. G., Seroczynski, A. D., Tram, J. M., et al. (2001). The development of multiple domains of child and adolescent self-concept: A cohort sequential longitudinal design. *Child Development, 72*, 1723–1746.

Coles, M., & Hall, C. (2002). Gendered readings: Learning from children's reading choices. *Journal of Research in Reading, 25*, 96–108.

Collins, W. A., & Laursen, B. (2006). Parent–adolescent relationships. In P. Noller & J. A. Feeney (Eds.), *Close relationships: Functions, forms and processes* (pp. 111–125). Hove, UK: Psychology Press/Taylor & Francis.

Collins, W. A., & Russell, G. (1991). Mother–child and father–child relationships in middle childhood and adolescence: A developmental analysis. *Developmental Review, 11*, 99–136.

Connolly, J., Craig, W., Goldberg, A., & Pepler, D. (1999). Conceptions of cross-sex friendships and romantic relationships in early adolescence. *Journal of Youth and Adolescence, 28*, 481–494.

Coontz, S. (1992). *The way we never were: American families and the nostalgia trap*. Scranton, PA: Harper/Collins.

Costa, P. T., Terracciano, A., & McCrae, R. R. (2001). Gender differences in personality traits across cultures: Robust and surprising findings. *Journal of Personality and Social Psychology, 81*, 322–331.

Costello, E. J., Mustillo, S., Erkanli, A., Keeler, G., & Angold, A. (2003). Prevalence and development of psychiatric disorders in childhood and adolescence. *Archives of General Psychiatry, 60*, 837–844.

Crick, N. R., Werner, N. E., O'Brien, K. M., Nelson, D. A., Grotpeter, J. K., & Markon, K. (1998). Childhood aggression and gender: A new look at an old problem. In D. Bernstein (Ed.), *Nebraska symposium on motivation, vol. 45. Gender and motivation* (pp. 75–151). Lincoln: University of Nebraska Press.

Crick, N. R., & Zahn-Waxler, C. (2003). The development of psychopathology in females and males: Current progress and future challenges. *Development and Psychopathology, 15*, 719–742.

Crouter, A. C., Helms-Erikson, H., Updegraff, K., & McHale, S. M. (1999). Conditions underlying parents' knowledge about children's daily lives in middle childhood: Between- and within-family comparisons. *Child Development, 70*, 246–259.

Crouter, A. C., Manke, B. A., & McHale, S. M. (1995). The family context of gender intensification in early adolescence. *Child Development, 66*, 317–329.

Crouter, A. C., Whiteman, S. D., McHale, S. M., & Osgood, D. W. (2007). Development of gender attitude traditionality across middle childhood and adolescence. *Child Development, 78*, 911–926.

Cunningham, M. (2001). Parental influences on the gendered division of housework. *American Sociological Review, 66*, 184–203.

De Bellis, M. D., Keshavan, M. S., Beers, S. R., Hall, J., Frustaci, K., Masalehdan, A., et al. (2001). Sex differences in brain maturation during childhood and adolescence. *Cerebral Cortex, 11*, 552–557.

Deaux, K., & Major, B. (1987). Putting gender into context: An interactive model of gender related behavior. *Psychological Review, 94*, 369–389.

DeLoache, J. S., Simcock, G., & Macari, S. (2007). Planes, trains, automobiles—and tea sets: Extremely intense interests in very young children. *Developmental Psychology, 43*, 1579–1586.

Demetriou, A., Christou, C., Spanoudis, G., & Platsidou, M. (2002). The development of mental processing: Efficiency, working memory, and thinking. *Monographs of the Society for Research in Child Development, 67* (1, serial no. 268).

Dessens, A. B., Slijper, F. M. E., & Drop, S. L. S. (2005). Gender dysphoria and gender change in chromosomal females with congenital adrenal hyperplasia. *Archives of Sexual Behavior, 34*, 389–397.

Di Pietro, J. A. (1981). Rough and tumble play: A function of gender. *Developmental Psychology, 17*, 50–58.

Diamond, L. M. (2000). Sexual identity attractions, and behavior among young sexual-minority women over a 2-year period. *Developmental Psychology, 36*, 241–250.

Diamond, L. M. (2003). New paradigms for research on sexual-minority and heterosexual youth. *Journal of Clinical Child and Adolescent Psychology, 32*, 490–498.

Diamond, L. M. (2008). Female bisexuality from adolescence to adulthood: Results from a 10-year longitudinal study. *Developmental Psychology, 44*, 5–14.

Diamond, L. M., & Dube, E. M. (2002). Friendship and attachment among heterosexual and sexual-minority youths: Does the gender of your friend matter? *Journal of Youth and Adolescence, 31*, 155–166.

Diekmann, A., & Schmidheiny, K. (2004). Do parents of girls have a higher risk of divorce? An eighteen-country study. *Journal of Marriage and the Family, 66*, 651–660.

Dohnt, H., & Tiggemann, M. (2006). The contribution of media and peer influences to the development of body satisfaction and self-esteem in young girls: A prospective study. *Developmental Psychology, 42*, 929–936.

Dorn, L. D., Dahl, R. E., Woodward, R., & Biro, F. (2006). Defining the boundaries of early adolescence: A user's guide to assessing pubertal status and pubertal timing in research with adolescents. *Applied Developmental Science, 10*, 30–56.

Drummond, K. D., Bradley, S. J., Peterson-Badali, M., & Zucker, K. J. (2008). A follow-up study of girls with gender identity disorder. *Developmental Psychology, 44*, 34–45.

Eagly, A. H. (1987). *Sex differences in social behavior: A social-role interpretation*. Hillsdale, NJ: Lawrence Erlbaum.

Eagly, A. H., & Steffen, V. J. (1986). Gender and aggressive behavior: A meta-analytic review of the social psychological literature. *Psychological Bulletin, 100*, 309–330.

Eagly, A. H., & Wood, W. (1999). The origins of sex differences in human behavior: Evolved dispositions versus social roles. *American Psychologist, 54*, 408–423.

Eaton, W. O., & Enns, L. R. (1986). Sex differences in human motor activity level. *Psychological Bulletin, 100*, 19–28.

Eccles, J. S. (2004). Schools, academic motivation, and stage-environment fit. In R. M. Lerner & L. Steinberg (Eds.), *Handbook of adolescent psychology* (2nd ed., pp. 125–153). Hoboken, NJ: John Wiley & Sons.

Eccles, J. S., Barber, B., & Jozefowicz, D. H. (1998). Linking gender to educational, occupational, and recreational choices: Applying the Eccles et al. model of achievement-related choices. In W. B. Swann, J. H. Langlois, & L. A. Gilbert (Eds.), *The many faces of gender: The multidimensional model of Janet Spence*. Washington, DC: APA Press.

Eccles, J. S., & Harold, R. D. (1992). Gender differences in educational and occupational patterns among the gifted. In N. Colangelo, S. G. Assouline, & D. L. Ambroson (Eds.), *Talent development: Proceedings from the 1991 Henry B. and Jocelyn Wallace National Research Symposium on Talent Development* (pp. 3–29). Unionville, NY: Trillium Press.

Eccles, J. S., Midgley, C., Wigfield, A., Buchanan, C. M., Reuman, D., Flanagan, C., et al. (1993). Development during adolescence: The impact of stage-environment fit on young adolescents' experiences in schools and in families. *American Psychologist, 48*, 90–101.

Eccles, J. S., Wigfield, A., & Schiefele, U. (1998). Motivation to succeed. In W. Damon (Series Ed.) & N. Eisenberg, (Vol. Ed.), *Handbook of child development,* vol. 3. *Social, emotional, and personality development* (5th ed., pp. 1017–1095). Hoboken, NJ: John Wiley & Sons.

Eckes, T., Trautner, H. M., & Behrendt, R. (2005). Gender subgroups and intergroup perception: Adolescents' views of own-gender and other-gender groups. *The Journal of Social Psychology, 145*, 85–111.

Egan, S. K., & Perry, D. G. (2001). Gender identity: A multidimensional analysis with implications for psychosocial adjustment. *Developmental Psychology, 37*, 451–463.

Else-Quest, N. M., Hyde, J. S., Goldsmith, H. H., & Van Hulle, C. A. (2006). Gender differences in temperament: A meta-analysis. *Psychological Bulletin, 132*, 33–72.

Ex, C. T. G.M., & Janssens, J. M. A. M. (1998). Maternal influences on daughters' gender role attitudes. *Sex Roles, 38*, 171–186.

Fabes, R. A., Martin, C. L., & Hanish, L. D. (2003). Young children's play qualities in same-, other-, and mixed-sex peer groups. *Child Development, 74*, 921–932.

Fabes, R. A., Martin, C. L., Hanish, L. D., Anders, M. C., & Madden-Derdich, D. A. (2003). Early school competence: The roles of sex-segregated play and effortful control. *Developmental Psychology, 39*, 848–858.

Farrington, D. P. (2004). Conduct disorder, aggression, and delinquency. In R. M. Lerner & L. Steinberg (Eds.), *Handbook of Adolescent Psychology* (2nd ed.; pp. 627–664). Hoboken, NJ: John Wiley & Sons.

Feingold, A. (1988). Cognitive gender differences are disappearing. *American Psychologist, 43*, 95–103.

Ferree, M. M. (1990). Beyond separate spheres: Feminism and family research. *Journal of Marriage and the Family, 52*, 866–884.

Fisher-Thompson, D. (1993). Adult toy purchases for children: Factors affecting sex-typed toy selection. *Journal of Applied Developmental Psychology, 14*, 385–406.

Fouts, G., & Burggraf, K. (1999). Television situation comedies: Female body images and verbal reinforcement. *Sex Roles, 40*, 473–481.

Fouts, G., & Burggraf, K. (2000). Television situation comedies: Female weight, male negative comments, and audience reactions. *Sex Roles, 42*, 925–952.

Fouts, G., & Vaughan, K. (2002). Television situation comedies: Male weight, negative references, and audience reactions. *Sex Roles, 46*, 439–442.

Fredricks, J. A., & Eccles, J. S. (2004). Parental influences on youth involvement in sports. In M. R. Weiss (Ed.), *Developmental sport and exercise psychology: A lifespan perspective* (pp. 145–164). Morgantown, WV: Fitness Information Technology.

Fuegen, K., Biernat, M., Haines, E., & Deaux, K. (2004). Mothers and fathers in the workplace: How gender and parental status influence judgments of job-related competence. *Journal of Social Issues, 60*, 737–754.

Funk, J. B., Baldacci, H. B., Pasold, T., & Baumgardner, J. (2004). Violence exposure in real-life, video games, television, movies, and the Internet: Is there desensitization? *Journal of Adolescence, 27*, 23–39.

Furman, W., & Buhrmester, D. (1992). Age and sex differences in perceptions of networks of personal relationships. *Child Development, 63*, 103–115.

Galambos, N. L., Almeida, D. M., & Petersen, A. C. (1990). Masculinity, femininity, and sex role attitudes in early adolescence: Exploring gender intensification. *Child Development, 61*, 1905–1914.

Galambos, N. L., Barker, E. T., & Almeida, D. M. (2003). Parents do matter: Trajectories of change in externalizing and internalizing problems in early adolescence. *Child Development, 74*, 578–594.

Garber, J., Keiley, M. K., & Martin, N. C. (2002). Developmental trajectories of adolescents' depressive symptoms: Predictors of change. *Journal of Consulting and Clinical Psychology, 70*, 79–95.

Gaulin, S. J. C. (1995). Does evolutionary theory predict sex differences in the brain? In M. S. Gazzaniga (Ed.), *The cognitive neurosciences* (pp. 1211–1225). Cambridge, MA: MIT Press.

Ge, X., Brody, G. H., Conger, R. D., Simons, R. L., & Murry, V. M. (2002). Contextual amplification of pubertal transition effects on deviant peer affiliation and externalizing behavior among African American children. *Developmental Psychology, 38*, 42–54.

Ge, X., Conger, R. D., & Elder, G. H. (1996). Coming of age too early: Pubertal influences on girls' vulnerability to psychological distress. *Child Development, 67*, 386–400.

Ge, X., Conger, R. D., & Elder, G. H., Jr. (2001). Pubertal transition, stressful life events, and the emergence of gender differences in adolescent depressive symptoms. *Developmental Psychology, 37*, 404–417.

Ge, X., Lorenz, F. O., Conger, R. D., Elder, G. H., Jr., & Simons, R. L. (1994). Trajectories of stressful life events and depressive symptoms during adolescence. *Developmental Psychology, 30*, 467–483.

Gentile, D. A., Lynch, P. J., Linder, J. R., & Walsh, D. A. (2004). The effects of violent video game habits on adolescent hostility, aggressive behaviors, and school performance. *Journal of Adolescence, 27*, 5–22.

Giedd, J. N. (2004). Structural magnetic resonance imaging of the adolescent brain. *Annals of the New York Academy of Sciences, 1021*, 77–85.

Giedd, J. N., Blumenthal, J., Jeffries, N. O., Castellanos, F. X., Liu, H., Zijdenbos, A., et al. (1999). Brain development during childhood and adolescence: A longitudinal MRI study. *Nature Neuroscience, 2*, 861–863.

Glick, P., & Fiske, S. T. (2001). An ambivalent alliance: Hostile and benevolent sexism as complementary justifications for gender inequality. *American Psychologist, 56*, 109–118.

Good, C. D., Johnsrude, I., Ashburner, J., Henson, R. N. A., Friston, K. J., & Frackowiak, R. S. J. (2001). Cerebral asymmetry and the effects of sex and handedness on brain structure: A voxel-based morphometric analysis of 465 normal adult human brains. *NeuroImage, 14*, 685–700.

Grabill, K. M., Lasane, T. P., Povitsky, W. T., Saxe, P., Munroe, G. D., Phelps, L. M., et al. (2005). Gender and study behavior: How social perception, social norm adherence, and structured academic behavior are predicted by gender. *North American Journal of Psychology, 7*, 7–24.

Green, R. (1974). *Sexual identity conflict in children and adults.* New York: Basic Books.

Greenfield, P., & Yan, Z. (2006). Children, adolescents, and the Internet: A new field of inquiry in developmental psychology. *Developmental Psychology, 42*, 391–394.

Grön, G., Wunderlich, A. P., Spitzer, M., Tomczak, R., & Riepe, M. W. (2000). Brain activation during human navigation: Gender-different neural networks as substrate of performance. *Nature Neuroscience, 3*, 404–408.

Grotevant, H. D. (1978). Sibling constellations and sex typing of interests in adolescence. *Child Development, 49*, 540–542.

Grumbach, M. M., Hughes, I. A., & Conte, F. A. (2002). Disorders of sex differentiation. In P. R. Larsen, H. M. Kronenberg, S. Melmed, & K. S. Polonsky (Eds.), *Williams textbook of endocrinology* (10th ed., pp. 842–1002). Philadelphia: W.B. Saunders.

Halpern, D. F. (2000). *Sex differences in cognitive abilities* (3rd ed.). Mahwah, NJ: Lawrence Erlbaum.

Hamann, S., & Canli, T. (2004). Individual differences in emotional processing. *Current Opinion in Neurobiology, 14*, 233–238.

Hamann, S., Herman, R. A., Nolan, C. L., & Wallen, K. (2004). Men and women differ in amygdala response to visual sexual stimuli. *Nature Neuroscience, 7*, 411–416.

Hamilton, S. F., & Hamilton, M. A. (2006). School, work and emerging adulthood. In J. J. Arnett & J. L. Tanner (Eds.), *Emerging adults in America: Coming of age in the 21st century* (pp. 257–277). Washington, DC: American Psychological Association.

Hampson, E. (2002). Sex differences in human brain and cognition: The influence of sex steroids in early and adult life. In J. B. Becker, S. M. Breedlove, D. Crews, & M. M. McCarthy (Eds.), *Behavioral endocrinology* (2nd ed., pp. 579–628). Cambridge, MA: MIT Press.

Hargreaves, D., & Tiggemann, M. (2002). The role of appearance schematicity in the development of adolescent body dissatisfaction. *Cognitive Therapy and Research, 26*, 691–700.

Harris, K. M., & Morgan, S. P. (1991). Fathers, sons, and daughters: Differential parental involvement in parenting. *Journal of Marriage and the Family, 53*, 531–544.

Harris, R. J., & Firestone, J. M. (1998). Changes in predictors of gender role ideologies among women: A multivariate analysis. *Sex Roles, 38*, 239–252.

Hedges, L. V., & Nowell, A. (1995). Sex differences in mental test scores, variability, and numbers of high-scoring individuals. *Science, 269*, 41–45.

Hernandez, D. J. (1997). Child development and the social demography of childhood. *Child Development, 68*, 149–169.

Hill, J. P., & Lynch, M. E. (1983). The intensification of gender-related role expectations during early adolescence. In J. Brooks-Gunn & A. C. Petersen (Eds.), *Girls at puberty: Biological and psychosocial perspectives* (pp. 201–228). New York: Plenum Press.

Hines, M., Ahmed, F., & Hughes, I. A. (2003). Psychological outcomes and gender-related development in complete androgen insensitivity syndrome. *Archives of Sexual Behavior, 32*, 93–101.

Hines, M., Brook, C., & Conway, G. S. (2004). Androgen and psychosexual development: Core gender identity, sexual orientation, and recalled gender role behavior in women and men with congenital adrenal hyperplasia (CAH). *Journal of Sex Research, 41*, 75–81.

Hines, M., Golombok, S., Rust, J., Johnston, K. J., Golding, J., & Avon Longitudinal Study of Parents and Children Study Team. (2002). Testosterone during pregnancy and gender role behavior of preschool children: A longitudinal, population study. *Child Development, 73*, 1678–1687.

Hoffman, M. L., Powlishta, K. K., & White, K. J. (2004). An examination of gender differences in adolescent adjustment: The effect of competence on gender role differences in symptoms of psychopathology. *Sex Roles, 50*, 795–810.

Huston, A. C. (1983). Sex-typing. In P. H. Mussen (Series Ed.) & E. M. Hetherington (Ed.), *Handbook of child psychology*, vol. 4. *Socialization, personality, and social development* (pp. 387–467). New York: John Wiley & Sons.

Hyde, J. S., Fennema, E., & Lamon, S. J. (1990). Gender differences in mathematics performance: A meta-analysis. *Psychological Bulletin, 107*, 139–155.

Hyde, J. S., & Frost, L. A. (1993). Meta-analysis in the psychology of women. In F. L. Denmark & M. A. Paludi (Eds.), *Psychology of women: A handbook of issues and theories* (pp. 67–103). Westport, CT: Greenwood Press.

Hyde, J. S., & Jaffee, S. R. (2000). Becoming a heterosexual adult: The experiences of young women. *Journal of Social Issues, 56*, 283–296.

Hyde, J. S., & Linn, M. C. (1988). Gender differences in verbal ability: A meta-analysis. *Psychological Bulletin, 104*, 53–69.

Ickes, W. (1993) Traditional gender roles: Do they make, and then break, our relationships? *Journal of Social Issues, 49*, 71–85.

Intons-Peterson, M. J. (1988). *Gender concepts of Swedish and American youth*. Hillsdale, NJ: Lawrence Erlbaum.

Jacobs, J. E. (1991). Influence of gender stereotypes on parent and child mathematics attitudes. *Journal of Educational Psychology, 83*, 518–527.

Jacobs, J. E., & Eccles, J. S. (1992). The impact of mothers' gender-role stereotypic beliefs on mothers' and children's ability perceptions. *Journal of Personality and Social Psychology, 63*, 932–944.

Jacobs, J. E., Lanza, S., Osgood, D. W., Eccles, J. S., & Wigfield, A. (2002). Changes in children's self-competence and values: Gender and domain differences across grades 1 through 12. *Child Development, 73*, 509–527.

Johnson, K. E., Alexander, J. M., Spencer, S., Leibham, M. E., & Neitzel, C. (2004). Factors associated with the early emergence of intense interests within conceptual domains. *Cognitive Development, 19*, 325–343.

Katz, P. A., & Ksansnak, K. R. (1994). Developmental aspects of gender role flexibility and traditionality in middle childhood and adolescence. *Developmental Psychology, 30*, 272–282.

Keating, D. P. (2004). Cognitive and brain development. In R. M. Lerner & L. Steinberg (Eds.), *Handbook of adolescent psychology* (2nd ed., pp. 45–84). Hoboken, NJ: John Wiley & Sons.

Kee, D. W., Gregory-Domingue, A., Rice, K., & Tone, K. (2005). A release from proactive interference analysis of gender schema encoding for occupations in adults and children. *Learning and Individual Differences, 15*, 203–211.

Kiecolt, K. J., & Acock, A. C. (1988). The long-term effects of family structure on gender-role attitudes. *Journal of Marriage and the Family, 50*, 709–717.

Killen, M., Lee-Kim, J., McGlothlin, H., & Stangor, C. (2002). How do children and adolescents evaluate gender and racial exclusion. *Monographs of the Society for Research in Child Development, 67* (4, serial no. 271).

Kim, J., McHale, S. M., Osgood, D. W., & Crouter, A. C. (2006). Longitudinal course and family correlates of sibling relationships from childhood through adolescence. *Child Development, 77*, 1746–1761.

Kimura, D. (1999). *Sex and cognition*. Cambridge, MA: MIT Press.

Klein, M. M, & Shulman, S. (1981). Adolescent masculinity–femininity in relation to parental models of masculinity-femininity and marital adjustment. *Adolescence, 16*, 45–48.

Kling, K. C., Hyde, J. S., Showers, C. J., & Buswell, B. N. (1999). Gender differences in self-esteem: A meta-analysis. *Psychological Bulletin, 125*, 470–500.

Klingenspor, B. (2002). Gender-related self discrepancies and bulimic eating behavior. *Sex Roles, 47*, 51–64.

Klomsten, A. T., Skaalvik, E. M., & Espnes, G. A. (2004). Physical self-concept and sports: Do gender differences still exist? *Sex Roles, 50*, 119–127.

Klump, K. L., Burt, S. A., McGue, M., & Iacono, W. G. (2007). Changes in genetic and environmental influences on disordered eating across adolescence: A longitudinal twin study. *Archives of General Psychiatry, 64*, 1409–1415.

Knickmeyer, R. C., Wheelwright, S., Taylor, K., Raggatt, P., Hackett, G., & Baron-Cohen, S. (2005). Gender-typed play and amniotic testosterone. *Developmental Psychology, 41*, 517–528.

Koch, H. L. (1956). Sissiness and tomboyishness in relation to sibling characteristics. *Journal of Genetic Psychology, 88*, 231–244.

Kohlberg, L. (1966). A cognitive-developmental analysis of children's sex-role concepts and attitudes. In E. E. Maccoby (Ed.), *The development of sex differences* (pp. 82–173). Stanford, CA: Stanford University Press.

Kolaric, G. C., & Galambos, N. L. (1995). Face-to-face interactions in mixed-sex adolescent dyads: Do girls and boys behave differently? *Journal of Early Adolescence, 15*, 363–382.

Krahé, B., Bieneck, S., & Scheinberger-Olwig, R. (2007). Adolescents' sexual scripts: Schematic representations of consensual and nonconsensual heterosexual interactions. *Journal of Sex Research, 44*, 316–327.

Krahé, B., & Möller, I. (2004). Playing violent electronic games, hostile attributional style, and aggression-related norms in German adolescents. *Journal of Adolescence, 27*, 53–69.

Kramer, J. H., Delis, D. C., & Daniel, M. (1988). Sex differences in verbal learning. *Journal of Clinical Psychology, 44*, 907–915.

La France, M., Hecht, M. A., & Levy Paluck, E. (2003). The contingent smile: A meta-analysis of sex differences in smiling. *Psychological Bulletin, 129*, 305–334.

Lansford, J. E., & Parker, J. G. (1999). Childrens' interactions in triads: Behavioral profiles and effects of gender and patterns of friendships among members. *Developmental Psychology, 35*, 80–93.

Larson, R. W., & Verma, S. (1999). How children and adolescents spend time across the world: Work, play and developmental opportunities. *Psychological Bulletin, 125*, 701–736.

Laursen, B., Coy, K. C., & Collins, W. A. (1998). Reconsidering changes in parent-child conflict across adolescence: A meta-analysis. *Child Development, 69*, 817–832.

Leahy, E., & Guo, G. (2001). Gender differences in mathematical trajectories. *Social Forces, 80*, 713–732.

Leaper, C., Anderson, K. J., & Saunders, P. (1998). Moderators of gender effects on parents' talk to their children: A meta-analysis. *Developmental Psychology, 34*, 3–27.

Leaper, C., & Smith, T. E. (2004). A meta-analytic review of gender variations in children's language use: Talkativeness, affiliative speech, and assertive speech. *Developmental Psychology, 40*, 993–1027.

Lenroot, R. K., & Giedd, J. N. (2006). Brain development in children and adolescents: Insights from anatomical magnetic resonance imaging. *Neuroscience and Biobehavioral Reviews, 30*, 718–729.

Lenroot, R. K., Gogtay, N., Greenstein, D. K., Wells, E. M., Wallace, G. L., Clasen, L. S., et al. (2007). Sexual dimorphism of brain developmental trajectories during childhood and adolescence. *Neuroimage, 15*, 1065–1073.

Leszczynski, J. P., & Strough, J. (2008). The contextual specificity of masculinity and femininity in early adolescence. *Social Development, 17*, 719–736.

Liben, L. S. (1995). Psychology meets geography: Exploring the gender gap on the national geography bee. *Psychological Science Agenda, 8*, 8–9.

Liben, L. S., & Bigler, R. S. (2002). The developmental course of gender differentiation: Conceptualizing, measuring, and evaluating constructs and pathways. *Monographs of the Society for Research in Child Development, 67* (2, serial no. 269).

Lindberg, S. M., Grabe, S., & Hyde, J. S. (2007). Gender, pubertal development, and peer sexual harassment predict objectified body consciousness in early adolescence. *Journal of Research on Adolescence, 17,* 723–742.

Linn, M. C., & Petersen, A. C. (1985). Emergence and characterization of sex differences in spatial ability: A meta-analysis. *Child Development, 56,* 1479–1498.

Lippa, R. (1998). Gender-related individual differences and the structure of vocational interests: The importance of the people-things dimension. *Journal of Personality and Social Psychology, 74,* 996–1009.

Lippa, R. A. (2002). *Gender, nature, and nurture.* Mahwah, NJ: Lawrence Erlbaum.

Lloyd, C. B., Grant, M., & Ritchie, A. (2008). Gender differences in time use among adolescents in developing countries: Implications of rising school enrolment rates. *Journal of Research on Adolescence, 18,* 99–120.

Lundy, B., Field, T., & McBride, C. K. (1998). Same-sex and opposite-sex best friend interactions among high school juniors and seniors. *Adolescence, 33,* 279–289.

Lutchmaya, S., Baron-Cohen, S., & Raggatt, P. (2002). Foetal testosterone and eye contact in 12-month-old human infants. *Infant Behavior and Development, 25,* 327–335.

Lytton, H., & Romney, D. M. (1991). Parents' differential socialization of boys and girls: A meta-analysis. *Psychological Bulletin, 109,* 267–296.

Ma, X., & Cartwright, F. (2003). A longitudinal analysis of gender differences in affective outcomes in mathematics during middle and high school. *School Effectiveness and School Improvement, 14,* 413–439.

Maccoby, E. E. (1990). Gender and relationships: A developmental account. *American Psychologist, 45,* 513–520.

Maccoby, E. E. (1998). *The two sexes: Growing apart and coming together.* Cambridge, MA: Harvard University Press.

Maccoby, E. E. (2002). Gender and group process: A developmental perspective. *Current Directions in Psychological Science, 11,* 54–58.

Maccoby, E. E., & Jacklin, C. N. (1975). *The psychology of sex differences.* London: Oxford University Press.

Maccoby, E. E., & Jacklin, C. N. (1987). Gender segregation in childhood. In E. H. Reese (Ed.), *Advances in child development and behavior* (Vol. 20, pp. 239–287). New York: Academic Press.

Mael, F., Alonso, A., Gibson, D., Rogers, K., & Smith, M. (2005). *Single-sex vs. coeducational schooling: A systematic review.* Retrieved April 1, 2008 from the U.S. Department of Education web site: www.ed.gov/rschstat/eval/other/single-sex/index.html.

Majeres, R. L. (1997). Sex differences in phonetic processing: Speed of identification of alphabetical sequences. *Perceptual and Motor Skills, 85,* 1243–1251.

Majeres, R. L. (1999). Sex differences in phonological processes: Speeded matching and word reading. *Memory and Cognition, 27,* 246–253.

Major, B., Barr, L., Zubek, J., & Babey, S. H. (1999). Gender and self-esteem: A meta-analysis. In W. B. Swann & J. H. Langlois (Eds.), *Sexism and stereotypes in modern society: The gender science of Janet Taylor Spence* (pp. 223–253). Washington, DC: American Psychological Association.

Maki, P. M., & Resnick, S. M. (2001). Effects of estrogen on patterns of brain activity at rest and during cognitive activity: A review of neuroimaging studies. *NeuroImage, 14,* 789–801.

Martin, C. L., & Fabes, R. A. (2001). The stability and consequences of young children's same-sex peer interactions. *Developmental Psychology, 37,* 431–446.

Martin, C. L., & Halverson, C. F. (1981). A schematic processing model of sex typing and stereotyping in children. *Child Development, 52,* 1119–1134.

Martin, C. L., & Ruble, D. (2004). Children's search for gender cues: Cognitive perspectives on gender development. *Current Directions in Psychological Science, 13,* 67–70.

Martin, C. L., Ruble, D. N., & Szkrybalo, J. (2002). Cognitive theories of early gender development. *Psychological Bulletin, 128,* 903–933.

May, A. L., Kim, J-Y., McHale, S. M., & Crouter, A. C. (2006). Parent–adolescent relationships and the development of weight concerns from early to late adolescence. *International Journal of Eating Disorders, 39,* 729–740.

Mayeux, L., Sandstrom, M. J., & Cillessen, A. H. N. (2008). Is being popular a risky proposition? *Journal of Research on Adolescence, 18,* 49–74.

McCoy, J. K., Brody, G. H., & Stoneman, Z. (1994). A longitudinal analysis of sibling relationships as mediators of the link between family processes and youths' best friendships. *Family Relations, 43,* 400–408.

McCrae, R. R, Costa, P. T., Jr., Terracciano, A., Parker, W. D., Mills, C. J., & De Fruyt, F. et al. (2002). Personality trait development from age 12 to age 18: Longitudinal, cross-sectional, and cross-cultural analyses. *Journal of Personality and Social Psychology, 83,* 1456–1468.

McHale, S. M, Crouter, A. C., & Tucker, C. J. (1999). Family context and gender socialization in middle childhood: Comparing girls to boys and sisters to brothers. *Child Development, 70,* 990–1004.

McHale, S. M, Crouter, A. C., & Tucker, C. J. (2001). Free time activities in middle childhood: Links with adjustment in early adolescence. *Child Development, 72,* 1764–1778.

McHale, S. M., Crouter, A. C., & Whiteman, S. D. (2003). The family contexts of gender development in childhood and adolescence. *Social Development, 12,* 125–148.

McHale, S. M., Kim, J. Y., Dotterer, A., Crouter, A. C., & Booth, A. (in press). The development of gendered interests and personality qualities from middle childhood through adolescence: A bio-social analysis. *Child Development.*

McHale, S. M., Kim, J. Y., Whiteman, S. D., & Crouter, A. C. (2004). Links between sex-typed time use in middle childhood and gender development in early adolescence. *Developmental Psychology, 40,* 868–881.

McHale, S. M., Shanahan, L., Updegraff, K. A., Crouter, A. C., & Booth, A. (2004). Developmental and individual differences in girls' sex-typed activities in middle childhood and adolescence. *Child Development, 75,* 1575–1593.

McHale, S. M., Updegraff, K. A., Helms-Erikson, H., & Crouter, A. C. (2001). Sibling influences on gender development in middle childhood and early adolescence: A longitudinal study. *Developmental Psychology, 37,* 115–125.

McHale, S. M., Updegraff, K. A., Shanahan, L., & Killoren, S. E. (2005). Siblings' differential treatment in Mexican American families. *Journal of Marriage and Family, 67,* 1259–1274.

McHale, S. M., Whiteman, S. D., Kim, J., & Crouter, A. C. (2007). Characteristics and correlates of sibling relationships in two-parent African American families. *Journal of Family Psychology, 21,* 227–235.

Meyer-Bahlburg, H. F. L. (2005). Gender identity outcome in female-raised 46,XY persons with penile agenesis, cloacal exstrophy of the bladder, or penile ablation. *Archives of Sexual Behavior, 34,* 423–438.

Meyer-Bahlburg, H. F. L., Dolezal, C., Baker, S. W., Ehrhardt, A. A., & New, M. I. (2006). Gender development in women with congenital adrenal hyperplasia as a function of disorder severity. *Archives of Sexual Behavior, 35,* 667–684.

Mischel, W. (1966). A social-learning view of sex differences in behavior. In E. E. Maccoby (Ed.), *The development of sex differences.* Stanford, CA: Stanford University Press.

Moen, P. A., Erickson, M. A., & Dempster-McClain, D. (1997). Their mothers' daughters? The intergenerational transmission of gender attitudes in a world of changing roles. *Journal of Marriage and the Family, 59,* 281–293.

Moffitt, T. E., Caspi, A., Rutter, M., & Silva, P. A. (2001). *Sex differences in antisocial behaviour: Conduct disorder, delinquency, and violence in the Dunedin Longitudinal Study.* Cambridge: Cambridge University Press.

Morgan, M. (1987). Television, sex-role attitudes, and sex-role behavior. *Journal of Early Adolescence, 7,* 269–282.

Neff, K. D., Cooper, C. E., & Woodruff, A. L. (2007). Children's and adolescents' developing perceptions of gender inequality. *Social Development, 16,* 682–699.

Neff, K. D., & Terry-Schmidt, L. N. (2002). Youths' attributions for power-related gender differences: Nature, nurture, or God? *Cognitive Development, 17,* 1185–1202.

Nelson, C., & Keith, J. (1990). Comparisons of female and male early adolescent sex role attitudes and behavior development. *Adolescence, 25,* 183–204.

Newcombe, N. (2007). Taking science seriously: Straight thinking about spatial sex differences In S. J. Ceci & W. M. Williams (Eds.), *Why aren't more women in science?* Washington, DC: APA Books.

Nordenström, A., Servin, A., Bohlin, G., Larsson, A., & Wedell, A. (2002). Sex-typed toy play behavior correlates with the degree of prenatal androgen exposure assessed by CYP21 genotype in girls with congenital adrenal hyperplasia. *Journal of Clinical Endocrinology and Metabolism, 87,* 5119–5124.

Otberg, N., Finner, A. M., & Shapiro, J. (2007). Androgenetic alopecia. *Endocrinology and Metabolism Clinics of North America, 36,* 379–398.

Parke, R. D., & Buriel, R. (1998). Socialization in the family: Ethnic and ecological perspectives. In W. Damon (Series Ed.) & N. Eisenberg (Vol. Ed.), *Handbook of child psychology: vol. 3. Social, emotional, and personality development* (5th ed., pp. 463–552). Hoboken, NJ: John Wiley & Sons.

Parke, R. D., Ornstein, P. A., Rieser, J. J., & Zahn-Waxler, C. (1994). *A century of developmental psychology.* Washington, DC: American Psychological Association.

Parsons, J. E., Kaczala, C. M., & Meece, J. L. (1982). Socialization of achievement attitudes and beliefs: Classroom influences. *Child Development, 53,* 322–339.

Parsons, T. (1974/1942). Age and sex in social structure. In R. L. Coser (Ed.), *The family: Its structures and functions* (pp. 243–355). New York: St. Martin's Press. (Originally published in *American Sociological Review, 7,* 604–616).

Parsons, T., & Bales, R. (1955). *Family, socialization, and interaction process.* Glencoe, IL:Free Press.

Pasterski, V. L., Geffner, M. E., Brain, C., Hindmarsh, P., Brook, C., & Hines, M. (2005). Prenatal hormones and postnatal socialization by parents as determinants of male-typical toy play in girls with congenital adrenal hyperplasia. *Child Development, 76,* 264–278.

Pasterski, V. L., Hindmarsh, P., Geffner, M., Brook, C., Brain, C., & Hines, M. (2007). Increased aggression and activity level in 3- to 11-year-old girls with congenital adrenal hyperplasia (CAH). *Hormones and Behavior, 52,* 368–374.

Paus, T. (2005). Mapping brain maturation and cognitive development during adolescence. *Trends in Cognitive Sciences, 9,* 60–68.

Pellegrini, A. D., & Smith, P. K. (1998). Physical active play: The nature and function of a neglected aspect of play. *Child Development, 69,* 577–598.

Phelps, L., Johnston, L. S., Jimenez, D. P., Wilczenski, F. L., Andrea, R. K., & Healy, R. W. (1993). Figure preference, body dissatisfaction, and body distortion in adolescence. *Journal of Adolescent Research, 8,* 297–310.

Phinney, J. S., & Alipuria, L. L. (1990). Ethnic identity in college students from four ethnic groups. *Journal of Adolescence, 13,* 171–183.

Phinney, J. S., & Chavira, V. (1992). Ethnic identity and self-esteem: An exploratory longitudinal study. *Journal of Adolescence, 15,* 271–282.

Polce-Lynch, M., Myers, B. J., Kliewer, W., & Kilmartin, C. (2001). Adolescent self-esteem and gender: Exploring relations to sexual harassment, body image, media influence, and emotional expression. *Journal of Youth and Adolescence, 30,* 225–244.

Powlishta, K. K. (1995). Intergroup processes in childhood: Social categorization and sex role development. *Developmental Psychology, 31,* 781–788.

Powlishta, K. K., Serbin, L. A., Doyle, A. B., & White, D. R. (1994). Gender, ethnic, and body type biases: The generality of prejudice in childhood. *Developmental Psychology, 30,* 526–536

Puts, D. A., McDaniel, M. A., Jordan, C. L., & Breedlove, N. J. (2008). Spatial ability and prenatal androgens: Meta-analyses of congenital adrenal hyperplasia and digit ratio (2D:4D) studies. *Archives of Sexual Behavior, 37,* 100–111.

Raz, N., Gunning-Dixon, F., Head, D., Rodrique, K. M., Williamson, A., & Acker, J. D. (2004). Aging, sexual dimorphism, and hemispheric asymmetry of the cerebral cortex: Replicability of regional differences in volume. *Neurobiology of Aging, 25,* 377–396.

Resnick, S. M. (2006). Sex differences in regional brain structure and function. In P. W. Kaplan (Ed.), *Neurologic disease in women* (2nd ed., pp. 15–26). New York: Demos Medical Publications.

Rheingold, H. L., & Cook, K. V. (1975). The contents of boys' and girls' rooms as an index of parents' behaviors. *Child Development, 46,* 459–463.

Rice, T. W., & Coates, D. L. (1995). Gender role attitudes in the southern United States. *Gender & Society, 9,* 744–756.

Richards, M. H., & Larson, R. (1989). The life space and socialization of the self: Sex differences in the young adolescent. *Journal of Youth and Adolescence, 18,* 617–626.

Richards, M. H., Crowe, P. A., Larson, R., & Swarr, A. (1998). Developmental patterns and gender differences in the experience of peer companionship during adolescence. *Child Development, 69,* 154–163.

Roberts, D. F., & Foehr, U. G. (2004). *Kids and media in America.* New York: Cambridge University Press.

Roberts, D. F., Henriksen, L., & Foehr, U. G. (2004). Adolescents and media. In R. M. Lerner & L. Steinberg (Eds.), *Handbook of adolescent psychology* (2nd ed., pp. 487–521). Hoboken, NJ: John Wiley & Sons.

Rodgers, J. L., & Rowe, D. C. (1988). Influence of siblings on adolescent sexual behavior. *Developmental Psychology, 24,* 722–728.

Roeser, R. W., Eccles, J. S., & Sameroff, A. J. (1998). Academic and emotional functioning in early adolescence: Longitudinal relations, patterns, and prediction by experience in middle school. *Development and Psychopathology, 10,* 321–352.

Rose, A. J. (2002). Co-rumination in the friendships of girls and boys. *Child Development, 73,* 1830–1843.

Rose, A. J., & Rudolph, K. D. (2006). A review of sex differences in peer relationship processes: Potential trade-offs for the emotional and behavioral development of girls and boys. *Psychological Bulletin, 132,* 98–131.

Rose, A. J., Carlson, W., & Waller, E. M. (2007). Prospective association of co-rumination with friendship and emotional adjustment: Considering the socioemotional trade-offs of co-rumination. *Developmental Psychology, 43,* 1019–1031.

Ross, J. L., Roeltgen, D., Kushner, H., Wei, F., & Zinn, A. R. (2000). The Turner syndrome-associated neurocognitive phenotype maps to distal Xp. *American Journal of Human Genetics, 67,* 672–681.

Ross, J., Roeltgen, D., & Zinn, A. (2006). Cognition and the sex chromosomes: Studies in Turner Syndrome. *Hormone Research, 65,* 47–56.

Rowe, R., Maughan, B., Worthman, C. M., Costello, E. J., & Angold, A. (2004). Testosterone, antisocial behavior, and social dominance in boys: Pubertal development and biosocial interaction. *Biological Psychiatry, 55,* 546–552.

Rowley, S., Mistry, R., & Feagans, L. (2007). Social status as a predictor of race and gender stereotypes in late childhood and early adolescence. *Social Development, 16,* 150–168.

Rubin, K. H., Bukowski, W. M., & Parker, J. G. (2006). Peer interactions, relationships, and groups. In W. Damon & R. M. Lerner (Series Eds.) & N. Eisenberg (Vol. Ed.), *Handbook of child psychology,* vol. 3. *Social, emotional, and personality development* (6th ed., pp. 571–645). Hoboken, NJ: John Wiley & Sons.

Ruble, D. N., & Martin, C. L. (1998). Gender development. In W. Damon (Series Ed.) & N. Eisenberg (Vol. Ed.), *Handbook of child psychology*, vol. 3. *Social, emotional, and personality development* (5th ed., pp. 933–1016). Hoboken, NJ: John Wiley & Sons.

Ruble, D. N., Martin, C. L., & Berenbaum, S. A. (2006). Gender development. In W. Damon & R. M. Lerner (Series Eds.) & N. Eisenberg (Vol. Ed.), *Handbook of child psychology*, vol. 3. *Social, emotional, and personality development* (6th ed., pp. 858–932). Hoboken, NJ: John Wiley & Sons.

Ruble, D. N., Taylor, L. J., Cyphers, L., Greulich, F. K., Lurye, L. E., & Shrout, P. E. (2007). The role of gender constancy in early gender development. *Child Development, 78*, 1121–1136.

Russell, A., & Saebel, J. (1997). Mother–son, mother–daughter, father–son, and father–daughter: Are they distinct relationships? *Developmental Review, 17*, 111–147.

Rust, J., Golombok, S., Hines, M., Johnston, K., Golding, J., & ALSPAC Study Team (2000). The role of brothers and sisters in the gender development of preschool children. *Journal of Experimental Child Psychology, 77*, 292–203.

Savin-Williams, R. C. (1979). Dominance hierarchies in groups of early adolescents. *Child Development, 50*, 923–935.

Savin-Williams, R. C., & Diamond, L. (2000). Sexual identity trajectories among sexual-minority youths: Gender comparisons. *Archives of Sexual Behavior, 29*, 607–627.

Sax, L. (2005). *Why gender matters: What parents and teachers need to know about the emerging science of sex differences.* New York: Doubleday.

Serbin, L. A., Powlishta, K. K., & Gulko, J. (1993). The development of sex-typing in middle childhood. *Monographs of the Society for Research in Child Development, 58* (2, serial no. 232).

Servin, A., Nordenström, A., Larsson, A., & Bohlin, G. (2003). Prenatal androgens and gender-typed behavior: A study of girls with mild and severe forms of congenital adrenal hyperplasia. *Developmental Psychology, 39*, 440–450.

Shanahan, M. J., & Flaherty, B. P. (2001). Dynamic patterns of time use in adolescence. *Child Development, 72*, 385–401.

Shanahan, L., McHale, S. M., Crouter, A. C., & Osgood, D. W. (2007). Warmth with mothers and fathers from middle childhood to late adolescence: Within- and between-families comparisons. *Developmental Psychology, 43*, 551–563.

Shanahan, L., McHale, S. M., Osgood, D. W., & Crouter, A. C. (2007). Conflict frequency with mothers and fathers from middle childhood to late adolescence: Within- and between-families comparisons. *Developmental Psychology, 43*, 539–550.

Shaywitz, B. A., Shaywitz, S. E., Pugh, K. R., Constable, R. T., Skudlarski, P., Fulbright, R. K., et al. (1995). Sex differences in the functional organization of the brain for language. *Nature, 373*, 607–609.

Sherriff, N. (2007). Peer group cultures and social identity: An integrated approach to studying masculinities. *British Educational Research Journal, 33*, 349–370.

Siegal, M. (1987). Are sons and daughters treated more differently by fathers than by mothers? *Developmental Review, 7*, 183–209.

Signorielli, N. (2001). Television's gender role images and contribution to stereotyping: Past, present, future. In D. G. Singer & J. L. Singer (Eds.), *Handbook of children and the media* (pp. 341–358). Thousand Oaks, CA: Sage.

Sinton, M. M., & Birch, L. L. (2006). Individual and sociocultural influences on pre-adolescent girls' appearance schemas and body dissatisfaction. *Journal of Youth and Adolescence, 35*, 165–175.

Sisk, C. L., & Zehr, J. L. (2005). Pubertal hormones organize the adolescent brain and behavior. *Frontiers in Neuroendocrinology, 26*, 163–174.

Slomkowski, C., Rende, R., Novak, S., Lloyd-Richardson, E., & Niaura, R. (2005). Sibling effects on smoking in adolescence: Evidence for social influence from a genetically informative design. *Addiction, 100*, 430–438.

Smetana, J. G., & Daddis, C. (2002). Domain-specific antecedents of parental psychological control and monitoring: The role of parenting beliefs and practices. *Child Development, 73*, 563–580.

Smetana, J. G., Metzger, A., & Campione-Barr, N. (2004). African American late adolescents' relationships with parents: Developmental transitions and longitudinal patterns. *Child Development, 75*, 932–947.

Smith, T. E., & Leaper, C. (2005). Self-perceived gender typicality and the peer context during adolescence. *Journal of Research on Adolescence, 16*, 91–103.

Steele, J., & Barling, J. (1996). Influences of maternal gender-role beliefs and role satisfaction on daughters' vocational interest. *Sex Roles, 34*, 637–648.

Steinberg, L.D., & Cauffman, E. (1995). The impact of employment on adolescent development. *Annals of Child Development, 11*, 131–166.

Steinberg, L., & Silk, J. S. (2002). Parenting adolescents. In M. H. Bornstein (Ed.), *Handbook of parenting*, vol. 1. *Children and parenting* (2nd ed., pp. 103–133). Mahwah, NJ: Lawrence Erlbaum.

Stewart, R. B., Kozak, A. L., Tingley, L. M., Goddard, J. M., Blake, E. M., & Cassel, W. A (2001). Adult sibling relationships: Validation of a typology. *Personal Relationships, 8*, 299–324.

Sulloway, F. J. (1996). *Born to rebel: Birth order, family dynamics, and creative lives.* New York: Pantheon Books.

Susman, E. J., Finkelstein, J. W., Chinchilli, V. M., Schwab, J., Liben, L. S., D'Arcangelo, M. R., et al. (1998). The effect of sex hormone replacement therapy on behavior problems and moods in adolescents with delayed puberty. *Journal of Pediatrics, 133*, 521–525.

Sutton-Smith, B., & Rosenberg, B. G. (1970). *The sibling.* Oxford, UK: Holt, Rinehart, & Winston.

Tajfel, H., & Turner, J. C. (1986). The social identity theory of intergroup behaviour. In S. Worchel & W. G. Austin (Eds.), *Psychology of intergroup relations* (pp. 7–24). Chicago: Nelson.

Tarrant, M. (2002). Adolescent peer groups and social identity. *Social Development, 11*, 110–123.

Tarrant, M., North, A. C., & Hargreaves, D. J. (2004). Adolescents' intergroup attributions: A comparison of two social identities. *Journal of Youth and Adolescence, 33*, 177–185.

Tenenbaum, H. R., & Leaper, C. (2002). Are parents' gender schemas related to their children's gender-related cognitions? A meta-analysis. *Developmental Psychology, 38*, 615–630.

Thompson, T., & Ungerleider, C. (2004). *Single sex schooling: Final report.* Retrieved April 1, 2008 from the Council of Ministers of Education web site: www.cmec.ca/stats/singlegender.en.pdf.

Tiggemann, M., Gardiner, M., & Slater, A. (2000). "I would rather be size 10 than have straight A's": A focus group study of adolescent girls' wish to be thinner. *Journal of Adolescence, 23*, 645–659.

Timmer, S. G., Eccles, J. S., & O'Brien, K. (1985). How children use time. In F. T. Juster & F. P. Stafford (Eds.), *Time, goods, and well-being* (pp. 353–382). Ann Arbor, MI: Institute for Social Research.

Trautner, H. M., Ruble, D. N., Cyphers, L., Kirsten, B., Behrendt, R., & Hartmann, P. (2005). Rigidity and flexibility of gender stereotypes in childhood: Developmental or differential? *Infant and Child Development, 14*, 365–381.

Trivers, R. L. (1972). Parental investment and sexual selection. In B. Campbell (Ed.), *Sexual selection and the descent of man, 1871–1971* (pp. 136–179). Chicago: Aldine-Atherton.

Twenge, J. M., & Nolen-Hoeksema, S. (2002). Age, gender, race, socioeconomic status, and birth cohort differences on the Children's Depression Inventory: A meta-analysis. *Journal of Abnormal Psychology, 111*, 578–588.

U.S. Department of Education. (1993). *The condition of education.* Washington, DC: National Center for Educational Statistics.

Udry, J. R. (2000). Biological limits of gender construction. *American Sociological Review, 65*, 443–457.

Updegraff, K. A., McHale, S. M., & Crouter, A. C. (2000). Adolescents' sex-typed friendship experiences: Does having a sister versus a brother matter? *Child Development, 71*, 1597–1610.

Updegraff, K., McHale, S. M., & Crouter, A. C. (1996). Gender roles in marriage: What do they mean for girls' and boy's school achievement? *Journal of Youth and Adolescence, 25*, 73–88.

Updegraff, K., McHale, S. M., Whiteman, S. D., Thayer, S. M., & Delgado, M. Y. (2005). Adolescent sibling relationships in Mexican American families: Exploring the role of familism. *Journal of Family Psychology, 19*, 512–522.

Van Beek, Y., van Dolderen, M. S. M., & Dubas, J. J. S. D. (2006). Gender-specific development of nonverbal behaviours and mild depression in adolescence. *Journal of Child Psychology and Psychiatry, 47*, 1272–1283.

Vaughan, K. K., & Fouts, G. T. (2003). Changes in television and magazine exposure and eating disorder symptomatology. *Sex Roles, 49*, 313–320.

Verkuyten, M., & Thijs, J. (2001). Ethnic and gender bias among Dutch and Turkish children in late childhood: The role of social context. *Infant and Child Development, 10*, 203–217.

Vogel, D. L., Tucker, C. M., Wester, S. R., & Heesacker, M. (1999). The impact of sex and situational cues on the endorsement of traditional gender-role attitudes and behaviors in dating couples. *Journal of Social and Personal Relationships, 16*, 459–473.

Voyer, D. (1996). On the magnitude of laterality effects and sex differences in functional lateralities. *Laterality, 1*, 51–83.

Wager, T. D., Phan, K. L., Liberzon, I., & Taylor, S. F. (2003). Valence, gender, and lateralization of functional brain anatomy in emotion: A meta-analysis of findings from neuroimaging. *NeuroImage, 19*, 513–531.

Ward, L. M., Hansbrough, E., & Walker, E. (2005). Contributions of music video exposure to black adolescents' sexual and gender schemas. *Journal of Adolescent Research, 20*, 143–166.

Washburn-Ormachea, J. M., Hillman, S. B., & Sawilowsky, S. S. (2004). Gender and gender-role orientation differences on adolescents' coping with peer stressors. *Journal of Youth and Adolescence, 33*, 31–40.

Watt, H. M. G. (2004). Development of adolescents' self-perception, values, and task perceptions according to gender and domain in 7th- through 11th-grade Australian students. *Child Development, 75*, 1556–1572.

Way, N., Reddy, R., & Rhodes, J. (2007). Students' perceptions of school climate during the middle school years: Associations with trajectories of psychological and behavioral adjustment. *American Journal of Community Psychology, 40*, 194–213.

Weichold, K., Silbereisen, R. K., & Schmitt-Rodermund, E. (2003). Short-and long-term consequences of early versus late physical maturation in adolescents. In C.Hayward (Ed.), *Puberty and psychopathology* (pp. 241–276). Cambridge, MA: Cambridge University Press.

Weisner, T. (2002). Ecocultural understanding of children's developmental pathways. *Human Development, 45*, 275–281.

Whiting, B. B., & Edwards, C. P. (1988). *Children of different worlds*. Cambridge, MA: Harvard University Press.

Wigfield, A., Eccles, J. S., Schiefele, U., Roeser, R. W., & Davis-Kean, P. (2006). Development of achievement motivation. In W. Damon & R. M. Lerner (Series Eds.) & N.Eisenberg (Vol. Ed.), *Handbook of child psychology,* vol. 3. *Social, emotional, and personality development* (6th ed., pp. 933–1002). Hoboken, NJ: John Wiley & Sons.

Wilgenbusch, T., & Merrell, K. W. (1999). Gender differences in self concept among children and adolescents: A meta-analysis of multidimensional studies. *School Psychology Quarterly, 14*, 101–120.

Williams, C. L., & Meck, W. H. (1991). The organizational effects of gonadal steroids on sexually dimorphic spatial ability. *Psychoneuroendocrinology, 16*, 155–176.

Wisniewski, A. B., Migeon, C. J., Meyer-Bahlburg, H. F. L., Gearhart, J. P., Berkovitz, G. D., Brown, T. R., et al. (2000). Complete androgen insensitivity syndrome: Long-term medical, surgical, and psychosexual outcome. *Journal of Clinical Endocrinology and Metabolism, 85*, 2664–2669.

Witelson, S. F., Glezer, I. I., & Kigar, D. L. (1995). Women have greater density of neurons in posterior temporal cortex. *Journal of Neuroscience, 15*, 3418–3428.

Wizemann, T. M., & Pardue, M.-L. (Eds.). (2001). *Exploring the biological contributions to human health: Does sex matter?* Washington, DC: National Academy Press.

Wood, W., & Eagly, A. H. (2002). A cross-cultural analysis of the behavior of women and men: Implications for the origins of sex differences. *Psychological Bulletin, 128*, 699–727.

Yee, M., & Brown, R. (1994). The development of gender differentiation in young children. *British Journal of Social Psychology, 33*, 183–196.

Zucker, K. J. (2004). Gender identity development and issues. *Child and Adolescent Psychiatric Clinics of North America, 13*, 551–568.

Zucker, K. J., & Bradley, S. J. (1995). *Gender identity disorder and psychosexual problems in children and adolescents*. New York: Guilford Press.

Zucker, K. J., Bradley, S. J., Oliver, G., Blake, J., Fleming, S., & Hood, J. (1996). Psychosexual development of women with congenital adrenal hyperplasia. *Hormones and Behavior, 30*, 300–318.

CHAPTER 11

Attachment and Autonomy During Adolescence

KATHLEEN BOYKIN McELHANEY, JOSEPH P. ALLEN, J. CLAIRE STEPHENSON, AND AMANDA L. HARE

Adolescence is often highlighted as being a phase of development during which there is particular tension between the struggle for autonomy and the strong attachment that teens have to their parents. Whereas, historically, these forces have been cast as diametrically opposed (such that achieving one meant sacrificing the other), more recent work has begun to examine the ways in which the drive to maintain close connections with parents, as well as the need to establish oneself as an autonomous individual, work together in complex—and not necessarily contradictory—ways. This chapter aims to examine both the theory and empirical findings from research on attachment and autonomy during adolescence, particularly with regard to the context of parent-adolescent relationships. Our goal is to more clearly elucidate how these processes may play out in the course of normative adolescent development; further, we will examine how variations in both attachment and autonomy may help to explain individual differences in adolescents' psychosocial adjustment.

We begin by outlining some of the major components of the theories of attachment relationships and autonomy development, including the historical roots of these constructs and the ways that they fit together to influence the course of development during adolescence. Included here is a review of the ways that attachment and autonomy processes have been defined and studied during adolescence, again particularly with regard to functioning within parent-adolescent relationships. We then consider the normative developmental changes in attachment relationships and autonomy processes during adolescence, and we subsequently move on to consider the nature of individual differences in attachment and autonomy processes. Here, we first examine how variations in attachment relationships and autonomy processes themselves are linked, and then turn to how variations in both of these two constructs are linked to a range of other outcomes for teens. Included in this final section is a consideration of how attachment and autonomy processes may be moderated by demographic factors such as gender and socioeconomic context.

THEORETICAL PERSPECTIVES ON ATTACHMENT AND AUTONOMY

Attachment Theory and Adolescence

Attachment theory has its roots in a diverse range of fields including psychoanalytic theory,

This chapter was completed with the assistance of grants from the National Institute of Mental Health. Requests for reprints should be sent to the second author at: Department of Psychology, Box 400400, University of Virginia, Charlottesville, VA 22904-4400 (allen@virginia.edu).

developmental psychology, evolutionary biology and ethology (Cassidy, 1999). Bowlby (1969/1982) initially developed attachment theory to explain why infants develop close relationships with their caregivers, as well as why and to what extent disruptions in such relationships affect later development. His theory provides a developmental framework that helps to explain both normative development and individual differences in social, emotional and behavioral outcomes over the course of infancy and early childhood. Within the past two decades, researchers have turned to questions related to the nature and function of the attachment system over the course of the life span, with a particular focus on adolescence (Allen & Land, 1999; Greenberg, Siegel, & Leitch, 1983; Kobak & Sceery, 1988; Rice, 1990).

The primary function of the attachment system during infancy is to maximize the safety and protection of the developing infant. Infants are predisposed to emit behaviors that promote proximity to caregivers, particularly during times of distress, and proximity to caregivers, in turn, provides the infant with protection from harm (Bowlby, 1969/1982). As children mature, they develop a larger repertoire of behaviors for achieving proximity to caregivers, and the focus on protection shifts somewhat to something more akin to emotional support. By adolescence, the outcome of activation of the attachment system is more towards "felt security" on the part of the teenager, rather than actual physical safety (Allen & Land, 1999; Allen, in press; Cummings & Davies, 1996). This felt security can be achieved in numerous ways, often without the literal physical presence of the attachment figure.

Thus, the emphasis on physical protection and proximity to caregivers decreases with increased maturity. This decrease occurs in part because older children and adolescents can achieve felt security without the physical presence of their attachment figures, and in part because their level of maturity allows them to

more capably interact with their environment on their own. Said differently, Bowlby (1980) noted that the attachment system is activated in response to two classes of factors that increase the need for presence of a caregiver: conditions of the child (e.g. illness, hunger, fatigue, pain) and conditions of environment (e.g., presence of threatening stimuli). During adolescence, increased cognitive, emotional and behavioral maturity dictates that teens are less likely to experience conditions that activate their need for their caregiver. Similarly, the environment is much less likely to be perceived as threatening to the degree to which teens require parents to help them manage those threats. For example, while sick teens may still want their parent(s) to care for them, if necessary they can also stay home from school by themselves without experiencing undue distress.

Before moving on to discuss theories of adolescent autonomy, it is worth noting that the concept of autonomy development is integrally embedded within the theory regarding the nature and function of attachment relationships. Bowlby (1980) and others proposed that there is a continual balance between stress-reducing behaviors that incorporate dependence on the caregiver and exploratory behaviors that function to increase knowledge of and mastery over the environment (Baltes & Silverberg, 1994; Bretherton, 1992). Similarly, Ainsworth's observations of infants suggested that the attachment system and exploratory system cannot be activated at the same time (Ainsworth, Blehar, Waters, & Wall, 1978). With regard to adolescent development, it becomes increasingly important for the exploratory system to be highly activated and fully developed; this activation corresponds to a decrease in the day-to-day reliance on attachment figures for comfort and support (Allen & Land, 1999; Allen, in press). Interestingly, it was Bowlby who first suggested that in adolescence it was the combination of *autonomy–relatedness* that was most linked to optimal outcomes in the parent–child relationship (Murphey, Silber, Coelho, Hamburg,

& Greenberg, 1963). Increased autonomous exploration (while utilizing parents as a secure base) allows adolescents to focus on the remaining tasks of social and emotional development: forming relationships with peers and romantic partners and regulating their own behavior and affective states.

Attachment theory further contains specific predictions regarding individual differences in the development of autonomy: independent, self-reliant functioning is facilitated by secure attachment relationships. When caregivers are both emotionally supportive and encouraging of autonomy, children develop the capacity to not only confidently approach and master novel situations and tasks, but also to ask for help when needed (Sroufe, 2005). Thus, in this formulation, autonomous functioning is not synonymous with complete independence from caregivers—children who are both secure and autonomous are expected to operate independently within the realms of their competence, but also to feel quite comfortable relying on others when necessary and appropriate. Further, this view of autonomy emphasizes the nature of the interpersonal context in which autonomy develops (namely, the parent–child relationship), but also postulates intraindividual traits that characterize an autonomous individual.

Autonomy During Adolescence

Most empirical work on autonomy processes during adolescence has its roots in a somewhat disparate, yet overlapping, set of theoretical frameworks. Much of the early interest in adolescent autonomy development stemmed from psychoanalytic theories that emphasized the need for adolescents to detach from parents and to relinquish childish ties to and conceptions of them (e.g., Freud, 1958). In this view, parent–adolescent conflict was viewed as normative and desirable, whereas, to a certain extent, close emotional ties between adolescents and their parents were considered an aberration. Neoanalytic theorists deemphasized

the role of detachment and conflict per se, and instead postulated that healthy adolescence involves a process of individuation, in which teens gradually come to see themselves as separate from parents (Blos, 1967). While Blos did not see individuation as involving detachment from parents, he did propose that teens must relinquish childish dependencies on parents in order to become fully autonomous. Along with individuating from parents, adolescents are also expected to undergo a process of deidealization, during which they begin to view their parents as imperfect versus all-knowing and all-powerful. In contrast to attachment theory, these propositions treat autonomy more clearly as an intraindividual construct, placing emphasis on intrapsychic development within the adolescent versus on the relational processes that surround this development.

However, this intrapsychic process is still being carried out within the interpersonal context of the parent–adolescent relationship, and some recent conceptualizations of autonomy development have highlighted the interpersonal nature of the autonomy process (Collins & Steinberg, 2006; Collins, 1990; Hill & Holmbeck, 1986). From this perspective, patterns of parent–child interaction are thought to shift as children enter adolescence, and as the underlying beliefs and expectations that surround those interactions change (Collins; Collins & Steinberg; Smetana 1988a, 1988b). These shifts may be seen in the increased conflict that occurs during adolescence, which signals to all the changes that are occurring within the parent–adolescent dyad. Although the process of individuation is still deemed important, this conceptualization places more emphasis on the quality of the relationship between parents and adolescents, and postulates that adolescent autonomy development is facilitated by parenting that is responsive and supportive. In healthy families, parent–adolescent relationships become transformed but not detached.

It should be noted that this perspective is actually quite close to the attachment theory model, in which healthy autonomy is achieved in the context of close and supportive relationships with parents. The normative changes in thoughts, feelings and behaviors that occur during adolescence may serve to "activate" the attachment system in ways that parallel the activation seen from physical separation from caregiver(s) in infancy. Ideally, this activation can act as a signal to parents and adolescents that adjustments need to be made within their relationship to accommodate the changes in teens' needs. Both the parental sensitivity that typically accompanies secure attachment and the level of openness and flexibility specifically with regard to evaluating (and reevaluating) the attachment relationship increase the chances that securely attached teens and their parents can successfully recognize and adapt to these developmental changes. Thus, a secure parent–teen relationship should allow both parent and teen to acknowledge the teen's autonomy strivings and to support them while also maintaining the relationship. Secure adolescents should also be better able to use their parents as a base from which to confidently and autonomously explore the world around them, returning to parents for comfort, support, and advice when the limits of their competence are reached (Belsky & Cassidy, 1994).

APPROACHES TO MEASURING ATTACHMENT AND AUTONOMY DURING ADOLESCENCE

Before we begin our review of normative development in attachment and autonomy processes during adolescence, it is important to outline the efforts to empirically define and measure these constructs. With regard to measurement of attachment, it is essential to understand the basis for the ways that attachment is assessed during adolescence, which differ from the ways that attachment is measured during infancy and early childhood. Specifically, research methods during infancy and early childhood are largely observational, focusing on dyadic processes that play out between parents and their children. In contrast,

attachment during adolescence is typically assessed via methods that are intended to capture underlying cognitive models of relationships, and thus by definition treat attachment as an intrapsychic construct and a characteristic of the individual. While secure versus insecure attachment models are thought to develop on the basis of dyadic interaction, the assumption is that these models are relatively fixed by adolescence.

It is also noteworthy that quite disparate methods have been utilized to purportedly capture adolescent attachment processes, and that while all methods may have merit, they are not equivalent or interchangeable. An additional source of confusion stems from the fact that the term *attachment* is often used more broadly, almost as a synonym for *relationship*, or to indicate the opposite of *detached* (e.g., adolescents remain *attached* to their parents). This usage differs from what is meant by an *attachment relationship* per se, which is defined as a relationship (usually with a caregiver) that fulfills specific functions, including providing comfort in times of distress and a secure base from which exploration can occur (Ainsworth, 1989).

A very similar set of issues is present in the literature examining adolescent autonomy development. At a basic level, researchers have differed as to whether they treat autonomy as an intraindividual characteristic of the adolescent, or focus on interpersonal context and dyadic processes surrounding autonomy (Collins & Steinberg, 2006; Hill & Holmbeck, 1986). Further, the term *autonomy* has often been used to capture a range of interrelated, but not necessarily equivalent, aspects of functioning, such as independence, competence, and self-reliance. As we will discuss further later in the chapter, the concept of autonomy in and of itself is also multifaceted, and numerous authors have proposed conceptual heuristics for defining and examining the various forms of autonomy that may exist (Douvan & Adelson, 1966; Collins & Steinberg; Goossens, 2006; Hill & Holmbeck).

Measurement of Attachment During Adolescence

The Beginning: Roots of Adolescent Attachment

Studies of attachment in young children primarily utilize Ainsworth's classic Strange Situation (Ainsworth et al., 1978), which focuses on the nature of individual differences in attachment behavior within the parent–child dyad. In this paradigm, the behaviors of infants and their caregiver(s) are observed during a series of separations and reunions that occur in a laboratory setting. The separations are intended to activate the attachment system, and variations in infants' use of the attachment figure(s) as a secure base are used to classify such behavior as secure or insecure. A securely attached child explores freely in the presence of his/her attachment figure, but shows distress and a cessation of exploration when the attachment figure departs; the secure infant also seeks contact with the attachment figure upon his/her return, and is comforted by his/her presence (Ainsworth, 1982, 1989). Insecurely attached infants are classified into one of two categories: insecure avoidant and insecure ambivalent. Insecure avoidant infants explore freely, but show minimal distress at the departure of their attachment figure(s), and generally not seek them out upon their return. Insecure ambivalent infants demonstrate inhibited exploration; they cling to their attachment figure(s) and strongly protest their departure. However, these infants show continued distress once their attachment figure(s) return, and demonstrate ambivalence toward them, for example, reaching up to be held but then arching away.

The Shift to Measuring Internal Working Models

Given that behavior during separations and reunions does not carry the same developmental implications later in life, attachment research with adolescents and adults has focused more on the concept of attachment representations or internal working models. It has been proposed that by adolescence, the attachment system can be assessed in terms of a single overarching attachment organization that is thought to be reflected in a "state of mind" regarding attachment (Allen & Land, 1999; Allen, in press; Hesse, 1999; Main, Kaplan, & Cassidy, 1985). These attachment representations are thought to be based on the sum of interactions with caregivers over time, and to consist of a person's beliefs and expectations about the ways that attachment relationships operate (Bowlby, 1980). Further, these representations are thought to provide guidelines for behavior as well as affective appraisal of experience. Thus, studies of attachment during adolescence have primarily focused on assessing internal working models of attachment, typically utilizing an adolescent version of the Adult Attachment Interview (AAI) (George, Kaplan, & Main, 1996; Main & Goldwyn, 1998; Ward & Carlson, 1995).

The Adult Attachment Interview

The AAI is a semistructured interview that probes individuals' descriptions of their childhood relationships with parents both in abstract terms and with requests for specific supporting memories. The adolescent version is almost identical to the adult version, though slight adaptations make the questions more natural and easily understood by an adolescent population (Ward & Carlson, 1995). These attachment interviews can be used to generate categorical attachment classifications that parallel those found in infancy (Main and Goldwyn, 1998), or can be evaluated using a Q-sort methodology that yields continuous scores (Kobak, Cole, Ferenz-Gillies, Fleming, & Gamble, 1993). In either case, transcripts of the interviews are rated according to a variety of factors, including coherence, valuing of attachment relationships and acknowledgment of the effects of attachment relationships.

Security in the AAI is manifested in coherent and believable accounts of past relationship experiences, *regardless of whether those experiences were positive or negative*. Not only are secure individuals able to provide a balanced perspective on their relationships, but also they express a high degree of valuing of attachment relationships, as well as insight into the ways in which these relationships have affected them. As with the Strange Situation coding system, insecure individuals fall into two major categories: The insecure–dismissing category parallels the infant insecure–avoidant classification, and the insecure–preoccupied classification is analogous to the infant insecure–ambivalent category. The descriptions of early experiences with caregivers provided by insecure dismissing individuals tend to be incoherent for a number of reasons, including a basic lack of information provided, a mismatch between semantic and episodic memories, and a denial of the impact of difficult experiences. Insecure–dismissing individuals tend to provide idealized descriptions of attachment figures and/or to devalue relationships with their attachment figures. Insecure–preoccupied individuals, however, provide descriptions of their attachment figures that tend to lack a sense of balance or perspective. For example, they may go on at great length in describing a seemingly trivial slight at the hands of a caregiver. Their discourse tends to be marked with either involved anger or passivity, and they are unable to cogently reflect on the ways that relationships may have affected their development (Main & Goldwyn, 1998).

Self-Report Measures of Attachment

Administering the AAI, transcribing the interviews, and then coding them is a time-intensive process that requires a great deal of training and experience. In part because of this issue, several alternate self-report methods have been developed to assess attachment in adolescents and adults. While these measures are often compared to the AAI in terms of validity, their focus and purpose is somewhat divergent from the AAI. Although their intention is often to tap into aspects of internal working models, these measures were not necessarily designed to capture the same patterns of attachment as seen in the Strange Situation, nor were they intended to predict the Strange Situation behavior of one's offspring, which was one of the defining features of the AAI when it was developed. One set of self-report measures of attachment that has recently been adapted for use with adolescents consists of measures of romantic attachment style that were originally developed for use with adults. These measures are based on the proposition that romantic love can be conceptualized and studied according to the tenets of attachment theory.

The primary example of such measures was developed by Hazan and Shaver (1987), and adopted and revised by Bartholomew and Horowitz (1991) as the Relationship Questionnaire (RQ). These measures provide raters with short descriptions of each of the primary attachment organizations, and ask them to classify (or rate) themselves according to which best describes their approach to romantic relationships. Whereas the AAI is thought to assess *states of mind* with regard to attachment, these self-report measures are generally referred to as assessing *attachment styles*. States of mind are assumed to be intrapsychic and generalized, and assessment via the AAI is thought to capture less conscious aspects of internal working models. In contrast, measures of self-reported attachment styles may assess more conscious aspects of internal working models, including attitudes, feelings, and behaviors with regard to *specific* close relationships. Most studies to date (primarily focusing on adults) have yielded only low (if any) association between the two measures (e.g., Crowell, Treboux, & Waters, 1999; de Hass, Bakermans-Kranenburg, & van Ijzendoorn, 1994; Mayseless & Sagi, 1994; Mayseless & Scharf, 2007; Shaver, Belsky, & Brennan, 2000). However, the few studies that have examined both attachment states of mind (as assessed by the AAI) and attachment styles (as assessed by questionnaire) have indicated that both measures contribute significantly to important outcomes (e.g., Mayseless & Scharf).[1]

Measurement of Attachment Hierarchies

As indicated above, efforts to define and measure attachment during adolescence have focused on capturing aspects of internal working models and on categorizing individual differences along secure and insecure dimensions. More recently, researchers have taken an alternative approach to the measurement of attachment processes by assessing attachment hierarchies. This model of assessment is focused on the normative development of attachment processes, and is based on the premise that individuals have organized preferences for multiple attachment figures that are likely to shift with development (Hazan, Hutt, Sturgeon, & Bricket, 1991). It has been proposed that adolescents can and will utilize other figures besides their primary attachment figures to fulfill attachment needs, and that there is a normative increase in this tendency to branch out from the primary attachment figure(s) during the teenage years.

More specifically, measures of attachment hierarchies aim to determine the people that adolescents and young adults may utilize to fulfill the primary functions of attachment relationships, including proximity seeking, safe haven, and secure base (Ainsworth, 1989; Hazan et al., 1991). Hazan and colleagues initially developed the WHOTO measure, which consists of three questions for each of these three attachment functions. For example, one of the questions related to proximity seeking is: Who is the person you don't like to be away from? Similarly, respondents are asked: Who is the person you most want to be with when you are feeling upset or down? (safe haven); and who is the person you feel you can always count on? (secure base). For each question, participants are either asked to choose one person from a set list (e.g., mother, father, best friend, girlfriend/boyfriend, self, other), or rate any number of persons for each one. There have been several revisions of the original WHOTO measure, including versions by Fraley and Davis (1997), Trinke and

Bartholomew (1997) (Attachment Network Questionnaire), and Rosenthal and Kobak (2007) (Important People Interview).

Measurement of Autonomy During Adolescence

Operational Definitions of Autonomy

As indicated previously, the study of adolescent autonomy functioning has been complicated by the varying ways in which autonomy has been operationally defined and measured, including whether autonomy is treated as an intraindividual or interpersonal construct and, relatedly, whether measurement focuses on autonomy as an end point or a process (Collins & Steinberg, 2006). Even when considering autonomy strictly as an interpersonal construct (primarily within the parent–adolescent relationship), there are still several facets of autonomy development, including cognitive autonomy, emotional autonomy and behavioral autonomy, that must be considered (Goossens, 2006; Hill & Holmbeck, 1986; Silverberg & Gondoli, 1996; Zimmer-Gembeck & Collins, 2003). *Cognitive autonomy* (sometimes termed *value autonomy*) can be construed as the ability to develop one's own thoughts, values, opinions, which may or may not correspond to those of parents (or peers). Verbal autonomy is the behavioral index of cognitive autonomy: the ability to clearly express and/or assert one's own thoughts and feelings within an interpersonal context. *Emotional autonomy* has been defined as involving decreased reliance on parents for emotion regulation as well as emotional support. However, this term has also been used to capture the process of reflecting on and evaluating parent-adolescent relationships, including the degree to which teens deidealize their parents. More recently, it has been proposed that emotional autonomy be more broadly construed to include adolescents' intraindividual and subjective sense of feeling separate, independent and/or "grown up" (Collins & Steinberg). A final component is *behavioral autonomy*, which is defined in terms of increased self-reliance and self-regulation, with most operational definitions referring specifically to functioning within the parent–adolescent relationship.[2]

Measures of Cognitive and Verbal Autonomy

While the measurement of other aspects of autonomy development has usually been accomplished via adolescents' self-reports, cognitive and verbal autonomy processes are often assessed using one of several observational coding systems aimed at rating parent–adolescent interactions. These systems view autonomy as an interfamilial construct, and as such they include ratings of both adolescents and their parents. They are usually applied to family interactions that occur in a laboratory setting around an assigned task, such as planning a trip or talking about an area of disagreement (either real or hypothetical). Given that during revealed differences tasks, stress is being applied by invoking normative developmental processes of facing disagreements, some authors have suggested that this paradigm presents a stage-salient task akin to the Strange Situation (Allen & Land, 1999; Kobak et al., 1993). The use of parents as secure base during adolescence may involve freedom to explore different ideas/points of view while still staying connected.

The Constraining and Enabling Coding System (CECS) (Hauser et al., 1984) builds upon Stierlin's (1974) theories about familial responses to adolescents' attempts at separation, and assesses the ways that parent–adolescent interactions may shape adolescent ego development. Family speeches during a discussion are categorized in terms of the extent to which they constrain (or interfere with) versus enable (or support) adolescents' autonomy during family discussions. The constructs of constraining and enabling are further divided into the cognitive and affective realms. Cognitive constraining includes behaviors that distract, withhold, or express indifference; affective constraining includes behaviors that are excessively gratifying, judging, or devaluing.

Cognitive enabling includes focusing, problem solving, curiosity, and explaining; affective enabling includes acceptance and empathy. In addition, an overall code for the balance that exists between constraining and enabling behaviors can be constructed by subtracting subjects' overall score for constraining statements from their overall enabling statements within a dyad (Hauser et al.).

The Family Interaction Coding System (FICS) was developed to capture processes of individuality and connectedness during family interactions (Grotevant & Cooper, 1985; Cooper, Grotevant, & Condon, 1983). This system defines individuality in terms of separateness, or the ability to differentiate oneself from others, and also in terms of self-assertion, or the clear expression of one's own point of view. Examples of separateness include statements that request an action from the other person or challenge his/her ideas. Examples of self-assertion include statements that directly and clearly express a point of view (e.g., I'd like to go to Italy). Connectedness is defined as mutuality, or being sensitive to and respecting others' points of view, and permeability, or being open and responsive to others' views. Examples of mutuality include statements that initiate compromise or state others' feelings; examples of permeability include statements that request information and those that acknowledge or incorporate the others' ideas.

Allen and colleagues (1994a; 2004) developed the Autonomy Relatedness Coding System (ARCS), in part based on the constructs outlined by the FICS described above. This coding system codes individual speeches into 10 possible subscales, which are in turn grouped on an a priori basis into four primary scales including Promoting Autonomy (akin to self-assertion and separateness from the FICS) and Promoting Relatedness (akin to permeability and mutuality from the FICS). Thus, individuals that are rated as high on autonomy and relatedness are able to confidently provide reasons for their points of view, while also remaining engaged in the discussion and expressing validation for what the other person has to say. However, this system added codes for negative behaviors in addition to positive ones, namely Undermining Autonomy and Undermining Relatedness. Behaviors that are undermining of autonomy make it more difficult for individuals to freely express themselves during the discussion; these behaviors include overpersonalizing a disagreement (inappropriately focusing on personal characteristics), recanting a position without being persuaded, and/or pressuring the other person to agree. Undermining relatedness includes making hostile and disrespectful statements, rudely interrupting the other person, and or blatantly ignoring him or her.

Measures of Emotional Autonomy

Measures of emotional autonomy are almost exclusively intraindividual, treating autonomy as a characteristic of the adolescent. These measures focus on the adolescent's intrapsychic autonomy development by asking adolescents questions about their perceptions of themselves, though typically still in the context of the quality of their relationships with parents. A primary example is Steinberg and Silverberg's (1986) Emotional Autonomy Scale (EAS). This measure was based on Blos's (1979) neoanalytic theory of adolescent development, discussed previously, which suggests that emotional autonomy involves a process of individuation and deidealization, such that adolescents come to perceive parents as separate and fallible individuals. Steinberg and Silverberg's (1986) original EAS consisted of 20 items divided into four subscales: Perceiving Parents as People, Parental Deidealization, Nondependency on Parents, and Individuation.

Steinberg and Silverberg's (1986) measure has generated a substantial amount of controversy. Some authors have criticized its construct validity. For example, it has been suggested that some of the items may measure detachment rather than emotional autonomy,

and that some items appear to have a pejorative and somewhat paranoid tone, suggesting alienation and distrust (Frank, Pirsch, & Wright, 1990; Ryan & Lynch, 1989; Schmitz & Baer, 2001). Others have asserted that this measure does capture emotional autonomy, but that having emotional autonomy as defined here is only adaptive under certain family contexts (Delaney, 1996; Fuhrman & Holmbeck, 1995; Lamborn & Steinberg, 1993; McClanahan & Holmbeck, 1992). However, there is further disagreement as to whether emotional autonomy is more adaptive in the context of negative vs. positive parent–adolescents relationships. Still others have noted that different versions of this measure, different samples, and divergent methods of analyses have been utilized across these various studies, which complicates interpretation of the findings (Beyers & Goossens, 1999; Beyers, Goossens, Vansant, & Moors, 2003; Beyers, Goossens, Van Calster, & Duriez, 2005). Despite the ongoing controversies surrounding this measure, many—if not most—of the self-report studies of adolescent autonomy have utilized the EAS.

There are at least two other commonly used self-report measures that attempt to capture intrapsychic processes of autonomy development, including emotional autonomy. These two measures have been developed to capture aspects of Mahler's childhood separation–individuation phases as applied to adolescence (Hoffman, 1984; Levine, Green, & Millon, 1986; Mahler & Furer, 1968). In developing the 138-item Psychological Separation Inventory (PSI), Hoffman extrapolated from infants' developmental tasks of psychological separation. The PSI assesses Functional Independence (managing and directing personal affairs), Attitudinal Independence (having own set of beliefs and values), Emotional Independence (freedom from excessive need for approval) and Conflictual Independence (freedom from excessive guilt and anxiety); thus, it is clear that the PSI captures aspects of both behavioral and cognitive autonomy, as well as emotional autonomy. In developing the Separation–Individuation Test of Adolescence (SITA), Levine, Green, and Millon were particularly interested in assessing both fixation points and milestones of healthy development. The SITA consists of scales assessing Nurturance–Succorance, Interpersonal Enmeshment, Engulfment Anxiety, Separation Anxiety, Need Denial, Self-Centeredness, and Healthy Separation. Unfortunately, the SITA has been the focus of numerous criticisms regarding its psychometric properties as well as content and construct validity (Anderson, LaVoie, & Dunkel, 2007; Holmbeck & McClanahan, 1994; McClanahan & Holmbeck, 1992), and it has generally been less widely used than the PSI. Further, there is stronger support for the construct validity of the PSI over the SITA (Hoffman, 1984; Kenny & Donaldson, 1992; Lapsley & Edgerton, 2002; Lapsley, Rice, & Shadid, 1989; Meeus, Iedema, Maassen, & Engels, 2005), with conflictual independence in particular being most consistently linked with adaptive outcomes.

One additional self-report measure, Epstein's (1983) Mother–Father–Peer scale, also contains a subscale that assesses deidealization of parents. As indicated previously, deidealization is considered to be an important component of the intrapsychic autonomy development throughout the analytic and neoanalytic literature, and involves shedding childhood conceptualizations of parents as all-knowing and all-powerful (Blos, 1979). This measure was originally developed for use with adults, and was constructed to assess the family origins of adult personality development (Ricks, 1985). The deidealization subscale of the Mother–Father–Peer scale contains seven items assessing presence or absence of unrealistically positive views of childhood relationships with parents (e.g., [my parent] "was close to the perfect parent" and "had not a single fault that I can think of"). Although this measure has not received very much empirical attention, it has been utilized recently with adolescents (Allen et al., 2003).[3]

Measures of Behavioral Autonomy

The term *behavioral autonomy* is widely used to capture a range of aspects of adolescent functioning, both within and outside of the parent–adolescent relationship. Measures of behavioral autonomy within parent–adolescent relationships include self-reports of aspects of those relationships, as well as of parents' behaviors either supporting or undermining autonomy. Thus, these measures are interfamilial, focusing on qualities of the parent–teen relationship that may support or undermine adolescent autonomy. The most commonly used measures of behavioral autonomy within the family context include assessment of patterns of family decision making and the degree and forms of parental monitoring and control.

With regard to decision making, measures typically ask respondents to estimate rates of conflict and then to report on who usually makes the final decisions for each conflict (parent, adolescent, both or neither). Parent-only decision making is usually taken to be indicative of autocratic or authoritarian parenting, which restricts autonomy; adolescent-only decision making is a sign of overly permissive parenting. Joint decision making, in which both parties contribute to the discussion and/or have a say in the final outcome, is thought to indicate more democratic parenting and thus to be most ideally supportive of adolescent autonomy. This latter style of autonomy promotion is also consistent with an authoritative parenting style, which balances responsiveness and demandingness and thus is characterized by firm control that still allows for negotiation and an open exchange of viewpoints regarding rules and consequences (Baumrind, 1991; Steinberg, Elmen, & Mounts, 1989).

Similarly, measures of parental monitoring and control over adolescents' behaviors can be construed as an assessment of behavioral autonomy. In these measures, adolescents and/or parents are asked to report on how much parents know about teens' day-to-day lives, as well as how much control parents exercise over adolescents' behaviors. It should be noted that measures that previously have been termed *parental monitoring* have more recently been recast as measures of parental knowledge. Researchers have suggested that such measures actually capture the degree to which adolescents are willing to share information with parents, as opposed to behaviors that parents may actively engage in to monitor and track adolescents' activities (Kerr & Stattin, 2000). With regard to behavioral control, the assessment can include the degree to which parents control teens' behavior in a number of areas (e.g., choice of friends), and/or the manner in which such control is exercised (e.g., rule setting, consequences). Whereas low levels of parental control are often considered indicative of overly permissive parenting, extremely high levels of parental control across multiple areas can be interpreted as authoritarian and overcontrolling, thus antithetical to autonomy development.

Parental use of psychological control overlaps (in an inverse sense) with the concept of emotional autonomy, given that methods of psychological control tend to include manipulation of emotions (e.g., guilt inducing), and are thought to impede emotional development (Barber, 1996). However, given that psychologically controlling parental behaviors are aimed at managing adolescents' behaviors, there is also overlap with behavioral autonomy. Psychologically controlling behaviors represent "control attempts that intrude into the psychological and emotional development of the child (e.g. thinking processes, self-expression, emotions and attachment to parents)" (Barber, p. 3296). These parental behaviors include manipulation of the love relationship between the parent and the child, and may involve gaining compliance through the use of guilt, love withdrawal, and criticism through shame (Barber; Schaefer, 1965). High levels of psychological control are thought to inhibit the child's ability to develop as an individual apart from the parent, both emotionally and behaviorally. To the extent that children are made to feel guilty and anxious in relation to attempts at separation from parents, they are likely to remain emotionally dependent on them and to have difficulty engaging in self-reliant behavior.

NORMATIVE DEVELOPMENT OF ATTACHMENT AND AUTONOMY

With a clearer understanding of the theoretical underpinnings of attachment and autonomy, as well as some sense of how such constructs have been operationalized, we now turn to a review of the normative development of these two processes during adolescence. As outlined earlier, the literature on these topics is somewhat uneven, varying in the level of emphasis placed on intraindividual versus interfamilial processes. Further, there is an imbalance regarding the extent of empirical attention that has been paid to possible changes in attachment relationships (or models) over the course of adolescence, versus the changes that occur with regard to autonomy processes—both in the intraindividual and interfamilial senses. The latter question has been relatively extensively examined, whereas data on the former question is scant. We will begin by reviewing the work that has been done regarding normative development of attachment during adolescence, then turn to the literature examining autonomy development.

Normative Development of Attachment

The focus of the majority of the research on adolescent attachment centers around the individual differences between teens who evidence secure versus insecure states of mind with regard to attachment. Relatively little empirical attention has been paid to questions of normative development, including whether and how attachment states of mind and/or attachment behaviors may change during this stage of life. Recently, there has been some work examining the extent to which attachment models appear to be stable versus unstable over the course of adolescence. There has also been recent interest in whether and to what extent adolescents begin to direct attachment behaviors toward peers and/or romantic partners, either instead of or in addition to their parents. This work overlaps conceptually with research documenting shifts in the emotional tone of parent–adolescent relationships.

With regard to stability, Bowlby (1980) proposed that there is a tendency toward continuity in attachment organization over time, and that internal working models may be relatively immune to revision after infancy. However, Bowlby further noted that there may be circumstances that arise that lead to a need to adjust existing models, specifically when the discrepancy between an individual's experiences and his/her internal working models becomes so great that the old models are no longer useful. In fact, research suggests that attachment classifications are relatively stable within infancy, and from infancy to early childhood (e.g., Main & Weston, 1981; Vaughn, Egeland, Sroufe, & Waters, 1979; Waters, 1978). However, the evidence for stability from childhood to adolescence is mixed (e.g., Becker-Stoll & Fremmer-Bombik, 1997; Hamilton, 2000; Lewis, Feiring, & Rosenthal, 2000).

It has been proposed that adolescence is a developmental period that is particularly ripe for revision of internal working models, especially given that teens are much better able than younger children to reflect on the thoughts, feelings, and experiences that comprise their internal working models (Ainsworth, 1989; Allen & Land, 1999; Kobak & Cole, 1994; Main, Kaplan, & Cassidy, 1985). Teens' increased perspective-taking and reasoning skills allow them to compare relationships with different attachment figures both to one another and to hypothetical ideals (Allen & Land; Allen, in press). The three existing studies to date have documented moderate stability in attachment security across both early and late adolescence (Allen et al., 2004; Ammaniti, van Ijzendoorn, Speranza, & Tambelli, 2000; Zimmermann & Becker-Stoll, 2002). Thus, while there is support for the contention that attachment models may become relatively resistant to revision by adolescence, the degree of stability documented to date indicates that models may still shift during this life stage.

Further research is clearly needed to understand how and to what extent shifts in internal working models may occur, as well as what contributes to possible changes in those models. While it is typically assumed that new experiences and increased perspective taking would result in a push toward attachment security, it is also possible that negative experiences during adolescence—particularly stressors around critical developmental tasks and/or intrapsychic stressors—could contribute to declines in attachment security over time (Allen et al., 2004). At least one study to date has examined whether and to what extent individual differences in adolescents' life experiences and/or internal processes might contribute to changes in their internal working models. This study found that negative shifts in attachment security were predicted by external stressors (poverty), conflicts around autonomy development within the mother–adolescent relationship, as well as adolescents' level of depressive symptoms (Allen et al.). Interestingly, another recent life-span study of attachment found a similar pattern in predicting attachment stability from infancy to late adolescence: The group that remained secure had lower levels of life stress, higher levels of observed support and collaboration during family discussions and problem solving tasks as assessed at age 13, and more positive infant temperament (Weinfield, Whaley, & Egeland, 2004). A key implication from both of these studies is that the quality of the parent–teen relationship, particularly with regard to the management of autonomy issues, is strongly linked to (and may continue to shape) the nature of internal working models during adolescence.

A growing body of work has begun to explore possible changes in attachment behaviors during adolescence. During infancy and childhood, proximity seeking is considered one of the hallmarks of the attachment relationship—under even modest stress, infants and young children seek physical closeness with their caregivers and protest involuntary separations from them. Consistent with the balance being tipped toward exploration, it is well documented that teens begin to physically spend less time with their parents as they enter adolescence (Dubas & Gerris, 2002; Larson & Richards, 1989, 1991; Larson, Richards, & Moneta, 1996; Montemayor & Brownlee, 1987; Repinski & Zook, 2005). At the same time, beginning in early adolescence, teens begin to express a preference for spending time with peers over parents. While approximately one-half of 4th graders list one of their parents as the person they would most like to spend time with, by 6th grade only 32% nominate a parent, and by 8th grade only 11% express a preference for spending time with parents over peers (Nickerson & Nagle, 2005). This trend continues into late adolescence and early adulthood, with the majority of respondents in older samples expressing a preference for being with peers and/or romantic partners over parents (Fraley & Davis, 1997; Rosenthal & Kobak, 2007; Markiewicz, Lawford, & Doyle, 2006).

At the same time that adolescents demonstrate a relative decrease in their desire to physically spend time with parents, there also tends to be an increase in emotional negativity and disengagement in the parent–teen relationship (Baer, 2002; Collins, 1990; Csikszentmihalyi & Larson, 1984; Gutman & Eccles, 2007; Kim, Conger, Lorenz, & Elder, 2001; Larson & Richards, 1991; Larson, Richards, & Moneta, 1996; Larson et.al, 1998; Pinquart & Silbereisen, 2002). Similarly, teens evidence a decreased need for emotional support from parents and are less likely to express a dependence on parents to help them solve their problems (Levpušcek, 2006; Lieberman, Doyle, & Markiewicz, 1999; Steinberg & Silverberg, 1986). This push away from parents corresponds to an increased tendency for adolescents to rely on friends and/or romantic partners for emotional support instead of (or at least in addition to) their parents. By mid-adolescence, interactions with peers have begun to take on many of the functions that they will

serve for the remainder of the lifespan— providing important sources of intimacy, feedback about social behavior, social influence and information, and ultimately attachment relationships and lifelong partnerships (Ainsworth, 1989; Collins & Laursen, 2000; Gavin & Furman, 1989; Gavin & Furman, 1996; Hartup, 1992). Thus, adolescents are not simply becoming more autonomous from their attachment figures; they are beginning the important process of *transferring* dependencies from parental to peer relationships (Allen, in press).

Although there is some debate regarding the extent to which peers ultimately serve as attachment figures, research suggests that attachment functions are increasingly directed at peers over the course of adolescence. For example, teens begin to utilize their peers more as "safe havens," seeking comfort and support from them in times of distress (Hazan & Ziefman, 1994; Markiewicz et al., 2006; Nickerson & Nagle, 1997). Whereas parents are primary sources of emotional support during childhood, beginning sometime between ages 12 and 15, teens report being equally likely to turn to their mother or a best friend for support and reassurance (Markiewicz et al., 2006; Nickerson & Nagle, 2005). By middle to late adolescence, teens report relying on either best friends or romantic partners for emotional support more often than parents (Markiewicz et al.; Nickerson & Nagle). Further, older teens are more likely than younger teens to identify a romantic partner as a "primary attachment figure"—someone who would be missed during a trip and who would be contacted following an accident (Rosenthal & Kobak, 2007).

Thus, as teens become more autonomous from parents, they disengage at least somewhat from parents and increasingly turn to peers and romantic partners for company and support. However, it appears that relationships with parents, particularly mothers, retain important attachment functions despite adolescents' increased push for autonomy. For example, even though proximity seeking is reduced during adolescence, it is still evident in some forms and in extreme circumstances. Teens may still "protest" separations (e.g., writing sad and homesick letters home from a sleep-away camp) and still seek their parents' company after an absence. Rosenthal & Kobak (2007) found that both adolescents and college students were likely to identify one of their parents (usually mothers) as the person they'd want contact with in an extreme emergency, and as the person they'd miss the most during a long trip. Further, while some data suggests that the secure base function (using the attachment figure as a base for exploration, to provide confidence in the face of challenge) is ultimately transferred to peers (Hazan & Ziefman, 1994), other studies suggest that parents retain this attachment function even into adulthood (Fraley & Davis, 1997; Markiewicz et al., 2006; Trinke & Bartholomew, 1997).

Research supports the notion that parents are maintained as attachment figures. For example, Markiewicz and colleagues (2006) found that across both adolescents and adults, mothers were identified most as "the person who will always be there for you." Similarly, Rosenthal & Kobak (2007) found that 68% of adolescents and 58% of first-year college students identified one of their parents as their primary attachment figure. Research on adolescents' responses to the loss of a parent also demonstrates that the very basic nature of the attachment relationship during this life stage is relatively unchanged. Similar to younger children, adolescents who lose a parent experience significant dysphoria over the parents' absence and increased anxiety about separation from remaining attachment figures (Dowdney, 2000). Further, teens who have lost parents often evidence attachment behaviors in the form of attempts to maintain a connection with the lost parent in some way, such as by talking to them, visiting their graves, and cherishing a possession of theirs (Silverman & Worden, 1992; Silverman, Nickman, & Worden, 1992; Stoppelbein & Greening, 2000; VanEerdewegh, Bieri, Parrilla, & Clayton, 1982; VanEerdewegh, Clayton, & VanEerdewegh, 1985).

In sum, what we know thus far regarding normative development of attachment relationships is that despite the degree of developmental change that occurs during adolescence, there is much that remains the same. Even though attachment relationships may be somewhat transformed by adolescents' increased autonomous functioning, attachment models appear to be relatively stable. Interestingly, the limited research to date on development of attachment models during adolescence suggests that the instability that does exist appears to be closely linked to negotiation of autonomy. In fact, most of what we know about how attachment relationships are transformed during adolescence must be implicitly drawn from more general research regarding how parent–adolescent relationships are transformed—a subtle but important distinction. We review the literature on how those relationships are transformed below, with a particular focus on autonomy processes.

Normative Development of Autonomy

In this section, we review normative development of autonomy during adolescence, first examining what is known about intraindividual development (largely with regard to emotional autonomy and value autonomy), and then research on interfamilial development (largely with regard to behavioral autonomy). We know very little about how verbal autonomy processes unfold within families over time. The research in this area is largely focused on individual differences—linking adolescent outcomes to familial support versus undermining of cognitive autonomy—which will be reviewed in the next section.

Intraindividual Changes: Emotional and Value Autonomy

Much of the research on autonomy development during adolescence focuses on intrapsychic changes within adolescents: changes in teens' perceptions, particularly of their parents and of themselves in relation to their parents. Both increased perspective taking and the advent of formal operational thinking have important implications for changes in the ways that adolescents think about their relationships. Adolescents can potentially reflect on and modify their perceptions of their parents, the relationships that they have with them, and their own role in those relationships. A close examination of the changes in the ways that adolescents think about their parents provides insight into the intersection between the intra-individual and interfamilial changes that occur during this stage of development.

With increased cognitive maturity, adolescents gain the capacity to revaluate and potentially "deidealize" their parents—to see them in both positive and negative ways (Blos, 1979; Steinberg, 2005). As discussed previously, this process of deidealization is a cornerstone of psychoanalytically oriented theories of adolescent autonomy development (Blos, 1979). There has been considerable debate in the literature over what this deidealization process should look like, and whether deidealization is healthy or even necessary for development to proceed normally (Steinberg & Silverberg, 1986; Ryan & Lynch, 1989). Despite these controversies, several studies have found normative changes in the degree to which adolescents idealize versus deidealize their parents. For example, middle to older adolescents (ages 15–17) are much less likely then younger adolescents or preteens to endorse items suggesting that their parents are perfect (Beyers & Goossens, 1999; Levpušcek, 2006). Similarly, increased deidealization with age is also seen in measures of "positive identification"; older teens are less likely than younger teens to report feelings of respect for parents and desire to be exactly like parents (Gutman & Eccles, 2007).

In addition to changes in levels of idealization of parents, teens' attitudes with regard to parental control versus autonomy granting show corresponding shifts over the course of adolescence. For example, as children enter early adolescence, they begin to rate discipline techniques such as physical punishment and power assertion more negatively (Paikoff, Collins, & Laursen, 1988; Seigel & Cowen, 1984). Older teens tend to be less accepting of parental directives than younger teens, particularly if those directives involve issues that are considered personal in nature (versus moral quandaries or practical matters) (Perkins & Turiel, 2007). Similarly, over the course of adolescence, teens become increasingly dissatisfied by the degree to which their parents grant them autonomy—discrepancies between ratings of actual parents and ideal parents are greater for adolescents versus preadolescents (Collins, 1990).

Adolescents not only gain the capacity to evaluate (and/or reevaluate) their relationships, but they also are better able to "think for themselves" and to establish a more consistent view of themselves as existing apart from interactions with caregivers (Selman, 1980). Thus, teens may develop opinions that diverge from those of their parents and/or other important adults, and this divergence is yet another index of the process of autonomous growth and separation that is seen during adolescence. For example, adolescents are more likely than children or preteens to endorse such statements as: "It's very important to me to be free to do what I want" and "I often find I have to question adults' decisions" (Frank, Schettini, & Lower, 2002). Similarly, adolescents become less likely than younger children to state that they always agree with or have the same opinions as their parents (Beyers & Goossens, 1999; Levpušcek, 2006; Steinberg & Silverberg, 1986). Further, adolescents increasingly conceptualize aspects of their day-to-day lives (e.g., cleaning their room and how they dress) as contingent on personal choice, and therefore not subject to parental control (Bosma et al., 1996; Smetana, 1988a, 1988b, 1989). Thus, adolescents increasingly define themselves as separate individuals, with their own agendas and corresponding thoughts, feelings, and actions.

In summary, changes in the ways that teens think about their parents, and about themselves in relation to their parents, are well documented. These normative developmental changes, sparked by the push for autonomy as well as adolescents' growing cognitive capacities, involve teens' realization that their parents are not perfect, their increased awareness of themselves as individuals, and their heightened desire for more say in how they live their lives. These transformations in adolescents' ways of thinking set the stage for autonomous adult functioning, in which close ties can be maintained with parents without the day-to-day dependence that characterizes earlier stages of development. However, it should be noted that despite the changes in conceptions of parents that occur during adolescence, such transformation rarely involves a complete rejection of parents or of parent-teen relationships. In contrast, research continues to suggest that overall, teens maintain positive views of their parents, respect their opinions, and agree with their general values (Douvan & Adelson, 1966; Offer, 1981).

Interfamilial Change: Behavioral Autonomy

Not surprisingly, changes in the ways that adolescents think about their parents tend to co-occur with changes in how adolescents (and parents) behave within their relationship. Adolescents begin to increasingly regulate their own activities, and at the same time the level of parental knowledge regarding their teens' daily lives tends to decrease. This increased self-regulation also frequently takes adolescents literally farther from home—as teens begin to function more autonomously, they engage in a wider range of activities and interact with a broadening social circle, all of which adds up to physically spending less time with parents. Finally, as adolescents begin to form their own thoughts, values, and opinions, they also begin to behaviorally "strike out on their own" more. The increased focus that adolescents have on their own agendas may take the form of increased challenges of parents' ideas, parent–teen conflicts, and at times an increased tendency to lie to and/or disobey parents.

It has long been documented that adolescents regulate their own daily activities more so than younger children (Douvan & Adelson, 1966), in part because they are granted the right to do so by their parents. More recent work continues to confirm that over the course of adolescence, teens are given increasing leeway to make their own decisions about their activities, and the range of activities that they are permitted to control similarly increases (Beyers & Goossens, 1999; Bosma et al., 1996; Gutman & Eccles, 2007). As teens make more of their own decisions, parents correspondingly know less about their daily lives; for example, older adolescents report disclosing less information to parents than younger teens (Finkenauer, Engels, & Meeus, 2002). Parents appear to view this increased privacy, corresponding to increased self-regulation, as developmentally appropriate. For example, parents rate older versus younger adolescents as significantly less obligated to disclose their activities related to a range of hypothetical issues to their parents, and as significantly more entitled to keep things private from their parents (Ruck, Peterson-Badali, & Day, 2002; Smetana, Metzger, Gettman, & Campione-Barr, 2006). Parents also report knowing much less about their older teens' experiences, whereabouts, and activities versus those of their younger siblings (Bumpus, Crouter, & McHale, 1998). Thus, a normative dyadic process unfolds in which adolescents begin to regulate themselves more and parents correspondingly reduce their vigilance regarding teens' moment-to-moment activities.

This process of gradually increasing self-regulation does not always occur smoothly, in part because teens do not always operate within the bounds of parental approval. Adolescents test the boundaries of their newly developed self-regulatory skills in numerous ways, including a tendency to express themselves more directly to parents: studies suggest that older teens are more likely than younger ones to defend and elaborate on their positions while discussing disagreements with their parents (Kreppner & Ulrich, 1998; Graber & Brooks-Gunn, 1999; Pinquart & Silbereisen, 2002). Adolescents' increased willingness to express disagreement and challenge their parents is implicit in the increased rate and intensity of parent–child conflict that occurs during early and middle adolescence (Bosma et al., 1996; Larson et al., 1998; Montemayor, 1983;1986). This increased conflict has often been attributed to adolescents' more autonomous thinking; in addition to increases in their willingness to express their opinions, they also become more likely to define areas of conflict as subject to their own personal choice versus parental control (Smetana, Braeges, & Yau, 1991). Adolescents may also challenge parents more indirectly—in addition to arguing more about rules, teens are also more willing to simply break them, by lying to and/or disobeying their parents (Darling, Cumsille, & Martinez, 2007; Perkins & Turiel, 2007). These "nonconformist" behaviors may serve as a way to establish a greater scope of thoughts and activities to which their parents do not have access (Jensen, Arnett, Feldman, & Cauffman, 2004). With regard to disobedience, it is well documented that adolescence marks a period of developmentally normative increase in deviant behavior. Several authors have proposed that this developmental trend in norm violations has its roots in the push for autonomy, and represents attempts to explore adult behavior and to gain skills and experiences that facilitate the transition away from the family unit (Moffitt, 1993; Spear, 2000).

To summarize, the behavioral changes that occur within the parent–adolescent relationship primarily involve the development of a new balance between attachment behaviors and the adolescents' needs for autonomous exploration. Adolescents are increasingly able to make their own choices and to regulate their own behaviors, and they do so more and more frequently without their parents' watchful eyes. Indeed, this increased self-regulation is often

sanctioned by parents—generally speaking, increasing maturity implies increased safety, which reduces the need for constant vigilance on the part of parents (Allen, in press). However, this process does not always proceed completely smoothly, as evidenced by heightened conflicts and increases in rates of lying and disobedience. The good news (perhaps not for parents) is that these perturbations in the ways that teens behave with parents are normative and equilibrium tends to be regained by early adulthood. For example, as adolescents get older, teens become once again less likely to lie to their parents and more likely to disclose information about things that are important to them—and parent–teen conflict also decreases (Jensen et al., 2004; Smetana et al., 2006). Said differently, this return to more a harmonious state corresponds with the achievement of autonomy that is seen by early adulthood.

INDIVIDUAL DIFFERENCES IN ATTACHMENT AND AUTONOMY PROCESSES

With some notion of the normative transformations that occur in attachment and autonomy processes during adolescence, we will now consider what we know about individual differences in the functioning of these systems. We will first review specific research findings with regard to predicting autonomous functioning from both secure and insecure adolescent attachment. Here, the literature has primarily examined links between attachment security and indices of cognitive or verbal autonomy, with a few studies examining how attachment security relates to more general measures of parental behaviors or parent–teen relationship quality. We will then examine predictions of other social, emotional, and behavioral outcomes from both attachment security versus insecurity and the expression of the various aspects of adolescent autonomy.

Attachment Security and the Push for Autonomy

The potential tension noted previously between the adolescents' developmental push to gain autonomy and the operation of the attachment system can give rise to important individual differences in the ways that this tension is managed. Just as the balance of exploration from a secure base has been highly informative about the nature of individual differences in infant attachments, the balance of attachment and autonomy in adolescence also has important implications for adolescents' long-term adjustment. Broadly speaking, the most adaptive outcomes are thought to follow from parent–adolescent relationship processes that provide sensitive, responsive, and supportive parenting while also appropriately promoting adolescents' increased autonomous exploration. Thus, securely attached teens (and their parents) are hypothesized to be especially able to successfully negotiate this balance between maintaining relatedness and supporting autonomy development.

Security of attachment during adolescence has generally been found to co-occur with a parenting style and parent–adolescent relationship qualities that support and promote autonomy. For example, secure teens and young adults (as assessed both with the AAI and attachment style questionnaires) perceive their families as more involved and supportive, and as granting them more psychological autonomy than insecure teens (Allen et al., 2003; Karavasilis, Doyle, & Markiewicz, 2003; Harvey & Byrd, 2000; Kobak & Sceery, 1988). Adolescents with secure attachment styles also report turning to their mothers (more than friends or romantic partners) to fulfill attachment functions, particularly the secure base function (Markiewicz, Lawford, & Doyle, 2006). One recent study also found security of attachment to be linked to high levels of maternal sensitivity, as measured by how well mothers were able to predict the ways that their teens would respond to a questionnaire about their own competence (Allen et al., 2003). Secure states of mind are also associated with warmer, more accepting, open, and engaged interactions with parents as observed from interactions and as reported by adolescents (Becker-Stoll, Delius, &

Scheitenberger, 2001; Ducharme, Doyle, & Markiewicz, 2002; Roisman, Madsen, Hennighausen, Sroufe, & Collins, 2001).

Thus, it is not surprising that one of the more consistent findings in the adolescent attachment literature is that when adolescents hold secure attachment states of mind, their interactions with their parents are characterized by healthy autonomy support, particularly as indexed by measures of cognitive and verbal autonomy. One long-term longitudinal study has demonstrated that infant security with mothers was more predictive of observed qualities of autonomy and relatedness in adolescent–mother interactions than it was of adolescent states of mind regarding attachment (Becker-Stoll & Fremmer-Bombik, 1997). These findings suggest that success in negotiating autonomy issues in adolescence may potentially be a stage-specific manifestation of a long-term secure attachment relationship with parents. Secure teens handle conflicts with parents by engaging in productive, problem-solving discussions that both allow for divergent opinions to be expressed, and also contain efforts to stay connected and engaged in the discussions (Allen & Hauser, 1996; Allen et al., 2003, 2004, in press; Becker-Stoll, Delius, & Scheitenberger, 2001; Becker-Stoll & Fremmer-Bombik, 1997; Ducharme, Doyle, & Markiewicz, 2002; Kobak et al., 1993). Secure teens (as rated by AAI as well as attachment style) also show less dysfunctional anger, less withdrawal and avoidance of problem solving, and fewer pressuring and/or overpersonalizing attacks while discussing an area of conflict with their mothers (Allen, Porter, McFarland, McElhaney, & Marsh, 2007; Becker-Stoll, Delius, & Scheitenberger, 2001; Kobak et al., 1993). Further, their discussions involve negotiation and compromise, such that both parties have the opportunity to express their thoughts and feelings (versus one member of the dyad's dominating the discussion) (Allen et al., 2003; Ducharme, Doyle, & Markiewicz, 2002).

There are further indications that a secure state of mind with regard to attachment is linked to healthy autonomy development. For example, security of attachment is linked to greater adolescent deidealization of their mothers; in other words, secure teens exhibit healthy autonomy development by being less likely to express *overly* positive and idealized beliefs about their mothers (Allen et al., 2003). Further, securely attached teens demonstrate more constructive coping strategies when presented with hypothetical separations from parents, both mild (e.g., joining a new class at school) and severe (e.g., a parent's going to the hospital) (Scharf, 2001). Beyond the hypothetical, it appears that security of attachment promotes healthier actual separations from parents: Securely attached teens are found to more successfully adjust to the developmental task of leaving home to attend college (Aspelmeier & Kerns, 2003; Bernier, Larose, & Whipple, 2005). In a sample primarily composed of college freshmen, a self-reported secure attachment style was associated with less self-reported anxiety about academic performance, more willingness to ask others for help, and higher levels of curiosity and willingness to seek out challenge (Aspelmeier & Kerns).

Attachment Insecurity and the Push for Autonomy

While the negotiation of attachment and autonomy issues may be at least somewhat challenging for all families at some point, this developmental task is likely to be particularly stressful for families with insecure adolescents. Before turning to the empirical findings, we will explicate some of the hypotheses underlying the links between attachment insecurity and autonomy struggles during adolescence. Insecure teens and their parents may not be able to adaptively manage the normative changes in their relationship that are brought on by the push for autonomy, and their struggles may be manifested in one or more aspects of these developmental transitions. For example, insecure teens may not be able to "step outside" of the attachment relationship in order to appropriately reevaluate their attachment figures. These teens (and/or their parents) may also be overwhelmed by the increased affective instability that tends to accompany autonomy strivings. Given that insecure adolescents may have a history of less-than-positive experiences with attachment figures in times of need, the increased uncertainties and insecurities that tend to accompany adolescence may propel them into a state of emotional and/or behavioral disturbance that is not easily assuaged by their caregivers (Allen & Land, 1999). Further, the push for autonomy may be experienced as a dangerous threat to either the parent–teen relationship overall or to parental authority in the relationship, or both.

The specific negative outcomes that follow from attachment insecurity and low autonomy support may vary according to whether the insecure adolescent holds a more dismissing versus preoccupied attachment organization. Dismissing adolescents may utilize their characteristic tendency to withdraw and disengage from caregivers when faced with the challenge of adapting to the new demands of autonomy. Rather than being able to reevaluate their attachment figures and maintain positive connections with them, they may reject and cut themselves off from parents (Allen & Land, 1999). Given that many (if not most) teens still need guidance to manage the social and developmental challenges they face, teens who withdraw from parents put themselves at risk for a range of negative outcomes, particularly with regard to risky behaviors. Preoccupied teens, whose attachment strategies include an angry, overinvolved stance toward attachment figures, may also be unable to appropriately separate during adolescence (Allen & Land). However, rather than withdrawing from and/or rejecting caregivers, these adolescents may remain overly engaged with them. This strategy may help to maintain connections with attachment figures, but at the cost of appropriate autonomy development.

Research evidence to date suggests that both insecure dismissing and insecure preoccupied adolescents and their parents struggle to manage autonomy issues, again largely with regard to cognitive and verbal autonomy. Studies have demonstrated that dismissing teens often fail to assert their points of view during discussions with their parents, and such discussions tend to be marked by a high level of disengagement and a lack of responsiveness (Becker-Stoll, Delius, & Scheitenberger, 2001; Becker-Stoll & Fremmer-Bombik, 1997; Kobak et al., 2003; Reimer et al., 1996). Dismissing adolescents tend to show the lowest levels of both autonomy and relatedness in interactions with parents of all attachment groups, and while discussing disagreements they tend to exhibit behaviors that discourage open communication, such as anger and turning away (Becker-Stoll & Fremmer-Bombik, 1997; Becker-Stoll, Delius, & Scheitenberger, 2001). Similarly, teens who demonstrated high levels of deactivation of thinking about attachment on the AAI (associated with dismissal of attachment) tended to have interactions with their mothers characterized by low levels of teen assertion coupled with high levels of maternal assertion (termed *maternal dominance*) (Kobak et al., 1993).

Insecure preoccupation, in contrast, appears to be associated with heightened and unproductive overengagement with parents, which restricts the autonomy process. For example, Allen and Hauser (1996) report that one indicator of preoccupation with attachment in young adulthood—use of passive thought processes, reflecting mental entanglement between self and caregivers—was predicted by adolescents' overpersonalized behaviors toward fathers in arguments 10 years earlier. This overengagement and difficulty with establishing autonomy appears to extend into late adolescence, as research also suggests that adolescents with insecure–preoccupied status have more difficulty leaving home successfully for college. They experience high levels of stress, anxiety, and loneliness when transitioning to college, as well as less willingness to seek out and trust potential supporters (Aspelmeier &

Kerns, 2003; Larose & Bernier, 2001). In contrast with secure teens, preoccupied teens who were leaving home for college reported having poorer quality of parent–adolescent relationships, including: lower trust, communication, and acceptance; higher rejection and alienation; and more negative expectations with regard to parental support. Despite being highly dissatisfied with their parents, however, preoccupied adolescents who had left home also had *increased* rates of contact with their parents (Bernier, Larose, & Whipple, 2005). Interestingly, these secure versus preoccupied differences were *not* found among the group of adolescents who were not leaving home for college, suggesting that the separation imposed by leaving home placed inordinate stress on the parent–adolescent relationship for those teens with a preoccupied state of mind (Bernier et al., 2005).

In summary, these studies demonstrate the important theoretically predicted links between security versus insecurity of attachment and the ways that autonomy is managed during adolescence. With a few exceptions, much of this literature has focused on linking adolescent security with interfamilial indexes of autonomy—more specifically, the ways that parents of secure versus insecure teens promote versus undermine their autonomy. We will now turn to the consideration of additional sequelae of individual variations in attachment and autonomy processes during adolescence. However, it is worth noting that, given that secure attachment and support for autonomy often go hand in hand, it is difficult to sort out the relative contributions of attachment security and interfamilial autonomy support with regard to adolescent outcomes. The relative contributions of attachment versus autonomy have rarely been addressed empirically, as very few studies have examined these constructs together within the same sample. Thus, we will first address correlates of secure versus insecure attachment, and then turn to outcomes associated with both intraindividual and interfamilial components of autonomy.

Correlates of Attachment Security Versus Insecurity During Adolescence

Attachment security is generally expected to be linked to more positive outcomes during adolescence, whereas attachment insecurity is expected to predict a range of social, emotional, and behavioral difficulties. Several specific sets of outcomes are particularly closely linked with the theoretical underpinnings of attachment security. Given the proposed association between a secure working model of attachment and views of others as more versus less trustworthy and accepting, attachment state of mind is especially expected to predict functioning within social relationships. Attachment security is also expected to be linked to style of emotion regulation via processes such as ability to identify, appropriately express, and manage a wide range of emotional states. Finally, attachment security versus insecurity is also predicted to be linked to views of the self as more versus less competent and worthy of love, suggesting predictions to outcomes such as self-concept and self-esteem. We will address each of these sets of outcomes in turn later. Further, we will demonstrate that the specific pattern of negative outcomes associated with insecurity tends to vary according to the specific type of insecurity (insecure dismissing versus insecure preoccupied). We should note a large body of literature has documented the associations between the nature and quality of parent–teen relationships and adolescent outcomes (see chapter 22 of this volume). Here, we focus exclusively on studies that utilize the AAI or attachment style measures to assess attachment states of mind, as opposed to examining parenting styles or behaviors that may promote versus undermine security of attachment.

Attachment and Adolescent Social Functioning

It is expected that security of attachment will facilitate adaptive psychosocial functioning during adolescence, particularly in terms of competence in social relationships. Secure working models are expected to provide positive expectations of relations with others, and also are predicted to guide affect and behavior within those relationships (Bowlby, 1969; Furman, 2001; Furman, Simon, Shaffer, & Bouchey, 2002). This may be particularly true during adolescence, when intimacy demands in relationships with peers increase; security of attachment is expected to be associated with abilities necessary to manage such intimacy successfully, such as the ability to seek and give care, to feel comfortable with an autonomous self and peer, and to negotiate disagreements (Belsky & Cassidy, 1994; Cassidy et al., 1996; Cassidy, 2001; Scharf, 2001). Further, the ability to maintain connections with parents but also appropriately separate from them should allow secure teens to move freely beyond parent–teen relationships in order to establish successful new relationships with peers as well as romantic partners (Gavin & Furman, 1996).

A rapidly increasing body of research confirms links between a secure adolescent attachment organization and a range of indexes of adaptive functioning with peers. Adolescent attachment security has been linked to measures of broader social competence such as overall friendship quality, popularity, and social acceptance (Allen, Moore, Kuperminc, & Bell, 1998; Allen et al., in press; Zimmermann, 2004), as well as to functioning within close friendships with peers (Bartholomew & Horowitz, 1991; Hazan & Shaver, 1987; Lieberman et al., 1999; Zimmermann). Both self-report, interview-based, and observational studies suggest that secure teens engage in high levels of prosocial and relationship maintaining behaviors with their friends, as well as low levels of negativity (e.g., Markiewicz, Doyle, & Brendgen, 2001; Wiemer, Kerns, & Oldenberg, 2004; Zimmermann, Maier, Winter, & Grossmann, 2001; Zimmermann, 2004). For example, secure teens exhibit high levels of support, respect, and acceptance when talking with their friends, and secure dyads are marked both by a "smooth conversational style" (e.g., low need for clarification of viewpoints) and by fewer statements challenging the other person (Weimer et al.). Similarly, when asked to work on a frustrating joint problem-solving task; secure teens engage in fewer disruptive behaviors such as ignoring their friends or rejecting their suggestions without discussion (Zimmerman et al.). Security of attachment with regard to parental relationships is also associated with having secure working models of friendships, as well as a greater capacity for both closeness and separateness in relationships with friends (Furman et al., 2002; Markiewicz et al., 2001; Mayseless & Scharf, 2007; Scharf, Mayseless, & Kivenson-Baron, 2004). Secure teens are also better able to rely on peers to fulfill attachment functions, including wanting to be near their friends (proximity seeking) and being able to turn to them for comfort and support (safe haven) (Fraley & Davis, 1997; Mayseless, 2004).

Attachment security also appears to be closely linked to behavior in romantic and sexual relationships in adolescence, though studies of this topic have focused almost exclusively on young adults, with only a few studies examining late adolescents. Secure states of mind with regard to attachment as well as secure attachment styles have been associated with a high capacity for romantic intimacy (e.g., high levels of trust), a greater capacity for both closeness and separateness in romantic relationships, and closer and more satisfying romantic relationships (Marston, Hare, Miga, & Allen, 2008; Mayseless & Scharf, 2007; Mikulincer & Erev, 1991; Scharf et al., 2004). Interestingly, research also suggests that younger teens with self-reported secure attachment styles report turning to romantic partners *less* often than mothers to fulfill attachment functions, which the authors consider to be a developmentally appropriate pattern for this age group (Markiewicz et al., 2006). In late adolescence, secure states of mind have also been linked to the subsequent quality of interactions with a romantic partner;

such interactions are characterized by willingness to express ideas, ability to resolve conflict, and mutual caring and pleasure in the other person (Roisman et al., 2001; 2005). Further, research with young adults indicates that security of attachment is linked to healthier sexual behavior: Securely attached young women are more likely to require some emotional commitment from partners before engaging in sex and are also likely to have somewhat less permissive attitudes toward sexuality (Januszewski, Turner, Guerin, & Flack, 1996).

Turning to insecure attachment organizations, an interesting pattern of results has begun to emerge with regard to preoccupation with attachment and social functioning. On the one hand, given their orientation toward valuing intimacy and seeking support from others, preoccupied individuals may fare better socially than those with dismissing orientations. On the other hand, preoccupied states of mind with regard to attachment are also likely to predispose individuals to feel anxious about their worth in close relationships as well as the degree to which others will be consistently available and supportive. The balance of the evidence indicates that while adolescents who are preoccupied are, in fact, generally more oriented toward relationships than their dismissing counterparts, they also generally function poorly in such relationships. For example, preoccupied adolescents report high levels of loneliness and distrust, as well as dissatisfaction and stress related to their close relationships (Larose & Bernier, 2001; Seiffge-Krenke, 2006). In addition, some studies indicate that preoccupation is also associated with higher levels of both interpersonal anxiety and hostility (Bartholomew & Horowitz, 1991; Cooper, Shaver, & Collins, 1998; Kobak & Sceery, 1988; Zimmermann, 2004). These difficulties also carry over to romantic relationships: insecure preoccupation in late adolescents and young adults has been associated with high levels of anxiety, dependence, and jealousy within romantic and sexual relationships, as well as low levels of satisfaction with such relationships (Collins & Read, 1990; Davila, Steinberg, Kachadourian, Cobb, & Fincham, 2004; Mayseless, Sharabany, & Sagi, 1997; Tracy, Shaver, Albino, & Cooper, 2003).

In the case of dismissal of attachment, defensive exclusion of information as well as discomfort with attachment-related affect and experiences may correspond to distorted communications, negative expectations about others, and rejection of and/or distancing from peers (Larose & Bernier, 2001; Spangler & Zimmermann, 1999). Adolescents with dismissing states of mind are consistently found to be less socially skilled and more socially isolated (Allen et al., 2002b). These teens engage in fewer active, support-seeking coping strategies, including turning to a friend to meet attachment needs (Fraley & Davis, 1997; Seiffge-Krenke & Beyers, 2005). Similarly, in samples of young adults, dismissal of attachment (as rated by the both AAI and self-report measures) is linked to low levels of sociability and high levels of peer-rated withdrawal, as well as to high levels of peer-rated hostility and "coldness" (Bartholomew & Horowitz, 1991; Kobak & Sceery, 1988; Larose & Bernier, 2001). While individuals who are dismissing of attachment tend not to describe themselves as hostile, they do tend to feel isolated and unsupported by others, self-reporting more loneliness and less support from families, peers, and teachers as compared to secure individuals (Kobak & Sceery; Larose & Bernier). A similar pattern emerges with regard to approaches to romantic relationships in late adolescents and young adults. As compared to those who are securely attached, dismissing individuals demonstrate more mistrust, lower levels of intimacy, and lower levels of closeness in romantic relationships, as reported and observed both concurrently (Guerrero, 1996) and longitudinally (Collins, Cooper, Albino, & Allard, 2002; Mayseless & Scharf, 2007).

In summary, attachment security versus insecurity—whether assessed with regard to overall state of mind or attachment style within specific relationships—has been consistently linked to social functioning. Secure teens evidence high levels of social competence and social skills, particularly in terms of the demands of negotiating the intimacy that becomes a more prominent feature of friendships during adolescence. Preoccupied teens appear to desire social relationships, but they also tend to be uncertain and anxious about whether those relationships will be satisfying, and perhaps highly demanding of relationship partners as a result—a pattern that also carries over into their romantic relationships. Dismissing teens appear to be relatively untrusting of others, and tend to be seen as withdrawn or "cold" by their peers. Overall, this pattern of empirical findings provides support for the theoretical role of internal working models in shaping adolescents' social and emotional ties with others. Individual differences with regard to emotion regulation and coping will be considered next.

Attachment, Emotion Regulation, and Coping with Stressors

Some researchers have suggested that the links between attachment security versus insecurity and functioning in close relationships with peers and romantic partners may be a result of generalized comfort in handling one's own emotional reactions in challenging situations (Kobak & Sceery, 1988; Zimmermann et al., 2001). Security of attachment is thought to be associated with the ability to be able to freely perceive and experience—as well as to openly express and communicate—both positive and negative feelings. This ability can thus help secure individuals in using their own appraisals of their emotional reactions to guide their behaviors, and also aids in clear and consistent communication of their emotional reactions to significant others (Spangler & Zimmermann, 1999). The degree to which attachment security maps onto emotion regulation outside of the attachment relationship has been studied in young children (e.g., Kirsh & Cassidy, 1997; Laible &

Thompson, 1998; Seuss, Grossmann, & Sroufe, 1992), and has recently been examined in adult samples (e.g. Roisman, 2006, 2007), but has rarely been studied in adolescents.

The evidence that does exist on attachment, emotion regulation, and coping suggests that secure teens differ from insecure teens with regard to their emotional perceptions, expressions, and styles of regulation. Both secure state of mind with regard to attachment and self-reported security of attachment have been linked to increased willingness to express emotions; clearer, more accurate, and more appropriate emotional expressions; as well as greater flexibility in emotional appraisals and behaviors (Ducharme et al., 2002; Spangler & Zimmermann, 1999; Zimmermann, 1999; Zimmermann et al., 2001). Secure teens display emotional reactions that are more consistently in tune with the emotional valence of film clips to which they are exposed (e.g., positive reactions in response to positive emotional events and negative responses to negative ones) (Spangler & Zimmermann). They also show higher concordance between emotional self-ratings and facial emotional expressions (e.g., frowning while also reporting a negative emotional experience) as assessed by both raters and facial electromyography (Spangler & Zimmermann; Zimmermann et al.). It should be noted that these results are based on relatively small sample sizes, and in most cases secure participants could only be differentiated from dismissing participants.

Recent research also suggests that secure individuals evidence more adaptive strategies when coping with relationship stressors. A recent longitudinal study that followed a sample of adolescents from age 14 to age 21 found that a secure state of mind with regard to attachment is associated with use of more self-reported active coping strategies (e.g., talking about problems and seeking emotional assistance), use of more internal coping strategies (e.g., searching for solutions, recognizing own limitations, willingness to accept compromises), and less use of withdrawal or avoidance

when faced with stressors (Seiffge-Krenke, 2006; Seiffge-Krenke & Beyers, 2005). In fact, secure teens show large developmental gains in both active and internal coping strategies over time, whereas the insecure groups do not demonstrate increases in these types of coping (Seiffge-Krenke & Beyers, 2005). Secure states of mind with regard to attachment are also associated with greater flexibility in assessing and generating responses to stressful social situations (in the form of hypothetical vignettes) (Zimmermann, 1999). More data is needed to further understand the interplay between attachment organization, emotion regulation, and coping strategies in teenagers, but the data that have been gathered to date support conclusions from studies of adults: security of attachment corresponds to more adaptive perception, labeling, and expression of emotions across a variety of situations, as well as more adaptive strategies for managing difficult situations.

Preoccupation with attachment is expected to be linked with high levels of negative emotionality, given that preoccupied individuals are easily overwhelmed by their negative emotions and have poor access to their own mood states (Spangler & Zimmermann, 1999). While they may try to turn to others for assistance when coping with negative emotions, they are not expected to be easily assuaged and are likely to be dissatisfied with their level of emotional support. Unfortunately, much of the research to date on emotion regulation in adolescence has been unable to examine effects of preoccupation due to small sample sizes. For example, in the study described above that exposed participants to positive versus negative film clips, the mean values for both positive and negative arousal were the highest for the preoccupied group, but this effect could not be demonstrated to be statistically reliable, likely as a result of the small number of preoccupied individuals (Spangler & Zimmermann). However, there is some evidence that a preoccupied state of mind is related to difficulties controlling one's emotions as well as rigid emotion-related behavior patterns (Zimmermann, 1999). Further, preoccupied teens report particularly high levels of stress across multiple contexts—especially as related to functioning in close relationships and during times of separation from caregivers—as well as maladaptive strategies for managing such stress (Larose & Bernier, 2001; Sieffge-Krenke & Beyers, 2005; Seiffge-Krenke, 2006). There is also some evidence that the combination of high levels of emotionality and poor resources for managing emotional stress at least partially account for the high levels of symptomatology often exhibited by individuals with a preoccupied state of mind, as will be discussed further later in the chapter (Sieffge-Krenke).

Dismissal of attachment is expected to be linked to restricted capacity regarding perception and communication of emotions, particularly when these emotions are negative (Spangler & Zimmermann, 1999). In addition, dismissing individuals are expected to cope with negative feelings by suppressing or ignoring them, and are not expected to seek out emotional support when distressed. For example, dismissing adolescents demonstrate biases toward idealization, a marker for distorted perception of emotional content: Dismissing teens are more likely than either secure or preoccupied teens to positively evaluate both positive and negative emotional content in film clips (Spangler & Zimmermann). In this study and others, dismissing individuals also show a mismatch between their self-reported mood states and their observed emotional expression, implying difficulties in their abilities to identify and/or communicate their affective experiences (Spangler & Zimmermann; Zimmermann et al., 2001). Cole-Detke and Kobak (1996) also report that eating-disordered individuals in a college population are more likely to use dismissing strategies, with the attention given to eating behaviors believed to distract from feelings of internal emotional distress. Similarly, as compared to secure teens, adolescents with dismissing states of mind report being less likely to seek out support from others when

distressed (Seiffge-Krenke, 2006; Seiffge-Krenke & Beyers, 2005). Dismissing adolescents also adapt less well to specific stressors, such as the transition to the military in an Israeli sample of late adolescent males, though only as assessed by peer reports, not by self-report (Scharf et al., 2004).

In summary, as with the links between security of attachment and social functioning, the growing body of research examining links between attachment and emotion regulation indicates that adolescents who are securely attached demonstrate more adaptive outcomes. Securely attached teens are better able to perceive, label and express their own emotions and are also more adept at managing difficult emotional experiences. They tend to engage in active coping strategies that often involve seeking support from others. In contrast, preoccupied teens appear to be both highly emotionally reactive and to have ineffective strategies for managing their emotions. However, it should be noted that small sample sizes often have precluded a thorough investigation of the links between preoccupation and emotion regulation. Finally, dismissing teens do not appear to recognize their own emotional reactions, nor can they effectively communicate their feelings to others. They engage in maladaptive coping strategies (e.g., distraction), fail to seek out support from others, and consequently do not adapt well to stressful situations. Next, we will turn to the links that have been found between attachment security versus insecurity and views of the self.

Attachment Security Versus Insecurity and Views of the Self

Security of attachment is in theory linked with a model of the self in relation to others that not only emphasizes trust in others to be responsive and helpful in times of need, but also confidence in one's own ability to face and manage challenges. In contrast, individuals with preoccupied attachments are expected to hold relatively negative views of themselves, although their views of others may be positive

(Bartholomew & Horowitz, 1991). Finally, the idealization processes that are associated with dismissing states of mind make it likely that dismissing individuals may not self-report high levels of negative self-concept, and some authors have pointed out that the defensive style of dismissing models are likely to involve relatively negative models of others but relatively positively models of the self (Bartholomew & Horowitz). Thus, it is expected that attachment security would predict various intrapsychic outcomes such as self-esteem and self-efficacy, as well as identity and ego development.

While there is some research with both child and adult samples to suggest links between attachment security and views of the self (Cassidy, 1988; Mikulincer & Florian, 1995, 1998), these topics have rarely been explored in adolescent samples. Further, results of existing studies are a bit mixed, and in part appear to depend on whether outcomes are assessed via self-reports versus peer reports or interview-based measures. Some studies have found no differences between secure versus dismissing adolescents on self-reported levels of self-esteem and/or descriptions of themselves (Mikulincer, 1995; Scharf et al., 2004). However, Cooper and colleagues (1998) found that teens with secure attachment styles had more positive self-concepts than either of the two insecure groups. Studies utilizing peer reports or coded interviews to assess outcomes (to circumvent the potential defensive bias in self-reports) suggest that secure teens have more positive and well-integrated views of self, though again with clearer contrasts between secure and preoccupied vs. secure and dismissing strategies. For example, a secure state of mind with regard to attachment in mid- to late adolescence has been linked to greater identity status achievement and higher levels of peer-rated ego resiliency (Kobak & Sceery, 1988; Manning, Stephenson, & Allen, 2008; Zimmermann & Becker-Stoll, 2002). Given the relative paucity of empirical work on this topic, there is clearly a need for additional research into the potential links between attachment security and models of the self during adolescence.

Insecure Attachment and Emotional and Behavioral Outcomes

A number of recent studies suggest the existence of substantial links between attachment security versus insecurity and both emotional and behavioral disturbances. Whereas secure adolescents demonstrate lower levels of both internalizing and externalizing symptoms (Allen et al., 1998; Allen et al., 2007), insecurity of attachment is consistently predictive of a range of emotional and behavioral difficulties. In fact, among the most highly disturbed adolescents—those requiring residential treatment—three studies have found links to either concurrent or future attachment insecurity, and to a heightened prevalence of insecure–unresolved attachment status (Allen & Hauser, 1996; Allen, Hauser, & Borman-Spurrell, 1996; Wallis & Steele, 2001). Interestingly, some authors have further suggested that it is the disruption of autonomy development per se that accounts for the development of psychopathology in these individuals (Ryan, Deci, Grolnick, & La Guardia, 2006). Regardless, both the preoccupied and dismissing strategies have been implicated in problems of psychosocial functioning, although the two are associated with somewhat different patterns of problems, as we will discuss in further detail below.

While adolescents' use of preoccupied strategies has been most closely linked to internalizing problems, research suggests that numerous psychosocial and environmental factors may interact with level of preoccupation in predicting mental health outcomes. Thus, while preoccupation of attachment often is directly linked to adolescents' self-reports of depression, anxiety, and distress (Allen et al., 1998; Bernier et al., 2005; Bartholomew & Horowitz, 1991; Cole-Detke & Kobak, 1996; Kobak et al., 1991; Kobak & Sceery, 1988; Larose & Bernier, 2001; Rosenstein & Horowitz, 1996; Seiffge-Krenke, 2006), this link appears particularly strong when preoccupied teens are exposed to intrapsychic states or environments that are confusing or enmeshed. For example, preoccupied adolescents display higher levels of depression when their mothers cannot display their own autonomy in discussions (i.e., appear passive and enmeshed) (Marsh, McFarland, Allen, McElhaney, & Land, 2003). Similarly, preoccupied teens whose friends exhibit high levels of enmeshed and overpersonalizing behaviors report increasing levels of depression over time, whereas those that experience high levels of conflict avoidance in their friends (which in this case may simply serve as nonenmeshed or distancing behavior) demonstrate decreasing levels of depression over time (Chango, McElhaney, & Allen, 2008). Researchers have speculated that the hyperactivation of the attachment system in preoccupied adolescents may correspond to extreme sensitivity to their social environments, thus accounting for this pattern of moderating effects.

In some circumstances, preoccupied teens have been found to be more likely to display externalizing symptoms as opposed to internalizing problems. For example, preoccupied adolescents display higher levels of drug use, precocious sexual activity, and increases in levels of delinquent behavior when their mothers exhibit extremely high levels of their own (maternal) autonomy in discussions (perhaps asserting themselves to the point of ignoring their adolescents) (Allen et al., 1998). Similarly, Marsh and colleagues (2003) found that adolescent preoccupation and mothers' focus on their own (as opposed to their adolescents') autonomy predicted adolescents' early sexual activity, whereas preoccupied adolescents whose mothers were relatively unfocused on their own autonomy had strikingly low rates of early sexual activity. Finally, when preoccupied adolescents are exposed to poverty (perhaps another situation in which their needs are likely to be ignored), there is also an increased likelihood of delinquent behavior (Allen et al., 2007).

Finally, in adaptive contexts, the increased orientation that preoccupied individuals have toward relationships may actually act as a protective factor for these teens. Though preoccupied teens tend to struggle socially, not all studies find significant differences in overall quality of social relationships between preoccupied versus secure adolescents (Weimer et al., 2004; Zimmermann, 2004). When preoccupied (and secure) teens are exposed to positive friendships, they exhibit lower concurrent risk for delinquent behavior (McElhaney, Immele, Smith, & Allen, 2006). In addition, when exposed to effective maternal behavioral control strategies, both preoccupied and secure teens exhibit lower levels of delinquent behavior than dismissing teens exposed to the same maternal behaviors (Allen et al., 1998). Taken together, these results suggest that when preoccupied adolescents are exposed to passivity or enmeshment, an internalizing, anxious/depressed pattern emerges; whereas when they are in situations where their attachment entreaties are more likely to be ignored or rebuffed, they react with externalizing behavior. In cases when preoccupied teens' hyperactivated attachment system brings them into contact with positive social interactions, it appears to leave the teen responsive to these as well.

In contrast to preoccupied adolescents, adolescents who are dismissing of attachment may take on symptoms that distract themselves and others from attachment-related cues (Cole-Detke & Kobak, 1996; Kobak & Cole, 1994). When examining psychiatrically hospitalized adolescents, almost all of whom were insecure, Rosenstein and Horowitz (1996) reported that dismissing strategies were associated with externalizing symptoms, including substance abuse and conduct disordered behavior. Similarly, Allen and colleagues report that dismissing attachment strategies were predictive of increasing delinquency and externalizing behavior over both short- and longer term spans of adolescence (Allen et al., 2002b; Allen et al., in press). Unlike preoccupied adolescents, dismissing adolescents also do not appear particularly sensitive to parental behaviors. For example, a factor such as parental control of adolescent behavior—which is well established as a buffer against delinquency—did not appear to serve this role for dismissing teens (Allen et al., 1998).

In summary, given that insecurity of attachment is associated with maladaptive social functioning, difficulties with emotion regulation, and negative views of the self, it is perhaps not particularly surprising that insecurity is also associated with more significant negative emotional and behavioral outcomes. Preoccupied adolescents appear to be particularly at risk for developing internalizing problems, including both depression and anxiety. However, the range of outcomes associated with preoccupied status is varied, and appears to at least partly depend on the nature of the social and emotional environment that the preoccupied teen experiences. Dismissal of attachment, in contrast, has been more consistently linked with a pattern of acting-out behavior that includes conduct problems and substance abuse. We will now turn to an examination of individual differences in autonomy functioning and outcomes during adolescence.

Adolescent Autonomy and Emotional and Behavioral Outcomes

Before beginning this section of our chapter, we return to the point that research on the consequences of secure versus insecure attachment and the consequences autonomy processes tends to be quite disparate in a number of ways. First, attachment research is more rooted in developmental psychology; autonomy research has tended to stem more from the work on personality and ego development, which in part has led to an examination of different sets of correlates of these two constructs. As a rough parallel to our earlier review of the attachment literature, we will specifically examine the outcomes of social functioning, views of self, and mental health outcomes. Unlike attachment research, links between autonomy processes

and emotion regulation have rarely—if ever—been examined. However, there is a small body of literature that examines the ways that autonomy development within parent–adolescent relationships is linked to coping with one specific developmental stressor: the adjustment to college. Second, attachment research focuses almost exclusively on the secure versus insecure adolescent as the starting point, whereas the literature on outcomes associated with autonomy development is largely focused on interfamilial processes that support versus undermine autonomy. One exception is the study of emotional autonomy, which treats autonomy as an intraindividual characteristic of the adolescent.

Autonomy Promotion and Social Functioning

Whereas there is definitive support for the links between attachment security and social competence during adolescence, the role of autonomy development with regard to adolescent peer relationships is less well studied. There is, however, a large body of research that has yielded definitive support for the role of interfamilial autonomy promotion in the social functioning of younger children (e.g., Maccoby & Martin, 1983). Given that autonomy development is such a central task of adolescence, issues of autonomy versus control may become even more central in shaping social competence as children move into adolescence (Amato, 1989). In fact, one study in particular compared parental promotion of autonomy in a sample of younger children (ages 8–9) and in an adolescent/young adult sample (ages 15 to early 20s) and found that there was a shift in the parent–child relationship variables that were associated with social competence in the two groups. For the younger sample, social competence was linked with both high parental support and high parental control, whereas in the adolescent sample, social competence was associated with high parental support and *low* parental control (Amato).

Adolescents from families that promote their autonomy while also maintaining limits on behaviors as well as close relational ties demonstrate better social adjustment. Observational studies of adolescents' expressions of autonomy during discussions with their parents (cognitive/verbal autonomy) suggest that these teens are both more interpersonally competent and more socially accepted, and they develop closer and more supportive relationships with their friends (Allen, Bell, & Boykin, 2000; Hall, 2002; McElhaney, 2000; McElhaney & Allen, 2001). In contrast, both self-report and observational studies demonstrate that undermining of autonomy within the parent–adolescent relationship is linked to a range of problems in social functioning, such as greater amounts of hostility in relationships with peers (Allen & Hauser, 1993; Allen, Hauser, O'Connor, & Bell, 2002b), more peer rejection (Marsh & McFarland, 2002), decreased interpersonal competence (Allen et al., 2000; McElhaney), and increasingly distant peer relationships (Tencer, Meyer, & Hall, 2003). These findings have been documented both concurrently and longitudinally. For example, fathers' behaviors undermining adolescents' cognitive/verbal autonomy (e.g., pressuring to agree) during family discussions at age 16 was found to predict peer ratings of adolescents' hostility approximately 10 years later, over and above initial levels of hostility (Allen et al., 2002a).

There are parallel findings in the self-report literature examining the concurrent and longitudinal correlates of parenting that promotes moderate behavioral autonomy and is also low in psychological control. For example, when teens view parents as highly authoritative and/or low in psychological control, they appear to be both more socially skilled and more closely connected to their peers, but also to be less "peer oriented" and more autonomous with their peers (Barber & Olson, 1997; Bednar & Fisher, 2003; Engels, Dekovic, & Meeus, 2002; Laible & Carlo, 2004; Steinberg, Elmen, & Mounts, 1989). In contrast, self-reports of high levels of parental psychological control and low support for behavioral autonomy have

been inversely linked to measures of competence, closeness and autonomy within peer relationships (Laible & Carlo, 2004; Lee & Bell, 2003; Soenens & Vansteenkiste, 2005). One particularly consistent finding is that teens who view their parents as controlling and restrictive of autonomy are more highly oriented toward their peers and also more likely to associate with deviant peers (Fuligni & Eccles, 1993; Goldstein, Davis-Kean, & Eccles, 2005).

In summary, the growing body of literature examining interfamilial promotion versus undermining of autonomy during adolescence demonstrates clear links between these processes and adolescents' social functioning. Results are most clear for cognitive/verbal autonomy, behavioral autonomy, and psychological control versus autonomy support. A family environment that supports adolescents' expressions of autonomy clearly promotes interpersonal competence, in terms of broad peer acceptance as well as the quality of close friendships. In contrast, parenting that is overly psychologically controlling and/or undermines cognitive or behavioral autonomy is linked to maladaptive social functioning. Undermining of cognitive autonomy appears to be linked to a relatively broad range of problems within peer relationships, whereas high levels of both behavioral and psychological control are most clearly linked to increased orientation toward peers as well as involvement with deviant peers.

Autonomy Processes, Views of the Self, and Internalizing Problems

To the extent that promotion of autonomy is linked with a sense of agency and confidence in one's own competence, parenting that supports autonomy during adolescence is also likely to promote more positive self-concepts. Consistent with these premises, research on autonomy processes within parent–teen relationships has yielded relatively consistent predictions from autonomy support to various indicators of intrapsychic competence and health. For example, observational research on family interactions indicates that adolescents' identity and ego development are positively linked with parental expressions of mutuality and enabling behavior (thought to promote cognitive/verbal autonomy), and negatively related to expressions of separateness and constraining behavior (thought to undermine cognitive/verbal autonomy) (Grotevant & Cooper, 1985; Hauser et al., 1984). Similarly, Allen and colleagues found that parental promotion of cognitive/verbal autonomy (defined as stating reasons for holding a differing position while also remaining open to others' views) is linked with higher levels of self-esteem and ego development (Allen et al., 1994b). Conversely, behaviors undermining autonomy and relatedness during interactions with mothers are linked to increases in depression during early adolescence (Allen et al., 2006). The self-report literature examining effects of parenting reveal a similar pattern: Adolescents' reports of psychological control versus autonomy support are cross-sectionally linked (in expected directions) to reports of self-concept, self-worth, and well-being (Aquilino & Supple, 2001; Frank et al., 2002; Laible & Carlo, 2004; Silk, Morris, & Kanaya, 2003; Soenens et al., 2007).

Given the links between parental autonomy support versus undermining and views of the self, it is perhaps not surprising that these constructs are also linked to psychological functioning, particularly with regard to internalizing symptoms. There is a relatively large body of research with younger children suggesting that those who experience psychological control are vulnerable to a range of developmental difficulties, particularly internalizing problems, and this same pattern of results is present in adolescent samples (Barber & Harmon, 2002). Parental psychological control during adolescence is linked to decreased self-confidence and self-worth, as well as increased maladaptive perfectionism, distress, and depressive symptoms both concurrently and over time (Barber, Olsen, & Shagle, 1994; Conger, Conger, & Scaramella,

1997; Garber, Robinson, & Valentiner, 1997; Gray & Steinberg, 1999; Petit, Laird, Dodge, Bates, & Criss, 2001; Soenens, Vansteenkiste, & Luyten, 2005; Soenens et al., 2007). Notably, research has further demonstrated that psychological control is uniquely predictive of internalizing problems over and above other dimensions of parenting, such as behavioral control and responsiveness (e.g. Soenens et al., 2005; Petit et al.). Conversely, self-report studies have indicated that parents' granting of psychological autonomy is linked with a range of positive emotional and behavioral outcomes, including less depressed affect and fewer externalizing problems both concurrently and longitudinally (Barber & Olson, 1997; Eccles, Early, Frasier, Belansky, & McCarthy, 1997; Herman, Dornbusch, Herron, & Herting, 1997; Silk et al., 2003). Similarly, observations of behavior promoting of cognitive/verbal autonomy while also maintaining relatedness during a family discussion have been linked to lower levels of adolescent depression over time, as rated by observers during a clinical interview (Allen et al., 1994a).

Autonomy Processes and Externalizing Behaviors

While undermining of cognitive/verbal autonomy and psychological control have been most closely linked with internalizing problems during adolescence, some studies have also found predictions to externalizing difficulties. At least one study has documented longitudinal prediction from observed behaviors undermining cognitive/verbal autonomy to self-reports of adolescents' externalizing behaviors (Allen et al., 1994b). Psychological control has been linked to increased rates of antisocial and externalizing behavior in late childhood and during adolescence in both cross-sectional and short-term longitudinal studies (Barber & Olson, 1997; Petit et al., 2001; Rogers, Buchanan & Winchel, 2003). Further, several studies have revealed links between dimensions of parental psychological control versus autonomy support and rates of substance use, as well as problems related to substance use during adolescence and young adulthood (Aquilino & Supple, 2001; Lee & Bell, 2003). Interestingly, at least one study has suggested that the links between perceptions of parental psychological control early in adolescence and engagement in problem behavior in late adolescence are mediated by engagement with risky peers during middle adolescence (Goldstein et al., 2005).

Research on parental monitoring, behavioral control and behavioral autonomy has indicated consistent links between high levels of monitoring and firm/consistent behavioral control and low levels of problems behaviors during adolescence (Barber et al., 1994; Galambos, Barker, & Almeida, 2003; Eccles et al., 1997; Gray & Steinberg, 1999; Hayes et al., 2004; Herman et al., 1997; Pettit, Laird, & Dodge, 2001). With regard to behavioral autonomy, adolescents appear to benefit from parenting that supports their participation in family decision making, but overly high levels of adolescent behavioral autonomy (as often occur with permissive and/or neglectful parenting) tend to be maladaptive for teens (Lamborn, Mounts, Steinberg, & Dornbusch, 1991; Steinberg, Lamborn, Darling, Mounts, & Dornbusch, 1994). Notably, some authors have recently called the concept of parental monitoring into question, highlighting the fact that operational definitions of parental monitoring have tended to focus more on adolescents' willingness to share information, versus parents' active tracking and checking of adolescents' behaviors (Kerr & Stattin, 2000). However, studies that have specifically examined aspects of actual parental monitoring, such as firmness of parental rules and closeness of parental supervision, confirm that adequate rules and close supervision have an inverse relationship to the level of adolescent problem behavior (Hayes et al., 2004).

In sum, undermining of cognitive/verbal autonomy and high levels of psychological control during adolescence are clearly linked to maladaptive outcomes for teens. This pattern is particularly found with regard to indices of self-concept and internalizing symptoms, although there is also some indication of links to externalizing behaviors. Notably, the association between psychological control and maladaptive outcomes does *not* appear to be attributable to other, more global aspects of the parent–teen relationship (e.g., warmth). Parenting that is manipulative, intrusive, and undermining of autonomy clearly has unique predictive power, suggesting that interference with this particular developmental task has serious and unique negative consequences for teens. However, a balance between moderate levels of behavioral control and opportunities for exercising behavioral autonomy appears to be beneficial for teens; firm control appears to play a particular protective role against engagement in risky and problematic behavior during adolescence. We will now turn to our final section examining individual differences with regard to autonomy processes and adjustment to college—one index of the ways that adolescents cope with a difficult developmental transition. This is one area of research that examines correlates of autonomy defined as an intrapsychic construct, as opposed to the preceding studies that focus on interfamilial indices of autonomy development.

Adolescent Autonomy and Adjustment to College

Unlike the attachment literature reviewed previously, autonomy development has not been directly examined in conjunction with emotion regulation and/or stress and coping. However, there is a relatively large body of evidence to suggest that autonomous teens adapt relatively well to one particular stressor: adjustment to college. Several studies of late adolescents and young adults have found links between various self-report measures of autonomy (particularly cognitive and emotional autonomy) and both concurrent and longitudinal adjustment to college, including both academic and personal–emotional outcomes (Beyers & Goossens, 2003; Frank et al., 1990; Haemmerlie, Steen, & Benedicto,

1994; Hoffman, 1984; Hoffman & Weiss, 1987; Holmbeck & Leake, 1999; Lapsley et al., 1989; Lopez, Campbell, & Watkins, 1988; Palladino & Blustein, 1994; Rice, 1992; Rice, Cole, & Lapsley, 1990). For example, one recent study that utilized the PSI and the EAS found positive predictions between self-reported autonomy from parents and a range of measures of adjustment to college (Beyers & Goossens). These authors conceptualized the autonomy process as involving both positive feelings about the separation from parents (emotional autonomy, in terms of freedom from guilt or anger) as well as various forms of independence from parents (e.g., functional or behavioral autonomy). The index of positive feelings about separation (emotional autonomy) was particularly strongly linked to measures of adjustment (Beyers & Goossens).

Emotional Autonomy and Adolescent Outcomes

It is clear from the previous review that interfamilial autonomy defined in terms of parental support for cognitive/verbal autonomy and lack of parental psychological control co-occurs with a range of positive outcomes for teens. The correlates of emotional autonomy, when conceptualized as increased deidealization and decreased reliance on parents, are complex, and thus we review them separately here. The bulk of studies using Steinberg & Silverberg's (1986) EAS have indicated that higher scores are linked with poorer quality parent–teen relationships (e.g., Beyers & Goossens, 1999; Delaney, 1996; Garber & Little, 2001; Ryan & Lynch, 1989; Power, Francis, & Hughes, 1992). In addition, particularly during early and middle adolescence, high scores on the EAS tend to be inversely linked with aspects of adolescents' functioning that should co-occur with healthy autonomy development, such as self-reliance and susceptibility to peer pressure (Steinberg & Silverberg). Other research has further documented that high scores on emotional autonomy as measured by the EAS are predictive of problems with both internalizing

symptoms (anxiety, depression, self-worth) and externalizing behaviors (substance use, minor delinquency, aggressive behavior) (Delaney; Power et al., 1992; Turner, Irwin, Tschann, & Millstein, 1993).

However, there may be some conditions under which higher levels of emotional autonomy are linked to more positive outcomes for teens. As outlined earlier, there are documented normative increases in emotional autonomy. This is especially true with regard to deidealization, as well as in other possible indicators of autonomous development within the parent–teen relationship (e.g., disengagement, secrecy, and conflict). While the majority of the empirical evidence suggests that adolescents who score highly on these measures relative to their peers are less well adjusted (e.g. Finkenauer et al., 2002; Steinberg & Silverberg, 1986; Montemayor, 1986), the one possible exception to this pattern is found in the studies of adjustment to college in *late* adolescence as outlined above. Further, at least one study has indicated positive correlates of emotional autonomy when parent–teen relationship quality is poor, although this sample was primarily composed of ethnic minority teens (e.g. Fuhrman & Holmbeck, 1995). One study that compared adolescents according to where they fell on a combination of closeness and emotional autonomy found the most adaptive outcomes for those classified as connected (high in closeness and low in emotional autonomy), and the worst outcomes for those classified as detached (low in closeness and high in emotional autonomy). Those that were both close *and* autonomous were classified as individuated, and this group tended to have average levels of adjustment, falling in between the other two groups in terms of their levels of self-worth and anxiety (Delaney, 1996).

Thus, while emotional autonomy and deidealization are normative processes, it may be that *precocious* autonomy development in this domain is neither normative nor adaptive. Further, optimal autonomy development appears to necessitate both individuation and a sense of closeness and connection with parents, perhaps particularly during early and middle adolescence. While measures of emotional autonomy tap into some important aspects of the autonomy process, they tend to focus primarily on the processes of separation and individuation. Finally, it should be noted that comparing results across studies utilizing the EAS is somewhat difficult, given that different versions of the measure are often used, and there are wide variations in the sample age range and demographic composition that might confound results and limit generalizability (Beyers et al., 2005). It may be, for example, that some components of the autonomy processes that are captured with the EAS scale are, in fact, normative and others are not (e.g., Chen & Dornbusch, 1998), and/or that some aspects may be adaptive for adolescents of certain ages (e.g., Frank et al., 1990) or sociocultural backgrounds (e.g., Fuhrman & Holmbeck, 1995).

Individual Differences: Gender and Socioeconomic Factors

Overall, neither the literature on attachment relationships nor studies of autonomy processes has tended to address the issues of gender and socioeconomic context. In many cases, particularly with regard to studies of attachment during adolescence, small sample sizes have precluded the examining of demographic effects. As we will review in more detail below, some studies have demonstrated differences in the distribution of patterns of security versus insecurity of attachment, according to both gender and socioeconomic context. However, neither gender nor socioeconomic context has been found to moderate the links between attachment security versus insecurity and outcomes for teens. The patterns of findings with regard to gender and socioeconomic context are somewhat more complex within the literature examining autonomy processes. As discussed below, there do appear to be some gender differences in the autonomy driven

shifts that occur in parent-teen relationships during adolescence, although the exact nature of those differences has been difficult to elucidate. Finally, the literature on socioeconomic context and autonomy development suggests both main effects and moderating effects of socioeconomic and contextual factors, as we will discuss below.

Attachment, Autonomy, and Gender

There are two main sets of questions to consider when examining the role of gender in parent–adolescent relationships. The first set concerns the possible differences between mother–adolescent and father–adolescent relationships, regardless of the gender of the teen. This area of research also includes whether there is differential prediction from qualities of mother–adolescent versus father–adolescent relationships. The second set of questions concerns possible differences in parent–teen relationships according to adolescents' gender, as well as possible moderating effects of adolescents' gender on the links between parent–teen relationship quality and adolescent outcomes. The examination of questions of gender effects is further complicated by methodological issues. With regard to attachment relationships, methods of assessment tend to focus on adolescents' overarching attachment models, and such methods supersede an examination of relationships with each parent separately. Similarly, one drawback to much of the self-report literature on autonomy development is that studies often assess adolescents' ratings of their relationships with both parents at once, rather than assessing the mother–adolescent and father–adolescent relationships separately (Eccles et al., 1997).

Results to date regarding effects of adolescent gender on attachment processes have been somewhat mixed. The majority of studies to date have not found gender differences with regard to distributions of secure, dismissing and preoccupied attachment representations, either as assessed via the AAI (Allen, Hauser, & Borman-Spurrell, 1996; Allen et al., 2004; Bernier et al., 2005;

Dykas, Woodhouse, Cassidy, & Waters, 2006; Scharf, 2001; Seiffge-Krenke, 2006; Spangler & Zimmermann, 1999; Zimmermann, 2004), or via self-report measures of attachment style (Hazan & Shaver, 1987; Schindler et al., 2005; Weimer et al., 2004). Studies that have found gender effects indicate that males may display higher levels of dismissing and deactivating tendencies, whereas females may demonstrate higher levels of preoccupation (Bartholomew & Horowitz, 1991; Kobak et al., 1993; Larose & Bernier, 2001). With regard to attachment hierarchies, studies have demonstrated that female adolescents tend to place mothers higher in their hierarchies than male adolescents, who tend to place fathers higher on their hierarchies than female adolescents (Markiewicz et al., 2006; Rosenthal & Kobak, 2007; Trinke & Bartholomew, 1997). However, gender does not appear to moderate links between attachment representations (or attachment hierarchies) and outcomes for teens: for both genders, secure attachment and reliance on parental figures (versus peers) for attachment needs is linked to more adaptive outcomes.

With regard to autonomy development, there is some support for the contention that mother–adolescent and father–adolescent relationships differ on a few dimensions, although not all students have found different patterns of interaction in mother–adolescent versus father–adolescent dyads. One relatively consistent finding is that the perturbations that occur in parent–adolescent relationships are somewhat more characteristic of mother-adolescent than father–adolescent dyads (Steinberg, 1987). Mothers are more likely than fathers to report problems in their relationships with their children as they enter adolescence, and mother–adolescent interactions become more conflictual and less supportive than father–adolescent interactions (Buchanan et al., 1990; Papini, Datan, & McClusky-Fawcett, 1988). However, adolescents tend to spend more time with their mothers, and are generally more likely to turn to mothers versus fathers for emotional support (Markiewicz et al., 2006; Rosenthal & Kobak, 2007; Trinke & Bartholomew, 1997).

With regard to autonomy and adjustment outcomes, some self-report research suggests that while both mothers' and fathers' approaches to autonomy support vs. inhibition have important implications for adolescents' adjustment, their relative contributions may depend both on both the outcomes being the examined and the gender of the adolescent (Conger, Conger, & Scaramella, 1997; Laible & Carlo, 2004). For example, one prospective study found gender differences in adolescent outcomes of variations in parental support versus inhibition of autonomy: autocratic parenting behaviors during preschool were associated with overcontrolled behavior in female late adolescents, but with undercontrolled behavior in male late adolescents (Kremen & Block, 1998). The observational research on autonomy and relatedness within parent–teen relationships has occasionally yielded results primarily for father–adolescent versus mother–adolescent dyads, but regardless of the adolescents' gender (Allen et al., 1994a; Grotevant & Cooper, 1985). Allen and colleagues (1994a) have hypothesized that fathers may take on a growing role in adolescence, and other authors have suggested that fathers play a particularly important role in shaping their children's relationships outside of the home (e.g., Crockenberg, Jackson, & Langrock, 1996; Youngblade & Belsky, 1995).

Results are even less clear regarding the moderating effects of adolescents' gender on the links between autonomy processes and adolescent outcomes. Studies often have revealed opposite conclusions, as well as complicated interactions between parents' and adolescents' gender, as suggested above. Studies have indicated, for example, that mother–*daughter* relationships become particularly disrupted and conflictual during adolescence (Buchanan et al., 1990; Holmbeck & Hill, 1991; Montemayor, 1982, 1986; Smetana, 1988a, 1989; Smetana, Daddis, & Chuang, 2003), although other research has not supported this pattern (Hill & Holmbeck, 1986; Smetana, Yau, & Hanson, 1991; Papini et al., 1988). There is additional evidence that adolescent girls perceive higher levels of autonomy support from parents, and are granted more input into family decision making (Beyers & Goossens, 1999; Brown & Mann, 1990; Flanagan, 1990; Fuligni & Eccles, 1993; Holmbeck & O'Donnell, 1991; Jacobs, Bennett, & Flanagan, 1993; Soenens et al., 2007). However, these differences may at least partially depend on the gender of the parent (Soenens & Vansteenkiste, 2005) and on other family characteristics, such as cultural context and parental attitudes toward gender roles (Bumpus, Crouter, & McHale, 1998; Daddis & Smetana, 2005). Further, as indicated above, most of the observational literature on autonomy development has not found any moderating effects of adolescent gender with regard to the concurrent and short-term links between parent–adolescent autonomy negotiation and adolescent outcomes (Allen et al., 1994a; 1994b; Allen et al., 1996; McElhaney & Allen, 2001).

In summary, there is some evidence that dyadic variations in parent–teen relationships do exist, though the exact nature of such variations is not entirely clear, and there are likely complex interactions between the gender of the adolescent and the gender of the parent. Mother–adolescent relationships may be most prone to the increased conflict and emotional distancing that has been described in the literature, though this may be purely a function of the nature and intensity of the different roles that mothers vs. fathers tend to play in their adolescents' daily lives. There is also some suggestion that fathers' approaches to autonomy support may be particularly important with regard to adolescents' social and emotional adjustment, though again there are inconsistencies in the data on this topic (e.g., Laible & Carlo, 2004). What does seem to be clear from the research to date is that attachment security versus insecurity does not generally vary according to gender, and that a secure state of mind with regard to attachment is linked to a range of positive outcomes for both genders. Further, promotion of autonomy

(particularly cognitive/verbal autonomy) also appears to be equally positive for both male and female teens (Allen et al., 1994a; Allen et al., 1996; McElhaney & Allen, 2001).

Attachment, Autonomy, and Socioeconomic Context

Studies of attachment processes during infancy and childhood show clear links between economic risk factors, including poverty, socioeconomic status and race/ethnic minority status and security vs. insecurity of attachment. Researchers have suggested that such factors impinge on attachment relationships via other classes of associated variables, including parental sensitivity and child maltreatment (e.g., Bakermans-Kranenburg, van Ijzendoorn, & Kroonenberg, 2004; Egelund & Sroufe, 1981). Similarly, during adolescence, both race/ethnic minority status and socioecomic status (SES) have been associated with security versus insecurity of attachment (Allen et al., 1996; Allen et al., 2003, 2004, 2007;). While some studies have not found SES differences in attachment security, these studies often have been comprised of mostly middle- to upper-income, two-parent households, thus with a relatively homogenous range of socioeconomic risk factors (e.g., Bernier et al., 2005; Seiffge-Krenke, 2006). However, despite the clear associations between these contextual risk factors and security of attachment, most studies to date have not found any moderating effects of these factors: Across all socioeconomic and racial groups, security of attachment is associated with positive outcomes.

A somewhat different picture emerges when examining the links between socioeconomic factors, autonomy processes, and outcomes. As suggested previously, parental responses to adolescent autonomy strivings require balancing the need to set limits on behavior and the need to provide adolescents with sufficient freedom to try out new behaviors and learn from mistakes (Allen, Kuperminc, & Moore, 1997; Holmbeck, Paikoff, & Brooks-Gunn, 1995). However, the appropriate balance between limit setting and encouragement of exploration may depend on contextual factors such as the level of complexity, challenge, and danger in the adolescent's environment (Bradley, 1995). Extensive anthropological theory and research suggests that parents' behaviors in socializing their children are strongly influenced by awareness of the traits that are considered necessary for survival and success (Barry, Child, & Bacon, 1959/67; Harkness & Super, 1995; Harrison, Wilson, Pine, Chan, & Buriel, 1990; Kohn, 1963, 1979; LeVine, 1980, 1988; Ogbu, 1981, 1988; Okagaki & Divecha, 1993). For example, parental appeals to prudential justifications—including concerns about health and safety—to resolve conflicts with their teens, have been found to be characteristic of certain subgroups of parents, particularly African American parents of male adolescents (Smetana et al., 2003).

Along those lines, it has been suggested that parental inhibition of autonomy—whether it is defined in behavioral terms (e.g., strict rules and consequences), and/or in cognitive terms (e.g., discouragement of individual expression)—is potentially more appropriate when greater independence may pose increased threats to the adolescent's well-being (Dubrow & Garbarino, 1989; Furstenberg, 1993; Smetana & Gaines, 1999). In less risky contexts, however, these same autonomy-inhibiting behaviors might be more likely to reflect a maladaptive parental reluctance to allow normative autonomy development to proceed (Baldwin, Baldwin, & Cole, 1990). Research focusing on parenting across social contexts does indicate that parents in high-risk contexts (e.g., lower SES) are more likely to use strategies emphasizing conformity and obedience, rather than those that promote independence and autonomy (Bartz & Levine, 1978; Dornbusch, Ritter, Leiderman, Roberts, & Fraleigh, 1987; Dubrow & Garbarino, 1989; Harkness & Super, 1995; Kelley, Sanchez-Hucles, & Walker, 1993). Even among a sample of middle-income African American families, for example, parental power assertion (and adolescents' acceptance of it) is more

common among the lower income ranges, whereas joint parent–adolescent decision making and adolescent rejection of parental authority are more common among the higher income families (Smetana, 2000; Smetana & Gaines, 1999). Parental approaches to autonomy granting have also been found to vary along ethnic and cultural lines, and the picture is further complicated when families from cultures that tend to place less emphasis on autonomy immigrate to places where autonomy is highly valued (Feldman & Quatman, 1988; Feldman & Wood, 1994; Fuligni, 1998; Rosenthal & Feldman, 1990).

Parental approaches to autonomy also appear to have different consequences for adolescent development in low versus high-risk contexts. Although results of this research have been somewhat mixed (Steinberg et al., 1991), several studies have found that adolescent reports of parents' authoritative parenting are *not* necessarily linked with positive outcomes in non-White, non-middle-class samples, whereas parenting styles involving a greater restriction of autonomy (i.e., authoritarian styles) are related to more positive child adjustment in these groups (Baumrind, 1972; Dornbusch et al., 1987; Dornbusch, Ritter, Mont-Reynaud, & Chen, 1990; Lamborn, Dornbusch, & Steinberg, 1996; Steinberg, Dornbusch, & Brown, 1992). Further, several recent surveys of parenting practices in primarily African American samples have demonstrated that the level of environmental risk moderates the links between parental restriction of autonomy and adolescent adjustment. In high-risk contexts within these samples, parental restriction of autonomy during early and middle adolescence is linked with positive indices of adjustment, including higher levels of academic competence, decreased externalizing behaviors, and more positive self-worth (Baldwin et al., 1990; Gonzales, Cauce, Friedman, & Mason, 1996; Mason, Cauce, Gonzales, & Hiraga, 1996; Smetana, Campione-Barr, & Daddis, 2004). Finally, one recent observational study found that adolescents from high-risk settings viewed mothers who were high on undermining of cognitive/verbal autonomy as more trustworthy and accepting; teens from low-risk settings, however, viewed highly undermining mothers as more psychologically controlling, and they reported feeling more alienated from them (McElhaney & Allen, 2001). In this same study, higher levels of adolescents' expressions of autonomy were linked to positive outcomes for low-risk teens (higher levels of competence with peers), but to negative outcomes for high-risk teens (higher levels of engagement in delinquent behaviors).

Social context clearly has important implications for both attachment and autonomy processes. The findings with regard to attachment relationships have been generally limited to main effects of socioeconomic factors on security versus insecurity of attachment states of mind. Research to date suggests that for all groups, secure attachment predicts more adaptive social and emotional functioning. In contrast, both main effects and moderating effects of socioeconomic context have been found with regard to the autonomy process. Parents who are raising teenagers in settings that pose increased risks to their health and well being tend to emphasize those issues more in their parenting, and exercise stricter controls over adolescents' autonomy. Further, in such high-risk contexts, this increased level of inhibition of autonomy generally does not appear to have the same negative correlates as are found in low-risk settings. It should be noted, however, that much of the work in this area is cross-sectional in nature, and has been conducted with samples of early to middle adolescents. It may be that restriction of autonomy does serve a protective function in the short term, which may or may not translate into adaptive outcomes later in life.

DIRECTIONS FOR FUTURE RESEARCH

Overall, there is empirical support for the integral nature of attachment security and autonomy development, and their importance both in terms of normative development and individual differences during adolescence. However, this field of research would benefit from further inquiry along a number of lines. With regard to normative development, very little research has examined stability versus instability in adolescent attachment security. More research is needed that examines the possible changes in attachment models that may occur during adolescence, including a closer examination of factors that may contribute to such changes.

Further, while research examining parent–adolescent relationships has yielded findings consistent with the notion that the balance in these relationships shifts toward increased autonomy and exploration, the variations in how autonomy has been conceptualized and operationally defined has complicated the research in this area. Studies rarely consider more than one aspect of autonomy development, and there is little exploration to date of how different types of autonomy are interrelated (e.g., intrapsychic and interfamilial), and/or whether they develop similarly within different interrpersonal contexts (e.g., within families versus within peer groups). Finally, the majority of the studies reported here focus on changes in aspects of parent–adolescent relationships that are more tangentially related to autonomy development, such as the nature and frequency of parent–teen conflict.

Further, while security of attachment and parental support for autonomy (across most facets) is clearly beneficial for most adolescents, there remain additional questions about the correlates of these important constructs. For example, small sample sizes have often precluded definitive conclusions about outcomes for preoccupied teens, and the pattern of moderating effects that has been found to date indicates that some of these teens may demonstrate adaptive outcomes in certain contexts. Along those lines, few studies have examined the joint effects of attachment security versus insecurity and autonomy processes in predicting adjustment outcomes for teens. Thus, the critical nature of establishing autonomy while maintaining relatedness largely remains untested. Finally, there is growing evidence the established links between parental support for autonomy and positive adaptation may be moderated by key aspects of adolescents' social, cultural and/or economic environments, though additional research in this area will help to specify which of those aspects may be most important. Whether and to what extent adolescents' gender plays a role in the nature and outcome of the autonomy process also has yet to be fully determined.

ENDNOTES

1. An additional self-report measure that has been utilized with adolescents is Armsden & Greenberg's Inventory of Parent and Peer Attachment (IPPA; 1987). The authors propose that adolescents' internal working models of attachment can be assessed by asking teens to report on how available and sensitive their caregivers are, as well as the degree to which teens experience anger or hopelessness as a result of unresponsiveness or inconsistency on the part of their caregivers. Although the IPPA has good psychometric properties and has been widely validated as a measure of parent–adolescent relationship quality, many attachment researchers do not consider it a measure of internal working models of attachment to parents. Most accurately, this measure appears to provide a general assessment of the current quality of the parent–adolescent relationship, without particular reference to attachment-relevant constructs (e.g., security, secure-base provision, caregiving under stress, etc.). Given these limitations, and the fact that the empirical overlap of this measure with other more widely validated measures of attachment organization (e.g., the AAI) is very low (Crowell, Treboux, & Waters, 1993; Zimmermann, 2004), studies primarily relying on the IPPA will not be reviewed here.

2. Some of the literature on behavioral autonomy also examines adolescents' functioning in peer relationships, encompassing such topics as peer pressure and peer influence. These topics are covered in chapter 16 of this volume, which provides an overview of adolescents' relationships with their peers.

3. At least one other questionnaire, the Adolescent Autonomy Questionnaire (Noom, Dekovic, & Meeus, 2001), has been developed for use with adolescents. This measure assesses attitudinal, emotional, and functional autonomy with no reference to the parent–adolescent relationship. Given our relational focus, this measure will not be reviewed here.

REFERENCES

Ainsworth, M. D. S. (1982). Attachment: Retrospect and prospect. In C. Parkes & J. Stevenson-Hinde (Eds.), *The place of attachment in human behavior*. New York: Basic Books.

Ainsworth, M. D. S. (1989). Attachments beyond infancy. *American Psychologist, 44*, 709–716.

Ainsworth, M. D. S., Blehar, M. C., Waters, E., & Wall, S. (1978). *Patterns of attachment: A psychological study of the strange situation*. Hillsdale, NJ: Lawrence Erlbaum.

Allen, J. P. (in press). The attachment system in adolescence. J. Cassidy & P. R. Shaver (Eds.), *Handbook of attachment theory and research* (2nd ed.). New York: Guilford Press.

Allen, J. P., Bell, K., & Boykin, K. A. (2000, March). *Autonomy in discussions vs. autonomy in decision-making as predictors of developing close friendship competence*. Paper presented at the Biennial Meetings of the Society for Research on Adolescence, Chicago, IL.

Allen, J. P., & Hauser, S. T. (1993, March). *Adolescent–family interactions: The unique roles of autonomy and relatedness as markers of development*. Paper presented at the Biennial Meeting of the Society for Research in Child Development, New Orleans, LA.

Allen, J. P., & Hauser, S. T. (1996). Autonomy and relatedness in adolescent–family interactions as predictors of young adults' states of mind regarding attachment. *Development & Psychopathology, 8*(4), 793–809.

Allen, J. P., Hauser, S. T., & Borman-Spurrell, E. (1996). Attachment theory as a framework for understanding sequelae of severe adolescent psychopathology: An 11-year follow-up study. *Journal of Consulting & Clinical Psychology, 64*(2), 254–263.

Allen, J. P., Hauser, S. T., Bell, K. L., McElhaney, K. B., Tate, D. C., Insabella, G. M., et al. (2000). *The autonomy and relatedness coding system*. Unpublished manuscript. University of Virginia.

Allen, J. P., Hauser, S. T., Bell, K. L., & O'Conner, T. G. (1994a). Longitudinal assessment of autonomy and relatedness in adolescent-family interactions as predictors of adolescent ego development and self-esteem. *Child Development, 65*, 179–194.

Allen, J. P., Hauser, S. T., Eickholt, C., Bell, K. L., & O'Conner, T. G. (1994b). Autonomy and relatedness in family interactions as predictors of adolescents' expressions of negative adolescent affect. *Journal of Research on Adolescence, 4*, 535–552.

Allen, J. P., Hauser, S. T., O'Conner, T. G., & Bell, K. L. (2002a). Prediction of peer-rated adult hostility from autonomy struggles in adolescent–family interactions. *Development and Psychopathology, 14*, 123–137.

Allen, J. P., Insabella, G. M., Porter, M. R., Smith, F. D., Land, D. J., & Phillips, N. (2006). A social-interactional model of the development of depressive symptoms in adolescence. *Journal of Consulting and Clinical Psychology, 74*(1), 55–65.

Allen, J. P., Kuperminc, G. P., & Moore, C. W. (1997). Developmental approaches to understanding adolescent deviance. In S. S. Luthar, J. A. Burack, D. Cicchetti, & J. Weisz (Eds.), *Developmental psychopathology: Perspectives on risk and disorder*. Cambridge: Cambridge University Press.

Allen, J. P., & Land, D. L. (1999). Attachment in adolescence. In J. Cassidy & P. R. Shaver (Eds.), *Handbook of attachment: Theory, research, and clinical applications* (pp. 319–335). New York: Guilford Press.

Allen, J. P., Marsh, P., McFarland, C., McElhaney, K. B., Land, D. J., Jodl, K. M., et al. (2002b). Attachment and autonomy as predictors of the development of social skills and delinquency during midadolescence. *Journal of Consulting & Clinical Psychology, 70*(1), 56–66.

Allen, J. P., McElhaney, K. B., Kuperminc, G. P., & Jodl, K. M. (2004). Stability and change in attachment security across adolescence. *Child Development, 75*, 1792–1805.

Allen, J. P., McElhaney, K. B., Land, D. J., Kuperminc, G. P., Moore, C. M., O'Beirne-Kelley, H., et al. (2003). A secure base in adolescence: Markers of attachment security in the mother–adolescent relationship. *Child Development, 74*, 292–307.

Allen, J. P., Moore, C., Kuperminc, G., & Bell, K. (1998). Attachment and adolescent psychosocial functioning. *Child Development, 69*(5), 1406–1419.

Allen, J. P., Porter, M. R., McFarland, F. C., McElhaney, K. B., & Marsh, P. A. (2007). The relation of attachment security to adolescents' paternal and peer relationships, depression, and externalizing behavior. *Child Development*, 78(4), 1222–1239.

Amato, P. R. (1989). Family processes and the competence of adolescents and primary school children. *Journal of Youth and Adolescence*, 18(1), 39–53.

Ammaniti, M., van Ijzendoorn, M. H., Speranza, A. M., & Tambelli, R. (2000). Internal working models of attachment during late childhood and early adolescence: An exploration of stability and change. *Attachment & Human Development*, 2, 328–346.

Anderson, B., LaVoie, J. C. & Dunkel, C. S. (2007). Individuation and parents as people: Measurement concerns regarding two aspects of autonomy. *Journal of Adolescence*, 30, 751–760.

Aquilino, W. S. & Supple, A. J. (2001). Long term effects of parenting practices during adolescence on well-being outcomes in young adulthood. *Journal of Family Issues*, 22, 289–308.

Armsden, G.,C., & Greenberg, M. T. (1987). The inventory of parent and peer attachment: Individual differences and their relationship to psychological well-being in adolescence. *Journal of Youth and Adolescence*, 16, 427–454.

Aspelmeier, J. E., & Kerns, K. A. (2003). Love and school: Attachment/exploration dynamics in college. *Journal of Social and Personal Relationships*, 20(1), 5–30.

Baer, J. (2002). Is family cohesion a risk or protective factor during adolescent development. *Journal of Marriage and Family*, 64(3), 668–675.

Bakermans-Kranenburg, M. J., van Ijzendoorn, M. H., & Kroonenberg, P. M. (2004). Differences in attachment security between African-American and white children: Ethnicity or socioeconomic status? *Infant Behavior & Development*, 27(3), 417–433.

Baldwin, A. L., Baldwin, C., & Cole, R. E. (1990). Stress-resistant families and stress-resistant children. In J. Rolf, A. S. Masten, D. Cicchetti, K. H. Nuechterlein, & S. Weintraub (Eds.), *Risk and protective factors in the development of psychopathology* (pp. 257–280). New York: Cambridge University Press.

Barber, B. K. (1996). Parental psychological control: Revisiting a neglected construct. *Child Development*, 67(6), 3296–3319.

Barber, B. K., & Harmon, E. (2002). *Violating the self:* Parental psychological control of children and adolescents. In B. K. Barber (Ed.), *Intrusive parenting: How psychological control affects children and adolescents*, pp. 15–52. Washington, DC: American Psychological Association.

Barber, B., & Olsen, J. (1997). Socialization in context: Connection, regulation, and autonomy in the family, school, and neighborhood with peers. *Journal of Adolescent Research*, 12(2), 287–315.

Barber, B. K., Olsen, J. E., & Shagle, S. C. (1994). Associations between parental psychological and behavioral control and youth internalized and externalized behaviors. *Child Development*, 65(4), 1120–1136.

Bartholomew, K., & Horowitz, L. M. (1991). Attachment styles among young adults: A test of a four-category model. *Journal of Personality and Social Psychology*, 61(2), 226–244.

Bartz, K. W., & Levine, E. S. (1978). Childrearing by Black parents: A description and comparison to Anglo and Chicano parents. *Journal of Marriage and the Family*, 40, 709–719.

Baltes, M. M., & Silverberg, S. B. (1994). The dynamics between dependency and autonomy: Illustrations across the life span. In D. L. Featherman, R. M. Lerner, & M. Perlmutter (Eds.), *Life span development and behavior*, vol. 12 (pp. 41–91). Mahwah, NJ: Lawrence Erlbaum.

Barry, H., III, Child, I. L., & Bacon, M. K. (1967). Relation of child training to subsistence economy. In C. S. Ford (Ed.), *Cross-cultural approaches: Readings in comparative research* (pp. 246–258). New Haven, CT: HRAF Press (Reprinted from *American Anthropologist*, 61, 51–63, 1959).

Baumrind, D. (1972). An exploratory study of socialization effects on Black children: Some Black–White comparisons. *Child Development*, 43, 261–267.

Baumrind, D. (1991). The influence of parenting style on adolescent competence and substance use. *Journal of Early Adolescence*, 11(1), 56–95.

Becker-Stoll, F., Delius, A., & Scheitenberger, S. (2001). Adolescents' nonverbal emotional expressions during negotiation of a disagreement with their mothers: An attachment approach. *International Journal of Behavioral Development*, 25(4), 344–353.

Becker-Stoll, F., & Fremmer-Bombik, E. (1997, April). *Adolescent–mother interaction and attachment: A longitudinal study.* Paper presented at the Biennial Meetings of the Society for Research in Child Development, Washington, DC.

Bednar, D. E., & Fisher, T. D. (2003). Peer referencing in adolescent decision making as a function of perceived parenting style. *Adolescence*, 38(152), 607–621.

Belsky, J., & Cassidy, J. (1994). Attachment: Theory and evidence. In M. Rutter & D. Hay (Eds.), *Development through life: A handbook for clinicians* (pp. 373–402). Oxford, UK: Blackbaum.

Bernier, A., Larose, S., & Whipple, N. (2005). Leaving home for college: A potentially stressful event for adolescents with preoccupied attachment patterns. *Attachment & Human Development*, 7(2), 171–185.

Beyers, W. & Goossens, L. (1999). Emotional autonomy, psychosocial adjustment and parenting: Interactions, moderating and mediating effects. *Journal of Adolescence*, 22(6), 753–769.

Beyers, W. & Goossens, L. (2003). Psychological separation and adjustment to university: Moderating effects of gender, age, and perceived parenting style. *Journal of Adolescent Research*, 18(4), 363–382.

Beyers, W., Goossens, L., Van Calster, B., & Duriez, B. (2005). An alternative substantive factor structure of the Emotional Autonomy Scale. *European Journal of Psychological Assessment*, 21(3), 147–155.

Beyers, W., Goossens, L., Vansant, I., & Moors, E. (2003). A structural model of autonomy in middle and late adolescence: Connectedness, separation, detachment and agency. *Journal of Youth and Adolescence*, 32(5), 351–365.

Blos, P. (1967). The second individuation process of adolescence. *Psychoanalytic Study of the Child*, 22,162–186.

Bosma, H. A., Jackson, S. E., Zijsling, D. H., Zani, B., Cicognani, E., Xerri, L., et al. (1996). Who has the final say? Decisions on adolescent behaviour within the family. *Journal of Adolescence*, 19(3), 277–291.

Bowlby, J. (1969/1982). *Attachment and loss*, vol. 1. New York: Basic Books.

Bradley, R. H. (1995). Environment and parenting. In M. H. Bornstein (Ed.), *Handbook of parenting: Biology and ecology of parenting*, vol. 2 (pp. 235–261). Mahwah, NJ: Lawrence Erlbaum.

Bretherton, I. (1992). The origins of attachment theory: John Bowlby and Mary Ainsworth. *Developmental Psychology*, 28(5), 759–775.

Brown, J. E., & Mann, L. (1990). The relationship between family structure and process variables and adolescent decision making. *Journal of Adolescence*, 13(1), 25–37.

Buchanan, C. M., Eccles, J. S., Flanagan, C. M., Midgely, C., Feldlaufer, J., & Harold, R. D. (1990). Parents' and teachers' beliefs about adolescents: Effects of sex and experience. *Journal of Youth and Adolescence*, 19, 363–394.

Bumpus, M. F., Crouter, A. C., & McHale, S. M. (1998). Parental autonomy granting during adolescence: Exploring gender differences in context. *Developmental Psychology*, 37(2), 163–173.

Cassidy, J. (1988). Child–mother attachment and the self in six-year-olds. *Child Development*, 59(1), 121–134.

Cassidy, J. (1999). The nature of the child's ties. In J. Cassidy & P. R. Shaver (Eds.), *Handbook of attachment: Theory, research, and clinical applications* (pp. 3–20). New York: Guilford Press.

Cassidy, J. (2001). Truth, lies, and intimacy: An attachment perspective. *Attachment & Human Development*, 3(2), 121–155.

Cassidy, J., Kirsh, S. J., Scolton, K. L., & Parke, R. D. (1996). Attachment and representations of peer relationships. *Developmental Psychology, 32*(5), 892–904.

Chango, J., McElhaney, K. B., & Allen, J. P. (2008, March). *Attachment organization and patterns of conflict resolution in friendships predicting adolescents' depressive symptoms over time.* Poster presented at the Biennial Meetings of the Society for Research on Adolescence, Chicago, IL.

Chen, Z., & Dornbusch, S. M. (1998). Relating specific aspects of adolescent emotional autonomy to academic achievement and deviant behavior. *Journal of Adolescent Research, 13,* 293–319.

Cole-Detke, H., & Kobak, R. (1996). Attachment processes in eating disorder and depression. *Journal of Consulting & Clinical Psychology, 64*(2), 282–290.

Collins, N. L., Cooper, M. F, Albino, A., & Allard, L. (2002). Psychosocial vulnerability from adolescence to adulthood: A prospective study of attachment style differences in relationship functioning and partner choice. *Journal of Personality, 70,* 965–1008.

Collins, N. L. & Read, S. J. (1990). Adult attachment, working models, and relationship quality in dating couples. *Journal of Personality and Social Psychology, 58*(4), 644–663.

Collins, W. A. (1990). Parent–child relationships in the transition to adolescence: Continuity and change in interaction, affect, and cognition. In R. Montemayor, G. R. Adams, & T. P. Gullotta (Eds.), *From Childhood to Adolescence: A Transitional Period? Advances in Adolescent Development,* vol.2 (pp. 85–106). Newbury Park: Sage.

Collins, W. A., & Laursen, B. (2000). Adolescent relationships: The art of fugue. In C. Hendrick & S. S. Hendrick (Eds.), *Close relationships: A sourcebook* (pp. 59–69). Thousand Oaks, CA: Sage.

Collins, W. A., & Steinberg, L. (2006). Adolescent development in interpersonal context. In N.Eisenberg, W.Damon, & R. M. Lerner (Eds.), *Handbook of child psychology,* vol. 3 (6th ed.; pp. 1003–1067). Hoboken, NJ: John Wiley & Sons.

Conger, K. J., Conger, R. D., & Scaramella, L. V. (1997) Parents, siblings, psychological control, and adolescent adjustment. *Journal of Adolescent Research. 12*(1), 113–138.

Cooper, C. R., Grotevant, H. D., & Condon, S. M. (1983). Individuality and connectedness in the family as a context for adolescent identity formation and role-taking skill. *New Directions for Child Development, 22,* 43–59.

Cooper, M. L., Shaver, P. R., & Collins, N. L. (1998). Attachment styles, emotion regulation, and adjustment in adolescence. *Journal of Personality & Social Psychology, 74*(5), 1380–1397.

Crockenberg, S., Jackson, S., & Langrock, A. M. (1996). Autonomy and goal attainment: Parenting, gender, and children's social competence. *New Directions for Child Development, 73,* 41–55.

Crowell, J., Treboux, D., & Waters, E. (1993, April). *Alternatives to the Adult Attachment Interview: Self-reports of attachment style and relationships with mothers and partners.* Paper presented at the biennial meetings of the Society for Research in Child Development, New Orleans, LA.

Crowell, J., Treboux, D., & Waters, E. (1999). The Adult Attachment Interview and the Relationship Questionnaire: Relations to reports of mothers and partners. *Personal Relationships, 6,* 1–18.

Csikszentmihalyi, M., & Larson, R. (1984). *Being adolescent: Conflict and growth in the teenage years.* New York: Basic Books.

Cummings, E. M., & Davies, P. (1996). Emotional security as a regulatory process in normal development and the development of psychopathology. *Development & Psychopathology, 8*(1), 123–139.

Daddis, C., & Smetana, J. (2005). Middle-class African American families' expectations for adolescents' behavioural autonomy. *International Journal of Behavioral Development, 29,* 371–381.

Darling, N., Cumsille, P., & Martinez, M. L. (2007) Adolescents as active agents in the socialization process: Legitimacy of parental authority and obligation to obey as predictors of obedience. *Journal of Adolescence, 30*(2), 297–311.

Davila, J., Steinberg, S. J., Kachadourian, L., Cobb, R., & Fincham, F. (2004). Romantic involvement and depressive symptoms in early and late adolescence: The role of a preoccupied relational style. *Personal Relationships, 11,* 161–178.

de Hass, M. A., Bakermans-Kranenburg, M. J., & van Ijzendoorn, M. H. (1994). The Adult Attachment Interview and questionnaires for attachment style, temperament and memories of parental behavior. *Journal of Genetic Psychology, 15,* 471–486.

Delaney, M. E. (1996). Across the transition to adolescence: Qualities of parent/adolescent relationships and adjustment. *Journal of Early Adolescence, 16*(3), 274–300.

Dornbusch, S. M., Ritter, P. L., Leiderman, P. H., Roberts, D. F., & Fraleigh, M. J. (1987). The relation of parenting style to adolescent school performance. *Child Development, 58,* 1244–1257.

Dornbusch, S. M., Ritter, P. L., Mont-Reynaud, R., & Chen, Z. (1990). Family decision-making and academic performance in a diverse high school population. *Journal of Adolescent Research, 5,* 143–160.

Douvan, E., & Adelson, J. (1966). *The adolescent experience.* New York: John Wiley & Sons.

Dowdney, L. (2000). Childhood bereavement following parental death. *Journal of Child Psychology and Psychiatry, 41*(7), 819–830.

Dubas, J. S., & Gerris, J. R. M. (2002). Longitudinal changes in the time parents spend in activities with their adolescent children as a function of child age, pubertal status and gender. *Journal of Family Psychology, 16*(4), 415–426.

Dubrow, N. F., & Garbarino, J. (1989). Living in the war zone: Mothers and young children in a public housing development. *Child Welfare, 68*(1), 3–20.

Ducharme, J., Doyle, A. B., & Markiewicz, D. (2002). Attachment security with mother and father: Associations with adolescents' reports of interpersonal behavior with parents and peers. *Journal of Social and Personal Relationships, 19*(2), 203–231.

Dykas, M. J., Woodhouse, S. S., Cassidy, J., & Waters, H. S. (2006). Narrative assessment of attachment representations: Links between secure base scripts and adolescent attachment. *Attachment & Human Development, 8*(3), 221–240.

Eccles, J. S., Early, D., Frasier, K., Belansky, E., & McCarthy, K. (1997). The relation of connection, regulation, and support for autonomy to adolescents' functioning. *Journal of Adolescent Research, 12*(2), 263–286.

Egeland, B., & Sroufe, L. A. (1981). Attachment and early maltreatment. *Child Development, 52*(1), 44–52.

Engels, R. C., Dekovic, M. E. & Meeus, W. (2002). Parenting practices, social skills and peer relationships in adolescence. *Social Behavior and Personality, 30*(1), 3–18.

Epstein, S. (1983). *Scoring and interpretation of the Mother–Father–Peer Scale.* Unpublished manuscript, University of Massachusetts, Department of Psychology, Amherst.

Feldman, S. S., & Quatman, T. (1988). Factors influencing age expectations for adolescent autonomy: A study of early adolescents and parents. *Journal of Early Adolescence, 8,* 325–343.

Feldman, S. S., & Wood, D. (1994). Parents' expectations for pre-adolescent sons' behavioral autonomy: A longitudinal study of correlates and outcomes. *Journal of Research on Adolescence, 4,* 45–70.

Finkenauer, C., Engels, R. C., & Meeus, W. (2002). Keeping secrets from parents: Advantages and disadvantages of secrecy in adolescence. *Journal of Youth and Adolescence, 31*(2), 123–136.

Flanagan, C. A. (1990). Change in family work status: Effects on parent-adolescent decision making. *Child Development, 61*(1), 163–177.

Fraley, R. C., & Davis, K. E. (1997). Attachment formation and transfer in young adults' close friendships and romantic relationships. *Personal Relationships, 4*, 131–144.

Frank, S., Schettini, A. M., & Lower, R. J. (2002). The role of separation–individuation experiences and personality in predicting externalizing and internalizing dimensions of functional impairment in a rural preadolescent and adolescent sample. *Journal of Clinical Child and Adolescent Psychology, 31*(4), 431–442.

Frank, S. J., Pirsch, L. A., & Wright, V. C. (1990). Late adolescents' perceptions of their relationships with their parents: Relationships among de-idealization, autonomy, relatedness, and insecurity, and implications for adolescent adjustment and ego identity status. *Journal of Youth and Adolescence, 19*, 571–589.

Freud, A. (1958). Adolescence. *Psychoanalytic Study of the Child, 13*, 255–278.

Fuhrmann, T., & Holmbeck, G. N. (1995). A contextual–moderator analysis of emotional autonomy and adjustment in adolescence. *Child Development, 66*(3), 793–811.

Fuligni, A. (1998). Authority, autonomy and parent–adolescent conflict and cohesion: A study of adolescents from Mexican, Chinese, Filipino and European backgrounds. *Developmental Psychology, 34*, 782–792.

Fuligni, A. J., & Eccles, J. S. (1993). Perceived parent–child relationships and early adolescents' orientation toward peers. *Developmental Psychology, 29*(4), 622–632.

Furman, W. (2001). Working models of friendships. *Journal of Social & Personal Relationships, 18*(5), 583–602.

Furman, W., Simon, V. A., Shaffer, L., & Bouchey, H. A. (2002). Adolescents' working models and styles for relationships with parents, friends, and romantic partners. *Child Development, 73*(1), 241–255.

Furstenberg, F. F. (1993). How families manage risk and opportunity in dangerous neighborhoods. In W. J. Wilson (Ed.), *Sociology and the public agenda* (pp. 231–257). Newbury Park, CA: Sage.

Galambos, N. L., Barker, E. T., & Almeida, D. M. (2003). Parents do matter: Trajectories of change in externalizing and internalizing problems in early adolescence. *Child Development, 74*(2), 578–594.

Garber, J., & Little, S. (2001). Emotional autonomy and adolescent adjustment. *Journal of Adolescent Research, 16*, 355–371.

Garber, J., Robinson, N. S., & Valentiner, D. (1997). The relation between parenting and adolescent depression: Self-worth as a mediator. *Journal of Adolescent Research, 12*(1), 12–33.

Gavin, L. A., & Furman, W. (1989). Age differences in adolescents' perceptions of their peer groups. *Developmental Psychology, 25*, 827–834.

Gavin, L. A., & Furman, W. (1996). Adolescent girls' relationships with mothers and best friends. *Child Development, 67*, 375–386.

George, C., Kaplan, N., & Main, M. (1996). *Adult Attachment Interview* (3rd ed.). Unpublished manuscript, Department of Psychology, University of California, Berkeley.

Goldstein, S. E., Davis-Kean, P. E., & Eccles, J. S. (2005). Parents, peers, and problem behavior: A longitudinal investigation of the impact of relationship perceptions and characteristics on the development of adolescent problem behavior. *Developmental Psychology, 41*(2), 401–413.

Gonzales, N. A., Cauce, A. M., Friedman, R. J., & Mason, C. A. (1996). Family, peer, and neighborhood influences on academic achievement among African-American adolescents: One-year prospective effects. *American Journal of Community Psychology, 24*(3), 365–387.

Goossens, L. (2006). The many faces of adolescent autonomy: Parent–adolescent conflict, behavioral decision-making, and emotional distancing. In S. Jackson & L. Goossens (Eds.), *Handbook of adolescent development* (pp. 135–153). New York: Psychology Press.

Graber, J. A., & Brooks-Gunn, J. (1999). "Sometimes I think that you don't like me." How mothers and daughter negotiate the transition into adolescence. In M. Cox and J. Brooks-Gunn

(Eds.), *Conflict and Cohesion in Families* (pp. 207–242). Mahwah, NJ: Lawrence Erlbaum.

Gray, M. R., & Steinberg, L. (1999). Unpacking authoritative parenting: Reassessing a multidimensional construct. *Journal of Marriage & the Family, 61*(3), 574–587.

Greenberg, M. T., Siegel, J. M., & Leitch, C. J. (1983). The nature and importance of attachment relationships to parents and peers during adolescence. *Journal of Youth and Adolescence, 12*(5), 373–386.

Grotevant, H. D., & Cooper, C. R. (1985). Patterns of interaction in family relationships and the development of identity exploration in adolescence. *Child Development, 56*, 415–428.

Guerrero, L. K. (1996). Attachment style differences in intimacy and involvement: A test of the four-category model. *Communication Monographs, 63*, 269–292.

Gutman, L. M., & Eccles, J. S. (2007). Stage–environment fit during adolescence: Trajectories of family relations and adolescent outcomes. *Developmental Psychology, 43*(2), 522–537.

Haemmerlie, F. M., Steen, S. C., & Benedicto, J. A. (1994). Undergraduates' conflictual independence, adjustment and alcohol use: The importance of the mother–student relationship. *Journal of Clinical Psychology, 50*, 644–650.

Hall, F. D. (2002, April). *African-American adolescents' observed autonomy and relatedness with their mothers as predictors of social competence.* Poster presented at the Biennial Meetings of the Society for Research on Adolescence, New Orleans, LA.

Hamilton, C. (2000). Continuity and discontinuity of attachment from infancy through adolescence. *Child Development, 71*, 690–694.

Harkness, S., & Super, C. M. (1995). Culture and parenting. In M. H. Bornstein (Ed.), *Handbook of parenting: Biology and ecology of parenting*, vol.2 (pp. 211–234). Mahwah, NJ: Lawrence Erlbaum.

Harrison, A. O., Wilson, M. N., Pine, C., Chan, S., & Buriel, R. (1990). Family ecologies of ethnic minority children. *Child Development, 61*(2), 347–362.

Hartup, W. W. (1992). Friendships and their developmental significance. In H. McGurk Ed.), *Childhood social development: Contemporary perspectives* (pp. 175–205). Hillsdale, NJ: Lawrence Erlbaum.

Harvey, M., & Byrd, M. (2000). Relationships between adolescents' attachment styles and family functioning. *Adolescence, 35*(138), 345–356.

Hauser, S. T., Powers, S. I., Noam, G. G., Jacobson, A. M., Weiss, B., & Follansbee, D. J. (1984). Familial contexts of adolescent ego development. *Child Development, 55*, 195–213.

Hazan, C., & Shaver, P. (1987). Romantic love conceptualized as an attachment process. *Journal of Personality and Social Psychology, 52*, 511–524.

Hazan, C., Hutt, M. J., Sturgeon, J., & Bricket, T. (1991, April). *The process of relinquishing parents as attachment figures.* Paper presented at the Biennial Meetings of the Social for Research in Child Development, Seattle, WA.

Hazan, C., & Ziefman, D. (1994). Sex and the psychological tether. In K. Bartholomew & D. Perlman (Eds.), *Attachment processes in adulthood* (pp. 151–178). London: Jessica Kingsley.

Herman, M. R., Dornbusch, S. M., Herron, M. C., & Herting, J. R. (1997). The influence of family regulation, connection, and psychological autonomy on six measures of adolescent functioning. *Journal of Adolescent Research, 12*(1), 34–67.

Hesse, E. (1999). The adult attachment interview: Historical and current perspectives. In J. Cassidy & P. R. Shaver (Eds.), *Handbook of attachment: Theory, research, and clinical applications* (pp. 395–433). New York: Guilford Press.

Hill, J. P., & Holmbeck, G. N. (1986). Attachment and autonomy during adolescence. *Annals of Child Development, 3*, 145–189.

Hoffman, J. A. (1984). Psychological separation of late adolescents from their parents. *Journal of Counseling Psychology, 31*, 170–178.

Hoffman, J. A., & Weiss, B. (1987). Family dynamics and presenting problems of college students. *Journal of Counseling Psychology, 34*, 157–163.

Holmbeck, G. N., & Hill, J. P. (1991). Conflictive engagement, positive affect, and menarche in families with seventh-grade girls. *Child Development, 62*(5), 1030–1048.

Holmbeck, G. N., & Leake, C. (1999). Separation–individuation and psychological adjustment in late adolescence. *Journal of Youth and Adolescence, 28*(5), 563–581.

Holmbeck, G. N., & McClanahan, G. (1994). Construct and content validity of the separation–individuation test of adolescence: A reply to Levine. *Journal of Personality Assessment, 62*, 168–172.

Holmbeck, G. N., & O'Donnell, K. (1991). Discrepancies between perceptions of decision making and behavioral autonomy. *New Directions for Child Development, 51*, 51–69.

Holmbeck, G. N., Paikoff, R. L., & Brooks-Gunn, J. (1995). Parenting adolescents. In M. H. Bornstein (Ed.), *Handbook of parenting,* vol.1: *Children and parenting* (pp. 91–118). Mahwah, NJ: Lawrence Erlbaum.

Januszewski, B., Turner, R., Guerin, L., & Flack, A. (1996, March). *Working models of attachment, sociosexual orientation, and sexual problems.* Paper presented at the Society for Research on Adolescence, Boston, MA.

Jensen, L. A., Arnett, J., Feldman, S. S., & Cauffman, E. (2004). The right to do wrong: Lying to parents among adolescents and emerging adults. *Journal of Youth and Adolescence, 33*(2), 101–112.

Karavasilis, L., Doyle, A. B., & Markiewicz, D. (2003). Associations between parenting style and attachment to mother in middle childhood and adolescence. *International Journal of Behavioral Development, 27*(2), 153–164.

Kelley, M. L., Sanchez-Hucles, J., & Walker, R. (1993). Correlates of disciplinary practices in working- to low-risk African American mothers. *Merrill-Palmer Quarterly, 39*, 252–264.

Kenny, M. E., & Donaldson, G. A. (1992). The relationship of parental attachment and psychological separation to the adjustment of first-year college women. *Journal of College Student Development, 33*(5), 431–438.

Kerr, M., & Stattin, H. (2000). What parents know, how they know it, and several forms of adolescent adjustment: Further support for a reinterpretation of monitoring. *Developmental Psychology, 36*(3), 366–380.

Kim, K. J., Conger, R. D., Lorenz, F. O., & Elder, G. H. (2001). Parent–adolescent reciprocity in negative affect and its relation to early adult social development. *Developmental Psychology, 37*(6), 775–790.

Kirsch, S. J., & Cassidy, J. (1997). Preschoolers' attention to and memory for attachment-related information. *Child Development, 68,* 1143–1153.

Kobak, R. R., & Cole, H. (1994). Attachment and meta-monitoring: Implications for adolescent autonomy and psychopathology. In D. Cicchetti & S. L. Toth (Eds.), *Disorders and dysfunctions of the self. Rochester symposium on developmental psychopathology,* vol. 5 (pp. 267–297). Rochester, NY: University of Rochester Press.

Kobak, R. R., Cole, H., Ferenz-Gillies, R., Fleming, W., & Gamble, W. (1993). Attachment and emotion regulation during mother–teen problem-solving: A control theory analysis. *Child Development, 64,* 231–245.

Kobak, R. R., & Sceery, A. (1988). Attachment in late adolescence: Working models, affect regulation and representations of self and others. *Child Development, 59,* 135–146.

Kohn, M. L. (1963). Social class and parent–child relationships: An interpretation. *American Journal of Sociology, 68*, 471–480.

Kohn, M. L. (1979). The effects of social class on parental values and practices. In D. Reiss & H. A. Hoffman (Eds.), *The American family: Dying or developing* (pp. 45–68). New York: Plenum Press.

Kremen, A. M., & Block, J. (1998). The roots of ego-control in young adulthood: Links with parenting in early childhood. *Journal of Personality and Social Psychology, 75*(4), 1062–1075.

Kreppner, K., & Ulrich, M. (1998). Talks to mom and dad and listen to what is in between: A differential approach to family communication and its impact on adolescent development. In M. Hofer, J. Younnis, & P. Noack (Eds.) *Verbal interaction and development in families with adolescents* (pp. 83–108). Stamford, CT: Ablex.

Laible, D., & Carlo, G. (2004). The differential relations of maternal and paternal support and control to adolescent social competence, self-worth, and sympathy. *Journal of Adolescent Research, 19*(6), 759–782.

Laible, D. J., & Thompson, R. A. (1998). Attachment and emotional understanding in preschool children. *Child Development, 34*, 1038–1045.

Lamborn, S. D., Dornbusch, S. M., & Steinberg, L. (1996). Ethnicity and community context as moderators of the relations between family decision making and adolescent adjustment. *Child Development, 67,* 283–301.

Lamborn, S. D., & Steinberg, L. (1993). Emotional autonomy redux: Revisiting Ryan and Lynch. *Child Development, 64*(2), 483–499.

Lamborn, S. D., Mounts, N. S., Steinberg, L., & Dornbusch, S. M. (1991). Patterns of competence and adjustment among adolescents from authoritative, authoritarian, indulgent and neglectful families. *Child Development, 62*, 573–582.

Lapsley, D. K., & Edgerton, J. (2002). Separation–individuation, adult attachment style, and college adjustment. *Journal of Counseling & Development, 80*(4), 484–492.

Lapsley, D. K., Rice, K. G., & Shadid, G. E. (1989). Psychological separation and adjustment to college. *Journal of Counseling Psychology, 36*, 286–294.

Larose, S., & Bernier, A. (2001). Social support processes: Mediators of attachment state of mind and adjustment in late adolescence. *Attachment & Human Development, 3*(1), 96–120.

Larson, R., Coy, K., & Collins, W. A. (1998). Reconsidering changes in parent–adolescent conflict across adolescence: A meta-analysis. *Child Development, 69,* 817–832.

Larson, R., & Richards, M. H. (1989). Introduction: The changing life space of early adolescence. *Journal of Youth and Adolescence,* Special issue: The changing life space of early adolescence, *18*(6), 501–509.

Larson, R., & Richards, M. H. (1991). Daily companionship in late childhood and early adolescence: Changing developmental contexts. *Child Development, 62*(2), 284–300.

Larson, R., Richards, M. H., & Moneta, G. (1996). Changes in adolescents' daily interactions with their families from ages 10 to 18: Disengagement and transformation. *Developmental Psychology, 32*(4), 744–754.

Lee, J., & Bell, N. J. (2003). Individual differences in attachment–autonomy configurations: Linkages with substance use and youth competencies. *Journal of Adolescence, 26*(3), 347–361.

LeVine, R. A. (1980). A cross-cultural perspectives on parenting. In M. D. Fantini & R. Cardenas (Eds.), *Parenting in a Multicultural Society* (pp. 17–26). New York: Longman.

LeVine, R. A. (1988). Human parental care: Universal goals, cultural strategies, individual behavior. In R. A. Levine, P. M. Miller, & M. M. West (Eds.), *Parental behavior in diverse societies,* New Directions for Child Development, No. 40, (pp. 3–11). San Francisco: Josey-Bass.

Levine, J. B., Green, C. J., & Millon, T. (1986). The Separation-Individuation Test of Adolescence. *Journal of Personality Assessment, 50*(1), 123–137.

Levpušcek, M. P. (2006). Adolescent individuation in relation to parents and friends: Age and gender differences. *European Journal of Developmental Psychology, 3*(3), 238–264.

Lewis, M., Feiring, C., & Rosenthal, S. (2000). Attachment over time. *Child Development, 71*, 707–720.

Lieberman, M., Doyle, A.-B., & Markiewicz, D. (1999). Developmental patterns in security of attachment to mother and father in late childhood and early adolescence: Associations with peer relations. *Child Development, 70*(1), 202–213.

Lopez, F. G., Campbell, V. L., & Watkins, C. E. (1988). Family structure, psychological separation and college adjustment: A canonical analysis and cross-validation. *Journal of Counseling Psychology, 35,* 402–409.

Maccoby, E. E., & Martin, J. A. (1983). Socialization in the context of the family: Parent–child interaction. In E. M.Hetherington (Vol. Ed.) & P.H. Mussen (Series Ed.), *Handbook of child psychology,* vol. 4: *Socialization, personality, and social development* (pp.1–101). New York: John Wiley & Sons.

Mahler, M. S., & Furer, M. (1968). *On human symbiosis and the vicissitudes of individuation: I. Infantile psychosis.* Oxford, England: International Universities Press.

Main, M., & Goldwyn, R. (1998). *Adult attachment scoring and classification system.* Unpublished manuscript, University of California at Berkeley.

Main, M., Kaplan, N., & Cassidy, J. (1985). Security in infancy, childhood, and adulthood: A move to the level of representation. In I. Bretherton & E. Waters (Eds.), *Growing points in attachment theory and research, Monographs of the society for research in child development, vol. 50* (serial no. 209), 66–104.

Main, M., & Weston, D. (1981). The quality of the toddler's relationship to mother and father: Related to conflict behavior and the readiness to establish new relationships. *Child Development, 52,* 932–940.

Manning, N., Stephenson, C., & Allen, J. P. (2008, March). *Early adolescent predictors of future ego resiliency.* Poster presented at the Biennial Meetings of the Society for Research on Adolescence, Chicago, IL.

Markiewicz, D., Doyle, A. B., & Brendgen, M. (2001). The quality of adolescents' friendships: Associations with mothers' interpersonal relationships, attachments to parents and friends, and prosocial behaviors. *Journal of Adolescence, 24,* 429–445.

Markiewicz, D., Lawford, H., & Doyle, A. B. (2006). Developmental differences in adolescents' and young adults' use of mothers, fathers, best friends, and romantic partners to fulfill attachment needs. *Journal of Youth and Adolescence, 35*(1), 127–140.

Marsh, P., McFarland, F. C, Allen, J. P., McElhaney, K. B., & Land, D. J. (2003). Attachment, autonomy, and multifinality in adolescent internalizing and risky behavioral symptoms. *Development and Psychopathology, 15*(2), 451–467.

Marsh, P. A., & McFarland, F. C. (2002, April). Adolescent sociometric status: Links to observational assessments of autonomy and relatedness with mothers and fathers. Poster presented at the Biennial Meetings of the Society for Research on Adolescence, New Orleans, LA.

Marston, E., Hare, A., Miga, E., & Allen, J. P. (2008, March). *Adolescent romantic relationships: The impact of rejection sensitivity and the moderating role of attachment security.* Poster presented at the Biennial Meetings of the Society for Research on Adolescence, Chicago, IL.

Mason, C. A., Cauce, A. M., Gonzales, N., & Hiraga, Y. (1996). Neither too sweet nor too sour: Problem peers, maternal control, and problem behavior in African-American adolescents. *Child Development, 67,* 2115–2130.

Mayseless, O. (2004). Home leaving to military service: Attachment concerns, transfer of attachment functions from parents to peers, and adjustment. *Journal of Adolescent Research, 19*(5), 533–558.

Mayseless, O., & Sagi, A. (1994). *The association between the Adult Attachment Interview and attachment patterns in romantic relationships.* Paper presented at the 7th International Conference on Personal Relationships, Groningen, Netherlands.

Mayseless, O., & Scharf, M. (2007). Adolescents' attachment representations and their capacity for intimacy in close relationships. *Journal of Research on Adolescence, 17*(1), 23–50.

Mayseless, O., Sharabany, R., & Sagi, A. (1997). Attachment concerns of mothers as manifested in parental, spousal, and friendship relationships. *Personal Relationships, 4*(3), 255–269.

McClanahan, G., & Holmbeck, G. N. (1992). Separation–individuation, family functioning, and psychological adjustment in college students: A construct validity study of the Separation–Individuation Test of Adolescence. *Journal of Personality Assessment, 59*(3), 468–485.

McElhaney, K. B. (2000). *Autonomy and relatedness in the transition to adulthood: Predictors of functioning in close relationships from age 16 to age 18.* Unpublished doctoral dissertation. University of Virginia, Charlottesville, VA.

McElhaney, K. B., & Allen, J. P. (2001). Autonomy and adolescent social functioning: The moderating effect of risk. *Child Development, 72,* 220–231.

McElhaney, K. B., Immele, A., Smith, F. D., & Allen, J. P. (2006). Attachment organization as a moderator of the link between peer relationships and adolescent delinquency. *Attachment & Human Development, 8,* 33–46.

Meeus, W., Iedema, J., Maassen, G., & Engels, R. (2005). Separation–individuation revisited: On the interplay of parent–adolescent relations, identity and emotional adjustment in adolescence. *Journal of Adolescence, 28*(1), 89–106.

Mikulincer, M. (1995). Attachment style and the mental representation of the self. *Journal of Personality and Social Psychology, 69,* 1203–1215.

Mikulincer, M., & Erev, I. (1991). Attachment style and structure of romantic love. *British Journal of Social Psychology, 30,* 273–291.

Mikulincer, M., & Florian, V. (1995). Appraisal of and coping with real-life stressful situations: The contributions of attachment styles. *Personality and Social Psychology Bulletin, 21,* 406–414.

Mikulincer, M., & Florian, V. (1998). The relationship between adult attachment styles and emotional and cognitive reactions to stressful events. In J. A. Simpson & W. S. Rhodes (Eds.), *Attachment theory and close relationships* (pp. 143–165). New York: Guilford Press.

Moffitt, T. E. (1993). Adolescence-limited and life-course-persistent antisocial behavior: A developmental taxonomy. *Psychological Review, 100,* 674–701.

Montemayor, R. (1982). The relationship between parent–adolescent conflict and the amount of time adolescents spend alone and with parents and peers. *Child Development, 53,* 1512–1519.

Montemayor, R. (1983). Parents and adolescents in conflict: All families some of the time and some families most of the time. *Journal of Early Adolescence, 3*(1), 83–103.

Montemayor, R. (1986). Family variation in parent–adolescent storm and stress. *Journal of Adolescent Research, 1*(1), 15–31.

Montemayor, R., & Brownlee, J. R. (1987). Fathers, mothers, and adolescents: Gender-based differences in parental roles during adolescence. *Journal of Youth and Adolescence, 16*(3), 281–291.

Murphey, E. B., Silber, E., Coelho, G. V., Hamburg, D. A., & Greenberg, I. (1963). Development of autonomy and parent–child interaction in late adolescence. *American Journal of Orthopsychiatry, 33,* 643–652.

Nickerson, A. B., & Nagle, R. J. (2005). Parent and peer attachment in late childhood and early adolescence. *Journal of Early Adolescence, 25*(2), 223–249.

Noom, M. J., Dekovic. M., & Meeus, W. (2001). Conceptual analysis and measurement of adolescent autonomy. *Journal of Youth and Adolescence, 30*(5), 577–595.

Ogbu, J. U. (1981). Origins of human competence: A cultural–ecological perspective. *Child Development, 52*(2), 413–429.

Ogbu, J. U. (1988). Cultural diversity and human development. *New Directions for Child Development, 42,* 11–28.

Okagaki, L., & Divecha, D. J. (1993). Development of parental beliefs. In T. Luster & L. Okagaki (Eds.), *Parenting: An ecological perspective* (pp. 35–67). Hillsdale, NJ: Lawrence Erlbaum.

Paikoff, R. L., Collins, W. A., & Laursen, B. (1988). Perceptions of efficacy and legitimacy of parental influence techniques by children and early adolescents. *Journal of Early Adolescence, 8*(1), 37–52.

Palladino, D. E., & Blustein, D. L. (1994). Role of adolescent–parent relationships in college student development and adjustment. *Journal of Counseling Psychology, 41,* 248–255.

Papini, D. R., Datan, N., & McCluskey-Fawcett, K. A. (1988). An observational study of affective and assertive family interactions during adolescence. *Journal of Youth and Adolescence, 17,* 477–492.

Perkins, S. A., & Turiel, E. (2007). To lie or not to lie: To whom and under what circumstances. *Child Development, 78*(2), 609–621.

Pettit, G. S., Laird, R. D., Dodge, K. A., Bates, J.E., & Criss, M.M. (2001). Antecedents and behavior-problem outcomes of parental monitoring and psychological control in early adolescence. *Child Development, 72*(2), 583–598.

Pinquart, M., & Silbereisen, R. K. (2002). Changes in adolescents' and mothers' autonomy and connectedness in conflict discussions: An observation study. *Journal of Adolescence, 25,* 509–522.

Power, T. G., Francis, T. J., & Hughes, S. O. (1992). *Is emotional autonomy really detachment? Another look.* Paper presented at the fourth biennial meeting of the Society for Research on Adolescence, Washington, DC.

Reimer, M. S., Overton, W. F., Steidl, J. H., Rosenstein, D. S., & Horowitz, H. (1996). Familial responsiveness and behavioral control: Influences on adolescent psychopathology, attachment, and cognition. *Journal of Research on Adolescence, 6*(1), 87–112.

Repinski, D. J., & Zook, J. M. (2005). Three measures of closeness in adolescents' relationships with parents and friends: Variations and developmental significance. *Personal Relationships, 12*(1), 79–102.

Rice, K. G. (1990). Attachment in adolescence: A narrative and meta-analytic review. *Journal of Youth and Adolescence, 19*(5), 511–538.

Rice, K. G. (1992). Separation–individuation and adjustment to college: A longitudinal study. *Journal of Counseling Psychology, 39,* 203–213.

Rice, K. G., Cole, D. A., & Lapsley, D. K. (1990). Separation–individuation, family cohesion and adjustment to college: Measurement validation and test of a theoretical model. *Journal of Counseling Psychology, 37,* 195–202.

Ricks, M. H. (1985). The social transmission of parental behavior: Attachment across generations. *Monographs of the Society for Research in Child Development, 50,* 211–227.

Rogers, K. N., Buchanan, C. M., & Winchel, M. E. (2003). Psychological control during early adolescence: Links to adjustment in differing parent/adolescent dyads. *Journal of Early Adolescence, 23*(4), 349–383.

Roisman, G. I. (2006). The role of adult attachment security in non-romantic, non-attachment-related first interactions between same-sex strangers. *Attachment and Human Development, 8*(4), 351–362.

Roisman, G. I. (2007). The psychophysiology of adult attachment relationships: Autonomic reactivity in marital and premarital interactions. *Developmental Psychology, 43*(1), 39–53.

Roisman, G. I., Madsen, S. D., Hennighausen, K. H., Sroufe, L. A., & Collins, W. A. (2001). The coherence of dyadic behavior across parent–child and romantic relationships as mediated by the internalized representation of experience. *Attachment & Human Development, 3*(2), 156–172.

Roisman, G. I., Collins, W. A., Sroufe, L. A., & Egeland, B. (2005). Predictors of young adults' representations of and behavior in their current romantic relationship: Prospective tests of the prototype hypothesis. *Attachment and Human Development, 7*(2), 105–121.

Rosenstein, D. S., & Horowitz, H. A. (1996). Adolescent attachment and psychopathology. *Journal of Consulting & Clinical Psychology, 64*(2), 244–253.

Rosenthal, D., & Feldman, S. (1990). The acculturation of Chinese immigrants: The effects on family functioning of length of residence in two cultural contexts. *Journal of Genetic Psychology, 151,* 493–514.

Rosenthal, N., & Kobak, R. R. (2007). *Assessment adolescent attachment hierarchies: Individual differences and developmental change.* Unpublished manuscript, University of Delaware.

Ruck, M. D., Peterson-Badali, M., & Day, D. M. (2002). Adolescents' and mothers' understanding of children's rights in the home. *Journal of Research on Adolescence, 12* (3), 373–398.

Ryan, R. M., Deci, E. L., Grolnick, W. S., & La Guardia, J. G. (2006). The significance of autonomy and autonomy support in psychological development and psychopathology. In D. Cicchetti & D. Cohen (Eds.), *Developmental psychopathology,* vol 1: *Theory and method* (2nd ed.; pp. 795–849). Hoboken, NJ: John Wiley & Sons.

Ryan, R. M., & Lynch, J. H. (1989). Emotional autonomy versus detachment: Revisiting the vicissitudes of adolescence and young adulthood. *Child Development, 60*(2), 340–356.

Schaefer, E. S. (1965). Children's reports of parental behavior: An inventory. *Child Development, 36,* 413–424.

Scharf, M. (2001). A "natural experiment" in childrearing ecologies and adolescents' attachment and separation representations. *Child Development, 72,* 236–251.

Scharf, M., Mayseless, O., & Kivenson-Baron, I. (2004). Adolescents' attachment representations and developmental tasks of emerging adulthood. *Developmental Psychology, 40*(3), 430–444.

Schindler, A., Thomasius, R., Sack, P., Gemeinhardt, B., Kustner, U., & Eckert, J. (2005). Attachment and substance use disorders: A review of the literature and a study in drug dependent adolescents. *Attachment & Human Development, 7*(3), 207–228.

Schmitz, M. F., & Baer, J. C. (2001). The vicissitude of measurement: A confirmatory factor analysis of the Emotional Autonomy Scale. *Child Development, 72*(1), 207–219.

Seiffge-Krenke, I. (2006). Coping with relationship stressors: The impact of different working models of attachment and links to adaptation. *Journal of Youth and Adolescence, 35*(1), 25–39.

Seiffge-Krenke, I., & Beyers, W. (2005). Coping trajectories from adolescence to young adulthood: Links to attachment state of mind. *Journal of Research on Adolescence, 15*(1), 561–582.

Seigel, M., & Cowen, J. (1984). Appraisals of intervention: The mother's versus the culprit's behavior as determinants of children's evaluations of discipline techniques. *Child Development, 55,* 1760–1766.

Selman, R. (1980). *The growth of interpersonal understanding: Developmental and clinical analyses.* New York: Academic Press.

Seuss, G., Grossmann, K. E., & Sroufe, L. A. (1992). Effects of infant attachment to mother and father on quality of adaptation in preschool: From dyadic to individual organization of self. *International Journal of Behavioral Development, 15,* 43–65.

Shaver, P. R., Belsky, J., & Brennan, K. A. (2000). The adult attachment interview and self-reports of romantic attachment: Associations across domains and methods. *Personal Relationships, 7,* 25–43.

Silk, J. S., Morris, A. S., & Kanaya, T. (2003). Psychological control and autonomy granting: Opposite ends of a continuum or distinct constructs? *Journal of Research on Adolescence, 13*(1), 113–128.

Silverberg, S. B., & Gondoli, D. M. (1996). Autonomy in adolescence: A contextualized perspective. In G. R. Adams, R. Montemayor, & T. P. Gullota (Eds.), *Psychosocial development during adolescence: Progress in developmental contextualism* (pp. 89–109). Thousand Oaks, CA: Sage.

Silverman, P. R., Nickman, S., & Worden, J. W. (1992). Detachment revisited: The child's reconstruction of a dead parent. *American Journal of Orthopsychiatry*, *62*(4), 494–503.

Silverman, P. R., & Worden, J. W. (1992). Children's reactions in the early months after the death of a parent. *American Journal of Orthopsychiatry*, *62*(1), 93–104.

Smetana, J. G. (1988a). Adolescents' and parents' conceptions of parental authority. *Child Development*, *59*, 321–335.

Smetana, J. G. (1988b). Concepts of self and social convention: Adolescents' and parents' reasoning about hypothetical and actual family conflicts. In M. Gunnar & W. A. Collins (Eds.), *Development during transition to adolescence: Minnesota symposia on child psychology*, vol. *21* (pp. 79–122). Hillsdale, NJ: Lawrence Erlbaum.

Smetana, J. G. (1989). Adolescents' and parents' reasoning about actual family conflict. *Child Development*, *60*, 1052–1067.

Smetana, J. G. (2000). Middle-class African American adolescents' and parents' conceptions of parental authority and parenting practices: A longitudinal investigation. *Child Development*, *71*(6), 1672–1686.

Smetana, J. G., Braeges, J. L, & Yau, J. (1991). Doing what you say and saying what you do: Reasoning about adolescent–parent conflict interviews and interactions. *Journal of Adolescent Research*, *6*(3), 276–295.

Smetana, J. G., Campione-Barr, N., & Daddis, C. (2004). Longitudinal development of family decision making: Defining healthy behavioral autonomy for middle-class African American adolescents. *Child Development*, *75*(5), 1418–1434.

Smetana, J. G., Daddis, C., & Chuang, S. S. (2003). "Clean your room!": A longitudinal investigation of adolescent–parent conflict and conflict resolution in middle-class African American families. *Journal of Adolescent Research*, *18*(6), 631–650.

Smetana, J. G., & Gaines, C. (1999). Adolescent–parent conflict in middle-class African American families. *Child Development*, *70*(6), 1447–1463.

Smetana, J. G., Metzger, A., Gettman, D. C., Campione-Barr, N. (2006). Disclosure and secrecy in adolescent–parent relationships. *Child Development*, *77*(1), 201–217.

Smetana, J. G., Yau, J. & Hanson, S. (1991). Conflict resolution in families with adolescents. *Journal of Research on Adolescence*, *1*(2), 189–206.

Soenens, B., & Vansteenkiste, M. (2005). Antecedents and outcomes of self-determination in 3 life domains: The role of parents' and teachers' autonomy support. *Journal of Youth and Adolescence*, *34*(6), 589–604.

Soenens, B., Vansteenkiste, M., Lens, W., Luyckx, K., Goossens, L., Beyers, W., et al. (2007). Conceptualizing parental autonomy support: Adolescent perceptions of promotion of independence vs. promotion of volitional functioning. *Developmental Psychology*, *43*(3), 633–646.

Soenens, B., Vansteenkiste, M., & Luyten, P. (2005). Maladaptive perfectionistic self-representations: The mediational link between psychological control and adjustment. *Personality and Individual Differences*, *38*(2), 487–498.

Spangler, G., & Zimmermann, P. (1999). Attachment representation and emotion regulation in adolescents: A psychobiological perspective on internal working models. *Attachment & Human Development*, *1*(3), 270–290.

Spear, L. P. (2000). Neurobehavioral changes in adolescence. *Current Directions in Psychological Science*, *9*(4), 111–114.

Sroufe, L. A. (2005). Attachment and development: A prospective, longitudinal study from birth to adulthood. *Attachment and Human Development*, *7*(4), 349–367.

Steinberg, L. (1987). Impact of puberty on family relations: Effects of pubertal status and pubertal timing. *Developmental Psychology*, *23*(3), 451–460.

Steinberg, L. (2005). *Adolescence*. New York: McGraw-Hill.

Steinberg, L., Dornbusch, S. M., & Brown, B. B. (1992). Ethnic differences in adolescent achievement: An ecological perspective. *American Psychologist*, *47*, 723–729.

Steinberg, L., Elmen, J. D., & Mounts, N. S. (1989). Authoritative parenting, psychosocial maturity, and academic success among adolescents, *Child Development*, *60*(6), 1424–1436.

Steinberg, L., Lamborn, S. D., Darling, N., Mounts, N. S., & Dornbusch, S. M. (1994). Over time change in adjustment and competence among adolescents from authoritative, authoritarian, indulgent, and neglectful families. *Child Development*, *65*, 754–770.

Steinberg, L., Mounts, N. S., Lamborn, S. D., & Dornbusch, S. M. (1991). Authoritative parenting and adolescent adjustment across varied ecological niches. *Journal of Research on Adolescence*, *1*, 19–36.

Steinberg, L., & Silverberg, S. B. (1986). The vicissitudes of autonomy in early adolescence. *Child Development*, *57*(4), 841–851.

Stierlin, H. (1974). *Separating parents and adolescents: A perspective on running away, schizophrenia, and waywardness*. Oxford, UK: Quadrangle.

Stoppelbein, L., & Greening, L. (2000). Posttraumatic stress symptoms in parentally bereaved children and adolescents. *American Academy of Child & Adolescent Psychiatry*, *39*(9), 1112–1119.

Tencer, H., Meyer, J., & Hall, F. (2003, April). *Maternal psychological control: Links to close friendship and depression in early adolescence*. Poster presented at the Biennial Meetings of the Society for Research in Child Development, Tampa, FL.

Tracy, J. L., Shaver, P. R., Albino, A. W., & Cooper, M. L. (2003). Attachment styles and adolescent sexuality. In P. Florsheim (Ed.), *Adolescent romantic relations and sexual behavior: Theory, research, and practical implications* (pp. 137–159). Mahwah, NJ: Lawrence Erlbaum.

Trinke, S. J., & Bartholomew, K. (1997). Heirarchies of attachment relationships in young adulthood. *Journal of Social and Personal Relationships*, *14*(5), 602–625.

Turner, R. A., Irwin, C. E., Tschann, J. M., & Millstein, S. G. (1993). Autonomy, relatedness and the intitiation of health risk behaviors in early adolescence. *Health Psychology*, *12*, 200–208.

VanEerdewegh, M. M., Bieri, M. D., Parrilla, R. H., & Clayton, P. J. (1982). The bereaved child. *British Journal of Psychiatry*, *140*, 23–29.

VanEerdewegh, M. M., Clayton, P. J., & VanEerdewegh, P. (1985). The bereaved child: Variables influencing early psychopathology. *British Journal of Psychiatry*, *147*, 188–194.

Vaughn, B., Egeland, B., Sroufe, L. A., & Waters, E. (1979). Individual differences in infant–mother attachment at twelve and eighteen months: Stability and change in families under stress. *Child Development*, *50*, 971–975.

Wallis, P., & Steele, H. (2001). Attachment representations in adolescence: Further evidence from psychiatric residential settings. *Attachment & Human Development*, *3*(3), 259–268.

Ward, M. J., & Carlson, E. A. (1995). Associations among adult attachment representations, maternal sensitivity, and infant-mother attachment in a sample of adolescent mothers. *Child Development*, *66*, 69–79.

Waters, E. (1978). The reliability and stability of infant–mother attachment. *Child Development*, *49*, 482–494.

Weimer, B. L., Kerns, K. A., & Oldenberg, C. M. (2004). Adolescents' interactions with a best friend: Associations with attachment style. *Journal of Experimental Child Psychology*, *88*(1), 102–120.

Weinfeld, N. S., Whaley, G. J. L., & Egeland, B. (2004). Continuity, discontinuity and coherence in attachment from infancy to late adolescence: Sequelae of organization and disorganization. *Attachment and Human Development*, *6*(1), 73–97.

Youngblade, L. M. & Belsky, J. (1995). From family to friend: Predicting positive dyadic interaction with a close friend at 5 years of age from early parent–child relations. In S. Shulman (Ed.), *Close Relationships and Socioemotional Development: Human Development*, vol.7. Norwood, NJ: Ablex.

Zimmer-Gembeck, M. J., & Collins, W. A. (2003). Autonomy development during adolescence. In G. R. Adams & M. D. Berzonsky (Eds.), *Blackwell handbook of adolescence* (pp. 175–204). Malden, MA: Blackwell.

Zimmermann. P. (1999). Structure and function of internal working models of attachment and their role for emotional regulation. *Attachment and Human Development*, *1*, 55–71.

Zimmermann, P. (2004). Attachment representations and characteristics of friendship relations during adolescence. *Journal of Experimental Child Psychology*, *88*(1), 83–101.

Zimmermann, P., & Becker-Stoll, F. (2002). Stability of attachment representations during adolescence: The influence of ego-identity status. *Journal of Adolescence, 25*(1), 107–124.

Zimmermann, P., Maier, M. A., Winter, M., & Grossmann, K. E. (2001). Attachment and adolescents' emotion regulation during a joint problem-solving task with a friend. *International Journal of Behavioral Development, 25*(4), 331–343.

CHAPTER 12

Schools, Academic Motivation, and Stage–Environment Fit

JACQUELYNNE S. ECCLES AND ROBERT W. ROESER

From the time individuals first enter school until they complete their formal schooling, children and adolescents spend more time in schools than in any other place outside their homes. Exploring all of the possible ways in which educational institutions influence motivation and development during adolescence is beyond the scope of a single chapter. In this chapter, we discuss the ways in which schools influence adolescents' social–emotional and behavioral development through organizational, social, and instructional processes ranging from those based in the immediate, proximal relation between students and the tasks they are asked to perform to the role that principals and the school boards play in setting school-level and district-level policies, which in turn influence the social organization of the entire school community.

Understanding the impact of schools on adolescent development requires a conceptual framework for thinking simultaneously about schools as contexts in which development takes place and about the changing developmental needs of students as they move through the school system. In the late 1980s, Eccles and Midgley proposed a model of stage–environment fit to guide research on the impact of school transitions on adolescent development (see Eccles & Midgley, 1989; Eccles et al., 1993). They argued that individuals have changing emotional, cognitive, and social needs and personal goals as they mature. Drawing on ideas related to person–environment fit and self-determination theory (Deci & Ryan, 2002;

Hunt, 1975), as well as more general ideas person–process–context models of human development (e.g., Lerner, 2002; Sameroff, 1983), they argued that schools need to change in developmentally appropriate ways if they are to provide the kind of social context that will continue to motivate students' interest and engagement as the students mature. To the extent that this does not happen, they predicted that students would disengage first psychologically and then physically from school as they matured into and through adolescence. This should be particularly true as the adolescents acquired more incentives and more power to control their own behavior. We say more about both of these psychological perspectives on the impact of classroom experiences later.

In 1999, we (see Eccles & Roeser, 1999) proposed a framework for thinking about school influences that conceptualized the school context into a series of hierarchically ordered, interdependent levels of organization beginning at the most basic level of the classroom and then moving up in complexity to the school as an organizational system embedded in a larger cultural system. In adopting this heuristic, we assumed that (1) schools are *systems* characterized by multiple levels of analysis composed of various regulatory processes (organizational, interpersonal, and instructional in nature); (2) these processes are interrelated across levels of analysis; (3) such processes are usually dynamic in nature, sometimes being worked out each day between the various social actors (e.g., teachers and students); (4) these processes change as children move through different school levels (elementary, middle, and high school); and (5) these processes regulate children's and adolescents' cognitive, social–emotional, and behavioral development. In this chapter, we focus on the interface between various theoretical frameworks that are consistent with these tenets of school influences. We begin with a summary of our multilevel description of school contexts.

AN ECOLOGICAL VIEW OF SCHOOLS AND THEIR IMPACT ON DEVELOPMENT DURING ADOLESCENCE

From the location of the school within macro-regulatory systems characterized by national, state, and school district laws and educational policies to the miniregulatory systems that involve the minute-to-minute interactions between teachers and individual students, schools are systems of complex, multilevel, regulatory processes. Eccles and Roeser (1999) described these different levels of the school environment in terms of their hierarchical ordering—moving from the student in a classroom to the school building itself, then to the school district, and finally to the larger communities in which school districts are located. Within each of these levels, we discussed those beliefs and practices that affect students' experiences on a daily basis. At the classroom level, we focused attention on teacher beliefs and instructional practices, teacher–student relationships, the nature and design of tasks and instruction, and the nature and structure of classroom activities and groups. At the level of the school building, we focused attention on organizational climate and such school-wide practices as academic tracking, school start time, and the provision of extracurricular activities. At the level of the school district, we focused on the between-school grade configurations that create particular school-transition experiences for students. Finally, at the level

of schools embedded in larger social systems, we discussed such issues as school resources, as well as the linkages of schools with parents and with the labor market.

We further assumed that in any given school setting these multilevel processes are highly interdependent. Relations between different levels of organization in the school may be complementary or contradictory and may influence students either directly or indirectly. For instance, a principal may decide that all of his or her teachers should use a particular practice such as cooperative learning or small learning communities. However, the impact of such a decision on the daily experiences of students depends on how well this practice is actually implemented at the classroom level. If done well, students should be seen working successfully in groups on complex, authentic problems. Such a well-implemented school policy is likely to produce gains in self-esteem, interethnic relationships, and achievement among students, especially those of low ability or status (Connell & Klem, 2000; Connell, 2003; Felner, Seitsinger, Brand, Burns, & Bolton, 2007; National Research Council [NRC], 2004; Slavin, 1990; Wigfield, Eccles, Schiefele, Roeser, & Davis-Kean, 2006). In contrast, if done poorly, classroom disorganization can result, leading to far less positive outcomes at the student level. How such a schoolwide instructional policy is implemented depends on many factors, including the morale within the school, the relationships between the principal and the teachers, the teachers' understanding and endorsement of the new instructional practice, the way in which the policy change was decided upon, the provision of adequate in-service training, the provision of adequate supports for implementation of new strategies, and the students' willingness to go along with the new practice. Recent debates about the No Child Left Behind policy provide another example of the complex ways in which a new policy—this time a national-level policy—can affect the daily experiences of teachers and students in the classroom and in the school building (Darling-Hammond & Bransford, 2005; NRC, 2004).

Eccles and Roeser (1999) also assumed that the processes associated with the different levels of the school environment interacting dynamically with each other, rather than static resources or characteristics of the curriculum, teachers, or school per se, influence adolescents' development. In addition, adolescents' own constructions of meaning and interpretations of events within the school environment are critical mediators between school characteristics and students' feelings, beliefs, and behavior.

Finally, in keeping with the stage–environment perspective proposed by Eccles and Midgely (1989), Eccles and Roeser (1999) assumed that these different school-related processes change across the course of children's and adolescents' development as they progress through elementary, middle, and high school. That is, not only are children and adolescents developing, but so too is the whole nature of the schools that they attend. For example, the organizational, social, and instructional processes in schools change as children move from elementary to middle school. Eccles and Midgley (1989) argued that these changes are often associated with declines in many adolescents' motivation and behavior. Understanding the interaction of different school features with the developmental needs of adolescents is critical to understanding the role of schooling in young people's development. In the next sections, we discuss those characteristics of each level of the school that are most likely to be important for understanding the impact of schools on adolescent development. We also discuss how school characteristics at each level may also influence group differences in adolescent development, paying particular attention to gender and ethnic group differences within the United States.

LEVEL 1: CLASSROOMS

The most immediate educational environment for the student is the classroom. This is also the level that has received the most attention from educational psychologists. In this section, we review some of what we know about teacher beliefs, classroom climate, the nature of the academic work itself, and experiences of racial–ethnic discrimination.

Teacher Beliefs

Teacher beliefs have received much attention in educational psychology. In this section, we focus on two types of beliefs: Teachers' general sense of their own teaching efficacy and teachers' expectations for specific students in their class.

Teachers' General Sense of Efficacy

When teachers hold high general expectations for student achievement and students perceive these expectations, students learn more, experience a greater sense of self-worth and competence as learners, feel more connected to their teacher and their school, and resist involvement in problem behaviors (Brophy, 2004; Lee & Smith, 2001; NRC, 2004; Roeser, Eccles, & Sameroff, 1998; Rutter, 1983; Weinstein, 1989; Wigfield, Byrnes, & Eccles, 2006). Alternatively, when teachers lack confidence in their teaching efficacy, they can engage in behaviors that reinforce feelings of incompetence and alienation in their students, increasing the likelihood that their students will develop learned helpless responses to failure in the classroom (see Roeser & Eccles, 2000). As we discuss in more detail later, the prevalence of teachers with a low sense of personal teaching efficacy is higher in junior high and middle schools than in elementary schools. Low teacher efficacy rates are also higher in schools that serve high proportions of ethnic minority and poor adolescents than in schools that serve more affluent and higher achieving adolescents (Darling-Hammond, 1997; Juvonen, Le, Kaganoff, Augustine, & Constant, 2004; Wigfield et al., 2006).

Differential Teacher Expectations

Equally important are the differential expectations teachers often hold for various individuals within the same classroom and the differential treatments that sometimes accompany these expectations. Many researchers have shown that undermining teacher-expectancy effects depend on how teachers structure activities differently, as well as interact differently with, high- and low-expectancy students and on how the students perceive these differences (Brophy, 2004; Cooper, 1979; Weinstein, 1989; Wigfield et al., 2006). Much of the work on teacher expectancy effects has focused on the negative effects of differential treatment related to gender, race–ethnic group, and/or social class (see Ferguson, 1998; Jussim, Eccles, & Madon, 1996; Valencia, 1991; Wigfield et al., 2006). Jussim et al. (1996) found that even though these effects are typically quite small, young women, African American adolescents, and students from poorer homes are more subject to both the positive and negative effects of teacher expectancy effects than are other students.

Researchers such as Steele and Aronson (1995) have linked this form of differential treatment, particularly for African American students, to school disengagement and disidentification (the separation of one's self-esteem from school-related feedback). Steele and Aronson argued that African American students become aware of the fact that teachers and other adults have negative stereotypes of African Americans' academic abilities. This awareness (labeled *stereotype threat* by Steele and colleagues; see Aronson & Steele, 2005) increases their anxieties, which in turn lead them to disidentify with the school context to protect their self-esteem. It is interesting that recent studies using the same theoretical notions and experimental techniques have shown that Asian students believe that teachers and adults expect them to perform very well and that this belief leads Asian students to perform better on tests when their ethnic identity is made salient (Shih, Pittinsky, & Ambady, 1999). Thus, the psychological processes associated with stereotype threat can either undermine or facilitate performance on standardized tests depending on the nature of commonly held stereotypes about the intellectual strengths and weaknesses of different social groups.

Classroom Climate

Classroom climate refers to the more general character of the classroom and teacher–student relationships within the classroom. In this section, we focus on the following aspects of classroom climate: Teacher–student relationships, classroom management, and motivational climate.

Teacher–Student Relationships

The quality of teacher–student relationships is a key aspect of the classroom climate. Teachers who trust, care about, and are respectful of students, and who care specifically about students' learning, provide the social–emotional and intellectual scaffolding that students need to approach, engage, and persist on academic learning tasks; to develop positive, achievement-related self-perceptions, values, and a sense of school belonging; and more generally to experience a sense of well-being when in school (Deci & Ryan, 2002; Goodenow, 1993; Midgley et al., 1989b; NRC, 2004; Roeser, Midgley, & Urdan, 1996; Wentzel, 2002; Wigfield et al., 2006). Feeling emotionally supported is one of the most important characteristics of developmental contexts like schools for fostering adolescents' positive development—people and feelings of belonging and support really matter. Declines in both adolescents' perception of emotional support from their teachers and in the adolescents' sense of belonging in their classrooms are quite common as adolescents move from elementary school into secondary schools (NRC, 2004; Roeser, Peck, & Nasir, 2006; Wigfield et al., 2006). This shift is particularly troublesome in our highly mobile society in which teachers represent one of the last stable sources of nonparental role models for adolescents. In addition to teaching, teachers in mobile societies such as the United States can provide guidance and assistance when social–emotional or academic problems arise.

This role is especially important for promoting developmental competence when conditions in the family and neighborhood cannot or do not provide such supports (Eccles, Lord, & Roeser, 1996; NRC, 2004; Simmons & Blyth, 1987).

Classroom Management

Work related to classroom management has focused on two general issues: orderliness/predictability and control/autonomy. With regard to orderliness and predictability, the evidence is quite clear: Student achievement and conduct are enhanced when teachers establish smoothly running and efficient procedures for monitoring student progress, providing feedback, enforcing accountability for work completion, and organizing group activities (e.g., Darling-Hammond & Bransford, 2005; Pintrich & Schunk, 1996; Roeser et al., 2008). Unfortunately, such conditions are often absent, particularly in highly stressed and underfunded schools with inexperienced teachers (Darling-Hammond, 1997; Darling-Hammond & Bransford, 2005; NRC, 2004).

Research on autonomy versus control is equally compelling. Many researchers believe that classroom practices that support student autonomy are critical for fostering intrinsic motivation to learn and for supporting socio-emotional development during childhood and adolescence (Deci & Ryan, 2002; Grolnick, Gurland, Jacob, & Decourcey, 2002). Support for this hypothesis has been found in both laboratory and field-based studies (Deci & Ryan, 2002; Grolnick et al., 2002; NRC, 2004). However, it is also critical that the teacher supports student autonomy in a context of adequate structure and orderliness (Wigfield et al., 2006). This issue is complicated by the fact that the right balance between adult-guided structure and opportunities for student autonomy changes as the students mature: Older students desire more opportunities for autonomy and less adult-controlled structure. To the extent that the students do not experience these changes in the balance between structure and opportunities for autonomy as

they pass through the K–12 school years, their school motivation should decline as they get older (Eccles et al., 1993).

Motivational Climate

Several teams of researchers have suggested that teachers engage in a wide range of behaviors that create a pervasive motivational climate in the classroom. For example, Rosenholtz and Simpson (1984) suggested a cluster of general teaching practices (e.g., individualized versus whole-group instruction, ability grouping practices, and publicness of feedback) that should affect motivation because these practices make ability differences in classrooms especially salient to students. They assumed that these practices affect the motivation of all students by increasing the salience of extrinsic motivators and ego-focused learning goals, leading to greater incidence of social comparison behaviors and increased perception of ability as an entity state rather than an incremental condition. All of these changes reduce the quality of students' motivation and learning. The magnitude of the negative consequences of these shifts, however, should be greatest for low-performing students: As these students become more aware of their relative low standing, they are likely to adopt a variety of ego-protective strategies that unfortunately undermine learning and mastery (Covington & Dray, 2002; NRC, 2004).

Researchers interested in goal theory have proposed a similar set of classroom characteristics (Maehr & Midgley, 1996; Midgley, 2002; NRC, 2004; Pintrich, 2000; Pintrich & Schunk, 2003). Goal theorists propose two major achievement goal systems: mastery-oriented goals and performance-oriented goals. Students with mastery-oriented goals focus on learning the material and on their own improvement over time. Students with performance-oriented goals focus on doing better than other students in their class. Goal theorists further argue that a mastery orientation sustains school engagement and achievement better than does a performance orientation (see Maehr & Midgley, 1996; Midgley, 2002). Evidence is quite strong for the first prediction and more mixed for the second: The desire to do better than others often has positive rather than negative consequences, whereas the fear of failing (performance-avoidance goal orientation) undermines school performance (see Midgley, 2002). Finally, these theorists suggest that the publicness of feedback, particularly social comparative feedback, and a classroom focus on competition between students undermine mastery motivation and increase performance motivation. The school-reform work of Midgley, Maehr, and their colleagues has shown that school reform efforts to reduce these types of classroom practices, particularly those associated with performance feedback, social comparative grading systems, and ego-focused, competitive motivational strategies have positive consequences for adolescents' academic motivation (e.g., Maehr & Midgley, 1996). Creating classroom climates that reframe student role identities in terms of cooperation, multiple intelligences, effort, and improvement toward attaining standards rather than in terms of competition and relative ability has been an important approach of school reform movements whose aim is to achieve equity and excellence in learning outcomes (e.g., Darling-Hammond, 1997; Maehr & Midgley, 1996).

The work on understanding group differences in achievement and achievement choices is another example of an attempt to identify a broad set of classroom characteristics related to motivation. The work on girls and math is one example of this approach. There are sex differences in adolescents' preference for different types of learning contexts that likely interact with subject area to produce sex differences in interest in different subject areas (Eccles, 1994; Hoffmann, 2002; Wigfield et al., 2006). Females appear to respond more positively to math and science instruction if it is taught in a cooperative or individualized manner rather than a competitive manner, if it is taught from an applied or person-centered perspective

rather than a theoretical or abstract perspective, if it is taught using a hands-on approach rather than a book-learning approach, and if the teacher avoids sexism in its many subtle forms. The reason given for these effects is the fit between the teaching style; the instructional focus; and females' values, goals, motivational orientations, and learning styles. The few relevant studies support this hypothesis (Eccles, 1994; Hoffmann, 2002; Wigfield et al., 2006). If such classroom practices are more prevalent in one subject area (e.g., physical science or math) than another (e.g., biological or social science), one would expect sex differences in motivation to study these subject areas. In addition, however, math and physical science do not have to be taught in these ways; more girl-friendly instructional approaches can be used. When they are, girls as well as boys are more likely to continue taking courses in these fields and to consider working in these fields when they become adults.

The girl-friendly classroom conclusion is a good example of person–environment fit. Many investigators have suggested that students are maximally motivated to learn in situations that fit well with their interests, current skill level, and psychological needs, so that the material is challenging, interesting, and meaningful (e.g., Ainley, Hidi, & Berndorff, 2002; Chen, Darst, & Pangrazi, 2001; Csikszentmihalyi, Rathunde, & Whalen, 1993; Eccles et al., 1993; Hidi, 2001; Hidi & Harackiewicz, 2000; Köller, Baumert, & Schnabel, 2001; NRC, 2004; Renninger, Ewen, & Lasher, 2002). Variations on this theme include aptitude by treatment interactions and theories stressing cultural match or mismatch as one explanation for group differences in school achievement and activity choices (e.g., Fordham & Ogbu, 1986; Ogbu, 1992; Okagaki, 2001; Suarez-Orozco; & Suarez-Orozco, 2001; Valencia, 1991). For example, Valencia (1991) concluded that a mismatch of both the values of the school and the materials being taught contributed to the poor performance and high dropout rates among Latino youth in the high school they studied. Deyhle and LeCompte (1999) made a similar argument in their discussion of the poor performance of Native American youth in traditional middle school contexts. The misfit between the needs of young adolescents and the nature of junior high school environments is another example of these person–environment fit dynamics.

The Nature of Academic Work

Academic work is at the heart of the school experience. Two aspects of academic tasks are important: the content of the curriculum and the design of instruction. The nature of academic content has an important impact on students' attention, interest, and cognitive effort. Long ago, Dewey (1902/1990) proposed that academic work that is meaningful to the historical and developmental reality of students' experiences will promote sustained attention, high investment of cognitive and affective resources in learning, and strong identification with educational goals and aims. In general, research supports this hypothesis: Content that provides meaningful exploration is critical given that boredom in school, low interest, and perceived irrelevance of the curriculum are associated with poor attention, diminished achievement, disengagement, and alienation from school (e.g., Finn, 1989, 2006; Jackson & Davis, 2000; NRC, 2004). Curricula that represent the voices, images, and historical experiences of traditionally underrepresented groups are also important (Valencia, 1991). Choosing materials that provide an appropriate level of challenge for a given class, designing learning activities that require diverse cognitive operations (e.g., opinion, following routines, memory, comprehension), structuring lessons so that they build on each other in a systematic fashion, using multiple representations of a given problem, and explicitly teaching students strategies that assist in learning are but a few of the design features that scaffold learning and promote effort investment, interest in learning, and achievement (Blumenfeld, 1992; Deci & Ryan, 2002; Wigfield et al., 2006).

Unfortunately, American secondary schools have problems providing each of these types of educational experiences. Larson and colleagues have documented the fact that adolescents are bored most of the time that they are in secondary school classrooms (see Larson, 2000). Culturally meaningful learning experiences are rare in many American secondary schools (Fine, 1991; Garcia-Coll et al., 1996; Graham & Taylor, 2002; Okagaki, 2001; Valencia, 1991; Wigfield et al., 2006). The disconnection of traditional curricula from the experiences of these groups can explain the alienation of some group members from the educational process, sometimes eventuating in school dropout (Fine, 1991; Sheets & Hollins, 1999). Appropriately designed tasks that adequately scaffold learning are also rare in many inner-city and poor schools (Darling-Hammond, 1997). In addition, from a developmental perspective, there is evidence that the nature of academic work too often does not change over time in ways that are concurrent with the increasing cognitive sophistication, diverse life experiences, and identity needs of adolescents as they move from the elementary into the secondary school years (Carnegie Council on Adolescent Development, 1989; Juvonen et al., 2004; Lee & Smith, 1993, 2001).

For example, middle school students report the highest rates of boredom when doing schoolwork, especially passive work (e.g., listening to lectures) and in particular classes such as social studies, math, and science (Larson & Richards, 1989). There is also evidence that the *content* of the curriculum taught in schools does not broaden to incorporate either important health or social issues that become increasingly salient as adolescents move through puberty and deal with the identity explorations associated with adolescence (Carnegie Council, 1989; Juvonen et al., 2004) It may be that declines in some adolescents' motivation during the transition to secondary school in part reflect academic work that lacks challenge and meaning commensurate with adolescents' cognitive and emotional needs

(Eccles & Midgley, 1989). Recent efforts at middle school reform support this hypothesis: Motivation is maintained when middle schools and junior high schools introduce more challenging and meaningful academic work (Jackson & Davis, 2000). We discuss this in more detail later.

Experiences of Racial–Ethnic Discrimination

Researchers interested in the relatively poor academic performance of adolescents from some ethnic-racial groups have suggested another classroom-based experience as critical for adolescent development, namely, experiences of racial–ethnic discrimination (Brody et al., 2006; Essed, 1990; Fordham & Ogbu, 1986; Garcia Coll et al., 1996; Graham & Taylor, 2002; Harris-Britt, Valrie, Kurtz-Costes, & Rowley, 2007; Ruggiero & Taylor, 1995; Sellers, Caldwell, Schmeelk-Cone, & Zimmerman, 2003; Taylor, Casten, Flickinger, Roberts, & Fulmore, 1994; Wong, Eccles, & Sameroff, 2003). Two types of discrimination have been discussed: (1) anticipation of future discrimination in the labor market, which might be seen as undermining the long-term benefits of education (Fordham & Ogbu, 1986); and (2) the impact of daily experiences of discrimination on one's mental health and academic motivation (Essed, 1990; Sellers et al., 2003; Wong et al., 2003). Both types have been shown to adversely affect the development of ethnic minority adolescents. For example, Wong et al. (2003) found that anticipated future discrimination leads to increases in African American youths' motivation to do well in school, which in turn leads to increases in academic performance. In this sample, anticipated future discrimination appeared to motivate the youth to do their very best so that they would be maximally equipped to deal with future discrimination. In contrast, daily experiences of racial discrimination from their peers and teachers led to declines in school engagement and confidence in one's academic competence and grades, along with increases in depression

and anger. Interestingly, evidence is beginning to show that a strong positive ethnic identity has protective effects against the aversive effects of daily experiences of racial and ethnic discrimination (Chavous et al., 2003; Harris-Britt et al., 2007; Sellers et al., 2003; Wong et al., 2003).

Thus, educating for diversity and redressing discrimination are among two of goals secondary school educators can pursue in efforts to reduce achievement gaps. If young people from immigrant and ethnic minority backgrounds are afforded environments that offer them social support, the development of life skills and transfer of cultural capital, and strategies for addressing the twin challenges of racism and poverty, then such challenges can become sources of motivation and engagement that eventuate in the pursuit of a college education (Darling-Hammond, 1997). Providing access to equal educational opportunities also requires attention to the language in which instruction is provided. For many immigrant children, schools do not provide adequate linguistic supports to allow the children to master the material being taught in English (Padilla & Gonzalez, 2001).

LEVEL 1: SUMMARY

The studies of classroom-level influences suggest that development is optimized when students are provided with challenging tasks in a mastery-oriented environment that also provides good emotional and cognitive support, meaningful and culturally diverse material to learn and master, and sufficient support for their own autonomy and initiative. Connell and Wellborn (1991), as well as Deci and Ryan (2002), suggested that humans have three basic needs: to feel competent, to feel socially attached, and to have autonomous control in their lives. Further, they hypothesized that individuals develop best in contexts that provide opportunities for each of these needs to be met. Clearly, the types of classroom characteristics that emerge as important for both intellectual, motivational, and socioemotional development would provide such opportunities.

LEVEL 2: SCHOOL BUILDINGS

Schools are formal organizations and, as such, have characteristics and features that are super-ordinate to classroom characteristics. These aspects of the whole school environment should impact on adolescents' intellectual, social-emotional, and behavioral development. Important school-level organizational features include school climate and sense of commu-nity (Connell, 2003; Connell & Klem, 2000; NRC, 2004; Rutter & Maughan, 2002) and the relationships among the students themselves. School organizational features also include such schoolwide practices as curricular track-ing, start and stop times, and the availability of extracurricular activities.

General School Climate

Researchers have become interested in the gen-eral school climate or culture of the entire school. These researchers suggest that schools vary in the climate and general expectations regarding student potential, and that such variations affect the development of both teachers and students in very fundamental ways (e.g., Bandura, 2006; Bryk, Lee, & Holland, 1993; Darling-Hammond & Bransford, 2005; Jackson & Davis, 2000; NRC, 2004). For example, in their analysis of higher achievement in Catholic schools, Bryk et al. (1993) discussed how the culture within Catholic schools is fun-damentally different from the culture within most public schools in ways that positively affect the motivation of students, parents, and teachers. This culture (school climate) values academics, has high expectations that all stu-dents can learn, and affirms the belief that the business of school is learning. Similarly, Lee and Smith (2001) showed that between-school differences in teachers' sense of their own personal efficacy as well as their confidence in the general ability of the teachers at their school to teach all students accounted, in part, for between-school differences in adolescents' high school motivation and performance.

Maehr, Midgley, and colleagues argued that just as classroom practices give rise to certain achievement goals, so too do schools through particular policies and practices. A school-level emphasis on different achievement goals cre-ates a schoolwide psychological environment that affects students' academic beliefs, affects, and behaviors (e.g., Maehr & Midgley, 1996; Roeser et al., 1996). For example, schools' use of public honor rolls and assemblies for the highest achieving students, class rankings on report cards, differential curricular offerings for students of various ability levels, and so on all emphasize relative ability, competition, and social comparison in the school and cre-ate a school-level ability rather than mastery/task focus. However, through the recognition of academic effort and improvement, rewards for different competencies that extend to all students, and through practices that emphasize learning and task mastery (block scheduling, interdisciplinary curricular teams, cooperative learning), schools can promote a school-level focus on discovery, effort and improvement, and academic mastery.

In studies of adolescents, Roeser et al. (1996) found that students' perceptions of the school mastery goal structure predicted their own per-sonal mastery goals, which in turn were posi-tively predictive of their academic self-efficacy and positive affect in school. Students' percep-tions of the school performance goal structure were positively associated with their personal performance goal orientations, which in turn predicted their feelings of self-consciousness in school. What were interesting about this study were the correlations between indi-cators of the social climate (i.e., respectful and caring relationships between teachers and students) and the academic climate. Students reporting a strong performance-goal structure in their school were much less likely to report that their teachers cared for them, whereas those perceiving a task goal structure in the school were more likely to see their teachers as caring.

Roeser, Eccles, and Sameroff (1998) examined the relation of perceived school goal structures to longitudinal change in adolescent students' motivation to learn and well-being after controlling for adolescents' sex, race, parental education level, parental occupational prestige, and income. Adolescent students' perceptions of their school as performance oriented were related to diminished feelings of academic competence and valuing of school, increased feelings of emotional distress, and decreased grades over time, whereas perceived school task goal structures were associated with increased valuing of school and diminished emotional distress over time (Roeser et al., 1998). Using the same sample with person-centered techniques, they found that youth who were most engaged in school reported a cluster of positive school perceptions, including a mastery-oriented school climate and positive teacher–student relationships. In contrast, those who were most disengaged reported more of an ability-oriented school (Roeser, Eccles, & Sameroff, 2000). In this study and others, adolescents' perceptions of a school ability goal structure is found to be highly positively correlated (r around 0.60) with perceptions of racial discrimination in school among African- and Latin American youth (Roeser & Peck, 2003; Roeser, 2004).

Similarly, Kaplan and Maehr (1999) reported that perceptions of a mastery goal structure at the school level were associated with greater sense of well-being and less misconduct than when students perceived an emphasis on performance goals in the school. Fiqueira-McDonough (1986) reported related findings in a study of two high schools that were similar in intake characteristics and achievement outcomes but differed in their academic orientation and rates of delinquent behavior. The high school characterized by a greater emphasis on competition and high grades (ability orientation) had higher delinquency rates, and the students' grades were a major correlate of students' involvement in delinquent behavior (low grades predicted increased delinquent behavior).

Overall, these studies suggest that the general school climate, especially its academic goal structures, is associated with aspects of adolescents' academic motivation, well-being, achievement, and school conduct. They also suggest the importance of considering how certain academic cultures in schools may collude with perceptions of racial discrimination, and may undermine students' perceptions of whether the school is a moral place and whether or not teachers actually care for students (see Roeser et al., 2008).

Academic Tracks and Curricular Differentiation

In the middle and high school years, between-class tracking becomes both more widespread and more broadly linked to the sequencing of specific courses for students bound for different post secondary school trajectories (college preparation, general education, and vocational education). As curriculum differentiation practices intensify in public schools during secondary school, students of different ability levels get exposed to (often very) different kinds of academic work, classmates, teachers, and teaching methods (Eccles & Roeser, 1999; Oakes, 2005).

A general consensus on the overall effects of curriculum differentiation as an educational practice remains elusive (Eccles & Roeser, 1999). Research suggests that students who are placed in high tracks evidence some educational benefits; whereas low tracks placements are associated with negative achievement outcomes (see Fuligni, Eccles, & Barber, 1995; Kao & Thompson, 2003; Oakes, Gamoran, & Page, 1992). As just one example, Hallinan and Kubitschek (1999) found that assignment to high track classes accelerated growth in school achievement, whereas assignment to a lower level or vocational track decelerated such growth. Studies have also demonstrated that lower track students report being labeled "dumb" by teachers and peers, feel less committed to school, and feel less successful academically (see Oakes et al., 1992). In our own work, we have found that youth who were in lower track math, English or ESL (English as a second language) courses saw themselves as less scholastically competent, perceived school as less valuable, and felt less of a sense of school belonging than students in higher track math and English (Roeser, 2005; Roeser et al., 1998). One factor that appears to explain some of these differential effects concerns teacher quality—those students who are placed in lower tracks during secondary school are often exposed to teachers with less qualifications, experience less constructivist teaching practices, and are exposed to what amounts to watered-down curricula (e.g., Darling-Hammond, 1997; Oakes, 2005).

In addition, ability grouping has an impact on students' peer groups: Between-classroom ability grouping and curricular tracking increase the extent of contact among adolescents with similar levels of achievement and engagement with school. For those doing poorly in school, tracking is likely to facilitate friendships among students who are similarly alienated from school and are more likely to engage in risky or delinquent behaviors (Dryfoos, 1990). Dishion, McCord, and Poulin (1999) showed experimentally how such collecting of alienated adolescents increases their involvement in problem behaviors. This collecting of adolescents with poor achievement or adjustment histories also places additional discipline burdens on the teachers who teach these classes (Oakes, 2005), making such classes unpopular with the teachers as well as the students and decreasing the likelihood that the teachers with the most experience will allow themselves to be assigned to these classes.

Given this accumulating evidence on the potential costs of tracking, educational scientists are now questioning the advisability of between class tracking. Concerns have also been raised about the ways in which students get placed in different classes and how difficult it is for students to change tracks once initial placements have been made. These issues are important both early in a child's school career (e.g., Entwisle & Alexander, 1993) and later in

adolescence, when course placement is linked directly to the kinds of educational options that are available to the student after high school. Poor children, among whom African American, Latino, and Native American children are overrepresented, are more likely than their wealthier and European- or Asian American peers to be placed in low-ability classrooms and in vocational track courses during secondary school (Oakes, 2005). Even in integrated schools, minority students tend to receive poor access to teaching resources through tracking practices (Oakes et al., 1992; Noguera & Wing, 2006). Furthermore, there is some evidence that students with limited English proficiency who are otherwise capable are placed in lower track classes (see Kao & Thompson, 2003). Finally, careful assessment of these types of track placements has shown that many of these youth are incorrectly assigned to these classes and tracks (Dornbusch, 1994; Oakes, 2005). Such misassignment has long-term consequences for students' ability to go to college once they complete secondary school.

Finally, concerns have also been raised about the marginalization and segregation of ESL students on middle and high school campuses (Olsen, 1997; Valdez, 2001). ESL programs are often housed on the periphery of regular school campuses and often fail to provide real opportunities for them to interact with native English speakers. Furthermore, similar to the misassignment of African American and Latino students to and lack of mobility out of low academic tracks, there is some evidence that ESL students often get reassigned to ESL programs following school transition events even though they may have graduated from such programs into mainstream classes in their previous schools (Valdez, 2001).

School Size

In 1964, Barker and Gump proposed that smaller schools afford young people greater opportunities for close relationships, make it easier for students to be monitored by adults, and have a favorable roles-to-people ratio with respect to school extracurricular activities that allows for widespread student participation in the life of the school. All of these factors enabled higher achievement, the theory went, by providing bonds between the student and the school (Barker & Gump, 1964). In recent studies, support for the positive influence of small school size has grown. For example, Lee and Loeb (2000) found that elementary school size in an urban Chicago sample of 264 (K–8) schools, 5000 teachers, and 23,000 students was correlated with both teacher beliefs and students' achievement gains. In the smaller schools (size < 400 students), teachers took greater responsibility for fostering students' learning and students showed greater 1-year gains in their mathematics test scores. Lee and Smith (1995) found a negative relation between school size and students' self-reported school engagement (e.g., positive attitudes toward classes, investing effort in school, feeling challenged) in the National Educational Longitudinal Study: 88 datasets of approximately 12,000 students in 830 high schools. Similarly, Elder and Conger (2000) reported that school size was associated with adolescent developmental outcomes among high school students in rural Iowa during the 1990s. Across a variety of measures of academic and social functioning (e.g., grades, problem behavior), results showed that adolescents attending smaller schools, on average, did better than the adolescents attending larger schools after sociodemographic factors were controlled.

In summarizing this work, Lee and Smith (1997) proposed that the most effective K–8 elementary schools with respect to student achievement gains are those that enroll 400 students or less, whereas the ideal 9–12 secondary school in this regard enrolls between 600 and 900 students. Students in elementary/middle schools that are larger than 400, and those in high schools smaller than 600 or larger than 2,100, learn less in reading and mathematics. These findings regarding optimal size were consistent regardless of the social class and racial composition of the school. Unfortunately, minority and poor adolescents are most likely to be concentrated in the most overcrowded and largest secondary schools (United Way, 2008).

Extracurricular and Out-of-School Activities

There is growing interest in the role of extracurricular activities in adolescent development (see chapter 7, vol. 2 of this *Handbook*). Some people are interested because these activities can fill time and thus decrease the time available for adolescents to get in trouble. For example, in communities where few structured opportunities for after-school activities exist (especially poor urban communities), adolescents are most likely to be involved in high-risk behaviors such as substance use, crime, violence, and sexual activity during the period between 2 and 8 PM. Providing structured activities either at school or within community organizations after school when many adolescents have no adults at home to supervise them is an important consideration in preventing adolescents from engaging in high-risk behaviors (Carnegie Council, 1989; Eccles & Gootman, 2001; Mahoney, Harris, & Eccles, 2006).

Others are interested in the potential benefits of such activities for adolescent development (Carnegie Corporation of New York, 1992; Eccles & Gootman, 2001; Eccles & Templeton, 2002; Mahoney et al., 2006; Mahoney, Larson, & Eccles, 2005). There is a positive link between adolescents' extracurricular activities and both educational outcomes (e.g., high school completion, adult educational attainment, occupation, and income) and positive youth development (better mental health and lower rates of involvement in delinquent activities), even after controlling for social class and ability (Barber, Eccles, & Stone, 2001; Eccles & Barber, 1999; Eccles, Barber, Stone, & Hunt, 2003; Mahoney & Cairns, 1997; McNeal, 1995; Peck, Roeser, Zarrett, & Eccles, 2007). Participation in sports, in particular, has been linked to lower likelihood of school dropout, higher rates of college attendance, greater educational attainment by age 25, and higher occupational attainment at least through the 20s, especially among low-achieving and blue-collar male athletes (Barber et al., 2001; Eccles & Barber, 1999; Eccles & Templeton, 2002; McNeal, 1995).

Participation in school-based extracurricular activities has also been linked to increases on such positive developmental outcomes as high school GPA, strong school engagement, and high educational aspirations (Eccles & Barber, 1999; Lamborn, Brown, Mounts, & Steinberg, 1992). Roeser and Peck (2003) found that among adolescents highly vulnerable to school disengagement, after-school activity involvement was associated with a twofold increase in college attendance rates. In a follow-up study, specific kinds of activity involvements were found to underlie this association – those associated with extracurricular activities at school, with religious activity, and with volunteering were particularly important for educational resilience (Peck et al., 2008). Similarly, participation in high school extracurricular activities and out-of-school volunteer activities predicts high levels of adult participation in the political process and other types of volunteer activities, continued sport engagement, and better physical and mental health (Youniss, McLellan, & Yates, 1997; Youniss, Yates, & Su, 1997). In contrast to these positive associations, sports has also been linked to increased rates of school deviance and drug and alcohol use (e.g., Eccles & Barber, 1999; Lamborn et al., 1992).

These results suggest that participation in organized extracurricular activities can have both positive and negative effects. Why? Summarizing research from several disciplines, Eccles and Templeton (2002) suggested the following possible mediating mechanisms: participation increases the association with academically oriented peers and exposure to academic and prosocial values; participation can lead to enhanced self-esteem and generalization of a high sense of personal efficacy; participation can increase exposure to

supportive adults and good mentoring, which, in turn can lead to superior career guidance and encouragement; participation can increase one's social networks and social capital; and finally participation can increase both soft skills and other skills needed for success in school and the transition to adulthood.

Investigators have been especially interested in the links among peer group formation, identity formation, and activity involvement (Eccles & Barber, 1999). For example, Eckert (1989) explored the link between the peer group identity formation and both in- and out-of-school activity involvement. As one moves into and through adolescence, individuals become identified with particular groups of friends or crowds (see also Brown, 1990). Being a member of one of these crowds helps structure both what one does with one's time and the kinds of values and norms to which one is exposed. Over time, the coalescence of one's personal identity, one's peer group, and the kinds of activities one participates in as a consequence of both one's identity and one's peer group can shape the nature of one's developmental pathway into adulthood.

This strong link between activity participation and peer group membership also provides an explanation for the negative influences of sports participation on drug and alcohol use. Knowing what an adolescent is doing often tells us a lot about who the adolescent is with: It is very likely that participation in organized activity settings directly affects adolescents' peer groups precisely because such participation structures a substantial amount of peer group interaction. One's coparticipants become one's peer crowd. And such peer crowds often develop an activity-based culture, providing adolescents with the opportunity to identify with a group having a shared sense of style and commitment. Involvement in a school organization or sports links an adolescent to a set of similar peers, provides shared experiences and goals, and can reinforce friendships between peers (see Mahoney et al., 2005). In turn, these experiences should influence identity formation as well as other aspects of adolescent development.

What is important from a school-building perspective is that schools differ in the extent to which they provide positive extracurricular activities for their students. Researchers who study the advantages of small schools often point to the fact that more students get to participate in extracurricular activities in small schools because there are fewer bodies to fill all of the available slots (Barker & Gump, 1964; Elder & Conger, 2000). Large schools have an overabundance of students to fill all of the available activity slots. The situation is even worse in poor, large secondary schools that have had to cut extracurricular activities to stay within their budgets. Recently, federal and state initiatives have emerged to help increase the availability of after-school programs that are housed in school buildings. Unfortunately, most of this money is going to elementary school and middle school programs rather than high schools (Eccles & Gootman, 2001).

Unsupervised Spaces

Another important physical dimension of school buildings to consider is the noninstructional space that adolescents move in and through before school, after school, and between classes. These spaces include the parking lots and the school grounds, the hallways and the bathrooms, the sports fields (if there are any), and the cafeteria(s). One example of the importance of considering noninstructional aspects of the school in studies of schooling and motivation comes from the work of Astor and colleagues (19981999). Astor's (1998) interest is in students' experiences of school violence and their related feelings of anxiety or safety while in school. Clearly, concerns about physical safety can undermine readiness and motivation to learn. These authors have found that even though students may respond affirmatively to a series of questions about how safe they feel in school in general, they still can show strong fears in particular areas of the school or school grounds at particular times of

the day where violence is most likely to occur. For example, in a recent study of students in five high school settings in southeastern Michigan, Astor and colleagues (1999) found that most violent events reported by students occurred in what the authors called the "undefined public spaces" of the school—spaces such as parking lots, bathrooms, particular hallways, and so on, where no adults assumed supervisory jurisdiction. These spaces were undefined in terms of adult monitoring of behavior in them, and thus were the frequent sites for fights, unwanted sexual attention, and so forth.

Fagan and Wilkinson (1998) reviewed theory and evidence that suggest several different functional goals that violence can serve for youth, including the securing of high status among peers, acquisition of material goods, dominance of others and retribution for insults to the self, defiance of authority, and a form of "rough justice" in situations in which there is little legitimate adult authority. All of these goals likely reflect responses to the frustration or anticipated frustration of basic needs for autonomy and security in social situations characterized by a lack of adult supervision and an absence of opportunities for wholesome learning, work, and recreation. In sum, understanding how undefined school spaces affect the motivation and well-being of students who are potential victims, as well as how particular school spaces offer disenfranchised victimizers a venue to express themselves in violent ways, can enhance our overall understanding of lives in school contexts.

School Start and Stop Times

School start time is another tangible school-level characteristic that can influence students' motivation, learning, and development. Research conducted by Carskadon (1990, 1997) has shown that as children progress through puberty, they need more sleep and their natural sleep cycles shift to a desire to go to sleep later in the evening and to wake up later in the morning. Unfortunately, secondary schools typically begin earlier in the morning than primary schools, necessitating earlier rise times for adolescents (Carskadon, 1997). In concert with other changes, such as the later hours at which adolescents go to bed, the earlier school start times of middle and high school create a "developmental mismatch" that can both promote daytime sleepiness and undermine adolescents' ability to make it to school on time, alert, and ready to learn. A study of 5th grade students in Israel, for example, compared of two groups: those in a school that started at 7:10 AM (early risers) and those in a school that started at 8:00 AM (regular risers). Results showed that early risers slept less, reported more daytime fatigue and sleepiness, and reported greater attention and concentration difficulties in school compared to their later rising counterparts (Epstein, Chillag, & Lavie, 1998). The implication is that the time that schools begin can have a profound effect on mood, energy, attention, and, therefore, motivation and learning.

The time at which school ends also has implications for students' motivation to learn and development. In communities where few structured opportunities for after-school activities exist, especially impoverished communities, young people are more likely to be involved in high-risk behaviors such as substance use, crime, violence, and sexual activity, and less likely to be engaged in productive or academically relevant activities during the period between 2 and 8 PM. Providing structured activities either at school or within community organizations after school when many young people have no adults at home to supervise them is an important consideration in preventing students from engaging in high risk behaviors (Eccles & Gootman, 2000) and for keeping educationally vulnerable students on track academically (Peck, Roeser, Zarrett, & Eccles, 2008).

SUMMARY OF SCHOOL-LEVEL EFFECTS

In this section, we reviewed the impact of several features of the whole school on adolescent development. These features included school climate, school size, curricular tracking practices, the availability of extracurricular activities, and the use of noninstructional spaces. There is very strong evidence that each of these schoolwide characteristics impacts adolescent development. Often, between-school variations on these characteristics result from school district policies or financial constraints that are beyond the control of the building's principal and staff. Reform efforts, however, have shown that changes can be created in each of these domains and that such changes can have a positive impact on the development of the adolescents attending the reformed school.

LEVEL 3: SCHOOL DISTRICTS AND SECONDARY SCHOOL TRANSITIONS

School transitions are an excellent example of how the multiple levels of schools interact to affect adolescent development. All school districts must decide how they will group the grade levels within the various school buildings. One common arrangement is to group children in kindergarten through 6th grade in elementary schools, young adolescents in grades 7–9 in junior high schools, and older adolescents in grades 10–12 in senior high schools. Another common arrangement places the transitions after grades 5 and 8, creating elementary schools, middle schools, and senior high schools. The third popular arrangement groups young people in grades K–8 in one school and then grades 9–12 in a high school. In each of these arrangements, the students typically move to a new and often larger building at each of the major transition points. These moves typically also involve increased bussing and exposure to a much more diverse student body. In this section, we discuss two of these transitions: the transition from elementary to middle or junior high school and the transition from middle or junior high school to high school. Because most of the empirical work has focused on the junior high–middle school transition, we emphasize this transition. Recent research, however, suggests quite similar developmentally inappropriate changes with the transition to high school.

The Middle-Grades School Transition

There is substantial evidence of declines in academic motivation and achievement across the early-adolescence and high school years (Dweck, 2002; Eccles & Midgley, 1989; Eccles et al., 1993; Finn, 2006; Fredricks & Eccles, 2002; Jacobs, Lanza, Osgood, Eccles, & Wigfield, 2002; Roeser, Eccles, & Freedman-Doan, 1999). These declines often coincide with the transition into either middle/junior high or high school. For example, there is a marked decline in some early adolescents' school grades as they move into junior high school (Simmons & Blyth, 1987). Similar declines occur for such motivational constructs as interest in school (Wigfield et al., 2006), intrinsic motivation (Gottfried, Fleming, & Gottfried, 2001; Harter, 1998; Harter, Whitesell, & Kowalski, 1992), self-concepts/self-perceptions and confidence in one's intellectual abilities (Wigfield, Eccles, MacIver, Reuman, & Midgley, 1991), mastery goal orientation (Anderman & Midgley, 1997), and a sense of belonging at school (Anderman, 1999). There are also increases in test anxiety (Wigfield et al., 2006), focus on self-evaluation and performance rather than task mastery (Anderman & Midgley, 1997), and both truancy and school dropout (Rumberger, 1995; Rumberger & Thomas, 2000). Furthermore, increasing evidence indicates that these declines predict subsequent school dropout and high school failure (Connell, Halpern-Felsher, Clifford, Crichlow, & Usinger, 1995; Connell, Spencer, & Aber, 1994; Finn, 2006; Roeser & Eccles, 1998; Roeser, Eccles, & Strobel, 1998). Although these changes are not extreme for most adolescents, there is sufficient evidence of declines in various indicators of academic motivation, behavior, and self-perception over the early adolescent years to make one wonder what is happening (see Eccles & Midgley, 1989; Ryan & Patrick, 2001). Further, although few studies have gathered information on ethnic

or social-class differences in these declines, academic failure and dropout are especially problematic among some ethnic groups and among youth from communities and families of low socioeconomic status. It is probable then that these groups are particularly likely to show these declines in academic motivation and self-perception as they move into and through the secondary school years.

Several explanations have been offered for these seemingly negative changes in academic motivation: Some point to the intrapsychic upheaval associated with young adolescent development (see Arnett, 1999). Others point to the simultaneous occurrence of several life changes. For example, Simmons and Blyth (1987) attributed these declines, particularly among females, to the coincidence of the junior high school transition with pubertal development. Still others point to the nature of the junior high school environment itself rather than the transition per se.

Extending person–environment fit theory (see Hunt, 1975) into a developmental perspective (stage–environment fit theory), Eccles and Midgley (1989) proposed that these negative developmental changes result from the fact that traditional junior high schools do not provide developmentally appropriate educational environments for young adolescents. The authors suggested that different types of educational environments are needed for different age groups to meet developmental needs and foster continued developmental growth. Exposure to the developmentally appropriate environment would facilitate both motivation and continued growth; in contrast, exposure to developmentally inappropriate environments, especially developmentally regressive environments, should create a particularly poor person–environment fit, which should lead to declines in motivation as well as detachment from the goals of the institution. What is critical to this argument is that the transition itself is *not* the cause of the declines; instead, it is the nature of the school into which the students move. Within this framework, the right kinds of middle school reforms can be quite effective at reducing these declines.

Two approaches have been used to study the middle school transition: one focused on more global school-level characteristics such as school size, degree of departmentalization, and extent of bureaucratization and the other on more specific classroom and motivational dynamics. The first type is best exemplified by the work of Simmons and Blyth (1987). They pointed out that most junior high schools are substantially larger than elementary schools and that instruction is more likely to be organized departmentally. As a result, junior high school teachers typically teach several different groups of students, making it very difficult for students to form a close relationship with any school-affiliated adult precisely at the point in development when there is a great need for guidance and support from nonfamilial adults. Such changes in student-teacher relationships are also likely to undermine the sense of community and trust between students and teachers, leading to a lowered sense of efficacy among the teachers, an increased reliance on authoritarian control practices by the teachers, and an increased sense of alienation among the students. Finally, such changes are likely to decrease the probability that any particular student's difficulties will be noticed early enough to get the student necessary help, thus increasing the likelihood that students on the edge will be allowed to slip onto negative motivational and performance trajectories, leading to increased school failure and dropout.

The latter is best exemplified by the work of Eccles and Midgley and by the studies on middle school reform initiated by the Carnegie Foundation after their report *Turning Points* (Carnegie Council, 1989; Jackson & Davis, 2000). These scholars have looked at several specific aspects of the classroom and school environment and have shown that negative changes in these aspects of student' experiences at school as they make the middle or junior high school transition are linked to the declines in school motivation and engagement. They have also shown that changing these aspects of the middle school environment can be effective in reducing the declines in school engagement often associated with this school transition (Anderman, Maehr, & Midgley, 1999; Maehr & Midgley, 1996).

Grade-Related Differences in Teacher Beliefs

Differences in all types of teacher beliefs have been shown in studies comparing elementary and middle grades teachers. For example, junior high school teachers on average have lower confidence in their own teaching efficacy than do elementary school teachers (i.e., their ability to teach and influence all of the students in their classes; Feldlaufer, Midgley, & Eccles, 1988; Midgley & Feldlaufer, 1987; Midgley, Feldlaufer, & Eccles, 1989a). An equally troubling difference occurs for teachers' views of their roles in their students' lives. For example, Roeser and colleagues found that with increasing grade level, middle school (6th–8th grades) teachers are less likely to endorse the notion that students' mental health concerns are part of the teacher role (Roeser & Midgley, 1997; Roeser, Marachi, & Gehlbach, 2000). Thus, at a time when adolescents need academic and social–emotional guidance and support from both parents and nonparental adults (i.e., during early adolescence), teachers appear less likely to be able to provide such support given the number of students they teach, their educational training, and the size of secondary schools. This creates holes in the safety net available to adolescents at a time when they are in particularly acute need of adult support and guidance (Simmons & Blyth, 1987). It is not surprising that the most at-risk youth often fall through these holes.

Grade-Related Differences in Authority Relationships

Despite the increasing maturity of students, junior high school teachers place a greater emphasis on teacher control and discipline and provide fewer opportunities for student decision making, choice, and self-management than do elementary school teachers (e.g., Feldlaufer et al., 1988; Midgley & Feldlaufer, 1987). Both stage–environment fit theory (Eccles et al., 1993) and self-determination theory suggest that these practices will create a mismatch between young adolescents' desires for autonomy and control and their perceptions of the opportunities in their learning environments; this mismatch is predicted to lead to a decline in the adolescents' intrinsic motivation and interest in school. Evidence supports this prediction (see Wigfield et al., 2006).

Grade-Related Differences in Affective Relationships

Junior high and middle school classrooms are often characterized by a less personal and positive teacher–student relationship than are elementary school classrooms (Feldlaufer et al., 1988; Midgley, Feldlaufer, & Eccles, 1988). Given the association of classroom climate and student motivation reviewed earlier, it should not be surprising that moving into a less supportive classroom leads to a decline in these young adolescents' interest in the subject matter being taught in that classroom, particularly among the low achieving students (Furrer & Skinner, 2003; Anderman & Anderman, 1999; Midgley et al., 1988).

Grade-Related Differences in Grading Practices

There is no stronger predictor of students' self-confidence and efficacy than the grades they receive (Guay, Marsh, & Boivin, 2003). If academic marks decline with the junior high or middle school transition, then adolescents' self-perceptions and academic motivation should also decline. In fact, junior high school teachers do use stricter and more social comparison–based standards than do elementary school teachers to assess student competency and to evaluate student performance, leading to a drop in grades for many young adolescents as they make the transition to junior high school

(Alspaugh, 1998; Eccles & Midgley, 1989; Finger & Silverman, 1966; Harter, Whitesell, & Kowalski, 1992; Simmons & Blyth, 1987). Imagine what such a decline in grades might do to young adolescents' self-confidence and motivation. Although Simmons and Blyth (1987) did not look at this specific question, they did document the impact of this grade drop on subsequent school performance and dropout. Even after controlling for a youth's performance prior to the school transition, the magnitude of the grade drop following the transition into either junior high school or middle school was a major predictor of leaving school early in both studies (see also Finn, 2006; Roderick, 1993; Roderick & Camburn, 1999).

Grade-Related Differences in Motivational Goal Context

Several of the changes just noted are linked together in goal theory. Classroom practices related to grading practices, support for autonomy, and instructional organization affect the relative salience of mastery versus performance goals that students adopt as they engage in the learning tasks at school. Given changes associated with these practices, it is not surprising that both teachers and students think that their school environment is becoming increasingly focused on competition, relative ability, and social comparison as the young adolescents progress from elementary to middle or junior high school (Midgley, Anderman, & Hicks, 1995). Midgley et al. (1995) found that both teachers and students indicated that performance-focused goals were more prevalent and task-focused goals were less prevalent in the middle school classrooms than in the elementary school classrooms. In addition, the elementary school teachers reported using task-focused instructional strategies more frequently than did the middle school teachers. Finally, at both grade levels the extent to which teachers were task-focused predicted the students' and the teachers' sense of personal efficacy. It is thus no surprise that personal efficacy was lower among the middle school participants than among the elementary school participants. Extending this work, Roeser et al. (2002) looked at how elementary and middle school teachers' motivational practices and perceptions of the learning environment for teachers was related to their perceptions of their own work environments using both self- and principal reports.

Results showed that teachers who were more performance-oriented based on self-reported instructional practices also (1) believed there was an emphasis on performance goals for students in the wider school environment; (2) worked in schools where their school principals reported greater use of performance-oriented practices and policies in the school as a whole; and (3) believed there was competition among staff and inequitable treatment of teachers by the administration (school performance goal structure for teachers). Similarly, teachers at both levels who reported a greater mastery orientation also (1) perceived a broader emphasis on such goals for students in the wider school culture and (2) perceived an emphasis on innovation and improvement for teachers among the staff and administration. These results suggest that the changing nature of the motivational climate for learning for students as they progress through school is paralleled by a changing motivational climate for teaching for teachers as well.

Anderman et al. (1999) also extended this work by comparing two groups of young adolescents: a group who moved into a middle school that emphasized task-focused instructional practices, and a group who moved into a middle school that emphasized more traditional performance/ability-focused instructional practices. Although these two groups of students did not differ in their motivational goals prior to the school transition, they did after the transition. As predicted, the adolescents who moved into the first type of middle school were less likely to show an increase in their extrinsic motivational and performance-oriented motivational goals.

Summary

Changes such as those just reviewed are likely to have a negative effect on many children's motivational orientation toward school at any grade level. However, Eccles and Midgley (1989) argued that these types of school environmental changes are particularly harmful at early adolescence given what is known about psychological development during this stage of life. Evidence from a variety of sources suggests that early adolescent development is characterized by increases in desire for autonomy, peer orientation, self-focus and self-consciousness, salience of identity issues, concern over heterosexual relationships, and capacity for abstract cognitive activity (see Brown, 1990; Eccles & Midgley, 1989; Simmons & Blyth, 1987; Wigfield, Byrnes, & Eccles, 2006). Simmons and Blyth (1987) argued that adolescents need safe, intellectually challenging environments to adapt to these shifts. In light of these needs, the environmental changes often associated with transition to junior high school are likely to be especially harmful in that they emphasize competition, social comparison, a performance-goal orientation rather than a mastery-goal orientation, and self-assessment of ability at a time of heightened self-focus; they decrease decision making and choice at a time when the desire for control is growing; and they disrupt the opportunity for a close relationship between students and teachers at a time when adolescents may be in special need of close adult relationships outside of the home. The nature of these environmental changes, coupled with the normal course of individual development, is likely to result in a developmental mismatch so that the fit between the young adolescent and the classroom environment is particularly poor, increasing the risk of negative motivational outcomes, especially for adolescents who are having difficulty succeeding in school academically.

The High School Transition

Although there is less work on the transition to high school, the existing work suggests quite similar problems (Coleman & Hoffer, 1987; Jencks & Brown, 1975; Roeser & Gonzalez, 1997; Wehlage, Rutter, Smith, Lesko, & Fernandez, 1989). For example, high schools are typically even larger and more bureaucratic than are junior high schools and middle schools. Lee and Smith (2001) provided numerous examples of how the sense of community among teachers and students is undermined by the size and bureaucratic structure of most high schools. There is little opportunity for students and teachers to get to know each other, and, likely as a consequence, there is distrust between them and little attachment to a common set of goals and values. There is also little opportunity for the students to form mentor-like relationships with nonfamilial adults, and little effort is made to make instruction relevant to the students. Such environments are likely to undermine further the motivation and involvement of many students, especially those not doing particularly well academically, those not enrolled in the favored classes, and those who are alienated from the values of the adults in the high school (e.g., Roeser et al., 1999). These hypotheses need to be tested.

The few available studies provide initial support (see Lee & Smith, 2001; Roeser et al., 1999). For example, Fine (1991) documented how secondary school practices cumulate to drive out students who are not doing very well academically. Similarly, studies of ethnic minority youth provide extensive evidence that alienating and noninclusive high school practices undermine the school engagement and achievement of students of color (e.g., Darling-Hammond, 1997; Deyhle & LeCompte, 1999; Ferguson, 1998; Jackson & Davis, 2000; Lee & Smith, 1993; Suarez-Orozco & Suarez-Orozco, 1995; Taylor et al., 1994; Valencia, 1991). Recent work by Midgley and colleagues provides additional support. In a longitudinal study of adolescents from elementary school to high school, they were able to look at the impact of both the middle school and the high school transition. They found less evidence of negative changes in school experiences as the students moved into middle school than when they moved into high school. As one would expect with the stage–environment fit theory, they found that the motivational declines were associated with the high school rather than the middle school transition (see Midgley, 2002, for relevant chapters). They concluded that middle school reform efforts have been effective in changing the middle school environment in ways that support rather than undermine the young adolescents' school engagement and motivation. Further, they concluded that reform is now needed at the high school level. These reforms look very much like the reforms that were advocated for the middle school years. Most large public high schools also organize instruction around curricular tracks that sort students into different groups. As a result, there is even greater diversity in the educational experiences of high school students than of middle grades students; unfortunately, this diversity is often associated more with the students' social class and ethnic group than with differences in the students' talents and interests (Lee & Smith, 2001).

Consequently, curricular tracking has served to reinforce social stratification rather than foster optimal education for all students, particularly in large schools (Dornbusch, 1994; Lee & Smith, 2001). Lee and Smith documented that average school achievement levels do not benefit from this curricular tracking. Quite the contrary—evidence comparing Catholic high schools with public high schools suggests that average school achievement levels are increased when all students are required to take the same challenging curriculum. This conclusion is true even after one has controlled for student selectivity factors. A more thorough examination of how the organization and structure of our high schools influence cognitive, motivational, and achievement outcomes is needed.

Summary

In this section we summarized the evidence related to the impact of school transitions on development. As one would expect, given what we now know about the ecological nature of the junior high school transition, many early adolescents, particularly the low achievers and the highly anxious, experience great difficulty with this transition. In many ways, this transition can be characterized as a developmentally regressive shift in one's school context. Consistent with our stage–environment fit perspective, such a shift has negative consequences for many youths' school engagement and performance. Also consistent with our stage–environment fit perspective, there are now an increasing number of intervention studies showing that the junior high school transition does not have to yield negative consequences for vulnerable youth. Educational institutions for the middle grades can be designed in a developmentally progressive manner; when they are, the majority of early adolescents gain from this school transition. Finally, emerging evidence on the senior high school transition suggests that reforms are badly needed at this level.

LEVEL 4: SCHOOLS AS EMBEDDED ORGANIZATIONS IN THE LARGER COMMUNITY

The most distal aspect of school influence on adolescent development lies in the fact that schools are embedded in much larger social systems. Characteristics of the communities and the nations in which schools are placed influence everything about what goes on in the school building itself. Discussing all of the macro influences is beyond the scope of a single chapter. In this section we focus on two macro characteristics: private versus public schools and school resources.

Public Versus Private Schools

The question of whether public versus private schools do a better job motivating adolescent students and reducing achievement gaps between those from different social backgrounds is long-standing. Because of their record with socially disadvantaged students in particular, various researchers have commented on the "religious schools effect" of Catholic schools in terms of student achievement and educational attainments, especially among adolescent non-Catholics, those of lower socioeconomic status, and African Americans and Latinos living in urban areas (Bryk et al., 1993; Coleman, Hoffer, & Kilgore, 1982; Jeynes, 2002). In a meta-analysis of the effects of Catholic religious school attendance and personal religious commitment on academic achievement and school conduct, for instance, Jeynes (2002) found that, after accounting for socioeconomic status and gender, the effect sizes for religious school attendance were between 0.20 and 0.25 of a standard deviation for both academic achievement and school conduct. These effects were particularly evident for Black and Hispanic secondary school students. Although some suggest these effects are due to Catholic schools selecting superior students, others have suggested that this claim is overdrawn and that the effects of a Catholic school education on achievement are quite robust (e.g., Bryk et al., 1993; Sander, 1995).

Three core features of the culture of these schools have been examined as instrumental in the reduction of inequality that are relevant here: a communal organization, a philosophy of human dignity, and a restricted range of curricular offerings (Bryk et al., 1993). First, Catholic secondary schools tend to be somewhat smaller than public secondary schools and have strong communal culture grounded in a rich array of rituals and activities outside of the classroom where teachers and students get to know one another beyond their school-related roles. This community environment provides a social basis for motivating school learning—a set of caring relationships and corresponding sense of community become faculty, staff and students become major motivators of in-school behavior.

In addition, these secondary schools are characterized by a set of shared moral commitments and a spiritual ideology that emphasize the dignity of each individual and a corresponding ethic of care. These shared beliefs are grounded in a religious theology (Christian personalism) in which social justice and the desire to provide a humanistic education for all individuals are paramount, and in which the dignity of the individual as having moral worth is preeminent to a view in which worth is accorded to individuals based on relative social and academic statuses. Thus, the school culture is one that bridges two worlds for individuals—a moral–spiritual one in which the dignity of all individuals is recognized and acknowledge as primary; and a pragmatic one in which individuals are prepared for the demands of economic and civic life in a capitalist democracy. It is our view that this moral center and related humanistic approach to education that characterizes the culture of Catholic schools affords young people a non-status-based foundation of worth and a sense of belonging and corresponding sense of dignity that disrupts pervasive negative images in the wider culture that may afflict ethnic minority youth and undermine their perceptions of themselves as successful students.

The final, related feature of Catholic secondary schools is their "delimited technical core" (Bryk et al., 1993, p. 297). Students in these schools have many required classes and less electives. Generally, all students are exposed to a common curriculum that the faculty expect them to learn. Although administrative sorting still occurs, there are less "tracks" and less differentiation of curricula by such tracks. The message to students is that every student is not only capable of, but is expected to, learn the core curriculum.

Similarly, Eccles, Lord, and Midgley (1991) found that student outcomes, as rated by both teachers and students, were better in those attending K–8 schools than those who made a transition into a middle or junior high school during grade 6, 7, or 8. Students in K–8 schools were less likely to be truant, violent, or use substances at school, and were more likely to say they felt prepared for and interested in their classwork compared to students

in middle or junior high schools. Furthermore, students in the K–8 schools reported higher self-concepts and greater locus of control, received higher grades, and did better on standardized achievement tests than those in the middle grades schools. These K–8 schools were predominantly private religious schools (74%) and were smaller size. Both sector (religious) and size (small) were identified by Eccles et al. (1991) as factors that could explain why students in K–8 schools showed greater student commitment and engagement than those who were in middle schools or junior high schools during these grades.

School Resources

School resources in terms of adequate materials, a safe environment, and continuity of teaching staff are often considered important for adolescents' learning and well-being. Early studies of school effects on adolescents' development and achievement were based on economic models in which the relation of so-called tangible school inputs (e.g., school resources or size) to student outputs (e.g., achievement and attainments) was the focus. Although the central question of how much school resources matter for raising achievement and reducing inequality in student outcomes is still being debated, school district–level variations in such school resources are likely a major contributor to the continuing inequity in educational outcomes for several minority groups in the United States.

Evidence does show that tangible physical plant of the school can affect students' behavioral conduct in school. In their study of 12 London area secondary schools, Rutter and colleagues (1979) found that although the age of the school buildings was not significantly related to achievement or behavioral outcomes in students, the cleanliness and use of plants, pictures, and other decorations inside the school buildings was a significant predictor of the level of behavioral misconduct students displayed in the school (after accounting for their social background). The more inhospitable and cold the school was, the greater the misconduct of students. This finding may reflect the "broken windows" theory (Wilson & Kelling, 1982) of delinquency and crime in relation to school physical environments. The basic thesis is that abandoned and dirty physical spaces connote a message of a lack of ownership and monitoring, and therefore become seedbeds for criminal activity and violence. It may be harder to value school and feel good about oneself as a learner in a broken-down, leaky school building that communicates a serious lack of societal value for teachers and students (Kozol, 2006). It also may be harder for an adolescent to be intrinsically motivated in a school environment in which poor lighting, crowding, noise, and debris are features that are as common as technology, books, and adequate desks and chairs (e.g., Clark et al., 2006; Evans, 2004).

Unfortunately, about 37% of African American youth and 32% of Latino youth, compared to 5% of European American and 22% of Asian youth, are enrolled in the 47 largest city school districts in this country; in addition, African American and Latino youth attend some of the poorest school districts in this country. In turn, 28% of the youth enrolled in city schools live in poverty, and 55% are eligible for free or reduced-cost lunch, suggesting that class may be as important (or more important) as race in the differences that emerge. Teachers in these schools report feeling less safe than do teachers in other school districts, dropout rates are highest, and achievement levels at all grades are the lowest (Council of the Great City Schools, 1992; United Way, 2008). Finally, schools that serve these populations are less likely than schools serving more advantaged populations to offer either high-quality remedial services or advanced courses and courses that facilitate the acquisition of higher order thinking skills and active learning strategies. Even adolescents who are extremely motivated may find it difficult to perform well under these educational circumstances (United Way, 2008).

SECONDARY SCHOOL REFORM EFFORTS

We want to end our chapter with a discussion of several promising efforts at secondary school reforms. As noted earlier, in 1989 the Carnegie Corporation issued the report *Turning Reports* calling for the reform of education for early adolescents. Based in part on notions linked to stage environment fit as well as linked to the needs of early adolescent children, they suggested that the middle grades should have the following characteristics:

- Create small learning communities that will allow close relationships to emerge between teachers and students.
- Teach a core academic program to everyone that includes opportunities for service.
- Ensure success for all by eliminating tracking, using cooperative learning, providing flexible scheduling and adequate resources to meet the learning needs of all students.
- Empower teachers and administrators to take control of and responsibility for their schools.
- Staff schools with teachers who are trained to teach early adolescents.
- Foster health and fitness.
- Reengage families.
- Connect schools with communities.

Similar recommendations have been offered by several other scholars, including Connell and colleagues at the Institute for Research and Reform in Education (Connell, 2003), Roderick (1993), Juvonen et al. (2004), Lehr, Johnson, Bremer, Cosio, Thompson (2004), as well as the many professionals interested in the "Middle School Philosophy" (see Felner et al., 1997; Jackson & Davis, 2000; Lipsitz, Mizell, Jackson, & Austin, 1997; MacIver & Plank, 1997; MacIver, Young, & Washburn, 2002; Midgley & Edelin, 1998). An increasing number of scholars and student advocates have argued for a return to the K–8 format because it seems to create more developmentally suitable environments for the early adolescent years (e.g., Juvonen et al., 2004; Simmons & Blyth, 1987).

The importance of small schools, schools within schools, or small learning communities has been stressed in many reform proposals, along with the need to provide rigorous, challenging, and high-quality instruction. Small learning communities are likely to be particularly important during this developmental period because they support the emergence of strong teacher–student relationships that will allow students some autonomy within a very tight support network. These characteristics should support stronger engagement and identification with the school institution. When engagement is accompanied by high-quality instruction then academic failure should be preventable. Interestingly, there are calls for quite similar reforms at the high school level.

Not surprisingly, the Carnegie Corporation report stimulated a major reassessment of schooling for early adolescents throughout the country. The results have been disappointing. Many districts changed from a junior high school format to a middle school format based on the fact that middle school philosophy includes many of the components outlined in the Carnegie Corporation report. Unfortunately, many of these changes failed to produce truly successful middle schools. Often, the new middle schools looked a lot like the old junior high schools except for the fact that they contained grades 6–8 rather than grades 7–9 (Jackson & Davis, 2001; Juvonen et al., 2004).

In 2000, Jackson and Davis (2000) summarized the findings of these many middle school reform efforts. They concluded that the following middle grade school characteristics support both learning and positive youth development:

- A curriculum grounded in rigorous academic standards and current knowledge about how students learn best and is relevant to the concerns of adolescents
- Instructional methods designed to prepare all students to achieve at the highest standards

- Organizational structures that support a climate of intellectual development and a caring community with shared educational goals
- Staff who are trained experts at teaching young adolescents
- Ongoing professional development opportunities for the staff
- Democratic governance that involves both the adults and the adolescents
- Extensive involvement of parents and the community
- High levels of safety and practices that support good health

Similar conclusions were reached by Juvonen and colleagues (2004), Lehr et al. (2004), and the NRC (2004) in their reviews of well-studied intervention and reform efforts. Juvonen et al. (2004) also argued that K–8 structures might be more successful at implementing the types of classroom characteristics and building-level opportunities most supportive of continued academic engagement and positive youth development.

Together, these recommendations fit very nicely with the stage–environment fit perspective we outlined earlier. They are consistent with both the developmental needs of early adolescence and what we know about high-quality instruction. We would like to provide a brief description of four promising programs as examples of changes that can be made at various levels within the secondary school context that could support these types of changes: the Coca-Cola Valued Youth Program (CCVYP, www.idra.org/CCVYP/default.htm#vyp), the Teen Outreach Program (www.cornerstone .to), Oyserman's possible selves intervention (Oyserman, Terry, & Bybee, 2002) and the First-Things-First whole school reform program (Institute for Research and Reform in Education [IRRE], 2004). We pick these particular programs because they relate directly to the developmental needs during adolescence.

The CCVYP took unique advantage of adolescents' desire to make a difference in their community. It offers 7th- through 12th-grade students considered to be at risk for dropping out of school an opportunity to tutor elementary school students who were also identified as being at risk. The tutors are provided with training and support by teacher coordinators. Such a program is unique in its attention to providing adolescent youth with a meaningful and authentic opportunity to "matter" in their school community. By allowing them to tutor younger children, the program also provides academically challenged youths with an opportunity to feel good about their academic skills and their ability to help other children do well in school. Finally, it provides an unobtrusive and respectful means for the tutors' teachers to become both mentors and protectors.

The Teen Outreach Program (TOP; Allen, Kuperminc, Philliber, & Herre, 1994; Allen, Philliber, Herrling, & Kuperminc, 1997), a national volunteer service program, is designed to both help adolescents understand and evaluate their future life options and develop life skills and autonomy in a context featuring strong social ties to adult mentors. The three program components are supervised community service, classroom-based discussions of service experiences, and classroom-based discussion and activities related to social–developmental tasks of adolescence. Participants choose their volunteer activities with the assistance of trained staff who help match the individual's interests and skills with community needs. TOP sites typically offer a minimum of 20 hours per year of volunteer service for each participant. In one evaluated program, participants averaged 45.8 hours of volunteer service during their 9 months of involvement.

The Teen Outreach Curriculum provides a framework for classroom meetings that include structured discussions, group exercises, role-playing exercises, guest speakers and informational presentations. These discussions are designed to help students prepare for, and learn from, their service experiences by dealing with topics such as lack of self-confidence, social skills, assertiveness, and self-discipline. Trained facilitators lead discussions of such topics as values clarification, managing family relationships, and handling close relationships. Participants are encouraged to discuss their feelings and attitudes.

Several evaluation studies have been done on TOP (Allen et al., 1994, 1997). The students who performed more volunteer service were at lower risk for course failure while they were involved in the program; they were also less likely to be suspended from school and to get pregnant. Also, implementation quality of the TOPS curriculum did not significantly influence program outcomes (Allen, Philliber & Hoggson, 1990), suggesting that it is the community service and possibly the mentoring components that are the most important program.

The intervention work by Oyserman and colleagues (Oyserman, Gant, & Ager, 1995) is based on the importance of group and individual differences in possible selves for students' engagement in school. Oyserman et al. (1995) found that African American students are more motivated to invest time and energy in mastering school learning materials if they include academic success in their future possible selves and if these African American adolescents included academic success in their view of what it means to be a successful African American (Oyserman et al., 1995). Subsequently, Oyserman and colleagues have developed and tested school-based interventions designed to increase the salience of academic achievement in both individuals' possible selves and ethnic identity. For example, using a randomized treatment intervention design, Oyserman et al. (2002) provided a group of African American adolescents with a series of experiences designed to help them expand both their views of themselves in various future occupations and the means of obtaining these various occupational goals. These means included increased commitment to educational success. Those students who were part of the treatment reported greater bonding with school and greater concern with doing well in school than the controls. They also evidenced better school attendance.

First Things First, created by the Institute for Research and Reform in Education, entails three basic strategies: the creation of small learning communities, the creation of strong connections between family and school, and the provision of high-quality instruction. These strategies were selected because they facilitate the following four experiences for students:

1. "Continuity of care" and strong student–teacher relationships
2. "Flexible scheduling that allows for additional instructional time and attention to individual learning needs"
3. "High, clear and fair standards for academics and conduct"
4. Exposure to "enriched and diverse learning opportunities"

To accomplish these goals, IRRE works with districts to provide the following three experiences for the teachers and staff: (1) "equip, empower, and expect staff to implement effective instructional practices"; (2) flexibility to redirect resources to meet emerging needs; and (3) "ensuring collective responsibility." (All quotes are from pages 6 and 7 of IRRE, 2004). All three of these features require school districts to put together teams of teachers that work with the same students over time and across school years. These teams are provided with common planning time and with remedial curricular materials that can be used to help students succeed. The teams are also provided with resources for their own continued development as high-quality teachers and mentors. All students are provided with a family advocate who works with 15–20 students and their families over time to help the students succeed. This reform has been implemented in many school districts across the country and has been carefully evaluated in the Kansas City, Kansas, school district. The results of this evaluation are quite positive for both the middle and senior high school grades. The program both reduces high school dropout and increases academic performance, as well

as closing the gap in academic performance between White and Black students.

SUMMARY AND CONCLUSIONS

We have outlined many ways in which schools affect the development of adolescents and stressed the need to take both a systems-level and a developmental perspective on schools. We began by pointing out how the multiple levels of school organization interact to shape the day-to-day experiences of adolescents and teachers. We also stressed the interface of schools as complex changing institutions with the developmental trajectories of individuals. To understand how schools influence development, one needs to understand change at both the individual and the institutional level. Stage–environment fit theory provides an excellent example of the linking of these two developmental trajectories. Imagine two trajectories: one at the school level and one at the individual level. Schools change in many ways over the grade levels. The nature of these changes can be developmentally appropriate or inappropriate in terms of the extent to which they foster continued development toward the transition into adulthood and maturity. Youth travel through this changing context as they move from grade to grade and from school to school. Similarly, youths develop and change as they get older. They also have assumptions about their increasing maturity and the privileges it ought to afford them. Optimal development is most likely when these two trajectories of change are in synchrony with each other—that is, when the changes in the context mesh well with, and perhaps even slightly precede, the patterns of change occurring at the individual level.

We also discussed the many ways in which experiences at school are influenced by the larger cultural and social milieu in which schools are nested. Culturally shared beliefs influence how we fund our schools, what and how we teach, and how we design school policy at all levels. These policies, in turn, influence the types of connections that schools have with families, communities, higher educational institutions, the labor market, and the daily experiences of youths in the schools they attend. On some levels, our schools are succeeding very well in supporting both learning and positive youth development for many groups of people. At other levels, schools are not supporting optimal learning or preparation for adult development for many young people. Adolescents of color, particularly African Americans, Latinos, and Native Americans, still perform less well than European Americans and some groups of Asian Americans (for discussions, see, e.g., Jencks & Phillips, 1998; Steinberg, Dornbusch, & Brown, 1992; Suarez-Orozco & Suarez-Orozco, 1995; Valencia, 1991).

REFERENCES

Ainley, M., Hidi, S., & Berndorff, D. (2002). Interest, learning, and the psychological processes that mediate their relationship. *Journal of Educational Psychology, 94*, 545–561.

Allen, J. P., Kuperminc, G., Philliber, S., & Herre, K. (1994). Programmatic prevention of adolescent problem behaviors: The role of autonomy, relatedness, and volunteer service in the Teen Outreach Program. *American Journal of Community Psychology, 22*(5), 617–638.

Allen, J. P., Philliber, S., & Hoggson, N. (1990). School-based prevention of teen-age pregnancy and school dropout: Process evaluation of the national replication of the Teen Outreach Program. *American Journal of Community Psychology, 18*(4), 505–524.

Allen, J. P., Philliber, S., Herrling, S., & Kuperminc, G. P. (1997). Preventing teen pregnancy and academic failure: Experimental evaluation of a developmentally based approach. *Child Development, 68*(4), 729–742.

Alspaugh, J. W. (1998). Achievement loss associated with the transition to middle school and high school. *The Journal of Educational Research, 92*, 20–26.

Anderman, E. M., & Midgley, C. (1997). Changes in achievement goal orientation, perceived academic competence, and grades across the transition to middle level schools. *Contemporary Educational Psychology, 22*, 269–298.

Anderman, E. M., Maehr, M. L., & Midgley, C. (1999). Declining motivation after the transition to middle school: Schools can make a difference. *Journal of Research and Development in Education, 32*, 131–147.

Anderman, L. H. (1999). Classroom goal orientation, school belonging and social goals as predictors of students' positive and negative affect following the transition to middle school. *Journal of Research and Development in Education, 32*, 90–103.

Anderman, L. H., & Anderman, E. M. (1999). Social predictors of changes in students' achievement goal orientations. *Contemporary Educational Psychology, 25*, 21–37.

Arnett, J. J. (1999). Adolescent storm and stress, reconsidered. *American Psychologist, 54*, 317–326.

Aronson, J., & Steele, C. M. (2005). Stereotypes and the fragility of academic competence, motivation, and self-concept. In A. J. Elliot & C. S. Dweck (Eds.), Handbook of competence and motivation, (pp. 436–456). New York: Guilford Press.

Astor, R. A., Meyer, H. A., Behre, W. J. (1999). Unowned places and times: Maps and interviews about violence in high schools. *American Educational Research Journal, 36*, 3–42.

Astor, R. A. (1998). Moral reasoning about school violence: Informational assumptions about harm within school subcontexts. *Educational Psychologist, 33*, 207–221.

Bandura, A. (2006). Toward a psychology of human agency. *Psychological Science, 1*, 164–180.

Barber, B. L., Eccles, J. S., & Stone, M. R. (2001). Whatever happened to the Jock, the Brain, and the Princess? Young adult pathways linked to adolescent activity involvement and social identity. *Journal of Adolescent Research, 16*, 429–455.

Barker, R. G., & Gump, P. (1964). *Big school, small school.* Stanford, CA: Stanford University Press.

Blumenfeld, P. C. (1992). Classroom learning and motivation: Clarifying and expanding goal theory. *Journal of Educational Psychology, 84*, 272–281.

Brody, G. H., Chen, Y-F., Murry, V. M., Simons. R. L., Ge, X., Gibbons, F. X., et al. (2006). Perceived discrimination and the adjustment of African American youths: A five-year longitudinal analysis with contextual moderation effects. *Child Development, 77*(5), 1170–1189.

Brophy, J. E. (2004). *Motivating students to learn* (2nd ed.). Mahwah, NJ: Lawrence Erlbaum.

Brown, B. B. (1990). Peer groups and peer culture. In S. S. Feldman & G. R. Elliott (Eds.), *At the threshold: The developing adolescent* (pp. 171–196). Cambridge, MA: Harvard University Press.

Bryk, A. S., Lee, V. E., & Holland P. B. (1993). *Catholic schools and the common good.* Cambridge, MA: Harvard University Press.

Carnegie Corporation of New York. (1992). *A matter of time: Risk and opportunity in the non school hours.* New York: Author.

Carnegie Council on Adolescent Development (1989). *Turning points: Preparing American youth for the 21st century.* Washington, DC: Author.

Carskadon, M. A. (1990). Patterns of sleep and sleepiness in adolescents. *Pediatrician, 17*, 5–12.

Carskadon, M. A. (1997, April). *Adolescent sleep: Can we reconcile biological needs with societal demands?* Lecture given at Stanford University, April 21, 1997.

Chavous, T.M., Bernat, D. H., Schmeelk-Cone, K., Caldwell, C. H. Kohn-Wood, L., & Zimmerman, M. A. (2003). Racial identity and academic attainment among African American adolescents. *Child Development, 74*(4), 1076–1090.

Chen, A., Darst, P. W., & Pangrazi, R. P. (2001). An examination of situational interest and its sources. *British Journal of Educational Psychology, 71*, 383–400.

Clark, C. Martin, R., van Kempen, E., Alfred, T., Head, J., Davies, H.W., et al. (2006). Exposure–effect relations between aircraft and road traffic noise exposure at school and reading comprehension. *American Journal of Epidemiology, 163*, 27–37.

Coleman, J. S., & Hoffer, T. (1987). *Public and private high schools: The impact of communities.* New York: Basic Books.

Coleman, J. S., Hoffer, T., & Kilgore, S. (1982). Cognitive outcomes in public and private schools. *Sociology of Education, 55*(2/3), 65–76.

Connell, J. P. (2003). *Getting off the dime: First steps toward implementing First Things First.* Reported prepared for the U.S. Department of Education. Philadelphia: Institute for Research and Reform in Education.

Connell, J. P., Halpern-Felsher, B. L., Clifford, E., Crichlow, W., & Usinger, P. (1995). Hanging in there: Behavioral, psychological, and contextual factors affecting whether African-American adolescents stay in high school. *Journal of Adolescent Research, 10*, 41–63.

Connell, J. P., & Klem, A. M. (2000), You can get there from here: Using a theory of change approach to plan urban education reform. *Journal of Educational and Psychological Consultation, 11*, 93–120.

Conneil, J. P., Spencer, M. B., & Aber, J. L. (1994). Educational risk and resilience in African American youth: Context, self, and action outcomes in school. *Child Development*, *65*, 493–506.

Connell, J. P., & Wellborn, J. G. (1991). Competence, autonomy, and relatedness: A motivational analysis of self-system processes. In R. Gunnar & L. A. Sroufe (Eds.), *Minnesota symposia on child psychology*, vol. *23* (pp. 43–77). Hillsdale, NJ: Lawrence Erlbaum.

Cooper, H. M. (1979). Pygmalion grows up: A model for teacher expectation communication and performance influence. *Review of Educational Research 49*(3), 389–410.

Council of the Great City Schools. (1992). *National urban education goals: Baseline indicators, 1990–91*. Washington, DC: Author.

Covington, M. V., & Dray, E. (2002). The developmental course of achievement motivation: A need-based approach. In A. Wigfield & J. S. Eccles (Eds.), *Development of achievement motivation* (pp. 33–56). San Diego: Academic Press.

Csikszentmihalyi, M., Rathunde, K., & Whalen, S, (1993). *Talented teenagers: The roots of success and failure*. New York: Cambridge University Press.

Darling-Hammond, L. (1997). *The right to learn: A blueprint for creating schools that work*. San Francisco: Jossey-Bass.

Darling-Hammond, L., & Bransford, J. (Eds.). (2005). *Preparing teachers for a changing world: What teachers should learn and be able to do*. San Francisco: Jossey-Bass.

Deci, E. L., & Ryan, R. M. (2002). Self-determination research: Reflections and future directions. In E. L. Deci & R. M. Ryan (Eds.), *Handbook of self-determination theory research* (pp. 431–441). Rochester, NY: University of Rochester Press.

Deyhle, D., & LeCompte, M. (1999). Cultural differences in child development: Navaho adolescents in middle schools. In R. H. Sheets & E. R. Hollins (Eds.), *Racial and ethnic identity in school practices: Aspects of human development* (pp. 123–140). Mahwah, NJ: Lawrence Erlbaum.

Dewey, J. (1990). *The child and the curriculum*. Chicago: University of Chicago Press. (Original work published 1902.)

Dishion, T. J., McCord, J., & Poulin, F. (1999). When interventions harm: Peer groups and problem behavior. *American Psychologist*, *54*(9), 755–764.

Dornbusch, S. M. (1994). *Off the track*. Presidential address at the biennial meeting of the Society for Research on Adolescence, San Diego, CA.

Dryfoos, J. G. (1990). *Adolescents at risk: Prevalence and prevention*. Oxford, UK: Oxford University Press.

Dweck, C. S. (2002). The development of ability conceptions. In A.Wigfield & J. S. Eccles (Eds.), *Development of achievement motivation* (pp. 57–88). San Diego: Academic Press.

Eccles, J. S. (1994). Understanding women's educational and occupational choices. *Psychology of Women Quarterly*, *18*, 585–609.

Eccles, J. S., & Barber, B. L. (1999). Student council, volunteering, basketball, or marching band: What kind of extracurricular involvement matters? *Journal of Adolescent Research*, *14*, 10–43.

Eccles, J. S., Barber, B. L., Stone, M., & Hunt, J. (2003). Extracurricular activities and adolescent development. *Journal of Social Issues*, *59*, 865–889.

Eccles, J. S., & Gootman, J. (2001). *Community programs to promote youth development*. Washington, DC: National Academy Press.

Eccles, J. S., & Midgley, C. (1989). Stage/environment fit: Developmentally appropriate classrooms for early adolescents. In R. Ames & C. Ames (Eds.), *Research on motivation in education*, vol. *3* (pp. 139–181). New York: Academic Press.

Eccles, J. S., & Roeser, R. (1999). School and community influences on human development. In M. Bornstein & M. Lamb (Eds.), *Developmental psychology: An advanced textbook* (4th ed., pp. 503–554). Mahwah, NJ: Lawrence Erlbaum.

Eccles, J. S., & Templeton, J. (2002). Extracurricular and other after-school activities for youth. In W. S. Secada (Ed.), *Review of Educational Research*, voi. *26* (pp.113–180). Washington DC: American Educational Research Association Press.

Eccles, J. S., Lord, S. E., & Roeser, R. W. (1996). Round holes, square pegs, rocky roads, and sore feet: The impact of stage/environment fit on young adolescents' experiences in schools and families. In S. L. Toth & D. Cicchetti (Eds.), *Adolescence: Opportunities and challenges*, vol. *7* (pp. 49–93). Rochester, NY: University of Rochester Press.

Eccles, J. S., Midgley, C., Wigfield, A., Buchanan, C. M., Reuman, D., Flanagan, C., et al. (1993). Development during adolescence: The impact of stage–environment fit on adolescents' experiences in schools and families. *American Psychologist*, *48*, 90–101.

Eccles, J., Lord, S., & Midgley, C. (1991). What are we doing to early adolescents? The impacts of educational contexts on early adolescents. *American Educational Journal*, August, 521–542.

Eckert, P (1989). *Jocks and burnouts: Social categories and identity in the high school*. New York: Teacher College Press.

Elder, G. H., Jr., & Conger, R. D. (2000). *Children of the land*. Chicago: Chicago University Press.

Entwisle, D. R., & Alexander, K. L. (1993). Entry into school: The beginning school transition and educational stratification in the United States. *Annual Review of Sociology*, *19*, 401–423.

Epstein, R., Chillag, N., & Lavie, P. (1998). Starting times of school: Effects on daytime functioning of fifth-grade children in Israel. *Sleep*, *3*, 250–256.

Essed, P. (1990). *Everyday racism: Reports from women of two cultures*. Claremont, CA: Hunter House.

Evans, G. W. (2004). The environment of childhood poverty. *American Psychologist*, *59*, 77–92.

Fagan, J., & Wilkinson, D. L. (1998). Guns, youth violence and social identity. In M.Tonry & M. H. Moore (Eds.), *Youth violence* (pp. 373–456). Chicago: University of Chicago Press.

Feldlaufer, H., Midgley, C., & Eccles, J. S. (1988). Student, teacher, and observer perceptions of the classroom environment before and after the transition to junior high school. *Journal of Early Adolescence*, *8*, 133–156.

Felner, R. D., Jackson, A. W., Kasak, D., Mulhall, P., Brand, S., & Flowers, N. (1997). The impact of school reform for the middle years: Longitudinal study of a network engaged in Turning Points–based comprehensive school transformation. *Phi Delta Kappan*, *78*, 528–532, 541–550.

Felner, R. D., Seitsinger, A. M. Brand, S., Burns, A, & Bolton, N., (2007). Creating small learning communities: Lessons from the project on high performing learning communities about "what works" in creating productive, developmentally enhancing, learning contexts. *Educational Psychologist*, *42*(4), 209–221.

Ferguson, R. F. (1998). Teachers' perceptions and expectations and the Black–White test score gap. In C. Jencks & M. Phillips (Eds.), *The Black–White test score gap* (pp. 273–317). Washington, DC: Brookings Institute Press.

Fine, M. (1991). *Framing dropouts: Notes on the politics of an urban public high school*. Albany: State University of New York Press.

Finger, J. A., & Silverman, M. (1966). Changes in academic performance in the junior high school. *Personnel and Guidance Journal*, *45*, 157–164.

Finn, J. D. (1989). Withdrawing from school. *Review of Educational Research*, *59*, 117–142.

Finn, J. D. (2006). *The adult lives of at-risk students: The roles of attainment and engagement in high school*. Report to National Center of Educational Statistics, Washington DC: U.S. Department of Education (NCES 2006–328).

Fiqueira-McDonough, J. (1986). School context, gender, and delinquency. *Journal of Youth and Adolescence*, *15*, 79–98.

Fordham, S., & Ogbu, J. U. (1986). Black students' school success: Coping with "the burden of 'acting white.'"*Urban Review*, *18*, 176–206.

Fredricks, J., & Eccles, J. S. (2002). Children's competence and value beliefs from childhood through adolescence: Growth trajectories in two male sex-typed domains. *Developmental Psychology*, *38*, 519–533.

Fuligni, A. J., Eccles, J. S., & Barber, B. L. (1995). The long-term effects of seventh-grade ability grouping in mathematics. *Journal of Early Adolescence*, *15*(1), 58–89.

Furrer, C., & Skinner, E. (2003). Sense of relatedness as a factor in children's academic engagement and performance. *Journal of Educational Psychology*, *95*, 148–162.

Garcia Coll, C. T., Crnic, K., Hamerty, G., Wasik, B. H., Jenkins, R., Vazquez Garcia, H., et al. (1996). An integrative model for the study of developmental competencies in minority children. *Child Development*, *20*, 1891–1914.

Goodenow, C. (1993). Classroom belonging among early adolescent students: Relationships to motivation and achievement. *Journal of Early Adolescence*, *13*(1), 21–43.

Gottfried, A. E., Fleming, J. S., & Gottfried, A. W. (2001). Continuity of academic intrinsic motivation from childhood through late adolescence: A longitudinal study. *Journal of Educational Psychology*, *93*, 3–13.

Graham, S., & Taylor, A. Z. (2002). Ethnicity, gender, and the development of achievement values. In A.Wigfield & J. S. Eccles (Eds.), *Development of achievement motivation* (pp. 123–146). San Diego: Academic Press.

Grolnick, W. S., Gurland, S. T., Jacob, K. F., & Decourcey, W. (2002). The development of self-determination in middle childhood and adolescence. In A. Wigfield & J. S. Eccles (Eds.), *Development of achievement motivation* (pp. 147–171). San Diego: Academic Press.

Guay, F., Marsh, H. W., & Boivin, M. (2003). Academic self-concept and academic achievement: Developmental perspectives on their causal ordering. *Journal of Educational Psychology*, *95*, 124–136.

Hallinan, M. T., & Kubitschek, W. N. (1999). Curriculum differentiation and high school achievement. *Social Psychology of Education*, *3*, 41–62.

Harris-Britt, A., Valrie, C. R., Kurtz-Costes, B., & Rowley, S. J. (2007). Perceived racial discrimination and self-esteem in African American youth: Racial socialization as a protective factor. *Journal of Research on Adolescence*, *17*(4), 669–682.

Harter, S. (1998). The development of self-representations. In W. Damon (Series Ed.) & N. Eisenberg (Vol. Ed.), *Handbook of child psychology*, vol. *3* (5th ed., pp. 553–617). New York: John Wiley & Sons.

Harter, S., Whitesell, N. R., & Kowalski, P. (1992). Individual differences in the effects of educational transitions on young adolescents' perceptions of competence and motivational orientation. *American Educational Research Journal*, *29*, 809–835.

Hidi, S. (2001). Interest, reading, and learning: Theoretical and practical considerations. *Educational Psychology Review*, *13*, 191–209.

Hidi, S., & Harackiewicz, J. (2000). Motivating the academically unmotivated: A critical issue for the 21st century. *Review of Educational Research*, *70*, 151–180.

Hoffmann, L. (2002). Promoting girls' interest and achievement in physics classes for beginners. *Learning and Instruction*, *12*, 447–465.

Hunt, D. E. (1975). Person–environment interaction: A challenge found wanting before it was tried. *Review of Educational Research*, *45*, 209–230.

Institute for Research and Reform in Education. (2004). *First Things First*. Internal working document. Philadelphia: Author.

Jackson, A. W., & Davis, G. A. (2000). *Turning Points 2000: Educating adolescents in the 21st century*. New York: Teachers College Press.

Jacobs, J., Lanza, S., Osgood, D. W., Eccles, J. S., & Wigfield, A. (2002). Ontogeny of children's self-beliefs: Gender and domain differences across grades one through 12. *Child Development*, *73*, 509–527.

Jencks, C. L., & Brown, M. (1975). The effects of high schools on their students. *Harvard Educational Review*, *45*, 273–324.

Jencks, C. L., & Phillips, M. (Eds.). (1998). *The Black-White test score gap*. Washington, DC: Brookings Institute Press.

Jeynes, W. H. (2002). A meta-analysis of the effects of attending religious schools and religiosity on Black and Hispanic academic achievement. *Education and Urban Society*, *35*, 27–49.

Jussim, L. Eccles, J. S., & Madon, S. (1996). Social perception, social stereotypes, and teacher expectations: Accuracy and the quest for the powerful self-fulfilling prophecy. In L. Berkowitz (Ed.), *Advances in experimental social psychology* (pp. 281–388). New York: Academic Press.

Juvonen, J., Le, V. N., Kaganoff, T., Augustine, C., & Constant, L. (2004). *Focus on the wonder years: Challenges facing the American middle school*. Santa Monica, CA: Rand Corporation.

Kao, G., & Thompson, J. S. (2003). Racial and ethnic stratification in educational achievement and attainment. *Annual Review of Sociology*, *29*, 417–442.

Kaplan, A., & Maehr, M. (1999) Achievement goals and student well-being. *Contemporary Educational Psychology*, *24*, 330–358.

Köller, O., Baumert, J.& Schnabel. K. (2001). Does interest matter? The relationship between academic interest and achievement in mathematics. *Journal of Research in Mathematics Education*, *32*, 448–470.

Kozol, J. (2006). *Shame of the nation*. NYC: Three Rivers Press.

Lamborn, S. D., Brown, B. B., Mounts, N. S., & Steinberg, L. (1992). Putting school in perspective: The influence of family, peers, extracurricular participation, and part-time work on academic engagement. In F. M. Newmann (Ed.), *Student engagement and achievement in American secondary schools* (pp. 153–181). New York: Teachers College Press.

Larson, R. W. (2000). Toward a psychology of positive youth development. *American Psychologist*, *55*(1), 170–183.

Larson, R. & Richards, M. (Eds.). (1989). The changing life space of early adolescence. *Journal of Youth and Adolescence*, *18* (6), 501–626.

Lee, V. E. & Loeb, S, (2000). School size in Chicago elementary schools: Effects on teachers' attitudes and students' achievement. *American Educational Research Journal*, *37*, 3-31.

Lee, V. E., & Smith, J. B. (1993). Effects of school restructuring on the achievement and engagement of middle-grade students. *Sociology of Education*, *66*, 164–187.

Lee, V. E., & Smith, J. B. (1995). Effects of high school restructuring and size on early gains in achievement and engagement. *Sociology of Education*, *68*(4), 241–270.

Lee, V. E., & Smith, J. B. (1997). High school size: Which works best, and for whom? *Educational Evaluation and Policy Analysis*, *19*(3), 205–227.

Lee, V. E., & Smith, J. B. (2001). *Restructuring high schools for equity and excellence: What works*. New York: Teacher's College Press.

Lehr, C. A., Johnson, D. R., Bremer, C. D., Cosio, A., & Thompson, M. (2004). *Essential tools: Increasing rates of school completion: Moving from policy and research to practice*. Minneapolis. MN: ICI Pulications Office.

Lerner, R. M. (2002). *Concepts and theories of human development*. Mahwah, NJ: Lawrence Erlbaum.

Lipsitz, J., Mizell, M. H., Jackson, A. W., & Austin, L. M. (1997). Speaking with one voice: A manifesto for middle-grades reform. *Phi Delta Kappan*, *78*, 533–540.

MacIver, D. J., & Plank, J. B. (1997). Improving urban schools: Developing the talents of students placed at risk. In J. L. Irvin (Ed.), *What current research says to the middle level practitioner* (pp. 243–256). Columbus, OH: National Middle School Association.

MacIver, D. J., Young, E. M., & Washburn, B. (2002). Instructional practices and motivation during middle school (with special attention to science). In A. Wigfield & J. S. Eccles (Eds.), *The development of achievement motivation* (pp. 333–351). San Diego: Academic Press.

Maehr, M. L., & Midgley, C. (1996). *Transforming school cultures to enhance student motivation and learning*. Boulder, CO: Westview Press.

Mahoney, J. L., & Cairns, R. B. (1997). Do extracurricular activities protect against early school dropout? *Developmental Psychology, 33,* 241–253.

Mahoney, J. L., Harris, A. L., & Eccles, J. S. (2006). Organized activity participation, positive youth development, and the over-scheduling hypothesis. *Social Policy Report, 20,* 1–30.

Mahoney, J. L., Larson, R. W., & Eccles. J. S. (Eds.) (2005). *Organized activities as contexts of development: Extracurricular activities, after-school and community programs.* Mahwah, NJ: Lawrence Erlbaum.

McNeal, R. B. (1995). Extracurricular activities and high school dropouts. *Sociology of Education, 68,* 62–81.

Midgley, C. (2002). *Goals, goal structures, and patterns of adaptive learning.* Mahwah, NJ: Lawrence Erlbaum.

Midgley, C., Anderman, E., & Hicks, L. (1995). Differences between elementary and middle school teachers and students: A goal theory approach. *Journal of Early Adolescence, 15,* 90–113.

Midgley, C., & Edelin, K. C. (1998). Middle school reform and early adolescent well-being: The good news and the bad. *Educational Psychologist, 33,* 195–206.

Midgley, C., & Feidlaufer, H. (1987). Students' and teachers' decision-making fit before and after the transition to junior high school. *Journal of Early Adolescence, 7,* 225–241.

Midgley, C., Feldlaufer, H., & Eccles, J. S. (1988). The transition to junior high school: Beliefs of pre- and post-transition teachers. *Journal of Youth and Adolescence, 17,* 543–562.

Midgley, C. M., Feldlaufer, H., & Eccles, J. S. (1989a). Changes in teacher efficacy and student self- and task-related beliefs during the transition to junior high school. *Journal of Educational Psychology, 81,* 247–258.

Midgley, C. M., Feldlaufer, H., & Eccles, J. S. (1989b). Student/teacher relations and attitudes toward mathematics before and after the transition to junior high school. *Child Development, 60,* 981–992.

National Research Council (2004). *Engaging schools: Fostering high school students' motivation to learn.* Washington, DC: National Academies Press.

Noguera, P. A., & Wing, J. Y. (Eds.). (2006). *Unfinished business: Closing the achievement in our schools.* San Francisco: Jossey-Bass.

Oakes, J. (2005). *Keeping track: How schools structure inequality* (2nd ed.). New Haven, CT: Yale University Press.

Oakes, J., Gamoran, A., & Page, R. N. (1992). Curriculum differentiation: Opportunities, outcomes, and meanings. In P. Jackson (Ed.), *Handbook of Research on Curriculum* (pp. 570–608). New York: MacMillan.

Ogbu, J. (1992). Understanding cultural diversity and learning. *Educational Researcher, 21,* 5–14.

Okagaki, L. (2001). Triarchic model of minority children's school achievement. *Educational Psychologist, 36,* 9–20.

Olsen. L. (1997). *Made in America: Immigrant students in our public schools.* New York: New Press.

Oyserman, D., Gant, L., Ager, J. (1995). A socially contextualized model of African American identity: Possible selves and school persistence. *Journal of Personality and Social Psychology, 69,* 1216–1232.

Oyserman, D., Terry, K., & Bybee, D., (2002). A possible selves intervention to enhance school involvement. *Journal of Adolescence, 24,* 313–326.

Padilla, A. M., & Gonzalez, R. (2001). Academic performance of immigrant and U.S. born Mexican-heritage students: Effects of schooling in Mexico and Bilingual/English language instruction. *American Educational Research Journal, 38,* 727–742.

Peck, S., Roeser, R. W., Zarrett, N. R. & Eccles, J. S. (2007). Exploring the roles of extracurricular quantity and quality in the educational resilience of vulnerable adolescents: Variable- and pattern-centered approaches. *Journal of Social Issues, 64,* 135–155.

Pintrich, P. R. (2000). Multiple pathways, multiple goals: The role of goal orientation in learning and achievement. *Journal of Educational Psychology, 92,* 554–555.

Renninger, K. A., Ewen, E., & Lasher, A. K. (2002). Individual interest as context in expository text and mathematical word problems. *Learning and Instruction, 12,* 467–491.

Roderick, M. (1993). *The path to dropping out: Evidence for intervention.* Westport, CT: Auburn House.

Roderick, M., & Camburn, E. (1999). Risk and recovery from course failure in the early years of high school. *American Educational Research Journal, 36,* 303–344.

Roeser, R. W. (2004). Competing schools of thought in achievement goal theory? In M. L. Maehr & P. R. Pintrich (Eds.), *Advances in motivation and achievement,* vol. 13: *Motivating students, improving schools* (pp. 265–299). New York: Elsevier.

Roeser, R. W. (2004, July). *The diversity of selfways in school during adolescence project.* Paper presented at the annual meeting of William T. Grant Faculty Scholars Program, Vail, CO.

Roeser, R. W., & Eccles, J. S. (1998). Adolescents' perceptions of middle school: Relation to longitudinal changes in academic and psychological adjustment. *Journal of Research on Adolescence, 88,* 123–158.

Roeser, R. W., & Eccles, J. S., (2000). Schooling and mental health. In A. J. Sameroff, M. Lewis, & S. M. Miller (Eds.), *Handbook of developmental psychopathology* (2nd ed.; (pp. 135–156). New York: Plenum.

Roeser, R. W., Eccles, J. S., & Freedman-Doan, C. (1999). Academic functioning and mental health in adolescence: Patterns, progressions, and routes from childhood. *Journal of Adolescent Research, 14,* 135–174.

Roeser, R. W., Eccles, J. S., & Sameroff, A. J. (1998). Academic and emotional functioning in early adolescence: Longitudinal relations, patterns, and prediction by experience in middle school. *Development and Psychopathology, 10,* 321–352.

Roeser, R. W., Eccles, J. S., & Sameroff, A. J. (2000). School as a context of social–emotional development: A summary of research findings. *Elementary School Journal, 100,* 443–471.

Roeser, R. W., Eccles, J. S. & Strobel, K. (1998). Linking the study of schooling and mental health: Selected issues and empirical illustrations at the level of the individual. *Educational Psychologist, 33,* 153–176.

Roeser, R. W., & Gonzalez, R. (!997). *Research on transitions into and out of the middle school years.* Working paper for the National Institute on the Education of At-Risk Students of the Office of Educational Research and Improvement, Washington, DC.

Roeser, R. W., & Midgley, C. M. (1997). Teachers' views of aspects of student mental health. *Elementary School Journal, 98*(2), 115–133.

Roeser, R. W., Marachi, R., & Gelhbach, H. (2002). A goal theory perspective on teachers' professional identities and the contexts of teaching. In C. M. Midgley (Ed.), *Goals, goal structures, and patterns of adaptive learning* (pp. 205–241). Mahwah, NJ: Lawrence Erlbaum.

Roeser, R. W., Midgley, C. M., & Urdan, T. C. (1996). Perceptions of the school psychological environment and early adolescents' psychological and behavioral functioning in school: The mediating role of goals and belonging. *Journal of Educational Psychology, 88,* 408–422.

Roeser, R. W., & Peck, S. C. (2003). Patterns and pathways of educational achievement across adolescence: A holistic–developmental perspective. In W. Damon (Series Ed.) & S. C. Peck & R. W. Roeser (Vol. Eds.), *New directions for child and adolescent development,* vol. 101: *Person-centered approaches to studying development in context* (pp. 39–62). San Francisco: Jossey-Bass.

Roeser, R. W., Peck, S. C. & Nasir, N. S. (2006). Self and identity processes in school motivation, learning, and achievement. In P. A. Alexander & P. H. Winne, (Eds.), *Handbook of educational psychology,* 2nd ed.; (pp. 391–424). Mahwah, NJ: Lawrence Erlbaum.

Rosenholtz, S. J., & Simpson, C. (1984). The formation of ability conceptions: Developmental trend or social construction? *Review of Educational Research, 54*, 31–63.

Ruggiero, K. M., & Taylor, D. M. (1995). Coping with discrimination: How disadvantaged group members perceive the discrimination that confronts them. *Journal of Personality and Social Psychology, 68*, 826–838.

Rumberger, R. W. (1995). Dropping out of middle school: A multilevel analysis of students and schools. *American Educational Research Journal, 32*, 583–625.

Rumberger, R. W., & Thomas, S. L. (2000). The distribution of dropout and turnover rates among urban and suburban high schools. *Sociology of Education, 73*, 39–67.

Rutter, M. (1983). School effects on pupil progress: Research findings and policy implications. *Child Development, 54*, 1–29.

Rutter, M. & Maughan, B. (2002). School effectiveness findings 1979–2002. *Journal of School Psychology, 40*, 451–475.

Rutter, M., Maughan, B., Mortimore, P., & Ouston, J. (1979). *Fifteen thousand hours: Secondary schools and their effects on children*. Cambridge, MA: Harvard University Press.

Ryan, A. M., & Patrick, H. (2001). The classroom social environment and changes in adolescents' motivation and engagement during middle school. *American Educational Research Journal, 38*, 437–460.

Sameroff, A. J. (1983). Developmental systems: Contexts and evolution. In W. Kessen (Ed.), *Handbook of child psychology, vol. 1: History, theory, and methods* (pp. 237–294). New York: John Wiley & Sons.

Sellers, R. M., Caldwell, C. H., Schmeelk-Cone, K. H., & Zimmerman, M. A. (2003). Racial identity, racial discrimination, perceived stress, and psychological distress among African American young adults. *Journal of Health and Social Behavior, 44*(3), 302–317.

Sheets, R. H., & Hollins, E. R. (Eds.). (1999). *Racial and ethnic identity in school practices: Aspects of human development*. Mahwah, NJ: Lawrence Erlbaum.

Shih, M., Pittinsky, T. L., & Ambady, N. (1999). Stereotype susceptibility: Identity salience and shifts in quantitative performance. *Psychological Science, 10*, 80–83.

Simmons, R. G., & Blyth, D. A. (1987). *Moving into adolescence: The impact of pubertal change and school context*. Hawthorn, NY: Aldine de Gruyter.

Slavin, R. E. (1990). Achievement effects of ability grouping in secondary schools: A best-evidence synthesis. *Review of Educational Research, 60*, 471–499.

Steele, C. M., & Aronson, J. (1995). Stereotype threat and the intellectual test performance of African-Americans. *Journal of Personality and Social Psychology, 9*, 797–811.

Steinberg, L., Dornbusch, S., & Brown, B. (1992). Ethnic differences in adolescents achievements: An ecological perspective. *American Psychologist, 47*, 723–729.

Suarez-Orozco, C. & Suarez-Orozco, M. (2001). *Children of Immigration*. Cambridge: Harvard University Press.

Suárez-Orozco, C., & Suárez-Orozco, M. (1995). *Transformations: Immigration, family life, and achievement motivation among Latino adolescents*. Stanford, CA: Stanford University Press.

Taylor, R. D., Casten, R., Flickinger, S., Roberts, D., & Fulmore, C. D. (1994). Explaining the school performance of African-American adolescents. *Journal of Research on Adolescence, 4*, 21–44.

United Way. (2008). *Seizing the middle ground: Why middle school creates the pathway to college and the workforce*. Los Angeles: United Way of Greater Los Angeles.

Valdez, G. (2001). *Learning and not learning English: Latino students in American schools*. New York: Teachers College Press.

Valencia, R. R. (Ed.) (1991). *Chicano school failure and success: Research and policy agendas for the 1990s*. London: Falmer Press.

Wehlage, G., Rutter, R., Smith, G., Lesko, N., & Fernandez, R. (1989). *Reducing the risk: Schools as communities of support*. Philadelphia: Falmer Press.

Weinstein, R. (1989). Perceptions of classroom processes and student motivation: Children's views of self-fulfilling prophecies. In C. Ames & R. Ames (Eds.), *Research on motivation in Education,* vol. 3: *Goals and cognitions* (pp. 13–44). New York: Academic Press.

Wentzel, K. (2002). Are effective teachers like good parents? Teaching styles and student adjustment in early adolescence. *Child Development, 73*, 287–301.

Wigfield, A., Byrnes, J. B., & Eccles, J. S. (2006). Adolescent development. In P. A. Alexander & P. Winne (Eds.), *Handbook of educational psychology* (2nd ed.; pp. 87–113). Mahwah, NJ: Lawrence Erlbaum.

Wigfield, A., Eccles, J. S., MacIver, D., Reuman, D., & Midgley, C. (1991). Transitions at early adolescence: Changes in children's domain-specific self-perceptions and general self-esteem across the transition to junior high school. *Developmental Psychology, 27*, 552–565.

Wigfield, A., Eccles, J. S., Schiefele, U., Roeser, R., Davis-Kean, P. (2006). Motivation. In N. Eisenberg (Ed.), *Handbook of child psychology*, vol. 3 (6th ed.). Hoboken, NJ: John Wiley & Sons.

Wilson, J. Q., & Kelling, G. L. (1982). Broken windows, *Atlantic Monthly*, March.[Available at www.TheAtlantic.com.]

Wong, C. A., Eccles, J. S., & Sameroff, A. J. (2003). The influence of ethnic discrimination and ethnic identification on African-Americans adolescents' school and socioemotional adjustment. *Journal of Personality, 71*, 1197–1232.

Youniss, J., McLellan, J. A., & Yates, M. (1997). What we know about engendering civic identity. *American Behavioral Scientist, 40*, 619–630.

Youniss, J., Yates, M., & Su, Y. (1997). Social integration: Community service and marijuana use in high school.

CHAPTER 13

Religion and Spirituality in Adolescent Development

PAMELA EBSTYNE KING AND ROBERT W. ROESER

This chapter marks the first time that the topic of adolescent religiousness and spirituality has appeared in the *Handbook of Adolescent Psychology*. Although significant attention was devoted to the religious development of adolescents in the early part of the twentieth century (e.g., Hall, 1904), and again in the 1960s and 1970s (see Spilka, Hood, Hunsberger, & Gorsuch, 2003), this topic was relatively neglected for much of the latter part of the twentieth century. It is only relatively recently that renewed interest in the topic of religious and spiritual development during adolescence has developed within the developmental sciences (e.g., Barrett & Richert, 2003; Bloom, 2007; Lerner, Roeser, & Phelps, 2008; Roehlkepartain, King, Wagener, & Benson, 2006).

Benson, Roehlkepartain, and Rude (2003) documented this recent lack of attention to religious and spiritual development during childhood and adolescence by reviewing the frequency of publications on these topics in six top-tiered journals (*Child Development, Developmental Psychology, International Journal of Behavioral Development, Journal of Adolescent Research, Journal of Early Adolescence,* and *Journal of Research on Adolescence*). Of the 3,123 articles published in these journals between 1990 and July 2002, only 27 or 0.9% referenced "religion," "religious development," "spirituality," or "spiritual

development" as key words. Repeating this search for the period from August 2002 to January 2008, we found that only 20 of the 1530 published articles, or 1.3%, referenced these key words.

These searches document that religion and spirituality are still rare topics of inquiry in the field of developmental science. Nonetheless, interest is increasing. The Society for Research on Adolescence's Study Group on Adolescence in the 21st Century, for instance, noted that one of the areas most in need of research "across all nations" is the development of spiritual and religious values and identities during adolescence (Larson, Wilson, & Mortimer, 2002). As noted in Roehlkepartain et al. (2006), special issues on the topic have also appeared recently in peer-reviewed journals such as the *Journal of Adolescence, Annals of Behavioral Medicine, Applied Developmental Science, Review of Religious Research, Journal of Health Psychology, Journal of Personality, New Directions for Youth Development,* and *American Psychologist* (special section). Another indicator of emerging interest in this area is the inclusion of chapters on spiritual and religious development in prominent handbooks in the field of developmental science such as this handbook. For example, for the first time since its original publication in 1946, the sixth edition of the *Handbook of Child Psychology* included a chapter on

The authors thank Casey Clardy, Kayla Davidson, Jennifer Davison, Lauren White, Sonia Issac, and Jenel Ramos for their invaluable assistance on this manuscript.

spiritual development (Oser, Scarlett, & Bucher, 2006). In addition, comprehensive synthesis of existing research and theory in the *Handbook of Spiritual Development in Childhood and Adolescence* (Roehlkepartain et al., 2006) and the *Encyclopedia of Religious and Spiritual Development in Childhood and Adolescence* (Dowling & Scarlett, 2006) have recently been published.

Given this emerging area of interest in the study of adolescence, we pursue four aims in this chapter. First, as a way of demonstrating the importance of the growing scholarly attention to religiosity and spirituality, we provide a demographic portrait of the role of religion and spirituality in the lives of adults and adolescents in the United States in particular. We present facts that show religion/spirituality to be an important part of the everyday lives of tens of millions of Americans young and old. To ignore this domain of study in human development as has been the case historically (Donelson, 1999) is thus to ignore something rather central to adolescent development (e.g., Lerner et al., 2008; Roehlkepartain et al., 2006), to the life of our nation (e.g., Pew Forum on Religion and Public Life, 2008d) to the global challenges of our times (e.g., Harris, 2004). After presenting a case for the importance of religion and spirituality in adolescent development, we review theoretical perspectives on religious and spiritual development during adolescence with a particular emphasis on a developmental system, social ecological perspective. This perspective provides a framework for organizing our review of extant evidence regarding how different social contexts influence religious and spiritual development during adolescence, as well as the role of religion and spirituality in broader aspects of adolescent development such as health, subjective well-being, education, risk behavior, and civic engagement. Finally, we examine the problematic and sometimes pathological role of religion/spirituality in adolescent development. We conclude with suggestions for future research.

THE ROLE OF RELIGION AND SPIRITUALITY IN ADOLESCENTS' LIVES: DEMOGRAPHIC TRENDS

In 1999, Gallup International (1999) surveyed over 50,000 people in 60 countries across the world about their religious beliefs. The sample represented approximately 1.25 billion people. Results showed that 87% of respondents self-identified with a collective religious tradition, and approximately two-thirds reported that "God" was very important in their lives. These trends were particularly strong in West Africa, Latin America, and North America. These findings and others document that: (1) religion/spirituality is a central part of the lives of a majority of the people across the world, particularly in developing nations; (2) the United States stands out as one of the most religious nations in the developed world, especially compared to western European countries; and China remains much less religious than other developing nations (Pew Forum, 2002).

U.S. Adult Trends in Religious and Spiritual Self-Identification

According to the Pew Forum on Religion and Public Life (2008), the religious affiliations of the U.S. adult population are changing in dramatic ways. Currently, the adult population identifies religiously as 51% Protestant Christian; 24% Catholic Christian; 16% unaffiliated with a religion; >2% Jewish, >2% Mormon, and >1% Muslim. About 4% were affiliated with other major faiths, and 1% refused to answer or didn't know.

These numbers reflect five basic trends in American religious life. First, for the first time in the history of the United States, a nation founded on Protestant Christianity, Protestantism represents only a slight religious majority (51%) or may even now be less than 50% of the country (Portes & Rumbaut, 2007) due to long-term declines in church membership. Second, a small but increasingly significant number of Americans identify religiously as Muslim, Hindu, Buddhist, or Orthodox Christian (e.g., Eck, 2007). Third, despite declines in church membership among U.S.-born Catholics, the membership of the Catholic church has remained stable (24%) in the United States due to immigrants, mostly from Latin America, the Philippines, and, to some extent, Vietnam, who identify as Catholic (Portes & Rumbaut). Fourth, an increasing proportion of Americans identify themselves as unaffiliated with any religious tradition. That approximately 14%–16% of American adults affiliate with no religious tradition, and that this percentage has increased over the past decade and a half, is taken as evidence of an increasing but still minority trend toward secularization in the United States (Portes & Rumbaut).

Finally, evidence suggests that there is great fluidity among American adults with respect to their religious affiliations. The Pew Forum study (2007) found that more than one-quarter of American adults (28%) have left the faith in which they were raised during childhood in favor of another religion or no religion at all. If one included switching churches within the Protestant faith in estimates of fluidity, this percentage of changing denominations rises to 44%. Add to this kind of fluidity Americans' tolerance for exploring practices beyond their tradition and the increase in interreligious marriages, and the religious context in America seems fluid indeed.

U.S. Adolescent Trends in Religious and Spiritual Self-Identification

Given the high levels of religiosity among American adults, it is not surprising that representative studies of American youth have documented that the vast majority of adolescents in the United States tend to affiliate with one particular religious group (84%–87%; Smith & Denton, 2005; Wallace, Forman, Caldwell, & Willis, 2003). In addition, a significant minority of young people today do not identify with any religion (13%–16%; Smith & Denton; Wallace et al.). Similar to the findings for adults (Pew, 2008), the number of religiously unaffiliated adolescents seems to be rising (Wallace et al.).

In terms of specific religious identifications, results of the National Study of Youth and Religion (NSYR) show that religious affiliations among adolescents parallel those of adults (Smith & Denton, 2005). Results documented that most youth in the United States self-identify as *Christian* (75%); mainly *Protestant* (52%) and *Catholic* (23%). In addition, 2.5% self-identity religiously as *Mormon*, 1.5% as *Jewish*, 0.5% as *Muslim*, and another 1%–2% identify with other religions (e.g., Jehovah's Witnesses, Hindus, Buddhists, Eastern Orthodox Christian, Unitarian Universalist, etc.). Furthermore, results showed that approximately 3% of adolescents self-identify with two different religions, likely due to the increase in interreligious marriages in U.S. society (Eck, 2007). The rest of adolescents in the NSYR, reflective of a substantial minority of adolescents (16%), did not report any collective religious identity (see also Wallace et al., 2003). These youth were labeled *nonreligious* (Smith & Denton, p. 31). Among adolescents whom Smith and Denton called *nonreligious*, most self-identified themselves as "just not religious" (10%), "atheist" (1.5%), or "agnostic" (1.5%). The remaining 3% of the 16% "nonreligious youth" seemed uncertain about their religious identity, suggesting a small percentage of young people may have relatively "unexplored" religious identities in adolescence (Smith & Denton). Some of these young people who did not identify with a religion in fact were raised in a household where there was religion. The main reason why U.S. adolescents raised in a religion said they were nonreligious was, by far, intellectual skepticism and disbelief (Smith & Denton).

Religious Importance and Attendance Among U.S. Adolescents

Perhaps the most studied variables indexing religiosity beyond religious self-identification is individuals' self-rated importance of religion to themselves (or in their lives) and religious attendance—usually frequency of attendance or time spent in religious services. These measures are often combined and called religiosity or religiousness—an unfortunate mixing of what can be considered psychological identity beliefs and religious behavior. Nonetheless, using these measures, several nationally representative studies in the last 10 years suggest that between 50%–60% of American adolescents can be considered "strongly religious" (Benson et al., 2003; Wallace et al., 2003). Smith and Denton (2005) report that about half of all U.S. adolescents (ages 13–17 years) indicate a strong, positive orientation to matters of religion, faith and religious experience in their lives. They point out that this means "the other half of U.S. teenagers express weak or no subjective attachment to religion and have fewer or no religious experiences" (p. 68).

Interestingly, Benson et al. (2003) also found sizeable proportions of youth who reported high attendance at religious services also reported low personal importance of religion. They speculated that parental pressures to attend services or voluntary youth attendance for the social rather than the religious aspect of religious activities with same-aged peers are the primary motivators behind such adolescents' attendance at religious programs, activities, and services. These results highlight the importance of (1) conducting research on the role of religion and spirituality in the lives of adolescents; (2) attending to the diversity of motives youth have for such attendance; and furthermore (3) allowing for the possibility in such research that in fact religion/spirituality plays little to no role in the development of some youth.

Age Differences

Research on age-related differences in indicators of religious attendance and salience is equivocal. Findings from one longitudinal study showed widespread continuous levels of religious attendance and importance across adolescence. In a study of 370 youth, Benson, Scales, Sesma, and Roehlkepartain (2005) found that about two-thirds showed continuous levels of religious importance from the middle to high school years. Nonetheless, that finding means that the other third of their sample showed a discontinuity during this period with attitudes changing from both favorable to unfavorable and vice versa. Wallace et al. (2003) reported less attendance among older adolescence and Smith and Denton (2005) reported minor age-related differences in various indicators of religiosity in their cross-sectional, national study of 13–17 year olds. These authors posit that declines in religiosity noted in other studies may begin after age 17.

Cohort Differences

Using data from the 1976–1999 panels of the Monitoring the Future Study, Wallace et al. (2003) found a decline in religious attendance among high school seniors across the 1970s and 1980s, and a stabilization of attendance among 12th graders across the 1990s. A conservative interpretation of their findings, the authors write, is that "religiosity has been fairly stable for over a decade among 8th and 10th graders and for more than a quarter century among 12th graders" (Wallace et al., p. 121).

Sex Differences

Several studies have shown that sex differences in religiosity are evident among adolescents (Smith & Denton, 2005; Wallace et al., 2003). Smith and Denton reported that, compared to adolescent boys, adolescent girls aged 13–17 years old (1) attend religious services more frequently; (2) see religion as shaping their daily lives more; (3) are more likely to have made a personal commitment to live life for God; (4) are involved more often in religious youth groups; (5) pray more alone; and (6) feel closer to God. These gender differences, consistent but fairly small in magnitude, remain after accounting for youths' social backgrounds. Furthermore, such sex differences persist into adulthood (Batson, Schoenrade & Ventis, 1993; Donahue & Benson, 1995).

Geographic Trends

There are also geographic differences in the level of religiosity among adolescents. Smith and Denton (2005) found that adolescents in the Northeast were generally the least religious, those in the South the most religious, and those in the Midwest and West fell in between. Wallace et al. (2003) reported slightly different findings from data collected in the late 1990s. Among this cohort of adolescents, those living in the South indeed reported the most attendance and highest centrality of religion to self and those in the Midwest showed intermediate levels of religiosity. These findings corroborate those of Smith and Denton. However, youth in the Monitoring the Future study in 1999 who lived in the West and the Northeast were found to be less religious on these measures than those in the South and Midwest. These findings concerning youth growing up in Western states differ from the NSYR findings. It may be that 10 years of immigration in Western states, especially immigration of Latin Americans who tend to be very religious, may account for this difference (Eck, 2007).

In addition to these major geographical differences, research shows that adolescents who live in the most rural and sparsely populated counties in the United States tend to be more religious than those living in more populated, urban environments (Smith & Denton, 2005; Wallace et al., 2003). Furthermore, studies within rural communities in Iowa show that European American adolescents living on farms had stronger ties to religious institutions and were more committed to religious values than their peers who do not live on farms (King, Elder, & Whitbeck, 1997).

In sum, demographic evidence in the United States shows that formal religious participation is important in about 50% of U.S. adolescents' lives, with some decline in religiousness among older adolescents. There are also sex differences in which female adolescents are more religious than their male peers. There is also evidence to suggest that living in the South, the Midwest, and to some degree the West, as well as the less densely populated and more rural areas of the country, is associated with greater religiousness among youth. These levels of

youth religious involvement may impact the development of adolescents. Such influences would, of course, depend at least in part on the nature of religious and spiritual development. Accordingly, in the next section, we provide an overview of theories of religious and spiritual development during adolescence.

CONCEPTS AND THEORIES OF RELIGIOUS AND SPIRITUAL DEVELOPMENT IN ADOLESCENCE

The study of religion and spirituality in developmental science hinges on whether it is possible to formulate *good* theories from which scientists derive clear and scientifically tractable definitions of what religion and spirituality *are* substantively, what they *do* functionally (Emmons & Paloutzian, 2003; Weaver, Pargament, Flannelly, & Oppenheimer, 2006), and how they *develop* systematically over ontogenetic time (cf. Lerner et al., 2008; Oser et al., 2006; Roehlkepartain et al., 2006). Indeed, the challenge of having "good" theories is one that has historically plagued the study of the psychology of religion (Batson, 1997). Having good theory remains a significant challenge in the contemporary study of religious and spiritual development (RSD) during adolescence.

Nonetheless, several key theoretical strands can be discerned in current research on religious and spiritual development (RSD) during adolescence. Specifically, RSD has been discussed in terms of (1) a relational system affording security and anxiety reduction; (2) a meaning system affording existential answers in the context of life's "boundary conditions" (e.g., death) and unexplainable life events; (3) the development of cognitive schemas indexing conceptions of religious phenomena such as prayer and God; (4) an identity-motivation system organized around particular religious and spiritual goals, values, and ultimate concerns; (5) states and stages of awareness that transcend ego-consciousness and its boundedness in time and space (e.g., mystical experiences, construct-aware stages of functioning); and (6) a dynamic developmental systems perspective in which RSD is seen in relation to multiple contexts, people, symbol systems, and opportunities and risks that foster or frustrate such development across the life span. In addition, not all current scholarship about RSD is theoretically framed. Accordingly, we begin this discussion by describing two atheoretical definitions that nevertheless have served as a point of departure for more theoretical approaches.

Atheoretical Approaches and the Study of Religion and Spirituality

A proliferation of atheoretical, descriptive taxonomies of RSD and of the question of how to distinguish religion and spirituality in human development characterize the field of the psychology of religion and spirituality today (Paloutzian & Park, 2005). Traditionally, the field of psychology of religion subsumed the terms *religion* and *spirituality* under the construct of religion (Spilka et al., 2003). However, recent years have seen a divergence in these constructs, both in the culture as well as in the sciences (Koenig, McCullough, & Larson, 2001; Zinnbauer & Pargament, 2005). Thus, debate over the substantive and functional distinctions between *religiousness* and *spirituality* is one of a number of central conceptual challenges in the psychology of religion today, and one that bears centrally on developmental science theories of religious and spiritual development.

One prominent atheoretical approach to distinguishing between religion and spirituality is to conceptualize religion at the level of an organized sociocultural–historical system, and spirituality at the level of individuals' personal quests for meaning, happiness, and wisdom. For instance, in chapter 1, Definitions, of the *Handbook of Religion and Health* (Koenig et al., 2001), religion is defined substantively and functionally as:

> . . . an organized system of beliefs, practices, rituals, and symbols that serve (a) to facilitate individuals' closeness to the sacred or

transcendent other (i.e., God, higher power, ultimate truth) and (b) to bring about an understanding of an individual's relationship and responsibility to others living together in community. (p.18)

In contrast, spirituality is defined as:

> . . . a personal quest for understanding answers to ultimate questions about life, about meaning, and about relationship to the sacred or transcendent, which may (or may not) lead to or arise from the development of religious rituals and the formation of community. (p. 18)

This perspective is close to Pargament's (2007) view of personal religiousness or spirituality as a "quest for the sacred" in which the "sacred" is defined in terms of individuals' "concepts of God, the divine and transcendent reality, as well as other aspects of life that take on divine character and significance by virtue of their association with, or representation of, divinity" (Pargament, 2007, p. 32). Koenig et al. posit that there are five "types" of (individual-level) spiritualities that are either "moored" or "unmoored" to an established (social-level) religious tradition. For the vast majority, they posit that the spiritual life is "moored" or tied to a formal religious tradition. Nonetheless, Koenig et al. (2001) also acknowledge the existence of individuals who search for meaning to ultimate questions through unmoored spiritualities such as "humanist spirituality" in which the focal concerns center on humanity as a whole, universal ethics, and the cultivation of human potential rather than around a Transcendent God or Transcendental Reality. This approach of assigning religion to the level of context and spirituality to the level of the person as a means of differentiating religion from spirituality is somewhat elegant. Rather than having to then decide if the person is religious or spiritual at the individual level (which tells one little about the meaning and functional significance of these terms), Koenig et al. propose that researchers focus attention on "religiously moored" or "religiously unmoored" forms of spirituality at the individual level. As mentioned earlier, given that nearly a half of adolescents report no formal religious engagement, and more and more are identifying with no religion, a focus on unmoored forms of spirituality during these years is warranted in the future.

The notion of "moored spiritualities" is akin to the situation when individuals identify as "religious." The notion of "unmoored spiritualities" is akin to the situation in which individuals identify as "spiritual, not religious." Zinnbauer and Pargament (2005) summarize research on adults that also applies to U.S. adolescents with respect to identifications as "religious and spiritual" and "spiritual, not religious." They suggest that:

1. Most people identify as both religious and spiritual.
2. A minority of people identify as "spiritual not religious," sometimes using this identification as a repudiation of institutional religion (e.g., Hood, 2003).
3. Religiousness and spirituality are constructs that overlap in the United States and are very similar, but not identical.
4. The terms are both multidimensional and multilevel constructs crossing biological, mental, and social levels of analysis.
5. Both religiosity and spirituality develop and change over time at the level of individuals and groups.
6. Religiousness and spirituality are developing different connotations in U.S. culture and science, with a trend toward religion being associated with the social system or group level, and spirituality being associated with the individual level of analysis.

For purposes of this chapter, we use the generic term *religious and spiritual development* (RSD) to capture the development of both moored and unmoored forms of spirituality during adolescence. This general notion provides a point of departure for discussing several theories of the development of religiously moored and unmoored spiritualities.

Religion and the Development of Relational Security

Freud saw religion as a "universal obsessional neurosis" derived from infantile human wishes for love, comfort and security (Freud, 1961, p. 43). Religion was an "opiate" derived across human evolution to provide an illusory sense of safety and security against the frailty of life and the ubiquity of suffering. Despite the fact that psychoanalytic accounts of religion have been criticized thoroughly on a number of grounds (see Spilka et al., 2003), Freud's "opiate theory" of religion informed and was transformed by subsequent object relations and attachment theorists.

With respect to Object Relations Theory, Rizzuto (1979) argued that representations of God are a universal outcome of a child's relationships with their parents or other caretakers. According to object relations theory, individuals internalize affectively charged representations of their relationships with significant others such as parents as "psychic objects." Internalized images of parents become "templates" for comprehending and understanding the development of God images and relationships in individuals.

For Rizzuto and other object relations theorists, God images are posited to serve as "transitional objects" that can reduce attachment insecurity as the child develops more independence from caregivers (e.g., Dickie et al., 1997), and at other times in the life course characterized by significant life change and stress. Of course, one such time in the life course is adolescence and its suite of biopsychosocial changes. Evidence shows that many young people in the United States and around the world report relationships with God (Gallup, 1999) and that as distance from parents increase, intimacy with God increases (Dickie et al.). Furthermore, there is some evidence of important changes in conceptions of God toward a more relational view during adolescence. In one study, Deconchy (1965) found three stages in such development from ages 7 to 16 years among French Catholics. In the first stage, from about 7 to 11 years, God was seen as having concrete anthropomorthic attributes. From 11 to 14 years, these attributes of God became more abstract, following general trends in cognitive development. Interestingly, from 14 onward, youth reported more abstract and relational conceptions of God—focusing on their personal relationships with God in terms of themes of love and trust. These findings suggest that conscious relational images of God may become more salient during adolescence. Similarly, evidence suggests that in adolescents' prayer life, there is a development from instrumental forms of prayer towards a dialogic style of prayer in which attempting to get closer to God is central (Scarlett & Perriello, 1991).

A related view of RSD comes from an adaptation of the evolution-based theory of parent-child attachments put forth by Bowlby (1988). Kirkpatrick (1997) likened individuals' relationships with God to their relational attachments to parents and also posited that the parent–child relationship serves as a template for the kind of God image children develop. Such attachment schemas, in both cases, are assumed to serve the functions of protection and comfort during times of stress. Kirkpatrick and Shaver (1990) posited two main hypotheses. First, they forwarded the compensation hypothesis in which individuals with insecure parental attachments are hypothesized to develop a belief in a loving, personal, and available God as a means of compensating for the absence of relational security in infancy. Second, they presented the mental model hypothesis, in which attachments, secure or insecure, provide a mental model upon which individuals base their later religious beliefs and relational images of God.

In a study of adults, Kirkpatrick and Shaver (1990) found that the relation between attachment style and individuals' own religiosity was moderated by their mothers' religiosity.

Among those who reported growing up with religious mothers, those with any of three types of attachment styles were more highly religious. Those with secure attachments to "nonreligious" mothers reported less religiosity themselves later. These findings were interpreted as examples of basic "mental modeling effects." The study also showed that those with avoidant attachments to "nonreligious" mothers reported more of an orientation toward religion, more religious activity, and greater closeness to God later. This finding was interpreted as a "compensation effect." These individuals were also more likely to report having had a "sudden conversion experience" as well. Kirkpatrick and Shaver note, "religion may function in a compensatory role for those with a (retrospectively) reported history of avoidant attachment; that is, God may serve as a substitute attachment figure" (1990, p. 315). Those individuals with ambivalent attachments fell in between, but were more like the securely attached in that they followed the role of their mother in religion. Other research with adults has also appeared more to support the correspondence hypothesis—that individuals develop attachments with God that are similar to their attachment with parents (Piedmont, 2005).

Research with youth utilizing the attachment theory perspective on religion has been conducted in Sweden, where the evidence suggested support for the compensation hypothesis. Youths with insecure early attachments were more likely to believe in a loving God (Granqvist, 2002). These results suggest a number of possibilities for adolescents. Those with secure attachments to parents are likely to adopt the faith and God images (or lack thereof) of their parents (e.g., Hertel & Donahue, 1995). However, those with insecure attachments are likely to seek security by joining a religious organization and seeking social support in that setting. Alternatively, they may reject their parents' religion altogether as a function of their distant or difficult relationships with parents (e.g., Smith, 2003b).

In sum, several of the notions originally discussed in psychodynamic theories of religion live on in the contemporary study of religious and spiritual development in adolescence in spirit if not specific content. One is the focus on the relational elements of religious faith. The notion of religious or spiritual development as involving the development of a relationship with that which is perceived as the Transcendent (i.e., God) or that of transcendental value is present in many definitions of religion today (e.g., Pargament, 2007). Indeed, in a sense, William James's (1902) view of religion was relational in that he defined *personal religion* as "the feelings, acts, and experiences of individual men in their solitude, as far as they apprehend themselves to stand in relation to whatever they may consider the divine" (p. 32). In sum, one way of understanding RSD is in terms of the elaboration and internalization of specific God images, with specific affective tones, across time that serve nonconscious relational functions, such as anxiety reduction. The research on such conjectures suffers from methodological weaknesses however, such as the relative lack of ability of researchers to accurately measure unconscious "God images" (Piedmont, 2005).

Religion as a Meaning/Coping System

Another related way that scholars have conceptualized RSD is in terms of the development of an attributional meaning system that addresses certain kinds of life events, experiences, and existence writ large. Meaning systems can be defined as "personal beliefs or theories [individuals] have about themselves, about others, about the world of situations they encounter, and their relations to it. These beliefs or theories form idiosyncratic meaning systems that allow individuals to give meaning to the world around them and to their experiences, as well as to set goals, plan activities, and order their behavior" (Silberman, 2005, p. 644.). Religions provide individuals with meaning-enhancing capabilities in the face of unexplainable events by providing individuals with a ready set of religious attributions for such purposes—God's grace, karma, sin, salvation, and so on. Evidence suggests that religious attributions for events are more likely in circumstances in which naturalistic attributions (e.g., to people, physical events, chance, etc.) prove unsatisfactory (Spilka, Shaver, & Kirkpatrick, 1997). Such events usually involve "boundary conditions" in life such as inexplicable suffering, moral transgressions, and death. According to psychologists of religion, the motivational impetus for religious attributional processes in the face of such unexplained events and the consequent meaning systems that evolve from them includes the need to establish meaning, personal control, and a sense of well-being (Spilka et al., 2003). Over developmental time, attributional processes are both contributory to and a function of religious beliefs systems. Such systems develop across the life span, beginning with intuitive or folk belief systems and changing toward more abstract belief systems during adolescence (e.g., Bloom, 2005; Park, 2005).

Bering (2003) hypothesized that there exists a unique attributional meaning system he called the "existential domain" whose function is to ascertain the meaning of events that happen to oneself. As such, Bering described this domain as an abstract ontological domain within which the subjective narrative self is said to be contained and whose function is said to be to make meaning of, in order of developmental complexity and abstractness, one's life events, one's experience, and one's existence in totality. This domain is hypothesized to be independent of both the physical domain, and its function in explaining the movements and dynamics of inanimate objects, and the social domain and its function in the comprehension of intentional agents and other minds. It is also hypothesized to be independent of the biological domain and its function in explaining animate objects and their dynamics of growth and decay. Nonetheless, the domain often involves elements of these other meaning making systems. The triggers for meaning making through the existential rather than the physical, social, and biological domains of mental life, according to Bering, are events whose causes are not easily interpretable through these other domains and whose causes therefore demand some form of alternative interpretation. For instance, individuals who have a close encounter with death and can find no logical explanation for their good fortune may invoke attributions about invisible forces (karma) and intentional agents (God) as a means of establishing existential meaning. Furthermore, Bering sees this system as tied to a more general intentional system that has been documented to tend toward the attribution of teleological purpose to an abstract agency (i.e., God) that is envisioned to be responsible for events personal and otherwise (e.g, Bloom, 2005). Such a system, if proven to exist, would have significant implications for religious and spiritual development during adolescence, insofar as identity development and questions about purpose and existence become focal during these years (Damon, 2008).

Smith and Denton (2005) described the prevailing religious meaning system among adolescents in the United States today—the vast majority of whom self-identify as Christian—in terms of Moralistic Therapeutic Deism (MTD). They suggested that MTD among adolescents in the United States is "diesm" because it is centered on a diety—an ultimate being called "God" (or, less so in America, "Allah" and "Yahweh") who created the universe, orders it with divine moral laws, and then watches over human life on earth. Given the central role of God in such a worldview, questions about "What, in the end, does God want for us and want for us to do?" and "What is the way to God and happiness?" arise. The MTD worldview is "moralistic" in that it teaches that living a good and happy life on earth requires that one be a good and moral person. Adolescents in the United States believe that God wants them to be happy, and that the way to happiness is by being morally good and obeying the moral laws laid down in religious

scriptures. Being morally good not only leads to happiness, but in general, youth believe that "good people go to Heaven when they die" (Smith & Denton, p. 163). Third, the MTD worldview is "therapeutic" in that it frames God as an ultimate and benevolent being who assists us in feeling good and happy about ourselves and our lives through grace and the scriptures. Finally, Smith and Denton suggested that the "God" of MTD is "not one who is particularly personally involved in one's affairs— especially affairs in which one would prefer not to have God involved" (p. 164). This "distant God," they suggest, is selectively available for taking care of needs, coping with stress, and providing meaning to otherwise unexplainable personal experiences and events.

Another area of study that builds on this religion as a meaning system perspective is what Pargament (2007) refers to "religious coping." Religious coping is defined as "a search for significance in times of stress in ways related to the sacred." This definition means that some individuals will use religious and spiritual knowledge and imagery in their search for the causes of and ways of responding to life stress. For instance, some individuals interpret the causes of certain life stressors in terms of "sanctification"—a challenging experience that is "God given" in some sense. Other people use religious responses as a means of addressing life stress—for instance, not only attributing life stressors as "God given" but reframing them in a positive light such that they are spiritual tests or learning experiences associated with suffering.

Despite the burgeoning literature on religious coping among adults (Pargament, 2007), research on religious coping among adolescents is not very well developed at this time (Mahoney, Pendleton, & Ihrke, 2006). In one of the few studies done on religious coping with youth to date, Dubow, Pargament, Boxer, and Tarakeshwar (2000) found that Jewish adolescents used three different kinds of religious coping strategies in the face of stressors: asking God for help in times of need, seeking support from Jewish culture and social relationships, and seeing one's difficulties in a spiritual light.

Religion as a meaning system can also serve as a buffer against the effects of racial and ethnic discrimination on minority and immigrant youth (Eck, 2007). For example, the use of Afrocentric coping strategies involving spirituality has been an important coping resource for the African American community for much of its history (McCrae, Thompson, & Cooper, 1999). In a sample of 106 African American high school–aged adolescents, Constantine, Donnell, and Myers (2002) found that the use of religious coping strategies was greatest among those with a secure sense of their African American identity. In a different sample of 50 African American high school–aged adolescents, Brega and Coleman (1999) found that those who were more religious were less likely to internalize stigmatizing messages in the wider society about African Americans.

In sum, a second way of understanding RSD is in terms of the elaboration and internalization of a specific meaning system and worldview that provides answers to the existential questions of life that defy naturalistic explanations. In turn, questions take on emergent significance during the adolescent years as young begin to conceptualize the world in increasingly abstract ways and encounter increasingly adult-like life experiences, such as unjust treatment at the hands of others.

Religion as Cognitive/Conceptual Development

Another notion of RSD is one that sees religion as involving a distinct representational domain with its own focal psychological content, functions, and stage structures (see Oser et al., 2006, for a review of such approaches). In contrast to psychoanalytic and objects relations theories that focused on religion in relation to basic motives of the personality and the quality of caregiver relationships, stage-structure theories drew upon notions of constructivism and Piaget's theory of cognitive development.

These theories focus on age-related changes in the kinds of mental representations that young people could construct around religious topics and issues, as well as their functional implications for the motivation and regulation of behavior across development. Focal content includes elements such as the development of conceptions of prayer and God concepts over time (e.g., Spilka et al., 2003). Stage-structure theories have shown that, from childhood to adolescence, religious concepts generally followed the Piagetian stages of representational development from more concrete and single domain to more abstract and multidimensional representations (see Oser et al. for details).

Faith Development Theory

One of the most comprehensive and enduring stage-structure theories of religious development was offered by James Fowler (1981). Fowler's Faith Development Theory is rooted in genetic structuralism and describes development that leads from the particular to the universal and from heteronomy to autonomy. Fowler's theoretical approach establishes significant age trends and the stages, drawing heavily from Piaget, Erikson, and Kohlberg. Faith Development Theory offers a framework for understanding the ontogeny of how people conceptualize God, or a Higher Being, and how the influence of the divine has an impact on core values, beliefs, and meanings in their personal lives and in their relationships with others. Erikson's stage theory greatly contributed to the development of Faith Development Theory (1981; also see Fowler & Dell, 2006). Thus, Fowler (1981) contends that faith has broadly recognizable patterns of development. He describes this unfolding pattern in terms of developing emotional, cognitive, and moral interpretations and responses (for a discussion of all six stages of his theory see Fowler or Fowler & Dell).

Fowler (1981) described the substance of *religious faith* as an individual's personal way of responding to that of "transcendent value and power as perceived and grasped through the forms of the cumulative tradition" (Fowler, p. 9). Fowler describes faith as an "orientation of the total person" involving an "alignment of the will" and "a resting of the heart" in accordance with "a vision of transcendent value and power, one's ultimate concern" (p. 14). Faith, as such, is "the human quest for relation to transcendence" (p. 14) and to "that which is universal" (p. 15). Functionally, Fowler hypothesized that religious faith serves "to give purpose and goal to one's hopes and strivings, thoughts and actions" (p. 14). Although Fowler's theory has been criticized for its strong cognitive basis and for its suggestion that children are limited to less mature forms of faith (e.g., Balswick, King, & Reimer, 2005), it put the study of religion, spirituality, and faith on a serious developmental footing.

Specifically during adolescence, Fowler attributes developments in cognitive functioning as the basis for faith development. Based on Piaget's conception of early formal operational thinking, Fowler suggests in this *synthetic-conventional stage,* that adolescents are capable of abstract thinking and begin to reflect upon their own thinking and their stories and to name and synthesize their understandings into higher order, abstract concepts, and conceptual systems. In addition, Fowler also credits the emergence of mutual interpersonal perspective taking (e.g., Selman, 1980) as an important influence on faith development at this stage. He suggests that a young person's capacity to be aware of what other people think of them can make youth very sensitive to the evaluations they have of others and the evaluations others might have of them. In addition, because some adolescents may lack "third person" perspective taking, they are over dependent on the responses and evaluations of others.

Because of these cognitive developments, identity development becomes a more self-reflective process. Fowler contends that at this stage youth construct transcendent understandings in terms of the personal and the relational. God representations often have personal qualities such as love, understanding, loyalty, and

support. During this stage, young people commit to beliefs, values, and aspects of identity that link them to significant others in their lives. Within this synthetic-conventional stage, normative to adolescence, dependence on others for confirmation and clarity about one's sense of self and meaning can trap the adolescent in the "tyranny of the they." At this stage, ideology is lived and asserted, and only in later stages it is critically reflected on.

Cognitive–Cultural Foundations

A cognitive science approach to religion has arisen that in some ways challenges and also extends constructivist notions such as Faith Development Theory with respect to religious and spiritual development (Bloom, 2007). In contrast to Piaget's conception that children are confused about religious/spiritual things until they have acquired the ability to think abstractly and differentiate reality from fantasy, current cognitive–developmental research points to young people's seemingly inherent intuitive capacities to differentiate objects into those of natural and supernatural kinds (Bloom, 2005). The conjecture underlying the development of such an intuitive capacity is that it evolved from cognitive features designed for other evolutionary tasks. These features, when combined together, give rise to new and unexpected things—in this case, beliefs in souls, Gods, and supernatural phenomena more generally (Bloom, 2007). Mithen (1996), for instance, traces the emergence of spirituality to *cognitive flexibility*—the connection of previously separate domains of intelligence.

Alternatively, according to Bloom (2007), the existence of different intuitive cognitive mechanisms for understanding physical reality and social reality present at or near birth give rise to a fundamental dualistic outlook in human functioning and to the universal themes of religion as well. These mechanisms evolved separately and allow humans to distinguish between a world of material things, on the one hand, and the world of immaterial things like goals, desires and agency, on the other. Johnson and Boyatzis

(2006) note the human attraction to representations of agents that combine the ordinary with the extraordinary, as in the case of God. In support of these ideas, studies show that very young children all over the world, often despite their parents' own beliefs, seem to generate concepts of God (Barrett & Keil, 1996; Barrett & Richert, 2003). Young people (and adults) often view God in concrete, anthropomorphic terms. Nevertheless, they also see God as special and someone who is not limited by the laws of nature. The coapplication of these mechanisms to ourselves and other humans, according to this view, causes us to believe our bodies, as material things, are different in kind from our minds or our souls, as immaterial things.

According to Bloom (2007), the intersection of these mechanisms gives rise to the ideas of bodies without souls, souls without bodies, and the possibility of "life after death." Contrary to the popular belief that children cannot fully grasp the concept of death, recent research (Bering & Bjorklund, 2004; Boyer, 2001) points to afterlife beliefs held even by youngsters. Young people can appreciate the cessation of physical functioning. However, they simultaneously struggle with death's elimination of mental functioning, due to the application of different information processing modules to understand the body and the mind.

In addition, the application of our social information processing module to non-social events causes human beings to be hypersensitive to signs of agency in the natural world and to over impute intentionality to complex phenomena like the weather or the design of nature. The consequence of this cognitive functioning is to read agency into events in the form of Gods and other supernatural beings that are intuited to control events and personal experiences. Studies by Evans (2000, 2001), for instance, reveal that 7- to 9-year-old children typically hold creationist views whether or not they grow up in secular or fundamentalist Christian homes. Children, that is, tend to explain the origin of things in teleological, creationist ways.

A key point in both classic Piagetian and new cognitive science accounts of RSD during adolescence is that with the development of abstract symbolic representation and metacognition during these years, intuitive religious beliefs from earlier life and the insights that they have provided children about nature, human nature and God can be challenged by new inquiries and doubts and by new sources of information from school, the media, peers, and so on. Elkind (1997), for instance, posited adolescence to be a period in which cognitive development heralds a new "search for comprehension." With respect to religion, Elkind saw adolescents' emergent desire for comprehension as leading to two possibilities—a deepening commitment to faith and its ability to render life comprehensible; or a reflective inquiry into and perhaps a repudiation of the articles of faith that were assimilated earlier. Given the widespread belief in souls, angels, afterlives and so on among many adults in the United States and the world, it seems these early mechanisms are more often then not coopted into the shape of traditional religious beliefs and doctrines than questioned in any serious manner that leads to a new kind of inner spiritual life for individuals (see Bloom, 2005, for discussion). Nonetheless, it is clear that adolescence represents a time of spiritual questioning, doubting, and questing (see Hunsberger, Pratt, & Pancer, 2002).

In sum, a third way of understanding RSD is in terms of the elaboration or repudiation of intuitive religious concepts concerning faith, God, the supernatural, creation, and so on, in terms of the new information-processing capacities that normatively emerge during adolescence.

Religion as Identity System

A fourth and related way that scholars have defined RSD in adolescence is in terms a domain or set of domains of identity development (Allport, 1950; Roeser et al., 2008a; Templeton & Eccles, 2008). Such conceptualizations often are founded on the notion that religion, like any other salient domain of social experience, constitutes an important source of individual differences in the kinds of social–cognitive–affective self-schemas or representations that are elaborated across development as a function of experience (e.g., Epstein, 1990; Harter, 2006).

One early scholar who conceptualized religion as part of one's broader psychosocial development was Erik Erikson (1968). In contrast to early psychoanalytic perspectives, Erikson was interested in the objective relationships between the person (ego) and their social and cultural environments (ethos), and the implications of these person–context relations for psychosocial identity development.

In his epigenetic theory of psychosocial development, Erikson (1950) gave considerable attention to the role of religion and spirituality in development. According to Erikson, identity development during adolescence involved a more or less conscious recycling through and reworking of prior developmental task resolutions from infancy, toddlerhood, and childhood. Erikson proposed that earlier task resolutions associated with security and belonging (e.g., trust versus mistrust), self and will (e.g., autonomy and initiative versus shame, doubt, and guilt), and personal and social competence (e.g., industry versus inferiority) were reworked during adolescence in the process of identity exploration and commitment and in the context of (emerging) adult roles, relationships, institutions, and ideological systems. Specifically, earlier task resolutions around trust were said to be renegotiated during adolescence in terms of the kinds of people, role models, cultural ideals, and social institutions in which the growing young person could (or could not) have *faith*; earlier task resolutions around issues of autonomy and initiative were renegotiated in terms of the self-images, purposes, and corresponding activities and ideologies to which youth could (or could not) freely choose to commit; and previous task resolutions around issues of industry were renegotiated in terms of desired social,

occupational roles in which youth could (or could not) expect to excel. Depending on the relative fit or mismatch of the social contexts of adolescents development with respect to accomplishing the general stage-salient task of identity development, and the specific stage-salient task involving a renegotiation of issues of trust and faith as a key facet of identity development, Erikson posited subsequent paths of positive and problematic development, respectively, in terms of well-being, achievement, and social integration and participation.

Erikson suggested that the successful resolution of the first stage of development in infancy (trust versus mistrust) shaped the life virtue of hope, which "is the enduring belief in the attainability of fervent wishes" (1964, p. 118). Hopefulness is linked to beliefs about whether the social, natural, and supernatural worlds are trustworthy or not. Fowler (1981) described the substance of *religious faith* as an individual's personal way of responding to "transcendent value and power as perceived and grasped through the forms of the cumulative tradition" (Fowler, p. 9). Fowler describes faith as an "orientation of the total person" involving an "alignment of the will" and "a resting of the heart" in accordance with "a vision of transcendent value and power, one's ultimate concern" (p. 14). Faith, as such, is "the human quest for relation to transcendence" (p. 14) and to "that which is universal" (p. 15). Functionally, Fowler hypothesized that religious faith serves "to give purpose and goal to one's hopes and strivings, thoughts and actions" (p. 14). Thus, for both Erikson and Fowler, religion was conceptualized as an institution that confirms and supports individuals' hopes throughout the life span.

Religion not only provides a transcendent worldview, moral beliefs, and behavioral norms, but religious traditions also embody these ideological norms in a community of believers who can act as role models for youth (Erikson, 1968). For many youth, it is clear that religion and spirituality represent important sources of hope, ideals, worldviews and role models that influence the course of identity development during adolescence (King, 2003, 2008; Roeser, Issac, Abo-Zena, Brittian, & Peck, 2008; Smith & Denton, 2005). One of the shortcomings of Erikson's work, however, was the lack of a clear empirical basis for his views on identity and the general lack of a more domain-specific approach to identity-related phenomena (e.g., gender identity, religious identity, etc.). Neo-Piagetian views of identity have been more helpful in this regard (e.g., Harter, 2006) and have recently been applied to the question of how to differentiate between religious and spiritual development.

Roeser et al. (2008a) recently proposed a new conceptualization in which they posited that religious identities as primarily cultural and collective in nature (see also Templeton & Eccles, 2006), and spiritual identities as primarily transcultural and contemplative in nature (see also Ho & Ho, 2007). From this perspective, the core of a religious identity is a personal identification of oneself with a social collective (group) characterized by a particular cultural–historical–religious tradition (Ashmore, Deaux, & McLaughlin-Volpe, 2004; Templeton & Eccles). Individuals who claim membership in a particular religious tradition share in common with other group members collective sacred worldviews and their associated "beliefs, practices, rituals, and symbols designed (1) to facilitate closeness to the sacred or transcendent (God, higher power, or ultimate truth/reality) and (2) to foster an understanding of one's relationship and responsibility to others in living together in a community" (Koenig et al., 2001, p. 18). Self-identification with a particular religious group; the meaning of that identification to the person in terms of his or her representations of self, world, life purpose, and the (prescribed) good life; the centrality of the identification to a person's overall sense of identity; and shared religious practices and the nature and number of social bonds with group members are all key substantive aspects of a *collective religious identity*. Functionally, collective religious identities

fulfill individuals' basic needs for meaning and purpose, social belonging, esteem, self-understanding, transcendence, and contribution to something greater than the self through organized cultural forms (cf. Fowler, 1981).

In contrast to a religious identity, Roeser et al. (2008a) posited that the core of a spiritual identity is a personal identification of oneself with that which is pan-human and transcultural, in terms of shared humanity and universal values, ethics, and wisdom concerning life's ultimate existential questions that are relevant to all human beings (Ho & Ho, 2007). These ultimate concerns focus on the nature of life and death, on how to lead a good and satisfying life, and on the nature of human identity and our relationality with all that is "not self" (or not only "my in-groups" which is "ego-self" extended socially; Roeser et al.). The spiritual domain of identity development can evolve from, co-evolve with, or evolve independent of the religious domain of identity development. That is, individuals can self-identify as spiritual, religious, both, or neither. The function of a spiritual identity is to foster an embodied realization of identification with that greater whole of being, whether conceived of in terms of an ultimate being, an ultimate state of being, or an ultimate reality that represents the (hypothesized) unity behind the apparent diversity of being (e.g., Piedmont, 1999). This functional definition is consistent with the view of James (1902), who noted that the function of personal religion was to motivate individuals to realize a more satisfying existence. "Not God, but life, more life, a larger richer, more satisfying life, is, in the last analysis, the end of religion. The love of life, at any and every level of development, is the religious impulse" (p. 453). For James the core of religion/spirituality at the individual level is fundamentally about being whole, being wholly human, and being part of the whole that is existence.

The conceptualization of religion and spirituality in identity-related terms is consistent with other contemporary scholarly movements aimed at defining religion at the individual level of analysis in terms of idiosyncratic meaning systems (e.g., Silberman, 2005). By operationalizing religion and spirituality at the individual level of analysis in terms of cognitive-affective belief systems concerning the self and the world (e.g., Epstein, 1990) that function to afford meaning and to motivate and regulate behavior, scholars have successfully been able to relate such religious meaning systems to issues of engagement in religious practices (e.g., Roeser, Rao, Shah, Hastak, Gonsalves, & Berry, 2006); contribution to others (e.g., Roeser et al., 2008b), prejudice (e.g., Hunsberger & Jackson, 2005), terrorism (Silberman, Higgins, & Dweck, 2005), coping (Park, 2005), parenting and discipline practices (Mahoney, 2005), and so on. Thus, framing religion and spirituality in terms of identity and meaning systems regarding self and world is one scientifically useful way to study both the common and divergent functions and correlates of these two facets of human development.

RSD as Evolution of Awareness

Another way RSD has been discussed is in relation to spiritual experiences and corresponding phenomenological states of awareness—those that transcend the limits of normal, everyday, waking, ego-consciousness (King, 2003, 2008; Roeser, 2005, 2008a). Ego-consciousness is, by definition, centered in the ego (on "Me"). According to the contemplative traditions of the world (Wilbur, 2006), the state of ego-consciousness is said to be permeated with a sense of uniqueness, separation, lack, fear, desire, and division. States of awareness that transcend ego-consciousness are often labeled "religious," "spiritual," "mystical," or "non-ordinary" (Hood, 2003) because they transcend this limited state and bring one temporarily into communion with "something more." Such states are often accompanied by particularly powerful emotions such as awe, wonder, elevation, and love that signal experiences beyond the limits of self that often have transformative value (Haidt, 2003).

Boyatzis (2005) has pointed out the commonness of spiritual experiences of children and the lack of their study in the development of beliefs and faith. The same situation holds for adolescents who, as a function of developmental changes in brain, mind, and social worlds may be even more likely to have such experiences that inform their religious and spiritual development (Good & Willoughby, 2008).

Conceptions of spirituality as "transcendence" often rest upon this notion of spirituality as "states of consciousness" that may, through practice, become "traits of consciousness." The capacity to turn transient states of ego-transcendence into enduring traits of awareness in which a stable and clear state is continually realized is a core goal of spiritual development from a contemplative perspective (Wilbur, 2006). This perspective is associated with wisdom (Roeser, 2005).

Developmental Systems Theories

Stage-structural theories, once so prominent in developmental science, have been subject to greater levels of criticism with regard to human development in general (Kagan, 1996) and RSD in particular (Spilka et al., 2003). Developmental scholars have been moving away from attempts to identify universal and invariant stages of development and toward an understanding of developmental pathways, lines of development, and the role of culture and context in the process of development. Developmental Systems Theory (DST) shifts the focus from individuals to transactions between individuals and their various embedded sociocultural contexts of development (Bronfenbrenner, 1979; Lerner, 2006; Sameroff, 1983). In the rest of the chapter, we use DST as a key theoretical frame to discuss the contexts and processes involved in RSD during adolescence.

Central to DST are the roles of plasticity, context, and developmental regulation (Lerner, 2006). *Plasticity* refers to the potential for individuals to change systematically in both positive and negative ways throughout his or her life. Such plasticity is important in that it legitimates the optimistic search for characteristics of people and their contexts that promote positive development generally and RSD during adolescence in particular. Although people have the capacity to develop along a vast array of possible trajectories, the number of actual developmental trajectories is constrained by both individual and contextual factors.

Also foundational to DST is the significance of *context* and person-by-context transactions. From a developmental systems perspective, spiritual development is also located not in the person but in the ongoing transactions between the person and her or his multiple embedded sociocultural contexts of development (Lerner et al., 2008). It is the goodness of fit between person and environment that is of primary concern in determining different developmental trajectories. In particular, optimal development occurs when the mutual influences between person and environment maintain or advance the well-being of the individual and context. This bidirectional relation is referred to as *adaptive developmental regulation*. From a DST perspective, RSD is best characterized by the transactions between individuals and their various embedded contexts over time, as well as the fit of the developmental affordances of those contexts with the salient developmental needs of adolescents (e.g., Eccles, Lord, & Roeser, 1996). If the transactions of the young person and their context leads to adaptive developmental regulation, Lerner et al. (2008) posit that youth will gain a growing sense of transcendence—a sense of connection to something beyond themselves as well as a growing sense of self or identity. This experience of transcendence is hypothesized to motivate a growing commitment to contributing to the well being of the world beyond themselves.

Positive Youth Development and Spirituality

A developmental systems approach has been useful in studying positive youth development. Based on the notion that the central task of adolescence is identity development (Erikson, 1968), researchers have used a DST perspective to hypothesize that youth whose interactions with their contexts are adaptive—mutually beneficial to the young person and society—are more likely to commit to a sense of identity that promotes reciprocity with their family, community, and society (Lerner, Alberts, Anderson, & Dowling, 2006). This idea was originally Erikson's (1968), in that he hypothesized that youth who successfully resolve the identity crisis gain a sense of fidelity—a sense of loyalty to an ideology that engages the young person in the world beyond themselves (Furrow, King, & White, 2004; King & Furrow, 2004; Youniss, McLellan, & Yates, 1999). Such an understanding of spirituality is more than a feeling of transcendence, but a motivational force that propels individuals to care for self and others and contribute to something greater than themselves. As such, spirituality nurtures a sense of thriving (see Lerner et al., 2006; King & Benson, 2006) in young people by providing the awareness of responsibility and the passion to initiate and sustain commitment to agency.

This perspective is an important lens for spirituality, but it is also important to note that adolescents are often co-opted into and become faithful to things that are actually destructive to others beyond the in group as in the case of child soldiers or Hitler's youth movement during World War II (Erikson, 1950). Thus, it is important to note that a developmental systems theory provides a helpful framework for thinking about negative spiritual development as well. Just as a youth may interact with their family, peers, and society in such a way that brings about a moral spiritual sensitivity, transactions between individuals and their contexts may bring about deleterious forms of spirituality. For example, families may interpret and enact religious ideologies to create cultures of abuse (i.e. "Spare the rod, spoil the child) or cultivate generosity and a spirit of gratitude and contribution.

History is full of examples where youth have been socialized with an immoral and destructive spiritual sensitivity, and such issues are discussed more at the end of the chapter. In the next section, we review evidence about the core tenet of a DST perspective on RSD during adolescence—that the nature of social contexts really matter for RSD.

THE ECOLOGY OF ADOLESCENT RELIGIOUS AND SPIRITUAL DEVELOPMENT

From a developmental systems perspective, religious and spiritual development, similar to other domains of development, are embedded within networks of social relationships in proximal and more distal social settings across the life span. Nonetheless, as Regnerus, Smith, & Smith (2004) note in their review article on the state of this research:

> Social scientists know more about which American teenagers are religiously active than how they got to be that way. We know less about the social environment in which religious development occurs, apart from the parent–child relationship . . . scholars have often appeared less concerned about the role of ecology and social relationships than about personality, emotions, and stages in the religious development of the individual. (p. 27)

In this section, we review existing evidence on how relationships with parents, peers, and mentors, and experiences in families and schools can shape religious and spiritual development during adolescence. We then offer a macrosystemic analysis of religion and spirituality as cultural phenomena and consider the role of ethnicity and culture in RSD. We discuss the role of religious institutions in adolescents' RSD in a later section.

Family Influences

Parents play an important role in the religious and spiritual development of adolescents (e.g., Boyatzis, 2005; Spilka et al., 2003). Similar to research in other areas of socialization, parents are posited to be key interpreters of religion for young people, and parental beliefs and practices are thought to provide the foundation for young people's development of their own religious beliefs and practices (Ozorak, 1989), both directly through explicit socialization practices, and indirectly through the influence of religion on parenting behaviors (Spilka et al.). Dollahite and Marks (2005) found that families foster religious and spiritual development in children through processes such as formal teaching, parent–child discussion, role modeling, and coparticipation in prayer and other rituals.

The quality of the parent–adolescent relationship is key to the religious socialization process. Studies in the United States and Scotland have shown that family cohesiveness is related to stability of religious participation of sons and daughters over time (Ozorak, 1989). Parent–child relationships characterized by frequent interaction and a high degree of trust have been linked to greater religious socialization (King & Furrow, 2004), and warm close relationships are also linked to greater correspondence of offspring's religious beliefs with those of their parents (Hoge, Petrillo & Smith, 1982). Bao, Whitbeck, Hoyt, & Conger (1999) found that parental acceptance (trust, care, absence of fault finding) was important for the socialization of religious beliefs and practices from parents to children with greater acceptance leading to greater influence. Other studies indicate that greater parent–child closeness leads to less religious rebellion over time (Wilson & Sherkat, 1994). This literature suggests that warm, supportive relationships with religious parents is a means of enhancing the RSD of adolescents.

There is some indication that mothers may be more important in the religious socialization of adolescents than fathers (Boyatzis, Dollahite & Marks, 2006; Erickson, 1992; Hertel & Donahue, 1995), although the research in this area is somewhat equivocal (Mahoney & Tarakestwar, 2005; Spilka et al., 2003). The apparent greater impact of mothers, makes sense, given that women traditionally have been called upon to organize the religious education of children in the home (Slonim, 1991). However, mothers who experience depression are less able to carry out this role in the intergenerational transmission of religion (Gur, Miller, Warner, Wickramaratne, & Weissman, 2005).

Other studies have looked at parental religious socialization and have found that daughters are more influenced by their parents than are sons. For instance, in a study of highly religious parents, results showed that parental efforts to control their adolescent sons with respect to problem behavior involvement can backfire, whereas such strategies are more effective with daughters (Mahoney & Tarakeshwar, 2005). On the other hand, Bao et al. (1999) found that parents who were perceived as accepting had equal influence on both sons and daughters in the religious domain. These findings suggest that controlling parenting practices, in conjunction with religious teachings, may be particularly problematic with adolescent sons, whereas support for autonomy and warmth can facilitate religious socialization in sons and daughters equally well during adolescence.

Another way parents can socialize adolescents in the religious domain has to do with engagement in family rituals around religion. For instance, results of the NSYR showed that 54% of U.S. families engaging in "giving thanks before or after meals," and 44% of youths said they talked with their families about God, the scriptures, prayer, or religious and spiritual matters one or more days a week. Family prayer is very common in conservative Protestant, African American Protestant, and Mormon families and likely is one major way that parents socialize religious practices in their offspring (e.g., Ozorak, 1989). In a national Seven-Day Adventist population, Lee, Rice, and Gillespie (1997) found that family worship patterns that involved a high degree of adolescent participation was positively linked with active adolescent faith scores. Erickson (1992) found that parental religious

participation with adolescents was more efficacious than mere parental religiousness. Similarly, another study on Protestant youth found that talking with parents about religious issues and participating in religious activities together predicted an adolescent's experience of God and their report of the importance of religion (King, Furrow, & Roth, 2002).

Although many studies have documented the importance of parents, some longitudinal findings have failed to support the importance of family life in long-term patterns of religiosity in children. For instance, O'Connor, Hoge, and Alexander (2002) found no relation between various indicators of religious socialization taken when adolescents were 16 years of age and their religious participation at age 38. The relative dearth of longitudinal studies on this topic make inferences about the long-term effects of parenting on the religion of offspring, especially given the considerable fluctuation of religious affiliations noted earlier (e.g., Pew Forum, 2007), unclear at this time. In addition, other sources of influence in the family, including siblings, aunts and uncles, and grandparents are important to consider in the religious development of youth (Boyatzis et al., 2006). Despite the importance of family in RSD, adolescence is clearly a time when religious and spiritual doubts increase (Levenson, Aldwin, & D'Mello, 2005). Factors other than the family, such as peers and mentors, are likely important in this developmental trend.

Peer Influences

The research on the effects of peers on adolescent religiosity is still in a nascent stage and results are not yet conclusive. Several findings are worth mentioning at this point. First, according to NSYR results (Smith & Denton, 2005), American youth generally report having peers that share their religious beliefs. When youths are asked to report on characteristics of their five closest friends, between two to three of these friends, on average, are said to "hold similar religious beliefs" to the target adolescent; in turn about one of these friends, on average is said to "be involved in the same religious group." Conservative, African American Protestant, and Mormon teens were more likely to have friends in their same religious group (Smith & Denton, 2005). King and Furrow (2004) found that compared to their less religious peers, religious youth reported higher levels of positive social interaction, shared values, and trust with their closest friends.

These findings suggest the existence of both selection effects (youth pick religiously similar peers) and socialization effects (peers shape each other). For instance, in a longitudinal study of children from ages 7 to 22 years of age, results showed that the best childhood and adolescent predictors of religiosity during early adulthood were ethnicity and peers' church attendance during high school (Gunnoe & Moore, 2002). Similarly, Regnerus et al. (2004) found that peer church attendance was an important predictor of youth church attendance. Hoge and Petrillo (1978) found that friends have at least moderate influence on religious practices (e.g., youth group attendance, enjoyment of that participation). Having friends who verbally talk about religion and spirituality has been found to be associated with higher self-reported religious belief and commitment among individuals, compared to those with friends who did not talk about their faith (Schwartz, Bukowski, & Aoki, 2006). In addition, Schwartz (2006) found that not only did friends' spiritual modeling and dialogue account for significant variance in adolescent religious belief and commitment, but that these factors actually mediated the influence of parents on religiousness. Similarly, King et al. (2002) found that talking with friends about religion and participating with friends in informal religious activities (i.e., studying religious or sacred texts, listening to religious music, or attending religious camp), explained significant variance in religious commitment over and above parental influences (King et al.). Similarly, in a large sample of Christian

adolescents aged 16 years, Schwartz (2006) found that perceived faith support from Christian friends was one of the most important influences on adolescents' faith net of family variables.

Mentors and Gurus

Despite the known role of adult mentors in the lives of youth (see Rhodes & Lowe, vol. 2 of this *Handbook*), only a small body of literature examines the roles of adult RS mentors and teachers in adolescent RSD. Some research has documented that the relational quality of the mentor–mentee relationship impacts the level of influence on spiritual development. One study of more that 3,000 Christian adolescents conducted by Schwartz (2006) found that when a young person described their relationship with their youth pastor as including strong religious instruction, spiritual modeling, and being known (i.e., intimacy), these relationships contributed significantly to youths' perceptions of their own spiritual development. Another study found relationships between youth pastors and their youth that are characterized by both relational intentionality and spiritual focus, result in spiritual development, as is indicated by outcomes such as personal relationship with God, moral responsibility, hopeful and positive attitudes, and engaging in mission and service (Strommen & Hardel, 2000). In a rare comparison study, Cannister (1999) found modest support for mentoring as supportive of the maturing spiritual development of adolescents. The study compared first-year college students who had a formal mentoring relationship with a professor who was intent on nurturing spiritual growth and those who did not have such a relationship. Those who were being intentionally mentored reported enhanced spiritual development.

Although only a few studies exist, research suggests that the presence of intimate and interactive relationships with spiritual mentors may provide a rich context for spiritual development. These studies and others demonstrate the importance of non-parental roles models in the RSD of adolescent youth. Not only are relationships important within the developmental systems of RSD, but institutions play an important part as well.

School Influences

A few studies have examined how schooling may affect the religious and spiritual development of young people. In one strand of research, the focus has been on the direct effects of attending a religious school on adolescents' academic development. In a second strand of work the focus has been on understanding how the religious composition of the student body may exert indirect effects on adolescents' religious lives. Oddly, rarely have studies looked at the religious and spiritual developmental effects of religious schooling (Spilka et al., 2003). Thus, this is an area ripe for future research.

Benson, Yeager, Wood, Guerra, and Manno (1986) found that Catholic high schools serving large proportions of low income youth affected the religious development of youth if they stressed both academics and religion simultaneously. In a study of an African American Muslim school, Nasir (2004) documented how a shared religious ideology allowed teachers and staff ideational and relational resources by which they could offer a positive identity to students. Specifically, teachers viewed a particular student as a spiritual being waiting to be developed rather than as a behavioral problem worthy of diagnosis and labeling. This social positioning based on a spiritual ideology afforded these young people a unique set of supports and a unique identity position from which to move forward despite adversity.

In a case-comparative study of eleven private, English-medium religious secondary schools in India, Roeser (2005) found a relation between aspects of adolescents' student and religious identities and the nature of their school culture. Through examining Hindu and Christian schools, they found that students reported views of spirituality and self consistent with the underlying religious philosophy and practices in their schools. This finding was true even when students attended schools with a different faith tradition than their own.

Other studies have examined the "religious climate" of schools. Regnerus et al. (2004) used National Longitudinal Data of Adolescents Health data to examine how the mean level of adolescents' schoolmates' inclinations toward religion were associated with adolescents' own religious service attendance and perceived importance of religion. Findings indicated that the level of religiosity among classmates predicated individual religiosity, even after accounting for family religiosity, peer religiosity, and a host of demographic factors. In fact, these authors found that aggregate student body religiosity was a more powerful predictor of individual religiosity than was attending a religious school. These effects make sense given the power of peer influences in schools specifically, and the more general influence of climate variables over school sector variables in mediating school effects generally.

Barrett, Pearson, Muller, and Frank (2007) posited that the private religiosity of schoolmates, especially popular ones, may create a climate and discourse community in which religious matters are normative and valued. In addition, the authors posited that to the extent youth are motivated to conform to such norms due to their level of shared denominational affiliations with schoolmates, and due to religiosity of high status peers in the school, student-body religiosity may affect personal religiosity.

Culture, Diversity, and Ethnicity

There exist additional macro-level contextual influences on RSD. Adolescence is a particularly important time in which cultural influences in the shaping of the religious and spiritual development of young people "show through" in the forms of rituals and ceremonies marking the transition from child to adult status in the eyes of the religious community. For instance, in some Protestant Christian communities, voluntary baptism during this stage marks a moment of sacred rebirth, inclusion, and adult membership in one's church. Similarly, the Bar- and Bat-Mitzvahs are transitional ceremonies in which youth move from childhood to adult religious status within the Jewish cultural–religious tradition. In still other contexts, children may go through formal rites of transition in which physically painful rituals are used to evoke courage and emphasize the passage from one life stage to another (Magesa, 1997). Such initiation rites are important cultural opportunities to teach youth about self-sacrifice, cooperation, and survival; and provide an opportunity for adolescents' to acknowledge to willingly participate in serving the community.

Unfortunately, biases in the field of study concerned with religion in psychology have limited our knowledge of religious and spiritual development among diverse religious, ethnic and culture groups within and beyond the United States (Mattis, Ahuluwalie, Cowie, & Kirkland-Harris, 2006). Leaders in the field of the psychology of religion, for instance, have acknowledged that the field has been dominated by a largely Protestant Christian orientation to date (see Hill & Pargament, 2003). What is less acknowledged is that this orientation includes a tacit emphasis on dualist metaphysics (spirit versus matter, sacred versus profane, soul versus body); theistic conceptions of divinity (God as a Being); singular pathways of spiritual development (e.g., devotion to God); and specific Western cultural issues in the study of religion and spirituality (Roeser et al., 2006).

Specific cultural issues that are intertwined with Western Christian religious traditions include a focus on the sinful nature of human beings and the Veneer Theory of morality with its impact on economics, law and government (de Waals, 2007); concern with differentiating between whether one is spiritual or religious (e.g., Fuller, 2001); and a focus on racial differences in religiosity (e.g., Mattis et al.,

2006). The fact of the matter is that religions are deeply cultural in nature, reflecting large scale national, historical, ethnic/racial and geographical influences (Geertz, 1973). Thus, to study religion without regard to culture is to miss something fundamental about its origins and manifestations.

Non-Western, Abrahamic forms of spirituality also diverge significantly from the assumptive frameworks and worldviews of Western Christianity. In some cultural contexts, for instance, spiritual development is assumed to begin prior to birth. In some communities in which reincarnation is accepted, adults may believe children inherit the spirit/soul of a dead ancestor; thus, children are born with spiritual powers, wisdom, and even physical attributes that can reflect their spiritual maturity. In addition, the early stages of a child's spiritual development are usually perceived as times of spiritual vulnerability in such cultures due to the evil eye phenomenon (Leach & Fried, 1972; Obermeyer, 2000). Some believe that malevolent and benevolent forces exist and manifest themselves in the child's immediate family and extended community, impacting all aspects of the child's new life. Consequently, the child's survival and healthy development depend on others' protection from spiritual harm. Thus, in cultures that believe in the existence of the evil eye and its power, rituals are performed to protect children from malevolent forces (Ruble, O'Nell, & Collando Ardán, 1992).

In sum, although it is evident that adolescent religious and spiritual development occurs within the developmental–contextual systems in which young people live, the processes by which this development occurs have been less explored. In the following section, we provide an overview of the theoretical explanations for how religious congregational and youth group contexts may influence not only religious and spiritual development of youth, but also wider aspects of development during adolescence. Many of the processes discussed in this section are also relevant to other social contextual influences on RSD outside religious institutions.

RELIGIOUS INSTITUTIONAL INFLUENCES ON ADOLESCENT RSD AND POSITIVE YOUTH DEVELOPMENT

Erikson (1950, 1964, 1968) pointed to religious institutions as important parts of the sociohistorical–cultural matrix in which identity development takes place. He argued that religion was an important institution in the promotion of fidelity during adolescence—defined as commitment and loyalty to an ideology. This may still be true today for perhaps half of all American youths who regularly attend services (Smith & Denton, 2005). In this section, we explore the role of religious congregations in shaping RSD and positive development through a variety of mechanisms involving social relationships, identity and skill development, and opportunities for transcendence through spiritual practices. Nonetheless, we note at the outset that only a little is known about how the dynamics of participation in religious congregations and how they affect youth spiritual development.

The term *congregation* refers to an organized community associated with a religion such as a church, parish, or cathedral (Christian); synagogue (Jewish); masjid/mosque (Muslim); temple (Buddhist, Hindu, Jewish), ward (Latter-Day Saint); gurdwara (Sikh); or assembly (Bahai). According to the NYSR, 48% of American youth attend religious services once a week or more, with another 27% attending at least many times a year. Of these attending youth, 89% find that their congregations usually or sometimes make them think about important things and 94% report that their congregation is usually or sometimes a welcoming place for youth. About 38% of the sample are currently involved in a religious youth group, and 69% are presently or have previously been involved (Smith & Denton, 2005).

Congregations have been linked to promoting faith maturity (Roehlkepartain & Patel, 2006), which refers to the degree to which a person exemplifies the priorities, commitments, and perspectives indicative of "vibrant and life-transforming faith" (Benson, Donahue, & Erickson, 1993, p. 3). Search Institute conducted a series of studies that examined the relationships between congregational dynamics, religious education, and faith maturity in mainline Protestant Christian churches. The findings suggested that personalized educational practices, caring and effective leaders, a climate of warmth and caring, a thinking culture, support for families, engagement in practical life issues, and opportunities to serve others were important for faith development (Benson & Elkin, 1990). Similar findings resulted from replication studies in other Christian faith traditions, including Seventh-Day Adventists, Catholics, and the Lutheran Church–Missouri Synod (see Roehlkepartain & Patel), suggesting that the multifaceted educational, relational, and emotional nature of congregations may promote spiritual development, at least as operationalized by faith maturity.

Secondary analysis of the Survey of Youth and Parents yielded results substantiating the claim that religious congregations provide rich settings for increasing closure in networks involving youth (Smith, 2003a). These relational ties may operate as extra familial resources, reinforcing parental influence and oversight. Similarly, in an ethnically diverse sample of urban youth, research found that religious youth reported higher levels of network closure and social capital resources including social interaction, trust and shared values among parents, close friends, and a nonparental adult (King, 2004; King & Furrow, 2004). As such, religious institutions provide unique support systems for youth that have the potential to influence religious and spiritual development.

Other types of religious organizations besides congregations such as paracongregational youth programs and organizations, faith-based social services, (nonreligious) youth organizations, camps, and schools can also affect RSD in adolescents. Sometimes these organizations intentionally promote adolescent religious and spiritual development and sometimes these ends are accomplished unintentionally.

Larson, Hansen, and Moneta (2006) found that students participating in faith-based youth groups reported significantly higher rates of identity work. About 66% of the students in faith-based activities endorsed the item "This activity got me thinking about who I am," compared to 33% of youths in other types of organized activities. Others have shown that religious youth organizations help integrate adolescents into a community of youths and adults (see Regnerus, 2000; Smith, 2003b). Larson et al. (2006) also found that youth involved in faith-based youth programs were significantly more likely to be engaged in positive relationships and in adult networks than youth not engaged in faith-based programs. For example, 75% of youths in faith-based programs reported that "We discussed morals and values," compared with 24% of youths involved in other organized activities. Furthermore, significantly more youths in faith-based activities stated that the activities improved their relationships with parents/guardians and helped them form new connections with nonparental adults in their faith community.

Theories of Religious Congregational Influence

Smith (2003b) theorized that there are three different ways that religious institutions can exert positive, constructive influences on youth development:

1. By providing youths with resources in the form of moral and religious worldviews (i.e., seeking reconciliation instead of vengeance, treating body as temple of Holy Spirit, respecting mother and father), spiritual experiences (e.g., experience of profound peace and belonging), and role models and mentors
2. By providing opportunities for skill development (i.e., leadership and coping skills) and cultural knowledge development (e.g., Biblical events)

3. By providing social capital in the form social ties across differently aged peers, nonparental adults, and members of wider communities and society.

In short, religious institutions afford adolescents resources that provide moral guidance, meaning, and purpose; learning opportunities that provide coping and life skills; and social relationships that provide support, social capital, and network closure. In addition to discussing potential ideological and contextual resources embedded within religion and spirituality, the spiritual practices often associated with RSD offer unique benefits to youth.

Ideological Context

Relationships and contexts that provide youth with ideological and moral directives provide adolescents with a structural framework of normative beliefs and values that reinforce their existing belief system. Young people strive to make sense of the world and to assert their place in it. The beliefs, worldview, and values of religious traditions provide an ideological context in which a young person can generate a sense of meaning, order, and place in the world that is crucial to adolescent development (King, 2003, 2008). Religion intentionally offers beliefs, moral codes, and values from which a young person can build a personal belief system (Smith, 2003b). Benson (2006) indicated the function of spiritual development is to make sense of one's life by weaving the self into a larger tapestry of connection and meaning. Spirituality entails the intentional identification and integration of beliefs, narrative, and values in the process of making meaning. Whether this process is one of personal construction or socialization, the intentional act of relying on personal, religious, or cultural ideology is central to spirituality and crucial to the development of identity, meaning, and purpose—all foundational to positive youth development.

Relationships, organizations, and institutions that intentionally provide clear ideology provide important contexts in which young people can internalize moral directives, clarify their beliefs, integrate a prosocial identity, and find meaning and make sense of the world (Lerner et al., 2006). Such environments nurture religious and spiritual development as well as other important aspects of adolescent development. In addition to providing ideology, such developmental systems provide social contexts that nurture adolescent religiousness and spirituality as well as overall positive adolescent development.

Social Context

Religion not only provides a transcendent world view and morality, but religious faith community members more or less embody these ideological norms in a community setting and thereby act as role models for youth (Erikson, 1968). Although religion and spirituality do not exclusively offer these social resources, research documents that they may very effectively offer social capital, helpful networks, social support, and mentors.

Social Capital

Social capital models posit that religion's constructive influence on young people may be accounted for by the nature and number of relationships—and the benefits associated with them. For instance, through religious involvement young people have access to intergenerational relationships that are recognized as rich sources of social capital (King & Furrow, 2004; Putnam, 2000; Smith, 2003a). Few other social institutions afford the opportunity to build trustworthy cross-generational relationships and link youth to sources of helpful information, resources, and opportunities. King and Furrow (2004) found that religiously engaged youth reported significantly higher levels of social capital resources than less active youth. They found that relationships characterized by social interaction, trust, and shared values are most strongly related to positive youth outcomes. Social support available through religion may be particularly effective

for promoting adolescent thriving. In addition, religious institutions and the relationships that they afford may promote *network closure*, providing relatively dense networks of relationships within which youth are embedded, providing oversight of and information about youth to their parents (Smith, 2003b).

Social Channeling

Religious institutional involvement also involves social channeling, conscious process on the part of adults to steer their children toward particular individuals positioned to discourage negative behaviors and to promote positive life practices among young people (Smith, 2003b). In addition, social channeling is a major way that parents socialize their children's religious development—they put them into groups, activities, and contexts that reinforce their own efforts at religious socialization (e.g., Martin, White, & Perlman, 2001; Wallace & Williams, 1997). For youths in urban, low-income neighborhoods, Regnerus and Elder (2003) have shown that church attendance is particularly important because it channels youths into relationships with those who support academics and who help them build "a transferable skill set of commitments and routines" (p. 646) useful for success in school. Similarly, Schreck, Burek, and Clark-Miller (2007) found that religious involvement serves as a protective factor for adolescents by encouraging less contact with deviant peers and more contact with parents and school officials.

Social Support and Coping

Religious institutions and the relationships they afford also provide forms of social support that are particularly important to adolescent coping, resilience, and well-being. For instance, the coping resources offered in a religious setting may include group level shows of support through prayer. A study of young adolescents showed the social support of religious community members was the strongest negative predictor of depressive symptoms

(Pearce, Little, & Perez, 2003). These findings were replicated in a sample of over 3,000 16-year-old adolescent girls at various stages of pubertal development (Miller & Gur, 2002). Specifically, findings showed that not only was the expectation of social support from religious congregations in times of need associated with less depressive symptoms among youth, but also the expectation that religious congregations were critical of teenagers generally was associated with increased depressive symptoms (Pearce et al.). Thus, religious communities can be sources of social support or socioemotional distress based on the ways adults in those communities perceive and relate to youth.

Spiritual Modeling

Spiritual modeling and mentorship are two other ways theorists have discussed how adults socialize young people's religious and spiritual identities in the direction of the beliefs, norms, and expectations of a particular religious group (Cornwall, 1988; Oman, Flinders, & Thoresen, 2008). Spiritual modeling refers to emulating another in order to grow spiritually. This effect occurs through observing and imitating the life or conduct of a spiritual example or model who may be a living or historic example of religious or spiritual ideology and values. Spiritual modeling is based on social modeling and observational learning in the acquisition and maintaining of human behaviors (Bandura, 1986, 2003). Foundational to this approach is the notion that the people with whom we regularly associate, either by force or by choice, shape the behavioral patterns that will be repeatedly observed and learned most thoroughly. Acknowledging the complexity of spiritual development involving the acquisition of beliefs, attitudes, and skills, Bandura (2003) argues that spirituality is difficult to teach and is better understood when exemplified or embodied.

Mentors and Gurus   Spiritual mentors provide opportunities for young people to experience being a part of something beyond

themselves (see Schwartz et al., 2006). Mentors or gurus often occur within a religious context. For example, within the Hindu religion, gurus are teachers that are widely considered to be self-realized masters and embodiments of the divine (Martignetti, 1998). In such relationships, followers of such teachers often treat devotion or service to this teacher as a major focus of their lives. In some forms of Judaism, sages serve as important role models who illustrate right living and wisdom. In the Christian tradition, young people are often discipled by youth pastors or adult volunteers at churches. Whether a young person perceives himself or herself as a being a follower or by being mentored or discipled, these individuals connect the young person to a larger whole and enables the youth to identify with a community beyond himself or herself. Furthermore, the worldviews provided by spiritual models and mentors are powerful cultural resources that can inform adolescents' quests for a sense of meaning, order, and their place in the world (King, 2003, 2008). This is particularly true during adolescence and puberty when one's body, thoughts and feelings, and social relationships are all changing and creating both possibility and uncertainty.

Developmental Assets   The developmental asset framework also provides a similar account of the resources available to youth through religious involvement. Through secondary analyses, Search Institute assessed the developmental resources embedded within a congregation that may contribute to positive outcomes in young people. Using a subsample of 20,020 randomly selected 6th–12th graders of youth in the United States, Wagener, Furrow, King, Leffert, and Benson (2003) found that the positive benefits of adolescent religiousness was partially mediated through developmental resources available to these youths.

These developmental resources are based on Search Institute's framework of developmental assets, which includes eight categories consisting of support, empowerment, boundaries and expectations, constructive use of time, commitment to learning, positive values, social competencies, and positive values. Although the study found that religious variables do have some independent effect on risk behaviors, the study showed that the positive benefits of religion are significantly mediated by these assets. The authors contended that religious influence might be better understood by the network of relationships, opportunities, and shared values common to religious congregations. These findings suggest that the developmental assets or social nutrients available through congregations promote thriving. The outcomes examined in this study were not homogenous with religious or spiritual development, and are better described as indicators of aspects of spiritual development, such as positive values and helping others. Nevertheless, this study sheds light on how congregations may influence RSD among young people not through mere participation, but through the provision of developmental resources such as caring adults, boundaries and expectations, and opportunities to serve others.

Spiritual Context   Congregations not only provide important developmental resources and social relationships that may nurture RSD and positive development, but they also provide opportunities for spiritual experiences. Religion and spirituality provide opportunities for transcendence when young people can experience something greater than themselves.

Spiritual Practices   Specifically, a process that shapes RSD during adolescence involves patterns of participation in spiritual practices. Spiritual practices can be defined as everyday, deliberate activities, engaged in solitude or in the company of others, in which individuals seek to explore and extend their relationship with some conception of the sacred or divinity. Thus, spiritual practices may enrich one's spiritual life; such practices can also have

beneficial side effects through their relation to coping and resilience.

Prayer is one such practice. In a study of a community-based sample of 155 men and women aged 25–45 years of age, researchers found that the use of religious coping strategies such as trusting in God, seeking God's help, praying, and taking comfort in religion in the face of stressors, was associated with reduced ambulatory blood pressure among African American, but not European American adults (Steffen, Hinderliter, Blumenthal, & Sherwood, 2001).

Another practice is meditation. In a national study of religion and spirituality, Smith and Denton (2005) found that 10% of all youth reported "practicing religious or spiritual meditation not including prayer" during the prior year. What is the effect of such practices on adolescent development (Roeser & Peck, 2008)? Barnes, Johnson, and Treiber (2004), for instance, found the practice of meditation was associated with reduced ambulatory blood pressure among African American adolescents.

In sum, the various environments in which youth live will foster positive development insofar as they offer clear ideology, social resources, and transcendent, spiritual experiences. Whether secular or faith-based, settings can promote spiritual development by "helping young people along the quest for self-awareness, meaning, purpose—shaping their core identity and their place in their families, communities, and the larger world" (Benson & Roehlkepartain, in press). Relationships, programs, and institutions that provide clear beliefs, moral directives, and values; peer and adult relationships that model and reinforce these prosocial norms; and experiences that move young people beyond their daily concerns and connect them with something beyond themselves are apt to nurture youth on such a quest. Such influences may therefore enhance adolescent development more generally. Accordingly, we next discuss some of the impact of adolescent RSD on overall adolescent development.

DEVELOPMENTAL CORRELATES OF RELIGION AND SPIRITUALITY DURING ADOLESCENCE

Adolescent religion and spirituality have gained increased attention within the academy largely due to the growing evidence suggesting that religion serves as a protective factor, buffering young people against health-compromising behavior and promoting their engagement in health-promoting behavior through many of the mechanisms just reviewed (e.g., Benson et al., 2003; Kerestes & Youniss, 2003; Smith, 2003b; Spilka et al., 2003). Studies have generally revealed that measures of religious attendance and religious importance are negatively correlated with indicators of risk behavior such as delinquency, substance abuse, violence, sexual activity, and suicide. Furthermore, these reviews reveal a positive relationship between religiousness and positive outcomes like life satisfaction, wearing seat belts, and civic engagement. In the following section, we examine studies of RSD during adolescence and indicators of both positive and problematic development.

Health

Evidence shows a strong correlation between denominational religious involvement and health in adults (Koenig et al., 2001) and adolescents (Gottlieb & Green, 1984; Oman & Thoresen, 2005). Jessor, Turbin, and Costa (1998), in an ethnically and racially diverse, longitudinal sample, found that adolescents' frequency of church attendance and the reported importance of religious teachings and values was strongly correlated with their engagement in healthy lifestyle behaviors such as keeping a nutritious diet, getting enough sleep, keeping up with dental hygiene, using seatbelts, and exercising.

Similarly, using Monitoring the Future data from nationally probability samples of 15,000 to 19,000 high school seniors collected annually since 1975, Wallace and Forman (1998) found that more highly religious adolescents (as measured by reported importance, attendance, and denominational affiliation) reported higher levels of health-promoting behaviors such as consuming breakfast, fruit, and green vegetables, in addition to obtaining seven hours or more of sleep per night.

Psychological Distress and Well-Being

The relationship between religiosity and mental health has also been clearly demonstrated in adults (Hackney & Sanders, 2003) and adolescents (Cotton, Zebracki, Rosenthal, Tsevat, & Drotar, 2006). For instance, adolescent religiosity, assessed in terms of church attendance and reported importance of religion, was inversely related with feelings of depression, hopelessness, and loneliness (Pearce et al., 2003b; Schapman & Inderbitzen-Nolan, 2002; Sinha, Cnaan, & Gelles, 2007; Smith & Denton, 2005; Wright, Frost, & Wisecarver, 1993) and positively related to life satisfaction (Varon & Riley, 1999).

In studies in Germany, Spain, and the United States, adolescent religiosity, assessed in terms of church attendance and reported importance of religion, was positively related to self-esteem (Donahue & Benson, 1995; Smith, Weigert, & Thomas, 1979). In a study of 615 ethnically and denominationally diverse adolescents, Kelley and Miller (2007) found that frequency of spiritual experiences in the context of daily life (e.g., seeing the sacred in others) was associated with life satisfaction. In a study of 134 college students, Leake, DeNeve, and Greteman (2007) found that youth who reported spiritual strivings (see Emmons, 1999) were more likely to experience positive emotions such as vitality and zest, in addition to greater psychological health as operationalized by tendencies toward self-actualization and achieved identity status. The one exception to these trends are pregnant adolescent girls who may be more likely to experience feelings of guilt and shame due to their pregnancy and its incongruence with religious–moral teachings (Sorenson, Grindstaff, & Turner, 1995).

These studies documenting a relationship between religious involvement, less psychological distress, and greater positive emotional experience, esteem, and life satisfaction also extend to immigrant youth. In a national study of adolescent health, Harker (2001) found that 1.5 generation immigrant adolescents experience less depression and greater positive well-being than their native-born peers from similar demographic and family backgrounds.

Suicide

Adolescents who experience feelings of worthlessness and depression are at heightened risk for suicide. Population analyses point to a relationship between having a religious affiliation and lower rates of suicide in both male and female adolescents (e.g., Baker & Gorsuch, 1982; Gartner, Larson, & Allen, 1991; Sturgeon & Hamley, 1979; Trovato, 1992). Other studies have shown indicators of religiosity (attendance, importance) are associated with lower levels of fatalism and suicidal ideation and fewer suicide attempts in large representative samples of American adolescents in grades 6–12 (Donahue & Benson, 1995; Jamieson & Romer, 2008; Nonnemaker, McNeely, & Blum, 2003). In a cross-sectional sample of 1,456 American Indian tribal members (ages 15–57 years old) living in Northern Plains reservations, orientation to traditional spiritual practices was associated with reduced suicide attempts (Garroutte et al., 2003).

Risk-Taking Behaviors

A solid body of evidence documents a negative relationship between adolescent RSD and risk-taking behavior (Smith & Faris, 2003). It is not that religious or spiritual youths are not taking risks or engaging in dangerous activities; rather, research has suggested that they do so to a lesser extent (e.g., Bridges & Moore, 2002; Donahue & Benson, 1995).

Substance Use

Adolescents RSD is negatively related to their use of marijuana, tobacco, steroids, and alcohol (e.g., Bartkowski & Xu, 2007; Regnerus & Elder, 2003; Sinha et al., 2007; Wallace & Forman, 1998; Yarnold, 1998). Cross-sectional

research shows that religious adolescents are significantly less likely to smoke cigarettes regularly, to drink alcohol weekly, or to get drunk, whereas less religious adolescents are likely to smoke marijuana (Smith & Denton, 2005). In native populations of Native American adolescents, orientation to indigenous spiritual beliefs and practices has been associated with reduced substance use among (Garouette et al., 2003). Longitudinal research that followed adolescents from grades 7 through 10 showed that religiosity reduced the subsequent impact of stress on substance use initiation and on the rate of growth in substance use over time (Wills, Yaeger, & Sandy, 2003).

The inverse relationship between religion and substance abuse is not as clear among gay, lesbian, bisexual, and transgendered adolescent populations. Rostosky, Danner, and Riggle (2007) cautioned against overgeneralizing the protective effects of religion to all adolescent populations, as their study of sexual minority adolescents found that religiosity was not protective against substance abuse for these youth in the way it was for heterosexual adolescents.

Sexual Activity

Evidence also documents that adolescent religiosity is associated with increased age of sexual debut and decreased number of sexual partners. Although religious youths engage in sexual behaviors, they tend to be less sexually active and have fewer sexual partners than their less religious peers (Donahue & Benson, 1995; Holder et al., 2000; McBride, 1996). Adolescent religiosity has also been found to be inversely correlated with risky sexual behaviors (Lammers, Ireland, Resnick, & Blum, 2000; Murray, 1994; Thornton & Camburn, 1989). Smith and Denton (2005) documented striking differences in teens' sexual attitudes based on their level of religious involvement and religious commitment that likely are behind these behavioral differences. Almost all religiously devoted youths believed in sexual abstinence until marriage. Only 3% of religiously devoted teens agreed that as long as teenagers were emotionally ready for sex, it was okay to engage in it. By comparison, 56% of religiously unengaged youths endorsed this position.

Similarly, Bridges and Moore (2002) found that adolescents who attended church, valued religion, and held strong religious beliefs had lower levels of sexual experience and held conservative attitudes about sexual activity. These findings have been replicated among Latin American, African American, and European American populations of youth (Edwards, Fehring, Jarrett & Haglund, 2008). However, females who considered themselves highly religious were less likely to use contraception during their initial sexual experience, which leads to higher risk in sexually transmitted diseases and pregnancy. Similar reports were found among males in which those who associated more with religiosity were less likely to partake in sexual activity at early ages and hold more conservative sexual attitudes and beliefs in one 13- to 16-year old sample.

In a national longitudinal study of 3,691 adolescents assessed at age 15 (time 1) and age 21 (time 2), Rostosky, Regnerus, and Wright (2003) found that adolescent religiosity at age 15 predicted delayed onset of coital debut for both males and females assessed at time 2 after accounting for adolescents' demographic background and number of romantic partners.

Delinquency

The inverse relationship between religiosity and delinquent behavior among adolescents has also been well established (Baier & Wright, 2001). Adolescent religiosity has also been linked to lower delinquent and violent problem behavior (Donahue & Benson, 1995; Johnson, Jang, Larson, & Li, 2001; Regnerus & Elder, 2003) and has increasingly become a focus of research for criminologists seeking to explore the mediating factors of crime deterrence, particularly in juveniles (Evans, Cullen, Dunaway, & Burton, 1995). For instance, Sloane and Potvin (1986), in a national probability sample, found that youth ages 13-18 who considered religion to be of considerable influence in their lives and attended church frequently were 50% less likely to engage in serious fighting than their nonreligious peers.

Johnson et al. (2001) found that adolescent religiosity was negatively correlated with adolescents' attitudes toward delinquent behaviors, their association with delinquent peers, and their engagement in delinquent behaviors after controlling for their sociodemographic backgrounds. Pearce, Jones, Schwab-Stone, and Ruchkin (2003) found that frequent exposure to religious content (e.g., reading, watching, or hearing religious information) decreased the likelihood of antisocial practices, witnessing violence, or being the victim of violence. In a nationally representative sample of youth in grades 7–12, Regnerus (2003) found evidence for a cyclical trend in the relationship between adolescent religiosity and delinquency. In this sample, religiosity was related to a slight decrease in delinquent behaviors in early adolescence, disappeared as a predictor of delinquent behaviors during middle adolescence, and finally emerged as a stronger negative predictor in late adolescence.

In sum, the current literature paints a clear picture of the protective relationship between adolescent religiosity and various risk behaviors. Participating in various forms of religion is clearly linked to a reduction in dangerous activities among young people. However, this buffering effect is less explored with specifically spiritual variables. Do these salutary impacts of religiosity and spirituality exists as well when we turn from problem behaviors to positive ones? In the next section, we examine the relationship between adolescent religiosity and spirituality and positive developmental outcomes.

Positive Development and Thriving

A growing body of literature has documented associations between adolescent RSD and various indicators of positive youth development and thriving. A thriving young person, as defined in this chapter, is one who is developing a positive identity and a meaningful and satisfying life, who experiences a sense of well-being, and who develops personal competencies. In addition to these things, however, a key attribute of thriving is an individual's contributions to the well-being of his or her family, community, and society (King et al., 2005; Lerner et al., 2006; Scales, Benson, Leffert, & Blyth, 2000). As such, the term *thriving* has referred to positive development that is characterized over time by a pattern of functioning indicative of the individual's ability to adapt to environmental opportunities, demands, and restrictions in a way that satisfies individual's developmental needs and the needs of others and society. This section examines the empirical work that supports the claim that spirituality and religion are associated with indicators of positive youth development and thriving.

Thriving

Dowling et al. (2004) found that adolescents' spirituality (defined as experiencing transcendence and defining self in relationship to others and having genuine concern for others) and religiosity (defined as institutional affiliation and participation with a religious tradition and doctrine) had direct effects on an omnibus measure of thriving (defined as a concept incorporating the absence of problem behaviors and the presence of healthy development). In addition, adolescent spirituality mediated the effects of religion on thriving. These findings suggest that both spirituality and religiousness may play roles in the development of thriving. Although most existing research has confirmed the positive role of religion, this study demonstrated that spirituality may have an influence on youth thriving beyond that of religion. In another study, Benson et al. (2005) found that religious salience and importance were positive predictors of eight thriving indicators across sex and racial/ethnic subgroups of youth.

Meaning and Identity

Adolescent RSD can contribute to thriving by influencing psychosocial identity development and the broader search for purpose, meaning, and fidelity characteristic of adolescence (Damon, 2008; Roeser et al., 2008; Templeton & Eccles, 2006). However, research using Marcia's identity statuses paradigm has yielded equivocal findings. For instance, Markstrom-Adams, Hoftstra, and Dougher (1994) examined the relationship of religious participation to Marcia's (1966) identity commitments. They found that identity commitments of foreclosure and achievement were related to church attendance. Subsequent studies showed that intrinsically religiously motivated youth were most likely to have attained Marcia's stage of identity achievement (Fulton, 1997; Markstrom-Adams & Smith, 1996). Other studies have shown identity diffusion has been associated with lower levels of religious importance and participation, orthodoxy of Christian beliefs, and intrinsic religious commitment (Markstrom-Adams et al., 1994). However, Hunsberger, Pratt, and Pancer (2001), however, found only weak associations between religious commitment and achieved identity status. Clearly, better conceptualization of RSD as well as "identity development' is needed to clarify the interaction of these domains of development. What has proven more fruitful is the focus on how RSD affects adolescents' sense of meaning, hope, and purpose.

It is not surprising that religion has been shown to have a positive impact on adolescents' development of a sense of personal meaning (Chamberlain & Zika, 1992). For instance, a national probability sample of U.S. adolescents showed that their religious and spiritual commitments are positively associated with their overall sense of meaning and hope for the future (Smith & Denton, 2005). Tzuriel (1984) and Francis (2000) found that religiously involved youth reported higher levels of commitment and purpose when compared to less religiously engaged youth. Furrow et al. (2004) found that youth reporting a strong religious identity were more likely to have a meaning framework that added direction and purpose to their lives than their nonreligious peers. It has also been shown that youths participating in religious communities are more likely to report having a sense of purpose indicative of a commitment to a personal philosophy (Markstrom, 1999). Also consistent with these findings, Showalter and Wagener (2000) found among youths attending a Christian summer camp that religion served as a productive source of meaning.

Contribution

Several studies have indicated a positive relationship between religion and indicators such as community service and altruism. For instance, Youniss and colleagues found that religious youth were more involved in community service compared to those adolescents reporting little religious activity (e.g., Kerestes, Youniss, & Metz, 2004; Youniss et al., 1999). Using Monitoring the Future data, Youniss et al. reported that students who believe that religion is important in their lives were almost three times more likely to participate in community service than those who do not believe that religion is important. Similarly, Smith and Denton (2005) reported that religiously devoted youth committed twice the national average of acts of service to homeless and needy people and significantly more acts than less religious youth.

Tracking religious development from the sophomore year to the senior year, Kerestes et al. (2004) found that civic integration, measured by participation in civic activities such as working on a political campaign and demonstrating for a cause, and willingness to perform volunteer service, were positively associated with stable or upward religious developmental trajectories among a sample of predominately white, socioeconomically middle- to upper-class students. Religious salience (Crystal & DeBell, 2002) and religious values (Serow & Dreyden, 1990; Smith, 1999) have both shown to be associated with various forms of civic engagement.

Teenagers' religious commitment and attendance has been associated with free time activity involvement and peer characteristics. Youth who reported greater importance of religion in their lives and who attended public religious services more were involved in constructive after-school activities. Furthermore, these youth were more likely to have friends with similar religious commitments and conventional value profiles, and who were similarly involved in formal religion and constructive free-time activities (Jessor & Jessor, 1977; Smith & Denton, 2005). In turn, Hart & Fegley (1995) noted the positive role of religion in the lives of youth nominated for their commitment to caring and contributions to others. For many, caring values, attitudes, and behaviors were not independent of their spirituality. Rather, all aspects of their morality were governed by their religious beliefs and experiences, which informed their goals of service and care and were closely related to their identity.

In summary, although the research just reviewed is suggestive of how RSD in adolescence is associated with other positive developmental outcomes (Wallace & Williams, 1997; Frank & Kendall, 2001; Regnerus, Smith, & Fritsch, 2003). Furthermore, work with national longitudinal research designs and samples, rather than cross-sectional, correlational designs and samples of convenience are needed to strengthen our knowledge base in this area. Nonetheless, the reviewed findings do point to potential avenues for further research.

Negative Outcomes of Adolescent RSD

It is important to consider adolescent RSD in its entirety, lest we identify religion and spirituality as a social panacea. Although there is ample evidence to make the case for the beneficial role of religion and spirituality in adolescence, RSD may also lead to problematic social outcomes and developmental forms of psychopathology (see Oser et al., 2006; Silberman et al., 2005; Wagener & Maloney, 2006). The notions of developmental systems theory concerning transactions, contexts, plasticity and different forms of person–environment fit in different sociocultural and historical environments is useful for understanding both positive and negative forms of religion and spirituality.

For instance, the change of Tibet from a nation of warriors to a nation of Buddhist contemplatives necessitates a complex, multilevel sociocultural-contextual and historical systems analysis to understand. A similar lens is needed to comprehend Nazi Germany and the religion of German youth generally and the Hitler youth (Hitler Jugend) in particular. Both societies transformed themselves in the direction of spiritual worldviews, one becoming a place in which the ethics of universal compassion and nonviolence thrived, and the other one where pseudospeciation and the holocaust unfolded. Indeed, the notion of "meaning systems" at the level of institutions and communities of religion, and "identity systems" at the level of individuals, have proven very fruitful for applying systems concepts to both spiritual thriving and pathology (e.g., Altemeyer & Hunsberger, 2005; Roeser et al., 2008a; Silberman et al., 2005).

We assume that optimal religion and spirituality affirms both individual development and engenders social contribution. This balance is important, for if one violates the other, healthy development does not occur. For example, if a religious tradition emphasizes the faith community, without valuing the uniqueness of its members, youths may not have the necessary opportunities to explore different aspects of identity. When youths are not given the freedom to explore, and are either forced or pressured into adopting a specific ideology, social group, or expression of spirituality, identity foreclosure is a risk.

Taken to the extreme, cults can be understood from this perspective as spiritual expressions that devalue the individuality of their members in order to elevate the ideology and group. This is graphically illustrated by spiritual groups that demand that their members all dress alike. In addition, recent current events such as suicide bombings illustrate devastation caused by religious groups that value the goals

and ends of the religion more than an individual's life.

However, some traditions might not leverage their potential as being conducive to promoting positive development because they emphasize the individual, over and above promoting a sense of community and belonging. For example, some conservative traditions within Christianity emphasize the individual believer's relationship with God to the extent that they do not expend time or resources on promoting a sense of community or contribution to larger society. When this occurs, although youths are reinforced about their personal worth, they lose out on both the support and accountability of a faith community and the value of learning what it means to belong and to contribute to a greater good. In addition, individual forms of spirituality that are not connected with a group of followers also have the potential to leave youths without the web of support present in spiritual traditions associated with a intentional group of followers.

These manifestations of spirituality are not necessarily deleterious for youth development or for society. Rather, they lack the rich social context that is so effective for optimal development. Forms of spirituality that do not connect youth with a social group or a transcendent experience of other may not promote a self-concept that fully integrates a moral, civic, and spiritual identity. However, taken to the extreme, forms of religion and spirituality that exalt the individual over a greater good can promote a sense of narcissism, entitlement, and lack of connectedness and contribution to society.

A developmental systems perspective highlights not only the goodness of fit between an individual and a religious/spiritual tradition, but also between a religious/spiritual tradition and the greater society. If such a spiritual tradition causes detriment to others, such as the case with prejudice (Hunsberger, 1995) and terrorism, then spirituality has gone awry. Numerous research studies have linked religious fundamentalism to right-wing authoritarianism, which in turn is related to ethnocentrism and many forms of prejudice (Hunsberger & Jackson, 2005). Understanding the developmental antecedents to such deleterious religious commitments is an important aspect of development science.

It is important to note that although a specific religious group might point to certain behaviors as indicators of thriving from within that group's perspective, these behaviors do not always represent "constructive development" from the perspective of developmental science. For example, as Silberman (2003) points out, the September 11, 2001, attacks on the United States can be viewed from very different perspectives, which engender different assumptions about desirable kinds of world change and violence or peace as legitimate means of achieving world change. According to one meaning perspective, the attacks were religiously legitimated. From another meaning perspective, these attacks were seen as violent assaults on innocent civilians that are prohibited by religion. How to tip the "double-edged sword" of religion away from its violent world change ideological forms and toward its peaceful world change ideological forms is the challenge facing the faith communities of the world today (Silberman et al., 2005). Such change may also be a force of future theory and research in developmental science.

DIRECTIONS FOR FUTURE THEORY AND RESEARCH

The role of religion and spirituality in informing and shaping the development of adolescents is only beginning to be explored in the developmental sciences with respect to a systems views of development in which biology, psychology, and social ecology play equally important, transacting roles. Research now shows that religion and spirituality are important for the course of youth development (Smith & Denton, 2005). However, more nuanced knowledge is required to better elucidate the precise individual and contextual relations that account for youth RSD and its

positive outcomes. In this section, we highlight what we see as a few key areas for future research that would strengthen this emerging area of scholarship.

The scientific study of religion and spirituality in human health and development necessitates definitional clarity of key concepts of religion, religiousness, spirituality, and spiritual. In the wake of stage-structural theories falling out of favor in the developmental sciences, there is a need for renewed theory in the area of what constitutes religious and spiritual development during adolescence. Innovative new approaches that incorporate and expand on these previous works exist (e.g., Wilbur, 2006), but have yet to be examined during adolescence.

Why are individuals religious or spiritual in the first place (e.g., Bloom, 2005)? Does adolescence represent a sensitive period in religious and spiritual formation (e.g., Good & Willoughby, 2008)? What processes mark "authentic" and "inauthentic" forms of development in these domains and what are the best candidate mechanisms for explaining the relation of religiosity or spirituality to various aspects of human development? How should we study religion and spirituality at the individual level – as domains of development generally, as domains of identity development in particular, etc. (Roeser et al., 2008)? In sum, it is with respect to issues of theory, construct definition, and the elucidation of mechanisms of influence where we see the most room for innovation and creativity in this emerging area of study.

There is also a great need for longitudinal research in this area. Understanding the developmental precursors and sequelae of various religious/spiritual identities and behaviors will be critical for untangling patterns of influence and pathways of continuity and change in this aspect of human development. Some of the most comprehensive studies to date remain cross-sectional in design (e.g., Benson et al., 2005; Lerner et al., 2008; Smith & Denton, 2005). A focus on particular subgroups of interest such as those who are particularly spiritually precocious, those who undergo conversion experiences, or those who leave religion and decide they are atheists, may be one way that such studies may advance understanding of not only normative but diverse patterns of religious and spiritual development across adolescence (e.g., King, Ramos, & Clardy, 2008).

The employment of non-self-report measures of behavior and behavioral sequelae will also be important in this work. For instance, little work on the development of prejudicial attitudes with respect to religion during adolescence, using implicit measures of attitudes has been conducted (e.g., Greenwald & Banaji, 1995). In addition, in order to understand the effect of religious attendance on positive behaviors during adolescence, such as service to others, it is necessary to gain multiple informants' perspectives and to use observational methods. Recent work on the neural underpinnings of spiritual experience, as well as on basic self-regulatory functions associated with particular practices like meditation, provide other new kinds of measures that move from first person to second person to third person in nature (e.g., Newberg & Newberg, 2006; Urry & Poey, 2008).

In addition, understanding the role of social factors in religious and spiritual development in a world plagued by religious violence, as it is today, seems essential. Thus, one key direction for future research on religious and spiritual development during adolescence involves a more thorough examination of the kinds of people, opportunities, and social settings that nurture healthy and authentic forms of spirituality (see King & Furrow, 2004; King et al., 2008). As in any other domain of development, we believe religious and spiritual development is scaffolded and linked to the kinds of social worlds and people with whom adolescents "come of age" (e.g., Rogoff, 2003). It is the developmentally instigative role of these social contexts in religious and spiritual development that require more research in this field of study (Regnerus, 2003).

Adolescence, with its characteristic changes in thinking and feeling, is a prime time for young people to be exposed to, and engaged in, dialogue about ideas and philosophies bearing on ultimate existential questions of identity, purpose, and meaning. Spiritual mentors, in such a context, can take on considerable importance in the lives of youth (e.g., Issac, Roeser, Abo-Zena, & Lerner, 2007). Unfortunately, recent work on youth purpose highlights the relative absence of such conversations about meaning in the lives of young people at least in the U.S. today (Damon, 2008). What happens to youths when they experience a significant absence of discussions of purpose and meaning? What is the net effect of this absence on the quality and richness of the inner spiritual lives of youths? Do violence, risk behavior, and anomie provide channels for frustrated or misdirected spiritual longings?

In summary, the preceding conceptual questions are important, general issues that should be addressed in further research. In addition to these more general issues, there are more specific contextual and individual variables that require greater empirical attention.

Race, Culture, and Ethnicity

Given that religion and spirituality are key facets of ethnicity, race, and culture (Mattis et al., 2006; Slonim, 1991), a key direction for future research concerns the intersectionality among, young people's developing ethnic/racial, cultural, and religious and spiritual identities in shaping patterns of positive or problematic youth development. Virtually no research has examined the intersectionality among such identities with adolescents (e.g., Abo-Zena, Roeser, Issac, & Lerner, 2007; Abo-Zena et al., 2008; Juang & Syed 2008). New research in this area would enhance our understanding of the roles that religion and spirituality can play in the positive development of ethnically, racially, and culturally diverse youth (e.g., Nicolas & DeSilva, 2008).

For instance, despite the centrality of the church in African American history, "almost no research focuses specifically on Black adolescents" with respect to religion and development today (Taylor, Chatters, & Levin, 2004, p. 46). What is known is that African American youths place more importance on religion than their European American peers (Donahue & Benson, 1995; Wallace et al., 2003) and that religion deters deviant behavior among African American youths. But what about its role in enhancing positive development? In addition, most existing research on adolescent religion and spirituality is based on North American samples; little research takes into consideration the role of spirituality in developing nations (King et al., 2008).

Immigrants

Similarly, we believe that religion and spirituality play a key role in the development of immigrants and their families (Abo-Zena et al., 2007; Jensen, 2008; Juang & Syed, 2008; Roeser, Lerner, Jensen, & Alberts, 2008). How might religious institutions provide a "context of reception" for newcomers to the United States? How might spiritual beliefs support immigrants in their efforts to assimilate and bridge to the mainstream of American cultural and economic life? How might being an ethnic–minority immigrant who is also a member of the religious majority of the country affect youth development? Future studies examining such issues would increase our understanding of the development of immigrant youths in the United States as well.

Sexual and Religious Minorities

The role of religion and spirituality in the development of youths who are sexual or religious minorities is also important. For instance, research has documented the important influence social environments can have on the sexual identity development of gay and lesbian youths (Ream & Savin-Williams, 2004). As the research on proscribed and nonproscribed sources of prejudice in religious traditions illustrates (Hunsberger & Jackson, 2005), sexual minorities remain targets for religious-based discrimination. Examining the effect of

such discrimination on the identity formation of gay and lesbian youths during adolescence is important.

Similarly, what is the role of religion in ameliorating or even exacerbating the risks associated with being a religious minority in the United States today (Abo-Zena et al., 2008)? How can religious practices such as wearing a headscarf differentially expose certain youths to risk factors like discrimination, while engagement in such practices provides a buffer against such experiences at the same time?

Worldviews and Violence

Another area for future research concerns the development of religious and spiritual worldviews during adolescence and early adulthood and their functional significance for well-being and life choices (e.g., Arnett, 2008). How do young people's knowledge and understanding (or lack of knowledge and understanding) of the world's religions shape their own worldviews? How can we help all young people achieve a deep appreciation for the plurality of religions and wisdom traditions that characterize different facets of humanity today and, in doing so, promote greater mutual understanding and civil society (Roeser & Lerner, 2008)? Which religious and spiritual worldviews are differentially associated with positive and problematic forms of human development (e.g., Feldman, 2008). Why are young males so vulnerable to the influence of violent worldviews and attendant forms of actual violence in nations all around the world (Wagener & Maloney, 2006)? What social ecological conditions foster such vulnerability? How can worldview beliefs be used to differentiate religious terrorism from positive forms of development (Silberman, 2005)?

Life Event Catalysts of RSD

More research on the life event catalysts of religious and spiritual development is also needed. At the time of writing, King et al. (2008) were in the process of analyzing in depth interviews of 32 adolescent spiritual exemplars from spiritually and culturally diverse backgrounds around the globe. An emerging finding as a key factor thought to affect the emergence of a reflective and intentional approach to life, in which happiness and a more satisfying life are sought, is the experience of suffering and an inability to address it sufficiently through prevailing identity commitments and worldviews (Corbett, 2000). From this perspective, spiritual development is said to be triggered when "traditional religious beliefs and images from childhood no longer offer comfort from suffering or provide adequate reasons for injustices in the world" (Templeton & Eccles 2006, p. 255). The resultant loss of meaning and desire for livable solutions to questions of ultimate meaning (e.g., the existence of suffering) catalyze new existential questioning, exploration, and seeking. More generally, understanding how life events may trigger spiritual doubts, identity explorations, and ongoing commitments is an important topic of inquiry.

Mediating Factors

Although the relationship between religion/spirituality and positive outcomes for youth is well documented at this writing, the mechanisms behind this association have not been well explored. Although there is evidence that social support, such as social capital or developmental assets may mediate the effect of religious participation or religious salience on positive development in young people, further research is needed to clarify how social support might work for different youths in different settings. For instance, do adolescents with varying amounts of parental support benefit differently from religious social support? Research demonstrates that young people in diverse contexts benefit from social capital differently (King, 2004).

Other questions about mediating factors exist as well. Do the ideology, worldviews, and moral order available through religion and spirituality help young people navigate through the waters of adolescence (King, 2008)? Is there a significant interaction between ideology and social support available through religious or spiritual contexts (King, 2008)? Was Erikson (1959) correct in suggesting that youths who are embedded in a social context that affords and models a particular worldview and moral order have advantages when forming an identity? Longitudinal studies exploring these issues are needed to understand causational effects of these potential mediating factors.

CONCLUSIONS

There is renewed interest in the study of religious and spiritual development. For far too long the field of developmental science overlooked these important aspects of being an adolescent. As the field moves toward consensus on the conceptualization of spirituality and religiousness, social scientists will be able to advance the operationalization of these complex constructs. Our hope is that the not-too-distant future will see the rise of creative and rigorous methodologies that will begin to answer some of the questions raised in this chapter.

Varying approaches to data gathering and analysis will allow scholars to examine the presence, development, and impact of spirituality and religion in the lives of diverse young people. Increased understanding will elucidate how spirituality may serve as a potentially potent aspect of the developmental system, through which young people can gain a greater understanding of themselves and their connections to the greater world in ways that fosters a sense of responsibility and compassion to the greater good.

REFERENCES

Abo-Zena, M. M., Roeser, R. W., Issac, S. S., Alberts, A. E., Du, D., Phelps, E., et al. (2008, March). *Religious identity development among religious majority and minority youth in the United States*. Poster presented at the Society for Research on Identity Formation, Chicago, Illinois.

Abo-Zena, M. M., Roeser, R. W., Issac, S. S., & Lerner, R. M. (2007, October). On religion in the development of immigrant youth: A descriptive and functional analysis. Poster to be presented at the *On New Shores: Understanding Immigrant Children* conference, the University of Guelph, Guelph, Ontario.

Allport G. W. (1950). *The individual and his religion*. New York: MacMillan.

Altemeyer, B., & Hunsberger, B. (2005). Fundamentalism and authoritarianism. In R. F. Paloutzian & C. L. Park (Eds.), *Handbook of the psychology of religion* (pp. 378–393). New York: Guilford Press.

Arnett, J. J. (2008). From "worm food" to "infinite bliss": Emerging adults' views of life after death. In R. M. Lerner, R. W. Roeser, & E. Phelps (Eds.), *Positive youth development and spirituality: From theory to research* (pp. 231–243). West Conshohocken, PA: Templeton Foundation Press.

Ashmore, R. D., Deaux, K., & McLaughlin-Volpe, T. (2004). An organizing framework for collective identity: Articulation and significance of multidimensionality. *Psychological Bulletin, 130,* 80–114.

Baier, C. J., & Wright, B. R. E. (2001). "If you love me, keep my commandments": A meta-analysis of the effect of religion on crime. *Journal of Research in Crime and Delinquency, 38,* 3–21.

Baker, M., & Gorsuch, R. (1982). Trait anxiety and intrinsic–extrinsic religiousness. *Journal for the Scientific Study of Religion, 21,* 119–122.

Balswick, J. O., King, P. E., & Reimer, K. S. (2005). *The reciprocating self: Human development in theological perspective.* Downer's Grove, IL: InterVarsity Press.

Bandura, A. (1986). *Social foundations of thought and action: A social cognitive theory.* Englewood Cliffs, NJ: Prentice Hall.

Bandura, A. (2003). On the psychosocial impact and mechanisms of spiritual modeling. *International Journal for the Psychology of Religion, 13,* 167–173.

Bao, W. N., Whitbeck, L. B., Hoyt, D. R., & Conger, R. D. (1999). Perceived parental acceptance as a moderator of religious transmission among adolescent boys and girls. *Journal of Marriage and the Family, 61,* 362–374.

Barnes, V. A., Treiber, F. A. & Johnson, M. H. (2004). Impact of Transcendental Meditation on ambulatory blood pressure in African-American adolescents. *American Journal of Hypertension, 17,* 366–369.

Barrett, J. B., Pearson, J., Muller, C., & Frank, K. A. (2007). Adolescent religiosity and school contexts. *Social Science Quarterly, 88,* 1024–1037.

Barrett, J. L., & Keil, F. C. (1996). Anthropomorphism and God concepts: Conceptualizing a non-natural entity. *Cognitive Psychology, 31,* 219–247.

Barrett, J. L., & Richert, R. A. (2003). Anthropomorphism or preparedness? Exploring children's God concepts. *Review of Religious Research, 44,* 300–312.

Bartkowski, J. P., & Xu, X. (2007). Religiosity and teen drug use reconsidered: A social capital perspective. *American Journal of Preventive Medicine, 32,* 182–194.

Batson, C. D. (1997). An agenda item for psychology of religion: Getting respect. In B. Spilka & D. N. McIntosh (Eds.), *Psychology of religion: Theoretical approaches* (pp. 3–10). Boulder, CO: Westview.

Batson, C. D., Schoenrade, P., & Ventis, W. L. (1993). *Religion and the individual: A social–psychological perspective.* New York: Oxford University Press.

Benson, P. L. (2006). The science of child and adolescent spiritual development: Definitional, theoretical, and field-building issues. In E. C. Roehlkepartain, P. E. King, L. M. Wagener, & P. L. Benson (Eds.), *The handbook of spiritual development in childhood and adolescence* (pp. 484–498). Newbury Park, CA: Sage.

Benson, P. L., Donahue, M. J., & Erickson, J. A. (1989). Adolescence and religion: A review of the literature from 1970 to 1986. *Research in the Social Scientific Study of Religion, 1,* 153–181.

Benson, P. L., Donahue, M. J., & Erickson, J. A. (1993). The faith maturity scale: Conceptualization, measurement, and empirical validation. *Research in the Social Scientific Study of Religion, 5,* 1–26.

Benson, P. L., & Elkin, C. H. (1990). *Effective Christian education: A national study of Protestant congregations.* Minneapolis, MN: Search Institute.

Benson, P. L., & Roehlkepartain, E. C. (2008). Spiritual development: A mission priority in youth development. In E. C. Roehlkepartain, P. L. Benson, & K. L. Hong (Eds.), *New directions for youth development: Special issue on spiritual development.* San Francisco: Jossey-Bass.

Benson, P. L., Roehlkepartain, E. C., & Rude, S. P. (2003). Spiritual development in childhood and adolescence: Toward a field of inquiry. *Applied Developmental Science, 7*(3), 204–212.

Benson, P. L., Scales, P. C., Sesma, A., Jr., & Roehlkepartain, E. C. (2005). Adolescent spirituality. In K. A. Moore & L. H. Lippman (Eds.), *What do children need to flourish? Conceptualizing and measuring indicators of positive development* (pp. 25–40). New York: Springer.

Benson, P. L, Yeager, P. K., Wood, M. J., Guerra, M. J. & Manno, B. V. (1986). *Catholic high schools: Their impact on low-income students.* Washington, DC: National Catholic Education Association.

Bering, J. M. (2003). Towards a cognitive theory of existential meaning. *New Ideas in Psychology, 21,* 101–120.

Bering, J. M., & Bjorklund, D. F. (2004). The natural emergence of reasoning about the afterlife as a developmental regularity. *Developmental Psychology, 40,* 217–233.

Bloom, P. (2005, December). Is God an accident? *Atlantic Monthly.*

Bloom. P. (2007) Religion is natural. *Developmental Science, 10,* 147–151.

Bowlby, J. (1988). *A secure base: Parent–child attachment and healthy human development.* New York: Basic Books.

Boyatzis, C. J. (2005). Children's religious and spiritual development. In Paloutzian & Park (Eds.), *Handbook of the psychology of religion and spirituality* (pp. 123–143). Guilford Press.

Boyatzis, C. J., Dollahite, D., & Marks, L. (2006). The family as a context for religious and spiritual development in children and youth. In E. C. Roehlkepartain, P. E. King, L. Wagener, & P. L. Benson (Eds.), *Handbook of spiritual development in childhood and adolescence* (pp. 297–309). Thousand Oaks, CA: Sage.

Boyer, P. (2001). *Religion explained: The evolutionary origins of religious thought.* New York: Basic Books.

Brega, A. G., & Coleman, L. M. (1999). Effects of religiosity and racial socialization on subjective stigmatization in African-American adolescents. *Journal of Adolescence, 22* (2), 223–242.

Bridges, L. J., & Moore, K. A. (2002). *Religious involvement and children's well-being: What research tells us (and what it doesn't).* Washington DC: Child Trends.

Bronfenbrenner, U. (1979). *The ecology of human development .* Cambridge, MA: Harvard University Press.

Cannister, M. W. (1999). Mentoring and the spiritual well-being of late adolescents. *Adolescence, 34,* 769–799.

Chamberlain, K., & Zika, S. (1992). Religiosity, meaning in life and psychological well-being. In J. F. Schumaker (Ed.). *Religion and mental health* (pp. 138–148). New York: Oxford University Press.

Constantine, M. G., Donnell, P. C., & Myers, L. J. (2002). Collective self-esteem and Afri-cultural coping systems in African-American adolescents. *Journal of Black Studies, 32,* 698–710.

Corbett, L. (2000). A depth psychological approach to the sacred. In D. P. Slattery & L. Corbett (Eds.), *Depth psychology: Meditations in the field* (pp. 73–86). Carpenteria, CA: Pacifica Graduate Institute.

Cornwall, M. (1988). The influence of three aspects of religious socialization: Family, church, and peers. In D. L. Thomas (Ed.), *The religion and family connection: Social science perspectives* (pp. 207–231). Provo, UT: Brigham Young University Press.

Cotton, S., Zebracki, K., Rosenthal, S. L., Tsevat, J., & Drotar, D. (2006). Religion/spirituality and adolescent health outcomes: A review. *Journal of Adolescent Health, 38,* 472–480.

Crystal, D. S., & DeBell, M. (2002). "Sources of civic orientation among American youth: Trust, religious valuation, and attributions of responsibility." *Political Psychology, 23,* 113–132.

Damon, W. (2008). *The path to purpose.* New York: Free Press.

de Waals, F. (2007). *Primates and philosophers: How morality evolved.* Princeton, NJ: Princeton University Press.

Deconchy, J. P. (1965). The idea of God: Its emergence between 7 and 16 years of age. In A. Godin (Ed.), *From religious experience to religious attitude* (pp. 97–108). Chicago: Loyola University Press.

Dickie, J. R., Eshleman, A. K., Merasco, D. M., Shepard, A., Vander Wilt, M., & Johnson, M. (1997). Parent–child relationships and children's images of God. *Journal for the Scientific Study of Religion, 36,* 25–43.

Dollahite, D. C., & Marks, L. D. (2005). How highly religious families strive to fulfill sacred purposes. In V. Bengtson, A. Acock, K. Allen, P. Dillworth-Anderson, & D. Klein (Eds.), *Sourcebook of family theory and research* (pp. 533–541). Thousand Oaks, CA: Sage.

Donahue, M. J., & Benson, P. L. (1995). Religion and the well being of adolescents. *Journal of Social Issues, 51,* 145–160.

Donelson, E. (1999). Psychology of religion and adolescents in the U.S. *Journal of Adolescence, 22,* 187–204.

Dowling, E. M., Gestsdottir, S., Anderson, P. M., von Eye, A., Almerigi, J., & Lerner, R. M. (2004). Structural relations among spirituality, religiosity, and thriving in adolescence. *Applied Developmental Science, 8,* 7–16.

Dowling, E. M., & Scarlett, W. G. (Eds.). (2006). *Encyclopedia of spiritual and religious development in childhood and adolescence.* Thousand Oaks, CA: Sage.

Dubow, E. F., Pargament, K. I., Boxer, P., & Tarakeshwar, N. (2000). Initial investigation of Jewish early adolescents' ethnic identity, stress, and coping. *Journal of Early Adolescence, 20,* 418–441.

Eccles, J.S., Lord, S., & Roeser, R.W. (1996). Round holes, square pegs, rocky roads, and sore feet: A discussion of stage-environment fit theory applied to families and school. In D. Cicchetti & S. L. Toth (Eds.), *Rochester Symposium on Developmental Psychopathology, Volume VII: Adolescence: Opportunities and Challenges* (pp. 47–92). Rochester, NY: University of Rochester Press.

Eck, D. (2007). Religion. In M. C. Waters & R. Ueda (Eds.), *The new Americans: A guide to immigration since 1965* (pp. 214–227). Cambridge, MA: Harvard University Press.

Edwards, L. M., Fehring, R. J., Jarrett, K. M, & Haglund, K. A. (2008). The influence of Religiosity, gender, and language preference acculturation on sexual activity among Latino/a adolescents. *Hispanic Journal of Behavioral Sciences, 30,* xx–yy.

Elkind, D. (1997). The origins of religion in the child. In B. Spilka & D. N. McIntosh (Eds.), *The psychology of religion* (pp. 97–104). Boulder, CO: Westview Press.

Emmons, R. A. (1999). *The psychology of ultimate concerns: Motivation and spirituality in personality.* New York: Guilford Press.

Emmons, R. A., & Paloutzian, R. F. (2003). The psychology of religion. *Annual Review of Psychology, 54,* 377–402.

Epstein, S. (1990). Cognitive–experiential self-theory. In L. A. Pervin (Ed.), *Handbook of personality: Theory and research* (pp. 165–192). New York: Guilford Press.

Erikson, E. H. (1950). *Childhood and society.* New York: W. W. Norton.

Erikson, E. H. (1959). Late adolescence. In D. H. Funkenstein (Ed.), *The student and mental health.* Cambridge, MA: Riverside Press.

Erikson, E. H. (1964). *Insight and responsibility.* New York: W.W. Norton.

Erikson, E. H. (1965). *Childhood and society* (2nd ed.). Harmondsworth, UK: Penguin.

Erikson, E. H. (1968). *Identity: Youth and crisis.* New York: W. W. Norton.

Erickson, J. A. (1992). Adolescent religious development and commitment: A structural equation model of the role of family, peer group, and educational influences. *Journal for the Scientific Study of Religion, 31,* 131–152.

Evans, E. M. (2000). *Beyond Scopes:* Why creationism is here to stay. In K. S. Rosengren, C. N. Johnson, & P. L. Harris (Eds.), *Imagining the impossible: Magical, scientific, and religious thinking in children* (pp. 305–333). New York: Oxford University Press.

Evans, E. M. (2001). Cognitive and contextual factors in the emergence of diverse belief systems: Creation versus evolution. *Cognitive Psychology, 42,* 217–266.

Evans, T. D., Cullen, F. T., Dunaway, R. G., & Burton, V. S. (1995). Religion and crime reexamined: The impact of religion, secular controls, and social ecology on adult criminality. *Criminology, 33,* 195–224.

Feldman, D. H. (2008). The Role of Developmental Change in Spiritual Development. In R. M. Lerner, R. W. Roeser, & E. Phelps (Eds.). *Positive youth development and spirituality: From theory to research* (pp. 167–196). West Conshohocken, PA: Templeton Foundation Press.

Fowler, J. (1981). *Stages of faith: The psychological quest for human meaning.* San Francisco: Harper.

Fowler, J. W., & Dell, M. L. (2006). Stages of faith from infancy through adolescence: Reflections on three decades of Faith Development Theory. In E. C. Roehlkepartain, P. E. King, L. M. Wagener, & P. L.Benson (Eds.), *The handbook of spiritual development in childhood and adolescence* (pp. 34–45). Newbury Park, CA: Sage.

Francis, L. J. (2000). The relationship between bible reading and purpose in life among 13–15 year olds. *Mental Health, Religion & Culture, 3,* 27–36.

Frank. N. C., & Kendall, S. J. (2001). Religion, risk prevention and health promotion in adolescents: A community-based approach. *Mental Health, Religion, & Culture, 4,* 133–148.

Freud, S. (1961). *The future of an illusion.* In J. Strachey (Ed. & Trans.), New York: W.W. Norton. (Original work published 1927.)

Fuller, R. C. (2001). *Spiritual, but not religious: Understanding unchurched America.* Oxford: Oxford University Press.

Fulton, A. S. (1997). Identity status, religious orientation, and prejudice. *Journal of Youth and Adolescence, 26,* 1–11.

Furrow, J. L., King, P. E., & White, K. (2004). Religion and positive youth development: Identity, meaning, and prosocial concerns. *Applied Developmental Science, 8,* 17–26.

Gallup International Association. (1999). Gallup international millennium survey. Accessed on February 20, 2008, from www.gallup-international.com/surveys1.htm.

Garroutte, E. M., Goldberg, J., Beals, J., Herrell, R., Manson, S. M., & the AI-SUPERPFP Team. Spirituality and attempted suicide among American Indians. *Social Science and Medicine, 56,* 1571–1579.

Gartner, J., Larson, D. B., & Allen, G. D. (1991). Religious commitment and mental health: A review of the empirical literature. *Journal of Psychology & Theology, 19,* 6–25.

Geertz, C. (1973). *The interpretations of cultures.* New York: Basic Books.

Good, M., & Willoughby, T. (2008). Adolescence as a sensitive period for spiritual development. *Child Development Perspectives, 2,* 32–37.

Gottlieb, N. H., & Green, L. W. (1984). Life events, social network, life-style, and health: An analysis of the 1979 National Survey of Personal Health Practices and Consequences. *Health Education Quarterly, 11,* 91–105.

Granqvist, P. (2002). Attachment and religiosity in adolescence: Cross-sectional and longitudinal evaluations. *Personality and Social Psychology Bulletin, 28,* 260–270.

Greenwald, A. G., & Banaji, M. R. (1995). Implicit social cognition: Attitudes, self-esteem, and stereotypes. *Psychological Review, 102,* 4–27.

Gunnoe, M. L. and K. A. Moore. (2002). Predictors of religiosity among youth aged 17–22: A longitudinal study of the National Survey of Children. *Journal for the Scientific Study of Religion, 41,* 613–622.

Gur, M., Miller, L., Warner, V., Wickramaratne, P., & Weissman, M. (2005). Maternal depression and the intergenerational transmission of religion. *Journal of Nervous and Mental Disease, 193,* 338–345.

Hackney, C. H., & Sanders, G. S. (2003). Religiosity and mental health: A meta-analysis of recent studies. *Journal for the Scientific Study of Religion, 42,* 43–55.

Haidt, J. (2003). Elevation and the positive psychology of morality. In C. L. M. Keyes & J. Haidt (Eds.), *Flourishing: Positive psychology and the well-lived life* (pp. 275–289). Washington, DC: American Psychological Association.

Hall, G. S. (1904). *Adolescence: Its psychology and its relations to psychology, anthropology, sociology, sex, crime, religion, and education.* New York: Appleton.

Harker, K. (2001). Immigrant generation, assimilation and adolescent psychological well being. *Social Forces, 79,* 969–1004.

Harris, S. (2004). *The end of faith: Religion, terror, and the future of reason.* New York: W. W. Norton.

Hart, D., & Fegley, S. (1995). Altruism and caring in adolescence: Relations to moral judgment and self-understanding. *Child Development, 66,* 1346–1359.

Harter, S. (2006). The self. In W. Damon & R. M. Lener (Series Eds.) & N. Eisenberg (Volume Ed.), *Handbook of Child Psychology* (6th ed.), vol. 3: *Social, emotional, and personality development* (pp. 505–570). Hoboken, NJ: John Wiley & Sons.

Hertel, B. R., & Donahue, M. J. (1995). Parental influences on God images among children: Testing Durkheim's metaphoric parallelism. *Journal for the Scientific Study of Religion, 34,* 186–199.

Hill, P. C., & Pargament, K. I. (2003). Advances in the conceptualization and measurement of religion and spirituality: Implications for physical and mental health research. *American Psychologist, 58,* 64–74.

Ho, D. Y. F., & Ho, R. T. H. (2007). Measuring spirituality and spiritual emptiness: Toward ecumenicity and transcultural applicability. *Review of General Psychology, 11,* 62–74.

Hoge, D. R., & Petrillo, G. H. (1978) Determinants of church participation and attitudes among high school youth. *Journal for the Scientific Study of Religion, 17,* 359–379.

Hoge, D. R., Petrillo, G. H., & Smith, E. I. (1982). Transmission of religious and social values from parents to teenage children. *Journal of Marriage and the Family, 44,* 569–580.

Holder, D. W., Durant, R. H., Harris, T. L., Daniel, J. H., Obeidallah, D., & Goodman, E. (2000). The association between adolescent spirituality and voluntary sexual activity. *Journal of Adolescent Health, 26,* 295–302.

Hood, R. W., Jr. (2005). Mystical, spiritual, and religious experiences. In R. F. Paloutzian & C. L. Park (Eds.), *Handbook of the psychology of religion* (pp. 348–364). New York: Guilford Press.

Hunsberger, B. (1995). Religion and prejudice: The role of religious fundamentalism, quest, and right-wing authoritarianism. *Journal of Social Issues, 51,* 113–129.

Hunsberger, B., & Jackson, L. M. (2005). Religion, meaning, and prejudice. *Journal of Social Issues, 61,* 807–826.

Hunsberger, B., Pratt, M., & Pancer, S. M. (2001). Adolescent identity formation: Religious exploration and commitment. *Identity: An International Journal of Theory and Research, 1,* 365–387.

Hunsberger, B., Pratt, M., & Pancer, S. M. (2002). A longitudinal study of religious doubts in high school and beyond: Relationships, stability, and searching for answers. *Journal for the Scientific Study of Religion, 41,* 255–266.

Issac, S. S., Roeser, R. W., Abo-Zena, M. M., & Lerner, R. M. (2007, August). *Understanding the influence of positive and negative models in adolescent spiritual development.* Poster presented at the European Conference on Developmental Psychology, Jena, Germany.

James, W. (1902). *The varieties of religious experience: A study in human nature.* New York: Longmans, Green. (Repr. in *William James: Writings 1902–1910.* New York: Library of America, 1987.)

Jamieson, P. E., & Romer, D. (2008). Unrealistic fatalism in U.S. youth ages 14 to 22: Prevalence and characteristics. *Journal of Adolescent Health, 42,* 154–160.

Jensen, L. A. (2008). Immigrant civic engagement and religion: The paradoxical roles of religious motives and organizations. In R. M. Lerner, R. W. Roeser, & E. Phelps (Eds.). *Positive youth development and spirituality: From theory to research* (pp. 247–261). West Conshohocken, PA: Templeton Foundation Press.

Jessor, R., & Jessor, S. L. (1977). *Problem behavior and psychosocial development: A longitudinal study of youth.* New York: Academic Press.

Jessor, R., Turbin, M., & Costa, F. (1998). Risk and protection in successful outcomes among disadvantaged adolescents. *Applied Developmental Science, 2,* 194–208.

Johnson, B. R., Jang, S. J., Larson, D. B., & Li, S. D. (2001). Does adolescent religious commitment matter? A reexamination of the effects of religiosity on delinquency. *Journal of Research in Crime and Delinquency, 38,* 22–43.

Johnson, C. N., & Boyatzis, C. J. (2006). Cognitive–cultural foundations of spiritual development. In E. C. Roehlkepartain, P. E. King, L. M. Wagener, & P. L. Benson (Eds.), *Handbook of spiritual development in childhood and adolescence* (pp. 211–223). Thousand Oaks, CA: Sage.

Juang, L., & Syed, L. M. (2008). Ethnic identity and spirituality. In R. M. Lerner, R. W. Roeser, & E. Phelps (Eds.). *Positive youth development and spirituality: From theory to research* (pp. 262–284). West Conshohocken, PA: Templeton Foundation Press.

Kagan, J. (1996). Three pleasing ideas. *American Psychologist, 51,* 901–908.

Kelley, B. S., & Miller, L. (2007). Life satisfaction and spirituality in adolescents. *Research in the Social Scientific Study of Religion, 18,* 233–261.

Kerestes, M., & Youniss, J. E. (2003). Rediscovering the importance of religion in adolescent development. In R. M. Lerner, F. Jacobs, & D. Wertlieb (Eds.), *Handbook of applied developmental science,* vol. 1: *Applying developmental science for youth and families.* Thousand Oaks, CA: Sage.

Kerestes, M., Youniss, J., & Metz, E. (2004). Longitudinal patterns of religious perspective and civic integration. *Applied Developmental Science, 8,* 39–46.

King, P. E. (2003). Religion and identity: The role of ideological, social, and spiritual contexts. *Applied Developmental Sciences, 7,* 196–203.

King, P. E. (2004). The religious social context of Korean and American youth. In H. Alexander (Ed.), *Spirituality and ethics in education: Philosophical, theological, and cultural perspectives.* East Sussex, UK: Sussex Academic Press.

King, P. E. (2008). Spirituality as fertile ground for positive youth development. In R. M. Lerner, R. W. Roeser, & E. Phelps (Eds.). *Positive youth development and spirituality: From theory to research* (pp. 55–73). West Conshohocken, PA: Templeton Foundation Press.

King, P. E., & Benson, P. L. (2006). Spiritual development and adolescent well-being and thriving. In E. C. Roehlkepartain, P. E. King, L. M. Wagener, & P. L. Benson (Eds.), *The handbook of spiritual development in childhood and adolescence.* Newbury Park, CA: Sage.

King, P. E., Dowling, E. M., Mueller, R. A., White, K., Schultz, W., Osborn, P., et al. (2005). Thriving in adolescence: The voices of youth-serving practitioners, parents, and early and late adolescents. *Journal of Early Adolescence, 25,* 94–112.

King, P. E., & Furrow, J. L. (2004). Religion as a resource for positive youth development: Religion, social capital, and moral outcomes. *Developmental Psychology, 40,* 703–713.

King, P. E., & Furrow, J. L., Roth, N. H. (2002). The influence of families and peers on adolescent religiousness. *Journal of Psychology and Christianity, 21,* 109–120.

King, P. E., Ramos, J., & Clardy, C. (2008). *Adolescent spiritual exemplars: An exploratory study of spiritual thriving.* Paper presented at the Biannual Meeting of the International Society for the Study of Behavioral Development, Wurtzburg, Germany.

King, V., Elder, G. H., & Whitbeck, L. B. (1997). Religious Involvement among rural youth: An ecological and life course perspective. *Journal of Research on Adolescence, 7,* 431–456.

Kirkpatrick, L. A. (1997). An Attachment-theory approach to the psychology of religion. In B. Spilka & D. N. McIntosh (Eds.), *Psychology of religion: Theoretical approaches* (pp. 114–133). Boulder, CO: Westview.

Kirkpatrick, L. A., & Shaver, P. R. (1990). Attachment theory and religion: Childhood attachments, religious beliefs, and conversion. *Journal for the Scientific Study of Religion, 29,* 315–334.

Koenig, H. G., McCullough, M. E., & Larson, D. B. (2001). *Handbook of religion and health.* New York: Oxford University Press.

Lammers, C., Ireland, M., Resnick, M., & Blum, R. (2000). Influences on adolescents' decision to postpone onset of sexual intercourse: A survival analysis of virginity among youths aged 13 to 18 years. *Journal of Adolescent Health, 26,* 42–48.

Larson, R., Hansen, D., & Moneta, G. (2006). Differing profiles of developmental experiences across types of organized youth activities. *Developmental Psychology, 42,* 849–863.

Larson, R. W., Wilson, S., Mortimer, J. T. (2002). Conclusions: Adolescents' preparation for the future. *Journal of Research on Adolescence, 12,* 159–166.

Leach, M., & Fried, J. (Eds). (1972). *Funk & Wagnalls standard dictionary of folklore, mythology and legend.* San Francisco: Harper.

Leake, G. K., DeNeve, K. M, & Greteman, A. J. (2007). The relationship between spirituality, assessed through self-transcendent goal strivings, and positive psychological attributes. *Research in the Social Scientific Study of Religion, 18,* 263–279.

Lee, J. W., Rice, G. T., & Gillespie, V. B. (1997). Family worship patterns and their correlation with adolescent behavior and beliefs. *Journal for the Scientific Study of Religion, 36,* 372–381.

Lerner, R. M. (2006). Developmental science, developmental systems, and contemporary theories of human development. In R. M. Lerner (Ed.). *Handbook of child psychology* (6th ed.), vol. 1: *Theoretical models of human development* (pp. 1–17). (Editors-in-chief: W. Damon & R. M. Lerner.) Hoboken, NJ: John Wiley & Sons.

Lerner, R. M., Alberts, A. E., Anderson, P. M., & Dowling, E. M. (2006). *On making humans human: Spirituality and the promotion of positive youth development.* In E. C. Roehlkepartain, P. E. King, L. Wagener, & P. L. Benson (Eds.). *The handbook of spiritual development in childhood and adolescence* (pp. 60–72). Thousand Oaks, CA: Sage.

Lerner, R. M., Roeser, R. W., & Phelps, E. (Eds.). (2008). *Positive youth development and spirituality: From theory to research.* West Conshohocken, PA: Templeton Foundation Press.

Levenson, M. R., Aldwin, C. M., & D'Mello, M. (2005). Religious development from adolescence to middle adulthood. In R. F. Paloutzian & C. L. Park (Eds.). *The psychology of religion and spirituality* (pp. 144–161). New York: Guilford Press.

Magesa, L. (1997). *African religion: The moral traditions of abundant life.* Maryknoll, NY: Orbis Books.

Mahoney, A. (2005). Religion and conflict in marital and parent-child relationships. *Journal of Social Issues, 61,* 689–706.

Mahoney, A., & Tarakeshwar, N. (2005). Religion's role in marriage and parenting in daily life and during family crises. In R. F. Paloutzian & C. L. Park (Eds.), *Handbook of the psychology of religion and spirituality* (pp. xx-yy). New York & London: Guilford Press.

Mahoney, A., Pendleton, S., & Ihrke, H. (2006). Religious coping by children and adolescents: Unexplored territory in the realm of spiritual development. In E. C. Roehlkepartain, P. E. King, L. Wagener, & P. L. Benson (Eds.), *The handbook of spiritual development in childhood and adolescence* (pp. 341–354). Thousand Oaks, CA: Sage.

Marcia, J. E. (1966). Development and validation of ego identity status. *Journal of Personality and Social Psychology, 3,* 551–558.

Markstrom, C. A. (1999). Religious involvement and adolescent psychosocial development. *Journal of Adolescence, 22,* 205–221.

Markstrom-Adams, C., Hofstra, G., & Dougher, K. (1994). The ego virtue of fidelity: A case for the study of religion and identity formation in adolescence. *Journal of Youth and Adolescence, 23,* 453–469.

Markstrom-Adams, C., & Smith, M. (1996). Identity formation and religious orientation among minority and majority high schools students from the United States and Canada. *Journal of Adolescence, 19,* 247–261.

Martignetti, C. A. (1998). Gurus and devotees: Guides or God? Pathology or faith? *Pastoral Psychology, 47,* 220–236.

Martin, T. F., White, J. M., & Perlman, D. (2001). Religious socialization: A test of the channeling hypothesis of parental influence on adolescent faith maturity. *Journal of Adolescent Research, 18,* 169–187.

Mattis, J. S., Ahluwalia, M. K, Cowie, S. E., & Kirkland-Harris, A. M. (2006). *Ethnicity, culture, and spiritual development.* In E. C. Roehlkepartain, P. E. King, L.Wagner, & P. L. Benson (Eds.), *The handbook of spiritual development in childhood and adolescence* (pp. 283–296). Thousand Oaks, CA: Sage.

McBride, V. M. (1996). An ecological analysis of coital timing among middle-class African-American adolescent females. *Journal of Adolescent Research, 11,* 261–279.

McCrae, M. B., Thompson, D. A., Cooper, S. (1999). Black churches as therapeutic groups. *Journal of Multicultural Counseling and Development, 78,* 137–144.

Miller, L., & Gur, M. (2002). Religiousness and sexual responsibility in adolescent girls. *Journal of Adolescent Health, 31,* 401–406.

Mithen, S. (1996). *The prehistory of the mind.* London: Thames & Hudson.

Murray, V. (1994). Black adolescent families: A comparison of early versus late coital initiators. *Family Relations, 43,* 342–348.

Nasir, N. (2004). "Halal-ing" the child: Reframing identities of opposition in an urban Muslim school. *Harvard Educational Review, 74,* 153–174.

Newberg, A. B., & Newberg, S. K. (2006). A neuropsychological perspective on spiritual development. In E. C. Roehlkepartain, P. E. King, L. Wagener, & P. L. Benson (Eds.), *The handbook of spiritual development in childhood and adolescence* (pp. 183–196). Thousand Oaks, CA: Sage.

Nicolas, G., & DeSilva, A. M. (2008). Spirituality research with ethnically diverse youth. In R. M. Lerner, R. W. Roeser, & E. Phelps (Eds.). *Positive youth development and spirituality: From theory to research* (pp. 305–321). West Conshohocken, PA: Templeton Foundation Press.

Nonnemaker, J. M., McNeely, C. A., Blum, R. W. (2003). Public and private domains of religiosity and adolescent health risk behaviors: Evidence from the National Longitudinal Study of Adolescent Health. *Social Science & Medicine, 57,* 2049–2054.

O'Connor, T. P., Hoge, D. R., & Alexander, E. (2002). The relative influence of youth and adult experiences on personal spirituality and church involvement. *Journal for the Scientific Study of Religon, 41,* 723–732.

Obermeyer, C. M. (2000). Pluralism and pragmatism: Knowledge and practice of birth in Morocco. *Medical Anthropology Quarterly, 14,* 180–201.

Oman, D., Flinders, T., & Thoresen, C. E. (in press). Integrating spiritual modeling into education: A college course for stress management and spiritual growth. *International Journal for the Psychology of Religion.*

Oman, D., & Thoresen, C. E. (2005). Do religion and spirituality influence health? In R. F. Paloutzian & C. L. Park (Eds.), *The handbook of the psychology of religion* (pp. 435–459). New York: Guilford Press.

Oser, F. K., Scarlett, W. G., & Bucher, A. (2006). Religious and spiritual development throughout the lifespan. In W. Damon & Richard M. Lerner (Series Eds.) & R.M. Lerner (Volume Ed.), *Handbook of child psychology* (6th ed.), vol. 1: *Theoretical models of human development* (pp. 942–998). Hoboken, NJ: John Wiley & Sons.

Ozorak, E. (1989). Social and cognitive influences on the development of religious beliefs and commitment in adolescence. *Journal for the Scientific Study of Religion, 28,* 448–463.

Paloutzian, R. F., & Park, C. L (2005). *Handbook of the psychology of religion and spirituality.* New York: Guilford Press.

Pargament, K. I. 2007. *Spiritually integrated psychotherapy: Understanding and addressing the sacred.* New York: Guilford.

Park, C. L. (2005). *Religion and meaning.* In R. F. Paloutzian & C. L. Park (Eds.), *Handbook of the psychology of religion* (pp. 295–314). New York: Guilford Press.

Pearce, M. J., Jones, S. M., Schwab-Stone, M. E., & Ruchkin, V. (2003a). The protective effects of religiousness and parent involvement on the development of conduct problems among youth exposed to violence. *Child Development, 74,* 1682–1696.

Pearce, M. J., Little, T. D. & Perez, J. E. (2003b). Religiousness and depressive symptoms among adolescents. *Journal of Clinical Child and Adolescent Psychology, 32,* 267–276.

Pew Forum on Religion and Public Life. (2002). *Global attitudes project.* Washington, DC: Pew Research Center.

Pew Forum on Religion and Public Life. (2008). *U.S. religious landscape survey.* Washington DC: Pew Research Center.

Piedmont, R. L. (1999). Does spirituality represent the sixth factor of personality? Spiritual transcendence and the five-factor model. *Journal of Personality, 67,* 985–1013.

Piedmont, R. L. (2005). *The role of personality in understanding religious and spiritual constructs.* In R. F. Paloutzian & C. L. Park (Eds.), *Handbook of the psychology of religion* (pp. 253–273). New York: Guilford Press.

Portes, A., & Rumbaut, R. G. (2006). *Immigrant America.* Berkeley and Los Angeles: University of California Press.

Putnam, R. (2000). *Bowling alone: The collapse and revival of American community.* New York: Simon & Schuster.

Ream, G. L., & Savin-Williams, R. C. (2004). Religion and the educational experiences of adolescents. In T. Urdan & F. Pajares (Eds.), *Educating adolescents: Challenges and strategies* (pp. 255–286), Greenwich, CT: Information Age Publishing.

Regnerus, M. D. (2000). Shaping schooling success: A multilevel study of religious socialization and educational outcomes in urban public schools. *Journal for the Scientific Study of Religion, 39,* 363–370.

Regnerus, M. D. (2003). Linked lives, faith, and behavior: An intergenerational model of religious influence on adolescent delinquency. *Journal for the Scientific Study of Religion, 42,* 189–203.

Regnerus, M. D., & Elder, G. H. (2003). Staying on track in school: Religious influences in high- and low-risk settings. *Journal for the Scientific Study of Religion, 42*(4), 633–649.

Regnerus, M. D., Smith, C., & Fritsch, M. (2003). *Religion in the lives of American adolescents: A review of the literature.* A Research Report of the National Study of Youth and Religion, No. 3. Chapel Hill: University of North Carolina.

Regnerus, M. D., Smith, C. S., & Smith, B. (2004). Social context in the development of adolescent religiosity. *Applied Developmental Science, 8,* 27–38.

Rizzuto, A. M. (1979). *The birth of the living God.* Chicago: University of Chicago Press.

Roehlkepartain, E. C., & Patel, E. (2006). Congregations: Unexamined crucibles for spiritual development. In E. C. Roehlkepartain, P. E. King, L. Wagener, & P. L. Benson (Eds.), *The handbook of spiritual development in childhood and adolescence* (pp. 324–336). Thousand Oaks, CA: Sage.

Roehlkepartain, E. C., King, P. E., Wagener, L. M., & Benson, P. L. (2006). *The handbook for spiritual development in childhood and adolescence.* Newbury Park, CA: Sage.

Roeser, R. W. (2005). An introduction to Hindu India's contemplative spiritual views on human motivation, selfhood, and development. In M. L. Maehr & S. A. Karabenick (Eds.), *Advances in motivation and achievement,* vol. 14: *Religion and motivation* (pp. 297–345). New York: Elsevier.

Roeser, R. W., Issac, S. S., Abo-Zena, M., Brittian, A., Peck, S. J. (2008a). Self and identity processes in spirituality and positive youth development. In R. M. Lerner, R. W. Roeser, & E. Phelps (Eds.). *Positive youth development and spirituality: From theory to research* (pp. 74–105). West Conshohocken, PA: Templeton Foundation Press.

Roeser, R. W., Berry, R., Hastak, Y., Shah, M., Rao, M. A., Gonsalves, A., & Bhatewara, S. (2006, April). *Exploring the varieties of moral and spiritual education in India: Implications for adolescents' spiritual development.* Paper presented at the annual meeting of the American Educational Research Association, San Francisco.

Roeser, R. W., & Lerner, R. M. (2008, January). *Youth religious pluralism and positive spiritual development spiritual identities in a pluralistic world.* Paper presented in a symposium on Spirituality in and Youth Development in a Pluralistic World (Organizer: G. Roehlkepartain) at the World Congress on Psychology and Spirituality, Delhi, India.

Roeser, R. W., & Peck, S. (2008). *An education in awareness: Human identity in contemplative perspective.* Manuscript under review.

Roeser, R. W., Lerner, R. M., Jensen, L. A., & Alberts, A. (2008b, April). Exploring the role of spirituality and religious involvement in patterns of social contribution among immigrant youth. Paper submitted as part of a symposium (R. W. Roeser, Organizer). *On the role of spirituality and religion in the lives of immigrant youth and their families.* Symposium submitted to biennial meeting of the Society for Research on Adolescence, Chicago, IL.

Roeser, R. W., Peck, S. C., & Nasir, N. S. (2006). Self and identity processes in school motivation, learning, and achievement. In Alexander, P. A., Pintrich, P. R., & Winne, P. H. (Eds.) *Handbook of educational psychology* (2nd ed.; pp. 391–424). Mahwah, NJ: Lawrence Erlbaum.

Roeser, R. W., Rao, M. A., Shah, M., Hastak, Y., Gonsalves, A., & Berry, R. (2006, March). *A return to the varieties of religious experience: Research notes from India.* Paper presented as part of a symposium, "Theoretical issues in the study of adolescent spiritual development," at the biennial meeting of the Society for Research on Adolescence, San Francisco.

Rogoff, B. (2003). *The cultural nature of human development.* New York: Oxford University Press.

Rostosky, S., Danner, F., & Riggle, E. (2007). Is religiosity a protective factor against substance use in young adulthood? Only if you're straight! *Journal of Adolescent Health, 40,* 440–447.

Rostosky, S. S., Regnerus, M. D., & Wright, M. L. C. (2003). Coital debut: The role of religiosity and sex attitudes in the add health survey. *Journal of Sex Research, 40,* 358–367.

Ruble, A. J., O'Nell, C. W., & Collando Ardán, R. (1992). Introducción al susto [Introduction to fright]. In R. Campos (Ed.), *La antropología médica en Mexico* [Medical anthropology in Mexico] (pp. 105–120). Mexico City: Universidad Autónoma Metropolitana.

Sameroff, A. J. (1983). Developmental systems: Contexts and evolution. In W. Kessen (Ed.), *History, theory, and methods,* vol. 1 (4th ed., pp. 237–294). New York: John Wiley & Sons.

Scales, P., Benson, P., Leffert, N., & Blyth, D. A. (2000). The contribution of developmental assets to the prediction of thriving among adolescents. *Applied Developmental Science, 4*, 27–46.

Scarlett, W. G., & Perriello, L. (1991). The development of prayer in adolescence. In F. K. Oser & W. G. Scarlett (Eds.), *Religious development in childhood and adolescence*, vol. 52: *New directions for child development* (pp. 63–76). San Francisco: Jossey-Bass.

Schapman, A. M., & Inderbitzen-Nolan, H. M. (2002). The role of religious behavior in adolescent depressive and anxious symptomatology. *Journal of Adolescence, 25*, 631–643.

Schreck, C. J., Burek, M. W., Clark-Miller, J. (2007). He sends rain upon the wicked: A panel study of the influence of religiosity on violent victimization. *Journal of Interpersonal Violence, 22*, 872–893.

Schwartz, K. D. (2006). Transformations in parent and friend faith support predicting adolescents' religious faith. *International Journal for the Psychology of Religion, 16*(4), 311–326.

Schwartz, K. D., Bukowski, W. M., & Aoki, W. T. (2006). Mentors, friends, and gurus: Peer and nonparent influences on spiritual development. In E. C. Roehlkepartain, P. E. King, L. Wagener, & P. L. Benson (Eds.), *The handbook of spiritual development in childhood and adolescence* (pp. 310–323). Thousand Oaks, CA: Sage.

Selman, R. L. (1980). *The growth of interpersonal understanding: Developmental and clinical analyses*. New York: Academic Press.

Serow, R., & Dreydon, J. (1990). Community service among college and university students: Individual and institutional relationships. *Adolescence, 25*, 553–566.

Showalter, S. M., & Wagener L. M. (2000). Adolescents' meaning in life: A replication of DeVogler and Ebersole (1983). *Psychological Reports, 87*, 115–126.

Silberman, I. (2003). Spiritual role modeling: The teaching of meaning systems. *The International Journal for the Psychology of Religion, 13*, 175–195.

Silberman, I. (2005). Religious violence, terrorism, and peace: A meaning-system analysis. In R. F. Paloutizian & C. L. Park (Eds.), *Handbook of the psychology of religion and spirituality* (pp. 529–549). New York: Guilford Press.

Silberman, I., Higgins, E. T., & Dweck, C. S. (2005). Religion and world change: Violence and terrorism versus peace. *Journal of Social Issues, 61*, 761–784.

Sinha, J. W., Cnaan, R. A., & Gelles, R. J. (2007). Adolescent risk behaviors and religion: Findings from a national study. *Journal of Adolescence, 30*, 231–249.

Sloane, D. M., & Potvin, R. H. (1986). Religion and delinquency: Cutting through the maze. *Social Forces, 65*, 87–105.

Slonim, M. (1991). *Children, culture, and ethnicity*. New York: Garland.

Smith, C. (1999). The effects of investments in the social capital of youth on political and civic behavior in young adulthood: A longitudinal analysis. *Political Psychology, 20*, 553–580.

Smith, C. (2003a). Religious participation and network closure among American adolescents. *Journal for the Scientific Study of Religion, 42*(2), 259–267.

Smith, C. (2003b). Theorizing religious effects among American adolescents. *Journal for the Scientific Study of Religion, 42*(1), 17–30.

Smith, C., & Denton, M. (2005). *Soul searching: The religious and spiritual lives of American teenagers*. New York: Oxford University Press.

Smith, C., & Faris, R. (2003). *Religion and American adolescent delinquency, risk behaviors, and constructive social activities.* A research report from the National Youth and Religion Study, Chapel Hill, NC.

Smith, C. B., Weigert, A. J., & Thomas, D. L. (1979). Self-esteem and religiosity: An analysis of Catholic adolescents from five cultures. *Journal for the Scientific Study of Religion, 18*, 51–60.

Sorenson, A. M., Grindstaff, C. F., & Turner, R. J. (1995). Religious involvement among unmarried adolescent mothers: A source of emotional support? *Sociology of Religion, 56*, 71–81.

Spilka, B., Hood, R. W., Hunsberger, B., & Gorsuch, R. (2003). *Psychology of religion: An empirical approach* (3rd ed.). New York: Guilford Press.

Spilka, B., Shaver, P. R., & Kirkpatrick, L. A. (1997). A general attribution theory for the psychology of religion. In B. Spilka & D. N. McIntosh (Eds.), *Psychology of religion: Theoretical approaches* (pp.153–170). Boulder, CO: Westview.

Steffen, P. R., Hinderliter, A. L., Blumenthal, J. A., & Sherwood, A. (2001). Religious coping, ethnicity and ambulatory blood pressure. *Psychosomatic Medicine, 63*, 523–530.

Strommen, M. P., & Hardel, R. A. (2000). *Passing on the faith: A radical new model for youth and family ministry*. Winona, MN: St. Mary's Press.

Sturgeon, R. S., & Hamley, R. W. (1979). Religiosity and anxiety. *Journal of Social Psychology, 108*, 137–138.

Taylor, R. J., Chatters, L. M. & Levin, J. (2004). *Religion in the lives of African Americans: Social, psychological and health perspectives*. Thousand Oaks, CA: Sage.

Templeton, J. L., & J. S.Eccles. (2008). The relation between spiritual development and identity processes. In E. C. Roehlkepartain, P. E. King, L. M.Wagener, and P. L. Benson (Eds.), *The handbook of spiritual development in childhood and adolescence* (pp. 252–265). Thousand Oaks, CA: Sage Publications.

Templeton, J. L. & Eccles, J. S. (2008). Spirituality, "Expanding Circle Morality," and Positive Youth Development. In R. M. Lerner, R. W. Roeser & E. Phelps (Eds.). *Positive youth development and spirituality: From theory to research (pp. 197–209)*. West Conshohocken, PA: Templeton Foundation Press.

Thornton, A., & Camburn, D. (1989). Religious participation and adolescent sexual behavior and attitudes. *Journal of Marriage and the Family, 51*, 641–653.

Trovato, F. (1992). A Durkheimian analysis of youth suicide: Canada, 1971 and 1981. *Suicide and Life-Threatening Behavior, 22*, 413–427.

Tzuriel, D. (1984). Sex role typing and ego identity in Israeli, Oriental, and Western adolescents. *Journal of Personality and Social Psychology, 46*, 440–457.

Urry, H. L., & Poey, A. P. (2008). How religious/spiritual practices contribute to well-being: The role of emotion regulation. In R. M. Lerner, R. W. Roeser, & E. Phelps (Eds.). *Positive youth development and spirituality: From theory to research (pp. 145–163)*. West Conshohocken, PA: Templeton Foundation Press.

Varon, S. R., & Riley, A. W. (1999). Relationship between maternal church attendance and adolescent mental health and social functioning. *Psychiatric Services, 50*, 799–805.

Wagener, L. M., & Maloney, H. N. (2006). Spiritual and religious pathology in childhood and adolescence. In E. C. Roehlkepartain, P. E. King, L. M. Wagener & P. L. Benson (Eds.), *The handbook of spiritual development in childhood and adolescence* (pp. xx-yy). Newbury Park, CA: Sage.

Wagener, L. M., Furrow, J. L., Ebstyne King, P., Leffert, N., & Benson, P. (2003). Religious involvement and developmental resources in youth. *Review of Religious Research, 44*, 271–284.

Wallace, J. M., Jr., & Forman, T. A. (1998). Religion's role in promoting health and reducing risk among American youth. *Health Education & Behavior, 25*, 721–741.

Wallace, J. M., Forman, T. A., Caldwell, C. H., & Willis, D. S. (2003). Religion and American youth: Recent patterns, historical trends and sociodemographic correlates. *Youth and Society, 35*, 98–125.

Wallace, J. M., Jr., & Williams, D. R. (1997). Religion and adolescent health compromising behavior. In J. Schulenberg, J. L. Maggs, & K. Hurrelmann (Eds.), *Health risks and developmental transitions during adolescence* (pp. 444–468). New York: Cambridge University Press.

Weaver, A. J., Pargament, K. I., Flannelly, K. J., & Oppenheimer, J. E. (2006). Trends in the scientific study of religion, spirituality, and health: 1965–2000. *Journal of Religion and Health, 45,* 208–214.

Wilbur, K. (2006). Integral Spirituality: A startling new role for religion in the modern and postmodern world. Boston: Shambhala.

Wills, T. A., Yaeger, A. M., & Sandy, J. M. (2003). Buffering effect of religiosity for adolescent substance use. *Psychology of Addictive Behaviors, 17,* 24–31.

Wilson, J., & Sherkat, D. E. (1994). Returning to the fold. *Journal for the Scientific Study of Religion, 33*:148–161.

Wright, L. S., Frost, C. J., & Wisecarver, S. J. (1993). Church attendance, meaningfulness of religion, and depressive symptomatology among adolescents. *Journal of Youth and Adolescence, 22,* 559–568.

Yarnold, B. M. (1998). Steroid use among Miami's public school students, 1992: Alternative subcultures: Religion and music versus peers and the "body cult."*Psychological Reports, 82,* 19–24.

Youniss, J. A., McLellan, J., & Yates, M. (1999). Religion, community service, and identity in American youth. *Journal of Adolescence, 22,* 243–253.

Zinnbauer, B., & Pargament, K. I. (2005). Religiousness and spirituality. In R. Paloutzian & C. Parks (Eds.), *Handbook of psychology and religion* (pp. 21–42). New York: Guilford Press.

CHAPTER 14

Adolescent Sexuality

LISA M. DIAMOND AND RITCH C. SAVIN-WILLIAMS

All adolescents have sex lives, whether they are sexually active with others, with themselves, or seemingly not at all. The question is whether they are going to have healthy experiences, at any or every level of sexual activity. (Ponton, 2000, p. 2)

In America today, it is nearly impossible to publish a book that says children and teenagers can have sexual pleasure and be safe too, . . . [yet sex] is a vehicle to self-knowledge, love, healing, creativity, adventure, and intense feelings of aliveness. (Levine, 2002, pp. xix, 225)

These two popular books question accepted wisdom regarding the role of sexuality in adolescents' lives. Thirty years ago one of the first systematic studies of adolescent sexuality echoed these concerns, asking researchers and educators to help adolescents "integrate the biological, social, and psychological aspects of their sexuality into all aspects of their lives" so that they can "realize their potential as whole human beings" (Chilman, 1978, p. 1). This goal remains unrealized, perhaps because nearly 80% of U.S. adults believe teenage sex is always or almost always wrong (Laumann, Gagnon, Michael, & Michaels, 1994, p. 322) and because adolescent sexual activity is commonly associated with a host of negative by-products, including pregnancy, sexually transmitted infections (STIs), abortions, substance use, delinquency, and bad grades. Youths encounter "educational" scare tactics admonishing them to avoid sex, yet also encounter ubiquitous and typically exploitative depictions of sexuality in mainstream American culture.

Contemporary research reflects a similarly conflicted approach to adolescent sexuality. Although developmental scientists have amassed an incredible amount of data on which adolescents pursue sexual activity, at what ages, how often, and with what types of partners, researchers have shied away from collecting in-depth information on the *qualitative* aspects of adolescents' developing sexual desires and early sexual experiences. Consequently, we know little about how adolescents *develop* their conceptualizations of sex, how they negotiate between conflicting motivations for and against different sexual activities, how they experience and interpret their sexual thoughts and fantasies, and how the subjective and symbolic meaning of sexuality is shaped by their culture and social–cognitive–biological maturation. Thus, even after decades of research on adolescent sexuality, many fundamental questions about normative sexual development from prepubescence to young adulthood remain unanswered.

It is with these caveats that we offer the present review. We begin by calling attention to the implicit and explicit conceptual frameworks shaping the questions asked, the methods used, and hence the answers offered about adolescent sexuality. We then review the most reliable contemporary data on the "who, what, and when" of teenage sexuality, highlighting overarching themes, emerging trends, and underinvestigated questions. Our review follows a rough trajectory from inside to outside, beginning with a youth's internal sexual desires and motivations, moving to solitary and then partnered sexual activities, and finally addressing in a more limited fashion the diverse array of individual and contextual factors that moderate adolescent sexual expression. In the interests of space, certain areas that have developed their *own* extensive literatures over the years are not addressed, including legal aspects of adolescent sexuality (Levesque, 2000); romantic relationships (Florsheim, 2003; Furman, Brown, & Feiring, 1999); the biology of sexual maturation (Brooks-Gunn & Reiter, 1990); and the influence of contextual factors such as family characteristics, friendships, community milieu, and demography (e.g., social class, region, and ethnicity) on the timing and frequency of sex (Buhi & Goodson, 2007; Manlove et al., 2001; Moore & Rosenthal, 1993). Our intent is to delineate where we are in the study of adolescent sexuality and where we have yet to go in our continuing attempts to build sophisticated scientific models of adolescent sexual development that capably represent its variety and complexity.

RISK FACTORS AND PROBLEM BEHAVIORS

Contemporary Western culture portrays teenage sexual expression as a dangerous activity that should be delayed as long as possible or prevented altogether until marriage, rather than as a normative, integral aspect of development with the potential to promote growth and well-being. As one sex advice columnist warned, "I don't care how far exactly it goes; that kind of behavior means moving into an intimacy that kids are simply not prepared for . . . and most experts believe that kids under 16 do not have the psychological and neurological development necessary to satisfactorily manage these feelings" (Pinsky, 2002, p. 6). Research mirrors this perspective, generally adopting a medicalized, reductionist, and implicitly moralizing view of adolescent sexuality as a collection of risk behaviors that threaten both individual development and public health (Carpenter, 2001; Leitenberg & Saltzman,

2000; Sonenstein, Ku, & Pleck, 1997). Indeed, the primary motivation for investigating adolescent sex has been to intervene and prevent an array of negative outcomes associated with early sexual initiation, such as pregnancy, STIs, low educational aspirations, and substance use (Alan Guttmacher Institute, 1994; Crockett, Bingham, Chopak, & Vicary, 1996; Davis & Lay-Yee, 1999; Halpern, Joyner, Udry, & Suchindran, 2000; Kirby, 2002; Laumann et al., 1994; Leitenberg & Saltzman, 2000; Manlove et al., 2001; Miller et al., 1997; Resnick et al., 1997).

The notion that *some* types and contexts of adolescent sexual activity might be more strongly associated with these negative outcomes than others is insufficiently addressed, and thus intervention often consists of one solution: delaying *all* adolescent sexual activity as long as possible with the hope that social, cognitive, and moral maturity will eventually allow youth to manage the complexities and risks of sexual interactions (Dittus, Jaccard, & Gordon, 1997; Gardner & Wilcox, 1993). Indeed, adolescent sex is considered so intrinsically and uniformly dangerous that some have characterized sexually inexperienced youth as "virgin *survivors*" (Costa, Jessor, Donovan, & Fortenberry, 1995, emphasis added), as if they have successfully navigated a battlefield. Notably, this negative emphasis is also manifested in our culture's ambivalence about— and corresponding inattention to—*childhood* sexuality. Although many researchers readily acknowledge that prepubertal children experience and enjoy sexual feelings and engage in sexual exploration and stimulation, research ethics and cultural norms (at least in the United States—for an exception, see Schoentjes, Deboutte, & Friedrich, 1999) essentially preclude the collection of data on such experiences (de Graaf & Rademakers, 2006; Gullotta, Adams, & Montemayor, 1993; Ponton, 2000; Okami, Olmstead, & Abramson, 1997).

The negative cast of contemporary research on adolescent sexuality has received increasing criticism in recent years (Ehrhardt, 1996;

Savin-Williams, 2001, 2005; Tolman, 2002; Tolman & Diamond, 2001; Wright, 1998). This shift away from an exclusively "sex-negative" focus reflects, in part, the emergence of "positive psychology" as a new paradigm in psychological science, emphasizing factors that promote *optimal* human emotional, cognitive, and social functioning instead of focusing exclusively on antecedents of dysfunction and pathology (Eisenberg, Fabes, & Spinrad, 2006; Keyes, 2005; Myers, 2000; Seligman & Csikszentmihalyi, 2000). Research on adolescent sexuality would profit from a similarly expanded approach—a topic we revisit at the end of this chapter.

This shift in emphasis, however, will likely prove a thorny battle. As scholars have long noted, national politics often dictates the kind of scientific research deemed worthy of receiving public support and funding. Given cultural squeamishness about adolescent sexuality, political support for adolescent sex research is generally predicated on the necessity of averting or ameliorating public health problems such as STIs and teenage pregnancy (Carpenter, 2001; di Mauro, 1997; Sonenstein et al., 1997). This risk-centric approach limits our understanding of normative adolescent sexual development and, paradoxically, has hampered efforts at sexual health promotion. As reviewed by Wright (1998), conventional "risk" research tends to paint *all* adolescent sexual activity with a somewhat pathological cast, fostering feelings of shame and guilt among sexually active youths. Such feelings are potent obstacles to constructive and open communication about sex, making it *less* likely that youths will take active steps toward safe and responsible sexual decision making. Hence, although the societal denigration of adolescent sexuality has been predicated on protecting youths' health and well-being, it might actually do more harm than good.

Critics such as Erhardt (1996) and Wright (1998) have argued that researchers should instead focus on normalizing and contextualizing adolescents' sexual feelings, emphasizing sexual responsibility and giving youths the safety to consider multiple forms of intimate expression, including celibacy. Wright specifically argued that researchers and policy makers should set aside the notion that adolescent sexual behavior is the product of rational decision making and instead acknowledge that sexuality has "its own rationality" (p. 14) and symbolic meaning; treat the sexual dyad rather than the individual as the unit of research and intervention; acknowledge the dynamic, changing nature of sexual needs and opportunities instead of treating individuals and their predispositions as static; and give greater attention to the social–cultural context of sexual interactions. European researchers have begun to adopt these changes; it remains to be seen whether American researchers will follow suit.

As it stands now, conventional adolescent sex research has a host of methodological shortcomings that pose obstacles to the correctives Wright recommended. Understanding the nature and implications of these limitations is critical for evaluating and interpreting contemporary data on adolescent sexuality.

Methodological Issues

A considerable cottage industry has developed around methodological issues in sex research, particularly research on adolescents (Bancroft, 1997; Catania, 1999; Catania, Gibson, Chitwood, & Coates, 1990; Goodson, Evans, & Edmundson, 1997; Moore & Rosenthal, 1993; Schwarz, 1999; Wiederman, 1999). One chief critique is the paucity of empirical data on the reliability and validity of techniques assessing the development and prevalence of adolescent sexual behavior (Catania et al.). A recent comprehensive review of survey research on sensitive topics such as drug use, abortion, and sexual behavior found evidence for systematic misreporting of these experiences (Tourangeau and Yan, 2007). Furthermore, the extent of misreporting was moderated by both situational factors (survey design, response format, experimenter presence, reminders of confidentiality) and motivational processes related to self-presentation. The degree to which such processes are developmentally sensitive is poorly understood. Another problem is that research designs are often simplistic, rarely taking advantage of the more complex perspectives afforded by multimethod, cross-disciplinary collaborations, and rarely attempting to integrate findings across multiple disciplines (di Mauro, 1997; Sonenstein et al., 1997). In addition to these fairly broad shortcomings, researchers have identified a number of more specific problems: *what* is studied, *who* is studied, and *how* it is studied.

What Is Studied? The Definition and Meaning of Sex

When researchers use the term *sex,* they nearly always mean sexual intercourse—more specifically, penile–vaginal intercourse. Despite the obvious fact that this is only one among many forms of adolescent sexual expression, researchers often adopt the larger culture's preoccupation with this form of sexual activity (Schwartz, 1999), ostensibly because it is the riskiest (Schuster, Bell, & Kanouse, 1996). This, of course, is a matter of perspective. If youth are less likely to refrain from noncoital activities or to use protection during such activities because they are perceived as safer, then such behaviors introduce greater rather than lesser risk.

But the problem runs deeper. The widespread, unquestioned equation of penile–vaginal intercourse with sex reflects a failure to examine systematically "whether the respondent's understanding of the question matches what the researcher had in mind" (Schwarz, 1999, p. 94). The full pragmatic and erotic meaning of the youth's sexual world is not elicited by the simple question, "Have you had sex?" As Reinisch and Sanders (1999, p. 1918) noted, answers to this question depend on (unmeasured) factors such as "consent, cohort, the potential costs and benefits of labeling a behavior, socioeconomic status, subculture, geography, and the demands of polite society."

A number of feminist scholars have questioned the gender neutrality of the sex-as-intercourse equation, believing the parallel is more in the minds of males than females (Peplau & Garnets, 2000; Rodríguez Rust, 2000; Rose, 2000; Rothblum, 2000). In reality, researchers rarely include measures other than intercourse, they fail to define sex, or they see little need to resolve potential discrepancies in definitions of sex. Thus, it is common to encounter statements such as, "The majority of the students reported having sex at least once a month" (Prince & Bernard, 1998, p. 17), without knowing just what respondents meant by "having sex." Other studies use the even vaguer term *sexually active.* To researchers' credit, their hands are often tied by school officials, parents, funding agencies, and institutional review boards that require that sex questions avoid explicit terminology and descriptions of specific sex acts (Crockett et al., 1996).

Substantial evidence indicates that contemporary adolescents and young adults do not have uniform or consistent conceptualizations of sex and sexual activity (Peterson & Muehlenhard, 2007). Based on surveys of college students from the U.S. Midwest (Sanders & Reinisch, 1999) and the United Kingdom (Pitts & Rahman, 2001), practically all youth consider penile–vaginal intercourse to be sex, but they disagree regarding other sex acts. For example, Sanders and Reinisch found that 81% of respondents considered penile–anal intercourse to be sex, and approximately 20% counted manual and oral stimulation. Notably, these proportions varied by gender, with males generally adopting more flexible definitions of sex. In a qualitative study of 15- to 19-year-old boys (Sonenstein et al., 1997), one respondent claimed that touching a female breast counted as having sex, whereas another said that sex involved going on a date and kissing. Some boys asserted that the term *sex* was reserved for any and all sexual activities pursued within an emotionally invested relationship.

All college students in one study considered penile–vaginal intercourse sex, including some self-identified virgins who nevertheless had had intercourse. Just over half agreed that performing or receiving oral sex also constituted sex; one-third reported that having your genitals fondled by another person was sex; and about one quarter said anal intercourse and fondling another's person's genitals qualified as sex (Peterson & Muehlenhard, 2007). Those who rated these behaviors as "almost but not quite sex" did so because these behaviors failed the penile–vaginal criterion. Besides oral sex, the most controversial behavior (with regard to its labeling as sex) was brief or partial penile–vaginal penetration—some considered it "not quite sex" whereas others called it "just barely sex."

These findings reflect the inconsistency of definitions of sexual activity, and the extent to which personal values and motives play a role in such definitions. Peterson and Muehlenhard (2007) noted that many of their midwestern college students did not label their sexual activities as "sex" even if these activities fit the student's own personal definition of sex. Notably, the motives underlying these labeling discrepancies varied by gender. Young women resisted labeling their sexual activities as "sex" to avoid negative self-evaluations, and also to maintain the image that they were virgins; young men did so to avoid damaging specific friendships in which they were pursuing sexual activity and to avoid acknowledging that they might have had sex with the "wrong person" (p. 266). Other frequently noted motives for "uncategorizing" sexual activity included avoiding the negative perceptions of peers, avoiding acknowledging infidelity, and avoiding violations of religious tenets.

In some cases, these motivations prompt youth to *retract* their own disclosures of sexual activity: 11% of youth in the National Longitudinal Study of Adolescent Health (Add Health) retracted reports of intercourse that they had made one year previously. Notably, many were born-again Christians who had taken a virginity pledge (Rosenbaum, 2006). As described by Peterson and Muehlenhard

(2007), by reinterpreting the study's definition of sexual intercourse they regained their prized status as virgins. Certainly, there is sufficient variability in definitions of virginity loss to make such reversals tenable. For example, some studies have found that about half of young adults do not consider heterosexual anal sex to "count" as virginity loss (Carpenter, 2001). These flexible definitions have critically important implications for sexual health. If certain sexual acts are not viewed as "real sex," then youth may (incorrectly) presume that condoms or birth control are unnecessary. One example is the virginity pledgers in the Add Health study—their STD rates were not lower, perhaps because they were "less likely than others to use condoms at sexual debut and to be tested and diagnosed with STDs" (Brückner & Bearman, 2005, p. 271).

The question of orgasm also plays a role in youth's definitions (Bogart, Cecil, Wagstaff, Pinkerton, & Abramson, 2000; Peterson & Muehlenhard, 2007), depending on the relational context and on "who does what to whom." Some heterosexual college students believe that a man who penetrates a woman anally has only had sex if he experiences orgasm, whereas *vaginal* penetration is usually considered sex even if the man does not have an orgasm (Bogart et al.). Of course, vaginal penetration is always considered to be sex for the *woman*, regardless of whether she experiences orgasm, testifying to the historical inattention to women's experiences of sexual desire and satisfaction. As for oral sex, few heterosexuals consider the giver of oral stimulation to have had sex, but the recipient is often viewed as having had sex *if* he/she had an orgasm (Sanders & Reinisch, 1999).

As these diverse findings attest, adolescents use no single standard to certify particular activities as sex. Consequently, two different adolescents with identical sexual histories might check different boxes on a questionnaire asking whether they have "had sex." This methodological conundrum was lucidly critiqued by Frye (1990), who emphasized the impossibility of comparing heterosexual and lesbian respondents' answers to the seemingly simply question, "How often do you have sex?"

> [Some lesbians] might have counted a two- or three-cycle evening as one "time" they "had sex"; some might have counted it as two or three "times." Some may have counted as "times" only the times both partners had orgasms; some may have counted as "times" occasions on which at least one had an orgasm; those who do not have orgasms or have them far more rarely than they "have sex" may not have figured orgasms into the calculations; perhaps some counted as a "time" every episode in which both touched the other's vulva more than fleetingly and not for something like a health examination. . . . But this also raises the questions of how heterosexuals counted their sexual acts. By orgasm? By whose orgasms? If the having of sex by heterosexual married couples did take on the average eight minutes, my guess is that in a very large number of those cases the women did not experience orgasms. (p. 244)

In response to such problems, some have called for more systematic specificity in survey language (Schwarz, 1999), whereas others have called for greater *qualitative* investigation into youths' subjective experiences and interpretations of different forms of sexual expression (Tolman, 2002). This is the position of Peterson and Muehlenhard (2007), who concluded that definitional inconsistencies are masked or ignored in typical surveys. They recommended interview assessments drawing out the context of respondents' real-life experiences (as opposed to presenting youth with a range of hypothetical scenarios and eliciting their responses). Numerous researchers have, in fact, taken up the challenge of conducting nuanced and labor-intensive interviews with youth about their subjective experiences and interpretations of sexual desires, fantasies, and behaviors (Diamond, 2008a; Savin-Williams, 1998, 2004, 2007; Thompson, 1995; Tolman, 2002). However, such research receives far less attention than do large-scale surveys of sexual

activity because it produces no generalizable facts and figures about national rates of risky behavior, no easy sound bites for consumption by policy makers and media outlets. Rather, qualitative interviews go "underneath" the facts and figures on adolescent sex to reveal youths' multifaceted motives for different types of sexual experiences, their subjective appraisals and interpretations of these experiences, and the gradual unfolding of youth's psychosexual developmental trajectories. Given the evidence for systematic inaccuracies in large-scale survey data on adolescent sexuality (Tourangeau & Yan, 2007), smaller-scale investigations of the *meaning*, rather than the frequency, of youths' sexual experiences can make a critical contribution to the development of accurate, nuanced models of adolescent sexual experience.

Specifically, such investigations can reveal the numerous factors impinging on youths' physical, emotional, and cognitive experiences of sexual activity, as well as their emerging symbolic *interpretation* of these phenomena. For example, the constellation of personal, social, and cultural factors making one youth's experience and interpretation of same-sex activity notably different from that of his/her partner can be revealed only through in-depth assessments (Savin-Williams 1998, 2004). The simple tabulation of isolated behaviors is fundamentally limited in what it can reveal about the changing forms and meanings of erotic experience during adolescence; their moderation by sex, ethnicity, relationship status, sexual orientation, and family background; and their implications for psychosocial development.

Who Is Studied? Target Populations, Sampling Problems, and Missing Data

Another problem facing scientists concerns the composition of our research samples. At the broadest level, the majority of contemporary research on adolescent sexuality published in high-impact journals is conducted in the United States or in other Western industrialized nations. Yet, cross-cultural comparisons of adolescent sexual behavior can obviously play an important role in debunking myths and assumptions about which types of behaviors and developmental timetables are "natural" and "normal" during the teenage years. Although an increasing number of rigorous, provocative cross-cultural studies are being conducted (Fineran, Bennett, & Sacco, 2003; Lam et al., 2004; Nieto, 2004; Schalet, 2007; Vazsonyi, Trejos-Castillo, & Huang, 2006; Yoon, 2005), their overall visibility in the broader landscape of social scientific research and thought on adolescent sexual development (as evidenced by their relatively low citation counts) remains low.

Within U.S. culture, identification of study populations is additionally problematic. In a notable contrast to virtually all other areas of research on adolescence, investigations of adolescent sexuality (especially studies of sexual decision making, contraception, and safer sex) have focused disproportionately on girls—particularly poor girls and girls of color (Fordham, 1993; Tolman & Higgins, 1996). This reflects the widespread notion that girls are the gatekeepers of adolescent sexuality and are therefore the primary sites for investigations of sexual risk and intervention (Thompson, 1995; Tolman, 2002) and that sexuality is more of a "problem" for poor and ethnic-minority youth than for privileged European American youth. Although data suggest that these groups do, in fact, often pursue riskier sexual trajectories than do wealthy European American youth, the reductionist nature of most sex research precludes sensitive analyses of the multiple mechanisms mediating this association. Thus, the pathways through which subsets of adolescents track different patterns of sexual behavior remain insufficiently elaborated, leaving only broad-based stereotypes about race, poverty, and sex, and ill-informed efforts at intervention.

Systematic inattention to sexual-minority adolescents has been another persistent problem. Note that we use the descriptor *sexual-minority* rather than *lesbian, gay,* or *bisexual* to emphasize the fact that all youth

with same-sex desires or behaviors deserve systematic research attention, regardless of whether they identify as lesbian, gay, or bisexual. Although there has been a steady increase in research on sexual-minority youth over the past two decades, this research has developed on a relatively separate "track" from research on mainstream heterosexual youth (Diamond, 2003b). Investigators typically recruit exclusively heterosexual or exclusively sexual-minority samples on the assumption that the experiences of these two groups are so fundamentally distinct that they cannot be meaningfully compared. This certainly overstates the case. Although researchers' efforts to develop separate sexual-developmental models for sexual-minority youth has been useful in highlighting their unique psychosocial challenges (and was, in our opinion, a necessary starting point for research on this long-understudied population), we now require systematic *integration* of research on sexual-minority and heterosexual youth. Our overarching goal should be the formulation and testing of rigorous, comprehensive models of adolescent sexual development that account for *both* same-sex and other-sex experiences and their immediate and long-term implications.

Progress toward this goal has, in fact, been made, most discernibly with regard to the increased attention to questions about same-sex sexuality in large-scale, mainstream surveys (Savin-Williams, 2008). For example, questions about same-sex sexuality can be found in a recent Canadian investigation of youth resilience and lifestyle choices (Busseri, Willoughby, Chalmers, & Bogaert, 2008), in a Texas longitudinal study of alcohol and risk behavior (Hatzenbuehler, Corbin, & Fromme, 2008), and in an Amsterdam study of school outcomes (Bos, Sandfort, de Bruyn, & Hakvoort, 2008). Investigators have used a range of creative and innovative techniques to recruit and define sexual-minority populations, many of which would have been nearly impossible a decade ago (such as Internet-based sampling strategies). Sexual minorities are also more willing to participate in contemporary research than was true in the past, increasing opportunities for longitudinal and prospective studies (Balsam, Beauchaine, Rothblum, & Solomon, 2008; Diamond, 2008a; Hatzenbuehler et al.; Rieger, Linsenmeier, Gygaz, & Bailey, 2008). Both conventional and novel research designs can be found, ranging from rigorous multimethod, multi-informant studies (Roisman, Clausell, Holland, Fortuna, & Elieff, 2008), to those employing siblings as a matched heterosexual reference group (Balsam et al.) and using innovative materials such as home videos (Rieger et al.).

Notably, however, the laudable efforts by researchers to integrate questions about same-sex sexuality into their survey and interview assessments raises perplexing—albeit inevitable—questions about just what phenomenon is being tapped by these questions: Sexual orientation? Sexual identity? Sexual experimentation? What is the relative importance of a youth's sexual attractions and behaviors to same-sex peers versus *emotional* attachments? Consider, for example, a heterosexually identified adolescent girl who reports no conscious awareness of same-sex attractions, but reports consistently falling in love with her female best friends. To what extent are her experiences comparable to those of a girl who has experienced consistent same-sex attractions and behaviors since age 13? Do these girls belong in the same sexual-minority category on the basis of their deviations from conventional heterosexual scripts, or do their differences outweigh their similarities? In particular, does the first girl's propensity for same-sex emotional attachment "count" as evidence of a potentially nonheterosexual orientation, or should we emphasize only clear-cut sexual attractions? Should we even bother trying to assess "orientation"?

The picture becomes even more complicated when the element of time is included. Recent research suggests that boundaries between sexual populations are relatively plastic over the lifespan (Diamond, 2002, 2003a, 2003c) and may be particularly permeable during the adolescent years. For example, the vast majority of Add Health high school students who reported a same-sex romantic attraction during one wave of data collection did *not* make such a report at a subsequent wave (Savin-Williams & Ream, 2007; Udry & Chantala, 2005). The developmental relevance of such transitions is not clear. Do they represent bona fide changes in attractions or changes in youth's *interpretations* of their feelings (Goodson et al., 1997)? Is it possible that some youth were intentionally falsifying their initial reports (Fan et al., 2006), or that they simply did not remember the previous encounter (Catania, 1999)?

We have little opportunity to probe the true variability of same-sex and other-sex experience over the course of adolescence given that the very youth who are most important to study—those with the most shifting and perplexing patterns of identification, desire, and behavior—are probably the *least* comfortable describing such experiences to researchers. Numerous studies have found that adolescents who are uncomfortable discussing sexual matters or who are self-conscious about potentially "weird" or "different" patterns of sexuality simply self-select themselves out of research samples, or their parents do it for them by denying parental consent (Trivedi & Sabini, 1998; Wiederman, 1999). Thus, accurate assessments of the full range of contemporary adolescents' sexual lives are exceedingly difficult to obtain. Fortunately, we can develop estimates of sampling biases by comparing findings from small studies of sexual-minority youth with large-scale investigations using random, representative samples, such as Add Health (www.cpc.unc.edu/projects/addhealth). A notable strength of Add Health is that it asks *all* youth to report their romantic attractions and sexual/romantic relationships with females and males, making it possible to determine the extent to which broadly defined populations of sexual-minority youth (i.e., those with any experience of same-sex sexuality) resemble more restrictively defined populations (i.e., those who are recruited into research studies on the basis of identifying as lesbian, gay, or bisexual).

Yet even in the largest, most representative studies, methodological hurdles remain. One of the most important concerns missing data. As every researcher knows, respondents frequently skip questions they do not understand or feel uncomfortable answering (Tourangeau and Yan, 2007), and different investigators handle this problem in different ways. Some delete the data of all respondents providing incomplete responses; others make such deletions question by question, so that each analysis contains a different subset of the total sample. When the amount of missing data is small and not systematically related to key variables of interest, differences between these strategies may have little import. In sexuality research, however, this is unlikely to be the case. Respondents are particularly likely to skip questions or misreport answers on sensitive topics such as sexuality (Tourangeau & Yan). The more sensitive and socially undesirable the topic at hand (masturbation, same-sex sexuality, abortion), the more likely for data to be missing.

Sophisticated techniques have been developed to impute missing data on the basis of respondents' total profile of responses on every other variable under analysis; simulation studies have found that these techniques greatly increase the validity of analyses, compared to deleting respondents with missing data or simply imputing the missing values with sample means, and computer programs for validly conducting such imputations have become increasingly sophisticated and easy to use (Graham & Hofer, 2000; Schafer, 2001; Schafer & Graham, 2002). Yet, the use of these techniques remains inconsistent, making it difficult to compare the findings of different studies. Additionally, the extent to which the missing data problem has systematically biased the *existing* body of research findings on adolescent sexuality remains unknown.

How Is Sex Studied?

The overwhelming majority of sex research relies on self-reports of sexual feelings and behaviors, and the limitations of this methodology are well known (Schwarz, 1999). In addition to problems with vaguely worded questions about "having sex" and the under-utilization of in-depth, qualitative interviews, there is the straightforward problem of validity (Tourangeau & Yan, 2007). Quite simply, how do we know whether reports of sexual behavior are accurate? Several investigators have used longitudinal assessments to examine the veracity of adolescent reports of sexual behavior. Newcomer and Udry (1988), for example, found that during a second wave of data collection, 10% of respondents reported having misrepresented their behavior at Time 1. Specifically, boys tended to overreport the amount of sex they had, whereas girls tended to say that they were virgins when they were not. Similar sex differences have been reported in other studies. Siegel, Aten, and Roghmann (1998) found that 8% of high school girls understated their sexual experience, whereas 14% of boys overstated their sexual experience. Boys and girls clearly understand the broader implications of different patterns of sexual behavior in the eyes of their peers, their parents, and society at large; accordingly, boys tend to exaggerate sexual activity to measure up to perceived standards of sexual prowess, whereas girls tend to minimize sexual experiences so as not to appear irresponsible or promiscuous (Catania, 1999; Siegel et al.).

Further complicating matters is the fact that responses to questions about sexual behavior vary according to methods used to ask those questions (Tourangeau & Yan, 2007). For example, a comparison of the 1990 and 2000 national surveys of British sexual behavior (Copas et al, 2002) found that use of a computer-assisted self-interviewing (CASI) format elicited higher reports of sensitive sexual behavior than did face-to-face interviews. Adult women's reports of same-sex behavior increased from 7% to 9.7% and men's from 6.7% to 8.4% when CASI was used in lieu of interviews. Among adolescent males, reports of having ever had sex with a prostitute, having been masturbated by another male, having had receptive oral sex, and having had receptive anal sex were three to seven times more frequently reported with audio CASI than with self-administered questionnaires (Turner et al., 1998). Researchers assessing adolescent sexuality must devote extra attention to designing questionnaires that accentuate ease of response, contain clear and nonjudgmental wording, and provide clear-cut assurances of confidentiality (Tourangeau & Yan).

Irregularities in self-reports are also influenced by qualities of the adolescents and their environments. Youth of different cohorts and educational levels or with different types of family, community, economic, and cultural backgrounds may have remarkably different motives for concealing and revealing aspects of their sexual lives (Catania, 1999; Grov, Bimbi, Nanin, & Parsons, 2006; Oliver & Hyde, 1993). Older adolescents are generally more embarrassed than are younger adolescents about being virgins—and thus more likely to misrepresent this fact (Carpenter, 2001). With regard to ethnicity, Latina female adolescents might feel pressure to adhere to *simpatía,* which involves pleasing others and being likable, and might therefore underestimate sexual activities that violate family or peer expectations. A Latino male adolescent, by contrast, might feel pressure to conform to *machismo,* involving hypermasculine appearance, stalwart rejection of homosexuality, and grandiose assessments of heterosexual behavior.

Finally, practically every study conducted on adolescent sexuality has treated the individual as the unit of analysis (Wright, 1998), even though partnered sexual interactions are inherently dyadic phenomena (see reliability data in Ochs & Binik, 1999). Thus, in attempting to predict an adolescent's pattern of sexual activity from his or her *individual* biology, personality, motives, environment, or personal history, we are effectively assuming that *partners* are blank slates without biological predispositions, personalities, motives, environments, or personal histories of their own. Of course,

the well-known problem of statistical non-independence between reports of partners in a dyad has historically made it difficult to conduct valid and interpretable dyadic analyses (Gable & Reis, 1999). In recent years, however, techniques for analyzing dyadic and other forms of nested data, such as structural equation modeling and multilevel random coefficient modeling (sometimes called hierarchical linear modeling), have become more widely accessible. Such techniques make it possible, for example, to test hypotheses about the degree to which each adolescent's personal characteristics contribute to characteristics of the sexual dyad (e.g., latency to begin sexual activity within a particular relationship). Greater attention to these sophisticated analyses is likely to become increasingly important in sex research.

With these methodological caveats in mind, we move on to consider some of the most important and widely investigated domains of adolescent sexual experience, reviewing what is known and suggesting directions for future study. We begin with the domain of *sexual desire.* Despite its status as an obvious "building block" for adolescent sexual experience, it has been historically underinvestigated (Tolman & Diamond, 2001).

SEXUAL DESIRE

Sexual desire is often presumed to be a fairly uniform experience propelling adolescents toward a diverse array of sexual behaviors, much the same way that hunger is presumed to be a uniform experience propelling one toward a diverse array of foods. This presumption has circumscribed the types of questions asked about adolescents' desires and the manner in which they are asked. Thus, although data are available on first sexual desire, we do not have sufficiently detailed information on the subjective quality of this experience, hampering attempts to systematically model trajectories of sexual motivation from childhood to young adulthood or to understand their links to sexual behavior.

Such blind spots reflect the tendency for developmental researchers to emphasize the nuts and bolts of sexual maturation at the expense of investigating the experiential aspects of this process (Brooks-Gunn & Paikoff, 1997). These blind spots also expose society's deep-seated ambivalence regarding early manifestations of sexuality and the need to control and monitor sexual behavior rather than promote positive sexual self-concepts (Fine, 1988; Fine & McClelland, 2006). If the overarching goal of research is simply to prevent risky sexual behaviors, then questions about the subjective quality of a youth's desires might appear to be irrelevant. We, of course, disagree. A brief review of what is and is not known about the development of sexual desire suggests that this may be one of the most promising areas for future research on adolescent sexuality.

What Is Desire and When Does It Start?

Although considerable debate has raged over how to define sexual desire, most investigators subscribe to a conceptualization resembling the following: "an interest in sexual objects or activities or a wish, need, or drive to seek out sexual objects or to engage in sexual activities" (Regan & Berscheid, 1995, p. 346). Note, however, that this definition combines two phenomena that are not entirely equivalent: an *interest* in sexual objects and a drive to *seek* sexual objects. This subtle but critical distinction is well known to those familiar with the sexual behavior of nonhuman primates (Hrdy, 1987), but it rarely receives substantive attention in discussions of human sexuality (Bancroft, 1989; Fisher, 1998; Wallen, 1995). These two types of sexual desires are denoted *proceptivity,* the basic urge to seek and initiate sexual activity, and *receptivity* (arousability), the capacity to become interested in sex when encountering certain eliciting stimuli (Bancroft; Beach, 1976; Wallen). It is important to note that although variability in proceptive sexual desire is tightly linked to variability in gonadal

hormones (specifically, testosterone in men and both testosterone and estrogen in women), variability in arousability is not (reviewed in Tolman & Diamond, 2001).

This difference might explain the fact that although sharp increases in pubertal gonadal hormone levels correspond to sharp increases in the frequency and intensity of self-reported sexual desires (Halpern, Udry, Campbell, & Suchindran, 1993; Udry & Billy, 1987; Udry, Talbert, & Morris, 1986), this is not the onset of sexual desire. Children report first awareness of sexual desires and attractions as early as 9 years, perhaps linked to the maturation of the adrenal gland (McClintock & Herdt, 1996), and some experiment with self-stimulation as early as 6 (Friedrich, Grambsch, Broughton, Kuiper, & Beilke, 1991)—these findings hold true for children with same-sex attractions as well (Savin-Williams, 2005). Perhaps these early childhood experiences of desire (and occasionally sexual behavior) stem from hormone-independent arousability, whereas the classic pubertal surges in self-reported sexual desire reflect the hormonally mediated development of proceptivity. If so, this supports McClintock and Herdt's (1996) argument that sexuality does not suddenly "switch on" at puberty, but develops gradually over the course of childhood and adolescence through a subtle and gradual intertwining of erotic and social experiences. Specifically, the existing literature on distinctions between arousability and proceptivity suggests that although young children might become aroused in response to erotic stimuli, many do not experience strong urges to act on those feelings until puberty.

It is difficult to test this model because so little information is available on how early sexual feelings are experienced. In fact, we cannot even be sure that adolescents are describing the same thing when they talk about sexual desire, given that few studies provide participants with an operationalization of "desire" or "attraction" or solicit qualitative descriptions of these feelings and the contexts in which they were experienced. Correspondingly, little is known about potential developmental changes in subjective experiences of desire, and whether such transitions have implications for understanding developmental transitions in sexual behavior.

Sex Differences in Desire

Such information would be particularly valuable for understanding well-documented sex differences in sexual desire. As exhaustively reviewed by Baumeister, Catanese, and Vohs (2001), empirical data (as well as conventional wisdom) have long suggested that women experience less frequent and insistent sexual desires than do men. Although the vast majority of this research has focused on adults, data indicate that these differences are also observed during childhood and adolescence. For example, regardless of sexual orientation, boys become aware of their sexual interests and impulses several years earlier than girls do (Knoth, Boyd, & Singer, 1988; Savin-Williams & Diamond, 2000), and boys report more frequent sexual arousal (several times a day versus once a week). Boys also report their sexual arousal to be more intense and distracting than do girls (Knoth et al.).

The origin of such differences remains a topic of active debate. Some researchers attribute them to the large sex differences in circulating androgens that come about after pubertal maturation, given that variability in androgen levels in both sexes has been found to be reliably associated with variability in self-reported sexual motivation (reviewed in Bancroft, 1978; Udry, 1988). Correspondingly, differences between male and female experiences of sexual desire—specifically, the fact that women report fewer spontaneous sexual urges than do men (Knoth et al., 1988; Laumann et al., 1994), fewer purely sexual fantasies (Ellis & Symons, 1990; Leitenberg & Henning, 1995), lower rates and frequencies of masturbation (Leitenberg, Detzer, & Srebnik, 1993), and less motivation to seek or initiate sexual activity (Laumann et al.; O'Sullivan & Byers, 1992)—have been attributed to (and in the most extreme cases, fundamentally reduced to) the well-known sex differences in testosterone levels.

Yet other researchers have argued that cultural and social factors are equally or more important, highlighting the powerful social forces that restrict female experiences of desire by casting girls in the role of "sexual gatekeepers" whose primary task is to fend off boys' sexual overtures in order to guard themselves against pregnancy and STIs. Fine (1988) powerfully identified and critiqued this cultural framework 20 years ago in a seminal review article on school-based sex education discourses, and has recently noted that this framework remains just as pervasive and stifling today (Fine & McClelland, 2006). Specifically, girls receive powerful and consistent messages from social and religious institutions, schools, media, and family that women do not want or "need" sexual activity as much as men, and that sexuality is appropriate only within committed, monogamous relationships.

As a result, girls may progressively learn to discount their own bodily experiences of sexual desire and to dismiss their own motives for sexual contact (Tolman, 2002). It should not be surprising, then, that the number one form of sexual dysfunction among American women— reported by more than a third of women over the age of 18—is *low or nonexistent sexual desire* (Laumann, Paik, & Rosen, 1999). How are girls supposed to consistently suppress and deny their sexual desires from childhood through adolescence, and then suddenly blossom into healthy, lusty, sexually self-confident adults at the magical age of 18? Some evidence suggests that the negative messages girls receive about female sexuality impedes their developing awareness of their own physical experiences of sexual arousal. Less than half of female teenagers report that they can always detect their sexual arousal, compared to nearly all of male teenagers (Knoth et al., 1988), and studies using physiological measures of genital blood flow has found that women often show distinct discrepancies between their degree of physical arousal and their subjective feelings of arousal (Chivers & Bailey, 2005; Chivers, Rieger, Latty, & Bailey, 2005; Heiman, 1975; Laan, Everaerd, van Bellen, & Hanewald, 1994; Brody, Laan, & van Lunsen, 2003).

Sexual "Plasticity"

Undoubtedly, *both* hormonal and social factors contribute to sex differences in sexual desire (Tolman & Diamond, 2001; Udry, Talbert, & Morris,1986), and some research suggests that the distinction between proceptivity and arousability is important for appropriately interpreting their interplay. Specifically, variability in proceptive sexual motivation appears directly linked to variability in gonadal hormone levels (androgens in men and both androgens and estrogen in women), whereas variability in arousability is hormone-independent (Wallen, 1995). Because females have a fundamentally different pattern of day-to-day gonadal hormone activation than do males, they should have a different pattern of day-to-day sexual motivation. As is well known, female levels of circulating androgens are substantially lower than those of males, and females experience high estrogen levels only a few days per month. Males, by contrast, have consistently high levels of circulating androgens. Thus, as noted by Wallen in his research on rhesus monkeys, females can be conceptualized as experiencing a brief period of high sexual motivation around the time of ovulation and lower levels of sexual motivation the rest of the month, whereas males have relatively higher, constant levels of sexual motivation.

Yet, one should not necessarily conclude that women have weaker libidos than men, because when women *do* experience strong initiatory urges for sexual contact, the strength and intensity of these urges appears comparable to those of men (reviewed by Wallen, 1995). Wallen therefore drew an important distinction between *low* sex drive and *periodic* sex drive. Even more interesting, however, are the implications of women's potentially more periodic sex drive for the relative role of arousability. If the hormone-dependent

component of women's sexual desire is more frequently quiescent than men's, then a greater proportion of the sexual desire they do experience will be predominantly situation dependent. Accordingly, variability in women's exposure to specific sexual stimuli, their internalization of particular sexual scripts, and their immersion in particular interpersonal and sociocultural contexts may therefore have a more persistent influence on their day-to-day experiences of sexual arousal than men's (as well as their behavior, as demonstrated by Udry & Billy, 1987). This may therefore explain why situation and context appear to play a greater role in structuring women's than men's sexual desires and behaviors, a phenomenon that has been exhaustively documented by Baumeister (2000) and described as female sexual plasticity.

By "plasticity," Baumeister (2000) means that female sexuality is more malleable and mutable than male sexuality, more responsive to cultural, social, and interpersonal factors, more subject to change in response to external circumstances, and more variable within the life course of any particular woman. Among the voluminous evidence he marshaled in support of this view were data indicating that women show less consistency between their sexual attitudes and behaviors (perhaps because women's sensitivity to situational context leads them to act in ways that contradict their attitudes) and evidence that women show greater temporal and developmental variation than men in what they desire (type of sex partner and activity), their degree of desire (frequency of sex and fantasy), and the way they express their desires (patterns of sexual activity). Importantly, there have been no systematic attempts to investigate the potential implications of sexual plasticity for adolescent female sexual development, despite the tremendous potential of this model to explain extant sex differences. Yet interestingly, the notion that female sexuality is particularly sensitive to cultural, social, and interpersonal context is notably consistent with data demonstrating that *the timing of female sexual maturation* is also sensitive to such factors. A number of researchers have suggested different evolutionary theories regarding these well-documented associations, suggesting that they represent an evolved strategy for adapting reproductive behavior to social conditions (Belsky, 2007).

Ellis (2004, 2005) comprehensively reviewed this literature, and argued for an "integrated life history approach" to girls' sexual maturation, which conceptualizes girls' pubertal timing as the end point of an evolved developmental strategy that functions to *lengthen* her total period of childhood dependency if she is lucky enough to enjoy a high-quality rearing environment with involved, engaged parents, but to *shorten* this period if the rearing environment is neglectful or conflictual. According to Ellis, the links between pubertal timing and contextual–psychosocial factors should be stronger for girls than boys because of the high energy demands of pregnancy and nursing, which make for a stark trade-off between allocating resources to one's own physical growth and allocating resources to one's offspring. Support for this evolutionary–developmental perspective comes from numerous cross-sectional and longitudinal studies showing that parental warmth, positivity, and investment during childhood is associated with delayed puberty, whereas conflict with parents, high levels of independence from parents, and father absence are associated with earlier puberty (see the detailed and exhaustive review in Ellis, 2004). One intriguing possibility is that the same mechanisms that provide for this contextual and psychosocial modulation of the hormonal changes of menarche (and even adrenarche – see Ellis & Essex, 2007) also play a role in modulating women's sexual desires and experiences over the life span.

Sex differences in plasticity also have notable implications for women's versus men's experiences of same-sex sexuality. Specifically, women may have a greater capacity than men to experience bisexual patterns of attraction (at least under certain conditions).

Chivers and Bailey (2005) measured the physiological and self-reported arousal of four different groups: gay men, heterosexual men, lesbian women, and heterosexual women. Participants viewed videos of women having sex with women, men having sex with men, men having sex with women, and some neutral videos of landscapes, as a control condition. Results revealed that gay men were most physiologically and subjectively aroused by the male–male videos, and heterosexual men were most physiologically and subjectively aroused by the female–female videos. Women, however, showed a completely different pattern. On average, women had roughly equivalent genital responses to the different sexual videos, regardless of their self-described sexual orientation (although this was not true to the same degree for each and every woman). The authors concluded that women's arousal patterns were fundamentally "nonspecific," whereas men's arousal patterns were more specifically targeted toward one sex or the other. Women's *self-reported* arousal, however, was more in line with their self-described identities: lesbians reported the greatest arousal to the female–female video, and heterosexual women reported the greatest arousal to the female–male video.

Research by Lippa (2006, 2007) provides further evidence for these sex differences. In a cross-national study, Lippa found that on average, men's attractions were more polarized than those of women, such that the negative correlation between same-sex and other-sex attractions was twice as large among men than among women. This suggests that for women, same-sex and other-sex attractions are more likely to coexist, whereas for men, one type of attraction tends to preclude the other. This is notably consistent with the results of several large-scale, representative studies which have found that women are more likely than men to report concurrent sexual attractions to *both* sexes (Laumann et al, 1994; Mosher, Chandra, & Jones, 2005). Lippa (2007) also examined the association between sex *drive* and the direction of women's and men's attractions. According to classic drive theory, high levels of sex drive should increase individuals' desires for the types of sexual partners that they usually desire, and not just desires for "anyone." This is exactly what Lippa's studies found among men, but not women. For most women (with the exception of the lesbian subsample in one of his studies), high sex drive was associated with increased sexual attraction to *both* men and women. Lippa suggested that there may be a fundamental difference between the way sexuality and sexual orientation are organized for women versus men, and specifically that most women may possess a latent capacity for attractions to both sexes.

What might this suggest for adolescents? None of the studies directly comparing the malleability of desires have been conducted among adolescents, but longitudinal research on changes in young women's attractions and behaviors provide further evidence for female sexual plasticity or "fluidity" (Diamond, 1998, 2000a, 2003a, 2005, 2007, 2008a, 2008b). Specifically, some young women experienced sexual attractions and relationships during their adolescent years that proved to be highly specific to particular environments and relationships, and often directly contradicted their previous and future patterns of desire and experience. Notably, women did not describe these experience as "phases" (2008b), but instead described them as singular events born of highly particular circumstances, especially their emotional bonds to specific individuals (2007, 2008a). Clearly, additional longitudinal research tracking childhood, adolescent, and adult experiences of *both* proceptive and receptive sexual desires, in *both* girls and boys, for *both* same-sex and other-sex partners, would make critical contributions to our presently impoverished understanding of the developmental phenomenology of desire. Such research would also allow for systematic investigation of *within-sex* variability in desire, another topic that has been woefully

understudied in developmental research on sexuality. Although numerous studies have focused on within-sex variability in the timing of pubertal maturation (Belsky et al., 2007; Ge, Natsuaki, Neiderhiser, & Reiss, 2007), variability in the outcomes of maturation—at least with respect to sexual urges and arousability—has received scant attention. As noted earlier, this reflects the implicit but incorrect presumption that sexual desire is a relatively uniform substrate for sexuality that is simply switched on at puberty. Although we know that some adolescents have more frequent and intense sexual desires and fantasies than do others (Udry, 1990), little is known about the origin of such interindividual differences, their longitudinal stability, and their implications for sexual behavior over the life course. Investigating such questions requires longitudinal assessments of links between children's changing hormone levels, social experiences, sociocultural environments, and the quality and context of their sexual feelings.

SEXUAL MOTIVES

Sexual desire is one thing. Behavior is quite another. Sexual *motives* can be conceptualized as providing the link between them. Numerous factors may explain why a particular adolescent does or does not act on his/her sexual desires, and understanding these motives is critical to a systematic analysis of adolescent sexual development. Quite tellingly, sexual intentions are among the strongest predictors of an adolescent's future sexual behavior (Buhi & Goodson, 2007; Kinsman, Romer, Furstenberg, & Schwartz, 1998). Furthermore, intraindividual and interindividual differences in adolescents' motives for pursuing sex are systematically related to the *types* of sexual contact pursued: committed versus casual, planned versus unplanned, protected versus unprotected, and with a single partner versus multiple partners (Cooper, Shapiro, & Powers, 1998; Levinson, Jaccard, & Beamer, 1995).

In their exhaustive survey of "why humans have sex," Meston and Buss (2007) reported 4 main explanatory factors (and 13 subfactors):

- *Physical:* stress reduction, pleasure, physical desirability, and experience seeking
- *Goal attainment:* resources, social status, revenge, and utilitarian concerns
- *Emotional:* the experience and expression of love and commitment
- *Insecurity:* low self-esteem, duty/pressure, and mate guarding

Although the sexes were remarkably similar on motives for having sex, men listed more items than did women. Women were more likely to endorse emotional reasons for having sex; men were more likely to emphasize the physical appearance and desirability of a partner, the seeking of sexual experience, and establishing social status ("bragging rights"). Men also reported that the mere opportunity for having sex was a major motive.

These are the motives of adults. Do adolescents share these sexual motivations? As should be clear from the preceding section, sexual desire itself is an obvious and important motive for sexual activity. Although pubertal hormonal changes do not create sexual desire and arousal *de novo*, they do imbue sexual feelings with newfound force and impetus. In addition, postpubertal adolescents receive multiple social cues from parents, peers, and the media that they are now expected to desire and seek sexual activity. They may consequently become increasingly attuned to the vicissitudes in their own states of sexual arousal. Thus, simple sexual release is clearly a salient motive for adolescent sexual activity.

Another important motivation is straightforward curiosity and experimentation, fueled in part by the increasing visibility of explicit depictions and discussions of sexuality in mainstream films, television shows, and the Internet (Boyce et al., 2006; Brown, 2002; Greenfield, 2004; Hawk, Vanwesenbeeck, de Graaf, & Bakker, 2006). Other than friends

and parents, the media are often sources for how adolescents learn about, and perhaps act on, their sexuality (Sutton, Brown, Wilson, & Klein, 2002). Controlling for respondent characteristics, teenagers who viewed more sexual content, whether consisting of sex talk or depictions of actual sex, at baseline were more likely to initiate intercourse and "advanced noncoital sexual activities" during the subsequent year (Collins et al., 2004). Although the media provide considerable and increasing exposure to adolescents about sex, little is known about how the media actually affect adolescent sexual behavior (Brown). Ward and Rivadeneyra (1999) found that television likely shapes adolescent sexual behavior indirectly, by first depicting permissible sexual attitudes, normative expectations, and a view of sexual reality. This is supported by research that found perceived support from the media for teen sexual behavior explained 13% of the variance in middle school youth's intentions to initiate sexual intercourse in the near future and 8%–10% of the variance in light and heavy sexual behaviors, after taking into account other contextual influences (L'Engle, Brown, & Kenneavy, 2006).

The achievement of social status is another important motive for adolescent sexual contact, signaling to oneself and others the realization of a much desired adult sexual status (O'Sullivan, Meyer-Bahlburg, & Watkins, 2000). Notably, among girls it is often not just sexual activity that confers popularity and mature status, but the entire complex of relationship phenomena associated with sex, such as having a boyfriend and being in love (Boyce et al., 2006; O'Sullivan & Meyer-Bahlburg, 2003). Thus, regardless of whether adolescents encounter implicit or explicit peer pressure to engage in sex, they may be motivated to pursue such activity simply to stay on course with what they perceive to be the normative sexual-developmental schedule. For example, urban 6th-grade students who initiated sexual intercourse during the school year were disproportionately likely to believe that most of their friends were already sexually experienced, and to associate sexual activity with social gains (Kinsman et al., 1998). Having sex might also function to establish independence from parents or to signal rejection of parental, religious, or community norms. In such cases, the strength or frequency of sexual desires might be a nonissue.

Romantic relationships also provide numerous motives and opportunities for sexual activity. In a national Canadian study of youth, 9th- and 11th-grade students reported "love for the person" as the primary motive for having sexual intercourse (Boyce et al., 2006). Love proved a more important motive for females than for males and for older than for younger adolescents. Perhaps most obviously, romantic relationships also afford frequent occasions to become sexually aroused and to act on those desires, consistent with the fact that the earlier and more frequently youths begin dating, the earlier and more frequently they engage in sexual activity (Blum et al., 2000; Halpern, Joyner, et al., 2000). In addition, youths tend to pursue a broader range of sexual behaviors with romantic partners to whom they report more emotional commitment (Miller & Benson, 1999). However, it is difficult to determine whether the emotional feelings that youth experience in these relationships are themselves sexual motivators or whether they simply provide an appropriate context in which to act on sexual feelings. Although it is commonly expected in U.S. culture that romantic and affectionate feelings precede thinking about and pursuing sex with a partner (Miller & Benson), little systematic data exist on the extent to which this is true, reflecting the overall dearth of research on the psychological and biobehavioral links between experiences of emotional affection and sexual desire (Diamond, 2003c). Miller and Benson argued that the role of emotional intimacy as a motivator for sex is changing and that, conversely, adolescents are increasingly using body-centered sexual experiences as a means of *establishing* intimacy. This may explain the

seemingly paradoxical finding that although adolescents perceive sexual activity at an early age to be more acceptable within a serious relationship than a casual relationship, they are more likely to *engage* in early sexual activity within a casual relationship than a serious one (Feldman, Turner, & Araujo, 1999; Vrangalova & Savin-Williams, 2008a).

Romantic relationships are particularly critical for understanding adolescent girls' sexual activity. As noted earlier, young women are more likely than young men to describe love and affection as causes of sexual desire (Regan & Berscheid, 1995); to associate sexual activity with partner-focused relationship phenomena, such as an opportunity to express love, intimacy, and commitment (Blumstein & Schwarz, 1983; Boyce et al., 2006; Oliver & Hyde, 1993; Patrick, Maggs, & Abar, 2007; Peplau & Garnets, 2000; Rodríguez Rust, 2000; Rose, 2000; Rothblum, 2000); to report that emotional involvement is a prerequisite for sex (Carroll, Volk, & Hyde, 1985); and to engage in sex in order to enhance emotional intimacy (Brigman & Knox, 1992). These sex differences, however, diminish somewhat as youths mature; as girls gain more confidence and experience during later adolescence, they feel less compelled to justify their sexual desires and behaviors by locating them within a serious relationship (Feldman et al., 1999). Young men, conversely, report more self-focused reasons to engage in sex—to feel loved, for pleasure, and to see what sex is like (Patrick et al.). However, males become more interested in having sex within an intimate relationships as they become more emotionally mature and socially skilled, and as both the novelty of sexual activity and its implications for social status begin to wane (Patrick et al.).

Finally, research suggests that another important motive for adolescent sexual activity is emotion regulation. The pleasure and release associated with sexual activity can attenuate or distract from negative emotions, helping youths to cope with troublesome events

(Brigman & Knox, 1992; Levinson et al., 1995). Although such motives are not as common as intimacy- and pleasure-based motives for sexual activity, they deserve substantive attention, given that adolescents with emotion-regulation motives are less likely to pursue sexual activity within committed relationships and tend to have a greater number of sexual partners and riskier sexual practices (Cooper et al., 1998). Emotion-regulating motives for sex are particularly important when considering the well-established correlations between compromised family and community environments and problematic adolescent sexual behavior (Miller et al., 1997). Specifically, adolescents whose environments have provided them with few opportunities to master emotion regulation skills, or whose exposure to environmental stressors regularly overwhelms their emotion regulation capacities, might be particularly likely to turn to sexual activity, as well as other mood-regulating behaviors such as substance use, to manage day-to-day negative emotions. Female youths with inadequate emotional support might construe both early sex *and* early motherhood—whether consciously or unconsciously—as routes to emotional closeness and nurturance (Musick, 1993).

With the multiple interacting underpinnings of sexuality more clearly in focus, we can more capably interpret the extant data on what contemporary adolescents are actually *doing* sexually, as well as the numerous factors that influence their sexual behavior—from autoerotic activity to same-sex sexuality throughout their life course.

THE STATE OF ADOLESCENT SEX

Premarital sexual intercourse is clearly the modal pattern among American youth (Finer, 2007; Halpern, Waller, Spriggs, & Hallfors, 2006), and is occurring at progressively younger ages. The average age for first sexual intercourse is currently 17 for boys and 16 for girls (Alan Guttmacher Institute, 1994; Centers for Disease Control [CDC], 2002), and a random representative sample of American adults found that only 12% of men and 6% of women aged 18–24 were still virgins (Laumann et al, 1994). In contrast to the 1950s and 1960s, when premarital sex was uniformly frowned upon, contemporary society has shifted toward a standard of "permissiveness with affection," in which premarital sexual activity is acceptable within the context of a loving and enduring relationship. Overall, multiple social institutions ranging from families to schools to religious groups have become more tolerant of adolescent premarital sexual behavior and have reduced sanctions against it. These attitudinal changes have been accompanied by social structural changes involving a greater variety of family types (in contrast to the traditional "nuclear" model) and reductions in parental supervision (Hopkins, 2000).

When contemplating the implications of these cultural shifts for contemporary adolescent sexual behavior, it is critical to consider boys and girls separately. In general, adolescent boys are more likely than girls to have sexually permissive attitudes, to be sexually experienced at earlier ages, to have more sex (including same-sex behavior), to have had sex more recently, and to count more sex partners (Browning, Kessler, Hatfield, & Choo, 1999; Manlove et al., 2001; Mosher et al., 2005; Vrangalova, & Savin-Williams, 2008a). Although mean age differences between boys and girls have decreased, the proportion of adolescent boys with sexual experience is generally equal to that of girls one year older (Alan Guttmacher Institute, 1994). Also, and perhaps most importantly, the sexual double standard continues to exist, such that sexual behavior—especially with multiple partners—is considered more acceptable for young men than women (Crawford & Popp, 2003; Milhausen & Herold, 2001).

Yet, notably, gender differences have been steadily decreasing in many aspects of sexual behavior, including attitudes toward premarital sex, number of sex partners, frequency of sexual intercourse, and masturbation (Oliver & Hyde, 1993; Sawyer & Smith, 1996). Data suggest that gender differences are largest during the beginning of a youth's sexual-developmental trajectory, but decrease over time as girls "catch up" to boys. For example, although more 15-year-old boys (43%) than 15-year-old girls (34%) report sexual contact with the opposite sex, by age 17 they are equal (64%) and by age 18 girls slightly *exceed* boys, 78%–74% (Mosher et al., 2005).

Although research on these historic changes and their implications for adolescent health and development has focused on penile–vaginal intercourse, it is important to consider the full range of sexual behaviors that youths pursue from childhood through adolescence, the developmental context of these behaviors, and the ways in which they are interpreted and experienced. This broad perspective is particularly valuable given ongoing debates about whether greater tolerance of noncoital sexual activity might help adolescents to delay coitus and therefore reduce their risks for pregnancy and STIs (Kegan, 1996). We therefore begin with a discussion of autoerotic activity in childhood and adolescence, followed by noncoital partnered activity, coitus, and same-sex behavior. We then turn to questions of *context* and the diverse relationship structures in which adolescent sexual activity is embedded.

Autoerotic Activity

Exceptionally little is known about prepubertal solitary sexual activities, making it difficult to determine a normative developmental trajectory of autoerotic behavior from childhood through puberty and young adulthood (for a history of masturbation, see Laqueur, 2003). The limited empirical data suggest that both boys and girls pursue a variety of solitary sexual behaviors, often at relatively high frequencies. A retrospective study of Swedish high school seniors (Larsson & Svedin, 2002) found that by age 12, more than three-fourths reported that they had engaged in autoerotic activities, including self-examination, self-stimulation, and viewing sexually explicit pictures or videos. Nearly twice as many boys than girls had masturbated and reached orgasm. Studies of

U.S. children have found fewer instances of autoerotic activity, perhaps because of methodological differences. Relying on mothers' reports of sexual behavior (Friedrich et al., 1991), 11% of 6- to 12-year-olds had masturbated by hand or object, although a much larger percentage (36% of boys and 18% of girls) had "touched their sex parts at home."

Despite this evidence, most adolescents and adults believe that the normative and acceptable time to initiate such activities is puberty (Bauserman & Davis, 1996). Certainly, rates of masturbation increase after puberty. In a representative sample of 8th–10th graders, Udry (1988) found that 32% of boys and 26% of girls reported masturbation; among 18- to 24-year olds, these figures rose to 61% of men and 36% of women (Laumann et al., 1994). However, prevalence estimates vary considerably, with respondents far more likely to report adolescent masturbation when asked about it retrospectively than when asked about current behavior. For example, one study (Halpern, Udry, Suchindran, & Campbell, 2000) found that less than one-third of 13-year-old boys reported masturbating. When these boys were reinterviewed as young adults, however, more than twice as many admitted having masturbated during early adolescence. Adolescents are more likely to skip or give inconsistent responses to questions about masturbation than about any other sexual activity, reflecting the pervasive stigma attached to this activity (Rodgers, Billy, & Udry, 1982). Indeed, nearly 60% of young adults felt guilty after masturbation (Laumann et al., 1994), and over 80% of adolescents in another study viewed masturbation as a harmful activity (Halpern et al., 1993). One of the worst insults a Greek adolescent can hurl at another is to say the equivalent of "you masturbate" (Papadopoulos, Stamboulides, & Triantafillou, 2000).

We do not know exactly why these attitudes are held. Some youths apparently believe that admitting to masturbation means that they are not having real sex, are oversexed, or are out of control (Halpern, Udry, et al., 2000). Others may have heard, or inferred, negative attitudes about masturbation from their parents. Gagnon (1985) interviewed nearly 1,500 parents about the possibility that their 3- to 11-year-old children had masturbated. Most parents accepted that it took place, but less than half wanted their children to have a positive attitude toward it. Not surprisingly, strongly religious parents were less accepting of masturbation.

Parents generally perceived boys to be more likely than girls to masturbate, and on this point they appear to be correct, as far as can be ascertained through self-report data (Kinsey, Pomeroy, & Martin, 1948; Kinsey, Pomeroy, Martin, & Gebhard, 1953; Laumann et al., 1994). In their review of the literature on sexual behavior, Oliver and Hyde (1993) concluded that gender differences in masturbation were among the largest and most reliable in the empirical literature. For example, one study of college students found that only 15% of males reported never having masturbated, compared to 63% of females (Schwartz, 1999), and similar gender differences have been found in other studies (Larsson & Svedin, 2002; Weinberg et al., 1995). Notably, these studies do not generally detect gender differences in rates of other noncoital activities, such as kissing and oral sex, suggesting that the gender differences in masturbation are not attributable to a generalized sexual reticence among women. Rather, they are generally interpreted as reflecting the fact that masturbation continues to be disproportionately stigmatized for women. Without more systematic qualitative data on adolescents' motives, interpretations, and experiences of autoerotic activity, it is impossible to reliably discern the extent to which variations in these activities reflect individuals' personal desires versus social controls and norms.

Partnered, Noncoital Activity

Similar to solitary sexual activities, partnered noncoital sexual activities (i.e., "petting" or "fooling around") prior to adolescence are common but seldom documented. Okami et al. (1997) reported that almost half of

young adult women and men had engaged in partnered noncoital sexual activities (excluding solitary masturbation) prior to age 6. In another sample, three-quarters of both sexes had engaged in such behaviors before age 12 (Larsson & Svedin, 2002). The most frequent activities included talking about sex, kissing and hugging, watching or reading pornography (primarily boys), and humping or feigning intercourse. Masturbating with a friend was reported by 14% of boys and 7% of girls. Even less common were showing one's genitals, watching others in a sexual way, having another child touch one's genitals, and exploring another child's genitals.

What is the meaning and developmental relevance of these activities? Limited empirical evidence suggests that if an early onset of partnered sexual contact (whether with the same or other sex) is not experienced as abusive or coercive, then it has a positive impact on adolescent and adult sexual arousal, pleasure, satisfaction, and acceptance of various sexual behaviors for self and others (Bauserman & Davis, 1996; Rind, 2001; Sandfort, 1992; Savin-Williams, 1998, 2004, 2007). Of course, given the degree of sex negativity in U.S. culture, not all adults view these as desirable outcomes. As for general social adjustment, little evidence suggests that childhood sexual activity is associated with either developmental benefits or deficits (Okami et al., 1997), yet this topic has received little systematic study.

Clearly, to understand the role of childhood sexual activity for adolescent sexual and social development, we need better data on which children engage in such activities, the context in which they are pursued, and the personal meanings that children attach to these activities. Given the difficulties conducting research on childhood sexuality, it may be some time before answers are obtained. Until that time, data reviewed by Okami et al. (1997) suggest caution in interpreting children's sexual activity. Although it seems intuitive to view such behaviors as rehearsals for pubertal sexual behavior, no direct empirical support exists for this interpretation. An alternative possibility is that childhood sexual activity is an altogether different phenomenon than pubertal sexual activity, with distinct motives, qualities, and functions corresponding to children's particular levels of social, cognitive, and biological maturation.

As for adolescent noncoital sexual activity, an increasing body of research testifies to its prevalence. One study found that over 80% of youths had participated in noncoital, partnered sexual activities (typically mutual masturbation and oral–genital contact) before age 16 (Bauserman & Davis, 1996). Over 60% of such activities were pursued with partners of roughly the same age and 92% were heterosexual in nature. In a national study of U.S. adolescents and young adults, 64% of 15- to 19-year-olds had engaged in any opposite-sex contact, with the most frequent for both sexes being oral sex (55%) and the least, anal sex (11%). Boys were more likely than girls to receive oral sex (51% versus 50%) oral sex; girls, more likely than boys to give oral sex (44% versus 39%).

Do adolescents engage in such behaviors as a "lead-up" to intercourse? This has certainly been a long-standing question among researchers, parents, and adolescents alike. Empirical data addressing this question are contained in the Add Health survey, which documents the first incidences of various noncoital behaviors. Findings suggest the following sequence: holding hands, kissing, necking (kissing for a long time), feeling breasts over clothes, feeling breasts under clothes or with no clothes on, feeling a penis over clothes, feeling a penis under clothes or with no clothes on, feeling a vagina over clothes, feeling a vagina under clothes or with no clothes on, and engaging in penile–vaginal intercourse (Halpern, Joyner, et al., 2000). Whether this progression characterizes a particular encounter or represents a series of unfolding activities across many encounters is undocumented.

Of course, this sequence may not be complete. Most notably missing, but included in other sequences, are oral sex (Rosenthal &

Smith, 1997; Weinberg, Lottes, & Shaver, 1995) and anal contact (Ochs & Binik, 1999). Weinberg et al. found that over 70% of undergraduates had engaged in active and receptive oral sex, and 16% had engaged in heterosexual anal intercourse. Among younger populations, recent data suggest that 30%–40% of American adolescents have given or received oral sex (Mosher et al., 2005). Some variability exists in whether adolescents consider oral sex to be more or less "advanced" than coitus or simply a safer alternative to coitus. Adolescents' first participation in oral sex sometimes follows first coitus (Weinberg et al.) and sometimes precedes it (Schwartz, 1999; Boekeloo & Howard, 2002), and youths report having a greater number of oral sex partners than intercourse partners (Boekeloo & Howard; Halpern-Felsher, Cornell, Kropp, & Tschann, 2005; Prinstein, Meade, & Cohen, 2003). Qualitative research on adolescents' motives for oral sex has found that youth pursue this behavior for a variety of reasons, including physical release, the establishment of intimacy, intoxication, avoidance of risks associated with intercourse, and avoidance of the reputation consequences of intercourse (Cornell & Halpern-Felsher, 2006). Because they perceive oral sex to be a "safer" sexual activity, they are less likely to use STI protection (Prinstein et al.).

The extent to which the timing and ordering of youth's noncoital behaviors vary systematically as a function of personal or social factors is currently unclear (Halpern, Joyner, et al., 2000; Rosenthal & Smith, 1997; Weinberg et al., 1995). Studies have found that youth with earlier timetables tend to be disproportionately likely to believe in early autonomy, to use sexually explicit media, and to abuse substances (Rosenthal & Smith), but such data do not reveal whether such factors lead to or result from early sexual behavior. Another important unanswered question concerns how youths understand and interpret their experiences. Where do they acquire their notions of which behaviors are more or less intimate or advanced? How do they negotiate this sequence with their partners? What are the repercussions of progressing at different rates, in different orders? Although studies have found that earlier participation in noncoital sexual activity is associated with earlier participation in coitus (Bauserman & Davis, 1996), the extent to which adolescents *continue* to pursue noncoital activities after progressing to coitus is unknown, as are individual and social factors that might predict such participation. More qualitative, experiential research is sorely needed to elucidate the multiple meanings attached to noncoital activity among contemporary adolescents.

Coitus

Mainstream media convey the impression that contemporary youth pursue sexual intercourse at much earlier ages than have previous historical cohorts, and research tends to bear this out, particularly among girls (Mosher et al., 2005; Davis & Lay-Yee, 1999; DeLamater & Friedrich, 2002; Laumann et al., 1994). Of course, our previous cautions regarding ambiguity in language must be borne in mind: Some studies have carefully and specifically asked about penile–vaginal intercourse, whereas others (usually in an attempt to use language that will be familiar and comfortable for adolescents) have asked about "having sex." With this limitation in mind, studies generally find an average age for first coitus of 16 for boys and 17 for girls; the most recent National Survey of Family Growth found that 30% of youths 17 and under and 71% of youths 19 and under have had penile–vaginal intercourse (Santelli, Lindberg, Finer, & Singh, 2007). Other notable historic changes concern marital status. In the early 1950s, about half of female teenagers were unmarried when they experienced first coitus; recent data from the Add Health study indicate that almost 90% of individuals between 18 and 27 have had premarital coitus (Halpern et al., 2006), and data from the National Survey of Family Growth has found that 75% of individuals do so before the age of 20 (Finer, 2007).

Given these patterns, researchers no longer ask *whether* American adolescents will have premarital sex, but instead *when* they will start doing so. Numerous studies suggest that the timing of sexual debut is developmentally significant. Early onset of sexual intercourse has been found to be associated with a lower likelihood of contraceptive use (Coker et al., 1994) a greater number of sexual partners in both adolescence and adulthood (Durbin, DiClemente, Siegel, & Krasnovsky, 1993; Laumann et al., 1994) and higher rates of extramarital sexual activity as adults (White, Cleland, & Carael, 2000; Treas & Giesen, 2000).

However, are these phenomena attributable to the experience of early debut itself or to the many other risk factors that have been found to co-occur with early sexual timing? For example, studies have found that adolescents with early sexual debut are more likely to have undergone early puberty (Flannery, Rowe, & Gulley, 1993; Halpern, Kaestle, & Hallfors, 2007; Halpern et al., 1993); to score higher on sensation seeking and unconventionality (Arnett, 1998; Neumark-Sztainer, Story, French, & Resnick, 1997); to score lower on self-efficacy and religiosity (Buhi & Goodson, 2007; Halpern et al., 2006); to come from lower-income or single-parent families (Paul, Fitzjohn, Herbison, & Dickson, 2000; Wu & Thomson, 2001); and to report lower family rule setting, parental involvement, and closeness (Catalano & Hawkins, 1996; Miller, 2002; Metzler et al., 1994). One seminal study (Bingham & Crockett, 1996) followed a group of adolescents from a single school district in a rural community from 9th through 12th grade and found that the correlation between the timing of sexual debut and youths' eventual psychosocial adjustment was completely mediated by their 9th-grade levels of adjustment. Hence, to the extent that consistent associations are observed between early coitus and a range of problem behaviors and risk factors, these associations are likely due to preexisting or concurrent characteristics of adolescents and their families rather than to the experience of early coitus itself. Another example is provided by Meier (2007), who found that the association between adolescent sexual debut and subsequent depressive symptoms was contingent on the longevity of the relationship after debut, rather than sexual debut per se.

The longitudinal, biosocial research of Udry and colleagues (Udry, 1988, 1990; Udry, Kovenock, Morris, & Vandenberg, 1995; Udry et al., 1986) has focused on disentangling the relative impact of hormonal and social factors on girls' and boys' coital timing, using data on maturational changes in hormone levels in concert with detailed data on a wide range of social–attitudinal factors, such as friends' participation in sexual activity, peer popularity, grades, sexual permissiveness, future orientation, parents' education, and locus of control. The results revealed notably gender-specific patterns. Specifically, maturational changes in free testosterone levels were directly related to initiation of coitus for White males, to the exclusion of all social variables save for popularity among other-sex friends. Importantly, the pattern of results was the opposite among White girls. Hormones had *no* direct effect on girls' first coitus (although hormone levels proved to be significantly related to girls' sexual thoughts and fantasies), and instead *every* social variable emerged as a significant and unique predictor of first intercourse. A different pattern of results was observed for African American girls. The single strongest predictor of sexual behavior was whether a girl *looked* physically mature to peers.

A number of additional studies (reviewed in Halpern, 2003) across cultures and cohorts have yielded similar findings regarding the greater sensitivity of young women than men to social and environmental influences on intercourse (which, of course, supports the aforementioned argument for greater sexual plasticity in women than in men; Baumeister, 2000). For example, among Chinese adolescents, early maturation predicted an early onset of dating and coitus among boys, but not among girls (Lam, Shi, Ho, Stewart, & Fan, 2002).

The authors speculated that boys are freer to act on hormonally driven changes in sexual motivation because they face less postpubertal parental monitoring than do girls. The consistency of this gender difference is particularly noteworthy given that during the past 50 years, cultural changes in sexual norms and attitudes have been far more pronounced with regard to female than to male sexuality.

Another important factor to consider, according to Udry et al. (1986), is that although adolescent boys face a nearly uniformly positive environment with regard to sexual behavior (which should ostensibly clear the way for hormonally mediated sexual motivation to predict coital onset straightforwardly), adolescent girls face inconstant, highly differentiated environments that send an array of conflicting and confusing messages about the desirability and costs of sexual behavior. Thus, it should not be surprising that under such circumstances, girls' hormonal maturation predicts changes in their sexual thoughts and motivation, but not coital onset.

Contraception and Safer Sex

Adolescent participation in coitus poses inevitable risks regarding STIs and pregnancy. Approximately half of all STIs occur among youths between the ages of 15 and 24, and adolescents face particular risks for HIV, chlamydia, and gonorrhea (Centers for Disease Control, 2005; Mosher et al., 2005). Each year, nearly 750,000 teen girls aged 15–19 become pregnant (Alan Guttmacher Institute, 2006), and 78% of these pregnancies are unplanned (Henshaw, 1998). Notably, the United States has a disproportionately high rate of adolescent pregnancy in comparison to other Western industrialized nations, despite the fact that U.S. teens engage in coitus at approximately the same rates and ages as do youths in other Western industrialized countries (Sandfort, Hubert, Bajos, & Bus, 1998; Teitler, 2002). According to the United Nations Population Fund (2008), in 2007 there were 49 births per 1,000 women aged 15–19 in the United States, compared to 23 in the United Kingdom, 12 in Canada, 12 in Ireland, 14 in Israel, 11 in the Czech Republic, 9 in Germany, 8 in Greece, 7 in Italy, 4 in the Netherlands, and 1 in France.

One piece of good news is that there has been a significant *decline* in the U.S. teen birth rate within all 50 states in the last decade, and research suggests that 86% of this decline can be attributed to improved use of condoms and other forms of contraception (Santelli et al., 2007). Condoms remain the most popular method, preferred by approximately 60% of sexually active young couples, followed by the birth control pill, preferred by approximately 20% (Everett et al., 2000). Yet rates of inconsistent use and nonuse remain high (Sundet, Magnus, & Kvalem, 1989; Tyden, Olsson, & Bjorkelund-Ylander, 1991). Approximately one-fourth of sexually active young women and one-third of young men report not using condoms or other forms of contraception during the first time they had intercourse (Kahn, Huang, Rosenthal, Tissot, & Burk, 2005; Manning, Longmore, & Giordano, 2000), and approximately 20%–30% of adolescents report not doing so the most recent time that they had sex (Hoefferth, 1990; Santelli, Lowry, Brener, & Robin, 2000). Then, of course, there is the gold standard of dual usage: Because birth control pills cannot protect against STIs and HIV, usage of both methods simultaneously is a highly effective way to prevent both pregnancy and STIs, but this appears to be an elusive goal. One study used daily diaries to track girls' sexual activity over a 2-month period, and found that even the most consistent and reliable contraceptive users (who comprised less than half of the sample) used birth control pills *with* condoms during only 45% of their intercourse experiences.

What are the obstacles to youths' consistent use of contraception and condoms? Lack of availability remains at the top of the list. Studies consistently demonstrate that one of the key predictors of adolescent contraceptive behavior is whether youths have access to a free, confidential family-planning facility

(Averett, Rees, & Argys, 2002; Blake et al., 2003; Ryan, Franzetta, & Manlove, 2007). The ability to obtain such services without the knowledge and consent of one's parents also plays an important role: One study found that teen pregnancies and childbearing rose significantly after a local clinic began requiring that adolescents obtain parental consent in order to obtain contraception (Zavodny, 2004), and another study found that 20% of sexually active teenagers would stop using contraceptives if they had to notify their parents in order to get them (Jones, Purcell, Singh, & Finer, 2005). Only 7% said that they would actually stop having sex.

Another barrier to reliable contraceptive use is low levels of knowledge about the " nuts and bolts" of fertility and contraception (Ryan et al., 2007). Without understanding exactly how or why birth control pills work, youths cannot be expected to realistically appraise the risks of missing "just one pill." It is also critical to consider adolescents' underdeveloped cognitive skills, particularly regarding long-range planning, evaluation of hypothetical probabilities, and future-oriented thinking (Eccles, Wigfield, & Byrnes, 2003; Lehalle, 2006). Such factors contribute to youths' poor estimation (or lack of estimation altogether) of their own risks for pregnancy and STIs, providing them with little motive for consistent contraceptive and condom use. As an example, one study found that adolescents who discovered after a pregnancy test that they were *not* pregnant were actually *less* likely to report consistent contraceptive use afterward (Zabin, Sedivy, & Emerson, 1994). Similarly, adolescents who do find themselves pregnant or who contract STIs do not report more consistent subsequent contraceptive and condom use (Davies et al., 2006). Clearly, adolescents do not appear to be drawing on rational calculations of cause and effect when making real-time decisions about contraceptive and condom use. Nor do they appear to be carefully evaluating the risks of their own behavior; rather, one study showed that adolescents are actually more motivated by the potential *benefits* of contraceptive/condom nonuse (such as immediate pleasure, feelings of physical and emotional connection to the partner) than by the attendant risks (Parsons, Halkitis, Bimbi, & Borkowski, 2000).

Another obstacle is youths' ability and willingness to realistically and honestly assess their own sexual behavior. Taking proactive steps to plan for sexual activity and use appropriate protection requires admitting that one is sexually active, an admission that may be particularly difficult for girls or those raised in conservative environments (Miller & Moore, 1990). Notably, youths who report feelings of guilt and shame about sex are less likely to use effective contraception (Gerrard, 1987), as are youths from extremely conservative religions (Miller & Gur, 2002; Studer & Thornton, 1987) and those who find themselves breaking previous "virginity pledges" (Brückner & Bearman, 2005).

On the positive side, factors that *promote* effective and consistent condom and contraceptive use include youths' motivations for doing so, their commitment to avoiding pregnancy (Bartz, Shew, Ofner, & Fortenberry, 2007), their knowledge about condoms and contraception (Ryan et al., 2007), their feelings of efficacy regarding condom/contraceptive use (Impett, Schooler, & Tolman, 2006; Longmore, Manning, Giordano, & Rudolph, 2003) and their ability and willingness to communicate openly about these issues with their partners (Jemmott, Jemmott, Fong, & McCaffree, 1999; Tschann & Adler, 1997; Widman, Welsh, McNulty, & Little, 2006).

Some youth advocates, of course, have argued that given the multiple risks associated with adolescent sexual activity, it is more appropriate and effective to promote 100% abstinence among adolescents than to provide them with comprehensive contraceptive information and access. In the past decade, numerous "abstinence only" programs have been developed and implemented across the country, as well as programs encouraging adolescents to take "virginity pledges" until marriage. Several comprehensive reviews of the effectiveness of these programs have been conducted. One recent such effort summarized the results of 13 scientifically rigorous trials involving over 16,000 youths (Underhill, Montgomery, & Operario, 2007). The results? *None* of these programs had significant effects on adolescents' age of sexual initiation, their rates of participation in unprotected vaginal sex, their number of sexual partners, or their condom and contraceptive use. Similar null effects have been found in other studies (Kohler, Manhart, & Lafferty, 2008). Even when positive effects of these programs have been found, the effects are fleeting, and typically disappear at follow-up assessments (Jemmott, Jemmott, & Fong, 1998). In contrast, programs offering comprehensive sexual education have been found to be associated with reduced risks of pregnancy and STIs (Kohler et al.), and survey data suggest that the majority of parents support teaching comprehensive sex education *in concert with* encouraging abstinence (Eisenberg, Bernat, Bearinger, & Resnick, 2008).

As for virginity pledges, they too appear unsuccessful in changing rates of pregnancy and STIs. A recent study of Add Health respondents used urine samples to compare rates of human papillomavirus, chlamydia, gonorrhea, and trichomoniasis among youths who did or did not take a virginity pledge. The results revealed that virginity pledgers had infection rates equal to nonpledgers. The authors speculated that virginity pledgers might be at particular risk for condom nonuse at sexual debut, and might also be less likely to be tested, diagnosed, and treated for sexually transmitted diseases. Hence, they concluded that adopting a virginity pledge does not appear to be an effective approach to preventing pregnancy and STIs (Brückner & Bearman, 2005).

Same-Sex Sexuality

Practically all research on same-sex behavior has been conducted with youths who self-identify as lesbian, gay, or bisexual, even though such youths comprise only a small subset of the total number of adolescents with same-sex attractions, fantasies, romances, or sexual activities (Savin-Williams, 2006, 2008). Furthermore, these different components of same-sex sexuality do not necessarily coincide. Quite simply, not all adolescents who experience same-sex desires identify as lesbian, gay, or bisexual, and not all of these individuals engage in same-sex activities during adolescence (Anderson, 2008; Diamond, 2000a, 2003a, 2008; Golden, 1996; Savin-Williams, 2005, 2006; Weinberg, Williams, & Pryor, 1994). Given our primitive understanding of how sexual orientation and sexual behavior link up with etiology and experience (Diamond, 2003c), we can learn more about the nature and long-term significance of different facets of same-sex sexuality by assessing and interpreting them separately. Even if youths with same-sex attractions never act on them, never identify as gay, and never come out to friends or family, the development of such youths might follow notably different trajectories than the development of youths who never have such feelings.

How many such youths are there? Among Wave 3 Add Health respondents, 13% of girls and 6% of boys reported same-sex attractions, a same-sex relationship, or a nonheterosexual sexual orientation identity (Savin-Williams, 2005). For comparison, Laumann et al.'s (1994) similarly random, representative survey of American adults found that nearly 9% of women and 10% of men reported same-sex attractions or behaviors. However, identifying as lesbian, gay, or bisexual during adolescence varies across various cultures, from less than 2% (Eskin, Kaynak-Demir, & Demir, 2005; Garofalo, Wolf, Wissow, Woods, & Goodman, 1999) to over 5% (Mosher et al., 2005; Wichstrøm & Hegna, 2003). Identifying as "something else" can add another 5% and "no report" can add 2% (Mosher et al., 2005).

In terms of same-sex behavior, proportions have been difficult to ascertain because of stigma attached to such behaviors. One study of junior high school students (Halpern et al., 1993) found that despite a confidential questionnaire, only a handful of youths reported same-sex contact by age 16. Among Greek (Papadopoulos et al., 2000), British (Copas et al., 2002), and U.S. (Garofalo et al., 1999) young adults, about 3% reported same-sex activities. By contrast, using audio CASI technology, 5% of U.S. boys and 11% of U.S. girls reported same-sex contact (Mosher et al., 2005). Age, cohort, and sexual experience are important factors when interpreting differential rates of same-sex behavior. The fraction of adolescent boys reporting same-sex sexual contact was 0.4% at age 12 but nearly 3% by age 18 in Minnesota (Remafedi, Resnick, Blum, & Harris, 1992). Nationally, the 2% of 15-year-old boys with same-sex behavior (oral or anal sex) tripled by age 19; among girls, same-sex experience doubled from 7% at age 15 to 14% at age 19 (Mosher et al., 2005). Age of "same-gender sexual debut" among women declined from age 28 among those at least 55 years old to age 17 among those 18–24 years old; among men, the cohort differential was far less marked, from 19 to 16 years old (Grov et al., 2006). In a Vermont study, the proportion of youth reporting same-sex contact rose from 1% to nearly 9% of young men and 5% of young women when the sample was restricted to youths who had heterosexual coitus (DuRant, Krowchuk, & Sinal, 1998).

Experimentation or Orientation?

Some developmental researchers might presume that adolescents who engage in same-sex contact are simply experimenting, and that they will eventually identify as heterosexual. For example, Maccoby (1998, p. 191) asserted that "a substantial number of people experiment with same-sex sexuality at some point in their lives, and a small minority settle into a lifelong pattern of homosexuality." Yet, it is unknown whether same-sex activity peaks during adolescence or is more characteristic of other points of the life course. We do know that one of the best predictors of an eventual gay, lesbian, or bisexual identity is childhood and adolescent same-sex behavior (Bell, Weinberg, & Hammersmith, 1981). At the same time, we also know that the majority of adolescents pursuing same-sex behavior consider themselves to be heterosexual. For example, half of youths reporting same-sex behavior on the Massachusetts Youth Risk Behavior Survey (YRBS) (Garofalo et al., 1999) were heterosexually identified; a study of Minnesota public school students found that over 60% reporting same-sex behavior identified as heterosexual (Remafedi et al., 1992); and across the United States, of individuals with same-sex sexual activities, 49% of boys and 65% of girls identified as heterosexual (Mosher et al., 2005). Note as well that many young men who pursue same-sex behavior in childhood and adolescence report that their *partners* identified as heterosexual (Savin-Williams, 1998).

Do such discrepancies between current and future behavior and identity simply reflect adolescent confusion or flightiness? If so, one would expect to see fewer such discrepancies among adults, but this is not the case. Although only about 3% of adults identify as lesbian, gay, or bisexual, *three times as many* report having had at least one same-sex sexual experience since puberty (Laumann et al., 1994). Clearly, contrary to the widespread notion that desire, behavior, and identity coalesce neatly in adolescence and young adulthood to signal an unambiguously heterosexual or homosexual orientation, the reality is much more complicated. Same-sex behavior may serve a variety of purposes for different youths; for some, it may provide the context for discovering a same-sex orientation and claiming a same-sex identity; for others, it may reflect a general sexual "openness" and a desire to experiment. It is impossible to determine its long-term significance simply on the basis of when and/or how often it occurred. Given cultural heterocentric assumptions and active sexual prejudice against sexual minorities (Herek, 2000), it should not be surprising that most adolescents with same-sex contact claim to be heterosexual. With the dearth of longitudinal research on

sexual orientation, behavior, and identity, we simply do not know for certain what proportion of adolescent same-sex behavior represents a precursor of adult same-sex sexuality. The only prospective study of female sexual-minority youth (Diamond, 2000b, 2003a, 2005, 2008a, 2008b) found that at the end of 10 years, 9% of the women who had previously considered themselves to be nonheterosexual claimed a heterosexual label. Notably, however, all of these women still reported experiencing same-sex attractions, and only one young woman called her previous sexual-minority identification a phase. Their motives for reclaiming a heterosexual label often revolved around their satisfaction with a current heterosexual relationship and their perception that future ties to women were exceedingly unlikely.

Retrospective data collected from adults (Laumann et al., 1994) suggest notable sex differences in patterns of adolescent same-sex behavior. Among adult male respondents who had ever had same-sex contact, 42% engaged in such contact during adolescence *only*. In other words, nearly half of their same-sex behavior occurred during the teenage years. In stark contrast, practically all female respondents with adolescent same-sex contact pursued such contact into adulthood, indicating that adolescent same-sex behavior was a better predictor of adult same-sex sexuality among women than among men. However, this does not suggest that same-sex behavior is always a marker of sexual orientation among women; rather, when heterosexual women pursue same-sex behavior, they do so at later ages, often in college rather than high school. This may reflect the historic fact that women have had fewer opportunities and social license to experiment sexually during their adolescent years (Gagnon & Simon, 1973).

Are there factors that researchers might use to distinguish experimental same-sex behavior from that which signals an underlying same-sex orientation? One possibility is that youths with an underlying same-sex orientation pursue such behavior more consistently than do heterosexual youths and that they choose it over opportunities for other-sex contact—although this is less true of bisexual youths. In the Vermont YRBS study, over half of males with a same-sex experience reported having had more than four different male partners, and most of these individuals also reported never having had sex with a female (DuRant et al., 1998). This might be construed as a prehomosexual trajectory, but at the current time no direct evidence exists to confirm or disconfirm this possibility. In her longitudinal study of young women, Diamond (2000b, 2003a, 2005) found that factors such as age of first same-sex attractions, first sexual questioning, and first same-sex contact failed to distinguish women who relinquished their sexual-minority identities from those who did not. The only significant predictor of future identity 5 and 10 years down the line was initial ratio of same-sex to other-sex attractions, which remained relatively stable over time (Diamond, 2008b).

Further complicating matters, a small number of contemporary investigators who assess multiple components of sexuality along a continuum, from exclusively other-sex to exclusively same-sex sexual or romantic attraction, fantasy, or identity have identified a "new" sexual-minority group—the "mostly straight" or those who identify as heterosexual but have significant same-sex attractions (Dickson, Paul, & Herbison, 2003; Hoburg, Konik, Williams, & Crawford, 2004; Kinnish, Strassberg, & Turner, 2005; Morgan Thompson & Morgan, 2008; Savin-Williams & Ream, 2007; Vrangalova & Savin-Williams, 2008b). These populations and their diverse experiences pose new dilemmas for investigators: Should they be classified as heterosexual based on their predominant (and sometimes exclusive) other-sex behavior, or should they be classified as sexual minorities based on their experience of periodic same-sex attractions and fantasies? Historically, such individuals have been deleted from research samples because of precisely these complications, but increasingly it has become clear that any substantive model of sexuality and sexual

orientation needs to account for *all* experiences of same-sex sexuality over the life course, even these perplexing and shifting ones (Diamond, 2008a).

Cultural factors must also be considered. European American men and women across age cohorts are more likely than African American, Asian/Pacific Islander, and Latino/a individuals to be out to parents, but not necessarily to self or to others (Grov et al., 2006). More specifically, paradoxical attitudes toward male–male sexual exploits are common in many Latino cultures. Carballo-Diéguez (1997) noted that Latin cultures tend to permit males to choose other males as sex partners providing that it is a private choice undertaken solely to satisfy sexual urges rather than a public acknowledgment of a gay identity encompassing both sex and love. Furthermore, strong links are perceived between men's behavioral roles in same-sex activity and their sexual and gender identity. A Latino man may pursue same-sex activity without threatening his heterosexual identity if he assumes the inserter role in oral and anal sex, maintains a highly masculine demeanor, and expresses no tender feelings toward his partner (no kissing). Men who allow themselves to be penetrated are considered intrinsically effeminate and are ridiculed as *jotos* (faggots) (Carrier, 1995).

Of course, investigations into the diverse meanings that adolescents attach to their same-sex behavior and the degree of emotional and physical satisfaction they experience in these interactions relative to other-sex interactions might predict future identification. However, such investigations have not been undertaken because it is sufficiently difficult for researchers to find heterosexually identified adolescents who report same-sex behavior, much less answer detailed questions about why they engage in such behavior and how satisfying these experiences are. Perhaps the best strategy is to pose such questions retrospectively. The combination of greater maturity and the cessation of same-sex behavior might render such respondents more willing to speak openly and honestly about their prior same-sex experiences.

In regard to youth who identify as lesbian, gay, or bisexual, the average age of first same-sex activity for females ranges from 14 (Rosario et al., 1996) to 18 (Diamond, 1998); for males, the range is narrower, usually averaging between ages 13 and 15 (D'Augelli, 2005; Herdt & Boxer, 1993; Rosario et al., 1996; Savin-Williams, 1998). The typical context for a first same-sex experience varies according to its timing. One retrospective study (Savin-Williams, 1998, 2004) found that prepubertal same-sex contact among boys often occurred during play activities with a same-age friend or relative; if during early adolescence, it was also likely pursued with close friends, but in these cases less playful and more explicitly sexual; if it occurred during the high school years, it was often with a notably older partner, a stranger, or a dating acquaintance. Among girls, close friends were common first partners at all ages, and young women were much more likely to have their first same-sex contact within the context of a full-fledged love affair, rather than with a stranger or a passing acquaintance (Savin-Williams, 2007). Some of these early affairs began as ambiguously passionate, platonic friendships that spilled over into sexual desire and activity (Diamond, 2000a).

Over half of gay and bisexual men and about 80% of lesbian and bisexual women also report other-sex experiences during adolescence. Herdt and Boxer (1993) reported that more lesbian and bisexual adolescent girls had other-sex *before* same-sex sexual activity, whereas boys followed the opposite pattern. This finding has been replicated in some (D'Augelli, 2005; Savin-Williams, 1998, 2004) but not all (Rosario et al., 1996) studies. Given that a sexual-minority youth's other-sex activities usually take place within the context of a dating relationship, this might reflect greater social pressures on teenage girls to date (Weinberg et al., 1994), as well as the greater likelihood that sexual-minority women are authentically attracted to both sexes (Baumeister,

2000; Diamond, 2005). Many sexual-minority youths report that their other-sex relationships are deeply satisfying—sometimes only emotionally, but sometimes both emotionally and physically (Diamond, 1998; Savin-Williams & Diamond, 2000). Of course, some youths report that other-sex activities were obligatorily pursued (Savin-Williams, 1998, 2004), which surely characterizes some heterosexuals' other-sex activities as well.

The sexes also differ regarding the sequencing of same-sex behavior and sexual identification. Whereas same-sex activity typically occurs one to two years prior to a gay or bisexual identification among males (Herdt & Boxer, 1993; Rosario et al., 1996; Savin-Williams & Diamond, 2000), sexual-minority females are more likely to have their first same-sex contact after identifying as lesbian or bisexual (Diamond, 1998; Savin-Williams & Diamond, 2000). As noted, this might stem from the greater sexual license granted to adolescent boys than girls. Yet this gender difference may be fading as contemporary sexual-minority boys question their sexual identities at increasingly earlier ages. An increasing number of young men now adopt a gay or bisexual label before ever having had same-sex contact. Dubé (2000), for example, found that young sexual-minority men were more likely than an older cohort (56% versus 38%) to have their first same-sex experience after identifying as gay or bisexual. Overall, these gender-differentiated sequences suggest that interpersonal and situational factors exert a greater press on sexual-minority women's than men's psychosexual development (Diamond, 2003c), a pattern that also characterizes heterosexual youths (Udry & Billy, 1987; Udry et al., 1986).

The Interpersonal Context of Adolescent Sexuality

Historically, investigations of adolescent sexuality have devoted far more attention to tabulating the number and timing of youths' sexual behaviors rather than their interpersonal context. Thankfully, this has now changed, and a considerable body of research addresses the diverse types of relationships in which youth pursue sexual activity (e.g., Crouter & Booth, 2006). Common questions include *how many* different partners youths have, *what types* of relationships they are forming, and *with whom?*

The answer to the "who" question depends on whether we are examining childhood sex play versus adolescent and young adult sexual activity. Partners for childhood sex play tend to be friends and playmates, although occasionally cousins or siblings. Only rarely do children pursue sexual activity with unacquainted peers or adults (Larsson & Svedin, 2002; Savin-Williams, 1998, 2004). Among older youths, however, the majority (especially girls) pursue their first sexual experiences with steady romantic partners (Abma, Chandra, Mosher, Peterson, & Piccinino, 1997; Cooksey, Mott, & Neubauer, 2002; Manning et al., 2000). Boys are more likely than girls to have their first sexual experiences with acquaintances, or girls that they are "just dating" (de Gaston, Jensen, & Weed, 1995; Papadopoulos et al., 2000; Weinberg et al., 1995; Zani, 1991). The same gender difference has emerged in retrospective surveys of adults. Laumann et al. (1994) found that 75% of young adult women had first sex with a spouse or someone they loved, compared with 41% of young men, who were more likely than women to report that their first partner was someone they knew well but did not love (37% versus 17%) or someone they did not know well, had just met, or had paid (21% versus 7%). Of course, these findings directly reflect aforementioned gender differences in the extent to which interpersonal relationships and emotional feelings—in contrast to straightforward sexual desires—function as motivators for adolescents' sexual activity.

Gender differences also exist in expectations regarding coital timing within an ongoing relationship. As Maccoby (1998) noted, girls typically want to prolong the early stages of dating and to delay intercourse, whereas boys typically want to accelerate the pace at which sexual intimacy progresses. This is consistent with research on adults. Within an ongoing relationship, men tend to push for sex while women set limits (Browning et al., 1999). One study found that college men expected sex at about the 10th date, whereas women expected sex after the 16th date (Cohen & Shotland, 1996). Both sexes believed that men wanted sex irrespective of physical attraction or emotional involvement and that women did not. In reality, both men and women expected sex only when they were attracted to the person, although men were more likely to expect sex in the absence of emotional closeness.

As for the number of sexual partners, one thing is certain: The 1950s model in which adolescents had *only one* serious romantic and sexual relationship during their high school years, and proceeded to marry that individual when they reached their early 20s, is long gone. Some researchers argue that this was probably never an optimal developmental trajectory to begin with, and that it likely failed to adequately prepare youths for the realities of adult marriage and commitment (Arnett, 2004). What number of partners, then, is optimal during the teen years, and what are the current norms?

The data are conflicting; some studies report that the average high school senior has had more than one intercourse partner (Alan Guttmacher Institute, 1994), whereas others report that the majority of youths have one or fewer partners by the end of high school (de Gaston et al., 1995; Mosher et al., 2005; Prince & Bernard, 1998). Findings from the Add Health study (Kelley, Borawski, Flocke, & Keen, 2003) showed that among 15- to 18-year-olds reporting *any* sexual activity in the past 18 months, 35% had more than one partner. Laumann et al. (1994) found that 55% of women and 44% of men between the ages of 18 and 24 had thus far had only one partner, and national data indicated that the median number of lifetime female partners was 1.9 among 15- to 19-year-old young men, higher than the 1.4 median male partners among comparable young women (Mosher et al., 2005). Sex differences in reports of partner number are observed across cohorts and cultures and are generally larger in more restrictive, traditional societies (Laumann et al., 1994; Papadopoulos et al., 2000; Prince & Bernard). However, it is important not to conflate the number of coital partners with overall frequency of sexual activity. Because young women are more likely than men (73% versus 38%) to report that their current sexual relationship is an ongoing relationship (de Gaston et al.), they tend to report higher rates of sexual activity, albeit with the same person, whereas young men have more infrequent sex with a variety of different individuals (Prince & Bernard).

Multiple sexual partners do appear to be associated with other developmental risks, including less consistent condom use (CDC, 1990) and greater rates of substance use and delinquency (Fortenberry, 1997; Kelley et al., 2003; Uttenbroek, 1994). Notably, youths in the Add Health study with more than one sexual partner in the past 18 months were more likely to report regretting one of their sexual experiences due to the influence of alcohol (Kelley et al., 2003). The mechanisms underlying these associations are not clear. Some evidence suggests that having multiple partners might simply be a marker for broader risk trajectories, given that youths with multiple partners tend to have begun sexual activity at earlier ages (Kupek, 2001; Moore & Rosenthal, 1993), and that early coitus is associated with a range of temperamental and familial predictors stretching back to late childhood (Bingham & Crockett, 1996).

Similar to declines in age of first coitus among girls, changes in partner number reflect historic transformations in attitudes and norms regarding female sexuality. In previous eras, having sex at all—especially with multiple partners—would have been scandalous for any girl hoping eventually to marry, as it would have labeled her a "slut." Although having multiple partners is still less acceptable for girls than for boys, the stigma attached to such behavior has

significantly declined (Milhausen & Herold, 2001). This is particularly true if a girl's multiple sexual relationships are full-fledged, committed romances, rather than casual liaisons. A related issue is whether youths pursue sexual activity with multiple partners concurrently or sequentially. Among the subset of Add Health youths who had multiple partners in the past 18 months, 42% reported that at least some of these relationships were pursued at the same time (Kelley et al., 2003). Notably, youths reporting concurrent relationships had the highest numbers of partners overall, were less likely to report condom use, and had lower self-efficacy than the other youths. Furthermore, having multiple concurrent sexual partners proved to be a stronger predictor of STI risk than having multiple sequential partners.

What Types of Relationships?

One recent and intriguing line of research on the interpersonal context of adolescent sexuality concerns the types of relationships in which sexual activity is pursued. To some extent this reflects growing concern by parents, educators, and health professionals that rates of casual, uncommitted sex are on the rise (Denizet-Lewis, 2004; Levin, 2005; Stepp, 2007). Although the majority of youth have their first sexual experiences within romantic relationships (Abma et al., 1997; Manning et al., 2000), research suggests that increasing numbers of adolescents and young adults are pursuing sexual activity outside of conventional dating relationships, for example, with ex-boyfriends or ex-girlfriends, people they date "once in awhile," people they have just met ("hook-ups"), or friends and acquaintances, sometimes denoted "friends with benefits" (Furman & Hand, 2006; Grello, Welsh, & Harper, 2006; Grello, Welsh, Harper, & Dickson, 2003; Hughes, Morrison, & Asada, 2005; Kan & Cares, 2006; Levinson et al., 1995; Manning et al, 2000; Paul & Hayes, 2002; Vrangalova & Savin-Williams, 2008a).

Do these patterns have implications for later social and sexual development? A 1-year longitudinal study (Grello et al., 2003) found that youths whose first sex took place within a casual rather than a romantic relationship were disproportionately likely to report depressive symptoms and delinquent behaviors, both before and after the transition. The fact that these youths reported greater psychosocial problems even before engaging in casual sex is important because it highlights the fact that casual sex may not "do" anything detrimental to youths; rather, the types of youths who self-select themselves into casual sexual relationships may already be predisposed to psychological and social difficulties. This may explain the range of psychosocial problems associated with casual sex, including early sex, sex with multiple partners, attachment insecurity, and alcohol and drug use (Cooper, Shaver, & Collins, 1998; Grello et al., 2006; Regan & Dreyer, 1999). Further evidence that casual sex is a correlate—but not a cause—of adjustment problems is provided by a recent analysis of Add Health data, which found that although youths in casual relationships had disproportionately high depressive symptoms compared to virgins, these differences *predated* their sexual debut, and ended up dissipating over time (Monahan & Lee, 2008).

Associations between casual sex and poor psychological adjustment appear to be particularly strong for women, most likely reflecting the double standard that disproportionately stigmatizes women for casual sex. For example, Grello, Welsh, and Harper (2006) found that males who engaged in casual sex reported the fewest symptoms of depression, whereas females who had a history of casual sex reported the *most* depressive symptoms. Other studies have found that for young women, casual sex is associated with decreased self-esteem, increased depressive symptoms, greater fear of losing one's individuality, self-perceived unattractiveness, as well as feelings of guilt, regret, disappointment, and a loss of control (Grello et al., 2003, 2006; Paul & Hayes, 2002). Gender differences have also been detected in youths' motives for pursuing casual or uncommitted sex. Although the primary motive is one of sexual pleasure for both sexes, relational motives factor prominently in women's decisions to engage in casual sex, including the hope for developing a future romantic relationship, finding the "right" partner, and testing sexual compatibility. Men include among their motives the attainment of social status, the expression of independence, and the development and display of sexual skill. Women, not surprisingly, are also more likely to report being coerced or "tricked" into casual sexual activity (Allen, 2004; Greiling & Buss, 2000; Regan & Dreyer, 1999; Weaver & Herold, 2000).

Importantly, however, some researchers suggest that sexual behavior occurring in nonromantic contexts need not be problematic, and that such relationships may have just as much potential as romantic relationships to be positive, empowering, and developmentally adaptive. For example, the lack of a romantic context may reduce the pressure that youths perceive to engage in certain behaviors. This may explain Kaestle and Halpern's (2007) finding that youth in Add Health who reported loving their partner "very much" were more likely to report participating in oral and anal sex. Caruthers (2006) found that many women actually perceived that they had *more* control in nonromantic relationships than in traditional romantic relationships. Her qualitative study revealed that many young women who pursued sex within nonromantic relationships were characterized by high self-esteem and sexual assertiveness, and felt that such relationships allowed them to express and satisfy their sexual desires on their own terms. Giordano, Manning, and Longmore (2006) noted that "friends with benefits" relationships often allow youth to seek sexual gratification within a familiar, stable, egalitarian relationship, escaping the potential volatility and power differentials that often accompany conventional romantic ties. Finally, studies conducted among *adults* suggest no consistent relations between casual sex and mental health problems (Arvidson, Kallings, Nilsson, Hellberg, & Mardh, 1997; Clark, 2006; Reise & Wright, 1996; Schmitt, 2005; Weeden & Sabini, 2007), suggesting that such behavior cannot be uniformly considered "good" or "bad." Rather, it appears to be the specific developmental, motivational, and interpersonal contexts of such activities that prove important for understanding their implications for youths' mental and sexual well-being. Greater research on the constellation of factors that mediate and moderate associations between "nonrelational" sex and various psychological and behavioral outcomes is clearly necessary.

THE EVALUATION OF SEXUAL EXPERIENCES

Given the tremendous buildup that sex receives, it is bound to disappoint some youth when it finally happens. However, little is known concerning how adolescents evaluate their sexual experiences, and most of the available data focus exclusively on intercourse. One notable exception is the research of Larsson and Svedin (2002), who examined the autoerotic and noncoital sexual activities of 11- to 12-year-olds. The most prevalent evaluations were extremely positive, including "pleasant body sensations," "excitement,""natural feeling," "silly," and "sexually stimulated." Less than 5% evaluated their sexual experiences as "frightening," "bad,""unpleasant body sensation," or "angry." Feelings of guilt were rare, although slightly more common among girls than boys. When followed up as high school seniors, over 90% described their earlier sexual experiences as "normal" or "good," and all but 4% said they had either a positive or a neutral effect on them. Notably, the exceptions were often individuals who had coercive early experiences.

Intercourse, however, is another matter, particularly for girls. Moore and Rosenthal (1993) concluded in a review of the extant literature that first coitus is often not pleasurable for adolescent girls. For example, Italian adolescent girls were often so disappointed by their first sexual experiences that they refrained from sexual activity altogether for lengthy periods of time (Zani, 1991). Adolescent boys evaluated their early intercourse experiences more positively, and data collected from young adults indicate that young men were more likely than women to have consistent orgasms with their primary partner (Laumann et al., 1994). Although 70% rated sexual intercourse as highly appealing, young men were more likely than women to evaluate a variety of other sexual activities as appealing, such as watching one's partner undress (50% and 31%), receiving oral sex (47% and 35%), and giving oral sex (32% and 15%). It is interesting to consider the degree to which the young women's dissatisfaction might be moderated by their partners' experience, considerateness, and familiarity with the female body. Such factors, or at least youth's perceptions of them, have not been studied systematically.

Another potential moderator of sexual satisfaction might be simultaneous feelings of guilt, shame, or regret about sexual activity, which are more common among young women than among men (Benda & DiBlasio, 1994; Crockett et al., 1996; de Gaston et al., 1995). Such feelings might be an inevitable consequence of the restrictive ways in which girls are socialized to think about their sexuality, making them disproportionately sensitive to the risks presented by sexual behavior, whereas boys focus on the rewards associated with sex (Benda & DiBlasio; Crockett et al.). Such factors likely play a critical role in shaping the subjective quality of adolescents' early sexual experiences.

The relational context of adolescent sexual activity also plays an important evaluative role. Adolescent girls are more likely to report a positive experience if sex occurs within the confines of a steady relationship, particularly one characterized by good communication (Donald, Lucke, Dunne, & Raphael, 1995) and high intimacy and engagement (Thompson, 1995). Relational contexts are important for boys, as well. One study of Swedish and American youth found that over 90% of both young men and women expressed greater happiness, more satisfaction, and less guilt about their most recent sexual intercourse when it was pursued within the context of a significant relationship (Weinberg et al., 1995; see also Zani, 1991). Nonetheless, the difference between the perceived quality of relationship sex versus nonrelationship sex was greater for women. Note, too, that despite their lower rates of orgasm frequency, the young adult women in Laumann et al.'s (1994) study were just as likely as were their male counterparts to describe their current sexual relationship as emotionally *and* physically satisfying.

Clearly, adolescents' evaluations of their sexual experiences depend greatly on their initial expectations as well as on the context in which they occur. Those who naively assume that all sexual activities, and sexual intercourse in particular, will be as uniformly satisfying as they appear to be in the media are bound to be let down by reality. Nevertheless, parents rarely communicate to their children that good sex is a skill to be learned like any other and that it often takes time to master. Youths who appreciate this fact will have more realistic expectations about the satisfaction they can expect from their initial sexual experiences and will therefore be in a better position to evaluate how positive or negative sexual experiences bear on their self-concept, current relationships, and sexual identity.

ADOLESCENT SEXUAL VIOLENCE

Up until now, our discussion has generally presumed that the sexual activity pursued by adolescents is of their choosing. Sadly, of course, this is not always the case. Many children and adolescents have been victims of coerced sexual activity, at the hands of relatives, friends, neighbors, and intimate partners. National data suggests that rates of victimization among children have declined slightly in the past 20 years, while those among adolescents have increased (Casey & Nurius, 2006). A recent representative phone survey of nearly 10,000 American adults found that 10.6% of women reported at least one incidence of forced sex during their lifetime, and the most common age range for such experiences (comprising 35% of accounts) was between 12 and 17 (Basile, Chen, Black, & Saltzman, 2007). Studies of adolescents have documented rates of forced sexual intercourse ranging between 7% and 18% (Howard & Wang, 2005; Howard, Wang, & Yan, 2007; Raghavan, Bogart, Elliott, Vestal, & Shuster, 2004). Adolescent girls are substantially more likely than boys to report experiences of sexual coercion (Foshee, Benefield, Ennett, Bauman, & Suchindran, 2004; Foster, Hagan, & Brooks-Gunn, 2004), but it is not known whether some of this difference is attributable to underreporting by boys (Wekerle & Wolfe, 1999). It is also important to remember that these statistics underrepresent experiences of sexual pressure that fall somewhat short of conventional definitions of "force." Notably, Laumann and colleagues (1994) found that 25% of women (and 8% of men) described their first intercourse experience as *not wanted, but not coerced*. This fascinating, liminal category receives little attention in research on contemporary adolescents, but raises important questions about the ways youths think about sexual consent, and also whether the difference between "pressure" and "force" is a difference of degree versus kind.

The implications of adolescent sexual coercion are serious. Youths who have experienced sexual coercion report greater hopelessness, sadness, suicidality, and a range of additional risk behaviors, such as alcohol or drug use (Coker et al., 2000; Harvey & Spigner, 1995; Howard & Wang, 2005; Howard et al., 2007). Among girls, forced sex is also associated with more romantic involvement, greater overall exposure to violence, emotional distress, earlier initiation of coitus, multiple sexual partners, and nonuse of contraceptives and protection against STIs (Howard et al., 2007; Raghavan et al., 2004; Upchurch & Kusunoki, 2004). Notably, one study detected a significant association between history of sexual coercion and rates of infection with the human papilloma virus, and further showed that this association was mediated by high numbers of sexual partners (Kahn et al., 2005).

In response to these chilling findings, a number of researchers have worked to develop antiviolence interventions that seek to reduce adolescent sexual violence and dating violence more generally (Foshee et al., 2000). Yet it is important to remember that sexual and dating violence do not simplistically "cause" these negative outcomes, but are usually part of complex, long-standing trajectories of psychosocial risk that stretch back to early childhood, often involving violence in the family of origin (Capaldi & Clark, 1998; Sears, Byers, & Price, 2007; Simons, Lin, & Gordon, 1998) and violence in their current neighborhoods and relationships (Howard et al., 2007). Youths who perpetrate and are victims of sexual coercion typically inhabit broadly maladaptive social environments which contain multiple risks and stressors and provide limited social resources, increasing their odds of dysfunction not only with respect to sexual coercion, but with respect to a wide range of negative social and psychological outcomes (Harvey & Spigner, 1995). Hence, reducing rates of sexual violence requires that we reduce *overall* social–psychological–interpersonal risks. Correspondingly, promoting *healthy and adaptive* sexual relationships requires a similarly broad, "whole-person" approach to adolescent development, as we address next.

POSITIVE SEXUAL DEVELOPMENT

Most researchers attest to the dramatic changes in age of coital onset, number of sex partners, and frequency of sexual intercourse, as well as to the tolerance—if not acceptance—of diverse sexual behaviors and identities (Browning et al., 1999; Feldman et al., 1999; Miller & Benson, 1999; Savin-Williams, 2005). In reviewing the historical record, Maccoby (1998) concluded that the legendary sexual revolution involved a realization by youth that they have a right to

sexual pleasure and fulfillment, a decline in the influence of earlier generations' dictates concerning good versus bad sexual behavior, and an increase in the visibility of explicit sexuality in daily life. Although the availability of contraceptives fueled the changes, Feldman and associates (1999, p. 46) argued that in addition, "the feminist movement, with its insistence that women's sexual desire and gratification be recognized, together with media representation of women's overt sexuality, have succeeded in permitting women to openly acknowledge their sexuality in a way similar to men." Traditional sex roles and morality were challenged, and sex for women became less shameful, less mysterious, and more a personal than a family decision (Hopkins, 2000). Reproductive sex was replaced by recreational sex, giving license for girls to behave in the way that boys always have (Levine, 2002).

Although permissiveness with affection and commitment is the prominent contemporary standard, sex differences in sexual behavior persist, and some would argue that the total eradication of such differences is neither justifiable nor ideal (Weinberg et al., 1995). After all, despite the historic changes in conceptions of female sexuality, adolescents continue to judge a girl's sexual behavior more harshly than a boy's (Maccoby, 1998; Milhausen & Herold, 2001; Crawford & Popp, 2003; Weinberg et al., 1995). Within this context, it is difficult to discern what a positive, empowering, and healthy model of female sexual development should look like. Certainly, questions of female sexual pleasure and entitlement are missing from current agendas for adolescent sex education. As Fine (1988) noted, young women are consistently reminded of the negative consequences of sexuality, especially sexual behavior pursued outside the context of a serious relationship. They have been indoctrinated to believe that it is *their* job to suppress sexual desire, to serve as sexual gatekeepers, and to avoid the physical, emotional, moral, reproductive, and financial costs of rape, disease, and pregnancy. According to this perspective, there is no positive model of female adolescent sexuality. Only adult woman are granted sexual agency.

Tolman (1994, 2000; Tolman, Spencer, Harmon, Rosen-Reynoso, & Striepe, 2004) and O'Sullivan (O'Sullivan & Meyer-Bahlburg, 2003; O'Sullivan, Meyer-Bahlburg, & Watkins, 2001) have illustrated and expanded Fine's points in interviews with adolescents. Taught to inhibit, censure, or deny sexual desire, arousal, and pleasure, young adolescent girls reported relinquishing sexual agency. Society encourages boys to explore their sexuality fully, but leaves girls mystified about what it means when they feel sexual desire or pleasure (O'Sullivan et al., 2000). Tolman's (2000, p. 70) radical corrective was to adopt and communicate to adolescents a normative expectation that girls "can and should experience sexual desire—not that they should or will necessarily act on these feelings, but that they should be able to recognize and acknowledge what is a part of the self."

Importantly, some would argue that the aforementioned gender differences are not as inevitable and pervasive as they are portrayed. Girls are more sexually oriented and boys more romantically oriented than previous research might indicate. Kalof (1995) reported that teenagers of both sexes seek both physical and emotional pleasure from their sexual activity, disputing the myth that young women participate in sex only to achieve closeness and not because of desire. Indeed, a *New York Times* article, "She's Got to Be a Macho Girl" (Kuczynski, 2002), quoted one teenage boy as reporting that girls are now the sexual aggressors: "They [girls] have more attitude. They have more power. And they overpower guys more. I mean, it's scary." In addition, emotional intimacy and self-disclosure are as important for some young men as they are for young women. Tolman et al. (2004) echoed these sentiments in interviews with young men. Heterosexual initiation was more than belt notches, more than raging hormones bent on one objective. Similar to girls, adolescent boys also desire romance, companionship, sharing, and trust, and they ably distinguish romantic from recreational sex.

In scholarly circles, however, these longings must appear surprising. Given the impetus to avert or forestall the so-called treacherous sexual activities of adolescents, research addressing how adolescent sexuality can be positive and growth-promoting is nearly absent from the empirical literature. There are, however, some promising exceptions. For example, Smiler, Ward, Caruthers, and Merriwether (2005), while not ignoring the negative aspects of first coitus among young adults, also documented youths' positive experiences of first coitus, typically revolving around feelings of pleasure, empowerment, and love. They showed that such positive experiences, for both sexes, were associated with use of contraception and with longer-term relationship involvement prior to coitus, and concluded that the conventional "just say no" philosophy should be abandoned in favor of sexual health approaches that encourage and foster youths' maturity, commitment, and mutuality. Along the same lines, Meier (2007) noted that a substantial majority of the Add Health adolescents who had sex did not experience negative changes in mental health.

Of course, definitions of "positive" sexuality are likely to remain controversial. For example, studies have shown that adolescents who pursue early and frequent sex are less conventional, more independent, more autonomous, and less religious; they view themselves as attractive and successful in forming romantic relationships and have less traditional attitudes toward sex roles (Costa et al., 1995; Crockett et al., 1996; Davis & Lay-Yee, 1999; Jessor & Jessor, 1975; McLaughlin, Chen, Greenberger, & Biermeier, 1997; Moore & Rosenthal, 1993). Some adults view such traits as positive precursors to the development of an empowered, agentic, creative, and adventurous adult, whereas others view these traits as harbingers of rebelliousness, deviance, and risk. With regard to the relationship between self-evaluative traits and sexual behavior, research has been mixed. Youth with high self-esteem report high sexual restraint (Lynch, 2001; Paul et al., 2000), yet sex during childhood and adolescence among gay youths is not associated with lower self-esteem (Rind, 2001; Savin-Williams, 1998); indeed, one study of heterosexual boys found that early sexual debut was associated with *higher* levels of self-esteem (Jessor & Jessor, 1975). Perhaps high self-esteem buffers some boys against the risk of sexual rejection, rendering them more likely to seek or respond to sexual opportunities; furthermore, success with gaining a sex partner is socially rewarding and might raise a youth's self-regard over time (Paul et al., 2000). For girls, engaging in casual sex might decrease her self-worth if she views it as violating social expectations. Overall, it appears misguided to view early coitus as a cause of psychosocial maladjustment; to the contrary, well-adjusted, socially competent youth might be the most successful at finding sexual partners (Crockett et al., 1996).

These findings support former Surgeon General Jocelyn Elders's call to end the "conspiracy of silence" about adolescent sexuality and her advocacy for teaching children and teenagers self-respect and sexual self-esteem by reducing misinformation, scare tactics, and hysteria. Elders argued that "treating sex as dangerous is dangerous in itself" (Levine, 2002, p. x). Similarly, Carpenter (2001, p. 128) noted that "sexuality constitutes a central feature of identity: individuals are to a great degree defined by themselves and others, both socially and morally, in terms of their sexuality." The popular books quoted at the outset of this review, should remind scholars of the exhilarating, growth-promoting possibilities of adolescent sexuality (Levine, 2002; Ponton, 2000). If teenagers find themselves emotionally or cognitively unprepared for sex, this is due in large part to the failures of adults. O'Sullivan et al. (2001, p. 288) noted that parents "rarely acknowledged the positive aspects of sexuality outside the context of harm. It appears that their communication efforts ultimately deter their daughters from confiding in them about their sexual interest or participation." The impact among their African American and Latina families was straightforward: Girls turned increasingly to others, not parents, for advice on psychosexual issues central for making wise healthy sexual choices.

We agree with Tolman (1994), who advocated unhitching adolescent sexuality from notions of deviance and instead reconceptualizing it to encompass multiple forms of erotic and affectional ideation and experience. Our goal should be to encourage adolescents "to know their sexuality as feelings as well as actions, feelings to which they are entitled, feelings that are in fact not necessarily the same as actions" (p. 268). Extending Tolman's (2000, p. 78) mandate to boys, we are further obliged to teach adolescents not only of "the physical and emotional risks of sexuality, but also of the ways in which our sexuality can make us more resilient and more alive and about our entitlement to an erotic voice." If we want to guide adolescent sexual development along the most positive trajectories possible, total denial is as untenable as total freedom. Rather, we should help adolescents develop the cognitive, emotional, and interpersonal skills necessary for them to assess appropriately the pleasures and dangers of sexuality so that they can make informed sexual choices that keep them safe and foster positive sexual self-concepts.

REFERENCES

Abma, J., Chandra, A., Mosher, W., Peterson, L., & Piccinino, L. (1997). Fertility, family planning, and women's health: New data from the 1995 National Survey of Family Growth. *Vital Health Statistics* (Vol. 23). Hyattsville, MD: National Center for Health Statistics.

Alan Guttmacher Institute. (1994). *Sex and America's teenagers.* Washington DC: Author.

Alan Guttmacher Institute. (2006). *U.S. teenage pregnancy statistics: National and state trends and trends by race and ethnicity.* New York: Author.

Allen, L. (2004). "Getting off" and "getting out": Young people's conceptions of (hetero)sexual relationships. *Culture, Health, and Sexuality, 6,* 463–481.

Anderson, E. (2008). "Being masculine is not about who you sleep with...:" Heterosexual athletes contesting masculinity and the one-time rule of homosexuality. *Sex Roles, 58,* 104-115.

Arnett, J. J. (1998). Risk behavior and family role transitions during the twenties. *Journal of Youth and Adolescence, 27,* 301–320.

Arnett, J. J. (2004). *Emerging adulthood: The winding road from the late teens through the twenties*. New York: Oxford University Press.

Averett, S. L., Rees, D. I., & Argys, L. M. (2002). The impact of government policies and neighborhood characteristics on teenage sexual activity and contraceptive use. *American Journal of Public Health, 92*, 1773–1778.

Arvidson, M., Kallings, I., Nilsson, S., Hellberg, D., & Mardh, P-A. (1997). Risky behavior in women with history of casual travel sex. *Sexually Transmitted Diseases, 24*, 418–421.

Balsam, K. F., Beauchaine, T. P., Rothblum, E. D., & Solomon, S. E. (2008). Three-year follow-up of same-sex couples who had civil unions in Vermont, same-sex couples not in civil unions, and heterosexual married couples. *Developmental Psychology, 44*, 102–116.

Bancroft, J. (1978). The relationships between hormones and sexual behavior in humans. In J. B. Hutchison (Ed.), *Biological determinants of sexual behavior*. Chichester, UK: John Wiley & Sons.

Bancroft, J. H. (1989). Sexual desire and the brain. *Sexual and Marital Therapy, 3*, 11–27.

Bancroft, J. H. (Ed.). (1997). *Researching sexual behavior: Methodological issues*. Bloomington, IN: Indiana University Press.

Bartz, D., Shew, M., Ofner, S., & Fortenberry, J. D. (2007). Pregnancy intentions and contraceptive behaviors among adolescent women: A coital event level analysis. *Journal of Adolescent Health, 41*, 271–276.

Basile, K. C., Chen, J., Black, M. C., & Saltzman, L. E. (2007). Prevalence and characteristics of sexual violence victimization among U.S. adults, 2001–2003. *Violence and Victims, 22*, 437–448.

Baumeister, R. F. (2000). Gender differences in erotic plasticity: The female sex drive as socially flexible and responsive. *Psychological Bulletin, 126*, 247–374.

Baumeister, R. F., Catanese, K. R., & Vohs, K. D. (2001). Is there a gender difference in strength of sex drive? Theoretical views, conceptual distinctions, and a review of relevant evidence. *Personality and Social Psychology Review, 5*, 242–273.

Bauserman, R., & Davis C. (1996). Perceptions of early sexual experiences and adult sexual adjustment. *Journal of Psychology and Human Sexuality, 8*, 37–59.

Beach, F. A. (1976). Sexual attractivity, proceptivity, and receptivity in female mammals. *Hormones and Behavior, 7*, 105–138.

Bell, A. P., Weinberg, M. S., & Hammersmith, S. K. (1981). *Sexual preference: Its development in men and women*. Bloomington: Indiana University Press.

Belsky, J. (2007). Experience in childhood and the development of reproductive strategies. *Acta Psychologica Sinica, 39*, 454–468.

Belsky, J., Steinberg, L. D., Houts, R. M., Friedman, S. L., DeHart, G., Cauffman, E., et al. (2007). Family rearing antecedents of pubertal timing. *Child Development, 78*, 1302–1321.

Benda, B. B., & DiBlasio, F. A. (1994). An integration of theory: Adolescent sexual contacts. *Journal of Youth and Adolescence, 23*, 403–420.

Bingham, C. R., & Crockett, L. J. (1996). Longitudinal adjustment patterns of boys and girls experiencing early, middle, and late sexual intercourse. *Developmental Psychology, 32*, 647–658.

Blake, S. M., Ledsky, R., Goodenow, C., Sawyer, R., Lohrmann, D., & Windsor, R. (2003). Condom availability programs in Massachusetts high schools: Relationships with condom use and sexual behavior. *American Journal of Public Health, 93*, 955–962.

Blum, R. W., Beuhring, T., Shew, M. L., Bearinger, L. H., Sieving, R. E., & Resnick, M. D. (2000). The effects of race/ethnicity, income, and family structure on adolescent risk behaviors. *American Journal of Public Health, 90*, 1879–1884.

Blumstein, P., & Schwarz, P. (1983). *American couples: Money, work, sex*. New York: Morrow.

Boekeloo, B. O., & Howard, D. E. (2002). Oral sexual experience among young adolescents receiving general health examinations. *American Journal of Health Behavior, 26*, 306–314.

Bogart, L. M., Cecil, H., Wagstaff, D. A., Pinkerton, S. D., & Abramson, P. R. (2000). Is it "sex"? College students' interpretations of sexual behavior terminology. *Journal of Sex Research, 37*, 108–116.

Bos, H. M. W., Sandfort, T. G. M., de Bruyn, E. H., & Hakvoort, E. M. (2008). Same-sex attraction, social relationships, psychosocial functioning, and school performance in early adolescence. *Developmental Psychology, 44*(1), 59-68.

Boyce, W., Doherty-Poirier, M., MacKinnon, D., Fortin, C., Saab, H., King, M., & Gallupe, O. (2006). Sexual health of Canadian youth: Findings from the Canadian Youth, Sexual Health and HIV/AIDS Study. *Canadian Journal of Human Sexuality, 15*(2), 59–68.

Brigman, B., & Knox, D. (1992). University students' motivations to have intercourse. *College Student Journal, 26*, 406–408.

Brody, S., Laan, E., & van Lunsen, R. H. W. (2003). Concordance between women's physiological and subjective sexual arousal is associated with consistency of orgasm during intercourse but not other sexual behavior. *Journal of Sex & Marital Therapy, 29*, 15–23.

Brooks-Gunn, J., & Paikoff, R. (1997). Sexuality and developmental transitions during adolescence, part II. In J.Schulenberg, J.Maggs, & K. Hurrelmann (Eds.), *Health risks and developmental transitions during adolescents* (pp. 190–219). London: Cambridge University Press.

Brooks-Gunn, J., & Reiter, E. (1990). The role of pubertal processes. In S. S. Feldman & G. E. Elliott (Eds.), *At the threshold: The developing adolescent* (pp. 16–23). Cambridge, MA: Harvard University Press.

Brown, J. D. (2002). Mass media influences on sexuality. *Journal of Sex Research, 39*, 42–45.

Browning, J. R., Kessler, D., Hatfield, E., & Choo, P. (1999). Power, gender, and sexual behavior. *Journal of Sex Research, 36*, 342–347.

Brückner, H., & Bearman, P. (2005). After the promise: The STD consequences of adolescent virginity pledges. *Journal of Adolescent Health, 36*, 271–278.

Buhi, E. R., & Goodson, P. (2007). Predictors of adolescent sexual behavior and intention: A theory-guided systematic review. *Journal of Adolescent Health, 40*, 4–21.

Busseri, M. A., Willoughby, T., Chalmers, H., & Bogaert, A. R. (2008). On the association between sexual attraction and adolescent risk behavior involvement: Examining mediation and moderation. *Developmental Psychology, 44*, 69–80.

Capaldi, D. M., & Clark, S. (1998). Prospective family predictors of aggression toward female partners for at-risk young men. *Developmental Psychology, 34*, 1175–1188.

Carballo-Diéguez, A. (1997). Sexual research with Latino men who have sex with men. In J. Bancroft (Ed.), *Researching sexual behavior: Methodological issues* (pp. 134–144). Bloomington: Indiana University Press.

Carpenter, L. M. (2001). The ambiguity of "having sex": The subjective experience of virginity loss in the United States. *Journal of Sex Research, 38*, 127–139.

Carrier, J. (1995). *De los ostros: Intimacy and homosexuality among Mexican men*. New York: Columbia University Press.

Carroll, J. L., Volk, K. D., & Hyde, J. S. (1985). Differences between males and females in motives for engaging in sexual intercourse. *Archives of Sexual Behavior, 14*, 131–139.

Caruthers, A. S. (2006). *"Hookups" and "friends with benefits": Nonrelational sexual encounters as contexts of women's normative sexual development*. Unpublished doctoral dissertation, University of Michigan, Ann Arbor.

Casey, E. A., & Nurius, P. S. (2006). Trends in the prevalence and characteristics of sexual violence: A cohort analysis. *Violence and Victims, 21*, 629–644.

Catalano, R. F., & Hawkins, J. D. (1996). The social development model: A theory of antisocial behavior. In J. D. Hawkins (Ed.), *Delinquency and crime: Current theories*. (pp. 149–197). New York: Cambridge University Press.

Catania, J. A. (1999). A framework for conceptualizing reporting bias and its antecedents in interviews assessing human sexuality. *Journal of Sex Research, 36*, 25–38.

Catania, J. A., Gibson, D. R., Chitwood, D. D., & Coates, T. J. (1990). Methodological problems in AIDS behavioral research: Influences on measurement error and participation bias in studies of sexual behavior. *Psychological Bulletin, 108*, 339–362.

Centers for Disease Control (1990). Selected behaviors that increase risk for HIV infection among high school students: United States. *Morbidity and Mortality Weekly Report, 41*(231), 237–240.

Centers for Disease Control. (2002). Trends in sexual risk behaviors among high school students —United States, 1991–2001. *Morbidity and Mortality Weekly Report, 51*, 856–859.

Centers for Disease Control. (2005). Youth risk behavior surveillance—United States, 2005. *Morbidity and Mortality Weekly Report, 55*, 19–22.

Chilman, C. S. (1978). *Adolescent sexuality in a changing American society: Social and psychological perspectives*. Bethesda, MD: National Institutes of Health.

Chivers, M. L., & Bailey, J. M. (2005). A sex difference in features that elicit genital response. *Biological Psychology, 70*, 115–120.

Chivers, M. L., Rieger, G., Latty, E., & Bailey, J. M. (2005). A sex difference in the specificity of sexual arousal. *Psychological Science, 15*, 736–744.

Clark, A. P. (2006). Are the correlates of sociosexuality different for men and women? *Personality and Individual Differences, 41*, 1321–1327.

Cohen, L. L., & Shotland, R. L. (1996). Timing of first sexual intercourse in a relationship: Expectations, experiences, and perceptions of others. *Journal of Sex Research, 33*, 291–299.

Coker, A. L., McKeown, R. E., Sanderson, M., Davis, K. E., Valois, R. F., & Huebner, E. S. (2000). Severe dating violence and quality of life among South Carolina high school students. *American Journal of Preventive Medicine, 19*, 220–227.

Coker, A. L., Richter, D. L., Valois, R. F., McKeown, R. E., Garrison, C. Z., & Vincent, M. L. (1994). Correlates and consequences of early initiation of sexual intercourse. *Journal of School Health, 64*, 372–377.

Collins, R. L., Elliott, M. N., Berry, S. H., Kanouse, D. E., Kunkel, D., Hunter, S. B., & Miu, A. (2004). Watching sex on television predicts adolescent initiation of sexual behavior. *Pediatrics, 114*, e280–e289.

Cooksey, E. C., Mott, F. L., & Neubauer, S. A. (2002). Friendships and early relationships: Links to sexual initiation among American adolescents born to young mothers. *Perspectives on Sexual and Reproductive Health, 34*(3), 118–126.

Cooper, M. L., Shapiro, C. M., & Powers, A. M. (1998). Motivations for sex and risky sexual behavior among adolescents and young adults: A functional perspective. *Journal of Personality and Social Psychology, 75*, 1528–1558.

Cooper, M. L., Shaver, P. R., & Collins, N. L. (1998). Attachment styles, emotion regulation, and adjustment in adolescence. *Journal of Personality and Social Psychology, 74*, 1380–1397.

Copas, A. J., Wellings, K., Erens, B., Mercer, C. H., McManus, S., Fenton, K. A., Korovessis, C., Macdowall, W. Nanchahal, K., & Johnson, A. M. (2002). The accuracy of reported sensitive sexual behaviour in Britain: Exploring the extent of change 1990–2000. *Sexual Transmission and Infection, 78*, 26–30.

Cornell, J. L. & Halpern-Felsher, B. L. (2006). Adolescents tell us why teens have oral sex. *Journal of Adolescent Health, 38*, 299–301.

Costa, F. M., Jessor, R., Donovan, J. E., & Fortenberry, J. D. (1995). Early initiation of sexual intercourse: The influence of psychosocial unconventionality. *Journal of Research on Adolescence, 5*, 93–121.

Crawford, M., & Popp, D. (2003). Sexual double standards: A review and methodological critique of two decades of research. *Journal of Sex Research, 40*, 13–26.

Crockett, L. J., Bingham, C. R., Chopak, J. S., & Vicary, J. R. (1996). Timing of first sexual intercourse: The role of social control, social learning, and problem behavior. *Journal of Youth and Adolescence, 25*, 89–111.

Crouter, A. C., & Booth, A. (2006). *Romance and sex in adolescence and emerging adulthood: Risks and opportunities*. Mahwah, NJ: Lawrence Erlbaum.

D'Augelli, A. R. (2005). Developmental and contextual factors and mental health among lesbian, gay, and bisexual youths. In A. Omoto & H. Kurtzman (Eds.), *Sexual orientation and mental health: Examining identity and development in lesbian, gay, and bisexual people* (pp. 37-53). Washington, DC: American Psychological Association.

Davies, S. L., DiClemente, R. J., Wingood, G. M., Person, S. D., Dix, E. S., Harrington, K., et al. (2006). Predictors of inconsistent contraceptive use among adolescent girls: Findings from a prospective study. *Journal of Adolescent Health, 39*, 43–49.

Davis, P., & Lay-Yee, R. (1999). Early sex and its behavioral consequences in New Zealand. *Journal of Sex Research, 36*, 135–144.

de Gaston, J. F., Jensen, L., & Weed, S. (1995). A closer look at adolescent sexual activity. *Journal of Youth and Adolescence, 24*, 465–479.

de Graaf, H., & Rademakers, J. (2006). Sexual development of prepubertal children. *Journal of Psychology and Human Sexuality, 18*(1), 1–21.

DeLamater, J., & Friedrich, W. N. (2002). Human sexual development. *Journal of Sex Research, 39*, 10–14.

Denizet-Lewis, B. (2004, May 30). Friends, friends with benefits and the benefits of the local mall. *New York Times Magazine*.

Diamond, L. M. (1998). Development of sexual orientation among adolescent and young adult women. *Developmental Psychology, 34*, 1085–1095.

Diamond, L. M. (2000a). Passionate friendships among adolescent sexual-minority women. *Journal of Research on Adolescence, 10*, 191–209.

Diamond, L. M. (2000b). Sexual identity, attractions, and behavior among young sexual-minority women over a two-year period. *Developmental Psychology, 36*, 241–250.

Diamond, L. M. (2002). "Having a girlfriend without knowing it": The relationships of adolescent lesbian and bisexual women. *Journal of Lesbian Studies, 6*, 5–16.

Diamond, L. M. (2003a). Was it a phase? Explaining changes in women's same-sex sexuality over a 5-year period. *Journal of Personality and Social Psychology, 84*, 352–364.

Diamond, L. M. (2003b). New paradigms for research on sexual-minority and heterosexual youth. *Journal of Clinical Child and Adolescent Pschology, 32*, 490–498.

Diamond, L. M. (2003c). What does sexual orientation orient? A biobehavioral model distinguishing romantic love and sexual desire. *Psychological Review, 110*, 173–192.

Diamond, L. M. (2005). What we got wrong about sexual identity development: Unexpected findings from a longitudinal study of young women. In A. Omoto & H. Kurtzman (Eds.), *Sexual orientation and mental health: Examining identity and development in lesbian, gay, and bisexual people* (pp. 73–94). Washington, DC: American Psychological Association.

Diamond, L. M. (2007). A dynamical systems approach to female same-sex sexuality. *Perspectives on Psychological Science, 2*, 142–161.

Diamond, L. M. (2008a). *Sexual fluidity: Understanding women's love and desire*. Cambridge, MA: Harvard University Press.

Diamond, L. M. (2008b). Female bisexuality from adolescence to adulthood: Results from a 10-year longitudinal study. *Developmental Psychology, 44*, 5–14.

Dickson, N., Paul, C., & Herbison, P. (2003). Same-sex attraction in a birth cohort: Prevalence and persistence in early adulthood. *Social Science & Medicine, 56*, 1607–1615.

di Mauro, D. (1997). Sexuality research in the United States. In J. Bancroft (Ed.), *Researching sexual behavior: Methodological issues* (pp. 3–8). Bloomington, IN: Indiana University Press.

Dittus, P. J., Jaccard, J., & Gordon, V. V. (1997). The impact of African American fathers on adolescent sexual behavior. *Journal of Youth and Adolescence, 26,* 445–465.

Donald, M., Lucke, J., Dunne, M., & Raphael, B. (1995). Gender differences associated with young people's emotional reactions to sexual intercourse. *Journal of Youth and Adolescence, 24,* 453–464.

Dubé, E. M. (2000). Sexual identity and intimacy development among two cohorts of sexual-minority men. The role of sexual behavior in the identification process of gay and bisexual males. *Journal of Sex Research, 37,* 123–132.

DuRant, R. H., Krowchuk, D. P., & Sinal, S. H. (1998). Victimization, use of violence, and drug use at school among male adolescents who engage in same-sex sexual behavior. *Journal of Pediatrics, 132,* 113–118.

Durbin, M., DiClemente, R. J., Siegel, D., & Krasnovsky, F. (1993). Factors associated with multiple sex partners among junior high school students. *Journal of Adolescent Health, 14,* 202–207.

Eccles, J. S., Wigfield, A., & Byrnes, J. (2003). Cognitive development in adolescence. In R. M. Lerner, M. A. Easterbrooks & J. Mistry (Eds.), *Handbook of psychology: Developmental psychology,* vol. 6 (pp. 325–350). Hoboken, NJ: John Wiley & Sons Inc.

Ehrhardt, A. A. (1996). Our view of adolescent sexuality: A focus on risk behavior without the developmental context. *American Journal of Public Health, 86,* 1523–1525.

Eisenberg, M. E., Bernat, D. H., Bearinger, L. H., & Resnick. M. D. (2008). Support for comprehensive sexuality education: Perspectives from parents of school-age youth. *Journal of Adolescent Health, 42,* 352–359.

Eisenberg, N., Fabes, R. A., & Spinrad, T. L. (2006). Prosocial development. In N. Eisenberg (Ed.), *Handbook of child psychology, vol. 3: Social, emotional, and personality development* (6th ed.) (pp. 646–718). Hoboken, NJ: John Wiley & Sons.

Ellis, B. J. (2004). Timing of pubertal maturation in girls: An integrated life history approach. *Psychological Bulletin, 130,* 920–958.

Ellis, B. J. (2005). Determinants of pubertal timing: An evolutionary developmental approach. In B. J. Ellis & D. F. Bjorklund (Eds.), *Origins of the social mind: Evolutionary psychology and child development.* (pp. 164–188). New York: Guilford Press.

Ellis, B. J., & Essex, M. J. (2007). Family environments, adrenarche, and sexual maturation: A longitudinal test of a life history model. *Child Development, 78,* 1799–1817.

Ellis, B. J., & Symons, D. (1990). Sex differences in sexual fantasy: An evolutionary psychological approach. *Journal of Sex Research, 27,* 527–555.

Eskin, M., Kaynak-Demir, H., & Demir, S. (2005). Same-sex sexual orientation, childhood sexual abuse, and suicidal behavior in university students in Turkey. *Archives of Sexual Behavior, 34,* 185–195.

Everett, S. A., Warren, C. W., Santelli, J. S., Kann, L., Collins, J. L., & Kolbe, L. J. (2000). Use of birth control pills, condoms, and withdrawal among U.S. high school students. *Journal of Adolescent Health, 27,* 112–118.

Fan, X., Miller, B. C., Park, K. E., Winward, B. W., Christensen, M., Grotevant, H. D., et al. (2006). An exploratory study about inaccuracy and invalidity in adolescent self-report surveys. *Field Methods, 18,* 1–22.

Feldman, S. S., Turner, R. A., & Araujo, K. (1999). Interpersonal context as an influence on sexual timetables of youths: Gender and ethnic effects. *Journal of Research on Adolescence, 9,* 25–52.

Fine, M. (1988). Sexuality, schooling, and adolescent females: The missing discourse of desire. *Harvard Educational Review, 58,* 29–53.

Fine, M., & McClelland, S. I. (2006). Sexuality education and desire: Still missing after all these years. *Harvard Educational Review, 76,* 297–338.

Finer, L. B. (2007). Trends in premarital sex in the United States, 1954–2003. *Public Health Reports, 122,* 73–78.

Fineran, S., Bennett, L., & Sacco, T. (2003). Peer sexual harassment and peer violence among adolescents in Johannesburg and Chicago. *International Social Work, 46,* 387–401.

Fisher, H. E. (1998). Lust, attraction, and attachment in mammalian reproduction. *Human Nature, 9,* 23–52.

Flannery, D. J., Rowe, D. C., & Gulley, B. L. (1993). Impact of pubertal status, timing, and age on adolescent sexual experience and delinquency. *Journal of Adolescent Research, 8,* 21–40.

Florsheim, P. (Ed.). (2003). *Adolescent romantic relations and sexual behavior: Theory, research, and practical implications.* Mahwah, NJ: Erlbaum.

Fordham, S. (1993). "Those loud black girls": (Black) women, silence, and gender "passing" in the academy. *Anthropology and Education Quarterly, 24,* 3–32.

Fortenberry, J. D. (1997). Number of sexual partners and adolescent health lifestyle: Use of the AMA's Guidelines for Adolescent Preventive Services to address a basic research question. *Archives of Pediatric and Adolescent Medicine, 151,* 1139–1143.

Foshee, V. A., Bauman, K. E., Greene, W. F., Koch, G. G., Linder, G. F., & MacDougall, J. E. (2000). The safe dates program: 1-year follow-up results. *American Journal of Public Health, 90,* 1619–1622.

Foshee, V. A., Benefield, T., Ennett, S. T., Bauman, K. E., & Suchindran, C. (2004). Longitudinal predictors of serious physical and sexual dating violence victimization during adolescence. *Preventive Medicine, 19,* 220–227.

Foster, H., Hagan, J., & Brooks-Gunn, J. (2004). Age, puberty, and exposure to intimate partner violence in adolescence. In J.Devine, J.Gilligan, K. A.Miczek, R.Shaikh, & D.Pfaff (Eds.), *Youth violence: Scientific approaches to prevention.* (pp. 151–166). New York: New York Academy of Sciences.

Friedrich, W. N., Grambsch, P., Broughton, D., Kuiper, J., & Beilke, R. L. (1991). Normative sexual behavior in children. *Pediatrics, 88,* 456–464.

Frye, M. (1990). Lesbian "sex." In J. Allen (Ed.), *Lesbian philosophies and cultures.* Albany: State University of New York Press.

Furman, W., Brown, B. B., & Feiring, C. (Eds.). (1999). *The development of romantic relationships in adolescence.* New York: Cambridge University Press.

Furman, W., & Hand, L. S. (2006). The slippery nature of romantic relationships: Issues in definition and differentiation. In A. C. Crouter & A.Booth (Eds.), *Romance and sex in adolescence and emerging adulthood: Risks and opportunities.* (pp. 171–178). Mahwah, NJ: Lawrence Erlbaum.

Gable, S. L., & Reis, H. T. (1999). Now and then, them and us, this and that: Studying relationships across time, partner, context, and person. *Personal Relationships, 6,* 415–432.

Gagnon, J. H. (1985). Attitudes and responses of parents to preadolescent masturbation. *Archives of Sexual Behavior, 14,* 451–466.

Gagnon, J. H., & Simon, W. (1973). *Sexual conduct: The social sources of human sexuality.* Chicago: Aldine.

Gardner, W., & Wilcox, B. L. (1993). Political intervention in scientific peer review: Research on adolescent sexual behavior. *American Psychologist, 48,* 972–983.

Garofalo, R., Wolf, R. C., Wissow, L. S., Woods, E. R., & Goodman, E. (1999). Sexual orientation and risk of suicide attempts among a representative sample of youth. *Archives of Pediatrics and Adolescent Medicine, 153,* 487–493.

Ge, X., Natsuaki, M. N., Neiderhiser, J. M., & Reiss, D. (2007). Genetic and environmental influences on pubertal timing: Results from two national sibling studies. *Journal of Research on Adolescence, 17,* 767–788.

Gerrard, M. (1987). Emotional and cognitive barriers to effective contraception: Are males and females really different? In K.Kelley (Ed.), *Females, males, and sexuality: Theories and research.* (pp. 213–242). Albany: State University of New York Press.

Giordano, P. C., Manning, W. D., & Longmore, M. A. (2006). Adolescent romantic relationships: An emerging portrait of their nature and developmental significance. In A. C. Crouter & A. Booth (Eds.), *Romance and sex in adolescence and emerging adulthood: Risks and opportunities* (pp. 127–150). Mahwah, NJ: Lawrence Erlbaum.

Golden, C. (1996). What's in a name? Sexual self-identification among women. In R. C. Savin-Williams & K. M. Cohen (Eds.), *The lives of lesbians, gays, and bisexuals: Children to adults* (pp. 229–249). Fort Worth, TX: Harcourt Brace.

Goodson, P., Evans, A., & Edmundson, E. (1997). Female adolescents and onset of sexual intercourse: A theory-based review of research from 1984 to 1994. *Journal of Adolescent Health, 21,* 147–156.

Graham, J. W., & Hofer, S. M. (2000). Multiple imputation in multivariate research. In T. D. Little & K. U. Schnabel (Eds.), *Modeling longitudinal and multilevel data: Practical issues, applied approaches, and specific examples.* (pp. 201-218, 269-281). Mahwah, NJ: Lawrence Erlbaum.

Greenfield, P. M. (2004). Inadvertent exposure to pornography on the Internet: Implications of peer-to-peer file-sharing networks for child development and families. *Journal of Applied Developmental Psychology, 25,* 741–750.

Grello, C. M., Welsh, D. P., Harper, M. S., & Dickson, J. W. (2003). Dating and sexual relationship trajectories and adolescent functioning, *Adolescent and Family Health, 3,* 103–111.

Grello, C. M., Welsh, D. P., & Harper, M. S. (2006). No strings attached: The nature of casual sex in college students. *Journal of Sex Research, 43,* 255–267.

Greiling, H., & Buss, D. M. (2000). Women's sexual strategies: The hidden dimension of extra-pair mating. *Personality and Individual Differences, 28,* 929–963.

Grov, C., Bimbi, D. S., Nanin, J. E., & Parsons, J. T. (2006). Race, ethnicity, gender, and generational factors associated with the coming-out process among gay, lesbian, and bisexual individuals. *Journal of Sex Research, 43,* 115–121.

Gullotta, T. P., Adams, G. R., & Montemayor, R. (Eds.). (1993). *Adolescent sexuality.* Newbury Park, CA: Sage.

Halpern, C. T. (2003). Biological influences on adolescent romantic and sexual behavior. In P. Florsheim (Ed.), *Adolescent romantic relations and sexual behavior: Theory, research, and practical implications.* Mahwah, NJ: Lawrence Erlbaum.

Halpern, C. T., Joyner, K., Udry, J. R., & Suchindran, C. (2000). Smart teens don't have sex (or kiss much either). *Journal of Adolescent Health, 26,* 213–225.

Halpern, C. T., Kaestle, C. E., & Hallfors, D. D. (2007). Perceived physical maturity, age of romantic partner, and adolescent risk behavior. *Prevention Science: The Official Journal of the Society for Prevention Research, 8,* 1–10.

Halpern, C. T., Udry, J. R., Campbell, B., & Suchindran, C. (1993). Testosterone and pubertal development as predictors of sexual activity: A panel analysis of adolescent males. *Psychosomatic Medicine, 55,* 436–447.

Halpern, C. T., Udry, J. R., Suchindran, C., & Campbell, B. (2000). Adolescent males' willingness to report masturbation. *Journal of Sex Research, 37,* 327–332.

Halpern, C. T., Udry, J. R., Campbell, B., & Suchindran, C. (1993). Testosterone and pubertal development as predictors of sexual activity: A panel analysis of adolescent males. *Psychosomatic Medicine, 55,* 436–447.

Halpern, C. T., Waller, M. W., Spriggs, A., & Hallfors, D. D. (2006). Adolescent predictors of emerging adult sexual patterns. *Journal of Adolescent Health, 39,* e1–e10.

Halpern-Felsher, B. L., Cornell, J. L., Kropp, R. Y., & Tschann, J. M. (2005). Oral versus vaginal sex among adolescents: perceptions, attitudes, and behavior. *Pediatrics, 115,* 845–851.

Harvey, S. M., & Spigner, C. (1995). Factors associated with sexual behavior among adolescents: A multivariate analysis. *Adolescence, 30,* 253–264.

Hatzenbuehler, M. L., Corbin, W. R., & Fromme, K. (2008). Trajectories and determinants of alcohol use among LGB young

adults and their heterosexual peers: Results from a prospective study. *Developmental Psychology, 44*(1), 81–90.

Hawk, S. T., Vanwesenbeeck, I., de Graaf, H., & Bakker, F. (2006). Adolescents' contact with sexuality in mainstream media: A selection-based perspective. *Journal of Sex Research, 43,* 352–363.

Heiman, J. R. (1975). The physiology of erotica: Women's sexual arousal. *Psychology Today, 8,* 90–94.

Henshaw, S. K. (1998). Barriers to access to abortion services. In L. J. Beckman & S. M. Harvey (Eds.), *The new civil war: The psychology, culture, and politics of abortion.* (pp. 61–80). Washington, DC: American Psychological Association.

Herdt, G., & Boxer, A. M. (1993). *Children of Horizons: How gay and lesbian teens are leading a new way out of the closet.* Boston: Beacon Press.

Herek, G. M. (2000). The psychology of sexual prejudice. *Current Directions in Psychological Science, 9,* 19–22.

Hoefferth, S. L. (1990). Trends in adolescent sexual activity, contraception, and pregnancy in the United States. In J. H. Bancroft & J. M. Reinisch (Eds.), *Adolescence and puberty* (pp. 217–233). New York: Oxford University Press.

Hopkins, K. W. (2000). Testing Reiss's autonomy theory on changes in non-marital coital attitudes and behaviors of U.S. teenagers: 1960–1990. *Scandinavian Journal of Sexology, 3,* 113–125.

Howard, D. E., & Wang, M. Q. (2005). Psychosocial correlates of U.S. adolescents who report a history of forced sexual intercourse. *Journal of Adolescent Health, 36,* 372–379.

Howard, D. E., Wang, M. Q., & Yan, F. (2007). Prevalence and psychosocial correlates of forced sexual intercourse among U.S. high school adolescents. *Adolescence, 42,* 629–643.

Hrdy, S. B. (1987). The primate origins of human sexuality. In R. Bellig & G. Stevens (Eds.), *The evolution of sex* (pp. 101–132). San Francisco: Harper & Row.

Hughes, M., Morrison, K., & Asada, K. J. K. (2005). What's love got to do with it? Exploring the impact of maintenance rules, love attitudes, and network support on friends with benefits relationships. *Western Journal of Communication, 69,* 49–66.

Impett, E. A., Schooler, D., & Tolman, D. L. (2006). To be seen and not heard: Femininity ideology and adolescent girls' sexual health. *Archives of Sexual Behavior, 35,* 131–144.

Jemmott, J. B. I., Jemmott, L. S., & Fong, G. T. (1998). Abstinence and safer sex HIV risk-reduction interventions for African American adolescents. *JAMA: Journal of the American Medical Association, 279,* 1529–1536.

Jemmott, J. B. I., Jemmott, L. S., Fong, G. T., & McCaffree, K. (1999). Reducing HIV risk-associated sexual behavior among African American adolescents: Testing the generality of intervention effects. *American Journal of Community Psychology, 27,* 161–187.

Jessor, S. L., & Jessor, R. (1975). Transition from virginity to nonvirginity among youth: A social–psychological study over time. *Developmental Psychology, 11,* 473–484.

Jones, R. K., Purcell, A., Singh, S., & Finer, L. B. (2005). Adolescents' reports of parental knowledge of adolescents' use of sexual health services and their reactions to mandated parental notification for prescription contraception. *Journal of the American Medical Association, 293,* 340–348.

Kaestle, C., & Halpern, C. T. (2007). What's love got to do with it? Sexual behaviors of opposite sex couples through emerging adulthood. *Perspectives on Sexual and Reproductive Health, 39,* 134–140.

Kahn, J. A., Huang, B., Rosenthal, S. L., Tissot, A. M., & Burk, R. D. (2005). Coercive sexual experiences and subsequent human papillomavirus infection and squamous intraepithelial lesions in adolescent and young adult women. *Journal of Adolescent Health, 36,* 363–371.

Kalof, L. (1995). Sex, power, and dependency: The politics of adolescent sexuality. *Journal of Youth and Adolescence, 24,* 229–249.

Kan, M. L., & Cares, A. C. (2006). From "friends with benefits" to "going steady": New directions in understanding romance and sex in adolescence and emerging adulthood. In A. C. Crouter & A. Booth (Eds.), *Romance and sex in adolescence and emerging adulthood: Risks and opportunities.* (pp. 241–258). Mahwah, NJ: Lawrence Erlbaum.

Kegan, R. (1996). Neither "safe sex" nor "abstinence" may work—now what? Toward a third norm for youthful sexuality. In D. Cicchetti & S. L. Toth (Eds.), *Adolescence: Opportunities and challenges. Rochester symposium on developmental psychopathology*, vol. 7 (pp. 125–147). Rochester, NY: University of Rochester Press.

Kelley, S. S., Borawski, E. A., Flocke, S. A., & Keen, K. J. (2003). The role of sequential and concurrent sexual relationships in the risk of sexually transmitted diseases among adolescents. *Journal of Adolescent Health, 32*, 296–305.

Keyes, C. L. M. (2005). Mental illness and/or mental health? Investigating axioms of the complete state model of health. *Journal of Consulting and Clinical Psychology, 73*, 539–548.

Kinnish, K. K., Strassberg, D. S., & Turner, C. W. (2005). Sex differences in the flexibility of sexual orientation: A multidimensional retrospective assessment. *Archives of Sexual Behavior, 34*, 173–183.

Kinsey, A. C., Pomeroy, W. B., & Martin, C. E. (1948). *Sexual behavior in the human male*. Philadelphia: W. B. Saunders.

Kinsey, A. C., Pomeroy, W. B., Martin, C. E., & Gebhard, P. H. (1953). *Sexual behavior in the human female*. Philadelphia: W. B. Saunders.

Kinsman, S. B., Romer, D., Furstenberg, F. F., & Schwartz, D. F. (1998). Early sexual initiation: The role of peer norms. *Pediatrics, 102*, 1185–1192.

Kirby, D. (2002). The impact of schools and school programs upon adolescent sexual behavior. *Journal of Sex Research, 39*, 27–33.

Knoth, R., Boyd, K., & Singer, B. (1988). Empirical tests of sexual selection theory: Predictions of sex differences in onset, intensity, and time course of sexual arousal. *Journal of Sex Research, 24*, 73–89.

Kohler, P. K., Manhart, L. E., & Lafferty, W. E. (2008). Abstinence-only and comprehensive sex education and the initiation of sexual activity and teen pregnancy. *Journal of Adolescent Health, 42*, 344–351.

Kuczynski, A. (2002, November 3). She's got to be a macho girl. *New York Times*, section 9, pp. 1, 12.

Kupek, E. (2001). Sexual attitudes and number of partners in young British men. *Archives of Sexual Behavior, 30*, 13–27.

Laan, E., Everaerd, W., van Bellen, G., & Hanewald, G. (1994). Women's sexual and emotional responses to male- and female-produced erotica. *Archives of Sexual Behavior, 23*, 153–170.

Lam, T. H., Shi, H. J., Ho, L. M., Stewart, S. M., & Fan, S. (2002). Timing of pubertal maturation and heterosexual behavior among Hong Kong Chinese adolescents. *Archives of Sexual Behavior, 31*, 359–366.

Lam, T. H., Stewart, S. M., Leung, G. M., Lee, P. W. H., Wong, J. P. S., & Ho, L. M. (2004). Depressive symptoms among Hong Kong adolescents: Relation to atypical sexual feelings and behaviors, gender dissatisfaction, pubertal timing, and family and peer relationships. *Archives of Sexual Behavior, 33*, 487–496.

Laqueur, T. W. (2003). *Solitary sex: A cultural history of masturbation*. New York: Zone Books.

Larsson, I., & Svedin, C. G. (2002). Sexual experiences in childhood: Young adults' recollections. *Archives of Sexual Behavior, 31*, 263–273.

Laumann, E. O., Gagnon, J. H., Michael, R. T., & Michaels, S. (1994). *The social organization of sexuality: Sexual practices in the United States*. Chicago: University of Chicago Press.

Laumann, E. O., Paik, A., & Rosen, R. C. (1999). Sexual dysfunction in the United States: Prevalence and predictors. *Journal of the American Medical Association, 281*, 537–544.

Lehalle, H. (2006). Cognitive development in adolescence: Thinking freed from concrete constraints. In S. Jackson & L. Goossens (Eds.), *Handbook of adolescent development*. (pp. 71–89). New York: Psychology Press.

Leitenberg, H., Detzer, M. J., & Srebnik, D. (1993). Gender differences in masturbation and the relation of masturbation experience in preadolescence and/or early adolescence to sexual behavior and sexual adjustment in young adulthood. *Archives of Sexual Behavior, 22*, 87–98.

Leitenberg, H., & Henning, K. (1995). Sexual fantasy. *Psychological Bulletin, 117*, 469–496.

Leitenberg, H., & Saltzman, H. (2000). A statewide survey of age at first intercourse for adolescent females and age of their male partners: Relation to other risk behaviors and statutory rape implications. *Archives of Sexual Behavior, 29*, 203–215.

L'Engle, K.L., Brown, J. D., Kenneavy, K. (2006). The mass media are an important context for adolescents' sexual behavior, *Journal of Adolescent Health, 38*, 186–192.

Levesque, R. J. R. (2000). *Adolescents, sex, and the law: Preparing adolescents for responsible citizenship*. Washington, DC: American Psychological Association.

Levin, D. E. (2005). So sexy, so soon: The sexualization of childhood. In S. Olfman (Ed.), *Childhood lost: How American culture is failing our kids*. (pp. 137–153). Westport, CT: Praeger Publishers/Greenwood Publishing Group.

Levine, J. (2002). *Harmful to minors: The perils of protecting children from sex*. Minneapolis: University of Minnesota Press.

Levinson, R. A., Jaccard, J., & Beamer, L. (1995). Older adolescents' engagement in casual sex: Impact of risk perception and psychosocial motivations. *Journal of Youth and Adolescence, 24*, 349–364.

Lippa, R. A. (2006). Is high sex drive associated with increased sexual attraction to both sexes? It depends on whether you are male or female. *Psychological Science, 17*, 46–52.

Lippa, R. A. (2007). The relation between sex drive and sexual attraction to men and women: A cross-national study of heterosexual, bisexual, and homosexual men and women. *Archives of Sexual Behavior, 36*, 209–222.

Longmore, M. A., Manning, W. D., Giordano, P. C., & Rudolph, J. L. (2003). Contraceptive self-efficacy: Does it influence adolescents' contraceptive use? *Journal of Health and Social Behavior, 44*, 45–60.

Lynch, C. O. (2001). Risk and protective factors associated with adolescent sexual activity. *Adolescent and Family Health, 2*, 99–107.

Maccoby, E. E. (1998). *The two sexes: Growing up apart and coming together*. Cambridge, MA: Belknap Press.

Manlove, J., Terry-Humen, E., Papillo, A. R., Franzetta, K., Williams, S., & Ryan, S. (2001). *Background for community-level work on positive reproductive health in adolescence: Reviewing the literature on contributing factors*. Washington, DC: Child Trends.

Manning, W. D., Longmore, M. A., & Giordano, P. C. (2000). The relationship context of contraceptive use at first intercourse. *Family Planning Perspectives, 32*, 104–110.

McClintock, M. K., & Herdt, G. (1996). Rethinking puberty: The development of sexual attraction. *Current Directions in Psychological Science, 5*, 178–183.

McLaughlin, C. S., Chen, C., Greenberger, E., & Biermeier, C. (1997). Family, peer, and individual correlates of sexual experience among Caucasian and Asian American late adolescents. *Journal of Research on Adolescence, 7*, 33–53.

Meier, A. M. (2007). Adolescent first sex and subsequent mental health. *American Journal of Sociology, 112*, 1811–1847.

Meston, C. M., & Buss, M. P. (2007). Why humans have sex? *Archives of Sexual Behavior, 36*, 477–507.

Metzler, C. W., Noell, J., Biglan, A., Ary, D., & et al. (1994). The social context for risky sexual behavior among adolescents. *Journal of Behavioral Medicine, 17*, 419–438.

Milhausen, R. R., & Herold, E. S. (2001). Reconceptualizing the sexual double standard. *Journal of Psychology and Human Sexuality, 13*, 63–83.

Miller, B., & Moore, K. (1990). Adolescent sexual behavior, pregnancy, and parenting: Research through the 1980's. *Journal of Marriage and the Family, 52*, 1025–1044.

Miller, B. C. (2002). Family influences on adolescent sexual and contraceptive behavior. *Journal of Sex Research, 39*, 22–26.

Miller, B. C., & Benson, B. (1999). Romantic and sexual relationship development during adolescence. In W. Furman, B. B.Brown, & C. Feiring (Eds.), *The development of romantic relationships in adolescence* (pp. 99–121). New York: Cambridge University Press.

Miller, B. C., Norton, M. C., Curtis, T., Hill, E. J., Schvaneveldt, P., & Young, M. H. (1997). The timing of sexual intercourse among adolescents: Family, peer, and other antecedents. *Youth and Society, 29*, 54–83.

Miller, L., & Gur, M. (2002). Religiousness and sexual responsibility in adolescent girls. *Journal of Adolescent Health, 31*, 401–406.

Monahan, K. C., & Lee, J. M. (2008). Adolescent sexual activity: Links between relational context and depressive symptoms. *Journal of Youth and Adolescence, 37*, 917–927.

Moore, S., & Rosenthal, D. (1993). *Sexuality in adolescence*. New York: Routledge.

Morgan Thompson, E., & Morgan, E. M. (2008). "Mostly straight" young women: Variations in sexual behavior and identity development. *Developmental Psychology, 44*, 15–21.

Mosher, W. D., Chandra, A., & Jones, J. (2005, September 15). Sexual behavior and selected health measures: Men and women 15–44 years of age, United States, 2002. *Advance Data: Vital and Health Statistics,* Number 362. Hyattsville, MD: U.S. Department of Health and Human Services, Centers for Disease Control and Prevention, National Center for Health Statistics.

Musick, J. S. (1993). *Young, poor, and pregnant: The psychology of teenage motherhood*. New Haven, CT: Yale University Press.

Myers, D. G. (2000). The funds, friends, and faith of happy people. *American Psychologist, 55*(1), 56–67.

Neumark-Sztainer, D., Story, M., French, S. A., & Resnick, M. D. (1997). Psychosocial correlates of health compromising behaviors among adolescents. *Health Education Research, 12*, 37–52.

Newcomer, S., & Udry, J. R. (1988). Adolescents' honesty in a survey of sexual behavior. *Journal of Adolescent Research, 3*, 419–423.

Nieto, J. A. (2004). Children and adolescents as sexual beings: Cross-cultural perspectives. *Child and Adolescent Psychiatric Clinics of North America, 13*, 461–477.

Ochs, E. P., & Binik, Y. M. (1999). The use of couple data to determine the reliability of self-reported sexual behavior. *Journal of Sex Research, 36*, 374–384.

Okami, P., Olmstead, R., & Abramson, P. R. (1997). Sexual experiences in early childhood: 18-year longitudinal data from the UCLA family lifestyles project. *Journal of Sex Research, 34*, 339–347.

Oliver, M. B., & Hyde, J. S. (1993). Gender differences in sexuality: A meta-analysis. *Psychological Bulletin, 114*, 29–51.

O'Sullivan, L., & Byers, E. S. (1992). College students' incorporation of initiator and restrictor roles in sexual dating interactions. *Journal of Sex Research, 29*, 435–446.

O'Sullivan, L. F., & Meyer-Bahlburg, H. F. L. (2003). African American and Latina inner-city girls' reports of romantic and sexual development. *Journal of Social and Personal Relationships, 20*, 221–238.

O'Sullivan, L. F., Meyer-Bahlburg, H. F. L., & Watkins, B. X. (2000). Social cognitions associated with pubertal development in a sample of urban, low-income, African-American and Latina girls and mothers. *Journal of Adolescent Health, 27*, 227–235.

O'Sullivan, L. F., Meyer-Bahlburg, H. F. L., & Watkins, B. X. (2001). Mother-daughter communication about sex among urban African American and Latino families. *Journal of Adolescent Research, 16*, 269–292.

Papadopoulos, N. G., Stamboulides, P., & Triantafillou, T. (2000). The psychosexual development and behavior of university students: A nationwide survey in Greece. *Journal of Psychology and Human Sexuality, 11*, 93–110.

Parsons, J. T., Halkitis, P. N., Bimbi, D., & Borkowski, T. (2000). Perceptions of the benefits and costs associated with condom use and unprotected sex among late adolescent college students. *Journal of Adolescence, 23*, 377–391.

Patrick, M. E., Maggs, K. L., & Abar, C. C. (2007). Reasons to have sex, personal goals, and sexual behavior during the transition to college. *Journal of Sex Research, 44*(3), 240–249.

Paul, C., Fitzjohn, J., Herbison, P., & Dickson, N. (2000). The determinants of sexual intercourse before age 16. *Journal of Adolescent Health, 27*, 136–147.

Paul, E. L., & Hayes, K. A. (2002). The causalities of 'casual' sex: A qualitative exploration of the phenomenology of college students' hookups. *Journal of Social and Personal Relationships, 19*, 639–661.

Peplau, L. A., & Garnets, L. D. (2000). A new paradigm for understanding women's sexuality. *Journal of Social Issues, 56*, 329–350.

Peterson, Z. D., & Muehlenhard, C. L. (2007). What is sex and why does it matter? A motivational approach to exploring individuals' definitions of sex. *Journal of Sex Research, 44*, 256–268.

Pinsky, D. (2002, August 23–25). The sex lives of kids. *USA Weekend* (pp. 6–7).

Pitts, M., & Rahman, Q. (2001). Which behaviors constitute "having sex" among university students in the UK? *Archives of Sexual Behavior, 30*, 169–176.

Ponton, L. (2000). *The sex lives of teenagers: Revealing the secret world of adolescent boys and girls*. New York: Penguin Putman.

Prince, A., & Bernard, A. L. (1998). Sexual behaviors and safer sex practices of college students on a commuter campus. *Journal of American College Health, 47*, 11–21.

Prinstein, M. J., Meade, C. S., & Cohen, G. L. (2003). Adolescent oral sex, peer popularity, and perceptions of best friend's sexual behavior. *Journal of Pediatric Psychology, 28*, 243–249.

Raghavan, R., Bogart, L. M., Elliott, M. N., Vestal, K. D., & Shuster, M. A. (2004). Sexual victimization among a national probability sample of adolescent women. *Perspectives on Sexual and Reproductive Health, 36*, 225–232.

Regan, P. C., & Berscheid, E. (1995). Gender differences in beliefs about the causes of male and female sexual desire. *Personal Relationships, 2*, 345–358.

Regan, P. C., & Dreyer, C. S. (1999). Lust? Love? Status? Young adults' motives for engaging in casual sex. *Journal of Psychology and Human Sexuality, 11*, 1–24.

Reinisch, J. M., & Sanders, S. A. (1999). Attitudes toward and definitions of having sex: In reply. *Journal of the American Medical Association, 282*(20), 1918–1919.

Reise, S. P., & Wright, T. M. (1996). Brief report: Personality traits, cluster B personality disorders, and sociosexuality. *Journal of Research in Personality, 30*, 128–136.

Remafedi, G., Resnick, M., Blum, R., & Harris, L. (1992). Demography of sexual orientation in adolescents. *Pediatrics, 89*, 714–721.

Resnick, M. D., Bearman, P. S., Blum, R. W., Bauman, K. E., Harris, K. M., Jones, J., Tabor, J., Beuhring, T., Sieving, R. E., Shew, M., Ireland, M., Bearinger, L. H., & Udry, J. R. (1997). Protecting adolescents from harm, findings from the national longitudinal study on adolescent health. *Journal of American Medical Association, 278*, 823–832.

Rieger, G., Linsenmeier, J. A. W., Gygaz, L., & Bailey, J. M. (2008). Sexual orientation and childhood nonconformity: Evidence from home videos. *Developmental Psychology, 44*(1), 46–58.

Rind, B. (2001). Gay and bisexual adolescent boys' sexual experiences with men: An empirical examination of psychological correlates in a nonclinical sample. *Archives of Sexual Behavior, 30*, 345–368.

Rodgers, J. L., Billy, J. O. G., & Udry, J. R. (1982). The rescission of behaviors: Inconsistent responses in adolescent sexuality data. *Social Science Research, 11*, 280–296.

Rodríguez Rust, P. C. (2000). Bisexuality: A contemporary paradox for women. *Journal of Social Issues, 56*, 205–221.

Roisman, G. I., Clausell, E. Holland, A., Fortuna, K., & Elieff, C. (2008). Adult romantic relationships as contexts of human development: A multimethod comparison of same-sex couples with opposite-sex dating, engaged, and married dyads. *Developmental Psychology, 44*(1), 91–101.

Rosario, M., Meyer-Bahlburg, H. F., Hunter, J., Exner, T. M., Gwadz, M., & Keller, A. M. (1996). The psychosexual development of urban lesbian, gay, and bisexual youths. *Journal of Sex Research, 33*, 113–126.

Rose, S. (2000). Heterosexism and the study of women's romantic and friend relationships. *Journal of Social Issues, 56*, 315–328.

Rosenbaum, J. E. (2006). Reborn a virgin: Adolescents' retracting of virginity pledges and sexual histories. *American Journal of Public Health, 96*, 1078–1103.

Rosenthal, D. A., & Smith, A. M. A. (1997). Adolescent sexual timetables. *Journal of Youth and Adolescence, 26*, 619–636.

Rothblum, E. D. (2000). Sexual orientation and sex in women's lives: Conceptual and methodological issues. *Journal of Social Issues, 56*, 193–204.

Ryan, S., Franzetta, K., & Manlove, J. (2007). Knowledge, perceptions, and motivations for contraception: Influence on teens' contraceptive consistency. *Youth & Society, 39*, 182–208.

Sanders, S. A., & Reinisch, J. M. (1999). Would you say you "had sex" if…? *Journal of the American Medical Association, 281*, 275–277.

Sandfort, T. G. M. (1992). The argument for adult-child sex: A critical appraisal and new data. In W. O'Donohue & J. H. Geer (Eds.), *The sexual abuse of children, vol. 1: Theory and research* (pp. 38–48). Hillside, NJ: Lawrence Erlbaum.

Sandfort, T. G. M., Hubert, M., Bajos, N., & Bus, H. (1998). Sexual behavior and HIV risk: Common patterns and differences between European countries. In M. Hubert, N. Bajos & T. G. M. Sandfort (Eds.), *Sexual Behavior and HIV/AIDS in Europe* (pp. 403–426). London: UCL Press.

Santelli, J. S., Lindberg, L. D., Finer, L. B., & Singh, S. (2007). Explaining recent declines in adolescent pregnancy in the United States: The contribution of abstinence and improved contraceptive use. *American Journal of Public Health, 97*, 150–156.

Santelli, J. S., Lowry, R., Brener, N. D., & Robin, L. (2000). The association of sexual behaviors with socioeconomic status, family structure, and race/ethnicity among US adolescents. *American Journal of Public Health, 90*, 1582–1588.

Savin-Williams, R. C. (1998). *"…and then I became gay": Young men's stories*. New York: Routledge.

Savin-Williams, R. C. (2001). A critique of research on sexual-minority youths. *Journal of Adolescence, 24*, 15–23.

Savin-Williams, R. C. (2004). Boy-on-boy sexuality. In N. Way & J. Y. Chu (Eds.), *Adolescent boys: Exploring diverse cultures of boyhood* (pp. 271–292). New York: New York University Press.

Savin-Williams, R. C. (2005). *The new gay teenager*. Cambridge, MA: Harvard University Press.

Savin-Williams, R. C. (2006). Who's gay? Does it matter? *Current Directions in Psychological Science, 15*, 40–44.

Savin-Williams, R. C. (2007). Girl-on-girl sexuality. In B. J. R. Leadbeater & N. Way (Eds.), *Urban girls revisited: Building strengths* (pp. 301–318). New York: New York University Press.

Savin-Williams, R. C. (2008). Then and now: Recruitment, definition, diversity, and positive attributes of same-sex populations. *Developmental Psychology, 44*(1), 135–138.

Savin-Williams, R. C., & Diamond, L. M. (2000). Sexual identity trajectories among sexual-minority youths: Gender comparisons. *Archives of Sexual Behavior, 29*, 419–440.

Savin-Williams, R. C., & Ream, G. L. (2007). Prevalence and stability of sexual orientation components during adolescence and young adulthood. *Archives of Sexual Behavior, 36*, 385–394.

Sawyer, R. G., & Smith, N. G. (1996). A survey of situational factors at first intercourse among college students. *American Journal of Health Behavior, 20*, 208–217.

Schafer, J. L. (2001). Multiple imputation with PAN. In L. M. Collins & A. G. Sayer (Eds.), *New methods for the analysis of change* (pp. 357–377). Washington, DC: American Psychological Association.

Schafer, J. L., & Graham, J. W. (2002). Missing data: Our view of the state of the art. *Psychological Methods, 7*, 147–177.

Schalet, A. (2007). Adolescent sexuality viewed through two different cultural lenses. In M. S. Tepper & A. F. Owens (Eds.), *Sexual health Vol 3: Moral and cultural foundations* (pp. 365–387). Westport, CT: Praeger Publishers/Greenwood Publishing.

Schmitt, D. P. (2005). Is short-term mating the maladaptive result of insecure attachment? A test of competing evolutionary perspectives. *Personality and Social Psychology Bulletin, 31*, 747–768.

Schoentjes, E., Deboutte, D., & Friedrich, W. (1999). Child sexual behavior inventory: A Dutch-speaking normative sample. *Pediatrics, 104*(4), 885–893.

Schuster, M. A., Bell, R. M., & Kanouse, D. E. (1996). The sexual practices of adolescent virgins: Genital sexual activities of high school students who have never had vaginal intercourse. *American Journal of Public Health, 86*, 1570–1576.

Schwartz, I. M. (1999). Sexual activity prior to coital initiation: A comparison between males and females. *Archives of Sexual Behavior, 28*, 63–69.

Schwarz, N. (1999). Self-reports: How the questions shape the answers. *American Psychologist, 54*, 93–105.

Sears, H. A., Byers, E. S., & Price, E. L. (2007). The co-occurrence of adolescent boys' and girls' use of psychologically, physically, and sexually abusive behaviours in their dating relationships. *Journal of Adolescence, 30*, 487–504.

Seligman, M. E. P., & Csikszentmihalyi, M. (2000). Positive psychology: An introduction. *American Psychologist, 55*, 5–14.

Siegel, D. M., Aten, M. J., & Roghmann, K. J. (1998). Self-reported honesty among middle and high school students responding to a sexual behavior questionnaire. *Journal of Adolescent Health, 23*, 20–28.

Simons, R. L., Lin, K.-H., & Gordon, L. C. (1998). Socialization in the family of origin and male dating violence: A prospective study. *Journal of Marriage & the Family, 60*, 467–478.

Smiler, A. P., Ward, L. M., Caruthers, A. & Merriwether, A. (2005). Pleasure, empowerment, and love: Factors associated with a positive first coitus. *Sexuality Research and Social Polity, 3*(2), 41–55.

Sonenstein, F. L., Ku, L., & Pleck, J. H. (1997). Measuring sexual behavior among teenage males in the United States. In J. Bancroft (Ed.), *Researching sexual behavior: Methodological issues* (pp. 87–105). Bloomington: Indiana University Press.

Stepp, L. S. (2007). *Unhooked: How young women pursue sex, delay love and lose at both*. New York: Riverhead Books.

Studer, M., & Thornton, A. (1987). Adolescent religiosity and contraceptive usage. *Journal of Marriage & the Family, 49*, 117–128.

Sundet, J. M., Magnus, P., & Kvalem, I. L., et al. (1989). Number of sexual partners and use of condoms in the heterosexual population of Norway: Relevance to HIV infection. *Health Policy, 13*, 159–167.

Sutton, M. J., Brown, J. D., Wilson, K. M., & Klein, J. D. (2002). Shaking the tree of knowledge for forbidden fruit: Where adolescents learn about sexuality and contraception. In J. D. Brown, J. R. Steele, & K. Walsh-Childers (Eds.), *Sexual teens, sexual media* (pp. 25–55). Mahwah, NJ: Lawrence Erlbaum.

Teitler J. O. (2002). Trends in youth sexual initiation and fertility in developed countries: 1960–1995. *Annals of the American Academy of Political Science, 580*, 134–152.

Thompson, S. (1995). *Going all the way: Teenage girls' tales of sex, romance and pregnancy*. New York: Hill and Wang.

Tolman, D. L. (2002). *Dilemma of desire: Teenage girls and sexuality.* Cambridge, MA: Harvard University Press.

Tolman, D. L. (2000). Object lessons: Romance, violation, and female adolescent sexual desire. *Journal of Sex Education and Therapy, 25,* 70–79.

Tolman, D. L. (1994). Adolescent girls' sexuality: Debunking the myth of the urban girl. In B. J. R. Leadbeater & N.Way (Eds.), *Urban girls: Resisting stereotypes, creating identities* (pp. 255–271). New York: New York University Press.

Tolman, D. L., & Diamond, L. M. (2001). Desegregating sexuality research: Combining cultural and biological perspectives on gender and desire. *Annual Review of Sex Research, 12,* 33–74.

Tolman, D. L., & Higgins, T. (1996). How being a good girl can be bad for girls. In N. B. Maglin & D. Perry (Eds.), *Good girls/ bad girls: Women, sex, violence and power in the 1990s* (pp. 205–225). New Brunswick, NJ: Rutgers University Press.

Tolman, D. L., Spencer, R., Harmon, T., Rosen-Reynoso, & Striepe, M. (2004). Getting close, staying cool: Early adolescent boys' experiences with romantic relationships. In N.Way & J. Y. Chu (Eds.), *Adolescent boys: Exploring diverse cultures of boyhood* (pp. 235–255). New York: New York University Press.

Tourangeau, R. & Yan, T. (2007). Sensitive questions in surveys. *Psychological Bulletin, 133,* 859–883.

Treas, J., & Giesen, D. (2000). Sexual infidelity among married and cohabiting Americans. *Journal of Marriage & the Family, 62,* 48–60.

Trivedi, N., & Sabini, J. (1998). Volunteer bias, sexuality, and personality. *Archives of Sexual Behavior, 27,* 181–195.

Tschann, J. M., & Adler, N. E. (1997). Sexual self-acceptance, communication with partner, and contraceptive use among adolescent females: A longitudinal study. *Journal of Research on Adolescence, 7,* 413–430.

Turner, C. F., Ku, L., Rogers, S. M., Lindberg, L. D., Pleck, J. H., & Sonenstein, F. L. (1998). Adolescent sexual behavior, drug use, and violence: Increased reporting with computer survey technology. *Science, 280,* 867–873.

Tyden, T., Olsson, S., & Bjorkelund-Ylander, C. (1991). Female university students in Sweden: Sex, contraception and STDs. *Advances in Contraception, 7,* 165–171.

Udry, J. R. (1988). Biological predispositions and social control in adolescent sexual behavior. *American Sociological Review, 53,* 709–722.

Udry, J. R. (1990). Hormonal and social determinants of adolescent sexual initiation. In J. Bancroft & J. M. Reinisch (Eds.), *Adolescence and puberty* (pp. 70–87). New York: Oxford University Press.

Udry, J. R., & Billy, J. O. G. (1987). Initiation of coitus in early adolescence. *American Sociological Review, 52,* 841–855.

Udry, J. R., & Chantala, K. (2005). Risk factors differ according to same-sex and opposite-sex interest. *Journal of Biosocial Science, 37,* 481–497.

Udry, J. R., Kovenock, J., Morris, N. M., & Vandenberg, B. J. (1995). Childhood precursors of age at first intercourse for females. *Archives of Sexual Behavior, 24,* 329–337.

Udry, J. R., Talbert, L. M., & Morris, N. M. (1986). Biosocial foundations for adolescent female sexuality. *Demography, 23,* 217–230.

Upchurch, D. M., & Kusunoki, Y. (2004). Associations among forced sex, sexual and protective practices, and sexually transmitted diseases among a national sample of adolescent girls. *Women's Health Issues, 14,* 75–84.

Underhill, K., Montgomery, P., & Operario, D. (2007). Sexual abstinence only programmes to prevent HIV infection in high income countries: Systematic review. *British Medical Journal, 335,* 248.

United Nations Population Fund (2008). State of World Population 2007: Indicators: Births per 1000 women (15–19 years). www.unfpa.org/swp/2007/english/notes/indicators.html Retrieved February 29, 2008.

Uttenbroek, D. G. (1994). The relationships between sexual behavior and health lifestyle. *AIDS Care, 6,* 237–447.

Vazsonyi, A. T., Trejos-Castillo, E., & Huang, L. (2006). Risky sexual behaviors, alcohol use, and drug use: A comparison of Eastern and Western European adolescents. *Journal of Adolescent Health, 39,* e1–e11.

Vrangalova, S., & Savin-Williams, R. C. (2008a). Casual sex: A sexual orientation, a context-dependent behavior, or a personal pathology? Manuscript submitted for publication. Cornell University, Ithaca, NY.

Vrangalova, S., & Savin-Williams, R. C. (2008b). How straight are straight people? Correlates of same-sex sexuality in heterosexually-identified young adults. Manuscript submitted for publication. Cornell University, Ithaca, NY.

Wallen, K. (1995). The evolution of female sexual desire. In P. R. Abramson & S. D. Pinkerton (Eds.), *Sexual nature/sexual culture* (pp. 57–79). Chicago: University of Chicago Press.

Ward, L. M., & Rivadeneyra, R. (1999). Contributions of entertainment television to adolescents' sexual attitudes and expectations: The role of viewing amount versus viewer involvement. *Journal of Sex Research, 36,* 237–249.

Weaver, S. J., & Herold, E. S. (2000). Casual sex and women: Measurement and motivational issues. *Journal of Psychology & Human Sexuality, 12,* 23–41.

Weeden, J. & Sabini, J. (2007). Subjective and objective measures of attractiveness and their relation to sexual behavior and sexual attitudes in university students. *Archives of Sexual Behavior, 36,* 79–88.

Weinberg, M. S., Lottes, I. L., & Shaver, F. M. (1995). Swedish or American heterosexual college youth: Who is more permissive? *Archives of Sexual Behavior, 24,* 409–437.

Weinberg, M. S., Williams, C. J., & Pryor, D. W. (1994). *Dual attraction: Understanding bisexuality.* New York: Oxford University Press.

Wekerle, C., & Wolfe, D. A. (1999). Dating violence in mid-adolescence: Theory, significance, and emerging prevention initiatives. *Clinical Psychology Review, 19,* 435–456.

White, R., Cleland, J., & Carael, M. (2000). Links between premarital sexual behaviour and extramarital intercourse: A multi-site analysis. *AIDS, 14,* 2323–2331.

Wichstrøm, L., & Hegna, K. (2003). Sexual orientation and suicide attempt: A longitudinal study of the general Norwegian adolescent population. *Journal of Abnormal Psychology, 112,* 144–151.

Widman, L., Welsh, D. P., McNulty, J. K., & Little, K. C. (2006). Sexual communication and contraceptive use in adolescent dating couples. *Journal of Adolescent Health, 39,* 893–899.

Wiederman, M. W. (1999). Volunteer bias in sexuality research using college student participants. *Journal of Sex Research, 36,* 59–66.

Wright, M. T. (1998). Beyond risk factors: Trends in European safer sex research. *Journal of Psychology and Human Sexuality, 10,* 7–18.

Wu, L. L., & Thomson, E. (2001). Race differences in family experience and early sexual initiation: Dynamic models of family structure and family change. *Journal of Marriage & the Family, 63,* 682–696.

Yoon, G. J. (2005). Predicting Korean adolescents' sexual behavior: Individual, relationship, family, and extra-family factors. In G. W. Peterson, S. K. Steinmetz & S. M. Wilson (Eds.), *Parent–youth relations: Cultural and cross-cultural perspectives.* (pp. 313–338). New York: Haworth Press.

Zabin, L. S., Sedivy, V., & Emerson, M. R. (1994). Subsequent risk of childbearing among adolescents with a negative pregnancy test. *Family Planning Perspectives, 26,* 212–217.

Zani, B. (1991). Male and female patterns in the discovery of sexuality during adolescence. *Journal of Adolescence, 14,* 163–178.

Zavodny, M. (2004). Fertility and parental consent for minors to receive contraceptives. *American Journal of Public Health, 94,* 1347–1351.

CHAPTER 15

Positive Youth Development

JACQUELINE V. LERNER, ERIN PHELPS, YULIKA FORMAN, AND EDMOND P. BOWERS

The positive youth development (PYD) perspective moves beyond the negative, deficit view of youth that dominated the fields of developmental science, psychology, sociology, education, public health, and other fields through the twentieth century, toward a view of the strengths of youth and the positive qualities and outcomes we wish our youth to develop. This orientation to young people originated from interest among developmental scientists in using developmental systems, or dynamic models of human behavior and development in understanding, first, the plasticity of human development and, second, the importance of relations between individuals and their real-world ecological settings as the bases of variation in the course of human development (Baltes, Lindenberger, & Staudinger, 2006; Lerner, 2005; Silbereisen & Lerner, 2007). The PYD perspective has arisen as well through the development and, in some cases the evaluation, of interventions designed and delivered within community-based, youth-serving programs that have worked to counter what have been seen as steady states across the past five to six decades of substantial incidences of risk behaviors among adolescents.

Hermann Ebbinghaus (in Boring, 1929, p. ix) said "Psychology has a long past, but only a short history." We can think of PYD in this way. That is, the language of positive psychology and positive youth development has been in the literature for decades, but efforts to validate the theoretical ideas empirically have only recently appeared in publications. In addition, there is considerable variability among the views of different scholars. For example, the roots and emergence of a PYD perspective were not linked to work in positive psychology or resilience, two distinct research traditions that focus on positive outcomes, but which were also independent of each other. Instead, the PYD perspective emerged from the work of comparative psychologists (e.g., Gottlieb, 1997; Schneirla, 1957) and biologists (e.g., Novikoff, 1945a, 1945b; von Bertalanffy, 1933, 1969) who had been studying the plasticity of developmental processes that arose from the "fusion" (Tobach & Greenberg, 1984) of biological and contextual levels of organization. The use of these ideas about levels of integration that shape ontogenetic change began to appear in research and theory in the human developmental sciences in the 1970s (Cairns, 2006; Gottlieb, Wahlsten, & Lickliter, 2006; Lerner, 2002, 2006; Overton, 1998, 2006). Examples are theoretical papers by Overton (1973) and by Lerner (1978) on how the nature–nurture controversy may be resolved by taking an integrative, relational perspective about genetic and contextual influences on human development.

As research about adolescent development began to proliferate during the 1970s and 1980s (Lerner & Steinberg, 2004; this *Handbook*), and as this research continued to point to the plasticity of adolescent development, developmental scientists who were studying adolescents and adolescence began to explore the use and implications of the ongoing work in comparative psychology and biology for devising a new theoretical frame for the study of adolescence. In turn, developmental scientists interested in other portions of the life span (e.g., adulthood and aging) were drawn to the methods of study of adolescence

because of its use as an ontogenetic laboratory (e.g., Lerner, Freund, De Stefanis, &
Habermas, 2001). The exploration of adolescence by developmental scientists interested
in developmental systems theory resulted in
the elaboration of the PYD perspective that
is adopted by the authors of this chapter and
the research group at the Institute for Applied
Research in Youth Development (IARYD) at
Tufts University.

We are not able to include in this chapter
every scholar or researcher who uses the term
PYD in their work. We have chosen to describe
first, several of the positive approaches to
human development currently under way in
developmental science. We review scholars
who have investigated human strengths and the
multiple contexts and characteristics of those
contexts that promote positive youth development. We give an overview of the issues that
are central to each perspective and we report
the supporting empirical evidence. We then
outline the key features of systems theories
and how they lead to the PYD approach that
we adopt. Finally, we provide an empirical
account of our theoretical approach by using
the 4-H study of Positive Youth Development
as an exemplar. Throughout, we emphasize
that the PYD perspective is most useful in
understanding adolescent development within
multiple contexts, and in promoting PYD
through community-based interventions or
social policy.

One challenge to reviewing and understanding the body of research on PYD is the lack of
a common definition of the term within and
across fields of study. Readers of the extant literature will encounter a variety of theoretical
origins of the concept with resulting variability in operational definitions and substantive
implications. To give only a few examples, the
term *positive youth development* has been used
as equivalent to empowerment (To, 2007),
healthy adjustment (Shek, Siu, & Lee, 2007),
positive well-being (Moore & Glei, 1995),
effective development (Weissberg & O'Brien,
2004), positive behaviors (Flay, 2002) and

youth development (Larson, 2006; Nicholson,
Collins, & Holmer, 2004). Many authors use the
term without defining it (e.g., see Park, 2004a,
2004b; To, 2007). When a definition is provided, it often lacks empirical validation (e.g.,
see Catalano, Berglund, Ryan, Lonczak, &
Hawkins, 2004; Larson; To). Furthermore,
often no clear distinction is made between
positive youth development and prevention of
high-risk behaviors, such as substance abuse
(e.g., see Tebes et al., 2007).

In the next sections, we review work of several major researchers whose focus on human
strengths and positive youth development falls
into several broad areas. First, we consider
researchers working in the field of positive psychology, positive purpose, and mental health.
Then, we discuss those researchers who focus
on the role of programs, communities, and
societies as contexts for positive youth development. We proceed to discuss the work in the
field of resilience and then present the details
of our theoretical and empirical work.

INDIVIDUAL STRENGTHS AND POSITIVE DEVELOPMENT

Some scholars interested in positive development have focused on individual strengths
and the role they play in the development of
positive purpose and in overall mental health.
We highlight the work of three of these
scholars in this section—Martin Seligman and
colleagues, Corey Keyes, and William Damon
and colleagues.

Martin Seligman

One area of work that focuses on individual
strengths is in the field of positive psychology. The goal of positive psychology is to
increase individual happiness (Seligman,
2003a) and the research has followed three
main paths: (1) the study of positive experiences, such as happiness, gratification, fulfillment, well-being and pleasure; (2) the study
of strengths and virtues (Seligman, 2003b),
such as character, talents, interests, values that
enable positive experiences; and (3) the study

of positive institutions, such as schools, families, businesses, communities, societies that enable positive traits and therefore positive experiences (Seligman & Csikszentmihalyi, 2000). In this work, individuals are viewed as active decision makers with choices, preferences (Seligman, 2002), and the ability to enhance their own well-being.

An influential and representative example of this approach is the work of Martin Seligman, who views human strengths as buffering mental illness (Seligman, 2002) and contributing to well-being (Park, Peterson, & Seligman, 2004). Following this view, the task of the science of prevention is to cultivate character strengths and virtues such as courage, future-mindedness, optimism, interpersonal skills, faith, work ethic, hope, honesty, perseverance, and the capacity for flow and insight. Some theoretical literature in the field (Park, 2004a, 2004b) links character strengths and subjective well-being to PYD, but this position has had little elaboration to date.

Seligman suggests preventive and treatment interventions using the cognitive behavioral approach as a way of teaching cognitive and problem-solving skills, such as disputing one's own catastrophic thoughts and assertiveness (Gillham et al., 2006). One of the goals is to prevent depression and anxiety in children and adults through learning optimism. Another goal is to amplify the strengths of individuals as a means to prevent mental illness and enhance social–emotional competence and health.

An example of a preventive intervention is the Penn Resiliency Program for Children and Adolescents (PRP-CA) (Gillham, Jaycox, Reivich, Seligman, & Silver, 1990; Shatte, Seligman, Gillham, & Reivich, 2003), a cognitive behavioral intervention for school-aged children to prevent depression and anxiety. Its evaluation, however, demonstrated inconsistent results (Gillham et al., 2007). When combined with a parent intervention component, PRP-CA was shown to prevent depression and anxiety in early adolescents in a pilot study with a small sample (Gillham et al., 2006). Reivich, Gillham, Chaplin, and

Seligman (2005) suggest that PRP can also be used as a universal intervention, for example, to promote general resiliency in children.

The field of positive psychology evolved as a complement to the field of clinical psychology, which in the second half of the twentieth century was focused on psychopathology and treatment of mental illness (Seligman, 2002). Its major contribution to the field is providing a counterbalance to this deficit-driven approach and, instead, undertaking the study of the "good life" (Seligman, 2004; Seligman & Csikszentmihalyi, 2000).

Corey Keyes

Corey Keyes (Keyes, 2005, 2006) also critiques the long-standing deficit model approach to development, and focuses on the study, conception, and measurement of mental health. Keyes argues that prior research defined mental health as the absence of mental illness and therefore assumed that individuals without a diagnosed mental illness are mentally healthy (Keyes, 2006). To balance this view, he developed a dual-factor model to posit that good mental health does not necessarily mean the absence of mental illness, while mental illness does not imply the lack of mental health (Keyes, 2005). This model calls for assessments of both mental health and mental illnesses (Keyes, 2007).

Applying a positive mental health approach, Keyes examines the presence of positive feelings and functioning in one's life. Keyes describes the presence of mental health as flourishing, and the absence of mental health as languishing. Individuals who are neither flourishing nor languishing are deemed to be moderately mentally healthy. The symptoms marking positive mental health were derived from the work of subjective well-being researchers and come from two traditions, hedonic well-being and eudaimonic well-being. The hedonic tradition focuses on emotional well-being, viewing mental health as professed happiness and satisfaction in life or the experience of positive emotions.

The eudaimonic approach views mental health as positive functioning in psychological and social dimensions of life. Social well-being is measured using Keyes's (1998) multidimensional model indicating how well individuals perceive their relationships with other people, their neighborhoods, and society. Based on the presence and level of symptoms of emotional well-being and positive functioning, an individual is diagnosed as flourishing, languishing, or moderately mentally healthy.

Although applied primarily to adult populations, Keyes's dual-factor model also has been examined in an adolescent population (Keyes, 2006). Results revealed that while flourishing was the most common diagnosis among 12- to 14-year-olds, moderate mental health was the most common diagnosis among 15- to 18-year-olds. Increases in mental health in adolescents were associated with decreases in depressive symptoms and conduct problems such as truancy, substance use, and arrest, and with increases in psychosocial functioning such as self-concept, self-determination, closeness to others, and school integration (Keyes, 2006).

William Damon

A key scholar who has made a major contribution to the development of the PYD perspective is William Damon. Damon approaches PYD through an examination of the development of noble purpose in youth and young adults (Damon, 2003, 2004, 2008; Mariano & Damon, 2008). Damon's position is that a central indicator of PYD and youth *thriving* (i.e., exemplary positive development, Scales, Benson, Leffert, & Blyth, 2000; Lerner, 2004b) is engagement in pursuits that serve the common welfare, and make meaningful contributions to communities. In his work, Damon assesses the ways in which youth go beyond their own self-centered needs and extend outward to the pursuit of goals that benefit the world beyond. An important concept in this work is the idea of "youth purpose."

In their program of research at the Stanford Center on Adolescence, Damon and colleagues have examined youth purpose through a series of studies with youth across the United States. To understand adolescents' potential sources of purpose, they surveyed a diverse group of youth from grades 6, 9, 12, and college, and asked respondents to indicate their level of dedication to 18 categories of purpose. A "category" refers to a life area that individuals find important, and in which they may be psychologically and actively invested. The categories included: family, country, personal growth, sports, academic achievement, good health, looking good, arts, making lots of money, lifework, general leadership, romance, political or social issues, happiness, religious faith or spirituality, community service, friends, and personal values.

In addition to the surveys, interviews were conducted with 12 "purpose exemplars." These purpose exemplars were young people who had demonstrated an extraordinary and long-term commitment to some cause. They were between the ages of 12 and 23, and needed to fulfill four criteria:

1. Dedication to some specific cause for two years or more
2. Rationales for involvement clearly included intention to contribute to the world beyond themselves
3. High levels of active engagement in their purpose
4. Concrete future plans around their purpose (Mariano & Damon, 2008).

In addition to asking about youth purpose, Damon and colleagues focused on the nature of the associations between spirituality and purpose in adolescence. Damon's findings suggest that many adolescents today are thinking about religion and spirituality in profound ways, and that in some cases spirituality and religion are influencing their purposes in life. The findings suggest that spirituality and religious faith may play very different roles in supporting youth purpose for some adolescents than for others. In fact, the relationship between spirituality, purpose, and different aspects of positive youth development may reflect different pathways, or models, for different groups of adolescents. Damon (Mariano & Damon, in press) proposes three models from this work:

Model 1: Spirituality guides young people toward an intention to contribute (purpose), which in turn leads to contribution

Model 2: Spirituality invests young people's personal goals with value and meaning, which in turn contributes to these goals becoming inspiring purposes

Model 3: Spirituality supports young people's intentions to develop character (moral purpose), which in turn supports character development

While Damon has viewed purpose as an indicator of PYD, he notes that a next step in this investigation will require a deeper understanding of the ways that young people are purposeful. Purposeful young people may indeed be contributing to something beyond themselves, but whether it is for self-serving reasons and social approval, or whether that contribution is an end in itself may be important for their development. Finally, Damon notes that an important issue for the study of PYD in general is under what circumstances an involvement in the spiritual life leads to contribution.

The approaches of Seligman, Keyes, and Damon highlight the importance of personal strengths as indicators of PYD, but they also underscore the need for a more systemic perspective of PYD. The presence of well-being, mental health, and purpose are related to a lower incidence of maladaptive outcomes and higher rates of positive development such as contribution and good relationships. The research reviewed in the following section emphasizes the role that context and community play in PYD.

PROGRAMS, COMMUNITIES AND SOCIETIES AS CONTEXTS FOR PYD

Scholars and practitioners agree that environment plays an important role in positive youth development, yet they may have different ways of characterizing what aspects of contexts are good for youth. In line with the scholars reviewed above, they have also articulated what they believe to be the internal assets or strengths of youth and assert that these can combine with the external or contextual assets that surround youth to promote development. In this section we present the work of several researchers who look at those contextual influences on various levels, from programmatic to societal, and who focus on different types of assets.

Developmental Assets: The Search Institute

Peter Benson and his colleagues at the Search Institute (Benson, 1997, 2003, 2007) have been integral in providing the vocabulary and vision about the strengths of youth. With its focus on what Benson has called "developmental assets," this approach emphasizes the talents, energies, strengths, and constructive interests that every young person possesses. Benson and his colleagues at Search have examined "external" assets (e.g., support or boundaries and expectations) and "internal" assets (e.g., personal values). In a series of studies, they found these assets to be predictive of seven behavioral indicators of *thriving,* including: (1) school success, (2) leadership, (3) helping others, (4) maintenance of physical health, (5) delay of gratification, (6) valuing diversity, and (7) overcoming adversity (Leffert et al., 1998; Scales et al., 2000). For example, achievement motivation and school engagement, which are internal assets, in combination with time spent in youth programs, which is an external asset, significantly predicted school success for six different racial/ethnic groups of 6th- to 12th-grade students.

The work of the Search Institute in the last two decades has been useful in helping communities to develop long-term goals for positive youth development. Today, more than 300 communities across the country have incorporated the asset-building framework, and scholars

(Lerner et al., 2005) have used the developmental assets in their PYD research. Benson and those influenced by his work engage in efforts that focus on sustaining the positive strengths of youth and building upon them, rather than on eliminating risk behaviors. The developmental implications of the assets approach are significant and we discuss them in a later section of this chapter. This view addresses key aspects of youth development that are invisible to those who have concentrated their efforts on the "Problems of Youth." According to Lerner, Fisher, and Weinberg (2000), who are leading proponents of the PYD approach, preventing disease or behavioral problems does not constitute the provision of health or the actualization of positive development.

Youth Assets and Positive Developmental Settings

The external developmental assets articulated by Benson can be found in many community programs for youth. Many scholars agree that these programs are key settings in which positive youth development can be fostered. In a report on program design, implementation and evaluation of community programs for youth (Eccles & Gootman, 2002), the Committee on Community-Level Programs for Youth conceptualizes positive youth development in terms of a range of skills and knowledge, as well as other personal and social assets required to successfully move from healthy adolescence into competent adulthood. These scholars maintain that community-based activities that provide opportunities for acquisition of those assets put youth at the center of neighborhood life and bring together caring adults to support them, thus increasing community support that has been weakened by the major social shifts of the twentieth and twenty-first centuries. This work is based on a comprehensive review and evaluation of the literature on community interventions, and programs aiming to promote positive development in adolescents.

Eccles and colleagues defined four domains of individual assets that represent health and well-being in adolescence. These four domains are: (1) physical development, (2) intellectual development, (3) psychological and emotional development, and (4) social development (see Table 15.1 for details).

In this view, positive development does not require possession of all assets in Table 15.1. Having more assets, however, is better than having fewer, and it is beneficial to have assets in all four domains. Eccles and Gootman (2002) note that these assets do not exist in

TABLE 15.1   Personal and Social Assets that Facilitate Positive Youth Development

Physical development
Good health habits
Good health risk management skills

Intellectual development
Knowledge of essential life skills
Knowledge of essential vocational skills
School success
Rational habits of mind—critical thinking and reasoning skills
In-depth knowledge of more than one culture
Good decision-making skills
Knowledge of skills needed to navigate through multiple cultural contexts

Psychological and emotional development
Good mental health including positive self-regard
Good emotional self-regulation skills
Good coping skills
Good conflict resolution skills
Mastery motivation and positive achievement motivation
Confidence in one's personal efficacy
"Planfulness"—planning for the future and future life events
Sense of personal autonomy/responsibility for self
Optimism coupled with realism
Coherent and positive personal and social identity
Prosocial and culturally sensitive values
Spirituality or a sense of a "larger" purpose in life
Strong moral character
A commitment to good use of time

Social development
Connectedness—perceived good relationships and trust with peers; and some other adults
Sense of social place/integration—being connected and valued by larger social networks
Attachment to prosocial/conventional institutions, such as school, church, nonschool youth programs
Ability, to navigate in multiple cultural contexts

a vacuum and do not in themselves ensure the well-being of adolescents. As mentioned above, youth need access to contexts that facilitate their development through exposure to positive experiences, settings, and people, and to contexts that provide opportunities to develop and refine real-life skills. It is important for every community to have an array of programs for youth that, taken together, offer all features of positive developmental settings. In this case, redundancy would contribute to PYD.

Some of the features that characterize such positive developmental settings include physical and psychological safety, appropriate structure and positive social norms. These contexts provide opportunities to enjoy supportive relationships, to belong, to build skills, and to feel empowered by experiencing efficacy and mattering. Moreover, these settings need to be synergistic with efforts and perspectives of the adolescents' families, as well as with the communities in which both the programs and the adolescents reside.

The contribution of this group of researchers involves taking stock of the current state of research on youth development programs and identifying additional work that needs to be done. In addition, their work provides concrete direction for communities striving to effectively support their youth. We now turn to a review of researchers who have "dug deeper" into the characteristics of programs that promote PYD.

The "Big Three" of Youth Development Programs

Roth and Brooks-Gunn investigated community-based programs, arguing that these programs should aim at "youth preparation and development" rather than "problem prevention and deterrence" (Roth and Brooks-Gunn, 2003a,b, p. 94). In this work, Roth and Brooks-Gunn addressed the need to understand what exactly is meant by the term *youth development program,* and identified the "big three" critical characteristics programs should have.

Based on the existing literature, Roth and Brooks-Gunn (2003a,b) concluded that (1)

specific program activities, (2) atmosphere, and (3) goals are the three defining aspects of youth development programs that differentiate them from other programs for adolescents. The goals of youth development programs go beyond prevention to include promotion of positive development. They are characterized by an atmosphere of hope, caring, safety, cultural appropriateness, and respect for adolescents' abilities to make choices and bear responsibility. Program activities provide opportunities for active involvement and meeting new challenges.

The authors surveyed 71 highly visible and well-regarded youth development programs to determine whether or not the "big three" are found in real life programs. Among the goals listed by these programs, the most frequently mentioned was prevention of high-risk behaviors; this was followed by skill and competency building, and connections to others. Program atmosphere was defined as presence of supportive relationships, youth empowerment, and expectations for positive behavior. The majority of the surveyed programs offered opportunities for building supportive relationships with adults and peers through counseling and mentoring. Almost all of the programs offered at least one empowering activity such as leadership training, opportunities for decision making, and community service, and over half offered all three. Most programs encouraged positive behavior through incentives for participation, and over half imposed sanctions for breaking the rules.

Program activities were considered in terms of the opportunities offered to participants. All programs offered skill-building activities, most provided real challenges, and all except one exposed youth to new places, people, and situations. Youth development programs focused on positive development in a way that paralleled theoretical descriptions of the concept, yet they emphasized social competence more than other aspects of positive development. The authors found that a significant minority of the programs did not provide an atmosphere of hope, caring, safety, cultural appropriateness, and respect for adolescents' abilities to make choices and bear responsibility.

In terms of organizational context, programs with higher intensity of programming; programs affiliated with a state, national, or religious organization; and programs serving more disadvantaged youth were found to be in greater alignment with the philosophy of youth development than other programs. This work provides an important link between research and practice, assessing a landscape of youth development programs in view of theoretical literature dedicated to the topic. The "big three" provides both researchers and practitioners with a simple yet powerful framework for thinking about quality of youth development programming.

Motivation, Active Engagement, and Real-Life Challenges

For Reed Larson (Larson, 2006), PYD is "a process in which young people's capacity for being motivated by challenge energizes their active engagement in development" (p. 677). For positive development to take place, the motivational system must become activated and remain engaged in multiple domains of development while young people deal with everyday real-life challenges.

In his work, Larson looks at the match between the experiences of adolescents and the requirements of the adult world they are preparing for (Larson, 2002; Larson, Wilson, Brown, Furstenberg, & Verma, 2002; Mortimer & Larson, 2002). He does this in a contextualized way, by describing the diversity of developmental tasks, skills, and competencies adolescents need to develop to successfully transition into adulthood in different cultures (Larson & Wilson, 2004).

For example, American teenagers have more leisure time than their counterparts in Europe and East Asia (Larson & Seepersad, 2003; Larson & Verma, 1999). Most of that time is spent in unstructured activities with peers, a pastime that is often associated with increased

delinquent behavior and substance abuse (McHale, Crouter, & Tucker, 2001, as cited in Larson & Seepersad) rather than with positive development (Larson, 2001). Larson, Hansen, and Moneta (2006) found that while unstructured time with peers does not differ from structured activities in terms of developmental opportunities, it involves more risks of negative experiences.

Out-of-school time (OST) activities is one context Larson has looked at in depth. Programs with structured activities are seen as contexts in which youth can act as producers of their own positive development (Dworkin, Larson, & Hansen, 2003; Larson et al., 2004), by offering opportunities to develop skills and competencies necessary for negotiating the real world (Mahoney, Larson, Eccles, & Lord, 2005). These skills and competencies include taking initiative, developing leadership, and learning responsibility, as well as strategic and teamwork skills (Larson, & Hansen, 2005; Larson, Hansen, & Walker, 2005; Larson, Walker, & Pearce, 2005; Larson, 2000; Larson & Walker, 2006; Larson et al., 2006). At the same time, participation in structured activities is associated with negative experiences such as stress, inappropriate adult behavior, negative influences, social exclusion, and negative group dynamics.

Participation in organized activities is viewed in contrast to spending unstructured time with peers, (Larson, 2001; Larson & Seepersad, 2003), as well as a complement to other contexts, such as school and family, in which adolescents spend their time. Larson reports strikingly high levels of boredom in modern adolescents across all of these contexts (Larson & Richards, 1991), a phenomenon that he views as absence of being invested in one's own future, a state synonymous with absence of positive development.

While this research does not yet offer a universal theory of change relevant to PYD in organized programs, there are separate studies offering possible models. For example, through interviewing and observing 34 youth as well as several adult leaders in three high-quality youth programs, Larson et al. (2004) described developmental processes that occur in five domains of development within organized youth programs and lead to a positive change in youth. These processes were reported to be development of initiative, transformations in motivation, acquiring social capital, learning to deal with human differences, and becoming responsible. Larson and Walker (2006) conducted 75 interviews with 12 youths over a 12-week engagement in an urban arts program consisting of a preparation course and such real-life challenges as internship and work on commissioned murals. In this study, learning real-life skills and competencies followed a developmental trajectory from dissonance to challenge to active adaptive learning. In a theory-generating study focused on developmental transactions that facilitate acquisition of teamwork skills in youth, Larson (2007) followed activities of 22 high school students enrolled in a 10-week program teaching high-tech skills. The process of change within a youth development program progressed from egocentric stage to learning the benefits of reciprocity, to developing group norms for teamwork, and then to applying the new teamwork skills outside of the program (Larson, 2007).

Consistent with the findings of Roth and Brooks-Gunn (2003a, 2003b), in all types of programs, adults were found to play an important role in facilitating positive development (Larson & Hansen, 2005; Larson, Walker, & Pearce, 2005; Larson & Walker, 2006; Larson et al., 2004). Successful adult leaders use techniques such as following youths' lead, cultivating a culture of youth input, monitoring, creating intermediate steps in task management, and stretching and pushing youth (Larson et al., 2004).

Larson's contribution to the field is the close attention he has paid to the specific aspects of youth development programs, such as developmental opportunities and actions of adults that contribute to positive development. His focus on the developmental processes that

occur within youth in successful programs elucidates possible intrapersonal pathways toward positive youth development.

Positive School-to-Work Transitions

Stephen Hamilton is a scholar whose work has helped us to understand the positive connections between adolescents and an important context and transition—the school-to-work transition (Hamilton, 1994; Hamilton & Hamilton, 1999, 2004; see also chapter 14, vol. 2 of this *Handbook*). Hamilton's scholarship provides theory and research that helps frame our understanding of the issues faced by youth trying to connect school and work. In addition, Hamilton offers ideas for policies and programs useful for enhancing the school to work connection for all youth and, in particular, for those adolescents who seek full-time employment immediately after completion of high school.

Hamilton's (1994; Hamilton & Hamilton, 1999, 2005, 2006; Hamilton & Lempert, 1997) research has involved the study of adolescents and young adults from seven nations: United States, Germany, Japan, Austria, Switzerland, Denmark, and Sweden. He observes that adolescents' expectations about the "payoff" in the labor market for achievement in secondary school motivates youth to work hard in high school and forges a connection between the educational and work contexts of life. He points out that "adolescents who believe their current efforts will bring them closer to a desirable future are far more likely to work hard in school and avoid self-destructive behavior than those who are either unable to think about the future or who believe their prospects are beyond their control" (Hamilton, 1994, pp. 267–268).

Hamilton (1994) explains that to attain the link they desire between their adolescent school context and their young adult work context, adolescents must consider two key facets of the worlds of education and work/career: transparency and permeability. Transparency describes the extent to which young people can "see through" the intricacies of the stated and the unstated rules of the educational system and the labor market and, using this understanding, plan a course of action to move from where they are in the present (e.g., a senior in high school) to a goal they have for the future (e.g., employment as an electrical engineer, as an accountant, or as a beautician). To the extent that these pathways are clear and may be learned by any student interested in knowing them, the education–work/career system is transparent.

In turn, permeability refers to the ease of movement from one part of the education–labor market system to another. Permeability involves the amount of effort needed to move from, say, a plan involving becoming an electrical engineer to a plan involving becoming an orthodontist or to a plan involving becoming a sales clerk if one has decided that one is no longer interested in becoming a beautician. A completely permeable system would be one in which, after years of planning to be a beautician after high school, and working within the educational–work/career system to reach this goal, there would be no problems encountered and it would be equally easy to now switch one's goal to electrical engineering, brain surgery, rocket science, or forestry.

Hamilton (1994) explains that formal credentials, or qualifications, are important in understanding both the transparency and the permeability of the education–work/career system. He notes that there is an inverse relation between transparency and permeability (Hamilton, 1994). That is, the more that there are particular and clearly specified qualifications for a given type of employment (e.g., 4 years of college, followed by 4 years of medical school, a 1-year internship, a 3-year residency in surgery, and a 3-year subspecialty residency in brain surgery for employment as a brain surgeon) the greater the transparency of the system. However, to the extent that the qualifications are difficult to obtain, the system, although transparent, is not permeable (Hamilton, 1994).

In the United States, the education–career/work system is, overall, not very transparent; it is, instead, opaque. For instance, there are no precise pathways that can be specified for becoming a rock star or movie star, the CEO of a Fortune 500 company, a successful lawyer and spouse/mother or father, or the proprietor of a successful e-commerce business. However, the education–work/career system in the Unites States is quite permeable (Hamilton, 1994). For example, Hamilton notes that it is possible to switch from the career of auto mechanic to the career of chef. Similarly, lawyers become entrepreneurs, teachers become store owners, and athletes become actors.

In other countries studied by Hamilton (1994), there are different connections between transparency and permeability. For example, in Germany, the relation between credentials and employment is completely transparent. Youth are directed into particular educational paths that will lead either to a particular vocation (e.g., a machinist, a printer, or an electrician) or to university training and subsequent professional activity (e.g., as a physician, scientist, lawyer, or professor). Hamilton underscores the need for programs that enhance youth's ability to understand the links between education and the world of work. He and his colleagues implemented the Youth Apprenticeship Demonstration Project in Broome County, New York, a program that influenced the School-to-Work Opportunities Act of 1994. Their subsequent work has addressed the creation of school-to-work systems and the teaching and mentoring of youth in workplaces. The contribution of this work has been to raise awareness of the importance of mentoring youth in their communities so that they are better prepared to enter the world of work.

From the preceding, we see that the contexts within which youth develop can contribute to their positive development in a number of important ways. The people and other assets found in these contexts are essential ingredients for PYD. Several researchers have examined how positive development occurs in contexts that are marked by high risk and adversity and focus on the resilience of youth. We turn to a consideration of these scholars next.

RESILIENCE AND POSITIVE YOUTH DEVELOPMENT

Emerging from the broader perspective of developmental psychopathology is the resilience work of Emmy Werner and colleagues (1995; Werner & Smith, 2001). Resilience is defined as the positive adaptation within the context of high-risk or adversity. Werner and Smith, in their seminal study of risk and resilience, followed nearly 700 children growing up in Kauai with risk factors (one-third of who had multiple risk factors) from birth to adulthood. Following this cohort of youth, Werner and Smith (1992, 2001) discovered that the children at risk grew increasingly more like their peers without risk factors. These findings have come up in contradiction to a belief of many risk-focused social scientists—that risk factors for the most part predict negative outcomes. Findings from resilience research suggest that risk factors are predictive of negative outcomes for only about 20 to 49 percent of a given high-risk population (Rutter, 1987, 2000; Werner & Smith, 2001). In contrast, "protective factors," the supports and opportunities that buffer the effect of adversity and enable development to proceed, appear to predict positive outcomes in anywhere from 50% to 80% of a high-risk population. These buffers (i.e., protective factors, assets) make a more profound impact on the life course of children who grow up under adverse conditions than do specific risk factors or stressful life events. Werner and Smith (2001) note that these findings offer us a more optimistic outlook than the perspective that can be offered from the literature on the negative consequences of perinatal trauma, caregiving deficits, and chronic poverty. Out of Werner's work comes the idea that the supports and opportunities serving as protective factors for youth facing adversity apply equally to all young people.

Following in the tradition of Werner and Smith, Ann Masten underscores the potential for plasticity in person–context relations in examining resilience. Her work involves "understanding behavior problems in the full context of human development . . . focus(ing) on variations in adaptation" (Masten, 2004, p. 311). In focusing on these variations, she believes that research on positive and maladaptive functioning and development are mutually informative (Masten, 2004, 2006).

To be considered "resilient," an individual must not only be identified as experiencing adversity, but he or she must also be deemed as doing "good" or "okay" in terms of the quality of adaptation or developmental outcome (Masten, 2001; Masten & Coatsworth, 1998). Masten and colleagues' work on determining what constitutes positive adaptation focuses on competence in age-salient developmental tasks (Masten, 2001; Masten & Curtis, 2000; Masten & Coatsworth, 1998; Masten et al., 1999; Masten & Obradović, 2006). This is a dynamic construct, as developmentally appropriate tasks vary according to the age of the individual as well as to the cultural and historical context in which the individual was raised. This measure of adaptation is also multidimensional, as there are multiple tasks during any given developmental stage in any given place at any given time. For example, during early childhood, children would be expected to develop an attachment relationship with their caregivers and begin to control their behavior and observe parental rules; in adolescence, forming close friendships and successful academic achievement would become salient developmental tasks. Maladaptive development would be operationalized as failure to meet the expectations of a given society for several domains of development or one major domain (Masten & Curtis, 2000).

As it is operationalized, competence could vary with the person, place, and time. However, in her work with Project Competence, Masten identified a smaller set of standards that traverse families, communities, and culture that reflect major tasks of adaptation across development (Masten & Coatsworth, 1998). These developmental tasks represent several broad domains of competence and have been shown to have continuity across development to varying degrees (Masten et al., 1995). Supporting earlier studies by Harter indicating that competence is a multidimensional construct (Harter, 1982, 1985a, 1985b, 1986), results of factor analyses indicated that during adolescence competence has at least five distinct dimensions: academic achievement, conduct, social competence, romantic competence, and job competence (Masten et al., 1995). Therefore, in determining adaptive development in the face of adversity, Masten considers how well adolescents are performing in these five areas.

Developmental task theory also suggests that performance in one task dimension results in cascading consequences that lead to success or failure in other dimensions of adaptation (Masten & Obradović, 2006). This conjecture was supported in work by Masten and colleagues using data from the Project Competence study (Masten et al., 1995, 2005) as research over the first 10 years found that compliance and rule-abidance predicted academic achievement (Masten et al., 1995). Subsequent testing of a series of nested cascade models based on the first twenty years of the study indicated that externalizing problems during childhood negatively affected academic competence during adolescence, which then led to more internalizing problems in young adulthood (Masten et al., 2005). Externalizing problems in childhood seemed to predict, directly and indirectly, problems in academic and internalizing domains regardless of gender, IQ, socioeconomic status, or parenting. Consistent with developmental systems theory (Granic & Patterson, 2006), the nature and strength of these cascades are expected to change as different tasks become more relevant to positive adaptation (e.g., peer social relations in adolescence versus parent–child relations in childhood).

The effect of success in early developmental tasks on later positive adaptation in other domains can also be seen in Obradović

and Masten's (2007) work linking adolescent competence to civic engagement in young adulthood. Civic engagement was operationalized as citizenship (e.g., voting, serving jury duty, following current events) and volunteering. Results showed that measures of adaptive functioning of academic and social competence in adolescence significantly predicted citizenship and volunteering in young adulthood. These same measures of competence in emerging adulthood still predicted citizenship in young adulthood after controlling for their parallel adolescent measures. Results also indicated that adolescent and emerging adult competence mediated the relation between activity involvement and subsequent civic engagement in young adulthood. Young adults who have shown competence in age-salient development tasks are more likely to be active citizens in young adulthood (Obradović & Masten, 2007).

In determining what could explain success in these developmental tasks, Masten indicates that several factors have been consistently identified as related to more favorable outcomes within the research literature (Masten, 2004, 2007; Masten & Coatsworth, 1998). These factors range from individual level characteristics such as good intellectual functioning and an easygoing disposition to family factors such as authoritative parenting and socioeconomic advantages to "extrafamilial contexts" such as effective schools (Masten & Coatsworth, 1998). Deeming these factors a "short list," Masten posits that these factors are suggestive of fundamental adaptive systems that play a role in positive development not only in cases of resilience, but also more broadly in normative development (Masten & Obradović, 2006). Good intellectual functioning and good parenting are critical to competence in normal development just as they are in resilient individuals. Therefore, resilience is not due to unique or amazing qualities of competent adolescents at risk, rather it is the result of the operation of basic human adaptive systems, or "ordinary magic" (Masten, 2001).

As long as these fundamental adaptive systems are not compromised, positive development will occur regardless of an individual's risk status (Masten & Coatsworth, 1995, 1998).

In her own work with the Project Competence group (Masten et al., 1999) and reviews of the resilience literature (Masten & Coatsworth, 1998), Masten implicates three adaptive systems as crucial to the development of competence: parenting, self-regulation skills, and cognitive functioning. For example, in the 10-year assessment of their urban sample (Masten et al., 1999), Masten and colleagues sought to test the hypotheses that parenting resources, cognitive functioning, and psychological well-being were related to more positive outcomes in three major age-salient developmental tasks (academic achievement, conduct, and peer social competence). Using a variable-focused approach, IQ and parenting were related to positive outcomes across the domains and these resources specifically played a protective role for antisocial behavior even at high levels of adversity. Person-focused analyses found that resilient individuals and competent individuals who experienced low adversity did not differ in terms of IQ, parenting, and psychological well-being; however, they did differ from maladaptive individuals who also experienced high levels of risk in IQ, parenting, and emotionality. Both methods of analysis supported the position that cognitive functioning and parenting quality are fundamental adaptational systems as they predicted current and future adaptation in children and adolescents.

Youth of Color

Some scholars have used the resilience models of Werner and Smith (1992, 2001) and Masten (2001, 2004) to specifically study the characteristics of the development of youth of color (e.g., Fisher, Jackson, & Villarruel, 1998; Lerner, Sparks, & McCubbin, 1999; McAdoo, 1995, 1999; Spencer, 1990, 1995, 1999, 2006b; Spencer, Dupree, & Hartmann, 1997). These scholars have discussed the resiliency, or "adaptive modes" (e.g., McAdoo, 1995;

Spencer, 1990) used by adolescents of color and their family and community contexts to promote positive development, especially in economically poor communities. To underscore the potential for positive youth development among poor youth of color constitutes a significant innovation in developmental research (e.g., Benson, 1997; Leffert et al., 1998; Scales et al., 2000), since race is the single best predictor of poverty and its behavioral outcomes (Huston, 1991; McLoyd, 1998).

There are numerous "success stories" of positive developmental outcomes reported among poor youth of color (Allison, 1993; McAdoo, 1995, 1999). African American male adolescents are arguably the group with the highest probability of experiencing the problematic behaviors associated with race and poverty in America (Mincy, 1994), yet there are many instances of positive development among this group. Researchers who have focused on this group note that the bases of the positive development of these youth and their ability to "overcome the odds" (Werner & Smith, 1992) lie in combinations of individual and ecological characteristics. In some of this work, Luster and McAdoo (1994, 1996) found that assets associated with the individual (cognitive competence, academic motivation, and personal adjustment in kindergarten) and the context (parental involvement in schools) were associated longitudinally with academic achievement and educational attainment.

Sociologist Carl Taylor saw that the power of the assets perspective of the Search Institute (Benson, 1997, 2000) may be coupled with the developmental systems idea—that all young people have strengths that, if capitalized on, can further their positive development. His view was that one could search *in any community context* for the combinations of individual and ecological assets that may be associated with positive development.

To test these ideas, Taylor and colleagues (Taylor et al., 2002a, 2002b, 2003, 2004) launched a qualitative study of the pathways to positive development among African

American adolescent male gang members. The differences between gang and nongang adolescents are underscored in the literature, but findings also point to the comparability in family, teacher, and peer resources for positive development between at least some gang members (e.g., about 20%; Patton, 1998) and their nongang counterparts. Titled "Overcoming the Odds" (OTO) and thus acknowledging Emmy Werner's influence (Werner & Smith, 1992, 2001), the research group attempted to identify the individual and contextual conditions that may provide comparable resources for positive development among both gang and nongang youth. It is these resources that Taylor and colleagues assert may protect diverse African American male adolescents from the actualization of risk (i.e., that allow them to "overcome the odds") and, in turn, may promote positive healthy, successful development.

For three years, the researchers studied African American male adolescents who were either (1) involved in gangs engaged in criminal behavior (e.g., drug use, violence) or (2) participating in non-gang-related community groups (e.g., 4-H clubs, church-related organizations). OTO compared the development of the gang youth with the development of African American youth from the same neighborhoods as the gang youth but who are involved in community-based organizations (CBOs) aimed at promoting youth development. However, the core idea in OTO is that, if and when, over time, gang youth approach the levels of developmental assets possessed by CBO youth, then their developmental trajectories will increasingly resemble those of CBO youth. On an absolute level, gang youth with high levels of developmental assets should, over time, show evidence that they are overcoming the odds existing against their positive development and, in fact, thrive.

They found that a substantial proportion of gang youth do maintain across a 3-year period stable levels of developmental assets and that, for a substantial proportion of these youth, these levels reflect relatively high levels of these assets (i.e., "high" here refers to "above the mean level of assets for gang youth"). Although the actual number of assets in the lives of gang youth is lower than the corresponding value for CBO youth, the assets and thriving are linked, and this is particularly the case within the third wave of testing for the young gang youth. Nevertheless, despite this finding for the third wave of testing, there was no systematic age variation within the two groups for assets, thriving, or their covariation.

The Taylor research underscores the developmental systems ideas that all youth may possess the bases for positive development (e.g., Benson, 1997; Lerner, 2004a,b; Spencer, 2006b; Taylor, 1996, 2001). Moreover, given the relationships found among thriving, developmental assets, and asset stability among the gang members, there is support within the Taylor study for the ideas of Benson (2003) and others (e.g., McAdoo, 1995) that thriving may be advanced when youth develop within a context possessing the internal and ecological resources promoting positive development.

Margaret Spencer's PVEST Model

Spencer's phenomenological variant of ecological systems theory (PVEST) is a dynamic and systemic framework for studying development that takes into account structural factors, cultural influences, and individual experiences, as well as individuals' perceptions of these features (Dupree, Spencer, & Fegley, 2007). A central feature of this model is an emphasis on the ways in which youth make sense of their contexts, and the role that these understandings play in their perceptions of events, people, and opportunities in their environments. The work of Spencer and her colleagues and students has especially focused on how youth respond to their environments when they are seen as reflecting social inequities or injustices, using PVEST as a framework for interpreting their findings. An important theoretical consequence of this model for the study of positive youth development is that different youth will experience the same events and settings through different lenses, which can yield different interpretations and effects. Thus, while an after-school homework club might promote academic competence for some youth, for others the same context might invoke reminders of earlier unavailability of resources such as access to books and teacher help. The effectiveness of this asset, then, is likely to vary according to youth's perceptions of this setting. While attention has been paid to the importance of bidirectional interactions of individual characteristics and ecological contexts, Spencer argues that the role of structural inequality must be considered as well. The framework of PYD and thriving is intended to be a general theory of human development that should be applicable to all youth. Spencer's model provides a way to include the systematic effects of shared contexts on youth's perceptions of their environments in the transactional study of PYD.

While PVEST is a general model, Spencer's own work with it focused especially on youth of color and poor youth, and is, in part, a critique of researchers' "failure to consider their unique human development experiences in socially constructed and culturally unique contexts" (Spencer, Swanson, & Cunningham, 1991; Spencer, 2006a, p. 271). The contexts of underserviced neighborhoods, impoverished communities, and families under stress that often characterize urban and, frequently, African American children, and the lifelong structural effects of these contexts are generally ignored or characterized as random error in developmental models (Spencer, Noll, Stoltzfus, & Harpalini (2001). In addition,

The deviance emphasizing and pathologizing of poor economic status youngsters (i.e., assumed always to be diverse youth of color) and the problematizing of their experiences (except for narrow self-esteem emphases), deviance, and failure continue to represent the "problem-focused" questions posed about non-White diverse American youth. (Spencer, 2006a, p. 272)

Thus, this work points directly at the need to study positive outcomes for all youth, defined within the cultures and contexts in which youth and their families find themselves. The PVEST model provides a sufficiently complex structure in which to do this, in part because the everyday experiences of race that include both overt and subtle racism with which people of color must learn to cope, in addition to the demands of socialization which all youth face, are explicitly acknowledged and modeled (Lee, Spencer, & Harpalini, 2003).

Identifying the "achievement gap" as a significant problem for educational reform in the United States, researchers usually end up attributing performance differences of poor students and students of color to personal attributes such as motivation to attend school and perform well. This tendency ignores how normal developmental processes interact with family, school, and cultural—that is, ecological—factors, as well as poverty-related stigma and other forms of structural inequality. In a major study, Spencer and colleagues evaluated a project that provided monetary incentives to help students achieve in school, specifically high-achieving, low-resource, urban high school youth (Spencer, Noll, & Cassidy, 2005). Rather than providing more school funding for infrastructure improvements and administrator and teacher salaries, the program took the opposite approach of providing stipends directly to students from poor families to support them in maintaining a high academic standing. From the PVEST perspective, monetary incentives may influence and/or reinforce choices made by youth in certain contexts, thus affecting educational outcomes.

Because PVEST takes into account the relationship between stressors and supports in adolescents' lives, it will be useful in framing hypotheses about how monetary incentives may pay a supportive role in the lives of . . . youth by helping them deal with financial stress, enhancing their positive identity development, and freeing them to focus on academic tasks. (Spencer et al., 2005, p. 204)

In order to be able to provide empirical evidence of the effects of stipends, a two-group randomized trial was conducted in the 1999–2000 school year, with 9th–11th graders in a northeastern urban school district. The sample consisted of 534 ethnically diverse youth (45% Black, 23% Asians, 12% Latino/a, 11% White, and 9% other; 69% female). Families of students were required to meet the guidelines for the Federal Free Lunch Program (130% of the poverty line) and students had to have all As and Bs in major subjects to qualify. In addition to collecting information about grades, a survey was administered before the start of the project, annually during high school, and post high school. This survey covered information about family composition and neighborhood, student and family employment, out-of-school activities, how the stipend was used, and several scales, including measures of positive self-identity and acceptance of one's responsibility for learning.

It is not possible here to do justice to the breadth of findings obtained in this study, which continue to be analyzed. After 1 year of the program, students who received stipends were 10% more likely to retain their high academic standing (As and Bs) than students who did not receive stipends (61% versus 51%) and the differences for males and females, and for the different ethnic groups were not significant. However, the percentages of students who maintained grades of As and Bs increased significantly from 9th to 10th to 11th grade (44%, 59%, and 68%, respectively). In addition, students in good standing at the end of the first year had higher mean baseline scores on both the Positive Self-Concept and Learning Responsibility measures.

This study is a rare example of an experimental approach to the study of PYD. The researchers were able to test the effectiveness of one aspect of the context on promoting positive outcomes, while at the same time comparing youth from comparable backgrounds with similar opportunities and barriers to their development. In addition, the incentivizing process was evaluated in an already existing ecology rather than introduced as a new idea. Also unique is the perspective of viewing positive outcomes and potential assets for promoting these outcomes from within the existing culture and context of the youth and their families.

Another example that is consistent with PVEST and the incentivizing project is an educational program rather than a research project that takes seriously the notion that how PYD and assets are defined and identified needs to be contextualized. The Algebra Project (AP) was developed by Robert Moses (Moses & Cobb, 2001) to integrate the learning of algebra with an understanding of the relationships with and responsibilities to communities by demonstrating the ways that using mathematics can be used to improve communities. Algebraic concepts are presented and expressed in terms of everyday experiences of students; older students take on leadership roles by teaching younger students. Students engage in the politics of their schools, create products that may produce economic benefits, and work with adults to obtain resources and learn algebra (Lee et al., 2003).

The work of Spencer and colleagues expands the frame of risk and resiliency research beyond looking at contexts of risk and identifying protective and promotive factors by incorporating notions of injustice and inequality into our models. Structural inequity, racism, and poverty are not individual characteristics, nor are they context specific. They are pervasive facts of American life that affect the segments of the population in various complex ways. At the same time, the actual experience is perceived at the individual level. What one adolescent experiences as stress may not affect his or her neighbor or sibling in the same way (Spencer, 2006b). Spencer argues that in order to effectively promote thriving, these factors will need to be understood better and incorporated into the models and methods of PYD.

The works of the researchers who focus on the resilience of youth highlight the need to view the dynamic relations between the person and context in the study of positive youth development. This reiterates our point above in using developmental systems, or dynamic models of human behavior and development in understanding, first, the plasticity of human development and, second, the importance of relations between individuals and their real-world ecological settings as the bases of variation in the course of human development (Baltes et al., 2006; Lerner, 2005; Silbereisen & Lerner, 2007). We turn now to an overview of the link between PYD and developmental systems theory.

POSITIVE YOUTH DEVELOPMENT AND DEVELOPMENTAL SYSTEMS THEORY

Earlier in this chapter, we noted our approach to the PYD perspective as an orientation to young people that has arisen because of interest among developmental scientists in using developmental systems, or dynamic, models of human behavior and development for understanding, first, the plasticity of human development and, second, the importance of relations between individuals and their real-world ecological settings as the bases of variation in the course of human development. Thus, our research emerges out of the concepts and models associated with developmental systems theories (Cairns & Cairns, 2006; Gottlieb et al., 2006; Lerner, 2002, 2006; Overton, 2006). The roots of these theories may be linked to ideas in developmental science that were presented at least as early as the 1930s and 1940s (e.g., Maier & Schneirla, 1935; Novikoff, 1945a, 1945b; von Bertalanffy, 1933), if not even significantly earlier, for example, in the concepts used by late nineteenth-century and early twentieth-century founders of the study of child development (see Cairns & Cairns, 2006). There are nine defining features of developmental systems theories (drawn from Lerner, 2006) These include:

1. **A relational metatheory**. Predicated on a postmodern philosophical perspective that transcends Cartesian dualism, developmental systems theories are framed by a relational metatheory for human development. There is, then, a rejection of all splits between components of the ecology of human development (e.g., between nature- and nurture-based variables), and between continuity and discontinuity and between stability and instability. Systemic syntheses or integrations replace dichotomizations or other reductionist partitions of the developmental system.

2. **The integration of levels of organization**. Relational thinking and the rejection of Cartesian splits is associated with the idea that all levels of organization within the ecology of human development are integrated, or fused. These levels range from the biological and physiological through the cultural and historical.

3. **Developmental regulation across ontogeny involves mutually influential individual $\leftrightarrow$ context relations**. As a consequence of the integration of levels, the regulation of development occurs through mutually influential connections among all levels of the developmental system, ranging from genes and cell physiology through individual mental and behavioral functioning to society, culture, the designed and natural ecology and, ultimately, history. These mutually influential relations may be represented generically as Level 1 $\leftrightarrow$ Level 2 (e.g., family $\leftrightarrow$ community) and, in the case of ontogeny may be represented as individual $\leftrightarrow$ context.

4. **Integrated actions, individual $\leftrightarrow$ context relations, are the basic unit of analysis within human development**. The character of developmental regulation means that the integration of actions—of the individual on the context and of the multiple levels of the context on the individual (individual $\leftrightarrow$ context)—constitutes the fundamental unit of analysis in the study of the basic process of human development.

5. **Temporality and plasticity in human development.** As a consequence of the

fusion of the historical level of analysis—and therefore temporality—within the levels of organization comprising the ecology of human development, the developmental system is characterized by the potential for systematic change, by plasticity. Observed trajectories of intraindividual change may vary across time and place as a consequence of such plasticity.

6. **Relative plasticity**. Developmental regulation may both facilitate and constrain opportunities for change. Thus, change in individual ↔ context relations is not limitless, and the magnitude of plasticity (the probability of change in a developmental trajectory occurring in relation to variation in contextual conditions) may vary across the life span and history. Nevertheless, the potential for plasticity at both individual and contextual levels constitutes a fundamental strength of all human's development.

7. **Intraindividual change, interindividual differences in intraindividual change, and the fundamental substantive significance of diversity.** The combinations of variables across the integrated levels of organization within the developmental system that provide the basis of the developmental process will vary at least in part across individuals and groups. This diversity is systematic and lawfully produced by idiographic, group differential, and generic (nomothetic) phenomena. The range of interindividual differences in intraindividual change observed at any point in time is evidence of the plasticity of the developmental system, and makes the study of diversity of fundamental substantive significance for the description, explanation, and optimization of human development.

8. **Optimism, the application of developmental science, and the promotion of positive human development**. The potential for and instantiations of plasticity legitimate an optimistic and proactive search for characteristics of individuals and of their ecologies that, together, can be arrayed to promote positive human development across life. Through the application of developmental science in planned attempts (i.e., interventions) to enhance (e.g., through social policies or community-based programs) the character of humans' developmental trajectories, the promotion of positive human development may be achieved by aligning the strengths (operationalized as the potentials for positive change) of individuals and contexts.

9. **Multidisciplinarity and the need for change-sensitive methodologies**. The integrated levels of organization comprising the developmental system require collaborative analyses by scholars from multiple disciplines. Multidisciplinary knowledge and, ideally, interdisciplinary knowledge is sought. The temporal embeddedness and resulting plasticity of the developmental system requires that research designs, methods of observation and measurement, and procedures for data analysis be change-sensitive and able to integrate trajectories of change at multiple levels of analysis.

Conclusions

The possibility of adaptive developmental relations between individuals and their contexts and the potential plasticity of human development that is a defining feature of onto-genetic change within the dynamic, developmental system (Baltes et al., 2006; Gottlieb et al., 2006; Thelen & Smith, 2006) stand as distinctive features of the developmental systems approach to human development and, as well, provide a rationale for making a set of methodological choices that differ in design, measurement, sampling, and data analytic techniques from selections made by researchers using split or reductionist approaches to developmental science. Moreover, the emphasis on how the individual acts on the context to contribute to the plastic relations with the context that regulate adaptive development (Brandtstädter, 2006) fosters an interest in person-centered (as compared to variable-centered) approaches to the study of human development (Magnusson & Stattin, 2006; Overton, 2006; Rathunde & Csikszentmihalyi, 2006).

Furthermore, given that the array of individual and contextual variables involved in these relations constitute a virtually open set (e.g., there are over 70 trillion potential human genotypes and each of them may be coupled across life with an even larger number of life course trajectories of social experiences; Hirsch, 2004), the diversity of development becomes a prime, substantive focus for developmental science (Lerner, 2004b; Spencer, 2006b). The diverse person, conceptualized from a strength-based perspective (in that the potential plasticity of ontogenetic change constitutes a fundamental strength of all humans; Spencer), and approached with the expectation that positive changes can be promoted across all instances of this diversity as a consequence of health-supportive alignments between people and settings (Benson et al., 2006), becomes the necessary subject of developmental science inquiry.

It is in the linkage between the ideas of plasticity and diversity that a basis exists for the extension of developmental systems thinking to the field of adolescence and for the field of adolescence to serve as a "testing ground" for ideas associated with developmental systems theory. This synergy has had at least one key outcome, i.e., the forging of a new, strength-based vision of and vocabulary for the nature of adolescent development. In short, the plasticity–diversity linkage within developmental systems theory and method provided the basis for the formulation of the PYD perspective.

FEATURES OF THE PYD PERSPECTIVE

Beginning in the early 1990s, and burgeoning in the first half-decade of the twenty-first century, a new vision and vocabulary for discussing young people has emerged. These innovations were framed by the developmental

systems theories that were engaging the interest of developmental scientists, some of whom were reviewed earlier in this chapter. The focus on plasticity within such theories led in turn to an interest in assessing the potential for change at diverse points across ontogeny, ones spanning from infancy through the 10th and 11th decades of life (Baltes et al., 2006). Moreover, these innovations were propelled by the increasingly more collaborative contributions of researchers focused on the second decade of life (e.g., Benson et al., 2006; Damon, 2004; Lerner, 2004b), practitioners in the field of youth development (e.g., Floyd & McKenna, 2003; Little, 1993; Pittman, Irby, & Ferber, 2001; Wheeler, 2003), and policy makers concerned with improving the life chances of diverse youth and their families (e.g., Cummings, 2003; Gore, 2003). These interests converged in the formulation of a set of ideas that enabled youth to be viewed as resources to be developed, and not as problems to be managed (Roth & Brooks-Gunn, 2003a, 2003b). These ideas may be discussed in regard to two key hypotheses (from Lerner, 2005). Each hypothesis is associated with two subsidiary hypotheses.

Hypothesis 1: Youth-Context Alignment Promotes PYD

Based on the idea that the potential for systematic intraindividual change across life (i.e., for plasticity) represents a fundamental strength of human development, the hypothesis was generated that, if the strengths of youth are aligned with resources for healthy growth present in the key contexts of adolescent development—the home, the school, and the community—then enhancements in positive functioning at any one point in time (i.e., well-being; Bornstein, Davidson, Keyes, Moore, & Center for Child Well-Being, 2003) may occur; in turn, the systematic promotion of positive development will occur across time (i.e., thriving; e.g., Dowling et al., 2004; Lerner, 1978, 2004b; Lerner et al., 2005).

Hypothesis 1A: Contextual Alignment Involves Marshaling Development Assets

A key subsidiary hypothesis to the notion that aligning individual strengths and contextual resources for healthy development is that there exist, across the key settings of youth development (i.e., families, schools, and communities), at least some supports for the promotion of PYD. As noted earlier in this chapter, these resources are termed developmental assets (Benson, Scales, Hamilton, & Semsa, 2006), and constitute the social and ecological "nutrients" for the growth of healthy youth (Benson, 2003). There exists some controversy in the literature about the number of developmental assets that may exist in different social ecologies. For instance, are there 40 developmental assets (half having their locus within the individual and the other half having their locus in the social ecology) as initially suggested by Search Institute (e.g., Benson, Leffert, Scales, & Blyth, 1998), or are there only 14 developmental assets (half associated with the individual and half associated with the social ecology), as recently reported by colleagues from the Institute for Applied Research in Youth Development and Search Institute (Theokas et al., 2005). There exist questions as well about whether developmental assets should be measured via youth reports, or perceptions, as is done in the survey research of Search Institute (e.g., Benson et al., 1998; Leffert et al., 1998; Scales et al., 2000) and/or through objective assessment of the actual ecology of youth development, as is done in the work of the Institute for Applied Research in Youth Development (Theokas & Lerner, 2006).

Moreover, a question exists about whether, from both theoretical and measurement standpoints, individual developmental assets can be differentiated from constructs related to indicators of PYD (which we discuss below, in Hypothesis 2, as the "Five Cs" of PYD; Eccles & Gootman, 2002; Lerner, 2004b); and, if such differentiation is not feasible conceptually or empirically, then through what processes does the youth contribute to the developmental regulations driving developmental changes (Lerner et al., 2005; Jelicic, Bobek, Phelps, Lerner, & Lerner, 2007; Phelps et al., 2007)? As we discuss later as well, one path taken in research is to explore the use of processes of intentional self-regulations, for instance the goal directed processes of selection, optimization, and compensation studied by Margaret and Paul Baltes and their colleagues (e.g., Baltes & Baltes, 1990; Baltes et al., 2006; Freund, Li, & Baltes, 1999), as a means of individual contribution to the developmental regulatory process linking an individual with ecological assets (Gestsdottir & Lerner, 2007).

Finally, there remains a question about whether the mere accumulation of assets, whatever their source (family, school, or community) is the best predictor of PYD or, in turn, whether there exist particular assets that are of specific salience for youth living in specific communities. While there is a good deal of evidence for the idea that "more is better" (e.g., Benson et al., 2006), this notion has been tested primarily through assessing only youth perceptions of developmental assets. However, there is both some theory, pertinent to the development of African American youth living in urban areas (e.g., Spencer, 2006b; Taylor, 2003; Taylor et al., 2003, reported earlier in this chapter), and some data (Theokas & Lerner, 2006), involving the objective assessment of assets, indicating that there are in fact specific developmental assets in specific settings that are most important as predictors of PYD.

Hypothesis 1B: Community-Based Programs are a Vital Source of Developmental Assets

Despite this controversy about the nature, measurement, and impact of developmental assets, there is broad agreement among researchers and practitioners in the youth development field that the concept of developmental assets is important for understanding what needs to be marshaled in homes, classrooms, and community-based programs to foster PYD. In fact, a key impetus for the interest in the PYD perspective among both researchers and youth program practitioners and, thus, a basis for the collaborations that exist among members of these two communities, is the interest that exists in ascertaining the nature of the resources for positive development that are present in youth programs, for example, in the literally hundreds of thousands of after-school programs delivered either by large, national organizations, such as 4-H, Boys and Girls Clubs, Scouting, Big Brothers/Big Sisters, YMCA, or Girls, Inc., or by local organizations. The focus on youth programs is important not only for practitioners in the field of youth development, however. In addition, the interest on exploring youth development programs as a source of developmental assets for youth derives from theoretical interest in the role of the macrolevel systems effects of the ecology of human development on the course of healthy change in adolescence (Bronfenbrenner & Morris, 2006); interest derives as well from policy makers and advocates, who believe that at this point in the history of the United States community-level efforts are needed to promote positive development among youth (e.g., Cummings, 2003; Gore, 2003; Pittman et al., 2001).

As we discussed earlier in this chapter, there are data suggesting that, in fact, developmental assets associated with youth programs, especially those that focus on youth development (i.e., programs that adopt the ideas associated with the PYD perspective; Roth & Brooks-Gunn, 2003a, 2003b), are linked to PYD. For instance, Scales et al. (2000) found that youth reports of three or more hours a week of participation in sports, clubs, or organizations at school or in the community was the single developmental asset (of the 40 assets they surveyed) that was most linked to thriving outcomes among the adolescents in the Search Institute sample. Lerner (2004b) hypothesized that this relationship emerges due to what he calls the "Big Three" features of optimal youth development programs, that is, (1) positive and sustained (for at least 1 year; Rhodes, 2002) adult–youth relationships; (2) skill building activities; and (3) opportunities to use these

skills by participating in, and leading, community-based activities. Although reviews by Blum (2003); Eccles and Gootman (2002); Larson, Walker, and Pearce (2005); and Roth and Brooks-Gunn (2003a, 2003b) differ in the number of attributes they propose as important for the conduct of youth programs effective in promoting PYD, all of these scholars endorse the importance of the three attributes of after-school activities noted by Lerner (2004a, b) as crucial for promoting exemplary positive development. In addition, Roth and Brooks-Gunn (2003b), in making the above-noted differentiation between youth programs and youth development programs, report that findings of evaluation research indicate that the latter programs are more likely than the former ones to be associated with the presence of key indicators of PYD.

Given the findings above, we raise the question of what are in fact the indicators of PYD. Addressing this question involves the second key hypothesis of the PYD perspective.

Hypothesis 2: PYD is Comprised of Five Cs

Based on both the experiences of practitioners and on reviews of the adolescent development literature (Eccles & Gootman, 2002; Lerner, 2004a, b; Roth & Brooks-Gunn, 2003b), "Five Cs"—competence, confidence, connection, character, and caring—were hypothesized as a way of conceptualizing PYD (and of integrating all the separate indicators of it, such as academic achievement or self-esteem). These five Cs were linked to the positive outcomes of youth development programs reported by Roth and Brooks-Gunn (2003a). In addition, these "Cs" are prominent terms used by practitioners, adolescents involved in youth development programs, and the parents of these adolescents in describing the characteristics of a "thriving youth" (King et al., 2005).

The Five Cs are described in Table 15.2. Briefly, competence includes having a positive view of one's actions in domain specific areas including social, academic, cognitive, physical

TABLE 15.2 The "Five Cs" of Positive Youth Development

Competence: Positive view of one's actions in specific areas, including social, academic, cognitive, health, and vocational. Social competence refers to interpersonal skills (e.g., conflict resolution). Academic competence refers to school performance as shown, in part, by school grades, attendance, and test scores. Cognitive competence refers to cognitive abilities (e.g., decision making). Health competence involves using nutrition, exercise, and rest to keep oneself fit. Vocational competence involves work habits and explorations of career choices.

Confidence: An internal sense of overall positive self-worth and self-efficacy.

Connection: Positive bonds with people and institutions that are reflected in exchanges between the individual and his or her peers, family, school, and community in which both parties contribute to the relationship.

Character: Respect for societal and cultural norms, possession of standards for correct behaviors, a sense of right and wrong (morality), and integrity.

Caring/Compassion: A sense of sympathy and empathy for others.

and vocational domains. Confidence has been operationalized as reflecting an internal sense of overall positive self-worth and self-efficacy, that is, one's global self-regard. Having respect for societal and cultural rules, possession of standards for correct behaviors, a sense of right and wrong (i.e., morality), and integrity are dimensions characterizing character. Connection characterizes having positive bonds with people and institutions that are reflected in healthy, bidirectional exchanges between the individual and peers, family, school, and community, in which both parties contribute to the relationship. And caring or compassion reflects the degree of sympathy and empathy a person demonstrates, or the extent to which individuals feel sorry for the distress of others.

Hypothesis 2A. Contribution is the "6th C"

A hypothesis subsidiary to the postulation of the "Five Cs" as a means to operationalize PYD is that, when a young person manifests the Cs across time (when the youth is thriving), he or she will be on a life trajectory toward an "idealized adulthood" (Csikszentmihalyi & Rathunde, 1998; Rathunde & Csikszentmihalyi, 2006). Theoretically, an ideal adult life is marked by integrated and mutually reinforcing contributions to self (e.g., maintaining one's health and one's ability therefore to remain an active agent in one's own development) and to family, community, and the institutions of civil

society (Lerner, 2004a, b). An adult engaging in such integrated contributions is a person manifesting adaptive developmental regulations (Brandtstädter, 1998, 1999). In addition, life can be viewed as a search for meaning: Why do I do what I do? Why do any of us? What will any of it accomplish in the end? One answer is that our purpose is to make the world a better place for those who come after us (Damon, 2005; Mariano & Damon, in press). Youth who develop positively and reach high levels of the Five Cs are well positioned to aspire to and become active contributors to the world around them.

Thus, an important tenet of this conceptualization of PYD is that youth who exhibit high levels of the Five Cs will engage also in contributions to the world around themselves. Contribution can take many forms on several levels, but is a necessary activity for, and a responsibility of, all citizens in democratic societies. Because of this, promoting PYD in all by providing the means and opportunities is a responsibility of all citizens and institutions in a democracy. Further, contribution to others and to society is the glue that creates and supports healthy human development. When we contribute to a world that supports the rights and welfare of all individuals, we are at the same time building a better life for ourselves by enhancing the lives of others. To survive and prosper, people and society must be inextricably linked in mutually beneficial ways, because unless both the individual and society flourish together, both fail (Lerner, 2007).

Teens can contribute to their families by helping out at home and to their schools by participating in school arts or athletic events, clubs, or school government. They can contribute to their communities by serving on town boards and commissions or by volunteering at local helping organizations such as food banks, nursing homes, and homeless shelters. In participating in activities such as these, youth learn how to contribute and begin to reap the benefits. Youth report many benefits that accrue from their participation. Among these are feeling deeply valued, learning responsibility, gaining new skills, innovating, engaging with a broader range of people, learning organization skills, and perhaps financial management.

Youth activism is a particular form of the sixth C, which implies some critique of the status quo. Specifically, we contend that there are fundamental structural inequities in the distribution of familial, institutional, and community opportunities to contribute, indeed to grow and thrive (Flanagan, Syvertsen, & Wray-Lake, 2007).

Thus, a young person enacts behaviors indicative of the Five Cs by contributing positively to family, community, and ultimately, civil society (Lerner, 2004a, b). Such contributions are envisioned to have both a behavioral (action) component and an ideological component (beliefs that it is one's responsibility to act on one's moral and civic obligations; Lerner, Dowling, & Anderson, 2003). In other words, when youth believe that they should contribute, and when they act on these beliefs, they will both reflect and promote further advances in their own positive development and, also, the health of their social world. Theoretically, there will be adaptive individual ↔ context developmental regulations. The developmental course of the ideological and behavioral components of contributions to society remains to be determined.

In order for the Five Cs to coalesce and lead to the sixth C, contribution, opportunities for giving to others need to exist. There are many mechanisms through which this can occur and we mention briefly three that are frequently available to youth in the United States. There is reason to believe that both positive development and youth contributions to family, community, and society are likely to take place in the context of community-based YD programs. Scales et al. (2000; see also Blum, 2003; Roth & Brooks-Gunn, 2003a, 2003b) have identified participation in youth programs as the key asset linked to exemplary positive development, or thriving, among contemporary American youth. In addition, YD programs promote youth contribution by assuring that the young person has a sustained relationship with at least one committed adult, who provides skill-building opportunities to the youth and acts to enhance the young person's healthy and active engagement with the community (Lerner, 2004a, b). Roth and Brooks-Gunn (2003a, 2003b) indicate that participation in such programs is likely to result in a competent, confident, and caring youth, who has character and positive social connections. Lerner (2004a, b) proposes that such a young person will be oriented to making integrative contributions to family, community, and civil society.

The school-based practice of service learning is another avenue for youth to become engaged with their communities and provide service. This is a teaching strategy in schools in which students learn curricular objectives by providing service that meets real community needs. In many programs, students have considerable voice in determining activities and teachers facilitate knowledge and skill acquisition (Camino & Zeldin, 2002). Service learning is provided in half of all public high schools (Skinner & Chapman, 1999) and 80% of private schools (Pritchard, 2002). Recent evidence suggests that service learning helps students develop knowledge of community needs, commit to an ethic of service, develop more sophisticated understandings of politics and morality, gain a greater sense of civic responsibility, heighten feelings of efficacy, and increase their desire to become active contributors to society (Billig, 2004; Billig, Root, & Jesse, 2005; Westheimer & Kahne, 2000; Youniss & Yates, 1997; Youniss, McLellan, & Yates, 1997).

A third context where opportunities to contribute are readily available to American youth is in religious organizations. For many, spirituality refers to a universal human capacity for transcendence or connectedness beyond the self. In this view, spiritual development is seen as a process of growing the intrinsic human capacity for self-transcendence, recognizing that the self is embedded in something greater than the self and has a responsibility to contribute (King, 2007). A central activity in most religious organizations is providing for those who are less fortunate, and youth are typically introduced to opportunities at young ages (Youniss, 1993; Youniss et al., 1999). Hodgkinson and Weitzman (1997) asked teenagers to indicate the means by which they got involved in service and found that the most frequent categories were school and church, particularly through religious youth groups. Nolin, Chaney, Chapman, & Chandler (1997) reported that students who attended church-affiliated schools were much more likely to do service regularly than students attending public schools.

There are several ways to try to study the specific characteristics of youth that comprise PYD and the characteristics of the contexts that predict positive growth and decreased risk during adolescence. The most powerful approach is to conduct a longitudinal study. We used this approach in the 4-H Study of Positive Youth Development, which we detail next.

EMPIRICAL STATUS OF THE PYD PERSPECTIVE: THE 4-H STUDY OF POSITIVE YOUTH DEVELOPMENT

In order to test the ideas presented in this chapter, the authors and the research group at the IARYD at Tufts University launched the 4-H Study of Positive Youth Development in the fall of 2001. We now turn to a discussion of the study and our findings.

The Model and the Methods of the 4-H Study of Positive Youth Development

The 4-H Study of Positive Youth Development is a longitudinal investigation supported by a grant from the National 4-H Council. The 4-H study is designed to test our theoretical model about the role of developmental assets in promotion of PYD, as conceptualized by the "Five Cs" of PYD (competence, confidence, connection, character, and caring) and of the "sixth C" of contribution, and in the diminution of problem and risk behaviors (Lerner et al., 2005). Figure 15.1 provides an illustration of this theoretical model.

The 4-H Study is an active longitudinal study, with data continuing to be collected annually (at this writing—Fall 2008—we are at the end of the sixth wave of data collection, which focuses on 10th-grade youth). The sampling approach of the 4-H Study was to study youth in their actual environments rather than conducting randomized controlled trials. In these environments, youth and their parents, rather than research investigators, make decisions about how they spend their time. Youth grow and develop in our cities, towns, counties; in our homes, schools, and communities; in OST activities, and so on.

The methodology will be described very briefly here; full details of the methodology of the 4-H Study have been presented in Lerner et al., 2005; Theokas & Lerner, 2006; see also Jelicic et al., 2007). The data collection approach uses a form of longitudinal sequential design. Fifth graders, gathered during the 2002–2003 school year (which was Wave 1 of the study), were the initial cohort within this design. To maintain at least initial levels of power for within-time analyses and to permit assessing the affects of retesting, subsequent waves of the study involved the addition of a new cohort (of youth of the current grade level of the initial cohort); this new cohort is

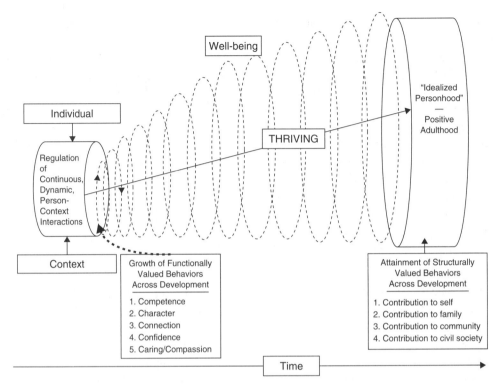

FIGURE 15.1   A Developmental Contextual View of PYD.
NOTE: PYD = Positive youth development.

then followed longitudinally. Overall, across four waves of study over 4,000 youth and 2,000 of their parents from 34 states have been surveyed. At all four waves, the sample varied in race, ethnicity, socioeconomic status, family structure, rural/urban location, geographic region, and program participation experiences. Data are scheduled to continue through at least Wave 8 (grade 12), and most likely through Waves 9 and 10 (post high school).

Data were collected through the use of a student questionnaire (SQ), a parent questionnaire (PQ), and—to assess facets of the settings within which youth develop—from school district administrators and from Web-based or census tract data, for example, about community and school resources and school climate. These data collection tools enable the 4-H Study to obtain information about the Five Cs of PYD, contribution, and risk and problem behaviors (e.g., smoking, drinking, bullying, or depression).

In addition, through obtaining information about the young person's abilities to select positive goals in life (S), to optimize the availability of the resources needed to reach these goals (O), and to compensate (C) when goals are lost or blocked, we are able to assess the individual strengths of adolescents to interact in families, schools, and communities to both develop the Cs and contribution and to diminish the likelihood of risks and problems. Moreover, our data collection procedures enable us identify the resources, or developmental assets, that exist in these settings of youth.

Finally, measures include assessments of several other individual characteristics (demographic variables, identity, puberty, and behavioral and social engagement with schools). We assessed patterns of participation in OST activities (e.g., "ever participated," intensity of participation, or duration across years of participation); these activities include YD programs, such as 4-H, Boys & Girls Clubs, Scouts, YMCA, and Big Brothers/Big Sisters, sports, arts and crafts, interest clubs, religious clubs, performing arts organizations, or service organizations. We gathered information about civic engagement/civic contribution; future aspirations and expectations; relationships with parents, friends, and other adults; and values. We also asked parents about the nature and composition of their household, their parenting style, and their education, employment, and neighborhood.

Key Discoveries to Date

Both the initial findings of the 4-H study, and the more recent findings, have brought empirical data to bear on several key ideas within the PYD perspective. As such, the 4-H Study has helped change research and practice in youth development. We discuss several discoveries about the key premises of the PYD perspective and, as well, about the conceptualization of such development as involving "Five Cs" that, in turn, predict the development of youth contribution. These findings that are based on scholarly publications (books, chapters, and peer-reviewed articles), or presentations at scholarly meetings or conferences, and on doctoral dissertations or master's theses completed at Tufts University.

The Structure and Function of PYD Using data from Wave 1 (grade 5) of the 4-H Study, structural equation modeling procedures provided evidence for five first-order latent factors representing the "Five Cs" of PYD (competence, confidence, connection, character, and caring) and for their convergence on a second-order PYD latent construct. A theoretical construct, youth contribution, was also created and examined. Both PYD and YD program participation were related to contribution (Lerner et al., 2005).

In turn, the expectation that PYD leads to both community contributions and lessened likelihood of risk/problem behaviors was assessed longitudinally by examining whether PYD in grade 5 predicted both youth contributions and risk behaviors and depression in grade 6 (Jelicic et al., 2007). Results of random effects regression and structural equation models indicated that, as expected, PYD in grade 5 predicted higher youth contributions and lower risk behaviors and depression in grade 6. There were significant sex differences for contribution (girls had higher scores) and for risk behaviors (boys had higher scores), but not for depression. In turn, the structural model fit was equivalent for boys and girls.

The Strengths of Youth Through use of data from 5th and 6th graders in the 4-H Study, structural equation modeling procedures, reliability analyses, and assessments of convergent, divergent, and predictive validity indicated that a global, nine-item form of the selection, optimization, and compensation (SOC) measure was a valid index of intentional self-regulation in early adolescence (Gestsdottir & Lerner, 2007), as measured by adolescents' scores for SOC. Indicative of youth abilities to engage in beneficial and positive relations with their social world, positive scores for SOC were related to indicators of positive and negative development in predicted directions, that is, high SOC was associated within and across grades with higher PYD and contribution scores and with lower risk/problem scores.

In turn, using data from grades 5, 6, and 7 of the 4-H Study, we again found that a nine-item index of SOC was valid (Zimmerman, Phelps, & Lerner, 2007). Results of hierarchical linear modeling analysis indicated that statistically significant but substantively minor changes in SOC scores existed across the three grades; these findings supported the use of the grade 5 SOC scores as predictors of subsequent development. Accordingly, grade 5 SOC scores positively predicted grade 7 scores on the Five Cs of PYD and negatively predicted grade 7 depression, delinquency, and risk behaviors. No gender effects were found in regard to changes in SOC scores.

Ecological Assets and PYD The relations among observed ecological assets in the families, schools, and neighborhoods of youth with positive and negative developmental outcomes were assessed with 5th-grade youth from the 4-H Study (Theokas & Lerner, 2006). The majority of participants were Latino (37.5%) or European American (35.5%) and lived in two-parent families. Ecological asset indicators were categorized into four dimensions—individuals, institutions, collective activity, and accessibility—and were measured equivalently across the three contexts. Different dimensions of the family, school, and neighborhood settings had the most comprehensive impact on the different developmental outcomes, specifically collective activity in the family, accessibility in school, and human resources in the neighborhood. However, in all settings, assets associated with individuals were the most potent predictors of PYD. Family assets were most important in the lives of youth. One of the strongest predictors of PYD was eating dinner together as a family.

Youth Development (YD) Programs are Key Developmental Assets   Using data from the 4-H Study, the 983 youth studied in both grades 5 and 6 were found to engage in structured OST activities at high levels (Balsano, Phelps, Theokas, Lerner, & Lerner, in press; Theokas, Lerner, Lerner, & Phelps, 2006). Fewer than 12% did not participate in any activities. Participation in multiple activities was the norm for these youth, and the configuration of activities changed between grades.

In turn, through use of all 5th and 6th graders participating in the 4-H Study (not only longitudinal participants), adolescents participating in YD programs were found to also engage in other types of programs. In Grades 5 and 6, 44.1% and 35.8% of youth, respectively, participated in YD-related programs, but typically in combination with other program types. The most frequent OST program in which youth participated was sports (Balsano et al., in press; Theokas et al., 2006).

Accordingly, using longitudinal data from 1,622 youth (56.8% female) from the first three waves (grades 5, 6, and 7) of the 4-H Study, we employed a pattern-centered approach to assess differences in adolescent functioning depending on what types of OST activities youth were participating in along with their sports participation (Zarrett, Fay, et al., in preparation; Zarrett et al., 2007, 2008). Our findings suggest that youth benefit from their sports participation differently depending on what other types of additional activities they participate in during their OST. In particular, the participation pattern characterized by high participation in sports and YD programs was found to be one of the most effective activity profiles for promoting PYD and preventing youth problems.

Promoting PYD is Not Equivalent to Preventing Risk/Problem Behaviors   Using data from grades 5, 6, and 7 from the 4-H Study, we assessed among 1,184 youth (58.5% female) the patterns of change associated with indicators of PYD and of risks/problem behaviors (Phelps, et al., 2007). Results indicated that five PYD trajectories represent change across grades, four trajectories were associated with indicators of internalizing problems, and three trajectories were associated with indicators of externalizing problems. Although theoretical expectations associated with the study of both child and adolescent resilience and PYD led to the expectation that most youth across the early adolescent period would show change marked by the coupling of increases in PYD and decreases in risk/problem behaviors, only about one-sixth of all youth in the sample manifested this particular pattern of change. Other youth remained stable over time, showed increases in PYD and risk, and declined in PYD. The multiplicity of patterns of conjoint trajectories for PYD and risks/problem behaviors constitutes a challenge for both developmental theory and applications aimed at enhancing resilience and positive development among adolescents.

School Bullying and PYD   School bullying has negative implications for adolescent academic competence, making it important to explore what factors promote such competence for adolescents who bully and who are bullied (Ma, 2007; Ma, Phelps, Lerner, & Lerner, in press). Data derived from grades 5 and 6 of the 4-H Study indicated that being a bully negatively impacted academic competence above and beyond the adolescents' demographic background, including sex and maternal education, and prior year academic competence. Random effects hierarchical regression analyses of a subsample of 250 adolescents suggested that educational expectations and school engagement interacted in fostering academic competence for bullies and victims.

In turn, data derived from grades 5, 6, and 7 of the 4-H Study, suggested that being a bully predicted lower self-reported grades over time, and being a bully was more detrimental for girls than for boys. Being a bully and being a victim negatively predicted self-perceived academic competence, but these predictive effects did not change over time or differ by sex.

Several selected contextual and individual variables acted as developmental assets for academic competence in the context of bullying. Teacher support positively predicted self-reported grades, and the effect was stronger for victims than for a comparison group of nonvictims. Greater parent support and teacher support independently predicted higher self-perceived academic competence. Greater educational expectations and school engagement independently predicted higher self-reported grades, while these two predictors positively interacted in explaining self-perceived academic competence. Unexpectedly, peer support negatively predicted self-reported grades for victims, and it also negatively predicted self-perceived academic competence for bullies.

School Engagement and Academic Competence Relations between school engagement and academic competence were assessed through the use of grades 5 and 6 data from the 4-H Study (Li, 2007). Factor analyses provided evidence for two school engagement components, behavioral and emotional. The results of hierarchical linear regression analyses indicated that several individual and contextual factors predicted both facets of school engagement: Youth who had higher scores

for intentional self-regulation, who perceived mothers as being warmer, and perceived their school atmosphere as being more positive reported higher levels of behavioral and emotional school engagement. There were sex differences (favoring girls) for both behavioral and emotional school engagement, but not for perceived academic competence. Behavioral school engagement at grade 5 predicted higher perceived academic competence in grade 6, after demographic and individual variables were controlled. Emotional school engagement did not predict perceived academic competence.

Civic Identity and Civic Engagement in 8th Grade Using findings from the 8th-grade wave of data collected from the 4-H Study, exploratory factor analysis identified eight indicators of civic identity/civic engagement (neighborhood social capital/social trust, peer social capital/social trust, adult social capital/social trust, civic duty, civic information, civic voice, civic helping, and civic activities) and, as well, an overall civic identity/civic engagement (CICE) score (Bobek, 2007). Participation in youth development organizations was used to predict scores on the resulting indicators. Table 15.3 lists these measurements.

Results indicated that participation in youth development programs had a positive impact on civic identity. For seven of the eight factors of civic identity and for civic identity overall, young people who participated in these organizations had higher scores than young people who did not participate in these organizations.

TABLE 15.3   Civic Identity and Civic Engagement (CICE) Factors

1. Neighborhood Social Capital/Social Trust
2. Peer Social Capital/Social Trust
3. Adult Social Capital/Social Trust
4. Civic Duty
5. Civic Information
6. Civic Voice
7. Civic Helping
8. Civic Activities

Based on Bobek (2007).

In summary, we believe that the results of the 4-H study of PYD have allowed us to gain powerful and practical insights into what constitutes PYD and what other individual and contextual factors guide an adolescent on a positive trajectory. We believe that the systems approach we have taken has been useful in understanding, first, the plasticity of human development and, second, the importance of relations between adolescents and their real-world ecological settings.

CONCLUSIONS AND FUTURE DIRECTIONS

In the past two decades we have seen a surge of research focused on the positive view of human development. In the adolescent literature, this focus has been aimed primarily at replacing the deficit view of youth as "problems to be managed" with the view that youth are "resources to be developed." Scholars have focused on the strengths of the individual, the factors in the context that support and promote those strengths, and the relationships between the two.

In terms of the contextual factors that promote PYD, we believe that the role of the context needs to be taken more seriously as well as the bidirectional effects that occur between the person and the context. Scholars should also aim to adopt a common language and system of measurement for individual and contextual assets. There is a need to differentiate individual assets from indicators of PYD since constructs can be seen as both outcomes and predictors. In addition, the characteristics of the contexts other than youth development programs and of the adults who promote PYD in youth should also be studied. In terms of the individual, factors related to the brain, hormones, genes, and gene–environment interactions need to be included in future work.

The extent to which the concept of PYD applies cross-culturally is an important question yet to be considered. Two program evaluations conducted in the United States, one in a Vietnamese community (Kegler, Young, Marshall, Bui, & Rodine 2005) and another in a Chicano-Latino community (Bloomberg, Ganey, Alba, Quintero, & Alcantara, 2003), suggest that concepts of PYD, such as confidence, connection, competence and contribution, are culturally relevant and viewed within the respective cultures as related to positive outcomes in youth. Research on the topic is needed with diverse groups in the United States, as well as internationally, both in Western and non-Western cultures. For example, what does PYD look like for males versus females; in racial/ethnic groups; and among gay, lesbian, bisexual, and transgendered (GLBT) youth and immigrant youth? Does it look different and should it be defined differently? In addition, a focus on the ideological, behavioral, and motivational components of PYD would add depth to our understanding of the overall development of all youth.

Furthermore, it is necessary to broaden the scope of contexts of PYDs that are being investigated. Currently, the role of community-based programs in promoting PYD receives substantial attention in the literature. There are other important contexts, such as families, schools and workplaces, where young people spend large portions of their time. The assets and developmental opportunities available in these contexts need to be considered by researchers for further elaboration of the ecological influences on PYD. On the level of practice, professionals working with families and schools, as well as employers who hire youth, would benefit from being educated about possible applications of PYD perspective in these settings.

The idea that the development of positive behaviors will lead to the reduction of negative ones should continue to be part of the research agenda, and as the 4-H study results reveal, youth who are developing positively are also engaging in some level of risk behaviors. This means that risk behaviors need to be studied along with positive ones. The multiple trajectories of development seen in the 4-H study support the idea that efforts should be aimed at understanding the factors that contribute to these individual differences. Scholars who work in both resilience and PYD have taken a systems view of the developing adolescent and have included individual, contextual and relational variables into their models (See the work of Spencer, Taylor, Masten, Lerner and colleagues. It is in these relationships that the focus of research should be placed.

To expand the above, if the 5 Cs are a good representation of PYD, are they equivalent across the second decade of life and for the different groups listed above? To address the questions above, we can use models such as PVEST (See Spencer) and thriving models (See Lerner and colleagues) to frame future research. Finally, there is a need to look at longer term outcomes of PYD as youth enter adulthood.

To reiterate what we noted earlier in the chapter, the diverse person, conceptualized from a strength-based perspective (in that the potential plasticity of ontogenetic change constitutes a fundamental strength of all humans; Spencer, 2006b), and approached with the expectation that positive changes can be promoted across all instances of this diversity as a consequence of health-supportive alignments between people and settings (Benson et al., 2006), becomes the necessary subject of developmental science inquiry.

REFERENCES

Allison, K. W. (1993). Adolescents living in "non-family" and alternative settings. In R. M. Lerner (Ed.), *Early adolescence: Perspectives on research, policy, and intervention* (pp. 37–50). Hillsdale, NJ: Lawrence Erlbaum.

Balsano, A., Phelps, E., Theokas, C., Lerner, J. V., & Lerner, R. M. (in press). Patterns of early adolescents' participation in youth developing programs having positive youth development. *Journal of Research on Adolescence*.

Baltes, P. B., & Baltes, M. M. (1990). Psychological perspectives on successful aging: The model of selective optimization with compensation. In P. B. Baltes & M. M. Baltes (Eds.), *Successful aging: Perspectives from the behavioral sciences* (pp. 1–34). New York: Cambridge University Press.

Baltes, P. B., Lindenberger, U., Staudinger, U. (2006). Life span theory in developmental psychology. In R. M. Lerner (Ed.). *Handbook of child psychology* (6th ed.), vol. 1: *Theoretical models of human development*. (pp. 569–664). (Editors-in-chief: W. Damon & R. M. Lerner.) Hoboken, NJ: John Wiley & Sons.

Benson, P. (1997). *All kids are our kids: What communities must do to raise caring and responsible children and adolescents*. San Francisco: Jossey- Bass.

Benson, P. L. (2003). Developmental assets and asset-building community: Conceptual and empirical foundations. In R. M. Lerner & P. L. Benson (Eds.), *Developmental assets and asset-building communities: Implications for research, policy, and practice* (pp. 19–43). New York: Kluwer Academic/Plenum Press.

Benson, P. (2007). Developmental assets: An overview of theory, research, and practice. In R. K. Silbereisen & R. M. Lerner (Eds.), *Approaches to positive youth development*. Thousand Oaks, CA: Sage.

Benson, P. L., Leffert, N., Scales, P. C., & Blyth, D. A. (1998). Beyond the "village" rhetoric: Creating healthy communities for children and adolescents. *Applied Developmental Science*, 2, 138–159.

Benson, P. L., Scales, P. C., Hamilton, S. F., & Semsa, A., Jr. (2006). Positive youth development: Theory, research, and applications. In R. M. Lerner (Ed.), *Handbook of child psychology* (6th ed.), vol. 1: *Theoretical models of human development*. (pp. 894–941). (Editors-in-chief: W. Damon & R. M. Lerner.) Hoboken, NJ: John Wiley & Sons.

Billig, S. H. (2004). Heads, hearts, hands: The research of K–12 service-learning. In J. Kielsmeier, M. Neal, & M. McKinnon (Eds.), *Growing to greatness: The state of service-learning projects* (pp. 12–25). St Paul, MN: National Youth Leadership Council.

Billig, S. H., Root, S., & Jesse, D. (2005). *The impact of participation in service-learning on high school students' civic engagement*. Circle Working Paper 33.

Bloomberg, L., Ganey, A., Alba, V., Quintero, G., Alcantara, L. A. (2003). Chicano–Latino Youth Leadership Institute: An asset-based program for youth. *American Journal of Health Behavior*, 27, S45–S54.

Blum, R. W. (2003). Positive youth development: A strategy for improving adolescent health. In R. M. Lerner, F. Jacobs, & D. Wertlieb (Eds.), *Handbook of applied developmental science: Promoting positive child, adolescent, and family development through research, policies, and programs*, vol. 2. *Enhancing the life chances of youth and families: Public service systems and public policy perspectives* (pp. 237–252). Thousand Oaks, CA: Sage.

Bobek, D. (2007). *Maintaining civil society and democracy: The role of youth development organizations in promoting civic identity development*. Doctoral dissertation, Tufts University, Medford, MA.

Boring, E. G. (1929). *A history of experimental psychology* (2nd ed.). New York: Century.

Bornstein, M. H., Davidson, L., Keyes, C. M., Moore, K., & Center for Child Well-Being (Eds.). (2003). *Well-being: Positive development across the life course*. Mahwah, NJ: Lawrence Erlbaum.

Brandtstädter, J. (1998). Action perspectives on human development. In W. Damon & R. M. Lerner (Eds.), *Handbook of child psychology*, vol. 1. *Theoretical models of human development* (5th ed., pp. 807–863). New York: John Wiley & Sons.

Brandtstädter, J. (1999). The self in action and development: Cultural, biosocial, and onotgenetic bases of intentional self-development. In J. Brandtstädter & R. M. Lerner (Eds.), *Action and self-development: Theory and research through the life-span* (pp. 37–65). Thousand Oaks, CA: Sage.

Brandtstädter, J. (2006). Action perspectives on human development. In R. M. Lerner (Ed.), *Handbook of child psychology* (6th ed.), vol. 1: *Theoretical models of human development*. (pp. 516–568). (Editors-in-chief: W. Damon & R. M. Lerner). Hoboken, NJ: John Wiley & Sons.

Bronfenbrenner, U., & Morris, P. A. (2006). The bioecological model of human development. In R. M. Lerner (Ed.), *Handbook of child psychology* (6th ed.), vol. 1: *Theoretical models of human development*. (Editors-in-chief: W. Damon & R. M. Lerner). Hoboken, NJ: John Wiley & Sons.

Camino, L., & Zeldin, S. (2002) From periphery to center: Pathways for youth civic engagement in the day-to-day life of communities. *Applied Developmental Science*, 6, 213–220.

Cairns, R. B., & Cairns, B. D. (2006). The making of developmental psychology. In R. M. Lerner (Ed.). *Handbook of child psychology* (6th ed.), vol. 1: *Theoretical models of human development* (pp. 89–165). (Editors-in-chief: W. Damon & R. M. Lerner.) Hoboken, NJ: John Wiley & Sons.

Catalano, R. S., Berglund., L. M., Ryan, J. A. M., Lonczak, H. S., & Hawkins, J. D. (2004). Positive youth development in the United States: Research findings on evaluations of positive youth development programs. *Annals of the American Academy of Political and Social Science*, 594, 98–124.

Csikszentmihalyi, M., & Rathunde, K. (1998). The development of the person: An experiential perspective on the ontogenesis of psychological complexity. In W. Damon (Series Ed.) & R. M. Lerner (Volume Ed.), *Handbook of child psychology*, vol. 1: *Theoretical models of human development* (5th ed.; 635–684). New York: John Wiley & Sons.

Cummings, E. (2003). Foreword. In D. Wertlieb, F. Jacobs, & R. M. Lerner (Eds.), *Promoting positive youth and family development: Community systems, citizenship, and civil society:* vol. 3. *Handbook of applied developmental science: Promoting positive child, adolescent, and family development through research, policies, and programs* (pp. ix–xi). Thousand Oaks, CA: Sage.

Damon, W. (2003). *Noble purpose: The joy of living a meaningful life*. West Radnor, PA: Templeton Foundation Press.

Damon, W. (2004). What is positive youth development? *Annals of the American Academy of Political and Social Science*, 591, 13–24.

Damon, W. (2008). *The path to purpose: Helping our children find their calling in life*. New York: Simon & Schuster.

Dowling, E., Gestsdottir, S., Anderson, P., Von Eye, A., Almerigi, J., & Lerner, R. M. (2004). Structural relations among spirituality, religiosity, and thriving in adolescence. *Applied Developmental Science*, 8, 7–16.

Dupree, D., Spencer, M. B., & Fegley, S. (2007). Perceived social inequity and responses to conflict among diverse youth of color: The effects of social and physical context on youth behavior and attitudes. In R. K. Silbereisen & R. M. Lerner (Eds.), *Approaches to positive youth development*. Thousand Oaks, CA: Sage.

Dworkin, J. B., Larson, R., & Hansen, D. (2003). Adolescents' accounts of growth experiences in youth activities. *Journal of Youth and Adolescence* 32, 17–26.

Eccles, J., & Gootman, J. A. (Ed.). (2002). *Community programs to promote youth development/Committee on Community-Level Programs for Youth*. Washington, DC: National Academy Press.

Fisher, C. B., Jackson, J. F., & Villarruel, F. A. (1998). The study of African American and Latin American children and youth. In R. M. Lerner (Ed.), *Handbook of child psychology*, vol. 1: *Theoretical models of human development* (5th ed., pp. 1145–1207). New York: John Wiley & Sons.

Flanagan, C., Syvertsen, A., & Wray-Lake, L. (2007). Youth political activism: Sources of public hope in the context of globalization. In R. K. Silbereisen & R. M. Lerner (Eds.), *Approaches to positive youth development*. Thousand Oaks, CA: Sage.

Flay, B. R. (2002). Positive youth development requires comprehensive health promotion programs. *American Journal of Health Behavior*, 26, 407–424.

Floyd, D. T., & McKenna, L. (2003). National youth serving organizations in the United States: Contributions to civil society. In R. M. Lerner, F. Jacobs, & D. Wertlieb (Eds.), *Handbook of applied developmental science: Promoting positive child, adolescent, and family development through research, policies, and programs*, vol. 3: *Promoting positive youth and family development: Community systems, citizenship, and civil society*. (pp. 11–26). Thousand Oaks, CA: Sage.

Freund, A. M., Li, K. Z. H., & Baltes, P. B. (1999). The role of selection, optimization, and compensation in successful aging. In J. Brandtstädter & R. M. Lerner (Eds.), *Action and development: Origins and functions of intentional self-development* (pp. 401–434). Thousand Oaks, CA: Sage.

Gestsdottir, S., & Lerner, R. M. (2007). Intentional self-regulation and positive youth development in early adolescence: Findings from the 4-H Study of Positive Youth Development. *Developmental Psychology*, 43, 508–521.

Gillham, J. E., Jaycox, L. H., Reivich, K. J., Seligman, M. E. P., & Silver, T. (1990). *The Penn Resiliency Program*. Unpublished manual, Philadelphia: University of Pennsylvania.

Gillham, J. E., Reivich, K. J., Freres, D. R., Lascher, M., Litzinger, S., Shatte, A., et al. (2006). School-based prevention of depression and anxiety symptoms in early adolescence: A pilot of a parent intervention component. *School Psychology Quarterly*, 21, 323–348.

Gillham, J. E., Reivich, K. J., Freres, D. R., Chaplin, T. M., Shatte, A. J., Samuels, B., et al. (2007). School-based prevention of depressive symptoms: A randomized controlled study of the effectiveness and specificity of the Penn Resiliency Program. *Journal of Consulting and Clinical Psychology*, 75, 9–19.

Gore, A. (2003). Foreword. In R. M. Lerner & P. L. Benson (Eds.), *Developmental assets and asset-building communities: Implications for research, policy, and practice* (pp. xi–xii). Norwell, MA: Kluwer.

Gottlieb, G. (1997). *Synthesizing nature–nurture: Prenatal roots of instinctive behavior*. Mahwah, NJ: Lawrence Erlbaum.

Gottlieb, G., Wahlsten, D., & Lickliter, R. (2006). The significance of biology for human development: A developmental psychobiological systems perspective. In R. M. Lerner (Ed.), *Handbook of child psychology* (6th ed.), vol. 1: *Theoretical models of human development*. (pp. 210–257). (Editors-in-chief: W. Damon & R. M. Lerner.) Hoboken, NJ: John Wiley & Sons.

Granic, I., Patterson, G. R. (2006). Toward a comprehensive model of antisocial development: A dynamic systems approach. *Psychological Review*, 113, 101–131.

Hamilton, S. F. (1994). Employment prospected as motivation for school achievement: Links and gaps between school and work in seven countries. In R. K. Silbereisen & E. Todt (Eds.), *Adolescence in context: The interplay of family, school, peers, and work in adjustment* (pp. 267–303). New York: Springer.

Hamilton, S. F., & Hamilton, M. A. (1999). *Building strong school-to-work systems: Illustrations of key components*. Washington, DC: National School-to-Work Office.

Hamilton, S.F., & Hamilton, M.A. (2004). Contexts for mentoring. In R.M. Lerner & L. Steinberg (Eds.), *Handbook of adolescent psychology*. Hoboken, NJ: John Wiley & Sons.

Hamilton, M. A., & Hamilton, S. F. (2005). Work and service-learning. In D. L. Dubois & M. K. Karcher (Eds.), *Handbook of youth mentoring* (pp. 348–363). Thousand Oaks, CA: Sage.

Hamilton, S. F., & Hamilton, M. A. (2006). School, work, and emerging adulthood. In J. J. Arnett & J. L. Tanner (Eds.), *Emerging adults in America: Coming of age in the 21st century* (pp. 257–277). Washington, DC: American Psychological Association.

Hamilton, S. F., & Lempert, W. (1997). The impact of apprenticeship on youth: A prospective analysis. *Journal of Research on Adolescence*, 6, 427–455.

Harter, S. (1982). The perceived competence scale for children. *Child Development*, 53, 87–97.

Harter, S. (1985a). Competence as a dimension of self-evaluation: Toward a comprehensive model of self-worth. In R. L. Leahy (Ed.), *The development of the self* (pp. 55–121). Orlando, FL: Academic Press.

Harter, S. (1985b). *The self-perception profile for children: Revision of the perceived competence scale for children*. Unpublished manuscript. Denver, CO: University of Denver.

Harter, S. (1986). *Manual: Self-perception profile for adolescents*. Unpublished manuscript. Denver, CO: University of Denver.

Hirsch, J. (2004). Uniqueness, diversity, similarity, repeatability, and heritability. In C. Garcia Coll, E. Bearer, & R. M. Lerner (Eds.), *Nature and nurture: The complex interplay of genetic and environmental influences on human behavior and development* (pp. 127–138). Mahwah, NJ: Lawrence Erlbaum.

Hodgkinson, V. A., & Weitzman, M. S. (1997). *Volunteering and giving among American teenagers 14 to 17 year of age.* Washington, DC: Independent Sector.

Huston, A. C. (1991). *Children in poverty: Child development and public policy.* Cambridge, UK: Cambridge University Press.

Jelicic, H., Bobek, D., Phelps, E. D., Lerner, J. V., Lerner, R. M. (2007). Using positive youth development to predict contribution and risk behaviors in early adolescence: Findings from the first two waves of the 4-H Study of Positive Youth Development. *International Journal of Behavioral Development, 31,* 263–273.

Kegler, M., Young, K., Marshall, L., Bui, D., & Rodine, S. (2005). Positive youth development linked with prevention in a Vietnamese American community: Successes, challenges, and lessons learned. *Journal of Adolescent Health, 37,* S69–S79.

Keyes, C. L. M. (1998). Social well being. *Social Psychology Quarterly, 61,* 121–140.

Keyes, C. L. M. (2005). Mental health and/or mental illness? Investigating axioms of the complete state model of health. *Journal of Consulting and Clinical Psychology, 73,* 539–548.

Keyes, C. L. M. (2006). Mental health in adolescence: Is America's youth flourishing. *American Journal of Orthopsychiatry, 76,* 395–402.

Keyes, C. L. M. (2007). Promoting and protecting mental health as flourishing: A complementary strategy for improving national mental health. *American Psychologist, 62,* 95–108.

King, P. E. (2007). Adolescent spirituality and positive youth development: A look at religion, social capital, and moral functioning. In R. K. Silbereisen & R. M. Lerner (Eds.), *Approaches to positive youth development.* Thousand Oaks, CA: Sage.

King, P. E., Dowling, E. M., Mueller, R. A., White, K., Schultz, W., Osborn, P., et al. (2005). Thriving in adolescence: The voices of youth-serving practitioners, parents, and early and late adolescents. *Journal of Early Adolescence, 25,* 94–112.

Larson, R. W. (2000). Toward a psychology of positive youth development. *American Psychologist, 55,* 170–183.

Larson, R. (2001). How U.S. children and adolescents spend time: What it does (and doesn't) tell us about their development. *Current Directions in Psychological Science, 10,* 160–164.

Larson, R. W. (2002). Globalization, societal change, and new technologies: What they mean for the future of adolescence. *Journal of Research on Adolescence, 12,* 1–30.

Larson, R. (2006). Positive youth development, willful adolescents, and mentoring. *Journal of Community Psychology, 34,* 677–689.

Larson, R. W. (2007). From "I" to "we": Development of the capacity for teamwork in youth programs. In R. K. Silbereisen & R. M. Lerner (Eds.). *Approaches to positive youth development* (pp. 277–292). London: Sage.

Larson, R., & Hansen, D. (2005). The development of strategic thinking: Learning to impact human systems in a youth activism program. *Human Development, 48,* 327–349.

Larson, R. W., Hansen, D. M., & Moneta, G. (2006). Differing profiles of developmental experiences across types of organized youth activities. *Developmental Psychology, 42,* 849–863.

Larson, R., Hansen, D., & Walker, K. (2005). Everybody's gotta give: Development of initiative and teamwork within youth program. In J. L. Mahoney, R.W. Larson, & J. S. Eccles, (Eds.), *Organized activities as contexts of development: Extracurricular activities, after-school and community programs.* Mahwah, NJ: Lawrence Erlbaum.

Larson, R., & Seepersad, S. (2003). Adolescents' leisure time in the United States: Partying, sports, and the American experiment. *New Directions for Child and Adolescent Development 2003,* 53–64.

Larson, R. W., & Richards, M. H. (1991). Boredom in the middle school years: Blaming schools versus blaming students. *American Journal of Education, 99,* 418–443.

Larson, R. W., & Verma, S. (1999). How children and adolescents spend time across the world: Work, play, and developmental opportunities. *Psychology Bulletin, 125,* 701–736.

Larson, R. W., & Walker, K. C. (2006). Learning about the "real world" in an urban arts youth program. *Journal of Adolescent Research, 21,* 244–268.

Larson, R., Walker, K., & Pearce, N. (2005). A Comparison of youth-driven and adult-driven youth programs: Balancing inputs from youth and adults. *Journal of Community Psychology, 33,* 57–74.

Larson, R. W., & Wilson, S. (2004). Adolescence across place and time: Globalization and the changing pathways to adulthood. In R. M. Lerner, & L. Steinberg (Eds.), *Handbook of adolescent psychology* (2nd ed., pp. 299–331). Hoboken, NJ: John Wiley & Sons.

Larson, R. W., Wilson, S., Brown, B. B., Furstenberg, F. F., Jr., & Verma, S. (2002). Changes in adolescents' interpersonal experiences: Are they being prepared for adult relationships in the twenty-first century? *Journal of Research on Adolescence, 12,* 31–68.

Larson, R., Jarrett, R., Hansen, D., Pearce, N., Sullivan, P., Walker, K., et al. (2004). Organized youth activities as contexts of positive development. In P.A. Linley & S. Joseph (Eds.), *Positive psychology in practice* (pp. 540–560). Hoboken, NJ: John Wiley & Sons.

Lee, C. D., Spencer, M. B., & Harpalani, V. (2003). "Every shut eye ain't sleep": Studying how people live culturally. *Educational Researcher, 32,* 6–13.

Leffert, N., Benson, P., Scales, P., Sharma, A., Drake, D., & Blyth, D. (1998). Developmental assets: Measurement and prediction of risk behaviors among adolescents. *Applied Developmental Science, 2,* 209–230.

Lerner, R. M. (1978). Nature, nurture, and dynamic interactionism. *Human Development, 21,* 1–20.

Lerner, R. M. (2002). *Concepts and theories of human development* (3rd ed.). Mahwah, NJ: Lawrence Erlbaum.

Lerner, R. M. (2004a). *Liberty: Thriving and civic engagement among America's youth.* Thousand Oaks, CA: Sage.

Lerner, R. M. (2004b). Diversity in individual ↔ context relations as the basis for positive development across the life span: A developmental systems perspective for theory, research, and application. *Research in Human Development, 1,* 327–346.

Lerner, R. M. (2005, September). *Promoting positive youth development: Theoretical and empirical bases.* White paper prepared for the Workshop on the Science of Adolescent Health and Development, National Research Council/Institute of Medicine. Washington, DC: National Academies of Science.

Lerner, R. M. (2006). Developmental science, developmental systems, and contemporary theories of human development. In R. M. Lerner (Ed.), *Handbook of child psychology* (6th ed.), vol. 1: *Theoretical models of human development.* (pp. 1–17). (Editors-in-chief: W. Damon & R. M. Lerner.) Hoboken, NJ: John Wiley & Sons.

Lerner, R. M. (2007). *The good teen: Rescuing adolescents from the myths of the storm and stress years.* New York: Crown.

Lerner, R. M., Dowling, E. M., & Anderson, P. M. (2003). Positive youth development: Thriving as a basis of personhood and civil society. *Applied Developmental Science, 7,* 172–180.

Lerner, R. M., Fisher, C. B., & Weinberg, R. A. (2000). Toward a science for and of the people: Promoting civil society through the application of developmental science. *Child Development, 71,* 11–20.

Lerner, R. M., Freund, A. M., De Stefanis, I., & Habermas, T. (2001). Understanding developmental regulation in adolescence: The use of the selection, optimization, and compensation model. *Human Development, 44,* 29–50.

Lerner, R. M., Lerner, J. V., Almerigi, J., Theokas, C., Phelps, E., Gestsdottir, S., et al. (2005). Positive youth development, participation in community youth development programs, and community contributions of fifth grade adolescents: Findings from the first wave of the 4-H Study of Positive Youth Development. *Journal of Early Adolescence, 25,* 17–71.

Lerner, R. M., Sparks, E. S., & McCubbin, L. (1999). *Family diversity and family policy: Strengthening families for America's children.* Norwell, MA: Kluwer Academic.

Lerner, R. M., & Steinberg, L. (Eds.). (2004). *Handbook of adolescent psychology.* Hoboken, NJ: John Wiley & Sons.

Li, Y. (2007). *School engagement and academic competence: The roles of individual and contextual assets. Master's thesis.* Medford, MA: Tufts University.

Little, R. R. (1993). *What's working for today's youth: The issues, the programs, and the learnings.* Paper presented at the ICYF Fellows Colloquium, Michigan State University.

Luster, T., & McAdoo, H. P. (1994). Factors related to the achievement and adjustment of young African American children. *Child Development, 65,* 1080–1094.

Luster, T., & McAdoo, H. P. (1996). Family and child influences on educational attainment: A secondary analysis of the High/Scope Perry Preschool data. *Developmental Psychology, 32,* 26–39.

Ma, L. (2007). *The development of academic competence among adolescents who bully and who are bullied.* Doctoral dissertation. Medford, MA: Tufts University.

Ma, L., Phelps, E., Lerner, J. V., & Lerner, R. M. (In press). Longitudinal research on school bullying: Adoelscents who bully and who are bullied. In D. Buchanan, C. B. Fisher, & L. Gable (Eds.). *Ethical & legal Issues in research with high risk populations: Addressing Threats of Suicide, Child Abuse, and Violence.* Washington, DC: APA Books.

Magnusson, D., & Stattin, H. (2006). The person in the environment: Towards a general model for scientific inquiry. In R. M. Lerner (Ed.), *Handbook of child psychology* (6th ed.), vol. 1: *Theoretical models of human development* (pp. 400–464). (Editors-in-chief: W. Damon & R. M. Lerner.) Hoboken, NJ: John Wiley & Sons.

Mahoney, J. L., Larson, R.W., Eccles, J.S., & Lord, H. (2005). Organized activities as developmental contexts for children and adolescents. In J. L. Mahoney, R.W. Larson, & J. S. Eccles (Eds.), *Organized activities as contexts of development: Extracurricular activities, after-school and community programs.* Mahwah, NJ: Lawrence Erlbaum.

Maier, N. R. F., & Schneirla, T. C. (1935). *Principles of animal behavior.* New York: McGraw-Hill.

Mariano, J. M., & Damon, W. (2008). The role of spirituality in supporting purpose in adolescence. In R. Roeser, E. Phelps, & R. M. Lerner (Eds.), *Positive youth development and spirituality: From theory to research* (pp. 210–230). West Conshohocken, PA: Templeton Foundation Press.

Masten, A. S. (2001). Ordinary magic: Resilience processes in development. *American Psychologist, 56,* 227–238.

Masten, A. S. (2004). Regulatory processes, risk and resilience in adolescent development. *Annals of the New York Academy of Sciences, 1021,* 310–319.

Masten, A. S. (2006). Developmental psychopathology: Pathways to the future. *International Journal of Behavioral Development, 31,* 46–53.

Masten, A. S. (2007). Resilience in developing systems: Progress and promise as the fourth wave rises. *Development and Psychopathology, 19,* 921–930.

Masten, A. S., & Coatsworth, J. D. (1995). Competence, resilience, and psychopathology. *Risk, Disorder, and Adaptation, 2,* 715–752.

Masten, A. S., & Coatsworth, J. D. (1998). The development of competence in favorable and unfavorable environments: Lessons from research on successful children. *American Psychologist, 53,* 205–220.

Masten, A. S., Coatsworth, J. D., Neeman, J., Gest, S. D., Tellegen, A., & Garmezy, N. (1995). The structure and coherence of competence through adolescence. *Child Development, 66,* 1635–1659.

Masten, A. S., & Curtis, W. J. (2000). Integrating competence and psychopathology: Pathways toward a comprehensive science of adaptation in development. *Development and Psychopathology, 12,* 529–550.

Masten, A. S., Hubbard, J., Gest, S. D., Tellegen, A., Garmezy, N., & Ramirez, M. (1999). Adversity, resources and resilience: Pathways to competence from childhood to late adolescence. *Development and Psychopathology, 11,* 143–169.

Masten, A. S., Long, J. D., Roisman, G. I., Burt, K. B., Obradovic, J., & Roberts, J. M. (2005). Developmental cascades: Linking academic achievement, externalizing and internalizing symptoms over 20 years. *Developmental Psychology, 41,* 733–746.

Masten, A. S., & Obradović, J. (2006). Competence and resilience in development. *Annals of the New York Academy of Sciences, 1094,* 13–27.

McAdoo, H. P. (1995). Stress levels, family help patterns, and religiosity in middle- and working class African American single mothers. *Journal of Black Psychology, 21,* 424–449.

McAdoo, H. P. (1999). Diverse children of color. In H. E. Fitzgerald, B. M. Lester, & B. S. Zuckerman (Eds.), *Children of color: Research, health, and policy issues* (pp. 205–218). New York: Garland Publishing.

McHale, S. M, Crouter, A. C., & Tucker, C. J. (2001). Free time activities in middle childhood Links with adjustment in early adolescence. *Child Development, 72,* 1764–1778.

McLoyd, V. C. (1998). Children in poverty: Development, public policy, and practice. In W. Damon (Series Ed.), I. Sigel, & K. A. Renninger (Eds.), *Handbook of child psychology,* vol 4: *Child psychology in practice* (5th ed., pp. 135–208). New York: John Wiley & Sons.

Mincy, R. B. (1994). *Nurturing young Black males: Challenges to agencies, programs, and social policy.* Washington, DC: Urban Institute.

Moore, K. A., & Glei, D. (1995). Taking the plunge: An examination of positive youth development. *Journal of Adolescent Research, 10,* 15–40.

Mortimer, J., & Larson, R. (2002). Macrostructural trends and the reshaping of adolescence. In J. L. Mortimer, R. (Ed.), *The changing adolescent experience: Societal trends and the transition to adulthood.* New York: Cambridge University Press.

Moses, R., & Cobb, C. (2001). *Radical equations: Math literacy and civil rights.* Boston: Beacon Press.

Nicholson, H. J., Collins, C., & Holmer, H. (2004). Youth as people: The protective aspects of youth development in after-school settings. *Annals of the American Academy of Political and Social Science, 591,* 55–71.

Nolin, M. J., Chaney, B., Chapman, C., & Chandler, K. (1997). *Student participation in community service activity.* Washington, DC: National Center for Educational Statistics.

Novikoff, A. B. (1945a). The concept of integrative levels and biology. *Science, 101,* 209–215.

Novikoff, A. B. (1945b). Continuity and discontinuity in evolution. *Science, 101,* 405–406.

Obradović, J. & Masten, A. S. (2007). Developmental antecedents of young adult civic engagement. *Applied Developmental Science, 11,* 2–19.

Overton, W. F. (1973). On the assumptive base of the nature-nurture controversy: Additive versus interactive conceptions. *Human Development, 16,* 74–89.

Overton, W. F. (1998). Developmental psychology: Philosophy, concepts, and methodology. In R. M. Lerner (Volume Ed.) & W. Damon (Editor-in-Chief), *Handbook of child psychology,* vol. 1: *Theoretical models of human development* (5th ed., pp. 107–187). New York: John Wiley & Sons.

Overton, W. F. (2006). Developmental psychology: Philosophy, concepts, methodology. In R. M. Lerner (Ed.), *Handbook of child psychology* (6th ed.), vol. 1: *Theoretical models of human development* (pp. 18–88). (Editors-in-chief: W. Damon & R. M. Lerner.) Hoboken, NJ: John Wiley & Sons.

Park, N. (2004a). Character strengths and positive youth development. *Annals of the American Academy of Political and Social Science, 591,* 40–54.

Park, N. (2004b). The role of subjective well-being in positive youth development. *Annals of the American Academy of Political and Social Sciences, 591*, 25–39.

Park, N., Peterson, C., & Seligman, M. (2004). Strengths of character and well-being. *Journal of Social and Clinical Psychology, 23*, 603–606.

Patton, P. L. (1998). The gangstas in our midst. *Urban Review, 30*, 49–76.

Phelps, E., Balsano, A., Fay, K., Peltz, J., Zimmerman, S., Lerner, R., M., et al. (2007). Nuances in early adolescent development trajectories of positive and of problematic/risk behaviors: Findings from the 4-H Study of Positive Youth Development. *Child and Adolescent Clinics of North America, 16*, 473–496.

Pittman, K., Irby, M., & Ferber, T. (2001). Unfinished business: Further reflections on a decade of promoting youth development. In P. L. Benson & K. J. Pittman (Eds.), *Trends in youth development: Visions, realities and challenges* (pp. 4–50). Norwell, MA: Kluwer.

Pritchard, I. (2002). Community service and service-learning in America: The state of the art. In A. Furco & S. H. Billig (Eds.), *Service-learning: The essence of the pedagogy* (pp. 3–21). Greenwich, CT: Information Age Publishers.

Rathunde, K., & Csikszentmihalyi, M. (2006). The developing person: An experiential perspective. In R. M. Lerner (Ed.), *Handbook of child psychology* (6th ed.), vol. 1: *Theoretical models of human development*. (Editors-in-chief: W. Damon & R. M. Lerner.) Hoboken, NJ: John Wiley & Sons.

Reivich, K. J., Gillham, J. E., Chaplin, T. M., & Seligman, M. E. P. (2005). From helplessness to optimism: The role of resilience in treating and preventing depression in youth. In S. Goldstein & R. B. Brooks (Eds.), *Handbook of resilience in children* (pp. 223–237). New York: Kluwer Academic/Plenum Press.

Rhodes, J. E. (2002). *Stand by me: The risks and rewards of mentoring today's youth*. Cambridge, MA: Harvard University Press.

Roth, J. L., & Brooks-Gunn, J. (2003a). What is a youth development program? Identification and defining principles. In. F. Jacobs, D. Wertlieb, & R. M. Lerner (Eds.), *Handbook of applied developmental science: Promoting positive child, adolescent, and family development through research, policies, and programs,* vol. 2: *Enhancing the life chances of youth and families: Public service systems and public policy perspectives* (pp. 197–223). Thousand Oaks, CA: Sage.

Roth, J. L., & Brooks-Gunn, J. (2003b). What exactly is a youth development program? Answers from research and practice. *Applied Developmental Science, 7*, 94–111.

Rutter, M. (1987). Psychosocial resilience and protective mechanisms. *American Journal of Orthopsychiatry, 57*, 216–331.

Rutter, M. (2000). Resilience reconsidered: Conceptual considerations, empirical findings, and policy implications. In J. P. Shonkoff & S. J. Meisels (Eds.), *Handbook of early intervention* (2nd ed., pp. 651–681). New York: Cambridge University Press.

Scales, P., Benson, P., Leffert, N., & Blyth, D. A. (2000). The contribution of developmental assets to the prediction of thriving among adolescents. *Applied Developmental Science, 4*, 27–46.

Schneirla, T. C. (1957). The concept of development in comparative psychology. In D. B.Harris (Ed.), *The concept of development* (pp. 78–108). Minneapolis: University of Minnesota.

Seligman, M. E. P. (2002). Positive psychology, positive prevention, and positive therapy. In C. R. Snyder & S. J. Lopez (Eds.), *Handbook of positive psychology*. Oxford, UK: Oxford University Press.

Seligman, M. E. P. (2003a). Positive psychology: Fundamental assumptions. *Psychologist, 16*, 126–127.

Seligman, M. E. P. (2003b). The past and future of positive psychology. In C. L. M. Keyes & J. Haidt (Eds.), *Flourishing: Positive psychology and the life well-lived* (pp. xi–xx). Washington, DC: American Psychological Association.

Seligman, M. E. P. (2004). *Authentic happiness: Using the new positive psychology to realize your potential for lasting fulfillment*. New York: Free Press

Seligman, M. E. P., & Csikszentmihalyi, M. (2000). Positive psychology: An introduction. *American Psychologist, 55*, 5–14.

Shatte, A. J., Seligman, M. E. P., Gillham, J. E., & Reivich, K. (2003). The role of positive psychology in child, adolescent, and family development. In R. E. Lerner, F. Jacobs, & D. Wertlieb (Eds.), *Handbook of applied developmental science: Promoting positive child, adolescent, and family development through research, policies, and programs*. Thousand Oaks, CA: Sage.

Shek, D. T. L., Siu, A. M. H., & Lee, T. Y. (2007). The Chinese positive youth development scale: A validation study. *Research on Social Work Practice, 17*, 380–391.

Silbereisen, R. K., & Lerner, R. M. (2007). Approaches to positive youth development: A view of the issues. In R. K. Silbereisen & R. M. Lerner (Eds.), *Approaches to positive youth development* (pp. 3–30). London: Sage.

Skinner, B., & Chapman, C. (1999). *Service-learning and community service in K–12 public schools*. Washington, DC: U.S. Department of Education, National Center for Education Statistics.

Spencer, M. B. (1990). Development of minority children: An introduction. *Child Development, 61*, 267–269.

Spencer, M. B. (1995). Old issues and new theorizing about African American youth: A phenomenological variant of ecological systems theory. In R. L. Taylor (Ed.), *Black youth: Perspectives on their status in the United States* (pp. 37–69). Westport, CT: Praeger.

Spencer, M. B. (1999). Social and cultural influences on school adjustment: The application of an identity-focused cultural ecological perspective. *Educational Psychologist, 34*, 43–57.

Spencer, M. B. (2006a). Commentary on "Studying Diverse Lives." *Research in Human Development, 3*, 271–280.

Spencer, M. B. (2006b). Phenomenology and ecological systems theory. Development of diverse groups. In W. Damon & R. M. Lerner (Eds.), *Handbook of child psychology*, vol. 1 (6th ed., pp. 829–893). Hoboken, NJ: John Wiley & Sons.

Spencer, M. B., Dupree, D., & Hartmann, T. (1997). A phenomenological variant of ecological systems theory (PVEST): A self-organization perspective in context. *Development and Psychopathology, 9*, 817–833.

Spencer, M. B., Noll, E., & Cassidy, E. (2005). Monetary incentives in support of academic achievement: Results of a randomized field trial involving high-achieving, low-resource, ethnically diverse urban adolescents. *Evaluation Review, 29*, 199–222.

Spencer, M. B., Noll, E., Stolzfus, J., & Harpalani, V. (2001). Identity and school adjustment: Revisiting the "acting white" assumption. *Educational Psychologist, 36*, 21–30.

Spencer, M. B., Swanson, D. P., & Cunningham, M. (1991). *Journal of Negro Education, 60*, 366–387.

Taylor, C. S. (1996, April). *The unintended consequences of incarceration: Youth development, the juvenile corrections systems, and crime*. Paper presented at the Vera Institute Conference, Harriman, New York.

Taylor, C. S. (2001). Youth gangs. In N. J. Smelser & P. B. Baltes (Eds.), *International encyclopedia of the social and behavioral sciences* (pp. 16,664–16,668). Oxford, UK: Elsevier.

Taylor, C. (2003). Youth gangs and community violence. In R. M. Lerner, F. Jacobs, & D. Wertlieb (Eds.), *Handbook of applied developmental science: Promoting positive child, adolescent, and family development through research, policies, and programs*, vol. 2: *Enhancing the life chances of youth and families: Public service systems and public policy perspectives* (pp. 65–80). Thousand Oaks, CA: Sage.

Taylor, C. S., Lerner, R. M., von Eye, A., Balsano, A. B., Dowling, E. M., Anderson, P. M., et al. (2002a). Stability of attributes of positive functioning and of developmental assets among African American adolescent male gang and community-based organization members. In R. M. Lerner, C. S. Taylor, & A. von Eye (Eds.), *New directions for youth development: Theory, practice and research: Pathways to positive development among diverse youth*, vol. 95 (pp. 35–56). (G. Noam, Series Ed.) San Francisco: Jossey-Bass.

Taylor, C. S., Lerner, R. M., von Eye, A., Balsano, A. B., Dowling, E. M., Anderson, P. M., et al. (2002b). Individual and ecological assets and positive developmental trajectories among gang and community-based organization youth. In R. M. Lerner, C. S. Taylor, & A. von Eye (Eds.), *New directions for youth development: Theory, practice and research: Pathways to positive development among diverse youth*, vol. 95 (pp. 57–72). (G. Noam, Series Ed.) San Francisco: Jossey-Bass.

Taylor, C. S., Lerner, R. M., von Eye, A., Bobek, D., Balsano, A. B., Dowling, E., et al. (2004). Internal and external developmental assets among African American male gang members. *Journal of Adolescent Research, 19*, 303–322.

Taylor, C. S., Lerner, R. M., von Eye, A., Bobek, D., Balsano, A., Dowling, E., et al. (2003). Positive individual and social behavior among gang and non-gang African American male adolescents. *Journal of Adolescent Research, 18*, 547–574.

Tebes, J. K., Feinn, R., Vanderploeg, J.J., Chinman, M.J., Shepard, J., Brabham, T., et al. (2007). Impact of a positive youth development program in urban after-school settings on the prevention of adolescent substance use. *Journal of Adolescent Health, 41*, 219–220.

Thelen, E., & Smith, L. B. (2006) Dynamic systems theories. In W. Damon (Editor), R. M. Lerner (Volume Editor), *Handbook of child psychology*, vol. 1: *Theoretical models of human development* (6th ed.; pp. 258–312.) Hoboken, NJ: John Wiley & Sons.

Theokas, C., Almerigi, J., Lerner, R. M., Dowling, E., Benson, P., Scales, P. C., et al. (2005). Conceptualizing and modeling individual and ecological asset components of thriving in early adolescence. *Journal of Early Adolescence, 25*, 113–143.

Theokas, C., & Lerner, R. M. (2006). Promoting positive development in adolescence: The role of ecological assets in families, schools, and neighborhoods. *Applied Developmental Science, 10*, 61–74.

Theokas, C., Lerner, J. V., Lerner, R. M. & Phelps, E. (2006). Cacophony and change in youth after school activities: Implications for development and practice from the 4-H Study of Positive Youth Development. *Journal of Youth Development: Bridging Research and Practice, 1*.

To, S. (2007). Empowering school social work practices for positive youth development: Hong Kong experience. *Adolescence, 42*, 555–567.

Tobach, E., & Greenberg, G., (1984). The significance of T. C. Schneirla's contribution to the concept of levels of integration. In G. Greenberg & E. Tobach (Eds.), *Behavioral evolution and integrative levels* (pp. 1–7). Hillsdale, NJ: Lawrence Erlbaum.

von Betralanffy, L. (1933). *Modern theories of development*. London: Oxford University Press.

von Bertalanffy, L. (1969). *General systems theory*. New York: Braziller Press.

Weissberg, R. P., & O'Brien, M. U. (2004). What works in school-based social and emotional learning programs for positive youth development. *Annals of the American Academy of Political and Social Science, 591*, 86–97.

Werner, E. (1995). Resilience in development. *Current Directions in Psychological Science, 4*, 81–85.

Werner, E., & Smith, R. (1992). *Overcoming the odds: High risk children from birth to adulthood*. Ithaca, NY: Cornell University Press.

Werner, E., & Smith, R. (2001). *Journeys from childhood to midlife. Risk, resilience, and recovery*. Ithaca: Cornell University Press.

Westheimer, J., & Kahne, J. (2000, January 26). Service learning required: But what exactly do students learn? *Education Week*, Back Page Commentary.

Wheeler, W. (2003). Youth leadership for development: Civic activism as a component of youth development programming and a strategy for strengthening civil society. In R. M. Lerner, F. Jacobs, & D. Wertlieb (Eds.), *Handbook of applied developmental science: Promoting positive child, adolescent, and family development through research, policies, and programs*, vol. 2: *Enhancing the life chances of youth and families: Public service systems and public policy perspectives* (pp. 491–505). (F. Jacobs, D. Wertlieb, & R. M. Lerner, Volume Editors.) Thousand Oaks, CA: Sage.

Youniss, J. (1993). Integrating culture and religion into developmental psychology. *Family Perspective, 26*, 171–188.

Youniss, J., McLellan, J. A., & Yates, M. (1997). What we know about engendering civic identity. *American Behavioral Scientist, 40*, 620–631.

Youniss, J., & Yates, M. (1997). *Community service and social responsibility*. Chicago: University of Chicago Press.

Zarrett, N., Fay, K., Carrano, J., Li, Y., Phelps, E., & Lerner, R. M. (in preparation). *More than child's play: Variable- and pattern-centered approaches for examining effects of sports participation on youth development*.

Zarrett, N., Lerner, R. M., Carrano, J., Fay, K., Peltz, J. S., & Li, Y. (2008). Variations in adolescent engagement in sports and its influence on positive youth development. In N. L. Holt (Ed.), *Positive youth development through sport* (pp. 9–23). Oxford, UK: Routledge.

Zarrett, N., Peltz, J. S., Fay, K., Li, Y., Lerner, R. M., & Lerner, J. V. (2007). Sports and youth development programs: Theoretical and practical implications of early adolescent participation in multiple instances of structured out-of-school (OST) activity. *Journal of Youth Development, 2*.

Zimmerman, S., Phelps, E., & Lerner, R. M. (2007). Intentional self-regulation in early adolescence: Assessing the structure of selection, optimization, and compensations processes. *European Journal of Developmental Science, 1*, 272–299.

PART III

Challenges to Healthy Development

CHAPTER 16

Processes of Risk and Resilience During Adolescence

BRUCE E. COMPAS AND KRISTEN L. REESLUND

Adolescence is a unique period of development for understanding processes that place individuals at risk for psychopathology, illness, and adverse developmental outcomes. Most adolescents traverse this developmental period successfully without encountering significant psychological, social, or health problems. However, adolescence also marks the increase in the incidence of a number of mental health problems and threats to physical health. Several psychiatric disorders increase significantly in incidence and prevalence during adolescence, most notably depression, conduct disorder, and eating disorders. Threats to physical health through smoking, substance abuse, and unprotected sex increase dramatically during this period. The prediction of which individuals will follow a successful path versus those who will encounter significant problems during adolescence is critical for preventing psychopathology and illness and promoting health and successful development.

Processes of risk and resilience are central to understanding adaptive and maladaptive paths of development during adolescence. Understanding risk factors and processes of risk is crucial to the identification of those adolescents most in need of early intervention, whereas clarification of protective factors and processes of resilience can inform interventions to strengthen those at greatest risk. In the pursuit of these goals, risk and resilience research has focused on several levels of analysis, including broad social contextual processes, proximal environments (especially the family), and individual psychological and biological processes. Furthermore, some important sources of risk and resilience precede adolescence and are linked to processes that occur or begin in childhood and continue into adolescence, whereas others arise in adolescence, and their effects either may be limited to adolescence or continue into adulthood. Integration of these different levels of analysis and developmental trajectories is essential for a comprehensive adolescent model of risk and resilience (Steinberg, 2002).

A large body of evidence has emerged on contextual and individual sources of risk and resilience in adolescence; however, a comprehensive review of this work spanning the diverse problems of adolescence is beyond the scope of this review. Rather, we begin by highlighting some of the broad issues in the development of a comprehensive, integrated perspective on adolescent risk and resilience. Then we consider processes related to stress, stress reactivity, and coping and emotion regulation as central constructs for understanding risk and resilience. Finally, we examine research on depression during adolescence as an exemplar of progress and continued challenges to research on risk and resilience during adolescence.

A major impediment to increasing our understanding of risk and resilience has been the failure to integrate contextual and individual levels of analysis. Research on social contextual factors such as poverty and significant disruptions and stress within families has rarely been coupled with methods to measure individual processes of risk and resilience in adolescents faced with these significant sources of adversity. Similarly, research on individual sources of resilience, including coping and emotion regulation, during adolescence has often ignored the broader context in which development occurs. A comprehensive understanding of risk and resilience during adolescence requires an integration of multiple levels and methods of analysis of contextual and individual factors (Cicchetti & Blender, 2006; Cicchetti & Dawson, 2002). Moreover, concepts are needed that can provide linkages across these different levels. Stress and the ways that individuals respond to and cope with stress continue to be important processes that can facilitate a multilevel approach to adolescent risk and resilience. Proximal stressors, especially stressors within the family, mediate the effects of distal contextual risk factors. The effects of proximal stressors are further mediated by the ways that adolescents react to and cope with stress. And both automatic stress responses and effortful coping responses may be influenced by individual development, as well as the effects of stress on psychological and biological processes related to stress reactivity and coping, during adolescence.

DEFINING KEY TERMS AND CONCEPTS

A number of concepts and terms have been used to describe processes of risk and resilience. This terminology is important beyond the level of semantics, as it conveys important differences regarding the nature of who will develop problems and disorders during adolescence and who will survive relatively unscathed. However, confusion over the definitions of key terms and over the sheer number of different terms that have been employed has been problematic. Many of the central issues and challenges facing the field were articulated by Kraemer et al. (1997) over a decade ago and continue to be unresolved and limit progress in the field.

Risk

The term *risk* refers to the increased probability of a negative outcome in a specified population (Kraemer et al., 1997; Kraemer, Stice, Kazdin, Offord, & Kupfer 2001). Thus, risk (or *degree of risk*) is a quantitative concept that is reflected as either an odds ratio when outcomes are measured categorically or as some variant of a regression weight when the outcomes are continuous or quantitative. For example, the odds of developing a mood disorder (major depressive disorder or dysthymic disorder) or a disruptive behavior disorder (oppositional defiant disorder or conduct disorder) can be calculated as a function of characteristics of the individual (e.g., age, gender), family factors (e.g., harsh parenting, parental psychopathology), and neighborhood characteristics (e.g., violence, inadequate housing). A *risk factor* is an agent or characteristic of the individual or the environment that is related to the increased probability of a negative outcome. For example, Rolf and Johnson (1990) defined risk factors as variables that "have proven or presumed effects that can directly increase the likelihood of a maladaptive outcome" (p. 387). The degree of risk associated with a given risk factor can be calculated at various levels, including the degree of risk for an individual person, a family, a classroom, a school, or a community. When outcomes are dichotomous, a risk factor can be used to divide the population into two groups, high risk and low risk, which comprise the total population (Kraemer et al., 1997). Quantitative measures of risk distinguish individuals along a continuum from high to low.

In addition to distinguishing levels of risk, temporal precedence must be established between risks and outcomes; that is, the presence of or exposure to the risk factor must precede evidence of the development of the outcome. Kraemer et al. (2001) addressed the issue of temporal precedence within a typology of risk factors. If a factor is simply associated with an outcome at a single point in time, it is identified as a *correlate*. A correlate that has been shown to precede the outcome is a *risk factor,* and a risk factor that can be changed or changes with development is a *variable risk factor*. Finally, if manipulation of the risk factor changes the outcome, it is a *causal risk factor*. Thus, the final step in risk research is likely to involve preventive interventions designed to change established risk factors in order to determine their possible causal role.

Cumulative risk refers to the co-occurrence of more than one risk factor for a given individual or within a population (Sameroff & Rosenblum, 2006). As the number of risk factors increases, the mental and physical health and development of adolescents decline (Friedman & Chase-Lansdale, 2002). For example, poverty and economic hardship are associated with multiple additional risks, including neighborhood crime and violence, lack of access to quality schools, single parenthood, and family conflict (e.g., Chen, 2007; Evans & Kim, 2007). Similarly, parental psychopathology, another important risk factor throughout childhood and adolescence, is linked with family conflict and discord and possible genetic risks for psychopathology (e.g., Goodman, 2007). Negative outcomes increase additively or exponentially as the number of risk factors increases.

A concept closely related to risk is that of *vulnerability* (e.g., Blum, McNeely, & Nonnemaker, 2002). Vulnerability is typically distinguished from risk in that it implies a focus on differences in the degree to which risk factors are associated with negative outcomes for specific individuals. That is, vulnerability addresses the question of why some individuals who are exposed to risk are more likely to develop a negative outcome. For example, it is clear that negative psychological outcomes ensue for some but certainly not all adolescents who experience parental divorce (Sandler, Tein, Mehta, Wolchik, & Ayers, 2000). Individual differences in vulnerability to parental divorce are related to child characteristics (e.g., age and gender) and to the level of conflict and hostility between the

parents, even after separation and divorce have occurred. Thus, vulnerability factors or markers encompass those factors that exacerbate the negative effects of the risk condition.

Unfortunately, the distinction between risk and vulnerability has generally failed to reach its promise, as the designation of factors that are sources of risk versus vulnerability is often quite arbitrary. Conceptually, the importance of this distinction lies in the ability to identify characteristics of the person or the environment that make some individuals more likely to develop adverse outcomes when exposed to sources of risk. Vulnerability factors are therefore tested as statistical interactions. However, a significant statistical interaction term alone does not identify how one factor (the source of vulnerability) acts on a second factor (the risk factor).

Kraemer et al. (2001) spelled out rather precise conditions in which one risk factor (A) moderates the effects of a second risk factor (B) on an outcome (O). For A to function as a moderator of B, A must precede B, A and B must not be correlated, and A cannot influence B directly. However, the strength of the effect of B in O must be affected by the level of A. For example, there is an interaction between gender and pubertal timing in predicting depression in adolescence, such that girls with early onset puberty have an increased likelihood of a major depressive episode (e.g., Angold, Costello, & Worthman, 1998; Ge, Conger, & Elder, 2001). Following the principles outlined by Kraemer et al., in this case gender (A) precedes pubertal timing (B), gender is uncorrelated with pubertal timing, and both are related to depression (O). However, the strength of the association between early onset puberty and depression is greater for girls than for boys; that is, pubertal timing moderates the relation between gender and depression. Thus, pubertal timing is a source of increased vulnerability to depression among girls but not among boys. Greater precision of the relations among risk factors and their moderating effects will contribute to greater clarity in distinguishing between risk factors and sources of vulnerability.

Resilience

Similar attention has been given to defining the concept of *resilience*. Luthar and Cicchetti (2000) defined resilience as a "dynamic process wherein individuals display positive adaptation despite experiences of significant adversity or trauma" (p. 858). Similarly, Masten (2001) defined resilience as "a class of phenomena characterized by good outcomes in spite of threats to adaptation or development" (p. 228). Resilience does not merely imply a personality trait or an attribute of the individual; rather, it is intended to reflect a process of positive adaptation in the presence of risk that may be the result of individual factors, environmental factors, or the interplay of the two (Luthar, 2006; Luthar & Cicchetti, 2000). Resilience research is concerned with identifying mechanisms or processes that might underlie evidence of positive adaptation in the presence of risk. Masten (2001) distinguished among several models of resilience. Variable-focused models of resilience test relations among quantitative measures of risk, outcomes, and potential characteristics of the individual or the environment that may serve a protective function against the adverse effects of risk. Within this approach, researchers can test for mediators and moderators of risk that can provide evidence of protection or resilience. Person-focused models of resilience examine individuals in an attempt to identify and compare those who display patterns of resilience (as evidenced by positive outcomes) and those who succumb to risk (as reflected in negative outcomes).

Closely related to the concept of resilience are *protective factors,* which are conceptualized as aspects of the individual or the environment that are related to resilient outcomes. In one of the original conceptualizations, Garmezy (1983) defined protective factors as "those attributes of persons, environments, situations, and events that appear to temper predictions of psychopathology based on an individual's at-risk status" (p. 73). In this sense, protective factors are the converse of vulnerability factors: Protective factors are characteristics of the individual or the environment that are associated with positive outcomes in the face of risk, whereas vulnerability factors are associated with negative outcomes in at-risk individuals.

Risk and Resilience

Although there is merit to distinguishing between risk and resilience (and between vulnerability and protective factors), there are challenges in the conceptualization of these two sets of factors and processes. Foremost is the difficulty of determining whether risk and resilience are distinct constructs or whether they exist on a continuum whose bipolar ends represent risk and resilience. In some instances, high levels of a factor protect individuals from risk whereas low levels of the same factor amplify risk (Luthar, Sawyer, & Brown, 2006). For example, high IQ may serve as a protective factor in the face of socioeconomic adversity, but low IQ may increase the potency of the effects of poverty. Thus, IQ may both increase (a vulnerability factor) and decrease (a protective factor) risk associated with socioeconomic hardship. In other instances, high levels of a factor are protective, but low levels are neutral or benign in relation to the source of risk. For example, the temperamental characteristics of negative affectivity and positive affectivity, respectively, are risk and resilience factors for emotional problems (Compas, Connor-Smith, & Jaser, 2004). However, these two traits are orthogonal, as low negative affectivity does not denote positive affectivity. Thus, low negative affectivity indicates the absence of this vulnerability factor, but it does not serve as a protective factor.

To address some of the confusion between risk and protective factors, Sameroff (2000) used the term *promotive factors* to refer to those characteristics of individuals and environments that are associated with positive outcomes irrespective of risk; that is, they are associated with positive outcomes in both high- and low-risk populations (Gutman, Sameroff, & Eccles, 2002; Sameroff, 2000). In contrast, protective factors would be expected to have no effect in low-risk populations or to be magnified in the presence of high risk (Gutman et al., 2002; Rutter, 1987).

The situation is further complicated in that some risk and protective factors are stable, whereas others change with development. For example, some temperamental characteristics emerge in infancy and remain stable throughout childhood and adolescence. Stable individual differences in temperament may function as either risk or protective factors in adolescence, depending on the characteristic in question. Similarly, some features of the environment may be stable sources of risk or protection throughout childhood and adolescence (e.g., chronic poverty, a supportive and structured family environment). Other factors may emerge during adolescence as sources of risk and protection and can be defined as developmental risk and protective factors. For example, some aspects of cognitive and brain development change dramatically during early adolescence and mark this as a period of heightened risk for many adolescents (Spear, 2000a, 2000b; Steinberg, 2005). Similarly, it appears that the effects of certain types of stressful events are relatively benign during childhood but are much more likely to be associated with negative outcomes during adolescence (Hankin & Abramson, 2001).

METHODOLOGICAL ISSUES

Risk and resilience research is compromised by a number of methodological issues. These include the use of cross-sectional versus longitudinal research designs and challenges in the measurement of sources of risk, vulnerability, resilience, and developmental outcomes. An understanding of risk and resilience is dependent in part of successful resolution of these issues.

Research Design

As noted earlier, the temporal precedence of a factor in relation to an outcome must be present in order to establish risk (Kraemer et al., 1997, 2001). Thus, true risk research requires the use of prospective longitudinal designs. In reality, however, risk research often unfolds sequentially, beginning with cross-sectional studies that are useful in identifying candidate risk factors that warrant attention in more costly longitudinal studies. Cross-sectional studies are a cost-effective step in the identification of risk and protective factors, as they require much less time, effort, and money than do prospective studies. However, they cannot provide evidence of the role of individual or environmental factors as predictors of negative outcomes (evidence of increased risk) or of positive outcomes in the presence of risk factors (resilience). Further, mediation effects identified in cross-sectional research that suggest processes of risk and resilience may actually be misleading as the results can provide biased estimates of longitudinal parameters (Maxwell & Cole, 2007). Thus, cross-sectional tests of processes of risk and resilience must be interpreted with considerable caution.

The identification of *processes* of risk and resilience, as opposed to the identification of risk or protective *factors,* requires attention to the both mediation and moderation of risk and resilience factors. Process research is required to explain *how* specific characteristics of the person or the environment lead to negative outcomes or to positive outcomes that are against the odds. For example, it is clear that growing up in poverty is an enormous risk factor for negative developmental outcomes in adolescence (Chen, 2007; Evans & Kim, 2007; Friedman & Chase-Lansdale, 2002; McLoyd, 1998; see also chapter 13, vol. 2 of this *Handbook*). However, process research is needed to identify the mediators of the relation between poverty and negative outcomes. These include neighborhood, school, and family factors that play out in the daily lives of poor adolescents. Similarly, moderators may explain why some adolescents are more vulnerable to the effects of some sources of stress and adversity. For example, gender and personality characteristics have been found to be important moderators of stressful events during adolescence (e.g., Papadakis, Prince, Jones, & Strauman, 2006). However, the identification of a moderator may require further research on the mediators that account for observed moderation effects. For example, adolescent girls may be more vulnerable to the effects of interpersonal stress, but the reason is the ways that they appraise and cope with such events and not because of their gender per se (Compas & Wagner, 1991; Hankin & Abramson, 2001).

Measurement

A number of issues and challenges arise in the measurement of risk and protective factors, processes of risk and resilience, and positive and negative developmental outcomes. Inherent in the constructs of both risk and resilience is the need to operationalize negative and positive adolescent developmental outcomes, including emotional, psychological, and physical problems, as well as overall health, well-being, and presence of disorders. There are, however, a number of challenges to the conceptualization and measurement of these outcomes.

Definitions of resilience require attention to the nature of positive adaptation, which is typically defined in terms of manifestations of social competence or success at meeting stage-relevant developmental tasks (Luthar, 2006; Luthar & Cicchetti, 2000). Successful adaptation in the face of risk can also be reflected in positive mental health during adolescence, which can be operationalized along two primary dimensions reflecting the skills and capacity to manage adversity and the capacity to involve oneself in personally meaningful activities (Compas, 1993). Thus, positive mental health is reflected in the ability to overcome risk. It is more than this, however, as positive mental health also includes the ability to engage oneself in relationships and activities that are personally meaningful and productive. Positive mental health and positive development are relative concepts and depend

on a number factors, including cultural context, developmental level, and differences in the perspective of various interested parties including adolescents, parents, teachers, and health professionals (Compas, 1993).

Resilience may also be manifested in physical health and healthy development, which, like positive mental health, include more than the absence of disease. Health is defined as a state of physical, mental, and social well-being and not merely the absence of disease (Richmond, 1993). Current biopsychosocial models of development consider health in terms of personal experiences of general well-being (quality of life), the capacity to perform developmentally expected roles and tasks (adaptive functioning), and fulfilling one's health potential (Millstein, Petersen, & Nightingale, 1993). Some indicators of poor health in adolescence do not immediately manifest themselves in disease or illness but are linked to later poor health outcomes. For example, obesity during adolescence may not result in any immediate health problems but is a strong risk factor for later cardiovascular disease and adult-onset diabetes. Although not related to disease and illness during adolescence, obesity may be related to impairment in current physical functioning and decreased quality of life. Thus, although obesity is not an illness or a disease, it is also not reflective of a state of health.

Social competence, particularly as reflected in relationships with peers, also plays a prominent role in resilience of at-risk youth. Peer relationships have been recognized as having a significant impact on development and the course of psychopathology (Masten, 2005). From a developmental psychopathology perspective, peers play many roles in the onset and maintenance of disorders in childhood and adolescence, and peer relationships have been targeted in prevention and treatment. Given that psychopathology is assumed to arise from a complex interaction between the individual and the many social systems with which the individual comes into contact, it is not surprising that peer groups and friendships have a significant impact as they comprise a major system that children and adolescents interact with through adulthood (Ladd, 2005; Masten, Rubin, Bukowski, & Parker, 2006). Issues regarding social competence become particularly salient as individuals move into adolescence.

The challenges of measuring negative outcomes are even greater than those involved in documenting positive adaptation. Most studies of risk and emotional and behavioral problems in adolescence have relied on measures of negative emotional states or checklists that are used to assess syndromes of emotional and behavioral problems. These have included measures of symptoms associated with specific internalizing problems such as depressive symptoms and anxiety and the broad factors of internalizing and externalizing problems (e.g., Achenbach & Rescorla, 2001). Risk researchers also use structured diagnostic interviews to assess psychiatric disorders as represented in the *Diagnostic and Statistical Manual of Mental Disorders, Fourth Edition* (*DSM-IV;* American Psychiatric Association, 1994). These two approaches are not incompatible, however, as quantitative variations in symptoms have been shown to be related to categorical diagnoses for several disorders (e.g., Achenbach & Dumenci, 2001; Gerhardt, Compas, Connor, & Achenbach, 1999; Jensen et al., 1996). Further, taxometric analyses indicate that depression in particular is best conceptualized as a dimensional rather than a categorical construct (Hankin, Fraley, Lahey, & Waldman, 2005). Both elevated scores on dimensional measures of symptoms or syndromes and diagnoses of categorical disorders of depression are associated with significant impairment and problems in functioning (e.g., Gotlib, Lewinsohn, & Seeley, 1995; Lengua, Sadowski, Friedrich, & Fisher, 2001). Therefore, *both* are viable perspectives on psychopathology in young people.

The assessment of symptoms as opposed to categorical diagnoses has implications for the type of research design required, as well as the types of research questions that can be answered. Studies of symptoms or quantitative variations on syndromes of psychopathology are typically used in variable-focused studies that are concerned with the linear relation between the level of risk (or resilience) and the number, level, or severity of psychological symptoms. Because symptoms are continuous and quantitative, researchers are not typically concerned with the timing of the onset of symptoms or the point at which symptoms exceed a specific threshold. The focus is on the degree to which changes in levels of risk account for changes in symptoms over time, as tested in variants of multiple regression models (e.g., Carter, Garber, Ciesla, & Cole, 2006; Hankin, Mermelstein, & Roesch, 2007).

The relation between risk factors and categorical diagnoses of disorder has been tested somewhat less often, in part because of the greater demands involved in the administration of clinical interviews. In addition, when the focus is on categorical diagnoses based on *DSM-IV* criteria, the emphasis is on the onset, duration, and remission of a disorder. Therefore, researchers must carefully document the timing of risk factors in relation to changes in diagnostic status. This requires the use of measures of both risk and psychopathology that are sensitive to timing and duration and research designs that are able to identify the specific timing of the onset of risk factors in relation to the onset or termination of an episode of disorder. Structured interviews are currently the best, albeit most labor-intensive, approach for accomplishing these goals in the assessment both of risk factors, such as stressful experiences, and psychological disorder (e.g., Rudolph & Hammen, 2000).

In addition to consideration of the method used to measure outcomes, it is also critical to account for the source of the data. The relatively low level of concordance in the reports of different informants on child and adolescent maladjustment and psychopathology is widely recognized (Achenbach, Dumenci, & Rescorla, 2002; Achenbach, McConaughy, & Howell,

1987). Although low rates of correspondence are potentially problematic, the general consensus is that different informants provide equally valid perspectives on adolescent problems, with specific perspectives particularly valid for specific types of symptoms (Garber, Keiley, & Martin, 2002). For example, teachers and parents may be better informants of externalizing symptoms, and children and adolescents may be better informants of internalizing symptoms. Most research on adolescent risk has failed to give careful attention to the informant effects in reports of risk factors and outcomes. Several studies have noted, however, that adolescent reports of risk factors are more strongly associated with their own reports of symptoms of psychopathology than with parental reports of symptoms (e.g., Compas et al., 1989). This suggests that common method variance in the assessment of both stressors and symptoms may contribute to the association between these two variables. The use of latent indicators that combine parent and adolescent reports can be used to overcome some of the problems inherent in shared method variance. For example, Compas et al. (2006) used structural equation modeling with latent variables to confirm a model of the role of adolescents' coping in relation to internalizing symptoms.

The measurement of negative outcomes is further complicated by the tendency of symptoms of psychopathology and psychiatric disorders to co-occur or to be comorbid in adolescence (e.g., Measelle, Stice, & Hogansen, 2006). This presents risk researchers with a challenge in their efforts to identify specificity in the association between particular types of stressors and particular psychological problems. When an association is found between a particular risk factor and symptoms of a particular disorder (e.g., depression), this association may not be unique to that disorder. Rather, the risk factor may serve as a relatively nonspecific risk factor for psychopathology because psychopathology often occurs in relatively nonspecific patterns. Thus, researchers need to include broad-based assessments of a range

of different types of psychopathology if they are to adequately capture the types of problems that are associated with stressors and to determine the degree to which particular risk factors are specifically related to particular outcomes (McMahon, Grant, Compas, Thurm, & Ey, 2003). Specificity requires careful consideration of both contextual factors and individual differences (see Steinberg & Avenevoli, 2000).

Summary

Theory and research on adolescent risk and resilience are fraught with multiple overlapping terms and concepts. At its core, however, this area is characterized by two observations that, regardless of the terms used, are relatively simple and enduring. First, some adolescents suffer poor health and psychological outcomes during this developmental period, and factors associated with a greater likelihood of negative outcomes need to be identified. Second, once predictors of increased risk for negative outcomes have been identified, it is clear that some adolescents evidence positive outcomes despite exposure to known risks. The challenge is in the identification of the processes that lead from risk and protective factors to good and bad outcomes. Perhaps the best source of illumination on these processes comes from a somewhat weathered set of concepts: stress, stress responses, and coping (Compas & Grant, 2002; Compas, Jaser, & Benson, in press).

STRESS, STRESS RESPONSES, AND COPING: UNIFYING CONCEPTS FOR UNDERSTANDING RISK AND RESILIENCE

Research on exposure to stressful events and circumstances and the ways that adolescents respond to and cope with stress has provided essential information on the linkages between contextual and individual processes of risk and resilience. Specifically, exposure to stressful events and circumstances is a primary pathway through which distal risk factors exert effects on adolescent mental and physical health, including the generation of stressors in neighborhood, school, peer, and family environments. Furthermore, individual differences in automatic and controlled responses to stress are crucial mediators of the effects of both distal and proximal sources of stress. Stress, stress responses, and coping are now considered as they relate to processes of risk and resilience.

Stress

Exposure to stressful life events, minor events and hassles, and chronic stressful circumstances represent significant sources of risk to the development of adolescents. However, lingering issues in the definition and measurement of stress continue to present challenges to research on these important processes.

Defining Stress

Stress is an old concept that will neither die nor fade away. In spite of strong criticism of the construct (e.g., Lazarus, 1993), stress remains a centrally important factor in understanding risk factors and processes. Prevailing definitions of stress all include environmental circumstances or conditions that threaten, challenge, exceed, or harm the psychological or biological capacities of the individual. Definitions of stress differ, however, in the degree to which they emphasize psychological processes that are implicated in determining what is and is not stressful to a given individual. Transactional approaches posit that the occurrence of stress is dependent on the degree to which individuals *perceive* environmental demands as threatening, challenging, or harmful (Lazarus & Folkman, 1984). Alternatively, environmental perspectives emphasize the importance of *objectively* documenting the occurrence of environmental events and conditions independent of the potential confounds of cognitive appraisals (Cohen, Kessler, & Gordon, 1995).

Although the transactional definition of stress is widely embraced, it poses problems for stress research with adolescents. Research on stress during infancy and early childhood indicates clear negative effects of maternal

separation, abuse, and neglect on infants (e.g., Field, 1995; Perry, Pollard, Blakley, Baker, & Vigilante, 1995). Whether or not these events are subjectively experienced as stressful, it is clear that adverse effects can occur in young children without the complex cognitive appraisals that are central to the transactional approach. In addition, research indicates that cognitive appraisal processes do not interact with stressful events in the prediction of symptoms until late childhood or early adolescence and that appraisals increase in their significance during this period (e.g., Cole et al., 2008; Nolen-Hoeksema, Girgus, & Seligman, 1992; Turner & Cole, 1994).

As conceptual models of adolescent developmental psychopathology have become more sophisticated, greater emphasis has been placed on moderating and mediating processes that influence or explain the relation between stress and psychopathology (Cicchetti & Cohen, 1995; Grant, Compas, Stuhlmacher, Thurm, & McMahon, 2003). Models of stress that fail to distinguish psychosocial stressors from mediating and moderating processes, including cognitive appraisal processes, are problematic. To understand fully how stressful experiences, moderating factors, and mediating processes relate to one another in the prediction of psychopathology and adjustment, it is important to define and measure each of these processes clearly. The single essential element of the concept of stress that is conceptually distinct from moderators–mediators, psychological symptoms, and other risk factors is the occurrence of external, environmental threat to the individual (Cohen et al., 1995).

Given the limitations with transactional definitions of stress for research with adolescents, this chapter presents a definition that focuses on external, environmental changes or conditions. Specifically, we adopt the Grant et al. (2003) definition of stressors that emphasizes objective environmental events or chronic conditions that threaten adolescents' physical and/or psychological health or well-being of youth. This definition is consistent with traditional stimulus-based definitions of stress and more recent definitions of stressors and objective stress (e.g., Rudolph & Hammen, 2000). Events or chronic circumstances can threaten the well-being of an individual without leading to a negative outcome. Thus, stressful events and conditions are defined independent of their effects or outcomes. Moreover, this definition allows for positive outcomes in the face of objectively threatening circumstances; that is, it allows for resilience.

In spite of the need for clarity in the definition of stress, in a recent review of stress measurement, methods used in research with children and adolescents (Grant, Compas, Thurm, McMahon, & Gipson, 2004) found wide variability in the ways that stress was conceptualized and measured. Of those researchers utilizing cumulative stress scales or interviews (as opposed to measures of specific stressors such as sexual abuse), fewer than 10% used a well-validated measure. About 45% reported that they developed their own measure, and the remaining authors used one of the approximately 50 currently available measures of cumulative stress (Grant et al., 2004). Psychometric data on most measures were not provided, and few of the authors who developed their own scales provided information about their method of measurement development or the items comprised in their scales (Grant et al., 2004).

One promising method for improving precision in stress research involves the use of structured interviews for the assessment of stressors experienced by adolescents (e.g., Goodyer & Altham, 1991a, 1991b; McQuaid, Monroe, Roberts, Kupfer, & Frank, 2000; Rudolph et al., 2000). Interviews are used to identify stressors that have been encountered and the conditions that surround these events. Probes for each event include a description of what occurred, when it occurred, the context of the event or ongoing circumstances, and the consequences of the event. External raters then evaluate and rate the level of threat associated with each event and condition based on the context of the stressor. For example, the objective

threat rating given to the stressor "death of a grandmother" would be higher for an adolescent for whom the grandmother was a primary caretaker than for an adolescent whose grandmother lived far away and was seen only occasionally (Rudolph et al., 2000). Ratings are then summed to form an index of the stressors that each adolescent has encountered.

Stressors and Adolescent Psychopathology

Stressors remain central to current etiological theories of child and adolescent psychopathology. This is evident in the more than 1,500 empirical investigations of the relation between stressors and psychological symptoms among youth identified by Grant et al. (2004). However, the level of interest in the relation between stressors and psychological problems in adolescence has not been matched by progress in the field. As described earlier, variability in the conceptualization and operationalization of stress and stressors has created significant problems (Grant et al.).

Underlying these specific measurement concerns is the broader issue that most studies of the relation between stressors and psychological problems in children and adolescents have not been theory driven beyond the general theoretical notion that stressors pose a risk factor for psychopathology (Grant et al., 2003; Steinberg & Avenevoli, 2000). Grant et al. proposed a framework to guide research on stress during childhood and adolescence. This general model includes five central hypotheses:

1. Stressors are a significant source of risk for psychopathology during childhood and adolescence.
2. Moderators influence the relation between stressors and psychopathology.
3. Mediators explain or account for the relation between stressors and psychopathology.
4. Relations among stressors, moderators, mediators, and psychopathology are reciprocal and dynamic.

5. There is specificity in the relations among stressors, moderators, and mediators.

These hypotheses reflect many of the core issues and assumptions in research on risk factors, protective factors, and processes of vulnerability and resilience.

The first hypothesis of this model, that stressors are a significant risk for negative psychological and health outcomes, provides the conceptual basis for all studies of the relation between stressors and psychological problems in children and adolescents. Nonetheless, Grant et al. (2004) identified comparatively few studies (about 60) that have tested this hypothesis using prospective designs. Although the number of prospective studies is disappointing at this stage of research on stress in adolescence, it reflects significant progress from 20 years earlier (see Compas, 1987a, 1987b). Furthermore, Grant et al. found evidence in 53 studies that stressful life experiences predict psychological problems in children and adolescents over time. Thus, evidence indicates that the cumulative effect of stressful events meets the criterion for a risk factor (Kraemer et al., 1997, 2001).

Potential moderators of the relation between stressors and psychopathology have been examined in numerous studies (Grant et al., 2006). Moderators may be conceptualized as vulnerabilities or protective factors, as they represent preexisting characteristics that increase or decrease the likelihood that stressors will lead to psychopathology. Moderators may also be viewed as the mechanisms that explain why similar processes may lead to various outcomes (multifinality) and varying processes may lead to similar outcomes (equifinality; Cicchetti & Rogash, 1996; Curtis & Cicchetti, 2003). Potential moderating variables include age, gender, temperament, stress (autonomic) reactivity, the presence of supportive relationships, and stable cognitive styles. Research on moderators and mediators is central to identifying processes of risk and resilience.

Although some variables may serve either a moderating or mediating function, mediators are conceptually distinct from moderators. Whereas moderators are characteristics of adolescents or their social networks prior to stressors, mediators are activated, set off, or caused by the current stressful experience and conceptually and statistically account for the relation between stressors and negative outcomes (Baron & Kenny, 1986; Holmbeck, 1997). Mediators may include variables such as coping responses, cognitive style, and family processes. In our recent review of the literature on mediators of the association between stressors and psychological problems in young people, we found promising evidence of mediating effects, particularly in regard to mediators of the effects of poverty on adolescent outcomes (Grant et al., 2003).

The hypothesis that relations among stressors, moderators, mediators, and health and psychological outcomes are reciprocal and dynamic has received relatively little attention in research on stress during adolescence (Grant et al., 2003). However, those studies that have examined this issue have found evidence that symptoms do predict increases in stressful events over time (e.g., Carter et al., 2006; Cole, Nolen-Hoeksema, Girgus, & Paul, 2006; Compas et al., 1989; DuBois, Felner, Meares, & Krier, 1994; Sandler, Tein, & West, 1994). Thus, some stressful events (referred to as dependent events) during adolescence are generated by symptoms and other characteristics of adolescents themselves. Some of the risk associated with stressful events can be self-generated and contribute to a vicious cycle in which stress may trigger initial behavioral and emotional problems, which in turn lead to more stress (e.g., Cole et al., 2006).

The final hypothesis in this model is that there is specificity in relations among particular stressors, moderators, mediators, and psychological outcomes. Evidence of specificity requires that a particular type of stressor (e.g., interpersonal rejection) is linked with a particular type of psychological problem (e.g., depression) via a particular mediating process (e.g., ruminative coping) in the context of a particular moderating variable (e.g., female gender, adolescent age). In a recent review, McMahon et al. (2003) failed to identify any studies that had examined a full specificity model including specific mediating and moderating processes in the relation between particular stressors and particular outcomes (see also Steinberg & Avenevoli, 2000). With a few notable exceptions (e.g., Sandler, Reynolds, Kliewer, & Ramirez, 1992), studies capable of examining specificity effects (i.e., studies that included more than one type of stressor and more than one type of psychological outcome) tested only a subset of the features of specificity, and a consistent pattern of specific effects failed to emerge (McMahon et al.). Thus, current evidence indicates that stressful events and circumstances are a general, nonspecific risk for psychopathology. However, this is in part a result of the failure of most studies to include the elements necessary to test for specificity.

Coping and Self-Regulation

A major source of variation in the effects of stress during adolescence is the result of the ways that adolescents react to stress and cope with stress and the degree to which they are able to regulate their emotions, behaviors, thoughts, and physiological responses to stress (Compas, in press).

Distinguishing Among Competence, Resilience, and Coping

Although the terms *coping, competence,* and *resilience* are often used interchangeably, they reflect distinct aspects of successful development and adaptation (e.g., Compas, Connor-Smith, Saltzman, Thomsen, & Wadsworth, 2001; Masten & Coatsworth, 1998; Masten & Obradovic, 2006). The primary distinction is that coping refers to *processes* of adaptation, competence refers to the *characteristics and resources* that are needed for successful adaptation, and resilience is reflected in *outcomes* for which competence and coping have been effectively put into action in response to stress and adversity. Therefore, coping

can be viewed as efforts to enact or mobilize competence or personal resources, and resilience as the successful outcome of these actions. Coping includes the behaviors and thoughts that are implemented by individuals when faced with stress without reference to their efficacy, whereas resilience refers to the results of the coping responses of competent individuals who have been faced with stress and have coped in an effective and adaptive manner. However, not all coping efforts represent the enactment of competence, and not all outcomes of coping are reflected in resilience; indeed, some coping efforts fail.

Definitions of Coping

Two challenges are foremost in generating a definition of coping to guide research with adolescents. The first is the need for a definition that reflects the nature of developmental processes. It is unlikely that the basic characteristics or the efficacy of coping are the same for a young child as for an adolescent, and any definition of coping should reflect such changes. Second, it is important to distinguish coping from other aspects of the ways that individuals respond to stress, as the utility of any definition of coping depends in part on the degree of specificity that is conveyed.

In those instances in which coping has been defined in research with adolescents, investigators frequently have drawn on definitions from models of adult coping; conceptualizations of coping that are explicitly concerned with adolescence (and childhood) have emerged only recently. The most widely cited definition is that of Lazarus and Folkman (1984), which is derived from their adult model of stress, cognitive appraisal, and coping. This conceptualization of coping has been the basis for numerous investigations of coping in adolescence (e.g., Compas, Malcarne, & Fondacaro, 1988; Lengua & Sandler, 1996; Steele, Forehand, & Armistead, 1997). Lazarus and Folkman defined coping as "constantly changing cognitive and behavioral efforts to manage specific external and/or internal demands that are appraised as taxing or exceeding the resources of the person" (p. 141). Coping is viewed as an ongoing dynamic process that changes in response to the changing demands of a stressful encounter or event. Furthermore, coping is conceptualized as purposeful responses that are directed toward resolving the stressful relationship between the self and the environment (problem-focused coping) or toward palliating negative emotions that arise as a result of stress (emotion-focused coping).

Perspectives on coping that are more explicitly concerned with childhood and adolescence include those outlined by Weisz and colleagues (Rudolph, Dennig, & Weisz, 1995; Weisz, McCabe, & Dennig, 1994), Skinner and colleagues (e.g., Skinner & Zimmer-Gembeck, 2007), and Eisenberg and colleagues (e.g., Eisenberg, Fabes, & Guthrie, 1997; see Compas et al., 2001, for a review of these perspectives). A central issue in defining coping during adolescence (and childhood) is whether coping includes all responses to stress, particularly both controlled and automatic responses. Skinner's (1995) original definition of coping included both volitional and involuntary or automatic responses to manage threats to competence, autonomy, and relatedness, and although Eisenberg et al. acknowledged that coping and emotional regulation are processes that typically involve effort, coping is not always conscious and intentional. There is now increasing consensus that coping is best understood within the context of the development of self-regulatory processes (Skinner & Zimmer-Gembeck, in press).

We view coping as one aspect of a broader set of processes that are enacted in response to stress (Compas et al., 2001; Compas, in press). Specifically, we define coping as "conscious volitional efforts to regulate emotion, cognition, behavior, physiology, and the environment in response to stressful events or circumstances" (Compas et al., p. 89). These regulatory processes both draw on and are constrained by the biological, cognitive, social, and emotional development of the individual.

An individual's developmental level both contributes to the resources that are available for coping and limits the types of coping responses the individual can enact. Coping is a subset of broader self-regulatory processes, with coping referring to regulatory efforts that are volitionally and intentionally enacted specifically in response to stress. Furthermore, coping is limited to responses that are controlled and volitional and is distinct from automatic stress response processes.

Although coping refers to the ways that an individual attempts to manage and adapt to stress, coping is a process that is embedded in and draws on social relationships. Some coping efforts involve obtaining information, emotional support, tangible forms of help, and guidance from others. Sources of support for adolescents include parents, siblings, peers, teachers, and other significant adults in their lives. Thus, coping is an important process that can lead to resilient outcomes, but it is not limited to the characteristics of individuals; coping is frequently a social process.

Dimensions and Categories of Coping

Coping research has been hindered by confusion and a lack of consensus about the dimensions of categories (Skinner, Edge, Altman, & Sherwood, 2003). We have proposed that stress responses can be distinguished along two broad dimensions: voluntary (controlled) versus involuntary (automatic) and engagement versus disengagement (Compas, in press; Compas et al., 2001; Connor-Smith, Compas, Thomsen, Wadsworth, & Saltzman, 2000). The inclusion or exclusion of automatic stress responses within the definition of coping is to a certain degree one of semantics, as both perspectives recognize the importance of the two broad categories of controlled or voluntary responses and automatic or involuntary responses to stress. However, the degree to which these two components of stress responses are conceptualized and measured as distinct processes and the extent to which the relationship between them is understood are of fundamental importance in understanding processes of adaptation and resilience.

Regardless of how these concepts are mapped onto a definition of coping, it is important to distinguish between volitional and involuntary responses to stress for several reasons. First, this distinction avoids an overly broad and imprecise definition of coping in which coping includes everything that individuals do in response to stress (Lazarus & Folkman, 1984; Rudolph et al., 1995). Second, automatic and controlled processes are experienced as subjectively and qualitatively different: Individuals can distinguish between those aspects of their thoughts and behavior that they experience as under their personal control versus those that are beyond their control (Skinner, 1995). For example, the release of emotions can occur through an involuntary ventilation of emotions (crying) or through a controlled process such as writing, and the effects of these processes on emotions and physiology may be quite different (Pennebaker, 1997). Third, volitional and involuntary responses may emerge differently over the course of development, with involuntary responses present early in development (e.g., Rothbart, 1991), followed by the emergence of volitional responses in early childhood. Fourth, volitional and involuntary processes may differ in the ways they respond to interventions. Psychological interventions are often designed to teach individuals skills in managing those aspects of cognition and behavior that are under personal control, but they can only indirectly increase or decrease responses that are experienced as uncontrollable.

Regulatory processes, especially in response to stress, include both automatic and controlled processes (Compas et al., 2001). Automatic (or involuntary) processes occur either within or outside of conscious awareness but are not under conscious control, whereas controlled (or voluntary) responses to stress and regulatory processes are within conscious awareness and are experienced as under personal control. Dual-process theories that encompass automatic and controlled processes are pervasive in psychological science (Barrett, Tugade, & Engle, 2004). Dual-process models have been applied to social cognition (e.g., Lierberman, 2007), mental control (e.g., Wenzlaff & Wegner, 2000), emotions and emotional disorders (e.g., Mathews & McCleod, 2005), and self-regulation (e.g., Bargh & Ferguson, 2000). Empirical support for the distinction between controlled or volitional responses and automatic or involuntary responses is extensive. For example, attention to and responses to threatening cues in the environment, which are experienced as stressful and therefore may initiate coping behavior, are processed on both an automatic, uncontrolled level as well as on a controlled, strategic level (see Mathews & McCleod for a review of research with adults). Research has recently begun to examine these two levels of attentional processing and biases in children and adolescents (e.g., Boyer et al., 2006). Automatic and controlled processes are critical to coping and emotion regulation.

We have proposed that both automatic and controlled responses to stress can be further distinguished as engaging with a stressor or one's responses to the stressor, or disengaging from the stressor and one's responses (Compas et al., 2001). The origins of the engagement–disengagement dimension can be found in the concept of the fight (engagement) or flight (disengagement) response (e.g., Cannon, 1933, 1934; Gray, 1991) and in the contrast between approach and avoidance responses (Krohne, 1996). Voluntary or controlled responses (coping) that involve engagement can be further distinguished by their goals—oriented toward achieving primary control or secondary control (Connor-Smith, et al., 2000). The goals of achieving either primary or secondary control are fundamental in motivational models of coping and self-regulation (e.g., Weisz, 1990). However, these goals are pursued only as part of controlled efforts to engage with the stressor or one's thoughts, emotions, and physiological reactions to the stressor (Rudolph et al., 1995).

Empirical support for this model comes from confirmatory factor analyses in studies of adolescents from different cultural groups reporting on their responses to different domains of stress (interpersonal stress, economic strain, family conflict; Compas et al., 2006; Connor-Smith et al., 2000; Wadsworth, Benson, Reichman, & Compas, 2003). A first factor has been labeled primary control engagement coping (Connor-Smith et al., 2000; Rudolph, Dennig, & Weisz, 1995) or active coping (Ayers, Sandler, West, & Roosa, 1996; Walker, Smith, Garber, & Van Slyke, 1997) and is defined as coping intended to influence objective events or conditions or one's emotional responses to stress. This category includes not only problem solving and other coping efforts directed at changing the stressor but also direct efforts to change one's emotional reactions (Connor-Smith et al.). The second category has been labeled secondary control engagement coping (Connor-Smith et al.; Rudolph et al., 1995) and accommodative coping (Ayers et al.; Walker et al.) and encompasses coping efforts aimed at maximizing one's fit to current conditions. Examples include acceptance, cognitive restructuring, and distraction. A third category is disengagement (Connor-Smith et al., 2000) or avoidance (Ayers et al.; Walker et al.) coping, which is defined as an effort to disengage cognitively or behaviorally from the source of stress or one's emotions.

Studies of coping and emotional distress during adolescence suggest that primary control coping is associated with better adjustment in response to stressors that are objectively controllable or are perceived as controllable (Compas et al., 2001). Secondary control coping is better suited for uncontrollable stressors, as indicated by lower levels of symptoms when these strategies are used in uncontrollable situations (Compas et al.). Disengagement or avoidance coping has consistently been found to be associated with poorer adjustment (higher levels of symptoms) regardless of the nature of the stressor.

Coping, Temperament, and Stress Reactivity

Coping is linked to but also distinct from several aspects of temperament, including the constructs of reactivity (response) and self-regulation (Compas, in press; Compas et al., 2001). Reactivity encompasses individual differences in physiological and emotional responses to stress. Physiological reactivity includes the threshold, dampening, and reactivation of autonomic arousal (e.g., Boyce, Barr, & Zeltzer, 1992). Although the characteristics of reactivity may vary across different emotions (e.g., fear versus anger), highly reactive individuals have a lower threshold of initial response, are slower in recovery or returning to baseline, and display greater reactivation of arousal with repeated exposure to stress. High reactivity is generally associated with inhibited temperament, whereas low reactivity is associated with uninhibited temperament. Individual differences in reactivity and temperament are related to coping, as they affect the individual's initial automatic response to stress and may constrain or facilitate certain types of coping responses (Compas, 1987b). For example, the temperamental characteristics of behavioral inhibition (e.g., Kagan, Reznick, & Snidman, 1987; Kagan & Snidman, 1991) and attentional control (e.g., Posner & Rothbart, 1994; Rothbart, Posner, & Hershey, 1995) are related to individual differences in reactivity to stress. Behavioral inhibition includes the tendency to experience high levels of arousal in novel, threatening, or stressful situations and may be related to the use of avoidance and withdrawal as coping methods, whereas uninhibited temperament is expected to be related to more active and approach-oriented coping responses. Individual differences in the capacity for attentional control (the ability to sustain attention as well as to shift attention) may be related to the ability to use strategies such as distraction to cope with negative emotions.

As noted earlier, coping is also related to or is an aspect of self-regulation. From infancy, individuals are capable of regulating aspects of their physiological arousal, behavior, and emotions (Gunnar, 1994; Rothbart, 1991). However, regulation is achieved initially through involuntary, biologically based processes (e.g., Blass & Ciaramitaro, 1994). These regulatory capacities are augmented early in development by responses that are acquired through learning and experience but are under the control of contextual cues that elicit and maintain behavior (Rothbart, 1991). Therefore, some important aspects of self-regulation precede the development of the capacity for the conscious volitional efforts that comprise coping. Features of responses to stress in infancy that precede coping include individual differences in self-soothing behaviors (e.g., Gunnar). These behaviors develop prior to the skills needed for conscious volitional self-regulation, yet they are important aspects of the ways that infants regulate themselves in response to stress. Coping is influenced by the emergence of cognitive and behavioral capacities for regulation of the self and the environment, including the emergence of intentionality, representational thinking, language, metacognition, and the capacity for delay.

RISK AND RESILIENCE: EXEMPLARS FROM RESEARCH ON STRESS, COPING AND DEPRESSION

Research on sources of risk and resilience during adolescence has addressed an impressive array of contextual and individual factors. To exemplify important issues in adolescent risk and resilience, we focus here on examples of risk and resilience in adolescence that are linked to the development of depression. Depression provides a useful example of risk and resilience because it increases dramatically in prevalence during adolescence and there is now a substantial body of work identifying stress as a significant source of risk, stress reactivity as a potential vulnerability factor, and coping as a source of resilience. Further, adolescents whose parents experience one or more episodes of depression are exposed to a

significant source of risk for depression and other mental health problems.

Depression

The high prevalence of depression in the general population represents a significant mental health problem in the United States. As reported in the National Comorbidity Survey Replication, Kessler et al. (2003) found the lifetime prevalence of major depressive disorder to be 16.9%. It is expected that 32–35 million adults in the United States will experience an episode of depression over the course of their lifetime. Depression also increases significantly from childhood to adolescence. Longitudinal studies suggest that middle adolescence (age 15–16 years old) is the peak time for the onset of major depression (e.g., Hankin et al., 1998). Depression is also a highly recurrent disorder, as more than 80% of depressed individuals experience more than one episode and about 50% of those who undergo an episode experience a recurrence within 2 years of recovery (Belsher & Costello, 1988). An initial onset of depression during adolescence predicts a more severe and recurrent course of the disorder and higher levels of impairment (e.g., Hammen, Brennan, Kennan-Miller, & Herr, 2008).

Rates of depression in women are highest in young adulthood, during childbearing years, and among women with children (Kessler et al., 1994, 2003). In a similar pattern, rates of depression are higher in males younger than age 45 than men age 45 and older (Blazer, Kessler, McGonagle, & Swartz, 1994). As Kane and Garber (2004) noted, this age group of men is also likely to have children. Thus, it is quite apparent that a significant number of children and adolescents are repeatedly exposed to symptoms of depression—both when their parents are in and out of episode. The significant number of mothers who experience clinical depression during their children's lifetimes is particularly problematic, as maternal depression is linked to significant negative developmental outcomes in children (Goodman, 2007; Goodman & Gotlib, 1999).

Rates of depression in school-aged offspring of depressed mothers have been estimated to be as high as 40%, in comparison to an estimated lifetime prevalence rate between 18% and 24% in the general population of children and adolescents (Goodman; Lewinsohn, Hops, Roberts, Seeley, & Andrews, 1993). Extensive research has documented the impact of maternal depression on children, but paternal depression has also been shown to strongly correlate with child and adolescent psychopathology (e.g., Connell & Goodman, 2002; Kane & Garber).

Parental depression in both mothers and fathers affects child and adolescent adjustment in a variety of ways. When compared to same-age children of nondepressed parents, offspring of depressed parents not only have higher rates of depression, but they also experience earlier onset of the disorder, greater functional impairment, and a higher likelihood of recurrence (Hammen, Shih, Altman, & Brennan, 2003; Keller et al., 1986; Warner, Weissman, Fendrich, Wickramarante, & Moreau, 1992).

Having established that parental depression is a significant risk factor for depression in children and adolescents, it is important to understand the mechanisms and processes by which this risk affects offspring. In addition, as not all offspring of depressed parents develop psychopathology, understanding the protective processes that lead to resilience are also important to consider.

Risk Processes

The effects of parental depression on offspring are likely transmitted through multiple mechanisms, including the heritability of depression; innate dysfunctional neuroregulatory mechanisms; exposure to negative maternal cognitions, behaviors, and affect; and the stressful context of the adolescent's life (Goodman & Gotlib, 1999). Of particular relevance to this paper are the disrupted interpersonal interactions that depressed individuals experience, as they may greatly influence parenting. Parenting is a complex form of social interaction

that is significantly impaired by depression (Coyne, Downey, & Boergers, 1991). Parent–child interactions serve as critical mechanisms through which children are exposed to risk factors associated with parental depression—particularly negative parental affect and cognitions, as well as stressful family exchanges (Garber & Martin, 2002; Lovejoy, Graczyk, O'Hare, & Neuman, 2000). In addition, coping may be a particularly important protective factor in shielding against the effects of psychosocial risk processes associated with parental depression.

Research indicates that exposure to stressful parent–child interactions is one of the primary psychosocial mechanisms through which parental depression exerts its effects on children (e.g., Jaser et al., 2005; Jaser et al., 2007; Jaser et al., in press; Langrock, Compas, Keller, Merchant, & Copeland, 2002). For example, Adrian and Hammen (1993) reported that children of unipolar depressed women experienced higher rates of family stress than children of bipolar, medically ill, or control women, and that family stress was an important predictor of both internalizing and externalizing problems in children. Another study conducted by Hammen, Brennan, and Shih (2004) found that, in a community sample, adolescents with mothers meeting criteria for current depression, past depression, or dysthymia all experienced increased levels of conflict and stress when compared to children of women without psychopathology. Furthermore, when examining adolescents exposed to similar levels of parent–child conflict, rates of depression were higher in offspring of depressed mothers than nondepressed mothers. Therefore, not only do offspring of depressed parents experience more stressful parent–child relationships, these children also may be more reactive to or affected by stressful circumstances (Hammen et al.). Children of depressed parents tend to experience more negative exchanges with their parents, either through verbal communication (e.g., criticism or blaming) or actions (e.g., ignoring or punishing), contributing to a chronically stressful environment. For example, Cummings and Davies (1994) found that dysfunctional parenting skills, particularly inconsistent discipline, displayed by depressed parents may be perceived as stressful and are likely to result in a negative cycle of child behavior problems.

Parenting in Depressed Parents

Depression significantly impairs parents' ability to effectively support and nurture children, leading to disruptions in parenting. Most of the research on parenting in depressed parents has concentrated on parenting difficulties associated with the physical, cognitive, and emotional symptoms of depression (e.g., sad mood, irritability, lack of interest, fatigue, or difficulty concentrating; Lovejoy et al., 2000). Specifically, studies have documented parental withdrawal (e.g., avoidance or unresponsiveness to their children's needs) and parental intrusiveness (e.g., irritability toward their children or excessive involvement in their children's lives) as characteristic of depressed parents in their interactions with their children (e.g., Cummings, DeArth-Pendley, DuRocher-Schudlich, & Smith, 2001; Malphurs, Field, Larraine, Pickens, & Palaez-Nogueras, 1996).

Based on the symptoms of depression, such as anhedonia, sleep disturbance, and low energy, it has been hypothesized that parents with a history of the disorder are less able to maintain involvement, remain emotionally available, and meet the needs of their children. For example, Goodman and Brumley (1990) stated that depressed parents may be "emotionally unavailable and withdrawn to the extent that they may be less sensitive to child behavior" (Goodman & Brumley, 1990, p. 31). This hypothesis has been supported in research showing that, relative to nondepressed mothers, depressed mothers are less sensitive, attentive, and responsive in their parenting skills (Bettes, 1988; Field, Healy, Goldstein, & Guthertz, 1990). During interactions with their children, depressed mothers have also been shown to demonstrate lower rates of behavior

and of affective expression (Downey & Coyne, 1990). Less is known about these interaction patterns in depressed fathers inasmuch as most research focuses on mother–child interactions (e.g., Marchand & Hock, 1998). However, one study conducted by Jacob and Johnson (1997) observed parent–child interactions within families with a depressed mother, a depressed father, and normal control families. Results revealed that paternal and maternal depression were similarly associated with less positivity (e.g., agreement and approval) and congeniality (e.g., talking, laughing, and smiling), indicating that the presence of a depressed parent was associated with decreased affective expression regardless of parental gender.

Research also indicates that maternal depression is associated with more critical interactions between mothers and children, characterized by heightened levels of intrusiveness, negativity, and hostility (Breznitz & Friedman, 1988; Cohn, Cambell, Matias, & Hopkins, 1990; Harnish, Dodge, Valente, & Conduct Problems Prevention Research Group, 1995; Malatesta-Magai, 1991). The parenting behavior of depressed individuals is frequently characterized by high levels of criticism of their children (Goodman, Adamson, Riniti, & Cole, 1994). For example, Nelson, Hammen, Brennan, and Ullman (2003) conducted a study exploring the role of maternal criticism as a predictor of child symptoms and functioning in a sample of mothers, both with a history of depression and without. A subtype of expressed emotion (EE), which is thought to reflect the negative emotional atmosphere in a family and is increasingly being used as an indicator of parenting, was used to assess levels of maternal criticism. EE criticism, a construct including critical comments and statements expressed by the mother, is assessed through having the mother speak for five minutes about her child and their relationship. Mothers with a history of depression were determined to be more likely than nondepressed mothers to exhibit critical EE, being significantly more likely to make critical/hostile comments regarding their children (Nelson et al.).

In addition, interpersonal interactions between mothers while in a depressive episode and their offspring have been characterized as having higher levels of irritability when compared to such interactions involving well mothers or mothers not in episode (Tarullo, DeMulder, Martinez, & Radke-Yarrow, 1994).

In the longitudinal UCLA Family Stress Project, clinically depressed mothers were observed to be more irritable and critical and less positive than nondepressed mothers during mother–child interactions on a conflict-resolution task (Gordon, Burge, Hammen, & Adrian, 1989; Hammen, et al., 1987). Similar patterns have also been found in the context of paternal depression. In a study examining the stress of living with a depressed parent, Langrock et al. (2002) found that current parental depressive symptoms in both mothers and fathers were significantly related to both parental withdrawal and intrusive behaviors. Not only have stressful parent–child interactions been associated with depression in parents, but these interchanges also have been linked with child internalizing and externalizing symptoms.

Exposure to hostile, disengaged, and inconsistent parenting, as opposed to nurturing parenting, contributes to a chronically stressful and unpredictable environment for children and tends to result in increased symptoms in offspring of depressed parents. Recent studies have shown that children exposed to higher levels of parental intrusiveness/irritability and withdrawal have higher internalizing and externalizing symptoms. For example, Langrock et al. (2002) found that both parental intrusiveness and withdrawal were significantly correlated with higher levels of offspring anxiety/depression and aggression, according to parent reports. Jaser et al. (2005) extended those findings by using adolescent reports of family stress and adolescent psychological symptoms in combination with parent reports. Cross-informant correlations showed that adolescent reports of parental intrusive behaviors were significantly correlated with parent reports of adolescent internalizing and externalizing symptoms. Specifically, parental intrusiveness was positively correlated with anxiety/depression and aggression. Thus, when using cross-informant analyses of parent and adolescent reports to control for shared method variance in the measurement of parenting and adolescent adjustment, parental intrusiveness is associated with increased levels of psychological symptoms in offspring of depressed parents.

Studies of maternal speech samples that code for critical EE have yielded significant findings with respect to the effects of maternal criticism on children's adjustment. For example, Frye and Garber (2005) found that maternal criticism was significantly associated with both adolescents' internalizing and externalizing symptoms. Nelson et al. (2003) used structural equation modeling to demonstrate that critical maternal EE mediated the relationship between maternal history of depression and adolescents' externalizing symptoms and impaired functioning.

Potential Protective Factors

Through several risk processes, offspring of depressed parents are at increased risk for depression and other forms of psychopathology. However, research suggests that even under the stressful circumstances of having a parent with depression, some or even most children are resilient and adapt successfully. Attempts to explain resilience have focused on potential moderators. For some children and adolescents, the effect of parental depression may be significant, while for others the effect may be negligible. The ways that adolescents react to and cope with the stress of living with a depressed parent may serve as both mediators and moderators of the effects of this stress.

Coping

The way in which individuals respond to and deal with stress plays a critical role in the impact that stress has on their emotional and psychological well-being (Compas et al., 2001;

Skinner & Zimmer-Gembeck, 2007). The proposition that coping functions as a mediator or moderator between parental depression and child psychopathology leads to a series of questions regarding the ways in which children in these families of depressed parents may respond to and cope with stress, and how coping helps to buffer the stress of parental depression. First, how do children cope with the stress associated with parental depression? Second, how does depression in a parent constraint or alter the ways that children cope with stress related to parents' depression? Third, how do children's coping responses moderate the relationship between stress and children's adjustment in families of depressed parents?

Parents have a significant influence on the development of children's coping and stress responses (e.g., Kliewer, Sandler, & Wolchik, 1994; Power, 2004; Skinner & Edge, 2002). Not only do parents affect, in part, the types of stressors to which their children are exposed, but parents may also contribute to the development of children's coping resources and help children learn coping skills through modeling, teaching and coaching (Skinner & Zimmer-Gembeck, 2007). In spite of the evidence implicating stress processes as a risk factor for children in families of depressed parents, relatively little research has examined the effect that having a parent with depression has on children's coping. In the first research on this issue, Klimes-Dougan and Bolger (1998) compared coping strategies of children of depressed and well mothers but found no significant differences in the general coping styles between the two groups. The findings of this study are limited, however, in that the ways that children cope specifically with stressors associated with parental depression were not examined.

Research on adolescents' coping has been primarily devoted to identifying the link between individual differences in responding to stress and various outcomes in hopes of identifying adaptive and maladaptive coping patterns (Skinner & Zimmer-Gembeck, 2007). Coping is critical in fully understanding the effects of stress on adolescents as it both identifies the active role children can play in the presence of stressors in their lives and helps to predict how these experiences with adversity will shape future development (Compas et al., 2001; Skinner & Zimmer-Gembeck, 2007). As described above, living with a depressed parent is a substantial source of stress for children. Thus, the ways in which children and adolescents cope with this stress may play a significant role in their adjustment.

Our research group has studied coping and stress responses in three samples of adolescent offspring of depressed parents. First, we examined these processes in a sample of adolescents whose mother or father had a history of depression, and who had experienced at least one episode of depression in the adolescent's lifetime (Jaser et al., 2005; Jaser et al., 2007; Langrock et al., 2002). We found that adolescents' use of secondary control coping (i.e., positive thinking, distraction, acceptance, and cognitive restructuring) was related to lower symptoms of anxiety and depression, both within and across adolescents' and parents' reports of adolescents' coping and symptoms. Further, higher levels of stress reactivity (emotional and physiological arousal, intrusive thoughts) were related to higher symptoms of anxiety/depression. A troubling pattern was identified in these adolescents—as levels of stress (parental withdrawal and parental intrusiveness) increased, adolescents used less secondary control coping and reported higher levels of stress reactivity (Jaser et al., 2005; Langrock et al., 2002). That is, as stress increases and adaptive coping becomes more important, adolescents use less secondary control coping and experience higher levels of reactivity. This is consistent with the notion that stress contributes to dysregulation (heightened stress reactivity) and interferes with controlled self-regulation and coping, both of which lead to increased risk for depressive symptoms (Compas, 2006).

Second, we have examined coping and stress responses in adolescents whose mothers had a history of depression as compared with a demographically matched sample of adolescents whose mothers did not have a history of depression (Jaser et al., in press). As expected, adolescents of mothers with a history of depression were higher in depressive symptoms and externalizing problems than adolescents whose mothers did not have a history of depression. Further, adolescent children of mothers with a history of depression reported higher levels of stress reactivity (e.g., emotional and physiological arousal, intrusive thoughts) than children of mothers with no history of depression. Mothers' reports of their current depressive symptoms and observations of maternal sadness during parent–child interactions in the laboratory were both related to higher levels of adolescents' depressive symptoms and externalizing problems, higher stress reactivity, and lower levels of secondary control coping. Finally, adolescents' use of secondary control coping and stress reactivity accounted for the relation between maternal history of depression and adolescents depressive symptoms. These findings replicate those found by Jaser et al. (2005) and Langrock et al. (2002) but extend the previous studies by using direct observations to assess parental depressive symptoms and parent–adolescent interactions.

Third, we have examined stress and coping in adolescent offspring of mothers and fathers with a history of depression (Fear et al., 2008). In this sample our focus was on adolescents' coping with interparental conflict and a very similar pattern of findings emerged. Once again, we found support for secondary control coping as a predictor of lower internalizing and externalizing symptoms, after accounting for method variance in adolescent and parent reports of coping and symptoms. Further, secondary control coping partially or fully accounted for the association between interparental conflict and adolescent symptoms (Fear et al.).

Researchers have also begun to examine emotion regulation, a concept closely related to coping (see Compas et al., in press; Gross & Thompson, 2007) in children of depressed parents; however, studies with this population have not yet examined emotion regulation in adolescents. The most extensive work has been conducted by Kovacs and colleagues and has used direct observation methods to assess young children's (age 3 to 7 years old) emotion regulation in response to laboratory stress tasks and examined the relation between children's emotion regulation and their depressive symptoms (Forbes et al., 2006a, 2006b; Silk et al., 2006a, 2006b). Because of the relevance to understanding emotion regulation and depression in young people, these studies will be reviewed here. These studies are noteworthy for several reasons, including inclusion of a particularly high-risk sample, children whose mothers had themselves first experienced depression during childhood, and the use of direct observations and physiological measures of emotion regulation.

Silk et al. (2006a) observed children's responses to a delay of gratification task as an example of an emotionally arousing (frustration) context for children and their mothers. Silk et al. found that children of mothers with childhood-onset depression were more likely to focus on a delay object (a response that is similar to rumination in that it is a form of passive engagement with the source of stress or source of emotional arousal) than children of mothers without a history of depression. Further, the use of positive reward anticipation (displays of joy and information gathering, a component of problem solving and a form of primary control engagement coping) was related to fewer internalizing symptoms in children of mothers with childhood-onset depression and current depressive symptoms, but not for children of mothers without a history of depression (Silk et al., 2006b). These studies suggest that processes of coping and emotion regulation may develop during childhood and carry over into adolescence.

TOWARD AN INTEGRATIVE MODEL OF STRESS, COPING, RISK, AND RESILIENCE IN ADOLESCENCE

A comprehensive understanding of processes of risk and resilience during adolescence will require multiple levels of analyses of stable and changing aspects of individual adolescents and their environments. The research reviewed in this chapter points to several basic principles about risk and resilience during adolescence and highlights important directions for future research.

1. Processes of Risk and Resilience Operate at Multiple Levels During Adolescence

A comprehensive understanding of who is at risk for negative outcomes and who develops positively in spite of exposure to known levels of risk requires analysis of multiple levels of functioning. Risk and resilience processes include aspects of individuals and their social contexts. Contextual factors include the broad social circumstances in which adolescents develop. A compelling example of contextual risk can be seen in the effects of parental depression on adolescent development. The effects of risk factors such as parental psychopathology are the result of factors embedded in the immediate social environments of adolescents, including disruptions and strains that are evident in parent–adolescent interactions. The multiple levels of context are further complicated by levels of individual functioning, including cognitive, affective, and behavioral responses to stress and efforts to cope with stress. These response processes are affected by underlying biological development and functioning.

In spite of recognition of the need for multiple levels of analysis in risk and resilience research (Cicchetti & Dawson, 2002), there has been little progress in this regard. Most studies continue to focus on one level of analysis, be it molar or molecular. At the greatest extremes, investigations of biological development (including brain development) during adolescence have typically relied on samples of convenience and have not examined these important changes in adolescents who are exposed to greatest risk due to chronic sources of stress and adversity. Similarly, research on distal contextual factors, such as poverty, has typically failed to examine individual-level

processes that may exacerbate or protect adolescents from the effects of broad risk factors. Research is needed that examines how distal environmental risks get into behavior and under the skin. Similarly, studies of individual processes, including brain development and function, need to be conducted on those individuals in greatest need. Much more precise predictions of positive and negative developmental outcomes during adolescence can be made based on multiple levels of analysis.

2. Some Processes of Risk and Resilience are Stable from Childhood into Adolescence

Important sources of risk and protection from risk are in place prior to adolescence. Many sources of adversity in the environment, including parental psychopathology, emerge during childhood and continue unabated through adolescence. But there are also enduring resources in families, neighborhoods, and schools that also follow individuals through early development and into adolescence.

At the individual level, there are stable characteristics, such as temperament, that serve to make adolescents more vulnerable to or protect them from risk. Therefore, longitudinal research that begins prior to adolescence is needed to understand fully what places some adolescents at risk and what protects others from negative outcomes.

3. Some Processes of Risk and Resilience Change with Development During Adolescence

A model of risk and resilience in adolescence must include processes that emerge during adolescence and that may be unique to this developmental period. Changes in cognitive, emotional, social, and biological development bring with them a host of increased sources of risk and concomitant increases in protective factors. Some forms of interpersonal stress increase during adolescence, along with changes in cognitive processes that can contribute both to greater vulnerability and protection from stress.

Emerging evidence on brain development during adolescence also points to changes in brain function that may shape automatic and controlled responses to stress (see chapter 4, this volume). Research on these changes is in its earliest phases, however, and is a high priority for future research.

4. Trajectories of Adolescent Development are Shaped by Both Stable and Developmental Sources of Risk and Resilience

Healthy and problematic physical and psychological development during adolescence is not static and is best reflected in pathways or trajectories of development and change (Compas, Hinden, & Gerhardt, 1995; Garber et al., 2002; Moffitt & Caspi, 2001). In some instances, these trajectories have their onset well prior to adolescence, and adolescent development reflects the continuation of an increasing or decreasing slope.

In other cases, trajectories are changed significantly by contextual and individual development during adolescence. Distinguishing risk and resilience processes that contribute to stable versus changing trajectories is a high priority.

5. Stress and Stress Reactivity are Important Unifying Constructs for Understanding Processes of Risk

After decades of research and thousands of studies, the concepts of stress and stress reactivity continue to play a central role in research on risk processes during adolescence. Stress, or more accurately stressful events and circumstances, operate at multiple levels and are both stable and changing during adolescence. As exemplified in research on the effects of poverty, adolescents who lack economic resources are under chronic stress. However, the stress of poverty is best understood by examining the more proximal sources of stress that are manifested in adolescents' immediate environments.

Individual differences in temperament influence stress processes by shaping automatic physiological, emotional, cognitive, and behavioral responses to stress. Behavioral inhibition, positive and negative affectivity, and attentional control are examples of temperamental characteristics that may shape responses to stress and thereby contribute to vulnerability or protection from stress. Because of problems inherent in retrospective recall of early temperament, longitudinal studies are needed in which temperamental characteristics are measured in childhood and used as predictors of responses to stress and adversity in adolescence.

6. Coping is an Important Unifying Construct for Understanding Processes of Resilience

The ways that adolescents cope with stress and adversity represent an essential feature of resilience. This includes the skills that the individual develops to regulate reactions to stress and the social and interpersonal resources that are used to facilitate effective coping. Coping is one of the primary processes through which resilient outcomes are achieved.

Therefore, it is essential to develop a detailed accounting of the ways of coping that are associated with positive and negative outcomes in adolescence. The details of effective and ineffective coping form a foundation for interventions to enhance resilience and decrease the adverse effects of stress during adolescence (Compas, Forehand, & Keller, in press).

CONCLUSIONS

One key to understanding adolescent development lies in the identification of processes that place some adolescents at risk for negative developmental outcomes while other individuals navigate this period of development without encountering significant problems in psychological or physical health. Research on risk, vulnerability, resilience, and protective factors continues to offer significant promise for distinguishing between these two general paths of adolescent development. The broad constructs of stress, stress reactivity, and coping provide examples of work that can contribute to better understanding of how risk processes can threaten development but also how adolescents and their social environments can be strengthened to decrease the likelihood of adverse developmental outcomes during adolescence.

REFERENCES

Achenbach, T. M., & Dumenci, L. (2001). Advances in empirically based assessment: Revised cross-informant syndromes and new DSM-oriented scales for the CBCL, YSR, and TRF: Comment on Lengua, Sadowksi, Friedrich, and Fisher (2001). *Journal of Consulting and Clinical Psychology, 69,* 699–702.

Achenbach, T. M., Dumenci, L., & Rescorla, L. A. (2002). Ten year comparisons of problems and competencies for national samples of youth: Self, parent and teacher reports. *Journal of Emotional and Behavioral Disorders, 10,* 194–203.

Achenbach, T. M., McConaughy, S. M., & Howell, C. T. (1987). Child/adolescent behavior and emotional problems: Implications of cross-informant correlations for situational specificity. *Psychological Bulletin, 101,* 213–232.

Achenbach, T. M., & Rescorla, L. A. (2001). *Manual for ASEBA school-age forms & profiles.* Burlington: University of Vermont, Research Center for Children, Youth, & Families.

Adrian, C., & Hammen, C. (1993). Stress exposure and stress generation in children of depressed mothers. *Journal of Consulting and Clinical Psychology, 61,* 354–359.

American Psychiatric Association. (1994). *Diagnostic and statistical manual of mental disorders* (4th ed.). Washington, DC: Author.

Angold, A., Costello E. J., & Worthman, C. M. (1998). Puberty and depression: The roles of age, pubertal status, and pubertal timing. *Psychological Medicine, 28,* 51–61.

Ayers, T. S., Sandler, I. N., West, S. G., & Roosa, M. W. (1996). A dispositional and situational assessment of children's coping: Testing alternative models of coping. *Journal of Personality, 64,* 923–958.

Bargh, J. A., & Ferguson, M. J. (2000). Beyond behaviorism: On the automaticity of higher mental processes. *Psychological Bulletin, 126,* 925–945.

Baron, R. M., & Kenny, D. A. (1986). The moderator–mediator variable distinction in social psychological research: Conceptual, strategic, and statistical considerations. *Journal of Personality and Social Psychology, 51,* 1173–1182.

Barrett, L. F., Tugade, M. M., & Engle, R. W. (2004). Individual differences in working memory capacity and dual-process theories of the mind. *Psychological Bulletin, 130,* 553–573.

Belsher, G., & Costello, C. G. (1988). Relapse after recovery from unipolar depression: A critical review. *Psychological Bulletin, 104,* 84–96.

Bettes, B. A. (1988). Maternal depression and motherese: Temporal and intonational features. *Child Development, 59,* 1089–1096.

Blass, E. M., & Ciaramitaro, V. (1994). A new look at some old mechanisms in human newborns: Taste and tactile determinants of state, affect, and action. *Monographs of the Society for Research in Child Development, 59,* v–81.

Blazer, D. G., Kessler, R. C., McGonagle, K. A., & Swartz, M. S. (1994). The prevalence and distribution of depression of major depression in a national community sample. *American Journal of Psychiatry, 151,* 979–986.

Blum, R. W., McNeely, C., & Nonnemaker, J. (2002). Vulnerability, risk, and protection. *Journal of Adolescent Health, 31,* 28–39.

Boyce, W. T., Barr, R. G., & Zeltzer, L. K. (1992). Temperament and the psychobiology of childhood stress. *Pediatrics, 90,* 483–486.

Boyer, M. B., Compas, B. E., Stanger, C., Colletti, R. B., Konik, B., Morrow, S. B., et al. (2006). Attentional biases to pain and social threat in children with recurrent abdominal pain. *Journal of Pediatric Psychology, 31,* 209–220.

Breznitz, Z., & Friedman, S. L. (1988). Toddler's concentration: Does maternal depression make a difference? *Journal of Child Psychology and Psychiatry, 29,* 267–279.

Cannon, W. (1933). *The wisdom of the body.* New York: W. W. Norton.

Cannon, W. (1934). The significance of emotional level. *Scientific Monthly, 38,* 101–110.

Carter, J. S., Garber, J., Ciesla, J. E., & Cole, D. A. (2006). Modeling relations between hassles and internalizing and externalizing symptoms in adolescents: A four-year prospective study. *Journal of Abnormal Psychology, 115,* 428–442.

Chen, E. (2007). Impact of socioeconomic status on physiological health in adolescents: An experimental manipulation of psychosocial factors. *Psychosomatic Medicine, 69,* 348–355.

Cicchetti, D., & Blender, J. A. (2006). A multiple-levels-of-analysis perspective on resilience: Implications for the developing brain, neural plasticity, and preventive interventions. *Annals of the New York Academy of Sciences, 1094,* 248–258.

Cicchetti, D., & Cohen, D. (1995). Perspectives on developmental psychopathology. In D. Cicchetti & D. Cohen (Eds.), *Developmental psychopathology,* vol. 1: *Theory and methods* (pp. 3–20). New York: John Wiley & Sons.

Cicchetti, D., & Dawson, G. (2002). Editorial: Multiple levels of analysis. *Development and Psychopathology, 14,* 417–420.

Cicchetti, D., & Rogash, F. A. (1996). Equifinality and multifinality in developmental psychopathology. *Development and Psychopathology, 8,* 597–600.

Cohen, S., Kessler, R. C., & Gordon, L. U. (1995). *Measuring stress.* New York: Oxford University Press.

Cohn, J. F., Cambell, S. B., Matias, R., & Hopkins, J. (1990). Face-to-face interactions of postpartum depressed and nondepressed mother–infant pairs at 2 months. *Developmental Psychopathology, 26,* 15–23.

Cole, D. A., Ciesla, J. A., Dallaire, D. H., Jacquez, F. M., Pineda, A. Q., LaGrange, B., et al. (2008). Emergence of attributional style and its relation to depressive symptoms. *Journal of Abnormal Psychology, 117,* 16.

Cole, D. A., Nolen-Hoeksema, S., Girgus, J., & Paul, G. (2006). Stress exposure and stress generation in child and adolescent depression: A latent trait–state–error approach to longitudinal analyses. *Journal of Abnormal Psychology, 115,* 40–51.

Compas, B. E. (1987a). Coping with stress during childhood and adolescence. *Psychological Bulletin, 101,* 393–403.

Compas, B. E. (1987b). Stress and life events during childhood and adolescence. *Clinical Psychology Review, 7,* 275–302.

Compas, B. E. (1993). Promoting adolescent mental health. In S. G. Millstein, A. C. Peterson, & E. O. Nightengale (Eds.), *Promoting the health of adolescents: New directions for the 21st century.* New York: Oxford University Press.

Compas, B. E. (2006). Psychobiological processes of stress and coping: Implications for resilience in childhood and adolescence. *Annals of the New York Academy of Sciences, 1094,* 226–234.

Compas, B. E. (in press). Coping, regulation and development during childhood and adolescence. In E. Skinner & M. J. Zimmer-Gembeck (Eds.), *Coping and the development of regulation* (a volume for the series). (R. W. Larson & L. A. Jensen, Editors-in-Chief.) *New directions in child and adolescent development,* San Francisco: Jossey-Bass.

Compas, B. E., Boyer, M. C., Stanger, C., Colletti, R. B., Thomsen, A. H., Dufton, L. M., et al. (2006). Latent variable analysis of coping, anxiety/depression, and somatic symptoms in adolescents with chronic pain. *Journal of Consulting and Clinical Psychology, 74,* 1132–1142.

Compas, B. E., Connor-Smith, J. K., & Jaser, S. S. (2004). Temperament, stress reactivity, and coping: Implications for depression in childhood and adolescence. *Journal of Clinical Child and Adolescent Psychology, 33,* 21–31.

Compas, B. E., Boyer, M. C., Stanger, C., Colletti, R. B., Thomsen, A. H., Dufton, L. M., & Cole, D. A. (2006). Latent variable analysis of coping, anxiety/depression, and somatic symptoms in adolescents with chronic pain. *Journal of Consulting and Clinical Psychology, 74,* 1132–1142.

Compas, B. E., Connor-Smith, J. K., Saltzman, H., Thomsen, A. H., & Wadsworth, M. E. (2001). Coping with stress during childhood and adolescence: Progress, problems, and potential in theory and research. *Psychological Bulletin, 127,* 87–127.

Compas, B. E., Forehand, R., & Keller, G. (in press). Preventive intervention in families of depressed parents: A family cognitive–behavioral intervention. In T. J. Strauman, P. R. Costanzo, J. Garber, & L. Y. Abramson (Eds.), *Preventing depression in adolescent girls: A multidisciplinary approach.* New York: Guilford Press.

Compas, B. E., & Grant, K. E. (2002). Processes of risk and resilience in adolescence. In R. M. Lerner, F. Jacobs, & D. Wertlieb (Eds.), *Handbook of applied developmental science, vol. 1: Applying developmental science for youth and families: Historical and theoretical foundations.* Thousand Oaks, CA: Sage.

Compas, B. E., Hinden, B. R., & Gerhardt, C. A. (1995). Adolescent development: Pathways and processes of risk and resilience. *Annual Review of Psychology, 46,* 265–293.

Compas, B. E., Howell, D. C., Phares, V., Williams, R. A., Giunta, C. T., & Ledoux, N. (1989). Risk factors for emotional/behavioral problems in young adolescents: A prospective analysis of adolescent and parental stress and symptoms. *Journal of Consulting and Clinical Psychology, 57,* 732–740.

Compas, B. E., Jaser, S. S., & Benson, M. (in press). Coping and emotion regulation: Implications for understanding depression during adolescence. In S. Nolen-Hoeksema & L. Hilt (Eds.), *Handbook of Adolescent Depression.*

Compas, B. E., Malcarne, V. L., & Fondacaro, K. M. (1988). Coping with stressful events in older children and young adolescents. *Journal of Consulting and Clinical Psychology, 56,* 405–411.

Compas, B. E., & Wagner, B. M. (1991). Psychosocial stress during adolescence: Intrapersonal and interpersonal processes. In M. E. Colten & S. Gore (Eds.), *Adolescent stress: Causes and consequences—Social institutions and social change* (pp. 67–85). New York: de Gruyter.

Connell, A. M., & Goodman, S. H. (2002). The association between psychopathology in fathers versus mothers and children's internalizing and externalizing behavior problems: A meta-analysis. *Psychological Bulletin, 128,* 746–773.

Connor-Smith, J. K., Compas, B. E., Thomsen, A. H., Wadsworth, M. E., & Saltzman, H. (2000). Responses to stress: Measurement of coping and reactivity in children and adolescents. *Journal of Consulting and Clinical Psychology, 68,* 976–992.

Coyne, J. C., Downey, G., & Boergers, J. (1991). Depression in families: A systems perspective. In. D. Cicchetti, & S. L. Toth (Eds.), *Models and integrations: The Rochester symposium on developmental psychopathology,* vol. 3. Rochester, NY: University of Rochester Press.

Cummings, M. E., & Davies, P. T. (1994). Maternal depression and child development. *Journal of Child Psychology and Psychiatry and Allied Disciplines, 35,* 73–112.

Cummings, M. E., DeArth-Pendley, G., DuRocher-Schudlich, T., & Smith, D. A. (2001). Parental depression and family functioning: Toward a process-oriented model of children's adjustment. In S. R. Beach (Ed.), *Marital and family processes in depression: A scientific foundation for clinical practice* (pp. 89–110). Washington, DC: American Psychological Association.

Curtis, W. J., & Cicchetti, D. (2003). Moving research on resilience into the 21st century: Theoretical and methodological considerations in examining the biological contributors to resilience. *Development and Psychopathology, 15,* 773–810.

Downey, G., & Coyne, J. C. (1990). Children of depressed parents: An integrative review. *Psychological Bulletin, 108,* 50–76.

DuBois, D., Felner, R., Meares, H., & Krier, M. (1994). Prospective investigation of the effects of socioeconomic disadvantage, life stress, and social support on early adolescent adjustment. *Journal of Abnormal Psychology, 103,* 511–522.

Eisenberg, N., Fabes, R. A., & Guthrie, I. (1997). Coping with stress: The roles of regulation and development. In J. N. Sandler & S. A. Wolchik (Eds.), *Handbook of children's coping with common stressors: Linking theory, research, and intervention.* New York: Plenum Press.

Evans, G. W., & Kim, P. (2007). Childhood poverty and health: Cumulative risk exposure and stress dysregulation. *Psychological Science, 18,* 953–957.

Fear, J., Champion, J. E., Reeslund, K. L., Forehand, R., Colletti, C., Roberts, L., & Compas, B. E. (2008). *Parental depression and interparental conflict: Adolescents' self-blame and coping responses.* Manuscript under review.

Field, T. (1995). Infants of depressed mothers. *Infant Behavior and Development, 18*(1), 1–13.

Field, T., Healy, B., Goldstein, S., & Guthertz, M. (1990). Behaviors state matching and synchrony in mother–infant interactions of nondepressed versus depressed dyads. *Developmental Psychology, 26,* 7–14.

Forbes, E. E., Fox, N. A., Cohn, J. F., Galles, S. F., & Kovacs, M. (2006a). Children's affect regulation during disappointment: Psychophysiological responses and relation to parent history of depression. *Biological Psychology, 71,* 264–277.

Forbes, E. E., Shaw, D. S., Fox, N. A., Cohn, J. F., Silk, J. S., & Kovacs, M. (2006b). Maternal depression, child frontal asymmetry, and child affective behavior as factors in child behavior problems. *Journal of Child Psychology and Psychiatry, 47,* 79–87.

Friedman, R. J., & Chase-Lansdale, P. L. (2002). Chronic adversities. In M. Rutter & E. Taylor (Eds.), *Child and adolescent psychiatry* (4th ed., pp. 261–276). Oxford, UK: Blackwell Science.

Frye, A. A., & Garber, J. (2005). The relations among maternal depression, maternal criticism, and adolescents' externalizing and internalizing symptoms. *Journal of Abnormal Child Psychology, 33,* 1–11.

Garber, J., Keiley, M. K., & Martin, N. C. (2002). Developmental trajectories of adolescents' depressive symptoms: Predictors of change. *Journal of Consulting and Clinical Psychology, 70,* 79–95.

Garber, J., & Martin, N. C. (2002). Negative cognitions in offspring of depressed parents: Mechanisms of risk. In S. H. Goodman and I. H. Gotlib (Eds.), *Children of depressed parents: Mechanisms of risk and implications for treatment* (pp. 121–153). Washington, DC: American Psychological Association.

Garmezy, N. (1983). Stressors of childhood. In Garmezy, N., & Rutter, M. (Eds.), *Stress, coping, and development in children* (pp. 43–84). Baltimore, MD: Johns Hopkins University Press.

Ge, X., Conger, R. D., & Elder, G. H. (2001). Pubertal transition, stressful life events, and the emergence of gender differences in adolescent depressive symptoms. *Developmental Psychology, 37,* 404–417.

Gerhardt, C. A., Compas, B. E., Connor, J. K., & Achenbach, T. M. (1999). Association of a mixed anxiety–depression syndrome and symptoms of major depression. *Journal of Youth and Adolescence, 28,* 305–323.

Goodman, S. H. (2007). Depression in mothers. *Annual Review of Clinical Psychology, 3,* 107–135.

Goodman, S. H., Adamson, L. B., Riniti, J., & Cole, S. (1994). Mothers' expressed attitudes: Associations with maternal depression and children's self-esteem and psychopathology. *Journal of the American Academy of Child and Adolescent Psychiatry, 9,* 1265–1274.

Goodman, S. H., & Brumley, H. E. (1990). Schizophrenic and depressed mothers: Relational deficits in parenting. *Developmental Psychology, 26,* 31–39.

Goodman, S. H., & Gotlib, I. H. (1999). Risk for psychopathology in the children of depressed mothers: A developmental model for understanding mechanisms of transmission. *Psychological Review, 106,* 458–490.

Goodyer, I. M., & Altham, P. M. E. (1991a). Lifetime exit events and recent social and family adversities in anxious and depressed school-age children and adolescents: I. *Journal of Affective Disorders, 21,* 219–228.

Goodyer, I. M., & Altham, P. M. E. (1991b). Lifetime exit events and recent social and family adversities in anxious and depressed school-age children and adolescents: II. *Journal of Affective Disorders, 21,* 229–238.

Gordon, D., Burge, D., Hammen, C., & Adrian, C. (1989). Observations of interactions of depressed women with their children. *American Journal of Psychiatry, 146,* 50–55.

Gotlib, I. H., Lewinsohn, P. M., & Seeley, J. R. (1995). Symptoms versus a diagnosis of depression: Differences in psychosocial functioning. *Journal of Consulting and Clinical Psychology, 65,* 90–100.

Grant, K. E., Compas, B. E., Stuhlmacher, A., Thurm, A. E., & McMahon, S. D. (2003). Stressors and child/adolescent psychopathology: Moving from markers to mechanisms of risk. *Psychological Bulletin, 129,* 447–476.

Grant, K. E., Compas, B. E., Thurm, A. E., McMahon, S. D., & Gipson, P. Y. (2004). Stressors and child/adolescent psychopathology: Measurement issues and prospective effects. *Journal of Clinical Child and Adolescent Psychology, 33,* 412–425.

Grant, K. E., Compas, B. E., Thurm, A. E., McMahon, S. D., Gipson, P. Y., Campbell, A. J., et al. (2006). Stressors and child and adolescent psychopathology: Evidence of moderating and mediating effects. *Clinical Psychology Review, 26,* 257–283.

Gray, J. A. (1991). The neuropsychology of temperament. In J. Strelau & A. Angleitner (Eds.), *Explorations in temperament: International perspectives on theory and measurement* (pp. 105–128). New York: Plenum Press.

Gross, J. J., & Thompson, R. A. (2007). Emotion regulation: Conceptual foundations. In J. J. Gross (Ed.), *Handbook of emotion regulation* (pp. 3–24). New York: Guilford Press.

Gunnar, M. (1994). Psychoendocrine studies of temperament and stress in early childhood: Expanding current models. In J. E. Bates & T. D. Wachs (Eds.), *Temperament: Individual differences at the interface of biology and behavior* (pp. 25–38). Washington, DC: American Psychological Association.

Gutman, L. M., Sameroff, A. J., & Eccles, J. S. (2002). The academic achievement of African American students during early adolescence: An examination of multiple risk, promotive, and protective factors. *American Journal of Community Psychology, 30,* 367–400.

Hammen, C., Brennan, P. A., Kennan-Miller, D., & Herr, N. R. (2008). Early onset recurrent subtype of adolescent depression: Clinical and psychosocial correlates. *Journal of Child Psychology and Psychiatry, 49,* 433–440.

Hammen, C., Brennan, P. A., & Shih, J. H. (2004). Family discord and stress predictors of depression and other disorders in adolescent children of depressed and nondepressed women. *Journal of the American Academy of Child and Adolescent Psychiatry, 43,* 994–1002.

Hammen, C., Gordon, D., Burge, D., Adrian, C., Jaenicke, C., & Hiroto, D. (1987). Communication patterns of mothers with affective disorders and their relationship to children's status and social functioning. In M. J. Goldstein & K. Hahlweg (Eds.), *Understanding major mental disorder: The contribution of family interaction research* (pp. 103–119). New York: Family Process Press.

Hammen, C., Shih, J., Altman, T., & Brennan, P. A. (2003). Interpersonal impairment and the prediction of depressive symptoms in adolescent children of depressed and nondepressed mothers. *Journal of the American Academy of Child and Adolescent Psychiatry, 42,* 571–577.

Hankin, B. L., & Abramson, L. Y. (2001). Development of gender differences in depression: An elaborated cognitive vulnerability-transactional stress theory. *Psychological Bulletin, 127,* 773–796.

Hankin, B. L., Abramson, L. Y., Moffitt, T. E., McGee, R., Silva, P. A., & Angell, K. E. (1998). Development of depression from preadolescence to young adulthood: Emerging gender differences in a 10-year longitudinal study. *Journal of Abnormal Psychology, 107,* 128–140.

Hankin, B. L., Fraley, R. C. Lahey, B. B., & Waldman, I. D. (2005). Is depression best viewed as a continuum or a discrete category? A taxometric analysis of childhood and adolescent depression in a population-based sample. *Journal of Abnormal Psychology, 114,* 96–110.

Hankin, B. L., Mermelstein, R., & Roesch, L. (2007). Sex differences in adolescent depression: Stress exposure and reactivity models. *Child Development, 78,* 279–295.

Harnish, J. D., Dodge, K. A., Valente, E., & Conduct Problems Prevention Research Group (1995). Mother–child interaction quality as a partial mediator of the roles of maternal depressive symptomatology and socioeconomic status in the development of child behavior problems. *Child Development, 66,* 739–753.

Holmbeck, G. N. (1997). Toward terminology, conceptual, and statistical clarity in the study of mediators and moderators: Examples from the child-clinical and pediatric psychology literatures. *Journal of Consulting and Clinical Psychology, 65,* 599–610.

Jacob, T., & Johnson, S. L. (1997). Parent–child interaction among depressed fathers and mothers: Impact on child functioning. *Journal of Family Psychology, 11,* 391–409.

Jaser, S. S., Champion, J. E., Reeslund, K., Keller, G., Merchant, M. J., Benson, M., et al. (2007). Cross-situational coping with peer and family stressors in adolescent offspring of depressed parents. *Journal of Adolescence, 30,* 917–932.

Jaser, S. S., Fear, J. M., Reeslund, K. L., Champion, J. E. Reising, M. M., & Compas, B. E. (in press). Maternal sadness and adolescents' responses to stress in offspring of mothers with and without a history of depression. *Journal of Clinical Child and Adolescent Psychology.*

Jaser, S. S., Langrock, A. M., Keller, G., Merchant, M. J., Benson, M., Reeslund, K., et al. (2005). Coping with the stress of parental depression II: Adolescent and parent reports of coping and adjustment. *Journal of Clinical Child and Adolescent Psychology, 34,* 193–205.

Jensen, P. S., Watanabe, H. K., Richters, J. E., Roper, M., Hibbs, E. D., Salzberg, A. D., et al. (1996). Scales, diagnoses, and child psychopathology: II. Comparing the CBCL and DISC against external validators. *Journal of Abnormal Child Psychology, 24,* 151–168.

Kagan, J., Reznick, J. S., & Snidman, N. (1987). The physiology and psychology of behavioral inhibition in children. *Child Development, 58,* 1459–1473.

Kagan, J., & Snidman, N. (1991). Infant predictors of inhibited and uninhibited profiles. *Psychological Science, 2,* 40–44.

Kane, P., & Garber, J. (2004). The relations among depression in fathers, children's psychopathology, and father–child conflict: A meta-analysis. *Clinical Psychology Review, 24,* 339–360.

Keller, M. B., Beardslee, W. R., Dorer, D. J., Lavori, P. W., Samuelson, H., & Klerman, G. R. (1986). Impact of severity and chronicity of parental affective illness on adaptive functioning and psychopathology in children. *Archives of General Psychiatry, 43,* 930–937.

Kessler, R. C., Berglund, P., Demler, O., Jin, R., Koretz, D., Merikangas, K. R., et al. (2003). The epidemiology of major depressive disorder: Results from the National Comorbidity Survey Replication (NCS-R). *Journal of the American Medical Association, 289,* 3095–3105.

Kessler, R. C., McGonagle, K. A., Zhao, S., Nelson, C. B., Hughes, M., Eshleman, S., et al. (1994). Lifetime and 12-month prevalence of DSM-III-R psychiatric disorders in the United States: Results from the National Comorbidity Study. *Archives of General Psychiatry, 51,* 8–19.

Kliewer, W., Sandler, I., & Wolchik, S. (1994). Family socialization of threat appraisal and coping: Coaching, modeling, and family context. In K. Hurrelman & F. Nestmann (Eds.), *Social networks and social support in childhood and adolescence* (pp. 271–291). Berlin: de Gruyter.

Klimes-Dougan, B., & Bolger, A. K. (1998). Coping with maternal depressed affect and depression: Adolescent children of depressed and well mothers. *Journal of Youth and Adolescence, 27,* 1–15.

Kraemer, H. C., Kazdin, A. E., Offord, D. R., Kessler, R. C., Jensen, P. S., & Kupfer, D. J. (1997). Coming to terms with the terms of risk. *Archives of General Psychiatry, 54,* 337–343.

Kraemer, H. C., Stice, E., Kazdin, A., Offord, D., & Kupfer, D. (2001). How do risk factors work together? Mediators, moderators, and independent, overlapping, and proxy risk factors. *American Journal of Psychiatry, 158,* 848–856.

Krohne, H. W. (1996). Individual differences in coping. In M. Zeidner & N. S. Endler (Eds.), *Handbook of coping: Theory, research, and application* (pp. 381–409). New York: John Wiley & Sons.

Ladd, G. (2005). *Children's peer relations and social competence: A century of progress. Current perspectives in psychology.* New Haven, CT: Yale University Press.

Langrock, A. M., Compas, B. E., Keller, G., Merchant, M. J., & Copeland, M. E. (2002). Coping with the stress of parental depression: Parents' reports of children's coping, emotional, and behavioral problems. *Journal of Clinical Child and Adolescent Psychology, 31,* 312–324.

Lazarus, R. S. (1993). From psychological stress to the emotions: A history of changing outlooks. *Annual Review of Psychology, 44,* 1–21.

Lazarus, R. S., & Folkman, S. (1984). *Stress, appraisal and coping.* New York: Springer.

Lengua, L. J., Sadowski, C. A., Friedrich, W. N., & Fisher, J. (2001). Rationally and empirically derived dimensions of childrens' symptomatology: Expert ratings and confirmatory factor analyses of the CBCL. *Journal of Consulting and Clinical Psychology, 69,* 683–698.

Lengua, L., & Sandler, I. (1996). Self-regulation as a moderator of the relation between coping and symptomatology in children of divorce. *Journal of Abnormal Child Psychology, 24,* 681–701.

Lewinsohn, P. M., Hops, H., Roberts, R. E., Seeley, J. R., & Andrews, J. A. (1993). Adolescent psychopathology, I: Prevalence and incidence of depression and other *DSM-III-R* disorders in high school students. *Journal of Abnormal Psychology, 102,* 133–144.

Lieberman, M. D. (2007). Social cognitive neuroscience: A review of core processes. *Annual Review of Psychology, 58,* 259–289.

Lovejoy, M. C., Graczyk, P. A., O'Hare, E., & Neuman, G. (2000). Maternal depression and parenting: A meta-analytic review. *Clinical Psychology Review, 20,* 561–592.

Luthar, S. S. (2006). Resilience in development: A synthesis of research across five decades. In D. J. Cohen & D. Cicchetti (eds.), *Developmental psychopathology,* vol. 3: Risk, disorder and adaptation, 2nd ed. (pp. 739–795). Hoboken, NJ: Wiley.

Luthar, S. S., & Cicchetti, D. (2000). The construct of resilience: Implications for interventions and social policy. *Development and Psychopathology, 12,* 857–885.

Luthar, S. S., Sawyer, J. A., & Brown, P. J. (2006). Conceptual issues in studies of resilience: Past, present and future research. *Annals of the New York Academy of Sciences, 1094,* 105–115.

Malatesta-Magai, C. (1991). Emotional socialization: Its role in personality and developmental psychopathology. In D. Cicchetti & S. L. Toth (Eds.), *Internalizing and externalizing of dysfunctional: Rochester Symposium on Developmental Psychopathology,* vol. 2 (pp. 203–224). Hillside, NJ: Lawrence Erlbaum.

Malphurs, J. E., Field, T. M., Larraine, C., Pickens, J., Pelaez-Nogueras, M. (1996). Altering withdrawn and intrusive interaction behaviors of depressed mothers. *Infant Mental Health Journal, 17,* 152–160.

Marchand, J. F., & Hock, E. (1998). The relation of problem behaviors in preschool children to depressive symptoms in mothers and fathers. *Journal of Genetic Psychology, 159,* 353–366.

Masten, A. S. (2001). Ordinary magic: Resilience processes in development. *American Psychologist, 56,* 227–238.

Masten, A. S. (2005). Peer relationships and psychopathology in developmental perspective: Reflections on progress and promise. *Journal of Clinical Child and Adolescent Psychology, 34,* 87–92.

Masten, A. S., & Coatsworth, J. D. (1998). The development of competence in favorable and unfavorable environments: Lessons from research on successful children. *American Psychologist, 53,* 205–220.

Masten, A. S., & Obradovic, J. (2006). Competence and resilience in development. *Annals of the New York Academy of Sciences, 1094,* 13–27.

Mathews, A., & MacLeod, C. (2005). Cognitive vulnerability to emotional disorders. *Annual Review of Clinical Psychology, 1,* 167–195.

Maxwell, S. E., & Cole, D. A. (2007). Bias in cross-sectional analyses of longitudinal mediation. *Psychological Methods, 12,* 23–44.

McLoyd, V. C. (1998). Socioeconomic disadvantage and child development. *American Psychologist, 53,* 185–204.

McMahon, S. D., Grant, K. E., Compas, B. E., Thurm, A. E., & Ey, S. (2003). Stress and psychopathology in children and adolescents: Is there evidence for specificity? *Journal of Child Psychology and Psychiatry, 44,* 1–27.

McQuaid, J. R., Monroe, S. M., Roberts, J. E., Kupfer, D. J., & Frank, E. (2000). A comparison of two life stress assessment approaches: Prospective prediction of treatment outcome in recurrent depression. *Journal of Abnormal Psychology, 109,* 787–791.

Measelle, J. R., Stice, E., & Hogansen, J. M. (2006). Developmental trajectories of co-occurring depressive, eating, antisocial, and substance abuse problems in female adolescents. *Journal of Abnormal Psychology, 115,* 524–538.

Millstein, S. G., Petersen, A. C., & Nightingale, E. O. (1993). *Promoting the health of adolescents: New directions for the twenty-first century.* New York: Oxford University Press.

Moffitt, T. E., & Caspi, A. (2001). Childhood predictors differentiate life-course persistent and adolescence-limited antisocial pathways among males and females. *Development and Psychopathology, 13,* 355–375.

Nelson, C. B., Hammen, C., Brennan, P. A., & Ullman, J. B. (2003). The impact of maternal depression on adolescent adjustment: The role of expressed emotion. *Journal of Consulting and Clinical Psychology, 71,* 935–944.

Nolen-Hoeksema, S., Girgus, J. S., & Seligman, M. E. P. (1992). Predictors and consequences childhood depressive symptoms: A 5-year longitudinal study. *Journal of Abnormal Psychology, 101,* 405–422.

Papadakis, A. A., Prince, R. P., Jones, N. P., & Strauman, T. J. (2006). Self-regulation, rumination, and vulnerability to depression in adolescent girls. *Development and Psychopathology, 18,* 815–829.

Pennebaker, J. W. (1997). Writing about emotional experiences as a therapeutic process. *Psychological Science, 8,* 162–166.

Perry, B. D., Pollard, R. A., Blakley, T. L., Baker, W. L., & Vigilante, D. (1995). Childhood trauma, the neurobiology of adaptation, and "use-dependent" development of the brain: How "states" become "traits." *Infant Mental Heath Journal, 16,* 271–289.

Posner, M. I., & Rothbart, M. K. (1994). Attentional regulation: From mechanism to culture. In P. Bertelson, P. Eelen, & G. d'Ydewalle (Eds.), *International perspectives on psychological science,* vol. 1 (pp. 41–55). Hove, UK: Lawrence Erlbaum.

Power, T. G. (2004). Stress and coping in childhood: The parents' role. *Parenting Science Practice, 4,* 271–317.

Richmond, J. (1993). Health promotion in historical perspective. In S. G. Millstein, A. C. Peterson, & E. O. Nightingale (Eds.), *Promoting the health of adolescents: New directions for the twenty-first century* (p. v–vii). New York: Oxford University Press.

Rolf, J., & Johnson, J. (1990). Protected or vulnerable: The challenge of AIDS to developmental psychopathology. In J. Rolf,

A. S. Masten, D. Cicchetti, K. Nuechterlein, & S. Weinstraub (Eds.), *Risk and protective factors in the development of psychopathology* (pp. 384–404). Cambridge, UK: Cambridge University Press.

Rothbart, M. K. (1991). Temperament: A developmental framework. In J. Strelau & A. Angleitner (Eds.), *Explorations in temperament: International perspectives on theory and measurement* (pp. 61–74). New York: Plenum Press.

Rothbart, M. K, Posner, M. I., & Hershey, K. L. (1995) Temperament, attention, and developmental psychopathology. In D. Cicchetti & D. Cohen (Eds.), *Developmental psychopathology*, vol. 1: *Theory and methods* (pp. 315–340). New York: John Wiley & Sons.

Rubin, K. H., Bukowski, W., & Parker, J. G. (2006). Peer interactions, relationships, and groups. In N. Eisenberg (Ed.), *Handbook of child psychology*, vol 3: *Social, emotional, and personality development* (pp. 571–645). Hoboken, NJ: John Wiley & Sons.

Rudolph, K. D., Dennig, M. D., & Weisz, J. R. (1995). Determinants and consequences of children's coping in the medical setting: Conceptualization, review, and critique. *Psychological Bulletin, 118,* 328–357.

Rudolph, K. D., & Hammen, C. (2000). Age and gender determinants of stress exposure, generation, and reactions in youngsters: A transactional perspective. *Child Development, 70,* 660–677.

Rudolph, K. D., Hammen, C., Burge, D., Lindberg, N., Herzberg, D., & Daley, S. E. (2000). Toward an interpersonal life-stress model of depression: The developmental context of stress generation. *Development and Psychopathology, 12,* 215–234.

Rutter, M. (1987). Psychosocial resilience and protective mechanisms. *American Journal of Orthopsychiatry, 57,* 316–331.

Sameroff, A. J. (2000). Developmental systems and psychopathology. *Development & Psychopathology, 12,* 297–312.

Sandler, I. N., Reynolds, K. D., Kliewer, W., & Ramirez, R. (1992). Specificity of the relation between life events and psychological symptomatology. *Journal of Clinical Child Psychology, 21,* 240–248.

Sandler, I. N., Tein, J., & West, S. G. (1994). Coping, stress, and psychological symptoms of children of divorce: A cross-sectional and longitudinal study. *Child Development, 65,* 1744–1763.

Sandler, I. N., Tein, J., Mehta, P., Wolchik, S., & Ayers, T. (2000). Coping efficacy and psychological problems of children of divorce. *Child Development, 71,* 1099–1118.

Silk, J. S., Shaw, D. S., Forbes, E. E., Lane, T. L., & Kovacs, M. (2006a). Maternal depression and child internalizing: The moderating role of child emotion regulation. *Journal of Clinical Child and Adolescent Psychology, 35,* 116–126.

Silk, J. S., Shaw, D. S., Skuban, E. M., Oland, A. A., & Kovacs, M. (2006b). Emotion regulation strategies of childhood-onset depressed mothers. *Journal of Child Psychology and Psychiatry, 47,* 69–78.

Skinner, E. A. (1995). *Perceived control, motivation, and coping.* Thousand Oaks, CA: Sage.

Skinner, E. A., & Edge, K. (2002). Parenting, motivation, and the development of children's coping. In R. A. Dienstbier & L. J. Crockett (Eds.), *Nebraska symposium on motivation, vol. 48: Agency, motivation, and the life course* (pp. 77–143). Lincoln: Nebraska University Press.

Skinner, E. A., Edge, K., Altman, J., & Sherwood, H. (2003). Searching for the structure of coping: A review and critique of category systems for classifying words of coping. *Psychological Bulletin, 129,* 216–269.

Skinner, E. A., & Zimmer-Gembeck, M. J. (2007). The development of coping. *Annual Review of Psychology, 58,* 119–144.

Spear, L. P. (2000a). The adolescent brain and age-related behavioral manifestations. *Neuroscience and Biobehavioral Reviews, 24,* 417–463.

Spear, L. P. (2000b). Neurobehavioral changes in adolescence. *Current Directions in Psychological Science, 9,* 111–114.

Steele, R., Forehand, R., & Armistead, L. (1997). The role of family processes and coping strategies in the relationship between parental chronic illness and childhood internalizing problems. *Journal of Abnormal Child Psychology, 25,* 83–94.

Steinberg, L. (2002). Clinical adolescent psychology: What it is, and what it needs to be. *Journal of Consulting and Clinical Psychology, 70,* 124–128.

Steinberg, L. (2005). Cognitive and affective development in adolescence. *Trends in Cognitive Sciences, 9,* 69–74.

Steinberg, L., & Avenevoli, S. (2000). The role of context in the development of psychopathology: A conceptual framework and some speculative propositions. *Child Development, 71,* 66–74.

Tarullo, L. B., DeMulder, E. K., Martinez, P. E., & Radke-Yarrow, M. (1994). Dialogues with preadolescents and adolescents: Mother–child interaction patterns in affectively ill and well dyads. *Journal of Abnormal Child Psychology, 22,* 33–50.

Turner, J. E., Jr., & Cole, D. A. (1994). Developmental differences in cognitive diatheses for child depression. *Journal of Abnormal Child Psychology, 22,* 15–32.

Walker, L. S., Smith, C. A., Garber, J., & Van Slyke, D. A. (1997). Development and validation of the Pain Response Inventory for Children. *Psychological Assessment, 9,* 392–405.

Warner, V., Weissman, M. M., Fendrich, M., Wickramaratne, P., & Moreau, D. (1992). The course of major depression in the offspring of depressed parents: Incidence, recurrence, and recovery. *Archives of General Psychiatry, 49,* 795–801.

Weisz, J. R. (1990). Development of control-related beliefs, goals, and styles in childhood and adolescence: A clinical perspective. In K. W. Schaie, J. Rodin, and C. Schooler (Eds.), *Self-directedness: Cause and effects throughout the life course* (pp. 103–145). Hillsdale, NJ: Lawrence Erlbaum.

Weisz, J. R., McCabe, M. A., & Dennig, M. D. (1994). Primary and secondary control among children undergoing medical procedures: Adjustment as a function of coping style. *Journal of Consulting and Clinical Psychology, 62,* 324–332.

Wenzlaff, R. M., & Wegner, D. M. (2000). Thought suppression. *Annual Review of Psychology, 51,* 59–91.

CHAPTER 17

Adolescents with Developmental Disabilities and Their Families

PENNY HAUSER-CRAM, MARTY WYNGAARDEN KRAUSS, AND JOANNE KERSH

The preparation of this manuscript was partially supported by grants R40 MC 00333 and R40 MC 08956 from the Maternal and Child Health Bureau (Title V, Social Security Act), Health Resources and Services Administration, Department of Health and Human Services.

INTRODUCTION

A comprehensive understanding of adolescent development requires investigation into both normative patterns and individual differences in the full range of developmental domains. Extensive research in adolescent development has focused on delineating trajectories of typical development and understanding how those vary based on gender, culture, and socioeconomic context. Very few studies, however, consider such trajectories in adolescents with developmental disabilities (i.e., biologically based delays or impairments in one or more areas of development). Investigations of individuals with developmental disabilities usually require cross-disciplinary collaboration among such fields as psychology, sociology, biology, medicine, public health, special education, social work, and psychopathology, and therefore the study of adolescents with developmental disabilities has not found a primary home. Indeed, some researchers point out that adolescence is not even considered an actual subdiscipline within the field of intellectual impairment (Hodapp, Kazemi, Rosner, & Dykens, 2006). Cross-disciplinary work, however, can provide critical insight into such investigations.

For example, current research emanating from the fields of molecular biology and behavioral genetics has stimulated thinking about the complex interplay between genetic disorders (such as Down syndrome or fragile X syndrome) and developmental changes in individuals with those disorders (Inlow & Restifo, 2004). Such work is essential to mapping the variation within typical development, locating biological differences in atypical development (e.g., in the synthesis of proteins), and forming testable hypotheses about gene–environment interaction and potential therapeutic interventions (Gardiner, 2006). Currently, the growing knowledge base on the confluence of gene–environment complexity along with the biological changes and psychosocial demands that typically occur during the adolescent period makes the study of this developmental phase for individuals with developmental disabilities essential to a full understanding of adolescent development. For example, studies on those with fragile X syndrome, the most common form of hereditary intellectual disability, indicate that the disorder is due to a mutation of the *FMRI* gene on the X chromosome, a condition that has been simulated in mice. Restivo et al. (2005) conducted a study on such mice (termed *knockout mice* since the *FMRI* gene is deleted) comparing those reared in enriched and standard caged environment. They reported that the transgenic mice raised in the enriched environment showed fewer behavioral abnormalities (such as hyperactivity and lack of habituation) and displayed postmortem morphological advantages in dendritic length and branching in the visual cortex. Such studies on transgenic mice combined with growing knowledge on changes in the adolescent brain of humans, especially synaptic pruning and reorganization (Blakemore & Choudhury, 2006), suggest that investigations on adolescent development in those with developmental disabilities may lead to a greater understanding of gene–environment–development interactions during the adolescent phase of life.

In this chapter, we center on the current theoretical and empirical knowledge base about the adolescent period for individuals with developmental disabilities and their families. Although adolescents with developmental disabilities by definition display atypical trajectories with regard to some aspects of development, most still encounter life challenges and embark on life tasks typical of this developmental phase. In addition, like most parents of adolescents, their parents face issues about the adolescent's current and future well-being. The need to understand the way in which typical developmental issues emerge for these adolescents and those supporting them is increasingly highlighted both in discussions about daily practice as well as in policy discourse. Despite the accelerating public attention on developmental disabilities and current federal mandates, including the Individuals with Disabilities Education Act (IDEA) and the Americans with Disabilities Act (ADA), empirical information, while rich at the early childhood phase, is only slowly gaining momentum about the development, strengths, and needs of adolescents with disabilities and their families.

This chapter has five main sections. The first offers a description of developmental disabilities and current U.S. federal policies and statistical information relevant to adolescents with developmental disabilities. In the next section, we discuss special concerns related to adolescents with developmental disabilities, with attention to their health and well-being. We then provide a discussion of the applicability of current developmental theories and related empirical work to adolescents with developmental disabilities. Relationships within families often change in adolescence, and in the fourth section we review theory and research on the role and functioning of families, including siblings, of adolescents with developmental disabilities. In a concluding section, we discuss the implications of current work and offer directions for future research.

DEVELOPMENTAL DISABILITIES: DEFINITIONS AND FEDERAL POLICY

In this section, we present a definition of developmental disabilities along with data on the increasing incidence of such disabilities. As legislation affects the lives of adolescents with disabilities in critical spheres including education, employment, and health, we also review the major federal policies that are specific to those with disabilities in the United States.

Definition and Incidence of Developmental Disabilities

The term *developmental disabilities* is codified in Public Law (PL) 106-402, the Developmental Disabilities Assistance and Bill of Rights Act Amendments of 2000. It is defined as a condition attributable to a mental or physical impairment (or combination) that manifests before age 22 and is likely to continue indefinitely. It results in substantial functional limitation in three or more areas of major life activity, including self-care, receptive and expressive language, learning, mobility, self-direction, capacity for independent living, and economic self-sufficiency, and reflects an individual's need for ongoing care and/or services. Among the most common conditions included under the umbrella of developmental disabilities are autism, cerebral palsy, epilepsy, intellectual disability (formerly termed *mental retardation*), and other neurological impairments. Current estimates indicate that, in 2005, about 17% of U.S. youth receiving special education services did so because of a developmental disability (U.S. Department of Education, 2007c).

The rates of documented disability during childhood and adolescence have increased steadily over the past decade (U.S. Department of Education, 2007c). This trend appears to be particularly strong for adolescents. For youth aged 12–17 years, the U.S. Department of Education reported a disability prevalence rate of 9.77 per 10,000 in 1995; by 2005, this rate had increased to 11.69. This increase appears to be due, in some part, to an increase in the number of youth who are diagnosed with autism spectrum disorders (ASDs). While the prevalence of children and adolescents with an intellectual disability has decreased slightly, the identification of autism and its related disorders has seen a marked increase. In 1995, only 6,648 adolescents nationwide received special education services because of a primary diagnosis of autism; however, this number had increased to 71,889 in 2005 (U.S. Department of Education, 2007c). There has been some debate around whether this increase in prevalence actually reflects an increase in the *incidence* of autism in the population, an increase in the rate of identification, or an effect of changing diagnostic criteria. Based on a review of 37 studies, Fombonne (2005) concluded that existing epidemiological data were insufficient to support the hypothesis of a secular increase in the rate of autism. Rather, the available evidence suggests that increases in the prevalence of autism are largely attributable to changes in diagnostic criteria and broadened definitions (Fombonne, 2005). Shattuck and Grosse (2007) suggested that because special education data are based solely on primary classifications, the growing enrollment prevalence of autism might also reflect the increasing proportion of youth with dual diagnoses who are being classified as having an ASD, rather than by a coexisting disability.

Federal Legislation Related to Developmental Disabilities

The rights of youth with developmental disabilities are protected by a range of federally legislated mandates and policies. In this section, we discuss three areas of legislation that are particularly salient for adolescents with developmental disabilities. First, we will briefly discuss the federal legislation that protects the civil rights of individuals with disabilities in the United States. Next, we will talk about educational legislation and policies that are relevant to youth with developmental disabilities. Finally, we will discuss programs enacted under the Social Security Act that have been put in place to assist individuals with disabilities and their families.

Civil Rights Legislation

In 1973, the Rehabilitation Act (PL 93-112) was passed, making it the first federally enacted legislation that addressed the rights of people with disabilities. Section 504 specifically stated that no federally funded program or institution may exclude individuals from access or participation based solely on their disability status. In 1990, the Americans with Disabilities Act (PL101-336) extended these protections, providing comprehensive civil rights protection for people with disabilities. It mandated that local and state, as well as federal, programs must be accessible; that businesses make reasonable accommodations for workers with disabilities; and that various aspects of public life, such as transportation and communication, be accessible. Thus, by ensuring these protections and rights, the ADA has guaranteed a variety of opportunities for youth with developmental disabilities, such as competitive employment, independent living, and a high level of community involvement, that were not available two decades ago.

Educational Policy and Legislation

In 1975, the Education of All Handicapped Children Act (PL 94-142) mandated a free, appropriate public education for all children with disabilities. Aside from guaranteeing the education of all students, this act established regulations governing the terms of "Special Education." For example, it mandated that all students receiving special education services have an individualized education program

(IEP) that specifies current level of performance, annual goals, and services to be provided. More recent amendments also mandate that an IEP specify the extent to which the student will be included in the general education curriculum. In 1990, this act was amended and renamed the Individuals with Disabilities Education Act (IDEA; PL 101-476). Since then, the IDEA has been amended and reauthorized twice, in 1997 (PL 105-17) and, most recently, in 2004 (PL 108-446).

Since 1990, the IDEA has included specific language that addressed the preparation of students for the transition from school to adulthood. Specifically, it mandates that schools must provide adolescents with disabilities with instructional and experiential opportunities that foster the skills necessary to function successfully after high school. Transition services, as detailed in IDEA 2004, encompass a broad set of coordinated activities and services, including both academic instruction and community experiences, which are tailored to prepare students to meet their goals for adult life. For youth with developmental disabilities, primary transition goals most frequently include maximizing functional independence, enhancing social relationships, living independently, and working competitively in the community (National Longitudinal Transition Study 2, 2007a). A transition plan is developed in consideration of each child's individual strengths, interests, and preferences and must be included in the IEP by age 16.

Although schools in the United States have made significant progress in their ability to implement transition plans for their students with disabilities (National Center on Secondary Education and Transition, 2004), their success in helping students with more severe impairments has been marginal. Recent findings from the National Longitudinal Transition Study 2 (2007b) report that, for youth with intellectual disabilities, less than 25% are described as making "a lot of progress" toward transition goals, as compared to 50% of youth with learning disabilities.

No Child Left Behind   Other federal education legislation that has had particular relevance for youth with developmental disabilities is the No Child Left Behind Act of 2001 (NCLB; PL 107-110). The NCLB established a state accountability system that is monitored through standards-based testing for all students, including those who receive special education services. This act also gave the states flexibility to use alternate and/or modified methods of assessment (based on alternate and/or modified standards of achievement) to assess the progress of students with disabilities, thus aligning the NCLB with existing IDEA regulations that require all students to have access to the general education curriculum and to be included in general assessments. The inclusion of students with developmental disabilities under NCLB has placed additional emphasis on special education in the United States, providing both increased opportunities and increased challenges for students and teachers (Wakeman, Browder, Meier, & McColl, 2007).

Social Security

Additional federal programs that significantly impact the lives of youth with developmental disabilities are those of the Social Security Administration, specifically, Supplemental Security Income (SSI) and Medicaid. SSI is an income assistance program for people with disabilities whose income and assets are sufficiently low to meet eligibility requirements. A significantly larger proportion of individuals with developmental disabilities than in the general population experience economic hardship, including children and youth with developmental disabilities and their families (e.g., Parish, 2003). In 2005, over 2 million children and youth received SSI payments, and about half of these were adolescents (U.S. Social Security Administration, 2007). In most states, those who apply for and are eligible for SSI are automatically enrolled in Medicaid, the federal program providing medical benefits to people with disabilities; however, in some states, individuals must apply separately.

Although both SSI and Medicaid are designed to reduce poverty and offset disability-related expenditures, neither program provides sufficient support (Parish, 2003). In 2006, the maximum federal SSI payment fell several thousand dollars short of the national poverty threshold (U.S. Department of Health and Human Services, 2006). Furthermore, the linking of SSI and Medicaid programs has created additional challenges and barriers for many parents of youth with disabilities. Because eligibility is linked to asset and income criteria, parents who are employed but have low-paying jobs risk losing comprehensive Medicaid benefits for their children, regardless of whether their employers offer health care benefits (Parish, 2003; Turnbull et al., 2007). Moreover, children and youth with developmental disabilities often have complex health problems (Lotstein, McPherson, Stickland, & Newacheck, 2005), and some of these health concerns may increase or worsen during the adolescent years due to hormonal changes, making this a particularly challenging and stressful time for parents. To address this problem, the Deficit Reduction Act of 2005 (PL 109-171) included the Family Opportunity Act, which authorized states to allow families of children with disabilities who do not meet SSI income eligibility requirements to buy-in to Medicaid. The act allows states to offer this opportunity to families with incomes up to 300% of poverty, and it is projected that by 2010, all children under the age of 18 that meet eligibility requirements will be covered.

Although clearly there are policies in place to aid and support adolescents with disabilities and their families, accessing and coordinating these services can be a significant responsibility and a source of stress (Schneider, Wedgewood, Llewellyn, & McConnell, 2006). It is striking that presently there is little to no interagency collaboration, and therefore the integration of these rights and resources is left to the adolescent and his or her parents, many of whom may already have limited resources. A recent study found that this was one of the greatest challenges faced by families; parents spoke of the complexity of navigating multiple service delivery systems that was exacerbated by a dearth of available information and the lack of coordination between agencies and schools (Timmons, Whitney-Thomas, McIntyre, Butterworth, & Allen, 2004). Indicating that this is not a situation unique to families in the United States, an Australian study concluded that, "the frustrations, difficulties, and delays typically encountered in accessing many services appeared to add to, rather than alleviate, the pressure and workload of families" (Schneider et al., p. 932).

HEALTH AND WELL-BEING OF ADOLESCENTS WITH DEVELOPMENTAL DISABILITIES

Although health and well-being are important areas of concern for anyone focusing on adolescent development, they have increased salience when considering those with developmental disabilities. Particular health concerns emerge for adolescents with specific disabilities. For example, among adolescents with autism, the risk for the onset of seizure disorders during adolescence is at least 20 times that of the general population (Spector & Volkmar, 2006). Due to scientific advances in medicine, many children with developmental disabilities now have much longer survival rates, and some of their adolescent health care needs are only beginning to be understood (Bittles, 2002). Notably, children with Down syndrome now have a life expectancy well into the adult years, primarily due to major changes in surgical treatment of cardiac anomalies during early life and better health care services overall (Glasson, Sullivan, Hussain, Petterson, Montgomery, & Bittles, 2002).

Sleep disruption is an area of increasing attention for those with intellectual disability (Sajith & Clarke, 2007), and obesity and obesity-related secondary conditions tend to be a concern for many adolescents with developmental disabilities (Rimmer, Rowland, & Yamaki, 2007). There is also evidence that the symptoms of particular developmental disabilities change during the adolescent period. Shattuck et al. (2007) report that there is a gradual pattern of improvement in the core symptoms of autism during adolescence and adulthood, although residual levels of impairment remain clinically significant. The American Academy of Pediatrics (American Academy of Pediatrics, American Academy of Family Physicians, & American College of Physicians–American Society of Internal Medicine, 2002) has called for pediatricians and other health care providers to become better educated about the population of children with special health care needs as increasing numbers are moving into the adolescent and emerging adult periods.

Transition to Adult Health Care Services

The entry into the late-adolescent period brings with it a transition in health care services from the pediatric, family-focused system to the adult, specific-care system. The American Academy of Pediatrics and other medical professional organizations recommend that all adolescents with special health care needs have a written health care transition plan by the age of 14 years (American Academy of Pediatrics et al., 2002), yet empirical studies indicate that this rarely occurs (e.g., Scal & Ireland, 2005). Although all adolescents or young adults need to move from the pediatric to the adult health care system, those with special health care needs or with developmental disabilities and their parents experience more disruption with this transition at least partially because the pediatric and adult systems of care represent different subcultures (Reiss, Gibson & Walker, 2005). Some find the more fragmented services available for adults to lack a necessary focus on the well-being of the adolescent as a developing person. Others find it difficult to leave a pediatrician who has known the child and family since birth. Mitchell and Hauser-Cram (2008) reported that satisfaction with the health care of their adolescent with developmental disabilities predicted maternal psychological well-being. Consistent with family systems theory (Minuchin, 2002), the adolescent is not the only one affected by the relationship with the health care system providing services to him or her.

One indicator of an adolescent's readiness to make the transition to adult services is his or her knowledge of sexual health (Ledlie, 2007). Sexuality, however, is an area of well-being that has been neglected in the study of adolescents with developmental disabilities. This neglect may be due to societal discomforts and misperceptions (Gordon, Tschopp, & Feldman, 2004); but like all adolescents, those with developmental disabilities are sexual beings (Committee on Children with Disabilities, 1996). Some disabilities, such as cystic fibrosis, are associated with slower-than-typical pubertal development whereas others, such as spina bifida, are associated with precocious puberty (Holmbeck, 2002). Although parents, health providers, and, most importantly, the adolescents themselves need information on changes to expect during puberty, little syndrome-specific information is available and even less is known about the behavioral correlates of those pubertal changes.

A few studies, however, indicate that parents are concerned about sexual abuse of their adolescent with developmental disabilities (Wilgosh, 1993). Prevalence rates of being abused are higher among those with developmental disabilities, although rates vary widely (Hodapp et al., 2006). In particular, girls with Williams syndrome may be at increased risk for sexual abuse given their tendency toward social disinhibition, and at least one study indicates that abuse rates may be higher for this group (Davies, Udwin, & Howlin, 1998).

Mental Health and Behavior Problems

The study of children and adolescents with developmental disabilities is sometimes placed within the field of developmental psychopathology. Generally, those who have developmental disabilities can be classified by the system detailed by the *Diagnostic and Statistical Manual of Mental Disorders*, 4th edition

(DSM-IV) (American Psychiatric Association, 2000), and intellectual disability (formerly termed *mental retardation*) is included in the DSM-IV categorization of psychiatric diagnoses. Adolescents with intellectual and other developmental disabilities do not necessarily, however, have mental health issues. Therefore, the presumption of psychopathology as an inevitable correlate of having a developmental disability is unwarranted.

Nevertheless, the likelihood of behavior problems is known to be increased in this group. Some individuals have specific genotypic disabilities that are associated with specific behavior problems. For example, Prader-Willi syndrome is associated with extreme hyperphagia (i.e., overeating). In contrast, those with Down syndrome have fewer difficulties with mental health in comparison to individuals with other forms of intellectual disability (Mantry et al., 2007). Longitudinal studies of behavior problems in children and adolescents with developmental disabilities indicate a prevalence rate around 40% (Einfeld & Tonge, 1996; Stromme & Diseth, 2000). That rate is notably higher than reported for the typical population of adolescents (Roberts, Attkisson, & Rosenblatt, 1998). In reviewing prior longitudinal studies of children with developmental disabilities, Chadwick, Kusel, Cuddy, and Taylor (2005) note that although stability of behavior problems remains fairly strong across developmental periods, a decrease in such problems tends to occur during the adolescent years. Lounds, Seltzer, Greenberg, and Shattuck (2007) reported that nearly half of their sample of 140 adolescents and adults with autism decreased in the number of behavior problems manifested over a 3-year period. In results from their longitudinal study of those with severe intellectual disabilities, Chadwick et al. (2004) found that the rates of some behavior problems decreased, especially in areas of overactivity. Two longitudinal birth-cohort samples were used in the Dutch Mental Health Study, allowing comparisons to be made between those with

and without intellectual disabilities. In one such comparison, de Ruiter, Dekker, Verhulst, and Koot (2007) concluded that children with intellectual disabilities had higher rates of problem behaviors across all ages but showed greater decreases in these behaviors during the adolescent period in comparison to other adolescents. Problems with aggression and attention showed notable decreases in the adolescents with intellectual disabilities, but problems in social-relating areas increased. Given the importance of peer relationships during the adolescent period, such findings underscore the importance of considering distinct types of behavior problems rather than an aggregation of problem behaviors or a division into the general categories of internalizing and externalizing problems.

As in studies of typically developing adolescents, investigations of those with developmental disabilities indicate that behavior problems are not entirely biologically based. Emerson, Robertson, and Wood (2005) found higher levels of behavior problems among those adolescents with intellectual disabilities living in low-income areas; this relation was stronger among those with relatively higher intellectual functioning than in those with more severe intellectual disabilities. The levels of psychological distress experienced by parents as well as the management strategies used by parents (Emerson, 2003) are also correlates of behavior problems in children and adolescents with intellectual disabilities. The sociocultural factors associated with increased likelihood of behavior problems, such as aggression, in typically developing youth (Watson, Fischer, Andreas, & Smith, 2004) appear also to be operational among those with developmental disabilities, although such factors may possibly operate differently among those with low levels of cognitive skills.

For adolescents as a group, an increased rate of psychiatric disorders has been noted to occur during the adolescent period, particularly depression among females and specific mental health conditions, such as schizophrenia, which have their onset during the adolescent or early adult period (Rutter, 1990). The extent to which such disorders emerge during adolescence among those with developmental disabilities is not known. Based on only a few studies, an increased risk of psychiatric disorders has been found for adolescents on the autism spectrum. Tantam (2000), for example, reported that such adolescents were more likely to experience depression. In a longitudinal study of adolescents with severe intellectual disabilities, however, Chadwick et al. (2005) found only a few cases (<10%) of individuals developing psychiatric disorders *de novo* in adolescence. The reliability of psychiatric diagnosis in those with intellectual disabilities is uncertain, however, and concerns about individuals with a dual diagnosis of intellectual disability and a psychiatric disorder are mounting (Sturmey, Lindsay, & Didden, 2007). One basis for such concerns is the increasing awareness that the emotional needs of those with intellectual disabilities may have been overlooked by a focus on their cognitive limitations. A related concern, however, is the lack of strong evidence about productive interventions for this population of adolescents, although pharmaceutical, behavioral, and, to a lesser extent, other therapies are increasingly common and have met with some success (Hodapp et al., 2006; Lounds et al., 2007).

In summary, it would be erroneous to assume that all adolescents with developmental disabilities have psychopathological problems. Although the likelihood of behavior problems is clearly much higher in this population than in typically developing youth, over half of adolescents with developmental disabilities do not exhibit high levels of problematic behaviors. The risk of having psychiatric disorders is somewhat elevated; however, we know less about the onset and course of such disorders among adolescents with developmental disabilities. The importance of diagnosing and treating behavior problems and psychiatric disorders should not be diminished, as such concerns are likely to affect the adolescent's sense of self, interaction with peers and family, and ultimate well-being.

THEORETICAL MODELS OF ADOLESCENT DEVELOPMENT: APPLICATIONS TO ADOLESCENTS WITH DEVELOPMENTAL DISABILITIES

Several current themes in the scholarship on adolescent development have particular relevance to, and raise provocative questions about, adolescents with developmental disabilities. Adolescence is a time of identity exploration and the development of a deeper and more complex understanding of self. It is also a period of establishing greater connection to others, especially peers, while reconfiguring relationships with parents and siblings. Finally, integral to these psychological changes and concomitant challenges and accomplishments is the sense of personal agency that can promote or dampen positive developmental change. Given the cognitive and often social challenges of many adolescents with developmental disabilities, what do we know about their development of a sense of self, their construction of a peer network, and their enactment of agentic behaviors?

Development of a Sense of Self

Adolescence is traditionally seen as a time of identity formation, developing a coherent sense of self based on values and ideological commitments (Erikson, 1950). Although Erikson originally depicted a stagelike progression in the development of the ego, with identity formation as a core event in the life of the adolescent, current theory places such formation within a developmental systems model in which the individual attempts to "make meaning" of his or her experiences (Kunnen & Bosma, 2000). From the perspective of developmental systems theory, identity development is not independent of other developmental transitions as identity emerges in part from transitions in cognition and metacognition, likely corresponding with neurodevelopmental changes in the brain that result in an integrated, reflective consciousness (Keating, 2004). Much research reviewed in this volume indicates that adolescence is a time when strength in executive processing emerges, not just for cognitive tasks but also for social challenges. Gaining a perspective of oneself (albeit a changing one) is a hallmark of adolescence; yet research on self-perception among adolescents with developmental disabilities is extremely limited. How do adolescents with developmental disabilities "make meaning" of their experiences and view themselves?

In one of the few investigations on this topic, Davies and Jenkins (1997) conducted interviews with 53 young adults with intellectual disabilities and their caregivers. They found that only eight participants understood the terms traditionally applied to their disability (e.g., *mental handicap*) and that most parents and other caregivers reported choosing not to discuss the meaning of such terms with the young adults. Nevertheless, many of these young adults incorporated a sense of diminished personal agency and of many societal limitations into their view of self, created through their daily experiences with adults, including caregivers, parents, and employers, who had authority over them.

Given current policies in the United States, especially IDEA, that mandate the rights of adolescents to participate in meetings involving their educational future, parental decisions about whether or not to discuss an adolescent's disability with him or her may not limit the adolescent's actual knowledge of that disability. Glidden and Zetlin (1992) suggest that part of the identity struggle for adolescents with developmental disabilities is related to the need for and resistance to awareness of their differences, especially if they perceive such differences as likely to have an immediate effect on their daily lives. Examples of these differences—such as driving a car, leaving home to live elsewhere, and having a job—all contribute to social comparisons for adolescents with developmental disabilities, especially during mid and late adolescence.

There are indications, however, that genotypical variations exist in self-concept. For example, Begley (1999) found that the self-concept of individuals with Down syndrome appears to be more positive than those with other intellectual disabilities and to increase between middle childhood and adolescence. She further found that such students differentiated their sense of competence and their sense of acceptance, as they tended to rate themselves relatively lower on scales measuring the latter. Glenn and Cunningham (2001) also reported positive ratings of general self-worth for adolescents and young adults with Down syndrome with more discriminative distinctions among domains of self-perception with increasing mental age. Shields, Murdoch, Loy, Dodd, and Taylor (2006) conducted a systematic review of self-concept in children and adolescents with cerebral palsy in comparison to other children and found that adolescent females with cerebral palsy (in comparison to typically developing adolescent females) had a lower self-concept in the domains of social acceptance, physical appearance, and athletic and scholastic competence. As found for typically developing adolescents, social acceptance and physical appearance appear to be areas that relate heavily to overall sense of self (Harter, 1986).

Ironically, as Glenn and Cunningham (2001) note, if adolescents with developmental disabilities have immature levels of cognitive processing (i.e., below the mental age of 6–7 years), they tend to be more positive in their views of themselves. For example, in a study of children with spina bifida, Mincham et al. (1995) reported that children with lower cognitive performance gave themselves higher ratings in the area of self-worth. This may be because those with lower cognitive performance, like preschool-age children, lack the skills required to make social comparisons and tend to describe themselves based primarily on physical attributes (Selman, 1980). Moreover, traditional measures of self-esteem and self-concept require making fine distinctions, often on a Likert scale, that are not always apparent to those with intellectual disabilities.

Given the difficulties in using quantitative measures of self-concept, several studies have employed qualitative methodologies to describe the multiple tasks involved in developing a sense of self when one has a disability. In a study by Olney and Kim (2001), college students with cognitive or emotional disabilities explained the complex processes involved in self-definitions that included their limitations but did not simultaneously pathologize their differences. Unlike those with physical disabilities, they wrestled with whether and how to disclose their disabilities to others. Like others with disabilities, however, they worried about stigmatizing and patronizing attitudes of peers.

Mpofu and Harley (2006) propose that determinants of disability identity are similar to those of racial identity in that both types of identity are socially constructed phenomena. They maintain that those with a healthy disability identity view their disability difference as a resource for growth. Like resilient racial identity described by Spencer (2006), resilient disability identity might serve valuable protective, compensatory, and self-enhancement functions. Racial identity, as described by Cross (2001) and Helms (1995), however, is a staged process and the extent to which children and adolescent with disabilities emerge through different life phase understandings of themselves in relation to having a disability is not known.

Moving beyond a psychological approach to the question of identity development in adolescents with developmental disabilities to a philosophical one offers a different and provocative perspective. Much work in this area is based on Foucault's (1994) themes of power, knowledge, and subjectivity as activities that produce and maintain the concept of disability as an "impaired body." Even the term *disability* implies its opposite—ability—and, according to this social theory, establishes unnecessary dichotomies that impose on the self-surveillance of individuals as they construct an identity and a sense of self (Reeve,

2002). By shifting the emphasis on the phenomenon of identity development from the individual to the societal level, the adolescent need not accept the larger social model and instead can replace it with a view of self as a social actor (Block, Balcazar, & Keys, 2002). Empirical research is lacking, however, on whether and how such shifts occur for adolescents with developmental disabilities in their understanding of self.

Development of a Peer Network

Adolescence is a time when social networks often change both in breadth and in depth. During the adolescent period, friendships typically change from being activity oriented to being relationships with strong emotional ties (Buhrmester & Furman, 1987). Friendships during adolescence provide companionship but also promote important social cognitive advances in areas such as conflict resolution, reciprocity, intimacy, and dimensions of trust and loyalty (Hartup, 1993). Friendships, therefore, are important to an adolescent's sense of well-being but also serve to advance development in significant ways.

Because of federal mandates, adolescents with developmental disabilities are now included with typically developing adolescents in many school classes and activities. Nevertheless, research on social interaction between students with and without a disability, although extensive for the preschool age group, is lacking for the secondary school level. The few studies that have been conducted report similar findings and point to the small and often inadequate social networks of adolescents with disabilities.

In a comparison of adolescents with and without intellectual disabilities, Zetlin and Murtaugh (1988) found that those with intellectual disabilities not only had fewer friends but also tended to have more relatives in their friendship group. Moreover, their friendships tended to be less stable and to have more conflicts than those of typically developing adolescents. A study by Heiman (2000) indicated that high levels of "feeling alone" (three to four times higher) were reported by students with intellectual disabilities in comparison to other students. They also were less likely to meet their peers out of school. Orsmond, Krauss, and Seltzer (2004) reported that almost half of their sample of 235 adolescents and adults with autism were reported not to have any reciprocal peer relationships with same-aged persons.

The nature of friendships of adolescents with developmental disabilities has been explored in a few studies. Bottroff et al. (2002) conducted a small-scale study of adolescents and young adults with Down syndrome and classified their friendships according to Selman's (1980) model of developmental stages of friendship formation. They found that only 25% of their sample could be classified at a friendship level that indicated mutual trust and reciprocity, whereas more friendships were classified at the lower levels based on simple proximity. Several participants, however, reported having imaginary friends, possibly a compensation strategy for such adolescents. In an ethnographic study of friendship among adolescents with developmental disabilities, Matheson, Olsen, and Weisner (2007) found that participating in shared activities and being perceived as similar were common themes in determining friendships, as was an ability to be available over time. Unlike typically developing adolescents, however, the adolescents with disabilities stressed that attributes of friendships often involved mere proximity and being in a group together, whereas notions of trust and reciprocity were mentioned less frequently.

One reason for the lack of strong reciprocal friendships found among adolescents with intellectual disabilities is likely related to individual levels of social cognitive processes. Interpreting social cues, developing strategies for approaching and responding to peers, and self-evaluation and monitoring are all central processes required for productive social interaction. Research indicates that in each of these areas individuals with intellectual disabilities exhibit more difficulties than those developing typically (Leffert & Siperstein, 2002). Syndrome-specific patterns of relative strengths and weaknesses in areas of social cognition also exist. For example, children with Williams syndrome often orient to and prefer social stimuli and are relatively successful in identifying others, seeing others as approachable, and imitating their affective states (Bellugi, Adolphs, Cassady, & Chiles, 1999), whereas they are less successful in perspective taking and decision making based on affective cues (Fidler, Hepburn, Most, Philofsky, & Rogers, 2007).

In a review of studies of children and adolescents with Down syndrome, Wishart (2007) speculated that their heightened sociability may be misunderstood as having good interpersonal understanding. Highly sociable behavior may, in fact, distract those with Down syndrome from developing more complex social cognitive skills necessary to collaborate with and learn from others using joint engagement on tasks. Studies on children and adolescents with autism spectrum disorders indicate that they have pronounced difficulty in social perspective taking, and thus tend to be limited in their ability to perceive the world through the eyes of others (Spector & Volkmar, 2006). This deficit has been attributed to impairment in the "theory of mind," that is, the ability to impute mental states to oneself and others, and thus make inferences regarding the thoughts of others (Baron-Cohen, 1995). In general, the growing literature on syndrome-specific disabilities is likely to lead to a greater understanding of the various aspects of social cognition necessary for the development and sustainment of friendships during the adolescent years as well as guide the field toward more productive interventions for adolescents with developmental disabilities who lack specific skills and are either rejected or ignored by their peers.

Development of Self-Agency

From a developmental systems perspective, the individual is an instrument of self-agency and, therefore, to some extent promotes his or her own development (Lerner, 2002). The action psychology model of Brandstädter (1998) and the agentic model of Baltes (1997) are relevant to the development of all adolescents, but have especially important implications for those with developmental disabilities. Agency is indicated in an adolescent's motivated approach to problem-posing tasks and situations, and is revealed by the adolescent's overture to others, including family members, engagement in the world of work or further schooling, and attempts to develop self-sufficiency to the extent possible. Those whose agentic actions are intruded upon or usurped by others risk developing behaviors indicative of learned helplessness, a pattern that has been found to be typical of many young adults with developmental disabilities (Jenkinson, 1999).

Autonomy implies the ability to act according to one's preferences, interests, and abilities, and therefore requires knowledge of self (Wehmeyer, 1996) but also involves the opportunity for choice. The importance of self-agency, which is required for autonomous behavior, is a continuing theme in the literature on children with developmental disabilities. In our longitudinal study of children with Down syndrome, motor impairment, or developmental delay (Hauser-Cram, Warfield, Shonkoff, & Krauss, 2001), we found that children's early strivings for agency predicted their adaptive skill development over a 10-year period. From a systems perspective, positive skill development is likely to provide children and adolescents with additional opportunities for self-determination, which in turn compounds the positive effects of agency.

Wehmeyer has conducted a series of studies on self-determination in individuals with developmental disabilities. In an investigation of adolescents, he reported both a positive relation between self-determination and age as well as higher scores for typically developing adolescents in comparison to those with disabilities (Wehmeyer, 1996). Considering only individuals with intellectual disabilities,

Wehmeyer and Garner (2003) reported a low correlation between level of intelligence and self-determination scores with only opportunities for choice (not intellectual performance) predicting membership in a high self-determination group. Wehmeyer and Schwartz (1998) reported that adolescents with developmental disabilities who had higher levels of self-determination had more positive adult outcomes, including higher rates of employment.

Employment offers one opportunity for increased autonomy, since through employment adolescents often develop a sense of responsibility, increased self-reliance, and expanded social networks. The employment of adolescents and young adults with developmental disabilities has received more attention than any other aspect of this phase of life. Findings from the National Longitudinal Transition Study 2 (Wagner, Newman, Cameto, Levine, & Garza, 2006), a longitudinal survey–based study of adolescents with a wide range of disabilities, indicated that at the time of the survey more than 40% of youth were employed, compared to 63% of the same-age out-of-school youth in the general population. These rates of employment varied considerably, however, based on type of disability, with highest rates among those with learning disabilities and far lower rates among those with intellectual disabilities. Rates also varied based on ethnicity, with highest rates among whites and lowest rates among African Americans and Native Americans. These figures indicate generally more positive trends than found in data collected two decades ago, but they still accentuate lower rates for those with disabilities than for the typically developing population, and they mimic the social inequities by ethnicity. Wagner et al. (2006) found that the reliance on low-paying caregiving jobs for females has decreased and the percentage of jobs in the trades has increased among males. Despite such generally positive trends in engagement in employment for adolescents and young adults with disabilities, students with cognitive disabilities report that they have few opportunities to work in paid jobs in career areas of their choice (Powers et al., 2007).

One of the greatest changes over the last decade has been an increase in opportunities for youth with developmental disabilities to attend postsecondary education programs. Wagner et al. (2006) found that about 30% of youth with disabilities were enrolled in some type of postsecondary school. Although this rate is still lower than that among typically developing youth (41%), this figure illustrates the potential role of community colleges and other institutions in increasing their services to adolescents and young adults with disabilities. Howlin (2000) notes the expanding number of higher functioning adolescents with autism spectrum disorders who now attend college, especially smaller colleges, supported by a range of mental health and peer mentoring services. The need for such postsecondary programs is likely to continue to grow as adolescents with developmental disabilities who have experienced education under the support of the IDEA emerge from high schools and push for a range of future educational and employment training opportunities.

Transition in Relationships with Parents

One of the hallmarks of adolescence is a reconfiguration of relationships with parents from one of dependency toward one of greater mutuality. Although such reconfiguration often involves struggles on the part of both the adolescent and the parent, national data indicate that most adolescent–parent relationships are positive (Moore, Guzman, Hair, Lippman, & Garrett, 2004). Such close and positive adolescent–parent relationships are related to a wide range of benefits for adolescents, including better academic outcomes and fewer problem behaviors (Moore et al., 2004).

Most adolescents with disabilities also report having strong and positive relationships with their parents (Wagner et al., 2006). They differ from other adolescents, however, in that they report receiving a great deal of attention from their families, more so than that reported by other adolescents (Wagner et al., 2006). Although such attention may indicate high levels of protection, resulting in less development of autonomy, it may also be a response to the adolescent's need for support from a trusted adult. Collins and Laursen (2004) propose that adolescent–parent relationships often serve to modify the impact of deleterious sources of influence, such as difficulties at school or destructive peer relationships. Although this proposition has not been tested explicitly in relation to adolescents with disabilities, survey data from parents of adolescents or young adults with disabilities leaving high school indicate that parents are well aware of the dilemmas they face regarding their dual role in the promotion of independence and the protection from harm of their child (Thorin, Yovanoff, & Irvin, 1996). Protection may limit immediate opportunities for independence but may serve an intermediate function that, in turn, promotes autonomy. For example, Dixon and Reddacliff (2001) found that parental behaviors aimed at protecting their adolescent with developmental disabilities from difficulties and exploitation also led to more successful employment outcomes.

Current trends in the United States indicate that many young adults return to reside with their parents during some periods of their young adult life (Arnett, 2004; DaVanzo & Goldscheider, 1990). In contrast to returning to the family home for brief periods of time, many adolescents with developmental disabilities live with their parents consistently for many years (Fujiura & Braddock, 1992; Seltzer & Krauss, 1984). Seltzer, Greenberg, Floyd, Pettee and Hong (2001), using data from the Wisconsin Longitudinal Study, found that 57% of the sons and daughters with a developmental disability and 41% of those with multiple mental health problems continued to live with their parents, in contrast to only 16% of sons and daughters without disabilities. In a study of individuals with developmental disabilities who had attended special education programs,

Scuccimarra and Speece (1990) found that the majority resided with their parents, although over 75% of those individuals said they would prefer to live independently. Kraemer and Blacher (2001) investigated the living situations of young adults with low levels of intellectual functioning and found that the majority lived at home; furthermore, their parents did not identify leaving home as a primary goal for their child. Thus, the reasons that the young adult with developmental disabilities most likely continues to live at home appear to be multiply determined, based on a confluence of parental choice, whether living options are available, and the extent and the desire of the adolescent or young adult to advocate for such change.

Parents and other family members serve as a potentially strong support network for individuals with developmental disabilities but may also substitute for friends. In a study of young adults with mild to severe disabilities, McGrew, Johnson, and Bruininks (1994) reported that an inverse relation occurs between the number of family and non–family members in their social networks. Therefore, the parent–child relationship, although always complex, becomes increasingly so for adolescents with developmental disabilities, especially those who rely on parents for many aspects of their daily living and social activities.

FAMILIES OF ADOLESCENTS WITH DEVELOPMENTAL DISABILITIES

Although early studies of parents of children with disabilities focused on issues such as "chronic sorrow" of parents (Olshansky, 1962), and assumed deleterious functioning of the parents, current research provides a more nuanced view of families. Drawing from several perspectives, a broad understanding of the family and its tasks and functioning over time have guided current investigations.

Conceptual Perspectives in Family Research

There has been a surge of research in the past several decades on the influence of children with developmental disabilities on their families and the influence of families on the development of children with developmental disabilities (e.g., Greenberg, Seltzer, Hong & Orsmond, 2006; Hauser-Cram et al., 2001; Keogh, Garnier, Bernheimer, & Gallimore, 2000; Kersh, Hedvat, Hauser-Cram, & Warfield, 2006; Mink, Nihira, & Meyers, 1983; Parish, 2006; Seltzer & Heller, 1997). This body of research has roots in transactional theories of human development (Lerner, 2002; Sameroff & Fiese, 2000), models of the ecology of human development (Bronfenbrenner, 1979), family systems theory (Minuchin, 2002; Olson, Russell & Sprenkle, 1983), and family life cycle theory (Carter & McGoldrick, 1980). Common to all these theoretical roots are three core propositions:

1. Individual development is shaped by both the biological attributes of the individual and the multiple and complex environmental contexts over the life course in which the individual exists.

2. Changes in the individual and his/her environment affect other members of the individual's environment in reciprocal and iterative ways.

3. There are predictable stages in human and family development that shape the tasks, functions, and behaviors of individuals and other family members.

Although this chapter focuses on a particular life stage for individuals with developmental disabilities and, by extension, of their families, much of what conditions the development of the adolescent and his/her family during this protracted period is linked to prior periods of individual development and family patterns, and is affected by the anticipated outcomes for the adolescent during adulthood.

In order to provide a context for considering the family environment of adolescents with developmental disabilities, a brief discussion of family life cycle theory is provided. Family life cycle theory posits that just as individuals have stages of development, families as a collective unit pass through predictable stages over the life course. These stages are typically defined by the employment status of the head of the household, the entry into and exit of family members from the family, and the age of the oldest child in the family. Theorists of the family life cycle posit a variable number of stages, from as few as seven (Duvall, 1957) to as many as 24 (Rodgers, 1960). The most commonly used set of stages include the following: couple, childbearing, school age, adolescence, launching, postpubertal, and aging (Olson, McCubbin, Barnes, Larsen, Muxen, & Wilson, 1984). Within each stage, there are specific tasks and functions that families perform, including economic, physical, rest and recuperation, socialization, self-definition, affection, guidance, educational, and vocational (Turnbull, Summers, & Brotherson, 1986). For each stage, the priorities of these different functions vary and the roles that individual family members assume in the conduct of these functions reflect their individual developmental capabilities and needs. Particular functions may be heavily influenced by the age of the child.

For example, during the adolescent period, there is usually less emphasis by parents on the physical care of their child and greater emphasis on the child's vocational preparation. In contrast to the childbearing stage, when physical affection and contact is a dominant feature of the parent–child relationship, the adolescent stage is characterized by an emphasis on "letting go" and on reducing child dependency.

Contemporary Perspectives on Family Impacts

While there is scant research on the reciprocal influences of parents on their adolescents with developmental disabilities, there is a broader literature available on the life-span impacts on families of having a child with a developmental disability (Seltzer, Greenberg, Floyd, Pettee & Hong, 2001; Seltzer, Krauss, Orsmond, & Vestal, 2001). Research on the role of the family

for individuals with developmental disabilities acknowledges that the family occupies a central and enduring role over the life course and that taking a life-span perspective reveals undeniable stresses on parental well-being and health, as well as positively regarded accommodations to family life and values (Blacher & Baker, 2007; Heller, Hsieh, & Rowitz, 1997; Krauss & Seltzer, 1994).

Over the past several decades, there also has been a shift in perspectives on the impacts on families of having a son or daughter with a developmental disability. Decades ago, the common view among professionals and society at large was that having a child with a developmental disability was a burden on the family and was associated with deleterious outcomes for the parents and siblings (Hodapp, Ly, Fidler, & Ricci, 2001). Indeed, out-of-home placement of the affected child was commonly recommended (Seltzer & Krauss, 1984). With the advent of the parents' movement and changes in social policies ensuring educational and social services for persons with developmental disabilities since the 1960s, the role of and impacts on the family have been viewed from new perspectives that acknowledge the complex and multifaceted ways that families adapt to their caregiving responsibilities.

Helff and Glidden (1998) reviewed research on family impacts over a 20-year period (from the 1970s through the 1990s) and found that while there was a decrease in the "negativity" of the research, there was not a concomitant increase in perceived positivity of family impacts. Blacher and Baker (2007) provide an interesting three-level conceptual scheme for identifying positive impacts on families. The first is that positive impacts may be inferred by the absence of negative impacts (the "low negative" level). The second, called the "common benefits" level, refers to families experiencing the same joys and frustrations with their child as is typical of all families. The third, called the "special benefits" level, implies that there are unique benefits associated with having a child with a developmental disability.

Indeed, there is a growing body of literature that focuses on the resilience found among many families who have a child with a developmental disability. The concept of resilience implies more than just coping with a situation—it includes the capacity to withstand hardship and rebound from adversity. Scorgie and Sobsey (2000) examined parental views on the transformations they have experienced because of having a child with a developmental disability and found evidence of three major areas of transformational change: personal growth, improved relations with others, and changes in philosophical or spiritual values. Bayat (2007) surveyed 175 parents of children and adolescents with autism regarding factors contributing to "family resilience" and found evidence of family resilience such as family connectedness and closeness, positive meaning-making of the disability, and spiritual and personal growth. Grant, Ramcharan, and Flynn (2007) reported three core elements associated with resilience at the individual level—search for meaning, sense of control, and maintenance of valued identities.

Dykens (2005) reviewed contemporary literature with respect to happiness, well-being, and character strengths as outcomes in families, including siblings, of persons with intellectual disabilities. She notes that the "stress and coping" model used in many studies is useful in identifying why some families cope well with the common and unique stresses of having a child with a disability and others do not. Rather than assume that psychopathology is an inevitable outcome for such families, as was common decades ago (Olshansky, 1962; Solnit & Stark, 1961), studies now focus on why many families cope well and derive valued meanings from their experiences. Indeed, there is considerable evidence that mothers with problem-focused coping styles generally fare better than those with emotional coping styles (Kim, Greenberg, Seltzer & Krauss, 2003).

According to Dykens (2006), the burgeoning interest in "positive psychology" (Seligman, 2000) should be extended to studies of persons with intellectual disabilities (and their families), for whom she argues that emotional states such as happiness, gratifications, and flow are relevant outcomes worthy of empirical investigation. Thus, there is a growing interest within the research community studying impacts on families of having a child with a developmental disability to examine positive contributions of such children (Hastings, Beck, & Hill, 2005), transformational (and positive) impacts on family members (Scorgie & Sobsey, 2000), and factors associated with a "meaningful life."

Challenges to the Family in the Adolescent Period

The adolescent period is sometimes characterized by heightened turmoil for parents, who must cope with the effects of the biological, cognitive, social, and psychological maturation of their adolescent as well as parental transitions into the midlife period (Seltzer, Krauss, Choi, & Hong, 1996). Part of the transition from childhood to adulthood includes the "push and pull" of relinquishing parental roles of protectiveness, close supervision, and authority while adopting parenting styles that respect the adolescent's emerging needs for autonomy, independence, and more egalitarian relationships with the parents. When the adolescent has a developmental disability, however, the normative tasks of adolescence and the normative tasks of parents during this period may be experienced in ways that are both similar and distinct in comparison to families of typically developing adolescents. As Zetlin and Turner (1985) note, "although retarded individuals experience the same biological changes and drives as nonretarded youngsters, the issues associated with adolescence—emancipation, self concept, sexuality—are exacerbated by the presence of their handicap" (p. 571).

Turnbull et al. (1986) articulated the major stressors arising from different family life course stages and the transitions across them for families of children with developmental disabilities. With respect to the adolescent period, they note particular stressors such as the emotional adjustment to the chronicity of the handicapping condition and related issues such as peer isolation. Further, many families remain deeply involved in arranging for leisure-time activities as well as participating in educational and vocational planning tasks. Although some of these stressors are applicable to all families of adolescents (e.g., issues surrounding emerging sexuality, dealing with physical and emotional changes of puberty), some are relatively distinctive features of parenting a child with a developmental disability (e.g., future planning for vocational development, arranging for leisure-time activities, participation in IEP meetings). Indeed, as discussed below, parental roles in the transition of adolescents with developmental disabilities from school to work is one of the major areas of research on parental involvement during this life stage.

There is substantial evidence that the adolescent period has particular and specific stressful content for parents of children with developmental disabilities. The stressful content seems to span various dimensions, including sobering appraisals of the child's developmental status, awareness of the potential for continued dependence (rather than independence) on the family, parallel parental transitions into their own midlife phase (and its attendant psychological tasks) (Todd and Jones, 2005), and trepidation over the end of federally guaranteed rights to services as children leave the special education system. Schneider et al. (2006) conducted ecocultural interviews with families of adolescents with severe disabilities and found both internal and external challenges to the maintenance of a meaningful family routine. Internally, family roles and relationships underwent change, resulting in various strategies to accommodate these changes (e.g., dividing up family time, protecting some members from too much involvement and engaging others in family activities). Externally, service discontinuities associated with the adolescent period were accommodated by various strategies such as advocacy, coordinating

multiple services and forfeiting a desired alternative. Their research illustrates the dynamics within families of managing the needs of and impacts on the family as a unit during the adolescent period.

Baine, McDonald, Wilgosh, and Mellon (1993) conducted quantitative and qualitative research on sources of general and unique family stress among families of adolescents with severe disabilities. The most stressful issues included characteristics of the adolescent (i.e., dependency, lack of autonomy, individual vulnerability, physical size, severity of disability) and aspects of the service systems that support these individuals (i.e., transition from school to adult services, eligibility for government assistance, residential costs). The least stressful aspects related to family interpersonal dynamics (i.e., sibling relationships, parental philosophy). Follow-up interviews with a subsample of the families participating in the quantitative portion of their research revealed a deeper and wider range of concerns than were evident in the numerical ratings of the areas of potential stress. The authors (Baine et al., 1993) summarized parental concerns about individual characteristics of their adolescents with developmental disabilities as follows:

> The parents expressed particular concerns about long-term, family life-planning related to chronic dependency of the persons with disabilities; physical management problems related to the increasing size and strength of the individual; concerns related to cleanliness, grooming, aggression, and inappropriate age and gender related behavior (e.g., expression of affection), and the amount of care required ('we must plan everything around his needs'). (p. 185)

With respect to stressors for the family, the qualitative information revealed concerns about the costs of long-term care, often requiring family sacrifices, parental tension regarding the role or level of involvement of fathers, and the strain on parents of having to organize or create a social, educational, and supportive world for their adolescent child.

Harris, Glasberg, and Delmolino (1998) propose that for families of children with developmental disabilities, adolescence may signify the end of illusion. Parental aspirations and dreams about dramatic changes in their child's functional abilities may be tempered by a clearer awareness of the child's developmental trajectory. Bristol and Schopler (1983), for example, note that parents of adolescents with autism have a greater sense of realism and pessimism about their child's development in comparison to parents of younger children with this disorder.

Wikler (1986) suggests that there is a cyclical quality to family stress over different developmental stages. Her research indicates that stress is highest in families of a child with developmental disabilities who is just entering early adolescence or early adulthood, as compared to stress among families whose child with disabilities is in later adolescence or further into young adulthood. One explanation for the increased stress for families of adolescents with disabilities was attributed to the degree of community acceptance offered to children with developmental disabilities at different life stages.

DeMyer and Goldberg (1983) and Bristol (1984) note that as children with developmental disabilities age, their behaviors are less well tolerated by society and they are less socially acceptable than younger children who, despite their disabilities, may be seen as "cute" or whose atypical behaviors are less different from the range of behaviors of typically developing children. The lack of community acceptance for adolescents with developmental disabilities may translate into greater social isolation of their families, and may instill a greater rigidity of family routines, in comparison to families of typically developing adolescents for whom social acceptance issues are less pressing and for whom more relaxed family routines often emerge as a consequence of the increasing independence of their adolescent.

For many parents of children with developmental disabilities, there is a complex mixture of gratification and frustration encountered in the parenting experience, leading to what Larson (1998) calls the "embrace of paradox." Based on a study of Latina mothers of children with developmental disabilities, Larson (1998) explained this phenomenon as follows:

> Despite what would appear as multiple limitations in their daily lives due to the caretaking of a child with disability, these mothers shared hopeful maternal visions and profound personal growth that emerged because of this experience. What surfaced . . . was a life metaphor, the embrace of paradox, that was central to the mothers' maternal work. The embrace of paradox was the management of the internal tension of opposing forces between loving the child as he or she was and wanting to erase the disability, between dealing with the incurability while pursuing solutions, and between maintaining hopefulness for the child's future while being given negative information and battling their own fears. (p. 873)

Parental narratives of their lives with children with developmental disabilities echo Larson's description, particularly during the adolescent period, when the realignment of parental roles in the face of their child's efforts towards independence and autonomy constitutes a compelling family challenge (e.g., Dunsford, 2007; Kaufman, 1999; Park, 2001; Todd & Jones, 2005).

Zetlin and Turner (1985) conducted an ethnographic study of 25 young adults with mild intellectual disabilities about their adolescence. The study included in-depth participant observation and interviews with the young adults and extensive interviewing of their parents. Their results provide insights into the interactions between parents and adolescents with intellectual disabilities during a stage of life when, for some, the social consequences of their disabilities become painfully manifest. They concluded that:

> . . . it appears that both parents and sample members viewed the adolescent experience as more problematic than either the childhood

period or the adult years and generally agreed on the nature of the adolescent conflicts. For the most part, these retarded adolescents were concerned with the same issues that preoccupy nonretarded adolescents—personal identify and autonomy. They interpreted parental attitudes and practices as nonsupportive and issues of competence and self-definition as sources of frustration and self-conflict. . . . The implications of their handicapped status as well as their limitations were salient concerns for the first time, and many of their experiences—parental restrictiveness, peer rejection, expectancy-performance discrepancies—contributed to their uneasiness and discontent. (p. 578)

There is a growing body of literature that examines changes in the parent–child relationship during the adolescent period. Orsmond, Seltzer, Greenberg, and Krauss (2003) studied the mother–child relationship among 202 adolescents and adults with autism living at home and found that for most of their sample, the mother–child relationship was characterized as positive across multiple measures. They also found that greater positive affect and warmth from the mother to the child was predictive of fewer maternal caregiving strains and greater caregiving gains. In a subsequent analysis from this study, Lounds et al. (2007) reported that during the adolescent period, there was a dominant pattern of improvement in maternal well-being and a closer relationship with their son or daughter with autism. Interestingly, they found that mothers of daughters experienced significantly greater reduction in depressive symptoms and increasing closeness in the mother–child relationship over the 1.5-year study period than mothers of sons.

Planning as a Unique Task for Families of Adolescents

As noted earlier, one of the markers of the end of the adolescent period is the assumption of adult roles, including employment, self-sufficiency, and formation of independent family units. For many individuals with developmental disabilities, these roles are particularly problematic. Because of the ongoing and heightened responsibilities of parents in planning for the future of their adolescents with disabilities, parental involvement in shaping the future may be far more extensive than is the case among families of typically developing adolescents. Thorin, Yovanoff, and Irvin (1996) articulated the six most common dilemmas reported by parents of adolescents with developmental disabilities as wanting to:

- Create opportunities for independence for the young adult, especially in light of health and safety needs.
- Do whatever is necessary to assure a good life for him or her.
- Provide stability and predictability in the family life while meeting the changing needs of the young adult and family.
- Create a separate social life for the young adult.
- Avoid parental burnout.
- Maximize the young adult's growth and potential.

This enumeration of parental dilemmas underscores the fact that for many families of adolescents with developmental disabilities, the parental role intensifies rather than diminishes during the period of transition to adulthood. Parental involvement occurs in regard to fundamental issues of protecting their child's health and safety, to constructing or arranging environments in which their child's social and economic life can be supported, and to providing a context in which their child's capabilities are maximized. These tasks constitute an atypical agenda in comparison to the tasks of parents of typically developing adolescents.

Indeed, the degree of planning that families need to do—repeatedly—over the life cycle has been consistently underscored. Nadworny and Haddad (2007) propose that planning is a lifelong activity, providing opportunities for reassessing goals and roles that various family members (and extended support people) can assume. They also note that planning must take into account the needs of all family members, not just the member with a developmental disability. Finally, they note that there are specific "pressure points"—transitions in the service delivery system and age-related changes—that punctuate particular planning needs. These pressure points need to include an examination of family issues, emotional needs, financial issues, legal considerations, and government benefits.

One of the unique tasks facing families of adolescents with developmental disabilities is planning for their adolescent's transition from special education services to adulthood. There is considerable evidence that the prospect of losing the mandated educational and related services guaranteed by the IDEA when a child with a disability reaches the age of 22 is one of the most stressful aspects of the adolescent period for parents (Thorin & Irvin, 1992). Recent estimates suggest that over 2 million students between ages 14 and 21 receive special education services under the IDEA (U.S. Department of Education, 2007a). Of these, approximately 400,000 exit the school system each year and enter the adult world (U.S. Department of Education, 2007b). As indicated in an earlier section, a component of the Individuals with Disabilities Education Act (IDEA) of 1990 requires that an individualized transition plan be crafted as part of a student's IEP that identifies needed transition services. Parents are expected to be part of that planning process.

Studies of the "transition process" from school to work have found that parents of children with disabilities are significantly less involved in transition planning than they desire to be (McNair & Rusch, 1991), although it appears that parental involvement increases as the severity of the child's disability increases (Kraemer & Blacher, 2001). Because a hallmark of being an adult is being employed (leading to economic self-sufficiency), and because of the many social benefits attributed to being employed, there is a great deal of attention in the practice and research literature on efforts by parents and service systems to enhance the future employability of

adolescents with developmental disabilities. Parental expectations for the future vocational activities of their adolescents with disabilities are an important factor in such transition plans. In a study conducted by Kraemer and Blacher (2001), almost two-thirds of parents of children with severe intellectual disabilities expected their child to work, most commonly in a day activity center or sheltered workshop. Parent roles in achieving desired vocational outcomes were examined in a qualitative study that identified the following important family characteristics: moral support, practical assistance, role models of appropriate work ethic, protection from difficulties and exploitation, and family cohesion (Dixon & Reddacliff, 2001). Clearly, parents occupy a critical position in the lives of youth with developmental disabilities, and parents' engagement in planning activities for the adult life of their adolescent constitutes a major family task of the adolescent period.

Sibling Relationships

There is very little research that has focused specifically on the sibling relationships of youth with disabilities during the adolescent years. The few studies that have been conducted indicate that these relationships appear to be qualitatively different from those that exist between typically developing siblings. Krauss and Seltzer (2001) reported that siblings of brothers and sisters with disabilities often experience issues that are unique to their family situation and that may set them apart from their friends who do not have a sibling with a disability. The relationships among typically developing siblings are often characterized by two particular dimensions of involvement—affective involvement and instrumental involvement—and these dimensions have been studied, although to a lesser extent, among siblings when one has a developmental disability.

Affective Involvement

Research on the relationships shared by typically developing siblings often focuses on two affective components: the positive dimension of warmth and the negative dimension of conflict (Bowerman & Dobash, 1974; Furman & Buhrmester, 1985). The relationships between individuals with disabilities and their siblings are frequently characterized by warmth and affection across a range of ages and life-course stages, including adolescence and young adulthood (e.g., Bagenholm & Gillberg, 1991; Begun, 1989; Eisenberg, Baker, & Blacher, 1998; Gath, 1973; McHale, Sloan, & Simeonsson, 1986; Rivers & Stoneman, 2003; Stoneman, Brody, Davis, & Crapps, 1987b). Siblings of individuals with disabilities appear to demonstrate more nurturance, empathy, and emotional support for their brothers and sisters than do comparison siblings of typically developing individuals (Abramovitch, Stanhope, Pepler, & Corter, 1987; Cuskelly & Gunn, 2003; Hannah & Midlarsky, 2005; McHale & Gamble, 1987; McHale et al., 1986). This substantiates the depiction of the more dominant, "parentified" role these siblings appear to adopt in their relationships with their brothers and sisters across the life span.

Siblings of children with a variety of disabilities generally report comparatively low levels of conflict in their relationships with their brothers and sisters (Cuskelly & Gunn, 2003; Eisenberg et al., 1998; Fisman, Wolf, Ellison, & Freeman, 2000; Kaminsky & Dewey, 2001; McHale & Gamble, 1989; Roeyers & Mycke, 1995). They frequently describe the most negative aspect of their relationships in a very different manner; when asked about the negative aspects of having a sibling with a disability, many siblings mention worry (Eisenberg et al., 1998). In a Dutch study, 75% of typically developing brothers and sisters reported that they sometimes worried about the future and/or their sibling's health (Pit-ten Cate & Loots, 2000). Moderate levels of worry and concern have been documented in siblings of both adolescents (Kersh, 2007) and adults with developmental disabilities (Orsmond & Seltzer, 2000). Furthermore, meta-analysis has shown that anxiety is one area of psychological

adjustment where siblings of children with disabilities and comparison peers do seem to evidence real differences (Rossiter & Sharpe, 2001). It is possible that this documented anxiety is closely connected to feelings of worry about their brothers and sisters, and the future of their families in general.

These relationships may differ from the normative view of sibling relationships in other ways, as well. Dunn (2002) describes intensity and intimacy as dominant themes in the literature on normative sibling relationships. In contrast, there is evidence to suggest that sibling relationships in which one child has a disability are lacking in both those areas. Begun (1989) asked adolescent and adult females to rate their relationships with their siblings both with and without disabilities. Comparisons across 16 dimensions of sibling relationship revealed distinct differences between the relationships these women had with their siblings with intellectual disabilities and their relationships with their typically developing siblings. They described their relationships with their siblings with developmental disabilities as characterized by significantly greater nurturance of and dominance over their siblings and lower levels of admiration. They also rated these relationships as being less intimate, less competitive, and characterized by less perceived similarity between the two when compared to the relationships they shared with their typically developing brothers and sisters. Begun concluded that, despite some strong positive aspects, the relationships that these women shared with their brothers and sisters with disabilities appeared to be more affectively neutral (i.e., less intense) than their relationships with their siblings without disabilities.

Instrumental Involvement

A large body of research indicates that the siblings of children with disabilities spend more time involved in caregiving activities than their peers with typically developing brothers and sisters, regardless of age or birth order

(Hannah & Midlarsky, 2005; McHale & Gamble, 1989; Stoneman, Brody, Davis, Crapps, & Malone, 1991). In addition, these siblings are more directive in their interactions with their brothers and sisters when compared to siblings of typically developing youth (Dallas, Stevenson, & McGurk, 1993; Stoneman et al., 1987b). The durability of the sibling relationship has also been noted. In a survey of adult siblings of persons with intellectual disabilities, about a quarter indicated that they planned to coreside with their brother or sister when their parents could no longer take care of the family member (Krauss, Seltzer, Gordon, & Friedman, 1996).

It is generally acknowledged that these sibling relationships appear to follow an atypical pattern of development. In typically developing sibling pairs, the older sibling assumes a dominant role in the family hierarchy, but over time the relationship becomes more egalitarian, as both siblings approach adulthood (Buhrmester & Furman, 1990). In dyads in which one sibling has a disability, the typically developing sibling, regardless of birth order, generally assumes a dominant role that is characterized by high levels of helping and custodial behavior, and these relationships often become increasingly imbalanced over time (Abramovitch et al., 1987; Corter, Pepler, Stanhope, & Abramovitch, 1992; Dallas et al., 1993; Stoneman, Brody, Davis, & Crapps, 1987a).

The patterns of relationship that are evidenced in sibling pairs when one has a disability might be atypical; however, it does not necessarily follow that they are a source of risk. Although it is largely accepted that siblings bear greater responsibility in the home when there is a child with a disability in the family, it is not clear that this heightened responsibility leads to negative outcomes (e.g., Cuskelly & Gunn, 1993). Greater child care responsibilities have also been associated with greater empathy (Cuskelly & Gunn, 2003) and less sibling conflict (Stoneman et al., 1991). McHale and Gamble (1989) found that the amount of time spent in child care activities

was positively associated with anxiety, but not with depression, self-esteem, or conduct problems. Since the anxiety reported by this group of siblings did not approach clinical levels, the authors concluded that it might simply represent a normative response to the special care needs of a loved one. In other words, children and adolescents with more severe impairments require greater levels of care and may also simultaneously provoke more anxiety or worry in family members.

Kersh (2007) found that the functional level of adolescents with developmental disabilities was a powerful predictor of multiple aspects of sibling involvement. Siblings engaged in greater caregiving and supportive helping behaviors (e.g., providing emotional support) when their brothers and sisters had lower cognitive and adaptive abilities. They also expressed greater warmth and more worry and concern for their adolescent brothers and sisters with developmental disabilities who had lower functional skills. Given that the majority of the siblings in that study were also adolescents, perhaps the overall functional level of a brother or sister with a developmental disability has particular salience for youth at this stage of development. During this stage, teens are often in the process of renegotiating and redefining their roles and relationships within the family (Steinberg, 1990). It may be that the functional skills and level of need of a brother or sister with a disability are particularly instrumental in this process. Indeed, the work of Wilson, McGillivray, and Zetlin (1992) suggests that the predictive power of functionality (with regard to sibling involvement) may dissipate in the adult years.

Positive Impacts

Recently, there has been a greater emphasis on a range of positive outcomes for all family members of individuals with disabilities, including siblings (Dykens, 2005). Many young people acknowledge that they have benefited from having a sibling with a disability (Eisenberg et al., 1998; Kaminsky & Dewey, 2001; Pit-ten Cate & Loots, 2000; Roeyers & Mycke, 1995;

Van Riper, 2000). They have credited their siblings with helping them gain virtues such as patience, tolerance, benevolence, and appreciation of health and family (Eisenberg et al., 1998; Van Riper, 2000). In Grossman's (1972) landmark study, over half of the college-aged men and women interviewed about having a sibling with an intellectual disability demonstrated increased levels of altruism, idealism, and tolerance. Furthermore, in a survey of adult siblings of persons with intellectual disabilities, the vast majority described their experiences as "mostly positive" and noted the valuable lessons of compassion, tolerance, respect for differences, and patience that they had learned, despite their reflections on interpersonal turmoil during the adolescent period (Krauss et al., 1996).

Finally, there is some suggestion that the presence of a sibling with a disability can profoundly shape individuals' identity formation. There are a number of anecdotal reports (e.g., McHugh, 1999; Merrell, 1995), as well as several empirical studies (Burton & Parks, 1991; Cleveland & Miller, 1977), that suggest that having a sibling with a disability has played a role in shaping people's lives, with particular regard to choosing career paths in the helping professions. In a phenomenological case study, a 39-year-old woman with a brother with Down syndrome considered herself a lifelong "surrogate mother" to her brother and chose to enter the field of special education as a direct result of growing up with a sibling with a disability (Flaton, 2006).

FUTURE DIRECTIONS

The years since our last chapter in the *Handbook of Adolescent Psychology* (Hauser-Cram & Krauss, 2004) are noteworthy for the beginning of the inclusion of the study of adolescents with developmental disabilities and their families into a more comprehensive understanding of development. The inclusion is partially a result of increased work on the genetic origins of some disabilities, such as Down syndrome and Williams syndrome, and

the role of gene–environment interactions in human behavior. The inclusion is also a result of researchers discovering that theories applied to those with typical development, such as developmental systems theory, hold much promise for the study of those with developmental disabilities. Core aspects of development, such as agency, identity, and connectedness to peers, also appear to be assets for those with developmental disabilities. Thus, we can derive a deeper understanding of the development of such adolescents through the valuable models applied to the study of typical adolescents.

Despite such promising movement in the field more generally, and the impact of federal legislation on the rights of adolescents with disabilities which has provided more normative opportunities in education, employment, and social interaction, one approach that is notably absent from research on adolescents with developmental disabilities is the model of positive youth development (PYD) (Lerner, 2005). This "strength-based approach" (Lerner, 2005) stands in sharp contrast to more traditional paradigms of adolescent development that view adolescents in general as a group at risk for a variety of maladaptive and/ or dangerous behaviors and outcomes (e.g., substance abuse, delinquency, depression). Similarly, this perspective is distinctly different from one that assumes psychopathology based on developmental disability. Predicated on the notion that youth are a resource to be developed, PYD maintains that within each adolescent is the potential for successful, healthy development across five domains: competence, confidence, connection, character, and caring (Lerner, 2005). This is likely to be an effective frame work within which to consider the developmental assets of adolescents with disabilities and offers a cohesive and inclusive model with principles of development that apply to a wide range of adolescents.

In regard to families of adolescents with developmental disabilities, while the volume of research is not large, there is an emergence of several themes from this research that warrant additional study. Clearly, one of the major tasks for families during their child's adolescence is planning for the future—for the time when the child leaves the educational system and enters the adult services system. Given the increasing variety of employment and postsecondary educational options that are now available in many communities, the choices families and their adolescent have are more varied. Studies should be conducted to elucidate ways in which families and their adolescent make this transition a successful one.

We also noted that the adolescent period brings unique as well as common challenges and stressors to families of children with developmental disabilities. Research on how families manage their caregiving responsibilities has increasingly focused on factors affecting positive outcomes (e.g., maternal well-being, parent–child relationship quality) This shift in attention, from a deficit to a resilience perspective, promises to elucidate new knowledge about the complexity of this developmental period and to offer useful suggestions to service providers and families regarding ways in which family well-being can be supported. While there now is a larger body of research on families of adolescents with developmental disabilities than was available even 5 years ago, more research needs to focus on this critical period in the lives of adolescents and their families.

It is almost commonplace to note that the ethnic and racial diversity of American society is not reflected in the samples included in most research investigations. This situation seriously limits the power of the research base to guide practice for the millions of Americans who have adolescents with developmental disabilities who are not Caucasian (Ali, Fazil, Bywaters, Wallace, & Singh, 2001; Harry, 2002). There is a small but growing literature comparing Latino and Anglo families of individuals with developmental disabilities that focuses primarily on maternal impacts (Blacher & McIntyre, 2005; Eisenhower & Blacher, 2006; Magana & Smith, 2006). Far

more research is needed on ethnically diverse samples across the family life span.

CONCLUSIONS

The adolescent period for individuals with developmental disabilities remains understudied but is beginning to emerge in the literature as a critical life phase for both the individuals themselves and for their families. The role of the family does not diminish during this time as developmentally typical challenges occur for the adolescent who has been included in many classroom and school activities but may be struggling for inclusion in social networks, employment, and postsecondary educational opportunities.

Research can serve an important role in articulating these struggles and their moderators but also in locating ways families derive strengths and that the adolescents themselves engage in PYD. Finally, we contend that as a field, we can also understand the science of adolescent development more thoroughly by the study of adolescents with disabilities. It is only through the construction and testing of models that apply to the full range of human development that we will gain comprehensive perspectives on the development of adolescents.

REFERENCES

Abramovitch, R., Stanhope, L., Pepler, D., & Corter, C. (1987). The influence of Down's syndrome on sibling interaction. *Journal of Child Psychology and Psychiatry, 28*, 865–879.

Ali, Z., Fazil, Q., Bywaters, P., Wallace, L., & Singh, G. (2001). Disability, ethnicity and childhood: A critical review of research. *Disability & Society, 16*, 949–968.

American Academy of Pediatrics, American Academy of Family Physicians, & American College of Physicians–American Society of Internal Medicine. (2002). A consensus statement on health care transition for young adults with special health care needs. *Pediatrics, 110*, 1304–1306.

Americans with Disabilities Act of 1990, 42 U.S.C. § 12101 *et seq.* (Matthew Bender, 2007). Deficit Reduction Act of 2005, Pub. L. No. 109–171, 120 Stat. 4.

American Psychiatric Association (2000). *Diagnostic and statistical manual of mental disorders* (4th ed.). Washington, DC: Author.

Arnett, J. J. (2004). *Emerging adulthood: The winding road from the late teens through the twenties*. Oxford: Oxford University Press.

Bagenholm, A., & Gillberg, C. (1991). Psychosocial effects on siblings of children with autism and mental retardation: A population-based study. *Journal of Mental Deficiency Research, 35*, 291–307.

Baine, D., McDonald, L., Wilgosh, L., & Mellon, S. (1993). Stress experienced by families of older adolescents or young adults with severe disability. *Australia and New Zealand Journal of Developmental Disabilities, 18,* 177–188.

Baltes, P. B. (1997). On the incomplete architecture of human ontology: Selection, optimization, and compensation as foundation of developmental theory. *American Psychologist, 52,* 366–380.

Baron-Cohen, S. (1995). *Mindblindness: An essay on autism and theory of mind.* Cambridge, MA: Bradford Books/MIT Press.

Bayat, M. (2007). Evidence of resilience in families of children with autism. *Journal of Intellectual Disability Research, 51,* 702–714.

Begley, A. (1999). The self-perceptions of pupils with Down syndrome in relation to their academic competence, physical competence and social acceptance. *International Journal of Disability, Development, and Education, 46,* 515–529.

Begun, A. L. (1989). Sibling relationships involving developmentally disabled people. *American Journal of Mental Retardation, 93,* 566–574.

Bellugi, U., Adolphs, R., Cassady, C., & Chiles, M. (1999). Towards the neural basis for hypersociability genetic syndrome. *NeuroReport, 10,* 1–5.

Blacher, J., & Baker, B. L. (2007). Positive impact of intellectual disability on families. *American Journal on Mental Retardation, 112,* 330–348.

Blacher, J., & McIntyre, L. L. (2005). Syndrome specificity and behavioural disorders in young adults with intellectual disability: Cultural differences in family impact. *Journal of Intellectual Disability Research, 50,* 184–198.

Blakemore, S-J., & Choudhury, S. (2006). Development of the adolescent brain: Implications for executive function and social cognition. *Journal of Child Psychology and Psychiatry, 47,* 296–312.

Block, P., Balcazar, F. E., & Keys, C. B. (2002). Race poverty and disability: Three strikes and you're out! Or are you? *Social Policy, 33,* 34–38.

Bottroff, V., Brown, R., Bullitis, E., Duffield, V., Grantley, J., Kyrkou, M., & Thornley, J. (2002). Some studies involving individuals with Down syndrome and their relevance to a quality of life model. In M. Cuskelly, A. Jobling, & S. Buckley (Eds.), *Down syndrome across the life span* (pp. 121–138). London: Whurr.

Bowerman, C. E., & Dobash, R. M. (1974). Structural variation in inter-sibling affect. *Journal of Marriage and the Family, 36,* 48–54.

Brandtstädter, J. (1998). Action perspectives on human development. In W. Damon (Series Ed.) & R. M. Lerner (Vol. Ed.), *Handbook of child psychology,* vol. 1: *Theoretical models of human development* (5th ed., pp. 807–863). New York: John Wiley & Sons.

Bristol, M. M. (1984). Family resources and successful adaptation to autistic children. In E.Schopler & G. B. Mesibov (Eds.), *Issues in autism,* vol. III: *The effects of autism on the family* (pp. 289–310). New York: Plenum Press.

Bristol, M. M., & Schopler, E. (1983). Stress and coping in families of autistic adolescents. In E. Schopler & G. B. Mesibov (Eds.), *Autism in adolescents and adults* (pp. 251–278). New York: Plenum Press.

Bronfenbrenner, U. (1979). *The ecology of human development.* Cambridge, MA: Harvard University Press.

Buhrmester, D., & Furman, W. (1990). Perceptions of sibling relationships during middle childhood and adolescence. *Child Development, 61,* 1387–1398.

Burton, S. L., & Parks, A. L. (1991). The self-esteem, locus of control, and career aspirations of college-aged siblings of individuals with disability. *Social Work Research, 18,* 178–185.

Carter, E., & McGoldrick, M. (1980). The family life cycle and family therapy: An overview. In E. A. Carter & M. McGoldrick (Eds.), *The family life cycle: A framework for family therapy* (pp. 3–20). New York: Gardner Press.

Chadwick, O., Kusel, Y., Cuddy, M., & Taylor, E. (2005). Psychiatric diagnoses and behaviour problems from childhood to early adolescence in young people with severe intellectual disabilities. *Psychological Medicine, 35,* 751–760.

Cleveland, D. W., & Miller, N. (1977). Attitudes and life commitments of older siblings of mentally retarded adults. *Mental Retardation, 15,* 38–41.

Collins, W. A., & Laursen, B. (2004). Parent-adolescent relationships and influences. In R. M. Lerner & L. Steinberg (Eds.), *Handbook of adolescent development* (pp. 331–361). Hoboken, NJ: John Wiley & Sons.

Committee on Children with Disabilities. (1996). Sexuality education of children and adolescents with developmental disabilities. *Pediatrics, 97,* 275–278.

Corter, C., Pepler, D., Stanhope, L., & Abramovitch, R. (1992). Home observations of mothers and sibling dyads comprised of Down's syndrome and nonhandicapped children. *Canadian Journal of Behavioural Science, 24,* 1–13.

Cross, W. E., Jr. (2001). Encountering nigrescence. In J. G. Ponterotto, J. M. Casas, L. A. Suzuki, & C. M. Alexander (Eds.), *Handbook of multicultural counseling* (2nd ed., pp. 30–44). Thousand Oaks, CA: Sage.

Cuskelly, M., & Gunn, P. (1993). Maternal reports of behavior of siblings of children with Down syndrome. *American Journal of Mental Retardation, 97,* 521–529.

Cuskelly, M., & Gunn, P. (2003). Sibling relationships of children with Down syndrome: Perspectives of mothers, fathers, and siblings. *American Journal of Mental Retardation, 108,* 234–244.

Dallas, E., Stevenson, J., & McGurk, H. (1993). Cerebral-palsied children's interactions with siblings—II. Interactional structure. *Journal of Child Psychology and Psychiatry, 34,* 649–671.

DaVanzo, J,, & Goldscheider, F. (1990). Coming home again: Returns to the nest in young adulthood. *Population Studies, 44,* 241–255.

Davies, C. A., & Jenkins, R. (1997). 'She has different fits to me': How people with learning difficulties see themselves. *Disability and Society, 12,* 95–105.

Davies, M., Udwin, O., & Howlin, P. (1998). Adults with Williams syndrome. *British Journal of Psychiatry, 172,* 273–276.

DeMyer, M. K., & Goldberg, P. (1983). Family needs of the autistic adolescent. In E. Schopler & G. B. Mesibov (Eds.), *Autism in adolescents and adults* (pp. 225–250). New York: Plenum Press.

de Ruiter, K. P., Dekker, M. C., Verhulst, F. C., & Koot, H. M. (2007). Developmental course of psychopathology in youths with and without intellectual disabilities. *Journal of Child Psychology and Psychiatry, 48,* 498–507.

Developmental Disabilities Assistance and Bill of Rights Act Amendments of 2000, 42 U.S.C.S. § 12101 *et seq.* (Matthew Bender, 2007).

Dixon, R. M., & Reddacliff, C. A. (2001). Family contribution to the vocational lives of vocationally competent young adults with intellectual disabilities. *International Journal of Disability, Development and Education, 48,* 193–206.

Dunsford, C. (2007). *Spelling love with an X: A mother, a son, and the gene that binds them.* Boston: Beacon Press.

Dunn, J. (2002). Sibling relationships. In C. H. Hart (Ed.), *Blackwell handbook of childhood social development* (pp. 223–237). Malden, MA: Blackwell.

Duvall, E. (1957). *Family development.* Philadelphia: J. B. Lippincott.

Dykens, E. M. (2005). Happiness, well-being, and character strengths: Outcomes for families and siblings of persons with mental retardation. *American Journal on Mental Retardation, 43,* 360–364.

Dykens, E. M. (2006). Toward a positive psychology of mental retardation. *American Journal of Orthopsychiatry, 76,* 185–193.

Education of All Handicapped Children Act of 1975, Pub. L. No. 94–142, 89 Stat. 773.

Einfeld, S. L., & Tonge, B. J. (1996). Population prevalence of psychopathology in children and adolescents with intellectual disability. II: Epidemiological findings. *Journal of Intellectual Disability Research, 40,* 99–109.

Eisenberg, L., Baker, B. L., & Blacher, J. (1998). Siblings of children with mental retardation living at home or in residential placement. *Journal of Child Psychology and Psychiatry and Allied Disciplines, 39,* 355–363.

Eisenhower, A., & Blacher, J. (2006). Mothers of young adults with intellectual disability: Multiple roles, ethnicity, and well-being. *Journal of Intellectual Disability Research, 50,* 905–916.

Emerson, E. (2003). Mothers of children and adolescents with intellectual disabilities: Social and economic situation, mental health status and self-assessed social and psychological impact of child's difficulties. *Journal of Intellectual Disability Research, 47,* 385–399.

Emerson, E., Robertson, J., & Wood, J. (2005). Emotional and behavioural needs of children and adolescents with intellectual disabilities in an urban conurbation. *Journal of Intellectual Disability Research, 49,* 16–24.

Erikson, E. H. (1950). *Childhood and society.* New York: W. W. Norton.

Fidler, D. J., Hepburn, S. L., Most, D. E., Philofsky, A., & Rogers, S. (2007). Emotional responsivity in young children with Williams syndrome. *American Journal on Mental Retardation, 112,* 194–206.

Fisman, S., Wolf, L., Ellison, D., & Freeman, T. (2000). A longitudinal study of siblings of children with chronic disabilities. *Canadian Journal of Psychiatry, 45,* 369–375.

Flaton, R. A. (2006). "Who would I be without Danny?" Phenomenological case study of an adult sibling. *Mental Retardation, 44,* 135–144.

Fombonne, E. (2005). The changing epidemiology of autism. *Journal of Applied Research in Intellectual Disabilities, 18,* 281–294.

Foucault, M. (1994). Technologies of the self. In P. Rabinow (Ed.), *Michael Foucault ethics: Subjectivity and truth,* vol. 1 (pp. 223–251). New York: New Press.

Fujiura, G. T., & Braddock, D. (1992). Fiscal and demographic trends in mental retardation services: The emergence of the family. In L. Rowitz (Ed.), *Mental retardation in the year 2000* (pp. 316–338). New York: Springer-Verlag.

Furman, W., & Buhrmester, D. (1985). Children's perceptions of the qualities of sibling relationship. *Child Development, 56,* 448–461.

Gardiner, K. (2006). Transcriptional dysregulation in Down syndrome: Predictions for altered protein complex stoichiometries and post-translational modifications, and consequences for learning/behavior genes ELK, CREB, and the estrogen glucocorticoid receptors. *Behavior Genetics, 36,* 439–453.

Gath, A. (1973). The school age siblings of mongol children. *British Journal of Psychiatry, 123,* 161–167.

Glasson, E. J., Sullivan, S. G., Hussain, R., Petterson, B. A., Montgomery, P. D., & Bittles, A. H. (2002). The changing survival profile of people with Down's syndrome: Implications for genetic counseling. *Clinical Genetics, 62,* 390–393.

Glenn, S., & Cunningham, C. (2001). Evaluation of self by young people with Down syndrome. *International Journal of Disability, Development, and Education, 48,* 163–177.

Glidden, L. M., & Zetlin, A. G. (1992). Adolescence and community adjustment. In L. Rowitz (Ed.), *Mental retardation in the year 2000* (pp. 101–114). New York: Springer-Verlag.

Gordon, P. A., Tschopp, M. K., & Feldman, D. (2004). Addressing issues of sexuality with adolescents with disabilities. *Child and Adolescent Social Work Journal, 21,* 513–527.

Grant, G., Ramcharan, P., & Flynn, M. (2007). Resilience in families with children and adult members with intellectual disabilities: Tracing elements of a psycho-social model. *Journal of Applied Research in Intellectual Disabilities, 20,* 563–575.

Greenberg, J. S., Seltzer, M. M., Hong, J., & Orsmond, G. I. (2006). Bidirectional effects of expressed emotion and behavior problems and symptoms in adolescents and adults with autism. *American Journal of Mental Retardation, 111,* 229–249.

Grossman, F. K. (1972). *Brothers and sisters of retarded children: An exploratory study.* Syracuse, NY: Syracuse University Press.

Hannah, M. E., & Midlarsky, E. (2005). Helping by siblings of children with mental retardation. *American Journal on Mental Retardation, 110,* 87–99.

Harris, S. L., Glasberg, B., & Delmolino, L. (1998). Families and the developmentally disabled adolescent. In U. B.VanHassert & M. Hereson (Eds.), *Handbook of psychological treatment problems for children and adolescents* (pp. 519–548). Mahwah, NJ: Lawrence Erlbaum.

Harry, B. (2002). Trends and issues in serving culturally diverse families of children with disabilities. *The Journal of Special Education, 36,* 132–140.

Harter, S. (1986). Developmental processes in the construction of self. In T. D. Yawkey & J. E. Johnson (Eds.), *Integrative processes and socialization: Early to middle childhood* (pp. 45–78). Hillsdale, NJ: Lawrence Erlbaum.

Hartup, W. W. (1993). Adolescents and their friends. In B. Laursen (Ed.), *Close friendships in adolescence* (pp. 3–22). San Francisco: Jossey-Bass.

Hastings, R. P., Beck, A., & Hill, C. (2005). Positive contributions made by children with an intellectual disability in the family. *Journal of Intellectual Disabilities, 9,* 155–165.

Hauser-Cram, P., & Krauss, M. W. (2004). Adolescents with developmental disabilities and their families. In R. M. Lerner & L. Steinberg (Eds.), *Handbook of adolescent development* (pp. 697–719). Hoboken, NJ: John Wiley & Sons.

Hauser-Cram, P., Warfield, M.E., Shonkoff, J. S., & Krauss, M. W., with Sayer, A., & Upshur, C. C. (2001). Children with disabilities: A longitudinal study of child development and parent well-being. *Monographs of the Society for Research in Child Development, 66* (3, Serial No. 266).

Heiman, T. (2000). Quality and quantity of friendship. *School Psychology International, 21,* 265–281.

Heller, T., Hsieh, K., & Rowitz, L. (1997). Maternal and paternal caregiving of persons with mental retardation across the lifespan. *Family Relations, 46,* 407–415.

Helff, C. M., & Glidden, L. M. (1998). More positive or less negative? Trends in research on adjustment of families rearing children with developmental disabilities. *Mental Retardation, 36,* 457–464.

Helms, J. E. (1995). An update of Helms's white and people of color racial identity models. In J. G. Ponterotto, J. M. Casas, L. A. Suzuki & C. M. Alexander (Eds.), *Handbook of multicultural counseling* (pp. 181–198). Thousand Oaks, CA: Sage.

Hodapp, R. M., Kazemi, E., Rosner, B. A., & Dykens, E. M. (2006). Mental retardation. In D. A. Wolfe & E. J. Mash (Eds.), *Behavioral and emotional disorders in adolescents* (pp. 383–409).New York: Guilford Press.

Hodapp, R. M., Ly, T. M., Fidler, D. J., & Ricci, L. A. (2001). Less stress, more rewarding: Parenting children with Down syndrome. *Parenting: Science and Practice, 3,* 317–337.

Holmbeck, G. N. (2002). A developmental perspective on adolescent health and illness: An introduction to the special issues. *Journal of Pediatric Psychology, 27,* 409–415.

Howlin, P. (2000). Outcome in adult life for more able individuals with autism or Asperger syndrome. *Autism, 4,* 63–83.

Individuals with Disabilities Education Act of 1990, 20 USC § 1400 *et seq.* (Matthew Bender, 2007).

Individuals with Disabilities Education Act Amendments of 1997, Pub. L. No. 105–17, 111 Stat. 37.

Individuals with Disabilities Education Improvement Act of 2004, Pub. L. No. 108–446, 118 Stat. 2647, H.R. 1350.

Inlow, J. K., & Restifo, L. L. (2004). Molecular and comparative genetics of mental retardation, *Genetics, 166,* 835–881.

Jenkinson, J. C. (1999). Factors affecting decision-making by young adults with intellectual disabilities. *American Journal on Mental Retardation, 104,* 320–329.

Kaminsky, L., & Dewey, D. (2001). Sibling relationships of children with autism. *Journal of Autism and Developmental Disorders, 31,* 399–410.

Kaufman, S. Z. (1999). *Retarded isn't stupid, mom.* Baltimore, MD: Paul H. Brookes.

Keating, D. P. (2004). Cognitive and brain development. In R. M. Lerner & L. Steinberg (Eds.), *Handbook of adolescent development* (pp. 45–84). Hoboken, NJ: John Wiley & Sons.

Keogh, B. K., Garnier, H. E., Bernheimer, L. P., & Gallimore, R. (2000). Models of child–family interaction for children with developmental delays: Child-driven or transactional? *American Journal on Mental Retardation, 105,* 32–46.

Kersh, J. (2007). Understanding the relationship between siblings when one child has developmental disability (doctoral dissertation, Boston College, 2007). *Dissertation Abstracts International, 68,* 3425.

Kersh, J., Hedvat, T. T., Hauser-Cram, P., & Warfield, M. E. (2006). The contribution of marital quality to the well-being of parents of children with developmental disabilities. *Journal of Intellectual Disability Research, 50,* 883–893.

Kim, H., Greenberg, J. S., Seltzer, M. M., & Krauss, M. W. (2003). The role of coping in maintaining the psychological well-being of mothers of adults with mental retardation and mental illness. *Journal of Intellectual Disability Research, 47,* 313–327.

Kraemer, B. R., & Blacher, J. (2001). Transition for young adults with severe mental retardation: School preparation, parent expectations, and family involvement. *Mental Retardation, 39,* 423–435.

Krauss, M. W., & Seltzer, M. M. (1994). Taking stock: Expected gains from a life-span developmental perspective on mental retardation. In M. M. Seltzer, M. W. Krauss, & M. Janicki (Eds.), *Life course perspectives on adulthood and old age* (pp. 213–220). Washington, DC: American Association on Mental Retardation.

Krauss, M. W., & Seltzer, M.M. (2001). Having a sibling with mental retardation. In J. V. Lerner, R. M. Lerner, & J. Finkelstein (Eds.), *Adolescence in America: An encyclopedia* (pp. 436–440). Santa Barbara, CA: ABC-CLIO.

Krauss, M. W., Seltzer, M. M., Gordon, R., & Friedman, D. H. (1996). Binding ties: The roles of adult siblings of persons with mental retardation. *Mental Retardation, 34,* 83–93.

Kunnen, E. S., & Bosma, H. A. (2000). Development of meaning making: A dynamic systems approach. *New Ideas in Psychology, 18,* 57–82.

Larson, E. (1998). Reframing the meaning of disability to families: The embrace of paradox. *Social Science and Medicine, 47,* 865–875.

Ledlie, S. W. (2007). Methods of assessing health care needs. In C. L. Betz & W. M. Nehring (Eds.), *Promoting health care transitions for adolescents with special health care needs and disabilities* (pp. 119–135). Baltimore: Brookes.

Leffert, J. S., & Siperstein, G. N. (2002). Social cognition: A key to understanding adaptive behavior in individuals with mild mental retardation. *International Review of Research in Mental Retardation, 25,* 135–181.

Lerner, R. M. (2002). *Concepts and theories of human development* (3rd ed.). Mahwah, NJ: Lawrence Erlbaum.

Lerner, R. M. (2005). Promoting positive youth development: Theoretical and empirical bases. *National Research Council/ Institute of Medicine.* Washington, DC: National Academies of Science.

Lotstein, D. D., McPherson, M., Stickland, B., & Newacheck, P. W. (2005). Transition planning for youth with special health care needs: Results from the National Survey of Children with Special Health Care Needs. *Pediatrics, 115,* 1562–1568.

Lounds, J., Seltzer, M. M., Greenberg, J. S., & Shattuck, P. T. (2007). Transition and change in adolescents and young adults with autism: Longitudinal effects on maternal well-being. *American Journal on Mental Retardation, 112,* 401–417.

Magana, S., & Smith, M. J. (2006). Psychological distress and well-being of Latina and non-Latina white mothers of youth

and adults with an autism spectrum disorder: Cultural attitudes towards coresidence status. *American Journal of Orthopsychiatry, 76,* 346–357.

Mantry, D., Cooper, S.-A, Smiley, E., Morrison, J., Allan, L., Williamson, A., et al. (2007). The prevalence and incidence of mental ill-health in adults with Down syndrome. *Journal of Intellectual Disability Research, 52,* 1–16.

Matheson, C., Olsen, R. J., & Weisner, T. (2007). A good friend is hard to find: Friendship among adolescents with disabilities. *American Journal on Mental Retardation, 112,* 319–329.

McGrew, K. S., Johnson, D. R., & Bruininks, R. H. (1994). Factor analysis of community adjustment outcome measures for young adults with mild to severe disabilities. *Journal of Psychoeducational Assessment, 12,* 55–66.

McHale, S. M., & Gamble, W. C. (1987). Sibling relationships and adjustment of children with disabled brothers and sisters. *Journal of Children in Contemporary Society, 19,* 131–158.

McHale, S. M., & Gamble, W. C. (1989). Sibling relationships of children with disabled and nondisabled brothers and sisters. *Developmental Psychology, 25,* 421–429.

McHale, S. M., Sloan, J., & Simeonson, R. J. (1986). Sibling relationships of children with autistic, mentally retarded, and nonhandicapped brothers and sisters. *Journal of Autism and Developmental Disorders, 16,* 399–413.

McHugh, M. (1999). *Special siblings: Growing up with someone with a disability.* New York: Hyperion.

McNair, J., & Rusch, F. R. (1991). Parent involvement in transition programs. *Mental Retardation, 29,* 93–101.

Merrell, S. S. (1995). *The accidental bond: The power of sibling relationships.* New York: Times Books.

Mincham, P. E., Appleton, P. L., Lawson, V., Boll, V., Jones, P., & Elliott, C. E. (1995). Impact of functional severity on self concept in young people with spina bifida. *Archives of Disease in Childhood, 73,* 48–52.

Mink, I., Nihira, C., & Meyers, C. (1983). Taxonomy of family life styles: I. Homes with TMR children. *American Journal of Mental Deficiency, 87,* 484–497.

Minuchin, P. (2002). Looking toward the horizon: Present and future in the study of family systems. In J. P. McHale & W. S. Grolnick (Eds.), *Retrospect and prospect in the psychological study of families* (pp. 259–278). Mahwah, NJ: Lawrence Erlbaum.

Mitchell, D. B., & Hauser-Cram, P. (2008). The well-being of mothers of adolescents with developmental disabilities in relation to medical care utilization and satisfaction with health care. *Research in Developmental Disabilities, 29,* 97–112.

Moore, K. A., Guzman, L., Hair, E., Lippman, L., & Garrett, S. (2004). Parent–teen relationships and interactions: Far more positive than not. *Child Trends Research Briefs,* Publication # 2004–25. Washington, DC: Child Trends.

Mpofu, E., & Harley, D. A. (2006). Racial and disability identity: Implications for career counseling of African Americans with disabilities. *Rehabilitation Counseling Bulletin, 50,* 14–23.

Nadworny, J. W., & Haddad, C. R. (2007). *The special needs planning guide: How to prepare for every stage of your child's life.* Baltimore: Paul H. Brookes.

National Center on Secondary Education and Transition (2004). *Current challenges facing the future of secondary education and transition services for youth with disabilities in the United States.* Retrieved January 10, 2008, from www.ncset.org/publications/discussionpaper/.

National Longitudinal Transition Study 2 (2007a). NLTS2 Wave 2 Student School Program Survey: Transition support table 183: Post-high school primary goal for youth with transition plan. Retrieved December 20, 2007, from www.nlts2.org/data_tables/tables/9/npr2E4.html.

National Longitudinal Transition Study 2 (2007b). NLTS2 Wave 2 Student School Program Survey: Transition support table 185: Youth with transition plan: Progress toward goals for leaving secondary school. Retrieved December 20, 2007, from www.nlts2.org/data_tables/tables/9/npr2E4.html.

No Child Left Behind Act of 2001, Pub. L. No.107–110, 115 Stat. 1425.

Olney, M. F., & Kim, A. (2001). Beyond adjustment: Integration of cognitive disability into identity. *Disability & Society, 16,* 563–583.

Olshansky, S. (1962). Chronic sorrow: A response to having a mentally defective child. *Social Casework, 43,* 190–193.

Olson, D. H. McCubbin, H. I., Barnes, H., Larsen, A., Muxen, M., & Wilson, M. (1984). *One thousand families: A national survey.* Beverly Hills, CA: Sage.

Olson, D. H., Russell, C. S., & Sprenkle, D. H. (1983). Circumplex model VI: Theoretical update. *Family Process, 22,* 69–83.

Orsmond, G. I., Krauss, M. W., & Seltzer, M. M. (2004). Peer relationships and social and recreational activities among adolescents and adults with autism. *Journal of Autism and Developmental Disabilities, 34,* 245–256.

Orsmond, G. I., & Seltzer, M. M. (2000). Brothers and sisters of adults with mental retardation: Gendered nature of the sibling relationship. *American Journal on Mentaly Retardation, 105,* 486–508.

Orsmond, G. I., Seltzer, M. M., Greenberg, J. S., & Krauss, M. W. (2003). Mother–child relationship quality among adolescents and adults with autism. *American Journal on Mental Retardation, 111,* 121–137.

Parish, S. L. (2003). Federal income payments and mental retardation: The political and economic context. *Mental Retardation, 41,* 446–459.

Parish, S. L. (2006). Juggling and struggling: A preliminary work-life study of mothers of adolescents who have developmental disabilities. *Mental Retardation, 44,* 393–404.

Park, C. C. (2001). *Exiting Nirvana.* Boston: Little, Brown & Co.

Pit-ten Cate, I. M., & Loots, G. M. P. (2000). Experiences of siblings of children with physical disabilities: An empirical investigation. *Disability and Rehabilitation, 22,* 399–408.

Powers, L. E., Garner, T., Valnes, B., Squire, P., Turner, A., Couture, T., et al. (2007). Building a successful adult life: Findings from youth-directed research. *Exceptionality, 15,* 45–56.

Reeve, D. (2002). Negotiating psycho-emotional dimensions of disability and their influence on identity constructions. *Disability & Society, 17,* 493–508.

Rehabilitation Act of 1973, Pub. L. No. 93–112, 87 Stat. 355.

Reiss, J., Gibson, R., & Walker, L. (2005). Health care transition: Youth family and providers perspectives. *Pediatrics, 115,* 112–120.

Restivo, L., Ferrari, F., Passino, E., Sgobio, C., Bock, J., Oostra, B. A., et al. (2005). Enriched environment promotes behavioral and morphological recovery in a mouse model for the fragile X syndrome. *Proceedings of the National Academy of Sciences, 102,* 11557–11562.

Rimmer, J. H., Rowland, J. L., & Yamaki, K. (2007). Obesity and secondary conditions in adolescents with disabilities: Addressing the needs of an underserved population. *Journal of Adolescent Health, 41,* 224–229.

Rivers, J. W., & Stoneman, Z. (2003). Sibling relationships when a child has autism: Marital stress and support coping. *Journal of Autism and Developmental Disorders, 33,* 383–394.

Roberts, R. E., Attkisson, C. C., & Rosenblatt, A. (1998). Prevalence of psychopathology among children and adolescents. *American Journal of Psychiatry, 155,* 715–725.

Rodgers, R. (1960, August). *Proposed modifications of Duvall's family life cycle stages.* Paper presented at the American Sociological Association Meeting, New York.

Roeyers, H., & Mycke, K. (1995). Siblings of a child with autism, with mental retardation and with normal development. *Child: Care, Health and Development, 21,* 305–319.

Rossiter, L., & Sharpe, D. (2001). The siblings of individuals with mental retardation: A quantitative integration of the literature. *Journal of Child and Family Studies, 10,* 65–84.

Rutter, M. (1990). Changing patterns of psychiatric disorders during adolescence. In J. Bancroft & J. M. Reinisch. (Eds.), *Adolescence and puberty* (pp. 124–145). Oxford: Oxford University Press.

Sajith, S. G., & Clarke, D. (2007). Melatonin and sleep disorders associated with intellectual disability: A clinical review. *Journal of Intellectual Disability Research, 51,* 2–13.

Sameroff, A. J., & Fiese, B. H. (2000). Transactional regulation: The developmental ecology of early intervention. In J. P. Shonkoff & S. J. Meisels (Eds.), *Handbook of early childhood intervention* (2nd ed., pp. 135–159). New York: Cambridge University Press.

Scai, P., & Ireland, M. (2005). Addressing transition to adult health care for adolescents with special health care needs. *Pediatrics, 115,* 1607–1612.

Schneider, J., Wedgewoord, N., Llewellyn, G. & McConnell, D. (2006). Families challenged by and accommodating to the adolescent years. *Journal of Intellectual Disability Research, 50,* 926–936.

Scorgie, K., & Sobsey, D. (2000). Transformational outcomes associated with parenting children who have disabilities. *Mental Retardation, 38,* 195–206.

Scuccimarra, D. J., & Speece, D. L. (1990). Employment outcomes and social integration of students with mild handicaps: The quality of life two years after high school. *Journal of Learning Disabilities, 23,* 213–219.

Seligman, M. E. P. (2000). Positive psychology: An introduction. *American Psychologist, 55,* 5–14.

Selman, R. L. (1980). *The growth of interpersonal understanding.* New York: Academic Press.

Seltzer, M. M., Greenberg, J. S., Floyd, R. J., Pettee, Y., & Hong, J. (2001). Life course impacts of parenting a child with a disability. *American Journal on Mental Retardation, 106,* 282–303.

Seltzer, M. M., & Heller, T. (1997). Families and caregiving across the life course: Research advances on the influence of context. *Family Relations, 46,* 321–323.

Seltzer, M. M., & Krauss, M. W. (1984). Placement alternatives for mentally retarded children and their families. In J. Blacher (Ed.), *Severely handicapped children and their families: Research in review.* New York: Academic Press.

Seltzer, M. M., Krauss, M. W., Choi, S. C., & Hong, J. (1996). Midlife and later life parenting of adult children with mental retardation. In C. D. Ryff & M. M. Seltzer (Eds.), *The parental experience at midlife.* Chicago: University of Chicago Press.

Seltzer, M. M., Krauss, M. W., Orsmond, G. I., & Vestal, C. (2001). Families of adolescents and adults with autism: Uncharted territory. In L. M. Glidden (Ed.), *International review of research on mental retardation,* vol. 23 (pp. 267–294). San Diego: Academic Press.

Shattuck, P. T., & Grosse, S. D. (2007). Issues related to the diagnosis and treatment of autism spectrum disorder. *Mental Retardation and Developmental Disabilities Research Reviews, 13,* 129–135.

Shattuck, P. T., Seltzer, M. M., Greenberg, J. S., Orsmond, G. I, Bolt, D., Kring, S., Lounds, J., & Lord, C. (2007). Change in autism symptoms and maladaptive behaviors in adolescents and adults with an autism spectrum disorder. *Journal of Autism and Developmental Disorders, 37,* 1735–1747.

Shields, N., Murdoch, A., Loy, Y., Dodd, K. J., & Taylor, N. F. (2006). A systematic review of the self-concept of children with cerebral palsy compared with children without disability. *Developmental Medicine and Child Neurology, 48,* 151–157.

Solnit, A., & Stark, M. (1961). Mourning and the birth of a defective child. *The Psychoanalytic Study of the Child, 16,* 523–537.

Spector, S. G., & Volkmar, F. R. (2006). Autism spectrum disorders. In D. A., Wolfe, & E. J. Mash, (Eds.), *Behavioral and emotional disorders in adolescents* (pp. 444–460). New York: Guilford Press.

Spencer, M. B. (2006). Phenomenology and ecological systems theory: Development of diverse groups. In W. Damon (Series Ed.) & R. M. Lerner (Vol. Ed.), *Handbook of child psychology,* vol. 1: *Theoretical models of human development* (6th ed., pp. 829–893). Hoboken, NJ: John Wiley & Sons.

Steinberg, L. (1990). Autonomy, conflict, and harmony in the family relationship. In S. S. Feldman & G. R. Elliott (Eds.),

At the threshold: The developing adolescent (pp. 255–276). Cambridge, MA: Harvard University Press.

Stoneman, Z., Brody, G. H., Davis, C. H., & Crapps, J. M. (1987a). Mentally retarded children and their older siblings: Naturalistic in-home observations. *American Journal on Mental Retardation, 92,* 290–298.

Stoneman, Z., Brody, G. H., Davis, C. H., & Crapps, J. M. (1987b). Mentally retarded children and their same-sex siblings: Naturalistic in-home observations. *American Journal on Mental Retardation, 92,* 290–298.

Stoneman, Z., Brody, G. H., Davis, C. H., Crapps, J. M., & Malone, D. M.(1991). Ascribed role relations between children with mental retardation and their younger siblings. *American Journal of Mental Retardation, 95,* 537–550.

Stromme, P., & Diseth, T. H. (2000). Prevalence of psychiatric diagnoses in children with mental retardation: Date from a population-based study. *Developmental Medicine and Child Neurology, 42,* 266–270.

Sturmey, P., Lindsay, W. R., & Didden, R. (2007). Special issue: Dual diagnosis. *Journal of Applied Research in Intellectual Disabilities, 20,* 379–383.

Tantam, D. (2000). Psychological disorder in adolescents and adults with Asperger syndrome. *Autism, 4,* 47–62.

Thorin, E. J., & Irvin, L. K. (1992). Family stress associated with transition to adulthood of young people with severe disabilities. *Journal of the Association for Persons with Severe Handicaps, 17,* 31–39.

Thorin, E., Yovanoff, P., & Irvin, L. (1996). Dilemmas faced by families during their young adults' transitions to adulthood: A brief report. *Mental Retardation, 34,* 117–120.

Timmons, J. C., Whitney-Thomas, J., McIntyre, J. P., Butterworth, J., & Allen, D. (2004). Managing service delivery systems and the role of parents during their children's transitions. *Journal of Rehabilitation, 70,* 19–26.

Todd, S., & Jones, S. (2005). The challenge of the middle years of parenting a child with IDs. *Journal of Intellectual Disability Research, 49,* 389–404.

Turnbull, A. P., Summers, J. A., & Brotherson, M. J. (1986). Family life cycle: Theoretical and empirical implications and future directions for families with mentally retarded members. In J. J. Gallagher & P. Vietze (Eds.), *Families of handicapped persons: Research, programs, and policy issues* (pp. 45–66). Baltimore: Paul H. Brookes.

Turnbull, H. R., Stowe, M. J., Agosta, J., Turnbull, A. P., Schrandt, M. S., & Muller, J. F. (2007). Federal family disability policy: Special relevance for developmental disabilities. *Mental Retardation and Developmental Disabilities Research Reviews, 13,* 114–120.

U.S. Department of Education. (2007a). Table 1–1. Children and students served under IDEA, Part B, by age group and state: Fall 2006. Retrieved January 8, 2008, from www.ideadata.org/PartBTrendDataFiles.asp.

U.S. Department of Education. (2007b). Table 4–2. Students with disabilities served under IDEA, Part B, in the U.S. and outlying areas who exited school, by exit reason and age: Fall 2005–2006. Retrieved January 8, 2008, from www.ideadata.org/PartBTrendDataFiles.asp.

U.S Department of Education. (2007c). Table B2A. Children served in the 50 states and DC (including BIA schools) under IDEA, Part B, Ages 6–21 by age group and disability, 1991 through 2005, numbers, percentage distributions, and prevalence rates.

Part B Trend Data Tables. Retrieved December 16, 2007, from www.ideadata.org/PartBTrendDataFiles.asp.

U.S. Department of Health and Human Services. (2006). Annual update of the HHS poverty guidelines. 71 Fed. Reg. 3846 (Jan. 24, 2006). Retrieved December 28, 2007, from http://aspe.hhs.gov/poverty/06fedreg.htm.

U.S. Social Security Administration. (2007). Social Security Annual Statistical Supplement 2006. Retrieved December, 28, 2007, from www.socialsecurity.gov/policy/docs/statcomps/supplement.

Van Riper, M. (2000). Family variables associated with well-being in siblings of children with Down syndrome. *Journal of Family Nursing, 6,* 267–286.

Wagner, M., Newman, L., Cameto, R., Levine, P., & Garza, N. (2006). An overview of findings from wave 2 of the National Longitudinal Transition Study-2 (NLST-2) (NCSER 2007–3006). Menlo Park, CA: SRI International.

Wakeman, S. Y., Browder, D. M., Meier, I., & McColl, A. (2007). The implications of No Child Left Behind for students with developmental disabilities. *Mental Retardation and Developmental Disabilities Research Reviews, 13,* 143–150.

Watson, M. W., Fischer, K. W., Andreas, J. B., & Smith, K. W. (2004). Pathways to aggression in children and adolescents. *Harvard Educational Review, 74,* 404–430.

Wehmeyer, M. L. (1996). Self-determination as an educational outcome: Why is it important to children, youth and adults with disabilities? In D. J. Sands & M. L. Wehmeyer (Eds.), *Self-determination across the life-span: Independence and choice for people with disabilities* (pp. 17–36). Baltimore: Paul H. Brookes.

Wehmeyer, M. L., & Garner, N. W. (2003). The impact of personal characteristics of people with intellectual and developmental disability on self-determination and autonomous functioning. *Journal of Applied Research in Intellectual Disabilities, 16,* 255–265.

Wehmeyer, M. L., & Schwartz, M. (1998). The relationship between self-determination and quality of life for adults with mental retardation. *Education and Training in Mental Retardation and Developmental Disabilities, 33,* 3–12.

Wikler, L. M. (1986). Family stress theory and research on families of children with mental retardation. In J. J. Gallagher & P. Vietze (Eds.), *Families of handicapped persons: Research, programs, and policy issues* (pp. 167–196). Baltimore: Paul H. Brookes, 571–573.

Wilgosh, L. (1993). Sexual abuse of children with disabilities: Intervention and treatment issues for parents. *Developmental Disabilities Bulletin, 21,* 1–11.

Wilson, C. J., McGillivray, J. A., & Zetlin, A. G. (1992). The relationship between attitude to disabled siblings and ratings of behavioural competency. *Journal of Intellectual Disability Research, 36,* 325–336.

Wishart, J. G. (2007). Socio-cognitive understanding: A strength or weakness in Down's syndrome? *Journal of Intellectual Disability Research, 51,* 996–1005.

Zetlin, A. G., & Murtaugh, M. (1988). Friendship patterns of mildly learning handicapped high school students. *American Journal on Mental Retardation, 92,* 447–457.

Zetlin, A. G., & Turner, J. L. (1985). Transition from adolescence to adulthood: Perspectives of mentally retarded individuals and their families. *American Journal of Mental Deficiency, 89,* 570–579.

CHAPTER 18

Adolescent and Young Adult Health

From Basic Health Status to Clinical Interventions

ELIZABETH M. OZER AND CHARLES E. IRWIN, JR.

The major support for this document was provided by two national policy centers funded by the Maternal and Child Health Bureau: The National Adolescent Health Information Center & The Public Policy Analysis and Education Center for Middle Childhood, Adolescent and Young Adult Health (U45MC00002 & U45MC00023). The Centers are located in the Division of Adolescent Medicine, Department of Pediatrics, and the Philip R. Lee Institute for Health Policy Studies, School of Medicine at the University of California–San Francisco (UCSF). Additional support was provided for the first author by the Young Adult and Family Center, Department of Psychiatry, UCSF.

INTRODUCTION

The second decade of life is a time for developing competencies, emerging independence, and beginning to assume responsibility for one's own health. It is also a time of special vulnerabilities, health concerns, and barriers to accessing healthcare (Ozer, Macdonald, & Irwin, 2002; Ozer, Park, Paul, Brindis, & Irwin, 2003). During this period, health habits and behaviors are established. These patterns affect not only the immediate health of adolescents/ young adults, but lay the foundation for health status throughout the lifetime.

The majority of youth successfully navigate the important transitions of the second decade of life, and most adolescents and young adults are healthy when assessed by traditional medical markers, such as the presence or absence of chronic disease, use of health care services and hospitalization (Irwin, Burg, & Cart, 2002; National Academies, 2009). Yet high rates of preventable morbidity and mortality keep some adolescents from achieving their potential of becoming productive, caring, and committed adults. Behaviors often initiated during adolescence, such as substance use and abuse, early sexual behavior, and risky driving, are responsible for the majority of deaths and disabling conditions through the fourth decade of life (Ozer et al, 2002; Park, Mulye, Adams, Brindis, & Irwin, 2006; Rivara, Park & Irwin, in press).

Among the *Healthy People 2010* Objectives, *21 critical objectives* have been identified as priority areas for prevention/intervention in adolescent/young adult health (Centers for Disease Control & Prevention [CDC], 2004; U.S. Department of Health and Human Services, 2000). These objectives span six areas, including mortality, unintentional injury, violence, substance abuse and mental health, reproductive health, and prevention of adult chronic disease. A 2007 midcourse review of the 21 objectives documented that there is much progress to be made in achieving the 2010 targets in most areas (Park, Brindis, Chang, & Irwin, 2008). However, it is also important to note that there has been encouraging news in the areas of reproductive health, tobacco use, and safer driving practices (Park et al., 2008).

In this chapter, we have chosen to define adolescence and young adulthood as encompassing 10–24 years of age. This fourteen-year period includes early adolescents who are moving from middle childhood into adolescence (10–13), middle and late adolescents (14–18), and young adults (19–24). Late adolescence has traditionally been defined as ages 17–21. A more recent concept in the development of late adolescence/young adulthood is the theory of emerging adulthood (Arnett, 2000; Arnett & Tanner, 2006). Emerging adulthood focuses on the years from about 18 to 25, recognizing those years as distinct from the preceding adolescent years as well as the adult years that follow. While not all data sources separate adolescence/young adulthood in this way, we attempt to provide a perspective on health that covers the broad age range.

To understand the health and well-being of adolescents and young adults, we provide a review of the changing demographics of this age group, an overview of the mortality and morbidity, data on risk-taking behaviors that are initiated during this time period, an overview of access to health care, and opportunities for clinical preventive services that may facilitate improving the health and well-being of adolescents and young adults.

HEALTH PROFILE OF ADOLESCENTS/YOUNG ADULTS IN THE UNITED STATES

To set the context for the health of contemporary American adolescents, a brief demographic picture is important (CDC, 2007). In 2006, 63 million adolescents and young adults (ages 10–24) accounted for 21% of the population. Fifty-five percent of this population was non-Hispanic white, 17% Hispanic, 14% Black, 4% Asian/Pacific Islander, and 1% American Indian/Alaskan Native.

Over the past decade, the racial/ethnic diversity of the adolescent population has changed dramatically, with the Hispanic population increasing by 92%, and the Black and White populations increasing by 25% and 3%, respectively. Currently, the Hispanic population represents the largest minority group among adolescents/young adults. By 2020, the Hispanic population will grow to make up 22% of the adolescent population.

Adolescents/young adults represent a disproportionate share of the U.S. population living in poverty (U.S. Bureau of the Census, 2007). The poverty rates for Blacks and Hispanics far exceed those for non-Hispanic Whites and Asians. With poverty having a strong affect on health status, Blacks and Hispanics have poorer health status. Eleven percent of adolescents/young adults are immigrants or foreign-born (U.S. Bureau of the Census, 2004). Most of the 10- to 24-year-old immigrants are of either Hispanic or Asian/Pacific Islander background.

Numerous sources of United States data continue to document unacceptably high levels of intentional and nonintentional injuries, mental health disorders, poor eating habits, physical inactivity, substance use and abuse, sexually transmitted infections (STIs), unintended pregnancies, and lack of utilization of health care services among adolescents and young adults (MacKay & Duran, 2007; National Academies, 2009). (See Table 18.1 for overview list of data sources.) These problems are most prevalent among economically and socially disadvantaged groups (Goodman, 1999; Knopf, Park, Brindis, Paul Mulye, & Irwin, 2007).

However, these data alone do not provide a comprehensive profile of the health and well-being of youth. The growing field of positive youth development has focused on developing personal, environmental, and social assets that enable successful transition from childhood, through adolescence, and into adulthood (Larson, 2000; Lerner, 2001; Pittman, 2003; Roth & Brooks-Gunn, 2003). There is an increasing recognition about the importance of protective factors that mitigate the likelihood of negative health and social outcomes (Bernat & Resnick, 2006; Resnick et al, 1997). Focusing on decreasing risky behavior and enhancing protective factors is likely to affect

TABLE 18.1   Data Sources for Monitoring Adolescent and Young Adult Health

Name of Data Source (Abbreviation) Sponsor Website	Data Source	Type of Data Collected	Sample and Age Grouping	Periodicity
Data Collected by the Centers for Disease Control and Prevention (CDC)				
HIV/AIDS Surveillance CDC, National Center for HIV, STD and TB Prevention, Division of HIV/AIDS Prevention www.cdc.gov/hiv/dhap .htm	Surveillance	HIV and AIDS Cases	AIDS cases reported to CDC by 50 states and DC; HIV cases reported by 38 states & DC Age groupings vary by report	Annually from 1982–1992, bi-annually since 1993, most recent 2004
National Health and Nutrition Examination Survey (NHANES) CDC, National Center for Health Statistics www. cdc.gov/nchs/nhanes.htm	Interview, physical examination, clinical measurements and tests	BMI, weight, waist circumference	National probability sample Age grouping 20–29	11 surveys since 1960, most recent in 2002
National Health Interview Survey (NHIS) CDC, National Center for Health Statistics www.cdc.gov/nchs/nhis .htm	Personal household interview	Access to health services, insurance, and health-related behaviors	Nationally representative sample of households Age grouping 18–24, 25–34	Annually since 1957
National Hospital Discharge Survey (NHDS) CDC, National Center for Health Statistics www.cdc.gov/nchs/about/ major/hdasd/ nhds.htm	Medical records	Rates of discharge, length of stay	National sample of short-stay hospitals Age groupings 20–24;	Annually since 1965, most recent 2001
National Survey of Family Growth (NSFG) CDC, National Center for Health Statistics www. cdc.gov/nchs/nsfg.htm	Personal interview	Factors affecting pregnancy and women's health	Nationally representative sample of women ages 15–44 Age groupings 20–24; 25–29	1973, 1976, 1988, 1995, 2002
National Vital Statistics System (NVSS) CDC, National Center for Health Statistics www.cdc.gov/nchs/nvss .htm	Birth and death certificates	Mortality and Natality	All births and deaths Age groupings 20–24; 25–29	Annually since 1950
Sexually Transmitted Disease Surveillance (STDS) CDC, National Center for HIV, STD and TB Prevention, Division of Sexually Transmitted Diseases www.cdc. gov/std/	Surveillance	Sexually transmitted diseases	STD surveillance systems operated by state and local STD control programs Age groupings 20–24; 25–29	Ongoing surveillance, annual publication

(Continued)

TABLE 18.1   *(continued)*

Name of Data Source (Abbreviation) Sponsor Website	Data Source	Type of Data Collected	Sample and Age Grouping	Periodicity
Behavior Risk Factor Surveillance System (BRFSS) CDC, Division of Adolescent and School Health, National Center for Chronic Disease Prevention and Health Promotion www.cdc.gov/brfss/index.htm	Telephone survey	Health status, immunization, risky behaviors	Nationally representative sample of adults, 18+ years old, Age groupings 18–24, 25–34	Initiated in early 1980s, annually Interactive database available
Youth Risk Behavior Surveillance System (YRBSS) CDC, Division of Adolescent and School Health, National Center for Chronic Disease Prevention and Health Promotion www.cdc.gov/healthyyouth/yrbs/index.htm	Surveys administered in high schools	Health status, risky behaviors	National sample of high school students, Grades 9–12	Every 2 years since 1991
Other Federally Sponsored Surveys				
Census Bureau United States Department of Commerce, U.S. Bureau of the Census www.census.gov/	Questionnaire administered in homes	Population	National estimates and projections of the population count, and demographic variables Age groupings 22–24; 25–29	Decennial Census, periodic annual population surveys
Monitoring the Future (MTF) National Institute on Drug Abuse, National Institutes of Health (conducted by Institute for Social Research at University of Michigan) www.monitoringthefuture.org/	Self-administered questionnaire in schools	Substance use	Nationally representative sample of students in grades 8–12, college students, and long. follow-up through 45; young adults ages 19–28	Annually since 1975, most recent 2005
National Center for Statistics & Analysis (NCSA) National Highway Traffic Safety Administration, U.S. Dept. of Transportation www-nrd.nhtsa.dot.gov/departments/nrd-30/ncsa/	Records from fatal motor vehicle crashes and work-related fatalities	Demographics of persons involved, circumstances surrounding the crash	Records collected in multiple data sources (including GES & FARS) Age groupings 21–24; 25–34	Annually since 1975, most recent 2004
National Survey on Drug Use & Health (NSDUH) Substance Abuse & Mental Health Administration, Office of Applied Statistics www.drugabusestatistics.samhsa.gov/	Personal household interview	Substance use, mental health	Nationally representative sample, ages 12 and older Age groupings 18–25	Annually since 1971, most recent 2004

(Continued)

TABLE 18.1 (Continued)

Name of Data Source (Abbreviation) Sponsor Website	Data Source	Type of Data Collected	Sample and Age Grouping	Periodicity
National Longitudinal Study of Adolescent Health (AddHealth) National Institute of Child Health and Human Development (conducted by the University of North Carolina, Chapel Hill) www.cpc.unc.edu/projects/addhealth/	Self-administered questionnaire in schools	Health-related behaviors with emphasis on social context	Nationally representative original sample of students in grades 7–12, 3rd wave = ages 18–28	Wave 1: 1994–1995 Wave 2: 1996 Wave 3: 2001, 2002
National Survey of Adolescent Males (NSAM) The National Institute of Child Health and Human Development, National Institutes of Health (conducted by Urban Institute) www.urban.org/Template .cfm?NavMenuID=9 5&template=/Search/ SearchDisplay	Household-based survey	Demographics, family and educational history, sexual behavior and knowledge, substance use	Longitudinal data collection in 3 waves: males ages 15–19, 16–21, and 21–27	1988, 1990–1991, 1995

Source: Adapted from Park, M. J., Paul Mulye, T., Adams, S. H., Brindis, C. D., & Irwin, C. E., Jr. (2006). The health status of young adults in the United States. *Journal of Adolescent Health, 39*(3), 305–317.

both problem and positive behavior, promoting better outcomes for youth (Catalano, Hawkins, Berglund, Pollard, & Arthur, 2002). Translating preventive research findings into community prevention service systems is an important step toward improving adolescent behavior and health (Hawkins et al., 2008).

Within the health community, these concepts have been relatively slow to be adopted. Few health practitioners have included a focus on strengths and protective factors within their clinical acumen; however, within the adolescent health field, the focus may be shifting (Duncan et al., 2007). The new *Bright Futures* guidelines encourages the adoption of the concepts of positive youth development through encouraging clinicians to include strength-based assessments in their annual well visits for adolescents (Hagan, Shaw, & Duncan, 2008; Ozer, 2007).

At this time, however, the majority of national data sets employ traditional mortality and morbidity indicators, as well as an emphasis on health risk behaviors (MacKay & Duran, 2007). Current data collection systems also provide information primarily on behavior and outcomes, rather than on the social determinants that are the focus of more systematic prevention strategies (Patton, 2008). As such, the following sections describe the current status of adolescent health according to these more traditional indicators.

Mortality

In the United States, 72% of all deaths among adolescents/young adults result from four preventable causes: motor vehicle crashes, other unintentional injuries, homicide, and suicide

(National Center for Injury Prevention and Control, 2008) (see Figure 18.1). Mortality rates for adolescents and young adults have decreased dramatically over the past 25 years (from 1980 to 2005), yet the age-specific differences are disconcerting. A greater than 300% increase in mortality from early (10–14 years) to late adolescence (15–19 years) reflects the violent etiology of most deaths as a consequence of increased access to motor vehicles and firearms, combined with the use of alcohol. This trend worsens in young adulthood, with young adults (20–24 years) having five times the mortality rate of younger adolescents.

Adolescent males are more likely than females to die from each leading cause of death, and this gender difference increases with age. The most striking difference between males and females is in homicide rates: older adolescent and young adult males are about six times as likely as females to die from homicide. Although homicide rates have decreased

since their peak levels in the early 1990s, black, non-Hispanic male adolescents still have the highest rates of mortality, primarily due to homicide (NCIPC, 2008).

Unintentional Injuries

Unintentional injuries account for the greatest number of adolescent and young adult deaths (about 45%). The majority of these unintentional deaths involve motor vehicle crashes, which are the leading cause of mortality among adolescents and young adults, accounting for about a third of all deaths among this age group. Other fatal unintentional injuries include poisoning, drowning, fires/burns, and falls. Non-Hispanic American Indian/Alaska Native youth have the highest motor vehicle crash mortality rate, followed by White, non-Hispanic youth (CDC, 2007; National Adolescent Health Information Center, 2006; NCIPC, 2006). The peak time for vehicular

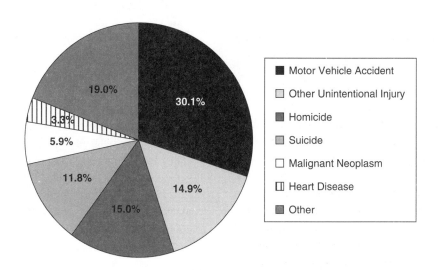

Source: National Center for Injury Prevention and Control (NCIPC). (2008). *Leading Causes of Death and Fatal Injuries Mortality Reports.* Atlanta, GA: Centers for Disease Control and Prevention. Retrieved on June 9, 2008, from www.cdc.gov/ncip/wisqars.

FIGURE 18.1   Leading Causes of Death, Ages 10–24, 2005

accidents among 15- to 19-year-olds occurs on weekends between 11 P.M. and 5 A.M. Factors such as inexperience leading to errors in judgment and poor decision making, fatigue, nonuse of seatbelts, alcohol use, high speed, inattention, and recklessness all contribute to motor vehicle accident mortality (NCIPC, 2006). Three in ten fatal vehicle crashes involve alcohol. Due to these factors, the implementation of graduated driver licensing (GDL) has become widely accepted in the United States over the past decade. Research has demonstrated that GDL reduces teenage driver crashes and fatalities. The GDL components of extended learner's permit holding periods, nighttime restrictions, and passenger restrictions have been found to be particularly effective in reducing accidents (Hedlund, 2007; National Research Council, Institute of Medicine and Transportation Research Board, 2007). Alcohol and other substances are also cofactors in injuries associated with bicycles, skateboards, boating, and swimming. While mortality rates for motor vehicle accidents among male adolescents have decreased significantly in the past decade, female high school students are still more likely to wear seat belts than same-age males; and male students are more likely than their female peers to drink and drive (CDC, 2008; Park et al., 2008).

Homicide

Homicide is the second leading cause of death in this age group, accounting for 14% of all deaths among adolescents and young adults in 2004. The homicide rate is 1 per 100,000 population for early adolescents (10–14 years), 9 per 100,000 for older adolescents (15–19 years), and 15 per 100,000 for young adults (20–24 years). Homicide is the leading cause of death for adolescent and young adult black males, accounting for 44.5% of all deaths among black, non-Hispanic males. Almost all of the deaths from homicide are related to guns (NCIPC, 2008).

Suicide

Suicide is the third leading cause of death in this age group, accounting for 13% of adolescent/young adult deaths. In 2005, the rate of suicide was seven times greater in late adolescence than early adolescence, and increased 10-fold between early adolescence and young adulthood. Adolescent/young adult males have a consistently higher suicide rate than females, averaging more than five times the rate of same-age females; and American Indian/Alaskan Native, non-Hispanics have the highest suicide rate. Firearms are the most common method of suicide for this age group. Over the past two decades, hanging and suffocation have become a more common method among all suicides and now it represents the most common method among females (CDC, 2007).

The most frequent nonviolent causes of mortality among adolescents and young adults, ages 10–24, are malignant neoplasms (5.9%) and heart disease (3.2%). Both of these have decreased over the past decade.

Morbidity/Health Status

As noted earlier, the majority of adolescents and young adults are healthy when assessed by traditional medical indicators such as disease, hospitalization, and out-patient health care utilization (National Academies, 2009). By both parent and adolescent/young adult self-report, most youth are in good or excellent health (Klein, Wilson, McNulty, Kapphahn, & Collins, 1999; McCraken, Jiles, & Blanck, 2007). In a recent analysis, 98% of adolescents and 96% of young adults considered themselves to be in good or excellent health (Policy Center, 2008).

However, some adolescents face multiple and complex challenges in managing their health. Adolescents with special health care needs are defined as "those who have or are at increased risk for a chronic, physical, developmental, behavioral, or emotional condition and who also require health and related services of a type or amount beyond that required by adolescents generally" (McPherson et al., 1998). Approximately 17% of adolescents have a special health care need (U.S. Department of Health and Human Services, 2008). These adolescents face an additional burden when they transition to young adulthood and have difficulty locating a usual source of health care and health insurance to pay for the services they require (Lotstein, Inkelas, Hays, Halfon, & Brook, 2008; Park & Irwin, 2008).

Chronic Illness

The most common causes of chronic illness in this age group include mental health disorders and diseases of the respiratory and musculoskeletal systems. Mental health disorders affect about 20% of adolescents, with about 10% experiencing significant impairment (Shaffer et al., 1996). The most common mental health disorders among adolescents include depression, anxiety disorders, attention-deficit/hyperactivity disorder, and substance use disorder. According to the World Health Organization, mental health disorders have a significant impact on functioning and well-being of all ages, including adolescents and young adults (National Academies, 2009; World Health Organization, 2004).

Most mental health problems begin in adolescence (Knopf, Park, & Mulye, 2008). Half of all lifetime mental health disorders start by age 14; and this number increases to three-fourths by age 24 (Kessler et al., 2005). About 20% of youth experience depression prior to turning 18 (DHHS, 1999), and 30% of teens report depressive symptoms at any given time (Rushton, Forcier, & Schectman, 2002). In the current Youth Risk Behavior Surveillance Survey (YRBSS), 28.5% of students reported that they felt sad or hopeless almost every day for 2 or more weeks in a row; and 14% reported that they had seriously considered attempting suicide during the 12 months before the survey (CDC, 2008).

Depression is a major risk factor for suicide, the third leading cause of death among adolescents (NCIPC, 2008). Using the concept of Disability Adjusted Life Year or DALY

(McKenna, Michaud, Murray, & Marks, 2005), which attempts to quantify the impact of an illness on a person's ability to fully function, depression accounts for the largest burden among individuals in the U.S. (WHO, 2004). Depression and depressive symptoms are also associated with unsafe health behaviors that are linked to morbidity and mortality among adolescents, such as substance use (Brown, Lewinsohn, Seeley, & Wagner, 1996; Kessler et al, 2002; Lewinsohn, Rohde, & Seeley, 1998), risky sexual behavior (Lehrer, Shrier, Gortmaker, & Buka, 2006), and fighting/weapon carrying (CDC, 2007).

There is a sharp increase in depression from childhood to adolescence (Kazdin, 1993), with reports of depression greater among adolescent girls than among boys (CDC, 2007; Kessler et al., 2005, 2007; Petersen et al., 1993; Schoen et al., 1997). Other psychological disorders that emerge or increase in prevalence during adolescence include anxiety disorders, schizophrenia, eating disorders, and substance use disorders (Kazdin, 1993).

These data suggest that mental health prevention and intervention efforts should target children and adolescents. Yet studies indicate that few youth experiencing emotional distress receive mental health evaluations or the mental health services that they need. Recent findings from studies utilizing national data sets indicate that only 10% of children and adolescents with symptoms of mental health problems received a specialty mental health evaluation or services (Kataoka, Zhang, & Wells, 2002); and that just 39% with significant mental health problems received mental health services (Howell, 2004).

Asthma is a major chronic illness in this age group, with about 16% of adolescents reported to have had asthma in their lifetime, and 10%–15% reported to have current asthma (Duncan, 2006). Diabetes is another common chronic illness that increases throughout adolescence (Institute of Medicine, 2005). The prevalence of both asthma and diabetes has increased in recent years. Additional causes of morbidity include skin problems associated with onset of puberty, reproductive health problems resulting from variants of normal physiological maturation and initiation of sexual activity, and orthopedic problems associated with skeletal growth and maturation.

Disordered Eating

The number of adolescents who are overweight and obese is of increasing concern (Ogden et al., 2006). The percentage of overweight adolescents has more than tripled over the past 25 years, with 17% of adolescents aged 12–19 considered overweight in 2004. Non-Hispanic Black girls have the highest prevalence of overweight at 25.4% (Ogden, Fryar, Carroll, & Flegal, 2004).

Over the past decade, numerous studies have documented the increase in number and type of calories being consumed and decrements in energy expenditure (Berkey, Rockett, Field, Gillman, & Colditz, 2004; Bowman, Gortmaker, Ebbeling, Pereira, & Ludwig, 2004; Ebbeling et al., 2004). Few adolescents engage in adequate physical activity—only 36% of high school students had levels of physical activity that were consistent with recommended levels (CDC, 2008). The health consequences of poor diet and physical inactivity among adolescents are immediate as well as long term. The immediate consequences are an increase in the number of adolescents with Type II diabetes mellitus. Other health outcomes for adolescents include metabolic syndrome, high cholesterol, and hypertension (Dietz, 1998; Liese et al., 2006). Longitudinal studies indicate that about 70% of overweight adolescents become overweight adults, with continuing health problems (Deshmukh-Taskar et al., 2006).

Disordered eating can cause both overweight/obesity and eating disorders, such as anorexia nervosa (AN) or bulimia nervosa (BN). AN, with a prevalence rate of 3% (Hoek & van Hoeken, 2003; Katzman, 2005), typically affects adolescent females during middle adolescence (ages 14–16). There are, however,

an increasing number of males being diagnosed with the condition. The features of AN are refusal to maintain a normal body weight, fear of gaining weight, and a disturbance in the perception of one's body (American Psychiatric Association [APA], 2005). Anorexia nervosa carries a very high mortality rate of 8% during the 10 years following the diagnosis (Keel et al., 2003). BN is an eating disorder affecting 2% of adolescent/young adults (Hoek & van Hoeken, 2003). The major features of BN are binge eating and inappropriate compensatory methods to prevent weight gain (e.g., purging and using laxatives) (APA, 2005). Bulimia nervosa generally has its onset at about 18 years of age and typically affects young women. There are increasing diagnoses of a category of eating disorders labeled Eating Disorders Not Otherwise Specified (EDNOS). These adolescents/young adults, who constitute the largest segment of eating disorders, do not meet all the *Diagnostic and Statistical Manual of Mental Disorders,* 4th edition (DSM-IV) criteria to be classified as either AN or BN but nonetheless evince clinically significant disordered eating. There are no good population-based estimates for the prevalence of this disorder.

HEALTH RISK BEHAVIOR

Risky health behaviors are important determinants of adolescent health status. The health behaviors established during adolescence have a major impact on the health and well-being of adolescents and young adults (CDC, 2008; Irwin et al., 2002; MacKay & Duran, 2007). It has been well established that adolescent engagement in risky behavior is embedded within a broader social context (National Academies, 2009; National Research Council, 1993; U.S. Congress, 1991).

More recently, there is evidence that changes in the brain during the second decade of life may also play a role in risky behavior. Giedd and others have hypothesized that the frontal lobe may play a role in inhibiting risky behavior (Giedd, 2008). Using magnetic resonance imaging to measure brain development from childhood through early adulthood, he has demonstrated that the prefrontal context is not fully developed until early adulthood. The definitive relationship between brain development and behavior during adolescence/young adulthood has yet to be confirmed, but the science of neuro-imaging provides further support for better understanding of the relationships between maturity and risky behavior (Steinberg, 2008).

Covariation Among Health Risk Behaviors

Risky health behaviors among adolescents co-vary or cluster in predictable ways (Jessor, 1999; Sales & Irwin, in press). The onset of one behavior may indicate that another behavior has a greater likelihood of being initiated. A considerable body of research has established links between adolescent substance use and other risky behaviors. The close association of alcohol and unintentional injury is well established (Elliott, 1993), with alcohol-related motor vehicle injuries the leading cause of death in late adolescence and early adulthood (Hingson, Heeren, Levenson, Jamanka, & Voss, 2002; Rivara, Garrison, Ebel, McCarty, Christakis, 2004). Alcohol and illicit drug use are also associated with engaging in fighting at school or at work (CDC, 2008; Hingson, Heeren, & Zakocs, 2001). Disordered eating is often associated with substance use and other mental health disorders (MacKay & Duran, 2007; CDC, 2008).

Substance use is related to early initiation of sexual activity, as well as sexual behaviors that place adolescents at increased risk for unintended pregnancy and sexually transmitted diseases (Davis, Hendershot, George, Norris, & Heiman, 2007; Goldstein, Barnett, Pedlow, & Murphy, 2007; Hingson, Heeren, Winter, & Wechsler, 2003; Lowry et al., 1994). The prevalence of sexual risk behaviors, such as multiple sex partners and not using condoms, is lowest among students who report no substance use, increases among students who use alcohol or cigarettes, and is greatest among

those students who use marijuana, cocaine, or other drugs. Within the area of substance use, there is a predictable developmental pattern (Kandel, 2002; see also the chapter by Chassin et al. in this *Handbook*). The use of alcohol and tobacco often occurs before the use of marijuana, and is followed by the use of other illicit substances, such as cocaine, psychedelics, heroin, and other nonprescribed stimulants, sedatives, and tranquilizers. The use of a substance farther along the trajectory generally implies ongoing use of the preceding substance, leading to a cumulative effect of all the substances (Grant et al, 2006; Kandel & Chen, 2000; Merrill, Kleber, Shwartz, Liu, & Lewis, 1999).

Although the passage to adolescence may involve engagement in risky behavior, to focus only on links among risky behaviors fails to explain factors that may reduce the likelihood of negative health and social outcomes (Bandura, 1997; Bernat & Resnick, 2007). For example, a sense of connectedness to family and school has been found to protect adolescents against multiple risky behaviors, including use of tobacco, alcohol and marijuana, and initiation of sexual activity (Resnick et al., 2007). Adolescents with the lowest risk profiles or clusters of risky behavior report high levels of protective factors in the areas of psychosocial adjustment, family, and school (Zweig, Phillips, & Lindberg, 2002).

Sexual Behavior

Sexual behavior during adolescence has decreased over the past 15 years, with fewer adolescents initiating sexual intercourse and more adolescents using effective contraception when they initiate (Ventura, Abma, Mosher, & Henshaw, 2006; see also the chapter in this volume by Diamond & Savin-Williams). The most recent 2007 survey on sexual behavior of youth between the ages of 15 and 19 shows that about half (48%) of high school students had experienced sexual intercourse at least once. The percentages are somewhat different by race and ethnicity: among Blacks,

61% for female and 75% for male teenagers; among Hispanics, 44% for female and 58% among male teenagers; and among Whites, 43% for female and 42% for male teenagers. Predictably, the higher the grade in school, the higher the percentage of students reporting sexual intercourse, with 9th graders at 20% and 12th graders at 53% (CDC, 2008). Among middle school students, rates of reported sexual intercourse are much lower, with 6% of girls and 8% of boys reporting having ever had intercourse (Abma, Martinez, Mosher, & Dawson, 2004). Of note is the significant increase between 8th and 9th grade, which should encourage increased prevention efforts focusing on the transition from middle to high school. Recently there has been an increasing interest in noncoital activities among adolescents. In an analysis of the National Survey of Family Growth, 54% of adolescent females and 55% of adolescent males reported that they had oral sex, and 1 in 10 reported anal sex. Both oral sex and anal sex were much more common in adolescents who had initiated vaginal sex as compared with virgins. Oral sex and vaginal intercourse tend to co-occur. Adolescents of White ethnicity and higher socioeconomic status were more likely than their peers to have ever had oral or anal sex (Lindberg, Jones, & Santelli, 2008). Data related to same-sex sexual activity are not included in the CDC's Youth Risk Behavior Survey, as many states opt out of these questions in their school-based surveys. There is national retrospective data, however, indicating that 5% of males and 11% of females age 15–19 report same-sex sexual contacts in their lifetime (Mosher, Chandra, & Jones, 2005).

Currently, about three-quarters of adolescents report using some form of contraception at first intercourse; and 62% report that either they or their partner used a condom at last intercourse (Abma et al, 2004). Trends are also positive related to adolescent pregnancy and childbearing. Between 1990 and 2000, pregnancy rates among 15- to 17-year-olds decreased 33%, the birth rate declined 42%

from 1991 to 2003, and abortion rates declined by more than half from the peak in 1987 to 2000 (Hamilton, Martin, & Ventura, 2007; Mosher et al., 2005).

An estimated 3 million adolescents are diagnosed with a sexually transmitted infection (STI) annually (Eng & Butler, 1997). Adolescents aged 15–19 years consistently demonstrate the highest age-specific rates of chlamydia and gonorrhea in the U.S., with sexually active African American adolescents having much higher rates than other ethnic/racial groups (CDC, 2006). Chlamydia rates among women aged 15–24 have increased over the past 5 years, while rates among 10- to 14-year-olds have decreased somewhat. This rate increase may not represent an actual increase in cases, but better case identification due to improved screening. AIDS cases among adolescents/young adults have increased since 1999, with a 7% increase among 13- to 19-year-olds and a 47% increase among 20- 24-year-olds. These data further reflect a need for ongoing preventive efforts in adolescents/young adults.

Substance Use

Tobacco Use

Although almost all tobacco-related deaths occur after 35 years of age, the majority of adults who are smokers began smoking during adolescence/young adulthood (Kandel & Chen, 2000; Mokdad, Marks, Stroup, & Gerberding, 2004). Since 1997 there has been a steady decline in the percentage of adolescents who regularly smoke tobacco, from 25% in 1997 to 12% in 2006. Among young adult smokers (19–28), after a decade of little change in daily smoking, there has been a decrease in smoking over the past 2 years, to a rate of 19% in 2006. Over 80% of adult smokers start smoking prior to 18 years, and it is rare to start smoking after age 25. Young adults (aged 18–25) have the highest prevalence of recent smoking (DHHS, 2007; Johnston, O'Malley, Bachman, & Schulenberg, 2008). New data suggests that nicotine addiction and symptoms of dependence begin soon after onset of smoking (Rubinstein, Thompson, Benowitz, Shiffman, & Moscicki, 2007). This lends further support to the need for preventive efforts during adolescence.

Alcohol Use

Patterns of drinking among adolescents have remained fairly stable in recent years (Johnston et al., 2008). Alcohol use is common during adolescence and peaks during young adulthood. Early onset of alcohol consumption increases the risk for later alcohol-dependence and the associated adverse effects from chronic heavy drinking. More than 40% of those who begin drinking at age 14 or younger develop alcohol dependence, compared with 10% of those who begin drinking at age 20 or older (Hingson, Heeren, & Winter, 2006). Alcohol use begins early in adolescence with 16% of 8th graders reporting that they had a drink in the previous month. By the time adolescents are in 12th grade, 44% report that they have had a drink in the previous month. More worrisome is the fact that 6% of 8th graders and 29% of 12th graders report that they have been drunk in the previous month. Binge drinking has dropped slightly for high school seniors over the past decade. Data focusing on young adults is less encouraging. According to the National Survey on Drug Use and Health, binge drinking has increased among 21- to 25-year-olds over the past 7 years. These data also highlight the fact that binge drinking peaks at 21 years old (Park et al, 2006; Rivara et al., in press).

Illicit Drugs

Over the past decade, illicit drug use has decreased among adolescents, although the rates remain unacceptably high. In 2007, 47% of high school seniors reported that they have used an illicit drug in their lifetime as compared to 19% of 8th graders. Marijuana use is reported by 42% of seniors in high school as compared with 14% of 8th graders. There continues to be concern about the use of prescription drugs and anabolic steroids, but these substances constitute a small percent of illicit drugs (Johnston et al., 2008).

Eating Behaviors and Physical Activity

As discussed in the earlier section on morbidity, there has been a dramatic increase in weight among adolescents and young adults. Data from the Youth Risk Behavior Surveillance Survey (YRBSS) continue to document an increase in risky behaviors among high school students associated with being overweight or obese: 35% of high school students report that they watched TV three or more hours a day, 77% report that they had not eaten fruits/vegetables five or more times a day, 34% had at least one serving of soda each day, and 65% had not met the recommended levels of physical activity (CDC, 2008). The health consequences of poor diet and physical inactivity among adolescents are immediate as well as long term. Longitudinal studies have documented that nearly all overweight adolescents become overweight adults (Deshmukh-Tashar et al., 2006).

There has also been concern among health care providers about the increasing number of adolescents and young adults with disordered eating, even though prevalence data for AN and BN do not reflect an increase in these disorders. Several studies report large numbers of adolescents and young adults with binge-eating or purging behaviors (Schneider, 2003; Zuckerman, Colby, & War, 1986). These trends have remained stable since the mid-1990s. Most recently, the YRBSS has documented behaviors associated with disordered eating among high school students—the only population-based data on disordered eating behaviors (CDC, 2008). In the 30 days before the survey, 5.9% had taken diet pills, powders, or liquids without a doctor's advice to lose weight or to keep from gaining weight; and 4.3% had vomited or taken laxatives to lose weight or keep from gaining weight.

ACCESS TO CARE AND HEALTH CARE UTILIZATION

Access to Care

The health concerns and health risk behavior among adolescents and young adults raise questions about access to health care and health care utilization. Adolescents/young adults require a range of preventive, diagnostic, and treatment services to respond to their diverse medical and psychosocial health needs. Close to one in five adolescents report incidences of forgone health care, in which they thought that they should seek medical care, but did not do so (Ford, Bearman, Peter, & Moody, 1999).

Assurance of confidentiality is an important factor in adolescents' willingness to seek medical care, disclose information to a provider, and return for subsequent visits (Cheng, Savageau, Sattler, & Dewitt, 1993; Ford, Millstein, Halpern-Felsher, & Irwin, 2002; National Academies, 2009; Society for Adolescent Medicine, 2004a). Adolescents are less likely to seek services in sensitive areas such as reproductive health, substance use, and mental health, if they have concerns about confidentiality (Ford & English, 2002; Klein et al., 1999; Reddy, Fleming, & Swain, 2002; Wissow, Fothergill, & Forman, 2002). Adolescents who are minors are authorized to give their own consent for health care in a variety of circumstances, including consultation about contraception and abortion. Some laws granting adolescent confidentiality have been strongly contested at the federal and state level, especially with regard to parental consent for abortion (English, 1999; English & Simmons, 1999; see also chapter 10, vol. 2 of this *Handbook*).

Other barriers to health care access for adolescents include transportation/inconvenient hours; the costs of copayments and deductibles; a fragmented, disconnected system; language/cultural barriers; and a shortage of providers trained in adolescent health (Brindis, VanLandeghem, Kirkpatrick, Macdonald, & Lee, 1999). Health insurance, however, is the primary determinant of whether adolescents will receive the health care services that they need.

Health Insurance

Insured adolescents have fewer unmet health needs and are more likely to have preventive health visits and a usual source of care than uninsured adolescents (Policy Center, 2008). Uninsured adolescents are almost three times more likely than their insured counterparts to use an emergency room or urgent care center as the usual setting to receive care (Newacheck et al., 1999).

As children grow older, they are less likely to have health insurance. Adolescents are among those with the lowest rates of insurance coverage, and this trend worsens after age 14 and into young adulthood (Adams, Newacheck, Park, Brindis, & Irwin, 2007). In 2005, 11% of adolescents aged 10–18 were not covered by any form of health insurance, whereas 31% of young adults aged 19–24 had no health insurance (NAHIC, 2008). Over 12.5 million adolescents and young adults or one in five were uninsured in 2007, accounting for 27% of the 47 million uninsured people in this country (Adams et al., 2007).

Lower-income and non-White adolescents are less likely to have health insurance and access to preventive care (Adams et al., 2007; Newacheck et al., 2003). Hispanic adolescents and young adults are the least likely to have health insurance: In 2006, only half of all Hispanic young adults were covered by health insurance (NAHIC, 2008). Ethnic differentials in health insurance coverage persist even after controlling for family income, employment, and family composition (Newacheck et al., 1999). This trend is disconcerting because Hispanic/Latino youth are rapidly increasing as a percentage of the adolescent population. Such projections portend that a greater number of young people will be uninsured and less likely to utilize primary care and preventive health care services.

In the past decade, there has been a substantial decline in private employer-based health insurance, while public insurance coverage has increased. Public insurance programs often have more generous eligibility requirements for young children than for adolescents, with coverage diminishing steadily after adolescence and into emerging adulthood (Newacheck,

1999; Adams et al., 2007). This is of concern because adolescence and young adulthood are key times for establishing positive, independent relationships with health care providers.

In 1997, the U.S. Congress took a major step to encourage the development and expansion of state-based health insurance programs for children and youth. The State Children's Health Insurance Program (CHIP) represented the first significant initiative to expand health insurance coverage for low-income adolescents since the creation of Medicaid in 1965 (Brindis et al., 1999). This allocation of funding is a large reason why the decrease in private insurance was offset by the increase in public insurance for the adolescent age group, and was an important step towards improving adolescents' access to care (Keane, Lave, Ricci, & LaVallee, 1999). There has been no similar program focused on young adults, however, which is especially troublesome, as trends suggest that the young adults who lose public health insurance do not regain health insurance later in adulthood (Adams et al., 2007).

Several states have passed laws to expand coverage of dependents up to age 24 or 25 under their parents' insurance policies. This policy change, in addition to two others—extending eligibility for public insurance programs beyond age 18 and insuring that colleges require and offer coverage to full and part time students—could help uninsured young adults gain coverage and prevent others from losing insurance (Kriss, Collins, Mahato, Gould, & Schoen, 2008).

Health Care Utilization

Because adolescents are generally healthy, the question arises as to when and where adolescents seek care. Second, when adolescents do use the health care system, are they utilizing the most appropriate health services?

Primary Care

Primary care includes office-based outpatient clinics, as well as community health clinics or hospital-affiliated primary care and, for a small percentage of teenagers, a school-based clinic. Most adolescents visit a primary care provider at least once per year. In 2005, 83% of adolescents aged 12–17 reported having visited a provider in the past year. Among young adults, aged 18–24, this percentage dropped to 67%. Hispanic adolescents and young adults were the least likely to have a provider visit (NAHIC, 2008).

Early adolescents are most likely to visit pediatricians, middle adolescents and late adolescent males are most likely to visit general and/or family physicians, and late adolescent females are most likely to visit obstetricians/gynecologists (Rand et al., 2007). Females have significantly more visits than males starting in middle adolescence (ages 15–17) and continuing through older adolescence (ages 18–21). This gender differential is the result of increased female visits for reproductive health issues such as pregnancy and sexually transmitted infections (Newacheck et al., 1999).

Despite the onset of depression and other emotional health problems during adolescence, many private and public health plans limit the mental health services eligible for reimbursement in primary care settings. For example, many plans do not cover counseling services that might extend care beyond the brief time allocated for a provider visit or the case management expenses associated with treating many behavioral problems (Fox, Limb, & McManus, 2007; Fox, McManus, & Reichman, 2003). Most health plans have "carve-outs," or separate insurance plans, for mental health treatment or substance abuse treatment. This can make it more difficult for adolescents and young adults to receive treatment or coordinated care (National Academies, 2009). Because most adolescents do not receive specialized mental health evaluations or services, these are missed opportunities in primary care.

Emergency Care

Adolescents rely heavily on emergency services for their primary care needs. In 2005, almost half of adolescents and young adults, aged 15–24, visited an emergency room. Over half of females (53%) and almost three-fourths of Blacks (74%) used emergency services (Nawar, Niska, & Xu, 2007). Across all age groups and both sexes, half of these visits were for nonurgent causes and few (3%–5%) resulted in hospitalization (Ziv, Boulet, & Slap, 1998).

Injury is the primary reason for an emergency room visit. After injury, the most common reasons for emergency services are for abdominal pain and for musculoskeletal and respiratory problems (Nawar et al, 2007). Among adolescent females over 15 years, pregnancy-related diagnoses account for a growing proportion of emergency department visits (Ziv, Boulet, & Slap, 1999). The low rate of hospitalization among adolescent emergency department patients and the similarity of the diagnoses with those seen in physician office visits suggest that many adolescents use emergency departments for their primary health care.

Inpatient Care

Adolescents and young adults have relatively low rates of hospitalization. In 2004, normal childbirth was the leading cause of hospitalization for adolescents and young adults aged 12–24. Mental disorders were the second leading cause, followed by injuries (Medical Expenditure Panel, 2007).

In summary, the majority of adolescents receive care from a provider at least once a year. Most of these visits take place in outpatient offices, although a significant number of adolescents appear to use emergency rooms for their primary care. Utilization trends suggest that adolescents and their families need further education about how to appropriately access the health care system. Gender and racial disparity in use of outpatient care suggests the need for focused outreach.

TRENDS IN THE PROVISION OF ADOLESCENT HEALTH SERVICES

The ability of an adolescent to access the health care system is the first step toward receiving effective health care. Because most adolescents visit a physician each year, there is an opportunity to integrate prevention into clinical encounters. The content and quality of the healthcare interaction then becomes fundamental. Is an adolescent's visit to a primary care provider utilized most effectively? Almost three-quarters of adolescents aged 12–17 had one or more preventive medical visits in 2003 (NAHIC, 2008; Rand, Auinger, Klein, & Weitzman, 2005). As repeated contacts with a primary care provider may occur over several years, many clinicians have multiple opportunities to screen and counsel an adolescent patient for risky health behaviors (Whitlock, Orleans, Pender, & Allan, 2002).

Guidelines specifically targeting the delivery of adolescent clinical preventive services were developed over a decade ago (Elster & Kuznets, 1994; Green & Palfrey, 2000; U.S. Preventive Services Task Force, 1996). In general, these guidelines recommend that all adolescents have an annual, confidential visit during which primary care providers should screen, educate, and counsel adolescent patients in a number of biomedical and sociobehavioral areas. Adolescents should be screened for risky health behaviors as well as reinforced for strengths and competencies. The updated *Bright Futures* guidelines (Hagan et al., 2008) specifically encourage the promotion of positive youth development through recommending that clinicians include a focus on strengths in their annual visits with adolescents. It is also recommended that health guidance be given to parents of adolescents to help them respond appropriately to the health needs of their child. This includes providing information about normative adolescent development, the signs and symptoms of disease and emotional distress, parenting behaviors that promote healthy adolescent adjustment, and methods to help adolescents avoid potentially harmful behaviors (e.g., parental monitoring).

To complement practice guidelines, measures have been developed to monitor the care provided to adolescents. For example, the

National Committee for Quality Assurance (NCQA) includes a strong focus on prevention it its health plan accreditation process. The Health Plan Employer Data and Information Set (HEDIS)—a set of quality indicators used to rank the performance of clinicians and health plans—tracks preventive measures for adolescents such as an annual preventive service visit, substance abuse counseling, and chlamydia screening (NCQA, 2008).

In addition to working toward definable prevention objectives with expected health benefits, prevention has also been seen as a means to reduce health care expenditures. Projections of clinical cost and resource savings suggest that even limited success in risk identification, behavioral change, and morbidity reduction would have significant effects on adolescent health and health care costs (Downs & Klein, 1995; Gans, Alexander, Chu, & Elster, 1995; Park et al., 2001).

THE IMPLEMENTATION OF ADOLESCENT CLINICAL PREVENTIVE SERVICES

With the linking of adolescent preventive screening and counseling to quality performance measures, substantial attention has focused on the integration of these services into adolescent health care. Yet despite evidence that adolescents and parents view providers as credible sources of information and are willing to talk with them about topics outlined in the guidelines (Blum, Beuhring, Wunderlich, & Resnick, 1996; Joffe, Radius, & Gall, 1988; Fisher, 1992; Orrell-Valente, Ozer, & Husting, 2004; Steiner & Gest, 1996), delivery of preventive services to adolescents is below recommended levels across health care settings (Halpern-Felsher et al., 2000; Ma, Wang, & Stafford, 2005; Mangione-Smith et al., 2007; Rand et al., 2005).

The barriers to guidelines have been well documented (Cabana et al., 1999) and include physician knowledge (lack of awareness or familiarity), physician attitudes (lack of self-efficacy), and external factors (time limitations, reimbursement, lack of reminder systems).

In an attempt to overcome these barriers, some health plans have developed their own training sessions, questionnaires, and charting forms to help facilitate the implementation of guidelines. One popular pediatric tool, HEADSS, is based on the biopsychsocial model. HEADSS is a screening acronym reminding clinicians to screen in a variety of domains, including Home, Education (or Employment), Activities, Drugs, Sexuality, Suicidality/Depression, and Strengths/Safety (Goldenring & Cohen, 1988).

Because screening often necessitates further discussion of risky behavior, the clinician needs to have a brief office based intervention for those engaging in risky behavior. One model, originally developed by the National Cancer Institute and recently modified by the U.S. Preventive Services Task Force as a framework for behavioral counseling interventions, is the 5 A's approach (Whitlock et al., 2002). The model is based on asking, advising, assessing the willingness to change, assisting in behavior change, and arranging for follow-up.

The lower-than-recommended levels of screening have prompted research into the development of primary care interventions to provide models for increasing the delivery of preventive services to adolescents. Recent research has established that clinicians with higher self-efficacy are more likely to deliver clinical services to adolescents across multiple risk areas (Ozer, et al., 2004), and that training and tools for primary care providers improves clinicians' self-efficacy (Buckelew, Adams, Irwin, & Ozer, 2008). Successful interventions to increase the delivery of adolescent preventive services have consistently involved skill-based learning for clinicians on how to incorporate preventive services into real-life clinical practice, and how to utilize screening and charting tools to assist with screening and documentation (Irwin, 2005; Klein, Allan, Hedberg, Stevens, & Elster, 1997; Klein et al., 2003; Lustig et al., 2001; Ozer et al., 2001; Ozer et al., 2005). The results from these studies are promising and indicate that it is possible to increase preventive services to teenagers.

Do Preventive Services Make a Difference?

Beyond the question of how to effectively implement preventive services is the question of whether clinical preventive services result in improved health for adolescents. Guidelines are based on the assumption that if services are delivered as recommended, a decrease in risk behavior will result. Yet despite the current trend toward emphasizing prevention, there are limited data on the efficacy of clinical preventive services on adolescent health (Park et al., 2001; Tylee, Haller, Graham, Churchill, & Sanci, 2007).

Evidence, though mixed, suggests that preventive interventions may show some success in improving adolescent behavior in certain risk areas. Brief office-based interventions have been shown to increase condom use among adolescents, but have not shown significant effects for changing rates of sexual activity (Boekeloo et al., 1999; Kamb et al., 1998); an intervention to reduce alcohol use found educational benefits, but no reduction in actual use of alcohol (Boekeloo et al., 2004); and a safety intervention was unable to detect behavioral changes in seat belt and bicycle helmet use after three months (Leverence et al., 2005).

Two clinical interventions that targeted more than one risk area had varying results: A pediatric intervention, in which practices were assigned to deliver either a substance use or safety intervention, showed increased bicycle helmet use at 3-year follow-up, but no significant effects for use of seat belts, alcohol, or tobacco (Stevens et al., 2002); and an emergency room intervention that randomized adolescents to receive counseling in a single risk area increased seatbelt and bicycle helmet use but did not change drinking-related risk behavior over a 6-month period (Johnston, Rivara, Droesch, Dunn, & Compass, 2002).

Because adolescent health risk behaviors tend to co-occur (Lindberg, Boggess, Porter, & Williams, 2000; Sales & Irwin, in press) and increase with age (Brener & Collins, 1998), practice guidelines recommend the delivery of services targeting a range of risk behaviors. Yet, the body of research on the effectiveness of preventive services is comprised almost entirely of studies that evaluate the outcome of preventive interventions that target a single risk area.

Our own program of research has focused on integrating a broad range of clinical services into primary care practice and then following adolescent patients longitudinally to assess the behavioral effects of adolescents receiving clinical preventive services. We found that a systems intervention—involving screening and brief counseling from a primary care clinician, followed by reinforcement and goal setting with a clinic health educator—resulted in positive behavioral outcomes, compared to cohort comparison groups, across multiple risk areas; the intervention had a strong effect on increasing helmet and seat belt use, showed promise of delaying the onset of sexual activity among younger teens, and suggested positive but inconsistent effects on adolescents' use of substances (Ozer et al., 2002).

Our intervention incorporated the 5 A's approach mentioned earlier and was guided theoretically by social cognitive theory with a focus on structuring prevention and risk reduction in ways that promote self-regulation. This involves helping individuals develop skills for regulating their own motivation and behavior through self-monitoring and setting short-term attainable goals to motivate and direct their efforts, and using positive incentives and social supports to support and sustain their efforts (Bandura, 1997). Clinicians were prompted to reinforce positive behavior in teenagers as well as to build on success experiences when discussing risky behavior (Ozer et al., 2001). Once empowered with skills and a belief in their capabilities, people are better able to adopt health-promoting behavior (Bandura, 1997). As such, an adolescent preventive services intervention should focus not only on the content of screening areas, but on the process of enhancing adolescents' perceived control and responsibility over their own health and well-being (Ozer, 2007; Duncan et al., 2007).

While results of this initial research are promising, more research is needed on the behavioral and health outcomes of brief office-based interventions with adolescents. Further, other recommended areas of screening, such as nutrition and physical activity (Barlow, 2007; U.S. Department of Health & Human Services, 2007), have not yet been incorporated into research focusing on the health outcomes of receiving comprehensive preventive services (Irwin, Garber, & Ozer, 2007).

Clinical practice guidelines have recently been developed specifically to assist primary care providers in the identification and management of adolescent depression (Zuckerbrot, Cheung, Jensen, Stein, & Laraque, 2007). Promising research indicates that an intervention within primary care was associated with improvements in adolescent depression (Arsarnow et al., 2005). Other recent research, indicating that routine physical exams are associated with receipt of counseling (Yu, Adams, Burns, Brindis, & Irwin, 2008), suggests that the primary care visit may provide an opportunity to screen and provide appropriate referral for mental health services. Yet a study of California adolescents indicates that only about 20% of adolescents are screened for emotional distress during a primary care visit (Ozer, Zahnd, Adams, Husting, Wibbelsman, Norman, & Smiga, in press). Given the high rates of emotional distress among adolescents, and that most teens seek care in primary care settings, further attention on models for screening and brief interventions within primary care are warranted.

SUMMARY

Most adolescents and young adults in the United States are healthy, but a significant number engage in behaviors that put them at risk for developing health problems during adolescence, young adulthood, and in later life (Irwin et al., 2002; Mackay & Duran, 2007; National Academies Press, 2009).

Many of the outcomes of the behaviors initiated during adolescence do not have discernable outcomes until adulthood. For example, unhealthy eating, insufficient physical activity, unsafe sexual behavior, and substance use not only have significant negative health outcomes during adolescence but may lead to chronic health conditions or premature death.

In spite of the focus on adolescent health and prevention over the past two decades, our midcourse review in 2007 suggests that most of the targeted outcomes for the 21 Critical Health Objectives of Healthy People 2010 will likely not be reached (CDC, 2004; Park et al., 2008). The areas that show the greatest improvement include reproductive health, safer practices while operating/riding in motor vehicles, and tobacco use. The areas that appear to be static, with little or no improvement, include overall mortality rates for 10- to 19-year-olds, binge drinking, marijuana use, and engaging in vigorous physical activity. Areas that have shown significant worsening include mortality among 20- to 24-year-olds, rates of chlamydia, and number of adolescents who are overweight or obese. In the area of preventing adult chronic disease, there is good news associated with decreased tobacco initiation but bad news reflected in an increase in the rate of obesity/overweight (Park et al., 2008).

Over the past two decades, there has been increasing emphasis on attempting to make the health care system more responsive to the needs of adolescents (Brindis et al., 1997; Irwin & Duncan, 2002; National Research Council, 1993; Society for Adolescent Medicine, 2004b; U.S. Congress, 1991). Through federal efforts to expand insurance coverage for low-income adolescents, one of the most critical barriers to access to health care for adolescents has been removed. Adolescents are making it into the health care system at least once a year on average. We now need to focus on eliminating the same barriers for young adults.

Health professional groups have made serious efforts to improve adolescent health through the development of guidelines to improve the content and the quality of health care for the annual visit (Hagan et al., 2008). These guidelines are based on the premise that a health care visit during adolescence should be focused on health damaging and protective behaviors initiated during this period of the life cycle, with an emphasis on both disease prevention and health promotion. Even with guidelines in place for over 10 years and embraced by the financing system, most adolescents are not receiving a full complement of the recommended preventive interventions, however. Given that we now have a series of studies documenting how we can improve clinician performance in the delivery of preventive services, the time has come to move forward on delivering these services to adolescents (Irwin, 2005; Klein et al., 2001; Ozer et al., 2004; Ozer et al., 2005). Clinicians continue to question whether the receipt of these services will improve the health status of the population being served. Until we have successful implementation of the services, the question of how they actually affect health outcomes will remain elusive at best.

One of the major problems with the health care system for adolescents is the fragmentation and separation of the physical and mental health care systems. For example, when a clinician is using the preventive guidelines and identifies a mental health problem, the "carve out" systems for mental health generally limit the content of the visit for the clinician. A new financing system is required to cover treatment for mental health problems. If we want a health care system that is truly health promoting, we need a system that integrates physical and emotional heath (Tylee et al., 2007).

Throughout this chapter we have attempted to draw attention to the critical importance of young adulthood, with documentation of young adults' health status, risk profile, and access to care. In the past, this age group has received little or no attention, yet by most measures of health status they fare worse than adolescents (Park et al., 2006). Beyond the usual health status indicators, young adults are less likely to have access to care because of inadequate insurance coverage, the lack of a common entry point into the health care system, and no guidelines for clinicians regarding the content of care for this age group. Currently, there are initiatives in place to attempt to improve health care financing, but there has been little emphasis on developing an overall system of care that would be responsive to young adults' needs (Adams et al., 2007; Holahan & Kenney, 2008; Kriss et al., 2008; Park et al., 2006).

We know it is possible to decrease adolescent morbidity and mortality and promote healthy development. Over the past two decades, there have been improvements in access to care, and the content and quality of services for adolescents. An environment that promotes continued improvement in the health and well-being of our adolescents will need to build upon these advances over the past two decades, and support federal, state, and community policies that encourage investments in systems that will reinforce these efforts.

REFERENCES

Abma, J. C., Martinez, G. M., Mosher, W. D., & Dawson, B. S. (2004). Teenagers in the United States: Sexual activity, contraceptive use, and childbearing, 2002. *Vital Health Statistics, 23,* 1–48.

Adams, S. H., Newacheck, P. W., Park, M. J., Brindis, C. D., & Irwin, C. E., Jr. (2007). Health insurance across vulnerable ages: Patterns and disparities from adolescence to the early 30s. *Pediatrics, 119,* e1033–e1039.

American Psychiatric Association. (2005). *Diagnostic and Statistical Manual of Mental Disorders,* 4th ed.Washington, DC: Author.

Arnett, J. J. (2000). Emerging adulthood: A theory of development from the late teens through the twenties. *American Psychologist, 55,* 469–480.

Arnett, J., & Tanner, J. L. (2006). *Emerging adults in America: Coming of age in the 21st century.* Washington, DC: APA Books.

Asarnow, J. R., Jaycox, L. H., Duan, N., LaBorde, A. P., Rea, M. M., Murray, P., et al. (2005). Effectiveness of a quality improvement intervention for adolescent depression in primary care clinics: A randomized controlled trial. *Journal of the American Medical Association, 293,* 311–319.

Bandura, A. (1997). *Self-efficacy: The exercise of control.* New York: W. H. Freeman & Company.

Barlow, S. E. (2007). Expert committee recommendations regarding the prevention, assessment, and treatment of child and adolescent overweight and obesity: Summary report. *Pediatrics, 120*(Suppl 4), S164–S192.

Berkey, C. S., Rockett, H. R., Field, A. E., Gillman, M. W., & Colditz, G. A. (2004). Sugar-added beverages and adolescent weight change. *Obesity Research, 12,* 778–788.

Bernat, D. H., & Resnick, M. D. (2006). Healthy youth development: Science and strategies. *Journal of Public Health Management,* Pract Suppl, S10–S16.

Blum, R. W., Beuhring, T., Wunderlich, M., & Resnick, M. D. (1996). Don't ask, they won't tell: The quality of adolescent health screening in five practice settings. *American Journal of Public Health*, 86, 1767–1772.

Boekeloo, B. O., Schamus, L. A., Simmens, S. J., Cheng, T. L., O'Connor, K., & D'Angelo, L. J. (1999). A STD/HIV prevention trial among adolescents in managed care. *Pediatrics*, 103, 107–115.

Boekeloo, B. O., Jerry, J., Lee-Ougo, W. I., Worrell, K. D., Hamburger, E. K., Russek-Cohen, E., et al. (2004). Randomized trial of brief office-based interventions to reduce adolescent alcohol use. *Archives of Pediatric and Adolescent Medicine*, 158, 635–642.

Bowman, S. A., Gortmaker, S. L., Ebbeling, C. B., Pereira, M. A., & Ludwig, D. S. (2004). Effects of fast-food consumption on energy intake and diet quality among children in a national household survey. *Pediatrics* 113, 112–118.

Brener, N., & Collins, J. (1998). Co-occurrence of health-risk behaviors among adolescents in the United States. *Journal of Adolescent Health*, 22, 209–213.

Brindis, C. D., Ozer, E. M., Handley, M., Knopf, D. K., Millstein, S. G., & Irwin, C. E., Jr. (1997). *Improving adolescent health: An analysis and synthesis of health policy recommendations.* San Francisco: University of California, National Adolescent Health Information Center.

Brindis, C. D., VanLandeghem, K., Kirkpatrick, R., Macdonald, T., & Lee, S. (1999). *Adolescents and the State Children's Health Insurance Program (CHIP): Healthy options for meeting the needs of adolescents.* Washington, D.C.: Association of Maternal and Child Health Programs, & San Francisco: University of California, Policy Information and Analysis Center for Middle Childhood and Adolescence, National Adolescent Health Information Center.

Brown, R. A., Lewinsohn, P. M., Seeley, J. R., & Wagner, E. F. (1996). Cigarette smoking, major depression, and other psychiatric disorders among adolescents. *Journal of the American Academy of Children and Adolescent Psychiatry*, 35, 1602–1610.

Buckelew, S. M., Adams, S. H., Irwin, C. E., Jr., & Ozer, E.M. (2008). Increasing clinician self-efficacy for screening and counseling adolescents for risky health behaviors: Results of an intervention. *Journal of Adolescent Health*, 43, 198–200.

Cabana, M. D., Rand, C. S., Powe, N. R., Wu, A. W., Wilson, M. H., Abboud, P. A., et al. (1999). Why don't physicians follow clinical practice guidelines? A framework for improvement. *Journal of the American Medical Association*, 282, 1458–1465.

Catalano, R. F., Hawkins, J. D., Berglund, M. L., Pollard, J. A., & Arthur, M. W. (2002). Prevention science and positive youth development: competitive or cooperative frameworks? *Journal of Adolescent Health*, 31, 230–239.

Centers for Disease Control and Prevention (2004). National Center for Chronic Disease Prevention and Health Promotion, Division of Adolescent and School Health; Health Resources and Services Administration, Maternal and Child Health Bureau, Office of Adolescent Health; National Adolescent Health Information Center, University of California, San Francisco. *Improving the health of adolescents and young adults: A guide for states and communities.* Atlanta, GA: Author. Retrieved on June 8, 2008, from http://nahic.ucsf.edu/2010guide.

Centers for Disease Control and Prevention. (2006). Youth Risk Behavior Surveillance—United States, 2007. *MMWR*, 57, SS-4.

Centers for Disease Control and Prevention. (2006). *Sexually transmitted disease surveillance, 2005.* Atlanta, GA: U.S. Department of Health and Human Services.

Centers for Disease Control and Prevention. (2007). *Bridged-Race Population Estimates, United States,* vol. 2007. Atlanta, GA: Author.

Centers for Disease Control and Prevention. (2007). *Compressed mortality file,* vol. 2007. Atlanta, GA: Author.

Centers for Disease Control and Prevention. (2007). Suicide trends among youth and young adults aged 10–24 years—United States, 1990–2004. *Morbidity and Mortality Weekly Report*, 56, 905–908.

Cheng, T. L., Savageau, J. A., Sattler, A. L., & DeWitt, T. G. (1993). Confidentiality in health care: A survey of knowledge, perceptions, and attitudes among high school students. *Journal of the American Medical Association*, 269, 1404–1407.

Davis, K. C., Hendershot, C. S., George, W. H., Norris, J., & Heiman, J. R. (2007). Alcohol's effects on sexual decision making: An integration of alcohol myopia and individual differences. *Journal of Studies on Alcohol and Drugs*, 68, 843–851.

Department of Health and Human Services. (2000). *Healthy people 2010* (Conference Edition, in Two Volumes). Washington, DC: Author.

Department of Health & Human Services, Health Resources & Services Administration & Maternal and Child Health Bureau. (1998). *Child health U.S.A.* Washington, DC: U.S. Government Printing Office.

Deshmukh-Taskar, P., Nicklas, T. A., Morales, M., Yang, S. J., Zakeri, I., & Berenson, G. S. (2006). Tracking of overweight status from childhood to young adulthood: The Bogalusa Heart Study. *European Journal of Clinical Nutrition*, 60, 48–57.

Dietz, W. H. (1998). Health consequences, of obesity in youth: Childhood predictors of adult disease. *Pediatrics*, 101, 518–525.

Downs, S. M., & Klein, J. D. (1995). Clinical preventive services efficacy and adolescents' risky behaviors. *Archives of Pediatrics and Adolescent Medicine*, 149, 374–379.

Duncan, G. E. (2006). Prevalence of diabetes and impaired fasting glucose levels among US adolescents: National Health and Nutrition Examination Survey, 1999–2002. *Archives of Pediatric and Adolescent Medicine*, 160, 523–528.

Duncan, P. M., Garcia, A. C., Frankowski, B. L., Carey, P. A., Kallock, E. A., Dixon, R. D., et al. (2007). Inspiring healthy adolescent choices: A rationale and guide to strength promotion in primary care. *Journal of Adolescent Health*, 41, 525–535.

Ebbeling, C. B., Sinclair, K. B., Pereira, M. A., Garcia-Lago, E., Feldman, H. A., & Ludwig, D. S. (2004). Compensation for energy intake from fast food among overweight and lean adolescents. *Journal of the American Medical Association*, 291, 2828–2833.

Elliott, D. S. (1993). Health enhancing and health-compromising lifestyles. In S. G.Millstein, A. C. Petersen, & E. O. Nightingale (Eds.), *Promoting the health of adolescents* (pp. 119–145). New York: Oxford University Press.

Elster, A. B., & Kuznets, N. J. (1994). *AMA Guidelines for Adolescent Preventive Services (GAPS): Recommendations and rationale.* Chicago, IL: American Medical Association.

Eng, T. R., & Butler, W. T. (Eds.). (1997). *The hidden epidemic: Confronting sexually transmitted diseases.* Washington, DC: National Academy Press.

English, A. (1999). Health care for the adolescent alone: A legal landscape. In J. Blustein, C. Levine, & N. N. Dubler (Eds.), *The adolescent alone: Decision making in health care in the United States* (pp. 78–99). Cambridge: Cambridge University Press.

English, A., & Simmons, P. S. (1999). Legal issues in reproductive health care for adolescents. *Adolescent Medicine: State of the Art Reviews*, 10, 181–194.

Fisher, M. (1992). Parents' views of adolescent health issues. *Pediatrics*, 90, 335–341.

Ford, C. A., Bearman, P. S., Peter, S., & Moody, J. (1999). Foregone health care among adolescents. *Journal of the American Medical Association*, 282, 2227.

Ford, C. A., & English, A. (2002). Limiting confidentiality of adolescent health services: What are the risks? *Journal of the American Medical Association*, 288, 752–753.

Ford, C. A., Millstein, S. G., Halpern-Felsher, B. L., & Irwin, C. E., Jr. (1997). Influence of physician confidentiality assurances on adolescents' willingness to disclose information and seek future health care. *Journal of the American Medical Association*, 278, 1029–1034.

Fox, H. B., McManus, M. A., & Reichman, M. B. (2003). Private health insurance for adolescents: Is it adequate? *Journal of Adolescent Health, 32*, 12–24.

Fox, H. B., Limb, S. J., & McManus, M. A. (2007). *Preliminary thoughts on restructuring Medicaid to promote adolescent health* (Issue Brief No. 1). Washington, DC: Incenter Strategies.

Gans, J. E., Alexander, B., Chu, R., & Elster, A. B. (1995). The cost of comprehensive preventive medical services for adolescents. *Archives of Pediatrics and Adolescent Medicine, 149*, 1226–1234.

Giedd, J. N. (2008). The teen brain: Insights from neuroimaging. *Journal of Adolescent Health 42*, 335–343.

Goldenring, J., & Cohen, E. (1988). Getting into adolescents heads. *Contemporary Pediatrics, 5*, 75–90.

Goldstein, A. L., Barnett, N. P., Pedlow, C. T., & Murphy, J. G. (2007). Drinking in conjunction with sexual experiences among at-risk college student drinkers. *Journal of Studies on Alcohol and Drugs, 68*, 697–705.

Goodman, E. (1999). The role of socioeconomic status gradients in explaining differences in U.S. adolescents' health. *American Journal of Public Health, 89*,1522–1528.

Grant, J. D., Scherrer, J. F., Lynskey, M. T., Lyons, M. J., Eisen, S. A., Tsuang, M. T., et al. (2006). Adolescent alcohol use is a risk factor for adult alcohol and drug dependence: Evidence from a twin design. *Psychological Medicine 36*, 109–118.

Green, M. E., & Palfrey, J. S. (2000). *Bright Futures: Guidelines for health supervision of infants, children, and adolescents* (2nd ed.). Arlington, VA: National Center for Education in Maternal and Child Health.

Hagan, J. F., Shaw, J. S., & Duncan, P. M. (Eds.). (2008). *Bright futures: Guidelines for health supervision of infants, children, and adolescents* (3rd ed.). Elk Grove Village, IL: American Academy of Pediatrics.

Halpern-Felsher, B. L., Ozer, E. M., Millstein, S. G., Wibbelsman, C. J., Fuster, C. D., Elster, A. B., et al. (2000). Preventive services in a health maintenance organization: How well do pediatricians screen and educate their adolescent patients? *Archives of Pediatrics and Adolescent Medicine, 154*, 173–179.

Hamilton, B. E., Martin, J. A., Ventura, S. J. (2007). Preliminary data for 2006. *National Vital Statistics Reports, 56*, 1–18.

Hawkins, J. D., Brown, E. C., Oesterle, S., Arthur, M. W., Abbott, R. D., & Catalano, R. F. (2008). Early effects of Communities That Care on targeted risks and initiation of delinquent behavior and substance use. *Journal of Adolescent Health, 43*, 15–22.

Hedlund, J. (2007). Novice teen driving: GDL and beyond. *Journal of Safety Research, 38*, 259–266.

Hingson, R., Heeren, T., Levenson, S., Jamanka, A., & Voss, R. (2002). Age of drinking onset, driving after drinking, and involvement in alcohol related motor-vehicle crashes. *Accident Analysis and Prevention, 34*, 85–92.

Hingson, R., Heeren, T., & Zakocs, R. (2001). Age of drinking onset and involvement in physical fights after drinking. *Pediatrics, 108*, 872–877.

Hingson, R., Heeren, T., Winter, M. R., & Wechsler, H. (2003). Early age of first drunkenness as a factor in college students' unplanned and unprotected sex attributable to drinking. *Pediatrics, 111*, 34–41.

Hingson, R., Heeren, T., Zakocs, R., Winter, M., & Wechsler, H. (2003). Age of first intoxication, heavy drinking, driving after drinking and risk of unintentional injury among U.S. college students. *Journal of Studies on Alcohol and Drugs, 64*, 23–31.

Hingson, R. W., Heeren, T., & Winter, M. R. (2006). Age of alcohol-dependence onset: Associations with severity of dependence and seeking treatment. *Pediatrics, 118*, e755–e763.

Hoek, H. W., & van Hoeken, D. (2003). Review of the prevalence and incidence of eating disorders. *International Journal of Eating Disorders, 34*, 383–396.

Holahan, J., & Kenney, J. (2008). *Health insurance coverage of young adults.* Washington, DC: Urban Institute. Retrieved on June 20, 2008, from www.urban.org/.

Howell, E. M. (2004). *Access to Children's Mental Health Services under Medicaid and SCHIP. New Federalism: National Survey of America's Families (Series B. No B-60).* Washington, DC: The Urban Institute. Retrieved on June 9, 2008, from http://www.urban.org/UploadedPDF/311053_B-60.pdf.

Institute of Medicine. (2005). *Preventing childhood obesity: Health in the balance.* Washington, DC: National Academies Press.

Irwin, C. E., Jr. (2005). Clinical preventive services for adolescents: Still a long way to go. *Journal of Adolescent Health, 37*, 85–86.

Irwin, C. E., Jr., Burg, S. J., & Cart, C. V. (2002). America's adolescents: Where have we been, where are we going? *Journal of Adolescent Health, 31*, 91–121.

Irwin, C. E., Jr., & Duncan, M. D. (2002). Health futures of youth II: Pathways to adolescent health, executive summary and overview. *Journal of Adolescent Health, 31*, 82–89.

Irwin, C. E., Jr., Garber, A., & Ozer, E. M. (2007). *Access to health care services: Implementing guidelines in systems of care.* Presented at the American Heart Association's Childhood Obesity Research Summit, Arlington VA.

Jessor, R. (1998) New perspectives on adolescent risk behavior. In Jessor, R. (Ed.). *New perspectives on adolescent risk behavior.* New York: Cambridge University Press.

Joffe, A., Radius, S., & Gall, M. (1988). Health counseling for adolescents: What they want, what they get, and who gives it. *Pediatrics, 82*, 481–485.

Johnston, L. D., O'Malley, P. M., Bachman, J. G., & Schulenberg, J. E. (2008). *Monitoring the future national results on adolescent drug use: Overview of key findings, 2007* (NIH Publication Number. 08–6418). Bethesda, MD: National Institute on Drug Abuse.

Johnston, B. D., Rivara, F. P., Droesch, R. M., Dunn, C., & Copass, M. K. (2002). Behavior change counseling in the emergency department to reduce injury risk: A randomized, controlled trial. *Pediatrics, 110*, 267–274.

Kamb, M. L., Fishbein, M., Douglas, J. M., Jr., Rhodes, F., Rogers, J., Bolan, G., et al. (1998). Efficacy of risk-reduction counseling to prevent human immunodeficiency virus and sexually transmitted diseases: a randomized controlled trial. Project RESPECT Study Group. *Journal of American Medical Association, 280,* 1161–1167.

Kandel, D. B., & Chen, K. (2000). Extent of smoking and nicotine dependence in the United States: 1991–1993. *Nicotine Tobacco Research, 2*, 263–274.

Kandel, D. B. E. (2002). *Stages of pathways of drug involvement.* Cambridge: Cambridge University Press.

Kataoka, S. H., Zhang, L., & Wells, K. B. (2002). Unmet need for mental health among U.S. children: Variation by ethnicity and insurance status. *American Journal of Psychiatry, 159*, 1548–1555.

Katzman, D. K. (2005). Medical complications in adolescents with anorexia nervosa: A review of the literature. *International Journal of Eating Disorders, 37* (Suppl), S52–S59; discussion S52–S59.

Kazdin, A. E. (1993). Adolescent mental health: Prevention and treatment programs. *American Psychologist, 48*, 127–141.

Keane, C. R., Lave, J. R., Ricci, E. M., & LaVallee, C. P. (1999). The impact of a children's health insurance program by age. *Pediatrics, 104*, 1051–1058.

Keel, P. K., Dorer, D. J., Eddy, K. T., Franko, D., Charatan, D. L., & Herzog, D. B. (2003). Predictors of mortality in eating disorders. *Archives of General Psychiatry, 60*,179–183.

Kessler, R. C., Andrews, G., Colpe, L. J., Hiripi, E., Mroczek, D. K., Normand, S., et al. (2002). Short screening scales to monitor population prevalences and trends in non-specific psychological distress. *Psychology Medicine, 32*, 959–976.

Kessler, R. C., Berglund, P., Demler, O., Jin, R., Merikangas, K. R., & Walters, E. E. (2005). Lifetime prevalence and age-of-onset distributions of DSM-IV disorders in the National Comorbidity Survey Replication. *Archives of General Psychiatry, 62*, 593–602.

Kessler, R. C., Amminger, G. P., Aguilar-Gaxiola, S., Alonso, J., Lee, S., & Ustun, T. B. (2007). Age of onset of mental disorders: A review of recent literature. *Current Opinion in Psychiatry, 20,* 359–364.

Klein, J. D., Allan, M. J., Hedberg, V. A., Stevens, D. A., & Elster, A. B. (1997). Implementing the guidelines for adolescent preventive services (GAPS) in community and migrant health centers. *Ambulatory Child Health,* 31, 66.

Klein, J. D., Sesselberg, T. S., Gawronski, B., Handwerker, L., Gesten, F., & Schettine, A. (2003). Improving adolescent preventive services through state, managed care, and community partnerships. *Journal of Adolescent Health, 32*(6 Suppl), 91–97.

Klein, J. D., Wilson, K. M., McNulty, M., Kapphahn, C., & Collins, K. S. (1999). Access to medical care for adolescents: Results for the 1997 Commonwealth Fund survey of the health of adolescent girls. *Journal of Adolescent Health, 25,* 120–130.

Knopf, D., Park, M. J., Brindis, C.D., Paul Mulye, T. & Irwin, C.E. Jr. (2007). What gets measured gets done: Assessing data availability for adolescent populations. *Maternal and Child Health Journal, 11,* 335–345.

Knopf, D., Park, M. J., & Paul Mulye, T. (2008). *A mental health profile of adolescents: 2008 brief.* National Adolescent Health Information Center, University of California, San Francisco.

Kriss, J. L., Collins, S. R., Mahato, B., Gould, E., & Schoen, C. (2008). *Rite of passage? Why young adults become uninsured and how new policies can help, 2008.* New York: Commonwealth Fund. Retrieved on June 29, 2008, from www.commonwealthfund.org.

Larson, R. W. (2000). Toward a psychology of positive youth development. *American Psychology, 55,* 170–183.

Lehrer, J. A., Shrier, L. A., Gortmaker, S., & Buka, S. (2006). Depressive symptoms as a longitudinal predictor of sexual risk behaviors among U.S. middle and high school students. *Pediatrics, 118,* 189–200.

Lerner, R. M. (2001). Promoting promotion in the development of prevention science. *Applied Developmental Science, 5,* 254–257.

Leverence, R. R., Martinez, M., Whisler, S., Romero-Leggott, V., Harji, F., Milner, M., et al. (2005). Does office-based counseling of adolescents and young adults improve self-reported safety habits? A randomized controlled effectiveness trial. *Journal of Adolescent Health, 36,* 523–528.

Lewinsohn, P. M., Rohde, P., & Seeley, J. R. (1998). Major depressive disorder in older adolescents: Prevalence, risk factors, and clinical implications. *Clinical Psychology Review, 18,* 765–794.

Liese, A. D., D'Agostino, R. B., Jr., Hamman, R. F., Kilgo, P. D., Lawrence, J. M., Liu, L. L., et al. (2006). The burden of diabetes mellitus among U.S. youth: Prevalence estimates from the SEARCH for Diabetes in Youth Study. *Pediatrics, 118,* 1510–1518.

Lindberg, L. D., Boggess, S., Porter, L., & Williams, S. (2000). *Teen risk taking: A statistical report.* Washington DC: Urban Institute.

Lindberg, L. D., Jones, R., & Santelli, J. S. (in press). Noncoital sexual activities among adolescents. *Journal of Adolescent Health.*

Lotstein, D. S., Inkelas, M., Hays, R. D., Halfon, N., Brook, R. (2008). Access to care for youth with special health care needs in the transition to adulthood. *Journal of Adolescent Health, 43,* 23–29.

Lowry, R., Holtzman, D., Truman, B. I., Kann, L., Collins, J. L., & Kolbe, L. J. (1994). Substance use and HIV-related sexual behaviors among U.S. high school students: Are they related? *American Journal of Public Health, 84,* 1116–1120.

Lustig, J. L., Ozer, E. M., Adams, S. H., Wibbelsman, C. J., Fuster, C. D.,Bonar, R. W., et al. (2001). Improving the delivery of adolescent clinical preventive services through skills-based training. *Pediatrics, 107,* 1100–1107.

Ma, J., Wang, Y., & Stafford, R. S. (2005). U.S. adolescents receive suboptimal preventive counseling during ambulatory care. *Journal of Adolescent Health, 36,* 441.

MacKay, A. P., & Duran, C. (2008). *Adolescent health in the United States, 2007,* National Center for Health Statistics.

Mangione-Smith, R., DeCristofaro, A. H., Setodji, C. M., Keesey, J., Klein, D. J., Adams, J. L., et al. (2007). The quality of ambulatory care delivered to children in the United States. *New England Journal of Medicine, 357,* 1515–1523.

McCraken, M., Jiles, R., & Blanch, H. M. (2007). Health behaviors of the young adult population: Behavioral risk surveillance system, 2003. *Preventing Chronic Disease Public Health and Research, Practice and Policy, 4,* A26.

McKenna, M. T., Michaud, C. M., Murray, C. J., & Marks, J. S. (2005). Assessing the burden of disease in the United States using disability-adjusted life years. *American Journal of Preventive Medicine, 5,* 415–423.

McPherson, M., Arango, P., Fox, H., Lauver, C., McManus, M., Newacheck, P., et al. (1998). A new definition of children with special health care needs. *Pediatrics, 102,* 137–140.

Medical Expenditure Panel Survey. (2007). *Household component summary tables: Medical Expenditure Panel survey.* Retrieved on June 6, 2008, from www.meps.ahrq.gov/mepsweb/data_stats/quick_tables.jsp.

Merrill, J. C., Kleber, H. D., Shwartz, M., Liu, H., & Lewis, S. R. (1999). Cigarettes, alcohol, marijuana, other risk behaviors, and American youth. *Drug Alcohol Dependency, 56,* 205–212.

Mokdad, A. H., Marks, J. S., Stroup, D. F., & Gerberding, J. L. (2004). Actual causes of death in the United States, 2000. *Journal of the American Medical Association, 291,* 1238–1245.

Mosher, W. D., Chandra, A., & Jones, J. (2005). Sexual behavior and selected health measures: Men and women 15–44 years of age, United States, 2002. *Advanced Data, 362,* 1–55.

National Adolescent Health Information Center. (2006). *Fact sheet on mortality: Adolescent and young adults.* San Francisco: University of California–San Francisco.

National Adolescent Health Information Center. (2007). *Fact sheet on unintentional injury: Adolescent and young adults.* San Francisco: University of California–San Francisco.

National Adolescent Health Information Center. (2008). *Fact sheet on health care access & utilization: Adolescents & young adults.* San Francisco: University of California–San Francisco.

National Center for Injury Prevention and Control (NCIPC). (2008). *Leading causes of death and fatal injuries mortality reports.* Atlanta, GA: Centers for Disease Control and Prevention. Retrieved on June 9, 2008, from www.cdc.gov/ncip/wisqars.

National Committee for Quality Assurance. (2008). HEDIS, 2008. Washington, DC: Author.

National Research Council. (1993). *Losing generations: Adolescents in high-risk settings.* Washington, DC: National Academies Press.

National Research Council, Institute of Medicine & Transportation Research Board. (2007). *Preventing teen crashes contributing from the behavioral and social sciences.* Washington, DC: National Academies Press.

National Research Council and Institute of Medicine (2009). *Adolescent health services: Missing opportunities.* Committee on Adolescent Health Care Services and Models of Care for Treatment, Prevention, and Healthy Development. Washington, DC: The National Academies Press.

Nawar, E. W., Niska, R. W., & Xu, J. (2007). National Hospital Ambulatory Medical Care Survey: 2005 emergency department summary. *Advanced Data, 386,* 1–32.

Newacheck, P. W., Brindis, C. D., Cart, C. U., Marchi, K., & Irwin, C. E., Jr. (1999). Adolescent health insurance coverage: Recent changes and access to care. *Pediatrics, 104,* 195–202.

Newacheck, P. W., Hung, Y. Y., Park, M. J., Brindis, C. D., & Irwin, C. E., Jr. (2003). Disparities in adolescent health and health care: does socioeconomic status matter? *Health Services Research, 38,* 1235–1252.

Ogden, C. L., Fryar, C. D., Carroll, M. D., & Flegal, K. M. (2004). Mean body weight, height, and body mass index, United States 1960–2002. *Advanced Data, 347,* 1–17.

Ogden, C. L., Carroll, M. D., Curtin, L. R., McDowell, M. A., Tabak, C. J., & Flegal, K. M. (2006). Prevalence of overweight and obesity in the United States, 1999–2004. *Journal of the American Medical Association, 295,* 1549–1555.

Orrell-Valente, J. K., Ozer, E. M., & Husting, S. R. (2004). Do parents of diverse sociodemographic backgrounds support clinical preventive services for adolescents? *Pediatric Research, 55,* 5A.

Ozer, E. M., Zahnd, E. G., Adams, S. H., Husting, B. A., Wibbelsman, C. J., Norman, K. P., Smiga, S. (in press). Are adolescents being screened for emotional distress in primary care? *Journal of Adolescent Health.*

Ozer, E. M. (2007). The adolescent primary care visit: Time to build on strengths. *Journal of Adolescent Health, 41,* 519–520.

Ozer, E. M., Adams, S. H., Gardner, L. R., Mailloux, D. E., Wibbelsman, C. J., & Irwin, C. E., Jr. (2004). Provider self-efficacy and the screening of adolescents for risky health behaviors. *Journal of Adolescent Health, 35,* 101–107.

Ozer, E. M., Adams, S. H., Lustig, J. L., Gee, S., Garber, A. K., Gardner, L. R., et al. (2005). Increasing the screening and counseling of adolescents for risky health behaviors: A primary care intervention. *Pediatrics, 115,* 960–968.

Ozer, E. M., Adams, S. H., Lustig, J. L., Millstein, S. G., Camfield, K., El-Diwany, S., Volpe, S., & Irwin, C. E., Jr. (2001). Can it be done? Implementing adolescent clinical preventive services. *Health Services Research, 36,* 150–165.

Ozer, E., Adams, S., Orrell-Valente, J., Lustig, J., Millstein, S., & Wibbelsman, C., Irwin, C. E., Jr. (2002). Does screening and counseling adolescents influence their behavior? [Abstract]. *Pediatric Research 55,* 2A.

Ozer, E. M., Macdonald, T., & Irwin, C. E., Jr. (2002). Adolescent Health Care in the United States: Implications and Projections for the New Millennium. In J. T. Mortimer & R. W. Larson (Eds.), *The changing adolescent experience: Societal trends and the transition to adulthood* (pp. 129–174). Cambridge: Cambridge University Press.

Ozer, E. M., Park, M. J., Paul, T., Brindis, C. D., & Irwin, C. E., Jr. (2003). *America's adolescents: Are they healthy?* San Francisco: University of California, National Adolescent Health Information Center.

Park, M. J., & Irwin, C. E., Jr. (2008). Youth with special health care needs: Facilitating a healthy transition to young adulthood. *Journal of Adolescent Health, 43,* 6–7.

Park, M. J., Paul Mulye, T., Adams, S. H., Brindis, C. D., & Irwin, C. E., Jr. (2006). The health status of young adults in the United States. *Journal of Adolescent Health, 39,* 305–317.

Park, M. J., Brindis, C. D., Chang, F., & Irwin, C. E., Jr. (2008). A midcourse review of the healthy people 2010: 21 critical health objectives for adolescents and young adults. *Journal of Adolescent Health, 42,* 329–334.

Park, M. J., Macdonald, T. M., Ozer, E. M., Burg, S. J., Millstein, S. G., & Brindis, C. D. (2001). *Investing in clinical preventive services for adolescents.* San Francisco: University of California–San Francisco, Policy Information and Analysis Center for Middle Childhood and Adolescence & National Adolescent Health Information Center.

Patton, G. C. (2008). Weighing an ounce of prevention. *Journal of Adolescent Health, 43,* 3–5.

Petersen, A. C., Compas, B. E., Brooks-Gunn, J., Stemmler, M., Ey, S., & Grant, K. E. (1993). Depression in adolescence. *American Psychologist, 48,* 155–168.

Pittman, K. (2003). *Preventing problems, promoting development, encouraging engagement: Competing priorities or inseparable goals?* Washington, DC: Forum for Youth Investment, Impact Strategies, Inc.

Policy Center, Public Policy Analysis and Education Center for Middle Childhood, Adolescent, and Young Adult Health. (2008). 2006 National Health Interview Survey [Private Data Run]: Retrieved on June 9, 2008, from www.cdc.gov/nchs/nhis.htm.

Rand, C. M., Auinger, P., Klein, J. D., & Weitzman, M. (2005). Preventive counseling at adolescent ambulatory visits. *Journal of Adolescent Health 37,* 87–93.

Rand, C. M., Shone, L. P., Albertin, C., Auinger, P., Klein, J. D., & Szilagyi, P. G. (2007). National health care visit patterns of adolescents: Implications for delivery of new adolescent vaccines. *Archives of Pediatric and Adolescent Medicine, 161,* 252–259.

Reddy, D. M., Fleming, R., & Swain, C. (2002). Effect of mandatory parental notification on adolescent girls' use of sexual health care services. *Journal of the American Medical Association, 288,* 710–714.

Resnick, M. D., Bearman, P. S., Blum, R. W., Bauman, K. E., Harris, K. M., Jones, J., et al. (1997). Protecting adolescents from harm: Findings from the National Longitudinal Study on Adolescent Health. *Journal of the American Medical Association, 278,* 823–831.

Rivara, F.P., Garrison, M.M., Ebel, B., McCarty, C.A., Christakis, D.A. (2004). Mortality attributable to harmful drinking in the United States, 2000. *Journal of Studies on Alcohol and Drugs, 65,* 530–536.

Rivara, F. R., Park, M. J., & Irwin, C. E., Jr. (in press). Trends in adolescent and young adult morbidity and mortality. In R. J. DiClemente & J.Santelli (Eds.), *Handbook of adolescent risk behavior.*

Roth, J. L., & Brooks-Gunn, J. (2003). Youth development programs: Risk, prevention and policy. *Journal of Adolescent Health, 32,* 170–182.

Rubinstein, M. L., Thompson, P. J., Benowitz, N. L., Shiffman, S., & Moscicki, A. B. (2007). Cotinine levels in relation to smoking behavior and addiction in young adolescent smokers. *Nicotine Tobacco Research 9,* 129–135.

Rushton, J. L., Forcier, M., & Schectman, R. M. (2002). Epidemiology of depressive symptoms in the National Longitudinal Study of Adolescent Health. *Journal of the American Academy of Child and Adolescent Psychiatry, 41,* 199–205.

Sales, J., & Irwin, C. E., Jr. (in press). Risk taking behaviors during adolescence. In R. DiClemente & J. Santelli (Eds.), *Handbook of adolescent risk behaviors.*

Schneider, M. (2003). Bulimia nervosa and binge-eating disorder in adolescents. *Adolescent Medicine, 14,* 119–131.

Schoen, C., Davis, K., Scott-Collins, K., Greenberg, L., Des Roches, C., & Abrams, M. (1997). *The Commonwealth Fund survey of adolescent girls.* New York: Commonwealth Fund.

Shaffer, D., Fisher, P., Dulcan, M. K., Davies, M., Piancentini, J., Schwab-Stone, M. E., et al. (1996). The NIMH Diagnostic Interview Schedule for Children Version 2.3 (DISC-2.3). Description, acceptability, prevalence rates, and performance in the MECA Study. Methods for the epidemiology of child and adolescent mental disorders study. *Journal of the American Academy of Child and Adolescent Psychiatry, 35,* 865–877.

Society for Adolescent Medicine. (2004a). Confidential health care for adolescents: Position paper of the Society for Adolescent Medicine. *Journal of Adolescent Health, 35,* 160–167.

Society for Adolescent Medicine. (2004). Access to care for adolescents and young adults: Position paper of the Society for Adolescent Medicine. *Journal of Adolescent Health, 35,* 342–344.

Stein, M. E. (1997). *Health supervision guidelines* (3rd ed.). Elk Grove Village, IL: American Academy of Pediatrics.

Steinberg, L. (2008). A social neuroscience perspective on adolescent risk-taking. *Developmental Review, 28,* 78–106.

Steiner, B. D., & Gest, K. L. (1996). Do adolescents want to hear preventive counseling messages in outpatient settings? *Journal of Family Practice, 43,* 375–381.

Stevens, M. M., Olson, A. L., Gaffney, C. A., Tosteson, T. D., Mott, L. A., & Starr, P. (2002). A pediatric, practice-based, randomized trial of drinking and smoking prevention and bicycle helmet, gun, and seatbelt safety promotion. *Pediatrics, 109,* 490–497.

Substance Abuse and Mental Health Services Administration. (2007). *Results from the 2006 National Survey on Drug Use and Health*. Rockville, MD: DHHS.

Tylee, A., Haller, D. M., Graham, T., Churchill, R., & Sanci, L. A. (2007). Youth-friendly primary-care services: How are we doing and what more needs to be done? *Lancet, 369*, 1565–1573.

U.S. Bureau of the Census. (2004). *Foreign born population of the U.S. by generation*, vol. 2007. Washington, DC: Author.

U.S. Bureau of the Census. (2007). *Current population survey, annual social and economic supplement, 2007*, vol. 2007. Washington, DC: Author.

U.S. Congress, Office of Technology Assessment. (1991). *Adolescent health*, vol. I: *Summary and policy options* [OTA-H-468]. Washington, DC: Government Printing Office.

U.S. Department of Health and Human Services. (1999). *Mental health: A report of the surgeon general*. Rockville, MD: Office of the Surgeon General, U.S. Public Health Service. Retrieved on February 4, 2008, from www.surgeongeneral.gov/library/mentalhealth/home.html.

U.S. Department of Health and Human Services. (2000). *Healthy People 2010: Understanding and improving health and objectives for improving health*, vols. 1 & 2. Washington, DC: U.S. Government Printing Office. Retrieved on June 18, 2008, from www.healthypeople.gov/document/tableof contents.htm.

U.S. Department of Health and Human Services. (2007). *The surgeon general's call to action to prevent and decrease overweight and obesity*. Retrieved on June 8, 2008, from www.surgeongeneral.gov/topics/obesity/calltoaction/fact_adolescents.htm [March 8, 2008]

U.S. Department of Health and Human Services, Health Resources and Services Administration, Maternal and Child Health Bureau. (2008). *The National Survey of Children with Special Health Care Needs chartbook 2005–2006*. Rockville, Maryland:

Author. Retrieved on June 13, 2008, from http://mchb.hrsa.gov/cshcn05/index.htm.

U.S. Preventive Services Task Force. (1996). *Guide to clinical preventive services* (2nd ed.). Alexandria, VA: International Medical Publishing.

Ventura, S. J., Abma, J. C., Mosher, W. D., & Henshaw, S. K. (2006). *Recent trends in teenage pregnancy in the United States, 1990–2002*: National Center for Health Statistics.

Whitlock, E. P., Orleans, C. T., Pender, N., & Allan, J. (2002). Evaluating primary care behavioral counseling interventions: an evidence-based approach. *American Journal of Preventive Medicine, 22*, 267–284.

World Health Organization. (2004). *Revised global burden of disease estimates, vol. 2007*. Geneva, Switzerland: Author.

Yu, J. W., Adams, S. A., Burns, J., Brindis, C. D., & Irwin, C. E., Jr. (2008). Use of mental health counseling as adolescents become young adults. *Journal of Adolescent Health, 43*, (3) 268–276.

Ziv, A., Boulet, J. R., & Slap, G. B. (1998). Emergency department utilization by adolescents in the United States. *Pediatrics, 101*, 987–994.

Ziv, A., Boulet, J. R., & Slap, G. B. (1999). Utilization of physician offices by adolescents in the United States. *Pediatrics, 104*, 35–42.

Zuckerbrot, R. A., Cheung, A. H., Jensen, P. S., Stein, R. E., & Laraque, D. (2007). Guidelines for adolescent depression in primary care (GLAD-PC): I.Identification, assessment, and initial management. *Pediatrics, 120*, e1299–e1312.

Zuckerman, D. M., Colby, A., Ware, N. C., & Lazerson, J. S. (1986). The prevalence of bulimia among college students. *American Journal of Public Health, 76*, 1135–1137.

Zweig, J. M., Phillips, S. D., & Lindberg, L. D. (2003). Predicting adolescent profiles of risk: Looking beyond demographics. *Journal of Adolescent Health, 31*, 343–353.

CHAPTER 19

Internalizing Problems During Adolescence

JULIA A. GRABER AND LISA M. SONTAG

The development of psychopathology during adolescence has been perhaps the single
most studied area in the field of adolescence
(Steinberg & Morris, 2001). Extensive focus has
been on depressive disorders, conduct disorder,
and related subclinical problems and symptoms;
multiple behaviors and problems fall generally under the categories of internalizing and
externalizing behaviors. Internalizing problems
are generally considered to be the subgroup of
psychopathology that involve disturbances in
emotion or mood, whereas externalizing problems have tended to refer to dysregulations in
behavior. However, the affect versus behavior
distinction between internalizing and externalizing is not clear cut, especially when considering such emotional experiences as anxiety and
anger, which are consistently considered when
discussing both internalizing and externalizing
problems. Regardless, the general identification of internalizing problems as focused on
emotional components such as sadness, guilt,
worry, and the like is consistent across several
definitions. More specifically, depression and
anxiety disorders and the subclinical problems
in these areas typically comprise discussions
of internalizing problems and disorders (see
Kovacs and Devlin, 1998; and Zahn-Waxler,
Klimes-Dougan, and Slattery, 2000, for recent
reviews of internalizing problems and disorders
in childhood and adolescence, and chapter 20,
this volume, for a discussion of externalizing
problems during adolescence).

Interestingly, the concept of internalization
has been investigated as a core task of early
childhood (Kochanska, 1993). In this case,
internalization is the incorporation into the
self of guiding principles (as values or patterns of culture) through learning or socialization. Stemming from psychoanalytic and
social learning theories, internalization is commonly thought of in the context of the regulation of moral behavior or the development
of conscience (Kochanska, 1993). Kochanska
suggests that internalization comes about in
early childhood through parent–child communication with a focus on developing feelings
of empathy, guilt, and prosocial affect such
as concern for others, and cause and effect of
behaviors (e.g., understanding how one's behavior makes others feel). In psychoanalytic theory,
anxiety and guilt are the internalized emotions that replace parental control of behavior
(Muuss, 1996). In the present usage, *internalizing* refers to problems or disorders of emotion
or mood; the dysregulation of emotion might
be thought of as overinternalization of certain
emotions such as guilt, anxiety, or overin-
volvement in the emotions of significant others (e.g., the inability to distinguish one's own
responsibility for another's emotional state
from non-self causes of distress in others).

Mood variability or emotionality has
historically been viewed as a defining characteristic of adolescence (e.g., Hall, 1904;
Muuss, 1996, for a review). However, the
literature on universal or typical changes in
mood or emotion during adolescence has
been limited (with a few exceptions such as
Larson, Csikszentmihalyi, & Graef, 1980) until

very recently (e.g., Weinstein, Mermelstein, Hankin, Hedeker, & Flay, 2007). In contrast, a vast literature exists on depressive disorders, subclinical problems, and symptoms during adolescence. As such, the goal of this chapter is not to provide a comprehensive review of that literature or even of the etiology or epidemiology of depression (see Costello, Foley, & Angold, 2006; Hammen, & Rudolph, 2003, for recent reviews). Instead, this chapter provides an overview of internalizing symptoms, problems, and disorders and their etiology throughout the adolescent period (approximately the second decade of life). The chapter focuses on models and factors that may be particularly salient to understanding which types of problems become prevalent during adolescence and on two specific questions that have long interested scholars of internalizing problems: "Why adolescence?" and "Why more girls?"

TRENDS IN STUDYING ADOLESCENCE AND INTERNALIZING

A surge of interest in adolescent development in the 1980s resulted in several longitudinal projects that spanned the middle school and sometimes high school or young adult periods. These studies grew from an interest in understanding the role of transitions on the course of development (e.g., Elder, 1985) as well as specific interest in the combined or transactional influences of biological, social, and psychological processes in determining pathways of adjustment (e.g., Petersen, 1984; Simmons & Blyth, 1987). It could be argued that these initial studies were undertaken to understand the typical or "normal" problems of adolescence with perhaps greater attention to variations in adjustment (e.g., moodiness, parent–adolescent conflict, academic achievement) rather than disorder per se. Such projects reported on the range and diversity of normative adolescent development but also delineated the nature of problems experienced by adolescents. A subsequent surge in the 1990s

of community and epidemiology based studies attempted to determine the severity of these problems by focusing on the assessment and experience of disorder.

Most developmental scientists agree that behavior and adjustment during adolescent transitions are dependent on the nature of the transitions and how they are navigated, as well as on developmental experiences prior to making the transitions (Graber & Brooks-Gunn, 1996; Rutter, 1994). In the study of internalizing problems, a few studies have examined childhood behaviors in connection with subsequent adjustment or behavior in adolescence, sometimes even accounting for a transitional experience (e.g., Caspi & Moffitt, 1991). More often, though, studies of childhood experiences conclude with suggestions that subsequent influences on adolescent internalizing behaviors would be expected, and studies of adolescence note that preexisting patterns, behaviors, and experiences were undoubtedly factors in who developed problems during adolescence. Notably, some comprehensive longitudinal studies have been initiated that allow for the examination of continuity and change from infancy or early childhood into adolescence (e.g., NICHD Study of Early Child Care; Belsky et al., 2007) and beyond (e.g., the Dunedin Longitudinal Study; Krueger, Caspi, Moffitt, & Silva, 1998).

PATHWAYS FOR CONTINUITY AND CHANGE

Differentiating who will and who will not develop serious problems, and differentiating normative experience from atypical, are central themes of the field of developmental psychopathology. In particular, under this rubric, describing pathways both to psychopathology and to normative, healthy, or competent development are essential for understanding etiology and treatment of problems (e.g., Cicchetti & Cohen, 1995; Masten & Curtis, 2000). Masten and her colleagues have defined competence as ". . . adaptational success in the developmental tasks expected of individuals of a given age in a particular cultural and historical context" (Masten & Curtis, 2000, p. 533). As such, the definition of competence is not static and not singular; that is, individuals may meet developmental challenges in some areas (e.g., academic achievement) but fail to demonstrate adaptational success in other domains (e.g., behavior or emotion regulation). When considering adaptive versus maladaptive development, competence has often been assessed as the absence of problems or significant deficits in an area. For mood disorders, Masten and Curtis (2000) note that the links between competence and pathology is complex and that direction of effects are difficult to determine. That is, individuals who do not successfully meet developmental challenges may experience increased symptoms as a result of this failure; or, in contrast, symptoms of disorders may interfere with successful adaptation. Of course, when viewed over time and across developmental challenges, both experiences are likely to occur.

As noted by others, in this volume and elsewhere, nearly all youth experience challenges during the transition into adolescence, and often throughout the adolescent decade. As such, all youth should have dramatic shifts in behavior and potentially damaging effects from the experience of simultaneous and cumulative challenges. Alternatively, these changes are endemic to the developmental process and all youth should have the appropriate resources to adapt to such normative challenges and sustain adaptive behavioral patterns. In reality, as has been repeated in nearly all discussions of continuity and change (e.g., Kagan, 1980; Rutter, 1994), some youth demonstrate continuity of either successful adaptation or psychopathology, whereas others evince change in the ability to meet developmental challenges.

The development of internalizing problems or disorders during adolescence is in many cases not about substantial behavioral change or new problems arising, but rather is dependent on individual characteristics that existed well before adolescence (Bandura, 1964). For some youth, the challenges of adolescence exacerbate or accentuate these characteristics, resulting in decreased functioning and serious dysregulation in mood. These preexisting characteristics, or vulnerabilities, are often traitlike and develop over the course of childhood and adolescence (Ingram & Luxton, 2005). In turn, for some youth, internalizing problems may emerge at this time of development in connection with more concurrent or recent experiences. Therefore, the meaningful developmental questions regarding internalizing problems in adolescence must focus on individual differences in development. The important issue regarding continuity and change is not whether the normative transitions of adolescence result in difficulties but rather *why* they result in difficulties for certain individuals but not others. However, prior to a discussion of why some individuals experience internalizing problems and others do not, it is useful to consider the rates of these problems during adolescence.

EPIDEMIOLOGY OF ANXIETY AND DEPRESSION IN ADOLESCENCE

Although internalizing problems or symptoms may broadly encompass disturbance in emotion or mood, discussions of internalizing problems are usually limited to the investigation of depression or anxiety, typically as distinct phenomena. Compas and colleagues (Compas, Ey, & Grant, 1993; Compas & Oppedisano, 2000; Petersen et al., 1993) have developed a framework for viewing depressive disorders and subclinical symptoms that is applicable to internalizing problems more generally. Within this framework, internalizing symptomatology can be classified into three levels or types: *disorders*, as determined by diagnostic criteria; *syndromes* or subclinical problems; and internalizing *moods* or dysregulated emotion or moods. In contrast, rather than clear qualitative distinctions between disorder and symptoms, others argue that depression exists on a continuum (i.e., individuals are more or less depressed; Hankin & Abela, 2005). Despite support for the latter perspective, many researchers continue to investigate disorder, subclinical symptoms, and mood separately.

Zahn-Waxler and colleagues (2000) note that theories and research on anxiety and depression in childhood and adolescence often have been separate lines of investigation. At the same time, as will be evident in the following discussion and in recent investigations (Compas & Oppedisano, 2000; Krueger et al., 1998), the extent to which anxiety and depression are distinct experientially or in the course of development is debatable. A review of prevalence rates in childhood versus adolescence for anxiety and depressive disorders sheds light on connections between the two domains. That is, whereas rates of some anxiety disorders clearly increase from childhood to adolescence, others are confined almost exclusively to early childhood or may be present at any point in development over the life span. In contrast, rates of depression are low in childhood and increase dramatically during adolescence. Despite differences in overall developmental trends, anxiety and depression share symptoms and have substantial co-occurrence or comorbidity. (*Comorbidity* refers to the occurrence of a second disorder in an individual with an existing disorder.) Hence, some joint processes of etiology are likely among internalizing problems and disorders.

Prevalence Rates for Internalizing Disorders

Detailed information on symptoms and criteria for diagnosis of disorders are found in the *Diagnostic and Statistical Manual of Mental Disorders,* 4th edition, Text Revision (DSM-IV-TR; American Psychiatric Association, 2000). Disorders must include significant impairment in daily functioning along with requisite symptom severity and duration in order for diagnostic criteria to be met. Criteria for impairment often have been more subjective and drawn from psychiatric interview. At the same time, these criteria are relatively

straightforward for adults (e.g., disruption in work, home life, interpersonal relationships). The challenge for practitioners or researchers conducting studies of disorder has been the identification of developmentally salient criteria for impairment for disorders in childhood and adolescence (Masten & Curtis, 2000). Difficulty in assessing severity or impairment may lead to an over- or underdiagnosis of disorder, ultimately leading to a misrepresentation of rates of incidence.

Anxiety Disorders

The DSM-IV-TR identifies six main subcategories of anxiety disorders that are applicable to children and adolescents: separation anxiety disorder, generalized anxiety disorder (GAD), obsessive-compulsive disorder, posttraumatic and acute stress disorder (PTSD), and specific phobias. Recent studies, both clinical and epidemiological, show that some anxiety disorders are more likely to emerge in childhood (separation anxiety disorder and specific phobias), whereas others usually begin in adolescence (social phobia and panic disorder; Costello, Foley, & Angold, 2006). Across investigations and collapsing across anxiety disorders, Costello, Egger, and Angold (2004) reported that prevalence rates for any anxiety disorder in children and adolescents ranged from 2.2% to 27%. However, prevalence rates varied dramatically by time criteria. As expected, studies with short assessment intervals and a single data wave had the lowest prevalence and studies using a lifetime criterion produced the highest rates. For example, studies with 3-month assessment periods reported a range of 2.2% to 8.6% prevalence; studies with a 6-month period reported a range of 5.5%–8.6%; studies with a 12-month period reported 8.6%–20.9%; studies assessing lifetime prevalence up to age 19 reported a range of 8.3%–27.0% (Costello et al., 2004). Reports suggest a slight trend for rates to increase with age (Costello & Angold, 1995), but such data must be interpreted with caution as it is based on "any anxiety disorder." Disparities in prevalence rates across studies are in part accounted for by whether or not the diagnostic criteria used included assessment of functional impairment. When impairment is considered, rates of anxiety disorder decrease (Vasey & Ollendick, 2000; Zahn-Waxler et al., 2000); more children and adolescents report the requisite symptoms of the disorder, but a smaller number indicate significant impairments in functioning along with these disorders.

In addition, girls have higher rates of several of the anxiety disorders with the possible exception of PTSD (Costello et al., 2006; Vasey & Ollendick, 2000). The gender difference in rates varies by type of anxiety disorder and for some anxiety disorders data are limited on whether gender differences are consistently demonstrated. For example, separation anxiety, which tends to be found in young children, demonstrates a 3-to-1, girls to boys, gender difference in rates. In contrast, GAD may have equal prevalence rates by gender or higher rates for boys than girls in

childhood, but among adolescents it is more prevalent in girls (Bowen, Offord, & Boyle, 1990; McGee et al., 1990). Criteria for GAD are shown in Table 19.1.

Depressive Disorder

Most discussions of mood disorders during adolescence focus on major depressive disorder (MDD), as this is the most commonly diagnosed mood disorder in childhood and adolescence. An overview of the criteria for a major depressive episode is listed in Table 19.1. A depressive episode is characterized by feelings of depression, sadness, and the like, or a loss of pleasure for a period of 2 weeks or more, coupled with a minimum number and frequency of the other symptoms listed. Typically, prevalence rates of MDD have ranged from 0.4%–8.3% among adolescents (Birmaher et al., 1996). Estimates of lifetime prevalence for MDD among children and adolescents range from 4% to 25% (Kessler, Avenevoli, & Merikangas, 2001)

TABLE 19.1   Selected *DSM-IV-TR* Criteria for General Anxiety Disorder and Major Depressive Episode[a]

Symptoms and Criteria for Generalized Anxiety Disorder

A   Excessive anxiety or worry on most days for 6 months about a number of events or activities

B   Difficulty controlling the worry

C   Anxiety and worry are associated with three or more of the following symptoms:
(1) Restlessness
(2) Easily fatigued
(3) Difficulty concentrating
(4) Irritability
(5) Muscle tension
(6) Sleep disturbance

Symptoms and Criteria for a Major Depressive Episode

A   Depressed mood or loss of interest for a 2-week period (or irritability among children and adolescents), plus

B   Four or more of the following symptoms in the same 2-week period:
(1) Weight loss or weight gain
(2) Insomnia or hypersomnia
(3) Being restless or being slow (psychomotor agitation or retardation)
(4) Fatigue or loss of energy
(5) Feelings of worthlessness or inappropriate guilt
(6) Inability to concentrate
(7) Recurrent thoughts of death or suicide ideations or plans

Additional Criteria for both GAD and MDD

A   Symptoms result in significant impairment in social and occupational functioning

B   Symptoms are not due to physical illness or drug use

[a]Criteria are adapted from *DSM-IV-TR* (APA, 2000).

but have been found to range from 15% to 20% for adolescents specifically (Birmaher et al., 1996; Lewinsohn & Essau, 2002). In comparison, prevalence of MDD in school age children is 1.5%–2.5%. Not only do rates of MDD increase dramatically from childhood to adolescence, but MDD is the most commonly occurring disorder among adolescents. As there are now several longitudinal studies of depression that have followed samples across adolescence into adulthood (e.g., the Oregon Adolescent Depression Project [OADP], the Great Smoky Mountain Study [GSM], the Dunedin Multidisciplinary Health and Development Study), detailed estimates of life-time prevalence, 1-year incidence, and rates of recurrence are available across studies.

DSM-IV TR diagnostic criteria for MDD in childhood and adolescence are similar to criteria in adulthood, with the primary exception being that, among children and adolescents, the DSM-IV-TR allows mood disturbance to manifest as irritability as well as sadness. Although diagnostic criteria may be equally applicable for MDD across age groups, some variations in symptoms experienced and sequelae of disorder may vary between depressed children and adolescents. Specifically, Yorbik and colleagues (2004) found that depressed adolescents had significantly more negative cognitions (hopelessness, helplessness, pessimism, and discouragement), fatigue, hypersomnia, weight loss, and suicidal ideations and acts compared to depressed children. In comparison to adults, adolescents often experience substantial comorbidity of MDD with other disorders (Rohde, Lewinsohn, & Seeley, 1991). Despite these differences in manifestation across the life span, MDD appears to be the same core disorder regardless of the age at which it is experienced.

As noted, rates of MDD are fairly low in childhood and begin to rise during early adolescence. In the OADP, the mean age of onset was 14.9 (Lewinsohn, Rohde, & Seeley, 1998). This age is consistent with other community-based studies, although studies of clinical samples tend to report earlier ages of onset for

first depressive episode (e.g., 11 years of age in Kovacs, Obrosky, Gatsonis, & Richards, 1997).

Studies of variations in rates by subgroups of the population have focused predominantly on gender. Whereas most studies find no gender differences in rates of MDD in childhood, by age 15, the gender difference in MDD is at the adult rate of about 2 to 1, girls to boys. Much less attention has been paid to sociodemographic and cultural variations in rates of disorders in childhood and adolescence. Sampling strategies have frequently not allowed for disentangling racial or ethnic variations from those variations due to poverty or other demographic factors (e.g., rural versus urban environments). In the GSM, White adolescents (ages 9–17) had higher rates of MDD than Black adolescents (Costello, Keeler, & Angold, 2001). Moreover, poverty was predictive of disorder among White but not Black youth.

Despite differences in rates of internalizing disorders as a function of gender, race, and socioeconomic status (SES), depression is clearly a significant concern when discussing the experience of internalizing disorders during adolescence across all groups; rates may also increase for anxiety, or at least for GAD, during this time period. At the same time, both types of disorders appear to be more common among girls than boys by mid-adolescence.

Pediatric Bipolar Disorder (PBPD)

Until recently, studies of depression and reviews of this literature have not included bipolar disorder. Bipolar disorder (previously referred to as manic depression) is characterized by dramatic mood swings from very high (i.e., mania) to very low (i.e., depression), with normal mood in between these episodes or cycles. Initial studies suggested that bipolar disorder did not emerge until late adolescence or adulthood and hence was less relevant to discussions of depression in adolescents (e.g., Birmaher et al., 1996). Recent epidemiological studies estimate that less than 1% of children and adolescents have PBPD (Kessler et al., 2001). In general, there is consensus that cases of bipolar disorder are evident in adolescents and children. Yet, controversy still exists over developmentally appropriate diagnostic criteria.

Very rarely do adolescents manifest bipolar disorder according to DSM-IV-TR criteria established for diagnosis in adults. In particular, adolescents frequently do not display distinct manic episodes or periods of relatively good functioning between episodes. Rather, adolescents generally exhibit chronic or ultradian cycles of mood shifts (cycling between manic and depressive states within a 24-hour period) that are frequently accompanied by irritability, rage, and aggression. In fact, symptoms of PBPD in adolescence, such as hyperactivity, distractibility, racing thoughts, pressure to talk, and impulsivity, overlap with those associated with other disorders (e.g., attention-deficit/ hyperactivity disorder [ADHD]), suggesting that the appearance of PBPD in childhood or adolescence may be an instance of comorbidity between depression and other disorders (Hammen & Rudolph, 2003). Recently, several key symptoms of mania have been identified that more concretely distinguish manic episodes or chronic mania in childhood from symptoms of other disorders, in particular, ADHD; these symptoms include elation, grandiosity, flight of ideas/racing thoughts, decreased need for sleep, and hypersexuality (Geller, Zimmerman, & Williams, 2002). Presence of these five symptoms aids in confirming PBPD as a distinct diagnosis rather than simply a manifestation of comorbid childhood depression and ADHD. Although there is increasing evidence supporting the notion of PBPD, little evidence exists to suggest that pediatric PBPD is associated with the occurrence of adult bipolar disorder. Moreover, insufficient information on the etiology of PBPD makes it difficult to consider commonalities with or distinct pathways from MDD. Future prospective studies are necessary to better understand the prognosis of adolescents diagnosed with PBPD.

Subclinical Problems, Syndrome, or Symptoms

In contrast to disorders, depressed or anxious mood are reports of emotional states that are not assessed in terms of their duration or in connection with other symptoms. As such, in studies of adolescent moods or symptoms, rates of depressed mood have varied dramatically; for example, some reports indicated as many as 40% of the sample experienced depressed mood (Compas et al., 1993; Petersen et al., 1993). Similar compilation of rates of anxious mood in different age ranges or across studies has not been made.

Measures of depressive symptoms typically report age and gender differences in elevated symptoms that parallel differences found for disorders. In a meta-analysis of the Children's Depression Inventory (CDI), Twenge and Nolen-Hoeksema (2002) found no gender difference in scores during childhood but a significant gender difference beginning at age 13, with higher scores among girls. Another study examining the rates of depressive symptoms in 8- to 17-year-olds found a small but highly significant interaction between age and gender such that boys and girls reported similar levels of depressive symptoms prior to age 12; but after age 12, scores increased among adolescent girls, whereas boys' scores fell slightly from childhood to adolescence (Angold, Erkanli, Silberg, Eaves, & Costello, 2002). In addition, in their meta-analysis, Twenge and Nolen-Hoeksema (2002) found no effects of sociodemographic status on depressive symptoms when analyzing data across studies, although this information was not available in all reports. Also, no differences in mean scores were found between White and Black children and adolescents. However, Hispanic children were found to have significantly higher scores than other children.

Syndromal classifications are based on endorsement of a constellation of symptoms that co-occur in a statistically consistent manner. Achenbach (e.g., 1993) has derived a syndrome that taps anxiety and depression and distinguishes referred from nonreferred adolescents across multiple cultures and nations (Ivanova et al., 2007). In this approach, about 5%–6% of adolescents evince anxious–depressive syndrome as determined by scores above/below a predetermined cut point (Compas et al., 1993; Petersen et al., 1993). The assessment of syndrome is based on statistical associations among a checklist of symptoms as rated by several reporters (i.e., parent, teacher, self). In this approach, separate distinct syndromes for depression and anxiety are not found; rather, these symptoms consistently co-occur, a point that is salient to the next section.

The syndromal, category as defined by Achenbach, is one approach to defining a subclinical internalizing problem based on a specific measure of symptoms. Several other measures have been developed to assess depressive and anxiety symptoms and problems. Many have established cutoff scores for identifying potential disorders. Such measures are useful for comparing the experience of symptoms among individuals in the general population of youth but also as screening instruments for identifying individuals who may have more serious disorders. In this case, individuals who exceed the determined cutoff score are the most likely to have a disorder if a full diagnostic protocol is used. However, such measures and cutoff scores are not identical to diagnostic interview protocols and often identify individuals with elevated symptoms who do not have a disorder. Community epidemiologic surveys of self-reported depressive symptoms have found that between 20% and 50% of individuals between the ages of 11 and 18 years exceed cutoff points for clinically significant depression (Kessler et al., 2001). As indicated, prevalence rates of MDD based on diagnostic interviews are considerably lower than these rates. This discrepancy may be due in part to an overreporting of mild mood disturbances or a large number of adolescents who experience subthreshold symptoms of depression. That is, individuals may endorse high levels of symptoms and be over an established cutoff point on a screening instrument but may not meet all necessary DSM-IV-TR criteria for diagnosis of a disorder.

Interestingly, in the development of the Center for Epidemiological Study Depression scale (CES-D), Radloff (1991) recommends different cutoff points for adolescents versus adults. On this measure, the cutoff point used to identify adults at high risk for depressive disorder is lower than that used to identify the comparable high risk group of adolescents. Such findings indicate that adolescents report greater numbers/frequency of symptoms of depression than adults even though the rates of disorder may not vary by mid- to late adolescence to adulthood. Avenevoli and Steinberg (2001) also suggest that adolescents have a "differential manifestation" of symptoms in comparison to other age groups due to unique developmental experiences of this period. As symptom measures typically include a range of symptoms related to depression or internalizing problems but not limited to the diagnostic criteria, there is evidence that symptom profiles differ for older versus younger adolescents, in particular among girls (Yorbik et al., 2004).

The particularly high rates of depressed mood and moderate rates of syndromes or problems have led to questions about the importance of these experiences in terms of concurrent difficulties or predictability to subsequent disorder. Numerous discussions have focused on whether there is merit in considering subclinical symptoms and factors that influence variations in mean scores on symptom and emotion scales. At one point in time, much of the literature was limited to assessments of affect or symptoms and did not include assessment of disorder (see Costello & Angold, 1995). As longitudinal studies that included diagnostic interviews were conducted, the literature expanded dramatically, with extensive information available on the predictors of disorder, continuity of disorder, and related issues. Such studies have shown that subclinical problems are particularly salient to identifying individuals who are most likely to develop a subsequent disorder. In the OADP, the best predictor of developing a depressive disorder over a 1-year period was having elevated symptomatology (i.e., over a cutoff on a screener) at the first assessment (Gotlib, Lewinsohn, & Seeley, 1995). Thus, at this end of the spectrum of symptoms, there seems to be greater continuity of symptomatology than among individuals with mid- or low-level symptoms. Moreover, for depressive symptoms (Gotlib et al., 1995) and other problems (e.g., eating problems and disorders; Graber, Tyrka, & Brooks-Gunn, 2002), individuals with elevated symptoms or problems but not disorder tend to have impairment in functioning that is similar to that seen among youth who meet criteria for disorder.

Thus, factors that predict disorder or predict progression on a pathway to internalizing disorder are central to the discussion of internalizing problems in adolescence. In contrast, factors that influence perturbations or minor changes in emotion or symptoms may hold promise for future investigation but may not be important in understanding who is at risk for serious dysfunction, or who may need treatment.

A More Nuanced View of Moodiness

As mentioned previously, extreme moodiness has historically been viewed as a defining feature of adolescence. This notion of adolescence as a period of "storm and stress" has been debunked by a burgeoning number of studies examining daily fluctuations in mood during adolescence. As a means of examining daily mood and what factors influence change, Larson and colleagues (Larson et al., 1980; Larson & Ham, 1993) used the experience sampling method (ESM; reports of mood at intervals throughout the day), in what is now considered to be seminal work in the field. They found that, although adolescents demonstrated more mood changes during the day than did adults and children, frequent shifts in mood were highly dependent on negative or positive daily experiences.

A new wave of ESM studies of adolescent mood is underway, examining the effects of gender and age on changes in specific moods as well as global positive and negative affect across adolescence. For example, Weinstein and colleagues (2007) studied young and mid-adolescent youth at 6-month intervals for 1 year. At each time, an ESM protocol was conducted as was a standard symptom questionnaire. As expected, mid-adolescents reported lower levels of positive affect compared to young adolescents. In contrast, global depressed mood (from the symptom questionnaire) did not change over time, and girls reported higher levels of depressed mood than boys in both age groups and across the year. These findings suggest that the declines in mood in adolescence, which are typical, may be driven by deteriorations in positive affect, rather than increases in negative affect (Weinstein et al., 2007). Other recent studies suggest that atypical fluctuations in mood may identify adolescents at risk for more serious symptomatology or disorder. Schneiders and colleagues (2006) found that adolescents at high risk for internalizing disorders (categorized based on internalizing and externalizing symptoms, self-esteem, loneliness, etc.) were more emotionally reactive to negative events, showing greater decreases in positive affect and greater increases in depressive symptoms, compared to low-risk adolescents. Together, these findings suggest that atypical peaks in negative mood may be a risk factor for more serious symptomatology. Thus, whereas some mood variability and even decline in positive mood may be normative in adolescence, particular patterns of mood, especially if they persist and begin to interfere with activities such as school, work, or interactions with peers, are not normative and may be indicators of potentially serious psychopathology.

Comorbidity or Co-occurrence of Anxiety and Depression

As we have already alluded to, internalizing problems and disorders do not occur in isolation of other disorders and problems. Unfortunately, many studies, most often of subclinical symptoms, focus on a single outcome. With the utilization and development of comprehensive diagnostic interviews that assess multiple disorders (see McClellan & Werry, 2000, for a special issue on these protocols), examination of co-occurrence or comorbidity has become more common. As indicated, comorbidity refers to the occurrence of a second disorder in an individual with an existing disorder; comorbidity may exist concurrently or over time. Comorbidity poses a special concern in the study of adolescent psychopathology. Caron and Rutter (1991) note that failure to identify comorbid conditions leads to two main problems. First, effects associated with the identified condition may be attributable to the other condition; and second, the experience of the other condition may influence the course of the first. Identifying comorbid conditions and the correlates of these conditions is essential for understanding the developmental processes of psychopathology across adolescence. Moreover, comorbidity may influence severity or impairment experienced by the individual and certainly impacts the course and outcomes of intervention.

It has been widely demonstrated that depression and depressive symptoms frequently co-occur with other symptoms and disorders (Kessler et al., 1996; Lewinsohn, Hops, Roberts, Seeley, & Andrews, 1993). Nearly half, or even two-thirds, of all adolescents who meet diagnostic criteria for depression have a comorbid condition (McGee et al., 1990; Rohde et al., 1991). Research also suggests that in most cases the other disorder preceded the depressive episode (Kessler et al., 1996; Rohde et al., 1991). For anxiety disorders, comorbidity is also commonly reported across studies (Kovacs & Devlin, 1998; Zahn-Waxler et al., 2000). Most importantly, comorbidity observed between anxiety and depression is quite high, with the OADP reporting a lifetime comorbidity of anxiety with MDD of 73.1% (Lewinsohn, Zinbarg, Seeley, Lewinsohn, & Sack, 1997). In particular, adolescent depression has frequently been preceded by childhood anxiety disorders.

As mentioned, Achenbach (1993) has demonstrated empirical evidence that questions whether childhood and adolescent anxious and depressive symptomatology are distinct. Compas and Oppedisano (2000) suggest that a lack of discrimination between anxiety and depression may also occur at the diagnostic level; examination of symptoms of MDD and GAD reveal several similarities—for example, symptoms of restlessness, fatigue, and irritability (see Table 19.1). Children and adolescents with mixed syndromes of anxious and depressive emotions and symptoms may be at heightened risk for development of subsequent disorders as well as for increased impairment in other areas (e.g., social interactions) than individuals with only elevated anxious or only elevated depressive symptoms.

In the Dunedin study, Krueger and his colleagues (1998) examined the extent to which specific disorders may actually be indicators of what they termed "stable, underlying core psychopathological processes." A two-factor model of internalizing versus externalizing disorders demonstrated the best fit at ages 18 and 21 years, and individuals demonstrated substantial continuity in their relative position on these latent constructs over this period. Such an approach may explain concurrent comorbidity rates within internalizing disorders (i.e., MDD and anxiety disorders) as well as the longitudinal links between prior anxiety disorders and subsequent adolescent depressive disorder.

In addition, subclinical internalizing symptoms and problems also demonstrate high rates of co-occurrence with other types of problems. For example, several studies report moderate to high correlations between scores for internalizing and externalizing symptoms (see Zahn-Waxler et al., 2000 for a brief review). In a study of subclinical eating problems and depressive symptomatology (Graber & Brooks-Gunn, 2001), individuals with co-occurring problems reported the greatest disturbances in family and peer relationships in comparison to individuals with only one or the other problem. Adolescent girls may be at particular risk not only for disorder but also for comorbidity of multiple disorders due to unique developmental issues surrounding pubertal maturation among females. A community study of young to mid-adolescent girls examined associations between early pubertal maturation and comorbidity in depression, substance use, and eating problems and found that early menarche in girls is associated with greater risk for comorbid depression and substance use (Stice, Presnell, & Bearman, 2001). Thus, co-occurrence of problems and comorbidity of disorder is fairly normative for adolescent psychopathology. This fact may partially explain why many risk factors for internalizing problems are not found to be specific to internalizing problems but rather are linked to various psychopathologies.

DEVELOPMENTAL MODELS FOR CHANGES IN INTERNALIZING SYMPTOMS AND DISORDERS DURING ADOLESCENCE

A number of models have been proposed to explain the development of internalizing problems, and more specifically depression, throughout the life span. Some models identify general processes that may lead to elevations in depressed or anxious mood or even disorder but do not specify why rates shift dramatically for depression during adolescence. Other models focus on adolescent development and internalizing problems but may or may not be applicable to general processes that lead to depression at other periods in the life span. For example, puberty is often included in models explaining increased internalizing problems during adolescence but rarely is mentioned in general process models of depression in adulthood. In the adolescence literature, focus has centered on models that incorporate developmental experiences in order to explain individual differences in behavioral and adjustment changes (e.g., Graber & Brooks-Gunn, 1996). The models stem from interactional or transactional approaches that might apply to development throughout the life span, but in these cases, particular transitions or experiences

of adolescence are focal to understanding adjustment or behavioral change at this time (Graber & Brooks-Gunn, 1996). Models that are particularly salient for understanding developmental changes and individual differences in internalizing problems during adolescence are: (a) diathesis-stress (Ingram & Luxton, 2005); (b) cumulative or simultaneous events (Petersen, Sarigiani, & Kennedy, 1991; Simmons & Blyth, 1987); (c) accentuation (Caspi & Moffitt, 1991; see also Susman & Dorn, this volume); and (d) differential sensitivity (Graber & Brooks-Gunn, 1996).

Diathesis-Stress Models

As noted in this chapter and throughout this volume, adolescence is remarkable as a developmental period because of the confluence of transitions and challenges that occur during this decade of life. General models of psychopathology, in particular, typically focus on the experience of stressful life events (Ingram & Luxton, 2005). That is, significant stressful occurrences commonly precede depressive episodes, and dysregulation of the physiological stress system occurs in the face of high levels of psychosocial stress. However, events in and of themselves rarely fully explain changes in affect or onset of disorder. Attention must also be given to the interplay of vulnerability, risk, and protective factors across developmental stages. As indicated, vulnerability, or "diathesis," refers to predispositional, usually intraindividual, factors that predict internalizing symptoms, (problems, or disorders, i.e., emotion regulation, physiological responses to stress, or temperament) that are in part shaped by experience but often become stable during childhood and adolescence (Ingram & Luxton, 2005). In contrast, risk factors are those factors associated with increased probability of internalizing problems but may not clearly be identified as causal (e.g., Ingram & Luxton, 2005). For example, gender is a risk factor for internalizing problems during adolescence because gender is associated with higher probability of developing these problems but does not explain why the problems occur more often for girls. Protective factors moderate or buffer the impact of risk factors and potentially impede the development of internalizing problems.

The diathesis-stress model of depression predicts that major transitions or negative events interact with prior vulnerabilities to psychopathology, resulting in increased problems or poor outcomes in the face of these stressors. In testing this model, the focus is typically on the identification and development of prior vulnerabilities to adjustment problems (e.g., poor emotion regulation skills, depressogenic cognitive styles, genetic markers). Ingram and Luxton (2005) note that these vulnerabilities must exist prior to the emergence of internalizing problems and as noted differ from risk factors of internalizing problems.

Cumulative or Simultaneous Events Models

Models of cumulative and simultaneous events posit that when individuals experience major events or transitions that typically occur during adolescence (e.g., school changes or pubertal development) either in close sequence (cumulatively) or simultaneously, they are more likely to have negative behavioral and emotional outcomes as a result of the confluence of events. Cumulative events may also be characterized by increasing numbers of stressful events that occur for adolescents commensurate with changes in peer groups, friendships, parental relationships, and school demands (e.g., the number of stressful events increases during early and mid-adolescence; Brooks-Gunn, 1991). Although conceptually the impact of simultaneously occurring events may differ from closely successive events, this is rarely, if ever, tested as most studies define events as simultaneous if they occur within a 6- to 12-month period (Graber & Brooks-Gunn, 1996). Of course, most adolescents effectively navigate the challenges and transitions of adolescence; however, in this model, coping resources may be overwhelmed by

the experience of multiple changes in close proximity, and thus internalizing symptoms increase. In essence, the experience of stressful events and their timing, as well as the increased likelihood that certain events will occur during adolescence are the critical factors predicting internalizing problems in this model.

Accentuation Models

Accentuation models posit that major developmental transitions accentuate preexisting problems or vulnerabilities, resulting in increased problems and poor outcomes after the transition (e.g., Elder & Caspi, 1990). Drawing on Piagetian theory, the model suggests that individuals will assimilate new information and experiences into preexisting behavioral, emotional, or cognitive patterns of response to challenging situations (Graber & Brooks-Gunn, 1996). Studies supporting such a model have found that preexisting behavioral problems are accentuated by major transitional events (e.g., puberty and parenthood; Caspi & Moffat, 1991; Cowan, Cowan, Hemming, & Miller, 1991). However, most tests of this model have been made 2–3 years after the time of transition, and the question of how subsequent transitions are negotiated is still unanswered (Graber & Brooks-Gunn, 1996). Note that accentuation models focus on major transitions that exacerbate preexisting problems or vulnerabilities, in contrast to diathesis-stress models that focus on prior vulnerabilities that interact with any type of stressful event.

Differential Sensitivity

Contrary to the previous models discussed, differential or heightened sensitivity models emphasize the potential for vulnerability within an individual to vary depending on the developmental period. That is, periods of transition may present increased vulnerability to the individual in how stress is experienced. Heightened sensitivity models have arisen from studies of women's reproductive transitions (puberty, pregnancy, menopause) and the connections between these transitions and changes in mental and physical health (e.g., Graber &

Brooks-Gunn, 1996). Biological systems may be more sensitive to environmental or contextual influences during times of rapid change, as seen in reproductive transitions. Similarly, models of differential sensitivity, also like accentuation or diathesis-stress models, suggest that individuals with preexisting characteristics are potentially more sensitive to developmental transitions and challenges. In this case, the transition period results in heightened vulnerability to stress resulting in poorer mental or physical health, but vulnerability may be less significant in nontransitional periods. Notably, one concern is that individuals who experience heightened vulnerability and enter a path for poorer health may continue on that trajectory after the transitional period ends.

Clearly, these models share many similarities and the distinctions are predominantly in the area of emphasis (stressful events versus vulnerabilities) and the extent to which they focus on developmental transitions as distinct from other stressful events. (Table 19.2 provides an overview of the primary emphases of these models.) These models will be revisited in the following sections in cases where they have been used to explain findings in the literature.

VULNERABILITY AND RISK FACTORS ASSOCIATED WITH INTERNALIZING PROBLEMS

In general, the etiology of internalizing problems can be organized around several vulnerability and risk factors. These include: stress;

psychological processing of stress including cognitive processes, personality, and related psychopathology; biology of stress, including markers of disorder, neurodevelopment, and hormones; genetics and gene environment interactions; and interpersonal relationships (e.g., Birmaher et al., 1996; Garber, 2000; Petersen et al., 1993). From a developmental perspective, such categorizations often fall short of examining integrative, transactional, or biopsychosocial processes; for example, genetic and parenting effects on depression are no doubt interactive (Collins, Maccoby, Steinberg, Hetherington, & Bornstein, 2000). Hence, consideration of how these factors influence each other and how they may be influenced by broader contextual factors (e.g., gender, transitional periods) will be taken into account. Also, within any particular study of adolescents, the subgroup experiencing an internalizing problem may be experiencing it for the first time or may have a recurrent or persistent problem. Recent longitudinal studies of depression find unique predictors of each (e.g., Lewinsohn et al., 1998). As noted, many more studies focus on the prediction and correlates of depression (MDD) and depressive symptoms, whereas much less in known about anxiety. Hence, the following sections most often apply to depressive problems and may not include literatures on all types of internalizing problems.

Stressful Events

As indicated, many models of the etiology of internalizing problems are based on the

TABLE 19.2   Models of the Development of Internalizing Problems

Model	Stress Associated With	Vulnerability
Diathesis-Stress	Stressful events	Traitlike characteristic that develops in childhood or during adolescence
Cumulative/Simultaneous Events	Developmental transition or multiple transitions	Conferred by timing of transition and overwhelming of psychological resources
Accentuation	Developmental transition or multiple transitions	Existence of prior internalizing problems
Differential Sensitivity	Stressful events	Develops during a transition due to some aspect of the transition

diathesis-stress model. Hence, stress or stressful events are critical risk factors for internalizing problems. Lazarus and Folkman (1984) define psychological stress as a "relationship between the person and the environment that is appraised by the person as taxing or exceeding his or her resources and endangering his or her well being," (p. 19). Garber (2000) defines stressful life events as "… circumstances characterized by either the lack or loss of a highly desirable and obtainable goal or the presence of a highly undesirable and inescapable event," (p. 475). As is demonstrated by these two highly cited definitions, numerous interpretations of stress exist within the psychological literature. Regardless of definitions, there is much consensus and evidence that events identified as stressful by the individual are linked to internalizing problems.

The adult and adolescent depression literatures frequently report retrospective associations between the experience of major life events and the experience of a depressive episode. Among adults, 60%–70% of individuals with MDD report a major stressful event in the preceding year, usually some type of loss; effects are more modest in studies of depressed children and adolescents (Birmaher et al., 1996). Traumatic loss, such as exposure to another's suicide, dramatically increases the risk for depression among adults and adolescents (Birmaher et al., 1996). Similarly, anxiety disorders may also be preceded by a stressful life event (Vasey & Ollendick, 2000). The events need not be associated with the anxiety problem directly, as in the case of PTSD, in which a precipitating event leads to the distress response, but instead, other anxiety disorders such as GAD may arise after family relocations, school changes, or other stressful life events.

The individual's assessments of the importance of the event, how negative the event is, what impact it has on other areas of the individual's life, and whether the event is controllable or uncontrollable are all factors affecting whether stressful events are associated with increased internalizing problems or disorder (Birmaher et al., 1996; Vasey & Ollendick, 2000). Compas Howell, Ledoux, Phares, and Williams (1989) report that major events in the family tend to increase the number of minor stressful events for family members, which leads to increased behavior problems (internalizing and externalizing symptoms) among young adolescents; thus, events in the broader context of an adolescent's life as well as immediately experienced events are salient to changes in internalizing symptoms. Furthermore, individual differences in terms of how events are interpreted or processed cognitively have been linked to onset and maintenance of internalizing problems (Kaslow, Adamson, & Collins, 2000; see subsequent section).

In general, such associations between stressful events and internalizing symptoms would apply to any point in the life course. As noted, cumulative or simultaneous event models suggest that internalizing symptoms increase during adolescence because adolescents are more likely to experience more stressful life events than individuals of other ages, given the nature of normative adolescent development; these events include puberty, school change, changes in family relationships, changes in peer relationships, and so on. Reports of stressful life events (both negative and positive events) have been found to increase during early to mid-adolescence, with higher rates of stressful events associated with increases in internalizing symptoms (Brooks-Gunn, 1991; Ge, Lorenz. Conger, Elder, & Simons, 1994).

In the few studies that have looked at the simultaneity or ordering of developmental events or transitions, the occurrence of peak pubertal development (as indexed by rapid change in physical growth) prior to school change was predictive of increased depressive symptoms several years later, at 12th grade (Petersen et al., 1991). Notably, this effect was found only among girls. Given the normative differences in pubertal timing between girls and boys, with girls showing physical changes of puberty earlier than boys, and the normative grades when young adolescents make school transitions, only girls had significant pubertal changes prior to making a school change. Hence, gender differences in internalizing symptoms over adolescence may in part be explained by the timing of developmental events and transitions.

In addition to greater likelihood of experiencing synchronous events and transitions, girls may be at greater risk for increases in internalizing symptoms because of the types of events that normatively occur in adolescence and how girls respond to them. Specifically, during the middle school years, adolescents frequently experience changes in their close relationships, endorsing events such as breaking up with a friend, having a fight with a parent, and so on. Girls, in comparison to boys, may be more likely to experience negative emotions in response to events in relationships, report more events that are relationship focused, and perseverate about events that have happened with peers (Kessler & McLeod, 1984; Rudolf, 2002). Because of girls' tendencies to rely heavily on peer relationships for emotional support and intimacy, these events may elicit more frequent or prolonged internalizing responses in girls, especially girls with vulnerabilities in interpersonal relationships (Rudolph, 2002; see subsequent section).

Overall, stressful events may increase in number due to changes in adolescent experience, may increase in magnitude in association with major developmental transitions, and may have a more deleterious effect due to the timing of events. The impact of events may vary due to psychological factors or biological factors. Acknowledging that neural processes are the basis of psychological factors, each will be discussed separately.

Psychological Factors: Cognitions, Emotion Regulation, and Temperament

Cognitions

As not all adolescents who experience challenge or stress develop internalizing problems, individual characteristics, skills, and capacities are often vulnerabilities that interact with stress increasing the likelihood of internalizing symptoms and problems. Cognitive changes during adolescence are a foundation of changes in self-evaluation and processing of the other challenges of adolescence (Harter, 1998). While cognitive abilities increase in several domains during adolescence, allowing for more nuanced reflections on the self, one's future, and the world (Keating, 2004), one question that remains is the extent to which adolescent changes in cognition are predictive of changes in internalizing symptoms. A well-documented literature demonstrates that cognitive styles or cognitive attribution biases are associated with depressive symptoms and that these styles and biases are often established prior to adolescence (Kaslow et al., 2000; Nolen-Hoeksema, 1994). Hypothetically, some cognitive-based vulnerabilities may develop during adolescence commensurate with cognitive development, whereas others may be preexisting, interacting with the developmental challenges of adolescence to lead to internalizing problems. For individuals with preexisting vulnerabilities, adolescence may be the first time in development when sufficient stressors have occurred to result in problems.

Kaslow and colleagues (2000) identify three primary areas of cognitive processing that are associated with depression: negative self-schemas (negative views of the self), faulty information processing (attributional biases), and negative expectancies (helplessness and hopelessness). As noted, changes in thinking about the self are part of adolescent development. Self-consciousness also seems to increase during early adolescence. In addition, assessments of self-image or esteem tend to demonstrate moderate to strong associations with internalizing symptoms, making it difficult to consider negative self-evaluations separately from these symptoms.

Appraisals of physical development or body image are areas of self evaluation that are particularly salient to adolescents and their risk for internalizing problems. Although most youth demonstrate increases in body esteem over adolescence, disturbances in body image are common during early adolescence (or at puberty) for both girls and boys (Graber, Petersen, & Brooks-Gunn, 1996), and in turn have been shown to prospectively predict increases in depressive symptomatology in adolescents (Paxton, Neumark-Sztainer, Hannan, & Eisenberg, 2006). At the same time, body image concerns seem to have a stronger impact on girls' internalizing symptoms as well as eating disorders and symptoms than on boys' symptoms (e.g., Allgood-Merten, Lewinsohn, & Hops, 1990; Rierdan, Koff, & Stubbs, 1989). In our own work in a longitudinal study of girls, many girls experienced a serious disturbance in body image at some point during adolescence (Ohring, Graber, & Brooks-Gunn, 2002). Body disturbance was concurrently associated with elevated internalizing and disturbed eating symptoms. However, girls with recurrent or persistent poor body image during adolescence not only had elevated depressive and eating symptoms during adolescence, but also reported more symptoms in young adulthood.

Nolen-Hoeksema (1994) postulated that gender differences in depression emerge during adolescence due to an interaction between how girls experience puberty and gender differences in the ways that adolescents experience and react to stress. Consistent with this proposition, we found that girls with persistent body dissatisfaction were also more likely to have gone through puberty earlier than their peers (Ohring et al., 2002). Thus, negative self evaluations (i.e., body dissatisfaction) were linked to puberty, and individual differences in puberty were important in determining who had continued negative self evaluations. In the limited literature on boys' body dissatisfaction, comparable individual differences are not found. Hence, the development during early adolescence of negative self-evaluations about the body may be an important factor explaining gender differences in depression, as well as explaining why some girls have more internalizing symptoms than other girls.

In contrast, faulty information processing and negative expectancies are cognitive vulnerabilities that are likely in place prior to adolescence. These factors are moderators of the experience of adolescent challenges in predicting not only internalizing symptoms, but also aggressive symptoms. In general, cognitive styles or faulty information processing usually reflect how social information or events are interpreted by the individual. Cognitive biases that attribute negative events to internal, stable, and global causes and biases that attribute positive events to external, unstable, and specific causes are linked to elevated depressive symptoms (Kaslow et al., 2000). The interpretation of the controllability of events in one's life has also been linked to both depressive and anxiety symptoms (Alloy & Abramson, 2007; Vasey & Ollendick, 2000). In particular, a sense of hopelessness (i.e., belief that events have internal, stable, and global causes that one can do little about) has been linked to depressive disorder.

Cognitive styles or attributions consistently differentiate youth with, versus without, disorders and those with elevated, versus normative, levels of internalizing symptoms (see Kaslow et al., 2000 for a review). However, a large meta-analysis did not find that attributional styles consistently interacted with life events to predict depression, as would be expected (Joiner & Wagner, 1995). Much of the research to date on this issue is cross-sectional, making it difficult to determine if cognitive styles develop or change substantially during adolescence. In analyses with the OADP, when youth were in high school, many adolescents demonstrated consistent cognitive styles over a 1-year period but subgroups of youth demonstrated change (Schwartz, Kaslow, Seeley, & Lewinsohn, 2000). Change in cognitive styles was associated with other cognitive factors; for example, better self-esteem at the initial assessment predicted change from maladaptive to an adaptive cognitive style over time.

Notably, certain attributions or cognitive styles may be more salient to the maintenance and recurrence of depression than to onset. For example, individuals who ruminate on negative emotions tend to have longer and more severe depressive episodes. Importantly, Nolen-Hoeksema (1994) suggests that girls are more likely to be ruminators than are boys. In her model, girls are not only more likely to experience normative developmental experiences negatively (i.e., form negative body images in response to the changes of puberty) but also girls are more likely to demonstrate an attributional style (i.e., rumination) that magnifies those negative feelings. Such an interactive model would address the question of why more girls become depressed or have elevated internalizing symptoms and problems. Alloy and Abramson (2007) lend further support to this model, postulating that changes in cognitive functioning due to brain development during adolescence result in improvements in attentional executive functions, increases in working memory skills, improved hypothetical thinking, and future orientation. These neural–cognitive changes serve as prerequisites for generating negative cognitions about stressful events, experiencing feelings of hopelessness, and rumination.

Along with attributions about events and expectations about one's ability to influence events, individuals also differ in the approaches they use to cope with the events. These factors are often related, as seen with ruminating styles. That is, when individuals ruminate, they focus on negative emotions rather than engage in problem solving or distraction, and thus respond to the emotions with continued perseveration about the negative emotions or events. More generally, cognitive beliefs about the extent to which one's actions can influence events, what can be done about events, or why the events occurred are in part the result of attributional biases. However, these biases also lead to subsequent behavioral responses to events and feelings. Hence, coping behaviors and cognitive processing are interactive in predicting the development of internalizing symptoms (Compas, Connor-Smith, Saltzman, Thomsen, & Wadsworth, 2001).

Emotion Regulation

As noted, internalizing problems are defined as dysregulations in mood and affect, and hence, by definition, are indications of difficulties in regulating negative emotions. Emotion regulation skills tend to develop substantially during early childhood (Rothbart & Bates, 2006; Zahn-Waxler et al., 2000), but also continue to develop in response to new demands of adolescent emotional experiences. Deater-Deckard (2001) identified emotion regulation and social cognitive skills as particularly salient to the peer relations of children and adolescents. For example, among young adolescents, better abilities to understand others' feelings or thoughts are associated with greater peer acceptance (Bosacki & Astington, 1999).

In some sense, emotion regulation and coping are similar constructs in that both involve managing one's reactions to negative and potentially stressful situations. Lazarus and Folkman (1984) define coping as an effort to manage specific external and/or internal demands that are appraised as taxing or exceeding the resources of the person. In addition to these active coping strategies, some individuals have vulnerabilities that impact emotion regulation and hinder effective adaptation to stressful experiences. These vulnerabilities may include temperamentally based and conditioned cognitive, behavioral, and physiological reactions to stress that may or may not be within conscious awareness and are not under personal control, such as physiological arousal, intrusive thoughts, and rumination.

Coping strategies aimed at removing the stressor or resolving the emotional, physiological, or cognitive distress (e.g., problem solving, seeking support, expressing emotions, reevaluating the situation, etc.) are typically associated with more positive adjustment and fewer internalizing problems (Compas et al., 2001; Sontag, Graber, Brooks-Gunn, & Warren, 2008). However, studies with adults have demonstrated that the effectiveness of coping strategies is dependent on the type of stressor and the cultural background of the individual (e.g., Compas et al., 2001; Utsey, Bolden, Lanier, & Williams, 2007). In recent work examining coping strategies, peer stress, and symptoms of psychopathology in young adolescent girls, we found that, compared to White girls, African American girls were less likely to use traditionally effective coping strategies, such as problem solving, emotional expression, and regulation (Sontag, Graber, & Brooks-Gunn, 2007). At the same time, exploratory analyses revealed that the tendency to use problem solving, emotional expression, and emotion regulation more often than other strategies mediated the association between stressful peer events and internalizing symptoms for African American girls only. Differences found between African American and White girls in use and impact of coping strategies suggest that standard measures of coping may not capture the full range of strategies used by adolescents from diverse ethnic groups.

Although it has been shown that more highly developed emotion regulation and coping skills in adolescents are associated with a lower incidence of internalizing problems, Zahn-Waxler and her colleagues (2000) have argued that promoting emotion regulation in early childhood may be linked subsequently to poor emotion regulation later in development. In particular, regulating externalizing behaviors (e.g., anger) is a primary task of early childhood. But individuals, particularly girls, who learn to overregulate these behaviors and emotions, may develop dispositions for internalizing emotions, such as fear and guilt. For example, parents can socialize children to be more or less anxious by encouraging regulation of fear via avoidance of the stimuli or situation versus encouraging a sense of control and self-efficacy (Vasey & Ollendick, 2000). Such findings speak to how attributional biases may develop with parents socializing children to develop different beliefs about control and efficacy in their environments (Zahn-Waxler et al., 2000). At the same time, attributions and emotion regulation skills may result from the interaction of biologically based (possibly with a genetic component) factors and socialization. Unfortunately, much of the research on emotion regulation effects on internalizing problems is based on cross-sectional comparisons of different age groups, and future longitudinal investigations are needed.

Temperament

As suggested in the discussion of attributional biases, many individuals have consistent ways of interacting with their social worlds, whereas for others, change in these constructs may occur across development. Temperament or personality may be one way of conceptualizing consistency in how individuals respond to their environments. A detailed discussion of how personality or temperament may be linked to internalizing problems over the course of development is beyond the scope of this chapter. However, a few brief examples support suggestions that these constructs may be important and understudied in their role in the development of psychopathology more generally.

Kagan and Fox (2006) view temperament as a stable way of responding to the environment, in particular, to unexpected events. Similarly, Block and Block (1980) describe ego control (impulse inhibition/expression) and ego resilience (flexibility to modify impulse control depending on the situation) as personality types, which reflect how an individual responds to environmental stress or frustration. Research based in each approach has found that children and adolescents who were inhibited or overcontrolled had higher rates of internalizing problems than those with other temperament or personality types (see Kagan and Fox, 2006, for a review). Perhaps the most compelling evidence in this area stems from Suomi's (1999) animal models of the interaction of temperament and rearing conditions. Selective breeding of highly reactive or inhibited monkeys produced offspring with these response patterns; however, rearing experiences had a profound impact on the behavioral adjustment of these monkeys over time.

Thus, compelling evidence from nonhuman primate and human studies indicate that temperament may be a vulnerability for internalizing problems, but that other factors mediate or moderate subsequent associations between this vulnerability and psychopathology. Such findings do not directly speak to why internalizing problems increase at adolescence in humans or why more girls than boys develop these problems. These factors likely play a role in answering these questions when temperament is examined along with developmental challenges and gender differences in stressful events. Furthermore, differential parenting practices of girls versus boys who are overcontrolled or inhibited/reactive may account in part for the gender differences in the development of particular attributional biases or coping responses.

"BIOLOGICAL MARKERS" OF DISORDER AND NEUROENDOCRINE PROCESSES OF STRESS

One scientific challenge has been to identify how experiences of stress translate into the behavioral and biological dysregulations observed in depressive and anxiety disorders. Investigations of biological mechanisms of disorder first focused on determining which neural and physiological systems differed between disordered and nondisordered individuals. More recently, process-oriented studies have considered how experiences interact with biological systems in the development of internalizing disorders.

Numerous studies of adults have documented altered or abnormal neuroendocrine functioning when comparing individuals with MDD or an anxiety disorder to individuals who do not have disorder, or have one or more non-affective disorders (see Dahl & Ryan, 1996; Meyer, Chrousos, & Gold, 2001 for reviews). In comparable pediatric studies of MDD, several of these findings have not been replicated among children and adolescents. Such discrepancies were puzzling, as children, adolescents,

and adults reported many similarities in the experience and symptoms of internalizing disorders. Discrepancies in neuroendocrine studies and pharmacological trials resulted in several tangential and occasionally nonproductive discussions as to whether children and adolescents were "really" depressed if they did not show biological markers of depression comparable to adults. For example, many of the drugs used to treat adulthood depression (e.g., tricyclics, lithium, and serotonin–norepinephrine reuptake inhibitors [SNRIs]) have been ineffective in treating MDD in children and adolescents. In contrast, efficacy trials of the present generation of drugs (primarily, selective serotonin reuptake inhibitors [SSRIs]), indicate that this class of drugs seems to be comparably effective in treating depression in children, adolescents, and adults (Singh, Pfeifer, Barzman, Kowatch, & DelBello, 2007). Notably, the neuroendocrine system is still undergoing substantial normative development in childhood and adolescence, making it likely that maturational factors account for some of the observed differences between adults versus children and adolescents. A comprehensive listing of which markers are or are not found in adolescents versus adults is beyond the scope of this chapter (see Dahl & Ryan, 1996; Meyer et al., 2001, for reviews). Most importantly, though, initial studies of differences between disordered and nondisordered individuals did not identify predictors of these disorders. Instead, such markers identify factors that need to be explained in the development of a disorder or possible systems that are disrupted by the disorder. Ultimately, the goal of neuroscience investigations is to link experiences to abnormal functioning of neurological or endocrine systems.

L-HPA and HPG Endocrine Systems

Two hormonal systems, the limbic–hypothalamus–pituitary–adrenal (L-HPA) axis and the hypothalamus–pituitary–gonadal (HPG) axis, appear to be central to the development of internalizing disorders, in part, stemming from studies of biological markers (see above), and in part from an interest in behavioral change with puberty (both the L-HPA and the HPG systems control hormonal changes of puberty). In addition, human and animal research demonstrates gene–environment interactions in the development of L-HPA functioning (e.g., Caspi et al., 2003; Francis, Champagne, Liu, & Meaney, 1999). The following provides a brief review of how changes in each system may be linked to internalizing problems.

The L-HPA Stress System

Activation of the L-HPA system occurs in response to novelty and stress, with a particular sensitivity to social stressors. During or briefly after exposure to the stimulus, hormones in the brain stimulate the pituitary to secrete adrenocorticotropic hormone (ACTH), which in turn stimulates the adrenal gland to secrete cortisol (see Gunnar, 2007; Meyer et al., 2001). About 20–30 minutes after the stressor, peak concentrations of cortisol are found in the system. Following this peak, the negative feedback loop of the L-HPA axis begins to reestablish homeostatic functioning by reducing the level of circulating cortisol. In parallel, as the individual assesses the threat level or copes with the challenge, cortisol levels also tend to decrease. For individuals who follow a typical day–night schedule, cortisol production rises during the last few hours of sleep, peaks just after awakening, declines rapidly throughout the morning, and then remains at relatively low and stable levels in the late afternoon and evening, with increases again during periods of sleep (Gunnar & Vazquez, 2001).

Interestingly, acute elevations of cortisol in response to stressful situations may promote cognitive processing of emotions; that is, humans and animals remember experiences that activate stress responses (McEwen, 2000). However, chronic production of cortisol appears to damage brain structures. Note that chronic cortisol production is not always due to exposure to chronic stressors. Dysregulation in the cortisol response to minor stressors, which most individuals experience on a frequent basis, can also play a role. While the majority of people adapt quickly to a minor stressful event, some individuals display longer lasting elevations in cortisol levels. The result is a seemingly chronic cortisol response to daily stressors, such as social hassles. Major life events can lead to chronic or overall greater net cortisol exposure and their potential damaging effects via this mechanism, by increasing the number of daily stressors experienced by these individuals (e.g., Compas et al., 1989).

Animal studies and recent work in humans have demonstrated that early experiences may result in long-term alterations in the L-HPA system. In rodents, studies of maternal separation in early development have revealed interesting effects of maternal behavior on the L-HPA axis (Boccia & Pedersen, 2001). Specifically, following a short separation, mothers engaged in increased care of their offspring; when exposed to other stressors, these offspring demonstrated smaller hormonal stress responses and quick recovery to baseline in comparison to nonseparated pups. In contrast, following long maternal separations, mothers decreased care of their offspring; when exposed to stressors, these offspring had higher and prolonged hormonal stress responses and greater anxiety and fear. Subsequent studies demonstrated that some mothers provided more or less care in the absence of the experimental separation condition. Effects on offspring were quite similar in comparisons of naturally occurring variations in maternal behavior with experimentally induced variations in maternal care. As indicated previously, the seminal work of Suomi (1999) and his colleagues has documented the interaction of genetic-based vulnerabilities for reactive, particularly high or sustained, responses to stress and maternal behavior in rhesus monkeys. In this work, reactive monkeys (those who demonstrate heightened responses to novelty and challenge) reared with less responsive or less nurturing caregivers were likely to develop symptoms and behaviors indicative of depression in response to stressors. In contrast, reactive monkeys who were reared by highly nurturing, patient mothers were likely to excel in the troupe social hierarchy, often becoming leaders in the group. The effects of parenting on the developing L-HPA system speak to how physiological vulnerabilities or perhaps invulnerabilities to stress may be established via early experience.

At present, there is a burgeoning of studies of the stress response in children, adolescents, and adults, including nonclinical samples. Across studies, adrenocortical activity as indicated by changes in basal levels and variations in response to stress have been associated with internalizing problems (Klimes-Dougan, Hastings, Granger, Usher, & Zahn-Waxler, 2001; Southwick, Vythilingam, & Charney, 2005). In one such study of young adolescents, Klimes-Dougan and colleagues (2001) found that maintaining an increased cortisol response to social challenges (i.e., public speaking task or conflict discussion task) was associated with both internalizing and externalizing symptoms; having a strong decrease in cortisol in response to the challenge was also associated with internalizing symptoms. However, within the child and adolescent literature, links between cortisol and internalizing problems have not been consistently found, especially in community rather than clinical studies (Klimes-Dougan et al., 2001). Hence, additional studies on how and why early vulnerabilities may eventually result in the dysregulations observed in depression among adults and whether dysregulations are specific to particular types of problems or disorders are warranted.

L-HPA and HPG Changes at Puberty and Depression   As noted, the HPG and L-HPA axes are both involved in pubertal development. As studies of pubertal hormones and internalizing symptoms are reviewed in detail by Susman and Dorn (chapter 5, this volume) and elsewhere (e.g., Graber, 2008), the present discussion is limited to main findings. Substantial maturation of these systems during puberty results in dramatically increasing hormonal levels, with some hormones (e.g., estradiol,

DHEAS) linked to changes in internalizing symptoms and disorders. Adrenarche, or maturation of the adrenal glands, involves the production of dehydroepiandrosterone (DHEA) and its sulfate (DHEAS) as well as other hormones, including testosterone. A different area of the adrenal gland is responsible for the secretion of cortisol. Walker, Walder, and Reynolds (2001) have found that the adrenal-cortisol areas mature linearly and continue to mature in the postpubertal period. They have also suggested that this maturation may be linked to expression of symptoms and disorder, most likely among individuals with vulnerabilities to these problems.

Initial studies of puberty and depression compared hormone profiles of depressed prepubertal and postpubertal individuals (Dahl & Ryan, 1996). Again, the physiological dysregulation observed in adult patients, was not observed in depressed children and adolescents. However, recent studies have identified altered diurnal patterns of cortisol secretion among children with anxiety disorders and adolescents with depression (Forbes, Silk, & Dahl, in press). Whereas the neuroendocrine dysregulation observed with MDD in adulthood is not fully present in children with MDD, diurnal alterations in cortisol may be an indication that pubertal maturation of the L-HPA is necessary before adult-type neuroendocrine concomitants of depression are observed. Of course, it should be remembered that even though neuroendocrine profiles of MDD differ between adolescents and adults, few differences in the experience of symptoms of depression are found from childhood into adulthood (e.g., Birmaher et al., 2004).

Along with puberty-related changes in the L-HPA system, evidence for links between HPG axis changes and internalizing problems has also been found. In particular, periods of puberty characterized by rapid increases in hormones as indexed by estradiol have been linked to higher levels of depressive symptoms among girls (Brooks-Gunn & Warren, 1989). Furthermore in the GSM, higher rates of

MDD were observed in girls who had attained a threshold level of estradiol, typical of the later stages of puberty (Angold, Costello, Erkanli, & Worthman, 1999). One problem with such findings is that ultimately all girls will attain the hormonal levels typical of adult reproductive functioning, but not all girls will become depressed. Subsequent analyses by Angold in the GSM indicate that other factors (i.e., maternal mental health) moderate these associations (Angold, Worthman, & Costello, 2003). It may be that depression is less likely to manifest prior to advanced or postpubertal development, at least in girls, an issue that will be discussed more fully in our review of the role of genetic factors. Notably, in the GSM, girls with estrogen levels indicative of later maturation were not more sensitive to depressogenic effects of life events than girls with lower levels of estrogen (Angold et al., 2003). In contrast, it may be that individual differences in postpubertal estrogen are more important than differences in estrogen as a function of pubertal stage. That is, some individuals do, in fact, have elevated gonadal hormonal levels postpubertally and in adulthood. A few studies (e.g., Lai, Vesprini, Chu, Jernström, & Narod, 2001) have reported that women who experienced menarche at earlier ages may have higher levels of estrogen in adulthood. In this case, propensity for elevated estrogen levels in women may be a vulnerability for depressive problems over the life course.

Of course, it is important to remember that the L-HPA and HPG systems are interconnected and that hormones do not function in isolation of one another. Interactions between these systems may result in experiencing the pubertal transition as a time of heightened sensitivity to environmental events or stressors. Walker (2002) has suggested that increases in gonadal hormones play an important role in the activation and regulation of the stress response and that the association between baseline hormone levels and behavior is nonlinear, emerging only after a certain threshold level of gonadal hormones has been reached. Lending support

to this hypothesis, Netherton, Goodyer, Tamplin, and Herbert (2004) found distinct gender differences in morning salivary cortisol levels in mid- to postpubertal adolescents, with girls exhibiting higher levels than boys; this difference did not emerge for pre- to beginning-pubertal boys and girls. In our lab, we have also found evidence that aspects of puberty (i.e., pubertal timing) and stress responses were associated in girls; in this case, early-maturing girls who also had high emotional arousal or high-for-development DHEAS levels had the highest levels of internalizing symptoms. Hence, the interaction of L-HPA and HPG systems may be most salient for understanding initial changes in internalizing symptoms in the early adolescent years (Graber, Brooks-Gunn, & Warren, 2006).

McEwen (1994) points out that gonadal hormones have effects in the brain beyond reproductive systems, including in the hippocampus, where many effects of stress are also observed. Taylor and her colleagues (2000) also identify behavioral responses to stress that may be more representative of female responses to stress, especially social stressors. Moreover, the physiological mechanisms underlying such responses involve female reproductive (gonadal) hormones and oxytocin, a hormone that is often associated with maternal caregiving behaviors as well as lactation. Advances in understanding gender differences in internalizing problems may be afforded by considering multiple "stress" systems and interactions across systems.

Pubertal Timing and Internalizing Problems

In addition to the role that hormones may play, increases in internalizing problems have also been linked to other aspects of puberty. Over the past 15 years, several studies have found that pubertal timing (going through puberty earlier, at about the same time, or later than one's peers) is associated with psychopathology during adolescence. In particular, earlier maturation among girls is associated with higher rates of depressive symptoms and disorders (e.g., Graber, Seeley, Brooks-Gunn, & Lewinsohn, 2004; Hayward et al., 1997; Stice et al., 2001), as well as externalizing (e.g., Graber, Lewinsohn, Seeley, & Brooks-Gunn, 1997; Sontag et al., 2008), and eating disorders and symptoms during adolescence (e.g., Graber, Brooks-Gunn, Paikoff, & Warren, 1994; Graber et al., 1997).

Findings are most consistent for early maturation effects in girls when looking at the disorder end of the continuum, although several studies find effects for subclinical symptoms (Graber, 2008). Of the studies that have examined disorder, three report an effect of early maturation on MDD or general internalizing disorders (Graber et al., 1997; Hayward et al., 1997; Stice et al., 2001); only one study did not find an effect (Angold, Costello, & Worthman, 1998). This inconsistency likely resulted from an unusual truncation of range in pubertal timing in the analyses (Graber, 2008). Of note is that these studies used a range of methods for assessing pubertal maturation and timing as well as diagnostic methods for assessing psychopathology.

More recently, we have also demonstrated that pubertal timing effects are maintained into young adulthood. Specifically, in the OADP, we found that early maturation and late maturation in girls were both associated with higher rates of MDD during the high school years. Notably, early-maturing girls also had elevated rates of many symptoms linked to depression at that time (Graber et al., 1997). In young adulthood, although late maturation was no longer associated with higher prevalence of MDD, early maturation effects were maintained, such that women who had been early maturers continued to have higher lifetime prevalence rates of MDD compared to on-time or late maturers (Graber et al., 2004).

For boys, pubertal timing has more often been linked to elevated symptoms rather than disorders, with early maturation associated with higher internalizing symptoms (e.g., Ge, Conger, & Elder, 2001; Graber et al., 1997),

as well as externalizing behaviors (e.g., Ge et al., 2001). Late maturation for boys also seems to confer some risk for psychopathology as reflected in higher rates of disruptive behavior disorders and increased alcohol use and/or abuse in young adulthood (Andersson & Magnusson, 1990; Graber et al., 2004).

Specific links between timing and adjustment within racial groups are just beginning to be studied. For example, Ge, Brody, Conger, and Simons (2006) reported similar effects of early maturation among both boys and girls on internalizing and externalizing behaviors and symptoms in a community sample of African American young adolescents. Recent studies have found comparable effects of early maturation on externalizing behaviors in African American and Latino youth (e.g., Lynne, Graber, Nichols, Brooks-Gunn, & Botvin, 2007). While limited, the emerging evidence indicates that early maturation is a risk for adjustment problems for European American, African American, and Latino youth and possibly other groups. Given the more pervasive and severe risk for internalizing problems among early-maturing girls, understanding the mechanisms or pathways for these effects may be particularly important in understanding why gender differences in internalizing disorders emerge in adolescence.

The aforementioned tests of simultaneous transition models have found that early maturing girls were at risk for increases in depressive symptoms across adolescence, as they were more likely than boys to experience rapid pubertal change at the same time as a school transition. In addition, two main hypotheses have been the foundation for these studies (Brooks-Gunn, Petersen, & Eichorn, 1985). An early maturation hypothesis suggests that being earlier than one's peers results in individuals entering into more "adultlike" behaviors commensurate with their physical appearance but prior to developing the skills or competencies needed to negotiate these situations. The result is that early maturers, potentially both girls and boys, may engage in more problem behaviors and experience greater distress during adolescence. However, no studies have actually examined this hypothesis; that is, no studies of pubertal timing have intensively assessed social cognitive abilities, social skills, and emotion regulation skills. Yet, as previously discussed, research suggests that these types of skills (and deficiencies in them) are important in the development of internalizing problems.

A separate hypothesis suggests that being "out-of-sync" with one's peers results in poor adjustment; in this case, early maturing girls and late maturing boys should be at risk for negative outcomes as their development is the most off-time given the relative gender difference in the timing of puberty. A caveat of this general hypothesis is that early maturing girls will seek out individuals more like themselves (e.g., older peers) and engage in problem behaviors at young ages (Stattin & Magnusson, 1990). As we and our colleagues have discussed previously (Graber & Sontag, 2006), tests of this hypothesis have focused on early maturing girls' associations with deviant peers or associations with boys, presumably romantic partners, both early maturing girls' and boys' association with deviant peers, and effects on externalizing behaviors (e.g., Ge, Brody, Conger, Simons, & Murry, 2002). For example, Marín, Coyle, Gómez, Carvajal, and Kirby (2000) found that girls with older boyfriends had more unwanted sexual advances, had more friends who were nonvirgins, and were more likely to have had intercourse than other girls. These experiences may or may not lead to internalizing problems (see subsequent section).

In the OADP, along with the striking rates of depressive and substance use disorders found among early maturing girls, these girls also report lower levels of social support from family and friends in mid-adolescence and young adulthood (Graber et al., 1997; Graber et al., 2004). Women who had been early maturers had higher rates of traits reflective of antisocial personality disorder at age 24,

a disorder associated with serious impairments in interpersonal relationships. Deficits in social interactions may be a pathway for girls to develop internalizing problems and possibly other problems; early maturation may be one component of this pathway. This hypothesis requires more detailed examinations of the quality of relationships among early-maturing girls as well as the type of individuals with whom they have relationships.

In fact, hypothetically, much of the effect of early timing on disorder in girls may be accounted for by exposure to unhealthy family relationships. Specifically, several studies have now demonstrated that stressful home environments and family interactions actually predict earlier maturation in girls (Belsky et al., 2007; Ellis & Garber, 2000, to name a few). These same family factors have been associated with the development of vulnerabilities for depression (Graber, 2008). Furthermore, youth who enter adolescence with poorer quality family relationships are likely to continue to have low-warmth and high-conflict relationships and higher risk for psychopathology during adolescence (Steinberg, 2001). It may be that both pubertal timing and family relationships have unique contributions as well as a combined contribution to the development of internalizing problems. As yet, no studies have fully examined family factors in childhood and adolescence in order to determine if early timing effects on depression are mediated by family relationships or other factors (Graber, 2008).

Genetic Factors and Family Aggregation

As with many disorders, genetic factors have been identified as important risk factors for internalizing problems. Note that genetic factors (vulnerabilities) confer greater risk for disorder via their interaction with environmental forces. Birmaher and colleagues (1996) suggest that, looking across twin and adoption studies, about 50% of the variance in mood disorders (e.g., MDD, dysthymic disorder, and bipolar disorder) is accounted for by genetic similarity. And children of depressed parents are about three times more likely to have a lifetime history of MDD even accounting for differences across study designs (Strober, 2001). Fewer family history, twin, or adoption studies have focused on anxiety problems and disorders in childhood or adolescence (Vasey & Ollendick, 2001); however, twin studies of adults find genetic similarity constitutes risk for GAD and other anxiety disorders (see Kendler, 2001, for a review). Interestingly, the impact of having a depressed parent is not confined to MDD among their offspring but is also associated with increased rates of anxiety and other disorders in offspring. Kendler (1995) has hypothesized that such findings may be explained by a genetic factor that is shared by depression and anxiety such that other environmental factors interact with or exacerbate this risk, resulting in one or the other disorder. Again, this inference is consistent with the position that anxiety and depression may not be distinct phenomena but rather have substantial shared characteristics, in terms of both their symptoms and their underlying genetics.

Genetic similarity and other familial factors may play a unique role in timing of onset of disorder, in particular, onset prior to adulthood (Jaffee & Poulton, 2006). In part, family context or parental behaviors may be more salient when individuals live with family members. At the same time, genetic similarity may be predictive of a vulnerability that results in earlier development of disorder. Drawing on the Virginia Twin Study of Adolescent Behavioral Development, Silberg and her colleagues (1999) found that genetic similarity was not important in explaining variance in symptoms in prepubertal children. Rather, genetic similarity was only significantly associated with depressive symptoms of pubertal and postpubertal adolescents. Consistent with other studies, Silberg et al. (1999) reported that negative life events were predictive of depressive symptoms in both boys and girls. But, among girls, depressive symptoms increased with age, even among girls who did not experience negative life events. Interestingly, genetic similarity accounted for variance in the reporting of negative life events. Thus, there is evidence for genetic similarity in twins with respect to vulnerability to report or to experience negative life events that covaries with depressive symptoms. Although genetic similarity likely plays a role in depression across the life span, this study points to the salience of such similarity in increases in depression at puberty, especially among girls.

Much of the literature on genetic factors has relied on family aggregation and twin studies which provide estimates of genetic influences but have several limitations. In contrast, with advances in the field of molecular genetics and drawing on animal models, recent studies have identified specific gene–environment interactions that may be linked to different disorders (Moffitt, Caspi, & Rutter, 2006). In the Dunedin project, a recent study examining the impact of gene–environment interactions on depression found that a functional polymorphism in the promoter region of the serotonin transporter (5-HTT) gene moderated the influence of stressful life events on depression (Caspi et al., 2003). This particular gene is thought to moderate serotonergic responses to stress. In this study, childhood maltreatment was more strongly linked to subsequent disorder in adolescence and young adulthood among individuals with the short allele of the gene in comparison to individuals homozygous for the long allele. Several, but not all, studies have replicated links between depression and the 5-HTT transporter gene (Moffitt et al., 2006).

The notion that genetic factors play a role in vulnerabilities via gene–environment interactions does not fit with a compartmentalized approach to predictors of disorder. Indeed, environmental influences have genetic components, especially when the environments include parents. Characteristics of parents, such as their own temperament or vulnerabilities to environmental stressors, influence not only the parent's likelihood of developing an internalizing problem but also their parenting behaviors. A fuller delineation of the processes through which genetic factors translate into vulnerabilities for internalizing symptoms and problems is needed and will likely emerge in the next several years (Collins et al., 2000).

Family Relations and Context

As indicated beyond linear genetic processes, family relationships, events, and interactions, as well as broader family contextual factors, have all been linked to changes in internalizing symptoms in childhood and adolescence. As noted, maltreatment in the family context interacts with genetic risk, and socialization behaviors of parents may influence the development of cognitive attributions and emotion regulation. The nature of parent–child interactions and attachments has been the focus of numerous theories of internalizing disorders (Bowlby, 1980; Zahn-Waxler et al., 2000). Freudian psychoanalytic theory identified the source of both anxiety and depression among adults as problems in early childhood relationships with parents.

In the work of Bowlby and Ainsworth on attachment, early parent–child interactions, as tapped by caregiver sensitivity and consistency, shape the child's expectations for the behavior of others and are the basis for a working model of relationships (see Thompson, 2006, for a review). Working models are not unchanging during development; subsequent changes in parental behaviors will also influence the child's working model over the course of development. During adolescence, nonfamilial relationships take on greater importance with initiation of romantic relationships and increasing intimacy in friendships (see chapter 3, vol. 2 of this *Handbook*); hence, working models may play a more significant role in social interactions at this time. In particular, working models defined by insecurity have been associated with depression in adolescents and adults (Garber, 2000). As mentioned, Suomi (1999) found that reactive monkeys reared with less responsive or less nurturing caregivers were

more likely to develop internalizing-like symptoms in response to stress. These findings suggest an interaction between parenting behaviors and temperament in predicting offspring behavior. Interestingly, there is no indication that a "working model" was a necessary conduit for this association. Specifically, it is unlikely that rhesus monkeys are cognitively capable of forming working models of relationships; rather, poor parenting behaviors influenced the stress system or emotion regulation skills, resulting in a vulnerability for internalizing problems.

Both increases in internalizing symptoms and depressive disorders in adolescence have been associated with increased family conflict, lower family warmth, parental rejection, and prior and concurrent maltreatment or abuse (Birmaher et al., 1996). Notably, Rueter, Scaramella, Wallace, and Conger (1999) examined the impact of parent–child conflict on internalizing symptoms and disorder over time. Both internalizing symptoms and parent–child conflict in early adolescence (age 12–13) predicted changes in internalizing symptoms and reports of history of disorder by young adulthood (ages 19–20). Specifically, prior parent–child disagreement influenced internalizing disorders via their indirect effect on subclinical symptoms rather than via a direct path to later disorder. In this study, gender differences in pathways were not assessed, although the rates of anxiety and depressive disorders demonstrated expected gender differences.

Other longitudinal projects have demonstrated that maternal adjustment and marital discord or divorce result in increases in internalizing symptoms over early to late adolescence in rural and urban youth (Crawford, Cohen, Midlarsky, & Brook, 2001; Forehand, Biggar, & Kotchick, 1998). Forehand and colleagues looked at the impact of multiple family risk factors (e.g., divorce, maternal depressive symptoms, mother–child relations) and found that when more than three risk factors were present during early adolescence, depressive symptoms were dramatically higher in late adolescence/young adulthood. However, the presence of more than three family risk factors also predicted poorer academic achievement or attainment by young adulthood. Steinberg and Avenevoli (2000) argue that findings such as these indicate a lack of specificity in the link between contextual stress and psychopathology. Also, gender was not consistently associated with cumulative risks; hence, risks were not explanatory of gender differences in this study. In contrast, Crawford and colleagues (2001) focused on the effects of maternal distress, as indexed by internalizing symptoms and marital discord. In this case, expected gender differences in internalizing symptoms emerged around age 13–14 and were predicted by maternal distress.

As noted, links between parental distress and adolescent internalizing symptoms may, in part, be accounted for by genetic similarity. At the same time, socialization and other factors may also play a role. Kessler and McLeod (1984) have suggested that women are more vulnerable than men to "network events," that is, stressful events that happen in one's network of close relationships. Gender differences in sensitivity to interpersonal stress have been attributed to biologically driven changes in affiliative relationship patterns (i.e., females display a stronger preference for intimacy and responsiveness within relationships). Specifically, research with animal models has shown that increases in the production of oxytocin triggered by female pubertal hormones are associated with the development of female affiliative behaviors (Cyranowski, Frank, Young, & Shear, 2000). This potential developmental process would be consistent with the age when gender differences emerged in the Crawford et al. (2001) study and with the finding that stressful life events influence depressive symptoms and have a genetic component (Silberg et al., 1999). Perhaps genetic similarity in the disposition to experience or to report stressful events is limited to stressful events within close social networks, such as

family and friends. Alternatively, vulnerability to network events may in part be associated with who is in one's network, in that adolescent girls who develop internalizing problems may be more likely to have female network members who share a genetic vulnerability to internalizing problems (i.e., mother, sister, etc.) and hence more distress in the network.

One concern about family influences on adolescent internalizing problems is that effects may not be unidirectional. Rather, having an adolescent with serious internalizing problems places additional strains on families and may result in increased conflict between parents and children, changes in expressions of warmth, communication problems among family members, and strain in the marital relationship of parents (Birmaher et al., 1996; Garber, 2000). Interestingly, Reuter and colleagues (1999) examined bidirectional influences of family conflict and internalizing symptoms over time and did not find support for internalizing symptoms predicting family conflict; however, they did find that conflict had an indirect effect on symptoms and disorder over time. In research on symptoms of eating disorders, quality of family relations predicted increased symptoms in young adolescents (Archibald, Graber, & Brooks-Gunn, 1999), and increasing symptoms of disturbed eating predicted declines in quality of family relations among mid- to late adolescents in separate studies that tested bidirectional influences (Archibald, Linver, Graber, & Brooks-Gunn, 2002). Quality of family relations may be more salient to younger adolescents or may have a greater impact on internalizing emotions during this developmental period. Additional studies modeling simultaneous change in family interactions and relationships and internalizing problems across developmental periods are needed.

Finally, stemming from ecological models (e.g., Bronfenbrenner, 1977), studies of family influences on internalizing problems have also examined how broader contextual factors influence children and families. Several studies have found that economic strain and persistent parental unemployment are predictive of internalizing symptoms among rural, White, and urban African American adolescents, usually via effects on parental mental health or parenting behaviors in parent–child interactions (Conger, Ge, Elder, Lorenz, & Simons, 1994; McLoyd, Jayaratne, Ceballo, & Borquez, 1994). Perceptions of economic hardship by youth, themselves, are also a factor in this process; adolescents who perceive that economic problems exist for the family are more likely to evince increasing internalizing symptoms over time (Conger, Conger, Matthews, & Elder, 1999). As with other family factors, contextual events and experiences do not uniformly predict internalizing symptoms in adolescence. Individual characteristics, such as the use of more problem-solving coping strategies or mastery, may be protective against perceiving strain in the first place (i.e., mastery predicted the likelihood of perceiving economic hardship; Conger et al., 1999) or may mediate effects of strain and family conflict on internalizing symptoms (Wadsworth, Raviv, Compas, & Connor-Smith, 2005).

Often, studies of economic influences on changes in internalizing symptoms during adolescence explain general effects on symptoms, usually well within the normal range of functioning, and have not shed light on why more girls develop these problems or even why increases happen during adolescence. To clarify, many of these studies have documented factors that predict changes for some individuals but not others in internalizing symptoms during adolescence. However, models might fit equally well in predicting changes in internalizing symptoms in childhood.

Peers

The impact of peer relationships on adjustment has been much less studied in adolescence than in childhood. In addition, much of the focus on peer relationships has been on aggression and externalizing problems. At the same time, withdrawal from social relationships and activities is often used as an indicator of impairment

among youth experiencing internalizing problems; for example, the diagnostic criteria for GAD and for MDD in the DSM-IV-TR both require that the anxious or depressive symptoms result in significant impairment in social or occupational functioning. Peer interactions and internalizing symptoms likely have bidirectional or transactional influences on each other; that is, poor relationships lead to poor emotional functioning, which in turn leads to poorer quality social interactions, and so on.

With entry into adolescence comes an increased focus on peer relationships and the greater importance of peers in one's daily life. Moreover, the quality of peer relationships changes, with greater focus on intimacy and trust (see chapter 3, vol. 2 of this *Handbook*; Cairns & Cairns, 1994; Rudolph, 2002). As noted, the report of stressful life events increases with age and is predictive of in-creased internalizing symptoms (Brooks-Gunn, 1991; Ge et al., 1994; Silberg et al., 1999). Peer-related events (e.g., a fight with a friend, breaking up with a friend, making a new friend) may account for a significant number of the events that adolescents experience (Brooks-Gunn, 1991), and appear to be more salient to girls than boys as part of the greater selience of social networks. Examination of the emotional impact of negative peer experiences includes victimization, rejection, and poor-quality peer relationships.

Victimization has been linked to poor emotional adjustment, poor school adjustment, and poor relationships with peers in community studies and cross-national research (Deater-Deckard, 2001; Nansel et al., 2004). Because of girls' tendencies to rely heavily on peers for emotional support and intimacy, victimization targeted at damaging one's social reputation and interpersonal relationships (i.e., relational aggression) is likely to create higher levels of stress in girls compared to boys, which in turn may contribute to higher rates of depression in girls (Rudolph, 2002). For example, Storch, Nock, Masia-Warner, and Barlas (2003) found that overt peer victimization was positively associated with depressive symptoms and aspects of social anxiety for both boys and girls, whereas, relational victimization was predictive of internalizing problems for girls only.

Certainly, prior relationship skills and patterns influence how well the challenges of new relationship demands are met by adolescents and may help to identify who will have greater difficulties during adolescence. Rejection by peers is often an indicator of skills. That is, peers may reject other children because the child is aggressive or because the child is withdrawn; however, rejection is also a source of stress and internalizing symptoms. Cross-sectional studies have indicated that, during childhood, peer rejection resulting from social withdrawal, rather than from aggression, has been linked to increased depressive symptoms and possibly disorder (Hecht, Inderbitzen, & Bukowski, 1998; Rubin & Burgess, 2001). In a longitudinal study from childhood into adolescence, Coie, Terry, Lenox, Lochman, and Hyman (1995) reported that boys who were rejected and aggressive in childhood increased in both externalizing and internalizing symptoms during early and mid-adolescence. In contrast, girls who were rejected in childhood regardless of the reason for rejection (withdrawal or aggression) had higher reports of internalizing symptoms in childhood and in early and mid-adolescence. These girls did not show increases in internalizing symptoms, but rather entered adolescence with already elevated symptoms. One implication of this finding is that within any group of adolescent girls with elevated internalizing symptoms, some will have had persistent internalizing problems and others will not have had preadolescent difficulties.

In other longitudinal work, London, Downey, and Bonica (2007) found that peer rejection predicted an increase over time in both anxious and angry expectations about rejection during early adolescence; expectations for future rejection, in turn, were associated with risk for internalizing and externalizing problems. Interestingly, London and colleagues (2007) found that anxious expectations of rejection

predicted increases over time in social anxiety and withdrawal, whereas angry expectations predicted decreases in social anxiety. Way (1996), in an ethnographic study of urban high school students, found that negative experiences with peers often resulted in negative emotions (e.g., distrust) about peers and close relationships. Significant periods of isolation or withdrawal from relationships with peers were also reported by several youth. Hence, both negative events and rejection shape adolescents' expectations about relationships, influencing subsequent relationship experiences and internalizing symptoms.

An extensive cross-sectional literature on bullying and victimization also suggests that children without peer supports who are victimized or rejected are more likely to have higher internalizing symptoms (Deater-Deckard, 2001). Both in childhood and in adolescence, better quality of a close friendship buffers negative effects of having few friends or difficulties in larger peer groups (Berndt, Hawkins, & Jiao, 1999). However, adolescents seem to associate with peers who have similar levels of internalizing symptoms (Hogue & Steinberg, 1995); in such cases, friends may reward less effective coping strategies for dealing with problems and maintain elevated symptoms or problems. Research has shown that friend-reported depressive symptoms are associated with increases in adolescent girls' self-reported depressive symptoms over time (Stevens & Prinstein, 2005). In addition, social anxiety and best friend's peer popularity moderate the association between best friend's and self-reported internalizing problems, such that only those adolescents high on social anxiety and those adolescents with popular friends exhibited the peer contagion effect (Prinstein, 2007).

Close peer relationships and peer group membership change frequently during the middle school years, with a tendency for greater stability by late high school (Cairns & Cairns, 1994). The turbulence and quality of peer relationships likely play a role in increases in internalizing problems during adolescence, especially in early to mid-adolescence. Also, emotion regulation and social cognitive skills influence competence in peer relationships, and are one source of individual differences in who does and does not experience poor peer relationships, and subsequent internalizing problems in the face of changing interpersonal demands. How peer events are experienced also varies based on these factors. Individuals with better skills may have fewer negative peer events (e.g., fight less often) or may deal with the emotional impact of negative events more effectively, either through better regulation skills or the buffering effect of having other positive relationships. Again, the salience of relationships to the emotional experience of adolescent girls coupled with instability of relationships during early adolescence may be important factors in explaining gender differences in internalizing problems (e.g., Rudolf, 2002).

Romantic and Sexual Relationships

The importance of romantic relationships in adolescent development has undergone a surge of attention both in understanding developmental process and in understanding problems and challenges faced by adolescents (e.g., Davila, 2008; Furman, Brown, & Feiring, 1999; Shulman & Collins, 1997). In the case of internalizing problems, the impact of romantic relationships, like peer relationships, often has been considered in terms of stressful life events, such as breaking up with a romantic partner, beginning dating, unrequited interest, and the like.

Although young adolescents, especially girls, strongly endorse the notion that it is desirable to be in love and have a romantic relationship (Simon, Eder, & Evans, 1992), experiences such as breaking up with a partner are stressful, particularly for young adolescents who may have difficulty regulating the strong emotions often coincident with the event. In turn, these negative experiences and emotions may lead to depressive symptoms, possibly even episodes (Joyner & Udry, 2000; Larson, Clore, & Wood, 1999). Although some studies

have suggested that positive romantic relationships may protect adolescents against feelings of social anxiety (La Greca & Harrison, 2006), Joyner and Udry (2000) found that initiating romantic relationships during adolescence was predictive of increased depressive symptoms over time among both boys and girls. In addition, becoming involved in a relationship had a larger negative effect on girls' than on boys' depressive symptoms. Negative effects were highest for younger girls who had repeated or continuous involvement in relationships. For boys, declines in school performance accounted for part of the effect of relationships on depressive symptoms, whereas for girls decreases in the quality of relationships with parents did so. The number and stability of relationships reported over time were also important in explaining the negative impact of involvement in romantic relationships, with more relationships and less stability leading to increases in depressive symptoms. Again, a distinctive feature of changes in symptoms for girls was their link to interpersonal factors (in the domain of partners and parents).

In general, gender differences in relationship goals, with girls being more likely than boys to focus on intimacy, make it particularly challenging for young adolescents to have relationships that meet their needs (Maccoby, 1998). Much like their tendencies in peer relationships, girls experience greater stress and internalize their experiences with romantic partners to a greater extent than do boys (Rudolf, 2002). Although empirical evidence on the impact of romantic involvements on adolescent adjustment is limited, parallel research on sexual behaviors sheds some light on this issue (see chapter 14, this volume).

Even though it is frequently noted that managing sexual feelings and interactions may tax emotion and behavior regulation skills, little attention has been given to this aspect of sexual behavior. (Actually, there is an enormous literature on the sexual activity of adolescents, but only recently has that literature been linked to relationships or with internalizing problems.) The emotional challenges of regulating sexual feelings and interactions may, in part, be embedded within the other emotional challenges of romantic relationships. However, it is likely that sexual experiences outside of relationships may also impact emotions and adjustment.

Adolescent girls are more likely than boys to have sexual partners who are older than they are at first intercourse, and are more likely to report that their first sexual experience was unwanted (Terry-Humen, Manlove & Cottingham, 2006). Individuals, especially girls, who have intercourse at younger ages are thought to be at greater risk for a number of sexual health–related problems and are more likely to transition to the next sexual partner more quickly than older girls (AGI, 1994). Again, higher number of relationships and relationships at younger ages have been linked to higher reports of depressive symptoms (e.g., Joyner & Udry, 2000).

As discussed previously, the negative effects reported for early-maturing girls may, in part, be due to their association with older or deviant peers. In fact, Halpern, Kaestle, and Hallfors (2007) reported that having a romantic partner was an important link between early maturation and risk for numerous internalizing symptoms and externalizing behaviors in both girls and boys. However, having an older partner was a unique risk for early maturing girls. As with prior research (e.g., Ge et al., 2002; Stattin & Magnusson, 1990), peers moderated the association between timing and adjustment, and the negative impact was not specific to internalizing problems but to externalizing problems as well.

Managing sexuality, relationships, or the interplay of both may all play a role in increases in internalizing symptoms during adolescence, but unique effects of each factor are difficult to delineate. For example, is the breakup of a relationship more stressful, eliciting more sadness, if the relationship included intercourse? The romantic relationships of adolescents are increasingly likely to include intercourse the longer the relationship lasts (Bearman, 2001). Another example of the challenges posed by relationships can be seen in studies of adolescent responses to sexual infidelity and betrayal in romantic relationships (Feldman & Cauffman, 1999; Thompson, 1994). In some cases, infidelity or betrayal leads to breakups and hence potential increases in internalizing symptoms. In fact, experience of breakups has been linked to suicide attempts among adolescents (Monroe, Rohde, Seeley, & Lewinsohn, 1999). But not all relationships that involve infidelity or betrayal result in breaking off the relationship. In either situation, many adolescents experience strong negative emotions such as sadness, despondency, and disillusionment in response to infidelities (Feldman & Cauffman, 1999; Thompson, 1994). In the narratives of an ethnically diverse sample of girls, Thompson (1994) found that girls who idealized romantic relationships described more fear of rejection and despondency at being "dumped."

Thus, rejection or betrayal in romantic and sexual relationships influences emotion, but as noted in peer relationships, these experiences also impact beliefs about relationships and future behaviors in relationships. In outlining the development of rejection sensitivity, Downey and colleagues (Downey, Bonica, & Rincon, 1999) note that past childhood experiences of rejection, initially from parents and then from peers, result in heightened sensitivity to rejection from romantic partners. Testing this model with young adolescent girls, Purdie and Downey (2000) found expectations of rejection from ambiguous peer and teacher interactions prospectively predicted heightened rejection fears from romantic partners. Rejection-sensitive individuals may shy away from romantic involvements out of increased fearfulness about close relationships or may find themselves seeking such involvements in order to gain acceptance that has previously been lacking. Individuals who seek acceptance may be overly willing to acquiesce in the relationship or place high value on it. In a study of adolescent couples, Harper, Dickson, and Welsh (2006) found that ability and comfort in voicing one's feelings or opinions partially mediated the association between rejection sensitivity and depressive symptoms in both boys and girls, suggesting that the fear of being rejected encourages adolescents in romantic relationships to stifle their emotions and fear voicing issues or concerns with the relationship. This type of dynamic in a romantic relationship puts both girls and boys at risk for internalizing problems. In addition, rejection-sensitive individuals tend to be highly jealous and hostile in their relationships; these feelings often lead to more conflict in the relationship, which subsequently leads to breakup (Downey et al., 1999). Whereas Downey and colleagues have suggested that rejection-sensitive women may be more likely to experience internalizing problems after a relationship breakup and rejection-sensitive men may be more likely to respond with aggression, recent studies have found that both boys and girls high in rejection sensitivity display greater levels of internalizing problems (Harper et al., 2006).

Our discussion has been based on findings across several literatures that seem to suggest that romantic and sexual relationships may be particularly challenging to adolescents and may be a source of increased internalizing problems for some youth. A recent increase in the number of empirical studies examining not only sexual behaviors but also more psychosocially based aspects of romantic relationships (i.e., rejection sensitivity, attachment, personality, pubertal development, peer relations, etc.) has helped the literature move away from focusing on adolescent romantic relationships as simply a risk for sexual promiscuity, pregnancy, and disease (see chapter 4, vol. 2 of this *Handbook*; Graber & Sontag, 2006). Unfortunately, many studies of sexual behaviors still focus heavily on teen pregnancy and health risks, such as sexually transmitted diseases, without considering interconnections with psychopathology. For example, poorer body image has been associated with fear of

abandonment, low rates of condom use during intercourse, and engaging in casual sex among African American girls (Wingood, DiClemente, Harrington, & Davies, 2002). Hence, health risks would be better understood if embedded in a broader developmental context.

Of course, emerging sexual feelings and behaviors as well as romantic interest and relationships are a normative part of adolescent development, and most youth meet these challenges with only temporary emotional upheaval. The importance of romantic and sexual experiences, the new emotion regulation challenges elicited by these experiences, the dramatic increase of these experiences around the time that internalizing problems increase (especially rates of MDD), and the potential for relationship experiences to account for gender differences in internalizing problems would all suggest that more nuanced investigations of how adolescents regulate relationships are warranted. Models, such as that of Downey on rejection sensitivity, that integrate childhood experiences, development of gender differences in response to these experiences, and interactions of vulnerabilities with challenges at adolescence are likely to be informative for understanding who is at risk for internalizing problems during adolescence.

TREATMENT OF INTERNALIZING DISORDERS

Given the severity and chronicity of internalizing problems and disorders during adolescence and the extension of these problems into adulthood, a large body of research has examined the efficacy of treatment for MDD in children and adolescents. We provide a brief overview here. Based on findings from efficacy studies, there are currently three empirically supported treatment methods for child and adolescent MDD—namely, interpersonal therapy, cognitive behavioral therapy (CBT), and antidepressant treatment (Wagner, 2003; Zalsman, Brent, & Weersing, 2006). Research examining treatment efficacy has found high response rate to placebo or brief supportive treatment in less clinically severe cases of MDD among adolescents, suggesting that it would be reasonable to begin treatment of mild depression with family education, supportive counseling, case management, and problem solving (Zalsman et al., 2006). However, for more persistent or severe depression, antidepressants, CBT, and interpersonal therapy have been shown to be more effective (Zalsman et al., 2006).

Interpersonal psychotherapy focuses on developmentally appropriate issues for adolescents, such as separation from parents, authority conflicts, peer pressures, and interpersonal relationships. In efficacy studies, interpersonal therapy has been effective at reducing depressive symptoms and improving social functioning and problem solving in adolescents (Wagner, 2003). At the same time, the majority of research has focused on the efficacy of CBT and antidepressants. CBT focuses on modifying cognitions, assumptions, beliefs, and behaviors as a way to reduce symptomatology. Despite being hailed as one of the more effective treatments for MDD in adolescents (Wagner, 2003), a recent meta-analysis of the effects of psychotherapy for child and adolescent treatment found that CBT trials were no more effective than non-cognitive-based treatments (e.g., relaxation training; Weisz, McCarty, & Valeri, 2006). In addition, a comparison of the SSRI fluoxetine, CBT, and their combination in the Treatment for Adolescent Depression Study (TADS, 2004) found that adolescents treated with CBT alone fared no better than those in the placebo condition, whereas adolescents treated with fluoxetine alone demonstrated outcomes superior to those in both the placebo and CBT alone condition. Using a combination of fluoxetine and CBT produced the most positive treatment response, indicating that combination treatments may be a very potent treatment tactic.

A particular challenge for parents and youth is that in many communities, specialized treatment of child and adolescent depression, such as CBT or interpersonal therapy, is not readily available. Although these communities often have treatment resources available for adults, the more generic types of psychotherapy that are often practiced with adults may not be helpful in the treatment of youth depression (Zalsman et al., 2006). When specialized psychotherapy is not available, an antidepressant is often recommended as a first-line treatment.

In fact, the first-line treatment for children with moderate to severe depressive symptoms or with impairment in functioning is pharmacotherapy, either alone or with CBT or interpersonal therapy. In general, SSRIs are effective for treating both children and adolescents with MDD as previously noted (Singh et al., 2007). Although there are a variety of SSRIs available in the market, fluoxetine is the only Food and Drug Administration (FDA)-approved antidepressant to treat MDD in children younger than 7 years of age (NIMH, 2008). SSRIs are well tolerated in adolescents with fewer side effects than the previous generation of drugs (e.g., tricyclic antidepressants) commonly used to treat MDD in adults. However, SSRIs have been shown to increase the risk for suicidal thoughts/behaviors, suggesting to clinicians and parents that these drugs be prescribed with caution to adolescents prone to these symptoms and that careful monitoring should ensue (Singh et al., 2007); that is, simply prescribing drugs with periodic monitoring by a psychiatrist or pediatrician may be risky in comparison to drug therapy plus regular psychotherapy sessions. With respect to other antidepressant drug options often employed in adult populations, studies find no difference in response rates between other antidepressants and placebo for the treatment of MDD in adolescents (Singh et al., 2007).

As noted, although studies have shown that SSRIs produce decreases in depressive symptoms in adolescents, the fact that many of the other drugs used to treat adult depression do not produce similar results in children suggests that the biology of depression (i.e., the role of neurotransmitters, dysregulations in brain systems) may differ between adolescents and adults. In addition, while studies have been conducted on treatment efficacy, especially clinical trials for medication, for MDD, very few studies have examined treatment protocols for less common disorders, such as PBPD, even though pharmacological treatments are actively prescribed for children and adolescents by a range of health practitioners.

Another concern for effective intervention is that engaging adolescents with mild or severe depression in treatment has proven to be difficult. The National Institute of Mental Health (NIMH) estimates that approximately 1 in 10 individuals under the age of 18 suffer from mental illness severe enough to cause impairment, but only 1 in 5 of these children and adolescents receives treatment (NIMH, 2004). Often, adolescents or their parents are reluctant to seek treatment, or, as noted, specialized treatment for youth is not available.

Because of the large number of adolescents who do not receive treatment for internalizing problems and the high costs associated with pediatric depression (i.e., increased concurrent occurrence of substance abuse, academic problems, aggression, physical health problems, etc.), interest in prevention programs has grown rapidly in the past 10–15 years (Horowitz & Garber, 2006). Programs designed to prevent the emergence of symptomatology typically fall within three broad categories: universal, selective, or indicated programs. *Universal* programs are administered to all members of a target population and typically involve large-group presentation or curricula that focus on cognitive restructuring, anxiety management, relaxation, problem-solving skills, emotion-focused coping, anticipating consequences, and assertiveness. Generally, universal programs are thought to be advantageous because of their ability to avoid the stigma of singling out individuals for treatment and their relatively low dropout rates. *Selective* interventions target individuals at elevated risk for depression (e.g., adolescents from divorced families, low SES, etc.) and often target multiple outcomes in addition to reducing depression.

Finally, *indicated* interventions are targeted at individuals who already demonstrate subclinical symptoms of depression. Similar to universal programs, most selective and indicated programs utilize some form of cognitive behavioral techniques.

While studies of prevention programs have shown a reduction in depressive symptoms in the short term, few studies have shown a reduction in the persistence of depressive disorder or symptoms (Horowitz & Garber, 2006; Merry, 2007). Unfortunately, most prevention programs do not follow up with participants beyond a 6- or 12-month period. In addition, many of the studies rely on self-report measures of depressive symptoms, which may not correspond to clinical assessment. Research comparing universal programs to more targeted programs has found that more targeted programs (both selective and indicated) are generally more effective at maintaining low levels of depression or reducing existing symptoms (Horowitz & Garber, 2006; Merry, 2007). However, Horowitz and Garber (2006), as well as others, caution that the apparent superiority of more targeted programs over universal may be partly explained by the differences in level of symptoms found in the control groups. That is, because universal programs target a normative sample with generally low initial levels of depression, effect sizes of change will ultimately be smaller.

Despite limitations of the programs, research suggests that more targeted prevention programs may be more cost-effective, practical, and beneficial in the long run than universal programs. Notably, Post, Leverich, Xing, and Weiss (2001) identify several reasons that treatment and prevention of internalizing disorders during adolescence should be a focus in research and practice. First, as we have noted, episodes of MDD are frequently untreated among adolescents. Second, there is evidence that recurrent episodes of disorder become harder to treat. And, finally, early treatment of disorders may be protective against recurrent episodes later in development. Thus, better identification of disordered youth and better access to services for them would substantially improve mental health in subsequent cohorts of adults.

IMPLICATIONS AND CONCLUSIONS

In the course of this chapter, the goal has been to consider the nature of internalizing symptoms, problems, and disorders during adolescence, as well as variations on the diathesis-stress model that explain why internalizing problems occur, why they increase during adolescence, and why more girls than boys experience these problems. As noted previously, it has been questioned whether subclinical problems are of importance. Clearly, in the developmental perspective taken here and elsewhere, subclinical problems are important as a pathway to disorder for some individuals. However, the literature on disorder and subclinical problems is incomplete in several areas. The extent to which findings regarding subclinical problems also apply to the develop of disorder or the extent to which dysregulations observed in disordered individuals also occur to a lesser, or even the same, extent in individuals with subclinical problems has often not been assessed.

Although rates of internalizing problems, especially MDD, change dramatically during adolescence, examination of development prior to adolescence in order to understand vulnerabilities and risk factors that influence the trajectory for adjustment is essential. Internalizing problems occur across the life span and exhibit much continuity, impacting later development in adulthood and being highly predictive from childhood symptomatology and experiences. The present discussion was limited to a single segment of the life course (albeit an important one). Internalizing symptoms, in particular depressive symptoms, seem to follow a curvilinear trend over the life span with highest symptom reports in adolescence and young adulthood, and rates of disorder being lowest among older adults (over age 65; Karel, 1997).

There is compelling evidence that preexisting biological and psychological vulnerabilities are an important factor affecting who develops internalizing problems during adolescence. Notably, socializing experiences and genetic factors interact in the development of vulnerabilities, and both contribute to the establishment of vulnerabilities prior to and during adolescence. Whereas different models place different emphasis on vulnerability versus stress, more attention has been given to unique stressors that may emerge during adolescence rather than determining how vulnerabilities change at this time. This trend is shifting, though, as evidenced by volumes devoted to specific constructs, how they develop, and potentially become vulnerabilities for internalizing problems; for example, Allen and Sheeber (2008) focused on emotional development and regulation as vulnerabilities for depression during adolescence.

Explaining why more girls experience internalizing problems has long been a focal point in research in this area and the mechanisms underlying this effect are emerging. Certainly, as Nolen-Hoeksema (1994) has asserted, there are unique challenges of adolescence and puberty that may exist for girls more so than for boys. In addition, studies of adolescent relationships have been particularly relevant to the issue of gender differences. Emotional responses to relationships and regulation of emotion or coping are also particularly salient to girls' experiences. Additional studies of relationships, how they are experienced (both psychologically and physiologically), and why some individuals may have particular difficulties with interpersonal relationships (e.g., early-maturing girls) would likely illuminate not only why more girls have internalizing problems but also why some boys experience these problems as well.

Across the correlates and possible predictors of internalizing problems discussed, it is clear that recent studies have been more integrative and have included multiple factors. Such approaches have made it feasible to compare relative influences of predictors on internalizing problems and their relative impact on other problems. No single study will be able to examine in depth each of the factors discussed in this review, but focused investigations that study pieces of different models and make comparative tests of models will continue to advance this area of research. Whereas several new findings have emerged in the past few years and certainly since the original studies of adolescence and adolescent disorder were begun, there are still numerous gaps in the literature, especially in terms of integration of constructs.

In concluding, it is probably useful to highlight what was not considered in this review. This review did not include all studies of internalizing problems and disorders but rather drew upon prior reviews and recent studies that seemed to advance the areas of interest here (i.e., those most salient to adolescence and individual differences). More importantly, this chapter provided only a brief discussion of prevention and treatment of problems and disorders. Certainly, the primary reason for understanding why these problems occur is to prevent them or treat them more effectively. Fortunately, several reviews consider the advances that have been made in treatment and prevention (e.g., Horowitz & Garber, 2006; Lewinsohn et al., 1998). Unfortunately, little or no research focuses on what treatments are actually being used in real-world settings versus those that are studied via clinical trials, especially for understudied disorders such as PBPD.

From the wealth of empirical evidence that has amassed in recent years, internalizing problems and disorders among adolescents are certainly a serious health concern, and these problems merit the attention they have been given and will likely continue to receive. At the same time, a fuller understanding of vulnerability and stress during adolescence would provide specific information for prevention programming. Whereas problems such as substance use initiation, use, and abuse have widespread prevention programming often

mandated by state or federal law, internalizing problems receive much less policy attention. Prevention measures focused on internalizing problems would likely yield societal benefits equal to or greater than those hoped for in other health domains.

REFERENCES

Achenbach, T. M. (1993). *Empirically based taxonomy*. Burlington: University of Vermont, Department of Psychiatry.

Alan Guttmacher Institute (AGI). (1994). *Sex and America's teenagers*. New York: Author.

Allen, N. B., & Sheeber, L. (2008). *Adolescent emotional development and the emergence of depressive disorders*. New York: Guilford Press.

Allgood-Merten, B., Lewinsohn, P. M., & Hops, H. (1990). Sex differences and adolescent depression. *Journal of Abnormal Psychology, 99*, 55–63.

Alloy, L. B., & Abramson, L. Y. (2007). The adolescent surge in depression and emergence of gender differences: A biocognitive vulnerability-stress model in developmental context. In D. Romer & E. F. Walker (Eds.), *Adolescent psychopathology and the developing brain: Integrating brain and prevention science* (pp. 284–312). Oxford: Oxford University Press.

American Psychiatric Association. (2000). *Diagnostic and statistical manual of mental disorders* (4th ed., Text Revision). Washington, DC: Author.

Andersson, T., & Magnusson, D. (1990). Biological maturation in adolescence and the development of drinking habits and alcohol abuse among young males: A prospective longitudinal study. *Journal of Youth and Adolescence, 19*, 33–41.

Angold, A., Costello, E. J., Erkanli, A., & Worthman, C. M. (1999). Pubertal changes in hormone levels and depression in girls. *Psychological Medicine, 29*, 1043–1053.

Angold, A., Costello, E. J., & Worthman, C. M. (1998). Puberty and depression: The roles of age, pubertal status, and pubertal timing. *Psychological Medicine, 28*, 51–61.

Angold, A., Erkanli, A., Silberg, J., Eaves, L., & Costello, E. J. (2002). Depression scale scores in 8–17-year-olds: Effects of age and gender. *Journal of Child Psychology and Psychiatry, 43*, 1052–1063.

Angold, A., Worthman, C., & Costello, J. E. (2003). Puberty and depression. In C. Hayward (Ed.), *Gender differences at puberty* (pp. 137–164). New York: Cambridge University Press,.

Archibald, A. B., Graber, J. A., & Brooks-Gunn, J. (1999). Associations among parent–adolescent relationships, pubertal growth, dieting and body image in young adolescent girls: A short term longitudinal study. *Journal of Research on Adolescence, 9*, 395–415.

Archibald, A. B., Linver, M. R., Graber, J. A., & Brooks-Gunn, J. (2002). Parent–adolescent relationships and girls' unhealthy eating: Testing reciprocal effects. *Journal of Research on Adolescence, 12*, 451–461.

Avenevoli, S., & Steinberg, L. (2001). The continuity of depression across the adolescent transition. In H. Reese & R. Kail (Eds.), *Advances in child development and behavior*, vol. 28 (pp. 139–173). New York: Academic Press.

Bandura, A. (1964). The stormy decade: Fact or fiction? *Psychology in the Schools, 1*, 224–231.

Bearman, P. (2001). Paper presented at the National Campaign to Prevent Teen Pregnancy conference, New York.

Belsky, J., Steinberg, L. D., Houts, R. M., Friedman, S. L., DeHart, G., Cauffman, E., et al. (2007). Family rearing antecedents of pubertal timing. *Child Development, 78*, 1302–1321.

Berndt, T. J., Hawkins, J. A., & Jiao, Z. (1999). Influences of friends and friendships on adjustment to junior high school. *Merrill-Palmer Quarterly, 45*, 13–41.

Birmaher, B., Ryan, N. D., Williamson, D. E., Dahl, R. E., Axelson, D. A., Kaufman, J., Dorn, L. D., et al. (2004). Clinical presentation and course of depression in youth: Does onset in childhood differ from onset in adolescence? *Journal of the American Academy of Child & Adolescent Psychiatry, 43*, 63–70.

Birmaher, B., Ryan, N. D., Williamson, D. E., Brent, D. A., Kaufman, J., Dahl, R. E., Perel, J., et al. (1996). Childhood and adolescent depression: A review of the past 10 years. Part I. *Journal of the American Academy of Child & Adolescent Psychiatry, 35*, 1427–1439.

Block, J. H., & Block, J. (1980). The role of ego-control and ego-resiliency in the organization of behavior. In W. A. Collins (Ed.), *Minnesota symposia on child psychology*, vol. 13 (pp. 39–101). Hillsdale, NJ: Lawrence Erlbaum.

Boccia, M. L., & Pedersen, C. (2001). Animal models of critical and sensitive periods in social and emotional development. In D. B. Bailey, Jr., J. T Bruer, F. J. Symons, & J. W. Lichtman (Eds.), *Critical thinking about critical periods* (pp. 107–127). Baltimore, MD: Brookes.

Bosacki, S., & Astington, J. W. (1999). Theory of mind in preadolescence: Relations between social understanding and social competence. *Social Development, 8*, 237–255.

Bowen, R. C., Offord, D. R., & Boyle, M. H. (1990). The prevalence of overanxious disorder and separation anxiety disorder: Results form the Ontario Child Health Study. *Journal of the American Academy of Child and Adolescent Psychiatry, 29*, 753–758.

Bowlby, J. (1980). *Attachment and loss*, vol. 3: *Loss, sadness, and depression*. New York: Basic Books.

Bronfenbrenner, U. (1977). Toward an experimental ecology of human development. *American Psychologist, 32*, 513–531.

Brooks-Gunn, J. (1991). How stressful is the transition to adolescence in girls? In M. E. Colten & S. Gore (Eds.), *Adolescent stress: Causes and consequences* (pp. 131–149). Hawthorne, NY: Aldine de Gruyter.

Brooks-Gunn, J., & Warren, M. P. (1989). Biological contributions to affective expression in young adolescent girls. *Child Development, 60*, 372–385.

Brooks-Gunn, J., Petersen, A. C., & Eichorn, D. (1985). The study of maturational timing effects in adolescence. *Journal of Youth and Adolescence, 14*, 149–161.

Cairns, R. B., & Cairns, B. D. (1994). *Lifelines and risks: Pathways of youth in our time*. New York: Cambridge University Press.

Caron, C., & Rutter, M. (1991). Comorbidity in child psychopathology: Concepts, issues and research strategies. *Journal of Child Psychology and Psychiatry, 32*, 1063–1080.

Caspi, A., & Moffitt, T. E. (1991). Individual differences are accentuated during periods of social change: The sample case of girls at puberty. *Journal of Personality and Social Psychology, 61*, 157–168.

Caspi, A., Sugden, K., Moffitt, T. E., Taylor, A., Craig, I. W., Harrington, H., et al. (2003). Influence of life stress on depression: Moderation by a polymorphism in the 5-HTT gene. *Science, 301*, 386–389.

Cicchetti, D., & Cohen, D. J. (1995). Perspectives on developmental psychopathology. In D. Cicchetti & D. J. Cohen (Eds.), *Developmental psychopathology*, vol. 1: *Theory and methods* (pp. 3–20). New York: John Wiley & Sons.

Coie, J., Terry, R., Lenox, K., Lochman, J., & Hyman, C. (1995). Childhood peer rejection and aggression as predictors of stable patterns of adolescent disorder. *Development and Psychopathology, 7*, 697–713.

Collins, W. A., Maccoby, E. E., Steinberg, L., Hetherington, E. M., & Bornstein, M. H. (2000). Contemporary research on parenting: The case for nature and nurture. *American Psychologist, 55*, 218–232.

Compas, B. E., Connor-Smith, J. K., Saltzman, H., Thomsen, A. H., & Wadsworth, M. (2001). Coping with stress during childhood and adolescence: Problems, progress, and potential in theory and research. *Psychological Bulletin, 127*, 87–127.

Compas, B. E., Ey, S., & Grant, K. E. (1993). Taxonomy, assessment, and diagnosis of depression during adolescence. *Psychological Bulletin, 114*, 323–344.

Compas, B. E., Howell, D. C., Ledoux, N., Phares, V., & Williams, R. A. (1989). Parent and child stress and symptoms: An integrative analysis. *Developmental Psychology, 25*, 550–559.

Compas, B. E., & Oppedisano, G. (2000). Mixed anxiety/depression in childhood and adolescence. In A. J. Sameroff, M. Lewis, & S. M. Miller (Eds.), *Handbook of developmental psychopathology* (2nd ed.; pp. 531–548). New York: Plenum Press.

Conger, R. D., Conger, K. J., Matthews, L. S., & Elder, G. H., Jr. (1999). Pathways of economic influence on adolescent adjustment. *American Journal of Community Psychology, 27*, 519–541.

Conger, R. D., Ge, X., Elder, G. H., Jr., Lorenz, F. O., & Simons, R. L. (1994). Economic stress, coercive family process, and developmental problems of adolescence. *Child Development, 65*, 541–561.

Costello, E. J., & Angold, A. (1995). Epidemiology. In J. S. March (Ed.), *Anxiety disorders in children and adolescents* (pp. 109–124). New York: Guilford Press.

Costello, E. J., Egger, H. L., & Angold, A. (2004). The developmental epidemiology of anxiety disorders. In T. Ollendick & J. March (Eds.), *Phobic and anxiety disorders in children and adolescents* (pp. 61–91). New York: Oxford University Press.

Costello, E. J., Foley, D. L., & Angold, A. (2006). Ten-year research update review: The epidemiology of child and adolescent psychiatric disorders: II. Developmental epidemiology. *Journal of the American Academy of Child and Adolescent Psychiatry, 45*, 8–25.

Costello, E. J., Keeler, G. P., Angold, A. (2001). Poverty, race/ethnicity, and psychiatric disorder: A study of rural children. *American Journal of Public Health, 91*, 1494–1498.

Cowan, C. P., Cowan, P. H., Hemming, G., & Miller, N. B. (1991). Becoming a family: Marriage, parenting, and child development. In P. A. Cowan, & M. Hetherington (Eds.), *Family transition* (pp. 79–109). Hillsdale, NJ: Lawrence Erlbaum.

Crawford, T. N., Cohen, P., Midlarsky, E., & Brook, J. S. (2001). Internalizing symptoms in adolescents: Gender differences in vulnerability to parental distress and discord. *Journal of Research on Adolescence, 11*, 95–118.

Cyranowski, J., Frank, E., Young, E., & Shear, K. (2000). Adolescent onset of the gender difference in lifetime rates of major depression. *Archives of General Psychiatry, 57*, 21–27.

Dahl, R. E., & Ryan, N. D. (1996). The psychobiology of adolescent depression. In D. Cicchetti & S. L. Toth (Eds.), *Rochester symposium on developmental psychopathology*, vol. 7: *Adolescence: Opportunities and challenges* (pp. 197–232). Rochester, NY: University of Rochester Press.

Davila, J. (2008). Depressive symptoms and adolescent romance: Theory, research, and implications. *Child Development Perspectives, 2*, 26–31.

Deater-Deckard, K. (2001). Annotation: Recent research examining the role of peer relationships in the development of psychopathology. *Journal of Child Psychology and Psychiatry, 42*, 565–579.

Downey, G., Bonica, C., & Rincon, C. (1999). Rejection sensitivity and adolescent romantic relationships. In W. Furman, B. B. Brown, & C. Feiring (Eds.), *Contemporary perspectives on adolescent relationships* (pp. 148–174). New York: Cambridge University Press.

Elder, G. H., Jr. (1985). Perspectives on the life course. In G. H. Elder, Jr. (Ed.), *Life course dynamics: Trajectories and transitions, 1968–1980* (pp. 23–49). Ithaca, NY: Cornell University Press.

Elder, G. H., Jr., & Caspi, A. (1990). Studying lives in a changing society: Sociological and personalogical explorations. In A. I. Rabin, R. A. Zucker, S. Frank, & R. A. Emmons (Eds.), *Studying persons and lives*. New York: Springer.

Ellis, B. J., & Garber, J. (2000). Psychosocial antecedents of variation in girls' pubertal timing: Maternal depression, stepfather presence, and marital and family stress. *Child Development, 71*, 485–501.

Feldman, S. S., & Cauffman, E. (1999). Sexual betrayal among late adolescents: Perspectives of the perpetrator and the aggrieved. *Journal of Youth and Adolescence, 28*, 235–258.

Forbes, E. E., Silk, J. S., & Dahl, R. E. (in press). Neurobiological processes in depressive disorders: Links with adolescent brain development. In N. B., Allen, & L. Sheeber, (Eds.), *Adolescent emotional development and the emergence of depressive disorders*. Cambridge: Cambridge University Press.

Forehand, R., Biggar, H., & Kotchick, B. A. (1998). Cumulative risk across family stressors: Short- and long-term effects for adolescents. *Journal of Abnormal Child Psychology, 26*, 119–128.

Francis, D. D., Champagne, F. A., Liu, D., & Meaney, M. J. (1999). Maternal care, gene expression, and the development of individual differences in stress reactivity. *Annals of the New York Academy of Sciences, 896*, 66–84.

Furman, W., Brown, B. B., & Feiring, C. (Eds.). (1999). Contemporary perspectives on adolescent relationships. New York: Cambridge University Press.

Garber, J. (2000). Development and depression. In A. J. Sameroff, M. Lewis, & S. M. Miller (Eds.), *Handbook of developmental psychopathology*, 2nd ed.; pp. 467–490). New York: Plenum Press.

Ge, X., Brody, G., Conger, R. D., & Simons, R. L. (2006). Pubertal maturation and African American children's internalizing and externalizing symptoms. *Journal of Youth and Adolescence, 35*, 531–540.

Ge, X., Brody, G. H., Conger, R. D., Simons, R. L., & Murry, V. M. (2002). Contextual amplification of pubertal transition effects on deviant peer affiliation and externalizing behavior among African American children. *Developmental Psychology, 38*, 42–54.

Ge, X., Conger, R. D., & Elder, G. H., Jr. (2001). The relationship between puberty and psychological distress in adolescent boys. *Journal of Research on Adolescence, 11*, 49–70.

Ge, X., Lorenz, F. O., Conger, R. D., Elder, G. H., Jr., & Simmons, R. L. (1994). Trajectories of stressful life events and depressive symptoms during adolescence. *Developmental Psychology, 30*, 467–483.

Geller, B., Zimmerman, B., & Williams, M. (2002). DSM-IV mania symptoms in a prepubertal and early adolescent bipolar disorder phenotype compared to attention-deficit hyperactive and normal controls. *Journal of Child and Adolescent Psychopharmacology, 12*, 11–25.

Gotlib, I. H., Lewinsohn, P. M., & Seeley, J. R. (1995). Symptoms versus a diagnosis of depression: Differences in psychosocial functioning. *Journal of Consulting and Clinical Psychology, 63*, 90–100.

Graber, J. A. (2008). Pubertal and neuroendocrine development and risk for depressive disorders. In N. B. Allen & L. Sheeber (Eds.), *Adolescent emotional development and the emergence of depressive disorders*. Cambridge: Cambridge University Press.

Graber, J. A., & Brooks-Gunn, J. (1996). Transitions and turning points: Navigating the passage from childhood through adolescence. *Developmental Psychology, 32*, 768–776.

Graber, J. A., & Brooks-Gunn, J. (2001). Co-occurring eating and depressive problems: An 8-year study of adolescent girls. *International Journal of Eating Disorders, 30*, 37–47.

Graber, J. A., Brooks-Gunn, J., Paikoff, R. L., & Warren, M. P. (1994). Prediction of eating problems: An eight year study of adolescent girls. *Developmental Psychology, 30*, 823–834.

Graber, J. A., Brooks-Gunn, J., & Warren, M. P. (2006). Pubertal effects on adjustment in girls: Moving from demonstrating effects to identifying pathways. *Journal of Youth and Adolescence, 35*, 413–423.

Graber, J. A., Lewinsohn, P. M., Seeley, J. R., & Brooks-Gunn, J. (1997). Is psychopathology associated with the timing of pubertal development? *Journal of the American Academy of Child and Adolescent Psychiatry, 36*, 1768–1776.

Graber, J. A., Petersen, A. C., & Brooks-Gunn, J. (1996). Pubertal processes: Methods, measures, and models. In J. A. Graber, J. Brooks-Gunn, & A. C. Petersen (Eds.), *Transitions through adolescence: Interpersonal domains and context* (pp. 23–53). Mahwah, NJ: Lawrence Erlbaum.

Graber, J. A., Seeley, J. R., Brooks-Gunn, J., & Lewinsohn, P. M. (2004). Is pubertal timing associated with psychopathology in young adulthood? *Journal of the American Academy of Child and Adolescent Psychiatry, 43*, 718–726.

Graber, J. A., & Sontag, L. M. (2006). Puberty and girls' sexuality: Why hormones aren't the complete answer. In R. Larson & L. Jensen (Series Ed.), L. M. Diamond (Vol. Ed.), *New directions for child and adolescent development*, vol. 112: *Rethinking positive adolescent female sexual development* (pp. 23–38). San Francisco: Jossey-Bass.

Graber, J. A., Tyrka, A. R., & Brooks-Gunn, J. (2002). How similar are correlates of different subclinical eating problems and bulimia nervosa? *Journal of Child Psychology and Psychiatry, 43*, 1–12.

Gunnar, M. R. (2007). Stress effects on the developing brain. In D. Romer & E. F. Walker (Eds.), *Adolescent psychopathology and the developing brain* (pp. 127–147). Oxford: Oxford University Press.

Gunnar, M. R., & Vazquez, D. M. (2001). Low cortisol and flattening of expected daytime rhythm: Potential indices of risk in human development. *Development and Psychopathology, 13*, 515–538.

Hall, G. S. (1904). *Adolescence: Its psychology and its relations to physiology, anthropology, sociology, sex, crime, religion, and education* (2 vols.). New York: Appleton.

Halpern, C. T., Kaestle, C. E., & Hallfors, D. D. (2007). Perceived physical maturity, age of romantic partner, and adolescent risk behavior. *Prevention Science, 8*, 1–10.

Hammen, C., & Rudolph, K. D. (2003). Childhood mood disorders. In E. J. Mash & R. A. Barkley (Eds.), *Child psychopathology* (pp. 233–278). New York: Guilford Press.

Hankin, B. L., & Abela, J. R. Z. (2005). Depression from childhood through adolescence and adulthood. In B. L. Hankin & J. R. Z. Abela (Eds.), *Development of psychopathology: A vulnerability-stress perspective* (pp. 245–288). Thousand Oaks, CA: Sage.

Harper, M. S., Dickson, J. W., & Welsh, D. P. (2006). Self-silencing and rejection sensitivity in adolescent romantic relationships. *Journal of Youth and Adolescence, 35*, 459–467.

Harter, S. (1998). The development of self-representations. In W. Damon (Series Ed.), & N. Eisenberg (Vol. Ed.). *Handbook of child psychology*, vol. 4: *Social, emotional, and personality development* (pp. 553–617). New York: John Wiley & Sons.

Hayward, C., Killen, J. D., Wilson, D. M., Hammer, L. D., Litt, I. F., Kraemer, et al. (1997). Psychiatric risk associated with early puberty in adolescent girls. *Journal of the American Academy of Child and Adolescent Psychiatry, 36*, 255–262.

Hecht, D. B., Inderbitzen, H. M., & Bukowski, A. L. (1998). The relationship between peer status and depressive symptoms in children and adolescents. *Journal of Abnormal Child Psychology, 26*, 153–160.

Hogue, A., & Steinberg, L. (1995). Homophily of internalizing distress in adolescent peer groups. *Developmental Psychology, 31*, 897–906.

Horowitz, J. L., & Garber, J. (2006). The prevention of depressive symptoms in children and adolescents: A meta-analytic review. *Journal of Consulting and Clinical Psychology, 74*, 401–415.

Ingram, R. E., & Luxton, D. D. (2005). Vulnerability-stress models. In B. L. Hankin & J. Abela (Eds.), *Development of psychopathology: Stress–vulnerability perspectives* (pp. 32–46). New York: Sage.

Ivanova, M. Y., Achenbach, T. M., Rescorla, L. A., Dumenci, L., Almqvist, F., Bilenberg, et al. (2007). The generalizability of the youth self-report syndrome structure in 23 societies. *Journal of Consulting and Clinical Psychology, 75*, 729–738.

Jaffee, S. R., & Poulton, R. (2006). Reciprocal effects of mothers' depression and children's problem behaviors from middle childhood to early adolescence. In A. C. Huston & M. N. Ripke (Eds.), *Developmental contexts in middle childhood: Bridges to adolescence and adulthood* (pp. 107–129). New York: Cambridge University Press.

Joiner, T. E., & Wagner, K. D. (1995). Attributional style and depression in children and adolescents: A meta-analytic review. *Clinical Psychology Review, 15*, 777–798.

Joyner, K., & Udry, J. R. (2000). You don't bring me anything but down: Adolescent romance and depression. *Journal of Health and Social Behavior, 41*, 369–391.

Kagan, J. (1980). Perspectives on continuity. In O. G. Brim, Jr., & J. Kagan (Eds.), *Constancy and change in human development* (pp. 26–74). Cambridge, MA: Harvard University Press.

Kagan, J., & Fox, N. A. (2006). Biology, culture, and temperamental bias. In W. Damon & R. M. Lerner (Series Eds.), & N. Eisenberg (Vol. Ed.). *Handbook of child psychology* (6th ed.), vol. 3: *Social, emotional, and personality development* (pp. 167–225). Hoboken, NJ: John Wiley & Sons.

Karel, M. J. (1997). Aging and depression: Vulnerability and stress across adulthood. *Clinical Psychology Review, 17*, 847–879.

Kaslow, N. J., Adamson, L. B., & Collins, M. H. (2000). A developmental psychopathology perspective on the cognitive components of child and adolescent depression. In A. J. Sameroff, M. Lewis, & S. M. Miller (Eds.), *Handbook of developmental psychopathology* (2nd ed.; pp. 491–510). New York: Plenum Press.

Keating, D. P. (2004). Cognitive and brain development. In R. M. Lerner & L. Steinberg (Eds.), *Handbook of adolescent psychology* (2nd ed.; pp. 45–84). Hoboken, NJ: John Wiley & Sons.

Kendler, K. S. (1995). Genetic epidemiology in psychiatry. Taking both genes and environment seriously. *Archives of General Psychiatry, 52*, 895–899.

Kendler, K. S. (2001). Twin studies of psychiatric illness. *Archives of General Psychiatry, 58*, 1005–1014.

Kessler, R. C., & Avenevoli, S., & Merikangas, K. R. (2001). Mood disorders in children and adolescents: An epidemiologic perspective. *Biological Psychiatry, 49*, 1002–1014.

Kessler, R. C., & McLeod, J. D. (1984). Sex differences in vulnerability to undesirable life events. *American Sociological Review, 49*, 620–631.

Kessler, R. C., Nelson, C. B., McGonagle, K. A., Liu, J., Swartz, M., & Blazer, D. G. (1996). Comorbidity of DSM-III-R major depressive disorder in the general population: Results from the U.S. National Comorbidity Survey. *British Journal of Psychiatry, 168*(Suppl.), 17–30.

Klimes-Dougan, B., Hastings, P. D., Granger, D. A., Usher, B. A., & Zahn-Waxler, C. (2001). Adrenocortical activity in at-risk and normally developing adolescents: Individual differences in salivary cortisol basal levels, diurnal variation, and responses to social challenges. *Development and Psychopathology, 13*, 695–719.

Kochanska, G. (1993). Toward a synthesis of parental socialization and child temperament in early development of conscience. *Child Development, 64*, 325–347.

Kovacs, M., & Devlin, B. (1998). Internalizing disorders in childhood. *Journal of Child Psychology and Psychiatry, 39*, 47–63.

Kovacs, M., Obrosky, D. S., Gatsonis, C., & Richards, C. (1997). First episode major depressive and dysthymic disorder in childhood: Clinical and sociodemographic factors in recovery. *Journal of the American Academy of Child and Adolescent Psychiatry, 36*, 777–784.

Krueger, R. F., Caspi, A., Moffitt, T. E., & Silva, P. A. (1998). The structure and stability of common mental disorders (DSM-III-R): A longitudinal-epidemiological study. *Journal of Abnormal Psychology, 107*, 216–227.

La Greca, A. M., & Harrison, H. M. (2005). Adolescent peer relations, friendships, and romantic relationships: Do they predict social anxiety and depression? *Journal of Clinical Child and Adolescent Psychology, 34*, 49–61.

Lai, J., Vesprini, D., Chu, W., Jernström, H., & Narod, S. A. (2001). CYP gene polymorphisms and early menarche. *Molecular Genetics and Metabolism, 74*, 449–457.

Larson, R. W., Clore, G. L., & Wood, G. A. (1999). The emotions of romantic relationships: Do they wreak havoc on adolescents?

In W. Furman, B. B. Brown, & C. Feiring (Eds.), *Contemporary perspectives on adolescent relationships* (pp. 19–49). New York: Cambridge University Press.

Larson, R. W., Csikszentmihalyi, M., & Graef, R. (1980). Mood variability and psychosocial adjustment of adolescents. *Journal of Youth and Adolescence, 9*, 469–490.

Larson, R., & Ham, M. (1993). Stress and "storm and stress" in early adolescence: The relationship of negative events with dysphoric affect. *Developmental Psychology, 29*, 130–140.

Lazarus, R. S., & Folkman, S. (1984). *Stress, appraisal, and coping.* New York: Springer.

Lewinsohn, P. M., & Essau, C. A. (2002). Depression in adolescents. In I. Gotlib & C. Hammen (Eds.), *Handbook of depression* (pp. 541–559). New York: Guilford Press.

Lewinsohn, P. M., Hops, H., Roberts, R. E., Seeley, J. R., & Andrews, J. A. (1993). Adolescent psychopathology: I. Prevalence and incidence of depression and other DSM-III-R disorders in high school students. *Journal of Abnormal Psychology, 102*, 133–144.

Lewinsohn, P. M., Rohde, P., Seeley, J. R. (1998). Major depressive disorder in older adolescents: Prevalence, risk factors, and clinical implications. *Clinical Psychology Review, 18*, 765–794.

Lewinsohn, P. M., Zinbarg, R., Seeley, J. R., Lewinsohn, M., & Sack, W. H. (1997). Lifetime comorbidity among anxiety disorders and between anxiety disorders and other mental disorders in adolescents. *Journal of Anxiety Disorders, 11*, 377–394.

London, B., Downey, G., & Bonica, C. (2007). Social causes and consequences of rejection sensitivity. *Journal of Research on Adolescence, 17*, 481–506.

Lynne, S. D., Graber, J. A., Nichols, T. R., Brooks-Gunn, J., & Botvin, G. J. (2007). Links between pubertal timing, peer influences, and externalizing behaviors among urban students followed through middle school. *Journal of Adolescent Health, 40*, 181.e7–181.e13.

Maccoby, E. E. (1998). *The two sexes: Growing up apart, coming together.* Cambridge, MA: Belknap Press/Harvard University Press.

Marín, B. V., Coyle, K. K., Gómez, C. A., Carvajal, S. C., & Kirby, D. B. (2000). Older boyfriends and girlfriends increased risk of sexual initiation in young adolescents. *Journal of Adolescent Health, 27*, 409–418.

Masten, A. S., & Curtis, W. J. (2000). Integrating competence and psychopathology: Pathways toward a comprehensive science of adaptation in development. *Development and Psychopathology, 12*, 529–550.

McClellan, J. M., & Werry, J. S. (Eds.). (2000). Introduction. [Special Section: Research psychiatric diagnostic interviews for children and adolescents]. *Journal of the American Academy of Child and Adolescent Psychiatry, 39*, 19–27.

McEwen, B. S. (2000). The neurobiology of stress: From serendipity to clinical relevance. *Brain Research, 886*, 172–189.

McEwen, B. S. (1994). How do sex and stress hormones affect nerve cells? *Annals of the New York Academy of Sciences, 743*, 1–18.

McGee, R., Fehan, M., Williams, S., Partridge, F., Silva, P. A., & Kelly, J. (1990). DSM-III disorders in a large sample of adolescents. *Journal of the American Academy of Child and Adolescent Psychiatry, 29*, 611–619.

McLoyd, V. C., Jayaratne, T. E., Ceballo, R., & Borquez, J. (1994). Unemployment and work interruption among African American single mothers: Effects on parenting and adolescent socioemotional functioning. *Child Development, 65*, 562–589.

Merry, S. N. (2007). Prevention and early intervention for depression in young people—practical possibility? *Current Opinion in Psychiatry, 20*, 325–329.

Meyer, S. E., Chrousos, G. P., & Gold, P. W. (2001). Major depression and the stress system: A life span perspective. *Development and Psychopathology, 13*, 565–580.

Moffitt, T. E., Caspi, A., & Rutter, M. (2006). Measured gene–environment interactions in psychopathology. Concepts, research strategies, and implications for research, intervention, and public understanding of genetics. *Perspectives on Psychological Science, 1*, 5–27.

Monroe, S. M., Rohde, P., Seeley, J. R., & Lewinsohn, P. M. (1999). Life events and depression in adolescence: Relationship loss as a prospective risk factor for first onset of major depressive disorder. *Journal of Abnormal Psychology, 108*, 606–614.

Muuss, R. E. (1996). *Theories of adolescence*. New York: McGraw-Hill.

Nansel, T. R., Craig, W., Overpeck, M. D., Saluja, G., & Ruan, W. J. (2004). Cross-national consistency in the relationship between bullying behaviors and psychosocial adjustment. *Archives of Pediatric and Adolescent Medicine, 158*, 730–736.

National Institute of Mental Health (NIMH). (2000). Treatment of children with mental disorders. Retrieved June 3, 2008, from www.nimh.nih.gov/health/publications/treatment-of-children-with-mental-disorders/summary.shtml.

National Institute of Mental Health (NIMH). (2008). Antidepressant medications for children and adolescents: Information for parents and caregivers. Retrieved June 3, 2008, from www.nimh.nih.gov/health/topics/child-and-adolescent-mental-health/antidepressant-medications-for-children-and-adolescents-information-for-parents-and-caregivers.shtml.

Netherton, C., Goodyer, I., Tamplin, A., & Herbert, J. (2004). Salivary cortisol and dehydroepiandrosterone in relation to puberty and gender. *Psychoneuroendocrinology, 29*, 125–140.

Nolen-Hoeksema, S. (1994). An interactive model for the emergence of gender differences in depression in adolescence. *Journal of Research on Adolescence, 4*, 519–534.

Ohring, R., Graber, J. A., & Brooks-Gunn, J. (2002). Girls' recurrent and concurrent body dissatisfaction: Correlates and consequences over 8 years. *International Journal of Eating Disorders, 31*, 404–415.

Paxton, S. J., Neumark-Sztainer, D., Hannan, P. J., & Eisenberg, M. E. (2006). Body dissatisfaction prospectively predicts depressive mood and low self-esteem in adolescent girls and boys. *Journal of Clinical Child and Adolescent Psychology, 35*, 539–549.

Petersen, A. C. (1984). The early adolescence study: An overview. *Journal of Early Adolescence, 4*, 103–106.

Petersen, A. C., Compas, B., Brooks-Gunn, J., Stemmler, M., Ey, S., & Grant, K. (1993). Depression in adolescence. *American Psychologist, 48*, 155–168.

Petersen, A. C., Sarigiani, P. A., & Kennedy, R. E. (1991). Adolescent depression: Why more girls? *Journal of Youth and Adolescence, 20*, 247–271.

Post, R. M., Leverich, G. S., Xing, G., & Weiss, S. R. B. (2001). Developmental vulnerabilities to the onset and course of bipolar disorder. *Development and Psychopathology, 13*, 581–598.

Prinstein, M. J. (2007). Moderators of peer contagion: A longitudinal examination of depression socialization between adolescents and their best friends. *Journal of Clinical Child and Adolescent Psychology, 36*, 159–170.

Purdie, V., & Downey, G. (2000). Rejection sensitivity and adolescent girls' vulnerability to relationship-centered difficulties. *Child Maltreatment, 5*, 338–349.

Radloff, L. S. (1991). The use of the Center for Epidemiologic Studies Depression Scale in adolescents and young adults. *Journal of Youth and Adolescence, 20*, 149–166.

Rierdan, J., Koff, E., & Stubbs, M. L. (1989). A longitudinal analysis of body image as a predictor of the onset and persistence of adolescent girls' depression. *Journal of Early Adolescence, 9*, 454–466.

Rohde, P., Lewinsohn, P. M., & Seeley, J. R. (1991). The comorbidity of unipolar depression: II. Comorbidity with other mental disorders in adolescents and adults. *Journal of Abnormal Psychology, 100*, 214–222.

Rothbart, M. K., & Bates, J. E. (2006). Temperament. In W. Damon & N. Eisenberg (Eds.), *Handbook of child psychology: Social, emotional, and personality development* (5th ed., pp. 99–166), vol. 3. Hoboken, NJ: John Wiley & Sons.

Rubin, K. H., & Burgess, K. (2001). Social withdrawal and anxiety. In M. W. Vasey & M. R. Dadds (Eds.), *The developmental psychopathology of anxiety* (pp. 407–434). London: Oxford University Press.

Rudolf, K. D. (2002). Gender differences in emotional responses to interpersonal stress during adolescence. *Journal of Adolescent Health, 30*(Suppl.), 3–13.

Rueter, M. A., Scaramella, L., Wallace, L. E., & Conger, R. D. (1999). First onset of depressive or anxiety disorders predicted by the longitudinal course of internalizing symptoms and parent-adolescent disagreement. *Archives of General Psychiatry, 56*, 726–732.

Rutter, M. (1994). Continuities, transitions and turning points in development. In M. Rutter & D. F. Hay (Eds.), *Development through life: A handbook for clinicians* (pp. 1–25). London: Blackwell Scientific Publications.

Schneiders, J., Nicolson, N. A., Berkhof, J., Feron, F. J., Van Os, J., & DeVries, M. W. (2006). Mood reactivity to daily negative events in early adolescence: Relationship to risk for psychopathology. *Developmental Psychology, 42*, 543–554.

Schwartz, J. A., Kaslow, N. J., Seeley, J. R., & Lewinsohn, P. M. (2000). Psychological, cognitive, and interpersonal correlates of attributional change in adolescents. *Journal of Clinical Child Psychology, 29*, 188–198.

Shulman, S., & Collins, W. A. (Vol. Eds.). (1997). *New directions for child development*, vol. 78: *Romantic relationships in adolescence: Developmental perspectives*. San Francisco: Jossey-Bass.

Silberg, J., Pickles, A., Rutter, M., Hewitt, J., Simonoff, E., Maes, H., et al. (1999). The influence of genetic factors and life stress on depression among adolescent girls. *Archives of General Psychiatry, 56*, 225–232.

Simmons, R. G., & Blyth, D. A. (1987). *Moving into adolescence: The impact of pubertal change and school context*. New York: Aldine.

Simon, R. W., Eder, D., & Evans, C. (1992). The development of feeling norms underlying romantic love among adolescent females. *Social Psychology Quarterly, 55*, 29–46.

Singh, M. K., Pfeifer, J. C., Barzman, D., Kowatch, R. A., & DelBello, M. P. (2007). Pharmacotherapy for child and adolescent mood disorders. *Psychiatric Annals, 37*, 465–476.

Sontag, L. M., Graber, J. A., & Brooks-Gunn, J. (2007, March). *Dealing with peer stress and the impact of ethnic differences in coping styles*. Paper presented at the biennial meeting of the Society for Research in Child Development, Boston, MA.

Sontag, L. M., Graber, J. A., Brooks-Gunn, J., & Warren, M. P. (2008). Coping with social stress: Implications for psychopathology in young adolescent girls. *Journal of Abnormal Child Psychology, 36*, 1159–1174.

Southwick, S. M., Vythilingam, M., & Charney, D. S. (2005). The psychobiology of depression and resilience to stress: Implications for prevention and treatment. *Annual Review of Clinical Psychology, 1*, 255–291.

Stattin, H., & Magnusson, D. (1990). *Paths through life*, vol. 2: *Pubertal maturation in female development*. Hillsdale, NJ: Lawrence Erlbaum.

Steinberg, L. (2001). We know some things: Parent–adolescent relationships in retrospect and prospect. *Journal of Research on Adolescence, 11*, 1–19.

Steinberg, L., & Avenevoli, S. (2000). The role of context in the development of psychopathology: A conceptual framework and some speculative propositions. *Child Development, 71*, 66–74.

Steinberg, L., & Morris, A. S. (2001). Adolescent development. *Annual Review of Psychology, 52*, 83–110.

Stevens, E. A., & Prinstein, M. J. (2005). Peer contagion and depressogenic attributional styles among adolescents: A longitudinal study. *Journal of Abnormal Child Psychology, 33*, 25–37.

Stice, E., Presnell, K., & Bearman, S. K. (2001). Relation of early menarche to depression, eating disorders, substance abuse, and comorbid psychopathology among adolescent girls. *Developmental Psychology, 37*, 608–619.

Storch, E. A., Nock, M. K., Masia-Warner, C., & Barlas, M. E. (2003). Peer victimization and social–psychological adjustment in Hispanic and African-American children. *Journal of Child and Family Studies, 12,* 439–452.

Strober, M. (2001). Family-genetic aspects of juvenile affective disorders. In I. M. Goodyer (Ed.), *The depressed child and adolescent* (2nd ed., pp. 179–203). Cambridge: Cambridge University Press.

Suomi, S. J. (1999). Attachment in rhesus monkeys. In J. Cassidy & P. R. Shaver (Eds.), *Handbook of attachment: Theory, research, and clinical applications* (pp. 181–197). New York: Guilford Press.

Taylor, S. E., Klein, L. C., Lewis, B. P., Gruenewald, T. L., Gurung, R. A. R., & Updegraff, J. A. (2000). Biobehavioral responses to stress in females: Tend-and-befriend, not fight-or-flight. *Psychological Review, 107,* 411–429.

Terry-Humen, E., Manlove, J., & Cottingham, S. (2006). Trends and recent estimates: Sexual activity among U.S. teens. *Child trends research brief.* Washington, DC: Child Trends.

Thompson, R. A. (2006). The development of the person: Social understanding, relationships, conscience, self. In W. Damon (Series Ed.), N. Eisenberg & R. M. Lerner (Vol. Eds.), *Handbook of child psychology* (6th ed.), vol. 3: *Social, emotional, and personality development* (pp. 25–104). Hoboken, NJ: John Wiley & Sons.

Thompson, S. (1994). Changing lives, changing genres: Teenage girls' narratives about sex and romance, 1978–1986. In A. S. Rossi (Ed.), *Sexuality across the life course* (pp. 209–232). Chicago: University of Chicago Press.

Treatment for Adolescents With Depression Study (TADS) Team. (2004). Fluoxetine, cognitive–behavioral therapy, and their combination for adolescents with depression: Treatment for Adolescents with Depression Study (TADS) randomized controlled trial. *Journal of the American Medical Association, 292,* 807–820.

Twenge, J. M., & Nolen-Hoeksema, S. (2002). Age, gender, race, socioeconomic status, and birth cohort differences on the Children's Depression Inventory: A meta-analysis. *Journal of Abnormal Psychology, 111,* 578–588.

Utsey, S. O., Bolden, M. A., Lanier, Y., & Williams, O. (2007). Examining the role of culture-specific coping as a predictor of resilient outcomes in African Americans from high-risk urban communities. *Journal of Black Psychology, 33,* 75–93.

Vasey, M. W., & Ollendick, T. H. (2000). Anxiety. In A. J. Sameroff, M. Lewis, & S. M. Miller (Eds.), *Handbook of developmental psychopathology* (2nd ed.; pp. 511–529). New York: Plenum Press.

Wadsworth, M. E., Raviv, T., Compas, B. E., & Connor-Smith, J. K. (2005). Parent and adolescent responses to poverty-related stress: Tests of mediated and moderated coping models. *Journal of Child and Family Studies, 14,* 283–298.

Wagner, K. D. (2003). Major depression in children and adolescents. *Psychiatric Annals, 33,* 266–270.

Walker, E. (2002). Adolescent neurodevelopment and psychopathology. *Current Directions in Psychological Science, 11,* 24–28.

Walker, E. F., Walder, D. J., & Reynolds, F. (2001). Developmental changes in cortisol secretion in normal and at-risk youth. *Development and Psychopathology, 13,* 721–732.

Way, N. (1996). Between experiences of betrayal and desire: Close friendships among urban adolescents. In B. J. R. Leadbeater & N. Way (Eds.), *Urban girls: Resisting stereotypes, creating identities* (pp. 173–192). New York: New York University Press.

Weinstein, S. M., Mermelstein, R. J., Hankin, B. L., Hedeker, D., & Flay, B. R. (2007). Longitudinal patterns of daily affect and global mood during adolescence. *Society for Research on Adolescence, 17,* 587–600.

Weisz, J. R., McCarty, C. A., & Valeri, S. M. (2006). Effects of psychotherapy for depression in children and adolescents: A meta-analysis. *Psychological Bulletin, 132,* 132–149.

Wingood, G. M., DiClemente, R. J., Harrington, K., & Davies, S. (2002). Body image and African American females' sexual health. *Journal of Women's Health and Gender-Based Medicine, 11,* 433–439.

Yorbik, O., Birmaher, B., Axelson, D., Williamson, D. E., & Ryan, N. D. (2004). Clinical characteristics of depressive symptoms in children and adolescents with major depressive disorder. *Journal of Clinical Psychiatry, 65,* 1654–1659.

Zahn-Waxler, C., Klimes-Dougan, B., & Slattery, M. J. (2000). Internalizing problems of childhood and adolescence: Prospects, pitfalls, and progress in understanding the development of anxiety and depression. *Development and Psychopathology, 12,* 443–466.

Zalsman, G., Brent, D. A., & Weersing, R. (2006). Depressive disorders in childhood and adolescence: An overview epidemiology, clinical manifestation, and risk factors. *Child and Adolescent Psychiatric Clinics of North America, 15,* 827–841.

CHAPTER 20

Conduct Disorder, Aggression and Delinquency

DAVID P. FARRINGTON

Within the limits of a short chapter, it is obviously impossible to provide an exhaustive review of all aspects of conduct disorder, aggression, and delinquency in adolescence. There are many extensive reviews of these topics (Anderson & Huesmann, 2003; Coie & Dodge, 1998; Connor, 2002; Farrington & Welsh, 2007; Hill & Maughan, 2001; Rutter, Giller, & Hagell, 1998). In this chapter, I will be very selective in focusing on what seem to me the most important findings obtained in the highest quality studies. I will particularly focus on risk factors discovered in prospective longitudinal surveys and on successful interventions demonstrated in randomized experiments. The major longitudinal surveys are detailed in Farrington and Welsh (2007, pp. 29–36) and Thornberry and Krohn (2003), while major experiments in criminology are reviewed by Farrington and Welsh (2006).

My emphasis is mainly on young people aged 10–17 and on research carried out in North America, Great Britain, and similar Western democracies. Most research has been carried out with males, but studies of females are included where applicable (Moffitt, Caspi, Rutter, & Silva, 2001; Moretti, Odgers, & Jackson, 2004; Pepler, Madsen, Webster, & Levine, 2005; Zahn et al., 2008). My focus is on substantive results rather than on methodological or theoretical issues.

In general, all types of antisocial behavior tend to coexist and are intercorrelated. I have chosen to concentrate on conduct disorder, aggression, and delinquency because

these are the most important types of adolescent antisocial behaviors studied in different fields: conduct disorder in clinical psychology and child/adolescent psychiatry, aggression in developmental psychology, and delinquency in criminology and sociology. While there is sometimes inadequate communication among different fields, it should be borne in mind that these behaviors are logically and empirically related, so that risk factors and successful interventions that apply to one of these types of antisocial behavior are also likely to apply to the other two types. Other types of antisocial behavior, such as drug use, will not be reviewed here. Although there is nowadays a great deal of interest in promotive and protective factors (e.g., Loeber, Farrington, Stouthamer-Loeber, & White, 2008), I do not have space to discuss them here. Before reviewing risk factors and successful interventions, I will briefly review the definition, measurement, and epidemiology of each type of antisocial behavior.

CONDUCT DISORDER

Definition and Measurement

Robins (1999) has traced the development of conduct disorder (CD) definitions over time. According to the *Diagnostic and Statistical Manual of Mental Disorders*, 4th edition (DSM-IV; American Psychiatric Association, 1994, p. 85), the essential feature of CD is a repetitive and persistent pattern of behavior in which the basic rights of others or major age-appropriate societal norms are violated.

Also, the disturbance of behavior must cause clinically significant impairment in social, academic or occupational functioning. According to the DSM-IV diagnostic criteria, 3 or more out of 15 specified behaviors, including aggression to people or animals, property destruction, stealing or lying, and violating rules (e.g., truancy, running away), must be present for CD to be diagnosed. The prevalence of CD is lower if evidence of impairment is required as well as specified behaviors (Romano, Tremblay, Vitaro, Zoccolillo, & Pagani, 2001). Frequent, serious, persistent behaviors that are shown in several different settings are most likely to be defined as symptoms of a disorder. Additions to the diagnostic protocol for CD in DSM-V were considered by Moffitt et al. (2008), including a childhood-limited subtype; callous–unemotional traits; female-specific criteria; and biomarkers. Overall, Moffitt and colleagues concluded that the current CD protocol was adequate and that the existing evidence base was not sufficiently compelling to justify alterations.

CD can be diagnosed by a clinician in a psychiatric interview with a child and the parents, or it can be assessed using a structured interview administered by a nonclinician, such as the Diagnostic Interview Schedule for Children (DISC; Shaffer et al., 1996) or Child and Adolescent Psychiatric Assessment (CAPA; Angold & Costello, 2000). Childhood antisocial behavior can also be assessed using rating scales or behavior problem checklists such as the Child Behavior Checklist (CBCL), typically completed by a parent, and its associated Teacher Report Form (TRF) and Youth Self-Report (YSR; Achenbach, 1993). These yield broadband scales such as "externalizing behavior" and more specific scales of aggression, delinquency, and hyperactivity, with impressive cross-cultural replicability (Achenbach, Verhulst, Baron, & Althaus, 1987). The aggression and delinquency scales are highly correlated (Pakiz, Reinherz, & Frost, 1992). The delinquency scale of the CBCL is closely related to the diagnosis of CD on the

DISC (Kasius, Ferdinand, van den Berg, & Verhulst, 1997).

Prevalence

Nottelmann and Jensen (1995) have usefully summarized findings obtained in epidemiological studies of conduct disorder. One problem in interpreting prevalence results concerns the time period to which they refer, which may be 3 months, 6 months, 12 months, or cumulatively over a period of years. Prevalence rates are greater among males than females and vary at different ages. Also, prevalence rates change as the DSM definitions change (Lahey et al., 1990). In the Great Smoky Mountains Study of Youth, only 79% of conduct-disordered youths had functional impairment (Costello et al., 1996). There is not space here to review measurement issues or changes in prevalence over time (e.g., Achenbach, Dumenci, & Rescorla, 2003; Collishaw, Goodman, Pickles, & Maughan, 2007).

The instantaneous (as opposed to cumulative) prevalence of CD is about 6%–16% of adolescent boys and about 2%–9% of adolescent girls (Mandel, 1997). For example, in the Ontario Child Health Study in Canada, the 6-month prevalence of CD at age 12–16 was 10% for boys and 4% for girls (Offord et al., 1987). In the New York State longitudinal study, the 12-month prevalence of CD for boys was 16% at both ages 10–13 and 14–16 (Cohen et al., 1993a). For girls, it was 4% at age 10–13 and 9% at age 14–16. Zoccolillo (1993) suggested that CD criteria may be less applicable to the behavior of girls than to the behavior of boys, and hence that gender-specific CD criteria should be developed. Gender differences in CD have been discussed by Lahey et al. (2006).

It is not entirely clear how the prevalence of CD varies over the adolescent age range, and this may depend on how CD is measured. For example, in the Methodology for Epidemiology of Mental Disorders in Children and Adolescents (MECA) study, which was a cross-sectional survey of 1,285 adolescents aged 9–17, the DISC was completed by parents and by adolescents (Lahey et al., 2000). The prevalence of CD (in the previous 6 months) did not vary significantly over this age range according to parents, but it increased with age according to adolescent self-reports. According to adolescents, the prevalence of CD increased for boys from 1.3% at age 9–11 to 6% at age 12–14 and 11% at age 15–17. For girls, prevalence increased from 0.5% at age 9–11 to 3% at age 12–14 and 4% at age 15–17. Hence, the male-to-female ratio for CD was greatest at age 15–17. In a large-scale study of over 10,000 British children aged 5–15, Maughan, Rowe, Messer, Goodman, and Meltzer (2004) found that the prevalence of CD increased with age for both boys and girls, and that the male preponderance in CD was most marked in childhood and early adolescence. The CD measure was derived from children, parents, and teachers.

In the Great Smoky Mountains Study of Youth, Maughan, Pickles, Rowe, Costello, and Angold (2000) investigated developmental trajectories of aggressive and nonaggressive conduct problems. Between ages 9 and 16, they found that there were three categories of adolescents, with stable high conduct problems, stable low conduct problems, and decreasing conduct problems. Boys were more likely to have stable high or decreasing conduct problems over time, whereas girls were more likely to have stable low conduct problems over time. Similarly, Shaw, Lacourse, and Nagin (2005) investigated trajectories of conduct problems between ages 2 and 10, and van Lier, van der Ende, Koot, and Verhulst (2007) studied such trajectories between ages 4 and 18.

Onset and Continuity

DSM-IV classified CD into childhood-onset versus adolescent-onset types. Childhood-onset CD typically begins with the emergence of oppositional defiant disorder (ODD), characterized by temper tantrums and defiant, irritable, argumentative, and annoying behavior (Hinshaw, Lahey, & Hart, 1993). Mean or median ages of onset for specific CD symptoms have been provided by various researchers, but they depend on the age of the child at measurement and the consequent cumulative prevalence of the symptoms. Retrospectively in the Epidemiological Catchment Area project, Robins (1989) reported that the mean age of onset (before 15) for stealing was 10 for males and females, while for vandalism it was 11 for males and females. However, ages of onset were generally later for girls than for boys.

While exact onset ages varied, some CD symptoms consistently appeared before others. This observation led Loeber et al. (1993) to postulate a model of three developmental pathways in disruptive childhood behavior. The overt pathway began with minor aggression (e.g., bullying) and progressed to physical fighting and eventually serious violence. The covert pathway began with minor nonviolent behavior (e.g., shoplifting) and progressed to vandalism and eventually serious property crime. The authority conflict pathway began with stubborn behavior and progressed to defiance and eventually authority avoidance (e.g., running away). Typically, progression in the overt pathway was accompanied by simultaneous progression in the covert pathway. Tolan and Gorman-Smith (1998) found that the hypothesized pathways were largely confirmed in the U.S. National Youth Survey and the Chicago Youth Development Study. The pathways model has also been replicated in Denver and Rochester (Loeber, Wei, Stouthamer-Loeber, Huizinga, & Thornberry, 1999), with African American and Hispanic adolescents (Tolan, Gorman-Smith, & Loeber, 2000), and with antisocial girls (Gorman-Smith & Loeber, 2005).

There is considerable continuity or stability in CD, at least over a few years. In the Ontario Child Health Study, 45% of children aged 4–12 who were CD in 1983 were still CD 4 years later, compared with only 5% of those who had no disorder in 1983 (Offord et al., 1992). CD was more stable than attention-deficit/hyperactivity disorder (ADHD) or emotional disorder. Also, stability was greater for children aged 8–12 (60% persisting) than for children aged 4–7 (25% persisting). However, the interpretation of results was complicated by comorbidity; 35% of those with CD in 1983 had ADHD 4 years later, and, conversely, 34% of those with ADHD in 1983 had CD 4 years later. In a Dutch follow-up study using the CBCL, Verhulst and van der Ende (1995) found a significant correlation (0.54) between externalizing scores over an 8-year period spanning adolescence.

Similar results have been reported by other researchers. In their New York State study, Cohen, Cohen, and Brook (1993b) found that 43% of CD children aged 9–18 were still CD 2.5 years later (compared with 10% of non-CD children). There were no significant age or gender differences in stability, but stability increased with the severity of CD. In the Developmental Trends Study, Lahey et al. (1995) reported that half of CD boys aged 7–12 were still CD 3 years later. Persistence was predicted by parental antisocial personality disorder (APD) and by low verbal IQ, but not by age, socioeconomic status (SES), or ethnicity. In the same study, CD in childhood and adolescence predicted APD in adulthood (Lahey, Loeber, Burke, & Applegate, 2005).

AGGRESSION

Definition and Measurement

Aggression is defined as behavior that is intended to, and actually does, harm another person (Coie & Dodge, 1998). Many different types of aggression have been distinguished, including physical versus verbal aggression, reactive versus proactive aggression, and hostile versus instrumental aggression (Raine et al., 2006; Vaillancourt, Miller, Fagbemi, Cote, & Tremblay, 2007). There is not space here to review special types of aggression such as soccer hooliganism (Farrington, 2006; Lösel & Bliesener, 2003). Instead, I will focus on school bullying, which is one of the most clearly defined and most researched types of adolescent aggression (Farrington, 1993b;

Smith, Pepler, & Rigby, 2004). Its definition typically includes physical, verbal, or psychological attack or intimidation that is intended to cause fear, distress, or harm to a victim; an imbalance of power, with the more powerful child oppressing the less powerful one; and repeated incidents between the same children over a prolonged time period.

Aggression is measured in a variety of ways, including self-reports, parent reports, teacher ratings, peer ratings, and school records. Solberg and Olweus (2003) argued that self-reports were the best method of measuring school bullying. Systematic observation is also used (e.g., Pepler & Craig, 1995). It is important to investigate the concordance of results obtained by these different methods, but these types of measurement issues will not generally be discussed in this chapter. Many aggressive acts committed by adolescents are not witnessed by teachers, parents, or peers. For example, in a Dublin study, O'Moore and Hillery (1989) found that teachers identified only 24% of self-reported bullies. In an observational study in Canada, Craig, Pepler, and Atlas (2000) discovered that the frequency of bullying was twice as high in the playground as in the classroom. However, Stephenson and Smith (1989) in England reported that teacher and peer nominations about which children were involved in bullying were highly correlated (0.8).

Prevalence

The prevalence of physical aggression (hitting) increases up to age 2 and then decreases between ages 2 and 4, when verbal aggression increases (Coie & Dodge, 1998). Most aggression at the preschool ages is directed against siblings or peers. The incidence of physical aggression continues to decrease in the elementary school years (Tremblay, 2000) as language and abstract thinking improve, children increasingly use words rather than aggressive actions to resolve conflicts, and internal inhibitions and the ability to delay gratification also improve. Research on the prevalence of physical aggression has been reviewed by Lee, Baillargeon, Vermunt, Wu, and Tremblay (2007).

In a cross-sectional survey of a large representative sample of Canadian children, Tremblay et al. (1999) found that the prevalence of hitting, kicking, and biting (as reported by mothers) decreased steadily from age 2 to age 11. Furthermore, in the Montreal longitudinal study, the prevalence of teacher-rated physical aggression of boys decreased steadily from age 6 to age 15. Nagin and Tremblay (1999) identified four different trajectories of aggression in the Montreal Longitudinal Experimental Study: consistently high, consistently low, high/decreasing, and moderate/decreasing. There have been many other studies of trajectories of physical aggression. Among the most important are the nationwide longitudinal study of Canadian children (Cote, Vaillancourt, LeBlanc, Nagin, & Tremblay, 2006) and the analysis of data from six sites in three countries by Broidy et al. (2003).

Interestingly, in a cross-sectional survey of a large sample of American children (Fitzpatrick, 1997), the prevalence of self-reported physical fighting decreased from grade 3 (age 8) to grade 12 (age 17). Also, in the Pittsburgh Youth Study, the prevalence of parent-rated physical aggression of boys decreased between ages 10 and 17 (Loeber & Hay, 1997). Similarly, in the large-scale British survey of Maughan et al. (2004), the only CD symptom that decreased between ages 8 and 15 was physical fighting. Of course, it is possible that the seriousness of aggression (e.g., according to injuries to participants) may increase between ages 10 and 17. Criminal violence will be discussed in the delinquency section.

The prevalence of bullying is often very high. For example, in the Dublin study of O'Moore and Hillery (1989), 58% of boys and 38% of girls said that they had ever bullied someone. The prevalence is lower when bullying is restricted to "sometimes or more often this term." With this definition, 11% of boys and 2.5% of girls were bullies in secondary schools in Norway (Olweus, 1991); and 8% of boys and 4% of girls were bullies in secondary schools in Sheffield, England (Whitney & Smith, 1991). The prevalence of bullying decreases with age from elementary to secondary schools, especially for girls. Cross-national comparisons of the prevalence of bullying have been published by Smith et al. (1999) and Due et al. (2005).

Gender differences in aggression are not very great in infancy and toddlerhood (Loeber & Hay, 1997), but they increase from the preschool years onward. Boys use more physical and verbal aggression, both hostile and instrumental. However, indirect or relational aggression—spreading malicious rumors, not talking to other children, excluding peers from group activities—is more characteristic of girls (Bjorkvist, Lagerspetz, & Kaukiainen, 1992; Crick & Grotpeter, 1995). Gender differences in aggression tend to increase in adolescence, as female physical aggression decreases more than male physical aggression (Fontaine et al., 2008).

Continuity

There is significant continuity in aggression over time. In a classic review, Olweus (1979) found that the average stability coefficient (correlation) for male aggression was 0.68 in 16 surveys covering time periods of up to 21 years. Huesmann, Eron, Lefkowitz, and Walder (1984) in New York State reported that peer-rated aggression at age 8 significantly predicted peer-rated aggression at age 18 and self-reported aggression at age 30. Similarly, in Finland, Kokko and Pulkkinen (2005) found that aggression at ages 8 and 14 predicted aggression at ages 36 and 42. Female aggression is also significantly stable over time; stability coefficients were similar for males and females in the Carolina Longitudinal Study (Cairns & Cairns, 1994, p. 63). However, Loeber and Stouthamer-Loeber (1998) pointed out that a high (relative) stability of aggressiveness was not incompatible with high rates of desistance from physical aggression (absolute change) from childhood to adulthood.

Olweus (1979) argued that aggression was a stable personality trait. However, theories of aggression place most emphasis on cognitive processes. For example, Huesmann and Eron (1989) put forward a cognitive script model, in which aggressive behavior depends on stored behavioral repertoires (cognitive scripts) that have been learned during early development. In response to environmental cues, possible cognitive scripts are retrieved and evaluated. The choice of aggressive scripts, which prescribe aggressive behavior, depends on the past history of rewards and punishments and on the extent to which adolescents are influenced by immediate gratification as opposed to long-term consequences. According to this theory, the persisting trait of aggressiveness is a collection of well-learned aggressive scripts that are resistant to change. A similar social information-processing theory was proposed by Dodge (1991) and updated by Dodge (2003). There is not space here to discuss other cognitive or decision-making theories of antisocial behavior.

DELINQUENCY

Definition and Measurement

Delinquency is defined according to acts prohibited by the criminal law, such as theft, burglary, robbery, violence, vandalism, and drug use. There are many problems in using legal definitions of delinquency. For example, the boundary between what is legal and what is illegal may be poorly defined and subjective, as when school bullying gradually escalates into criminal violence. Legal categories may be so wide that they include acts which are behaviorally quite different, as when "robbery" ranges from armed bank holdups carried out by gangs of masked men to thefts of small amounts of money perpetrated by one schoolchild on another. Legal definitions rely on the concept of intent, which is difficult to measure reliably and validly, rather than the behavioral criteria preferred by social scientists. Also, legal definitions change over time. However, their main advantage is that, because they have been adopted by most delinquency researchers, their use makes it possible to compare and summarize results obtained in different projects.

Delinquency is commonly measured using either official records of arrests or convictions or self-reports of offending. The advantages and disadvantages of official records and self-reports are to some extent complementary. In general, official records include the worst offenders and the worst offenses, while self-reports include more of the normal range of delinquent activity. In the Pittsburgh Youth Study, Farrington, Jolliffe, Loeber, and Homish (2007) found that there were 2.4 self-reported offenders per official court offender, and 80 self-reported offenses per officially recorded offense. The worst offenders may be missing from samples interviewed in self-report studies (Cernkovich, Giordano, & Pugh, 1985). Self-reports have the advantage of including undetected offenses, but the disadvantages of concealment and forgetting.

By normally accepted psychometric criteria of validity, self-reports of delinquency are valid (Junger-Tas & Marshall, 1999). For example, self-reported delinquency predicted later convictions among undetected boys in the Cambridge Study in Delinquent Development, which is a prospective longitudinal survey of 400 London boys (Farrington, 1989b). In the Pittsburgh Youth Study, the seriousness of self-reported delinquency predicted later court referrals (Farrington, Loeber, Stouthamer-Loeber, van Kammen, & Schmidt, 1996b). However, predictive validity was enhanced by combining self-report and parent and teacher information about offending. Similarly, in the Seattle Social Development Project, self-reported delinquency predicted later court referrals (Jolliffe et al., 2003).

The key issue is whether the same results are obtained with both self-reports and official records. For example, if both show a link between parental supervision and delinquency, it is likely that supervision is related to delinquent behavior (rather than to any biases in measurement). Generally, the worst offenders according to self-reports (taking account of frequency and seriousness) tend also to be the worst offenders according to official records (Huizinga & Elliott, 1986). In the Cambridge Study, the predictors and correlates of official and self-reported delinquency were very similar (Farrington, 1992c).

Prevalence

Even when measured by convictions, the cumulative prevalence of delinquency is substantial. In the Cambridge Study, 20% of males were convicted before age 17. The annual prevalence of convictions increased to a peak at age 17 and then declined (Farrington, 1992a). It was 1.5% at age 10, 5% at age 13, 11% at age 17, 6% at age 22, and 3% at age 30. According to national figures for England and Wales (Prime, White, Liriano, & Patel, 2001), about 15% of males and 3% of females born in 1953–1963 were convicted up to age 17 for a "standard list" offense (i.e., a more serious offense, excluding traffic infractions and drunkenness, for example).

Cumulative prevalence is also substantial in the United States. In a longitudinal study of over 27,000 persons born in Philadelphia in 1958, Tracy, Wolfgang, and Figlio (1985) found that 33% of males and 14% of females were arrested before age 18 for nontraffic offenses. The male-to-female ratio was greater for more serious (crime index) offenses: 18% of males versus 4% of females. Cumulative prevalence is surprisingly high even for the most serious offense of homicide. In the Pittsburgh Youth Study, 33 of the 1,500 males were convicted of homicide up to age 26 (Farrington, Loeber, Stallings, & Homish, 2008; Loeber et al., 2005). Weighting back to the population of Pittsburgh public schools, 2.7% of African American males were convicted of homicide, compared with 0.5% of Caucasian males.

National U.S. figures show that, in 2006, the male-to-female ratio for arrests under 18 was

4.7 for index violence and 2.1 for index property offenses (FBI, 2007, Table 33). The peak age for male index property and index violence offenses was about 17–18 (FBI, 2007, Table 39). The peak age for female index property offenses was about 16–17, while female index violence peaked later, at about age 18–21 (FBI, 2007, Table 40).

The prevalence of delinquency according to self-reports is higher than in official records. In the large-scale Denver, Rochester, and Pittsburgh longitudinal studies, the annual prevalence of "street crimes" (burglary, serious theft, robbery, aggravated assault, etc.) increased from less than 15% at age 11 to almost 50% at age 17 (Huizinga, Loeber, & Thornberry, 1993). Similarly, in the U.S. National Youth Survey, the annual prevalence of self-reported violence increased to a peak of 28% of males at age 17 and 12% of females at ages 15–17 (Elliott, 1994). Annual prevalence rates for specific acts have been provided by Loeber, Farrington, Stouthamer-Loeber, & van Kammen (1998, p. 94). For example, shoplifting increased from 10% of boys at age 10 to 19% at age 13. Carrying a weapon increased from 12% of boys at age 10 to 23% at age 13.

In both official records and self-reports, the age-crime curve—obtained cross-sectionally—usually increases to a peak in the late teenage years and then decreases (Kirk, 2006). In the Pittsburgh Youth Study, Loeber et al. (2008) presented age–crime curves obtained longitudinally rather than cross-sectionally. Whether based on official records or on reports by boys, mothers, and teachers, the curves usually peaked in the mid to late teenage years. The oldest cohort of boys (born about 1974) had a higher prevalence and frequency of offending than the youngest cohort (born about 1980), probably because the teenage years of the oldest boys coincided with a big increase in the violent crime rate (in Pittsburgh and in the United States) to a peak in 1993–1994 (Fabio et al., 2006).

There have been many studies of trajectories of offending at different ages, reviewed by Piquero (2008). While many offenders follow the traditional age–crime curve, with offending peaking in late adolescence and then declining, most studies also find groups of offenders with other developmental trajectories. For example, in the Cambridge Study there were a group of low-rate chronic offenders whose offending did not peak until the mid-20s (Piquero, Farrington, & Blumstein, 2007). In the Pittsburgh youth study, there was a group whose offending declined steadily from age 13 to age 24 (Loeber et al., 2008). Trajectories based on self-reports are sometimes different from trajectories based on official records (Wiesner, Capaldi, & Kim, 2007). Attempts have been made to investigate risk factors for different trajectory groups (e.g., Barker et al., 2007; Fergusson & Horwood, 2002; Harachi et al., 2006), but this topic will not be reviewed here.

The age distributions of CD, aggression, and delinquency seem somewhat inconsistent. While the prevalence of physical aggression (hitting and kicking) and bullying decrease from age 10 to age 17, the prevalence of CD and violent and property offenses generally increase over this age range. It may be that most children "grow out" of minor types of antisocial behavior, perhaps because of increasing internal inhibitions inculcated by parents, but that more serious types increase during adolescence, perhaps because of the increasing importance of peer influence (Farrington, 1986a).

Onset and Continuity

Criminal career research using official records of delinquency generally shows a peak age of onset between 13 and 16. In the Cambridge Study, the peak age of onset was at 14; 5% of the males were first convicted at that age (Farrington, 1992a). The onset curves up to age 25 of working-class males in London and Stockholm were quite similar (Farrington & Wikström, 1994). Sequences of onsets were studied for Montreal delinquents by LeBlanc and Frechette (1989). They discovered that shoplifting and vandalism tended to occur before adolescence (average age of onset, 11),

burglary and motor vehicle theft in adolescence (average onset, 14–15), and sex offenses and drug trafficking in the later teenage years (average onset, 17–19).

In the Seattle Social Development Project, delinquency career features were compared in official court records and self-reports (Farrington et al., 2003). The results showed that there was a sharp increase in the prevalence of court referrals between ages 12 and 13, probably reflecting the reluctance of the U.S. juvenile justice system to deal with very young offenders (Loeber & Farrington, 2001). An early age of onset predicted a high rate of offending in court referrals but not in self-reports, possibly because the very young offenders who were referred to court were an extreme group.

In the Cambridge Study, the males first convicted at the earliest ages (10–13) tended to become the most persistent offenders, committing an average of 9 offenses leading to convictions in an average criminal career lasting 13 years (Farrington et al., 2006). Similarly, Farrington and Wikström (1994), using official records in Stockholm, and LeBlanc and Frechette (1989) in Montreal, using both self-reports and official records, showed that the duration of criminal careers decreased with increasing age of onset. It is generally true that an early age of onset of antisocial behavior predicts a long and serious antisocial career (Loeber & LeBlanc, 1990).

Moffitt (1993a) distinguished between "life-course-persistent" offenders, who had an early onset and a long criminal career, and "adolescence-limited" offenders, who started later and had a short criminal career. Her analyses in the Dunedin (New Zealand) study generally confirmed the features of her postulated model (Moffitt, Caspi, Dickson, Silva, & Stanton, 1996). Childhood- and adolescent-onset cases differed in temperament as early as age 3. (For recent reviews of research on this theory, see Moffitt, 2003; Piquero & Moffitt, 2005.) Life-course-persistent and adolescence-limited offenders were identified using conviction records in the Cambridge Study (Nagin, Farrington, & Moffitt, 1995). However, according to self-reports, the apparent reformation of the adolescence-limited offenders was less than complete. At age 32, they continued to drink heavily, use drugs, get into fights, and commit criminal acts.

Several researchers have investigated factors that predict early versus late onset offending (Carroll et al., 2006). In the Cambridge Study, the strongest predictors were rarely spending leisure time with the father, troublesome school behavior, authoritarian parents and psychomotor impulsivity (Farrington & Hawkins, 1991). In contrast, late onset offenders tended to be nervous–withdrawn and anxious, suggesting that these factors may have protected children from offending at an early age (Zara & Farrington, 2007). In the Pittsburgh Youth Study, the strongest correlates of early onset were physical aggression, ODD, ADHD, truancy, peer delinquency, and poor parental supervision (Loeber, Stouthamer-Loeber, van Kammen, & Farrington, 1991). There is a great deal of criminological research on other criminal career features such as desistance, duration of careers, escalation and deescalation (Farrington, 1997a), but there is not space to review this here.

Generally, there is significant continuity between delinquency in one age range and delinquency in another. In the Cambridge Study, nearly three-quarters (73%) of those convicted as juveniles at age 10–16 were reconvicted at age 17–24, in comparison with only 16% of those not convicted as juveniles (Farrington, 1992a). Nearly half (45%) of those convicted as juveniles were reconvicted at age 25–32, in comparison with only 8% of those not convicted as juveniles. Furthermore, this continuity over time did not merely reflect continuity in police reaction to delinquency. For 10 specified offenses, the significant continuity between offending in one age range and offending in a later age range held for self-reports as well as official convictions (Farrington, 1989b). In the Seattle Social Development Project, there was also significant continuity in court referrals and self-reports (Farrington et al., 2003a).

Other studies show similar continuity in delinquency. For example, in Sweden, Stattin and Magnusson (1991) reported that nearly 70% of males registered (by police, social, or child welfare authorities) for committing a crime before age 15 were registered again between ages 15 and 20, and nearly 60% were registered between ages 21 and 29. Also, the number of juvenile offenses is an effective predictor of the number of adult offenses (Wolfgang, Thornberry, & Figlio, 1987). There was considerable continuity in offending between the ages of 10 and 25 in both London and Stockholm (Farrington & Wikström, 1994).

COMORBIDITY AND VERSATILITY

In general, CD adolescents tend also to be aggressive and delinquent. There is controversy about whether aggressive symptoms should be considered part of ODD or CD (Loeber, Burke, Lahey, Winters, & Zera, 2000). In the Christchurch Study in New Zealand, Fergusson and Horwood (1995) reported that 90% of children with three or more CD symptoms at age 15 were self-reported frequent offenders at age 16 (compared with only 17% of children with no CD symptoms). Fergusson, Horwood, and Ridder (2005) later showed that conduct problems at ages 7–9 predicted offending at ages 21–25. Similarly, in the Great Smoky Mountains Study, Copeland, Miller-Johnson, Keeler, Angold, and Costello (2007) found that CD under age 16 predicted serious and violent crimes between ages 16 and 21. In the Denver Youth Survey, Huizinga and Jakob-Chien (1998) found that about half of male and female self-reported violent offenders had a large number of externalizing symptoms on the CBCL. In Cyprus, Kokkinos and Panayiotou (2004) reported that CD adolescents were likely to be bullies.

Numerous studies show that aggression in childhood and adolescence predicts later delinquency and crime. For example, Hamalainen and Pulkkinen (1995, 1996) in Finland followed up nearly 400 children between ages 8 and 32 and found that early aggression and conduct problems predicted later criminal offenses. In the Cambridge Study, teacher ratings of aggression at age 12–14 (disobedient, difficult to discipline, unduly rough, quarrelsome and aggressive, overcompetitive) significantly predicted self-reported violence at age 16–18 (physical fighting) and convictions for violence up to age 32 (Farrington, 1991).

Generally, delinquents are versatile rather than specialized in their offending. In the Cambridge Study, 86% of violent offenders also had convictions for nonviolent offenses (Farrington, 1991). Violent and nonviolent but equally frequent offenders were very similar in their childhood and adolescent features in the Oregon Youth Study (Capaldi & Patterson, 1996) and in the Philadelphia Collaborative Perinatal Project (Piquero, 2000). Studies of transition matrices summarizing the probability of one type of offense following another show that there is a small degree of specificity superimposed on a great deal of generality in juvenile delinquency (Farrington, Snyder, & Finnegan, 1988).

The Cambridge Study shows that delinquency is associated with many other types of antisocial behavior. The boys who were convicted before age 18 (most commonly for offenses of dishonesty, such as burglary and theft) were significantly more antisocial than the nondelinquents on almost every factor that was investigated at that age (West & Farrington, 1977). The convicted delinquents drank more beer, got drunk more often, and were more likely to say that drinking made them violent. They smoked more cigarettes, had started smoking at an earlier age, and were more likely to be heavy gamblers. They were more likely to have been convicted for minor motoring offenses, to have driven after drinking at least 10 units of alcohol (e.g., 5 pints of beer), and to have been injured in road accidents.

The delinquents were more likely to have taken prohibited drugs such as marijuana or LSD, although few of them had convictions for drug offenses. Also, they were more likely to have had sexual intercourse, especially with a variety of different girls, and especially beginning at an early age, but they were less likely to use contraceptives. The delinquents were more likely to go out in the evenings, and were especially likely to spend time hanging about on the street. They tended to go around in groups of four or more, and were more likely to be involved in group violence or vandalism. They were much more likely to have been involved in physical fights, to have started fights, to have carried weapons, and to have used weapons in fights. They were also more likely to express aggressive and anti-establishment attitudes on a questionnaire (negative to police, school, rich people, and civil servants).

Because CD, aggression, and delinquency are overlapping problems, they tend to have the same risk factors, and interventions that are effective in reducing one of these types of antisocial behavior tend also to be effective in reducing the other two types. I will focus especially on risk factors for delinquency (for a review of risk factors for CD, see Burke, Loeber, & Birmaher, 2002). Less is known about early risk factors for aggression (Tremblay, 2008). Risk factors that are essentially measuring the same underlying constructs as CD, aggression, and delinquency (e.g., anger; Colder & Stice, 1998) are not reviewed here.

RISK FACTORS

Longitudinal data are required to establish the time ordering of risk factors and antisocial behavior. As mentioned, in this review I focus especially on results obtained in major prospective longitudinal studies. It is extremely difficult in correlational or cross-sectional studies to draw valid conclusions about cause and effect. Similarly, because of the difficulty of establishing causal effects of factors that vary only between individuals (e.g., gender and ethnicity), and because such factors have no practical implications for intervention (e.g., it is not practicable to change males into females), unchanging variables will not be reviewed here. In any case, their effects on offending are usually explained by reference to other, modifiable, factors. For example, gender differences in offending have been explained on the basis of different socialization methods used by parents with boys and girls, or different opportunities for offending of males and females. According to Rowe, Vazsonyi, and Flannery (1995), risk factors for delinquency are similar for boys and girls, but boys are generally exposed to more risk factors or higher levels of risk factors.

Risk factors will be discussed one by one; additive, interactive, independent, or sequential effects will not be exhaustively reviewed, although these are important issues (Waschbusch & Willoughby, 2008). Because of limitations of space, and because of their limited relevance for psychosocial interventions, biological factors are not reviewed. For example, one of the most replicable findings in the literature is that antisocial and violent adolescents tend to have low resting heart rates (Raine, 1993, p. 167). In the Cambridge Study, resting heart rate at age 18 was significantly related to convictions for violence and to self-reported violence, independently of all other variables (Farrington, 1997b). There is also little space to review theories of the causal mechanisms by which risk factors might have their effects on antisocial behavior.

It is plausible to suggest that risk factors influence the potential for aggression and antisocial behavior, and that whether this potential becomes the actuality in any situation depends on immediate situational factors such as opportunities and victims. In other words, antisocial acts depend on the interaction between the individual and the environment (Farrington, 1998). However, there is not space here to review immediate situational influences or situational crime prevention (Clarke, 1995).

Temperament and Personality

Personality traits such as sociability or impulsiveness describe broad predispositions to respond in certain ways, and temperament is basically the childhood equivalent of personality. Temperament is clearly influenced by biological factors but is not itself a biological variable like heart rate. The modern study of child temperament began with the New York longitudinal study of Chess and Thomas (1984). Children in their first 5 years of life were rated on temperamental dimensions by their parents, and these dimensions were combined into three broad categories of easy, difficult and "slow to warm up" temperament. Having a difficult temperament at age 3–4 (frequent irritability, low amenability and adaptability, irregular habits) predicted poor psychiatric adjustment at age 17–24.

Unfortunately, it was not very clear exactly what a "difficult" temperament meant in practice, and there was the danger of tautological conclusions (e.g., because the criteria for difficult temperament and ODD were overlapping). Later researchers have used more specific dimensions of temperament. For example, Kagan (1989) in Boston classified children as inhibited (shy or fearful) or uninhibited at age 21 months, and found that they remained significantly stable on this classification up to age 7 years. Furthermore, the children who were uninhibited at age 21 months were more likely to be identified as aggressive at age 13 years, according to self- and parent reports (Schwartz, Snidman, & Kagan, 1996).

Important results on the link between childhood temperament and later offending have been obtained in the Dunedin longitudinal study in New Zealand (Caspi, 2000). Temperament at age 3 years was rated by observing the child's behavior during a testing session. The most important dimension of temperament was being undercontrolled (restless, impulsive, with poor attention), and this predicted aggression, self-reported delinquency and convictions at age 18–21.

Studies using classic personality inventories such as the Minnesota Multiphasic Personality Inventory (MMPI) and the California Psychological Inventory (CPI; Wilson & Herrnstein,

1985, pp. 186–198) often seem to produce essentially tautological results, such as that delinquents are low on socialization. The Eysenck personality questionnaire has yielded more promising results (Eysenck, 1996). In the Cambridge Study, those high on both extraversion and neuroticism tended to be juvenile self-reported delinquents, adult official offenders, and adult self-reported offenders, but not juvenile official delinquents (Farrington, Biron, & LeBlanc, 1982). Furthermore, these relationships held independently of other variables such as low family income, low intelligence, and poor parental child-rearing behavior. However, when individual items of the personality questionnaire were studied, it was clear that the significant relationships were caused by the items measuring impulsiveness (e.g., doing things quickly without stopping to think).

Since 1990, the most widely accepted personality system has been the "Big Five" or five-factor model (McCrae & Costa, 2003). This suggests that there are five key dimensions of personality: neuroticism (N), extraversion (E), openness (O), agreeableness (A), and conscientiousness (C). Openness means originality and openness to new ideas, agreeableness includes nurturance and altruism, and conscientiousness includes planning and the will to achieve. It is commonly found that low levels of agreeableness and conscientiousness are related to offending (Heaven, 1996; John, Caspi, Robins, Moffitt, & Stouthamer-Loeber, 1994).

Impulsiveness

Impulsiveness is the most crucial personality dimension that predicts antisocial behavior (Lipsey & Derzon, 1998). Unfortunately, there are a bewildering number of constructs referring to a poor ability to control behavior. These include impulsiveness, hyperactivity, restlessness, clumsiness, not considering consequences before acting, a poor ability to plan ahead, short time horizons, low self-control, sensation-seeking, risk-taking, and a poor ability to delay gratification. Pratt, Cullen, Blevins, Daigle, and Unnever (2002) carried

out a meta-analysis of research on ADHD and delinquency, and concluded that they were strongly associated. Similar conclusions about impulsiveness were drawn by Jolliffe and Farrington (in press).

Many studies show that hyperactivity or ADHD predicts later offending. In the Copenhagen Perinatal project, hyperactivity (restlessness and poor concentration) at age 11–13 significantly predicted arrests for violence up to age 22, especially among boys experiencing delivery complications (Brennan, Mednick, & Mednick, 1993). Similarly, in the Orebro longitudinal study in Sweden, hyperactivity at age 13 predicted police-recorded violence up to age 26. The highest rate of violence was among males with both motor restlessness and concentration difficulties (15%), compared to 3% of the remainder (Klinteberg, Andersson, Magnusson, & Stattin, 1993). In the Seattle Social Development Project, hyperactivity and risk taking in adolescence predicted violence in young adulthood (Herrenkohl et al., 2000).

In the Cambridge Study, boys nominated by teachers as restless or lacking in concentration; those nominated by parents, peers, or teachers as the most daring or taking most risks; and those who were the most impulsive on psychomotor tests at age 8–10 all tended to become offenders later in life. Daring, poor concentration, and restlessness all predicted both official convictions and self-reported delinquency, and daring was consistently one of the best independent predictors (Farrington 1992c). Interestingly, Farrington, Loeber, and van Kammen (1990) found that hyperactivity predicted juvenile offending independently of conduct problems. Lynam (1996) proposed that boys with both hyperactivity and CD were most at risk of chronic offending and psychopathy, and Lynam (1998) presented evidence in favor of this hypothesis from the Pittsburgh Youth Study.

The most extensive research on different measures of impulsiveness was carried out in the Pittsburgh Youth Study by White et al. (1994). The measures that were most strongly related to self-reported delinquency at ages 10 and 13 were teacher-rated impulsiveness (e.g., acts without thinking), self-reported impulsiveness, self-reported undercontrol (e.g., unable to delay gratification), motor restlessness (from videotaped observations), and psychomotor impulsiveness (on the Trail Making Test). Generally, the verbal behavior rating tests produced stronger relationships with offending than the psychomotor performance tests, suggesting that cognitive impulsiveness was more relevant than behavioral impulsiveness. Future time perception and delay-of-gratification tests were only weakly related to self-reported delinquency. In the Developmental Trends Study, Burke, Loeber, Lahey, and Rathouz (2005) found that ADHD predicted ODD, which in turn predicted CD.

Low IQ and Low Educational Achievement

Low IQ and low school achievement are important predictors of CD, delinquency, and adolescent antisocial behavior (Moffitt, 1993b). In an English epidemiological study of 13-year-old twins, low IQ of the child predicted conduct problems independently of social class and of the IQ of parents (Goodman, Simonoff, & Stevenson, 1995). Low school achievement was a strong correlate of CD in the Pittsburgh Youth Study (Loeber et al., 1998). In both the Ontario Child Health Study (Offord, Boyle, & Racine, 1989) and the New York State longitudinal study (Velez, Johnson, & Cohen, 1989), failing a grade predicted CD. Underachievement, defined according to a discrepancy between IQ and school achievement, is also characteristic of CD children, as Frick et al. (1991) reported in the Developmental Trends Study.

Low IQ and low school achievement also predict youth violence. In the Philadelphia Biosocial project (Denno, 1990), low verbal and performance IQ at ages 4 and 7 and low scores on the California Achievement test at age 13–14 (vocabulary, comprehension, maths, language, spelling) all predicted arrests for

violence up to age 22. In Project Metropolitan in Copenhagen, low IQ at age 12 significantly predicted police-recorded violence between ages 15 and 22. The link between low IQ and violence was strongest among lower class boys (Hogh & Wolf, 1983).

Low IQ measured in the first few years of life predicts later delinquency. In a prospective longitudinal survey of about 120 Stockholm males, low IQ measured at age 3 significantly predicted officially recorded offending up to age 30 (Stattin & Klackenberg-Larsson, 1993). Frequent offenders (with 4 or more offenses) had an average IQ of 88 at age 3, whereas nonoffenders had an average IQ of 101. All of these results held up after controlling for social class. Similarly, low IQ at age 4 predicted arrests up to age 27 in the Perry Preschool Project (Schweinhart, Barnes, & Weikart, 1993) and court delinquency up to age 17 in the Collaborative Perinatal Project (Lipsitt, Buka, & Lipsitt, 1990).

In the Cambridge Study, twice as many of the boys scoring 90 or less on a nonverbal IQ test (Raven's Progressive Matrices) at age 8–10 were convicted as juveniles as of those scoring above 90 (West & Farrington, 1973). However, it was difficult to disentangle low IQ from low school achievement, because they were highly intercorrelated and both predicted delinquency. Low nonverbal IQ predicted juvenile self-reported delinquency to almost exactly the same degree as juvenile convictions (Farrington, 1992c), suggesting that the link between low IQ and delinquency was not caused by the less intelligent boys having a greater probability of being caught. Also, low IQ and low school achievement predicted offending independently of other variables such as low family income and large family size (Farrington, 1990), and were important predictors of bullying (Farrington, 1993b).

Low IQ may lead to delinquency through the intervening factor of school failure. The association between school failure and delinquency has been demonstrated repeatedly in longitudinal surveys (Maguin & Loeber,

1996). In the Pittsburgh Youth Study, Lynam, Moffitt, and Stouthamer-Loeber (1993) concluded that low verbal IQ led to school failure and subsequently to self-reported delinquency, but only for African American boys. An alternative theory is that the link between low IQ and delinquency is mediated by disinhibition (impulsiveness, ADHD, low guilt, low empathy), and this was also tested in the Pittsburgh Youth Study (Koolhof, Loeber, Wei, Pardini, & d'Escury, 2007).

A plausible explanatory factor underlying the link between low IQ and delinquency is the ability to manipulate abstract concepts. Children who are poor at this tend to do badly in IQ tests and in school achievement, and they also tend to commit offenses, mainly because of their poor ability to foresee the consequences of their offending. Delinquents often do better on nonverbal performance IQ tests, such as object assembly and block design, than on verbal IQ tests (Moffitt, 1993b), suggesting that they find it easier to deal with concrete objects than with abstract concepts. Similarly, Rogeness (1994) concluded that CD children had deficits in verbal IQ but not in performance IQ.

Impulsiveness, attention problems, low IQ, and low school achievement could all be linked to deficits in the executive functions of the brain, located in the frontal lobes. These executive functions include sustaining attention and concentration, abstract reasoning, concept formation, goal formulation, anticipation and planning, programming and initiation of purposive sequences of motor behavior, effective self-monitoring and self-awareness of behavior, and inhibition of inappropriate or impulsive behaviors (Moffitt & Henry, 1991; Morgan & Lilienfeld, 2000). Interestingly, in the Montreal longitudinal experimental study, a measure of executive functioning based on cognitive–neuropsychological tests at age 14 was the strongest neuropsychological discriminator between violent and nonviolent boys (Seguin, Pihl, Harden, Tremblay, & Boulerice, 1995). This relationship held independently of

a measure of family adversity (based on parental age at first birth, parental education level, broken family, and low SES). In the Pittsburgh Youth Study, the life-course-persistent offenders had marked neurocognitive impairments (Raine et al., 2005).

Other Individual Factors

Numerous other individual factors have been related to CD, aggression, and delinquency, including low self-esteem (Kokkinos & Panayiotou, 2004), depression (Burke et al., 2005), moral judgment (Stams et al., 2006), and social information processing (Lösel, Bliesener, & Bender, 2007). I will focus on empathy, which is related to other concepts such as having callous–unemotional traits (Frick & White, 2008) and being cold, manipulative, and Machiavellian (Sutton, Smith, & Swettenham, 1999).

A distinction has often been made between cognitive empathy (understanding or appreciating other people's feelings) and emotional empathy (actually experiencing other people's feelings). Jolliffe and Farrington (2004) carried out a systematic review of 35 studies comparing questionnaire measures of empathy with official record measures of delinquent or criminal behavior. They found that low cognitive empathy was strongly related to offending, but low affective empathy was only weakly related. Most importantly, the relationship between low empathy and offending was greatly reduced after controlling for IQ or SES, suggesting that they might be more important risk factors or that low empathy might mediate the relationship between these risk factors and offending.

Empathy has rarely been investigated in prospective longitudinal studies but there have been important large-scale cross-sectional surveys. In Australia, Mak (1991) found that delinquent females had lower emotional empathy than nondelinquent females, but that there were no significant differences for males. In Finland, Kaukiainen et al. (1999) reported that empathy (cognitive and emotional combined) was negatively correlated with aggression (both measured by peer ratings). In Spain, Luengo, Otero, Carrillo-de-la Pena, and Miron (1994) carried out the first project that related cognitive and emotional empathy separately to (self-reported) offending, and found that both were negatively correlated.

Jolliffe and Farrington (2006a) developed a new measure of empathy called the Basic Empathy Scale. An example of a cognitive item is "It is hard for me to understand when my friends are sad," and an example of an emotional item is "I usually feel calm when other people are scared." In a study of 720 British adolescents aged about 15, they found that low emotional empathy was related to self-reported offending and violence for both males and females, and to an official record for offending by females (Jolliffe & Farrington, 2007). Similar, they found that low emotional empathy (but not low cognitive empathy) was related to bullying (Jolliffe & Farrington, 2006b).

Child Rearing

In the Pittsburgh Youth Study, poor parental supervision was an important risk factor for CD (Loeber et al., 1998). Poor maternal supervision and low persistence in discipline predicted CD in the Developmental Trends Study (Frick et al., 1992), but not independently of parental APD. Rothbaum and Weisz (1994) carried out a meta-analysis and concluded that parental reinforcement, parental reasoning, parental punishments, and parental responsiveness to the child were all related to antisocial child behavior. There could be reciprocal relationships between parenting and child behavior, as Sheehan and Watson (2008) concluded for aggression.

Of all child-rearing factors, poor parental supervision is the strongest and most replicable predictor of delinquency (Smith & Stern, 1997), and harsh or punitive discipline (involving physical punishment) is also an important predictor (Haapasalo & Pokela, 1999). The classic longitudinal studies by McCord (1979) in Boston and Robins (1979) in St. Louis show

that poor parental supervision, harsh discipline, and a rejecting attitude all predict delinquency. In the Seattle Social Development Project, poor family management (poor supervision, inconsistent rules, and harsh discipline) in adolescence predicted violence in young adulthood (Herrenkohl et al., 2000). Similar results were obtained in the Cambridge Study. Harsh or erratic parental discipline; cruel, passive, or neglecting parental attitudes; and poor parental supervision, all measured at age 8, predicted later juvenile convictions and self-reported delinquency (West & Farrington, 1973). Generally, the presence of any of these adverse family background features doubled the risk of a later juvenile conviction.

Steinberg, Lamborn, Dornbusch, and Darling (1992) distinguished an authoritarian style of parenting (punitively emphasizing obedience) from an authoritative style (granting autonomy with good supervision). In the Cambridge Study (Farrington, 1994), having authoritarian parents was the second most important predictor of convictions for violence (after hyperactivity/poor concentration). Interestingly, having authoritarian parents was the most important childhood risk factor that discriminated between violent offenders and frequently convicted nonviolent offenders (Farrington, 1991). An authoritarian, punitive parenting style is also related to bullying (Baldry & Farrington, 1998).

Child Abuse

There seems to be significant intergenerational transmission of aggressive and violent behavior from parents to children, as Widom (1989) found in a longitudinal survey of abused children in Indianapolis. Children who were physically abused up to age 11 were significantly likely to become violent offenders in the next 15 years (Maxfield & Widom, 1996). Similarly, in the Rochester Youth Development Study, Smith and Thornberry (1995) showed that recorded child maltreatment under age 12 predicted self-reported violence between ages 14 and 18, independently of gender, ethnicity,

SES, and family structure. Keiley, Howe, Dodge, Bates, and Pettit (2001) reported that maltreatment under age 5 was more damaging than maltreatment between ages 6 and 9. The extensive review by Malinosky-Rummell and Hansen (1993) confirms that being physically abused as a child predicts later violent and nonviolent offending.

Possible causal mechanisms linking childhood victimization and adolescent antisocial behaviors have been reviewed by Widom (1994):

1. Childhood victimization may have immediate but long-lasting consequences (e.g., shaking may cause brain injury).
2. Childhood victimization may cause bodily changes (e.g., desensitization to pain) that encourage later aggression.
3. Child abuse may lead to impulsive or dissociative coping styles that, in turn, lead to poor problem-solving skills or poor school performance.
4. Victimization may cause changes in self-esteem or in social information-processing patterns that encourage later aggression.
5. Child abuse may lead to changed family environments (e.g., being placed in foster care) that have deleterious effects.
6. Juvenile justice practices may label victims, isolate them from prosocial peers, and encourage them to associate with delinquent peers.

Parental Conflict and Disrupted Families

There is no doubt that parental conflict and interparental violence predict adolescent antisocial behavior, as the meta-analysis of Buehler et al. (1997) shows. Also, parental conflict is related to childhood externalizing behavior, irrespective of whether the information about both comes from parents or children (Jenkins & Smith, 1991). In the Pittsburgh Youth Study, CD boys tended to have parents who had unhappy relationships (Loeber et al., 1998). Parental conflict also predicts delinquency (West & Farrington, 1973).

In the Christchurch Study in New Zealand, children who witnessed violence between their parents were more likely to commit both violent and property offenses according to their self-reports (Fergusson & Horwood, 1998). Witnessing father-initiated violence was still predictive after controlling for other risk factors such as parental criminality, parental substance abuse, parental physical punishment, a young mother, and low family income.

Parental separation and single parenthood predict CD in children. In the Christchurch Study, separations from parents in the first five years of a child's life (especially) predicted CD at age 15 (Fergusson, Horwood, & Lynskey, 1994). In the New York State longitudinal study, CD was predicted by parental divorce, but far more strongly by having a never-married lone mother (Velez et al., 1989). In the Ontario Child Health Study, coming from a single-parent family predicted CD, but this was highly related to poverty and dependence on welfare benefits (Blum, Boyle, & Offord, 1988). Also, children from single-parent female-headed households are two to three times as likely to be rated aggressive by teachers compared to other children (Pearson, Ialongo, Hunter, & Kellam, 1994).

In the Dunedin Study in New Zealand, boys from single-parent families disproportionally tended to be convicted; 28% of violent offenders were from single-parent families, compared with 17% of nonviolent offenders and 9% of unconvicted boys (Henry, Caspi, Moffitt, & Silva, 1996). Based on analyses of four surveys (including the Cambridge Study), Morash and Rucker (1989) concluded that the combination of teenage childbearing and a single-parent female-headed household was especially conducive to the development of offending in children. Later analyses of the Cambridge Study showed that teenage childbearing combined with a large number of children particularly predicted offending by the children (Nagin, Pogarsky, & Farrington, 1997).

Many studies show that broken homes or disrupted families predict delinquency (Wells &

Rankin, 1991). In the Newcastle (England) Thousand-Family Study, Kolvin, Miller, Fleeting, and Kolvin (1988) reported that marital disruption (divorce or separation) in a boy's first 5 years predicted his later convictions up to age 32. Similarly, in the Dunedin study in New Zealand, Henry, Moffitt, Robins, Earls, and Silva (1993) found that children who were exposed to parental discord and many changes of the primary caretaker tended to become antisocial and delinquent.

Most studies of broken homes have focused on the loss of the father rather than the mother, simply because the loss of a father is much more common. McCord (1982) in Boston carried out an interesting study of the relationship between homes broken by loss of the natural father and later serious offending of the children. She found that the prevalence of offending was high for boys reared in broken homes without affectionate mothers (62%) and for those reared in united homes characterized by parental conflict (52%), irrespective of whether they had affectionate mothers. The prevalence of offending was low for those reared in united homes without conflict (26%) and—importantly—equally low for boys from broken homes with affectionate mothers (22%). These results suggest that it is not so much the broken home that is criminogenic as the parental conflict that often causes it, and that a loving mother might in some sense be able to compensate for the loss of a father.

In the Cambridge Study, both permanent and temporary separations from a biological parent before age 10 (usually from the father) predicted convictions and self-reported delinquency, providing that they were not caused by death or hospitalization (Farrington, 1992c). However, homes broken at an early age (under age 5) were not unusually criminogenic (West & Farrington, 1973). Separation before age 10 predicted both juvenile and adult convictions (Farrington, 1992b) and predicted convictions up to age 32 independently of all other factors such as low family income or poor school attainment (Farrington, 1993a).

Explanations of the relationship between disrupted families and delinquency fall into three major classes. Trauma theories suggest that the loss of a parent has a damaging effect on a child, most commonly because of the effect on attachment to the parent. Life-course theories focus on separation as a sequence of stressful experiences, and on the effects of multiple stressors such as parental conflict, parental loss, reduced economic circumstances, changes in parent figures, and poor child-rearing methods. Selection theories argue that disrupted families produce delinquent children because of preexisting differences from other families in risk factors such as parental conflict, criminal or antisocial parents, low family income, or poor child-rearing methods.

Hypotheses derived from the three theories were tested in the Cambridge Study (Juby & Farrington, 2001). While boys from broken homes (permanently disrupted families) were more delinquent than boys from intact homes, they were not more delinquent than boys from intact high-conflict families. Interestingly, this result was replicated in Switzerland (Haas, Farrington, Killias, & Sattar, 2004). Overall, the most important factor was the postdisruption trajectory. Boys who remained with their mother after the separation had the same delinquency rate as boys from intact low-conflict families. Boys who remained with their father, with relatives, or with others (e.g., foster parents) had high delinquency rates. It was concluded that the results favored life-course theories rather than trauma or selection theories.

Antisocial Parents

It is clear that antisocial parents tend to have antisocial children (Lipsey & Derzon, 1998). In the Developmental Trends Study, parental APD was the best predictor of childhood CD (Frick et al., 1992) and parental substance use was an important predictor of the onset of CD (Loeber, Green, Keenan, & Lahey, 1995). Similarly, in the New York State longitudinal study, parental APD was a strong predictor of antisocial child behavior (Cohen, Brook, Cohen, Velez & Garcia, 1990). However, children of antisocial parents were almost as likely to develop internalizing disorders, as they were to develop externalizing disorders (Johnson, Cohen, Kasen, & Brook, 2006). In the Pittsburgh Youth Study, parents with behavior problems and substance use problems tended to have CD boys (Loeber et al., 1998).

In their classic longitudinal studies, McCord (1977) and Robins, West, and Herjanic (1975) showed that criminal parents tended to have delinquent sons. In the Cambridge Study, the concentration of offending in a small number of families was remarkable. Less than 6% of the families were responsible for half of the criminal convictions of all members (fathers, mothers, sons, and daughters) of all 400 families (Farrington, Barnes, & Lambert, 1996a). Having a convicted mother, father, brother, or sister significantly predicted a boy's own convictions. Same-sex relationships were stronger than opposite-sex relationships, and older siblings were stronger predictors than younger siblings. Furthermore, convicted parents and delinquent siblings were related to a boy's self-reported as well as official offending (Farrington, 1979). CD symptoms also tend to be concentrated in families, as shown in the Ontario Child Health Study (Szatmari, Boyle, & Offord, 1993).

Similar results were obtained in the Pittsburgh Youth Study. Arrests of fathers, mothers, brothers, sisters, uncles, aunts, grandfathers, and grandmothers all predicted the boy's own delinquency (Farrington, Jolliffe, Loeber, Stouthamer-Loeber, & Kalb, 2001). The most important relative was the father; arrests of the father predicted the boy's delinquency independently of all other arrested relatives. Only 8% of families accounted for 43% of arrested family members. In the Dunedin study in New Zealand, antisocial behavior of grandparents, parents, and siblings predicted antisocial behavior of boys (Odgers et al., 2007).

While arrests and convictions of fathers predicted antisocial behavior of boys, imprisonment of fathers before boys were aged 10 further increased the risk of later antisocial and delinquent outcomes in the Cambridge Study (Murray & Farrington, 2005). Interestingly, the effect of parental imprisonment in Sweden (in Project Metropolitan) disappeared after controlling for parental criminality (Murray, Janson, & Farrington, 2007). This cross-national difference may have been the result of shorter prison sentences in Sweden, more family-friendly prison policies, a welfare-oriented juvenile justice system, an extended social welfare system, or more sympathetic public attitudes toward prisoners.

Farrington et al. (2001) reviewed six different explanations for why offending and antisocial behavior were concentrated in families and transmitted from one generation to the next:

1. There may be intergenerational continuities in exposure to multiple risk factors such as poverty, disrupted families, and living in deprived neighborhoods.
2. Assortative mating (e.g., the tendency of antisocial females to choose antisocial males as partners) facilitates the intergenerational transmission of offending.
3. Family members may influence each other (e.g., older siblings may encourage younger ones to be antisocial).
4. The effect of a criminal parent on a child's offending may be mediated by environmental mechanisms such as poor parental supervision and inconsistent discipline.
5. Intergenerational transmission may be mediated by genetic mechanisms.
6. There may be labeling and police bias against known criminal families.

Large Families

Many studies show that coming from a large family predicts delinquency (Fischer, 1984). For example, in the English National Survey of Health and Development, Wadsworth (1979) found that the percentage of boys who were officially delinquent increased from 9% for families containing one child to 24% for families containing four or more children. In their

Nottingham study, the Newsons also concluded that large family size was one of the most important predictors of delinquency (Newson, Newson, & Adams, 1993). Large family size also predicts adolescent self-reported violence (Farrington, 2000).

In the Cambridge Study, a boy's having four or more siblings by his 10th birthday doubled his risk of being convicted as a juvenile (West & Farrington, 1973). Large family size predicted self-reported delinquency as well as convictions (Farrington, 1979), and adult as well as juvenile convictions (Farrington, 1992b). Also, large family size was the most important independent predictor of convictions up to age 32 in a logistic regression analysis (Farrington, 1993a). Large family size was similarly important in the Cambridge and Pittsburgh studies, even though families were on average smaller in Pittsburgh in the 1990s than in London in the 1960s (Farrington & Loeber, 1999).

Brownfield and Sorenson (1994) reviewed several possible explanations for the link between large families and delinquency, including those focusing on features of the parents (e.g., criminal parents, teenage parents), those focusing on parenting (e.g., poor supervision, disrupted families) and those focusing on socioeconomic deprivation or family stress. Another interesting theory suggested that the key factor was birth order: large families include more later born children, who tend to be more delinquent. Based on an analysis of self-reported delinquency in a Seattle survey, they concluded that the most plausible intervening causal mechanism was exposure to delinquent siblings. In the Cambridge Study, co-offending by brothers was surprisingly common; about 20% of boys who had brothers close to them in age were convicted of a crime committed with their brother (Reiss & Farrington, 1991, p. 386).

Socioeconomic Factors

It is clear that antisocial children disproportionally come from low SES families. In the Ontario Child Health Study, CD children tended to come from low-income families, with unemployed parents, living in subsidized housing and dependent on welfare benefits (Offord, Alder, & Boyle, 1986). In the New York State longitudinal study, low SES, low family income and low parental education predicted CD children (Velez et al., 1989). In the Developmental Trends Study, low SES predicted the onset of CD (Loeber et al., 1995); and, in the Pittsburgh Youth Study, family dependence on welfare benefits was characteristic of CD boys (Loeber et al., 1998).

In general, coming from a low SES family predicts adolescent violence. For example, in the U.S. National Youth Survey, the prevalence of self-reported assault and robbery were about twice as high among lower-class youth as among middle-class ones (Elliott, Huizinga, & Menard, 1989). In Project Metropolitan in Stockholm (Wikström, 1985) and in the Dunedin study in New Zealand (Henry et al., 1996), the SES of a boy's family—based on the father's occupation—predicted his later violent crimes. Several researchers have suggested that the link between a low SES family and adolescent antisocial behavior is mediated by family socialization practices. For example, Dodge, Pettit, and Bates (1994) found that about half of the effect of SES on peer-rated aggression and teacher-rated externalizing problems was accounted for by family socialization.

The relationship between low SES and delinquency varies according to whether SES is measured by income and housing or by occupational prestige. Numerous indicators of SES were measured in the Cambridge Study, both for the boy's family of origin and for the boy himself as an adult, including occupational prestige, family income, housing, and employment instability. Most of the measures of occupational prestige were not significantly related to offending. However, low SES of the family when the boy was aged 8–10 significantly predicted his later self-reported but not his official delinquency. More consistently, low family income and poor housing predicted official and self-reported, juvenile and adult, offending (Farrington, 1992b, 1992c).

It was interesting that the peak age of offending, at 17–18, coincided with the peak age of affluence for many convicted males. In the Cambridge Study, convicted males tended to come from low-income families at age 8 and later tended to have low incomes themselves at age 32 (West & Farrington, 1977, p. 62). However, at age 18, they were relatively well paid in comparison with nondelinquents. Whereas convicted delinquents might be working as unskilled laborers on building sites and getting the full adult wage for this job, nondelinquents might be in poorly paid jobs with prospects, such as bank clerks, or might still be students. These results show that the link between income and offending is quite complex.

Socioeconomic deprivation of parents is usually compared to offending by children. However, when the children grow up, their own socioeconomic deprivation can be related to their own offending. In the Cambridge Study, official and self-reported delinquents tended to have unskilled manual jobs and an unstable job record at age 18. Just as an erratic work record of his father predicted the later offending of the study boy, an unstable job record of the boy at age 18 was one of the best independent predictors of his convictions between ages 21 and 25 (Farrington, 1986b). Between ages 15 and 18, the Study boys were convicted at a higher rate when they were unemployed than when they were employed (Farrington, Gallagher, Morley, St. Ledger, & West, 1986), suggesting that unemployment in some way causes crime, and conversely that employment may lead to desistance from offending. Since crimes involving material gain (e.g., theft, burglary, robbery) especially increased during periods of unemployment, it seems likely that financial need is an important link in the causal chain between unemployment and crime.

Several researchers have suggested that the link between low SES families and antisocial behavior is mediated by family socialization practices. For example, Larzelere and Patterson (1990) in the Oregon Youth Study concluded that the effect of SES on delinquency was entirely mediated by parent management skills. In other words, low SES predicted delinquency because low SES families used poor child-rearing practices. In the Christchurch Health and Development Study, Fergusson, Swain-Campbell, and Horwood (2004) reported that living in a low SES family between birth and age 6 predicted self-reported and official delinquency between ages 15 and 21. However, this association disappeared after controlling for family factors (physical punishment, maternal care, and parental changes), conduct problems, truancy, and deviant peers, suggesting that these may have been mediating factors.

Peer Influences

The reviews by Zimring (1981) and Reiss (1988) show that delinquent acts tend to be committed in small groups (of two or three people, usually) rather than alone. Large gangs are comparatively unusual. In the Cambridge Study, the probability of committing offenses with others decreased steadily with age (Reiss & Farrington, 1991). Whereas the average crime before age 17 was committed with others, the average crime after age 17 was committed alone. Boys tended to commit their crimes with other boys similar in age and living close by.

The major problem of interpretation is whether young people are more likely to commit offenses while they are in groups than while they are alone, or whether the high prevalence of co-offending merely reflects the fact that, whenever young people go out, they tend to go out in groups. Do peers tend to encourage and facilitate offending, or is it just that most kinds of activities outside the home (both delinquent and nondelinquent) tend to be committed in groups? Another possibility is that the commission of offenses encourages association with other delinquents, perhaps because "birds of a feather flock together" or because of the stigmatizing and isolating effects of court appearances and institutionalization. Thornberry, Lizotte, Krohn, Farnworth, & Jang (1994) in the Rochester Youth Development Study and Elliott and

Menard (1996) in the National Youth Survey concluded that there were reciprocal effects, with delinquent peer bonding causing delinquency and delinquency causing association with delinquent peers.

In the Pittsburgh Youth Study, risk factors for delinquency were compared both between individuals and within individuals (Farrington, Loeber, Yin, & Anderson, 2002). Peer delinquency was the strongest correlate of delinquency in between-individual correlations but did not predict delinquency within individuals. In contrast, poor parental supervision, low parental reinforcement, and low involvement of the boy in family activities predicted delinquency both between and within individuals. It was concluded that these three family variables were the most likely to be causes, whereas having delinquent peers was most likely to be a correlate of the boy's offending.

It is clear that young people increase their offending after joining a gang. In the Seattle Social Development Project, Battin, Hill, Abbott, Catalano, and Hawkins (1998) found this, and also showed that gang membership predicted delinquency above and beyond having delinquent friends. In the Pittsburgh Youth Study, Gordon et al. (2004) reported not only a substantial increase in drug selling, drug use, violence, and property crime after a boy joined a gang, but also that the frequency of offending decreased to pregang levels after a boy left a gang. Thornberry, Krohn, Lizotte, Smith, & Tobin (2003) in the Rochester Youth Development Study and Gatti, Tremblay, Vitraro, and McDuff (2005) in the Montreal longitudinal experimental study also found that young people offended more after joining a gang. Several of these studies constrasted the "selection" and "facilitation" hypotheses and concluded that future gang members were more delinquent to start with but became even more delinquent after joining a gang. Gang membership in adolescence is a risk factor for later violence (Herrenkohl et al., 2000), but this may be because both are measuring the same underlying construct.

There is no doubt that highly aggressive children tend to be rejected by most of their peers (Coie, Dodge, & Kupersmidt, 1990; Dodge et al., 2003). In the Oregon Youth Study, Nelson and Dishion (2004) found that peer rejection at age 9–10 significantly predicted adult antisocial behavior. However, it is unclear to what extent peer rejection causes later aggression. Low popularity was only a marginal predictor of adolescent aggression and teenage violence in the Cambridge Study (Farrington, 1989a). Coie and Miller-Johnson (2001) found that it was the boys who were both aggressive and rejected by their classmates who became the self-reported and official delinquents. However, while aggressive children are rejected by conventional peers, they can be popular with other aggressive children (Cairns, Cairns, Neckerman, Gest, & Gariepy, 1988).

School Influences

It is also well established that delinquents disproportionately attend high delinquency rate schools, which have high levels of distrust between teachers and students, low commitment to the school by students, and unclear and inconsistently enforced rules (Graham, 1988). In the Cambridge Study, attending a high-delinquency-rate school at age 11 significantly predicted a boy's own delinquency (Farrington, 1992c). However, what is less clear is to what extent the schools themselves influence antisocial behavior, by their organization, climate and practices, or to what extent the concentration of offenders in certain schools is mainly a function of their intakes. In the Cambridge Study, most of the variation between schools in their delinquency rates could be explained by differences in their intakes of troublesome boys at age 11 (Farrington, 1972). However, reviews of American research show that schools with clear, fair, and consistently enforced rules tend to have low rates of student misbehavior (Gottfredson, 2001; Herrenkohl, Hawkins, Chung, Hill, & Battin-Pearson, 2001).

In the New York State Longitudinal Study, Kasen, Johnson, and Cohen (1990) investigated the effects of different dimensions of school climate on changes in children's conduct problems over time. They found that high school conflict (between students and teachers, or between students and other students) predicted increases in conduct problems. In contrast, a high academic focus in schools (e.g., emphasizing homework, academic classes, and task orientation) predicted decreases in conduct problems and hence might be regarded as a protective factor.

Community Influences

Many studies show that boys living in urban areas are more violent than those living in rural ones. In the U.S. National Youth Survey, the prevalence of self-reported assault and robbery was considerably higher among urban youth (Elliott, Huizinga, & Menard, 1989). Within urban areas, boys living in high-crime neighborhoods are more violent than those living in low-crime neighborhoods. In the Rochester Youth Development Study, living in a high-crime neighborhood significantly predicted self-reported violence (Thornberry, Huizinga, & Loeber, 1995). Similarly, in the Pittsburgh Youth Study, living in a bad neighborhood (either as rated by the mother or based on census measures of poverty, unemployment, and female-headed households) significantly predicted official and reported violence (Farrington, 1998).

Sampson, Raudenbush, and Earls (1997) studied community influences on violence in the Project on Human Development in Chicago Neighborhoods. The most important community predictors were concentrated economic disadvantage (as indexed by poverty, the proportion of female-headed families, and the proportion of African Americans), immigrant concentration (the proportions of Latinos or foreign-born persons), residential instability, and low levels of informal social control and social cohesion. They suggested that the "collective efficacy" of a neighborhood, or the willingness of residents to intervene to prevent antisocial behavior, might act as a protective factor against crime. In the same

project, Sampson, Morenoff, and Raudenbush (2005) concluded that most of the difference between African Americans and Caucasians in violence could be explained by racial differences in exposure to risk factors, especially living in bad neighborhoods. Similar conclusions were drawn by Farrington, Loeber, and Stouthamer-Loeber (2003b) in the Pittsburgh Youth Study.

It is clear that offenders disproportionately live in inner-city areas characterized by physical deterioration, neighborhood disorganization, and high residential mobility (Shaw & McKay, 1969). However, again, it is difficult to determine to what extent the areas themselves influence antisocial behavior and to what extent it is merely the case that antisocial people tend to live in deprived areas (e.g., because of their poverty or public housing allocation policies). Interestingly, both neighborhood researchers such as Gottfredson, McNeil, and Gottfredson (1991) and developmental researchers such as Rutter (1981) have argued that neighborhoods have only indirect effects on antisocial behavior through their effects on individuals and families. In the Chicago Youth Development Study, Tolan, Gorman-Smith, and Henry (2003) concluded that the relationship between community structural characteristics (concentrated poverty, racial heterogeneity, economic resources, violent crime rate) and individual violence was mediated by parenting practices, gang membership, and peer violence.

In the Pittsburgh Youth Study, Wikström and Loeber (2000) found an interesting interaction between types of people and types of areas. Six individual, family, peer, and school variables were trichotomized into risk, middle, or protective scores and added up. Boys with the highest risk scores tended to be delinquent irrespective of the type of area in which they were living. However, boys with high protective scores or balanced risk and protective scores were more likely to be delinquent if they were living in disadvantaged public housing areas. Hence, the area risk was most important when other risks were not high. In the same study,

Lynam et al. (2000) reported that impulsivity predicted delinquency most strongly in poor neighborhoods.

Clearly, there is an interaction between individuals and the communities in which they live. Some aspect of an inner-city neighborhood may be conducive to offending, perhaps because the inner city leads to a breakdown of community ties or neighborhood patterns of mutual support, or perhaps because the high population density produces tension, frustration, or anonymity. There may be many inter-related factors. As Reiss (1986) argued, high-crime-rate areas often have a high concentration of single-parent female-headed households with low incomes, living in low-cost, poor housing. The weakened parental control in these families—partly caused by the fact that the mother had to work and left her children largely unsupervised—meant that the children tended to congregate on the streets. In consequence, they were influenced by a peer subculture that often encouraged and reinforced offending. This interaction of individual, family, peer, and neighborhood factors may be the rule rather than the exception.

SUCCESSFUL INTERVENTIONS

As mentioned earlier, I will focus here especially on results obtained in randomized experiments with reasonably large samples, since the effect of any intervention on antisocial behavior can be demonstrated most convincingly in such experiments (Farrington, 1983; Farrington & Welsh, 2005). For more extensive reviews of the effects of interventions, see Wasserman and Miller (1998), Catalano, Arthur, Hawkins, Berglund, and Olson (1998), and Farrington and Welsh (2007). Most interventions target risk factors and aim to prevent antisocial behavior. However, it is equally important to strengthen protective factors and promote healthy adolescent development (Catalano, Hawkins, Berglund, Pollard, & Arthur, 2002).

A meta-analysis by Farrington and Welsh (2003) concluded that two main types of family-based programs—general parent education

(in the context of home visiting and parent education plus daycare services) and parent management training—were effective in preventing delinquency. Both types of programs also produce a wide range of other important benefits for families—improved school readiness and school performance on the part of children, greater employment and educational opportunities for parents, and greater family stability in general. There is some evidence that home visiting programs can pay back program costs and produce substantial monetary benefits for the government and taxpayers. Little is known about the economic efficiency of day care and parent management training programs.

Early Home Visiting

In New York State, Olds, Henderson, Chamberlain, and Tatelbaum (1986) randomly allocated 400 mothers either to receive home visits from nurses during pregnancy, or to receive visits both during pregnancy and during the first 2 years of life, or to a control group who received no visits. The home visitors gave advice about prenatal and postnatal care of the child, about infant development, and about the importance of proper nutrition and avoiding smoking and drinking during pregnancy.

The results of this experiment showed that the postnatal home visits caused a decrease in recorded child physical abuse and neglect during the first 2 years of life, especially by poor unmarried teenage mothers; 4% of visited versus 19% of nonvisited mothers of this type were guilty of child abuse or neglect. This last result is important because (as mentioned above) children who are physically abused or neglected tend to become violent offenders later in life. In a 15-year follow-up, the main focus was on lower class unmarried mothers. Among these high-risk mothers, those who received prenatal and postnatal home visits had fewer arrests than those who received prenatal visits or no visits (Olds et al., 1997). Also, children of these mothers who received prenatal and/or postnatal home visits had less than half as many arrests as children of mothers who received no visits (Olds et al., 1998). According to Aos, Phipps, Barnoski, and Lieb (2001a), the benefit-to-cost ratio for high risk mothers was 3.1, based on savings to crime victims and criminal justice. (For a recent review of home visiting programs, see Olds, Sadler, & Kitzman, 2007.)

Preschool Programs

One of the most successful early prevention programs has been the Perry preschool project carried out in Michigan by Schweinhart and Weikart (1980). This was essentially a "Head Start" program targeted on disadvantaged African American children. The experimental children attended a daily preschool program, backed up by weekly home visits, usually lasting two years (covering ages 3-4). The aim of the "plan-do-review" program was to provide intellectual stimulation, to increase thinking and reasoning abilities, and to increase later school achievement.

As demonstrated in several other Head Start projects, the experimental group showed gains in intelligence that were rather short-lived. However, the experimental children were significantly better in elementary school motivation, school achievement at age 14, teacher ratings of classroom behavior at ages 6–9, self-reports of classroom behavior at age 15, and self-reports of offending at age 15. A later follow-up of the Perry sample (Berrueta-Clement, Schweinhart, Barnett, Epstein, & Weikart, 1984) showed that, at age 19, the experimental group was more likely to be employed, more likely to have graduated from high school, more likely to have received college or vocational training, and less likely to have been arrested. By age 27, the experimental group had accumulated only half as many arrests on average as the controls (Schweinhart et al., 1993). Also, they had significantly higher earnings and were more likely to be homeowners. Hence, this preschool intellectual enrichment program led to decreases in school failure, to decreases in delinquency, and to decreases in other undesirable outcomes.

The most recent follow-up of this program at age 40 found that it continued to make an important difference in the lives of the participants (Schweinhart et al., 2005). Compared to the control group, those who received the program had significantly fewer lifetime arrests for violent crimes (32% vs. 48%), property crimes (36% vs. 56%), and drug crimes (14% vs. 34%), and they were significantly less likely to be arrested five or more times (36% vs. 55%). Improvements were also recorded in many other important life-course outcomes. For example, significantly higher levels of schooling (77% vs. 60% graduating from high school), better records of employment (76% vs. 62%), and higher annual incomes were reported by the program group compared to the controls.

Several economic analyses show that the financial benefits of this program outweighed its costs. The Perry project's own calculation (Barnett, 1993) included crime and noncrime benefits, intangible costs to victims, and even included projected benefits beyond age 27. This generated the famous benefit-to-cost ratio of 7 to 1. Most of the benefits (65%) were derived from savings to crime victims. The most recent cost-benefit analysis at age 40 found that the program produced $17 in benefits per $1 of cost.

Like the Perry project, the Child Parent Center (CPC) in Chicago provided disadvantaged children with a high-quality, active learning preschool supplemented with family support (Reynolds, Temple, Robertson, & Mann, 2001). However, unlike Perry, CPC continued to provide the children with the educational enrichment component into elementary school, up to age 9. Focussing on the effect of the preschool intervention, it was found that, compared to a control group, those who received the program were less likely to be arrested for both nonviolent and violent offenses by the time they were 18. The CPC program also produced other benefits for those in the experimental compared to the control group, such as a higher rate of high school completion.

Parent Training

Parent training is also an effective method of preventing delinquency (Piquero, Farrington, Welsh, Tremblay, & Jennings, 2008). Many different types of parent training have been used (Kazdin, 1997), but the behavioral parent management training developed by Patterson (1982) in Oregon is one of the most effective approaches. His careful observations of parent–child interaction showed that parents of antisocial children were deficient in their methods of child rearing. These parents failed to tell their children how they were expected to behave, failed to monitor their behavior to ensure that it was desirable, and failed to enforce rules promptly and unambiguously with appropriate rewards and penalties. The parents of antisocial children used more punishment (such as scolding, shouting, or threatening), but failed to make it contingent on the child's behavior.

Patterson's method involved linking antecedents, behaviors, and consequences. He attempted to train parents in effective child-rearing methods, namely noticing what a child is doing, monitoring behavior over long periods, clearly stating house rules, making rewards and punishments contingent on behavior, and negotiating disagreements so that conflicts and crises did not escalate. His treatment was shown to be effective in reducing child stealing and antisocial behavior over short periods in small-scale studies (Dishion, Patterson, & Kavanagh, 1992; Patterson, Chamberlain, & Reid, 1982; Patterson, Reid, & Dishion, 1992). However, the treatment worked best with children aged 3–10 and less well with adolescents. Also, there were problems of achieving cooperation from the families experiencing the worst problems. In particular, single mothers on welfare were experiencing so many different stresses that they found it difficult to use consistent and contingent child-rearing methods.

One of the most famous parent training programs was developed by Webster-Stratton (1998) in Seattle. She evaluated its success by randomly allocating 426 children aged 4 (most with single mothers on welfare) either to an experimental group that received parent training or to a control group that did not. The experimental mothers met in groups every week for 8 or 9 weeks, watched videotapes demonstrating parenting skills, and then took part in focused group discussions. The topics included how to play with your child, helping your child learn, using praise and encouragement to bring out the best in your child, effective setting of limits, handling misbehavior, how to teach your child to solve problems, and how to give and get support. The program was successful. Observations in the home showed that the experimental children behaved better than the control children (see also Webster-Stratton, 2000).

Sanders, Markie-Dadds, Tully, and Bor (2000), in Brisbane, Australia, developed the Triple-P Parenting program. This can either be delivered to the whole community in primary prevention using the mass media or can it be used in secondary prevention with high-risk or clinic samples. The success of Triple-P was evaluated with high-risk children aged 3 by randomly assigning them either to receive Triple-P or to a control group. The Triple-P program involves teaching parents 17 child management strategies, including talking with children, giving physical affection, praising, giving attention, setting a good example, setting rules, giving clear instructions, and using appropriate penalties for misbehavior ("time-out," or sending the child to his or her room). The evaluation showed that the Triple-P program was successful in reducing children's antisocial behavior.

Another parenting intervention, Functional Family Therapy, was evaluated in Utah by Alexander and Parsons (1973). This aimed to modify patterns of family interaction by modeling, prompting, and reinforcement; to encourage clear communication of requests and solutions between family members; and to minimize conflict. Essentially, all family members were trained to negotiate effectively, to set clear rules about privileges and responsibilities, and to use techniques of reciprocal reinforcement with each other. This technique halved the recidivism rate of minor delinquents in comparison with other approaches (client-centered or psychodynamic therapy). Its effectiveness with more serious delinquents was confirmed in a replication study using matched groups (Gordon, 1995; see also Sexton & Alexander, 2000).

The multidimensional treatment foster care (MTFC) program, evaluated in Oregon by Chamberlain and Reid (1998), also produced desirable results. In treatment foster care, families in the community were recruited and trained to provide a placement for delinquent youths. The MTFC youths were closely supervised at home, in the community, and in the school, and their contacts with delinquent peers were minimized. The foster parents provided a structured daily living environment, with clear rules and limits, consistent discipline for rule violations and one-to-one monitoring. The youths were encouraged to develop academic skills and desirable work habits. In the evaluation, 79 chronic male delinquents were randomly assigned to treatment foster care or to regular group homes where they lived with other delinquents. A 1-year follow-up showed that the MTFC boys had fewer criminal referrals and lower self-reported delinquency. Hence, this program seemed to be an effective treatment for delinquency.

Skills Training

The set of techniques variously termed *cognitive behavioral interpersonal social skills training* have proved to be successful (Lipsey & Wilson, 1998). For example, the "Reasoning and Rehabilitation" program developed by Ross and Ross (1995) in Ottawa, Canada, aimed to modify the impulsive, egocentric thinking of delinquents, to teach them to stop and think before acting, to consider the consequences of their behavior, to conceptualize alternative ways of solving interpersonal problems, and to consider the impact of their

behavior on other people, especially their victims. It included social skills training, lateral thinking (to teach creative problem solving), critical thinking (to teach logical reasoning), values education (to teach values and concern for others), assertiveness training (to teach nonaggressive, socially appropriate ways to obtain desired outcomes), negotiation skills training, interpersonal cognitive problem solving (to teach thinking skills for solving interpersonal problems), social perspective training (to teach how to recognize and understand other people's feelings), role playing and modeling (demonstration and practice of effective and acceptable interpersonal behavior). This program led to a large decrease in reoffending by a small sample of delinquents.

Tong and Farrington (2008) completed a systematic review of the effectiveness of "Reasoning and Rehabilitation" in reducing offending. They located 32 comparisons of experimental and control groups in four countries. Their meta-analysis showed that, overall, there was a significant 14% decrease in offending for program participants compared with controls.

Jones and Offord (1989) implemented a skills training program in an experimental public housing complex in Ottawa and compared it with a control complex. The program centered on nonschool skills, both athletic (e.g., swimming and hockey) and nonathletic (e.g., guitar and ballet). The aim of developing skills was to increase self-esteem, to encourage children to use time constructively and to provide desirable role models. Participation rates were high; about three-quarters of age-eligible children in the experimental complex took at least one course in the first year. The program was successful; delinquency rates decreased significantly in the experimental complex compared to the control complex. The benefit-to-cost ratio, based on savings to taxpayers, was 2.5.

Lösel and Beelman (2006) completed a systematic review of the effectiveness of skills training with children and adolescents. They located 89 comparisons of experimental and control groups. Their meta-analysis showed that, overall, there was a significant 10% decrease in delinquency in follow-up studies for children who received skills training compared with controls. The greatest effect was for cognitive-behavioral skills training, where there was an average 25% decrease in delinquency in seven follow-up studies. The most effective programs targeted children aged 13 or older and high-risk groups who were already exhibiting behavior problems.

Peer Programs

There are few outstanding examples of effective intervention programs for antisocial behavior targeted on peer risk factors. The most hopeful programs involve using high-status conventional peers to teach children ways of resisting peer pressure; this is effective in reducing drug use (Tobler, Lessard, Marshall, Ochshorn, & Roona, 1999). Also, in a randomized experiment in St. Louis, Feldman, Caplinger, and Wodarski (1983) showed that placing antisocial adolescents in activity groups dominated by prosocial adolescents led to a reduction in their antisocial behavior (compared with antisocial adolescents placed in antisocial groups). This suggests that the influence of prosocial peers can be harnessed to reduce antisocial behavior. However, putting antisocial peers together can have harmful effects (Dishion, McCord, & Poulin, 1999).

The most important intervention program whose success seems to be based mainly on reducing peer risk factors is the Children at Risk program (Harrell, Cavanagh, Harmon, Koper, & Sridharan, 1997), which targeted high-risk adolescents (average age 12) in poor neighborhoods of five cities across the United States. Eligible youths were identified in schools, and randomly assigned to experimental or control groups. The program was a comprehensive community-based prevention strategy targeting risk factors for delinquency, including case management and family counseling, family skills training,

tutoring, mentoring, after-school activities and community policing. The program was different in each neighborhood.

The initial results of the program were disappointing, but a one-year follow-up showed that (according to self-reports) experimental youths were less likely to have committed violent crimes and used or sold drugs (Harrell, Cavanagh, & Sridharan, 1999). The process evaluation showed that the greatest change was in peer risk factors. Experimental youths associated less often with delinquent peers, felt less peer pressure to engage in delinquency, and had more positive peer support. In contrast, there were few changes in individual, family or community risk factors, possibly linked to the low participation of parents in parent training and of youths in mentoring and tutoring (Harrell et al., 1997, p. 87). In other words, there were problems of implementation of the program, linked to the serious and multiple needs and problems of the families.

Community-based mentoring programs usually involve nonprofessional adult volunteers spending time with young people at risk for delinquency, dropping out of school, school failure, or other social problems. Mentors behave in a "supportive, nonjudgmental manner while acting as role models" (Howell, 1995, p. 90). Welsh and Hoshi (2006) identified seven community-based mentoring programs (of which six were of high quality) that evaluated the impact on delinquency. Since most programs found desirable effects, Welsh and Hoshi concluded that community-based mentoring was a promising approach in preventing delinquency. Similarly, a meta-analysis by Jolliffe and Farrington (2008) concluded that mentoring was often effective in reducing reoffending.

School Programs

An important school-based prevention experiment was carried out in Seattle by Hawkins, von Cleve, and Catalano (1991). This combined parent training, teacher training, and skills training. About 500 first-grade children (aged 6) were randomly assigned to be in experimental or control classes. The children in the experimental classes received special treatment at home and school, which was designed to increase their attachment to their parents and their bonding to the school, on the assumption that delinquency was inhibited by the strength of social bonds. Their parents were trained to notice and reinforce socially desirable behavior in a program called "Catch Them Being Good." Their teachers were trained in classroom management, for example, to provide clear instructions and expectations to children, to reward children for participation in desired behavior, and to teach children prosocial (socially desirable) methods of solving problems.

In an evaluation of this program 18 months later, when the children were in different classes, Hawkins et al. (1991) found that the boys who received the experimental program were significantly less aggressive than the control boys, according to teacher ratings. This difference was particularly marked for Caucasian boys rather than African American boys. The experimental girls were not significantly less aggressive, but they were less self-destructive, anxious, and depressed. In a later follow-up, Hawkins, Catalano, Kosterman, Abbott, and Hill (1999) found that, at age 18, the full intervention group (those receiving the intervention from grades 1 to 6) admitted less violence, less alcohol abuse and fewer sexual partners than the late intervention group (grades 5–6 only) or the controls. The benefit-to-cost ratio of this program according to Aos et al. (2001a) was 4.3. Other school-based programs have also been successful in reducing antisocial behavior (Catalano et al., 1998).

In Baltimore, Petras et al. (2008) evaluated the "Good Behavior Game" (GBG), which aimed to reduce aggressive and disruptive child behavior through contingent reinforcement of interdependent team behavior. First-grade classrooms and teachers were randomly assigned either to the GBG condition ($N = 238$) or to a control condition ($N = 165$), and the GBG was played repeatedly over 2 years. In trajectory analyses, the researchers found that the GBG decreased aggressive/disruptive behavior (according to teacher reports) up to grade 7 among the most aggressive boys, and also caused a decrease in APD at ages 19–21. However, effects on girls and on a second cohort of children were less marked.

There have been a number of comprehensive, evidence-based reviews of the effectiveness of school-based programs (Gottfredson, Wilson, & Najaka, 2006; Wilson, Gottfredson, & Najaka, 2001; Wilson & Lipsey, 2007). Meta-analyses identified four types of school-based programs that were effective in preventing delinquency: school and discipline management, classroom or instructional management, reorganization of grades or classes, and increasing self-control or social competency using cognitive behavioral instruction methods. Reorganization of grades or classes had the largest average effect size ($d = 0.34$), corresponding to a significant 17% reduction in delinquency.

After-school programs (e.g., recreation-based, drop-in clubs, dance groups, and tutoring services) are based on the belief that providing prosocial opportunities for young people in the after-school hours can reduce their involvement in delinquent behavior in the community. After-school programs target a range of risk factors for delinquency, including association with delinquent peers. Welsh and Hoshi (2006) identified three high-quality after-school programs with an evaluated impact on delinquency. Each had desirable effects on delinquency, and one program also reported lower rates of drug use for participants compared to controls.

Anti-Bullying Programs

Several school-based programs have been designed to decrease bullying. The most famous of these was implemented by Olweus (1994) in Norway. It aimed to increase awareness and knowledge of teachers, parents, and children about bullying and to dispel myths about it. A 30-page booklet was distributed to all schools in Norway describing what was known about bullying and recommending what steps schools and teachers could take to reduce it. Also, a 25-minute video about bullying was made available to schools. Simultaneously, the schools distributed to all parents a four-page folder containing information and advice about bullying. In addition, anonymous self-report questionnaires about bullying were completed by all children.

The program was evaluated in Bergen. Each of the 42 participating schools received feedback information from the questionnaire, about the prevalence of bullies and victims, in a specially arranged school conference day. Also, teachers were encouraged to develop explicit rules about bullying (e.g., do not bully, tell someone when bullying happens, bullying will not be tolerated, try to help victims, try to include children who are being left out) and to discuss bullying in class, using the video and role-playing exercises. Also, teachers were encouraged to improve monitoring and supervision of children, especially on the playground. The program was successful in reducing the prevalence of bullying by half.

A similar program was implemented in England in 23 Sheffield schools by Smith and Sharp (1994). The core program involved establishing a "whole-school" anti-bullying policy, raising awareness of bullying and clearly defining roles and responsibilities of teachers and students, so that everyone knew what bullying was and what they should do about it. In addition, there were optional interventions tailored to particular schools: curriculum work (e.g., reading books, watching videos), direct work with students (e.g., assertiveness training for those who were bullied), and playground work (e.g., training lunchtime supervisors). This program was successful in reducing bullying (by 15%) in primary schools, but had relatively small effects (a 5% reduction) in secondary schools.

Baldry and Farrington (2007) reviewed 16 major evaluations of programs to prevent school bullying, conducted in 11 different countries. Of these, eight yielded clearly desirable results and only two yielded undesirable negative effects on bullying. They concluded that the findings of existing evaluations were generally optimistic. Similarly optimistic conclusions were drawn in systematic reviews by Vreeman and Carroll (2007) and Ttofi, Farrington, and Baldry (2008).

Multimodal Programs

Multimodal programs including both skills training and parent training are more effective than either alone (Wasserman & Miller, 1998). An important multimodal program was implemented by Tremblay, Pagani-Kurtz, Vitaro, Masse, and Pihl (1995) in Montreal, Canada. They identified about 250 disruptive (aggressive/hyperactive) boys at age 6 for a prevention experiment. Between ages 7 and 9, the experimental group received training to foster social skills and self-control. Coaching, peer modeling, role playing, and reinforcement contingencies were used in small group sessions on such topics as "how to help," "what to do when you are angry," and "how to react to teasing." Also, their parents were trained using the parent management training techniques developed by Patterson (1982).

This prevention program was successful. By age 12, the experimental boys committed less burglary and theft, were less likely to get drunk, and were less likely to be involved in fights than the controls. Also, the experimental boys had higher school achievement. At every age from 10 to 15, the experimental boys had lower self-reported delinquency scores than the control boys. Interestingly, the differences in antisocial behavior between experimental and control boys increased as the follow-up progressed. A later follow-up showed that fewer experimental boys had a criminal record by age 24 (Boisjoli, Vitaro, Lacourse, Barker, & Tremblay, 2007).

Intervention programs that tackle several of the major risk factors for CD and delinquency are likely to be particularly effective. Henggeler, Melton, Smith, Schoenwald, and

Hanley (1993) in South Carolina evaluated multisystemic therapy (MST) for juvenile offenders, tackling family, peer, and school risk factors simultaneously in individualized treatment plans tailored to the needs of each family. MST was compared with the usual Department of Youth Services treatment, involving out-of-home placement in the majority of cases. In a randomized experiment with delinquents, MST was followed by fewer arrests, lower self-reported delinquency, and less peer-oriented aggression. Borduin et al. (1995) also showed that MST was more effective in decreasing arrests and antisocial behavior than was individual therapy. According to Aos, Phipps, Barnoski, and Lieb (2001b), MST had one of the highest benefit-to-cost ratios of any program. For every $1 spent on it, $13 was saved in victim and criminal justice costs.

MST was the most effective intervention in the review by Farrington and Welsh (2003). However, since that review two later meta-analyses have reached dramatically opposite conclusions about the effectiveness of MST; Curtis, Ronan, and Borduin (2004) concluded that it was effective, but Littell (2005) concluded that it was not. Therefore, we cannot be confident about the effectiveness of MST until this controversy is resolved by more evaluations.

CONCLUSIONS

A great deal is known about adolescent antisocial behavior from high-quality longitudinal and experimental studies. First, males are more antisocial than females. Second, all types (including CD, aggression, and delinquency) tend to coexist and are intercorrelated. Third, the most antisocial adolescents at one age tend also to be the most antisocial at a later age. Fourth, an early onset of antisocial behavior predicts a long and serious antisocial career. However, both the prevalence and the age of onset of antisocial behavior can vary dramatically according to its definition and how it is measured. Research is needed on a wider range of features of antisocial careers; not just prevalence and

onset but also frequency, seriousness, duration, escalation, deescalation, desistance, remission, motivation and situational influences. More studies are needed with multiple informants and frequent measurements.

How the prevalence and incidence of antisocial behavior varies between ages 10 and 17 is less well understood. The existing evidence suggests that the incidence of physical aggression decreases during adolescence but that the prevalence of CD and delinquency increase. More research is needed on the age distribution of different types of antisocial behavior, in order to explain these findings. Also, more research is needed on different types of developmental pathways and trajectories during this age range.

A great deal is known about the key risk factors for adolescent antisocial behavior, which include impulsiveness, low empathy, low IQ and low school achievement, poor parental supervision, child physical abuse, punitive or erratic parental discipline, cold parental attitude, parental conflict, disrupted families, antisocial parents, large family size, low family income, antisocial peers, high-delinquency-rate schools, and high-crime neighborhoods. However, the causal mechanisms linking these risk factors with antisocial outcomes are less well established. Larger developmental theories that explain broader patterns of results need to be formulated and tested (Lahey, Moffitt, & Caspi, 2003; Farrington, 2005). More research is needed on risk factors for persistence or escalation of antisocial behavior. To what extent risk factors are the same for males and females, for different ethnic groups, or at different ages needs to be investigated. More cross-national comparisons of risk factors, and more studies of promotive and protective factors, are needed.

The comorbidity and versatility of antisocial behavior poses a major challenge to scientific understanding. It is important to investigate to what extent research findings are driven by a minority of multiple-problem adolescents or chronic delinquents. Often, multiple risk factors lead to multiple-problem boys (Farrington,

2002; Loeber et al., 2001). To what extent any given risk factor generally predicts a variety of different outcomes (as opposed to specifically predicting one or two outcomes) and to what extent each outcome is generally predicted by a variety of different risk factors (as opposed to being specifically predicted by only one or two risk factors) is unclear. An increasing number of risk factors leads to an increasing probability of antisocial outcomes, almost irrespective of the particular risk factors included in the prediction measure, but more research is needed on this. There was insufficient space in this chapter to review theories explaining the links between risk factors and antisocial outcomes, but these have to be based on knowledge about the additive, independent, interactive, and sequential effects of risk factors.

There are many examples of successful intervention programs, including general parent education in home visiting programs, preschool intellectual enrichment programs, parent management training, cognitive behavioral skills training, anti-bullying and other school programs, mentoring and after-school programs, and multimodal programs including individual and family interventions. The meta-analysis by Farrington and Welsh (2003) concluded that the average effect size of family-based programs on delinquency was $d = 0.32$, corresponding to a decrease in the percentage convicted from 50% to 34%. However, many experiments are based on small samples and short follow-up periods. The challenge to researchers is to transport carefully monitored small-scale programs implemented by high-quality university personnel into routine large-scale use, without losing their effectiveness. Often, multimodal programs are the most successful, making it difficult to identify the active ingredient. Successful multimodal programs should be followed by more specific experiments targeting single risk factors, which could be very helpful in establishing which risk factors have causal effects.

More efforts are needed to tailor types of interventions to types of adolescents. Ideally, an intervention should be preceded by a screening or needs assessment to determine which problems need to be rectified and which adolescents are most likely to be amenable to treatment. It is important to establish to what extent interventions are successful with the most antisocial adolescents, in order to identify where the benefits will be greatest in practice. Also, more cost–benefit analyses are needed, to show how much money is saved by successful programs. Saving money is a powerful argument to convince policy makers and practitioners to implement intervention programs.

A great deal has been learned about adolescent antisocial behavior in the past 25 years, especially from longitudinal and experimental studies. More investment in these kinds of studies is needed in the next 25 years in order to advance knowledge about and decrease these troubling social problems.

Acknowledgments

I am very grateful to Rowell Huesmann, Ben Lahey, Rolf Loeber, Barbara Maughan, Terrie Moffitt, and Richard Tremblay for providing helpful comments and materials.

REFERENCES

Achenbach, T. M. (1993). *Empirically based taxonomy: How to use syndromes and profile types derived from the CBCL4–18, TRF and YSR*. Burlington, VT: University of Vermont Department of Psychiatry.

Achenbach, T. M., Dumenci, L., & Rescorla, L. A. (2003). Are American children's problems still getting worse? A 23-year comparison. *Journal of Abnormal Child Psychology, 31,* 1–11.

Achenbach, T. M., Verhulst, F. C., Baron, G. D., & Althaus, M. (1987). A comparison of syndromes derived from the child behavior checklist for American and Dutch boys aged 6–11 and 12–16. *Journal of Child Psychology and Psychiatry, 28,* 437–453.

Alexander, J. F., & Parsons, B. V. (1973). Short-term behavioral intervention with delinquent families: Impact on family process and recidivism. *Journal of Abnormal Psychology, 81,* 219–225.

American Psychiatric Association. (1994). *Diagnostic and statistical manual of mental disorders* (4th ed.). Washington, DC: American Psychiatric Association.

Anderson, C. A., & Huesmann, L. R. (2003). Human aggression: A social-cognitive view. In M. A. Hogg & J. Cooper (Eds.), *Sage handbook of social psychology* (pp. 296–323). London: Sage.

Angold, A. & Costello, E. J. (2000). The Child and Adolescent Psychiatric Assessment (CAPA). *Journal of the American Academy of Child and Adolescent Psychiatry, 39,* 39–48.

Aos, S., Phipps, P., Barnoski, R., & Lieb, R. (2001a). *The comparative costs and benefits of programs to reduce crime* (version 4.0). Olympia, WA: Washington State Institute for Public Policy.

Aos, S., Phipps, P., Barnoski, R., & Lieb, R. (2001b). The comparative costs and benefits of programs to reduce crime: A review of research findings with implications for Washington State. In B. C. Welsh, D. P. Farrington, & L. W. Sherman (Eds.), *Costs and benefits of preventing crime* (pp. 149–175). Boulder, CO: Westview Press.

Baldry, A. C., & Farrington, D. P. (1998). Parenting influences on bullying and victimization. *Legal and Criminological Psychology, 3,* 237–254.

Baldry, A. C., & Farrington, D. P. (2007). Effectiveness of programs to prevent school bullying. *Victims and Offenders, 2,* 183–204.

Barker, E. D., Seguin, J. R., White, H. R., Bates, M. E., Lacourse, E., Carbonneau, R., et al. (2007). Developmental trajectories of male physical violence and theft. *Archives of General Psychiatry, 64,* 592–599.

Barnett, W. S. (1993) Cost–benefit analysis. In L. J. Schweinhart, H. V. Barnes, & D. P. Weikart (Eds.), *Significant benefits: The High/Scope Perry Preschool Study through age 27* (pp. 142–173). Ypsilanti, MI: High/Scope Press.

Battin, S. R., Hill, K. G., Abbott, R. D., Catalano, R. F., & Hawkins, J. D. (1998). The contribution of gang membership to delinquency beyond delinquent friends. *Criminology, 36,* 93–115.

Berrueta-Clement, J. R., Schweinhart, L. J., Barnett, W. S., Epstein, A. S., & Weikart, D. P. (1984). *Changed lives.* Ypsilanti, MI: High/Scope Press.

Bjorkvist, K., Lagerspetz, K. M. J., & Kaukiainen, A. (1992). Do girls manipulate and boys fight? Developmental trends in regard to direct and indirect aggression. *Aggressive Behavior, 18,* 117–127.

Blum, H. M., Boyle, M. H., & Offord, D. R. (1988). Single-parent families: Child psychiatric disorder and school performance. *Journal of the American Academy of Child and Adolescent Psychiatry, 27,* 214–219.

Boisjoli, R., Vitaro, F., Lacourse, E., Barker, E. D., & Tremblay, R. E. (2007). Impact and clinical significance of a preventive intervention for disruptive boys. *British Journal of Psychiatry, 191,* 415–419.

Borduin, C. M., Mann, B. J., Cone, L. T., Henggeler, S. W., Fucci, B. R., Blaske, D. M., et al. (1995). Multisystemic treatment of serious juvenile offenders: Long-term prevention of criminality and violence. *Journal of Consulting and Clinical Psychology, 63,* 569–578.

Brennan, P. A., Mednick, B. R., & Mednick, S. A. (1993). Parental psychopathology, congenital factors, and violence. In S.Hodgins (Ed.), *Mental disorder and crime* (pp. 244–261). Newbury Park, CA: Sage.

Broidy, L. M., Nagin, D. S., Tremblay, R. E., Bates, J. E., Brame, B., Dodge, K. A., et al. (2003). Developmental trajectories of childhood disruptive behaviors and adolescent delinquency: A six-site, cross-national study. *Developmental Psychology, 39,* 222–245.

Brownfield, D., & Sorenson, A. M. (1994). Sibship size and sibling delinquency. *Deviant Behavior, 15,* 45–61.

Buehler, C., Anthony, C., Krishnakumar, A., Stone, G., Gerard, J., & Pemberton, S. (1997). Interparental conflict and youth problem behaviors: A meta-analysis. *Journal of Child and Family Studies, 6,* 233–247.

Burke, J. D., Loeber, R., & Birmaher, B. (2002). Oppositional defiant disorder and conduct disorder: A review of the past 10 years, part 2. *Journal of the American Academy of Child and Adolescent Psychiatry, 41,* 1275–1293.

Burke, J. D., Loeber, R., Lahey, B. B., & Rathouz, P. J. (2005). Developmental transitions among affective and behavioral disorders in adolescent boys. *Journal of Child Psychology and Psychiatry, 46,* 1200–1210.

Cairns, R. B. & Cairns, B. D. (1994). *Lifelines and risks: Pathways of youth in our time.* Cambridge: Cambridge University Press.

Cairns, R. B., Cairns, B. D., Neckerman, H. J., Gest, S. D., & Gariepy. J.-L. (1988). Social networks and aggressive behavior: Peer support or peer rejection? *Developmental Psychology, 24,* 815–823.

Capaldi, D. M., & Patterson, G. R. (1996). Can violent offenders be distinguished from frequent offenders? Prediction from childhood to adolescence. *Journal of Research in Crime and Delinquency, 33,* 206–231.

Carroll, A., Hemingway, F., Bower, J., Ashman, A., Houghton, S., & Durkin, K. (2006). Impulsivity in juvenile delinquency: Differences among early-onset, late-onset, and non-offenders. *Journal of Youth and Adolescence, 35,* 519–529.

Caspi, A. (2000). The child is father of the man: Personality continuities from childhood to adulthood. *Journal of Personality and Social Psychology, 78,* 158–172.

Catalano, R. F., Arthur, M. W., Hawkins, J. D., Berglund, L., & Olson, J. J. (1998). Comprehensive community and school based interventions to prevent antisocial behavior. In R. Loeber & D. P. Farrington (Eds.), *Serious and violent juvenile offenders: Risk factors and successful interventions* (pp. 248–283). Thousand Oaks, CA: Sage.

Catalano, R. F., Hawkins, J. D., Berglund, L., Pollard, J. A., & Arthur, M. W. (2002). Prevention science and positive youth development: Competitive or cooperative frameworks? *Journal of Adolescent Health, 31,* 230–239.

Cernkovich, S. A., Giordano, P. C., & Pugh, M. D. (1985). Chronic offenders: The missing cases in self-report delinquency research. *Journal of Criminal Law and Criminology, 76,* 705–732.

Chamberlain, P., & Reid, J. B. (1998). Comparison of two community alternatives to incarceration for chronic juvenile offenders. *Journal of Consulting and Clinical Psychology, 66,* 624–633.

Chess, S., & Thomas, A. (1984). *Origins and evolution of behavior disorders: From infancy to early adult life.* New York: Brunner/Mazel.

Clarke, R. V. (1995). Situational crime prevention. In M. Tonry & D. P. Farrington (Eds.), *Building a safer society: Strategic approaches to crime prevention* (pp. 91–150). Chicago: University of Chicago Press.

Cohen, P., Brook, J. S., Cohen, J., Velez, C. N., & Garcia, M. (1990). Common and uncommon pathways to adolescent psychopathology and problem behavior. In L. N. Robins & M. Rutter (Eds.), *Straight and devious pathways from childhood to adulthood* (pp. 242–258). Cambridge: Cambridge University Press.

Cohen, P., Cohen, J., & Brook, J. (1993b). An epidemiological study of disorders in late childhood and adolescence. II: Persistence of disorders. *Journal of Child Psychology and Psychiatry, 34,* 869–877.

Cohen, P., Cohen, J., Kasen, S., Velez, C. N., Hartmark, C., Johnson, J., et al. (1993a). An epidemiological study of disorders in late childhood and adolescence. I: Age and gender-specific prevalence. *Journal of Child Psychology and Psychiatry, 34,* 851–867.

Coie, J. D. & Dodge, K. A. (1998). Aggression and antisocial behavior. In W. Damon and N. Eisenberg (Eds.), *Handbook of child psychology* (5th ed.), vol. 3: *Social, emotional and personality development* (pp. 779–862). New York: John Wiley & Sons.

Coie, J. D., Dodge, K. A., & Kupersmidt, J. (1990). Peer group behavior and social status. In S. R. Asher & J. D. Coie (Eds.), *Peer rejection in childhood* (pp. 17–59). Cambridge: Cambridge University Press.

Coie, J. D., & Miller-Johnson, S. (2001). Peer factors and interventions. In R. Loeber & D. P. Farrington (Eds.), *Child delinquents: Development, intervention, and service needs* (pp. 191–209). Thousand Oaks, CA: Sage.

Colder, C. R., & Stice, E. (1998). A longitudinal study of the interactive effects of impulsivity and anger on adolescent problem behavior. *Journal of Youth and Adolescence, 27,* 255–274.

Collishaw, S., Goodman, R., Pickles, A., & Maughan, B. (2007). Modelling the contribution of changes in family life to time trends in adolescent conduct problems. *Social Science and Medicine, 65,* 2576–2587.

Connor, D. F. (2002). *Aggression and antisocial behavior in children and adolescents.* New York: Guilford Press.

Copeland, W. E., Miller-Johnson, S., Keeler, G., Angold, A., & Costello, E. J. (2007). Childhood psychiatric disorders and young adult crime: A prospective, population-based study. *American Journal of Psychiatry, 164,* 1668–1675.

Costello, E. J., Angold, A., Burns, B. J., Erkanli, A., Stangl, D. K., & Tweed, D. L. (1996). The Great Smoky Mountains Study of Youth: Functional impairment and serious emotional disturbance. *Archives of General Psychiatry, 53,* 1137–1143.

Cote, S. M., Vaillancourt, T., LeBlanc, J. C., Nagin, D. S., & Tremblay, R. E. (2006). The development of physical aggression from toddlehood to pre-adolescence: A nationwide longitudinal study of Canadian children. *Journal of Abnormal Child Psychology, 34,* 71–85.

Craig, W. M., Pepler, D., & Atlas, R. (2000). Observations of bullying in the playground and in the classroom. *School Psychology International, 21,* 22–36.

Crick, N. R., & Grotpeter, J. K. (1995). Relational aggression, gender, and social–psychological adjustment. *Child Development, 66,* 710–722.

Curtis, N. M., Ronan, K. R., & Borduin, C. M. (2004). Multisystemic treatment: A meta-analysis of outcome studies. *Journal of Family Psychology, 18,* 411–419.

Denno, D. W. (1990). *Biology and violence: From birth to adulthood.* Cambridge: Cambridge University Press.

Dishion, T. J., McCord, J., & Poulin, F. (1999). When interventions harm: Peer groups and problem behavior. *American Psychologist, 54,* 755–764.

Dishion, T. J., Patterson, G. R., & Kavanagh, K. A. (1992). An experimental test of the coercion model: Linking theory, measurement and intervention. In J. McCord & R. Tremblay (Eds.), *Preventing antisocial behavior* (pp. 253–282). New York: Guilford Press.

Dodge, K. A. (1991). The structure and function of reactive and proactive aggression. In D. J. Pepler & K. H. Rubin (Eds.), *The development and treatment of childhood aggression* (pp. 201–218). Hillsdale, NJ: Lawrence Erlbaum.

Dodge, K. A. (2003). Do social information-processing patterns mediate aggressive behavior? In B. B. Lahey, T. E. Moffitt, & A. Caspi (Eds.), *Causes of conduct disorder and juvenile delinquency* (pp. 254–274). New York: Guilford Press.

Dodge, K. A., Lansford, J. E., Burks, V. S., Bates, J. E., Pettit, G. S., Fontaine, R., et al. (2003). Peer rejection and social information-processing factors in the development of aggressive behavior problems in children. *Child Development, 74,* 374–393.

Dodge, K. A., Pettit, G. S., & Bates, J. E. (1994). Socialization mediators of the relation between socioeconomic status and child conduct problems. *Child Development, 65,* 649–665.

Due, P., Holstein, B. E., Lynch, J., Diderichsen, F., Gabhain, S. N., Scheidt, P., et al. (2005). Bullying and symptoms among school-aged children: International comparative cross-sectional study in 28 countries. *European Journal of Public Health, 15,* 128–132.

Elliott, D. S. (1994). Serious violent offenders: Onset, developmental course, and termination. *Criminology, 32,* 1–21.

Elliott, D. S., Huizinga, D., & Menard, S. (1989). *Multiple problem youth: Delinquency, substance use, and mental health problems.* New York: Springer-Verlag.

Elliott, D. S., & Menard, S. (1996). Delinquent friends and delinquent behavior: Temporal and developmental patterns. In J. D. Hawkins (Ed.), *Delinquency and crime: Current theories* (pp. 28–67). Cambridge: Cambridge University Press.

Eysenck, H. J. (1996). Personality and crime: Where do we stand? *Psychology, Crime and Law, 2,* 143–152.

Fabio, A., Loeber, R., Balasubramani, G. K.. Roth, J., Fu, W., & Farrington, D. P. (2006). Why some generations are more violent than others: Assessment of age, period and cohort effects. *American Journal of Epidemiology, 164,* 151–160.

Farrington, D. P. (1972). Delinquency begins at home. *New Society, 21,* 495–497.

Farrington, D. P. (1979). Environmental stress, delinquent behavior, and convictions. In I. G. Sarason & C. D. Spielberger (Eds.), *Stress and anxiety,* vol. 6 (pp. 93–107). Washington, DC: Hemisphere.

Farrington, D. P. (1983). Randomized experiments on crime and justice. In M. Tonry & N. Morris (Eds.), *Crime and justice,* vol. 4 (pp. 257–308). Chicago: University of Chicago Press.

Farrington, D. P. (1986a). Age and crime. In M. Tonry & N. Morris (Eds.), *Crime and justice,* vol. 7 (pp. 189–250). Chicago: University of Chicago Press.

Farrington, D. P. (1986b). Stepping stones to adult criminal careers. In D. Olweus, J. Block, & M. R. Yarrow (Eds.), *Development of antisocial and prosocial behavior* (pp. 359–384). New York: Academic Press.

Farrington, D. P. (1989a). Early predictors of adolescent aggression and adult violence. *Violence and Victims, 4,* 79–100.

Farrington, D. P. (1989b). Self-reported and official offending from adolescence to adulthood. In M. W. Klein (Ed.), *Cross-national research in self-reported crime and delinquency* (pp. 399–423). Dordrecht, Netherlands: Kluwer.

Farrington, D. P. (1990). Implications of criminal career research for the prevention of offending. *Journal of Adolescence, 13,* 93–113.

Farrington, D. P. (1991). Childhood aggression and adult violence: Early precursors and later life outcomes. In D. J. Pepler & K. H. Rubin (Eds.), *The development and treatment of childhood aggression* (pp. 5–29). Hillsdale, NJ: Lawrence Erlbaum.

Farrington, D. P. (1992a). Criminal career research in the United Kingdom. *British Journal of Criminology, 32,* 521–536.

Farrington, D. P. (1992b). Explaining the beginning, progress and ending of antisocial behavior from birth to adulthood. In J. McCord (Ed.), *Facts, frameworks and forecasts: Advances in criminological theory,* vol. 3 (pp. 253–286). New Brunswick, NJ: Transaction.

Farrington, D. P. (1992c). Juvenile delinquency. In J. C. Coleman (Ed.), *The school years* (2nd ed.; pp. 123–163). London: Routledge.

Farrington, D. P. (1993a). Childhood origins of teenage antisocial behavior and adult social dysfunction. *Journal of the Royal Society of Medicine, 86,* 13–17.

Farrington, D. P. (1993b). Understanding and preventing bullying. In M. Tonry & N. Morris (Eds.), *Crime and justice,* vol. 17 (pp. 381–458). Chicago: University of Chicago Press.

Farrington, D. P. (1994). Childhood, adolescent and adult features of violent males. In L. R. Huesman (Ed.), *Aggressive behavior: Current perspectives* (pp. 215–240). New York: Plenum Press.

Farrington, D. P. (1997a). Human development and criminal careers. In M. Maguire, R. Morgan, & R. Reiner (Eds.), *The Oxford handbook of criminology* (2nd ed.; pp. 361–408). Oxford: Clarendon Press.

Farrington, D. P. (1997b). The relationship between low resting heart rate and violence. In A. Raine, P. A. Brennan, D. P. Farrington, & S. A. Mednick (Eds.), *Biosocial bases of violence* (pp. 89–105). New York: Plenum Press.

Farrington, D. P. (1998). Predictors, causes and correlates of male youth violence. In M. Tonry & M. H. Moore (Eds.), *Youth violence* (pp. 421–475). Chicago: University of Chicago Press.

Farrington, D. P. (2000). Adolescent violence: Findings and implications from the Cambridge Study. In G. Boswell (Ed.), *Violent children and adolescents: Asking the question why* (pp. 19–35). London: Whurr.

Farrington, D. P. (2002). Multiple risk factors for multiple problem violent boys. In R. R. Corrado, R. Roesch, S. D. Hart, & J. K. Gierowski (Eds.), *Multi-problem violent youth: A foundation for comparative research on needs, interventions and outcomes* (pp. 23–34). Amsterdam: IOS Press.

Farrington, D. P. (Ed.). (2005). *Integrated developmental and life-course theories of offending: Advances in criminological theory,* vol. 14. New Brunswick, NJ: Transaction.

Farrington, D. P. (2006). Comparing football hooligans and violent offenders: Childhood adolescent, teenage and adult features. *Monatsschrift fur Kriminologie und Strafrechtsreform (Journal of Criminology and Penal Reform), 89,* 193–205.

Farrington, D. P., Barnes, G., & Lambert, S. (1996a). The concentration of offending in families. *Legal and Criminological Psychology, 1,* 47–63.

Farrington, D. P., Biron, L., & LeBlanc, M. (1982). Personality and delinquency in London and Montreal. In J. Gunn & D. P. Farrington (Eds.), *Abnormal offenders, delinquency, and the criminal justice system* (pp. 153–201). Chichester, UK: John Wiley & Sons.

Farrington, D. P., Coid, J. W., Harnett, L., Jolliffe, D., Soteriou, N., Turner, R., et al. (2006). *Criminal careers and life success: New findings from the Cambridge Study in Delinquent Development.* London: Home Office (Research Findings No. 281).

Farrington, D. P., Gallagher, B., Morley, L., St.Ledger, R. J., & West, D. J. (1986). Unemployment, school leaving, and crime. *British Journal of Criminology, 26,* 335–356.

Farrington, D. P., & Hawkins, J. D. (1991). Predicting participation, early onset, and later persistence in officially recorded offending. *Criminal Behaviour and Mental Health, 1,* 1–33.

Farrington, D. P., Jolliffe, D., Hawkins, J. D., Catalano, R. F., Hill, K. G., & Kosterman, R. (2003a). Comparing delinquent careers in court records and self-reports. *Criminology, 41,* 933–958.

Farrington, D. P., Jolliffe, D., Loeber, R., & Homish, D. L. (2007). How many offenses are really committed per juvenile court offender? *Victims and Offenders, 2,* 227–249.

Farrington, D. P., Jolliffe, D., Loeber, R., Stouthamer-Loeber, M., & Kalb, L. M. (2001). The concentration of offenders in families, and family criminality in the prediction of boys' delinquency. *Journal of Adolescence, 24,* 579–596.

Farrington, D. P., & Loeber, R. (1999). Transatlantic replicability of risk factors in the development of delinquency. In P. Cohen, C. Slomkowski & L. N. Robins (Eds.), *Historical and geographical influences on psychopathology* (pp. 299–329). Mahwah, NJ: Lawrence Erlbaum.

Farrington, D. P., Loeber, R., Stallings, R., & Homish, D. L. (2008). Early risk factors for young homicide offenders and victims. In M. J. Delisi & P. J. Conis (Eds.), *Violent offenders: Theory, research, public policy and practice* (pp. 79–96). Sudbury, MA: Jones and Bartlett.

Farrington, D. P., Loeber, R., & Stouthamer-Loeber, M. (2003). How can the relationship between race and violence be explained? In D. F. Hawkins (Ed.), *Violent crime: Assessing race and ethnic differences* (pp. 213–237). Cambridge: Cambridge University Press.

Farrington, D. P., Loeber, R., Stouthamer-Loeber, M. S., van Kammen, W., & Schmidt, L. (1996b). Self-reported delinquency and a combined delinquency seriousness scale based on boys, mothers and teachers: Concurrent and predictive validity for African Americans and Caucasians. *Criminology, 34,* 493–517.

Farrington, D. P., Loeber, R., & van Kammen, W. B. (1990). Long-term criminal outcomes of hyperactivity–impulsivity–attention deficit and conduct problems in childhood. In L. N. Robins & M. Rutter (Eds.), *Straight and devious pathways from childhood to adulthood* (pp. 62–81). Cambridge: Cambridge University Press.

Farrington, D. P., Loeber, R., Yin, Y., & Anderson, S. (2002). Are within-individual causes of delinquency the same as between-individual causes? *Criminal Behaviour and Mental Health, 12,* 53–68.

Farrington, D. P., Snyder, H. N., & Finnegan, T. A. (1988). Specialization in juvenile court careers. *Criminology, 26,* 461–487.

Farrington, D. P., & Welsh, B. C. (2003). Family-based prevention of offending: A meta-analysis. *Australian and New Zealand Journal of Criminology, 36,* 127–151.

Farrington, D. P., & Welsh, B. C. (2005). Randomized experiments in criminology: What have we learned in the last two decades? *Journal of Experimental Criminology, 1,* 9–38.

Farrington, D. P., & Welsh, B. C. (2006). A half century of randomized experiments on crime and justice. In M. Tonry (Ed.), *Crime and justice,* vol. 34 (pp. 55–132). Chicago: University of Chicago Press.

Farrington, D. P., & Welsh, B. C. (2007). *Saving children from a life of crime: Early risk factors and effective interventions.* Oxford: Oxford University Press.

Farrington, D. P., & Wikström, P.-O. H. (1994). Criminal careers in London and Stockholm: A cross-national comparative study. In E. G. M. Weitekamp & H. J. Kerner (Eds.), *Cross-national longitudinal research on human development and criminal behavior* (pp. 65–89). Dordrecht, Netherlands: Kluwer.

Federal Bureau of Investigation (2007). *Crime in the United States, 2006.* Washington DC: Author.

Feldman, R. A., Caplinger, T. E., & Wodarski, J. S. (1983). *The St. Louis conundrum.* Englewood Cliffs, NJ: Prentice Hall.

Fergusson, D. M., & Horwood, L. J. (1995). Predictive validity of categorically and dimensionally scored measures of disruptive childhood behaviors. *Journal of the American Academy of Child and Adolescent Psychiatry, 34,* 477–485.

Fergusson, D. M., & Horwood, L. J. (1998). Exposure to interparental violence in childhood and psychosocial adjustment in young adulthood. *Child Abuse and Neglect, 22,* 339–357.

Fergusson, D. M., & Horwood, L. J. (2002). Male and female offending trajectories. *Development and Psychopathology, 14,* 159–177.

Fergusson, D. M., Horwood, J., & Lynskey, M. T. (1994). Parental separation, adolescent psychopathology, and problem behaviors. *Journal of the American Academy of Child and Adolescent Psychiatry, 33,* 1122–1131.

Fergusson, D. M., Horwood, L. J., & Ridder, E. M. (2005). Show me the child at seven: The consequences of conduct problems in childhood for psychosocial functioning in adulthood. *Journal of Child Psychology and Psychiatry, 46,* 837–849.

Fergusson, D., Swain-Campbell, N., & Horwood, J. (2004). How does childhood economic disadvantage lead to crime? *Journal of Child Psychology and Psychiatry, 45,* 956–966.

Fischer, D. G. (1984). Family size and delinquency. *Perceptual and Motor Skills, 58,* 527–534.

Fitzpatrick, K. M. (1997). Fighting among America's youth: A risk and protective factors approach. *Journal of Health and Social Behavior, 38,* 131–148.

Fontaine, N., Carbonneau, R., Barker, E. D., Vitaro, F., Hebert, M., Cote, S. M., et al. (2008). Girls' hyperactivity and physical aggression during childhood and adjustment problems in early adulthood: A 15-year longitudinal study. *Archives of General Psychiatry, 65,* 320–328.

Frick, P. J., Kamphaus, R. W., Lahey, B. B., Loeber, R., Christ, M. A. G., Hart, E. L., et al. (1991). Academic underachievement and the disruptive behavior disorders. *Journal of Consulting and Clinical Psychology, 59,* 289–294.

Frick, P. J., Lahey, B. B., Loeber, R., Stouthamer-Loeber, M., Christ, M. A. G., & Hanson, K. (1992). Familial risk factors to oppositional defiant disorder and conduct disorder: Parental psychopathology and maternal parenting. *Journal of Consulting and Clinical Psychology, 60,* 49–55.

Frick, P. J., & White, S. F. (2008). The importance of callous–unemotional traits for developmental models of aggressive and antisocial behavior. *Journal of Child Psychology and Psychiatry, 49,* 359–375.

Gatti, U., Tremblay, R. E., Vitaro, F., & McDuff, P. (2005). Youth gangs, delinquency and drug use: A test of the selection, facilitation, and enhancement hypotheses. *Journal of Child Psychology and Psychiatry, 46,* 1178–1190.

Goodman, R., Simonoff, E., & Stevenson, J. (1995). The impact of child IQ, parent IQ and sibling IQ on child behavioral deviance scores. *Journal of Child Psychology and Psychiatry, 36,* 409–425.

Gordon, D. A. (1995). Functional family therapy for delinquents. In R. R. Ross, D. H. Antonowicz, & G. K. Dhaliwal (Eds.), *Going straight: Effective delinquency prevention and offender rehabilitation* (pp. 163–178). Ottawa, Canada: Air Training and Publications.

Gordon, R. A., Lahey, B. B., Kawai, E., Loeber, R., Stouthamer-Loeber, M., & Farrington, D. P. (2004). Antisocial behavior and young gang membership: Selection and socialization. *Criminology, 42,* 55–87.

Gorman-Smith, D., & Loeber, R. (2005). Are developmental pathways in disruptive behaviors the same for girls and boys? *Journal of Child and Family Studies, 14,* 15–27.

Gottfredson, D. C. (2001). *Schools and delinquency.* Cambridge: Cambridge University Press.

Gottfredson, D. C., McNeil, R. J., & Gottfredson, G. D. (1991). Social area influences on delinquency: A multilevel analyses. *Journal of Research in Crime and Delinquency, 28,* 197–226.

Gottfredson, D. C., Wilson, D. B., & Najaka, S. S. (2006). School-based crime prevention. In L. W. Sherman, D. P. Farrington, B. C. Welsh, & D. L. MacKenzie (Eds.), *Evidence-based crime prevention* (rev. ed.; pp. 56–164). London: Routledge.

Graham, J. (1988). *Schools, disruptive behaviour and delinquency.* London: Her Majesty's Stationery Office.

Haapasalo, J., & Pokela, E. (1999). Child-rearing and child abuse antecedents of criminality. *Aggression and Violent Behavior, 1,* 107–127.

Haas, H., Farrington, D. P., Killias, M., & Sattar, G. (2004). The impact of different family configurations on delinquency. *British Journal of Criminology, 44,* 520–532.

Hamalainen, M., & Pulkkinen, L. (1995). Aggressive and non-prosocial behavior as precursors of criminality. *Studies on Crime and Crime Prevention, 4,* 6–21.

Hamalainen, M., & Pulkkinen, L. (1996). Problem behavior as a precursor of male criminality. *Development and Psychopathology, 8,* 443–455.

Harachi, T. W., Fleming, C. B., White, H. R., Ensminger, M. E., Abbott, R. D., Catalano, R. F., et al. (2006). Aggressive behavior among girls and boys during middle childhood: Predictors and sequelae of trajectory group membership. *Aggressive Behavior, 32,* 279–293.

Harrell, A. V., Cavanagh, S. E., Harmon, M. A., Koper, C. S., & Sridharan, S. (1997). *Impact of the Children at Risk program: Comprehensive final report,* vol. 2. Washington, DC: Urban Institute.

Harrell, A. V., Cavanagh, S. E., & Sridharan, S. (1999). *Evaluation of the Children at Risk program: Results one year after the program.* Washington, DC: U.S. National Institute of Justice.

Hawkins, J. D., Catalano, R. F., Kosterman, R., Abbott, R., & Hill, K. G. (1999). Preventing adolescent health risk behaviors by strengthening protection during childhood. *Archives of Pediatrics and Adolescent Medicine, 153,* 226–234.

Hawkins, J. D., von Cleve, E., & Catalano, R. F. (1991). Reducing early childhood aggression: Results of a primary prevention program. *Journal of the American Academy of Child and Adolescent Psychiatry, 30,* 208–217.

Hawkins, J. D., Herrenkohl, T., Farrington, D. P., Brewer, D., Catalano, R. F., & Harachi, T. W. (1998). A review of predictors of youth violence. In R. Loeber & D. P. Farrington (Eds.), *Serious and violent juvenile offenders: Risk factors and successful interventions* (pp. 106–146). Thousand Oaks, CA: Sage.

Heaven, P. C. L. (1996). Personality and self-reported delinquency: Analysis of the "Big Five" personality dimensions. *Personality and Individual Differences, 20,* 47–54.

Henggeler, S. W., Melton, G. B., Smith, L. A., Schoenwald, S. K., & Hanley, J. H. (1993). Family preservation using multisystemic treatment: Long-term follow-up to a clinical trial with serious juvenile offenders. *Journal of Child and Family Studies, 2,* 283–293.

Henry, B., Caspi, A., Moffitt, T. E., & Silva, P. A. (1996). Temperamental and familial predictors of violent and non-violent criminal convictions: Age 3 to age 18. *Developmental Psychology, 32,* 614–623.

Henry, B., Moffitt, T., Robins, L., Earls, F., & Silva, P. (1993). Early family predictors of child and adolescent antisocial behavior: Who are the mothers of delinquents? *Criminal Behaviour and Mental Health, 2,* 97–118.

Herrenkohl, T. I., Hawkins, J. D., Chung, I.-J., Hill, K. G., & Battin-Pearson, S. (2001). School and community risk factors and interventions. In R. Loeber & D. P. Farrington (Eds.), *Child delinquents: Development, intervention and service needs* (pp. 211–246). Thousand Oaks, CA: Sage.

Herrenkohl, T. I., Maguin, E., Hill, K. G., Hawkins, J. D., Abbott, R. D., & Catalano, R. F. (2000). Developmental risk factors for youth violence. *Journal of Adolescent Health, 26,* 176–186.

Hill, J., & Maughan, B. (Eds.). (2001). *Conduct disorders in childhood and adolescence.* Cambridge: Cambridge University Press.

Hinshaw, S. P., Lahey, B. B., & Hart, E. L. (1993). Issues of taxonomy and comorbidity in the development of conduct disorder. *Development and Psychopathology, 5,* 31–49.

Hogh, E., & Wolf, P. (1983). Violent crime in a birth cohort: Copenhagen 1953–1977. In K. T. van Dusen & S. A. Mednick (Eds.), *Prospective studies of crime and delinquency* (pp. 249–267). Boston: Kluwer-Nijhoff.

Howell, J. C. (Ed.). (1995). *Guide for implementing the comprehensive strategy for serious, violent, and chronic juvenile offenders.* Washington, DC: U.S. Office of Juvenile Justice and Delinquency Prevention.

Huesmann, L. R., & Eron, L. D. (1989). Individual differences and the trait of aggression. *European Journal of Personality, 3,* 95–106.

Huesmann, L. R., Eron, L. D., Lefkowitz, M. M., & Walder, L. O. (1984). Stability of aggression over time and generations. *Developmental Psychology, 20,* 1120–1134.

Huizinga, D., & Elliott, D. S. (1986). Reassessing the reliability and validity of self-report measures. *Journal of Quantitative Criminology, 2,* 293–327.

Huizinga, D., & Jakob-Chien, C. (1998). The contemporaneous co-occurrence of serious and violent juvenile offending and other problem behaviors. In R. Loeber & D. P. Farrington (Eds.), *Serious and violent juvenile offenders: Risk factors and successful interventions* (pp. 47–67). Thousand Oaks, CA: Sage.

Huizinga, D., Loeber, R., & Thornberry, T. P. (1993). Longitudinal study of delinquency, drug use, sexual activity and pregnancy among children and youth in three cities. *Public Health Reports, 108,* 90–96.

Jenkins, J. M., & Smith, M. A. (1991). Marital disharmony and children's behavior problems: Aspects of a poor marriage that affect children adversely. *Journal of Child Psychology and Psychiatry, 32,* 793–810.

John, O. P., Caspi, A., Robins, R. W., Moffitt, T. E., & Stuthamer-Loeber, M. (1994). The "Little Five": Exploring the nomological network of the Five-Factor Model of personality in adolescent boys. *Child Development, 65,* 160–178.

Johnson, J. G., Cohen, P., Kasen, S., & Brook, J. S. (2006). A multiwave multi-informant study of the specificity of the association between parental and offspring psychiatric disorders. *Comprehensive Psychiatry, 47,* 169–177.

Jolliffe, D., & Farrington, D. P. (2004). Empathy and offending: A systematic review and meta-analysis. *Aggression and Violent Behavior, 9,* 441–476.

Jolliffe, D., & Farrington, D. P. (2006a). Development and validation of the Basic Empathy Scale. *Journal of Adolescence, 29,* 589–611.

Jolliffe, D., & Farrington, D. P. (2006b). Examining the relationship between low empathy and bullying. *Aggressive Behavior, 32,* 540–550.

Jolliffe, D., & Farrington, D. P. (2007). Examining the relationship between low empathy and self-reported offending. *Legal and Criminological Psychology, 12,* 265–286.

Jolliffe, D., & Farrington, D. P. (2008). *The influence of mentoring on reoffending.* Stockholm, Sweden: National Council for Crime Prevention.

Jolliffe, D., & Farrington, D. P. (in press). A systematic review of the relationship between childhood impulsiveness and later violence. In M. McMurran & R. Howard (Eds.), *Personality, personality disorder, and risk of violence.* Chichester, UK: John Wiley & Sons.

Jolliffe, D., Farrington, D. P., Hawkins, J. D., Catalano, R. F., Hill, K. G., & Kosterman, R. (2003). Predictive, concurrent, prospective, and retrospective validity of self-reported delinquency. *Criminal Behaviour and Mental Health, 13,* 179–197.

Jones, M. B., & Offord, D. R. (1989). Reduction of antisocial behavior in poor children by non-school skill-development. *Journal of Child Psychology and Psychiatry, 30,* 737–750.

Juby, H., & Farrington, D. P. (2001). Disentangling the link between disrupted families and delinquency. *British Journal of Criminology, 41,* 22–40.

Junger-Tas, J., & Marshall, I. H. (1999). The self-report methodology in crime research. In M. Tonry (Ed.), *Crime and justice,* vol. 25 (pp. 291–367). Chicago: University of Chicago Press.

Kagan, J. (1989). Temperamental contributions to social behavior. *American Psychologist, 44,* 668–674.

Kasen, S., Johnson, J., & Cohen, P. (1990). The impact of school emotional climate on student psychopathology. *Journal of Abnormal Child Psychology, 18,* 165–177.

Kasius, M. C., Ferdinand, R. F., van den Berg, H.& Verhulst, F. C. (1997). Associations between different diagnostic approaches for child and adolescent psychopathology. *Journal of Child Psychology and Psychiatry, 38,* 625–632.

Kaukiainen, A., Bjorkvist, K., Lagerspetz, K., Osterman, K., Salmivalli, C., Rothberg, S., et al. (1999). The relationships between social intelligence, empathy, and three types of aggression. *Aggressive Behavior, 25,* 81–89.

Kazdin, A. E. (1997). Parent management training: Evidence, outcomes and issues. *Journal of the American Academy of Child and Adolescent Psychiatry, 36,* 1349–1356.

Keiley, M. L., Howe, T. R., Dodge, K. A., Bates, J. E., & Pettit, G. S. (2001). The timing of child physical maltreatment: A cross-domain growth analysis of impact on adolescent externalizing and internalizing problems. *Development and Psychopathology, 13,* 891–912.

Kirk, D. S. (2006). Examining the divergence across self-report and official data sources on inferences about the adolescent life-course of crime. *Journal of Quantitative Criminology, 22.* 107–129.

Klinteberg, B. A., Andersson, T., Magnusson, D., & Stattin, H. (1993). Hyperactive behavior in childhood as related to subsequent alcohol problems and violent offending: A longitudinal study of male subjects. *Personality and Individual Differences, 15,* 381–388.

Kokkinos, C. M., & Panayiotou, G. (2004). Predicting bullying and victimization among early adolescents: Associations with disruptive behavior disorders. *Aggressive Behavior, 30,* 520–533.

Kokko, K., & Pulkkinen, L. (2005). Stability of aggressive behavior from childhood to middle age in women and men. *Aggressive Behavior, 31,* 485–497.

Kolvin, I., Miller, F. J. W., Fleeting, M., & Kolvin, P. A. (1988). Social and parenting factors affecting criminal-offence rates: Findings from the Newcastle Thousand Family Study (1947–1980). *British Journal of Psychiatry, 152,* 80–90.

Koolhof, R., Loeber, R., Wei, E. H., Pardini, D., & D'Escury, A. C. (2007). Inhibition deficits of serious delinquent boys of low intelligence. *Criminal Behaviour and Mental Health, 17,* 274–292.

Lahey, B. B., van Hulle, C. A., Waldman, I. D., Rodgers, J. L., D'Onofrio, B. M., Pedlow, S.,et al. (2006). Testing descriptive hypotheses regarding sex differences in the development of conduct problems and delinquency. *Journal of Abnormal Child Psychology, 34,* 737–755.

Lahey, B. B., Loeber, R., Burke, J. D., & Applegate, B. (2005). Predicting future antisocial personality disorder in males from a clinical assessment in childhood. *Journal of Consulting and Clinical Psychology, 73,* 389–399.

Lahey, B. B., Loeber, R., Hart, E. L., Frick, P. J., Applegate, B., Zhang, Q.,et al. (1995). Four-year longitudinal study of conduct disorder in boys: Patterns and predictors of persistence. *Journal of Abnormal Psychology, 104,* 83–93.

Lahey, B. B., Loeber, R., Stouthamer-Loeber, M., Christ, M. A. G., Green, S., Russo, M. F., et al. (1990). Comparison of DSM-3

and DSM-3R diagnoses for prepubertal children: Changes in prevalence and validity. *Journal of the American Academy of Child and Adolescent Psychiatry, 29,* 620–626.

Lahey, B. B., Moffitt, T. E., & Caspi, A. (Eds.) (2003). *Causes of conduct disorder and juvenile delinquency.* New York: Guilford Press.

Lahey, B. B., Schwab-Stone, M., Goodman, S. H., Waldman, I. D., Canino, G., Rathouz, P. J.,et al. (2000). Age and gender differences in oppositional behavior and conduct problems: A cross-sectional household study of middle childhood and adolescence. *Journal of Abnormal Psychology, 109,* 488–503.

Larzelere, R. E., & Patterson, G. R. (1990). Parental management: Mediator of the effect of socioeconomic status on early delinquency. *Criminology, 28,* 301–324.

LeBlanc, M., & Frechette, M. (1989). *Male criminal activity from childhood through youth.* New York: Springer-Verlag.

Lee, K-H., Baillargon, R. H., Vermunt, J. K., Wu, H-X., & Tremblay, R. E. (2007). Age differences in the prevalence of physical aggression among 5–11 year old Canadian boys and girls. *Aggressive Behavior, 33,* 26–37.

van Lier, P. A. C., van der Ende, J., Koot, H. M., & Verhulst, F. C. (2007). Which better predicts conduct problems? The relationship of trajectories of conduct problems with ODD and ADHD symptoms from childhood into adolescence. *Journal of Child Psychology and Psychiatry, 48,* 601–608.

Lipsey, M. W., & Derzon, J. H. (1998). Predictors of violent or serious delinquency in adolescence and early adulthood: A synthesis of longitudinal research. In R. Loeber & D. P. Farrington (Eds.), *Serious and violent juvenile offenders: Risk factors and successful interventions* (pp. 86–105). Thousand Oaks, CA: Sage.

Lipsey, M. W., & Wilson, D. B. (1998). Effective intervention for serious juvenile offenders: A synthesis of research. In R. Loeber & D. P. Farrington (Eds.), *Serious and violent juvenile offenders: Risk factors and successful interventions* (pp. 313–345). Thousand Oaks, CA: Sage.

Lipsitt, P. D., Buka, S. L., & Lipsitt, L. P. (1990). Early intelligence scores and subsequent delinquency: A prospective study. *American Journal of Family Therapy, 18,* 197–208.

Littell, J. H. (2005). Lessons from a systematic review of effects of multisystemic therapy. *Children and Youth Services Review, 27,* 445–463.

Loeber, R., Burke, J. D., Lahey, B. B., Winters, A., & Zera, M. (2000). Oppositional defiant and conduct disorder: A review of the past 10 years, part 1. *Journal of the American Academy of Child and Adolescent Psychiatry, 39,* 1468–1484.

Loeber, R., & Farrington, D. P. (Eds.). (2001). *Child delinquents: Development, intervention, and service needs.* Thousand Oaks, CA: Sage.

Loeber, R., Farrington, D. P., Stouthamer-Loeber, M., & van Kammen, W. B. (1998). *Antisocial behavior and mental health problems: Explanatory factors in childhood and adolescence.* Mahwah, NJ: Lawrence Erlbaum.

Loeber, R., Farrington, D. P., Stouthamer-Loeber, M., Moffitt, T. E., Caspi, A., & Lynam, D. (2001). Male mental health problems, psychopathy, and personality traits: Key findings from the first 14 years of the Pittsburgh Youth Study. *Clinical Child and Family Psychology Review, 4,* 273–297.

Loeber, R., Farrington, D. P., Stouthamer-Loeber, M., & White, H. R. (2008). *Violence and serious theft: Development and prediction from childhood to adulthood.* New York: Routledge.

Loeber, R., Green, S. M., Keenan, K., & Lahey, B. B. (1995). Which boys will fare worse? Early predictors of the onset of conduct disorder in a six-year longitudinal study. *Journal of the American Academy of Child and Adolescent Psychiatry, 34,* 499–509.

Loeber, R., & Hay, D. F. (1997). Key issues in the development of aggression and violence from childhood to early adulthood. *Annual Review of Psychology, 48,* 371–410.

Loeber, R., & LeBlanc, M. (1990). Toward a developmental criminology. In M. Tonry & N. Morris (Eds.), *Crime and justice,* vol. 12 (pp. 375–473). Chicago: University of Chicago Press.

Loeber, R., Pardini, D., Homish, D. L., Wei, E. H., Crawford, A. M., Farrington, D. P., et al. (2005). The prediction of violence and homicide in young men. *Journal of Consulting and Clinical Psychology, 73,* 1074–1088.

Loeber, R., & Stouthamer-Loeber, M. (1998). Development of juvenile aggression and violence: Some common misconceptions and controversies. *American Psychologist, 53,* 242–259.

Loeber, R., Stouthamer-Loeber, M., van Kammen, W. B., & Farrington, D. P. (1991). Initiation, escalation and desistance in juvenile offending and their correlates. *Journal of Criminal Law and Criminology, 82,* 36–82.

Loeber, R., Wei, E., Stouthamer-Loeber, M., Huizinga, D., & Thornberry, T. (1999). Behavioral antecedents to serious and violent offending: Joint analyses from the Denver Youth Survey, Pittsburgh Youth Study, and the Rochester Youth Development Study. *Studies on Crime and Crime Prevention, 8,* 245–263.

Loeber, R., Wung, P., Keenan, K., Giroux, B., Stouthamer-Loeber, M., & van Kammen, W. B. (1993). Developmental pathways in disruptive child behavior. *Development and Psychopathology, 5,* 101–132.

Lösel, F., & Beelmann, A. (2006). Child social skills training. In B. C. Welsh & D. P. Farrington (Eds.), *Preventing crime: What works for children, offenders, victims, and places* (pp. 33–54). New York: Springer.

Lösel, F., & Bliesener, T. (2003). Hooligan violence: A study on its prevalence, origins, and prevention. In F. Dunkel & K. Drenkhahn (Eds.), *Youth violence: New patterns and local responses—Experiences in East and West.* Monchengladbach, Germany: Forum Verlag Godesberg.

Lösel, F., Bliesener, T., & Bender, D. (2007). Social information processing, experiences of aggression in social contexts, and aggressive behavior in adolescents. *Criminal Justice and Behavior, 34,* 330–347.

Luengo, M. A., Otero, J. M., Carrillo-de-la-Pena, M. T., & Miron, L. (1994). Dimensions of antisocial behavior in juvenile delinquency: A study of personality variables. *Psychology, Crime and Law, 1,* 27–37.

Lynam, D. (1996). Early identification of chronic offenders: Who is the fledgling psychopath? *Psychological Bulletin, 120,* 209–234.

Lynam, D. R. (1998). Early identification of the fledgling psychopath: Locating the psychopathic child in the current nomenclature. *Journal of Abnormal Psychology, 107,* 566–575.

Lynam, D. R., Caspi, A., Moffitt, T. E., Wikström, P.-O. H., Loeber, R., & Novak, S. (2000). The interaction between impulsivity and neighborhood context on offending: The effects of impulsivity are stronger in poorer neighborhoods. *Journal of Abnormal Psychology, 109,* 563–574.

Lynam, D., Moffitt, T. E., & Stouthamer-Loeber, M. (1993). Explaining the relation between IQ and delinquency: Class, race, test motivation, school failure or self-control? *Journal of Abnormal Psychology, 102,* 187–196.

McCord, J. (1977). A comparative study of two generations of native Americans. In R. F. Meier (Ed.), *Theory in criminology* (pp. 83–92). Beverly Hills, CA: Sage.

McCord, J. (1979). Some child-rearing antecedents of criminal behavior in adult men. *Journal of Personality and Social Psychology, 37,* 1477–1486.

McCord, J. (1982). A longitudinal view of the relationship between paternal absence and crime. In J. Gunn & D. P. Farrington (Eds.), *Abnormal offenders, delinquency, and the criminal justice system* (pp. 113–128). Chichester, UK: John Wiley & Sons.

McCrae, R. R., & Costa, P. T. (2003). *Personality in adulthood: A five-factor theory perspective.* New York: Guilford Press.

Maguin, E., & Loeber, R. (1996). Academic performance and delinquency. In M. Tonry (Ed.), *Crime and justice,* vol. 20 (pp. 145–264). Chicago: University of Chicago Press.

Mak, A. S. (1991). Psychosocial control characteristics of delinquents and non-delinquents. *Criminal Justice and Behavior, 18,* 287–303.

Malinosky-Rummell, R., & Hansen, D. J. (1993). Long-term consequences of childhood physical abuse. *Psychological Bulletin, 114,* 68–79.

Mandel, H. P. (1997). *Conduct disorder and underachievement.* New York: John Wiley & Sons.

Maughan, B., Pickles, A., Rowe, R., Costello, E. J., & Angold, A. (2000). Developmental trajectories of aggressive and nonaggressive conduct problems. *Journal of Quantitative Criminology, 16,* 199–221.

Maughan, B., Rowe, R., Messer, J., Goodman, R., & Meltzer, H. (2004). Conduct disorder and oppositional defiant disorder in a national sample: Developmental epidemiology. *Journal of Child Psychology and Psychiatry, 45,* 609–621.

Maxfield, M. G., & Widom, C. S. (1996). The cycle of violence revisited six years later. *Archives of Pediatrics and Adolescent Medicine, 150,* 390–395.

Moffitt, T. E. (1993a). Adolescence-limited and life-course-persistent antisocial behavior: A developmental taxonomy. *Psychological Review, 100,* 674–701.

Moffitt, T. E. (1993b). The neuropsychology of conduct disorder. *Development and Psychopathology, 5,* 135–151.

Moffitt, T. E. (2003). Life-course-persistent and adolescence-limited antisocial behavior: A 10-year research review and a research agenda. In B. B. Lahey, T. E. Moffitt, & A. Caspi (Eds.), *Causes of conduct disorder and juvenile delinquency* (pp. 49–75). New York: Guilford Press.

Moffitt, T. E., Arseneault, L., Jaffee, S. R., Kim-Cohen, J., Koenen, K. C., Odgers, C. L., et al. (2008). DSM-V conduct disorder: Research needs for an evidence base. *Journal of Child Psychology and Psychiatry, 49,* 3–33.

Moffitt, T. E., Caspi, A., Dickson, N., Silva, P., & Stanton, W. (1996). Childhood-onset versus adolescent-onset antisocial conduct problems in males: Natural history from ages 3 to 18 years. *Development and Psychopathology, 8,* 399–424.

Moffitt, T. E., Caspi, A., Rutter, M., & Silva, P. A. (2001). *Sex differences in antisocial behavior.* Cambridge: Cambridge University Press.

Moffitt, T. E., & Henry, B. (1991). Neuropsychological studies of juvenile delinquency and juvenile violence. In J. S. Milner (Ed.), *Neuropsychology of aggression* (pp. 131–146). Boston: Kluwer.

Morash, M., & Rucker, L. (1989). An exploratory study of the connection of mother's age at childbearing to her children's delinquency in four data sets. *Crime and Delinquency, 35,* 45–93.

Moretti, M. M., Odgers, C. L., & Jackson, M. A. (Eds.). (2004). *Girls and aggression: Contributing factors and intervention principles.* New York: Kluwer/Plenum Press.

Morgan, A. B., & Lilienfeld, S. O. (2000). A meta-analytic review of the relation between antisocial behavior and neuropsychological measures of executive function. *Clinical Psychology Review, 20,* 113–136.

Murray, J., & Farrington, D. P. (2005). Parental imprisonment: Effects on boys' antisocial behavior and delinquency through the life-course. *Journal of Child Psychology and Psychiatry, 46,* 1269–1278.

Murray, J., Janson, C-G., & Farrington, D. P. (2007). Crime in adult offspring of prisoners: A cross-national comparison of two longitudinal samples. *Criminal Justice and Behavior, 34,* 133–149.

Nagin, D. S., Farrington, D. P., & Moffitt, T. E. (1995). Life-course trajectories of different types of offenders. *Criminology, 33,* 111–139.

Nagin, D. S., Pogarsky, G., & Farrington, D. P. (1997). Adolescent mothers and the criminal behavior of their children. *Law and Society Review, 31,* 137–162.

Nagin, D. S., & Tremblay, R. E. (1999). Trajectories of boys' physical aggression, opposition, and hyperactivity on the path to physically violent and nonviolent juvenile delinquency. *Child Development, 70,* 1181–1196.

Nelson, S. E., & Dishion, T. J. (2004). From boys to men: Predicting adult adaptation from middle childhood sociometric status. *Development and Psychopathology, 16,* 441–459.

Newson, J., Newson, E., & Adams, M. (1993). The social origins of delinquency. *Criminal Behaviour and Mental Health, 3,* 19–29.

Nottelmann, E. D., & Jensen, P. S. (1995). Comorbidity of disorders in children and adolescents: Developmental perspectives. In T. H. Ollendick & R. J. Prinz (Eds.), *Advances in clinical child psychology,* vol. 17 (pp. 109–155). New York: Plenum Press.

Odgers, C. L., Milne, B. J., Caspi, A., Crump, R., Poulton, R., & Moffitt, T. E. (2007). Predicting prognosis for the conduct-problem boy: Can family history help?*Journal of the American Academy of Child and Adolescent Psychiatry, 46,* 1240–1249.

Offord, D. R., Alder, R. J., & Boyle, M. H. (1986). Prevalence and sociodemographic correlates of conduct disorder. *American Journal of Social Psychiatry, 6,* 272–278.

Offord, D. R., Boyle, M. H., & Racine, Y. (1989). Ontario Child Health Study: Correlates of disorder. *Journal of the American Academy of Child and Adolescent Psychiatry, 28,* 856–860.

Offord, D. R., Boyle, M. H., Racine, Y. A., Fleming, J. E., Cadman, D. T., Blum, H. M., et al. (1992). Outcome, prognosis and risk in a longitudinal follow-up study. *Journal of the American Academy of Child and Adolescent Psychiatry, 31,* 916–923.

Offord, D. R., Boyle, M. H., Szatmari, P., Rae-Grant, N. I., Links, P. S., Cadman, D. T., et al. (1987). Ontario Child Health Study. II. Six-month prevalence of disorder and rates of service utilization. *Archives of General Psychiatry, 44,* 832–836.

Olds, D. L., Eckenrode, J., Henderson, C. R., Kitzman, H., Powers, J., Cole, R., et al. (1997). Long-term effects of home visitation on maternal life course and child abuse and neglect. *Journal of the American Medical Association, 278,* 637–643.

Olds, D. L., Henderson, C. R., Cole, R., Eckenrode, J., Kitzman, H., Luckey, D., (1998). Long-term effects of nurse home visitation on children's criminal and antisocial behavior: 15-year follow-up of a randomized controlled trial. *Journal of the American Medical Association, 280,* 1238–1244.

Olds, D. L., Henderson, C. R., Chamberlain, R., & Tatelbaum, R. (1986). Preventing child abuse and neglect: A randomized trial of nurse home visitation. *Pediatrics, 78,* 65–78.

Olds, D. L., Sadler, L., & Kitzman, H. (2007). Programs for parents of infants and toddlers: Recent evidence from randomized trials. *Journal of Child Psychology and Psychiatry, 48,* 355–391.

Olweus, D. (1979). Stability of aggressive reaction patterns in males: A review. *Psychological Bulletin, 86,* 852–875.

Olweus, D. (1991). Bully/victim problems among school children: Basic facts and effects of a school based intervention program. In D. J. Pepler & K. H. Rubin (Eds.), *The development and treatment of childhood aggression* (pp. 411–448). Hillsdale, NJ: Lawrence Erlbaum.

Olweus, D. (1994). Bullying at school: Basic facts and effects of a school based intervention program. *Journal of Child Psychology and Psychiatry, 35,* 1171–1190.

O'Moore, A. M., & Hillery, B. (1989). Bullying in Dublin schools. *Irish Journal of Psychology, 10,* 426–441.

Pakiz, B., Reinherz, H. Z., & Frost, A. K. (1992). Antisocial behavior in adolescence: A community study. *Journal of Early Adolescence, 12,* 300–313.

Patterson, G. R. (1982). *Coercive family process.* Eugene, OR: Castalia.

Patterson, G. R., Capaldi, D., & Bank, L. (1991). An early starter model for predicting delinquency. In D. J. Pepler & K. H. Rubin (Eds.), *The development and treatment of childhood aggression* (pp. 139–168). Hillsdale, NJ: Lawrence Erlbaum.

Patterson, G. R., Chamberlain, P., & Reid, J. B. (1982). A comparative evaluation of a parent training program. *Behavior Therapy, 13,* 638–650.

Patterson, G. R., Reid, J. B., & Dishion, T. J. (1992). *Antisocial boys.* Eugene, OR: Castalia.

Pearson, J. L., Ialongo, N. S., Hunter, A. H., & Kellam, S. G. (1994). Family structure and aggressive behavior in a population of urban elementary school children. *Journal of the American Academy of Child and Adolescent Psychiatry, 33,* 540–548.

Pepler, D. J., & Craig, W. M. (1995). A peek behind the fence: Naturalistic observations of aggressive children with remote audiovisual recording. *Developmental Psychology, 31,* 548–553.

Pepler, D. J., Madsen, K. C., Webster, C., & Levene, K. S. (Eds.) (2005). *The development and treatment of girlhood aggression.* Mahwah, NJ: Lawrence Erlbaum.

Petras, H., Kellam, S. G., Brown, C. H., Múthen, B. O., Ialongo, N. S., & Poduska, J. M. (2008). Developmental epidemiological courses leading to antisocial personality disorder and violent and criminal behavior: Effects by young adulthood of a universal preventive intervention in first and second grade classrooms. *Drug and Alcohol Dependence, 95S,* S45–S59.

Piquero, A. R. (2000). Frequency, specialization, and violence in offending careers. *Journal of Research in Crime and Delinquency, 37,* 392–418.

Piquero, A. R. (2008). Taking stock of developmental trajectories of criminal activity over the life course. In A. M. Liberman (Ed.), *The long view of crime: A synthesis of longitudinal research* (pp. 23–78). New York: Springer.

Piquero, A. R., Farrington, D. P., & Blumstein, A. (2007). *Key issues in criminal career research: New analyses of the Cambridge Study in Delinquent Development.* Cambridge: Cambridge University Press.

Piquero, A. R., Farrington, D. P., Welsh, B. C., Tremblay, R. E., & Jennings, W. (2008). *Effects of early family/parent training programs on antisocial behavior and delinquency: A systematic review.* Stockholm, Sweden: National Council for Crime Prevention.

Piquero, A. R., & Moffitt, T. E. (2005). Explaining the facts of crime: How the developmental taxonomy replies to Farrington's invitation. In D. P. Farrington (Ed.), *Integrated developmental and life-course theories of offending* (pp. 51–72). New Brunswick, NJ: Transaction.

Pratt, T. C., Cullen, F. T., Blevins, K. R., Daigle, L., & Unnever, J. D. (2002). The relationship of attention deficit hyperactivity disorder to crime and delinquency: A meta-analysis. *International Journal of Police Science and Management, 4,* 344–360.

Prime, J., White, S., Liriano, S., & Patel, K. (2001). *Criminal careers of those born between 1953 and 1978.* London: Home Office (Statistical Bulletin 4/01).

Pulkkinen, L. (1987). Offensive and defensive aggression in humans: A longitudinal perspective. *Aggressive Behavior, 13,* 197–212.

Raine, A. (1993). *The psychopathology of crime.* San Diego, CA: Academic Press.

Raine, A., Dodge, K., Loeber, R., Gatzke-Kopp, L., Lynam, D., Reynolds, C., et al. (2006). The Reactive-Proactive Aggression Questionnaire: Differential correlates of reactive and proactive aggression in adolescent boys. *Aggressive Behavior, 32,* 159–171.

Raine, A., Moffitt, T. E., Caspi, A., Loeber, R., Stouthamer-Loeber, M., & Lynam, D. (2005). Neurocognitive impairments in boys on the life-course-persistent antisocial path. *Journal of Abnormal Psychology, 114,* 38–49.

Reiss, A. J. (1986). Why are communities important in understanding crime? In A. J. Reiss & M. Tonry (Eds.), *Communities and crime* (pp. 1–33). Chicago: University of Chicago Press.

Reiss, A. J., & Farrington, D. P. (1991). Advancing knowledge about co-offending: Results from a prospective longitudinal survey of London males. *Journal of Criminal Law and Criminology, 82,* 360–395.

Reynolds, A. J., Temple, J. A., Robertson, D. L., & Mann, E. A. (2001). Long-term effects of an early childhood intervention on educational achievement and juvenile arrest: A 15-year follow-up of low-income children in public schools. *Journal of the American Medical Association, 285,* 2339–2346.

Robins, L. N. (1979). Sturdy childhood predictors of adult outcomes: Replications from longitudinal studies. In J. E. Barrett, R. M. Rose, & G. L. Klerman (Eds.) *Stress and mental disorder* (pp. 219–235). New York: Raven Press.

Robins, L. N. (1989). Epidemiology of antisocial personality. In J. O. Cavenar (Ed.), *Psychiatry*, vol. 3 (pp. 1–14). Philadelphia: Lippincott.

Robins, L. N. (1999). A 70-year history of conduct disorder: Variations in definition, prevalence and correlates. In P. Cohen, C. Slomkowski, & L. N. Robins (Eds.), *Historical and geographical influences on psychopathology* (pp. 37–56). Mahwah, NJ: Lawrence Erlbaum.

Robins, L. N., West, P. J., & Herjanic, B. L. (1975). Arrests and delinquency in two generations: A study of Black urban families and their children. *Journal of Child Psychology and Psychiatry, 16*, 125–140.

Rogeness, G. A. (1994). Biologic findings in conduct disorder. *Child and Adolescent Psychiatric Clinics of North America, 3*, 271–284.

Romano, E., Tremblay, R E., Vitaro, F., Zoccolillo, M., & Pagani, L. (2001). Prevalence of psychiatric diagnoses and the role of perceived impairment: Findings from an adolescent community sample. *Journal of Child Psychology and Psychiatry, 42*, 451–461.

Ross, R. R., & Ross, R. D. (Eds.). (1995). *Thinking straight: The reasoning and rehabilitation program for delinquency prevention and offender rehabilitation*. Ottawa, Canada: Air Training and Publications.

Rothbaum, F., & Weisz, J. R. (1994). Parental caregiving and child externalizing behavior in nonclinical samples: A meta-analysis. *Psychological Bulletin, 116*, 55–74.

Rowe, D. C., Vaszonyi, A. T., & Flannery, D. J. (1995). Sex differences in crime: Do means and within-sex variation have similar causes? *Journal of Research in Crime and Delinquency, 32*, 84–100.

Rutter, M. (1981). The city and the child. *American Journal of Orthopsychiatry, 51*, 610–625.

Rutter, M., Giller, H., & Hagell, A. (1998). *Antisocial behavior in young people*. Cambridge: Cambridge University Press.

Sampson, R. J., Morenoff, J. D., & Raudenbush, S. (2005). Social anatomy of racial and ethnic disparities in violence. *American Journal of Public Health, 95*, 224–232.

Sampson, R. J., Raudenbush, S. W., & Earls, F. (1997). Neighborhoods and violent crime: A multilevel study of collective efficacy. *Science, 277*, 918–924.

Sanders, M. R., Markie-Dadds, C., Tully, L. A., & Bor, W. (2000). The Triple-P Positive Parenting Program: A comparison of enhanced, standard and self-directed behavioral family intervention for parents of children with early onset conduct problems. *Journal of Consulting and Clinical Psychology, 68*, 624–640.

Schwartz, C. E., Snidman, N., & Kagan, J. (1996). Early childhood temperament as a determinant of externalizing behavior in adolescence. *Development and Psychopathology, 8*, 527–537.

Schweinhart, L. J., Barnes, H. V., & Weikart, D. P. (1993). *Significant benefits*. Ypsilanti, MI: High/Scope.

Schweinhart, L. J., Montie, J., Zongping, X., Barnett, W. S., Belfield, C. R., & Nores, M. (2005). *Lifetime effects: The High/Scope Perry Preschool Study through age 40*. Ypsilanti, MI: High/Scope Press.

Schweinhart, L. J., & Weikart, D. P. (1980). *Young children grow up*. Ypsilanti, MI: High/Scope.

Seguin, J., Pihl, R. O., Harden, P. W., Tremblay, R. E., & Boulerice, B. (1995). Cognitive and neuropsychological characteristics of physically aggressive boys. *Journal of Abnormal Psychology, 104*, 614–624.

Sexton, T. L., & Alexander, J. F. (2000). *Functional family therapy*. Washington, DC: U.S. Office of Juvenile Justice and Delinquency Prevention.

Shaffer, D., Fisher, P., Dulcan, M. K., Davies, M., Piacentini, J., Schwab-Stone, M. E., et al. (1996). The NIMH Diagnostic Interview Schedule for Children, version 2.3 (DISC-2.3): Description, acceptability, prevalence rates and performance in the MECA Study. *Journal of the American Academy of Child and Adolescent Psychiatry, 35*, 865–877.

Shaw, C. R., & McKay, H. D. (1969). *Juvenile delinquency and urban areas* (rev. ed.). Chicago: University of Chicago Press.

Shaw, D. S., Lacourse, E., & Nagin, D. S. (2005). Developmental trajectories of conduct problems and hyperactivity from ages 2 to 10. *Journal of Child Psychology and Psychiatry, 46*, 931–942.

Sheehan, M. J., & Watson, M. W. (2008). Reciprocal influences between maternal discipline techniques and aggression in children and adolescents. *Aggressive Behavior, 34*, 245–255.

Smith, C. A., & Stern, S. B. (1997). Delinquency and antisocial behavior: A review of family processes and intervention research. *Social Service Review, 71*, 382–420.

Smith, C. A., & Thornberry, T. P. (1995). The relationship between childhood maltreatment and adolescent involvement in delinquency. *Criminology, 33*, 451–481.

Smith, P. K., Morita, J., Junger-Tas, D., Olweus, D., Catalano, R., & Slee, P. T. (Eds.). (1999). *The nature of school bullying: A cross-national perspective*. London: Routledge.

Smith, P. K., Pepler, D., & Rigby, K. (2004). *Bullying in schools: How successful can interventions be?* Cambridge: Cambridge University Press.

Smith, P. K., & Sharp, S. (1994). *School bullying: Insights and perspectives*. London: Routledge.

Solberg, M., & Olweus, D. (2003). Prevalence estimation of school bullying with the Olweus Bully/Victim Questionnaire. *Aggressive Behavior, 29*, 239–268.

Stams, G. J., Brugman, D., Dekovic, M., van Rosmalen, L., van der Laan, P., & Gibbs, J. C. (2006). The moral judgment of juvenile delinquents: A meta-analysis. *Journal of Abnormal Child Psychology, 34*, 697–713.

Stattin, H., & Klackenberg-Larsson, I. (1993). Early language and intelligence development and their relationship to future criminal behavior. *Journal of Abnormal Psychology, 102*, 369–378.

Stattin, H., & Magnusson, D. (1991). Stability and change in criminal behavior up to age 30. *British Journal of Criminology, 31*, 327–346.

Steinberg, L., Lamborn, S. D., Dornbusch, S. M., & Darling, N. (1992). Impact of parenting practices on adolescent achievement: Authoritative parenting, school involvement and encouragement to succeed. *Child Development, 63*, 1266–1281.

Stephenson, P., & Smith, D. (1989). Bullying in the junior school. In D. Tattum & D. Lane (Eds.), *Bullying in schools*. Stoke-on-Trent, England: Trentham.

Sutton, J., Smith, P. K., & Swettenham, J. (1999). Social cognition and bullying: Social inadequacy or skilled manipulation? *British Journal of Developmental Psychology, 17*, 435–450.

Szatmari, P., Boyle, M. H., & Offord, D. R. (1993). Familial aggregation of emotional and behavioral problems of childhood in the general population. *American Journal of Psychiatry, 150*, 1398–1403.

Thornberry, T. P., Huizinga, D., & Loeber, R. (1995). The prevention of serious delinquency and violence: Implications from the program of research on the causes and correlates of delinquency. In J. C. Howell, B. Krisberg, J. D. Hawkins, & J. J. Wilson (Eds.), *Sourcebook on serious, violent and chronic juvenile offenders* (pp. 213–237). Thousand Oaks, CA: Sage.

Thornberry, T. P., & Krohn, M. D. (Eds.). (2003). *Taking stock of delinquency: An overview of findings from contemporary longitudinal studies*. New York: Kluwer/Plenum Press.

Thornberry, T. P., Krohn, M. D., Lizotte, A. J., Smith, C. A., & Tobin, K. (2003). *Gangs and delinquency in developmental perspective*. New York: Cambridge University Press.

Thornberry, T. P., Lizotte, A. J., Krohn, M. D., Farnworth, M., & Jang, S. J. (1994). Delinquent peers, beliefs and delinquent behavior: A longitudinal test of interactional theory. *Criminology, 32*, 47–83.

Tobler, N. S., Lessard, T., Marshall, D., Ochshorn, P., & Roona, M. (1999). Effectiveness of school-based drug prevention programs for marijuana use. *School Psychology International, 20*, 105–137.

Tolan, P. H., & Gorman-Smith, D. (1998). Development of serious and violent offending careers. In R. Loeber & D. P. Farrington (Eds.), *Serious and violent juvenile offenders: Risk factors and successful interventions* (pp. 68–85). Thousand Oaks, CA: Sage.

Tolan, P. H., Gorman-Smith, D., & Henry, D. B. (2003). The developmental ecology of urban males' youth violence. *Developmental Psychology, 39,* 274–291.

Tolan, P. H., Gorman-Smith, D., & Loeber, R. (2000). Developmental timing of onsets of disruptive behaviors and later delinquency of inner-city youth. *Journal of Child and Family Studies, 9,* 203–230.

Tong, L. S. J., & Farrington, D. P. (2008). Effectiveness of "Reasoning and Rehabilitation" in reducing offending. *Psicothema, 20,* 20–28.

Tracy, P. E., Wolfgang, M. E., & Figlio, R. M. (1985). *Delinquency in two birth cohorts.* Washington, DC: U.S. Office of Juvenile Justice and Delinquency Prevention.

Tremblay, R. E. (2000). The development of aggressive behavior during childhood: What have we learned in the past century? *International Journal of Behavioral Development, 24,* 129–141.

Tremblay, R. E. (2008). Understanding development and prevention of chronic physical aggression: Towards experimental epigenetic studies. *Philosophical Transactions of the Royal Society, B, 363,* 2613–2622.

Tremblay, R. E., Japel, C., Perusse, D., McDuff, P., Boivin, M., Zoccolillo, M., et al. (1999). The search for the age of onset of physical aggression: Rousseau and Bandura revisited. *Criminal Behavior and Mental Health, 9,* 8–23.

Tremblay, R. E., Pagani-Kurtz, L., Vitaro, F., Masse, L. C., & Pihl, R. D. (1995). A bimodal preventive intervention for disruptive kindergarten boys: Its impact through mid-adolescence. *Journey of Consulting and Clinical Psychology, 63,* 560–568.

Ttofi, M.M., Farrington, D.P., & Baldry, A.C. (2008) *Effectiveness of programmes to reduce school bullying.* Stockholm, Sweden: National Council for Crime Prevention.

Vaillancourt, T., Miller, J. L., Fagbemi, J., Cote, S., & Tremblay, R. E. (2007). Trajectories and predictors of indirect aggression: Results from a nationally representative longitudinal study of Canadian children aged 2–10. *Aggressive Behavior, 33,* 314–326.

Velez, C. N., Johnson, J., & Cohen, P. (1989). A longitudinal analysis of selected risk factors for childhood psychopathology. *Journal of the American Academy of Child and Adolescent Psychiatry, 28,* 861–864.

Verhulst, F. C., & van der Ende, J. (1995). The eight-year stability of problem behavior in an epidemiologic sample. *Pediatric Research, 38,* 612–617.

Vreeman, R. C., & Carroll, A. E. (2007). A systematic review of school-based interventions to prevent bullying. *Archives of Pediatrics and Adolescent Medicine, 161,* 78–88.

Wadsworth, M. (1979). *Roots of delinquency.* London: Martin Robertson.

Waschbusch, D. A., & Willoughby, M. T. (2008). Attention-deficit/hyperactivity disorder and callous–unemotional traits as moderators of conduct problems when examining impairment and aggression in elementary school children. *Aggressive Behavior, 34,* 139–153.

Wasserman, G. A., & Miller, L. S. (1998). The prevention of serious and violent juvenile offending. In R. Loeber & D. P. Farrington (Eds.), *Serious and violent juvenile offenders: Risk factors and successful interventions* (pp. 197–247). Thousand Oaks, CA: Sage.

Webster-Stratton, C. (1998). Preventing conduct problems in Head Start children: Strengthening parenting competencies. *Journal of Consulting and Clinical Psychology, 66,* 715–730.

Webster-Stratton, C. (2000). *The incredible years training series.* Washington, DC: U.S. Office of Juvenile Justice and Delinquency Prevention.

Wells, L. E., & Rankin, J. H. (1991). Families and delinquency: A meta-analysis of the impact of broken homes. *Social Problems, 38,* 71–93.

Welsh, B. C., & Hoshi, A. (2006). Communities and crime prevention. In L. W. Sherman, D. P. Farrington, B. C. Welsh, & D. L. MacKenzie (Eds.), *Evidence-based crime prevention* (rev. ed.; pp. 165–197). London: Routledge.

West, D. J., & Farrington, D. P. (1973). *Who becomes delinquent?* London: Heinemann.

West, D. J., & Farrington, D. P. (1977). *The delinquent way of life.* London: Heinemann.

White, J. L., Moffitt, T. E., Caspi, A., Bartusch, D. J., Needles, D. J., & Stouthamer-Loeber, M. (1994). Measuring impulsivity and examining its relationship to delinquency. *Journal of Abnormal Psychology, 103,* 192–205.

Whitney, I., & Smith, P. K. (1991). *A survey of the nature and extent of bullying in junior/middle and secondary schools (final report to the Gulbenkian Foundation).* Sheffield, UK: University of Sheffield, Department of Psychology.

Widom, C. S. (1989). The cycle of violence. *Science, 244,* 160–166.

Widom, C. S. (1994). Childhood victimization and adolescent problem behaviors. In R. D. Ketterlinus & M. E. Lamb (Eds.), *Adolescent problem behaviors* (pp. 127–164). Hillsdale, NJ: Lawrence Erlbaum.

Wiesner, M., Capaldi, D. M., & Kim, H. K. (2007). Arrest trajectories across a 17-year span for young men: Relation to dual taxonomies and self-reported offense trajectories. *Criminology, 45,* 835–863.

Wikström, P.-O. H. (1985). *Everyday violence in contemporary Sweden.* Stockholm, Sweden: National Council for Crime Prevention.

Wikström, P.-O. H., & Loeber, R. (2000). Do disadvantaged neighborhoods cause well-adjusted children to become adolescent delinquents? A study of male juvenile serious offending, individual risk and protective factors, and neighborhood context. *Criminology, 38,* 1109–1142.

Wilson, D. B., Gottfredson, D. C., & Najaka, S. S. (2001). School-based prevention of problem behaviors: A meta-analysis. *Journal of Quantitative Criminology, 17,* 247–272.

Wilson, J. Q., & Herrnstein, R. J. (1985). *Crime and human nature.* New York: Simon & Schuster.

Wilson, S. J., & Lipsey, M. W. (2007). School based interventions for aggressive and disruptive behavior: Update of a meta-analysis. *American Journal of Preventive Medicine, 33*(2S), 130–143.

Wolfgang, M. E., Thornberry, T. P. & Figlio, R. M. (1987). *From boy to man, from delinquency to crime.* Chicago: University of Chicago Press.

Zahn, M. A., Brumbaugh, S., Steffensmeier, D., Feld, B. C., Morash, M., Chesney-Lind, M., et al. (2008). *Violence by teenage girls: Trends and context.* Washington, DC: U.S. Office of Juvenile Justice and Delinquency Prevention.

Zara, G., & Farrington, D. P. (2007). Early predictors of late onset offenders. *International Annals of Criminology, 45,* 37–56.

Zimring, F. E. (1981). Kids, groups and crime: Some implications of a well-known secret. *Journal of Criminal Law and Criminology, 72,* 867–885.

Zoccolillo, M. (1993). Gender and the development of conduct disorder. *Development and Psychopathology, 5,* 65–78.

CHAPTER 21

Adolescent Substance Use

LAURIE CHASSIN, ANDREA HUSSONG, AND IRIS BELTRAN

Adolescence is often described as a time of experimentation with "risky" or "problem" behaviors (Steinberg, 2007), and substance use is one such behavior that is initiated during this age period. Substance use and addictive disorders are topics of considerable importance both because of their significance for adolescent development and because of their public health impact. For example, considering both adults and adolescents, recent estimates are that the use and abuse of alcohol, nicotine, and illegal drugs cost the United States approximately $441 billion per year, exceeding the costs associated with heart disease or cancer (American Cancer Society, 2007; American Heart Association, 2007; Office of National Drug Control Policy, 2001; U.S. Department of Health and Human Services [USDHHS], 2000; U.S. Department of Health and Human Services, 2004). Underage drinking cost the United States approximately 61 billion dollars in 2001, or $1 for each drink consumed by an underage drinker (Miller, Levy, Spicer, & Taylor, 2006). Substance use is also associated with the major sources of mortality and morbidity during the adolescent years, which are accidents, homicide, and suicide (USDHHS, 2007). Perhaps related to its public health impact and significance for adolescent development, the field of adolescent

substance use research has seen rapid and significant expansion in the past 3 decades.

This chapter will describe the prevalence and predictors of adolescent substance use and substance use problems, with particular emphasis on their relation to the developmental issues of adolescence. Given the wide scope of this field, we do not attempt a comprehensive review. For example, we do not consider issues of substance abuse treatment (see, e.g., Brown & D'Amico, 2003; Morral, McCaffrey, Ridgeway, Mukherji, & Beighley, 2006; Waldron & Kaminer, 2004; Rowe & Liddle, 2006) or prevention (Caulkins, Liccardo, Pacula, Paddock, & Chiesa, 2002; Faggiano et al., 2005; Gates, McCambridge, Smith, & Foxcroft, 2006). Rather, we will selectively emphasize recent empirical work, as well as studies that illustrate important general themes in adolescent substance use research.

In this chapter, we include studies of substances that are legal if consumed by adults (cigarettes and alcohol) as well as illegal drugs. Moreover, we include studies of substance "use" (i.e., the quantity and frequency of consumption) as well as studies of "substance use problems" or formal diagnoses of substance use disorders. The standard diagnostic taxonomy (*Diagnostic and Statistical Manual of Mental Disorders,* 4th edition [DSM-IV],

Preparation of this chapter was supported by Grants AA016213 from the National Institute on Alcohol Abuse and Alcoholism and DA13555, DA019697, and DA015398 from the National Institute on Drug Abuse. The content is solely the responsibility of the authors and does not necessarily represent the official views of the National Institute on Drug Abuse or the National Institutes of Health. We thank Manuel Barrera, Brooke Molina, Ryan Trim, and Jennifer Ritter for their contributions to the version of this chapter that appeared in the second edition of this volume.

American Psychiatric Association, 1994) distinguishes between two different substance use disorders: substance dependence and substance abuse. Although the adequacy of the diagnostic criteria has been questioned in terms of their appropriateness for adolescent populations (Caetano & Babor, 2006; Chung, Martin, & Winters, 2005; Deas, Riggs, Langenbucher, Goldman, & Brown, 2000; Fulkerson, Harrison, & Beebe, 1999; Martin, Kaczynski, Maisto, Bukstein, & Moss, 1995), current practice is to diagnose adolescents with the same criteria that are used for adults. According to the DSM-IV, substance dependence involves compulsive use (e.g., unsuccessful attempts to cut down). Other symptoms of substance dependence (although no one particular symptom is required for the diagnosis) include tolerance (needing increased amounts of the substance to achieve intoxication or experiencing reduced effects from the same amount of consumption) and withdrawal (cognitive and physiological changes upon discontinuing use). In contrast, substance abuse, involves repeated negative consequences of substance use, including failure to fulfill obligations at work, school, or home and use of substances in situations that are physically hazardous. Substance dependence and substance abuse are currently operationalized as two distinct disorders, with abuse being considered as less severe. However, research using item response theory methods with both adults (Saha, Chou, & Grant, 2006) and adolescents (Martin, Chung, Kirisci, & Langenbucher, 2006) suggests that the symptoms form a single underlying continuum of severity, and that some of the dependence symptoms may reflect less severity than some of the abuse symptoms.

Aside from questions of how to define clinical substance use disorders in adolescents, researchers have suggested that the antecedents of adolescent substance use differ from those of substance use problems or disorders (Colder & Chassin, 1999; Sartor, Lynskey, Heath, Jacob, & True, 2007; Shedler & Block, 1990). This implies that researchers need to distinguish among different substance use outcomes

(both different substances and different "stages" of use from initiation to clinical disorder). Accordingly, the current chapter includes both studies of adolescent substance use and substance use disorders, but we note the distinctions between them.

PREVALENCE OF ADOLESCENT SUBSTANCE USE AND SUBSTANCE USE DISORDERS

Epidemiological studies and most other studies of adolescent substance use rely on adolescents' self-reports, because parents are unlikely to be aware of their adolescents' use. Indeed, parent and adolescent reports show low levels of agreement (Cantwell, Lewinsohn, Rohde, & Seely, 1997; Fisher et al., 2006; Williams, McDermitt, Bertrand, & Davis, 2003; Winters, Anderson, Bengston, Stinchfield, & Latimer, 2000). Although it is beyond the scope of this chapter, a large literature has addressed the validity (and threats to validity) of these adolescent self-reports, including their validation with biological measures (e.g., Williams & Nowatzki, 2005; Buchan, Dennis, Tims, & Diamond, 2002). In general, these data suggest that self-reports can be valid if they are obtained under conditions of anonymity and privacy, and when there is little motivation to distort responses. Several studies have found that self-administered questionnaires tend to produce higher frequencies of reported sensitive behaviors than do interviewer-administered questionnaires (Aquilino & Wright, 1996; Fendrich & Yun-Soo-Kim, 2001; Rogers, Miller, & Turner, 1998).

Data from the Monitoring the Future (MTF) study, a national school-based survey, show that adolescent substance use is relatively common by the end of the high school years (Johnston, O'Malley, Bachman, & Schulenberg, 2007). For example, in 2006 approximately 48% of 12th graders used some illegal drug in their lifetimes, with 36.5% using in the past year. Marijuana is the most frequently used illegal drug, with 31.5% of 12th graders reporting some lifetime use (Johnston et al., 2007). The use of substances that are legal for adults (i.e., alcohol and tobacco) is even more common, with 73% of today's students having consumed alcohol by the end of high school and 45% of high school seniors reporting drinking in the past month (Johnston et al., 2007). Forty-seven percent of high school seniors report some experience with cigarette smoking, and 22% were current smokers in 2006 (Johnston et al., 2007). The use of different drugs is highly interrelated in both epidemiological and clinical samples of adolescents (Johnston, Bachman, & O'Malley, 2000). For example, in the 1985 National Household Survey on Drug Abuse (NHSDA) data, 24% of illicit drug users used multiple drugs simultaneously within the past year, and 43% had used alcohol along with an illicit drug (Clayton, 1992). Sneed, Morisky, Rotheram-Borusa, Lee, and Ebin (2004) found that males, older youth, and U.S.-born participants were more likely to report using multiple substances than females, younger youth, and foreign-born participants.

The MTF data also reveal interesting patterns of change over time. In general, adolescent substance use involvement reached a peak in the mid-1970s and early 1980s and then declined. Substance use rose again in the early 1990s but has since leveled off. Specific drugs show marked increases and decreases in use over time. For example, cocaine use among 12th graders peaked in the late 1970s, showed dramatic declines between 1986 and 1992 (to about one-fourth the rate), but then was on the increase again until 2000. As of 2007, there were declining trends for marijuana, amphetamines, methamphetamines, alcohol, and cigarettes, but increasing trends for ecstasy (MDMA). (Johnston et al., 2008). Among the drugs that did not show change in 2006 were LSD, powder cocaine, heroin, club drugs, and steroids.

One class of substances of recent concern is adolescents' nonmedical use of prescription drugs (Johnston et al., 2007; McCabe, Boyd, & Young, 2007). According to the MTF data, the proportion using any of the three classes of prescription drugs in their lifetime (sedatives/barbiturates, tranquilizers, or narcotics other than heroin) is 1 in 5 seniors, with 1 in 7 using in the prior year (Johnston et al., 2007). In 2007, the study found annual prevalence rates of 5.2% for OxyContin and 9.6% for Vicodin use among 12th graders. Misuse of prescription medication is correlated with use of alcohol and illegal drugs as well as elevated risk for substance use disorders (McCabe, Teter, & Boyd, 2004).

Over the past decade there has also been concern about adolescents' use of steroids. According to Johnston et al. (2007), anabolic steroid use reached peak levels by 2000 in 8th and 10th grades, and by 2002 in 12th grade. Since those peak levels were reached, declines began in 2001 among 8th graders, in 2003 among 10th graders, but not until 2005 among 12th graders. In 2007 the annual prevalence figures were 0.8% in 8th grade, 1.1% in 10th grade, and 1.4% in 12th grade.

Another substance that is gaining popularity is dextromethorphan (DXM), a cough suppressant found in many over-the-counter cough and cold remedies. Based on the Substance Abuse and Mental Health Administration's (SAMHSA's) National Survey on Drug Use and Health in 2006 (SAMHSA, 2008), about 3.1 million people aged 12–25 (5.3%) had ever used an over-the-counter (OTC) cough and cold medications to get high, and about 1 million people in the same age group (1.7%) had used it in the past year. People aged 18–25 were more likely than youth aged 12–17 to have used OTC cough and cold medications nonmedically in their lifetime (6.5% vs. 3.7%) but were less likely to do so in the past year (1.6% vs. 1.9%). Whites aged 12–25 (2.1%) were more likely than Hispanics (1.4%) and Blacks (0.6%) to have used an OTC cough and cold medication in the past year to get high. Johnston et al. (2008) found that 4%, 5.4%, and 5.8% of adolescents in grades 8, 10, and 12, respectively, reported having used DXM during the prior year for the purpose of getting high. Because this substance is available over the counter, young people may not fully recognize the dangers of using it, especially in high doses.

Interpreting these different time trends, Johnston et al. (2007) note that, as older drugs wane in popularity, new drugs replace them.

For example, phencyclidine (PCP) showed a rapid rise in the 1970s, crack and cocaine in the 1980s, and rophynol and ecstasy in the 1990s. Interestingly, the popularity of specific drugs often revives after a period of low use. Johnston et al. (2007) suggest that the use of a particular drug may make such a "comeback" because knowledge of its risks and negative effects gets lost from the adolescent culture after a period of nonuse. They refer to this phenomenon as "generational forgetting."

Substantial numbers of adolescents who use alcohol or drugs also report some problem associated with their substance use. For example, Ridenour, Lanza, Donny, and Clark (2006) found that 46.24% of adolescents in their sample first experienced a *Diagnostic and Statistical Manual of Mental Disorders,* 3rd edition (rev. ed.; DSM-III-R) abuse or dependence symptom 28 months after initiation of alcohol use. Of those who had used cocaine, 51.52% experienced a drug-related problem 28 months after initiation of cocaine use. However, the prevalence of diagnosable substance use disorders among adolescents is markedly lower, with point prevalences of 3%–4% for alcohol disorders and 2%–3% for drug use disorders among younger adolescents (13–16 years of age). For example, Fergusson, Horwood, and Lynskey (1993) found that 5.5% of their New Zealand birth cohort of 15-year-olds could be diagnosed with a lifetime history of substance use disorder (1.7% for illegal drugs and 3.5% for alcohol). The 2005 National Survey on Drug Use & Health (SAMHSA, 2006) found that in a sample of noninstitutionalized persons aged 12–17 residing within the United States, the lifetime prevalence rate for drug abuse or dependence was 4.7%, and the rate for alcohol abuse or dependence was 5.5%.

DEMOGRAPHIC CORRELATES OF USE, ABUSE, AND DEPENDENCE

Gender

Studies have documented gender differences in the use of certain substances, but the picture is very complex. In general, girls use fewer drugs with less frequency than do boys (Johnston et al., 2007). MTF data show that 12th-grade males report substantially higher prevalence rates in the annual use of inhalants, hallucinogens, OxyContin, Vicodin, Ritalin, Rohypnol, heroin, LSD, steroids, and smokeless tobacco, as well as in the daily use of marijuana and alcohol. At younger grades, however, males and females show similar rates for many drugs, and females have higher rates of annual use of cocaine, crack, methamphetamine, inhalants, tranquilizers, and amphetamines in 8th grade. These findings suggest that gender differences emerge in middle to late adolescence. Johnston, O'Malley, Bachman, & Schulenberg (2006) hypothesize that differences in early grades may result from girls' tendency to mature earlier than boys and, consequently, associate with older peers. Male and female adolescents may also be differentially exposed to some drugs. For example, the National Survey on Drug Use and Health (Office of Applied Studies, 2003) found that females aged 12–17 were more likely than males to report that LSD, cocaine, crack, and heroin were easy to obtain.

In addition to gender differences in use of substances, researchers have found that male and female adolescents have different trajectories of substance use over time. Ridenour et al. (2006) found that length of time for progression from initiation to first experience of a substance-related problem tends to be faster for females than males. The results from Ridenour et al.'s study suggest that males' liability to regular use is greater, but speed of transition to problem use may be greater for females.

Males and females may also use drugs for different reasons. For example, males report stronger social and enhancement motives for drinking than do females (Cooper, 1994; Jerez & Coviello, 1998). Younger females report stronger coping and conformity motives for drinking than do males, although this gender difference reverses at older ages (Cooper). Studies of tobacco use have found that females report stronger weight regulation and anxiety reduction motives than do males (Grunberg, Winders & Wewers, 1991).

Ethnicity

Several analyses of epidemiological data have concluded that there are ethnic differences in rates of adolescent substance use (see Barrera, Castro, & Biglan, 1999; and Kandel, 1995, for reviews). Kandel's broad conclusion from 14 epidemiological studies was that Asian American adolescents had the lowest lifetime prevalence of use and Native American adolescents showed the highest lifetime use. Of the other major ethnic groups, non-Hispanic Caucasians report the highest use, followed by Hispanics and African Americans, in that order.

However, the pattern of ethnic differences varies by other factors, such as geographical location and tribal affiliation of Native American adolescents (Stubben, 1997) or level of acculturation of Hispanic youth (Gil, Wagner, & Vega, 2000; Kulis, Marsiglia, & Hurdle, 2003). It also varies somewhat by the type of substance that is being considered. For example, in the MTF data, in 8th grade, African American students show lower use than Caucasians or Hispanics for almost all drugs. However, they have slightly higher rates of annual prevalence of marijuana use than Caucasian students (Johnston et al., 2006). In other studies, Asian youth exhibited lower rates of smoking than did Whites and Hispanics, but not African Americans (Epstein, Botvin, & Diaz, 1998; Chen, Unger, Cruz, & Johnson, 1999; Wallace et al., 2002). One study found that Asian/Pacific Islander American youth had higher rates of substance use indicators compared to African American adolescents (Choi & Lahey, 2006).

Moreover, ethnic differences seem to vary with age. For example, in 8th grade, Hispanic students report more use of illicit drugs, except for amphetamines, than do non-Hispanic Caucasians, but in 12th grade, Hispanics tend to have use rates that fall between Caucasians and African American adolescents. Caucasians may start using drugs later in adolescence and

eventually overtake the prevalence rates of Hispanics (Johnston et al., 2007), although this crossover may also be caused by the comparatively high school dropout rate of Hispanics.

Researchers have also found ethnic differences in the trajectories of substance use over time. Different developmental patterns have been found for Caucasian and African American adolescents in the use of alcohol (Flory et al., 2006) and marijuana (Brown, Flory, Lynam, Leukefeld, & Clayton, 2004). White, Nagin, Replogle, and Stouthamer-Loeber (2004) found that Caucasian adolescents began smoking earlier in life and had faster progressions to regular use than did their African Americans counterparts. Similarly, Ellickson and colleagues (Ellickson, Martino, & Collins, 2004) found that although Hispanic adolescents had smoking patterns similar to those of White adolescents, they were more likely to follow trajectories characterized by decreases in smoking in young adulthood. Additionally, several studies have shown that African American adolescents initiate smoking later than do Hispanics (e.g., Brook, Pahl, & Ning, 2006; Trinidad, Gilpin, Lee, & Pierce, 2004).

There are also ethnic differences in the prevalence of diagnosed adolescent substance use disorders. Several studies have reported that Native American adolescents were significantly more likely to receive a substance use disorder diagnosis than were Caucasian adolescents (Costello, Farmer, Angold, Burns, & Erkanli, 1997; Kilpatrick et al., 2000). Results from the Methodology for Epidemiology of Mental Disorders in Children and Adolescents (MECA) study (Kandel et al, 1997) showed that Caucasian and African American adolescents were more likely to be diagnosed with a substance use disorder than were Hispanic adolescents. It is important to note that, although rates of adolescent substance use vary by ethnicity, this conclusion may oversimplify a more complex picture in which interactions of gender and ethnicity could be influencing prevalence rates (Griesler & Kandel, 1998), and the correlated effects of ethnicity and socioeconomic status (SES) are difficult to disaggregate.

In addition to ethnic group differences in prevalence rates and trajectories of use, there have been some reports of ethnic differences in the correlates of adolescent substance use (see reviews by Newcomb, 1995; Resnicow, Soler, Braithwaite, Ahluwalia, & Butler, 2000). Previous research suggests racial/ethnic variations in four psychosocial and behavioral risk domains relevant to smoking: social bonds, exposure to pro-smoking social influences, engagement in problem behavior, and pro-smoking attitudes. For example, Ellickson et al. (2004) concluded that African American adolescents who initiate smoking are less likely to become regular smokers than are Whites or Hispanics because their social environment after age 13 is less supportive of smoking and because they do not develop pro-smoking attitudes. Resnicow et al. (2000) concluded that peers have a greater influence on the smoking of Hispanic and White youth than they do on the smoking of African Americans. They also concluded that parental influence on smoking is greater for African American youth than it is for Whites. Unger and colleagues (2001) concluded that the influence of friends' smoking behavior was stronger among Whites than among Pacific Islanders, African Americans, and Hispanics.

At the same time, there are several large studies that show more ethnic similarities than differences in the developmental processes underlying adolescent substance use. For example, Barrera, Biglan, Ary, and Li (2001) showed that adolescent substance use is correlated with antisocial behaviors and poor academic performance to form a problem behavior construct that is comparable for Latino, Native American, and Caucasian adolescents. This study also supported the ethnic equivalence of a model of family and peer influences on adolescent problem behavior. Other studies with large samples of adolescents from several different ethnic groups have also shown ethnic

similarities in the relation of alcohol use to risk and protective factors (Costa, Jessor, & Turbin, 1999) and to separation and individuation (Bray, Getz, & Baer, 2000). A study on White, African American, Puerto Rican, and Colombian adolescents found that a number of psychosocial risk factors (e.g., unconventionality, parental identification, peer deviance) predicted later marijuana use across the different groups, suggesting that the predictors were robust and generalizable across gender and ethnic background (Brook, Brook, Arencibia-Mireles, Richter, & Whiteman, 2001). Bersamin, Paschall, and Flewelling (2005) found several risk factors to be similarly associated with binge drinking in both White and Asian youth. In addition, Brown et al. (2004) found that the relation of antecedents, such as school, family, and peer factors, to substance use trajectory groups was not different for African American and Caucasian adolescents.

Although it is important to study whether ethnic groups differ significantly in their substance use behavior, it is equally important to investigate the development of use within groups. In recent years, a growing body of literature has been focusing on within-group variation and the social, cultural, and historical heterogeneity that exists within each ethnic group. Studies suggest that Hispanic and Asian subgroups can vary in their use of substances by national origin (e.g., Amaro, Whitaker, Coffman, & Heeren, 1990; SAMHSA, 2006), nativity (e.g., Turner & Gil, 2002), and assimilation into American society (e.g., Amaro et al., 1990; Vega, Alderete, Kolody, & Aguilar-Gaxiola, 1998). For example, the rate of past-month cigarette smoking is higher among Korean than Chinese adolescents (SAMHSA, 2006). Moreover, when compared to those of Chinese, Filipino, Korean, and Japanese origin, Asian Indian and Vietnamese adolescents had the highest risk of alcohol use based on past smoking history (Chen et al., 2002). Similarly, Delva et al. (2005) found higher rates of marijuana use among Mexican American and Puerto Rican 8th graders compared to Cuban American and other Latin American adolescents. In addition to identifying different patterns of alcohol use for Caucasian and African American adolescents, Flory et al. (2006) demonstrated that neither group is homogeneous in their use, thereby highlighting the need for research that takes a developmental, within-groups approach to examining the antecedents of different patterns among ethnic groups.

Socioeconomic Status

Research indicates that SES is associated with adolescent use of some licit and illicit drugs. Some studies have reported greater substance use in low SES populations (Chassin, Presson, Sherman, & Edwards, 1992; Droomers, Schrjvers, Casswell, & Mackenbach, 2003; Duncan, Duncan, Strycker, & Chaumeton, 2002; Office of Applied Studies, 2004; Wardle et al., 2003). However, recent studies have also found higher substance use among teens living in affluent suburban settings compared with teens living in less affluent rural or urban settings (Ennett, Flewelling, Lindrooth, & Norton, 1997; Falck, Siegal, Wang, & Carlson, 1999; Hanson & Chen, 2007; Lucas & Gilham, 1995; Luthar & D'Avanzo, 1999). Together, these studies suggest that the effect of SES on substance use is curvilinear, with high rates of use among adolescents in poverty and in affluence, and also depends on the type of substance under consideration. However, Hanson and Chen's review of the literature for the years 1970–2007 on the association between SES and cigarette smoking, alcohol use, and marijuana use in adolescents found that there was no clear relationship between SES and alcohol or marijuana use (Hanson & Chen, 2007). Their review suggests that the majority of studies find low SES to be associated with greater cigarette smoking. They hypothesize that patterns differ for smoking versus alcohol and marijuana use because parents are more likely to model smoking in front of the children than to model drug or alcohol use. Studies that have found a relation between SES and adolescent

substance use suggest that high and low SES adolescents use substances for similar reasons, but that the manifestation of these reasons may take somewhat different form for the two groups. For example, although both high and low SES adolescents may be isolated from parents, in high SES groups, this may be due to parents' high-powered jobs and frequent travel, whereas in low SES groups, this may be due to parents working multiple jobs and being preoccupied with coping with financial stress (Luthar & Latendresse, 2005).

Hanson and Chen's review of the literature suggests that the type of SES marker (e.g., family financial resources versus family education) is also important to consider when assessing the relation between SES and different substances. They found that lower SES may be more likely to be related to substance use if SES is measured using social status indicators, such as parental education. However, when indicators of family financial resources are used, higher SES adolescents are at greater risk for using certain substances, like marijuana.

AGE-RELATED TRAJECTORIES OF ADOLESCENT SUBSTANCE USE: RELATIONS TO DEVELOPMENTAL TRANSITIONS

Both substance use and substance use disorders show systematic age-related patterns from adolescence to adulthood that have led some researchers to view substance abuse and dependence as "developmental disorders" (Sher & Gotham, 1999; Tarter & Vanukov, 1994). Substance use is typically initiated in adolescence. For example, MTF data suggest that the typical time for alcohol use onset as well as for first intoxication is between 7th and 11th grade (Johnston et al., 2007). Adolescent substance use typically begins with the use of legal drugs (tobacco and alcohol), and rates of illegal drug use onset peak in the high school years (Johnston et al., 2007; Kandel, 1975).

Over the adolescent years, alcohol and drug use increase in quantity and frequency, peaking between ages 18–25. The prevalence of diagnosed substance abuse and dependence also peaks in this age period (e.g., Harford, Grant, Yi, & Chen, 2005). In the mid- to late 20s, the consumption of alcohol and illegal drugs begins to decline, perhaps in response to the demands of newly acquired adult roles such as marriage, work, and parenthood (Bachman, Wadsworth, O'Malley, Johnston, & Schulenberg 1997; Schulenberg, Bachman & O'Malley, 2005; Yamaguchi & Kandel, 1985). Substance use disorders that decline in young adulthood have been referred to as "developmentally limited" (Zucker, 2006).

Given that adolescent substance use typically onsets between 7th and 11th grade, it is interesting to speculate about its link with adolescence as a developmental stage, in terms of maturational processes in interaction with changes in environmental contexts.

Maturational Changes: The Neurobiology of Adolescence and Brain Changes

Research has suggested important developmental changes in brain systems that influence both reward sensitivity and cognitive control. Specifically, changes in dopaminergic systems, including changes in receptor densities in cortical and subcortical areas, occur early in adolescence and are thought to produce changes in sensation seeking and reward salience, including increases in the reward value of peer social interactions (Chambers, Taylor, & Potenza, 2003; Gardner & Steinberg, 2005; Spear, 2000). In contrast, the timing of developmental changes in cognitive control systems continues until the mid-20s. These changes include synaptic pruning in prefrontal regions; increases in white matter, which occur with myelination; and increased connections among cortical areas as well as between cortical and subcortical areas (Paus, 2005). The differing developmental age course in systems governing reward and motivation compared to systems governing cognitive control and self-regulation are theorized to create a gap, which places adolescents at elevated risk for risky behavior in general, including substance

use (Steinberg, in press). Thus, the typical ages of substance use initiation occur during times of biologically based increases in sensation seeking and reward salience (particularly the salience of social and peer reward) coupled with a less than fully mature cognitive control system. Later age-related declines in substance use in the mid-20s occur during a time of maturation of the cognitive control system.

In addition to developmental changes in neural systems governing self-regulation and reward, adolescents may also be particularly biologically vulnerable to substance use effects (Spear, 2000; Levin, Rezvani, Montoya, Rose, & Swartzwelder, 2003). These hypotheses predict not only that adolescence will be a period of substance use onset but that, because adolescents may derive greater positive effects (and/or less negative effects) from the use of tobacco, alcohol, or other drugs, that initiation of substance use during the adolescent years (compared to initiation in adulthood) will also be associated with more rapid increases in consumption. Because of their implications for escalating trajectories of substance use, these findings are described in more detail below, in the context of discussing heterogeneity in substance use trajectories.

The Pubertal Transition

Adolescent substance use has also been associated with the pubertal transition—specifically to early puberty among adolescent girls (Dick, Rose, Viken, & Kaprio, 2000; Ge et al., 2006; Stattin & Magnusson, 1990; Stice, Presnell, & Bearman, 2001). Girls who enter puberty earlier than their age-peers show an earlier onset of alcohol use and cigarette smoking (Stattin & Magnusson, 1990), increased substance experimentation in early adolescence (Ge et al., 2006), and a threefold increase for more advanced stages of substance use (Lanza & Collins, 2002), whereas late-maturing girls are more likely to abstain from substance use (Aro & Taipale, 1987). Importantly, these findings have been replicated in a sample of adolescent twin girls who were discordant for pubertal timing (Dick et al., 2000). This study is important because it demonstrates an effect of early pubertal timing on adolescent substance use even after controlling for confounding between-family factors that are associated with early maturation.

Findings for boys have been more mixed, with studies of European youth suggesting greater risk for substance use among early maturers (e.g., Andersson & Magnusson, 1990; Dick & Mustanski, 2006; Silbereisen & Kracke, 1993) and those of American youth finding effects for both early (Costello, Sung, Worthman, & Angold, 2007) and late maturers (e.g., Ge et al., 2006; Graber, Seeley, Brooks-Gunn, & Lewinsohn, 2004). Moreover, although studies show a "catch-up effect" in which the effects of early pubertal timing are reduced by late adolescence and early adulthood (Dick et al., 2000; Graber et al., 2004), longer term effects can still be detected. For example, Graber et al. (2004) found that early-maturing boys, though not girls, had a higher onset of substance disorders in the transition to adulthood, and Stattin and Magnusson (1990) found that late-maturing girls were still more likely than were early-maturing girls to be abstainers at age 25.

The effect of pubertal maturation on substance use appears due to morphological development rather than hormonal changes that occur early in this transition (Costello et al., 2007). Studies testing whether associations with older peers explained the association between early maturation and substance use in girls show inconsistent effects and no support in within-family analyses of a twin sample (Dick et al., 2000). However, several factors appear to increase risk for substance use among early maturing youth, including lax parental supervision (for girls) and a family history of drugs, crime, or psychiatric problems (for boys; Costello et al., 2007). Interestingly, Dick et al. (2000) found that the relation between early maturation and substance use was moderated by whether the family lived in an urban versus a rural environment, such that early maturation was related to substance use only for those who lived in an urban environment. The authors suggest that families in rural environments might have stronger parental

influences and/or less access to substances, so that the effects of early maturation are negated (Dick et al., 2000). These findings illustrate the importance of contextual influences as moderators of the relations between developmental transitions and adolescent substance use.

Psychosocial Transitions of Adolescence: School Transitions

Adolescents' school transitions involve a complex set of changes in the academic and social contexts of adolescents' lives, including less personal and positive student–teacher relationships and changes in the peer environment (Eccles, Lord, Roeser, Barber, & Jozefowicz, 1997). However, the link between these school transitions and adolescent substance use is complex. For example, Eccles et al. (1997) found that, among low-achieving adolescents, those whose self-esteem increased during the transition to middle school showed the most substance use in high school. However, among high-achieving adolescents, those whose self-esteem decreased during the transition to middle school showed increased substance use. Eccles et al. (1997) suggest that low-achieving adolescents whose self-esteem increased might have disengaged from academics and formed deviant peer affiliations that promoted substance use.

Role Transitions

Substance use also changes in relation to role transitions, including transitions to higher education, work, and romantic relationships (O'Malley, 2004). However, the ways in which these transitions are related to adolescent substance use involve multiple processes that Yamaguchi and Kandel (1985) term *role socialization* and *role selection.* Role selection refers to the fact that not all individuals select (or are selected into) the roles of work, higher education, and romantic relationships. Role selection encompasses the effects of adolescent substance use on role occupancy as well as the fact that characteristics associated with both adolescent drug use and social roles may explain the relation between them. For example, adolescents who use substances are less likely to go on to college (Bachman et al., 1997; Newcomb & Bentler, 1988a). This may be because their substance use is performance-impairing and/or because adolescents who are less motivated to succeed academically are also more likely to use drugs. In contrast, role socialization refers to the reverse direction of effect, that is, the effect of role responsibilities on substance use behavior. Because the demands and norms of adult roles are generally incompatible with substance use, adult role occupancy typically reduces alcohol and drug use.

Evidence for the impact of role transitions on the course of substance use during adolescence thus focuses on isolating the effects of role socialization, although few studies are able to do so definitively. The effects of role transitions can vary with age. For work roles, high school students who work more hours also report more substance use (Bachman, Safron, Sy, & Schulenberg, 2003; Steinberg & Dornbusch, 1991). However, in young adulthood, those who enter adult work roles decrease their substance use, perhaps because of the different working conditions and social norms of the work environment, as well as greater demands of adults' jobs as predicted by role socialization (Bachman et al., 1997).

During young adulthood, the assumption of marital roles is associated with reductions in substance use (Bachman et al., 1997; Gotham, Sher, & Wood, 2003; Schulenberg, Bachman, & O'Malley, 2005), with marriage in young adulthood predicting less drug use in the late 20s, especially among men (Flora & Chassin, 2005), and non-Hispanic Caucasians (Mudar, Kearns, & Leonard, 2002). Pregnancy also reduces substance use in women, though not in men, but the beginning of parenthood is perhaps the key event that prompts men to reduce their drinking (O'Malley, 2004). When these transitions occur in adolescence, however, the effects differ. For example, Little, Handley, Leuthe, and Chassin (2007) showed that early parenthood is associated with increases in substance use, whereas an older and more normative age of parenthood is associated with declines. Similarly, Bogart et al. (2005) showed that women who marry as adolescents only report less alcohol involvement in their late 20s than never-married women if they were not divorced; thus, the high divorce rate associated with adolescent marriage appears to wipe out the protective effect of marriage for these women.

Finally, although higher educational attainment is generally associated with reduced adolescent substance use (Hawkins, Catalano, & Miller, 1992), an exception occurs during the transition to college (especially for non-Hispanic Caucasians, Paschall, Bersamin, & Flewelling, 2005). Data from the MTF study (Bachman et al., 1997) show that college-bound high school seniors drank less than did their peers who were not college bound (consistent with a role selection effect). However, after the transition to college, those who were college students drank at higher levels than did their peers who did not attend college (see also Slutske et al., 2004). This effect is particularly true for those who live away from home to attend college (White et al., 2006). Bachman et al. (1997) attribute this pattern to the "new freedoms" of college life, including living arrangements independent of parental supervision and social norms that promote alcohol use.

These findings describe an overall age-related trajectory of adolescent onset, late-adolescent escalation, and adult decline in substance use. However, recent evidence suggests that it is useful to distinguish among multiple age-related trajectories. Because some type of substance use during adolescence is developmentally and statistically normative, it is necessary to distinguish developmental trajectories of substance use that are relatively benign from those that result in clinical impairment or diagnosable substance use disorders. Several studies have suggested that an early age of substance use onset is one predictor of subsequent course and clinical impairment. For example, alcohol use initiation before age 14 (Grant & Dawson, 1997) and illegal drug use before age 15 (Robins & Pryzbeck, 1985) are associated with elevated risk for the development of alcohol and drug disorders.

Empirically Identified Multiple Trajectories of Substance Use

Developments in statistical techniques of mixture modeling (Múthen & Shedden, 1999; Nagin, 1999) have allowed researchers to empirically identify multiple developmental trajectories of substance use. The studies that have used this method have identified a subgroup in which early age of onset is associated with a steeply escalating course of use and with the most problematic outcomes (including diagnosed abuse or dependence). This subgroup has been found for both cigarette smoking (Chassin, Presson, Pitts, & Sherman, 2000) and heavy drinking (Chassin, Pitts, & Prost, 2002; Hill, White, Chung, Hawkins, & Catalano, 2000). It has been found in studies of early adolescents (Abroms, Simons-Morton, Haynie, & Chen, 2005; Colder et al., 2001), middle adolescents (Wills, Resko, Ainette, & Mendoza, 2004), and later adolescents (Stanton, Flay, Colder, & Mehta, 2004). Sometimes this early-onset group shows stable but elevated levels of use (e.g., Windle & Wiesner, 2004) or even slight declines from a very high level of early use (Ellickson et al., 2004). These "early-escalating" or "stable high" subgroups have elevated profiles of psychosocial risk, including family history of substance use and high levels of conduct problems (Chassin et al., 2002; Costello, Erkanli, Federman, & Angold, 1999; Ellickson et al., 2004; Hill, Shen, Lowers, & Locke, 2000; Loeber, Stouthamer-Loeber, & White, 1999; Windle & Wiesner, 2004).

There are multiple reasons that early onset of substance use might be associated with increased risk for accelerating use and later substance use disorders. First, this might reflect selection effects, such that early onset is an epiphenomenon (Prescott & Kendler, 1999; McGue, Iacono, Legrand, Malone, & Elkins, 2001). That is, individuals with preexisting high-risk factors (e.g., high genetic load, disinhibited personality, greater propensity to develop dependence, high-risk family and peer environments) may be more likely to both initiate substance use at an early age and also develop a substance use disorder. King and Chassin (2007) found that early-onset drinking (before age 13) was not uniquely related to later alcohol dependence once preexisting risk factors and co-occurring early-onset drug use were controlled. However, early-onset alcohol and drug use was uniquely related to later drug dependence.

The idea that an early onset of substance use may be causally linked to greater consumption and later substance use disorders is also consistent with data from animal models that suggest that adolescents (as opposed to adults) may have differential sensitivity to the effects of substances. For example, adolescent animals are less sensitive to some of the negative effects of alcohol, such as sedation and hangover, perhaps allowing them to consume greater quantities. However, adolescents are more sensitive than are adults to some of the positive effects of alcohol, particularly social facilitation (see Spear & Varylinskaya, 2005, for a review). Similar findings of age-related differences in effects have been reported for nicotine (Belluzzi, Lee, Oliff, & Leslie, 2004; Levin, Rezvani, Montoya, Rose, & Swartzwelder, 2003; O'Dell, Brujinzeel, Ghozland, Markou, & Koob, 2004; see Slotkin, 2002, for a review). Adolescent exposure to nicotine (compared to adult exposure) has produced higher levels of self-administration (Levin et al., 2003). Taken together, these data suggest that adolescence may be a unique period of biological vulnerability, during which substance use exposure produces particularly rapid escalation in trajectories of consumption that may persist over time, as well as increased vulnerability for dependence because of differential sensitivity to substance use effects.

Of course, caution is required in generalizing from animal models to human adolescents given differences in methods of administration, dosages, and contextual factors such as the social and peer context of self-administration, and self-selection into substance use for human adolescents. Even in the rodent model, the empirical evidence concerning age differences in substance use response is not always clear-cut. For example, the nicotine data have shown variation with gender and with the task or paradigm that is used, as well as interactions with exposure to other substances (Faraday, Elliott, & Grunberg, 2001; Olmstead, 2006; Rezvani & Levin, 2004). More needs to be learned concerning the mechanisms underlying these age-dependent effects as well as their magnitude and persistence over time.

These animal models suggest that adolescence is a time of vulnerability to substance use onset because of a biologically driven vulnerability to substance use effects. As described earlier, another model (which is not necessarily competing or mutually exclusive) suggests that adolescence is a time of vulnerability to substance use onset because of a biologically driven disjunction between increases in reward sensitivity and sensation seeking, increased sensitivity to social (peer) reward, and less than fully developed capacities for self-regulation (Steinberg, 2007). These models suggest that adolescents will be vulnerable to risk-taking behaviors in general, not just to substance use. Finally, other psychosocial models suggest that adolescence is a time of vulnerability because of a desire for independence and adult-like status (Jessor & Jessor, 1977), as well as transitions in school, dating, and pubertal status (described earlier), all of which are stressful and also provide more opportunities and reinforcement for substance use. Although these various models are not necessarily competing in terms of suggesting that adolescence is a time of vulnerability for substance use onset, models that focus on biologically based age differences in substance use effects are the only ones to hypothesize that individual differences in age of onset are *causally* related to increases in consumption and risk for substance use disorders. Moreover, all of these models of adolescent vulnerability to substance use onset (with the exception of the hypothesis that age of onset is an epiphenomenon) have interesting implications for prevention. They suggest

that, if substance use onset can be delayed past adolescence, then the motivations for use and the consequences of use may be diminished, which could ultimately reduce the population prevalence of substance use disorders.

Conversely, studies have also identified a "late-onset" subgroup (at least late in the adolescent age period) whose substance use does not begin until after high school (Chassin et al., 2000; Chassin et al., 2002; Orlando, Tucker, Ellickson, & Klein, 2004). The description of later onset groups in terms of antecedent risk factors and later adult outcomes is somewhat less consistent in the literature. In terms of risk factors, antecedents may differ by the substance that is being considered. For example, late-onset cigarette smokers (Chassin et al., 2000) and late-onset alcohol users (Flory, Lynam, Milich, Leukefeld, & Clayton, 2004) showed lower levels of antecedent risk factors compared to early-onset groups. However, for marijuana use, Flory et al. (2004) found that both early- and late-onset groups differed from nonusers, and both early- and late-onset groups showed elevated psychosocial risk. Similarly, it is unclear whether early- versus late-onset groups have differing outcomes. For example, Orlando et al. (2004) found that, by age 23, early- and late-onset cigarette smoking trajectory groups converged into a single outcome of high-frequency smoking. However, Chassin et al. (2000) found that the late-onset group smoked at lower levels than did the early-onset group, even into the mid-30s. Whether different trajectories of use ultimately converge may vary both with the age of follow-up and the dependent measure that is studied (Jackson & Sher, 2005, 2006).

CONSEQUENCES OF ADOLESCENT SUBSTANCE USE

Adolescent substance use itself may affect the course of adolescent development and create significant consequences for later adult outcomes. In general, the immediate, short-term effects of substance use are related to its impact on judgment and performance. For example, even a single episode of heavy drinking has been associated with a risk for morbidity and mortality from impaired driving, accidents, and risky sexual behavior (USDHHS, 2007). Moreover, substance use during adolescence may have longer term effects on the maturing brain. Adolescents' use of alcohol, particularly heavy episodic or "binge" drinking that results in hangovers, is associated with negative consequences on neuropsychological performance (i.e., notably working memory and visuospatial functioning), brain structure (i.e., reduced hippocampal volume and white-matter integrity in the corpus callosum), and physiologic brain functioning (i.e., slowed P300 latencies and lowered blood oxygen levels in the cerebral cortex; Tapert, Caldwell & Burke, 2004–2005). In addition, evidence from animal and some human studies shows that moderate to heavy drinking disrupts female puberty, primarily by impacting hormone secretions (Emanuele, Wezeman, & Emanuele, 2002). Although increasing evidence suggests that these effects of alcohol may be causal, initial findings of similar deficits in high-risk youth with little alcohol involvement, such as children of alcoholic parents (e.g., Begleiter & Porjesz, 1999), indicate that at least part of this association may reflect preexisting neurological risks for alcohol and drug involvement.

As noted earlier, animal studies have also shown that adolescents experience different substance use effects than do adults. For example, heavy drinking during adolescence is associated with resistance to many of the acute intoxicating effects of alcohol (e.g., alcohol-induced motor impairment, social impairment, dysphoria, and sedation) that are thought to deter heavy use (Molina, Pelham, Gnagy, Thompson, & Marshal, 2007). Moreover, adolescent animals show increased social interaction following alcohol challenges (with low doses in familiar settings), whereas adults do not (Varlinskaya & Spear, 2002). As noted earlier, these findings suggest that a consequence of early-onset use will be greater risk for increased, escalating use and persistence of

use into adulthood. In fact, longitudinal studies suggest that the long-term consequence most consistently related to adolescent substance use is the continued use of the same substance (Kandel, Davies, Karus, & Yamaguchi, 1986). Long-term effects of adolescent substance use on psychosocial functioning are generally less clear. For example, Jessor, Donovan, and Costa (1991) found little impact of adolescent alcohol use on adult outcomes unless the alcohol use persisted into adulthood. Additionally, methodologically, it is difficult to disentangle the unique impact of adolescent substance use on developmental outcomes because substance use itself is correlated with numerous other risk factors, including conduct problems, poor parenting, and high-risk temperament, all of which are important determinants of later outcomes. For example, drinking among college students is correlated with educational attainment, but this relationship is attenuated when preexisting measures of high school aptitude and achievement are considered (Wood, Sher, Erickson, & DeBord, 1997).

Two hypotheses about the impact of adolescent substance use on adoption of adult roles posit opposing effects. The role incompatibility hypothesis (Yamaguchi & Kandel, 1985) suggests that the heavy use of substances into young adulthood will be incompatible with role acquisition and thus result in delayed entry into adult roles. However, the pseudomaturity hypothesis (Newcomb & Bentler, 1988a) indicates that strivings for adult status associated with adolescent substance use will lead to premature role entry, hastening entry into adult roles. Evidence to date provides support for both hypotheses, though favoring a role incompatibility interpretation (Chassin et al., 1992; Yamaguchi & Kandel, 1985). For example, after controlling for preexisting risk factors, adolescent substance use, particularly use that is prolonged into adulthood, is associated with a lower likelihood of marriage among high-risk youth (children of alcoholic parents; Flora, & Chassin, 2005) and among African American men (Green & Ensminger, 2006). However, heavy marijuana use in African American youth is associated with a greater risk of having children outside of marriage (Green & Ensminger, 2006).

Although substance use is associated with lower educational attainment (i.e., likelihood of high school or college degree completion, fewer years of education), prospective studies that control for selection effects show few unique effects of adolescent substance use on educational attainment in young adulthood (Gothan, Sher & Wood, 2003; King, Meehan, Trim, & Chassin, 2006). This effect, however, may be more evident for illicit drug use or in treatment samples. For example, Chatterji (2006) showed that marijuana and cocaine use in high school predicted fewer years of schooling by the mid-20s; King et al. (2006) showed that faster escalations in drug use predicted lower educational attainment; and McCarthy, Aarons, and Brown (2002) showed that more positive expectancies about drinking mediated the effect of alcohol use in high school and educational level in early adulthood in an adolescent-treatment but not community sample.

Prospective effects of adolescent substance use on occupational attainment (i.e., job prestige, hours worked per week, and annual salary) are generally weak, suggesting little relation between the two (Gotham, Sher & Wood, 2003; King et al., 2006; McCarthy et al., 2002). However, most studies that directly assess substance use predict occupational functioning in early adulthood (mid-20s), and longer follow-ups may be needed to see the long-term consequences of early substance use on this outcome, given that many young adults delay career entry beyond this point in development. In support of this possibility, Green and Ensminger (2006) showed that African American teens who used marijuana heavily (20 times or more) had higher rates of unemployment than their peers by their early 30s, an effect mediated by high school dropout.

Adolescent substance use may also impact the experience of leaving the family home. Although few studies have examined predictors of leaving home transitions, girls' early transitions out of the parental home have been associated with a history of substance use during adolescence (O'Connor, Allen, Bell, & Hauser, 1996; Stattin & Magnusson, 1996). Similarly, Hussong and Chassin (2002) found that adolescent risk behaviors, including substance use, predicted both earlier departures from home and greater difficulties in this transition such as leaving because of perceived unhappiness and leaving with less parental consultation.

Adolescent substance use has also been linked to later adult psychological distress and mental health problems. Longitudinal studies controlling for preexisting risk factors report a greater risk for anxiety disorders at age 22 for youth who smoked more than a pack of cigarettes a day at age 16 (Johnson et al., 2000) as well as higher levels of internalizing symptoms in young adults with either greater alcohol or drug use at age 13 or increasing in drug use during adolescence (Trim, Meehan, King, & Chassin, 2007). Interestingly, adolescent alcohol use may be an exception to this conclusion. Newcomb and Bentler (1988b) found that adolescent alcohol use was associated with enhanced positive self-feelings and improved social relationships in young adulthood. Leifman, Kuhlholm, Allebeck, Andreasson, and Romelsjo (1995) also reported that those who were light drinkers in late adolescence had better psychological status and sociability than did abstainers. The association between adolescent drinking and improved mood and social relationships may be related to the instrumental use of alcohol to obtain valued social goals in adolescence (Maggs, 1997).

Importantly, one key to understanding the long-term consequences of adolescent substance use may be better identifying individual vulnerabilities. For example, Caspi et al. (2005) showed that cannabis use increased likelihood for adult psychosis among those with a specific genetic risk (a functional polymorphism in the catechol-O-methyltransferase gene), possibly through an interactive effect initiating dopaminergic dysregulation. Underscoring the potential sensitivities of the adolescent brain to substance use, only adolescent-, not adult-, onset cannabis use was predictive of adult psychosis in these vulnerable individuals.

If adolescent drug use has a negative impact on adult outcomes, it is important to identify the mechanisms underlying these effects. First, the pharmacological effects of consumption might be performance impairing, for example, interfering with studying or performing on a job. Second, potentially toxic effects of substance use on neurobiological development could produce long-lasting damage to mechanisms underlying reward and self-regulation. Third, to the extent that adolescent substance use develops into physical and psychological dependence, then impaired functioning will result. Finally, adolescent substance use may influence adult psychosocial outcomes by influencing emerging developmental competency. Baumrind and Moselle (1985) suggested that adolescent substance use can produce a false sense of reality that interferes with the ability to evaluate and respond to environmental demands, while also permitting an avoidance of these demands. This will impair the development of effective coping. Similarly, Baumrind and Moselle (1985) proposed that adolescent drug use can create a false sense of autonomy and also undermine the development of intimate relationships. Baumrind's hypothesis that drug use during adolescence impairs emerging developmental competencies is important, but has had few empirical tests. Chassin, Pitts, and DeLucia (1999) found that adolescents' illegal drug use predicted lowered autonomy and less competence in positive activities in young adulthood (above and beyond earlier adolescent symptomatology). Moreover, drug-using adolescents have low levels of behavioral coping (Wills, 1986) although substance use in mid-adolescence was not associated with coping styles in young adulthood after controlling for adolescent coping patterns (Hussong & Chassin, 2004). However, whether or not adolescent drug use impairs emerging developmental competencies is largely unknown.

THEORETICAL MODELS

Theoretical models of adolescent substance use consider variables ranging from the intrapersonal to the macroenvironmental level (Hawkins et al., 1992; Petraitis, Flay, & Miller, 1995). Given the heterogeneity of substance use, it is unlikely that any one factor or etiological pathway could explain the development of substance use or substance use disorders. Rather, there are likely to be multiple pathways and multiple subtypes of substance use and substance use disorders. Some of the earliest theories consider adolescent substance use within a broader framework of behavioral deviance (e.g., Elliott, Huizinga, & Ageton, 1985; Hirschi, 1969; Jessor & Jessor, 1977). These theories draw upon the strong correlations between adolescent substance use and a broad range of other nonconventional behaviors that range from low aspirations for academic achievement and staying out past curfew, to theft and violence. Elliott's Social Control Theory (Elliott et al., 1985) emphasizes the causal role of weak bonds to conventional society including institutions (e.g., school, religion) and values, as well as lack of attachment to conventional role models (e.g., parents and teachers). Role strain, or poor fit between an adolescent's aspirations and perceptions of available resources to achieve the desired goals, is one contributor to the weak bonding with societal convention. As with Jessor and Jessor's Problem Behavior Theory (1977), attachment to like-minded peers results, and socialization into unconventional behavior, including substance use and abuse, follows. Empirical support for these general deviance models is plentiful (for a review, see Petraitis et al., 1995).

Although risk factors for substance use and problem behaviors overlap substantially (e.g., Fergusson, Lynsky, & Horwood, 1996a), it is not clear that substance use and other deviant behaviors reflect a single underlying construct of adolescent deviance (Willoughby, Chalmers, & Busseri, 2004). Recent data suggest that variability in substance use and other externalizing or delinquent behavior in adolescence are due to both shared and behavior-specific variance (Krueger et al., 2002; Mason & Windle, 2002). Some studies have shown specificity in the predictors of different problem behaviors (Maggs & Hurrelman, 1998; White, Pandina, & LaGrange, 1987). For example, Erickson, Crosnoe, and Dornbusch (2000) found stronger prospective prediction from social bonding variables (e.g., parent attachment, educational commitment) to substance use than to delinquent behavior. Loeber et al. (1999) found that bad neighborhoods predicted delinquency and aggression better than they predicted substance use. Although studies have not identified a consistent pattern of unique predictors of substance use compared to delinquency, the most prudent conclusion at this time is that substance use is both strongly related to, yet distinct in some ways from, other conduct problems.

Although much variability in substance use is explained by general deviance theories, these models do not directly address genetic and biological vulnerability toward substance use (Cloninger, 1987; Tarter, Alterman, & Edwards, 1985; Zucker, 1987). A particularly useful integration of theoretical models has been provided by Sher (1991), who identifies three (interrelated) pathways to substance use involvement and substance use disorders (a deviance-proneness pathway, a negative affect pathway, and an enhanced reinforcement pathway). Sher's models are particularly useful because they incorporate genetic and environmental risk; they link early childhood antecedents to later adult substance use disorders, and they respect the reality of transactional influences that may exacerbate risk (e.g., reciprocal influences between parenting behavior and personality). Sher's models were originally formulated to explain why individuals with a family history of substance use disorder are at elevated risk for substance use disorders. However, it is important to note that these same processes are hypothesized to produce substance use and substance use disorders among adolescents in general. They do not apply only to those with family history risk. Thus, our review is organized according to Sher's proposed pathways, after first describing family history of substance abuse or dependence use as a risk factor and the genetic and fetal exposure findings that may underlie family history effects.

Family History of Substance Abuse or Dependence

Adults with a family history of alcoholism are themselves at elevated risk for alcohol abuse or dependence (McGue, 1994; Russell, 1990), although the magnitude of the risk varies substantially across studies (from risk ratios of 2–3 in community samples to 9 in severely antisocial samples, McGue, 1994; Russell, 1990). There is also elevated risk (up to eightfold) for drug disorders among relatives of probands with drug disorders (Merikangas et al., 1998). In adolescence, family history risk is associated with an early onset of substance use (Chassin et al., 2000; Costello et al., 1999) with the persistence of substance use over time (Chassin et al., 2000), and with foreshortened time from onset to dependence diagnoses (Hussong, Bauer, & Chassin, in press). Studies of illegal drug use also suggest that there is familial aggregation (see Prescott, Madden, & Stallings, 2006). Twin studies suggest that this family history risk has both heritable and environmental mediators.

Genetics of Adolescent Substance Use

An exhaustive review of this literature is beyond the scope of this chapter, but recent reviews can be found in Hopfer, Crowley, and Hewitt (2003) and Prescott et al. (2006). Studies include both behavioral genetic methods (e.g., twin studies, extended family studies) and a smaller molecular genetic literature. In general, the behavior genetic literature suggests that both genetic and environmental influences are important. However, the magnitude of genetic influences varies across substances (with tobacco use having stronger genetic influences than does alcohol or marijuana use; Hopfer et al., 2003).

For example, in a study of 17-year-old twins, McGue, Elkins, and Iacono (2000) found that heritability for use and abuse of illegal drugs was 25%, whereas heritability for tobacco use and dependence was more powerful (40%–60%). Similarly, Han, McGue, and Iacono (1999) reported varying magnitudes of heritability estimates for tobacco (59%), alcohol (60%), and drug use (33%) in male adolescents, again suggesting that the importance of genetic and environmental influences may vary by the type of substance that is used.

The magnitude of genetic influence also varies by "stage" of substance use, with initiation generally showing weaker genetic influences than "problem" use (Fowler, Lifford, et al., 2007; but see McGue et al., 2000; and Maes et al., 2004, for some exceptions). Moreover, for adolescent substance use, there are also notable and significant effects of shared environment (more so for adult data; Han, McGue, & Iacono, 1999). Studies have also identified moderators of genetic influences, including religiosity (Timberlake et al., 2006), parenting and parent–adolescent relationships (Dick et al., 2007; Miles, Silberg, Pickens, & Eaves, 2005), and depression (Audrain-McGovern, Lerman, Wileyto, Rodriguez, & Shields, 2004). Because the attempt to identify moderators is relatively recent, there are few studies, and there is a need for replication of these findings.

Studies of the molecular genetics of substance abuse and dependence have proposed many possibilities for candidate genes (see Nestler, 2000; Reich, Hinrichs, Culverhouse, & Bierut, 1999; Uhl, 1999; Zucker, 2006, for reviews), but this work is still very new and findings are contradictory. Candidates genes that been proposed include both those that are involved in general pathways associated with internalizing and externalizing behaviors (e.g., experiences of reward and self-regulatory behaviors) such as those involving dopamine, serotonin, and gamma-aminobutyric acid (GABA), as well as those that involve the metabolism of specific substances like ethanol (e.g., alcohol dehydrogenase and aldehyde dehydrogenase) and nicotine (e.g., cytochrome P450 (CYP2A6)).

This distinction between general pathways and substance-specific pathways is an important one, and Sher's models (described earlier) recognize both substance-specific and general pathways (which are not mutually exclusive). That is, the "deviance proneness" and "stress-negative affect" pathways can explain "substance use" broadly, whereas "substance use effects" pathways are drug specific.

Several studies have investigated the genetic underpinnings of the association among different forms of adolescent substance use. Young, Rhee, Stallings, Corley, and Hewitt (2006) found that the correlation among substance use behaviors was driven by both common genetic and common environment factors, and that "problem" substance use showed stronger genetic correlations than did substance use without any associated consequences. Similarly, McGue, Iacono, and Krueger (2006) found a highly heritable factor that accounted for the association among multiple forms of disinhibitory psychopathology (including substance use). Yoon, Iacono, Malone, and McGue (2006) found that multiple forms of early substance use were linked to reduced P300 amplitude, which itself was highly heritable. They suggest that a failure in top-down control of behavior (as manifested by P300 amplitude) may be one endophenotype that accounts for genetic influences on adolescent substance use. Thus, an endophenotype associated with the "externalizing spectrum" (*deviance proneness* in Sher's terminology) may be one pathway that is associated with adolescent substance use.

Prenatal Exposure

Although twin and adoption studies indicate significant heritability for substance use and abuse in adolescence, family history risk can also exert influence through fetal exposure (see Glantz & Chambers, 2006, for a review). In human studies, it is difficult to isolate the effects of prenatal exposure from genetic risk and postnatal environmental risk (e.g., the environmental disruptions associated with ongoing parental substance use). However, animal models have found effects of prenatal exposure to alcohol on subsequent alcohol intake (Chotro, Arias, & Laviola, 2007), suggesting that there might be some unique effects of prenatal exposure (at least for alcohol). Baer et al. (1998, 2003) found that prenatal exposure to alcohol raised risk for adolescent and young adult drinking above and beyond a family history of alcoholism. Similarly, Cornelius, Leech, Goldschmidt, and Day (2000) found that prenatal tobacco exposure raised risk for offspring tobacco use in childhood. However, subsequent follow-up in adolescence (Cornelius, Leech, Goldschmidt, & Day, 2005) showed that the effects of prenatal exposure were no longer significant once co-occurring risk factors were considered. Glantz and Chambers' (2006) review concluded that prenatal exposure was best viewed as a modest direct contribution to vulnerability to drug abuse. Prenatal exposure may raise risk for adolescent substance use either through its effect on receptors, which then make the child more biologically sensitive to the effects of the substance, or by raising risk for temperamental underregulation and conduct problems, which are themselves risk factors for adolescent substance use (Glantz & Chambers).

Deviance Proneness Models

Sher's (1991) deviance proneness submodel suggests that the development of substance disorders occurs within a broader context of conduct problems and antisociality. Adolescents at risk for substance disorders are thought to be temperamentally "difficult" and prone to cognitive deficits, including verbal skill deficits and executive functioning deficits, that contribute to a lack of self-regulation. These adolescents are impulsive and sensation seeking. In addition, high-risk children are thought to receive inadequate parenting, and this combination of temperamental, cognitive, and environmental risk factors sets the stage for failure at school and ejection

from the mainstream peer group. This results in affiliation with deviant peers who provide opportunities, models, and approval for alcohol and drug use. Because these theories consider substance use within the broader context of antisocial behavior, they are quite similar to theories that attempt to explain the etiology of conduct problems more generally (e.g., Patterson, 1986). Empirical evidence for each of these links is reviewed below.

Temperament and Personality

A host of studies report that temperamental and personality traits reflecting behavioral undercontrol and poor self-regulation are associated with adolescent substance use problems. The personality characteristics most consistently associated with adolescent substance use include unconventionality, low ego control, sensation seeking, aggression, impulsivity, and an inability to delay gratification (Hawkins et al., 1992).

Longitudinal research has demonstrated that childhood temperamental characteristics reflecting undercontrolled behavior are predictive of later substance use problems. For instance, Block, Block, and Keyes (1988) found that adolescents who used marijuana at least weekly were characterized as children by heightened levels of behavioral undercontrol and interpersonal alienation, and these traits were observable as early as 3–4 years of age. Similarly, Caspi, Moffitt, Newman, and Silva (1996) found that 3-year-old boys described by others as impulsive, restless, and distractible were at increased risk for a diagnosis of drug dependence by age 21. Lerner and Vicary (1984) found that 5-year-old children with "difficult" temperamental profiles, including high levels of behavioral reactivity and emotionality and slow adaptability, were more likely than were non-"difficult" children to use substances in adolescence and young adulthood. Wong et al. (2006) found that children with slower rates of increase in behavioral control were more likely to use substances in adolescence.

Several biobehavioral markers of behavioral undercontrol, and risk for adolescent substance use problems, have been identified. One is a diminished P3 component in event-related brain potentials. Reductions in P3 amplitude have been reported for several forms of under-controlled behaviors, including antisocial personality disorder, attention-deficit/hyper-activity disorder (ADHD), and aggression, as well as substance use disorders (Begleiter & Porjesz, 1999; Iacono, Carlson, Taylor, Elkins, & McGue, 1999; Yoon et al., 2006). Moreover, young children of alcoholics also show reduced P3 amplitude even before the onset of drinking (Begleiter & Porjesz, 1999), and reduced P3 amplitude predicts drinking onset in this population (Hill, Shen et al., 2000; Iacono et al., 1999). Other candidate biobehavioral markers for behavioral undercontrol and risk for substance use include neurochemical and neuro-endocrine response and ability to modulate autonomic nervous system reactivity (Iacono et al., 1999; Tarter et al., 1999).

Data from twin studies further suggest that indicators of behavioral undercontrol have substantial heritability, and may serve to increase risk for substance use problems in adolescents, particularly in the context of familial alcoholism. The Minnesota Family Twin Study (Iacono et al., 1999) has found substantial heritability for a variety of indices of undercontrol, including reduced constraint, poor psychophysiological modulation in response to stress, and high levels of externalizing behavior. These traits were also more likely to characterize children with a family history of alcoholism. In turn, these risk factors were strongly associated with a diagnosis of adolescent substance dependence, even after controlling for effects of paternal alcoholism. Taken together, these findings support a genetic diathesis model for adolescent substance use problems, with the diathesis consisting of heritable individual differences in behavioral undercontrol. Consistent with these findings, high levels of impulsivity and low agreeableness partially mediated familial alcoholism effects on the development of substance use disorders (Chassin, Flora, & King, 2004).

Although rarely empirically tested, the effects of temperament on substance use are also presumed to be modified by the environment—particularly by the family environment. Wills, Sandy, Yaeger, and Shinar (2001a) and Stice and Gonzales (1998) examined moderating effects of temperament and parenting on adolescent substance use and found that parental risk factors and parenting behaviors differentially affected risk for substance use among adolescents with differing temperaments. King and Chassin (2004) found a "protective but reactive" interaction between parental support and adolescent behavioral undercontrol in predicting drug disorders. That is, parental support had buffered the effects of behavioral undercontrol, but this protective effect was lost at the highest levels of behavioral undercontrol. Thus, despite their heritable bases, the effects of temperamental characteristics on substance use outcomes may be either exacerbated or buffered by the type of parenting that the adolescent receives.

Cognitive Functioning

Additional evidence for deficient self-regulation as a risk factor for adolescent substance use and abuse may be found in studies of cognitive functioning. Specifically, adolescents with substance use problems are characterized by lower levels of executive functioning—that is, higher order cognitive processes that allow for future goal-oriented behavior. These processes include planning, organizational skills, selective attention, hypothesis generation, cognitive flexibility, maintenance of cognitive set, decision making, judgment, inhibitory control, and self-regulation (Lezak, 1995). These deficits make it difficult for children to create strategic and goal-oriented responses to environmental stimuli, and to use feedback to modify their behavior in response to environmental events (Peterson & Pihl, 1990). Such cognitive difficulties then produce heightened levels of behavioral undercontrol, such as impulsive and externalizing behavior, which raise risk for substance use and substance use disorders (Peterson & Pihl, 1990).

Deficits in cognitive function have been well documented in studies of adults with substance use disorders (Rourke & Loberg, 1996; Sher, Martin, Wood, & Rutledge, 1997), and emerging research suggests that these findings may also apply to adolescents with substance use problems. For example, Brown and colleagues reported that relative to youth without alcohol problems, a sample of alcohol-dependent adolescents was characterized by poorer retention of verbal and nonverbal information, poorer attentional capacities, and deficits in visual–spatial planning (Tapert & Brown, 1999). Similarly, Giancola and colleagues (Giancola, Mezzich, & Tarter, 1998) found that adolescent girls with a substance use disorder exhibited poorer executive functioning relative to controls. Banich et al. (2007) conducted a functional magnetic resonance imaging (fMRI) study comparing adolescents with and without severe substance use and conduct problems as they were performing a Stroop task. Although there were no between-group differences in task performance, the adolescents with substance use and conduct problems showed activation in a greater number of brain structures, suggesting that the underlying attentional processes of adolescent substance abusers may differ from those of normal controls.

Although these cross-sectional studies cannot determine whether executive functioning deficits are a cause or effect of substance use, other data suggest that executive functioning deficits are found in children of alcoholics, even at early ages, before alcohol problems have developed (e.g., Drejer, Theilgard, Teasdale, Schulsinger, & Goodwin, 1985; Giancola, Martin, Tarter, Pelham, & Moss, 1996; Harden & Pihl, 1995; Nigg et al., 2004; Peterson, Finn, & Pihl, 1992). These data suggest that executive functioning may be an antecedent risk factor rather than a result of alcohol consumption in this population. Moreover, Deckel and Hesselbrock (1996) found that children of alcoholics with poorer executive functioning showed greater increases in alcohol consumption over a 3-year period than did children of

alcoholics with higher levels of executive functioning, suggesting that executive functioning was a prospective predictor of substance use among high-risk adolescents. Similarly, Nigg et al. (2006) found that response inhibition prospectively predicted substance use outcomes in a high-risk sample, and Tapert, Baratta, Abrantes, and Brown (2002) found that executive functioning prospectively predicted substance use in a community sample.

Deficits in cognitive functioning among substance users include risky decision making that results in less advantageous outcomes on laboratory tasks such as the Iowa gambling task (Bechara et al., 2001; Stout, Rock, Campbell, Busemeyer, & Finn, 2005). Although mostly studied with adults, these riskier decisions have also been related to substance use in adolescents (Lejeuz et al., 2007) and to college student binge drinking (Goudriaan, Grekin, & Sher, 2007). Poorer decision making on these tasks has been linked to sensitivity to immediate rewards (Stout et al., 2005). Consistent with this interpretation, adolescent substance use has also been related to measures of delay discounting of rewards (Reynolds, Karraker, Horn, & Richards, 2003; Reynolds, Patak, & Shroff, 2007). For example, heavy-drinking adolescents show greater discounting of delayed monetary rewards than do light-drinking adolescents (Field et al., 2007). However, although decision-making measures are often viewed as indicators of behavioral impulsivity, performance on decision-making tasks is not necessarily correlated with impulsivity as measured by questionnaires (Goudriann et al., 2007). Moreover, the tasks themselves are quite complex, and task performance can be influenced by multiple factors other than a focus on immediate reward (Stout et al., 2005). The relation of these underlying cognitive processes to adolescent substance use is not yet well understood and is an important future direction.

Parenting and Socialization

Variations in several aspects of parenting, including nurturance, discipline, monitoring, and conflict, are related to adolescent substance use. Parenting that combines high levels of nurturance with consistent discipline has been associated with a lowered risk of adolescent substance use (see Hawkins et al., 1992, for a review). Stice and Barrera (1995) found that low levels of parental social support and discipline prospectively predicted increases in adolescent substance use over time. Similarly, low levels of parental monitoring have been shown to prospectively predict the onset of both substance use and heavy drinking in adolescence (Reifman, Barnes, Dintcheff, Farrell, & Uhteg, 1998; Simons-Morton & Chen, 2005; Steinberg, Fletcher, & Darling, 1994). Finally, high levels of family conflict (Webb & Baer, 1995), lack of family cohesion (Duncan, Tildesley, Duncan, & Hops, 1995), and parental divorce and single-parent families (Duncan, Duncan & Hops, 1998) have been associated with higher levels of adolescent substance use. Moreover, low levels of family harmony prospectively predict the development of substance use disorders (Zhou, King, & Chassin, 2006). Finally, as noted earlier, the quality of the parent–adolescent relationship moderates the heritability of adolescent substance use (Dick et al., 2007; Miles et al., 2005). Zhou et al. (2006) found that family harmony buffered the effects of family history density of alcoholism on young adults' substance use disorders, although the protective effect of family harmony was lost at the highest levels of family history density. Taken together, the effects of authoritative parenting, close parent–child bonds, and harmonious family climate in reducing the risk of adolescent substance use have led some researchers to call for family-focused intervention as a prevention strategy (Guyll, Spoth, Chao, Wickrama, & Russell, 2004; Spoth, Kavanagh, & Dishion, 2002).

Not only is adolescent substance use related to general parenting style, family climate, and parent–adolescent relationships, but data also suggest that adolescent substance use may be related to parents' specific socialization about the use of substances. Parents not only set general rules and expectations for adolescent behavior, but they set rules and policies about the use of tobacco, alcohol, and other drugs; they may discuss reasons not to use these substances, and they may punish substance use behavior. Cross-sectional studies have suggested that socialization that is specific to substance use may also deter adolescents' substance use behavior (Chassin, Presson, Todd, Rose, & Sherman, 1998; Jackson & Henrickson, 1997). However, some cross-sectional data have shown counterintuitive effects (Huver, Engels, & deVries, 2006), suggesting that the parenting practice may be a reaction to the adolescent's substance use. Moreover, prospective data have been less consistent (Huver, Engels, & deVries, 2006). Chassin et al. (2005) found that smoking-specific parenting practices prospectively predicted adolescent smoking, but only among families with nonsmoking parents. Van der Vorst, Engels, Meeus, and Dekovic (2006) found that strict rules against drinking were associated with postponed onset in adolescents, but only indirectly through earlier alcohol use.

Thus, available data suggest that parent socialization either in the form of general parenting and parent–adolescent relationships or in the form of specific attempts to deter substance use may influence the development of adolescent substance use behavior. Moreover, although data are not extensive, several mediational models suggest that the effects of parenting on adolescent substance use may be mediated through the effects of parenting on affiliations with deviant peer networks as specified in "deviance proneness models" (Chassin, Curran, Hussong, & Colder, 1996; Dishion, Patterson, & Reid, 1988; Nash, McQueen, & Bray, 2005; Simons-Morton & Chen, 2005). Finally, parenting can have important influences on adolescents' connections to broader social–contextual resources such as participation in after-school sports, religious organizations, and clubs which in turn can influence substance use outcomes (Scaramella & Keyes, 2001).

There are also some limitations to existing data on parental influences. Most noteworthy, adolescents who are rebellious, externalizing, and poorly regulated may be difficult to monitor and discipline, and they may also evoke parental rejection (Ge, McCambridge, Smith, & Foxcroft, 1996), and it may be these adolescent characteristics that raise risk for substance use rather than the parenting behavior per se. Reciprocal relations between adolescent problem behavior and parenting must be considered. Moreover, because parents provide both genetic and environmental influences, the correlations between parenting and adolescent substance use that are reported in the literature may inflate the magnitude of what appears to be environmental influence. In this regard, it is noteworthy that several studies of genetically informative samples (Dick et al., 2007; Miles et al., 2005) report parenting as a moderator of genetic influence. Finally, although there is a growing literature on diverse ethnic groups, it is still not known how the role of parenting and family environment factors might differentially affect adolescent substance abuse and dependence across different ethnic or cultural groups. Despite evidence for generalizability of familial influences across ethnic groups (Barrera et al., 2001), some studies have reported differential magnitudes of correlations between parenting and substance use across ethnicity (Broman, Reckase, & Freedman-Doan, 2006) or that the relations between authoritative parenting and adolescent "deviance proneness" might vary as a function of ethnicity and community context (Lamborn, Dornbusch, & Steinberg, 1996; Nowlin & Colder, 2007).

School Failure and Academic Aspirations

Children who are temperamentally poorly regulated, who receive poor parental nurturance and involvement and deficient parental monitoring and discipline, and who have cognitive deficits in executive and verbal functioning are at heightened risk for school failure (Patterson, 1986). Moreover, school failure itself may further elevate risk for the onset of adolescent substance use through several mechanisms. First, school failure is a source of stress and negative affect, which can raise risk for substance use to regulate that affect. Second, school failure can weaken school attachment (e.g., aspirations for higher education, values placed on academic success, participation in mainstream school activities). Estrangement from conventional mainstream social institutions makes adolescents more vulnerable to engaging in "problem" behaviors, including drug use, because they feel less bound by conventional social norms and values. Moreover, adolescents who are not committed to academic success will experience less role conflict between the demands of academic roles and the impairment produced by substance use, so that they have less reason to refrain from substance use. Third, school failure can increase risk for adolescent drug use because it raises risk for adolescents' rejection from a mainstream peer group, particularly if the school failure is associated with aggressive or underregulated behavior (Dishion, Patterson, Stoolmiller, & Skinner, 1991). Adolescents who are rejected from a mainstream peer group are more likely to affiliate with deviant peers, who model and approve of substance use behavior. Consistent with these mechanisms, available empirical evidence suggests that adolescents with poor grades (Cox, Zhang, Johnson, & Bender, 2007; Duncan, Duncan, Biglan, & Ary, 1998; Kandel, 1978), low educational aspirations (e.g., Paulson, Combs, & Richardson, 1990), poor school connectedness (Bond et al., 2007), and low value and expectations for attaining educational success (Jessor & Jessor, 1977) are more likely to use alcohol or drugs. Moreover, MTF data showed that poor school achievement prospectively predicted substance use (in this case, tobacco use) across ethnic groups, for both boys and girls (Bryant, Schulenberg, Bachman, O'Malley, & Johnston, 2000).

Peer Influences

A robust, widely replicated finding is that adolescent alcohol and drug use can be predicted from the alcohol and drug use behavior of their friends (Hawkins et al., 1992; Kandel, 1978), both close friends and larger friendship groups (Urberg, Degirmencioglu, & Pilgrim, 1997). Affiliation with a drug-using peer group elevates risk for adolescent substance use by providing models and opportunities for engaging in drug use as well as norms that approve of drug use behavior. Drug use is also related to membership in different adolescent "cliques" (e.g., "preppies," "jocks," etc.; Sussman, Dent, & McCullar, 2000), and it may serve to communicate particular social images that are characteristic of these peer groups (Barton, Chassin, Presson, & Sherman, 1982). Moreover, substance use by peers within each type of peer context (i.e., close friendships, peer groups, and social groups) contributes uniquely to adolescent substance use, and the presence of non-drug-using peers in one context (e.g., within close friendships) can offset risk associated with the presence of substance-using peers in another context (e.g., within larger peer groups, Hussong & Hicks, 2003). Finally, siblings can constitute a source of peer influence on adolescent drug use (East & Khoo, 2005; Rende, Slomkowski, Lloyd-Richardson, & Niaura, 2005). Correlations have been found between adolescent alcohol use and sibling alcohol use in both biological and adoptive sibling pairs, suggesting an environmental transmission mechanism (McGue, Sharma, & Benson, 1996).

However, even though peer use is typically the strongest predictor of adolescent substance use, researchers have also questioned the interpretation of this relation. Because most studies have the adolescent report on both his or her own use and the behavior of his or her friends, the magnitude of the correlation between peer use and adolescent use is inflated because adolescents who themselves use drugs systematically overestimate their friends' use (Bauman & Ennett, 1996). Correlations between adolescent and friends' drug use are lower (although still significant) when peers are surveyed directly (Kandel, 1978). Moreover, cross-sectional correlations reflect the contribution of two different processes: peer selection (in which drug-using adolescents seek out similar friends) and peer influence (in which drug-using peers influence adolescents' behavior). The contribution of peer selection further inflates the magnitude of the association between peer use and adolescent use (Bauman & Ennett, 1996), although longitudinal data suggest that both peer selection and peer influence processes are operative (Curran, Stice, & Chassin, 1997; Kandel, 1978). Moreover, genetically informative studies find that genetic influences explain a significant amount of the variation of twin reports of peers' substance use, and these findings suggest that peer selection processes are, in part, genetically influenced (Fowler et al., 2007).

Childhood Conduct Problems

A central assumption of the deviance proneness model is that adolescent substance use disorders are related to the broader development of conduct problems and antisociality, an assumption with robust empirical support (see Hawkins et al., 1992; and Zucker, 2006, for reviews). Conduct problems and aggression predict adolescent substance use (Henry et al., 1993; Kellam, Brown Rubin, & Ensminger, 1983), escalations in use over time (Hill, White et al., 2000; Hussong, Curran, & Chassin, 1998), shorter trajectories from drinking onset to alcohol disorder (Hussong, Bauer, & Chassin, in press), and later substance abuse and dependence diagnoses (Chassin et al., 1999; Fergusson, Horwood, & Ridder, 2007; Pardini, White, & Stouthamer-Loeber, 2007) among both boys and girls (Chassin et al., 1999; Costello et al., 1999; Disney, Elkins, McGue, & Iacono, 1999). The magnitude of the association with conduct problems is strongest for illicit drug use and substance use disorders as opposed to licit substance use (Disney et al., 1999). This may reflect the fact that licit drug use in adolescence can be normative and socially enhancing (Maggs & Hurrelman, 1998).

Whether ADHD contributes to risk for substance use in adolescence is less clear. A strong comorbidity between conduct disorder (CD) and ADHD complicates interpretation of findings (Fergusson et al., 2007). Childhood ADHD symptoms or diagnosis predict adolescent substance use and substance use disorder in clinic-referred (Barkley, 1990; Molina & Pelham, 2002) and some nonclinic samples (Disney et al., 1999; Lynsky & Fergusson, 1995), but not all (Costello et al., 1999). However, these effects are magnified for ADHD that is comorbid with CD (Flory, Milich, Lynam, Leukefeld, & Clayton, 2003) and often diminish to nonsignificance once CD or conduct problems are controlled (Fergusson et al., 2007; Pardini et al., 2007). August et al. (2006) found that children with ADHD without a comorbid externalizing disorder did not show elevated substance use later in adolescence. This may indicate that the relation between ADHD and substance use is spurious (due to CD as an underlying "third variable"). Alternatively, it may indicate a mediated process in which ADHD symptoms cause the development of later conduct problems, which in turn increase the likelihood of adolescent substance use. However, the relation of ADHD to substance use may be more complicated because at least one study has reported age specificity of ADHD effects on later substance use (Molina et al., 2007). The effects of ADHD may also vary for different substances. Interestingly, ADHD may confer unique risk for tobacco use, above and beyond the development of conduct problems (Burke, Loeber, & Lahey, 2001; Disney et al., 1999; Milberger, Biederman, Faraone, Chen, & Jones, 1997). Given the well-established beneficial effects of nicotine on attention in adults (Levin et al., 1998), adolescents with ADHD may smoke cigarettes as a way to self-medicate their attentional deficits. Consistent with this interpretation, Burke et al. (2007) found that inattention (but not hyperactivity–impulsivity) significantly predicted adolescent tobacco use.

Stress and Negative Affect Pathways

Theories about the role of stress and negative affect hypothesize that adolescents who are at risk for substance disorders experience a high level of stress and resulting negative affect and use alcohol or drugs as a way to decrease this negative affect (i.e., as a form of self-medication). Although this model is intuitively appealing, it has not enjoyed clear-cut empirical support.

Life Stress

There are consistent findings that adolescents who experience high levels of life stress are more likely to use alcohol or drugs, and to escalate the quantity and frequency of their use over time (Chassin et al., 1996; Hussong & Chassin, 2004; Wills, Vaccaro, McNamara, & Hirky, 1996). However, the literature on the stress–substance use relation in adolescence may overestimate the effects of stress because some measures of stress include items that may reflect the adolescents' conduct problems (e.g., items like "conflicts with teachers"). Nonetheless, even studies that restrict their stress items to uncontrollable life events still report significant prediction of adolescent substance use (e.g., Chassin et al., 1996; Newcomb & Harlow, 1986).

Some research suggests that the relation between stress and substance use may be developmentally sensitive. Alsetine and Gore (2000) showed a weakening of this relation with the transition to young adulthood. Moreover, the effect of stress on substance use appears stronger in youth who initiate drinking early (before age 14), consistent with the possibility that alcohol and stress sensitivities within the developing adolescent brain create a susceptibility to stress-reactive drinking when alcohol is introduced early in adolescence (Dawson, Grant, & Li, 2007).

Adolescents who are at risk for substance use may not only be exposed to heightened levels of stress, but they may also be characterized by abnormal stress responses. Adult children of alcoholics have been reported to exhibit elevated psychophysiological response to stress in the laboratory compared to those without parental alcoholism

(Conrod, Peterson, & Pihl, 1997). Similar findings have been obtained with a small sample of boys whose families had multiple alcoholic members (Harden & Pihl, 1995). These young boys showed greater heart rate increases and peripheral vasoconstriction during a mental arithmetic task than did boys without a family history of alcoholism, suggesting that substance use may provide a way to regulate stress response. In contrast, however, Moss, Vanyukov, Yao, and Irillova (1999) found that sons whose fathers had a substance use disorder had a decreased salivary cortisol response to an anticipated stressor, and that those boys with lower cortisol responses also showed more marijuana use. Moss et al. (1999) suggest that hyporeactivity in these boys may represent an adaptation to chronic exposure to high levels of stress. Finally, Iacono et al. (1999) suggest that adolescents at risk for substance use problems show poor modulation of stress responses, as reflected in an ability to control psychophysiological arousal in predictable versus unpredictable exposures to a laboratory stressor. Although the possibility that high-risk adolescents show abnormalities in stress response is potentially of great etiological importance, there have been very few empirical studies (particularly of girls), so conclusions must remain preliminary at this point.

The Role of Emotional Distress

The relation of emotional distress to adolescent substance use and substance use disorders has not been consistently upheld. Many studies have reported cross-sectional correlations between negative affect and adolescent substance use (Chassin, Pillow, Curran, Molina, & Barrera, 1993; Cooper, Frone, Russell, & Mudar, 1995), as well as substantial comorbidity between clinically diagnosed depression and adolescent nicotine dependence (Fergusson, Lynsky, & Horwood, 1996b), alcoholism (Rohde, Lewinsohn, & Seeley, 1996), and drug abuse or dependence (Armstrong & Costello, 2002; Deykin, Buka, & Zeena, 1992). However, other researchers have argued that negative

affectivity has only weak relations to adolescent substance use compared to factors such as peer affiliations, and that effects of emotional distress are weak and indirect (Swaim, Oetting, & Beauvais, 1989). Moreover, studies considering the role of negative affect have often failed to consider the effects of externalizing symptoms and conduct problems. Because there is considerable covariation between internalizing and externalizing symptoms, it has not been clearly established that negative affect has a unique relation to adolescent substance use (above and beyond co-occurring conduct problems). Those that have often fail to find unique effects of negative affect (Capaldi & Stoolmiller, 1999; Miller-Johnson, Lochman, Coie, Terry, & Hyman, 1998). However, because internalizing and externalizing symptoms become increasingly comorbid with adolescence, unique effects may be evident for only more chronic internalizing symptoms that predate adolescence.

Perhaps most important, longitudinal studies have not consistently confirmed that negative affectivity prospectively predicts the onset or escalation of adolescent substance use or the development of substance abuse and dependence (Hansell & White, 1991; see Hallfors, Waller, Bauer, Ford, & Halpern, 2005; Hill, White et al., 2000; and Hussong et al., 1998, for studies failing to support this relation). In fact, anxiety has been associated with delayed onset of gateway drug use such as cigarette smoking (Costello et al., 1999). In terms of clinical disorders, Chassin et al. (1999) found that adolescent internalizing symptoms did not prospectively predict young adult alcohol and drug diagnoses, and Rohde et al. (1996) did not find that depressive disorder preceded the development of adolescent alcohol abuse and dependence. This pattern of cross-sectional but not prospective relations between negative affect and adolescent substance use suggests that negative affect might be a result, rather than a cause, of adolescent substance use and substance use problems. Evidence for both the short-term and long-term impact of substance use on emotions and internalizing symptoms come from studies of adults (Sher & Grekin, 2007) and longitudinal studies of adolescents (Trim, Meehan, King, & Chassin, 2007).

Despite the inconsistent prospective findings, it might be premature to dismiss the role of negative affect in the development of adolescent substance use disorders for several reasons. First, some studies do find prospective effects (e.g., Mason, Hitchings, & Spoth, 2007; Repetto, Caldwell, & Zimmerman, 2005; Windle & Windle, 2001). Second, the time lag of measurement in most longitudinal studies (often a year or more) is not optimal for detecting self-medication. Recent studies using temporally informative designs (e.g., experience and event sampling, diary-based assessments) have shown short-term (within a day or over 1–4 days) covariation in mood and drinking in college and adult samples (Hussong, Hicks, Levy, & Curran, 2001; Park, Armeli, & Tennen, 2004). Microanalytic techniques, such as experience sampling methods, might reveal different findings in adolescents as well.

In addition, conflicting findings might be due to variation in the type of negative affect that is assessed. Support has been stronger for depression, irritability, and anger as prospective predictors of adolescent substance use than for anxiety (Block et al., 1988; Swaim et al., 1989). In prospective analyses, Kaplow, Curran, Angold, and Costello (2001) showed that generalized anxiety disorder predicted substance use initiation, whereas separation anxiety disorder decreased the likelihood of initiation. Anxious adolescents who fear social interaction and parental separation may be less likely to select into (or to be selected into) peer contexts that promote substance use, thus decreasing risk for substance use, whereas those anxious adolescents with more generalized fears may initiate substance use to self-medicate. In addition, findings from Shoal, Castaneda, and Giancola (2005) suggest that worry specifically may reduce risk for substance use in adolescents who are high in negative affect. However, because aggregated daily reports of greater anxiety

are positively associated with smoking and drinking in youth (Henker, Whalen, Jamner, & Delfino, 2002), and other researchers suggest that clinically diagnosed social phobia increases risk for substance use (Merikangas & Avenevoli, 2000), further studies of anxiety and social phobia are warranted. In short, variations in both the type of negative affect (depression, anger, irritability versus anxiety) and the severity of the distress (e.g., symptomatology versus actual clinical diagnosis) might produce differing findings.

Related to the distinction between the roles of anxiety and depression is the role of positive affect. Recent conceptualizations of the distinction between anxiety and depression suggest that anxiety may co-occur with positive affect, whereas depression is more likely correlated with low levels of positive affect (Watson, Clark, & Carey, 1988). Indeed, a motivation to use substances in order to increase positive affect has also been posited within affect regulation models (Cooper et al., 1995), although it has not been as widely studied as the motivation to reduce negative affect. Some researchers have suggested that adolescents who use substances to maintain or enhance positive affect may use at moderate levels of quantity and frequency, whereas those who use substances to relieve negative affect may show higher consumption (Labouvie, Pandina, White, & Johnson, 1990). In a 3-month diary study of marijuana-abusing adolescents not receiving treatment, 81% of moods experienced during periods of use were described as happy, relaxed, and tired (Smith, Koob, & Wirtz, 1985). Data also suggest that low levels of positive affect are particularly associated with adolescent substance use for those adolescents who are also highly impulsive (Colder & Chassin, 1997). Thus, affect regulation models should consider multiple states, including depression, anxiety, general distress, and positive affect.

Finally, the lack of consistent relations between negative affect and adolescent substance use may reflect the presence of moderator variables, such that negative affectivity produces risk for substance use under only certain circumstances. In Sher's (1991) submodel, one important potential moderator variable is coping style. Theoretically, adolescents should not react to emotional distress by turning to substance use if other, more adaptive coping mechanisms are available to them. Some data suggest that behavioral coping (e.g., "Make a plan and follow it") may serve such an adaptive function (Wills, 1986) but that "disengagement coping" (e.g., coping through anger, hanging out with friends) may actually amplify the effects of life stress events on growth over time in adolescent substance use (Wills, Sandy, Yaeger, Cleary, & Shinar, 2001b).

Similarly, Sher (1991) suggests that the relation between stress or emotional distress and substance use should be stronger for those who expect substance use to relieve their emotional distress, and this hypothesis has received some empirical support (Kushner, Sher, Wood, & Wood, 1994).

Individual differences may also moderate the relation between negative affectivity and adolescent substance use. For example, research in social development has suggested that low levels of temperamental self-regulation will amplify the relation between reactivity (a propensity to experience intense affective states) and conduct problems (Eisenberg et al., 2000). Thus, adolescents who are highly emotionally reactive may show particularly heightened risk for substance use or abuse or dependence when they also show low levels of temperamental self-regulation. Interestingly, some laboratory data also suggest that individuals who are temperamentally "underregulated" may derive the strongest psychophysiological stress response dampening benefits from consuming alcohol (Levenson, Oyama, & Meek, 1987). If behaviorally undercontrolled individuals derive greater stress response dampening effects from consuming alcohol and drugs, then this would be consistent with stronger links between stress or negative affect and substance use for individuals who are low in self-regulation. This notion of self-regulation as a moderator variable

in the relation between negative affect and substance use can serve to bridge "deviance proneness" models of adolescent substance use with "stress and negative affect" models of adolescent substance use. Although these two models have typically been conceptualized and studied in isolation of each other, the relation between these two pathways is worthy of future study. Finally, both gender and age may moderate the relation between negative affectivity and substance use disorders. Negative affect and self-medication motives may be more strongly linked to substance abuse and dependence that has late onset (later in adulthood) and among females (Cloninger, 1987).

Models of Substance Use Effects

The discussion of "deviance proneness" and "stress and negative affect" models serves to illustrate the importance of considering the functions that substance use might serve for adolescents. Deviance proneness models highlight the fact that adolescent substance use occurs in a broader social context of low behavioral constraint and drug use–promoting peer networks. Within these contexts, substance use may serve the function of communicating a social image of toughness and precocity and expressing an adolescent's actual or ideal self-concept (Barton et al., 1982; Gerrard, Gibbons, Stock, Lune, & Cleveland, 2005; Jessor & Jessor, 1977; Sussman et al., 2000). Stress and negative affect models highlight the affect-regulating functions that alcohol and drug use might serve for adolescents. However, in considering the multiple functions that substance use might serve for adolescents, it is important to remember that alcohol and drug consumption produces reinforcing pharmacological effects as well as social benefits. It is important to consider these pharmacological effects within etiological models of adolescent substance use and abuse. In substance use effects models, risk for substance disorders is thought to be associated with individual differences in sensitivity to the pharmacological effects of alcohol and other drugs. As individuals experience different effects of their alcohol and drug use, these experiences then influence their expectancies about the effects of future consumption, which in turn influence future substance use.

A large literature on substance use effects has examined the impact of alcohol and drug self-administration in both human and animal laboratory studies, and this literature is beyond the scope of the current chapter. Moreover, for ethical reasons, laboratory studies of self-administration have been largely confined to adult participants. Researchers who are interested in child and adolescent populations have more often studied beliefs or expectancies about substance use effects than actual effects experienced in the laboratory. These expectancies can be measured in young children even before substance use begins, become increasingly complex with age (Dunn & Goldman, 1996), and predict adolescent drug use (Aarons, Brown, Stice, & Coe, 2001; Smith, Goldman, Greenbaum, & Christiansen, 1995; Stacy, Newcomb, & Bentler, 1991). In addition to expectancies, researchers have examined self-reported retrospections of initial use episodes, and found that adolescents who report greater positive and/or fewer negative experiences in their initial use episodes are more likely to increase their use (Eissenberg & Balster, 2000).

Although laboratory studies have been largely confined to adult samples, they are certainly important for etiological theories of substance use. For example, these studies suggest that individuals with family histories of alcoholism derive greater cardiovascular stress response–dampening benefits from consuming alcohol in anticipation of a laboratory stressor (Levenson et al., 1987), and show greater increases in resting heart rate after drinking (which has been interpreted as reflecting greater reinforcement from the "psychostimulant" effects of alcohol; Conrod, Peterson, & Pihl, 1997). Thus, high-risk individuals may derive more reinforcement from drinking than do their low-risk peers (at least for men;

Croissant, Rist, Demmel, & Olbrich, 2006), and this might explain their greater alcohol involvement. Similarly, high-risk men experience less negative impact of alcohol consumption than do their low-risk peers (e.g., less body sway and less perceived intoxication), and a lowered response to the negative effects of alcohol prospectively predicts the development of alcohol use disorders 15 years later (Schuckit & Smith, 2000; Schuckit, Smith, Pierson, Danko, & Beltran, 2006). Individuals who experience little negative impact of drinking will have little reason to curtail their intake, thus raising their risk for high levels of consumption and subsequent alcohol use disorders. Taken together, these data suggest that individual differences in the positive or negative pharmacological effects of consumption may motivate future use, and thus influence risk for developing substance use disorders. Moreover, to the extent that these individual differences are heritable (e.g., Schuckit, Smith, & Kalmijn, 2004), they may mediate family history risk for later substance use disorders.

Macrolevel Influences: Neighborhoods and Schools

Sher's (1991) models do not focus on social influences that are broader than peer and family environments. However, there have been some efforts to understand the ways in which broader macrolevel factors such as school environments, neighborhoods, and state policies might influence adolescent substance use and substance use disorders. These factors could influence risk for substance use and abuse by providing social norms about the acceptability of use, affecting ease of access to substances, and providing punishment or sanctions for use.

The status of neighborhoods is often assessed with indicators of neighborhoods' SES, ethnic composition, and residential mobility (Leventhal & Brooks-Gunn, 2000). Surprisingly, although disadvantaged neighborhoods show more adolescent conduct problems and delinquency than do advantaged neighborhoods, the opposite has been found for adolescent substance use (Leventhal & Brooks-Gunn, 2000). For example, higher rates of adolescent substance use have been reported for neighborhoods with higher SES (Skager & Fisher, 1989), low rates of residential instability, high neighborhood attachment, and low density (Ennett, Flewelling, Lindrooth, & Norton, 1997), and higher prevalences of residents with professional or managerial occupations (Luthar & Cushing, 1999). However, findings are not entirely consistent. Smart, Adlaf, and Walsh (1994) found an inverse relation between neighborhood SES and adolescent substance use. Nowlin and Colder (2007) found that neighborhood poverty was related to smoking for White but not Black adolescents. The emerging pattern may suggest a nonlinear relation between social disadvantage and substance use, with both high and low social disadvantage increasing risk, though perhaps through different mechanisms.

Initial attempts to examine these mediators in socially disadvantaged neighborhoods show that adolescents' beliefs about drugs (i.e., lower perceived harm and greater approval of use) in part explain risk for substance use in African American urban youth, though a decreased sense of control resulting from the stress of living in such neighborhoods does not (Lambert, Brown, Phillips, & Ialongo, 2004). In addition, greater social disadvantage is related to lower neighborhood social cohesion and control, which in turn predict greater perceptions of neighborhood problems with youth alcohol and drug use as well as more youth alcohol and drug arrests (Duncan, Duncan, & Strycker, 2002). Moreover, other factors, such as parental absence or emphasis on achievements may similarly predict risk for adjustment problems in preadolescents in both affluent and disadvantaged neighborhoods (Luthar & Latendresse, 2005); however, whether this finding generalizes to predict risk for substance use is as of yet unclear.

More research is necessary to identify the mechanisms underlying these neighborhood effects, and also to examine ways in which they interrelate with other etiological factors such as personality characteristics and family environment. Although some research suggests that neighborhood influences serve to moderate the effects of personality characteristics on juvenile offending (Lynam et al., 2000), and that neighborhood influences on adolescent problem behaviors are mediated through family environment effects (Scaramella & Keyes, 2001; Simons, Johnson, Beamans, Conger, & Whitbeck, 1996), these types of analyses have not been applied to studies of adolescent substance use disorders as specific outcomes.

In addition to social disadvantage, researchers have suggested that schools and neighborhoods in which norms are more favorable to use, and in which there is greater availability and access to substances, are associated with higher use rates. For example, school norms have been related to adolescent substance use (Allison et al., 1999), and density of alcohol outlets has been related to alcohol use at the community level (Scribner, Cohen, & Fisher, 2000). For legal drugs such as alcohol and tobacco, findings such as these have been used to support public policies that aim to decrease adolescents' access to substances and change community norms (e.g., raising drinking ages, reducing sales to minors, increasing tobacco taxes, restricting advertising) as ways of reducing adolescent substance use (see Institute of Medicine, 1994, for a review). A meta-analysis of studies accessing effectiveness of laws restricting youth access to tobacco showed no effects of having such access laws, of level of merchant compliance with such laws, and of increased compliance with these laws over time on 30-day and regular youth smoking prevalence (Fichtenberg & Glantz, 2002). Other studies have shown such effects in the absence of controls for other state policies impacting youth smoking (e.g., clean air laws and media campaigns; Luke, Stamatakis, & Brownson, 2000) and policies to reduce access do decrease retail and vending machine purchases and self-service purchases (Johnston, O'Malley, & Terry-McElrath, 2004). Such findings may not be at odds, however, as access laws may indeed reduce sales but not uniquely impact smoking rates as youth seek out alternate, nonretail means of accessing tobacco products (e.g., friends, parents) when access laws are enforced.

CONCLUSIONS AND FUTURE DIRECTIONS

As illustrated by the preceding discussion, much is known about the nature of adolescent substance use and substance use disorders and their developmental antecedents. A large and diverse literature has produced consensus that a family history of substance abuse, childhood conduct problems, temperamental traits reflecting "behavioral undercontrol," and affiliations with drug-using peers all raise risk for substance use and substance use disorders.

However, there are also many unanswered questions and areas for future research. Basic descriptive studies are needed to distinguish among multiple trajectories of substance use in adolescence, to determine whether some are relatively benign, and to determine whether there are differential antecedents for trajectories that result in clinical impairment and addictive disorders. These studies may help to refine the phenotypes of adolescent substance use and identify underlying endophenotypes. Moreover, studies are needed to understand more about the neurobiological vulnerability of adolescents to substance use effects, and to understand the extent to which animal models of substance use effects can generalize to human adolescents. Similarly, studies are needed to examine the impact of adolescent substance use on a broad range of developmental outcomes, including emerging competencies and coping abilities. In terms of etiology, although the role of family history risk is well established, much less is known about the mechanisms underlying the intergenerational transmission of risk or about the protective factors that might buffer this risk (which could be useful targets for preventive intervention). Moreover, stress reactivity and negative affect regulation models of adolescent substance use disorders are in need of further study, and their effects are often difficult to identify because they can be obscured in the context of strong externalizing influences on substance use. Further research is needed to clarify the roles of different types of negative affect and the importance of moderating variables such as coping or behavioral undercontrol. Additional information on mediating mechanisms that underlie the relation between negative affect and substance use across development is also important. In terms of the deviance proneness pathway, research is needed to identify variables (if any) that are related specifically to substance use outcomes rather than to conduct problems in general, and to understand the roles of cognitive processes related to decision making (particularly decision making in "real-world" contexts in the presence of affective arousal and cues for reward). Implications of the neurobiology of adolescence in terms of brain systems underlying reward (particularly social reward) and self-regulation (and the discrepancies in the developmental courses of these systems) are important for increasing our understanding of adolescent substance use and risk behaviors more broadly. Across all the developmental models, more data are needed on ways in which existing findings might vary across particular gender and ethnic groups. There is a need for theories of adolescent substance use that include ethnicity, as well as data on the cultural and historical heterogeneity (e.g., immigration status, acculturation) that exists among people within an ethnic subgroup. Additionally, more research is needed on the influence of SES on substance use, taking into consideration curvilinear patterns and different types of SES markers. Moreover, this area is in need of stronger theory development that would help guide our interpretations of why particular risk or protective factors might operate in particular ways within certain gender or ethnic subgroups. Research is also needed to study the effects of neighborhood, school, and social policy influences as they interact with individual, family, and peer factors. Moreover, research is needed to provide richer descriptions of neighborhood contexts and the mediating mechanisms that explain their effects.

Given the heterogeneity of substance use behaviors and variation in their onset and course, it is clear that a single etiological pathway will not be capable of explaining the development of adolescent substance use and substance use disorders. Similarly, given the significant selection and transactional effects that confound risk processes and substance use outcomes over time, it remains difficult to parse factors that play an etiological role in substance disorders versus those that merely result from substance involvement. Thus, we are in need of studies and methods that are capable of differentiating among multiple pathways that might underlie different trajectories of substance use. Achieving this goal requires studies that are multilevel and multidisciplinary, and that embed studies of substance use and substance use disorders within a broader developmental perspective. Given the clinical and public health importance of adolescent substance use and substance use disorders, it is essential that the field continues to expand in these future directions.

REFERENCES

Aarons, G., Brown, S., Stice, E., & Coe, M. (2001). Psychometric evaluation of the marijuana and stimulant effect expectancy questionnaires for adolescents. *Addictive Behaviors, 26,* 219–236.

Abroms, L., Simons-Morton, B., Haynie, D., & Chen, R. (2005). Psychosocial predictors of smoking trajectories during middle and high school. *Addiction, 100,* 852–861.

Allison, K. W., Crawford, I., Leone, P., Trickett, E., Perez-Febles, A., Burton, L., et al. (1999). Adolescent substance use: Preliminary examinations of school and neighborhood context. *American Journal of Community Psychology, 27,* 111–141.

Amaro, H., Whitaker, R., Coffman, G., & Heeren, T. (1990) Acculturation and marijuana and cocaine use: Findings from the HHANES 1982–84. *American Journal of Public Health, 80,* 54–60.

American Cancer Society. (2007). *Cancer facts & figures 2007.* Atlanta, GA: Author.

American Heart Association. (2007). *Heart disease and stroke statistics—2007 update.* Dallas, TX: Author.

American Psychiatric Association. (1994). *Diagnostic and Statistical Manual of Mental Disorders* (4th ed.). Washington, DC: Author.

Andersson, T., & Magnusson, D. (1990). Biological maturation in adolescence and the development of drinking habits and alcohol abuse among young males: A prospective longitudinal study. *Journal of Youth and Adolescence, 19,* 33–41.

Aquilino, W. S., & Wright, D. L. (1996). Substance use estimates from RDD and area probability samples: Impact of differential screening methods and unit non-response. *Public Opinion Quarterly, 60,* 563–573.

Armstrong, T. D., & Costello, E. J. (2002). Community studies on adolescent substance use, abuse, or dependence and psychiatric comorbidity. *Journal of Consulting and Clinical Psychology* [Special Issue: Impact of childhood psychopathology interventions on subsequent substance abuse], *70,* 1224–1239.

Aro, H., & Taipale, V. (1987). The impact of timing of puberty on psychosomatic symptoms among fourteen to sixteen-year old Finnish girls. *Child Development, 58,* 261–268.

Aseltine, R. H., Jr., & Gore, S. L. (2000). The variable effects of stress on alcohol use from adolescence to early adulthood. *Substance Use and Misuse.* [Special Issue: Stress and substance use], *35,* 643–668.

Audrain-McGovern, J., Lerman, C., Wileyto, E., Rodriguez, D., & Shields, P. (2004). Interacting effects of genetic predisposition and depression on adolescent smoking progression. *American Journal of Psychiatry, 161,* 1224–1230.

August, G., Winters, K., Realmuto, G., Fahnhorst, T., Botzet, A., & Lee, S. (2006). Prospective study of adolescent drug use among community samples of ADHD and non-ADHD participants. *Journal of the American Academy of Child and Adolescent Psychiatry, 45,* 824–832.

Bachman, J. G., Safron, D. J., Sy, S. R., & Schulenberg, J. E. (2003). Wishing to work: New perspectives on how adolescents' part-time work intensity is linked to educational disengagement, substance use, and other problem behaviours. *International Journal of Behavioral Development, 27,* 301–315.

Bachman, J. G., Wadsworth, K., O'Malley, P., Johnston, L., & Schulenberg, J. (1997). *Smoking, drinking, and drug use in young adulthood: The impact of new freedoms and new responsibilities.* Mahwah, NJ: Lawrence Erlbaum.

Baer, J. S., Barr, H., Bookstein, F., Sampson, P., & Streissguth, A. (1998). Prenatal alcohol exposure and family history of alcoholism in the etiology of adolescent alcohol problems. *Journal of Studies on Alcohol, 59,* 533–543.

Baer, J. S., Sampson, P. D., Barr, H. M., Connor, P. D., & Streissguth, A. (2003). A 21 year longitudinal analysis of the effects of prenatal alcohol exposure on young adult drinking. *Archives of General Psychiatry, 60,* 377–385.

Banich, M., Crowley, T., Thompson, L., Jacobsen, B., Liu, X., Raymond, K., et al. (2007). Brain activation during the Stroop task in adolescents with severe substance and conduct problems: A pilot study. *Drug and Alcohol Dependence, 90,* 175–182.

Barkley, R. A. (1990). The adolescent outcome of hyperactive children diagnosed by research criteria: I. An 8-year prospective follow-up study. *Journal of the American Academy of Child and Adolescent Psychiatry, 29,* 546–557.

Barrera, M., Jr., Biglan, A., Ary, D., & Li, F. (2001). Modeling parental and peer influences on problem behavior of American Indian, Hispanic, and non-Hispanic Caucasian youth. *Journal of Early Adolescence, 21,* 133–156.

Barrera, M. B., Castro, F. G., & Biglan, A. (1999). Ethnicity, substance use, and development: Exemplars for exploring group differences and similarities. *Development and Psychopathology, 11,* 805–822.

Barton, J., Chassin, L., Presson, C., & Sherman, S. J. (1982). Social image factors as motivators of smoking initiation in early and middle adolescents. *Child Development, 53,* 1499–1511.

Bauman, K. E., & Ennett, S. T. (1996). On the importance of peer influence for adolescent drug use: Commonly neglected considerations. *Addiction, 91,* 185–198.

Baumrind, D., & Moselle, K. (1985). A developmental perspective on adolescent drug abuse. *Advances in Alcohol and Substance Abuse, 4,* 41–67.

Bechara, A., Dolan, S., Denburg, N., Hindes, A., Anderson, W., & Nathan, P. (2001). Decision-making deficits linked to a dysfunctional ventromedial prefrontal cortex, revealed in alcohol and stimulant abusers. *Neuropsychologia, 39,* 376–389.

Begleiter, H., & Porjesz, B. (1999). What is inherited in the predisposition toward alcoholism: A proposed model. *Alcoholism: Clinical and Experimental Research, 23,* 1125–1135.

Belluzzi, J. D., Lee, A. G., Oliff, H. S., & Leslie, F. M. (2004). Age-dependence effects of nicotine on locomotor activity and conditioned place preference in rats. *Psychopharmacology, 174,* 389–395.

Bersamin, M., Paschall, M. J., & Flewelling, R. L. (2005). Ethnic differences in relationships between risk factors and adolescent binge drinking: A national study. *Prevention Science, 6,* 127–137.

Block, J., Block, H., & Keyes, S. (1988). Longitudinally foretelling drug usage in adolescence: Early childhood personality and environmental precursors. *Child Development, 59,* 336–355.

Bogart, L. M., Collins, R. L., Ellickson, P. L., Martino, S. C., & Klein, D. J. (2005). Effects of early and later marriage on women's alcohol use in young adulthood: A prospective analysis. *Journal of Studies on Alcohol, 66,* 729–737.

Bond, L., Butler, N., Thomas, L., Carling, J., Glover, S., Bowes, G., et al. (2007). Social and school connectedness in early secondary school as predictors of late teenage substance use, mental health, and academic outcomes. *Journal of Adolescent Health, 40,* 357–366.

Bray, J. H., Getz, J. G., & Baer, P. E. (2000). Adolescent individuation and alcohol use in multi-ethnic youth. *Journal of Studies on Alcohol, 61,* 588–597.

Broman, C., Reckase, M., & Freedman-Doan, C. (2006). The role of parenting in drug use among black, Latino, and white adolescents. *Journal of Ethnicity and Substance Use, 5,* 39–50.

Brook, J. S., Brook, D. W., Arencibia-Mireles, O., Richter, L., & Whiteman, M. (2001). Risk factors for adolescent marijuana use across cultures and across time. *Journal of Genetic Psychology, 162,* 357–374.

Brook, J. S., Pahl, K., & Ning, Y. (2006). Peer and parental influences on longitudinal trajectories of smoking among African Americans and Puerto Ricans. *Nicotine & Tobacco Research, 8,* 639–651.

Brown, S., & D'Amico, E. (2003). Outcomes of alcohol treatment for adolescents. *Recent Developments in Alcoholism, 16,* 289–312.

Brown, T. L., Flory, K., Lynam, D. R., Leukefeld, C., & Clayton, R. R. (2004). Comparing the developmental trajectories of marijuana use of African American and Caucasian adolescents: Patterns, antecedents, and consequences. *Experimental and Clinical Psychopharmacology, 12*(1), 47–56.

Bryant, A., Schulenberg, J., Bachman, J., O'Malley, P., & Johnston, L. (2000). Understanding the links among school misbehavior, academic achievement and cigarette use: A national panel study of adolescents. *Prevention Science, 1,* 71–87.

Buchan, B. J., Dennis, M. L., Tims, F. M., & Diamond, G. S. (2002). Cannabis use: Consistency and validity of self-report, on-site urine testing and laboratory testing. *Addiction, 97*(Suppl.), 98–108.

Burke, J., Loeber, R., & Lahey, B. (2001). Which aspects of ADHD are associated with tobacco use in early adolescence? *Journal of Child Psychology and Psychiatry and Allied Disciplines, 42,* 493–502.

Burke, J., Loeber, R, White, H. R., Stouthamer-Loeber, M., & Pardini, D. (2007). Inattention as a key predictor of tobacco use in adolescence. *Journal of Abnormal Psychology, 116,* 249–258.

Caetano, R., & Babor, T. (2006). Diagnosis of alcohol dependence in epidemiological surveys: An epidemic of youthful alcohol dependence of a case of measurement error? *Addiction, 101* [Special Issue], 111–114.

Cantwell, D., Lewinsohn, P., Rohde, P., & Seeley, J. R. (1997). Correspondence between adolescent report and parent report of psychiatric diagnostic data. *Journal of the American Academy of Child and Adolescent Psychiatry, 36,* 610–619.

Capaldi, D. M., & Stoolmiller, M. (1999). Co-occurrence of conduct problems and depressive symptoms in early adolescent boys: III. Prediction to young-adult adjustment. *Development and Psychopathology, 11,* 59–84.

Caspi, A., Moffitt, T. E., Cannon, M., McClay, J., Murray, R., & Harrington, H., et al. (2005). Moderation of the effect of adolescent-onset cannabis use on adult psychosis by a functional polymorphism in the catechol-O-methyltransferase gene: Longitudinal evidence of a gene X environment interaction. *Biological Psychiatry, 57,* 1117–1127.

Caspi, A., Moffitt, T., Newman, D., & Silva, P. (1996). Behavioral observations at age 3 predict adult psychiatric disorders. *Archives of General Psychiatry, 53,* 1033–1039.

Caulkins, J., Liccardo, R., Pacula, S., Paddock, S., & Chiesa, J. (2002). *School-based drug prevention: What kind of drug use does it prevent?* Santa Monica, CA: Rand Corporation.

Chambers, R., Taylor, J., & Potenza, M. (2003). Developmental neurocircuitry of motivation in adolescence: A critical period of addiction vulnerability. *American Journal of Psychiatry, 160,* 1041–1052.

Chassin, L., Curran, P. J., Hussong, A. M., & Colder, C. R. (1996). The relation of parent alcoholism to adolescent substance use: A longitudinal follow-up study. *Journal of Abnormal Psychology, 105,* 70–80.

Chassin, L., Flora, D., & King, K. (2004). Trajectories of alcohol and drug use and dependence from adolescence to adulthood: The effects of familial alcoholism and personality. *Journal of Abnormal Psychology, 113,* 483–498.

Chassin, L., Pillow, D. R., Curran, P. J., Molina, B. S. G., & Barrera, M., Jr. (1993). Relation of parental alcoholism to early adolescent substance use: A test of three mediating mechanisms. *Journal of Abnormal Psychology, 102,* 3–19.

Chassin, L., Pitts, S., & DeLucia, C. (1999). The relation of adolescent substance use to young adult autonomy, positive activity involvement, and perceived competence. *Development and Psychopathology, 11,* 915–932.

Chassin, L., Pitts, S., & Prost, J. (2002). Heavy drinking trajectories from adolescence to young adulthood in a high risk sample: Predictors and substance abuse outcomes. *Journal of Consulting and Clinical Psychology, 70,* 67–78.

Chassin, L., Presson, C. C., Sherman, S. J., & Edwards, D. (1992). The natural history of cigarette smoking and young adult social roles. *Journal of Health and Social Behavior, 33,* 328–347.

Chassin, L., Presson, C. C., Pitts, S., & Sherman, S. J. (2000). The natural history of cigarette smoking from adolescence to adulthood in a midwestern community sample: Multiple trajectories and their psychosocial correlates. *Health Psychology, 19,* 223–231.

Chassin, L., Presson, C. C., Todd, M., Rose, J., & Sherman, S. J. (1998). Maternal socialization of adolescent smoking: The intergenerational transmission of parenting and smoking. *Developmental Psychology, 34,* 1189–1201.

Chassin, L., Presson, C., Rose, J., Sherman, S., Davis, M., & Gonzalez, J. (2005). Parenting style and smoking-specific parenting practices as predictors of adolescent smoking onset. *Journal of Pediatric Psychology, 30,* 333–344.

Chatterji, P. (2006). Illicit drug use and educational attainment. *Health Economics, 15,* 489–511.

Chen, X., Unger, J. B., Cruz, T. B., & Johnson, C. A. (1999). Smoking patterns of Asian-American youth in California and their relationship with acculturation. *Journal of Adolescent Health, 24,* 321–328.

Chen, X., Unger, J. B., Palmer, P., Weiner, M. D., Johnson, C. A., Wong, M. M., et al. (2002). Prior cigarette smoking initiation predicting current alcohol use: Evidence for a gateway drug effect among California adolescents from eleven ethnic groups. *Addictive Behaviors, 27,* 799–817.

Choi, Y., & Lahey, B. B. (2006). Testing the model minority stereotype: Youth behaviors across racial and ethnic groups. *Social Service Review, 80,* 419–452.

Chotro, M., Arias, C., & Laviola, G. (2007). Increased ethanol intake after prenatal ethanol exposure: Studies with animals. *Neuroscience Biobehavioral Reviews, 31,* 181–191.

Chung, T., Martin, C., & Winters, K. (2005). Diagnosis, course, and assessment of alcohol abuse and dependence in adolescents. *Recent Developments in Alcoholism, 17,* 5–27.

Clayton, R. (1992). Transitions in drug use: Risk and protective factors. In M. Glantz & R. Pickens (Eds.), *Vulnerability to drug abuse* (pp. 15–51). Washington, DC: American Psychological Association.

Cloninger, C. R. (1987). Neurogenetic adaptive mechanisms in alcoholism. *Science, 236,* 410–416.

Colder, C., & Chassin, L. (1997). Affectivity and impulsivity: Temperament risk for adolescent alcohol involvement. *Psychology of Addictive Behaviors, 11,* 83–97.

Colder, C., & Chassin, L. (1999). The psychosocial characteristics of alcohol users vs. problem users: Data from a student of adolescents at risk. *Development and Psychopathology, 11,* 321–348.

Colder, C., Mehta, P., Balanda, K., Campbell, R., Mayhew, K., Stanton, W., et al. (2001). Identifying trajectories of adolescent smoking: An application of latent growth mixture modeling. *Health Psychology, 20,* 127–135.

Conrod, P., Petersen, J., & Pihl, R. O. (1997). Disinhibited personality and sensitivity to alcohol reinforcement: Independent correlates of drinking behavior in sons of alcoholics. *Alcoholism: Clinical and Experimental Research, 21,* 1320–1332.

Cooper, M. L. (1994). Motivations for alcohol use among adolescents: Development and validation of a four-factor model. *Psychological Assessment, 6,* 117–128.

Cooper, M. L., Frone, M. R., Russell, M., & Mudar, P. (1995). Drinking to regulate positive and negative emotions: A motivational model of alcohol use. *Journal of Personality and Social Psychology, 69,* 990–1005.

Cornelius, M., Leech, S., Goldschmidt, L., & Day, N. (2000). Prenatal tobacco exposure: Is it a risk factor for early tobacco experimentation? *Nicotine and Tobacco Research, 2,* 45–52.

Cornelius, M., Leech, S., Goldschmidt, L., & Day, N. (2005). Is prenatal tobacco exposure a risk factor for early adolescent smoking? A follow-up study. *Neurotoxicology and Teratology, 27,* 667–676.

Costa, F. M., Jessor, R., & Turbin, M. S. (1999). Transition into adolescent problem drinking: The role of psychosocial risk and protective factors. *Journal of Studies on Alcohol, 60,* 480–490.

Costello, E. J., Erkanli, A., Federman, E., & Angold, A. (1999). Development of psychiatric comorbidity with substance abuse in adolescents: Effects of timing and sex. *Journal of Clinical Child Psychology, 28,* 298–311.

Costello, E. J., Farmer, E. M. Z., Angold, A., Burns, B. J., & Erkanli, A. (1997). Psychiatric disorders among American Indian and white youth in Appalachia: The Great Smoky Mountains Study. *American Journal of Public Health, 87,* 827–832.

Costello, E. J., Sung, M., Worthman, C., & Angold, A. (2007). Pubertal maturation and the development of alcohol use and abuse. *Drug and Alcohol Dependence, 88S,* S50–S59.

Cox, R., Zhang, L., Johnson, W., & Bender, D. (2007). Academic performance and substance use: Findings from a state survey of public high school students. *Journal of School Health, 77,* 109–115.

Croissant, B., Rist, F., Demmel, R., & Olbrich, R. (2006). Alcohol-induced heart rate response dampening during aversive and rewarding stress paradigms in subjects at risk for alcoholism. *International Journal of Psychophysiology, 61,* 253–261.

Curran, P. J., Stice, E., & Chassin, L. (1997). The relation between adolescent alcohol use and peer alcohol use: A longitudinal random coefficients model. *Journal of Consulting and Clinical Psychology, 65,* 130–140.

Deas, D., Riggs, P., Langenbucher, J., Goldman, M., & Brown, S. (2000). Adolescents are not adults: Developmental considerations in alcohol users. *Alcoholism: Clinical and Experimental Research, 24,* 232–237.

Deckel, A. W., & Hesselbrock, V. (1996). Behavioral and cognitive measurements predict scores on the MAST: A 3-year prospective study. *Alcoholism: Clinical and Experimental Research, 20,* 1173–1178.

Delva, J., Wallace, J., O'Malley, P., Bachman, J., Johnston, L., & Schulenberg, J. (2005). The epidemiology of alcohol, marijuana, and cocaine use among Mexican American, Puerto Rican, Cuban American, and other Latin American eighth-grade students in the United States: 1991–2002. *American Journal of Public Health, 95,* 696–702.

Deykin, E., Buka, S., & Zeena, T. (1992). Depressive illness among chemically dependent adolescents. *American Journal of Psychiatry, 149,* 1341–1347.

Dick, D. M., & Mustanski, B. S. (2006). *Pubertal development and health-related behavior.* New York: Cambridge University Press.

Dick, D. M., Viken, R., Purcell, S., Kaprio, J., Pulkkinen, L., & Rose, R. (2007). Parental monitoring moderates the importance of genetic and environmental influences on adolescent smoking. *Journal of Abnormal Psychology, 116,* 213–218.

Dick, D. M., Rose, R. J., Viken, R., & Kaprio, J. (2000). Pubertal timing and substance use: Associations between and within families across late adolescence. *Developmental Psychology, 36,* 180–189.

Dishion, T., Patterson, G. R., & Reid, J. R. (1988). Parent and peer factors associated with drug sampling in early adolescence: Implications for treatment. *NIDA Research Monograph, 77,* 69–93.

Dishion, T., Patterson, G. R., Stoolmiller, M., & Skinner, M. (1991). Family, school, and behavioral antecedents to early adolescent involvement with antisocial peers. *Developmental Psychology, 27,* 127–180.

Disney, E., Elkins, I., McGue, M., & Iacono, W. (1999). Effects of ADHD, conduct disorder, and gender on substance use and abuse in adolescence. *American Journal of Psychiatry, 156,* 1515–1521.

Drejer, K., Theilgard, A., Teasdale, T. W., Schulsinger, F., & Goodwin, D. W. (1985). A prospective study of young men at high risk for alcoholism: Neuropsychological assessment. *Alcoholism: Clinical and Experimental Research, 9,* 498–502.

Droomers, M., Schrijvers, C. T. M., Casswell, S., & Mackenbach, J. P. (2003). Occupational level of the father and alcohol consumption during adolescence; patterns and predictors. *Journal of Epidemiology & Community Health, 57,* 704–710.

Duncan, S. C., Duncan, T. E., Biglan, A., & Ary, D. (1998). Contributions of the social context to the development of adolescent substance use: A multivariate latent growth modeling approach. *Drug and Alcohol Dependence, 50,* 57–71.

Duncan, T. E., Duncan, S. C., & Hops, H. (1998). Latent variable modeling of longitudinal and multilevel alcohol use data. *Journal of Studies on Alcohol, 59,* 399–408.

Duncan, S. C., Duncan, T. E., & Strycker, L. A. (2002). A multilevel analysis of neighborhood context and youth alcohol and drug problems. *Prevention Science, 3,* 125–133.

Duncan, S. C., Duncan, T. E., Strycker, L. A., & Chaumeton, N. R. (2002). Relations between youth antisocial and prosocial activities. *Journal of Behavioral Medicine, 25,* 425–438.

Duncan, T. E., Tildesley, E., Duncan, S. C., & Hops, H. (1995). The consistency of family and peer influences on the development of substance use in adolescence. *Addiction, 90,* 1647–1660.

Dunn, M., & Goldman, M. (1996). Empirical modeling of an alcohol expectancy network in elementary-school children as a function of grade. *Experimental and Clinical Psychopharmacology, 4,* 209–217.

East, P., & Khoo, S. T. (2005). Longitudinal pathways linking family factors and sibling relationship qualities to adolescent substance use and sexual risk behaviors. *Journal of Family Psychology, 19,* 571–580.

Eccles, J. S., Lord, S. E., Roeser, R. W., Barber, B. L., & Jozefowicz, D. (1997). The association of school transitions in early adolescence with developmental trajectories through high school. In J. Schulenberg, J. Maggs, & K. Hurrelmann (Eds.), *Health risks and developmental transitions during adolescence* (pp. 283–320). Cambridge: Cambridge University Press.

Eisenberg, N., Guthrie, I., Fabes, S., Shepard, S., Losoya, S., Murphy, B., et al. (2000). Prediction of elementary school childrens' externalizing problem behaviors from attentional and behavioral regulation and negative emotionality. *Child Development, 71,* 1367–1382.

Ellickson, P., Martino, S., & Collins, R. L. (2004). Marijuana use from adolescence to young adulthood: Multiple developmental trajectories and their associated outcomes. *Health Psychology, 23,* 299–307.

Elliott, D. S., Huizinga, D., & Ageton, S. (1985). *Explaining delinquency and drug use.* Beverly Hills, CA: Sage.

Emanuele, M. A., Wezeman, F., & Emanuele, N. V. (2002). Alcohol's effects on female reproductive function. *Alcohol Health and Research World, 26,* 274–281.

Ennett, S., Flewelling, R., Lindrooth, R., & Norton, E. (1997). School and neighborhood characteristics associated with school rates of alcohol, cigarette, and marijuana use. *Journal of Health and Social Behavior, 38,* 55–71.

Epstein, J. A., Botvin, G. J., & Diaz, T. (1998). Ethnic and gender differences in smoking prevalence among a longitudinal sample of inner-city adolescents. *Journal of Adolescent Health, 23,* 160–166.

Erickson, K., Crosnoe, R., & Dornbusch, S. (2000). A social process model of adolescent deviance: Combining social control and differential association perspectives. *Journal of Youth and Adolescence, 29,* 395–425.

Faggiano, F., Vigna-Taglianti, F., Versino, E., Zambon, A., Borraccino, A., & Lemma, P. (2005). School-based prevention for illicit drug use. *Cochrane Database of Systematic Reviews, 18,* CD003020.

Falck, R. S., Siegal, H. A., Wang, J., & Carlson, R. G. (1999). Differences in drug use among rural and suburban high school students in Ohio. *Substance Use and Misuse* [Special Issue: Symposium on rural/urban continuum], *34,* 567–577.

Faraday, M., Elliott, B., & Grunberg, N. (2001). Adult versus adolescent rats differ in biobehavioral responses to chronic nicotine exposure. *Pharmacology, Biochemistry, and Behavior, 70,* 475–489.

Fendrich, M., & Yun-Soo-Kim, J. (2001). Multi-wave analysis of retest artifact in the National Longitudinal Survey of Youth drug use. *Drug and Alcohol Dependence, 6,* 239–253.

Fergusson, D. M., Horwood, L. J., & Lynskey, M. T. (1993). Prevalence and comorbidity of DSM-III-R diagnoses in a birth cohort of 15 year olds. *Journal of the American Academy of Child and Adolescent Psychiatry, 32,* 1127–1134.

Fergusson, D. M., Lynsky, M., & Horwood, L. J. (1996a). Alcohol misuse and juvenile offending in adolescence. *Addiction, 91,* 483–494.

Fergusson, D. M., Lynsky, M., & Horwood, L. J. (1996b). Comorbidity between depressive disorders and nicotine dependence in a cohort of 16 year olds. *Archives of General Psychiatry, 53,* 1043–1047.

Fergusson, D., Horwood, J., & Ridder, E. (2007). Conduct and attentional problems in childhood and adolescence and later substance use, abuse, and dependence: Results of a 25-year longitudinal study. *Drug and Alcohol Dependence, 88,* S14–S26.

Fichtenberg, C. M., & Glantz, S. A. (2002). Youth access interventions do not affect youth smoking. *Pediatrics, 109,* 1088–1092.

Field, M., Christiansen, P., Cole, J., & Goudie, A. (2007). Delay discounting and the alcohol stroop in heavy drinking adolescents. *Addiction, 102,* 579–586.

Fisher, S. L., Bucholz, K. K., Reich, W., Fox, L., Kuperman, S., Kramer, J.,et al. (2006). Teenagers are right—parents do not know much: An analysis of adolescent–parent agreement on reports of adolescent substance use, abuse, and dependence. *Alcoholism: Clinical and Experimental Research, 10,* 1699–1710.

Flora, D. B., & Chassin, L. (2005). Changes in drug use during young adulthood: The effects of parent alcoholism and transition into marriage. *Psychology of Addictive Behavior, 19,* 352–362.

Flory, K., Brown, T. L., Lynam, D. R., Miller, J. D., Leukefeld, C., & Clayton, R. R. (2006). Developmental patterns of African American and Caucasian adolescents' alcohol use. *Cultural Diversity and Ethnic Minority Psychology, 12,* 740–746.

Flory, K, Milich, R., Lynam, D., Leukefeld, C., & Clayton, R. (2003). Relation between childhood disruptive behavior disorders and substance use and dependence symptoms in young adulthood: Individuals with symptoms of attention-deficit/hyperactivity disorder and conduct disorder are uniquely at risk. *Psychology of Addictive Behaviors, 17,* 151–158.

Flory, K., Lynam, D., Milich, R., Leukefeld, C., & Clayton, R. (2004). Early adolescent through young adult alcohol and marijuana use trajectories: Early predictors, young adult outcomes, and predictive utility. *Development and Psychopathology, 16,* 193–218.

Fowler, T., Lifford, K., Shelton, K., Rice, F., Thapar, A., Neale, M., et al. (2007). Exploring the relationship between genetic and environmental influences on initiation and progression of substance use. *Addiction, 102,* 413–422.

Fowler, T., Shelton, K., Lifford, K., Rice, F., McBride, A., Nikolov, I., et al. (2007). Genetic and environmental influences on the relationship between peer alcohol use and own alcohol use in adolescents. *Addiction, 102,* 894–903.

Fulkerson, J. A., Harrison, P. A., & Beebe, T. J. (1999). DSM-IV substance abuse and dependence: Are there really two dimensions of substance use problems in adolescents. *Addiction, 94,* 495–506.

Gardner, M., & Steinberg, L. (2005). Peer influence on risk taking, risk preference, and risky decision making in adolescence and adulthood: An experimental study. *Developmental Psychology, 41,* 625–635.

Gates, S., McCambridge, J., Smith. L., & Foxcroft, D. (2006). Interventions for prevention of drug use by young people delivered in non-school settings. *Cochrane Database of Systematic Reviews, 25,* CD005030.

Ge, X., Conger, R., Cadoret, R., Neiderheiser, J., Yates, W., Troughton, E., et al. (1996). The developmental interface between nature and nurture: A mutual influence model of child antisocial behavior and parent behavior. *Developmental Psychology, 32,* 574–589.

Ge, X., Jin, R., Natsuaki, M. N., Gibbons, F. X., Brody, G. H., Cutrona, C. E., et al. (2006). Pubertal maturation and early substance use risks among African American children. *Psychology of Addictive Behaviors, 20,* 404–414.

Gerrard, M., Gibbons, F. X., Stock, M., Lune, L., & Cleveland, M. (2005). Images of smokers and willingness to smoke among African American pre-adolescents: An application of the prototype willingness model of adolescent health risk behavior to smoking initiation. *Journal of Pediatric Psychology, 30,* 305–318.

Giancola, P. R., Martin, C. S., Tarter, R. E., Pelham, W., & Moss, H. B. (1996). Executive cognitive functioning and aggressive behavior in preadolescent boys at high risk for substance abuse/dependence. *Journal of Studies on Alcohol, 57,* 352–359.

Giancola, P. R., Mezzich, A. C., & Tarter, R. E. (1998). Disruptive, delinquent and aggressive behavior in female adolescents with a psychoactive substance use disorder: Relation to executive cognitive functioning. *Journal of Studies on Alcohol, 59,* 560–567.

Gil, A. G., Wagner, E. F., & Vega, W. A. (2000). Acculturation, familism and alcohol use among Latino adolescent males: Longitudinal relations. *Journal of Community Psychology, 28,* 443–458.

Glantz, M., & Chambers, J. (2006). Prenatal drug exposure effects on subsequent vulnerability to drug abuse. *Development and Psychopathology, 18,* 893–922.

Gotham, J. J., Sher, K. J., & Wood, P. K. (2003). Alcohol involvement and developmental task completion during young adulthood. *Journal of Studies on Alcohol, 64,* 32–42.

Goudriaan, A., Grekin, E., & Sher, K. J. (2007). Decision making and binge drinking: A longitudinal study. *Alcoholism: Clinical and Experimental Research, 31,* 928–938.

Graber, J., Seeley, J. R., Brooks-Gunn, J., & Lewinsohn, P. M. (2004). Is pubertal timing associated with psychopathology in young adulthood? *Journal of the American Academy of Child and Adolescent Psychiatry, 43,* 718–726.

Grant, B. F., & Dawson, D. A. (1997). Age at onset of alcohol use and its association with DSM-IV alcohol abuse and dependence: Results from the National Longitudinal Epidemiologic Survey. *Journal of Substance Abuse, 9,* 103–110.

Green, K. M., & Ensminger, M. E. (2006). Adult social behavioral effects of heavy adolescent marijuana use among African Americans. *Developmental Psychology, 42,* 1168–1178.

Griesler, P. C., & Kandel, D. B. (1998). Ethnic differences in the correlates of adolescent cigarette smoking. *Journal of Adolescent Health, 23,* 167–180.

Grunberg, N., Winders, S., & Wewers, M. (1991). Gender differences in tobacco use. *Health Psychology, 10,* 143–153.

Guyll, M., Spoth, R., Chao, W., Wickrama, K., & Russell, D. (2004). Family-focused preventive interventions: Evaluating parental risk moderation of substance use trajectories. *Journal of Family Psychology, 18,* 293–301.

Hallfors, D. D., Waller, M. W., Bauer, D., Ford, C. A., & Halpern, C. T. (2005). Which comes first in adolescence—sex and drugs or depression? *American Journal of Preventive Medicine, 29,* 163–170.

Han, C., McGue, M., & Iacono, W. (1999). Lifetime tobacco, alcohol, and other substance use in adolescent Minnesota twins: Univariate and multivariate behavior genetic analyses. *Addiction, 94,* 981–983.

Hansell, S., & White, H. R. (1991). Adolescent drug use, psychological distress, and physical symptoms. *Journal of Health and Social Behavior, 32,* 288–301.

Hanson, M. D., & Chen, E. (2007). Socioeconomic status and substance use behaviors in adolescents: The role of family resources versus family social status. *Journal of Health Psychology, 12,* 32–35.

Harden, P., & Pihl, R. (1995). Cognitive function, cardiovascular reactivity, and behavior in boys at high risk for alcoholism. *Journal of Abnormal Psychology, 104,* 94–103.

Harford, T. C., Grant, B. F., Yi, H., & Chen, C. M. (2005). Patterns of DSM-IV alcohol abuse and dependence criteria among adolescents and adults: Results from the 2001 National Household Survey on drug abuse. *Alcoholism: Clinical and Experimental Research, 29,* 810–825.

Hawkins, J. D., Catalano, R., & Miller, J. (1992). Risk and protective factors for alcohol and other drug problems in adolescence and early adulthood: Implications for substance abuse prevention. *Psychological Bulletin, 112,* 64–105.

Henker, B., Whalen, C. K., Jamner, L. D., & Delfino, R. J. (2002). Anxiety, affect, and activity in teenagers: Monitoring daily life with electronic diaries. *Journal of the American Academy of Child & Adolescent Psychiatry, 41,* 660–670.

Henry, B., Feehan, M., McGee, R., Stanton, W., Moffitt, T., & Silva, P. (1993). The importance of conduct problems and depressive symptoms in predicting adolescent substance use. *Journal of Abnormal Child Psychology, 21,* 469–480.

Hill, K., White, H. R., Chung, I.-J., Hawkins, J. D., & Catalano, R. F. (2000). Early adult outcomes of adolescent binge drinking: Person- and variable-centered analyses of binge drinking trajectories. *Alcoholism: Clinical and Experimental Research, 24,* 892–901.

Hill, S., Shen, S., Lowers, L., & Locke, J. (2000). Factors predicting the onset of adolescent drinking in families at high risk for developing alcoholism. *Biological Psychiatry, 48,* 265–275.

Hirschi, T. (1969). *Causes of delinquency.* Berkeley: University of California Press.

Hopfer, C., Crowley, T., & Hewitt, J. (2003). Review of twin and adoption studies of adolescent substance use. *Journal of the American Academy of Child and Adolescent Psychiatry, 42,* 710–719.

Hussong, A. M., Bauer, D. J., & Chassin, L. (in press). Telescoped trajectories from alcohol initiation to disorder in children of alcoholic parents. *Journal of Abnormal Psychology.*

Hussong, A., & Chassin, L. (2002). Parent alcoholism and the leaving home transition. *Development and Psychopathology, 14,* 139–157.

Hussong, A. M., & Chassin, L. (2004). Stress and coping among children of alcoholic parents through the young adult transition. *Development and Psychopathology* [Special Issue: Transition from adolescence to adulthood], *16,* 985–1006.

Hussong, A., Curran, P., & Chassin, L. (1998). Pathways of risk for accelerated heavy alcohol use among adolescent children of alcoholic parents. *Journal of Abnormal Child Psychology, 26,* 453–466.

Hussong, A. M., & Hicks, R. E. (2003). Affect and peer context interactively impact adolescent substance use. *Journal of Abnormal Child Psychology, 31,* 413–426.

Hussong, A., Hicks, R., Levy, S., & Curran, P. (2001). Specifying the relations between affect and heavy alcohol use among young adults. *Journal of Abnormal Psychology, 110,* 449–461.

Huver, R., Engels, R., & deVries, H. (2006). Are anti-smoking parenting practices related to adolescent smoking cognitions and behavior? *Health Education Research, 21,* 66–77.

Iacono, W. G., Carlson, S. R., Taylor, J., Elkins, I. J., & McGue, M. (1999). Behavioral disinhibition and the development of substance-use disorders: Findings from the Minnesota Twin Family Study. *Development and Psychopathology, 11,* 869–900.

Institute of Medicine. (1994). *Growing up tobacco free: Preventing nicotine addiction in children and youths.* B. Lynch & R. Bonnie (Eds.). Washington, DC: National Academies Press.

Jackson, C., & Henriksen, L. (1997). Do as I say: Parent smoking, antismoking socialization, and smoking onset among children. *Addictive Behaviors, 22,* 107–114.

Jackson, K., & Sher, K. J. (2005). Similarities and differences of longitudinal phenotypes across alternate indices of alcohol involvement: A methodologic comparison of trajectory approaches. *Psychology of Addictive Behaviors, 19,* 339–351.

Jackson, K., & Sher, K. J. (2006). Comparison of longitudinal phenotypes based on number and timing of assessments: A systematic comparison of trajectory approaches. *Psychology of Addictive Behaviors, 20,* 373–384.

Jerez, S. J., & Coviello, A. (1998). Alcohol drinking and blood pressure among adolescents. *Alcohol, 16,* 1–5.

Jessor, R., Donovan, J., & Costa, F. (1991). *Beyond adolescence: Problem behavior and young adult development.* Cambridge: Cambridge University Press.

Jessor, R., & Jessor, S. (1977). *Problem behavior and psychosocial development: A longitudinal study of youth.* New York: Academic Press.

Johnson, J. G., Cohen, P., Pine, D., Klein, D., Kasen, S., & Brook, J. (2000). Association between cigarette smoking and anxiety disorders during adolescence and early adulthood. *Journal of the American Medical Association, 284,* 2348–2351.

Johnston, L., O'Malley, P., & Bachman, J. (2000). *Monitoring the Future: National survey results on drug use, 1975–1999.* (NIH Publication No. 00-4802). Bethesda, MD: National Institute on Drug Abuse.

Johnston, L., O'Malley, P., Bachman, J., & Schulenberg, J. E. (2006). *Monitoring the Future national survey results on drug use, 1975–2005, vol. I: Secondary school students.* (NIH Publication Number 06-5883). Bethesda, MD: National Institute on Drug Abuse.

Johnston, L. D., O'Malley, P. M., Bachman, J. G., & Schulenberg, J. E. (2007). *Monitoring the Future national results on adolescent drug use: Overview of key findings, 2006* (NIH Publication No. 07-6202). Bethesda, MD: National Institute on Drug Abuse.

Johnston, L. D., O'Malley, P. M., Bachman, J. G., & Schulenberg, J. E. (2008). *Monitoring the Future national results on adolescent drug use: Overview of key findings, 2007* (NIH Publication No. 08-6418). Bethesda, MD: National Institute on Drug Abuse.

Johnston, L. D., O'Malley, P. M., & Terry-McElrath, Y. M. (2004). Methods, locations, and ease of cigarette access for American youth, 1997–2002. *American Journal of Preventive Medicine, 27,* 267–276.

Kandel, D. B. (1975). Stages in adolescent involvement in drug use. *Science, 165,* 912–914.

Kandel, D. B. (1978). Convergences in prospective longitudinal surveys of drug use in normal populations. In D. B. Kandel (Ed.), *Longitudinal research on drug use: Empirical findings and methodological issues* (pp. 3–40). New York: John Wiley & Sons.

Kandel, D. B. (1995). Ethnic differences in drug use: Patterns and paradoxes. In G. J. Botvin, S. Schinke, & M. Orlandi (Eds.), *Drug abuse prevention with multi-ethnic youth* (pp. 81–104). Thousand Oaks, CA: Sage.

Kandel, D. B., Davies, M., Karus, D., & Yamaguchi, K. (1986). The consequences in young adulthood of adolescent drug involvement. *Archives of General Psychiatry, 43,* 746–754.

Kandel, D. B., Johnson, J. G., Bird, H. R., Canino, G., Goodman, S., Lahey, B., et al. (1997). Psychiatric disorders associated with substance use among children and adolescents: Findings from the Methods for the Epidemiology of Child and Adolescent Mental Disorders (MECA) study. *Journal of Abnormal Child Psychology, 25,* 121–132.

Kaplow, J. B., Curran, P. J., Angold, A., & Costello, E. J. (2001). The prospective relation between dimensions of anxiety and the initiation of adolescent alcohol use. *Journal of Clinical Child Psychology, 30,* 316–326.

Kellam, S., Brown, C., Rubin, B., & Ensminger, M. (1983). Paths leading to teenage psychiatric symptoms and substance use: Developmental epidemiological studies in Woodlawn. In S. B. Guze, J. Earls, & J. Barrett (Eds.), *Childhood psychopathology and development* (pp. 17–52), New York: W. W. Norton.

Kilpatrick, D. G., Acierno, R., Saunders, B., Resnick, H. S., Best, C. L., & Schnurr, P. P. (2000) Risk factors for adolescent substance abuse and dependence: data from a national sample. *Journal of Consulting Clinical Psychology, 68,* 19–30.

King, K., & Chassin, L. (2004). Mediating and moderated effects of adolescent behavioral undercontrol and parenting in the predicting of drug use disorders in emerging adulthood. *Psychology of Addictive Behaviors, 18,* 239–249.

King, K., & Chassin, L. (2007). A prospective study of the effects of age of initiation of alcohol and drug use on young adult substance dependence. *Journal of Studies on Alcohol and Drugs, 68,* 256–265.

King, K. M., Meehan, B. T., Trim, R. S., & Chassin, L. (2006). Marker or mediator? the effects of adolescent substance use on young adult educational attainment. *Addiction, 101,* 1730–1740.

Krueger, R., Hicks, B., Patrick, C., Carlson, R., Iacono, W., & McGue, M. (2002). Etiological connections among substance dependence, antisocial behavior, and personality: Modeling the externalizing spectrum. *Journal of Abnormal Psychology, 111,* 411–424.

Kulis, S., Marsiglia, F. F., & Hurdle, D. (2003). Gender identity, ethnicity, acculturation, and drug use: Exploring differences among adolescents in the southwest. *Journal of Community Psychology, 31,* 167–188.

Kushner, M., Sher, K. J., Wood, M., & Wood, P. (1994). Anxiety and drinking behavior: Moderating effects of tension-reduction expectancies. *Alcoholism: Clinical and Experimental Research, 18,* 852–860.

Labouvie, E., Pandina, R. J., White, J. R., & Johnson, V. (1990). Risk factors of adolescent drug use: An affect-based interpretation. *Journal of Substance Abuse, 2,* 262–285.

Lambert, S. F., Brown, T. L., Phillips, C. M., & Ialongo, N. S. (2004). The relationship between perceptions of neighborhood characteristics and substance use among urban African American adolescents. *American Journal of Community Psychology, 34,* 205–218.

Lamborn, S. D., Dornbusch, S. M., & Steinberg, L. (1996). Ethnicity and community context as moderators of the relations between family decision-making and adolescent adjustment. *Child Development, 67,* 283–301.

Lanza, S. T., & Collins, L. M. (2002). Pubertal timing and the onset of substance use in females during early adolescence. *Prevention Science, 3,* 69–82.

Leifman, H., Kuhlhorn, E., Allebeck, P., Andreasson, S., & Romelsjo, A. (1995). Abstinence in late adolescence: Antecedents to and covariates of a sober lifestyle and its consequences. *Social Science and Medicine, 41,* 113–121.

LeJeuz, C., Aklin, W., Daughters, S., Zvolensky, M., Kahler, C., & Gwadz, M. (2007). Reliability and validity of the youth version of the Balloon Analogue Risk Task (BART-Y) in the assessment of risk-taking behavior among inner-city adolescents. *Journal of Clinical Child and Adolescent Psychology, 36,* 106–111.

Lerner, J. V., & Vicary, J. R. (1984). Difficult temperament and drug use: Analyses from the New York Longitudinal Study. *Journal of Drug Education, 14,* 1–8.

Levenson, R., Oyama, O., & Meek, P. (1987). Greater reinforcement from alcohol for those at risk: Parental risk, personality risk, and sex. *Journal of Abnormal Psychology, 96,* 247–253.

Leventhal, T., & Brooks-Gunn, J. (2000). The neighborhoods they live in: The effects of neighborhood residence on child and adolescent outcomes. *Psychological Bulletin, 126,* 309–337.

Levin, E., Rezvani, A., Montoya, D., Rose, J., & Swartzwelder, S. (2003). Adolescent-onset nicotine self-administration modeled in female rats. *Psychopharmacology, 169,* 141–149.

Levin, E., Connors, C., Silva, D., Hinton, S., Meek, W., March, J., et al. (1998). Transdermal nicotine effects on attention. *Psychopharmacology, 140,* 135–141.

Lezak, M. D. (1995). *Neuropsychological assessment* (3rd ed.). New York: Oxford University Press.

Little, M., Handley, E. D., Leuthe, E., & Chassin, L. (2007, February). Early transition to parenthood and growth in emerging adult substance use: A dual pathway model of the impact of family history of alcoholism on early transition to parenthood and growth in emerging adult substance use. A poster presented at the biennial conference on Emerging Adulthood, Tucson, AZ.

Loeber, R., Stouthamer-Loeber, M., & White, H. R. (1999). Developmental aspects of delinquency and internalizing problems and their association with persistent juvenile substance use between ages 7 and 18. *Journal of Clinical Child Psychology, 28,* 322–332.

Lucas, W. L., & Gilham, S. A. (1995). Profiles of drug use and attitudes among young adolescents. *Journal of Child & Adolescent Substance Abuse, 4,* 41–60.

Luke, D. A., Stamatakis, K. A., & Brownson, R. C. (2000). State youth-access tobacco control policies and youth smoking behavior in the United States. *American Journal of Preventive Medicine, 19,* 180–187.

Luthar, S. S., & Cushing, G. (1999). Neighborhood influences and child development: A prospective study of substance abusers' offspring. *Development and Psychopathology, 11,* 763–784.

Luthar, S. S., & D'Avanzo, K. (1999). Contextual factors in substance use: A study of suburban and inner-city adolescents. *Development and Psychopathology* [Special Issue: Developmental approaches to substance use and abuse], *11,* 845–867.

Luthar, S. S., & Latendresse, S. J. (2005). Children of the affluent: Challenges to well-being. *Current Directions in Psychological Science, 14,* 49–53.

Lynam, D., Caspi, A., Moffitt, T., Wikstrom, P.-O., Loeber, R., & Novak, S. (2000). The interaction between impulsivity and neighborhood context on offending: The effects of impulsivity are stronger in poorer neighborhoods. *Journal of Abnormal Psychology, 109,* 563–574.

Lynsky, M. T., & Fergusson, D. M. (1995). Childhood conduct problems, attention deficit behaviors, and adolescent alcohol, tobacco and illicit drug use. *Journal of Abnormal Child Psychology, 23,* 281–302.

Maes, H., Sullivan, P., Bulik, C., Neale, M., Prescott, C., Eaves, L., et al. (2004). A twin study of genetic and environmental influences on tobacco initiation, regular tobacco use, and nicotine dependence. *Psychological Medicine, 34,* 1251–1261.

Maggs, J. L. (1997). Alcohol use and binge drinking as goal-directed action during the transition to post-secondary education. In J. Schulenberg, J. L. Maggs, & Klaus Hurrelmann (Eds.), *Health risks and developmental transitions during adolescence* (pp. 345–371). Cambridge University Press: Cambridge.

Maggs, J. L., & Hurrelmann, K. (1998). Do substance use and delinquency have differential associations with adolescents' peer relations? *International Journal of Behavioral Development, 22,* 367–388.

Martin, C., Chung, T., Kirisci, L., & Langenbucher, J. (2006). Item response theory analysis of diagnostic criteria for alcohol and cannabis use disorders in adolescents: Implications for DSM-V. *Journal of Abnormal Psychology, 115,* 807–814.

Martin, C. S., Kaczynski, N. A., Maisto, S. A., Bukstein, O. M., & Moss, H. B. (1995). Patterns of DSM-IV alcohol abuse and dependence in adolescent drinkers. *Journal of Studies on Alcohol, 56,* 672–680.

Mason, W. A., Hitchings, J. E., & Spoth, R. L. (2007). Emergence of delinquency and depressed mood throughout adolescence as predictors of late adolescent problem substance use. *Psychology of Addictive Behaviors, 21,* 13–24.

Mason, W., & Windle, M. (2002). Reciprocal relations between adolescent substance use and delinquency: A longitudinal latent variable analysis. *Journal of Abnormal Psychology, 111,* 63–76.

McCabe, S. E., Boyd, C. J., & Young, A. (2007). Medical and nonmedical use of prescription drugs among secondary school students. *Journal of Adolescent Health, 40,* 76–83.

McCabe, S. E., Teter, C. J., & Boyd, C. J. (2004). The use, misuse and diversion of prescription stimulants among middle and high school students. *Substance Use & Misuse, 39,* 1095–1116.

McCarthy, D. M., Aarons, G. A., & Brown, S. A. (2002). Educational and occupational attainment and drinking behavior: An expectancy model in young adulthood. *Addiction, 97,* 717–726.

McGue, M. (1994). Genes, environment, and the etiology of alcoholism. In R. Zucker, G. Boyd, & J. Howard (Eds.), *The development of alcohol problems: Exploring the biopsychosocial matrix of risk* (NIAAA Research Monograph 26, pp. 1–40). Washington, DC: U.S. Government Printing Office.

McGue, M., Elkins, I., & Iacono, W. (2000). Genetic and environmental influences on adolescent substance use and abuse. *American Journal of Medical Genetics, 96,* 671–677.

McGue, M., Iacono, W., & Krueger, R. (2006). The association of early adolescent problem behavior and adult psychopathology: A multivariate behavioral genetic perspective. *Behavioral Genetics, 36,* 591–602.

McGue, M., Iacono, W. G., Legrand, L. N., Malone, S., & Elkins, I. (2001). Origins and consequences of age at first drink. I. Associations with substance-use disorders, disinhibitory behavior and psychopathology, and P3 amplitude. *Alcoholism: Clinical and Experimental Research, 25,* 1156–1165.

McGue, M., Sharma, A., & Benson, P. (1996). Parent and sibling influences on adolescent alcohol use and misuse: Evidence from a U.S. adoption cohort. *Journal of Studies on Alcohol, 57,* 8–18.

Merikangas, K., & Avenevoli, S. (2000). Implications of genetic epidemiology for the prevention of substance use disorders. *Addictive Behaviors, 25,* 807–820.

Merikangas, K., Stolar, M., Stevens, D., Goulet, J., Preisign, M., Fenton, B., et al. (1998). Familial transmission of substance use disorders. *Archives of General Psychiatry, 55,* 973–979.

Milberger, S., Biederman, J., Faraone, S., Chen, L., & Jones, J. (1997). ADHD is associated with early initiation of cigarette smoking in children and adolescents. *Journal of the American Academy of Child and Adolescent Psychiatry, 36,* 37–44.

Miles, D., Silberg, J., Pickens, R., & Eaves, L. (2005). Familial influences on alcohol use in adolescent female twins: Testing for genetic and environmental interactions. *Journal of Studies on Alcohol, 66,* 445–451.

Miller, T. R., Levy, D. T., Spicer, R. S., & Taylor, D. M. (2006). Societal costs of underage drinking. *Journal of Studies on Alcohol, 67,* 519–528.

Miller-Johnson, S., Lochman, J. E., Coie, J. D., Terry, R., & Hyman, C. (1998). Comorbidity of conduct and depressive problems at sixth grade: Substance use outcomes across adolescence. *Journal of Abnormal Child Psychology, 26,* 221–232.

Molina, B. S. G., & Pelham, W. E. (2002). *Childhood predictors of substance use in a longitudinal sample of children with ADHD.* Manuscript under editorial review.

Molina, B., Pelham, W., Gnagy, E., Thompson, A., & Marshal, M. (2007). Attention-deficit hyperactivity disorder risk for heavy drinking and alcohol use disorder is age specific. *Alcoholism: Clinical and Experimental Research, 31,* 643–654.

Morral, A., McCaffrey, D., Ridgeway, G., Mukherji, A., & Beighley, C. (2006). *The relative effectiveness of 10 adolescent substance abuse treatment programs in the United States.* Rand Corporation Technical Report, TS-346-CSAT, Santa Monica, CA.

Moss, H. B., Vanyukov, M., Yao, J., & Irillova, G. (1999). Salivary cortisol responses in prepubertal boys: The effects of parental substance abuse and association with drug use behavior during adolescence. *Biological Psychiatry, 45,* 1293–1299.

Mudar, P., Kearns, J. N., & Leonard, K. E. (2002). The transition to marriage and changes in alcohol involvement among black couples and white couples. *Journal of Studies on Alcohol, 63,* 568–576.

Múthen, B., & Shedden, K. (1999). Finite mixture modeling with mixture outcomes using the EM Algorithm. *Biometrics, 55,* 463–469.

Nagin, D. (1999). Analyzing developmental trajectories: A semiparametric group-based approach. *Psychological Methods, 4,* 139–157.

Nash, S., McQueen, A., & Bray, J. (2005). Pathways to adolescent alcohol use: Family environment, peer influence, and parental expectations. *Journal of Adolescent Health, 37,* 19–28.

Nestler, E. (2000). Genes and addiction. *Nature Genetics, 26,* 277–281.

Newcomb, M. D. (1995). Drug use etiology among ethnic minority adolescents: Risk and protective factors. In G. J. Botvin, S. Schinke, & M. A. Orlandi (Eds.), *Drug abuse prevention with multiethnic youth* (pp. 105–129). Thousand Oaks, CA: Sage.

Newcomb, M., & Bentler, P. (1988a). *Consequences of adolescent drug use: Impact on the lives of young adults.* Newbury Park, CA: Sage.

Newcomb, M., & Bentler, P. (1988b). Impact of adolescent drug use and social support on problems of young adults: A longitudinal study. *Journal of Abnormal Psychology, 97,* 64-75.

Newcomb, M., & Harlow, L. (1986). Life events and substance use among adolescents: Mediating effects of perceived loss of control and meaninglessness in life. *Journal of Personality and Social Psychology, 51,* 564–577.

Nigg, J. T., Glass, J. M., Wong, M. M., Poon, E., Jester, J. M., Fitzgerald, H. E., et al. (2004). Neuropsychological executive functioning in children at elevated risk for alcoholism: Findings in early adolescence. *Journal of Abnormal Psychology, 113,* 302–314.

Nigg, J., Wong, M., Martel, M., Jester, J., Puttler, L., Glass, J., et al. (2006). Poor response inhibition as a predictor of problem drinking and illicit drug use in adolescents at risk for alcoholism and other substance use disorders. *Journal of the American Academy of Child and Adolescent Psychiatry, 45,* 468–475.

Nowlin, P., & Colder, C. (2007). The role of ethnicity and neighborhood poverty on the relationship between parenting and adolescent cigarette use. *Nicotine and Tobacco Research, 9,* 545–556.

O'Connor, T. G., Allen, J. P., Bell, K. L., & Hauser, S. T. (1996). Adolescent–parent relationships and leaving home in young adulthood. In J. A. Graver and J. S. Dubas (Eds.), *Leaving home: Understanding the transition to adulthood, vol. 71: New directions for child development* (pp. 39–52). San Francisco: Jossey-Bass.

O'Dell, L., Bruijnzeel, A., Ghozland, S., Markou, A., & Koob, G. (2004). Nicotine withdrawal in adolescent and adult rats. *Annals of the New York Academy of Sciences, 1021,* 167–74.

Office of Applied Studies. (2003). *Results from the 2002 national survey on drug use and health: National findings* (DHHS Publication NO. SMA 03383, NHSDA Series H-22). Rockville, MD: Substance Abuse and Mental Health Services Administration.

Office of Applied Studies. (2004). *Results from the 2003 national survey on drug use and health: National findings* (DHHS Publication NO. SMA 04-3964, NHSDA Series H-25). Rockville, MD: Substance Abuse and Mental Health Services Administration.

Office of National Drug Control Policy. (2001). *The economic costs of drug abuse in the United States, 1992–1998.* Washington, DC: Executive Office of the President (Publication No. NCJ-190636).

O'Malley, P. M. (2004). Maturing out of problematic alcohol use. *Alcohol Research and Health, 28,* 202–204.

Olmstead, M. C. 2006. Animal models of drug addiction: Where do we go from here? *Quarterly Journal of Experimental Psychology, 59,* 625–653.

Orlando, M., Tucker, J. Ellickson, P., & Klein, D. (2004). Developmental trajectories of cigarette smoking and their correlates from early adolescence to young adulthood. *Journal of Consulting and Clinical Psychology, 72,* 400–410.

Pardini, D., White, H., & Stouthamer-Loeber, M. (2007). Early adolescent psychopathology as a predictor of alcohol use disorders by young adulthood. *Drug and Alcohol Dependence, 88,* S38–S49.

Park, C. L., Armeli, S., & Tennen, H. (2004). The daily stress and coping process and alcohol use among college students. *Journal of Studies on Alcohol, 65,* 126–135.

Paschall, M. J., Bersamin, M., & Flewelling, R. L. (2005). Racial/ethnic differences in the association between college attendance and heavy alcohol use: A national study. *Journal of Studies on Alcohol, 66,* 266–274.

Patterson, G. R. (1986). Performance models for antisocial boys. *American Psychologist, 41,* 432–444.

Paus, T. (2005). Mapping brain maturation and cognitive development during adolescence. *Trends in Cognitive Science, 9,* 60–68.

Paulson, M., Combs, R., & Richardson, M. (1990). School performance, educational aspirations, and drug use among children and adolescents. *Journal of Drug Education, 20,* 289–303.

Peterson, J. B., Finn, P. R., & Pihl, R. O. (1992). Cognitive dysfunction and the inherited predisposition to alcoholism. *Journal of Studies on Alcohol, 53,* 154–160.

Peterson, J. B., & Pihl, R. O. (1990). Information processing, neuropsychological function, and the inherited predisposition to alcoholism. *Neuropsychology Review, 1,* 343–369.

Petraitis, J., Flay, B., & Miller, T. (1995). Reviewing theories of adolescent substance use: Organizing pieces in the puzzle. *Psychological Bulletin, 117,* 76–86.

Prescott, C., Madden, P., & Stallings, M. (2006). Challenges in genetic studies of the etiology of substance use and substance use disorders. *Behavior Genetics, 36,* 473–482.

Reich, T., Hinrichs, A., Culverhouse, R., & Bierut, L. (1999). Genetic studies of alcoholism and substance dependence. *American Journal of Human Genetics, 65,* 599–605.

Reifman, A., Barnes, G. M., Dintcheff, B. A., Farrell, M. P., & Uhteg, L. (1998). Parental and peer influences on the onset of heavier drinking among adolescents. *Journal of Studies on Alcohol, 59,* 311–317.

Rende, R., Slomkowski, C., Lloyd-Richardson, E., & Niaura, R. (2005). Sibling effects on substance use in adolescence: Social contagion and genetic relatedness. *Journal of Family Psychology, 19,* 611–618.

Repetto, P. B., Caldwell, C. H., & Zimmerman, M. A. (2005). A longitudinal study of the relationship between depressive symptoms and cigarette use among African American adolescents. *Health Psychology, 24,* 209–219.

Resnicow, K., Soler, R., Braithwaite, R. L., Ahluwalia, J. S., & Butler, J. (2000). Cultural sensitivity in substance use prevention. *Journal of Community Psychology, 28,* 271–290.

Reynolds, B., Karraker, K., Horn, K., & Richards, J. (2003). Delay and probability discounting as related to different stages of adolescent smoking and nonsmoking. *Behavioral Processes, 31,* 333–344.

Reynolds, B., Patak, M., & Shroff, P. (2007). Adolescent smokers rate delayed rewards as less certain than adolescent nonsmokers. *Drug and Alcohol Dependence, 90,* 301–303.

Rezvani, I., & Levin, E. (2004). Adolescent and adult rats respond differently to nicotine and alcohol: Motor activity and body temperature. *International Journal of Developmental Science, 22,* 349–354.

Ridenour, T. A., Lanza, S. T., Donny, E. C., & Clark, D. B. (2006). Different lengths of times for progressions in adolescent substance involvement. *Addictive Behaviors, 31,* 962–983.

Robins, L. N., & Pryzbeck, T. R. (1985). *Age of onset of drug use as a factor in drug and other disorders.* NIDA Research Monograph, No. 56, (pp. 178–192). Washington, DC: National Institute on Drug Abuse.

Rogers, S., Miller, H., & Turner, C. (1998). Effects of interview mode on bias in survey measurement of drug use: Do respondent characteristics make a difference? *Substance Use and Misuse, 33,* 2179–2220.

Rohde, P., Lewinsohn, P., & Seeley, J. (1996). Psychiatric comorbidity with problematic alcohol use in high school students. *Journal of the American Academy of Child and Adolescent Psychiatry, 35,* 101–109.

Rourke, S. B., & Loberg, T. (1996). Neurobehavioral correlates of alcoholism. In I. Grant & K. M. Adams (Eds.), *Neuropsychological assessment of neuropsychiatric disorders* (2nd ed.; pp. 423–485). New York: Oxford University Press.

Rowe, C., & Liddle, H. (2006). Family-based treatment development for adolescent alcohol abuse. *International Journal of Adolescent Medicine and Health, 18,* 43–51.

Russell, M. (1990). Prevalence of alcoholism among children of alcoholics. In M. Windle & J. Searles (Eds.), *Children of alcoholics: Critical perspectives* (pp. 9–38). New York: Guilford Press.

Saha, T., Chou, P., & Grant, F. (2006). Toward an alcohol use disorder continuum using item response theory: Results from the national epidemiologic survey on alcohol and related conditions. *Psychological Medicine, 36,* 931–941.

Sartor, C., Lynskey, M., Heath, A., Jacob, T., & True, W. (2007). The role of childhood risk factors in initiation of alcohol use and progression to alcohol dependence. *Addiction, 102,* 216–226.

Scaramella, L. V., & Keyes, A. W. (2001). The social contextual approach and rural adolescent substance use: Implications for prevention in rural settings. *Clinical Child and Family Psychology Review, 4,* 231–251.

Schuckit, M. A., & Smith, T. L. (2000). The relationships of a family history of alcohol dependence, a low level of response to alcohol and six domains of life functioning to the development of alcohol use disorders. *Journal of Studies on Alcohol, 61,* 827–835.

Schuckit, M., Smith, T., & Kalmijn, J. (2004). The search for genes contributing to the low level of response to alcohol: Pattern of findings across studies. *Alcoholism: Clinical and Experimental Research, 28,* 1449–1458.

Schuckit, M., Smith, T., Pierson, J., Danko, G., & Beltran, I. (2006). Relationships among the level of response to alcohol and the number of alcoholic relatives in predicting alcohol-related outcomes. *Alcoholism: Clinical and Experimental Research, 30,* 1308–1314.

Schulenberg, J. E., Bachman, J. G., & O'Malley, P. M. (2005). Early adult transitions and their relation to well-being and substance use. In R. A. Settersten, Jr., F. F. Furstenberg, & R. G. Rumbaut (Eds.), *On the frontier of adulthood: Theory, research, public policy* (pp. 417–453). Chicago: University of Chicago Press.

Scribner, R., Cohen, D., & Fisher, W. (2000). Evidence of a structural effect for alcohol outlet density: A multilevel analysis. *Alcoholism: Clinical and Experimental Research, 24,* 188–196.

Shedler, J., & Block, J. (1990). Adolescent drug use and psychological health: A longitudinal inquiry. *Psychological Bulletin, 45,* 612–630.

Sher, K. J. (1991). *Children of alcoholics: A critical appraisal of theory and research.* Chicago: University of Chicago Press.

Sher, K. J., & Gotham, J. J. (1999). Pathological alcohol involvement: A developmental disorder of young adulthood. *Development and Psychopathology, 11,* 933–956.

Sher, K. J., & Grekin, E. R. (2007). *Alcohol and affect regulation.* New York: Guilford Press.

Sher, K. J., Martin, E. D., Wood, P. K., & Rutledge, P. C. (1997). Alcohol use disorders and neuropsychological functioning in first-year undergraduates. *Experimental and Clinical Psychopharmacology, 5,* 304–315.

Shoal, G. D., Castaneda, J. O., & Giancola, P. R. (2005). Worry moderates the relation between negative affectivity and affect-related substance use in adolescent males: A prospective study of maladaptive emotional self-regulation. *Personality and Individual Differences, 38,* 475–485.

Silbereisen, R. K., & Kracke, B. (1993). *Variation in maturational timing and adjustment in adolescence.* Hillsdale, NJ: Lawrence Erlbaum.

Simons, R., Johnson, C., Beamans, J., Conger, R., & Whitbeck, L. (1996). Parents and peer group as mediators of the effect of community structure on adolescent problem behavior. *American Journal of Community Psychology, 24,* 145–171.

Simons-Morton, B., & Chen, R. (2005). Latent growth curve analyses of parent influences on drinking progression among early adolescents. *Journal of Studies on Alcohol, 66,* 5–13.

Skager, R., & Fisher, D. (1989). Substance use among high schoolers in relation to school characteristics. *Addictive Behaviors, 14,* 129–138.

Slotkin, T. A. (2002). Nicotine and the adolescent brain: Insights from an animal model. *Neurotoxicology and Teratology, 24,* 369–384.

Slutske, W., Hunt-Carter, E., Nabors-Oberg, R., Sher, K., Bucholz, K., Madden, P., et al. (2004). Do college students drink more than their non-college-attending peers? Evidence from a population-based longitudinal female twin study. *Journal of Abnormal Psychology, 113,* 530–540.

Smart, R. G., Adlaf, E. M., & Walsh, G. W. (1994). Neighborhood socio-economic factors in relation to student drug use and programs. *Journal of Child and Adolescent Substance Abuse, 3,* 37–46.

Smith, G. T., Goldman, M. S., Greenbaum, P. E., & Christiansen, B. A. (1995). Expectancy for social facilitation from drinking: The divergent paths of high-expectancy and low-expectancy adolescents. *Journal of Abnormal Psychology, 104,* 32–40.

Smith, T. E., Koob, J., & Wirtz, T. (1985). Ecology of adolescents' marijuana abuse. *International Journal of the Addictions, 20,* 1421–1428.

Sneed, C. D., Morisky, D. E., Rotheram-Borus, M. J., Lee, S.-J., & Ebin, V. J. (2004) Indices of lifetime polydrug use among adolescents. *Journal of Adolescents, 27,* 239–249.

Spear, L. P. (2000). Neurobehavioral changes in adolescence. *Current Directions in Psychological Science, 9,* 111–114.

Spear, L. P., & Varlinskaya, E. I. (2005). Adolescence. Alcohol sensitivity, tolerance, and intake. *Recent Developments in Alcoholism, 17,* 143–159.

Spoth, R., Kavanagh, K., & Dishion, T. (2002). Family-centered preventive intervention science: Toward benefits to larger populations of children, youth, and families. *Prevention Science, 3,* 145–152.

Stacy, A., Newcomb, M., & Bentler, P. (1991). Cognitive motivation and problem drug use: A 9 year longitudinal study. *Journal of Abnormal Psychology, 100,* 502–515.

Stattin, H., & Magnusson, D. (1990). *Pubertal maturation in female development, vol 2: Paths through life.* Hillsdale, NJ: Lawrence Erlbaum.

Stattin, H., & Magnusson, D. (1996). Leaving home at an early age among females. In J. A. Graver & J. S. Dubas (Eds.), *Leaving home: Understanding the transition to adulthood, vol. 71: New directions for child development* (pp. 53–70). San Francisco: Jossey-Bass.

Stanton, W., Flay, B., Colder, C., & Mehta, P. (2004). Identifying and predicting adolescent smokers' developmental trajectories. *Nicotine and Tobacco Research, 5,* 843–852.

Steinberg, L. (in press). A neurobiological perspective on adolescent risk-taking. *Developmental Review.*

Steinberg, L. (2007). Risk taking in adolescence: New perspectives from brain and behavioral science. *Current Directions in Psychological Science, 16,* 55–59.

Steinberg, L., & Dornbusch, S. M. (1991). Negative correlates of part-time employment during adolescence: Replication and elaboration. *Developmental Psychology, 29,* 171–180.

Steinberg, L., Fletcher, A., & Darling, N. (1994). Parental monitoring and peer influences on adolescent substance use. *Pediatrics, 93,* 1060–1064.

Stice, E., & Barrera, M. (1995). A longitudinal examination of the reciprocal relations between perceived parenting and adolescents' substance use and externalizing behaviors. *Developmental Psychology, 33,* 322–334.

Stice, E., & Gonzales, N. (1998). Adolescent temperament moderates the relationship of parenting to antisocial behavior. *Journal of Adolescent Research, 13,* 5–31.

Stice, E., Presnell, K., & Bearman, S. (2001). Relation of early menarche to depression, eating disorders, substance abuse, and comorbid psychopathology among adolescent girls. *Developmental Psychology, 37,* 608–619.

Stout, J., Rock, S., Campbell, M., Busemeyer, J., & Finn, P. (2005). Psychological processes underlying risky decisions in drug abusers. *Psychology of Addictive Behaviors, 19,* 148–157.

Stubben, J. (1997). Culturally competent substance abuse prevention research among rural American Indian communities. In E. B. Robertson, Z. Sloboda, G. M. Boyd, L. Beatty, & N. J. Kozel (Eds.), *Rural substance abuse: State of knowledge and issues.* NIDA Research Monograph 168 (pp. 459–483). Rockville, MD: National Institute on Drug Abuse.

Substance Abuse and Mental Health Services Administration. (2006). *Results from the 2005 national survey on drug use and health: National findings.* Office of Applied Studies, NSDUH Series H-30, DHHS Publication No. SMA 06-4194, Rockville, MD.

Substance Abuse and Mental Health Services Administration, Office of Applied Studies. (2008). *The NSDUH report: Misuse of over-the-counter cough and cold medications among persons aged 12 to 25.* Rockville, MD.

Substance Abuse and Mental Health Services Administration, Office of Applied Studies. (2006). *The NSDUH report: Past month cigarette use among racial and ethnic groups.* Rockville, MD.

Sussman, S., Dent, C., & McCullar, W. (2000). Group self-identification as a prospective predictor of drug use and violence in high-risk youth. *Psychology of Addictive Behaviors, 14,* 192–196.

Swaim, R., Oetting, E., Beauvais, F. (1989). Links from emotional distress to adolescent drug use: A path model. *Journal of Consulting and Clinical Psychology, 57,* 227–231.

Tapert, S., Baratta, M., Abrantes, A., & Brown, S. (2002). Attention dysfunction predicts substance involvement in community youth. *Journal of the American Academy of Child and Adolescent Psychiatry, 41,* 680–686.

Tapert, S. F., & Brown, S. A. (1999). Neuropsychological correlates of adolescent substance use: Four-year outcomes. *Journal of the International Neuropsychological Society, 5,* 481–493.

Tapert, S. F., Caldwell, L., & Burke, C. (2004–2005). Alcohol and the adolescent brain: Human studies. *Alcohol Research & Health, 28,* 205–212.

Tarter, R. E., Alterman, A. I., & Edwards, K. L. (1985). Vulnerability to alcoholism in men: A behavior–genetic perspective. *Journal of Studies on Alcohol, 46,* 329–356.

Tarter, R., & Vanyukov, M. (1994). Alcoholism: A developmental disorder. *Journal of Consulting and Clinical Psychology, 62,* 1096–2007.

Tarter, R., Vanukov, M., Giancola, P., Dawes, M, Blackson, T., Mezzich, A., et al. (1999). Etiology of early age onset substance use disorder: A maturational perspective. *Development and Psychopathology, 11,* 657–683.

Timberlake, D., Rhee, S., Haberstrick, B., Hopfer, C., Ehringer, M., Lessem, J., et al. (2006). The moderating effects of religiosity on the genetic and environmental determinants of smoking initiation. *Nicotine and Tobacco Research, 8,* 123–133.

Trim, R. S., Meehan, B. T., King, K. M., & Chassin, L. (2007). The relation between adolescent substance use and young adult internalizing symptoms: Findings from a high-risk longitudinal sample. *Psychology of Addictive Behaviors, 21,* 97–107.

Trinidad, D. R., Gilpin, E. A., Lee, L., & Pierce, J. P. (2004). Do the majority of Asian-American and African-American smokers start as adults? *American Journal of Preventive Medicine, 26,* 156–158.

Turner, R. J., & Gil, A. G. (2002). Psychiatric and substance use disorders in South Florida: Racial/ethnic and gender contrasts in a young adult cohort. *Archives of General Psychiatry, 59,* 43–50.

Uhl, G. R. (1999). Molecular genetics of substance abuse vulnerability: A current approach. *Neuropsychopharmacology, 20,* 3–9.

Unger, J. B., Rohrbach, L. A., Cruz, T. B., Baezconde-Garbanati, L., Howard, K. A., Palmer, P. H., et al. (2001). Ethnic variation in peer influences on adolescent smoking. *Nicotine and Tobacco Research, 3,* 167–176.

Urberg, K. A., Degirmencioglu, S. M., & Pilgrim, C. (1997). Close friend and group influence on adolescent cigarette smoking and alcohol use. *Developmental Psychology, 33,* 834–844.

U.S. Department of Health and Human Services. (2000). *National household survey on drug abuse: Main findings, 1999.* Washington, DC: Substance Abuse and Mental Health Services Administration.

U.S. Department of Health and Human Services. (2004). *The health consequences of smoking: A report of the surgeon general.* Atlanta, GA: USDHHS, Centers for Disease Control and Prevention, National Center for Chronic Disease Prevention and Health Promotion, Office on Smoking and Health

U.S. Department of Health and Human Services. (2007). *The surgeon general's call to action to prevent and reduce underage drinking.* Washington, DC: USDHHS, Office of the Surgeon General.

Van der Vorst, H., Engels, R., Meeus, W., & Dekovic, M. (2006). The impact of alcohol-specific rules, parental norms about early drinking, and parental alcohol use on adolescents' drinking behavior. *Journal of Child Psychology and Psychiatry, 47,* 1299–1306.

Varlinskaya, E. I., & Spear, L. P. (2002). Acute effects of ethanol on social behavior of adolescent and adult rats: Role of familiarity of the test situation. *Alcoholism: Clinical and Experimental Research, 26,* 1502–1511.

Vega, W. A., Alderete, E., Kolody, B., & Aguilar-Gaxiola, S. (1998). Illicit drug use among Mexicans and Mexican Americans in California: The effects of gender and acculturation. *Addiction, 93,* 1839–1850.

Waldron, H., & Kaminer, Y. (2004). On the learning curve: The ermging evidence supporting cognitive–behavioral therapies for adolescent substance abuse. *Addiction, 99,* 93–105.

Wallace, J. M., Bachman, J. G., O'Malley, P. M., Johnston, L. D., Schulenberg, J. E., & Cooper, S. M. (2002) Tobacco, alcohol, and illicit drug use: Racial and ethnic differences among U. S. high school seniors. *Public Health Reports, 117,* S67–S75.

Wardle, J., Jarvis, M. J., Steggles, N., Sutton, S., Williamson, S., Farrimond, H., et al. (2003). Socioeconomic disparities in cancer-risk behaviors in adolescence: Baseline results from the health and behaviour in teenagers study (HABITS). *Preventive Medicine: An International Journal Devoted to Practice and Theory, 36,* 721–730.

Watson, D., Clark, L. A., & Carey, G. (1988). Positive and negative affectivity and their relation to anxiety and depressive disorders. *Journal of Abnormal Psychology, 97,* 346–353.

Webb, J. A., & Baer, P. E. (1995). Influence of family disharmony and parental alcohol use on adolescent social skills, self-efficacy and alcohol use. *Addictive Behaviors, 20,* 127–135.

White, H. R., McMorris, B. J., Catalano, R. F., Fleming, C. B., Haggerty, K. P., & Abbott, R. D. (2006). Increases in alcohol and marijuana use during the transition out of high school into emerging adulthood: The effects of leaving home, going to college, and high school protective factors. *Journal of Studies on Alcohol, 67,* 810–822.

White, H. R., Nagin, D., Replogle, E., & Stouthamer-Loeber, M. (2004). Racial differences in trajectories of cigarette use. *Drug and Alcohol Dependence, 76,* 219–227.

White, H. R., Pandina, R. J., & LaGrange, R. L. (1987). Longitudinal predictors of serious substance use and delinquency. *Criminology, 25,* 715–739.

Williams, R., McDermitt, D., Bertrand, L., & Davis, R. (2003). Parental awareness of adolescent substance use. *Addictive Behaviors, 28,* 803–809.

Williams, R., & Nowatzki, N. (2005). Validity of adolescent self-report of substance use. *Substance Use and Misuse, 40,* 299–311.

Willoughby, T., Chalmers, H., & Busseri, M. (2004). Where is the syndrome? Examining co-occurrence among multiple problem behaviors in adolescence. *Journal of Consulting and Clinical Psychology, 72,* 1022–1037.

Wills, T. A. (1986). Stress and coping in early adolescence: Relationships to substance use in urban school samples. *Health Psychology, 5,* 503–529.

Wills, T. A., Resko, J. A., Ainette, M. G., & Mendoza, D. (2004). Smoking onset in adolescence: A person-centered analysis with time-varying predictors. *Health Psychology, 23,* 158–167.

Wills, T. A., Sandy, J. M., Yaeger, A., & Shinar, O. (2001a). Family risk factors and adolescent substance use: Moderation effects for temperament dimensions. *Developmental Psychology, 37,* 283–297.

Wills, T. A., Sandy, J., Yaeger, A., Cleary, S., & Shinar, O. (2001b). Coping dimensions, life stress, and adolescent substance use: A latent growth analysis. *Journal of Abnormal Psychology, 110,* 309–323.

Wills, T. A., Vaccaro, D., McNamara, G., & Hirky, A. (1996). Escalated substance use: A longitudinal grouping analysis from early to middle adolescence. *Journal of Abnormal Psychology, 105,* 166–180.

Windle, M., & Wiesner, M. (2004). Trajectories of marijuana use from adolescence to young adulthood: Predictors and outcomes. *Development and Psychopathology, 16,* 1007–1027.

Windle, M., & Windle, R. (2001). Depressive symptoms and cigarette smoking among middle adolescents: Prospective associations and intrapersonal and interpersonal influences. *Journal of Consulting and Clinical Psychology, 69,* 215–226.

Winters, K. C., Anderson, N., Bengston, P., Stinchfield, R. D., & Latimer, W. W. (2000) Development of a parent questionnaire for use in assessing adolescent drug abuse. *Journal of Psychoactive Drugs, 32,* 3–13.

Wong, M., Nigg, J., Zucker, R., Puttler, L., Fitzgerald, H. M., Jester, J., et al. (2006). Behavioral control and resiliency in the onset of alcohol and illicit drug use: A prospective study from preschool to adolescence. *Child Development, 77,* 1016–1033.

Wood, P., Sher, K. J., Erickson, D., & DeBord, K. (1997). Predicting academic problems in college from freshman alcohol involvement. *Journal of Studies on Alcohol, 58,* 200–210.

Yamaguchi, K., & Kandel, D. B. (1985). On the resolution of role incompatibility: A life event history analysis of family roles and marijuana use. *American Journal of Sociology, 90,* 1284–1325.

Yoon, H., Iacono, W., Malone, S., & McGue, M. (2006). Using the brain P300 response to identify novel phenotypes reflecting genetic variability for adolescent substance misuse. *Addictive Behaviors, 31,* 1067–1081.

Young, S., Rhee, S., Stallings, M., Corley, R., & Hewitt, J. (2006). Genetic and environmental vulnerabilities underlying adolescent substance use and problem use: General or specific. *Behavior Genetics, 36,* 603–615.

Zhou, Q., King, K., & Chassin, K. (2006). The roles of familial alcoholism and adolescent family harmony in young adults'

substance dependence disorders: Mediated and moderated relations. *Journal of Abnormal Psychology, 115,* 320–331.

Zucker, R. A. (1987). The four alcoholisms: A developmental account of the etiologic process. In P. C. Rivers (Ed.), *Nebraska symposium on motivation, 1986: Alcohol and addictive behavior* (pp. 27–83). Lincoln: University of Nebraska Press.

Zucker, R. A. (2006). Alcohol use and the alcohol use disorders: A developmental biopsychosocial systems formulation covering the life course. In D. Cicchetti & D. Cohen (Eds.), *Developmental psychopathology, vol. 3: Risk, disorder, and adaptation* (2nd ed.; pp. 620–656). Hoboken, NJ: John Wiley & Sons.

Author Index

B

Subject Index